Contemporary Issues in Bioethics

CONTEMPORARY
ISSUES IN
BIOETHICS

FOURTH EDITION

Edited by

Tom L. Beauchamp & LeRoy Walters

Kennedy Institute of Ethics and Department of Philosophy

Georgetown University

Wadsworth Publishing Company
Belmont, California
A Division of Wadsworth, Inc.

Philosophy Editor: Tammy Goldfeld
Senior Editorial Assistant: Kristina Pappas
Production: Ruth Cottrell
Print Buyer: Barbara Britton
Permissions Editor: Robert Kauser
Copy Editor: Sheryl Rose
Compositor: ColorType, San Diego
Printer: Maple-Vail Book Manufacturing Group

 *This book is printed on
acid-free recycled paper.*

 I(T)P ™

International Thomson Publishing
The trademark ITP is used under license.

Printed in the United States of America

2 3 4 5 6 7 8 9 10 — 98 97 96 95 94

Library of Congress Cataloging-in-Publication Data

Contemporary issues in bioethics / edited by Tom L.
Beauchamp & LeRoy Walters. — 4th ed.
       p. cm.

   Includes bibliographical references.
   1. Medical ethics. 2. Bioethics. I. Beauchamp, Tom L.
II. Walters, LeRoy. III. Title: Bioethics.
R724.C67 1994   93-40221
174'.2 — dc20
ISBN 0-534-22314-1

CONTENTS

CHAPTER 5: ABORTION AND MATERNAL-FETAL RELATIONS 271

PART IV Decisions About the End of Life

CHAPTER 6: THE RIGHT TO DIE   351

CHAPTER 7: ACTIVE EUTHANASIA AND ASSISTED SUICIDE   431

PART V Public Health, Biomedical Research, and Biomedical Technologies

PART VI Justice in Access to Health Care

CHAPTER 10: JUSTICE IN THE DISTRIBUTION OF HEALTH CARE   675

PREFACE

The objective of this anthology is to make students aware of complex situations in biology and medicine that require moral reflection, judgment, or decision, while also indicating how justified moral conclusions can be reached. The essays have been chosen on the basis of their clarity of conceptual and ethical reflection, their teachability, and their significance for current controversies. Whenever possible, the essays have been arranged in a debate-like format so that the reader may explore the strengths and weaknesses of alternative positions on an issue. Each chapter of readings is preceded by an editor's introduction, which sets the essays in context and surveys the major arguments on the chapter topic. At the end of each chapter we recommend readings and list bibliographical resources that contain additional citations.

This fourth edition of *Contemporary Issues in Bioethics* continues the focus in previous editions on moral problems generated by the biomedical fields. The third edition, published in 1989, involved major changes in the selections, and this fourth edition is as different from the third as the third was from the first two editions. The chapter on ethical theory has been thoroughly revised and includes new subsections under the section on types of ethical theory. Each of the remaining chapter introductions has been revised, and often expanded. A new structure of six parts organizes the volume, and we have added new chapters on reproduction, euthanasia and assisted suicide, AIDS, and human genetics. Other new material has been added on the topics of professional relationships to patients and subjects, abortion, the right to die, and justice in access to health care. In all, 88 selections are new, with 21 selections carried over from the previous edition. Nonetheless, some familiar landmarks remain. We have retained several chapter topics from the third edition, as well as most of the major divisions in those chapters.

We have received many helpful suggestions for improving this anthology. It is impossible to recognize them all, but special thanks should be given to a talented research staff that has assisted us for two years in the collection and evaluation of materials. Three undergraduate and graduate students—Catherine Marshall, Brian Tauscher, and Dianne Gokey Lidiak—provided invaluable advice that helped us make our selections more pertinent and the introductions more readable for students. Five other students helped with page proofs: Monique Bynoe, Tysha Lupe, Lisa Novak, Shirmel Richards, and Emily Wilson. Superb assistance was also provided through our university offices, where for several months drafts were faithfully prepared in what must have seemed an endless flow of editing, rewriting, proofing, and permission requests. We are especially indebted for this assistance to Moheba Hanif and Diane Michutka.

We have been generously aided in this edition by Ruth Cottrell, who has devoted meticulous attention to our book during every phase of editing, composition, and correction. We also wish to thank Tammy Goldfeld and Kristina Pappas of Wadsworth for their helpful editorial advice. We acknowledge with warm appreciation the assistance provided by the Kennedy Institute's bioethics library and information retrieval project, which kept us in touch with the most important literature and reduced the burdens of library research. In particular, we thank Doris Goldstein, Director of Library and Information Services, and her colleagues, Frances Abramson, Ariella Barrett, Laura Bishop, Mary Coutts, Lucinda Huttlinger, Joy Kahn, Pat McCarrick, Hannelore Ninomiya, Anita Nolen, Cecily Orr, Clementine Pellegrino, Kathleen Reynolds, Amy Sharon, and Sue Walters. And again we acknowledge the backing provided by the Kennedy Institute of Ethics and its Director, Robert Veatch. We also thank the following reviewers: Don Becker, University of Texas, Austin; Candace C. Gauthier, University of North Carolina, Wilmington; Richard T. Hull, SUNY Buffalo; Douglas C. Long, University of North Carolina, Chapel Hill; Lynn Lumbrezer, University of Toledo; and Lynn Pasquerella, University of Rhode Island.

Finally, we are grateful to our spouses, Ruth R. Faden and Sue Walters, for their constant encouragement, support, and love.

November 1993
Tom L. Beauchamp
LeRoy Walters
*Kennedy Institute of Ethics
and Department of Philosophy,
Georgetown University*

Part I

INTRODUCTION TO ETHICS

1.
Ethical Theory and Bioethics

The moral problems discussed in this book have emerged from professional practice in the fields of clinical medicine, biomedical research, nursing, and in some cases the social and behavioral sciences. The goal of this first chapter is to provide a basis in ethical theory sufficient for reading and criticizing the essays in the later chapters. This chapter focuses on ethical theory and refrains from exploring the history and nature of bioethics—two topics considered in later chapters.

FUNDAMENTAL PROBLEMS

THE STUDY OF MORALITY

Some Basic Definitions. The field of ethics includes the study of social morality as well as philosophical reflection on its norms and practices. The terms "ethical theory" and "moral philosophy" refer exclusively to philosophical reflection on morality. The purpose of theory is to introduce clarity, substance, and precision of argument into the domain of morality. The term "morality," by contrast, is used to refer to traditions of belief about right and wrong human conduct. Morality is a social institution with a history and a code of learnable rules. Like political constitutions and languages, morality exists before we are instructed in its relevant rules, and thus it has a trans-individual status as a body of guidelines for action. Individuals do not create their morality by making their own rules, and morality cannot be purely a personal policy or code, because it is a social code.

We learn the requirements of morality as we grow up. We learn moral rules alongside other important social rules, which is one reason it later becomes difficult to distinguish the two. For example, we are constantly reminded in our early years that we must observe social rules of etiquette such as saying "Please" when we want something and "Thank you" when we receive it, as well as more specific rules such as "A judge is addressed as 'judge.'" We are also taught rules of prudence, including "Don't touch a hot stove," as well as rules of housekeeping, dressing, and the like.

But the whole of these rules does not amount to morality. Morality enters the picture when certain actions ought or ought not to be performed because of the considerable impact these actions can be expected to have on the interests of other people. We first learn maxims such as "It is better to give than to receive" and "Respect the rights of others." These are elementary instructions in morality; they express what society expects of us and of everyone in terms of taking the interests of other people into account. We thus learn about moral instructions and expectations, and gradually we come to understand morality as a set of normative standards about doing good, avoiding harm, respecting others, keeping promises, and acting fairly—as well as standards of character and moral excellence.

Following this analysis, the terms "ethical" and "moral" are to be understood in this introduction as identical in meaning, and "ethics" will be used as a general term referring to *both* morality and ethical theory. The terms "moral philosophy," "ethical theory," and "philosophical ethics" will be reserved for philosophical theories.

Four Approaches to the Study of Ethics. Morality can be studied and developed in a variety of ways, only some of which can be correctly called "ethical theory." In particular, four ways of either studying moral beliefs or doing moral philosophy have been prominent in the literature of ethics. Two of these approaches describe and analyze morality without taking moral positions, and these approaches are therefore called "nonnormative"; two other approaches do involve taking moral positions, and are therefore "normative." These four approaches can be summarized as follows:

A. *Nonnormative approaches*
 1. Descriptive ethics
 2. Metaethics
B. *Normative approaches*
 3. General normative ethics
 4. Practical normative ethics

It would be a mistake to regard these categories as expressing rigid, sharply differentiated approaches. They are often undertaken jointly, and they overlap in goal and content. Nonetheless, when understood as broad polar contrasts exemplifying models of inquiry, these distinctions are important.

First among the two nonnormative fields of inquiry into morality is descriptive ethics, or the factual description and explanation of moral behavior and beliefs. Anthropologists, sociologists, and historians who study moral behavior employ this approach when they explore how moral attitudes, codes, and beliefs differ from person to person and from society to society. Their works often dwell in detail on matters such as professional codes and practices, codes of honor, and rules governing permissible killing in a society. Although philosophers do not typically engage in descriptive ethics in their work, some have combined descriptive ethics with philosophical ethics, for example, by analyzing the ethical practices of American Indian tribes or researching Nazi experimentation during World War II.

A second nonnormative field, metaethics, involves analysis of the meanings of central terms in ethics, such as "right," "obligation," "good," "virtue," and "responsibility." The proper analysis of the term "morality" and the distinction between the moral and the nonmoral are typical metaethical problems. Crucial terms in medical ethics, including "informed consent," "person," and "access" to health care, can be given the same kind of careful conceptual attention, and they are so treated in various chapters in this volume. (Descriptive ethics and metaethics may not be the only forms of nonnormative inquiry. In recent years there has been an active discussion of the biological bases of moral behavior and of the ways in which humans do and do not differ from animals.)

General normative ethics attempts to formulate and defend basic principles and virtues governing the moral life. Ideally, any ethical theory will provide a system of moral principles or virtues and reasons for adopting them, and will defend claims about the range of their applicability. In the course of this chapter the most prominent of these theories will be examined, as will various principles of respect for autonomy, justice, and beneficence, which have played a major role in some of these theories.

Principles found in general normative theories are often used to justify positions on particular moral problems such as abortion, widespread hunger, racial and sexual discrimination, and research involving human subjects. These attempts to use general theories and principles for specific problems are referred to as "practical ethics." Philosophical treatments of medical ethics, engineering ethics, journalistic ethics, jurisprudence, and business ethics often appeal to general ethical principles. Usually, however, no direct move can be made from theory or principles to particular judgments, and theory and principles therefore typically only *facilitate* the development of policies, action-guides, or judgments.

Substantially the same general ethical principles apply to problems across professional fields and in areas beyond professional ethics as well. One might appeal to principles of justice, for example, in order to illuminate and resolve issues of taxation, health care distribution, criminal punishment, and reverse discrimination. Similarly, principles of veracity (truthfulness) are invoked to discuss secrecy and deception in international politics, misleading advertisements in business ethics, balanced reporting in journalistic ethics, and the disclosure of the nature and extent of an illness to a patient in medical ethics.

MORAL DILEMMAS AND DISAGREEMENTS

In the teaching of ethics in professional schools, moral problems are often examined through case studies, which vividly display dilemmas that require students to identify the principles at issue and to confront problems of moral disagreement. We can approximate this method while examining the nature of moral dilemmas and disagreements.

Moral Dilemmas. In a case presented in Chapter 3, two judges became entangled in apparent moral disagreement when confronted with a murder trial. A woman named Tarasoff had been killed by a man who previously had confided to a therapist his intention to kill her as soon as she returned home from a summer vacation. Owing to obligations of confidentiality between patient and physician, a psychologist and a consulting psychiatrist did not report the threat to the woman or to her family, though they did make one unsuccessful attempt to commit the man to a mental hospital. One judge held that the therapist could not escape liability: "When a therapist determines, or pursuant to the standards of his profession should determine, that his patient presents a serious danger of violence to another, he incurs an obligation to use reasonable care to protect the intended victim against such danger." Notification of police and direct warnings to the family were mentioned as possible instances of due care. The judge argued that, although medical confidentiality must generally be observed by physicians, it was overridden in this particular case by an obligation to the possible victim and to the "public interest in safety from violent assault."

In the minority opinion, a second judge stated his firm disagreement. He argued that a patient's rights are violated when rules of confidentiality are not observed, that psychiatric treatment would be frustrated by nonobservance, and that patients would subsequently lose confidence in psychiatrists and would fail to provide full disclosures. He also suggested that violent assaults would actually increase because mentally ill persons would be discouraged from seeking psychiatric aid.[1]

The Tarasoff case is an instance of a moral dilemma, because strong moral reasons support the rival conclusions of the two judges. The most difficult and recalcitrant moral controversies that we encounter in this volume generally have at least some dilemmatic features. They involve what Guido Calabresi has called "tragic choices." Everyone who has been faced with a difficult decision—such as whether to have an abortion, to have a pet "put to sleep," or to commit a member of one's family to a mental institution—knows through deep anguish what is meant by a personal dilemma.

Dilemmas occur whenever good reasons for mutually exclusive alternatives can be cited; if any one set of reasons is acted upon, events will result that are desirable in some respects but undesirable in others. Here an agent morally ought to do one thing and also morally ought to do another thing, but the agent is precluded by circumstances from doing both. Although the moral reasons behind each alternative are good reasons, neither set of reasons clearly outweighs the other. Parties on both sides of dilemmatic disagreements thus can *correctly* present moral reasons in support of their competing conclusions. The reasons behind each alternative are good and weighty, and neither set of reasons is obviously the best set. If one acts on either set of reasons, one's actions will be morally acceptable in some respects but morally unacceptable in others. Most moral dilemmas therefore present a need to balance rival claims in untidy circumstances.

One possible response to the problem of public moral dilemmas and disputes is that we do not have and are not likely ever to have a single ethical theory or a single method for resolving public disagreements. In any pluralistic culture there may be many sources of moral value and consequently a pluralism of moral points of view on many issues; bluffing in business deals, providing national health insurance to all citizens, involuntarily committing the mentally disturbed, civil disobedience in pursuit of justice, and so on. If this response is correct, we can understand why there seem to be intractable moral dilemmas and controversies both inside and outside professional philosophy. However, there also are ways out of at least some dilemmas and disputes, as we shall now see.

The Resolution of Moral Disagreements. Can we hope — in light of complex dilemmas and other sources of dispute — to resolve moral disagreements? Probably no single set of considerations will prove consistently reliable as a means of ending disagreement and controversy (and resolutions of cross-cultural conflicts will always be especially elusive). Nonetheless, several methods for dealing constructively with moral disagreements have been employed in the past, and each deserves recognition as a method of easing and perhaps settling controversies. These methods can at least help us manage dilemmas, even if no entirely satisfactory resolution emerges.

1. *Obtaining Objective Information.* First, many moral disagreements can be at least facilitated by obtaining factual information concerning points of moral controversy. It has often been uncritically assumed that moral disputes are (by definition) produced solely by differences over moral principles or their interpretation and application, rather than by a lack of information. This assumption is too simple, however, because disputes over what morally ought or ought not to be done often have nonmoral elements as central ingredients. For example, debates about the allocation of health dollars to preventive and educational strategies (see Chapter 10) have often bogged down over factual issues of whether these strategies actually function to prevent illness and promote health.

In some cases new information facilitates negotiation and compromise. New scientific information about the alleged dangers involved in certain kinds of scientific research, for instance, have turned public controversies regarding the risks of science and the rights of scientific researchers in unanticipated directions. In several controversies over research with a high level of uncertainty, it has been feared that the research might create an irreversible and dangerous situation (for example, an organism of pathogenic capability that known antibodies would be unable to combat and that could produce widespread contagion).

Controversies about sweetening agents for drinks, toxic substances in the workplace, pesticides in agriculture, radiation therapies, IQ research, and vaccine dissemination, among others, have been laced with issues of both values and facts. Current controversies over whether there should be compulsory screening for AIDS often turn critically on factual claims about how HIV (human immunodeficiency virus) is transmitted, how much can be learned by screening, how many persons are threatened, whether health education campaigns can successfully teach safe sex practices, and the like. Related moral problems about whether nurses and other health professionals have a role obligation to feed, ambulate, or otherwise administer to an AIDS patient may also be resolvable only by recourse to the facts about AIDS transmission.

The arguments used by disagreeing parties in these cases *sometimes* turn on some dispute about liberty or justice and therefore *sometimes are* primarily normative, but they may also rest on purely factual disagreements. New information may have only a limited bearing on the resolution of some of these controversies, whereas in others it may have a direct and almost overpowering influence. The problem is that rarely, if ever, is all the information obtained that would be sufficient to settle factual disagreements.

2. *Providing Definitional Clarity*. Second, controversies have been settled by reaching conceptual or definitional agreement over the language used by disputing parties. In some cases stipulation of a definition or a clear explanation of what is meant by a term may prove sufficient, but in other cases agreement cannot be so conveniently achieved. Controversies over the morality of euthanasia, for example, are often needlessly entangled because disputing parties use different senses of the term and have invested heavily in their particular definitions. For example, it may be that one party equates euthanasia with mercy killing and another party equates it with voluntarily elected natural death. Some even hold that euthanasia is by definition *nonvoluntary* mercy killing. Any resulting moral controversy over "euthanasia" is ensnared in terminological problems (see Chapters 6–7), rendering it doubtful that the parties are discussing the same problem.

Some central concepts in bioethics have several incoherent meanings. For example, the central concept in the principle of respect for autonomy is autonomy, but the bioethics literature contains several inconsistent conceptions of autonomy, each of which has been ably defended. There is no common point of discussion and disagreement in those cases in which parties are addressing different issues as a result of their different conceptual assumptions. Under these conditions, it cannot reasonably be expected that the issues can be pushed forward. Nonetheless, conceptual analysis does often facilitate discussion of issues. For this reason, many essays in this volume dwell at some length on conceptual analysis.

3. *Adopting a Code*. Third, resolution of moral problems can be facilitated if disputing parties can come to agreement on a common set of moral guidelines. If this method requires a complete shift from one starkly different moral point of view to another, agreement will rarely be achieved. Differences that divide persons at the level of their most cherished principles are deep divisions, and conversions are infrequent. Various forms of discussion and negotiation can, however, lead to the adoption of a new or changed moral framework that can serve as a common basis for discussion.

For example, a national commission appointed to study ethical issues in research involving human subjects unanimously adopted a common framework of moral principles, which then provided a general background and starting point for deliberations about particular problems. Commissioners developed a framework of three moral principles: respect for persons, beneficence, and justice. These principles were analyzed in light of contemporary philosophical ethics and were then used, along with other considerations, to justify a position on a wide range of moral problems that confronted the commission.[2] This common framework of moral principles facilitated discussion of the controversies they addressed and opened up avenues of agreement that might otherwise not have been spotted.

Virtually every professional association in medicine and nursing has a code of ethics, and the reason for the existence of these codes is to give guidance in a circumstance of uncertainty or dispute. Their rules apply to all persons in the relevant professional roles in medicine, nursing, and research. These codes are very general and cannot be expected to cover every possible case, but agreed-upon general principles do provide an important starting point.

4. *Using Examples and Counterexamples*. Fourth, resolution of moral controversies can be aided by a constructive method of example and opposed counterexample. Cases or examples favorable to one point of view are brought forward, and counterexamples to these cases are thrown up against the examples and claims of the first. A longstanding debate over truth telling in medicine provides a typical case. (See Chapter 3.) The personal experiences of practitioners and some recent empirical research have provided a set of examples (both anecdotes and empirical evidence) about the consequences of telling the truth and of not telling the truth to seriously ill patients. Argument about the acceptability of withholding information can proceed by citing relevant cases and then presenting alternative cases (counterexamples) that support a different approach, on grounds that the counterexample shows the superiority of the second approach. This dialectical use of example and counterexample serves as a format for weighing the strength of alternative proposals and policies.

This form of debate occurred when the commission mentioned in the preceding section came to consider the level of risk that can justifiably be permitted in scientific research involving children as subjects, where no therapeutic benefit is offered to the child. On the basis of principles of acceptable risk used in their own previous deliberations, commissioners were at first inclined to accept the view that only low risk or "minimal risk" procedures could be justified in the case of children (where "minimal risk" refers analogically to the level of risk present in standard medical examinations of patients). Many examples were put forward of unnecessary risk presented to children in research. However, examples from the history of medicine were then cited that revealed how certain significant diagnostic, therapeutic, and preventive advances in medicine would have been unlikely, or at least slowed, unless procedures that posed a higher level of risk had been employed. Counterexamples of overzealous researchers who placed children at too much risk were then thrown up against these examples, and the debate continued in this way for several months.

Eventually a majority of commissioners abandoned their original view that nontherapeutic research involving more than minimal risk was unjustified. Instead, the majority accepted the position that a higher level of risk can be justified by the benefits provided to other children, as when a group of terminally ill children becomes the subject of research in the hope that something will be learned about their disease that can be applied to other children. Once a consensus on this particular issue crystallized, resolution was achieved on the primary moral controversy about the involvement of children as research subjects (although two commissioners never agreed).

5. *Analyzing Arguments*. Fifth and finally, one of the most important methods of philosophical inquiry, that of exposing the inadequacies, gaps, fallacies, and unexpected consequences of an argument, can also be brought to bear on moral disagreements. For example, if an argument rests on accepting two incoherent points of view, then pointing out the incoherence will require a change in the argument. There are many subtle ways of attacking an argument. For example, in Chapter 5 there are discussions of the nature of "persons," and these discussions are carried into later chapters dealing with problems of the right to die, euthanasia, and the definition of death. Some writers on these topics have not appreciated that their arguments about persons — used, for example, to discuss fetuses and those who are irreversibly comatose — were so broad that they carried important but unnoticed implications for both infants and animals. Their arguments implicitly provided reasons

they had not noticed for denying rights to infants (rights that adult have), or for granting (or denying) the same rights to fetuses that infants have, and in some cases for granting (or denying) the same rights to animals that infants have.

It may, of course, be correct to hold that infants have fewer rights than adults, or that fetuses and animals should be granted the same rights as infants. The present point is that if a moral argument leads to conclusions that a proponent is not prepared to defend and did not previously anticipate, part of the argument will have to be changed, and this process may reduce the distance between the parties who are disagreeing. This style of argument is often supplemented by one or more of the other four ways of reducing moral disagreement. Much of the work published in philosophical journals takes the form of attacking arguments, using counterexamples, and proposing alternative principles. To accept this ideal of philosophical criticism is not to assume that conflicts can always be eliminated. The moral life will always be plagued by some forms of conflict and incoherence that cannot be eradicated without producing some other form of incoherence or unacceptable outcome. Our pragmatic goal should be a method that helps in a circumstance of disagreement, not a method that will always resolve our problems.

Some moral disagreements therefore may not be resolvable by any of the five means discussed in this section. We need not claim that moral disagreements can always be resolved, or even that every rational person must accept the same method for approaching such problems. There is always a possibility of ultimate disagreement. However, if something is to be done about problems of justification in contexts of disagreement, a resolution is more likely to occur if the methods outlined in this section are used. These strategies are often found in the articles included in this anthology.

RELATIVISM AND OBJECTIVITY IN ETHICS

The fact of moral disagreement raises questions about whether there can be correct or objective moral judgments. Cultural differences and individual disagreements among friends over issues like abortion, euthanasia, and the right to health care have led many to doubt the possibility that there are correct and objective positions in morals. This doubt is fed by popular aphorisms asserting that morality is more properly a matter of taste than reason, that what one believes is a matter of choice, and that there is no neutral standpoint from which to view disagreements.

Tension between the belief that morality is purely a matter of personal or social convention and the belief that it has an objective grounding leads to issues of relativism in morals. Moral relativism is no newcomer to the scene of moral philosophy. Ancient thinkers were as perplexed by cultural and individual differences as moderns, as is evidenced by Plato's famous battle with a relativism popular in his day. Nevertheless, it was easier in former times to ignore cultural differences than it is today, because there was once greater uniformity within cultures, as well as less commerce between them. The contrast between ancient Athens and modern Manhattan is evident, and any contemporary pluralistic culture is saturated with individuality of belief and lifestyle. At the same time, we tend to reject the claim that this diversity compels us to tolerate racism, social caste systems, sexism, genocide, and a wide variety of inequalities of treatment that we deeply believe to be morally wrong but find sanctioned either in our own culture or in others. Which view, then, is correct?

Cultural Relativism. Relativists often start with and defend their position by appeal to anthropological data indicating that moral rightness and wrongness vary from place to place and that there are no absolute or universal moral standards that could apply to all persons at all times. They add that rightness is contingent on cultural beliefs and that the concepts of rightness and wrongness are therefore meaningless apart from the specific contexts in which they arise. The claim is that patterns of culture can only be understood as unique wholes and that moral beliefs about normal behavior are closely connected in a culture to other cultural characteristics, such as language and fundamental political institutions. Studies show, they maintain, that what is deemed worthy of moral approval or disapproval in one society varies, both in detail and as a whole pattern, from moral standards in other societies.

This form of relativism has plagued moral philosophy, and many arguments have been advanced in criticism of it. Among the best-known criticisms is that there is a universal structure of human nature, or at least a universal set of human needs, which leads to the adoption of similar or perhaps identical moral principles in all cultures. This factual argument rests on empirical claims about what actually is believed across different cultures. For example, some anthropologists have probed beneath what they considered to be surface moral disagreements and have claimed to discover agreement on more basic principles at deeper levels. Thus, although cultural practices and individual beliefs vary, it does not follow that people fundamentally disagree about ultimate moral standards. Two cultures may agree about an ultimate principle of morality yet disagree about *how to apply* the principle in a particular situation or practice. That is, the two cultures may agree about basic principles of morality, yet disagree about how to live by these principles in particular circumstances.

For example, if personal payments for special services are common in one culture and punishable as bribery in another, then it is undeniable that these customs are different, but it does not follow that the moral principles underlying the customs are relative. One culture may exhibit a belief that practices of grease payments produce a social good by eliminating government interference and by lowering the salaries paid to functionaries, while the people of another culture may believe that the overall social good is best promoted by eliminating all special favors. Both justifications rest on an appraisal of the overall social good, but the people of the two cultures apply this principle in disparate, indeed apparently competing ways.

This possibility suggests that a basic or fundamental conflict between cultural values can only occur if apparent cultural disagreements about proper principles or rules occur at the level of ultimate moral principles. Otherwise, the apparent disagreements can be understood in terms of, and perhaps be arbitrated by, appeal to deeper shared values. If a moral conflict were truly fundamental, then the conflict could not be removed even if there were perfect agreement about the facts of a case, about the concepts involved, and about background beliefs.

We need, then, to distinguish *relativism of judgments* from *relativism of standards:* Many different particular judgments can call upon the same general standards for their justification. Moreover, relativism of judgment is so pervasive in human social life that it would be foolish to deny it. When people differ about whether one policy for keeping hospital information confidential is more acceptable than another, they differ in their judgments but it does not follow that they have different moral standards of confidentiality. They may hold the same moral standard on protecting confidentiality, but differ over how to implement that standard.

A relativism of standards, then, may not be a correct account even if a relativism of judgment is correct. This possibility is worth serious consideration for two reasons. First, many prorelativism arguments are based on relativism of judgment, whose examples are claimed to support a relativism of standards. But if differing judgments were the only basis for a relativism of standards, the theory would be poorly supported. Second, many people react negatively to the idea that moral rules allow no flexibility for individual judgment. It seems to them that relativism is therefore preferable to an "iron law" set of binding rules. Relativism of judgment does allow flexibility, but it is consistent with a denial of the relativism of moral standards.

However, these observations do not decide whether a relativism of standards is true, and this shortcoming has been of major concern. Suppose, then, that disagreement exists at the deepest level of moral belief; that is, suppose that two cultures disagree on basic or fundamental norms. It still does not follow from a relativity of cultural standards that there is no ultimate norm or set of norms in which everyone *ought* to believe. Consider an analogy to religious disagreement: From the fact that people have incompatible religious or atheistic beliefs, it does not follow that there is no single correct set of religious or atheistic propositions. Nothing more than skepticism seems justified by the facts about religious belief that are adduced by anthropology; and nothing more than skepticism seems justified if fundamental conflicts of belief were present in ethics. Skepticism of course presents serious philosophical issues, but alone it does not support relativism; and skepticism leaves ethical theory free to try to determine which is the best set of moral beliefs.

Normative Relativism. Cultural relativists might reasonably be said to hold that "What is right at one place or time may be wrong at another." This statement is ambiguous, however, and can be interpreted as a second form of relativism. Some relativists interpret "What is right at one place or time may be wrong at another" to mean that *it is right* in one context to act in a way that *it is wrong* to act in another. This thesis is normative, because it makes a value judgment; it delineates *which standards or norms determine right and wrong behavior*. One form of this normative relativism asserts that one ought to do what one's society determines to be right (a group or social form of normative relativism), and a second form holds that one ought to do what one personally believes is right (an individual form of normative relativism).

This normative position has sometimes crudely been translated as "Anything is right or wrong whenever some individual or some group judges that it is right or wrong." However, less crude formulations of the position can be given, and more or less plausible examples can be adduced. One can hold the view, for example, that in order to be right something must be conscientiously and not merely customarily believed. Alternatively, it might be formulated as the view that whatever is believed to be right is right if it is part of a well-formed traditional moral code of rules in a society — for example, a medical code of ethics developed by a professional society.

The evident inconsistency of this form of relativism with many of our most cherished moral beliefs is one major reason to be doubtful of it. No general theory of normative relativism is likely to convince us that a belief is acceptable merely because others believe it in a certain way, although that is exactly the commitment of this theory. At least some moral views seem relatively more enlightened, no matter how great the variability of beliefs. For example, the idea that practices such as slavery cannot be evaluated across cultures by some common standard seems morally unacceptable, not morally enlightened. It is one thing to suggest that such beliefs might be *excused*, still another to suggest that they are *right*.

One can evaluate various (but not all) problems of relativism by focusing on (1) the objectivity of morals within cultures and (2) the stultifying consequences of a serious commitment to moral relativism. Because the first focus provides an argument against *individual* relativism and the second provides an argument against a *cultural* source of relativism, we will consider each independently.

We noted previously that morality is concerned with practices of right and wrong transmitted within cultures from one generation to another. The terms of social life are set by these practices, whose rules are pervasively acknowledged and shared in that culture. Within the culture, then, a significant measure of moral agreement (objectivity) exists, because morality by its nature does not exist through a person's individual preferences. Individuals cannot create it by stipulation or correctly call a personal policy a morality. Such moral individualism is as dubious as anarchism in politics and law, and few readily accept a declaration that a person's political and legal beliefs are legitimately determined by that person alone. For example, a hospital corporation cannot develop its professional ethics from whole cloth. No hospital chain can draw up a code that brushes aside the need for confidentiality of patient information or that permits surgeons to proceed without adequate consents from patients; and a physician cannot make up his or her individual "code" of medical ethics. If codes deviate significantly from standard or accepted rules, they will rightly be rejected as subjective and mistaken. Room for invention or alteration in morality is therefore restricted by the broader understanding of social morality. Beliefs cannot become *moral* standards simply because an individual so labels them. Because individual (normative) relativism claims that moral standards can be invented or labeled, the theory seems *factually* mistaken.

This critique of individual relativism does not count against cultural relativism, however, because a cultural relativist could easily accept this critique. Our discussion needs to shift, then, to the second argument, which is directed at cultural forms of normative relativism. This argument looks at the pragmatic consequences of accepting cultural normative relativism, especially the ways this form of relativism would prevent serious reflection on, and resolution of, moral problems. The problem is the following: In circumstances of disagreement, moral reflection is needed to resolve moral issues whether or not people accept very different and conflicting norms. When two parties argue about a serious, divisive, and contested moral issue — for example, conflicts of interest — most of us think that some fair and justified compromise may be reached despite the differences of belief causing the dispute. People seldom infer from the mere fact of a conflict between beliefs that there is no way to judge one view as correct or as better argued or fairer-minded than the other. The more implausible the position advanced by one party, the more convinced others become that some views are mistaken or require supplementation. People seldom conclude, then, that there is not a better and worse ethical perspective or a more reasonable form of negotiation. If cultural normative relativists deny the acceptability of these beliefs, they seem to give up too early on the possibility that moral agreement may be achieved.

MORAL JUSTIFICATION

Typically we have no difficulty in deciding whether to act morally. We make moral judgments through a mix of appeals to rules, paradigm cases, role models, and the like. These moral beacons work well as long as we are not asked to deliberate about or justify our judgments. However, when we experience moral doubt or uncertainty, we are led to moral deliberation, and often from there to a need to justify our beliefs. Deliberation is primarily a problem-solving context in which individuals or groups struggle to develop and assess their beliefs in order to reach a decision. As we deliberate, we usually consider which among the possible courses of action is morally justified, i.e., which has the strongest moral reasons behind it. The reasons we finally accept express the conditions under which we believe some course of action is morally justified.

A good case can be made that philosophy in general, in all of its fields, is primarily concerned with the criticism and justification of arguments and conclusions—whether the subject matter under discussion is religion, science, law, education, mathematics, or some other field. A good case can be made, then, that the central philosophical questions in ethics are those of justification. But what is required in order to justify a moral point of view?

Moral judgments are justified by giving reasons for them. The objective is to establish one's case by presenting a sufficient set of reasons for belief and action. Not all reasons, however, are good reasons, and even good reasons are not always sufficient for justification. There is, then, a need to distinguish a reason's *relevance* to a moral judgment from its final *adequacy* for that judgment; and also to distinguish an *attempted* justification from a *successful* justification. For example, a good reason for involuntarily committing certain mentally ill persons to institutions is that they present a clear and present danger to other persons. Many believe that this reason is also sufficient to justify various practices of involuntary commitment. By contrast, a reason for commitment that is sometimes offered as a good reason, but which many people consider a bad reason (because it involves a deprivation of liberty), is that some mentally ill persons are dangerous to themselves.

If someone holds that involuntary commitment on grounds of danger to self is a good reason and is solely sufficient to justify commitment, that person should be able to give some account of why this reason is good and sufficient. That is, the person should be able to give further justifying reasons for the belief that the reason offered is good and sufficient. The person might refer, for example, to the dire consequences for the mentally ill that will occur if no one intervenes. The person might also invoke certain principles about the moral importance of caring for the needs of the mentally ill. In short, the person is expected to give a set of reasons that amounts to an argued defense of his or her perspective on the issues. These appeals are usually either to a coherent group of moral principles or to consequences of actions, and they form the substantive basis of justification.

To this point, we have been concerned primarily with the justification of moral *judgments,* but philosophers are no less concerned with the justification of ethical theories. We start in ethical theory with our most confidently held moral judgments (also called self-evident norms, plausible intuitions, and considered judgments). These are accepted initially without argumentative support. We then construct a general theory comprised of principles that we hope to make coherent with our other moral beliefs. The resultant principles are then tested against a wide range of our confidently held moral beliefs to see if our beliefs are still incoherent in some way. If so, they are readjusted or given up, and the process of finding principles that are coherent and that cohere with our other beliefs is renewed. The goal is to attain a justified set of beliefs—or theory—by making all principles and basic beliefs coherent.

Which theory, then, is the best theory? Or do all theories fail tests for plausibility and coherence?

TYPES OF ETHICAL THEORY

If there is to be a meaningful ethics in the cultures of medicine and research, practitioners in these fields must be able to implement standards that are more than loose abstractions. We need a way to make moral theory of direct relevance to professional practice and public policy. Bringing theory directly to bear on issues of practice, professional responsibility, and public policy are largely the subjects of later chapters in this book. At present we are concerned primarily with the nature of the theories that either underlie our practices and policies or that could be used to revise practice and policy.

Some persons interested in ethics do not see the need for abstract theory or for any revisions of prevailing practices that might flow from a theory. They find present moral conventions and rules comfortable and adequate. However, other persons are concerned about relating ethical theory to practice, and they take the competing view that traditional or operative standards are often incomplete, poorly understood, and inconsistent—as well as suffering from the lack of a uniform theory that would make the body of rules coherent and relevant. Those who take this viewpoint are inclined to revise present practices and policies, and they often look to some system of ethical theory to provide a basis for revisions.

To deal with these issues, we should be prepared not only to understand ethical theory but also to make some assessment of its value for bioethics. Our objective in this section is not to show how ethical theory can resolve problems in health care, but only to present several types of ethical theory. These theories should be situated under the category that we earlier called general normative ethics. We will concentrate on several types of ethical theory: utilitarianism, Kantianism, character ethics, the ethics of care, and casuistry. Some knowledge of these theories is indispensable for reflective study in biomedical ethics, because a sizable part of the field's literature draws on methods and conclusions found in these theories. In almost every chapter in this volume at least one author relies upon or defends some version of one or more of these theories.

UTILITARIAN THEORIES

Utilitarianism is rooted in the thesis that an action or practice is right (when compared to any alternative action or practice) if it leads to the greatest possible balance of good consequences or to the least possible balance of bad consequences in the world as a whole. Utilitarians hold that there is one and only one basic principle of ethics: the principle of utility. This principle asserts that we ought always to produce the maximal balance of positive value over disvalue (or the least possible disvalue, if only undesirable results can be achieved). The classical origins of this theory are found in the writings of Jeremy Bentham (1748–1832) and John Stuart Mill (1806–1873).

Utilitarians invite us to consider the larger objective or function of morality as a social institution, where "morality" is understood to include our shared rules of justice and other principles of the moral life. The point of the institution or morality, they insist, is to promote human welfare by minimizing harms and maximizing benefits: There would be no point in having moral codes and understandings unless they served this purpose. Utilitarians thus see moral rules as the means to the fulfillment of individual needs as well as to the achievement of broad social goals.

Mill's Utilitarianism. In several types of ethical theory, classic works of enduring influence form the basis for development of the theory. The most influential exposition of utilitarianism is John Stuart Mill's book *Utilitarianism* (1863). In this work Mill refers to the principle of utility as the Greatest Happiness Principle: "Actions are right in proportion as they tend to promote happiness, wrong as they tend to produce the reverse of happiness, i.e., pleasure or absence of pain." Mill's view seems to be that the purpose of morality is at once to tap natural human sympathies so as to benefit others while at the same time controlling unsympathetic attitudes that cause harm to others. The principle of utility is conceived as the best means to these basic human goals.

For Mill and other utilitarians, moral theory is grounded in a theory of the general goals of life, which they conceive as the pursuit of pleasure and the avoidance of pain. The production of pleasure and pain assumes moral and not merely personal significance when the consequences of our actions affect the pleasurable or painful states of others. Moral rules and moral and legal institutions, as they see it, must be grounded in a general theory of value, and morally good actions are alone determined by these final values.

Essential Features of Utilitarianism. Several essential features of utilitarianism may be extracted from the reasoning of Mill and other utilitarians. In particular, four conditions must be satisfied in order to qualify as a utilitarian theory.

1. *The Principle of Utility: Maximize the Good.* First, actors are obliged to maximize the good: We ought always to produce the greatest possible balance of value over disvalue (or the least possible balance of disvalue, if only bad results can be achieved). But what is the good or the valuable? This question takes us to the second condition.

2. *A Theory of Value: The Standard of Goodness.* The goodness or badness of consequences is to be measured by items that count as the primary goods or utilities. Many utilitarians agree that ultimately we ought to look to the production of *agent-neutral* or intrinsic values, those that do not vary from person to person. That is, what is good in itself, not merely what is good as a means to something else, ought to be produced. Bentham and Mill are hedonists; they believe that only pleasure or happiness (which are synonymous terms in this context) can be intrinsically good. Pluralistic utilitarian philosophers, by contrast, believe that no single goal or state constitutes the good and that many values besides happiness possess intrinsic worth—for example, the values of friendship, knowledge, love, personal achievement, culture, freedom, and liberties can all qualify.

Both the hedonistic and the pluralistic approaches have nonetheless seemed to some recent philosophers relatively problematic for purposes of objectively aggregating widely different interests in order to determine where maximal value, and therefore right action, lies. Many utilitarians now interpret the good as that which is *subjectively* desired or wanted. The satisfaction of desires or wants is seen as the goal of our moral actions. To maximize an individual's utility is to maximize what he or she has chosen or would choose from the available alternatives.

3. *Consequentialism.* All utilitarian theories decide which actions are right and which wrong by the consequences of the actions. Consequentialism is the position that actions are morally right or wrong according to their consequences, rather than by virtue of any intrinsic moral features they may have, such as truthfulness or fidelity. Here the utilitarian need not demand that all future consequences or even all avoidable consequences be anticipated. A utilitarian demands only that we take account of what can reasonably be expected to produce the greatest balance of good or least balance of harm. In judging the *agent* of the action, we should assess whether the agent conscientiously attempts to produce the best utilitarian outcome.

4. *Impartiality (Universalism).* Finally, in a utilitarian theory the consequences affecting all parties must receive equal and impartial consideration. Utilitarianism thus stands in sharp contrast to egoism, which proposes maximizing consequences for oneself rather than for all parties affected by an action. In seeking a blinded impartiality, utilitarianism aligns good and mature moral judgment with moral distance from the choices to be made.

Act and Rule Utilitarianism. Utilitarian moral philosophers are conventionally divided into several types, and it is best to think of "utilitarianism" as a label designating a family of theories that use a consequentialist principle. A significant dispute has arisen among utilitarians over whether the principle of utility is to be applied to *particular acts* in particular circumstances or to *rules of conduct* that determine which acts are right and wrong. For the rule utilitarian, actions are justified by appeal to rules such as "Don't deceive" and "Don't break promises." These rules, in turn, are justified by appeal to the principle of utility. An act utilitarian simply justifies actions directly by appeal to the principle of utility. Act utilitarianism is thus characterized as a "direct" or "extreme" theory because the act utilitarian directly asks, "What good and evil consequences will result directly from this action in this circumstance?"—not "What good and evil consequences will result generally from this sort of action?"

Consider the following case, which occurred in the state of Kansas and which anticipates some issues about euthanasia encountered in Chapters 6 and 7. An elderly woman lay ill and dying. Her suffering came to be too much for her and her faithful husband of fifty-four years to endure, so she requested that he kill her. Stricken with grief and unable to bring himself to perform the act, the husband hired another man to kill his wife. An act utilitarian might reason that in this case hiring another to kill the woman was justified, although in general we would not permit persons to perform such actions. After all, only this woman and her husband were directly affected, and relief of her pain was the main issue. It would be unfortunate, the act utilitarian might reason, if our "rules" against killing failed to allow for selective killings in extenuating circumstances, because it is extremely difficult to generalize from case to case. The jury, as it turned out, convicted the husband of murder, and he was sentenced to twenty-five years in prison. An act utilitarian might maintain that a *rigid* application of rules inevitably leads to injustices and that rule utilitarianism cannot escape this problem of an undue rigidity of rules.

Many philosophers object vigorously to act utilitarianism, charging its exponents with basing morality on mere expediency. On act-utilitarian grounds, they say, it is desirable for a physician to kill babies with many kinds of birth defects if the death of the child would relieve the family and society of a burden and inconvenience and thus would lead to the greatest good for the greatest number. Many opponents of act utilitarianism have thus argued that strict rules, which cannot be set aside for the sake of convenience, must be maintained. Many of these apparently desirable rules can be justified by the principle of utility, so utilitarianism need not be abandoned if act utilitarianism is judged unworthy.

Rule utilitarians pick up on this point and hold that rules have a central position in morality and cannot be compromised by the demands of particular situations. Compromise would threaten rules, whose effectiveness is judged by determining whether the observance of a given rule would, in theory, maximize social utility better than would any substitute rule (or having no rule). Utilitarian rules are, in theory, firm and protective of all classes of individuals, just as human rights (as we will later see) firmly protect all individuals regardless of social convenience and momentary need.

Still, we should ask whether rule-utilitarian theories offer substantially more than act utilitarianism. Dilemmas often arise that involve conflicts among moral rules; for example, rules of confidentiality conflict with rules protecting individual welfare, as in the Tarasoff case found in Chapter 3. If there are no rules to resolve these conflicts, perhaps the rule utilitarian simply becomes an act utilitarian.

KANTIAN THEORIES

We have seen that utilitarianism conceives the moral life in terms of intrinsic value and the means to produce this value. A second type of theory departs significantly from this approach. Often called *deontological* (i.e., a theory that some features of actions other than or in addition to consequences make actions obligatory), this type is now increasingly called *Kantian*, because of its origins in the theory of Immanuel Kant (1724–1804).

Duties from Rules of Reason. Kant believes that an act is morally praiseworthy only if done neither for self-interested reasons nor as the result of a natural disposition, but rather from *duty.* That is, the person's motive for acting must be a recognition of the act as resting on duty. It is not good enough, in Kant's view, that one merely performs the morally correct action, because one could perform one's duty for self-interested reasons having nothing to do with morality. For example, if an employer discloses a health hazard to an employee only because he or she fears a lawsuit, and not because of a belief in the importance of truth telling, then this employer acts rightly but deserves no moral credit for the action.

Kant tries to establish the ultimate basis for the validity of moral rules in pure reason, not in intuition, conscience, or utility. Kant thinks all considerations of utility and self-interest secondary, because the moral worth of an agent's action depends exclusively on the moral acceptability of the rule on the basis of which the person is acting. An action has moral worth only when performed by an agent who possesses a good will, and a person has a good will only if moral duty based on a universally valid rule is the sole motive for the action. Morality, then, provides a rational framework of principles and rules that constrain and guide everyone, without regard to their personal goals and interests. Moral rules apply universally, and the ultimate basis of moral principles is in human reason.

Kant's supreme principle, also called "the moral law," is expressed in several ways in his writings. In what appears to be his favored formulation, the principle is stated as follows: "I ought never to act except in such a way that I can also will that my maxim should become a universal law." This Kantian principle has often been compared to the golden rule, but Kant calls it the "categorical imperative." He gives several examples of moral maxims required by this fundamental principle: "Help others in distress"; "Do not commit suicide"; and "Work to develop your abilities." The categorical imperative is categorical, he argues, because it admits of no exceptions and is absolutely binding. It is imperative because it gives instruction about how one must act.

Kant clarifies this basic moral law — the condition of morality, in his view — by drawing a distinction between a categorical imperative and a hypothetical imperative. A hypothetical imperative takes the form "If I want to achieve such and such an end, then I must do so and so." These prescriptions — so reminiscent of utilitarian thinking — tell us what we must do, provided that we already have certain desires, interests, or goals. An example would be "If you want to regain your health, then you must take this medication," or "If you want to improve infant mortality rates, then you must improve your hospital facilities." These imperatives are obviously not commanded for their own sake. They are commanded only as means to an end that has already been willed or accepted. Hypothetical imperatives are not moral imperatives in Kant's philosophy because moral imperatives tell us what must be done independently of our goals or desires.

Kant emphasizes the notion of "rule as universal law." Rules that determine duty are made correct by their universality, that is, the fact that they apply consistently to everyone. This criterion of universality offers some worthwhile lessons for bioethics. Some of the clearest cases of immoral behavior involve a person trying to make a unique exception of himself or herself purely for personal reasons. Obviously this conduct could not be made universal, or else the rules presupposed by the idea of "being an exception" would be destroyed. If carried out consistently by others, this conduct would violate the rules presupposed by the system of morality, thereby rendering the system inconsistent — that is, having inconsistent rules of operation.

Kant's view is that wrongful practices, including invasion of privacy, theft, cheating, and bribes, are "contradictory"; that is, they are not consistent with what they presuppose.

Consider cases of promising, information disclosure, and lying, as found in Chapter 3 of this volume. If one were consistently to recommend the rule "Lie when it works to your advantage," practices of truth telling would be inconsistent with such a rule. The universalization of rules that allow lying would entitle everyone to lie to you, just as you could lie to them. In this event, one could never tell if a person were telling the truth or lying. Such a rule would be inconsistent with the practice of truth telling it presupposes. Similarly, fraud in research is inconsistent with the practice of publishing the truth. How could one cheat in research if there were no criteria that assumed honesty? All such practices are inconsistent with a rule or practice that they presuppose.

The Requirement to Never Treat Persons as Means. Kant states his categorical imperative in another and distinctly different formulation (which many interpreters take to be a wholly different principle). This form is probably more widely quoted and endorsed in contemporary philosophy than the first form, and certainly it is more frequently invoked in bioethics. Kant's later formulation stipulates that "One must act to treat every person as an end and never as a means only." This imperative insists that one must treat persons as having their own autonomously established goals and that one must never treat them solely as the means to one's own personal goals.

It has been widely stated in contemporary textbooks that Kant is arguing categorically that we can never treat another as a means to our ends. This interpretation, however, misrepresents his views. He argues only that we must not treat another *exclusively* as a means to our own ends. When adult human research subjects are asked to volunteer to test new drugs, for example, they are treated as a means to someone else's ends (perhaps society's ends), but they are not exclusively used for others' purposes, because they do not become mere servants or objects. Their consent legitimates using them as means to the end of research.

Kant's imperative demands only that persons in such situations be treated with the respect and moral dignity to which all persons are entitled at all times, including the times when they are used as means to the ends of others. To treat persons merely as means, strictly speaking, is to disregard their personhood by exploiting or otherwise using them without regard to their own thoughts, interests, and needs. It involves a failure to acknowledge that every person has a worth and dignity equal to that of every other person.

Contemporary Kantian Ethics. Several writers in contemporary ethical theory have defended a Kantian account. One theory has been a major force in stimulating the use of Kantian insights in contemporary ethical theory. John Rawls argues that vital moral considerations, such as individual rights and the just distribution of goods among individuals, depend less on social factors, such as individual worth, self-respect, and autonomy.[3] Rawls uses a hypothetical social contract, in which valid principles are those to which we would all agree if we could freely consider the social situation from an impartial standpoint, which he calls the "original position." In the original position all individuals are equally ignorant of the individual characteristics and advantages they personally possess or will possess. Persons in the original position know that they live together in a cooperative venture, but they are blinded to their individual desires, interests, and objectives. In Kant's terms, they are purely rational agents behind what Rawls calls a "veil of ignorance."[4]

Rawls aligns his original position with the Kantian theory of reason and self-legislation: Individuals give themselves the law from the perspective of rationality alone. Autonomy is moral self-governance through a structure of reason and will that is common to all rational agents: Persons are autonomous in the original position, because they choose and give to themselves the moral law out of their nature as rational, independent, and mutually disinterested persons.

Rawls considers Henry Sidgwick's objection to Kant that the principles of the scoundrel and the principles of the saint could both be accepted autonomously. Rawls appropriately argues that this objection springs from a misunderstanding of Kantian theory. Although a free self *could* choose as a scoundrel would, this choice would be inconsistent with the choices that rational beings expressing their nature as such would make. For Rawls, any philosophy in which the right to individual autonomy legitimately outweighs the dictates of objective moral principles is unacceptable. Even courageous and conscientious actions do not merit respect unless they accord with objective moral principles. If society restricts conscientious actions that violate valid public principles, "there is no violation of our [moral] autonomy," because these acts are not morally autonomous—no matter how freely and conscientiously chosen.[5]

Although Rawls has expressed many important Kantian themes, he stops short of making a full commitment to Kant's moral theory. The same can also be said of many contemporary Kantians.

CONTEMPORARY CHALLENGES TO THE TRADITIONAL THEORIES

Thus far we have treated only two types of theory: utilitarianism and Kantianism. These theories combine a variety of moral considerations into a surprisingly systematized framework, centered around a single major principle. Much is attractive in these theories, and they have been the dominant models in ethical theory throughout much of the twentieth century. So dominant have the models been that they have sometimes been presented as the only types of ethical theory. From this perspective, one must choose between them, as if there were no available alternative. However, much recent philosophical writing has focused on weaknesses in these theories and on ways in which the two theories actually affirm a similar conception of the moral life oriented around universal principles and rules.

Critics of utilitarian and Kantian models believe that the contrast between the two types of theory has been overestimated and that they do not merit the attention they have received and the lofty position they have occupied. Three popular replacements for, or perhaps supplements to, utilitarian and Kantian theories are (1) virtue theories (based on character traits), (2) the ethics of care (which is relationship-based), and (3) casuistry (which is case-based). These are the topics of the next three sections.

VIRTUE ETHICS

In discussing utilitarian and Kantian theories, we have looked chiefly at obligations and rights. Beyond obligations and rights, we often reflect on the agents who perform actions, have motives, and follow principles. We commonly make judgments about good and evil character in persons. In recent years, several philosophers have proposed that ethics should redirect its preoccupation with principles of obligation and look to decision making by persons of good character, that is, virtuous persons.

Virtue ethics descends from the classical Hellenistic tradition represented by Plato and Aristotle. Here the cultivation of virtuous traits of character is viewed as morality's primary function. Aristotle held that virtue is neither a feeling nor an innate capacity, but rather a disposition bred from an innate capacity properly trained and exercised. People acquire virtues much as they do skills such as carpentry, playing an instrument, or cooking. They become just by performing just actions and become temperate by performing temperate actions. Virtuous character, says Aristotle, is neither natural nor unnatural; it is cultivated and made a part of the individual, much like a language or tradition.

But an ethics of virtue is more than habitual training. This approach relies even more than does Kant's theory on the importance of having a correct *motivational structure*. A person's *characteristic* motivational structure is central, because we are dealing with character. We try to look at the inner dimension of persons, rather than settling for the outer actions they perform. A just person, for example, not only has a disposition to act fairly, but has a morally appropriate desire to do so. The person characteristically has a moral concern and reservation about acting in a way that would be unfair. Having only the motive to act in accordance with a rule of obligation, as Kant demands, is not morally sufficient for virtue. Imagine a Kantian who always performs his or her obligation because it is an obligation, but intensely dislikes having to allow the interests of others to be of importance. Such a person, let us imagine, does not cherish, feel congenial toward, or think fondly of others, and respects them only because obligation requires it. This person can nonetheless, on a theory of moral obligation such as Kant's or Mill's, perform a morally right action, have an ingrained disposition to perform that action, and act with obligation as the foremost motive. It is possible (1) to be disposed to do what is right, (2) to intend to do it, and (3) to do it, while also (4) yearning to be able to avoid doing it. If the motive is improper, a vital moral ingredient is missing; and if a person *characteristically* lacks this motivational structure, a necessary condition of virtuous character is absent.

Consider a physician who meets his moral obligations but whose underlying motives and desires are morally inappropriate. This physician detests his job and hates having to spend time with every patient who comes through the door. He cares not at all about being of service to people or creating a better environment in the office. All he wants to do is make money and avoid malpractice suits. Although this man meets his moral obligations, something in his character is deeply defective morally. The admirable compassion guiding the lives of many dedicated health professionals is absent in this person, who merely engages in rule-following behavior.

There is another reason why virtue ethics may be of value for biomedical ethics. A morally good person with right desires or motives is more likely to understand what should be done, more likely to perform required acts, and more likely to form and act on moral ideals than a morally bad person. A person who is ordinarily trusted is one who has an ingrained motivation and desire to perform right actions, and who characteristically cares about morally appropriate responses. A person who simply follows rules of obligation and who otherwise exhibits no special moral character may not be trustworthy. Not the rule follower, then, but the person disposed by *character* to be generous, caring, compassionate, sympathetic, and fair is the one recommended, praised, and held up as a moral model.

A proponent of character ethics need not claim that analysis of the virtues subverts or discredits ethical principles and rules. It is enough to argue that ethical theory is more complete if the virtues are included and that moral motives deserve to be at center stage in a way some leading traditional theories have inadequately appreciated. Whenever the feelings, concerns, and attitudes of others are the morally relevant matters, rules and principles are not as likely as human warmth and sensitivity to lead us to notice what should be done. Even a seldom noticed virtue, such as cheerfulness or tactfulness, can be far more important than standard rules in some contexts. Also, forms of loyalty, reliability, and commitment to other persons can, across time, be more integral to an adequate or full moral life than following principles or rules.

THE ETHICS OF CARE

Related to virtue ethics in some respects is a relatively new body of moral reflection often called the "ethics of care." This theory develops some of the themes in virtue ethics about the centrality of character, but the ethics of care focuses on a set of character traits that people all deeply value in close personal relationships: sympathy, compassion, fidelity, love, friendship, and the like. Noticeably absent are universal moral rules and impartial utilitarian calculations such as those espoused by Kant and Mill. The origin of the ethics of care was predominantly in feminist writings, and many still consider the ethics of care to be a feminist theory.

To understand this approach, consider again the traditional theories' criterion of impartiality in moral judgment. This criterion of distanced fairness, equal rights, and treating similar cases similarly makes eminently good sense for courts, but does it make good sense of intimate moral relationships? The care perspective views this criterion as cutting away too much of morality in order to get to a standpoint of detached fairness. Lost in the traditional *detachment* of impartiality is *attachment*—that which we care about most and which is closest to us. In seeking blindness, we may be made blind and indifferent to the special needs of others. So, although impartiality is a moral virtue in some contexts, it may be a moral vice in others. The care perspective is especially important for roles such as parent, friend, physician, and nurse, where contextual response, attentiveness to subtle clues, and discernment are likely to be more important morally than impartial treatment.

An aversion to abstract principles of obligation—the instruments of impartiality—is also characteristic of the ethics of care. Defenders of the ethics of care find principles often to be irrelevant, vacuous, or ineffectual in the moral life. A defender of principles could say that principles of care, compassion, and kindness structure our understanding of when it is appropriate to respond in caring, compassionate, and kind ways, but there is something hollow about this claim. It seems truer to our moral experience to say that we rely on our emotions, our capacity for sympathy, our sense of friendship, and our knowledge of how caring people behave.

Principles can function to separate moral agents from the particularities of their individual lives and inappropriately separate moral problems from social and historical facts. Exponents of the ethics of care have similarly criticized the autonomous, unified, rational beings that typify both the Kantian and the utilitarian conception of the moral self. They argue that moral decisions often require a sensitivity to the situation, as well as an awareness of the beliefs, feelings, attitudes, and concerns of each of the individuals involved and of the relationships of those individuals to one another.

Firmly rejected, then, are contractarian models of ethics, with their emphasis on justice, rights, and *autonomous choice* among *free* and *equal* agents. Here the ethics of care offers a fundamental rethinking of the moral universe: The terms of social cooperation, especially in families and in communal decision making, are, as Annette Baier writes, *unchosen*, *intimate,* and among *unequals*. The contractarian model fails, Baier claims, to appreciate that parents and health professionals, for example, do not see their responsibilities to their children and patients in terms of contracts or universal rules, but rather in terms of care, needs, sustenance, and loving attachment.[6]

Additional reasons exist for thinking that a morality centered on care and concern cannot be squeezed into a morality of rules. For example, it seems very difficult to express the responsibilities of a health care professional adequately through principles and rules. We can generalize about how caring physicians and nurses respond in encounters with patients, but these generalizations do not amount to principles, nor will such generalizations be subtle enough to give sound guidance for the next patient. Each situation calls for a different set of responses, and behavior that in one context is caring seems to intrude on privacy or be offensive in another context.

The care ethic, then, suggests that we need a corrective to two centuries of system-building in ethical theory and to the tendency to neglect themes such as sympathy, the moral emotions, and women's experiences. A morality centered on care and concern can potentially serve health care ethics in a constructive and balanced fashion, because it is close to the processes of reason and feeling exhibited in clinical contexts. We have seen that human warmth, sympathy, friendliness, compassion, and trust cannot easily be brought under rules of behavior or even under a principle such as beneficence. Physician and nursing ethics have recently been presented in codes that express obligations and rights, but the ethics of care can retrieve basic commitments of caring and caretaking and help free health professionals from an unduly narrow conception of their role responsibilities.

Disclosures, discussions, and decision making in health care typically become a family affair, with support from a health care team. The ethics of care fits this context of relationships, whereas rights theory, for example, seems poorly equipped for it. The ethics of care frames responsibilities in terms of meeting the health as well as other human needs of patients and their families, role commitments, concerns about causing harm, protecting positive family relationships, and the like. This may help explain why rights and principled obligations do not always capture the moral essence of clinical encounters.

CASUISTRY

Joining character ethics and the ethics of care in objecting to traditional theories is a recent revival of an approach of impressive influence during the medieval and early modern periods. Labeled "casuistry," this approach focuses on practical decision making about particular cases in which the judgments made cannot simply be brought under general norms such as principles and rules. Casuists are skeptical of rules, rights, and theory divorced from history and circumstance: One can make successful moral judgments of agents and actions, casuists say, only when one has an intimate understanding of particular situations and an appreciation of treating similar cases similarly.

A major model for ethical theory in the nineteenth and twentieth centuries has been the model of a unified theory. The hope has been to find what is most general and universal, expressed in precise principles in which we have a high measure of confidence of the sort found in scientific theory. Casuists say ethics is not a science, but a matter of wisdom and prudence. It is not the person filled with moral certainty or the person of rigid principles that we trust; rather, it is the person ready to conform principles to circumstances by reasoning through particular cases and making judgments.

How exactly, the casuist asks, is a moral judgment made? Whatever the full answer, the casuist believes it cannot come through traditional appeals to general principles and rules, for at least two reasons. First, various forms of moral thinking and judgment do not involve appeals to rules, rights, or virtues. The casuist holds that we sometimes appeal to narratives or paradigm cases, to classification schemes, to precedents, and even to immediate intuition. Consider an analogy to the way a physician thinks in making a judgment and then a recommendation to a patient. Many individual factors, including the patient's medical history, the physician's successes with other similar patients, paradigms of expected outcomes, and the like will play a role in formulating a judgment and recommendation to this patient, which may be very different from the recommendation made to the next patient with the same malady. So it is with moral judgment and recommendation.

Second, although rules or principles need not be excluded from patterns of moral thinking, the casuist insists that moral judgments are made when there can be no further appeals to principles. For example, when principles, rules, or rights conflict, and appeal to higher principle, rule, or right has been exhausted, we still must make moral judgments. Again, we may invoke a paradigm, a model, a story, an analogy, an intuition, or a discerning insight; but we cannot rely purely on principles.

Casuists also see a link between judgments about particular cases and authoritative moral judgments. An analogy to law is helpful in understanding the casuist's point. In case law, the normative judgments of a majority of judges become authoritative, and it is reasonable to hold that these judgments are the primary normative judgments for later judges who assess other cases. Cases in ethics are similar: Normative judgments emerge through majoritarian consensus in society and in institutions because careful attention has been paid to the details of particular problem cases. That consensus then becomes authoritative and is extended to relevantly similar cases.

At first sight, casuistry seems strongly opposed to the framework of principles and rules at work in traditional moral theory. However, closer inspection of casuistry shows that its primary concern is with an *excessive* reliance in recent philosophy on impartial, universal action-guides. Two casuists, Albert Jonsen and Stephen Toulmin, write that "*good* casuistry . . . applies general principles to particular cases with discernment." An account with "general rules" is thus not a rival of "casuistry." Rather, the casuist holds that as a history of similar cases and similar judgments mounts, we become more confident in our judgments. A "locus of moral certitude" arises in the judgments, and the stable elements crystallize in the form of tentative principles. As confidence in these generalizations increases, they are accepted less tentatively and moral knowledge develops. Just as case law (legal rules) develops incrementally from legal decisions in actual cases, so the moral law (moral rules) develops incrementally.[7]

From the casuists' perspective, moral reasoning is similar to that of a physician in clinical diagnosis: Paradigms of proper treatment function as sources of comparison when new problem-cases arise. Recommendations are made by analogy to the paradigm. If the analogy is proper, a resolution of the problem and a recommendation will be achieved; but if there is no close analogy, uncertainty may remain. Presumably no prior appeal to principles or theory is needed. However, ethical theory is both possible and desirable: Case-based judgment that rests on plausible intuition is, as Baruch Brody puts it,

only the *first* stage in the process of coming to have moral knowledge. The *next* stage is that of theory formation. . . . The goal is to find a theory that systematizes these intuitions, explains them, and provides help in dealing with cases about which we have no intuitions. In the course of this systematization, it may be necessary to reject some of the initial intuitions on the grounds that they cannot be systematized into the theory.[8]

Today's casuists have resourcefully reminded us of the importance of analogical reasoning, paradigm cases, and practical judgment. Biomedical ethics, like ethical theory, has unduly minimized this avenue to moral knowledge. Casuists also have rightly pointed out that generalizations are often best learned, accommodated, and implemented by using cases, case discussion, and case methods. These insights can be utilized by connecting them to an appropriate set of concepts, principles, and theories that control the judgments we make about cases.

MAJOR ETHICAL PRINCIPLES

How are we to determine, in light of the preceding theories and analysis of justification, whether a particular action is morally acceptable? Understandably, this question is complex, and there is no way to answer it with confident finality. But this much seems reasonable to assume: If a particular act is wrong, then it will have certain similarities, certain shared features, with other wrong actions; conversely, if a particular act is morally required, it will share similar features with other actions that are morally required. Philosophers who have tried to develop a general normative theory of right and wrong have attempted to discover these shared features. Often they are formulated as *principles* that hold across a range of cases.

Despite the reservations about principles discussed in the previous section, if we are to take a reasoned approach to the range of problems in bioethics, we need principles that help us to take a consistent position on specific and related issues. Three general moral principles have proved to be serviceable as a framework of principles for bioethics: respect for autonomy, beneficence, and justice. These three principles should not be construed as jointly forming a complete moral system or theory, but they are sufficiently comprehensive to provide an analytical framework through which we can begin to reason about problems in bioethics.

However, one caution is in order about the nature and use of principles. Moral thinking and judgment, the formation of public policies, must take account of many considerations besides ethical principles and rules, because principles do not contain sufficient content. To be used in moral judgment, moral principles must be made more specific for a context and must also take account of problems of feasibility and political procedures. Principles provide a starting point for moral judgment and policy evaluation, but, as we saw in the previous section and will see below in the section on public policy, more content is needed than that supplied by principles alone. They are tested and reliable starting points, but they rarely are sufficient for moral thinking.

RESPECT FOR AUTONOMY

Respect for autonomy is a frequently mentioned moral principle in bioethics. It is a principle rooted in the liberal Western tradition of the importance of individual freedom and choice, but "autonomy" and "respect for autonomy" are terms loosely associated with several ideas, such as privacy, voluntariness, self-mastery, choosing freely, the freedom to choose, choosing one's own moral position, and accepting responsibility for one's choices.

Historically, the word "autonomy" is a legacy from ancient Greece, where *autos* (self) and *nomos* (rule or law) were joined to refer to political self-governance in the city-state. In moral philosophy personal autonomy has come to refer to personal self-governance: personal rule of the self by adequate understanding while remaining free from controlling interferences by others and from personal limitations that prevent choice. "Autonomy," so understood, has been analyzed in terms of freedom from external constraint and the presence of critical mental capacities such as understanding, planning, and deciding.

It is one thing to be autonomous and another to be *respected* as autonomous. Many issues in bioethics concern failures to respect autonomy, ranging from manipulative underdisclosure of pertinent information to nonrecognition of a refusal of medical interventions. To respect an autonomous agent is to recognize with due appreciation that person's capacities and perspective, including his or her right to hold certain views, to make certain choices, and to take certain actions based on personal values and beliefs. Such respect has historically been connected to the idea that persons possess an intrinsic value independent of special circumstances that confer value. As expressed in Kantian ethics, autonomous persons are ends in themselves, determining their own destiny, and are not to be treated merely as means to the ends of others. Thus, the burden of moral justification rests on those who would restrict or prevent a person's exercise of autonomy.

The moral demand that we respect the autonomy of persons can be formulated as a principle of respect for autonomy: *Autonomy of action should not be subjected to controlling constraint by others*. The principle provides the justificatory basis for the right to make decisions, which in turn takes the form of specific autonomy-related rights. For example, in the debate over whether autonomous, informed patients have the right to refuse self-regarding, life-sustaining medical interventions, the principle of respect for autonomy suggests a morally appropriate response. But the principle covers even simple exchanges in the medical world, such as listening carefully to patients' questions, answering the questions in the detail that respectfulness would demand, and not treating patients in a patronizing fashion.

To respect the autonomy of such self-determining agents is to recognize them as *entitled* to determine their own destiny, with due regard to their considered evaluations and view of the world. They must be accorded the moral right to have their own opinions and to act upon them (as long as those actions produce no moral violation). Thus, in evaluating the self-regarding actions of others, we are obligated to respect them as persons with the same right to their judgments as we possess to our own, and they in turn are obligated to treat us in the same way.

Medical and nursing codes have begun in recent years to include rules that are explicitly based on this principle. For example, the first principle of the American Nurses' Association *Code* reads as follows:

The fundamental principle of nursing practice is respect for the inherent dignity and worth of every client. Nurses are morally obligated to respect human existence and the individuality of all persons who are the recipients of nursing actions. . . . Truth telling and the process of reaching informed choice underlie the exercise of self-determination, which is basic to respect for persons. Clients should be as fully involved as possible in the planning and implementation of their own health care.[9]

The controversial problems with the noble-sounding principle of respect for autonomy, as with all moral principles, arise when we must interpret its significance for particular contexts and determine precise limits on its application and how to handle situations when it conflicts with such other moral principles as beneficence and justice. The best known problems of conflict involve overriding refusals of treatment by patients, as in Jehovah's Witnesses' refusals of blood transfusions.

Many controversies involve questions about the conditions under which a person's right to autonomous expression demands actions by others and also questions about the restrictions society may rightfully place on choices by patients or subjects when these choices conflict with other values. If an individual's choices endanger the public health, potentially harm another party, or involve a scarce resource for which a patient cannot pay, it may be justifiable to restrict exercises of autonomy. If restriction is in order, the justification will rest on some competing moral principle such as beneficence or justice. This issue of both *specifying* and *balancing* the demands made by conflicting moral principles can now be seen to apply to each of these principles.

BENEFICENCE

The welfare of patients is the goal of health care. This welfare objective is medicine's context and justification: Clinical therapies are aimed at the promotion of health by cure or prevention of disease. This value has long been treated as a foundational value — and sometimes as *the* foundational value — in medical and nursing ethics. Among the most quoted principles in the history of codes of medical ethics is the maxim *primum non nocere:* "Above all, do no harm." Although the origins of this abstract principle are obscure and its implications often unclear, it has appeared in many medical writings and codes, and it was present in nursing codes as early as Florence Nightingale's *Pledge for Nurses.* Many current medical and nursing codes assert that the health professional's "primary commitment" is to protect the patient from harm and to promote the patient's welfare.

Other duties in medicine, nursing, public health, and research are expressed in terms of a *more positive* obligation to come to the assistance of those in need of treatment or in danger of injury. In the International Code of Nursing Ethics, for example, it is said that "[T]he nurse shares with other citizens the responsibility for initiating and supporting action to meet the health and social needs of the public."[10] Various sections of the Principles of Medical Ethics of the American Medical Association express a virtually identical point of view.

The range of duties requiring abstention from harm and positive assistance may be conveniently clustered under the single heading of "beneficence." This term has a broad set of meanings, including the doing of good and the active promotion of good, kindness, and charity. But in the present context the principle of beneficence has a narrower meaning: It requires us to abstain from injuring others and to help others further their important and legitimate interests, largely by preventing or removing possible harms.[11] Presumably such acts are required when they can be performed with minimal risk to the actors; one is not under an obligation of beneficence in all circumstances of risk.

According to William Frankena, the principle of beneficence can be expressed as including the following four elements: (1) One ought not to inflict evil or harm (a principle of nonmaleficence). (2) One ought to prevent evil or harm. (3) One ought to remove evil or harm. (4) One ought to do or promote good.[12] Frankena suggests that the fourth element may not be an obligation at all (being an act of benevolence that is over and above obligation) and contends that these elements appear in a hierarchical arrangement so that the first takes precedence over the second, the second over the third, and the third over the fourth.

There are philosophical reasons for separating passive nonmaleficence (as expressed in 1) and active beneficence (as expressed in 2–4). Ordinary moral thinking often suggests that certain duties not to injure others are more compelling than duties to benefit them. For example, we do not consider it justifiable to kill a dying patient in order to use the patient's organs to save two others. Similarly, the obligation not to injure a patient by abandonment seems to many stronger than the obligation to prevent injury to a patient who has been abandoned by another (under the assumption that both are moral duties).

Despite the attractiveness of this hierarchical ordering rule, it is not firmly sanctioned by either morality or ethical theory. The obligation expressed in (1) may not *always* outweigh those expressed in (2)–(4). For example, the harm inflicted in (1) may be negligible or trivial, whereas the harm to be prevented in (2) may be substantial: Saving a person's life by a blood transfusion clearly justifies the inflicted harm of venipuncture on the blood donor. One of the motivations for separating nonmaleficence from beneficence is that they themselves conflict when one must *either* avoid harm *or* bring aid. In such cases, one needs a decision procedure for choosing one alternative rather than another. But if the weights of the two principles can vary, as they can, there can be no mechanical decision rule asserting that one obligation must always outweigh the other.

Such problems lead us to unify the moral demands that we should benefit and not injure others under a single general label, even though there may be more than one principle of beneficence. We should, then, take care to distinguish, as necessary, between strong and weak requirements of this principle. In its general form, then, the principle of beneficence requires us to abstain from intentionally injuring others and to further the important and legitimate interests of others.

One of the most vexing problems in ethical theory is the extent to which the principle of beneficence generates *general moral duties* that are incumbent on everyone — not because of a professional role but because morality itself makes a general demand of beneficence. Any analysis of beneficence, in the broad sense delineated above, would potentially demand severe sacrifice and extreme generosity in the moral life, for example, giving a kidney for transplantation or donating bone marrow. As a result, some philosophers have argued that this form of beneficent action is virtuous and a moral *ideal*, but not an obligation. From this perspective, the positive benefiting of others is based on professional obligations or personal ideals that are praiseworthy but not obligatory: We are not *required* by the general canons of morality to promote the good of persons, even if we are in a position to do so and the action is morally *justified*.

Several proposals have been offered in moral philosophy to resolve this problem by showing that beneficence *is* a principle of obligation, but these theoretical ventures are extraneous to our concerns here. The scope or range of acts required by the obligation of beneficence is an undecided issue, and perhaps an undecidable one. Fortunately, we do not need a resolution in the present context. That we are morally obligated on *some* occasions to assist others — at least in professional roles such as nursing, medicine, and research — is hardly a matter of moral controversy. Beneficent acts are demanded by the roles involved in fiduciary relationships between health care professionals and patients, lawyers and clients, researchers and subjects (at least in therapeutic research), bankers and customers, and so on.

We will treat the basic roles and concepts that give substance to the principle of beneficence in medicine as follows: The positive benefits the physician and nurse are obligated to seek all involve the alleviation of disease and injury, if there is a reasonable hope of cure. The harms to be prevented, removed, or minimized are the pain, suffering, and disability of injury and disease. In addition, the physician and nurse are of course enjoined from *doing* harm if interventions inflict unnecessary pain and suffering on patients.

Those engaged in both medical practice and research know that risks of harm presented by interventions must constantly be weighed against possible benefits for patients, subjects, and the public. The physician or nurse who professes to "do no harm" is not pledging never to cause harm, but rather to strive to create a positive balance of goods over inflicted harms. This is recognized in the Nuremberg Code, which enjoins: "The degree of risk to be taken should never exceed that determined by the humanitarian importance of the problem to be solved by the experiment." Such a balancing principle is essential to any sound moral system: Beneficence assumes an obligation to weigh and balance benefits against harms, benefits against alternative benefits, and harms against alternative harms. When a life is at stake, it may be justified to take high risks of harm and death.

Health care professionals and research investigators often disagree over how to weigh and balance the various factors, and there may be no objective evidence that dictates one course rather than another. In clinical contexts, this balancing can also present situations in which health care professionals and patients differ in their assessments of the professional's obligations. In some cases, benefit to a third party is involved, as, for example, when a pregnant woman refuses a physician's recommendation of fetal surgery. In other cases, the refusal may be exclusively self-regarding. Some health care professionals will accept a patient's refusal as valid, whereas others are inclined to ignore the fact that an informed consent to treatment has not been given, and so try to "benefit" the patient through a medical intervention.

This problem of whether to override the decisions of patients in order to benefit them or prevent harm to them is one dimension of the problem of medical paternalism, in which a parental-like decision by a professional overrides an autonomous decision of a patient. This problem of paternalism is treated in detail later in this introduction in the section on Law, Authority, and Autonomy. It is shown there how the problem of paternalism is generated by a conflict between principles of respect for autonomy and beneficence, each of which can be and has been conceived by different parties as the overriding principle in cases of conflict. This conflict between the demands of beneficence and respect for autonomy underlies a broad range of controversies in this volume.

JUSTICE

Every civilized society is a cooperative venture structured by moral, legal, and cultural principles that define the terms of social cooperation. Beneficence and respect for autonomy are principles in this fabric of social order, but *justice* has been the subject of more treatises on the terms of social cooperation than any other principle. A person has been treated justly if treated according to what is fair, due, or owed. For example, if equal political rights are due all citizens, then justice is done when those rights are accorded. Any denial of a good, service, or piece of information to which a person has a right or entitlement based in justice is an injustice. It is also an injustice to place an undue burden on the exercise of a right; for example, to make a piece of information owed to a person unreasonably difficult to obtain.

The term *distributive justice* refers to fair, equitable, and appropriate distribution in society determined by justified norms of distribution that structure part of the terms of social cooperation. Usually this term refers to the distribution of primary social goods, such as economic goods and fundamental political rights. But social burdens must also be considered. Paying taxes and being drafted into the armed services to fight a war are distributed burdens; Medicare checks and grants to do research are distributed benefits. Recent literature on distributive justice has tended to focus on considerations of fair economic distribution, especially unjust distributions in the form of inequalities of income between different classes of persons and unfair tax burdens on certain classes. But many problems of distributive justice exist besides issues about income and wealth, including the issues raised in prominent contemporary debates over health care distribution, as discussed in Chapter 10.

There is no single principle of justice. Somewhat like principles under the heading of beneficence, there are several principles of justice, each requiring specification in particular contexts. But common to almost all theories of justice is a minimal, beginning principle: Like cases should be treated alike, or, to use the language of equality, equals ought to be treated equally and unequals unequally. This elementary principle is referred to as the formal principle of justice, or sometimes as the formal principle of equality—formal because it states no particular respects in which people ought to be treated. It merely asserts that whatever respects are under consideration, if persons are equal in those respects, they should be treated alike. Thus, the formal principle of justice does not tell us how to determine equality or proportion in these matters, and it therefore lacks substance as a specific guide to conduct. Equality must here be understood as "equality in the relevant respects." Many controversies about justice arise over what should be considered the relevant characteristics for equal treatment. Principles that specify these relevant characteristics are often said to be *material* because they identify relevant properties for distribution.

Because the formal principle leaves space for differences in the interpretation of how justice applies to particular situations, philosophers have developed diverse theories of justice that provide material principles and that defend the choice of principles. These theories attempt to be more specific than the formal principle by elaborating how people are to be compared and what it means to give people their due. The following is a sample list of major candidates for the position of valid principles of distributive justice (though longer lists have been proposed): (1) To each person an equal share. (2) To each person according to individual need. (3) To each person according to acquisition in a free market. (4) To each person according to individual effort. (5) To each person according to societal contribution. (6) To each person according to merit. There is no obvious barrier to acceptance of more than one of these principles, and some theories of justice accept all six as valid. Most societies use several principles in the belief that different rules are appropriate to different situations.

Egalitarian theories of justice emphasize equal access to primary goods; libertarian theories emphasize rights to social and economic liberty; and utilitarian theories emphasize a mixed use of such criteria so that public and private utility are maximized. The utilitarian theory follows the main lines of the explanation of utilitarianism above, and thus economic justice is viewed as one among a number of problems concerning how to maximize value. The ideal economic distribution, utilitarians argue, is any arrangement that would have this maximizing effect.

Egalitarianism holds that distributions of burdens and benefits in a society are just to the extent they are equal, and deviations from equality in distribution are unjust. Most egalitarian accounts of justice are guardedly formulated, so that only *some* basic equalities among individuals take priority over their differences. In recent years an egalitarian theory discussed above in the section on Kantian theories has enjoyed wide currency: John Rawls's *A Theory of Justice*. This book has as its central contention that we should distribute all economic goods and services equally except in those cases in which an unequal distribution would actually work to everyone's advantage, or at least would benefit the worst off in society.

Sharply opposed to egalitarianism is the libertarian theory of justice. What makes libertarian theories *libertarian* is the priority afforded to distinctive processes, procedures, or mechanisms for ensuring that liberty rights are recognized in economic practice—typically the rules and procedures governing social liberty and economic acquisition and exchange in free market systems. Because free choice is the pivotal goal, libertarians place a premium on the principle of respect for autonomy. In some libertarian systems, this principle is the sole basic moral principle, and there thus are no other principles of justice. We will see in Chapter 10 that many philosophers believe that this approach is fundamentally wrong because economic value is generated through an essentially communal process that our health policies must reflect if justice is to be done.

Libertarian theorists, however, explicitly reject the conclusion that egalitarian patterns of distribution represent a normative ideal. People may be equal in a host of morally significant respects (for example, entitled to equal treatment under the law and equally valued as ends in themselves), but the libertarian contends that it would be a basic violation of *justice* to regard people as deserving of equal economic returns. In particular, people are seen as having a fundamental right to own and dispense with the products of their labor as they choose, even if the exercise of this right leads to large inequalities of wealth in society. Equality and utility principles, from this libertarian perspective, sacrifice basic liberty rights to the larger public interest by coercively extracting financial resources through taxation.

These three theories of justice all capture some of our intuitive convictions about justice, and each exhibits strengths as a theory of justice. Perhaps, then, there are several equally valid, or at least equally defensible, theories of justice and just taxation. This situation of competing and apparently viable theories has led some writers to note that there seem to be severe limits to philosophy's capacity to resolve public-policy issues through theories of distributive justice. They believe these theories are simply unsuited for public-policy formulation. Just as we must specify and interpret principles, so we must balance competing considerations of justice.

Prima Facie Principles. W. D. Ross, a prominent twentieth-century British philosopher, developed a theory intended to assist us in resolving problems of a conflict between principles. Ross's views are based on an account of what he calls prima facie duties, which he contrasts with actual duties. A prima facie duty is a duty that is always to be acted upon unless it conflicts on a particular occasion with an equal or stronger duty. A prima facie duty, then, is always right and binding, all other things being equal; it is conditional on not being overridden or outweighed by competing moral demands. One's *actual* duty, by contrast, is determined by an examination of the respective weights of competing prima facie duties.

Ross argues that several valid principles, all of which can conflict, express moral duties (that is, obligations). These principles do not derive from either the principle of utility or Kant's categorical imperative. For example, our promises create duties of fidelity, wrongful actions create duties of reparation, and the generous gifts of our friends create duties of gratitude. Ross defends several additional duties, such as duties of self-improvement, nonmaleficence, beneficence, and justice. Unlike Kant's system and the utilitarian system, Ross's list of duties is not based on any overarching principle. He defends it simply as a reflection of our ordinary moral conventions and beliefs.

The idea that moral principles are absolute values that cannot be overridden has had a long but troubled history. Both utilitarians and Kantians have defended their basic rule (the principle of utility and the categorical imperative) as absolute, but this claim to absoluteness has been widely challenged. For Ross's reasons, among others, many moral philosophers have with increasing frequency come to regard principles, duties, and rights not as unbending standards but rather as strong prima facie moral demands that may be validly overridden in circumstances of competition with other moral claims.

Although Ross admits that neither he nor any moral philosopher has been able to present a system of moral rules free of conflicts and exceptions, he argues that this implication of the theory is no more of a problem for him than for anyone else, because the complexity of the moral life simply makes an exception-free hierarchy of rules and principles impossible. There has been a Ross-inspired trend in recent moral theory to believe that many different moral principles—for example, utility, justice, and respect for autonomy—are *equally weighted* in abstraction from particular circumstances. This proposal has proven particularly controversial, however. This is because many philosophers believe that some principle—be it of respect for autonomy or utility or justice—is more basic or has greater weight than other principles. This problem of how to value or weight different moral principles remains unresolved in contemporary moral theory.

The final section of this chapter will look at possible ways in which moral reasoning might assist in the formulation of public policy, whether by appeal to principles or to some other form of moral reflection.

ETHICS, LAW, AND PUBLIC POLICY

Moral principles are often already embedded in public morality and public policies, but if these values are already in place, how can philosophical development of principles or philosophical theory assist us in the complicated task of forming and criticizing law and public policy?

ETHICS AND PUBLIC AFFAIRS

Public policies are almost always motivated by and incorporate moral considerations. A public policy is comprised of a set of normative, enforceable guidelines that govern a particular area of conduct and that have been accepted by an official public body, such as an agency of government or a legislature. Moral analysis is part of good policy formation, not merely a method for evaluating already formed policy.

Many articles in this volume are concerned with the use of ethical theory for the formulation of public affairs. Joel Feinberg has made a suggestive comment about one way in which the problems raised in these essays might *ideally* be viewed:

It is convenient to think of these problems as questions for some hypothetical and abstract political body. An answer to the question of when liberty should be limited or how wealth ideally should be distributed, for example, could be used to guide not only moralists, but also legislators and judges toward reasonable decisions in particular cases where interests, rules, or the liberties of different parties appear to conflict. . . . We must think of an ideal legislator as somewhat abstracted from the full legislative context, in that he is free to appeal directly to the public interest unencumbered by the need to please voters, to make "deals" with colleagues, or any other merely "political" considerations. . . . The principles of the ideal legislator . . . are still of the first practical importance, since they provide a target for our aspirations and a standard for judging our successes and failures.[13]

However, such use of ideals is not the only approach to ethics and public policy. Policy formation and criticism usually involve complex interactions between moral values and cultural and political values. A policy will be shaped by relevant empirical data and information in relevant fields such as medicine, economics, law, and the like. By taking into consideration factors such as efficiency and clientele acceptance, we interpret principles so that they provide a practical strategy for real-world problems involving the demands of political procedures, legal constraints, uncertainty about risk, and the like. Moral principles and theories thereby can be made to fit contexts of cultural pluralism, political representation, and uncertainty about risk.[14]

In this book we will consider policies pertaining to euthanasia, ethics committees mandated for hospitals, public allocations for health care, regulation of risk in the workplace, protection of animal and human subjects of research, legislative definitions of death, liability for failures of disclosure and confidentiality, policies to control developments in genetics, the control of epidemics, and a host of other problems of ethics and public policy.

A specific example of ethics at work in the formulation of public policy is found in the work of the previously mentioned National Commission for the Protection of Human Subjects of Biomedical and Behavioral Research, which was established by a federal law. Its mandate was to develop ethical guidelines for the conduct of research involving human subjects and to make recommendations to the Department of Health and Human Services (DHHS). To discharge its duties, the commission studied the nature and extent of various forms of research, its purposes, the ethical issues surrounding the research, present federal regulations, and the views of representatives of professional societies and federal agencies. The commission engaged in extensive deliberations on these subjects in public, a process in which moral reasoning played as central a role as the information and methods supplied from other fields.

Subsequent government regulations regarding research issued by the relevant agency (DHHS) were developed on the basis of work provided by the commission. These public laws show the imprint of the commission in virtually every clause. The regulations cannot be regarded as exclusively ethical in orientation, but much distinctive ethical material is found in the commission documents, and ethical analysis provided the framework for its deliberations and recommendations. The commission also issued one exclusively philosophical volume, which sets forth the moral framework that underlies the various policy recommendations it made. It is among the best examples of the use of moral frameworks for actual (not merely theoretical or programmatic) policy development and of a philosophical publication issued through a government-sponsored body.

Several U.S. federal branches, agencies, and courts regularly use ethical premises in the development of their health policies, rules, or decisions. These include the Centers for Disease Control (CDC), the National Institutes of Health (NIH), the Office of Technology Assessment (OTA), and the U.S. Supreme Court. Ethical analysis also often plays a prominent role in policy formation in bioethics. Examples include the widely examined work of the Oregon legislature on rationing in health care, the New York Task Force on Life and the Law, and the New Jersey Bioethics Commission. Such commission reports and legislative actions raise vital questions explored at various points in this book about the proper relation between government and professional groups in formulating standards of practice.

The policies of corporations, hospitals, trade groups, and professional societies also sometimes have a deep impact on public policy, but these policies are private rather than public (although these bodies are frequently regulated by public policies). A far closer connection exists between law and public policy, as we will now see.

MORALITY AND LAW

Public policy often has the force of law, and the "morality" of many actions that have a public impact is often gauged by whether the law prohibits that form of conduct. Law is often the public's agent for translating morality into explicit social guidelines and practices and for stipulating punishments for offenses. Both case law (judge-made law expressed in court decisions) and statutory law (federal and state statutes and their accompanying administrative regulations) set standards for science, medicine, and health care, and these sources have deeply influenced bioethics. In these forms law has forced many issues before the public. Case law, in particular, has established influential precedents that provide material for reflection on both legal and moral questions. Prominent examples include judicial decisions about informed consent and terminating life-sustaining treatment. The line of court decisions since the Karen Ann Quinlan case in the mid-1970s constitutes in itself a source of moral reflection. Most of the chapters in this book contain selections from case law, and often selections in the chapters will mention actual or proposed statutory law.

Moral evaluation is often very different from *legal* evaluation, even when the two intersect. Issues of legal liability, costs to the system, practicability within the litigation process, and questions of compensation demand that legal requirements be different from moral requirements. Despite a set of shared interests held in morals and law, the law is not the repository of our moral standards and values, even when the law is directly concerned with moral problems. A law-abiding person is not necessarily morally sensitive or virtuous, and from the fact that something is legally acceptable, it does not follow that it is morally acceptable. Numerous failures to fulfill promises do not involve legal violations of contract but may nonetheless involve serious moral violations. Questions are raised in later chapters about the morality of many actions in medicine and research, such as the proper form of interaction with patients, although such actions are not illegal.

Issues of law and morality are commonly treated in public debate as if the only matter of abiding concern worthy of public scrutiny is whether a person has conformed to or violated the law. One problem with this approach is what often forms its bottom line: Individuals' conduct and institutional policies are judged *acceptable* because (1) there is no legal violation and (2) there is no apparent need for new rules to hold persons legally liable. Ignored is the fact that the conduct may be inappropriate and condemnable by the standards of morality.

Law and morality should therefore be kept distinct. It is often not a straightforward move from a judgment that an act of a certain type is morally right (or wrong) to a judgment that a law promoting or prohibiting the act is morally right (or wrong). Factors such as the deprivation of liberty and the cost of enforcement must be considered. For example, one can consistently hold that abortion is morally wrong without holding that the law should prohibit it. The judgment that an act is morally acceptable also does not imply that the law should permit it. For example, the moral position that various forms of euthanasia are morally justified is consistent with the thesis that the government should legally prohibit these acts, on grounds that it would not be possible to control potential abuses.

Bioethics in the United States is currently involved in a complex and mutually stimulating relationship with law. The law often appeals to moral duties and rights, places sanctions on violators, and in general strengthens the social importance of moral beliefs. Morality and law share concerns over matters of basic social importance and often acknowledge the same principles, obligations, and criteria of evidence. Nevertheless, the law rightly backs away from attempting to legislate against everything that is morally wrong. In recent years the judges have been searching in their opinions for extra-legal mechanisms such as peer review, committees, codes of ethics, and self-regulatory procedural mechanisms that will promote morally sound judgments while also avoiding entanglement with legislatures, regulatory agencies, and the courts. As the courts and legislatures become more pressed for time, it seems inevitable that procedures to protect ethical interests that are outside the reach of the law will assume greater significance.

LEGAL AND MORAL RIGHTS

Much of the modern ethical discussion that we shall encounter throughout this volume turns on ideas about rights, and many public policy issues concern rights or attempts to secure rights. Our political tradition itself has developed from a conception of human rights. However, until the seventeenth and eighteenth centuries, problems of social and political philosophy were rarely discussed in terms of rights, perhaps because duties to lord, king, state, church, and God had been the dominant focus of political and ethical theory. New political views were introduced at this point in history, including the notion of universal natural (or human) rights. Thus, historically, the notion of rights emerged from a need to check the sovereign power of states. Rights quickly came to be understood as powerful assertions of claims that demand respect and status.

Substantial differences exist between moral and legal rights, because legal systems do not formally require reference to moral systems for their understanding or grounding, nor do moral systems formally require reference to legal systems. One may have a legal right to do something patently immoral, or have a moral right without any corresponding legal guarantee. Legal rights are derived from political constitutions, legislative enactments, case law, and the executive orders of the highest state official. Moral rights, by contrast, exist independently of and form a basis for criticizing or justifying legal rights. Finally, legal rights can be eliminated simply by lawful amendments to political constitutions, or by a coup d'etat, but moral rights cannot be eroded or banished by political votes, powers, or amendments.

Philosophers have often drawn a distinction between positive and negative rights. A right to well-being—generally the right to receive goods and services—is a positive right, and a right to liberty—generally a right not to be interfered with—is a negative right. The right to liberty is a negative right because no one has to do anything to honor it. Presumably all that must be done to honor negative rights is to leave people alone. The same is not true with respect to positive rights. To honor those rights someone has to provide something. For example, if a person has a human right to well-being and is starving, then someone has an obligation to provide that person with food.

This distinction between positive and negative rights has led those who include various rights to well-being on the list of human rights to argue that the obligation to provide for positive rights falls on the political state. Others, however, wish to limit the power of the state to regulate our affairs, and they regard the protection of negative rights as the sole prerogative and responsibility of state officials. This important distinction between positive and negative rights is analyzed in the introduction to Chapter 10 under the subject of the right to health care, which is a positive right (if it exists).

Because general negative rights are rights of noninterference, their direct connection to individual self-determination is apparent. General positive rights require that all members of the community yield some of their resources to advance the welfare of others by providing social goods and services, and there is a natural connection in theories that emphasize positive rights to a communitarianism or sense of "the commons" that limits the scope of individualism. To generalize, the broader the scope of positive rights in a theory, the more likely that theory is to emphasize a scheme of social justice that confers positive rights to redistributions of resources.

Accordingly, a moral system composed of a powerful set of general negative obligations and rights is antithetical to a moral system composed of a powerful set of general positive obligations and rights, just as a strong individualism is opposed to a strong communitarianism. Rights of privacy and the pursuit of one's autonomous projects will inevitably conflict with obligations to assist or provide resources for others. Many of the conflicts that we encounter throughout this book spring from these basic differences over the existence and scope of negative and positive rights and obligations, especially regarding the number, types, and weight of *positive* rights and obligations.

LAW, AUTHORITY, AND AUTONOMY

Various autonomy rights are often said to be fundamental rights, but no right is strong enough to entail a right to unrestricted exercises of autonomy in the public life. The notion of "acceptable liberty" refers to actions in which people ought to be free to engage. Although it would be difficult to determine a set of right and wrong exercises of autonomy, some valid restrictions on our liberty are appropriate. But how many restrictions are valid?

Liberty-Limiting Principles. Various "moral" principles have been advanced in the attempt to establish valid grounds for the limitation of autonomy. The following four "liberty-limiting principles" have been defended and have played a significant role in recent philosophical controversies:

1. *The Harm Principle:* A person's liberty is justifiably restricted to prevent harm to others caused by that person.
2. *The Principle of Paternalism:* A person's liberty is justifiably restricted to prevent harm to self caused by that person.
3. *The Principle of Legal Moralism:* A person's liberty is justifiably restricted to prevent that person's immoral behavior.
4. *The Offense Principle:* A person's liberty is justifiably restricted to prevent offense to others caused by that person.

Each of these four principles represents an attempt to balance liberty and other values. Although different people assess the weight of certain values differentially in the balancing process, the harm principle is universally accepted as a valid liberty-limiting principle (despite certain unclarities that surround the notion of a harm). However, much controversy surrounds the other three liberty-limiting principles, and their general validity is widely doubted.

Only one of these controversial principles is pertinent to the controversies that arise in this volume: paternalism. Here the central problem is whether this form of justification for a restriction of liberty may ever validly be invoked, and, if so, how the principle that stands behind this judgment is to be formulated. In order to answer this question, we must look more closely at the nature of paternalism.

Paternalism. The word "paternalism" refers to treating individuals in the way that a parent treats his or her child. But in ethical theory the word is more narrowly used to apply to treatment that restricts individual autonomy: Paternalism is the intentional limitation of the autonomy of one person by another, where the person who limits autonomy appeals exclusively to grounds of beneficence for the person whose autonomy is limited. The essence of paternalism is an overriding of the principle of respect for autonomy on grounds of the principle of beneficence.

Several writers have argued that paternalism is pervasively present in modern society; many actions, rules, and laws are commonly justified by appeal to a paternalistic principle. Examples in medicine include court orders for blood transfusions when patients have refused them, involuntary commitment to institutions for treatment, intervention to stop "rational" suicides, resuscitating patients who have asked not to be resuscitated, withholding medical information that patients have requested, denial of an innovative therapy to someone who wishes to try it, and some government efforts to promote health. Other health-related examples include laws requiring motorcyclists to wear helmets and motorists to wear seat belts and the regulations of governmental agencies such as the Food and Drug Administration that prevent people from purchasing possibly harmful or inefficacious drugs and chemicals. In all cases the motivation is the beneficent promotion of health and welfare.

It is often said that the patient-physician relationship, the regulation of food and drugs, and many other parts of the health care system are essentially paternalistic. This view is tempting, because patients can be so ill that their judgments or voluntary abilities are significantly affected, or because they are incapable of grasping important information about their case, thus being in no position to reach carefully reasoned decisions about their medical treatment or their purchase of drugs. Such paternalism has been under attack in recent years, especially by defenders of the autonomy rights of patients. The latter hold that physicians and government officials intervene too often and assume too much paternalistic control over patients' choices.

Philosophers and lawyers have tended to support the view that the autonomy of patients is the decisive factor in the patient-physician relationship and that interventions can be valid only when patients are in some measure unable to make voluntary choices or to perform voluntary actions. Physicians too have increasingly criticized authoritarianism in their profession. A recent draft of principles of ethics of the American Medical Association asserted that "paternalism by the profession is no longer appropriate."

Any careful proponent of a principle of paternalism will specify precisely which goods and needs deserve paternalistic protection and the conditions under which intervention is warranted. In several recent formulations, it has been argued that one is justified in interfering with a person's autonomy only if the interference protects the person against his or her own actions where those actions are extremely and unreasonably risky (for example, refusing a life-saving therapy in nonterminal situations) or are potentially dangerous and irreversible in effect (as some drugs and surgery are). According to this position, paternalism is justified if and only if the evils prevented from occurring to the person are greater than the evils (if any) caused by interference with his or her liberty and if it can be universally justified, under relevantly similar circumstances, always to treat persons in this way.

This moderate formulation of paternalism still leaves many critics resolutely opposed to all possible uses of this principle. Their arguments against paternalism turn on some defense of the importance of the principle of respect for autonomy, and we will many times encounter such appeals in this volume, especially as applied to rightful state intervention in order to benefit patients or subjects without their authorization.

One major source of the difference between supporters and opponents of paternalism rests on the emphasis each places on capabilities for autonomous action by patients making "choices." Supporters of paternalism tend to cite examples of persons of diminished or compromised capacity, for example, persons lingering on kidney dialysis, chronic alcoholics, compulsive smokers, and seriously depressed suicidal patients. Opponents of paternalism cite examples of persons who are capable of autonomous choice but have been socially restricted in exercising their capacities. Examples include those involuntarily committed to institutions largely because of eccentric behavior, prisoners not permitted to volunteer for risky research, and those who might rationally elect to refuse treatment in life-threatening circumstances. One critical element of this controversy thus concerns the quality of understanding and also of consent or refusal by the persons whose autonomy might be restricted by such policies.

Many articles in this volume deal with public policies that involve such substantive moral issues in which liberty-limiting principles are invoked. These policies affect not only doctor and patient, lawyer and client, and researcher and subject—they affect every individual in society.

CONCLUSION

This chapter has surveyed some central themes in philosophical ethical theory. Such theory should not be expected to resolve the many problems in medical practice and research discussed in this volume. Some controversies are largely factual, and, as seen in the next two chapters, some controversies are more conceptual than moral. Practical wisdom and sound judgment are also indispensable allies of theory.

T.L.B.

NOTES

1. *Tarasoff* v. *Regents of the University of California,* California Supreme Court (17 California Reports, 3d Series, 425. Decided July 1, 1976). Reprinted in Chapter 3.

2. These principles and their analysis by the National Commission for the Protection of Human Subjects of Biomedical and Behavioral Research have been published as *The Belmont Report: Ethical Principles and Guidelines for the Protection of Human Subjects of Research* (Washington, D.C.: U.S. Government Printing Office, DHEW Publication, 1978).

3. See *A Theory of Justice* (Cambridge: Harvard University Press, 1971), pp. 3–4, 26–31.

4. *A Theory of Justice,* pp. 102, 137, 252–55.

5. *A Theory of Justice,* pp. 252, 256, 515–19.

6. Annette Baier, "Hume, The Women's Moral Theorist?" in *Women and Moral Theory,* edited by Eva Feder Kittay and Diana T. Meyers (Totowa, N.J.: Rowman and Littlefield, 1987), pp. 38ff; and Baier, *Postures of the Mind* (Minneapolis: University of Minnesota Press, 1985), pp. 210–19.

7. Jonsen and Toulmin, *Abuse of Casuistry* (Berkeley: University of California Press, 1988), pp. 16–19, 66–67; Jonsen, "Casuistry and Clinical Ethics," *Theoretical Medicine* 7 (1986), 67, 71.

8. Brody, *Life and Death Decision Making* (New York: Oxford University Press, 1988), p. 13.

9. American Nurses' Association, *Code for Nurses with Interpretive Statements* (Kansas City, Mo.: ANA, 1985), pp. 2–3.

10. 1953 and 1973 International Codes of Nursing Ethics of the International Council of Nurses.

11. The conditions for X's having an obligation of beneficence to Y have been plausibly analyzed by Eric D'Arcy as follows. X has a duty of beneficence to Y if and only if: (1) Y is at risk of significant loss or damage; (2) X's action is necessary to prevent loss or damage; (3) X's action would probably prevent loss or damage; (4) X's own losses or damages would probably be minimal or negligible; (5) Benefit to Y will probably outweigh the harm to X. Eric D'Arcy, *Human Acts: An Essay in Their Moral Evaluation* (Oxford: Clarendon Press, 1963), pp. 56–57.

12. William Frankena, *Ethics,* 2d ed. (Englewood Cliffs, N.J.: Prentice-Hall, 1973), p. 47.

13. Joel Feinberg, *Social Philosophy* (Englewood Cliffs, N.J.: Prentice-Hall, 1973), pp. 2–3.

14. Dennis Thompson, "Philosophy and Policy," *Philosophy and Public Affairs* 14 (Spring 1985), 205–18.

SUGGESTED READINGS FOR CHAPTER 1

MORALITY AND MORAL PHILOSOPHY

Beauchamp, Tom L. *Philosophical Ethics.* 2d ed. New York: McGraw-Hill, 1991.

Holmes, Robert L. *Basic Moral Philosophy.* Belmont, CA: Wadsworth, 1993.

MacIntyre, Alasdair. *A Short History of Ethics.* New York: Macmillan, 1966.

Regan, Tom, ed. *Matters of Life and Death.* 3d ed. New York: Random House, 1992.

Singer, Peter. *Practical Ethics.* 2d ed. New York: Cambridge University Press, 1993.

Sinnot-Armstrong, Walter. *Moral Dilemmas.* Oxford: Basil Blackwell, 1988.

RELATIVISM AND DISAGREEMENT

Brandt, Richard B. "Ethical Relativism." In Edwards, Paul, ed. *Encyclopedia of Philosophy,* Vol. 3. New York: Macmillan, 1967, pp. 75–78.

Glover, Jonathan. *Causing Death and Saving Lives.* New York: Penguin Books, 1977, Chap. 2.

Krausz, Michael, ed. *Relativism: Interpretation and Confrontation.* Notre Dame, IN: University of Notre Dame Press, 1989.

Krausz, Michael, and Meiland, Jack W., eds. *Relativism: Cognitive and Moral.* Notre Dame, IN: University of Notre Dame Press, 1982.

Rachels, James. "Can Ethics Provide Answers?" *Hastings Center Report* 10 (June 1980), 32–40.

Stocker, Michael. *Plural and Conflicting Values.* Oxford: Clarendon Press, 1990.

Wallace, James D. *Moral Relevance and Moral Conflict.* Ithaca, NY: Cornell University Press, 1988.

JUSTIFICATION

Brandt, R. B. *Morality, Utilitarianism, and Rights.* Cambridge: Cambridge University Press, 1992.

Griffiths, A. Phillips. "Ultimate Moral Principles: Their Justification." In Edwards, Paul, ed. *Encyclopedia of Philosophy,* Vol. 8. New York: Macmillan, 1967, pp. 177–82.

The Monist 71 (July 1988). Special issue on "Justification."

Odegard, Douglas, ed. *Ethics and Justification.* Edmonton, Alberta: Academic Printing & Publishing, 1988.

Pennock, J. Roland, and Chapman, John W., eds. *NOMOS XXVIII: Justification.* New York: New York University Press, 1986.

UTILITARIANISM

Bentham, Jeremy. *An Introduction to the Principles of Morals and Legislation.* Oxford: Clarendon Press, 1970.

Frey, R. G., ed. *Utility and Rights.* Minneapolis, MN: University of Minnesota Press, 1984.

Gorovitz, Samuel, ed. *Mill: Utilitarianism, with Critical Essays.* New York: Bobbs-Merrill, 1971.

Griffin, James. *Well-Being: Its Meaning, Measurement and Moral Importance.* Oxford: Clarendon Press, 1986.

Kagan, Shelly. *The Limits of Morality.* Oxford: Clarendon Press, 1989.

Mill, John Stuart. *Collected Works of John Stuart Mill.* Toronto: University of Toronto Press, 1969.

Scheffler, Samuel, ed. *Consequentialism and Its Critics.* Oxford: Oxford University Press, 1988.

KANTIAN AND DEONTOLOGICAL THEORIES

Donagan, Alan. *The Theory of Morality.* Chicago: University of Chicago Press, 1977.

Guyer, Paul, ed. *The Cambridge Companion to Kant.* Cambridge: Cambridge University Press, 1992.

Kant, Immanuel. *Ethical Philosophy.* J. Ellington, ed. Indianapolis: Hackett, 1983.

O'Neill, Onora Nell. "Universal Laws and Ends-in-Themselves." *Monist* 72 (1989), 341–61.

Rawls, John. *A Theory of Justice.* Cambridge, MA: Harvard University Press, 1971.

_____. "The Priority of Right and Ideas of the Good." *Philosophy & Public Affairs* 17 (1988), 251–76.

_____. "Themes in Kant's Moral Philosophy." In Förster, Eckart, ed. *Kant's Transcendental Deductions.* Stanford: Stanford University Press, 1989.

Ross, William D. *The Right and the Good.* Oxford: Oxford University Press, 1930.

ETHICS OF CARE

Baier, Annette. "What Do Women Want in a Moral Theory?" *Nous* 19 (1985), 53–56.

Blustein, Jeffrey. *Care and Commitment: Taking the Personal Point of View.* New York: Oxford University Press, 1991.

Carse, Alisa. "The Voice of Care: Implications for Bioethical Education." *Journal of Medicine and Philosophy* 16 (1991), 5–28.

Gilligan, Carol. *In a Different Voice.* Cambridge, MA: Harvard University Press, 1982.

Holmes, Helen Bequaert, and Purdy, Laura M., eds. *Feminist Perspectives in Medical Ethics.* Bloomington, IN: Indiana University Press, 1992.

Journal of Clinical Ethics 3 (1992). Special issue: See Hilde L. Nelson, "Against Caring," Nel Noddings, "In Defense of Caring," and Toni M. Vezeau, "Caring: From Philosophical Concerns to Practice."

Noddings, Nel. *Caring: A Feminine Approach to Ethics and Moral Education.* Berkeley: University of California Press, 1984.

Sherwin, Susan. *No Longer Patient: Feminist Ethics and Health Care.* Philadelphia: Temple University Press, 1992.

VIRTUE ETHICS

Aristotle. *Nicomachean Ethics.* Terence Irwin, trans. Indianapolis: Hackett Publishing Co., 1985.

Flanagan, Owen, and Rorty, Amélie Oksenberg, eds. *Identity, Character, and Morality.* Cambridge, MA: MIT Press, 1990.

Hume, David. *A Treatise of Human Nature.* 2d ed. Oxford: Clarendon Press, 1978.

French, Peter A., Uehling, Theodore E., Jr., and Wettstein, Howard K. *Midwest Studies in Philosophy, Volume XIII—Ethical Theory: Character and Virtue.* Notre Dame, IN: University of Notre Dame Press, 1988.

MacIntyre, Alasdair. *After Virtue.* 2d ed. Notre Dame, IN: University of Notre Dame Press, 1984.

Nussbaum, Martha. *Love's Knowledge.* Oxford: Oxford University Press, 1990.

Sherman, Nancy. *The Fabric of Character: Aristotle's Theory of Virtue.* Oxford: Clarendon Press, 1989.

CASUISTRY

Arras, John. "Getting Down to Cases: The Revival of Casuistry in Bioethics." *Journal of Medicine and Philosophy* 16 (1991), 29–51.

Brody, Baruch. *Life and Death Decision Making*. New York: Oxford University Press, 1988.

Jonsen, Albert. "American Moralism and the Origin of Bioethics in the United States." *Journal of Medicine and Philosophy* 16 (1991), 113–30.

_____. "Casuistry as Methodology in Clinical Ethics." *Theoretical Medicine* 12 (1991), 295–307.

Jonsen, Albert, and Toulmin, Stephen. *The Abuse of Casuistry: A History of Moral Reasoning*. Berkeley: University of California Press, 1988.

Toulmin, Stephen. "The Tyranny of Principles." *Hastings Center Report* 11 (December 1981), 31–39.

MORAL PRINCIPLES

Beauchamp, Tom L., and Childress, James F. *Principles of Biomedical Ethics*. 4th ed. New York: Oxford University Press, 1994. Chaps. 3–6.

Christman, John, ed. *The Inner Citadel: Essays on Individual Autonomy*. New York: Oxford University Press, 1989.

Clouser, K. Danner, and Gert, Bernard. "A Critique of Principlism." *Journal of Medicine and Philosophy* 15 (1990), 219–36.

DeGrazia, David. "Moving Forward in Bioethical Theory: Theories, Cases, and Specified Principlism." *Journal of Medicine and Philosophy* 17 (1992), 511–539.

Engelhardt, H. Tristram, Jr. *The Foundations of Bioethics*. New York: Oxford University Press, 1986.

Gillon, Raanan, and Lloyd, Ann, eds. *Principles of Health Care Ethics*. London: John Wiley & Sons, 1993.

National Commission for the Protection of Human Subjects of Biomedical and Behavioral Research. *The Belmont Report*. Washington, D.C.: DHEW Publication No. OS 78-0012, 1978.

Pellegrino, Edmund, and Thomasma, David. *For the Patient's Good: The Restoration of Beneficence in Health Care*. New York: Oxford University Press, 1988.

Richardson, Henry. "Specifying Norms as a Way to Resolve Concrete Ethical Problems." *Philosophy & Public Affairs* 19 (1990), 279–310.

Schneewind, Jerome. "Moral Knowledge and Moral Principles." In Hauerwas, Stanley, and MacIntyre, Alasdair, eds. *Revisions: Changing Perspectives in Moral Philosophy*. Notre Dame, IN: University of Notre Dame Press, 1983.

Veatch, Robert M. *A Theory of Medical Ethics*. New York: Basic Books, 1981.

ETHICS AND PUBLIC POLICY

Areen, Judith, et al. *Law, Science, and Medicine*. Mineola, NY: Foundation Press, 1984. Supplementary volume, 1987.

Brock, Dan W. "Truth or Consequences: The Role of Philosophers in Policy-Making." *Ethics* 97 (1987), 786–91.

Thompson, Dennis. "Philosophy and Policy." *Philosophy & Public Affairs* 14 (1985), 205–18.

Weisbard, Alan J. "The Role of Philosophers in the Public Policy Process." *Ethics* 97 (1987), 776–85.

MORALITY AND LAW

Dworkin, Ronald. *Taking Rights Seriously*. Cambridge, MA: Harvard University Press, 1977.

Feinberg, Joel. *The Moral Limits of the Criminal Law*. 4 vols. New York: Oxford University Press, 1984–1987.

Lyons, David. *Ethics and the Rule of Law*. Cambridge: Cambridge University Press, 1984.

Meyer, Michael J., and Parent, W. A., eds. *The Constitution of Rights*. Ithaca, NY: Cornell University Press, 1992.

Winston, Morton E., ed. *The Philosophy of Human Rights*. Belmont, CA: Wadsworth, 1989.

LIBERTY, AUTHORITY, AND PATERNALISM

Beauchamp, Tom L., and McCullough, Laurence B. *Medical Ethics*. Englewood Cliffs, NJ: Prentice-Hall, 1984. Chap. 4.

Childress, James. *Who Should Decide? Paternalism in Health Care*. New York: Oxford University Press, 1982.

Feinberg, Joel. *The Moral Limits of the Criminal Law*. New York: Oxford University Press, 1984–87. Esp. Vol. 3, *Harm to Self*.

Kleinig, John. *Paternalism*. Totowa, NJ: Rowman and Allenheld, 1983.

Sartorius, Rolf, ed. *Paternalism*. Minneapolis: University of Minnesota Press, 1983.

VanDeVeer, Donald. *Paternalistic Intervention: The Moral Bounds on Benevolence*. Princeton, NJ: Princeton University Press, 1986.

BIBLIOGRAPHIES AND ENCYCLOPEDIAS WITH BIBLIOGRAPHIES

Basic Resources in Bioethics (1991); *Teaching Ethics in the Health Care Setting, Part I: Survey of the Literature* (1991). *Teaching Ethics in the Health Care Setting, Part II: Sample Syllabus* (1991). Bibliographies available from the National Reference Center for Bioethics Literature, Kennedy Institute of Ethics, Georgetown University, Washington, D.C. 20057. Published in the *Kennedy Institute of Ethics Journal,* beginning in 1991.

Bioethicsline: Computer Retrieval Service.

Encyclopedia of Bioethics, ed. Warren Reich. New York: Macmillan, 1994.

Encyclopedia of Ethics, ed. Lawrence Becker and Charlotte Becker. New York: Garland, 1992.

Lineback, Richard H., ed. *Philosopher's Index*. Vols. 1– . Bowling Green, Ohio: Philosophy Documentation Center, Bowling Green State University. Issued quarterly.

Part II

PROFESSIONAL RELATIONSHIPS TO PATIENTS AND SUBJECTS

2.
Rights and Responsibilities

INTRODUCTION

That medicine and nursing are applied sciences none would deny. But these practices also involve the common human transactions of contracts and services. Interesting responsibilities and rights emerge from this human side of medical and nursing research and practice. Professional obligations have long been recognized in codes of ethics, but only recently has much systematic thought been given to the moral and legal rights of patients and subjects. In this chapter both traditional conceptions of, and emerging problems in, the relationships between health professionals and patients or subjects are explored.

PROFESSIONAL CODES AND STATEMENTS

The first four selections included in this chapter are samples of numerous codes and statements that have been developed by health professionals in both ancient and modern times. The Hippocratic Oath took the form of a series of religious vows. More recent codes, including those of the American Nurses Association (ANA) and the World Medical Association, generally contain secular statements of moral rules. The central affirmation of such codes is that, in treating the (frequently vulnerable) patient or research subject, the health professional will not exploit his or her position of relatively controlling power and influence.

The statement entitled "Fundamental Elements of the Patient-Physician Relationship," written by the Council on Ethical and Judicial Affairs of the American Medical Association (AMA), represents a departure from earlier AMA codes and a synthesis of several diverse themes. Unlike the "Principles of Medical Ethics" (1980), which had enumerated the moral obligations of physicians, the "Fundamental Elements" focus primarily on patients' rights. In fact, one hears in the "Elements" reminiscences of a much earlier document, the 1972 "Statement on a Patient's Bill of Rights" by the American Hospital Association. The rights asserted on behalf of patients by the "Elements" are relatively robust and include the important welfare right to "adequate health care" (see Point 6). The "Fundamental Elements" also portray the physician as an advocate for patients, a role introduced for nurses in the 1976 ANA "Code for Nurses" and still present in the 1985 revision (see Section 3.1). A new theme presented by the "Fundamental Elements" is the shared responsibility of patients for their own health care and therefore, presumably, for their own health.

The Declaration of Helsinki, first adopted by the World Medical Association in 1964, reminds us that health professionals also interact with research subjects. The ANA "Code for Nurses" devotes a section (Section 7) to this topic, as well. Patients can be invited to participate in research that is directly related to the diagnosis or treatment of their illnesses;

this type of research is called "clinical research" by the Helsinki Declaration. The other major kind of biomedical research involves either healthy individuals, often called normal volunteers, or patients who are asked to participate in research that is not directly related to their illnesses. This type of research is called "non-clinical biomedical research" and is discussed in Part III of the Helsinki Declaration.

Two questions arise concerning the status of these codes and statements: (1) What is their relation to law? and (2) What is their relation to general ethical principles? The codes and statements, though quasi-legal in form, are self-legislative documents developed by particular professions. As such, they have only the force that the profession chooses to attribute to them. In most professions, including medicine and nursing, professional self-discipline or self-policing has usually been less than vigorous.

Two possible relationships between professional codes or statements and general ethical principles can be envisioned. The codes and statements may constitute autonomous, self-contained systems of ethics that are unrelated to external validating principles. Or, the codes and statements may be viewed as specific applications of universal ethical principles. According to the latter conception, the codes or statements consist primarily of moral rules or rights that implicitly appeal to general ethical principles, and perhaps even to particular ethical theories. On this view, the same canons of logical coherence and consistency that are applied to any other system of moral rights or rules can also be employed in the critical evaluation of the professional codes and statements. (See the discussion of moral rights and moral justification in Chapter 1.)

THE VIRTUES AND OBLIGATIONS OF PROFESSIONALS

This section of Chapter 2 elaborates several of the themes introduced by the professional codes and statements but discusses complementary emphases, as well. Central to most professional documents has been an emphasis on the moral obligations of each professional or the moral rights of each patient in their one-on-one relationship. But are there other approaches to ethics that focus less on moral rights and obligations? And what of the obligations of each professional (and each patient, for that matter) to third parties?

In his essay in this chapter Edmund Pellegrino distinguishes among three standards by which professional behavior might be judged. The first standard is the least stringent. It asks, "Has the professional violated any legal rules or administrative regulations in his or her treatment of the patient?" The second standard is the one employed in most essays in this chapter — and indeed in this book. This standard evaluates professional performance on the basis of its conformity with widely accepted ethical principles and moral rules, such as the principle of respect for the autonomy of persons. The third and most stringent standard is one that requires professionals not only to fulfill their moral obligations but to be virtuous as well. In what ways does virtue go beyond mere conformity with moral rules? First, a virtuous person performs morally right actions for the right reasons, as an expression of his or her genuine concern for the welfare of others. Second, in some cases a virtuous person will behave in a self-sacrificial way, going beyond the obligations that are imposed, for example, by the usual requirements of justice. Pellegrino is under no illusion that all health professionals are necessarily virtuous persons. However, he recommends the cultivation of character as an important adjunct to the clarification of moral concepts and the development of coherent theories of rights and obligations.

A second alternative approach to professional ethics focuses on care, or caring, rather than on virtue in general. Nancy Jecker and Donnie Self attempt to clarify the notion of care and to show how care has been, and ought to be, associated with the nursing and medical professions. Drawing on the research of Carol Gilligan and others, Jecker and Self note that caring has often been construed as a virtue that is especially characteristic of nurses. However, Jecker and Self also raise the question whether caring might be a moral obligation of both nurses and physicians. If caring is regarded as a moral obligation, one might ask a further question: How is such a moral obligation related to the general principles of bioethics discussed in Chapter 1, and particularly to the principles of beneficence and nonmaleficence?

At first glance, it might seem that the primary moral obligation of health professionals is always to promote the welfare (or respect the autonomy) of their patients. However, even at a purely descriptive level, we know that physicians and nurses must make decisions about how to allocate time among the multiple patients for whom they almost always bear responsibility. Further, both patients and health professionals live in complex webs of interrelationships outside the health care setting. There is no easy way for either patients or professionals to avoid taking these extra-medical relationships into account in their decision making. The remaining two essays in this section address the important topic of conflicts of obligations.

Normal Daniels's essay takes up the theme of patient advocacy introduced by the ANA code and the AMA "Fundamental Elements." According to Daniels, the traditional notion of the physician as patient advocate has included five important elements, of which the last two have become increasingly problematic. The first problematic element is that a physician's clinical decisions must be "free from consideration of the physician's interests"; the second is that his or her decisions must be "uninfluenced by judgments about the patient's worth." Daniels argues that a just health care system that would be compatible with these constraints can and should be constructed in the United States. Within such a system a physician acting as gatekeeper could continue to fulfill the role of Ideal Advocate for his or her patients.

Tom Beauchamp and Laurence McCullough focus their attention on the potentially conflicting roles of physicians and argue that physicians have a moral duty at least to consider third-party interests in their encounters with patients. In some cases the third parties are identifiable individuals or institutions, for example, a child of the patient or the patient's spouse, employer, or insurance company. In other cases, a vague entity often described as "the wider society" is the intended beneficiary of actions that involve the patient — medical education, biomedical research, or the reporting of communicable disease. According to Beauchamp and McCullough, one cannot stipulate in advance whether the moral obligations of physicians to patients will be stronger than, equivalent to, or weaker than their obligations to third parties.

PROFESSIONALS AND SPECIFIC PATIENT POPULATIONS

This section of Chapter 2 focuses on the moral obligations of health professionals toward four groups of patients: the homeless, women, the elderly, and the seriously mentally ill. In his brief commentary, David Hilfiker recounts the case of Mr. W., who was found unconscious on a street corner. For Hilfiker, Mr. W.'s situation raises broader questions about the moral obligation of physicians, and of society in general, to provide health care to poor people.

The treatment of women by health providers and their level of participation in clinical research are the principal foci of the essay by the AMA's Council on Ethical and Judicial Affairs. The Council notes that women are underrepresented in clinical research and that they are less likely than men to be offered several important diagnostic or therapeutic interventions, for example, kidney dialysis and kidney transplants. On the other hand, according to some studies, women's health complaints are more likely to be attributed to emotional causes than are similar complaints expressed by men. The Council's prescriptions for change include a reexamination of their attitudes toward patients by physicians and increasing participation by women in leadership roles in medicine.

In their essay "The Goals of Medicine in an Aging Society" Christine Cassel and Bernice Neugarten ask whether there is a natural life span that human beings ought not to exceed and question whether people aged sixty-five and older consume a disproportionate share of health care resources in the United States. Their answer to the first question is no; this answer is based on data showing that increasing numbers of Americans are remaining in relatively good health even as they live longer than people in earlier generations lived. Cassel and Neugarten provide a more nuanced answer to the second question, noting that only a small percentage of Medicare patients (about 17 percent) account for over 60 percent of Medicare payments. In their view, these relatively high payments on a relatively small number of patients are likely to be reduced in the future as patients make their wishes known through advance directives and as medicine achieves a better balance between heroic and humanistic patterns of practice.

Professional obligations to the seriously mentally ill are the focus of Paul Chodoff's essay. Chodoff, a psychiatrist, questions whether the emphasis on patients' rights has not been carried too far by civil liberties lawyers and their allies in the health professions. In the context of mental illness, and in cases involving persons of questionable competence to care for themselves, an overly zealous respect for the rights of patients may, in Chodoff's view, lead to unmitigated disaster. Thus, he argues, the temporary loss of freedom through involuntary commitment may sometimes be in the long-term best interest of patients.

MORAL QUANDARIES OF PROFESSIONALS

The final section of this chapter discusses problems that may arise in the care of mentally competent patients who do not belong to particular economic, ethnic, gender, or age groups. In the first essay Dan Brock, a philosopher, and Steven Wartman, a physician, consider how professionals should respond to apparently irrational choices of competent patients. In some cases, this quandary represents a classic conflict between the ethical principles of beneficence and respect for autonomy. More specifically, it illustrates the problem of paternalism, that is, intervention for the benefit of a competent person but against the wishes of that person. (Please see the discussion of these issues in Chapter 1.) In other cases, the welfare of a particular patient may come into conflict with the good of others. Brock and Wartman do not offer a simple solution to this important problem; instead, they provide a taxonomy of types of situations and recommend patience and sensitivity on the part of well-intentioned professionals.

Medical accidents and medical malpractice have, for the most part, been the subject of *legal* rather than ethical discussion. Frequently the debate has become polarized between the positions of trial lawyers and health professionals. In their essay on "Medical Ethics and Medical Injuries" Lynn Peterson and Troyen Brennan propose a new approach to this perennial problem. The authors summarize data from a comprehensive study of medical injury in which they both participated, the Harvard Medical Practice Study. These data suggest that accidental medical injury is a much more serious problem than is often acknowledged; in fact, the Harvard Study estimated that 1.5 million avoidable medical injuries occur each year in the United States and that approximately 200,000 deaths occur annually as a result of such injuries. Peterson and Brennan recommend an ethical response to this problem that begins with frank disclosure to all patients who are accidentally injured in the course of medical treatment. The authors go on to discuss the moral obligation of health professionals to assist policy makers in creating a system for the just compensation of patients who are harmed rather than helped by their health care providers.

L. W.

Professional Codes

The Hippocratic Oath

I swear by Apollo Physician and Asclepius and Hygieia and Panaceia and all the gods and goddesses, making them my witnesses, that I will fulfill according to my ability and judgment this oath and this covenant:

To hold him who has taught me this art as equal to my parents and to live my life in partnership with him, and if he is in need of money to give him a share of mine, and to regard his offspring as equal to my brothers in male lineage and to teach them this art—if they desire to learn it—without fee and covenant; to give a share of precepts and oral instruction and all the other learning to my sons and to the sons of him who has instructed me and to pupils who have signed the covenant and have taken an oath according to the medical law, but to no one else.

I will apply dietetic measures for the benefit of the sick according to my ability and judgment; I will keep them from harm and injustice.

Reprinted with permission of the publisher from "The Hippocratic Oath," in Ludwig Edelstein, *Ancient Medicine*, edited by Oswei Temkin and C. Lillian Temkin (Baltimore: Johns Hopkins University Press, 1967).

I will neither give a deadly drug to anybody if asked for it, nor will I make a suggestion to this effect. Similarly I will not give to a woman an abortive remedy. In purity and holiness I will guard my life and my art.

I will not use the knife, not even on sufferers from stone, but will withdraw in favor of such men as are engaged in this work.

Whatever houses I may visit, I will come for the benefit of the sick, remaining free of all intentional injustice, of all mischief and in particular of sexual relations with both female and male persons, be they free or slaves.

What I may see or hear in the course of the treatment or even outside of the treatment in regard to the life of men, which on no account one must spread abroad, I will keep to myself holding such things shameful to be spoken about.

If I fulfill this oath and do not violate it, may it be granted to me to enjoy life and art, being honored with fame among all men for all time to come; if I transgress it and swear falsely, may the opposite of all this be my lot.

AMERICAN MEDICAL ASSOCIATION, COUNCIL ON ETHICAL AND JUDICIAL AFFAIRS

Fundamental Elements of the Patient-Physician Relationship (1990)

From ancient times, physicians have recognized that the health and well-being of patients depends upon a collaborative effort between physician and patient. Patients share with physicians the responsibility for their own health care. The patient-physician relationship is of greatest benefit to patients when they bring medical problems to the attention of their physicians in a timely fashion, provide information about their medical condition to the best of their ability, and work with their physicians in a mutually respectful alliance. Physicians can best contribute to this alliance by serving as their patients' advocate and by fostering these rights:

1. The patient has the right to receive information from physicians and to discuss the benefits, risks, and costs of appropriate treatment alternatives. Patients should receive guidance from their physicians as to the optimal course of action. Patients are also entitled to obtain copies or summaries of their medical records, to have their questions answered, to be advised of potential conflicts of interest that their physicians might have, and to receive independent professional opinions.

2. The patient has the right to make decisions regarding the health care that is recommended by his or her physician. Accordingly, patients may accept or refuse any recommended medical treatment.

3. The patient has the right to courtesy, respect, dignity, responsiveness, and timely attention to his or her needs.

4. The patient has the right to confidentiality. The physician should not reveal confidential communications or information without the consent of the patient, unless provided for by law or by the need to protect the welfare of the individual or the public interest.

5. The patient has the right to continuity of health care. The physician has an obligation to cooperate in the coordination of medically indicated care with other health care providers treating the patient. The physician may not discontinue treatment of a patient as long as further treatment is medically indicated, without giving the patient sufficient opportunity to make alternative arrangements for care.

6. The patient has a basic right to have available adequate health care. Physicians, along with the rest of society, should continue to work toward this goal. Fulfillment of this right is dependent on society providing resources so that no patient is deprived of necessary care because of an inability to pay for the care. Physicians should continue their traditional assumption of a part of the responsibility for the medical care of those who cannot afford essential health care.

Reprinted by permission of the publisher from *Journal of the American Medical Association* 264 (1990), 3133. © 1990, American Medical Association.

AMERICAN NURSES ASSOCIATION

Code for Nurses (1985)

1

The nurse provides services with respect for human dignity and the uniqueness of the client, unrestricted by considerations of social or economic status, personal attributes, or the nature of health problems.

1.1 RESPECT FOR HUMAN DIGNITY

The fundamental principle of nursing practice is respect for the inherent dignity and worth of every client. Nurses are morally obligated to respect human existence and the individuality of all persons who are the recipients of nursing actions. Nurses therefore must take all reasonable means to protect and preserve human life when there is hope of recovery or reasonable hope of benefit from life-prolonging treatment.

Truth telling and the process of reaching informed choice underlie the exercise of self-determination, which is basic to respect for persons. Clients should be as fully involved as possible in the planning and implementation of their own health care. Clients have the moral right to determine what will be done with their own person; to be given accurate information, and all the information necessary for making informed judgments; to be assisted with weighing the benefits and burdens of options in their treatment; to accept, refuse, or terminate treatment without coercion; and to be given necessary emotional support. Each nurse has an obligation to be knowledgeable about the moral and legal rights of all clients and to protect and support those rights. In situations in which the client lacks the capacity to make a decision, a surrogate decision maker should be designated.

Reprinted with permission from *Code for Nurses with Interpretative Statements,* © 1985, American Nurses Association, Washington, DC.

Individuals are interdependent members of the community. Taking into account both individual rights and the interdependence of persons in decision making, the nurse recognizes those situations in which individual rights to autonomy in health care may temporarily be overridden to preserve the life of the human community; for example, when a disaster demands triage or when an individual presents a direct danger to others. The many variables involved make it imperative that each case be considered with full awareness of the need to preserve the rights and responsibilities of clients and the demands of justice. The suspension of individual rights must always be considered a deviation to be tolerated as briefly as possible.

1.2 STATUS AND ATTRIBUTES OF CLIENTS

The need for health care is universal, transcending all national, ethnic, racial, religious, cultural, political, educational, economic, developmental, personality, role, and sexual differences. Nursing care is delivered without prejudicial behavior. Individual value systems and life-styles should be considered in the planning of health care with and for each client. Attributes of clients influence nursing practice to the extent that they represent factors the nurse must understand, consider, and respect in tailoring care to personal needs and in maintaining the individual's self-respect and dignity.

1.3 THE NATURE OF HEALTH PROBLEMS

The nurse's respect for the worth and dignity of the individual human being applies, irrespective of the nature of the health problem. It is reflected in care given the person who is disabled as well as one without disability, the person with long-term illness as well as one with acute illness, the recovering patient as well as one in the last phase of life. This respect extends to all who require the services of the nurse for the promotion of health, the prevention of illness, the restoration of health, the alleviation of suffering, and the provision of supportive care of the dying. The nurse does not act deliberately to terminate the life of any person.

The nurse's concern for human dignity and for the provision of high quality nursing care is not limited by personal attitudes or beliefs. If ethically opposed to interventions in a particular case because of the procedures to be used, the nurse is justified in refusing to participate. Such refusal should be made known in advance and in time for other appropriate arrangements to be made for the client's nursing care. If the nurse becomes involved in such a case and the client's life is in jeopardy, the nurse is obliged to provide for the client's safety, to avoid abandonment, and to withdraw only when assured that alternative sources of nursing care are available to the client.

The measures nurses take to care for the dying client and the client's family emphasize human contact. They enable the client to live with as much physical, emotional, and spiritual comfort as possible, and they maximize the values the client has treasured in life. Nursing care is directed toward the prevention and relief of the suffering commonly associated with the dying process. The nurse may provide interventions to relieve symptoms in the dying client even when the interventions entail substantial risks of hastening death.

1.4 THE SETTING FOR HEALTH CARE

The nurse adheres to the principle of nondiscriminatory, nonprejudicial care in every situation and endeavors to promote its acceptance by others. The setting shall not determine the nurse's readiness to respect clients and to render or obtain needed services.

2

The nurse safeguards the client's right to privacy by judiciously protecting information of a confidential nature.

2.1 THE CLIENT'S RIGHT TO PRIVACY

The right to privacy is an inalienable human right. The client trusts the nurse to hold all information in confidence. This trust could be destroyed and the client's welfare jeopardized by injudicious disclosure of information provided in confidence. The duty of confidentiality, however, is not absolute when innocent parties are in direct jeopardy.

2.2 PROTECTION OF INFORMATION

The rights, well-being, and safety of the individual client should be the determining factors in arriving at any professional judgment concerning the disposition of confidential information received from the client relevant to his or her treatment. The standards of nursing practice and the nursing responsibility to provide high quality health services require that relevant data be shared with members of the health team. Only information pertinent to a client's treatment and welfare is disclosed, and it is disclosed only to those directly concerned with the client's care.

Information documenting the appropriateness, necessity, and quality of care required for the purposes of peer review, third-party payment, and other quality assurance mechanisms must be disclosed only under defined policies, mandates, or protocols. These written guidelines must assure that the rights, well-being, and safety of the client are maintained.

2.3 ACCESS TO RECORDS

If in the course of providing care there is a need for the nurse to have access to the records of persons not under the nurse's care, the persons affected should be notified and, whenever possible, permission should be obtained first. Although records belong to the agency where the data are collected, the individual maintains the right of control over the information in the record. Similarly, professionals may exercise the right of control over information they have generated in the course of health care.

If the nurse wishes to use a client's treatment record for research or nonclinical purposes in which anonymity cannot be guaranteed, the client's consent must be obtained first. Ethically, this ensures the client's right to privacy; legally, it protects the client against unlawful invasion of privacy.

3

The nurse acts to safeguard the client and the public when health care and safety are affected by incompetent, unethical, or illegal practice by any person.

3.1 SAFEGUARDING THE HEALTH AND SAFETY OF THE CLIENT

The nurse's primary commitment is to the health, welfare, and safety of the client. As an advocate for the client, the nurse must be alert to and take appropriate action regarding any instances of incompetent, unethical, or illegal practice by any member of the health care team or the health care system, or any action on the part of others that places the rights or best interests of the client in jeopardy. To function effectively in this role, nurses must be aware of the employing institution's policies and procedures, nursing standards of practice, the Code for Nurses, and laws governing nursing and health care practice with regard to incompetent, unethical, or illegal practice.

3.2 ACTING ON QUESTIONABLE PRACTICE

When the nurse is aware of inappropriate or questionable practice in the provision of health care, concern should be expressed to the person carrying out the questionable practice and attention called to the possible detrimental effect upon the client's welfare. When factors in the health care delivery system threaten the welfare of the client, similar action should be directed to the responsible administrative person. If indicated, the practice should then be reported to the appropriate authority within the institution, agency, or larger system.

There should be an established process for the reporting and handling of incompetent, unethical, or illegal practice within the employment setting so that such reporting can go through official channels without causing fear of reprisal. The nurse should be knowledgeable about the process and be prepared to use it if necessary. When questions are raised about the practices of individual practitioners or of health care systems, written documentation of the observed practices or behaviors must be available to the appropriate authorities. State nurses' associations should be prepared to provide assistance and support in the development and evaluation of such processes and in reporting procedures.

When incompetent, unethical, or illegal practice on the part of anyone concerned with the client's care is not corrected within the employment setting and continues to jeopardize the client's welfare and safety, the problem should be reported to other appropriate authorities such as practice committees of the pertinent professional organizations or the legally constituted bodies concerned with licensing of specific categories of health workers or professional practitioners. Some situations may warrant the concern and involvement of all such groups. Accurate reporting and documentation undergird all actions.

3.3 REVIEW MECHANISMS

The nurse should participate in the planning, establishment, implementation, and evaluation of review mechanisms that serve to safeguard clients, such as duly constituted peer review processes or committees, and ethics committees. Such ongoing review mechanisms are based on established criteria, have stated purposes, include a process for making recommendations, and facilitate improved delivery of nursing and other health services to clients wherever nursing services are provided.

4

The nurse assumes responsibility and accountability for individual nursing judgments and actions.

• • •

5

The nurse maintains competence in nursing.

• • •

6

The nurse exercises informed judgment and uses individual competency and qualifications as criteria in seeking consultation, accepting responsibilities, and delegating nursing activities.

• • •

7

The nurse participates in activities that contribute to the ongoing development of the profession's body of knowledge.

7.1 THE NATURE AND DEVELOPMENT OF KNOWLEDGE

Every profession must engage in scholarly inquiry to identify, verify, and continually enlarge the body of knowledge that forms the foundation for its practice. A unique body of verified knowledge provides both framework and direction for the profession in all of its activities and for the practitioner in the provision of nursing care. The accrual of scientific and humanistic knowledge promotes the advancement of practice and the well-being of the profession's clients. Ongoing scholarly activity such as research and the development of theory is indispensable to the full discharge of a profession's obligations to society. Each nurse has a role in this area of professional activity, whether as an investigator in furthering knowledge, as a participant in research, or as a user of theoretical and empirical knowledge.

7.2 PROTECTION OF RIGHTS
OF HUMAN PARTICIPANTS IN RESEARCH

Individual rights valued by society and by the nursing profession that have particular application in research include the right of adequately informed consent, the right to freedom from risk of injury, and the right of privacy and preservation of dignity. Inherent in these rights is respect for each individual's rights to exercise self-determination, to choose to participate or not, to have full information, and to terminate participation in research without penalty.

It is the duty of the nurse functioning in any research role to maintain vigilance in protecting the life, health, and privacy of human subjects from both anticipated and unanticipated risks and in assuring informed consent. Subjects' integrity, privacy, and rights must be especially safeguarded if the subjects are unable to protect themselves because of incapacity or because they are in a dependent relationship to the investigator. The investigation should be discontinued if its continuance might be harmful to the subject.

7.3 GENERAL GUIDELINES
FOR PARTICIPATING IN RESEARCH

Before participating in research conducted by others, the nurse has an obligation to (a) obtain information about the intent and the nature of the research and (b) ascertain that the study proposal is approved by the appropriate bodies, such as institutional review boards.

Research should be conducted and directed by qualified persons. The nurse who participates in research in any capacity should be fully informed about both the nurse's and the client's rights and obligations.

8

The nurse participates in the profession's efforts to implement and improve standards of nursing.

• • •

9

The nurse participates in the profession's efforts to establish and maintain conditions of employment conducive to high quality nursing care.

• • •

10

The nurse participates in the profession's effort to protect the public from misinformation and misrepresentation and to maintain the integrity of nursing.

• • •

11

The nurse collaborates with members of the health professions and other citizens in promoting community and national efforts to meet the health needs of the public.

11.1 COLLABORATION WITH OTHERS
TO MEET HEALTH NEEDS

The availability and accessibility of high quality health services to all people require collaborative planning at the local, state, national, and international levels that respects the interdependence of health professionals and clients in health care systems. Nursing care is an integral part of high quality health care, and nurses have an obligation to promote equitable access to nursing and health care for all people.

11.2 RESPONSIBILITY TO THE PUBLIC

The nursing profession is committed to promoting the welfare and safety of all people. The goals and values of nursing are essential to effective delivery of health services. For the benefit of the individual client and the public at large, nursing's goals and commitments need adequate representation. Nurses should ensure this representation by active participation in decision making in institutional and political arenas to assure a just distribution of health care and nursing resources.

11.3 RELATIONSHIPS WITH OTHER DISCIPLINES

The complexity of health care delivery systems requires a multidisciplinary approach to delivery of services that has the strong support and active participation of all the health professions. Nurses should actively promote the collaborative planning required to ensure the availability and accessibility of high quality health services to all persons whose health needs are unmet.

WORLD MEDICAL ASSOCIATION

Declaration of Helsinki
(Hong Kong, 1989)

Recommendations guiding physicians in biomedical research involving human subjects

INTRODUCTION

It is the mission of the physician to safeguard the health of the people. His or her knowledge and conscience are dedicated to the fulfillment of this mission.

The Declaration of Geneva of the World Medical Assembly binds the physician with the words, "The health of my patient will be my first consideration," and the International Code of Medical Ethics declares that, "A physician shall act only in the patient's interest when providing medical care which might have the effect of weakening the physical and mental condition of the patient."

The purpose of biomedical research involving human subjects must be to improve diagnostic, therapeutic and prophylactic procedures and the understanding of the aetiology and pathogenesis of disease.

In current medical practice most diagnostic, therapeutic or prophylactic procedures involve hazards. This applies especially to biomedical research.

Medical progress is based on research which ultimately must rest in part on experimentation involving human subjects.

In the field of biomedical research a fundamental distinction must be recognized between medical research in which the aim is essentially diagnostic or therapeutic for a patient, and medical research, the essential object of which is purely scientific and without

From *World Medical Association Recommendations Guiding Physicians in Biomedical Research Involving Human Subjects* (Ferney-Voltaire, France: World Medical Association, September 1989). Reprinted with permission of the World Medical Association.

implying direct diagnostic or therapeutic value to the person subjected to the research.

Special caution must be exercised in the conduct of research which may affect the environment, and the welfare of animals used for research must be respected.

Because it is essential that the results of laboratory experiments be applied to human beings to further scientific knowledge and to help suffering humanity, the World Medical Association has prepared the following recommendations as a guide to every physician in biomedical research involving human subjects. They should be kept under review in the future. It must be stressed that the standards as drafted are only a guide to physicians all over the world. Physicians are not relieved from criminal, civil and ethical responsibilities under the laws of their own countries.

I. BASIC PRINCIPLES

1. Biomedical research involving human subjects must conform to generally accepted scientific principles and should be based on adequately performed laboratory and animal experimentation and on a thorough knowledge of the scientific literature.

2. The design and performance of each experimental procedure involving human subjects should be clearly formulated in an experimental protocol which should be transmitted for consideration, comment and guidance to a specially appointed committee independent of the investigator and the sponsor provided that this independent committee is in conformity with the laws and regulations of the country in which the research experiment is performed.

3. Biomedical research involving human subjects should be conducted only by scientifically qualified persons and under the supervision of a clinically competent medical person. The responsibility for the human subject must always rest with a medically qualified person and never rest on the subject of the research, even though the subject has given his or her consent.

4. Biomedical research involving human subjects cannot legitimately be carried out unless the importance of the objective is in proportion to the inherent risk to the subject.

5. Every biomedical research project involving human subjects should be preceded by careful assessment of predictable risks in comparison with foreseeable benefits to the subject or to others. Concern for the interests of the subject must always prevail over the interests of science and society.

6. The right of the research subject to safeguard his or her integrity must always be respected. Every precaution should be taken to respect the privacy of the subject and to minimize the impact of the study on the subject's physical and mental integrity and on the personality of the subject.

7. Physicians should abstain from engaging in research projects involving human subjects unless they are satisfied that the hazards involved are believed to be predictable. Physicians should cease any investigation if the hazards are found to outweigh the potential benefits.

8. In publication of the results of his or her research, the physician is obliged to preserve the accuracy of the results. Reports of experimentation not in accordance with the principles laid down in this Declaration should not be accepted for publication.

9. In any research on human beings, each potential subject must be adequately informed of the aims, methods, anticipated benefits and potential hazards of the study and the discomfort it may entail. He or she should be informed that he or she is at liberty to abstain from participation in the study and that he or she is free to withdraw his or her consent to participation at any time. The physician should then obtain the subject's freely given informed consent, preferably in writing.

10. When obtaining informed consent for the research project the physician should be particularly cautious if the subject is in a dependent relationship to him or her or may consent under duress. In that case the informed consent should be obtained by a physician who is not engaged in the investigation and who is completely independent of this official relationship.

11. In case of legal incompetence, informed consent should be obtained from the legal guardian in accordance with national legislation. Where physical or mental incapacity makes it impossible to obtain informed consent, or when the subject is a minor, permission from the responsible relative replaces that of the subject in accordance with national legislation.

    Whenever the minor child is in fact able to give a consent, the minor's consent must be obtained in addition to the consent of the minor's legal guardian.

12. The research protocol should always contain a statement of the ethical considerations involved and should indicate that the principles enunciated in the present Declaration are complied with.

II. MEDICAL RESEARCH COMBINED WITH CLINICAL CARE (CLINICAL RESEARCH)

1. In the treatment of the sick person, the physician must be free to use a new diagnostic and therapeutic measure, if in his or her judgement it offers hope of saving life, reestablishing health or alleviating suffering.

2. The potential benefits, hazards and discomfort of a new method should be weighed against the advantages of the best current diagnostic and therapeutic methods.

3. In any medical study, every patient — including those of a control group, if any — should be assured of the best proven diagnostic and therapeutic method.

4. The refusal of the patient to participate in a study must never interfere with the physician-patient relationship.

5. If the physician considers it essential not to obtain informed consent, the specific reasons for this proposal should be stated in the experimen-

tal protocol for transmission to the independent committee ([see] I, 2).

6. The physician can combine medical research with professional care, the objective being the acquisition of new medical knowledge, only to the extent that medical research is justified by its potential diagnostic or therapeutic value for the patient.

III. NON-THERAPEUTIC BIOMEDICAL RESEARCH INVOLVING HUMAN SUBJECTS (NON-CLINICAL BIOMEDICAL RESEARCH)

1. In the purely scientific application of medical research carried out on a human being, it is the duty of the physician to remain the protector of the life and health of that person on whom biomedical research is being carried out.
2. The subjects should be volunteers — either healthy persons or patients for whom the experimental design is not related to the patient's illness.
3. The investigator or the investigating team should discontinue the research if in his/her or their judgement it may, if continued, be harmful to the individual.
4. In research on man, the interest of science and society should never take precedence over considerations related to the wellbeing of the subject.

The Virtues and Obligations of Professionals

EDMUND D. PELLEGRINO

The Virtuous Physician and the Ethics of Medicine

Consider from what noble seed you spring: You were created not to live like beasts, but for pursuit of virtue and of knowledge.

Dante, *Inferno* 26, 118–120

THE VIRTUOUS PERSON, THE VIRTUOUS PHYSICIAN

Virtue implies a character trait, an internal disposition, habitually to seek moral perfection, to live one's life in accord with the moral law, and to attain a balance between noble intention and just action. Perhaps C. S. Lewis has captured the idea best by likening the virtuous man to the good tennis player: "What you mean by a good player is the man whose eye and muscles and nerves have been so trained by making innumerable good shots that they can now be relied upon. . . . They have a certain tone or quality which is there even when he is not playing. . . . In the same way a man who perseveres in doing just actions gets in the end a certain quality of character. Now it is that quality rather than the particular actions that we mean when we talk of virtue" [1].

On almost any view, the virtuous person is someone we can trust to act habitually in a 'good' way — courageously, honestly, justly, wisely, and temperately. He is committed to *being* a good person and to the pursuit of perfection in his private, professional and communal life. He is someone who will act well

Reprinted from Earl E. Shelp (ed.), *Virtue and Medicine: Exploration in the Character of Medicine* (Philosophy and Medicine Series, No. 17), pp. 243–255. © 1985 by D. Reidel Publishing Company. Reprinted by permission of Kluwer Academic Publishers.

even when there is no one to applaud, simply because to act otherwise is a violation of what it is to be a good person. No civilized society could endure without a significant number of citizens committed to this concept of virtue. Without such persons no system of general ethics could succeed, and no system of professional ethics could transcend the dangers of self-interest. That is why, even while rights, duties, obligations may be emphasized, the concept of virtue has 'hovered' so persistently over every system of ethics.

Is the virtuous physician simply the virtuous person practicing medicine? Are there virtues peculiar to medicine as a practice? Are certain of the individual virtues more applicable to medicine than elsewhere in human activities? Is virtue more important in some branches of medicine than others? How do professional skills differ from virtue? These are pertinent questions propaedeutic to the later questions of the place of virtue in professional medical ethics.

I believe these questions are best answered by drawing on the Aristotelian-Thomist notion of virtues and its relationship to the ends and purposes of human life. The virtuous physician on this view is defined in terms of the ends of medicine. To be sure, the physician, before he is anything else, must be a virtuous person. To be a virtuous physician he must also be the kind of person we can confidently expect will be disposed to the right and good intrinsic to the practice he professes. What are those dispositions?

To answer this question requires some exposition of what we mean by the good in medicine, or more specifically the good of the patient — for that is the end the patient and the physician ostensibly seek. Any theory of virtue must be linked with a theory of the good because virtue is a disposition habitually to do the good. Must we therefore know the nature of the good the virtuous man is disposed to do? As with the definition of virtue we are caught here in another perennial philosophical question — what is the nature of the Good? Is the good whatever we make it to be or does it have validity independent of our desires or interest? Is the good one, or many? Is it reducible to riches, honors, pleasures, glory, happiness, or something else?

I make no pretense to a discussion of a general theory of the good. But any attempt to define the virtuous physician or a virtue-based ethic for medicine must offer some definition of the good of the patient. The patient's good is the end of medicine, that which

shapes the particular virtues required for its attainment. That end is central to any notion of the virtues peculiar to medicine as a practice.

I have argued elsewhere that the architectonic principle of medicine is the good of the patient as expressed in a particular right and good healing action [2]. This is the immediate good end of the clinical encounter. Health, healing, caring, coping are all good ends dependent upon the more immediate end of a right and good decision. On this view, the virtuous physician is one so habitually disposed to act in the patient's good, to place that good in ordinary instances above his own, that he can reliably be expected to do so.

But we must face the fact that the 'patient's good' is itself a compound notion. Elsewhere I have examined four components of the patient's good: (1) clinical or biomedical good; (2) the good as perceived by the patient; (3) the good of the patient as a human person; and (4) the Good, or ultimate good. Each of these components of patient good must be served. They must also be placed in some hierarchical order when they conflict within the same person, or between persons involved in clinical decisions [3].

Some would consider patient good, so far as the physician is concerned, as limited to what applied medical knowledge can achieve in *this* patient. On this view the virtues specific to medicine would be objectivity, scientific probity, and conscientiousness with regard to professional skill. One could perform the technical tasks of medicine well, be faithful to the skills of good technical medicine per se, but without being a virtuous person. Would one then be a virtuous physician? One would have to answer affirmatively if technical skill were all there is to medicine.

Some of the more expansionist models of medicine — like . . . that of the World Health Organization (total well-being) — would require compassion, empathy, advocacy, benevolence, and beneficence, i.e., an expanded sense of the affective responses to patient need [4]. Some might argue that what is required, therefore, is not virtue, but simply greater skill in the social and behavioral sciences applied to particular patients. On this view the physician's habitual dispositions might be incidental to his skills in communication or his empathy. He could achieve the ends of medicine without necessarily being a virtuous person in the generic sense.

It is important at this juncture to distinguish the virtues from technical or professional skills, as MacIntyre and, more clearly, Von Wright do. The latter defines a skill as 'technical goodness'—excellence in some particular activity—while virtues are not tied to any one activity but are necessary for "the good of man" ([5], pp. 139–140). The virtues are not "characterized in terms of their results" ([6], p. 141). On this view, the technical skills of medicine are not virtues and could be practiced by a non-virtuous person. Aristotle held *techne* (technical skills) to be one of the five intellectual virtues but not one of the moral virtues.

The virtues enable the physician to act with regard to things that are good for man, when man is in the specific existential state of illness. They are dispositions always to seek the good intent inherent in healing. Within medicine, the virtues do become in MacIntyre's sense acquired human qualities ". . . the possession and exercise of which tends to enable us to achieve those goods which are internal to practices and the lack of which effectively prevents us from achieving any such goods" ([7], p. 178).

We can come closer to the relationship of virtue to clinical actions if we look to the more immediate ends of medical encounters, to those moments of clinical truth when specific decisions and actions are chosen and carried out. The good the patient seeks is to be healed—to be restored to his prior, or to a better, state of function, to be made 'whole' again. If this is not possible, the patient expects to be helped, to be assisted in coping with the pain, disability or dying that illness may entail. The immediate end of medicine is not simply a technically proficient performance but the use of that performance to attain a good end—the good of the patient—his medical or biomedical good to the extent possible but also his good as he the patient perceives it, his good as a human person who can make his own life plan, and his good as a person with a spiritual destiny if this is his belief [8]. It is the sensitive balancing of these senses of the patient's good which the virtuous physician pursues to perfection.

To achieve the end of medicine thus conceived, to practice medicine virtuously, requires certain dispositions: conscientious attention to technical knowledge and skill to be sure, but also compassion—a capacity to feel something of the patient's experience of illness and his perceptions of what is worthwhile; beneficence and benevolence—doing and wishing to do good for the patient; honesty, fidelity to promises, perhaps at times courage as well—the whole list of virtues spelled out by Aristotle: ". . . justice, courage, temperance, magnificence, magnanimity, liberality, placability, prudence, wisdom" (*Rhetoric*, 1, c, 13666, 1–3). Not every one of these virtues is required in

every decision. What we expect of the virtuous physician is that he will exhibit them when they are required and that he will be so habitually disposed to do so that we can depend upon it. He will place the good of the patient above his own and seek that good unless its pursuit imposes an injustice upon him, or his family, or requires a violation of his own conscience.

While the virtues are necessary to attain the good internal to medicine as a practice, they exist independently of medicine. They are necessary for the practice of a good life, no matter in what activities that life may express itself. Certain of the virtues may become duties in the Stoic sense, duties because of the nature of medicine as a practice. Medicine calls forth benevolence, beneficence, truth telling, honesty, fidelity, and justice more than physical courage, for example. Yet even physical courage may be necessary when caring for the wounded on battlefields, in plagues, earthquakes, or other disasters. On a more ordinary scale courage is necessary in treating contagious diseases, violent patients, or battlefield casualties. Doing the right and good thing in medicine calls for a more regular, intensive, and selective practice of the virtues than many other callings.

A person who is a virtuous person can cultivate the technical skills of medicine for reasons other than the good of the patient—his own pride, profit, prestige, power. Such a physician can make technically right decisions and perform skillfully. He could not be depended upon, however, to act against his own self-interest for the good of his patient.

In the virtuous physician, explicit fulfillment of rights and duties is an outward expression of an inner disposition to do the right and the good. He is virtuous not because he has conformed to the letter of the law, or his moral duties, but because that is what a good person does. He starts always with his commitment to be a certain kind of person, and he approaches clinical quandaries, conflicts of values, and his patient's interests as a good person should.

Some branches of medicine would seem to demand a stricter and broader adherence to virtue than others. Generalists, for example, who deal with the more sensitive facets and nuances of a patient's life and humanity must exercise the virtues more diligently than technique-oriented specialists. The narrower the specialty the more easily the patient's good can be safeguarded by rules, regulations, rights and duties; the broader the specialty the more significant are the physician's character traits. No branch of medicine, however, can be practiced without some dedication to some of the virtues [9].

Unfortunately, physicians can compartmentalize their lives. Some practice medicine virtuously, yet are guilty of vice in their private lives. Examples are common of physicians who appear sincerely to seek the good of their patients and neglect obligations to family or friends. Some boast of being 'married' to medicine and use this excuse to justify all sorts of failures in their own human relationships. We could not call such a person virtuous. Nor could we be secure in, or trust, his disposition to act in a right and good way even in medicine. After all, one of the essential virtues is balancing conflicting obligations judiciously.

As Socrates pointed out to Meno, one cannot really be virtuous in part:

Why did not I ask you to tell me the nature of virtue as a whole? And you are very far from telling me this; but declare every action to be virtue which is done with a part of virtue; as though you had told me and I must already know the whole of virtue, and this too when frittered away into little pieces. And therefore my dear Meno, I fear that I must begin again, and repeat the same question: what is virtue? For otherwise, I can only say that every action done with a part of virtue is virtue; what else is the meaning of saying that every action done with justice is virtue? Ought I not to ask the question over again; for can any one who does not know virtue know a part of virtue? (*Meno*, 79)

VIRTUES, RIGHTS AND DUTIES IN MEDICAL ETHICS

Frankena has neatly summarized the distinctions between virtue-based and rights- and duty-based ethics as follows:

In an ED (ethics of duty) then, the basic concept is that a certain kind of external act (or doing) ought to be done in certain circumstances; and that of a certain disposition being a virtue is a dependent one. In an EV (ethics of virtue) the basic concept is that of a disposition or way of being— something one has, or if not, does—as a virtue, as morally good; and that of an action's being virtuous or good or even right, is a dependent one [10].

There are some logical difficulties with a virtue-based ethic. For one thing, there must be some consensus on a definition of virtue. For another there is a circularity in the assertion that virtue is what the good

man habitually does, and that at the same time one becomes virtuous by doing good. Virtue and good are defined in terms of each other and the definitions of both may vary among sincere people in actual practice when there is no consensus. A virtue-based ethic is difficult to defend as the sole basis for normative judgments.

But there is a deficiency in rights- and duty-ethics as well. They too must be linked to a theory of the good. In contemporary ethics, theories of good are rarely explicitly linked to theories of the right and good. Von Wright, commendably, is one of the few contemporary authorities who explicitly connects his theory of good with his theory of virtue. . . .

In most professional ethical codes, virtue- and duty-based ethics are intermingled. The Hippocratic Oath, for example, imposes certain duties like protection of confidentiality, avoiding abortion, not harming the patient. But the Hippocratic physician also pledges: ". . . in purity and holiness I will guard my life and my art." This is an exhortation to be a good person and a virtuous physician, in order to serve patients in an ethically responsible way.

Likewise, in one of the most humanistic statements in medical literature, the first century A.D. writer, Scribonius Largus, made *humanitas* (compassion) an essential virtue. It is thus really a role-specific duty. In doing so he was applying the Stoic doctrine of virtue to medicine [11].

The latest version (1980) of the AMA 'Principles of Medical Ethics' similarly intermingles duties, rights, and exhortations to virtue. It speaks of 'standards of behavior', 'essentials of honorable behavior', dealing 'honestly' with patients and colleagues and exposing colleagues 'deficient in character'. The *Declaration of Geneva*, which must meet the challenge of the widest array of value systems, nonetheless calls for practice 'with conscience and dignity' in keeping with 'the honor and noble traditions of the profession'. Though their first allegiance must be to the Communist ethos, even the Soviet physician is urged to preserve 'the high title of physician', 'to keep and develop the beneficial traditions of medicine' and to 'dedicate' all his 'knowledge and strength to the care of the sick'.

Those who are cynical of any protestation of virtue on the part of physicians will interpret these excerpts as the last remnants of a dying tradition of altruistic benevolence. But at the very least, they attest to the recognition that the good of the patient cannot be fully protected by rights and duties alone. Some degree of supererogation is built into the nature of the relationship of those who are ill and those who profess to help them.

This too may be why many graduating classes, still idealistic about their calling, choose the Prayer of Maimonides (not by Maimonides at all) over the more deontological Oath of Hippocrates. In that 'prayer' the physician asks: ". . . may neither avarice nor miserliness, nor thirst for glory or for a great reputation engage my mind; for the enemies of truth and philanthropy may easily deceive me and make me forgetful of my lofty aim of doing good to thy children." This is an unequivocal call to virtue and it is hard to imagine even the most cynical graduate failing to comprehend its message.

All professional medical codes, then, are built of a three-tiered system of obligations related to the special roles of physicians in society. In the ascending order of ethical sensitivity they are: observance of the laws of the land, then observance of rights and fulfillment of duties, and finally the practice of virtue.

A legally based ethic concentrates on the minimum requirements—the duties imposed by human laws which protect against the grosser aberrations of personal rights. Licensure, the laws of torts and contracts, prohibitions against discrimination, good Samaritan laws, definitions of death, and the protection of human subjects of experimentation are elements of a legalistic ethic.

At the next level is the ethics of rights and duties which spells out obligations beyond what law defines. Here, benevolence and beneficence take on more than their legal meaning. The ideal of service, of responsiveness to the special needs of those who are ill, some degree of compassion, kindliness, promise-keeping, truth-telling, and non-maleficence and specific obligations like confidentiality and autonomy, are included. How these principles are applied, and conflicts among them resolved in the patient's best interests, are subjects of widely varying interpretation. How sensitively these issues are confronted depends more on the physician's character than his capability at ethical discourse or moral casuistry.

Virtue-based ethics goes beyond these first two levels. We expect the virtuous person to do the right and the good even at the expense of personal sacrifice and legitimate self-interest. Virtue ethics expands the notions of benevolence, beneficence, conscientiousness, compassion, and fidelity well beyond what strict duty might require. It makes some degree of supererogation mandatory because it calls for standards of ethical

performance that exceed those prevalent in the rest of society [12].

At each of these three levels there are certain dangers from over-zealous or misguided observance. Legalistic ethical systems tend toward a justification for minimalistic ethics, a narrow definition of benevolence or beneficence, and a contract-minded physician-patient relationship. Duty- and rights-based ethics may be distorted by too strict adherence to the letter of ethical principles without the modulations and nuances the spirit of those principles implies. Virtue-based ethics, being the least specific, can more easily lapse into self-righteous paternalism or an unwelcome over-involvement in the personal life of the patient. Misapplication of any moral system even with good intent converts benevolence into maleficence. The virtuous person might be expected to be more sensitive to these aberrations than someone whose ethics is more deontologically or legally flavored.

The more we yearn for ethical sensitivity the less we lean on rights, duties, rules, and principles, and the more we lean on the character traits of the moral agent. Paradoxically, without rules, rights, and duties specifically spelled out, we cannot predict what form a particular person's expression of virtue will take. In a pluralistic society, we need laws, rules, and principles to assure a dependable minimum level of moral conduct. But that minimal level is insufficient in the complex and often unpredictable circumstances of decision-making, where technical and value desiderata intersect so inextricably.

The virtuous physician does not act from unreasoned, uncritical intuitions about what feels good. His dispositions are ordered in accord with that 'right reason' which both Aristotle and Aquinas considered essential to virtue. Medicine is itself ultimately an exercise of practical wisdom—a right way of acting in difficult and uncertain circumstances for a specific end, i.e., the good of a particular person who is ill. It is when the choice of a right and good action becomes more difficult, when the temptations to self-interest are most insistent, when unexpected nuances of good and evil arise and no one is looking, that the differences between an ethics based in virtue and an ethics based in law and/or duty can most clearly be distinguished.

Virtue-based professional ethics distinguishes itself, therefore, less in the avoidance of overtly immoral practices than in avoidance of those at the margin of moral responsibility. Physicians are confronted, in to-day's morally relaxed climate, with an increasing number of new practices that pit altruism against self-interest. Most are not illegal, or, strictly speaking, immoral in a rights- or duty-based ethic. But they are not consistent with the higher levels of moral sensitivity that a virtue-ethics demands. These practices usually involve opportunities for profit from the illness of others, narrowing the concept of service for personal convenience, taking a proprietary attitude with respect to medical knowledge, and placing loyalty to the profession above loyalty to patients.

Under the first heading, we might include such things as investment in and ownership of for-profit hospitals, hospital chains, nursing homes, dialysis units, tie-in arrangements with radiological or laboratory services, escalation of fees for repetitive, high-volume procedures, and lax indications for their use, especially when third party payers 'allow' such charges.

The second heading might include the ever decreasing availability and accessibility of physicians, the diffusion of individual patient responsibility in group practice so that the patient never knows whom he will see or who is on call, the itinerant emergency room physician who works two days and skips three with little commitment to hospital or community, and the growing over-indulgence of physicians in vacations, recreation, and 'self-development.'

The third category might include such things as 'selling one's services' for whatever the market will bear, providing what the market demands and not necessarily what the community needs, patenting new procedures or keeping them secret from potential competitor-colleagues, looking at the investment of time, effort, and capital in a medical education as justification for 'making it back', or forgetting that medical knowledge is drawn from the cumulative experience of a multitude of patients, clinicians, and investigators.

Under the last category might be included referrals on the basis of friendship and reciprocity rather than skill, resisting consultations and second opinions as affronts to one's competence, placing the interest of the referring physician above those of the patients, [and] looking the other way in the face of incompetence or even dishonesty in one's professional colleagues.

These and many other practices are defended today by sincere physicians and even encouraged in this era of competition, legalism, and self-indulgence. Some can be rationalized even in a deontological ethic. But it would be impossible to envision the physician committed to the virtues assenting to these practices. A virtue-based ethic simply does not fluctuate with what the dominant social mores will tolerate. It must interpret benevolence, beneficence, and responsibility in a way that reduces self-interest and enhances altruism. It is the only convincing answer the profession can give to the growing perception clearly manifest in the legal commentaries in the FTC [Federal Trade Commission] ruling that medicine is nothing more than business and should be regulated as such.

A virtue-based ethic is inherently elitist, in the best sense, because its adherents demand more of themselves than the prevailing morality. It calls forth that extra measure of dedication that has made the best physicians in every era exemplars of what the human spirit can achieve. No matter to what depths a society may fall, virtuous persons will always be the beacons that light the way back to moral sensitivity; virtuous physicians are the beacons that show the way back to moral credibility for the whole profession.

Albert Jonsen, rightly I believe, diagnoses the central paradox in medicine as the tension between self-interest and altruism [13]. No amount of deft juggling of rights, duties, or principles will suffice to resolve that tension. We are all too good at rationalizing what we want to do so that personal gain can be converted from vice to virtue. Only a character formed by the virtues can feel the nausea of such intellectual hypocrisy.

To be sure, the twin themes of self-interest and altruism have been inextricably joined in the history of medicine. There have always been physicians who reject the virtues or, more often, claim them falsely. But, in addition, there have been physicians, more often than the critics of medicine would allow, who have been truly virtuous both in intent and act. They have been, and remain, the leaven of the profession and the hope of all who are ill. They form the sea-wall that will not be eroded even by the powerful forces of commercialization, bureaucratization, and mechanization inevitable in modern medicine.

We cannot, need not, and indeed must not, wait for a medical analogue of MacIntyre's 'new St. Benedict' to show us the way. There is no new concept of virtue waiting to be discovered that is peculiarly suited to the dilemmas of our own dark age. We must recapture the courage to speak of character, virtue, and perfection in living a good life. We must encourage those who are willing to dedicate themselves to a "higher standard of self effacement" [14].

We need the courage, too, to accept the obvious split in the profession between those who see and feel the altruistic imperatives in medicine, and those who do not. Those who at heart believe that the pursuit of private self-interest serves the public good are very different from those who believe in the restraint of self-interest. We forget that physicians since the beginnings of the profession have subscribed to different values and virtues. We need only recall that the Hippocratic Oath was the Oath of physicians of the Pythagorean school at a time when most Greek physicians followed essentially a craft ethic [15]. A perusal of the Hippocratic Corpus itself, which intersperses ethics and etiquette, will show how differently its treatises deal with fees, the care of incurable patients, and the business aspects of the craft.

The illusion that all physicians share a common devotion to a high-flown set of ethical principles has done damage to medicine by raising expectations some members of the profession could not, or will not, fulfill. Today, we must be more forthright about the differences in value commitment among physicians. Professional codes must be more explicit about the relationships between duties, rights, and virtues. Such explicitness encourages a more honest relationship between physicians and patients and removes the hypocrisy of verbal assent to a general code, to which an individual physician may not really subscribe. Explicitness enables patients to choose among physicians on the basis of their ethical commitments as well as their reputations for technical expertise.

Conceptual clarity will not assure virtuous behavior. Indeed, virtues are usually distorted if they are the subject of too conscious a design. But conceptual clarity will distinguish between motives and provide criteria for judging the moral commitment one can expect from the profession and from its individual members. It can also inspire those whose virtuous inclinations need re-enforcement in the current climate of commercialization of the healing relationship.

To this end the current resurgence of interest in virtue-based ethics is altogether salubrious. Linked to a theory of patient good and a theory of rights and duties, it could provide the needed groundwork for a reconstruction of professional medical ethics as that work matures. Perhaps even more progress can be made if we take Shakespeare's advice in *Hamlet*: "Assume the virtue if you have it not. . . . For use almost can change the stamp of nature."

NOTES

1. Lewis, C.: 1952, *Mere Christianity*, Macmillan Co., New York.

2. Pellegrino, E.: 1983, 'The Healing Relationship: The Architectonics of Clinical Medicine', in E. Shelp (ed.), *The Clinical Encounter*, D. Reidel, Dordrecht, Holland, pp. 153–172.

3. Pellegrino, E.: 1983, 'Moral Choice, The Good of the Patient and the Patient's Good', in J. Moskop and L. Kopelman (eds.), *Moral Choice and Medical Crisis*, D. Reidel, Dordrecht, Holland.

4. Engel, G.: 1980, 'The Clinical Application of the Biopsychosocial Model', *American Journal of Psychiatry* 137: 2, 535–544.

5. Von Wright, G.: 1965, *The Varieties of Goodness*, The Humanities Press, New York.

6. Ibid.

7. MacIntyre, A.: 1981, *After Virtue*, University of Notre Dame Press, Notre Dame, Indiana.

8. Pellegrino, E.: 1979, 'The Anatomy of Clinical Judgments: Some Notes on Right Reason and Right Action', in H. T. Engelhardt, Jr., *et al.* (eds.), *Clinical Judgment: A Critical Appraisal*, D. Reidel, Dordrecht, Holland, pp. 169–194. Pellegrino, E.: 1979, 'Toward a Reconstruction of Medical Morality: The Primacy of the Act of Profession and the Fact of Illness', *Journal of Medicine and Philosophy* 4: 1, 32–56.

9. May, W.: Personal communication, 'Virtues in a Professional Setting', unpublished.

10. Frankena, W.: 1982, 'Beneficence in an Ethics of Virtue', in E. Shelp (ed.), *Beneficence and Health Care*, D. Reidel, Dordrecht, Holland, pp. 63–81.

11. Cicero: 1967, *Moral Obligations*, J. Higginbotham (trans.), University of California Press, Berkeley and Los Angeles. Pellegrino, E.: 1983, '*Scribonius Largus* and the Origins of Medical Humanism', address to the American Osler Society.

12. Reeder, J.: 1982, 'Beneficence, Supererogation, and Role Duty', in E. Shelp (ed.), *Beneficence and Health Care*, D. Reidel, Dordrecht, Holland, pp. 83–108.

13. Jonsen, A.: 1983, 'Watching the Doctor', *New England Journal of Medicine* 308: 25, 1531–1535.

14. Cushing, H.: 1929, *Consecratio Medici and Other Papers*, Little, Brown and Co., Boston.

15. Edelstein, L.: 1967, 'The Professional Ethics of the Greek Physician', in O. Temkin (ed.), *Ancient Medicine: Selected Papers of Ludwig Edelstein*, Johns Hopkins University Press, Baltimore.

NANCY S. JECKER
AND DONNIE J. SELF

Separating Care and Cure: An Analysis of Historical and Contemporary Images of Nursing and Medicine*

Care as a central organizing concept is a relative newcomer to moral theory (Blum, 1988; Kittay and Meyers, 1987; Noddings, 1984, 1987, 1989; Pearsall, 1986) and moral development theory (Gilligan, 1982, 1986; Gilligan and Wiggins, 1987; Lyons, 1983). However, its roots in American nursing trace back to nursing's early history. In the late nineteenth century, Florence Nightingale thought medical therapeutics and 'curing' were of less importance to patient outcome and willingly left this realm to the physician. Caring, the arena she considered of greatest importance, she assigned to the nurse (Reverby, 1987a, 1987b).[1]

Although the nurses and physicians entertain a more sophisticated picture of their professions today, the image of caring as the exclusive province of nurses continues to influence public perceptions. Because patients exert influence over professionals' self-perceptions, patients' attitudes have the potential to strengthen and reinforce traditional stereotypes, obstruct efforts to re-define professional relationships and provide political fuel for traditional hierarchies. In this way, the idea that 'doctors cure and nurses care' continues to exercise a pervasive influence on health professionals' self-images and inter-professional rela-

tionships. In addition to these practical consequences, the care-cure division easily can produce a lack of philosophical clarity regarding the concept of care itself. In particular, dissociating the labor of physicians from the realm of care narrows our understanding of care, while treating nursing work as an exclusive care paradigm encourages one-dimensional thinking about care.

This essay provides a philosophical critique of professional stereotypes in medicine. In the course of this critique, we also offer a detailed analysis of the concept of care in health care. More precisely, our aims are to (1) identify factors that contribute to viewing care as the exclusive province of nurses; (2) fine tune the concept of care by exploring alternative forms of care; and (3) illustrate, through the use of cases, diverse models of caring.

GENDER-BASED EXPLANATIONS OF PROFESSIONAL STEREOTYPES

In a popular text on nursing ethics, Andrew Jameton observes that "Physicians are . . . said to focus on the *cure* function, while nurses focus on the *care* functions" (1984, p. 10). Jameton goes on to explain that nurses are expected to perform such functions as follow hospital procedures, report significant incidents and mishaps to supervisors, and organize work on wards and hospital departments. Presumably, physicians order procedures, make medical decisions and take charge of wards and departments. What are the origins of this apparent division of labor? Why does the perception that nurses, and only nurses, perform care functions remain with us? Since nursing and medicine are largely gender segregated professions,

From *Journal of Medicine and Philosophy* 16 (1991), 285–306. © 1991 by Kluwer Academic Publishers. Reprinted by permission of Kluwer Academic Publishers.

*We wish to thank Sara T. Fry, Albert R. Jonsen and an anonymous reviewer of this journal for valuable comments. A version of this paper was presented at a University of Maryland School of Nursing conference on Ethics and Nursing Practice in May of 1990 and at a conference on The Politics of Caring held at the Emory University Institute for Women's Studies in October of 1990.

the answers to these questions may lie as much in gender-related tendencies as in the histories of nursing and medicine.

One explanation for this apparent division is suggested by Gilligan and Pollak (1989). They report that the association of danger with intimacy is a more salient feature in the fantasies of men than of women. In their study, men projected more danger into situations of close, personal affiliation than situations of impersonal achievement. For example, male subjects expressed "a fear of being caught in a smothering relationship or humiliated by rejection or deceit" (1989, p. 246). Females, by contrast, perceived more danger in situations of impersonal achievement than situations of personal affiliation. For instance, females "connected danger with the isolation that they associated with competitive success" (1989, p. 246). If male and female attitudes toward attachment and separation do cluster in the way this study suggests, this indicates one fairly obvious explanation for care and cure stereotypes in the health professions. Female nurses would tend to cultivate skill at caring activities, because these activities involve the intimacy and close personal affiliation that women, as a group, prefer. Curing activities would, on the whole, be shunned by nurses, because such activities involve forms of impersonal achievement that women, as a group, find threatening. The opposite tendency should occur in medicine, a male dominated profession, namely: physicians would be likely to stress scientific and technical achievement, while downplaying patient contact and physician-patient relationships.

Consistent with the above line of reasoning is a second possible explanation. According to this second account, the detached objectivity of scientific fields generally, and medical science in particular, discourages many women from excelling at them. Keller maintains that the goal of post-enlightenment science has been a method of perception that affirms empirical reality, while denying subjectivity (1985). This method of knowing implies a purely mechanical view of persons and objects: "no longer filling the void with living form," scientists in the modern age "learned to fill it with dead form" (Keller, 1985, pp. 69–70). In our culture, such a view of self and world is, according to Keller, pervasively associated with masculinity (1985, p. 71).

If Keller is correct about both the association between science and objectivity and the association between objectivity and masculinity, her analysis sheds light on the alleged cure-care division. Following Keller's analysis, once scientific medicine became the dominant mode of medicine in this country, a method of perception that denied the significance of subjectivity took hold. Such an approach focused attention on patients' physical signs and symptoms, while downplaying the significance of their subjective preferences, feelings and experiences. The masculine image this method portrayed in the culture induced males to practice medicine, but encouraged women to assume healing roles that fit better the culture's idea of femininity.

A third explanation of professional stereotypes in nursing and medicine also appeals to gender stereotypes. This explanation holds that our culture associates ethics and humanism with femininity rather than masculinity. For example, ethics and values frequently are referred to as being learned at mother's knee. Morantz-Sanchez (1985) traces this association between ethics and femininity to the early nineteenth century. She argues that during this time, the popular image of women shifted from the biblical and puritan idea of an innately sexual temptress to the idea of women as naturally passionless, spiritual and moral. When women were no longer seen as 'the inheritors of Eve's questionable legacy" (Morantz-Sanchez, 1985, p. 22), their prudery confined the social roles they were qualified to fill. In particular, women were judged unqualified to enter the medical profession because, unlike men, they could not restrain their natural sympathies as a physician must. For example, women could not be brought into the dissecting room and undergo other rigors of medical training without destroying their innate moral sensibilities.

Referring to the modern tradition, Jameton makes the point that it is "women [not men who] have carried the humane tradition in modern western cultures: they educate children, soften the blows of the world, nurture others and humanize modern life. Nursing and medicine have reified this stereotype" (1987, p. 67). Jameton also notes the longstanding tradition of ethics in the female dominated profession of nursing, and the comparatively weaker and more recent tradition of ethics in medicine. According to Jameton, since 1900 not a single decade has passed without publication of at least one basic text in nursing ethics. Moreover, in its very first volume (1901), *The American Journal of Nursing* published an article on ethics. In the 1920s and 1930s, the *Journal* carried a regular column of ethics cases. In addition to ethics publications, ethics courses have a long history in nursing: they were included in the first formal training programs for nurses. In medicine, by contrast, the tradition of ethics teaching in a sustained and consistent manner is much more recent. It was not until the 1970s that medicine incorporated a significant formal ethics curriculum into medical school classes, and even then "it resulted in large part from outside pressures" (Jameton, 1987, p. 67). Assuming Morantz-Sanchez's and Jameton's historical analyses are correct, they illuminate another possible source of professional stereotypes. If our culture associates ethical concern and response with femininity, one would expect females in general to gravitate toward roles that call upon these abilities. Men who wished to enter the health care profession would fill other roles.

It should be noted that all of the above explanations take for granted the idea that American nursing and medicine are gender segregated professions. This assumption is historically accurate, since a generation or more ago over ninety percent of medical students and physicians were white men (Relman, 1989), and nursing has long been dominated by women. Yet despite this historical precedence, today more men are becoming nurses and women are much more likely to enter the medical profession. In 1972, for example, 1,694 men graduated from American nursing schools, a fourfold increase over 1963, and in 1981 the number of men graduating from R.N. programs jumped to 3,492 (Rowland, 1984). Since women continue to dominate nursing, it is not surprising that overall they occupy more high-level administrative and supervisory positions than men. Yet, the percentage of male nurses who have reached administrative or supervisory positions is much larger than the percentage of female nurses who have reached administrative or supervisory positions (Rowland, 1984). Thus men who do enter nursing are more likely to be in positions where their presence and influence is felt.

Likewise, in the American medical profession, the percentage of female applicants and matriculants to medical school began to rise abruptly in 1970–1971. The number of applications from men, which had been rising steeply, reached a peak in 1974–1976 and has been falling ever since (Relman, 1989). Although few women serve on medical faculty (Eisenberg, 1989), and women are underrepresented in positions of power in academic institutions and as leaders in medical organizations (Levinson, Tolle, Lewis, 1989), their presence in medicine is growing and their influence in shaping medicine's professional identity is increasing.

For these reasons, the above explanations of professional stereotypes are incomplete as they stand. A more complete account would need to explain recent changes in the gender constitution of each profession, perhaps by appealing to shifts in the culture's gender ideals. For example, new gender ideals for men may lie behind changes currently underway in the medical profession. For example, the Association of American Medical Colleges has substantially revised its Medical College Admission Test (MCAT) to place greater emphasis on 'humanistic' skills in selecting physicians; the American Board of Internal Medicine has requested directors of residency programs to assess compassion, respect for patients and integrity in candidates for board certification; and the American Medical Association recently embarked on a major quality assurance initiative which will include research into attributes of 'interpersonal exchange' (Nelson, 1989). Alternatively, a fuller explanation might uncover ways in which traditional gender attitudes persist, despite greater integration of men in nursing and women in medicine. For example, despite greater numbers of male nurses, the American nursing profession is still overwhelmingly female: ninety-seven percent of the total nurse population is female (American Nurses' Association, 1987). Moreover, the majority (56.3 percent) of men cite employment availability as their reason for entering nursing, while most women (62.1 percent) cite interest in people (Rowland, 1984). This suggests that practical economic considerations, rather than a desire to enter a caring role, are more frequent motives among men. Furthermore, the fact that more men are entering nursing may simply indicate that more men are willing to challenge prevailing stereotypes, rather than indicating that these stereotypes and the expectations associated with them no longer apply. Evidence for this is that males who become nurses are more likely than female nurses to be viewed as gay or asked why they do not become doctors (Rowland, 1984). Male nurses also report greater difficulty than female nurses in telling others of their occupational choice: in one study, only sixty-six percent felt comfortable doing so, as compared with eighty-three percent of women (Rowland, 1984). Finally, although more men are choosing nursing, gender segregation reportedly persists between nursing specialties. Men's highest priorities after graduation are jobs in critical or acute care settings, whereas women prefer pediatric and public health fields (Rowland, 1984). In one study of nursing students, male students preferred, in rank order: emergency nursing, then outpatient, intensive care, medical-surgical, psychiatric, and coronary care nursing, and lastly, anesthesia. By contrast, female students ranked pediatric nursing first, then public health, medical-surgical, obstetrics/maternity, and psychiatric nursing (Rowland, 1984).

HISTORICAL EXPLANATIONS OF PROFESSIONAL STEREOTYPES

Another kind of explanation for the cure-care division has less to do with hypothesized gender differences and more to do with the unique histories of the nursing and medical professions. First, the history of nursing, and its domestic roots in particular, may shed light on the association of nursing with care. Although historians sometimes ignore these roots and begin the history of nursing with the introduction of formal training programs for nurses in the 1870s, a growing number of revisionist historians reject this approach. For example, Reverby makes the point that American nursing "did not appear *de novo* at the end of the nineteenth century . . . [instead,] nursing throughout the colonial era and most of the nineteenth century took place within the family" (1987a, p. 5). O'Brien also finds the roots of nursing "deep in the domestic world of the family" (1987). And Starr maintains that "care of the sick was part of the domestic economy for which the wife assumed responsibility. She would call on the networks of kin and community for advice and assistance when illness struck" (1982, p. 32, 1982).

According to these historians, the history of American nursing begins prior to the 1870s. During this earlier period, mothers, daughters and sisters nursed their families at home, sometimes aided by female neighbors who called themselves 'professed' or 'born' nurses and had previous experience caring for their own families (O'Brien, 1987, p. 13). So long as the locus of nursing remained domestic, its primary task was the nurturing of loved ones through ongoing feeding, clothing, bathing and comforting.

Increasingly, the nurturing tasks in which home-based nurses engaged during the colonial era were set apart from the responsibility of their physician counterparts. First, the medical manuals that domestic nurses consulted drew a sharp line between "what could be accomplished by a loving mother and nurse and what needed the skilled consultation of a physi-

cian" (O'Brien, 1987, p. 13). The popular 18th century book, *Domestic Medicine*, assured readers that physicians need be consulted rarely, and that most people underestimate their own abilities and knowledge (Buchanan, 1778). Second, the very fact that nurses lived with their patients and constantly were immersed in the practical activity of caring for them, meant that their job took on a distinctive character. In contrast to nurses, physicians made house calls or were visited by patients in offices. Patients were not primarily relatives, but neighbors and townspeople. The physician's job was to offer expert advice or perform specific medical procedures, while nurses carried out physicians' instructions. Thus, physicians used their presumed expertise to direct the caring process, while nurses who lived with patients carried out the actual tasks of ongoing care.

According to this account, the association of American nursing with care traces back to the time when nurses' chief task was caring for sick offspring in the home. Later in the nineteenth century, when nurses left the domestic front to care for patients in hospitals and during wartime, and when they attended the first professional training schools, these early domestic roots continued to shape nursing's identity. In these new locations, nurses' roles continued to include traditional domestic tasks, such as bed making, feeding and hygiene. Thus, a significant emphasis of early training programs was on practical skills. Later educational reforms which sought to introduce scientific content into the nursing curriculum stirred heated debate, attesting to the continued influence of the domestic tradition on the nursing profession.

While American nursing was linked intimately with caregiving activities, American physicians achieved professional status and identity by fashioning a separate sphere. Given the association between caring and 'women's work', physicians surely had little incentive to identify their own professional function as caring. As Benner and Wrubel note, "caring is devalued because caring is associated with women's work and women's work is devalued and most often unpaid" (1989, p. 368). During the colonial era, physicians had only part time medical practices. They earned a livelihood performing other tasks, such as clergy, teaching and farming (Conrad and Schneider, 1990). Not until the nineteenth century did medicine become a full time vocation, but during this period its dangerous and often unsuccessful therapies undermined its prestige.

According to Starr, "while some physicians were seeking to make themselves into an elite profession with a monopoly of practice, much of the public refused to grant them any such privileges" (1982, p. 31). In addition, physicians were fiercely competitive with homeopaths and other medical sects for a share of the medical market. Thus, much of American medicine's early history was characterized by repeated efforts to gain repute and professional standing. The first state licensing laws, which granted to physicians with special training and class sole authority to practice medicine, were repealed during the Jacksonian period (Starr, 1982). Later in the nineteenth century, with the formation of the American Medical Association, physicians were finally successful in their efforts to professionalize medicine and control medical markets. Medicine was credited with the decline in incidence and mortality of diseases, such as leprosy, malaria, smallpox and cholera, thereby increasing the public's faith in its healing powers. During the latter part of the nineteenth century, the rise of scientific medicine ushered in significant progress and ensured the continued prestige and dominance of the medical profession.

The early history of American medicine suggests a possible explanation for the association of medicine with cure, rather than care. The presence of fierce competition and marginal status during its early years forged a mission for medicine that focused on achieving cultural authority and an elite status for its practitioners. Efforts to gain authority and status required physicians to stand apart from laypersons and develop exclusive modes of language, technique and theory. This put physicians at odds with activities, such as patient empathy and care, that call upon abilities of engagement and identification with others. The scientific paradigm that became the language and practice of medicine further reinforced a separation between physician and patient. This paradigm pictured the human being as a machine, and disease as an objective entity that interfered with the human being's mechanical functioning. Such a perspective implied that the 'ghost in the machine' was superfluous to the healing process.

RETHINKING THE CONCEPT OF CARE

Having considered several possible explanations for the association of nursing with care, and medicine with cure, we need to consider next whether these common stereotypes are justified. To address this question, we now turn to a critical analysis of the concept of care. To begin with, it should be noted that the very idea of separating care from cure assumes that these ideas are distinct and non-overlapping. An alternative view sees caring as part of the very meaning of curing. According to this view, physicians who cure also care. Interestingly, the *Oxford English Dictionary* supports this interpretation of cure. Cure comes from the Latin word "curare" meaning "to care for, take care of". Cure refers to "care, heed, concern; to do one's (busy) care, to give one's care or attention to some piece of work; to apply one's self diligently". This definition renders the idea of a physician who cures without caring unintelligible. A person who heals a wound, or otherwise restores a patient to health, cures only if this outcome is the result of devoted caring.

On this reading, although curing entails applying one's care to some one or thing, caring does not imply curing. Thus, physicians can and often do *care* for patients, while suspending attempts to *cure* them. This occurs, for example, when physicians withdraw medical treatments they judge futile, while continuing palliative measures. Hauerwas notes the practical importance of acknowledging the possibility of caring *without* curing. Physicians who fail to recognize the possibility of caring without curing might attempt futile therapies, based on the false belief that efforts to cure patients are all they have to offer.

The *Oxford English Dictionary* distinguishes two distinct senses of care. First, care means "a burdened state of mind arising from . . . concern about anything . . . mental perturbation", and "serious or grave mental attention, the charging of the mind". In this first sense, to "have a care" or "keep a care" is to be in a subjective state of concern about something. Second, care refers to "oversight with view of protection, preservation, or guidance; hence to have the care of". In this second sense, care implies an activity of looking out for or safeguarding the interests of others.

We shall designate the first sense of care, 'caring about'. Caring about indicates an attitude, feeling, or state of mind directed toward a person or circumstance (Hauerwas, 1978, p. 145). To assert that 'My nurse cares about me' or that 'Everyone ought to care about the environment' refers to care in this first sense. The second sense of care involves the exercise of a skill, with or without a particular attitude or feeling toward the object upon which this skill is exercised. We shall refer to this as 'caring for'. For example, we use care in this sense when we say that 'Nurse

Jones is caring for your mother' or 'The mechanic down the street offered to take care of my car'. Caring in both senses is a relational term, referring to an attitude or skill directed to someone or something. One's concern about others may be more or less deep, and one's skill at caring for others may display more or less ability. Thus, we refer to the quality of caring to describe how deeply one feels, or how good or poor one is at caring for another. Whereas caring about can occur at a distance from its object, caring for usually requires direct contact with the one who is cared for. Excellence at caring for particular patients typically requires repeated contacts and skill in ascertaining each patient's particular needs. Thus, an expert caregiver learns "through repeated experience with patients . . . to perceive the particular rather than the typical, care becomes individualized rather than standardized and planning becomes anticipatory of change rather than simply responsive to change" (Benner and Wrubel, 1989, p. 382).

Applying these definitions of cure and care to the medical setting enables us to say that a health professional who cares *about* a patient makes a cognitive or emotional decision that the welfare of the patient is of great importance. Caring about requires keeping the patient's best interest in the forefront of mind and heart. By contrast, a health professional who cares *for* a patient engages in a deliberate and ongoing activity of responding to the patient's needs. Caring for, executed in an exemplary or excellent way, involves deciphering the patient's particular condition and needs. This calls upon verbal skills of questioning and listening and requires attending to and translating nonverbal cues. Caring for thus requires cultivating a capacity to understand others' subjective experiences. Understood in this light, caring for draws upon and teaches a way of knowing that involves "awareness of the complexities of a particular situation" and "inner . . . resources that have been garnered through experience in living" (Benoliel, 1987). The source of this knowledge tends to be participation in relationships with others and observation of others' actions, rather than verbal debate and conversation or the reading of texts (Benner, 1983). Knowledge in this form is practical and interpersonal (Schultz and Meleis, 1988). In the case of unconscious or mentally compromised patients and infants, caring for especially draws upon a person's skill at interpreting gestures, postures, sounds, grimaces, eye scans and bodily movements (Jecker, 1990a). For instance, through intimate engagement, a daughter who serves as a caretaker for a disoriented elderly parent may be able to decipher what counts as pain and comfort, or boredom and interest to the parent. Evidence is gleaned through partaking in daily rituals, such as bathing and feeding, and interpreting the parent's responses.

Caring *about* does not imply caring for. For example, a ward supervisor may care deeply about her patients, without being engaged in the activity of caring directly for them. Nor does caring *for* entail caring about. For instance, one who skillfully cares for patients may be meticulous in her efforts to interpret patients' needs, without actually caring about patients: she may regard them as just one more puzzle to be solved, excel at caring for its own sake, or simply seek to impress colleagues or a boss.

While it is fairly easy to tell who cares *for* a patient, it can be exceedingly difficult to construe who cares *about* a patient. Some professionals may prefer colleagues and supervisors to think they care about their patients, even if they in fact are preoccupied with other matters. Others may learn to cover up the fact that they do care about patients. For example, the idea of masculinity to which some aspire discourages outward expressions of care and concern for others. It would be difficult to gauge whether males who express masculinity in this way care about their patients. Still others may appear uncaring because they learn deference in conflict. For example, women or nurses who are taught to follow orders blindly may appear not to take a genuine interest in their patients. Historically, nurses were instructed to discharge medical orders in an obedient, unquestioning manner (Jameton, 1987), but this expectation does not necessarily entail the absence of caring about.

EXAMPLES OF CARE

In order to bring the concept of care into sharper focus, it is useful to review cases in which individuals exhibit care in different ways. In the course of this review, we shall consider in more detail the protective qualities associated with different kinds of care and the positive and negative forms these qualities can take.

1. CASE ONE: CARING FOR AND ABOUT A PATIENT

I was taking care of a 40-year-old female who had been hospitalized for 3 months in another hospital and came to our hospital the day before to have her abdominal fistulas [external openings for collecting bodily wastes] corrected.

The night before I met her, the bag collecting her drainage fell off three times and was reapplied the same way each time by her former nurse due to the patient's insistence that nothing else works. Her skin was very excoriated in spots and tender. When I removed the leaking bag I noticed that the problem was that she had a large crease between two recessed fistulas. I attempted to reapply it to avoid these. She was resistant to my suggestions, and protested my efforts to replace the bag. So I told her that she should trust me because I've had numerous similar situations with which I've had positive outcomes. I pointed out that if the bag was not replaced to avoid the fistulas it would continue to fall off and her pain and discomfort would only increase. She reconsidered. I told her that I was sure I could get a bag to stay on her for at least 24 hours, if not more. She said she'd love that to happen and told me I could do what I wanted. (Benner, 1984, pp. 138–139)

In this first case, a nurse appears to care both for and about a patient. Each effort calls upon a distinct set of responses. Caring *for* manifests itself in the activities of removing the leaking bag, locating the problem in adhering it to the patient's skin and replacing the bag. Caring *about* is shown by the *manner* in which the nurse cares for the patient, a manner which expresses concern and involves efforts to reassure and gain the patient's confidence.

Notice too the nurse's response to her patient's initial resistance. This response exhibits the nurse's ability to persuade a recalcitrant patient that a certain procedure (replacing the bag) is in the patient's best interest and that she can execute this procedure successfully. A different response would have been simply to say, 'you *must* let me do this'. The difference between these two responses reveals alternative forms of parentalism (Taylor, 1985). In the medical setting, parentalism is an attempt to justify performing (or omitting) an action that is contrary to a patient's expressed wishes, yet judged to be in a patient's best interest. Were the nurse in this situation to respond to the refusal of treatment by saying 'that's my final word', she would illustrate a kind of parentalism that justifies medical actions by presuming to abrogate a patient's *rights*. An alternative mode of parentalism invokes a morality of *responsibility*, rather than rights (Taylor, 1985; Ruddick, 1989). Here, one appeals to the patient's self-interest and personal responsibility, rather than invoking one's own authority to override the patient. For example, the nurse in case one displays this latter kind of parentalism by effectively lay-

ing out for the patient the consequences that attach to different alternatives: replacing the bag properly ensures that it will adhere; not doing so may result in the bag falling off and so heighten the patient's pain and discomfort. In this way, the patient is led to choose between taking responsibility for safeguarding her own interests, or behaving in a less responsible fashion.

Parentalism that is based on promoting the patient's sense of personal responsibility elicits our powers of practical persuasion, and it is often cultivated by those who care *for* others. This is because those charged with caring for others are more often in the position of having to gain others' cooperation. Those who care about, but not for, may need only to confirm in their *own* mind that a certain course of action is justified.

Both kinds of parentalism can be instantiated in positive and negative ways. For example, parentalism that fosters the patient's sense of responsibility can be a positive force. However, this kind of parentalism can also deteriorate into a manipulative tool, for example, when it is used merely to produce guilt in patients, block the expression of patients' feelings, or manipulate patients to acquiesce to decisions they do not prefer in order to gain petty conveniences for caregivers (Taylor, 1985).

The other form of parentalism, that appeals to the health professional's rights and authority over the patient, can represent both positive and negative approaches as well. Negative expressions include a doctor or nurse who knowingly assumes greater authority than she is morally entitled to claim. Or negative parentalism occurs when the justified exercise of authority is conjoined with callousness, e.g., bullying a patient or giving patients orders in an abrupt or cruel fashion. By contrast, an example of positive parentalism of this sort is overriding the rights of someone that one is close to in order to protect that person's interests. Hardwig, for example, notes that in the context of close personal relationships, parentalistic behavior is often warranted and failing to show parentalism can signal a failure to fulfill special responsibilities (Hardwig, 1984). Elsewhere (Jecker, 1989, 1990b, 1990c), it is argued that the responsibilities of individuals in close relationships are different and often greater than the responsibilities that exist between acquaintances or strangers. If this approach is correct, then whether or not abrogating others' rights is justified in the health care setting depends, in part, upon whether particular health professionals stand in close relationships with their patients. Between virtual strangers, interference with others for their own good is less often desirable and more apt to overstep moral boundaries between persons.

2. CASE TWO: CARING FOR, BUT NOT ABOUT A PATIENT

A demented thirty-year-old man had AIDS for eight months. His final admission to our hospital was prompted by the development of large decubitus ulcers. On the ward his oral intake was minimal, and the attending physician instructed me to administer parenteral nutrition. I didn't like taking care of this patient. I kept thinking that he had brought this fate upon himself by his gay lifestyle. Gays repulsed me, and I was unable to feel any compassion for this fellow. I also found his medical problems disgusting and resented the fact that caring for him exposed me to life threatening risks. The patient had copious diarrhea; the decubiti were oozing fluids; and administering parenteral nutrition was complicated by high, spiking fevers that twice necessitated removal of the central line. (Cooke, 1986)

In case two a nurse is involved in caring *for* a patient. Caring for is manifest in the activities of treating the patient's ulcers and administering parenteral nutrition. Although the nurse is engaged in the activity of caregiving, her negative feelings about the patient suggest that she lacks an attitude of caring *about* the patient. Mustering such an attitude would require the nurse to reject or subdue her negative responses to the patient. On the other hand, particular nurses will always dislike particular patients, and subduing negative feelings will not necessarily change or mitigate bad feelings. Attempting and failing to reduce negative feelings may simply compound a nurse's difficulties by festering guilt or lowering self-esteem. Where dislike for patients is likely to persist, it is important to keep separate the ideas of *dislike* and *disrespect*. A nurse who dislikes a particular patient may still express respect toward the patient as a fellow human being, for example, through her ongoing activity of caring *for* the patient. Thus, although the nurse may not care *about* the patient, she can still regard the patient in a positive manner and express this regard in action.

3. CASE THREE: CARING ABOUT, BUT NOT FOR A PATIENT

A twenty-seven-year-old model was admitted to the emergency room after an automobile accident that caused multiple fractures and burns over sixty-five percent of his body. Glass had penetrated both eyes so severely as to leave him blind, although a good chance for survival existed. In the emergency room, the patient was met by friends who candidly told him that his physician expects that his life can be saved. Later when I, the physician, met with the patient to discuss treatment, the patient bluntly told me that he had enjoyed a life in which he had identified with his body and physical pleasure and abilities. He had few intellectual or other interests. On these grounds, he flatly refused treatment and asked me to keep him comfortable. My only concern was to promote this patient's welfare. I had seen many burn patients begin with a negative attitude toward treatment and then undergo a change of heart. Based on these experiences I decided to order aggressive treatment and arranged for a psychiatric consult. (Brody and Engelhardt, 1987, pp. 327–328)

The third case is about a physician who cares about a patient, but may not be engaged, in an ongoing way, in caring for the patient. For example, the physician orders burn treatments, but may not be the one who actually will provide these treatments to the patient. Unlike the nurse in case one, the physician in this case does not need to gain the patient's cooperation immediately. Moreover, the physician expresses parentalism by appealing to her authority and presumed superior knowledge to justify overriding the patient's wishes. The justification she gives for this is the silent refrain: "I know better; I've seen many burn patients in this situation change their mind". A different kind of parentalism would involve persuading the patient, as well as herself, of the wisdom of continued treatment. The alternative response intends to justify an action *to the patient* through iteration of the consequences of different choices. By contrast, the physician in case three seeks to justify the action mainly *to herself*. Thus her reasoning is 'silent' and she does not attempt negotiation of a solution agreeable to the patient.

4. CASE FOUR: CARING NEITHER FOR NOR ABOUT A PATIENT

I supervise a ward of terminally ill cancer patients. I deliberately avoid getting emotionally involved with these patients because I realize it would be terribly depressing. Fortunately, most of my responsibilities involve management of nurses, paper work and general organization, so I by and large can steer clear of patients and families. Most of the time, I limit my contact with nursing staff while eschewing patient contact. This enables me to direct my energy toward problems I can solve effectively and prevents me from feeling overwhelmed and powerless about dying patients.[2]

The nurse in this last case does not assume the responsibility of caring *for* patients. Nor does she display an attitude of caring *about* patients on her ward. Instead, she strives to maintain a neutral or indifferent stance. Presumably, such a stance affords her a sense of control in an otherwise emotionally charged environment.

FORMS OF CARE
IN HEALTH CARE PROFESSIONS

The foregoing analysis of the concept of care places us in a better position to consider traditional stereotypes with a critical eye. In rethinking the idea that 'doctors cure and nurses care', it is helpful to be aware of four possible models of caring. These models parallel the cases discussed above:

1. Health professionals who care for and about their patients,
2. Health professionals who care for, but not about their patients,
3. Health professionals who care about, but not for their patients,
4. Health professionals who care neither for nor about their patients.

In the first model, health professionals care for and about patients. Since caring for is an ongoing and deliberate activity, a health professional whose patient contact is limited to brief visits or to discrete medical interventions, such as taking vital signs, does not fit the first model. Rather, to care in the sense defined by the first model a health professional must both carry out the tasks required to provide health care to the patient and possess an attitude of being concerned about what happens to the patient.

The difference between the first and second models of caring is that in the second it does not ultimately matter much to the professional what happens to patients. Nonetheless, it would be misleading to say that the second professional 'does not care'. After all, the second kind of health professional cares *all the time*: he or she is an ongoing caregiver, even though she lacks an attitude of caring *about* patients. This lack may impede her ability to care for patients, but (as noted above), it need not.

Similarly, it would be misleading to state that health professionals whose caring exemplifies the third model 'do not care.' Such professionals (who care about but not for their patients) may think about patients with great frequency, pray for their recovery and be deeply moved to witness it. These kinds of professionals do indeed care, but their care is more remote by virtue of being removed from the immediate context of the patient. This does not imply that caring *about* is 'intellectual' or 'cold', but it does represent a more abstract mode of caring.

The grounds for saying that a health professional 'does not care' can only be that the professional cares neither for nor about patients. In the fourth model, health professionals do not care in either sense. An *uncaring* health professional is neither a caregiver nor concerned about the welfare of patients. Multiple factors may contribute to health professionals' lacking an attitude of caring about patients. In the cases discussed in the previous section, the absence of caring is prompted, in part, by feeling superior, being emotionally indifferent, needing control, blaming the patient for the disease and disliking the patient. Caring neither for nor about patients often will be an unacceptable role for health professionals. Yet it also may represent a legitimate coping tool, for example, when one's responsibilities are experienced as overwhelming and the need to distance oneself emotionally is felt forcefully.

It is now time to ask how the above models can serve to deepen our understanding of nurses' and physicians' professional roles. To begin with, it is never correct to hold that nurses who function as caregivers do not care. Caring, in the sense of *caring for*, is an inextricable part of their role. The history of nursing is *essentially* a history of caring in this sense. In the colonial era, home-based nurses always cared in the sense of caring *for* family members. Nursing also has a caring tradition in the sense of caring *about* patients. As noted earlier, the first training programs for nurses sought to cultivate moral virtues, including devotion to the welfare of patients.

Despite the historical tradition of care by nurses, there are, and always have been, nurses who do not care much *about* patients in general, or *about* particular patients they nurse. Moreover, as more and more nurses become engaged in administrative and supervisory roles, they may do less caring *for* patients. On these grounds, it is misleading to accept the traditional stereotype that 'nurses care'. This stereotype obscures the fact that over time nursing has changed in its stratification and fields of specialization. These changes have meant that in some areas nurses have less direct patient contact and are less engaged in caring *for* patients. In addition, the traditional stereotype obscures the fact that there always have been nurses who do not care *about* patients.

Turning to physicians, a similar cautionary note is in order. Although some physicians may be less likely to care for patients, and so less likely to exemplify the first two models of caring, many physicians obviously care profoundly *about* patients. Moreover, physicians are a diverse group. In a universal hospital, medical students or residents-in-training may seek or be delegated a considerable amount of caring for responsibilities, while attendings or senior staff may assume very little. Likewise, in health maintenance organizations, physician assistants and nurse practitioners may be utilized to perform a majority of caring for activities. By contrast, in private practices, physicians may undertake most of the caring for responsibilities. Such physicians may establish ongoing relationships with each patient over several years, e.g., monitoring medications, performing regular check-ups and treating minor emergencies. However, regardless of whether physicians care directly *for* patients, they usually assume a stance of caring *about* patients. Attempting to *cure* a patient is ordinarily an expression of a physician's caring about the patient. It is unfortunate, as well as confusing, then, to assume that doctors cure, as *opposed* to care. Thus, to the extent that the care-cure distinction informs our present thinking, it wrongly denies to the medical profession a caring role and unfortunately clouds our conception of the complexities of nursing care.

CONCLUSION

In closing, this [essay] has intended to take a careful look at professional stereotypes in nursing and medicine. Doing so required clarifying the concept of care and articulating different models of caring. That the concept of care is multiform and the models of caring many should attune us to the dangers of buying into popular stereotypes. Holding tenaciously to traditional stereotypes can prevent us from seeing the evidence that both medicine and nursing are caring professions and both men and women care for and about their patients.

Appreciating the richness of the concept of care also should infuse new energy into research on care in health care and professional settings. The following are suggested research topics that merit further consideration. (1) How can cure and care be joined and integrated into the curriculum of both nursing and medical schools? (2) Is care a virtue? If so, under what circumstances might it deteriorate into a vice? Is care ever a duty or obligation? (3) Is caring a way of knowing? How do cure and care relate to both scientific and intuitive forms of knowledge? (4) What is the proper balance between cure and care in developing an ethic for specific patient groups, such as the elderly, the terminally ill and the chronically ill? Although answering these questions is a tall order, our analysis shows the importance and promise of further research in this area.

NOTES

1. Throughout this paper, we will use the terms 'care' and 'caring' interchangeably. There may be important shades of meaning unique to each term, but exploring this is beyond the scope of the present inquiry.

2. Whereas the previous cases are drawn from the medical ethics literature, we could find no cases in the literature to illustrate the fourth model. We believe this is significant if it represents a lack of attention to the ethical problems of health care workers who exemplify this model.

REFERENCES

American Nurses' Association: 1987, *Facts About Nurses*, American Nurses' Association, Kansas City, Missouri.

Benner, P.: 1983, 'Recovering the knowledge embedded in clinical practice', *Image: Journal of Nursing Scholarship* 15, 30–41.

Benner, P.: 1984, *From Novice to Expert: Excellence and Power in Clinical Nursing Practice*, Addison-Wesley Publishing Company, Menlo Park, California.

Benner, P., and Wrubel, J.: 1989, *The Primacy of Caring*, Addison-Wesley Publishing Company, Menlo Park, California.

Benoliel, J.Q.: 1987, 'Response to 'toward holistic inquiry in nursing: A proposal for synthesis of patterns and methods', *Scholarly Inquiry for Nursing Practice: An International Journal* 1, 147–152.

Blum, L.A.: 1988, 'Gilligan and Kohlberg: Implications for moral theory', *Ethics* 98, 472–491.

Brody, B.A., and Engelhardt, H.T.: 1987, *Bioethics: Readings and Cases*, Prentice-Hall, Englewood Cliffs, New Jersey.

Buchanan, W.: 1778, *Domestic Medicine, The Third American Edition*, John Trumbull, Boston.

Conrad, P., and Schneider, J.W.: 1990, 'Professionalization, monopoly, and the structure of medical practice', in P. Conrad and R. Kern (eds.), *The Sociology of Health and Illness: Critical Perspectives, Third Edition*, St. Martin's Press, New York, pp. 141–147.

Cooke, M.: 1986, 'Ethical issues in the care of patients with AIDS', *Quality Review Bulletin*, October, 343–346.

Eisenberg, C.: 1989, 'Medicine is no longer a man's profession', *New England Journal of Medicine* 321, 1542–1544.

Gilligan, C.: 1982, *In a Different Voice: Psychological Theory and Women's Development*, Harvard University Press, Cambridge, Massachusetts.

Gilligan, C.: 1986, 'Remapping the moral domain: New images of the self in relationship', in T.C. Heller, M. Sosna, and D.E. Wellbery (eds.), *Reconstructing Individualism: Autonomy, Individuality, and the Self in Western Thought*, Stanford University Press, Stanford, California, pp. 237–252.

Gilligan, C., and Wiggins, G.: 1987, 'The origins of morality in early childhood', in J. Kagan and S. Lamb (eds.), *The Emergence of Morality in Young Children*, University of Chicago Press, Chicago, pp. 277–305.

Gilligan, C., and Pollak, S.: 1989, 'The vulnerable and invulnerable physician', in C. Gilligan, J.V. Ward, and J.M. Taylor (eds.), *Mapping the Moral Domain*, Harvard University Press, Cambridge, Massachusetts, pp. 245–262.

Hardwig, J.: 1984, 'Should women think in terms of rights?,' *Ethics* 94, 441–455.

Hauerwas, S.: 1978, 'Care', in W.T. Reich (ed.), *The Encyclopedia of Bioethics*, Free Press, New York, Vol. 1, 145–150.

Levinson, W., Tolle, S., and Lewis, C.: 1989, 'Women in academic medicine', *New England Journal of Medicine* 321, 1511–1517.

Jameton, A.: 1984, *Nursing Practice: The Ethical Issues*, Prentice-Hall, Englewood Cliffs, New Jersey.

Jameton, A.: 1987, 'Physicians and nurses: A historical perspective', in B.A. Brody and H.T. Engelhardt, *Bioethics, Readings and Cases*, Prentice-Hall, Englewood Cliffs, New Jersey, pp. 66–73.

Jecker, N.S.: 1989, 'Are filial duties unfounded'? *American Philosophical Quarterly* 26, 73–80.

Jecker, N.S.: 1990a, 'The role of intimate others in medical decision making', *The Gerontologist* 30, 65–71.

Jecker, N.S.: 1990b, 'Conceiving a child to save a child: Reproductive and filial ethics', *The Journal of Clinical Ethics* 1, 99–103.

Jecker, N.S.: 1990c, 'Anencephalic infants and special relationships', *Theoretical Medicine* 11, 333–342.

Keller, E.F.: 1985, *Reflections on Gender and Science*, Yale University Press, New Haven, Connecticut.

Kittay, E.F., and Meyers, D.T. (eds.): 1987, *Women and Moral Theory*, Rowman and Littlefield, Totowa, New Jersey.

Lyons, N.P.: 1983, 'Two perspectives: On self, relationships, and morality', *Harvard Educational Review* 53, 125–145.

MacIntyre, A.: 1987, 'How virtues become vices', in B.A. Brody and H.T. Engelhardt (eds.), *Bioethics: Readings and Cases*, Prentice-Hall, Englewood Cliffs, New Jersey, pp. 100–101.

Morantz-Sanchez, R.M.: 1985, *Sympathy and Science: Women Physicians in American Medicine*, Oxford University Press, New York.

Nelson, A.R.: 1989, 'Humanism and the art of medicine: Our commitment to care', *Journal of the American Medical Association* 262, 1228–1230.

Noddings, N.: 1984, *Caring: A Feminine Approach to Ethics and Moral Education*, University of California Press, Berkeley.

Noddings, N.: 1987, 'Do we really want to produce good people?', *Journal of Moral Education* 16, 177–188.

Noddings, N.: 1989, *Women and Evil*, University of California Press, Berkeley.

O'Brien, P.: 1987, 'All a woman's life can bring: The domestic roots of nursing in Philadelphia, 1830–1885', *Nursing Research* 36, 12–17.

Pearsall, M. (ed.): 1986, *Women and Values*, Wadsworth Publishing Company, Belmont, California.

Relman, A.: 1989, 'The changing demography of the medical profession', *New England Journal of Medicine* 321, 1540–1542.

Reverby, S.: 1987a, 'A caring dilemma: Womanhood and nursing in historical perspective', *Nursing Research* 36, 5–11.

Reverby, S.: 1987b, *Ordered to Care: The Dilemma of American Nursing*, Cambridge University Press, New York.

Rowland, H.S.: 1984, *The Nurse's Almanac, 2nd edition*, Aspen Systems Corporation, Rockville, Maryland.

Ruddick, S.: 1989, *Maternal Thinking*, Beacon Press, Boston.

Schultz, P.R., and Meleis, A.I.: 1988, 'Nursing epistemology: Traditions, insights, questions', *Image: Journal of Nursing Scholarship* 20, 217–221.

Starr, P.: 1982, *The Social Transformation of American Medicine*, Basic Books, New York.

Taylor, S.G.: 1985, 'Rights and responsibilities: Nurse-patient relationships', *Image: Journal of Nursing Scholarship* 17, 9–13.

NORMAN DANIELS

The Ideal Advocate and Limited Resources

1. INTRODUCTION

Recently, a friend of mine confided to me that he is not sure he will be able to continue practicing medicine if current trends in the health care system continue. He complained that various reforms—actual and proposed—in the financing of health care make him feel that he will not be able to remain the unbiased agent or advocate for his patients. He feels he has always been such an advocate and that medical ethics requires him to be one. To represent his patient's best interests, he feels he must be free to make medical decisions aimed at the best treatments and outcome which are *medically possible* for his patient.

Of course, he knows he cannot be a completely autonomous agent. Though this was not part of his early medical training, he has learned that his patient should have the ultimate say in what is done and that he must act with his patient's informed consent. But my friend is now concerned about threats to his autonomy that come not from the patient, but from outside the doctor-patient relationship. He feels he cannot in good conscience comply with hospital pressures to discharge his Medicare patients before he thinks they are ready. He finds repugnant a recent capitation scheme proposed for physicians at his hospital. Under the plan, doctors would be financially rewarded for not ordering certain diagnoses or consultations. He insists these are threats to his "moral character" and to his "psyche" as a physician.

I do not think my friend's complaints are unfamiliar. Similar remarks can be heard in scrub rooms, hospital staff meetings, and letters columns in medical journals. Many physicians believe that the 'old' retrospective fee-for-service schemes facilitated acting as the unfettered agent of the patient, but that cost-containment schemes destroy morally essential features of the doctor-patient relationship by restricting physician autonomy. I want [to] explore some general questions underlying these reactions and beliefs. Specifically, I want to address these questions: What kinds of autonomy have been granted American physicians, and how do these fit with ethical constraints on how a physician may act concerning his patient? Do the pre-cost-containment arrangements many physicians prefer institutionally embody or facilitate the ideal doctor-patient relationship? Can we, or how can we, reconcile the fact of resource limitations with the plausible view that physicians should remain neutral advocates of their patients' best interests? In answering these questions, I shall argue that we can reconcile resource limitations with what I will call the Ideal Advocate model of the doctor-patient relationship, but that doing so requires that our health care institutions be just.

2. PHYSICIAN AUTONOMY AND IDEAL ADVOCACY

It will help to analyze briefly the dimensions of autonomy traditionally claimed by U.S. physicians. We can pick out four main dimensions: (1) Whom to treat, (2) Where to practice, (3) What to specialize in, and (4) How to treat?

Unlike their colleagues in many other countries, U.S. physicians retain the power to decide *whom* they will treat. They may consider facts about the individual patient or his method of reimbursement. Choices about both *where* to practice and *what* to specialize in

From *Theoretical Medicine* 8 (1987), 69–80. © 1987 by D. Reidel Publishing Company. Reprinted by permission of Kluwer Academic Publishers.

are of course subject to what might be called 'market' constraints. They are subject to facts about the availability of training positions, practices to enter, indebtedness, and other factors. But few of these market constraints are themselves the results of centralized planning, and so there is an extensive, unregulated space for physicians' choice.

These first three dimensions of autonomy are similar in that they all are responsive to physician interests — some would say physicians' 'rights' — rather than patient interests. Granting these dimensions of autonomy to physicians has a major negative impact, for example, on programs to improve access to health care for underserved groups. Thus, only a minority of physicians will treat Medicaid patients. But I am not chiefly interested here in these three dimensions of autonomy. Rather, it is the fourth dimension, *clinical autonomy*, autonomy in *how* to treat, that is most directly affected by the recent cost-containment measures.

Granting physicians clinical autonomy is justified by reference to the patient's interests, not the physician's. Thus autonomy in treatment decisions is constrained by what might be called an 'ethic of advocacy (or agency)', The autonomy we grant the physician is necessary precisely if he is to act in his patient's best interest, and for this reason it also includes some constraints on the physician. The clinical decisions must be: (A) competent: up to professional standards of care; (B) respectful of patient autonomy; (C) respectful of other patient rights, e.g., confidentiality; (D) free from consideration of the physician's interests; (E) uninfluenced by judgments about the patient's worth.

The first of these constraints, the competency constraint, is enforced by peer review and tort law. The four remaining constraints are special features of the kind of fiduciary relationship that holds between a physician, with his greater knowledge and skill, and the patient, on whose behalf the physician acts as agent or advocate. Much recent clinical medical ethics has focused on patient autonomy and rights [constraints (B) and (C)]. Because they have little to do with the problem of cost-containment, I will not talk about them here. But the "purity" constraints, as I will call constraints (D) and (E), are at the heart of the issue. Constraint (D) requires that the physician not allow consideration of his economic or career interests to influence his treatment of his patient. Constraint (E)

is interpreted by some to mean that the physician should not put a price on his patient's life — should not decide how much it is worth to save or extend a particular patient's life. More narrowly interpreted, constraint (E) bars a physician from considering facts other than medical need or likelihood of treatment success in making clinical decisions for a particular patient. I shall call the Ideal Advocate model the view that physicians should be autonomous in their clinical decision-making and pursuit of their patients' best interests, while abiding by constraints (A)–(E) of the ethic of agency.

An important loose-end remains here. Some people believe that the Ideal Advocate is necessarily also an Unrestricted Ideal Advocate. That is, the physician should be subject to no external constraints on treatments he can pursue for his patient. Our retrospective fee-for-service reimbursement schemes may have contributed to this belief. They give the appearance that no resource constraints affect clinical decision-making: just treat, and then bill. Of course, these arrangements hide the way in which rationing actually takes place, by ability to pay, that is, to buy insurance. But this form of rationing seems to leave the clinician untouched. There seem to be no direct incentives to physicians to consider their own interest or the relative worth of the patient in decisions about how to treat (though the physician can refuse to treat at all, which clearly has something to do with his interests and possibly with his assessment of patient worth). In reality, retrospective fee-for-service schemes contain incentives for physicians to treat too much. But this tendency has been viewed as a lesser evil than incentives to deny beneficial care.

Because pre-cost-containment arrangements seem to embody the virtues of the Unrestricted Ideal Advocate, many physicians may have come to think of them as the form medicine must take if it is to be morally acceptable. Similarly, because current cost-containment measures introduce a concern about resource limitations through incentives which threaten the purity constraints (D) and (E), it is easy for physicians to overgeneralize and to think that any challenge to the Unrestricted Ideal Advocate must undermine the Ideal Advocate. A glance at some history may put this issue in perspective.

3. A HISTORY LESSON

Paul Starr has recently described the rise of the American medical profession from an early period in which the medical profession lacked the cultural authority and power it now enjoys.[1] He shows that physicians did not acquire their cultural power merely because they were "healers" and society has always revered healers. He documents the ways in which physicians resisted "capture" by hospitals and other emerging institutions, because hospitals in the U.S. remained dependent on physicians for referrals. In contrast, in many European countries, physicians were often salaried employees of hospitals from early on. Consequently they too had an interest in undercutting the independence of non-hospital-based physicians. Starr also documents the ways in which physicians and their professional associations and lobbies resisted "capture" by institutions developed to improve access to health care through new financing and insurance schemes. For example, when Medicare and Medicaid were established, physicians retained the power to determine whether they would treat such patients and how many they would treat. They also retained the retrospective, fee-for-service reimbursement scheme that characterized private insurance schemes. If we add to this the control physicians retain over where they locate their practices and what specialties they enter, we arrive at a unique pattern of physician autonomy and power, one that has had a negative effect on access to care for important subgroups in the population.

By exposing the details of the idiosyncratic history that led to this result, Starr shows us that the arrangements we presently have [are] not the result of an "inner logic" or ethical necessity that characterizes the doctor-patient relationship. We should not transform features of the relationships and institutions that result from such a unique historical process into a "nature." We have not stumbled on the *natural form* of the professional-patient relationship. When we see the details of this history, we lose any inclination we might have had to believe that the autonomy and power that has been granted American physicians is based either on the inner necessities of the doctor-patient relationship or on a reasoned social calculation about how to guarantee equitable access to high-quality care at acceptable costs. Rather we see ingenious lobbying by the medical profession, strategic exercises of economic strength, and the effective use of cultural authority. The results have been a series of exasperating political compromises embedded in financing reforms throughout this century. But past political success on this uneven historical battleground is hardly a *justification* of the institutions which grant and protect the profession's power. Might does not make right, and the peculiarities and vagaries of the historical process undermine claims that it is procedurally fair. Moreover, the very idiosyncrasy of the profession's historical success undercuts claims that "legitimate" expectations would weigh in favor of preserving the status quo.

An important feature of the history Starr documents is the way in which some physicians, we must suppose quite sincerely, made explicitly ethical arguments in favor of the broad institutional powers and authority they sought. Starr cites the code of ethics the AMA adopted in 1934 which claimed it was "unprofessional" for a physician to permit making "a direct profit" from his work: "The making of a profit from medical work is beneath the dignity of professional practice, is unfair competition with the profession at large, is harmful alike to the profession of medicine and the welfare of the people, and is against sound public policy."[2] As Starr points out, it was unprofessional only for someone *other* than a doctor to make a profit from a physician's work. It was acceptable, however, for another doctor to make such a profit! How exquisitely refined this principle of professional ethics is! The first of ten principles for medical service adopted by the AMA in 1934 (current codes are less explicit about converting economic considerations into ethical ones) says that "All features of medical service in any method of medical practice should be under the control of the medical profession." The fifth claimed that the "medical profession alone can determine the adequacy and character" of the institutions involved in medical care, which should be construed as "but expansions of the equipment of the physician."[3] Starr notes that "the doctors took professional authority, patient confidentiality, and free choice to require a specific set of economic relations." For example, "However the cost of medical service may be distributed . . . the immediate cost should be borne by the patient if able to pay at the time the service is rendered."[4] Thus, as Starr concludes, "the AMA insisted that all health insurance plans accept the private physician's monopoly control of the medical market and complete authority over all aspects of medical institutions,"[5] and it did so by deriving these controls from its view of professional ethics.

Of course the fact that physicians later embraced many of the institutional arrangements which they earlier thought unethical does not mean they were morally inconsistent. Rather it suggests that their moral concerns about some features of the doctor-patient relationship had led them to make false claims about ethically acceptable institutional arrangements. Obviously, this is a pattern of which we must be wary. (I am not even considering the more cynical view that all these moral concerns are secondary to economic interests and are appealed to only to disguise bald self-interest; Starr is less generous.)

Let me summarize the argument I have been making in this historical section. First, the kinds of control physicians have in our society over whom they will treat, where they will locate, what they will specialize in, as well as the autonomy they retain within largely retrospective fee-for-service reimbursement schemes—this autonomy and power of physicians is the result of a very particular, even idiosyncratic series of historical events. When we examine the power struggles that yielded physicians these results, we find no evidence that the institutional arrangements were the product of a social consensus in which all parties agreed that the Ideal Advocate model necessitated such full-blown autonomy and powers. Second, at points in that history, some physicians sincerely believed that Ideal Advocacy did require that particular institutional arrangements be established and others opposed. Physicians later embraced institutions which they had earlier thought ethically unacceptable, suggesting that Ideal Advocacy had fewer implications for institutional arrangements than physicians had previously believed. Third, in view of this history, we should be very careful not to assume that important, morally desirable features of medical decision-making can be preserved only if we maintain the institutional arrangements with which we are familiar. These arrangements are not necessarily the historical product of respect for that moral core of the doctor-patient relationship. They have, if Starr is right, a less respectable birthright.

This history lesson brings me to a central claim. The shape of professional relationships, and thus the scope and content of professional ethics, should depend on what kinds of institutions are needed to guarantee the just distribution of the goods provided by those relationships. It is justice that should be primary here, as should other general moral principles, and professional ethics should govern roles circumscribed by just institutions. Professional ethics should not be the tail that wags the dog. Ludicrous professional codes, such as the 1934 AMA principles, are but an extreme result of reversing priorities in this way.

4. JUSTICE AND IDEAL ADVOCACY

To see how the ethic of agency and the Ideal Advocate model can fit within a just health care system, we must consider what justice requires. As we shall see, justice will require that we abandon the Unrestricted Ideal Advocate in favor of a more modest Ideal Advocate. I have provided elsewhere a detailed account of what a just health care system might look like.[6] Here I shall offer but a brief summary of that argument.

We can begin with the question, Is health care 'special'? Should we distinguish it from other goods, say video recorders, because of its special moral importance? And does that moral importance mean there are social obligations to distribute it in particular ways, ways which might not coincide with the results of market distribution? I believe the answer to all these questions is "yes".

Health care—I mean the term quite broadly—does many important things for people. Some extends lives, some reduces pain and suffering, some merely gives important information about one's condition. I have argued that a central, unifying function of health care is to maintain and restore functional organization, let us say 'functioning', that is typical or normal for our species. This central function of health care derives its moral importance from the following fact: normal functioning has a central effect on the opportunity open to an individual. More specifically, an individual's fair share of the normal opportunity range for his society is impaired when disease or disability impairs normal functioning. I believe this means there are social obligations to provide health care services that protect and restore normal functioning. In short, the principle of justice that should govern the design of health care institutions is a principle that calls for guaranteeing fair equality of opportunity.

This principle of justice has implications for access and resource allocation. It implies that there should be no financial, geographical or discriminatory barriers to a level of care which promotes normal functioning. It also implies that resources [should] be allocated in ways that are effective in promoting normal functioning. That is, we can use the effect on normal opportunity range as a crude way of ranking the moral importance of health care services. This does not mean that any technology which might have a positive impact on normal functioning for some individuals should be introduced: we must weigh new technologies against alternatives to judge the overall impact of introducing them on fair equality of opportunity — this gives a slightly new sense to the term 'opportunity cost'. The point is that social obligations to provide just health care must be met within the conditions of moderate scarcity that we face. This approach is not one which gives individuals a basic right to have all their health care needs met. Rather, there is a social obligation to provide individuals only with those services which are part of the design of a system that on the whole protects equal opportunity.

This view has implications for the autonomy and powers we might grant physicians. Specifically, institutions must give providers incentives that yield equitable access to care. This may mean restricting some of the powers now held by providers to choose whom they are willing to treat, what specialties they will enter, and where they will locate. These restrictions need violate no fundamental liberties of providers, though realistic options open to individual providers might be dramatically different from those enjoyed under current incentives. Similarly, providers will find themselves in a framework that restricts the resources that may be devoted to treating certain conditions in order that a more equitable distribution of resources overall results. There will be some things that providers cannot do for their patients — providers will not be able to be the unrestricted advocates of their patients, but will have to do the best they can for them under the restrictions that exist in the system.[7]

What is crucial to understand about these restrictions on the Ideal Advocate is their underlying justification. Under conditions of moderate resource scarcity, there will be some things we cannot do for certain classes of patients because doing them would mean we would not be able to meet the requirements of justice regarding other classes of patients. Notice that there are two central features underlying these kinds of rationing decisions. First, weighing the opportunity cost of one class of treatments or technologies against another must take place in a *closed* system. When beneficial care is denied it must be because the resources will be better used elsewhere in the system. Second, principles of justice must govern the decisions about priorities within this closed system — and thus define what counts as "better" uses of services. Thus, the just distribution of health care re-

sources implies that we cannot implement the Unrestricted Ideal Advocate model. Rather, we can now state how the Ideal Advocate model must be qualified: physicians should be the advocates of their patients, abiding by the ethic of agency, within the limits imposed by just resource allocation. The physician as Ideal Advocate cannot do things which would be unfair or unjust to other patients. This is the sense in which justice is primary, or provides the framework within which professional ethics can be elaborated.

Stringent — but just — rationing schemes need not threaten the ethic of advocacy. The purity constraint (D), which requires clinical decisions to be free from consideration of the physician's interests, is perfectly compatible with the just rationing of limited health care resources. British physicians, for example, who deny beneficial care that may be available to patients in the United States, do not do so because of any economic incentives that directly reward them for denying care.[8] It is possible to construct institutions in which physicians pursue their patients' best interests and respect fair resource limitations without their incentive for denying care deriving from economic incentives to them.

Similarly, a physician need not violate the constraint (E) that he avoid judgments about a patient's worth. Judgments about the just distribution of health care resources must be social and public ones. For example, the fair equality of opportunity principle I described might require us to forego treatments or technologies which consume resources more effectively used elsewhere to protect opportunity. But this principled social decision does not involve the physician in making any judgments of social worth. The physician acts as a "gatekeeper," but he is abiding by a just social decision, not his own determination that it is not worth the resources to treat a particular class of patients in a particular way. Physicians can still do the best they can for their patients within the limits imposed by justice, which is all that constraints (D) and (E) require.

We can now better see why American cost-containment measures have seemed so threatening to the idea that a physician must be the advocate for his patients. Constraints on physician autonomy embodied within current cost-restraint measures carry with them no such justification grounded in requirements of justice. In the United States, there is no assurance that when a patient is required to forego beneficial treatment, say a needed day in the hospital beyond the DRG [Diagnosis Related Group] standard, the saving in resources works to the advantage of other patients whom justice requires we treat instead. Rather, services that might well benefit one patient are foregone simply because it is not profitable to treat him compared to another, and the system of incentives has no principle guiding it other than the intention of reducing 'unnecessary' services. Indeed, decisions about the dissemination of new technologies are made without the system being closed at all: opportunity costs are not considered at all, let alone by reference to a principle of justice.

The Ideal Advocate who plays the role of "gatekeeper" in a just system can nevertheless reassure himself that his denials of care are *fair*. It is because this reassurance is most definitely lacking for the U.S. physician under existing cost-containment schemes that we hear the complaints my friend expressed. When he denies beneficial care, the American physician can be rather sure that the savings will not go to more urgently needed care elsewhere in the system. He may know, for example, the savings will be returned to investors for a for-profit hospital or be consumed elsewhere in a hospital budget which has never been examined to see what implicit assumptions about health care priorities govern it. To be compelled to play the role of "gatekeeper" under these circumstances may interfere with Ideal Advocacy in a morally unacceptable way. In the long run it can erode patient confidence that physicians will act as their advocates or agents. My physician friend was right to feel threatened by cost-containment measures with such implications.

5. A PALLIATIVE FOR COST-CONSTRAINTS?

The problem with current cost-containment measures is that they are not part of an overall effort to make the U.S. health care system more just. They compromise the physician, who must deny beneficial care for reasons other than those imposed by justice. The measures fail to preserve important features of the Ideal Advocate model, especially the purity constraints on clinical decisions. These are serious flaws, and only quite basic reforms — drastic reconstructive surgery — could eliminate them. Contrary to what many physicians believe, we would have to undertake more, not less, extensive planning within our health care system, and we would have to do so with a com-

mitment to justice. In the current political climate, no one seems ready to finance such measures, yet nothing short of them can let us preserve the Ideal Advocate model and face resource scarcity at the same time.

Since I am loathe to suggest a band-aid or palliative when only major interventions will produce real reform, I hesitate to advance the following suggestion. Nevertheless, one feature of the current situation that clearly exacerbates it is that physicians have no public way of resisting pressures to deny beneficial care. They have no way to appeal what they take to be unacceptable pressures in particular cases. Physicians — and other medical personnel — need some hearing board to which they can appeal against hospital policies and third-party restrictions. It is not clear what form such a board should take, but perhaps some expanded role for hospital ethics committees is in order. Instead of merely approving plug-pulling, they might consider the ethical issues involved in decision-making under cost-constraints. This would provide a broader, more public forum in which disputes between physicians and hospital administrators might be aired. It might also provide a setting in which evidence about the effects of the cost-constraints can be gathered — effects on access and quality of care, not just on costs.

Such appeals to ethics committees are costly and may be time-consuming. And it is difficult to imagine many hospitals surrendering authority over policies to such committees. Indeed, only about 10% of all hospitals have such committees at all. In contrast, it is easy to imagine physicians trying to do quiet end-runs around the cost-constraints instead, even if it involves some compromise to integrity. But some way of protecting the physician — and ultimately the patient — against policies which are aimed at profit, not fair allocation, is definitely in order. Such boards might give us a way to monitor the cost-containment process, but they are no substitute for careful research into effects on access to care and quality of care. Unfortunately, the government which was so quick to install DRGs — without full consideration of them — has taken only small steps to measure their real effects. Funding for this research is hard to come by.

I think there is another argument for establishing a mechanism for this type of review. The measures we have so far encountered may be mild compared to what we may encounter next — especially if there is no defined forum for appeal against what we already have. I am particularly concerned that our halfway measures in the direction of cost-containment will be seen as typical failures of "regulation" and that there will be a further push to make the health care market more competitive and entrepreneurial. This would only postpone facing the problem of rationing equitably in the face of resource limitations. Hearing boards might thus offer some preventive effects. In any case, they provide another context in which the physician can attempt to abide by the Ideal Advocate model, and this may slow the erosion of physician commitment to important moral ideals.

Acknowledgment: Research for this paper was funded by grants from the National Endowment for the Humanities Basic Research Program and the Retirement Research Foundation. I am indebted to David Ozar for editorially carving this paper out of a much longer take, "Are Physicians Treating Patients Too Well?" delivered at the Loyola-Strich School of Medicine, Loyola University of Chicago, April, 1985.

NOTES

1. Paul Starr, *Social Transformation of American Medicine* (New York: Basic Books, 1982). Material in this section draws on my review of Starr's book, "Understanding Physician Power," *Philosophy and Public Affairs* 13:4, pp. 347–357.

2. Starr, *Social Transformation,* p. 216.

3. Starr, *Social Transformation,* p. 299.

4. Starr, *Social Transformation,* p. 300.

5. Starr, *Social Transformation,* p. 300.

6. Norman Daniels, *Just Health Care* (New York: Cambridge University Press, 1985).

7. For further discussion of the relationship between provider liberties and the requirements of justice, see my *Just Health Care,* Ch. 6.

8. See my "Why Saying 'No' to Patients in the United States Is so Hard," *New England Journal of Medicine* 314 (May 22, 1986), 1381–1393; also see Henry Aaron and William Schwartz, *The Painful Prescription* (Washington: Brookings Institution, 1984).

TOM L. BEAUCHAMP AND LAURENCE B. McCULLOUGH

Third-Party Interests

. . . The rule that the patient always comes first has undoubted intuitive appeal, as well as the weight of medical tradition. On closer examination, however, this principle rests on the dubious, indeed indefensible, assumption that the patient-physician relationship never involves primary obligations to third parties. The physician's professional relationships are multi-leveled. It is not uncommon for a physician's initial contact with a patient to come through a third party, and the relationship may encompass several other levels. For example, a woman may request health care services from the family physician for her seriously ill husband. After examining the patient and assessing his needs, the physician in turn may contact a local visiting nurse, who visits the home to provide required services. In addition, the physician's fees, as well as those of the nurse, are often paid by third parties. Private insurance, health maintenance organizations, and publicly funded programs such as Medicare and Medicaid may place restrictions on payment for certain services.

There are compelling moral reasons why the physician must consider the interests of such third parties. For example, third parties such as spouses, parents, and guardians often have rights and responsibilities that cannot be ignored. They may be the patient's fiduciary no less than the physician, and they may

Reprinted with permission of the publisher from *Medical Ethics: The Moral Responsibilities of Physicians* (Englewood Cliffs, N.J.: Prentice-Hall, 1984), pp. 133–137, 138–140, 141–145, 148–154, 158–159, 164.

have legal authority to act to benefit the patient. At the same time, these parties may be significantly harmed if the physician acts in the best interests of the patient alone. The parents of a seriously ill infant may, for example, suffer overwhelming emotional, psychological, and financial consequences if their child is aggressively treated.[1]

Third parties also shape the physician's responsibilities because of the many roles the physician plays in contemporary medicine, particularly institutional roles. For example, the physician may be a research investigator or have public health responsibilities. Promoting the best interest of a patient—under the directives of the beneficence and autonomy models—may threaten or even harm the best interests of others the physician is expected to serve in these roles—for example, future patients and the local community. In these circumstances the general philosophical *principle* of beneficence (though not the beneficence *model*) directs the physician to promote the interests of third parties,[2] and this may generate obligations that conflict with or even override the physician's obligations to a patient.

Because they focus exclusively on the best interests of patients, the beneficence and autonomy models of moral responsibility in medicine are, by themselves, unable to take into account such obligations to third parties. At most, the two models have the moral power to determine that the physician must, *as a prima facie duty*, put the patient's best interests first. They do not tell the physician how to weigh the requirements of the models against a competing principle that would put some third party's best interests first. There is, therefore, no *a priori* ground for asserting that third-party obligations cannot be primary.

As a consequence, we argue in this [essay] that "The health of my patient will be my first consideration" is but *one* prima facie valid principle. It must yield on occasion to a more complex account of conflicts between obligations to patients and obligations to third parties. We shall see in this [essay] that these conflicts are resolvable in one of three ways: (1) In some instances obligations to patients justifiably override those to third parties. (2) In other instances the obligations owed to patients and third parties are equal in weight, and the physician faces a genuine moral dilemma—that is, a circumstance involving a conflict of obligations, where inevitably an outcome of great value will be lost by pursuing one obligation at the expense of another. (3) Finally, in still other cases, the weight of morality shifts in favor of third-party interests, and obligations owed to third parties override those owed to patients. . . .

THIRD PARTIES WITH FIDUCIARY OBLIGATIONS: PARENTS AND GUARDIANS

We begin with an analysis of the physician's conflicting obligations to patients and to their fiduciaries—in particular, parents and guardians. A physician must sometimes abide by the decisions of parents and guardians, and sometimes must accept them even if he or she believes the decisions are not in the best interests of the child. Indeed, some have argued that the *child* is the third party in such circumstances, because the physician's contract is with the fiduciary parents, a view we reject.[3] Such a context is rife with the potential for moral conflict. For example, parents sometimes make poor and even disastrous decisions for children, including circumstances of neglect and unjustified decisions to allow newborn infants to die. But the reverse may also be true: Adolescents may make disastrous decisions that they wish to shield from their parents—for example, decisions about sexual activity that eventuate in a need for medical care. The physician can have powerful obligations to both parents and children in such circumstances and may be trapped between competing obligations. As one court recently put it, there can be agonizing conflict between the "parental rights doctrine" and the "doctrine of the best interests of the child."[4]

We narrow our investigation here to conflicts involving the treatment of life-threatening conditions of infants and conflicts involving the control of confidential information about adolescent minors in sexual matters. Because the fiduciary—the parent or guardian—is expected to act to benefit the patient, we shall consider the obligations of the parent or guardian to protect the patient as well as the potential harm that may result if those obligations are discharged in certain ways. Our goal in each case is to determine whether the physician's obligations to avoid harm to the patient or to respect the rights of the patient outweigh conflicting obligations to avoid harm to the fiduciary or to respect the rights of the fiduciary.

CHILDREN WITH LIFE-THREATENING CONDITIONS

Raymond Duff and A. G. M. Campbell have reported that fourteen percent of the deaths recorded in the special-care nursery of the Yale–New Haven Hospital from January 1, 1970 through June 30, 1972, were associated with refusal, withholding, discontinuance, or withdrawal of treatment. The parents' decision was usually the decisive consideration, and Drs. Duff and Campbell view these parental decisions as generally legitimate.[5] By contrast, some institutions, such as Children's Hospital in Philadelphia, have a reputation for being much more aggressive.[6] They rarely discontinue or withhold treatment, irrespective of parental desires. Despite variations from institution to institution and physician to physician, questions remain about how the physician should respond if parents refuse permission for treatment of their seriously ill infant. This is but one instance of the more general problem of how the physician should weigh the interests of parents in determining his or her moral responsibilities. . . .

We begin our analysis with the following case: A baby girl is born with trisomy 21 (Down's syndrome), a genetic defect that involves varying and, at birth, unpredictable levels of mental retardation. The baby also has a life-threatening defect, an esophageal-tracheal fistula, an opening between the baby's airway and passage to the stomach. The danger of this anatomical malformation is that her lungs can become infected or even blocked as a result of contact with food regurgitated from her stomach into her lungs. As a consequence, this infant cannot be fed by mouth. If the defect is not corrected by surgical intervention to close the opening, or if the baby is not supplied with nutrients by artificial means, she will die by dehydration. In addition, if her anatomical malformation is not corrected, she is at risk of contracting aspiration pneumonia, which, if not treated, will take her life—probably before dehydration. The parents, George and Sandra Breckner, already have three children, ages two, five, and seven. Together they earn a moderate wage. They refuse treatment on the grounds that it would not be worth the effort and ultimate costs—neither for the child's sake, nor for theirs. The baby will be mentally retarded, they note, and raising a handicapped child would impose psychological, emotional, and serious financial burdens on them and their other children. . . .

In what respects, if any, do the interests of parents (and perhaps other family members) determine the physician's obligations in cases like that of baby girl Breckner?

To answer this question, we first need an understanding of parental obligations and interests. What obligations do Mr. and Mrs. Breckner have regarding the treatment of their infant? Are they morally free to refuse treatment for any reason they regard as sufficient? To the latter question the answer is decisively negative. From the legal as well as the moral point of view, the responsibility of parents toward their children is defined as that of the fiduciary: They are to act in the best interests of the child. While the common-law tradition treats children as chattels (personal property) of their parents, owing obedience to their dictates about education and medical intervention, it is also assumed in law that parents, as fiduciaries, always act in their children's best interests. The state is not to interfere until it and the parents disagree regarding some decision with potentially serious consequences for the child. For this reason, the state—which has fiduciary responsibilities it may assert in a petition for guardianship—has often intervened in cases like that presented by the Breckner baby.

The state traditionally has had the right to seize authority to act in the best interests of children, and incompetents generally, in order to protect them from serious harm that parents or guardians might cause or permit.[7] When the best interests test is applied by the courts to the parent as decision maker, the test sometimes has been treated in a highly malleable fashion, taking into account intangible factors of questionable importance. For example, in cases where parents seek court permission for a kidney transplant from an incompetent minor to a competent sibling, the best interests of the donor have occasionally taken into account projected psychological trauma resulting from the death of the sibling and psychological benefits of the unselfish act of donation.[8] Consideration of such factors can easily lead to abuse, and the safest application of the best interests standard should require reference to *tangible* factors, such as demonstrable and significant physical, financial, and psychological risks.

The Breckners, then, are bound by certain obligations that constitute the parental role, namely to see to it that their daughter's best interests are promoted by her physicians. Following the principle of beneficence (not, of course, the beneficence model), and assuming normal circumstances, their obligation is to authorize the required surgery. The obligations of the Breckners and the attending physicians coincide in protecting their daughter's best interests through vigorous medical intervention. Accordingly, it seems reasonably clear that this child's interests in medical treatment ought to override the interests of the parents, and if the parents reach an unacceptable decision, the physician should attempt to overrule it. The physician's obligation in such cases is primarily to the patient. However, this conclusion can be escaped if it is genuinely in the best interests of the child *not* to have the surgery, as it is in some cases of very severe abnormalities and problems. This could be the case if the treatment is futile because death is imminent or the patient is irreversibly dying, or if the burdens of treatment clearly outweigh the benefits to the patient.[9] . . .

In sum, we have seen in this section that in cases involving life-threatening conditions of children the physician faces conflicting obligations. In those cases in which it is in the patient's best interests to be treated, parents usually have an obligation to authorize treatment, an obligation that tends to override personal interests they might have. In such circumstances, the "weight of morality" resides with the normal obligation of the physician to provide treatment. We also saw that decisions for or against treatment are not the whole of the matter in cases involving life-threatening conditions. If treatment is provided, other obligations may have to be determined, especially regarding the continued care and support of the child. The physician faces genuine dilemmas, in some cases between obligations to the child and obligations to parents, and in still other cases the obligations to parents justifiably override what the physician recognizes to be the patient's best interests.

ADOLESCENT SEXUALITY AND PRIVACY

Conflicts between the patient's interests and those of the parents increase in complexity when older children are involved. In recent years older children have ever more frequently been recognized as developing in autonomy and not as mere chattels of their parents (or the state, in the case of wards). These children are now acknowledged as having legal and moral rights (and responsibilities) unimagined in earlier times. There is currently a legal trend toward the explication and expansion of children's rights, some of which are referred to as "rights of self-determination." Similarly, many child psychologists view autonomy on a sliding scale from no autonomy to more or less full autonomy, as the child develops from birth to late adolescence.[10] The problem is how full an older child's au-

tonomy must be before the child's decisions and the obligations they create override obligations to respect the decisions of their parents or guardians.

This problem is especially difficult in cases where minor children seek medical treatment without their parents' knowledge or consent. Ordinarily, parental decisions for the benefit of their children require access to information in the sole possession of their children's physician. Obligations to maintain a very young child's confidentiality are usually not given overriding authority, but as autonomy grows in presence and importance, obligations to maintain the child's privacy and confidentiality also increase in weight.

These autonomy-based considerations are given additional weight from the perspective of the beneficence model. Irresponsible parents—for example, those who drink heavily and abuse the child—create grounds for protecting the child's confidentiality that are not otherwise present. Also, young people may not trust the physician without assurances of confidentiality. With such assurances, the adolescent patient is more likely to be open and honest, a key condition in the pursuit of the goods highlighted in the beneficence model. These reasons underlie laws in virtually every state in the U.S. allowing physicians to treat venereal disease in adolescents without parental consent.[11] At some point, the parent loses all rights of special access. But at what point?

Leading cases emerged in *Planned Parenthood of Central Missouri v. Danforth* and *Bellotti v. Baird*,[12] where the United States Supreme Court invalidated state statutes requiring parental consent, consultation, or notification in cases of abortions for minors. The Court ruled that the statutes were impermissible because they restricted the *competent* minor's constitutional rights of privacy and imposed an undue burden on the right to seek an abortion. The Court, however, did not set out a relevant test for "competence"—a major consideration, especially if legal and moral demands of informed consent are pertinent. . . . Other medical interventions that some minors may request without parental consent include treatment for venereal disease, addiction, pregnancy, consultation for contraception, treatment for psychological disturbance, blood donation, treatment for emergency, "necessary services," and treatment for reportable disease. Legal accessibility to these treatments varies from state to state, and moral views are no less settled than the legal situation.

If *Danforth* and *Bellotti* were accepted as the final word, one might be tempted to draw the following conclusion: In the case of adolescents and their autonomous decisions about their own sexuality (not merely a choice for abortion), "Put the patient's interests first" is an absolute principle, one that in every case overrides the principle that the parents' interests in their child should come first. This view is consistent with the demands of both models, which seem to converge on a strong obligation of confidentiality. It is not difficult, however, to imagine circumstances in which this obligation of confidentiality to the adolescent patient is weaker. This obligation would clearly be weakened if a profound threat to health or life were present, but it would be weakened in less dramatic cases as well.

Suppose that an adolescent requesting an abortion is deeply and perhaps irrationally fearful of her parents' possibly negative reaction to her decision. The physician may detect that the patient in these circumstances takes this view primarily because of the views of her friends and not because she has made a thoughtful assessment of her parents' likely response. In addition, the physician may know her parents and have good reason to believe that while they would not necessarily accept her choice or the values it expresses, they would be concerned to help her reach an autonomous decision. If her parents are excluded from helping her reach a thoughtful decision, the relationship between them may be damaged, especially if the parents discover the truth later. In short, the patient's choice for an abortion may reflect a degree of reduced autonomy, her parents might be an invaluable resource for an autonomous decision, and her parents might be harmed by being excluded.

Because the interests of the parents coincide with the patient's best interest, it would be unreasonable to exclude her parents altogether. To be sure, including them might unduly influence the patient, and in such circumstances the physician might be faced with a genuine dilemma. However, consider the following case: The young woman's parents know that she is pregnant. She believes that they want her to have an abortion, but the physician has spoken with them and knows that they do not. The young woman very much wants to keep her baby and tells the physician that she thinks her parents do not understand her at all and are wrong and insensitive to want her to have an abortion. In the physician's judgment, the patient's growing bitterness and anger toward her parents could severely damage an otherwise positive relationship with them. The only way to avoid damaging the relationship irreparably would be to involve the parents in the patient's decisions about her pregnancy, even if she did not believe that doing so would be in her best interests.[13]

The physician, then, must carefully weigh all competing obligations when dealing with conflicts between obligations to minors who are patients and obligations to their parents. Broad declarations of parents' rights or of children's rights do a disservice, rather than a service, and may unnecessarily squeeze the physician into an untenable position. Distinctive virtues such as compassion or tact may serve the physician more steadily than moral principles of duty or assertions of rights. If the adolescent's confidentiality merits rigid protection, considerable tact and compassion may be demanded, because the physician may have to deflect well-intended — and very direct — parental inquiries concerning the source and nature of the child's problem.

THIRD PARTIES WITH NONFIDUCIARY OBLIGATIONS

The physician has potentially conflicting obligations to third parties other than fiduciaries such as parents and guardians. Some of these third parties — e.g., health care institutions and employers — may have some limited fiduciary obligations to the patient. But they also have competing obligations and interests. Unlike parents, whose *primary* charge is to act as the patient's fiduciary, these third parties have primary responsibilities that are sometimes remote from serving the patient's interests. In this section we explore how the physician should weigh obligations based in such interests.

HEALTH CARE INSTITUTIONS

Physicians practice ever less frequently in the solo style of one patient–one physician. Increasingly, they provide care to patients in institutional settings such as group practices, clinics, health maintenance organizations (HMOs), private (nonprofit and profit) hospitals, nursing homes, and hospices. In a group practice, for example, a patient is seen primarily by one physician but also, on occasion, by other physicians in the group, especially in multi-specialty group practices. In clinics and HMOs the physician practices alongside many health care professionals, and in hospitals the patient is seen and treated by a sometimes bewildering train of physicians, nurses, and other health care professionals, including medical students and physicians in training. As the number of highly specialized practitioners increases, the individual responsibilities they have for patients tend to decrease. Sometimes the patient may not have a single physician in charge of the case—and no one to turn to for information and comfort.

The institutional organization of medical care has expanded in novel directions in order to provide a quantity and quality of care that the individual physician cannot provide.[14] While health care institutions are committed to the well-being of patients, their large scale and complexity generate commitments to other values as well. These tend to cluster around considerations of efficiency, with special emphasis on cost-effectiveness and cost-reduction, and, increasingly, profit. Goods and harms understood from the perspective of medicine can conflict with broader, though related, institutional perspectives. The patient, too, may not accept such an institutional perspective, and this produces conflicts between obligations based in beneficence generally and obligations based in the autonomy model. . . .

MEDICAL RESEARCH AND EDUCATION

A major goal of medicine is to provide for medical care to future generations of patients by training physicians and by producing new knowledge, skills, medicines, and technologies. These enterprises, however, can be a source of conflict of obligations for clinicians engaged in both patient care and research or teaching.

Medical Research. Consider the role of the clinician-researcher. He or she has a dual responsibility that easily produces a conflict of obligations: The physician is obligated to act in the patient's best interests and is also obligated to carry out research according to strict canons of scientific methodology. Controlled clinical trials require accurate confirmation of a scientific hypothesis. They can involve the random assignment of therapies and even placebos to patients, as well as other maneuvers intended to eliminate bias in the research. While in theory patients do not receive treatments that are known to be less safe or less

effective than other available treatments, preliminary data occasionally indicate an increased efficacy of one therapy, and animal studies sometimes indicate efficacy prior to initiation of the trial.

In any event, it would be inconsistent with the beneficence model to *randomly* select a treatment for a patient *unless* he or she were involved in a clinical trial. As Arthur Schafer puts it, "Regardless of whether a patient benefits from agreeing to become a research subject, the physician who attempts to combine the traditional role of healer with the modern role of scientist places himself in a situation that contains a potential conflict of values. His commitment can no longer be exclusively and unequivocally to promote the interests of his patients."[15] To preserve the integrity of the research protocol, physicians involved in clinical research would be obligated to make recommendations about care that the nonresearch physician would not make. How should the physician weigh these competing obligations?

To illustrate these concerns, consider the following case. Gloria Wallace is an eighteen-year-old woman with Hodgkin's disease, a form of cancer. She is presently at stage II of the disease, for which the standard therapy is radiation. This treatment carries the risk of secondary cancer. An alternative treatment, still in the experimental stage, is "combined therapy": narrowly focused radiation (to reduce the secondary risk of cancer) combined with chemotherapy. The latter causes nausea and in some cases hair loss. Gloria's physician is part of a multisite research project that is examining the relative efficacy of this treatment, as compared with standard radiation treatment, in a randomized clinical trial. When presented with the information that she might receive combined therapy in the clinical trial if she should choose to participate in the project as a research subject, Gloria elects not to participate. Her reason is that she does not want to be disfigured.

If the role of the physician in this case is regarded as that of clinician alone, matters are unclouded: Ms. Wallace has been offered and has accepted the standard therapy. She has exercised her autonomy in an informed decision. . . . Moreover, she has chosen a mode of treatment known to be effective for her disease. Thus, the physician's obligation to Ms. Wallace, based in both models of moral responsibility, is explicit. For the clinician who is also a research scientist, however, matters are more complex. The research in which Ms. Wallace is invited to participate is based on a morally justified goal—to develop for patients with her disease a form of therapy that possibly will reduce the risks of secondary cancer, while maintaining as much or greater efficacy in treating the disease than radiation alone.

This consideration is not irrelevant to the clinician's role: Without the new therapy, he or she will have no choice but to treat future patients by standard radiation therapy, which for some patients results in yet another form of cancer. The risk of secondary cancer is not eliminated with combined therapy, but it is hoped that its frequency will be reduced. When the two modes of treatment are viewed from the perspective of the beneficence model, the new, combined therapy—*if* shown to be as effective in combating the primary disease as the standard therapy—is the one that should be used, because it presents a lower level of risk. Here the dual roles of clinician and researcher produce a genuine moral dilemma. On the one hand, the physician as *clinician* is obligated to provide treatment that serves the patient's best interests, as directed by the beneficence and autonomy models. This obligation is most satisfactorily discharged by use of standard therapy because the experimental therapy has not yet been shown to be of equal or greater benefit. On the other hand, the principle of beneficence generates an obligation for the physician as *researcher* to benefit future patients with effective therapies that carry the lowest possible risks. The investigator also has institutional obligations to perform the research. He or she will not be able to discharge these obligations unless sufficient numbers of present patients participate in the experimental protocol. This might not occur if the physician were to act exclusively in the best interests of the patient. The physician in the dual role of clinician *and* researcher thus faces equally compelling claims on the part of present patients and those of future patients.[16] . . .

Medical Education. A similar range of conflicts is present in medical education. Patients who receive their medical care in clinics and hospitals that are teaching institutions are seen by medical students and physicians-in-training, as well as by practicing physicians. When so informed by their physician, some patients adamantly insist that they be examined and treated by their physician alone. Based on the autonomy model, it would seem that the physician's obligation is to respect the patient's wishes. The physician engaged in medical education, however, has the addi-

tional responsibility of assisting in the education of the next generation of physicians in order to serve the interests of future patients. If patients do not consent to be "teaching material" for students and others new to medical "practice," this important goal cannot be realized. The consequence might be that levels of care now enjoyed by patients will not be available to future patients. Thus, the academic physician faces a conflict of equally compelling interests: those of the patient presently in his or her care, and those of future patients who will be cared for by the students and physicians-in-training for whose education he or she also is responsible.

Consider the following case. Dr. Sean O'Malley is chief of cardiology in a university teaching hospital. In his educational role, Dr. O'Malley is responsible for the training of medical residents—physicians who have completed their medical degrees and are taking specialty training. Among the procedures that they must learn is how to thread a catheter (a hollow tube) into a patient's heart as part of a complex diagnostic procedure. This diagnostic intervention poses significant risk, even when performed by a physician with many years of experience. These risks increase if a relatively inexperienced resident performs the procedure. Dr. O'Malley is also the physician in charge of the care of patients who become "teaching material" for the residents. As the patient's physician, Dr. O'Malley would not be justified in placing the patient in a position where the risks involved when a resident performs catheterization fall below a minimally acceptable level of professional skill. As residents learn, incurring the possibility of such risk is inevitable. Yet if residents are not given the opportunity to learn, they will not be as competent to benefit future patients as they would be as the result of many such learning opportunities.

Ordinarily, this problem is handled by providing close supervision of physicians-in-training and medical students. At best, this approach reduces increased risk to the patients, but it does not always reduce risk to an acceptable minimum level.[17] Such risk is justifiably incurred, however, in the interests of future patients. If physicians are not provided with adequate training, they may well subject their patients to risks higher than those that present patients encounter at the hands of their physicians—an unacceptable balancing of goods and harms under the principle of beneficence.

Obligations to such patients override those of present patients, who are themselves the beneficiaries of former teaching exercises on other patients.

Problems of Persuasion and Manipulation. Institutional commitment to teaching and research facilities can also raise subtle questions about the limits of persuasion and manipulation as means to gain the cooperation of patients in medical research and education. Concerns about manipulation are of course ubiquitous in life — as testified by popular debates about whether or not various forms of advertising are manipulative. These are usually concerns about whether we are being played upon by devious or unfair techniques — whether or not that is the intention of the manipulator. Problems of manipulation and perhaps even coercion can be of importance in medicine because patients are often abnormally weak, dependent, and surrender-prone. Influences that can normally be resisted might become irresistible.

Dr. Franz Ingelfinger argued that "some element of coercion" is present in virtually every circumstance in which a physician asks a patient to join an experimental investigation. Ingelfinger characterized what he took to be a *typical* situation of influence as follows: "Incapacitated and hospitalized because of illness, frightened by strange and impersonal routines, and fearful for his health and perhaps life, the patient is far from exercising a free power of choice when the person to whom he anchors all his hopes asks, 'Say, you wouldn't mind, would you, if you joined some of the other patients on this floor and helped us to carry out some very important research we are doing?' . . . Here the thumb screws of coercion are . . . relentlessly applied . . . to the patient with disease."[18] The point to be extracted from such examples is that the physician could compel compliance both in education and in research by playing upon desperation, anxiety, boredom, hope, and a wide variety of human emotions so poignantly present in the life of the hospitalized or seriously ill patient. Thus, what the physician regards as an attempt at truly rational persuasion may have the effect of irrational persuasion or manipulation because of the way in which the words tug at such patients' vulnerabilities.[19]

Education, advertising, and propaganda (to take some distant analogies) can certainly be used as rationally persuasive and quite acceptable techniques, but they can also easily glide into unjustifiable means of "persuasion," especially if a powerful authority figure employs them. Similarly, the influence of a physician may be welcomed by the patient and may be perfectly appropriate — up to a limiting point. Just as educators, advertising agencies, and propagandists can inadvertently (or advertently) move from persuasion to manipulation to coercion, so can physicians. It can be agonizingly difficult to pinpoint the conditions under which a surrender-prone patient, desperately needing an authority, willingly submits to the physician's authority, as distinct from the conditions under which a physician uses authority for undue, even exploitative, advantage.

It does not follow from these problems of medical practice that physicians *do* routinely manipulate or exploit the psychological vulnerabilities of patients. It follows only that patients are vulnerable to such forms of influence and that due care must be taken to cultivate virtues of restraint and compassion that avoid or minimize manipulation and coercion, especially in implementing obligations based on third-party interests in medical research and education.[20]

EMPLOYERS

The third-party interests discussed thus far have generally not been altogether remote from those of serving the patient's interests. The patient's health and well-being are expectably at the forefront, even if they are not always foremost for the health care, research, and academic institutions. Some third-party interests, however, diverge sharply from those of the patient. This is commonly the case in some dimensions of occupational medicine. For example, physicians who contract to examine job applicants or employees, physicians who are employed in industry, prisons, and the military to provide medical care for employees, or physicians who are employed to develop health-education and preventive-medicine programs regularly confront conflicts between the individual worker's best interests and the interests of an employer to whom the physician owes a contractual obligation.

The employer's best interests are not captured by the objectives of the beneficence model. Efficiency, cost-reduction, and profitability are among the employer's primary interests; maintaining the health and welfare of employees may often be a remote interest. The contract between physician and employer may, for example, require disclosure to the employer and records open to the company (and sometimes to unions). The occupational physician's obligation to disclose to employees the nature of health hazards that may exist in their workplace can be in direct conflict with these contractual commitments. . . .

THE LOCAL COMMUNITY AND THE STATE

Physicians have long accepted obligations to protect the health and welfare of the communities in which they reside. The first *Code of Ethics* of the American Medical Association, for example, contains a lengthy section on the obligations of physicians to "the public," including the care of those who are sick and poor, as well as general public health responsibilities.[21] This position had been defended in the previous century by Johann Peter Frank, a German physician who held high posts in government and academia. His view of the physician's obligations to the community stems from a strong general principle of beneficence directed toward public health: "Medical police [Frank's term for the public health role of physicians] . . . is an art of defense, a model of protection of people and their animal helpers against the deleterious consequences of dwelling together in large numbers, but especially of promoting their physical well-being so that people will succumb as late as possible to their eventual fate from the many physical illnesses to which they are subject."[22] In a more recent article in the *New England Journal of Medicine*, Dr. Fitzhugh Mullan similarly argues that primary care and community medicine should be united in what he terms "community-oriented primary care."[23] Under this proposal, the physician is obligated not only to care for his or her patients but to attend to "the overall problems of the community," including activities to "promote health and prevent disease."[24]

CONCLUSION

We conclude that the principle, "The best interests of my patient come first" is not absolute. It is a rebuttable presumption that must sometimes give way to the principle, "The interests of third parties come first." Although there is no well-developed *model* of moral responsibility to third parties, any adequate account of the physician's moral responsibilities must accommodate interests of parties such as the family, health care institutions, medical education and research, future generations of patients, employers, the local community, and the state. For each, a range of conflicts is present for the physician. Some forms of conflict are best resolved in favor of the patient, others

present genuine dilemmas, and still others are best resolved in favor of the third party. . . .

NOTES

1. See Natalie Abrams, "Scope of Beneficence in Health Care," in *Beneficence and Health Care,* ed. Earl Shelp (Boston: D. Reidel, 1982), p. 194. For a compelling account of these issues from the parental perspective, see Robert and Peggy Stinson, *The Long Dying of Baby Andrew* (Boston: Atlantic–Little, Brown, 1983).

2. Others have analyzed the physician's moral conflict differently. Robert Veatch, for example, insists on a lexical order that places a principle of justice over that of beneficence. This leads him to a quite different account of how conflicts based in third-party interests might be resolved. See his *A Theory of Medical Ethics* (New York: Basic Books, 1982), Chapters 6, 12, and 13.

3. In "Involuntary Euthanasia of Defective Newborns: A Legal Analysis," *Stanford Law Review* 27 (1975), John Robertson argues that the infant is effectively a third-party beneficiary by virtue of the parents' contract with the physicians.

4. *Guardianship of Becker,* Superior Court of Santa Clara, California, 1981, no. 101981, p. 1. This wardship case involves a Down's child with an at-birth ventricular septal defect of the heart and possible need for life-prolonging surgery. The court asserts that the case has "floundered on the rock of parental rights."

5. R. S. Duff and A. G. M. Campbell, "Moral and Ethical Dilemmas in the Special Care Nursery," *The New England Journal of Medicine* 289 (1973): 890–94. See also "On Deciding the Care of Severely Handicapped or Dying Persons with Particular Reference to Infants," *Pediatrics* 57 (1976): 487–93; and "Counseling Families and Deciding Care of Severely Defective Children," *Pediatrics* 67 (1981): 315–20. This perspective has clearly been influential in American medicine. See *Current Opinions of the Judicial Council of the A.M.A.,* Article 2. 10 (Chicago: American Medical Association, 1982).

6. See D. C. Drake, "Keeping Infants Alive Is Only Half the Battle," *Philadelphia Inquirer* (September 24, 1978): 16.

7. Every state in the U.S. requires parents to provide necessary medical assistance, and any failure to do so that causes death may result in prosecution for manslaughter or murder. Many forms of medical neglect may result in criminal charges. A physician who accepts such a parental decision may also be criminally liable, because he or she, too, has breached a legal duty of care. See John A. Robertson and Norman Fost, "Passive Euthanasia of Defective Newborn Infants: Legal Considerations," *Journal of Pediatrics* 88 (1976): 883–89.

8. The precedent case for many later cases is *Strunk v. Strunk,* 445 S.W. 2d 145 (Ky. 1969). See also *Hart v. Brown,* 289 A2d 386 (Conn. 1972). Contrast *Lausier v. Pescinski,* 67 Wis. 2d 4, 226 N.W. 2d 180 (1975). See also John A. Robertson, "Organ Donations by Incompetents and the Substituted Judgment Doctrine," *Columbia Law Review* 76 (1976), esp. pp. 57–65.

9. These justifying conditions are explored in detail in Tom L. Beauchamp and James Childress, *Principles of Biomedical Ethics,* 2d ed. (New York: Oxford University Press, 1983), Chapter 4. For important related arguments, see Terrence F. Ackerman, "Meningomyelocele and Parental Commitment: A Policy Proposal Regarding Selection for Treatment," *Man and Medicine* 5 (1980): 291ff.; "The Limits of Beneficence," *Hastings Center Report* 10 (August 1980): 13–18; Albert R. Jonsen and Michael J. Garland,

"A Moral Policy for Life/Death Decisions in the Intensive Care Nursery," in *Ethics of Newborn Intensive Care,* ed. Albert R. Jonsen and Michael J. Garland (Berkeley: University of California, Institute of Governmental Studies, 1976); H. Tristram Engelhardt, Jr., "Ethical Issues in Aiding the Death of Young Children," in *Beneficent Euthanasia,* ed. Marvin Kohl (Buffalo, N.Y.: Prometheus Books, 1975); R. B. Zachary, "Ethical and Social Aspects of Treatment of Spina Bifida," *Lancet* 2 (3 August 1968): 274–76; John M. Freeman, "To Treat or Not to Treat: Ethical Dilemmas of Treating the Infant with a Myelomeningocele," *Clinical Neurosurgery* 20 (1973): 134–46; John Lorber, "Selective Treatment of Myelomeningocele: To Treat or Not to Treat?" *Pediatrics* 53 (1974): 307–8; several articles in Chester Swinyard, ed., *Decision Making and the Defective Newborn* (Springfield, Ill.: Charles C Thomas, 1978); and President's Commission for the Study of Ethical Problems in Medicine and Biomedical and Behavioral Research, *Deciding to Forego Life-Sustaining Treatment* (Washington, D.C.: U.S. Government Printing Office, 1983), pp. 6–8 and 197–229. These problems are often discussed in law and ethics alike in terms of the confusing distinction between withholding ordinary means and withholding extraordinary means.

10. See Lucy Rau Ferguson, "The Competence and Freedom of Children to Make Choices Regarding Participation in Biomedical and Behavioral Research," in *Research Involving Children, Appendix* (Washington, D.C.: DHHS for the National Commission for the Protection of Human Subjects, 1977), pp. 4–1 to 4–42.

11. See H. F. Pilpel, "Minors' Rights to Medical Care," *Albany Law Review* 36 (1972): 462ff.

12. *Planned Parenthood of Central Missouri v. Danforth*, 428 U.S. 52 (1976) and *Bellotti v. Baird*, 443 U.S. 622 (1979). See also *Carey v. Population Services Int'l.*, 431 U.S. 678 (1977)—a contraception case—and contrast *H. L. v. Matheson*, 101 S.Ct. 1164 (1981) to all three of the above.

13. A convincing case of an 11-year-old girl whose confidentiality about venereal disease was not broken, but probably should have been, is found in Norman Fost, "Ethical Problems in Pediatrics," *Current Problems in Pediatrics* 6 (October 1976): 25. Fost argues that "an unnecessary and often harmful isolation from the parents" can be created by rules of confidentiality.

14. For an important analysis of the impact of the institutionalization of medicine, see Paul Starr, *The Social Transformation of American Medicine* (New York: Basic Books, 1982).

15. Arthur Schafer, "The Ethics of the Randomized Clinical Trial," *New England Journal of Medicine* 307 (16 September 1982): 720.

16. A similar problem is identified by D. Mark Mahler et al. regarding research on medical cost containment. See D. Mark Mahler, Robert M. Veatch, and Victor W. Seidel, "Ethical Issues in Informed Consent: Research on Medical Cost Containment," *Journal of the American Medical Association* 247 (22–29 January 1982): 481–85.

17. For a moving account of how important it was to one leukemia patient to have the intravenous nurse-team draw blood, see Morris B. Abram, *The Day Is Short* (New York: Harcourt Brace Jovanovich, 1982), p. 209.

18. Franz J. Ingelfinger, "Informed (But Uneducated) Consent," *New England Journal of Medicine* 288 (31 August 1972): 465–66. See also Henry W. Riecken and Ruth Ravich, "Informed Consent to Biomedical Research in Veterans' Administration Hospitals," *Journal of the American Medical Association* 248 (16 July 1982): 344–48.

19. A complicating factor here—and elsewhere in medical practice—is conflict of interest for the physician. Thus, for example, the young clinical-researcher seeking tenure and other signs of recognition may allow ambition to override his or her moral responsibilities. The topic of conflicts of interests in medicine is a large one and, unfortunately, beyond the scope of this [essay].

20. For concrete recommendations, see President's Commission for the Study of Ethical Problems in Medicine and Biomedical and Behavioral Research, *Making Health Care Decisions* (Washington, D.C.: U.S. Government Printing Office, 1982), Chapter 6, pp. 129–49.

21. American Medical Association, "Code of Ethics," in *Proceedings of the National Medical Convention, 1846–1847,* reprinted in *Ethics in Medicine*, ed. Stanley Reiser et al. (Cambridge: MIT Press, 1977), pp. 33–34.

22. Johann Peter Frank, *A System of Complete Medical Police,* trans. Erna Lesky (Baltimore: Johns Hopkins University Press, 1976), p. 12.

23. Fitzhugh Mullan, "Community-Oriented Primary Care," *New England Journal of Medicine* 307 (21 October 1982): 1076–78.

24. Ibid., 1077.

DAVID HILFIKER

Unconscious on a Corner . . .

The police brought Mr W. to the emergency room. They had found him unconscious on a corner in Washington, DC, one more drunk littering the city, disturbing our view. Fifty-two years old, black, dressed in rags, homeless, he was no different from the countless other tragedies that find their way to the ER. But Mr W. was not drunk. His jaw had previously been broken and—at another emergency room—wired shut to heal, whereupon he had been discharged back to the streets. He couldn't eat or drink enough to keep himself going, and so it was that the police found him, severely dehydrated, unconscious, close to death.

Mr W. was initially rehydrated with intravenous solutions, but his condition deteriorated, and he was readmitted to the intensive care unit. Tests were ordered, examinations repeated, consults held. At last it was clear: Mr W. had the syndrome of inappropriate antidiuretic hormone secretion with life-threatening hyponatremia. Fluids were limited to 800 mL per day, his physicians went out of their way to find demeclocycline (an expensive medication not routinely available at the hospital), and Mr W. was slowly and painstakingly nursed back to health.

Without reference to the chart, his physicians explained to me in detail his prognosis and continuing treatment; clearly they knew their patient well. Mr W. would be returning to a city shelter in a few days and the medical team would follow him up in the outpatient clinic. And as I reviewed the chart, I was impressed with our city hospital. Compassionate, competent care had obviously been rendered this homeless man without reference to his finances, social class, or culture. In my work with the poor, I was used to stories that ended differently; Mr W.'s story gave me hope for the wounded of our society.

As I walked into Mr W.'s room, however, my hopes dimmed. I was shocked by his emaciation, by the emptiness in his eyes, by the light slowly but definitely extinguishing. He was confused. Now "ready for discharge," he could not remember the day of the week, the month, or even guess the year; he seemed unaware he was in a hospital. Clearly Mr W. was demented.

How could he be discharged to a shelter? How would he manage to take his medicines if he couldn't even remember the day of the week? How would he limit his fluid intake if he couldn't understand instructions? How could these obviously compassionate physicians send this man back to an overnight shelter from which he would be sent out into the street to forage for himself every day? Mr W. had been well treated initially; why was he being abandoned now that his treatable condition had been corrected?

I talked to his physicians, trying to understand. No, they didn't really know what the shelters were like. They didn't know that there was essentially no supervisory staff, that meals were unavailable, that ten men would be herded together in one room shared with cockroaches and other vermin, that alcoholism and random violence were uncontrollable. Without a conscious decision, it has become policy in our city to consider overnight shelters as places of disposition for emergency rooms, jails, prisons, and hospitals. I could hardly blame Mr W.'s physicians for following usual policy.

Reprinted by permission of the publisher from *Journal of the American Medical Association* 258 (1987), 3155–3156. © 1987, American Medical Association.

The issue, however, was deeper. When Mr W. first entered the hospitals, there was indeed something that his physicians could *do* for him. They had the knowledge, they had the resources, and they could *do some good*. But now that time was over and he was "cured." There were no more diseases to treat. Furthermore, there was no place to send him. In Washington, nursing home placement for the indigent can take over six months, and the physicians knew there would be intense pressure to discharge their patient from his expensive hospital bed. They knew no other options. So, their honest compassion had no place of expression and they had withdrawn. They hardened themselves to the reality of Mr W.'s plight and talked about discharge to a shelter as if that were a legitimate plan for a demented old man who needed constant supervision.

Are not many of us like Mr W.'s physicians? Within us are deep wells of compassion that — given the right set of circumstances — can be tapped to generate enormous generosity and creativity. But the truly broken — the chronically schizophrenic, the alcoholic, the homeless, the very poor — seem beyond our caring. Their needs are overwhelming, the structures that reach out to them so few. We don't know what to do, and so we turn away, offering nothing. Compassion is exiled.

After four years of working in the inner city, it is clear to me that medicine has largely abandoned the poor. Private medicine in Washington is inaccessible without insurance coverage. We called at random 50 private primary care physicians; less than half accept Medicaid for payment. Fewer than 10% have any provision for reducing fees or for deferred payment for uninsured, indigent patients. Unless one can pay the $75 to $150 office visit fee in advance, there is simply no way to get in the door.

And so the poor must rely on the public sector, on the good will of a society that has no use for them. Government budget cuts are no longer news, and an aging, fragmented bureaucracy delivers distinctly second-class care.

The reasons are multiple and complex, but the final reality is painfully obvious. The poor are denied access to adequate health care. Every day we see the scars among our patients: an ataxic, demented alcoholic who can barely balance with a walker is discharged to live on the streets; a hypertensive woman suffers a stroke because she cannot afford her medicines; a one-legged man with the remaining foot frostbitten is discharged from an emergency room with instructions to soak what is ultimately shown to be osteomyelitis. What has happened? How can the richest nation in the history of the world permit such tragedies?

The "monetarization"[1] of private medical care and the inadequacy of the public system are certainly the most important reasons for the abandonment of the poor. It is difficult for us physicians to maintain our average $108,000 annual salary and still provide care to the indigent. Medicine is quickly changing from a servant profession into a business and it is the poor who are most deeply affected. And it is also easy to blame a public system in which only 31% of the poor even *qualify* for Medicaid,[2] of which bureaucracy and second-class care are the hallmarks. But there are more subtle reasons than money and an unresponsive bureaucracy for the medical abandonment of the poor.

I would suggest that it is difficult to be a highly trained physician and work with the poor. Most of us come from a different culture and do not understand, for instance, that the very poor are often so overwhelmed by the emotional, social, and financial stresses in their lives that they simply cannot comply with our evaluation or treatment. If a patient cannot articulate his history, has a fourth-grade education, compounds his hypertension with alcoholism, cannot afford laboratory evaluation or medications, is unable to return for consistent follow-up because of problems at home, and cannot afford a place to live, we who are trained to treat diseases[3] will feel at sea. The physicians who treated Mr W. could express their compassion by diagnosing and treating his rare hormonal disorder, but they were deeply frustrated by his dementia and his homelessness, by the years of despair that had left him without resources. We who are used to the efficiency and power of conventional doctoring find this new work very demanding emotionally.

Most frustrating is the absence of self-esteem among my patients. Because so many come out of generations of poverty, they *know* that they have little value in our society; it has been demonstrated to them over and over again. There is little sense that anything they can do will make a real difference in their lives. . . .

What can be done? Clearly our institutions need to change. Clearly some form of national health coverage available to all the poor is required. Without guaranteed health insurance, nothing else will be of much use. But, given the current social and political atmosphere, that change will be a long time coming. There is the danger that by focusing exclusively on what needs to happen in the political system, we will avoid the deeper, more personal transformation that is also necessary.

Can we who are in private medicine open, say, 15% of our practice to those who cannot afford the full fee? Can we accept Medicaid—with all its paperwork, discounts, and headaches—joyfully as an opportunity to participate with our society in ministry to the poor and oppressed? Can we who belong to medical institutions press our employers to do the same?

The first step must be to bring the poor into our practices. In our city, over 200 private consultants—coordinated by the Archdiocese of Washington—have volunteered to serve as a referral network for indigent patients; radiology and laboratory services have been similarly offered. It is only a beginning, of course, but it opens us to the possibility.

I am beginning to realize that we in medicine need the poor to bring us back to our roots as a servant profession. Medicine drifts understandably yet ominously toward the technical and the economically lucrative, and we find it difficult to resist. Perhaps we *need* the poor at this very moment to bring us back to ourselves. The nature of the healer's work is to be with the wounded in their suffering. Can the poor in their very vulnerability show us how?

NOTES

1. Ginzberg E: The monetarization of medical care. *N Engl J Med* 1984; 310: 1162–1165.

2. *No Room in the Marketplace: The Health Care of the Poor.* St. Louis, Catholic Health Association's Task Force on Health Care of the Poor, 1986, p. 2.

3. Baron R: An introduction to medical phenomenology: I can't hear you while I'm listening. *Ann Intern Med* 1985; 103: 606–611.

COUNCIL ON ETHICAL AND JUDICIAL AFFAIRS, AMERICAN MEDICAL ASSOCIATION

Gender Disparities in Clinical Decision Making

Recent evidence has raised concerns that women are disadvantaged because of inadequate attention to the research, diagnosis, and treatment of women's health care problems. In 1985, the US Public Health Service's Task Force on Women's Health Issues reported that the lack of research data on women limited understanding of women's health needs.[1]

One concern is that medical treatments for women are based on a male model, regardless of the fact that women may react differently to treatments than men

Reprinted by permission of the publisher from *Journal of the American Medical Association* 266 (1991), 559–562.© 1991, American Medical Association.

or that some diseases manifest themselves differently in women than in men. The results of medical research on men are generalized to women without sufficient evidence of applicability to women.[2–4] For example, the original research on the prophylactic value of aspirin for coronary artery disease was derived almost exclusively from research on men, yet recommendations based on this research have been directed to the general populace.[4]

Some researchers attribute the lack of research on women to women's reproductive cycles. Women's menstrual cycles may constitute a separate variable affecting test results.[5] Also, researchers are reluctant to perform studies on women of childbearing age, because experimental treatments or procedures may affect their reproductive capabilities. However, the task force pointed out that it is precisely because medications and other therapeutic interventions have a differential effect on women according to their menstrual cycle that women should not be excluded from research.[6] Research on the use of antidepressant agents was initially conducted entirely on men, despite apparently higher rates of clinical depression in women.[6,7] Evidence is emerging that the effects of some antidepressants vary over the course of a woman's cycle, and as a result, a constant dosage of an antidepressant may be too high at some points in a woman's cycle, yet too low at others.[2,3]

In response to the task force, the National Institutes of Health promised to implement a policy ensuring that women would be included in study populations unless it would be scientifically inappropriate to do so.[4] However, in June 1990, the General Accounting Office reported that the National Institutes of Health had made little progress in implementing the policy and that many problems remained.[4]

In addition to these general concerns raised by the task force about women's health, recent studies have examined whether a patient's gender inappropriately affects the access to and use of medical care. Three important areas in which evidence of gender disparities exists are (1) access to kidney transplantation, (2) diagnosis and treatment of cardiac disease, and (3) diagnosis of lung cancer. Other studies have also revealed gender-based differences in patterns of health care use. Although biological factors account for some differences between the sexes in the provision of medical care, these studies indicate that nonbiological or nonclinical factors may affect clinical decision making. There are not enough data to identify the exact nature of nonbiological or nonclinical factors. Nevertheless, the existence of these factors is a cause for concern that the medical community needs to address.

EVIDENCE OF DISPARITIES

GENDER DIFFERENCES IN HEALTH CARE USE

Some evidence indicates that, compared with men, women receive more health care services overall. In general, women have more physician visits per year and receive more services per visit.[8] Several studies have examined the issue of differences in health care use between men and women.[8–14] The results of these studies vary and some are contradictory. One of the most extensive studies on gender differences in the use of health care services found that when medical care differs for men and women (in approximately 30% to 40% of cases), the usual result is more care for women than for men. Women seem to receive more care even when both men and women report the same type of illness or complaint about their health.[8] Women undergo more examinations, laboratory tests, and blood pressure checks and receive more drug prescriptions and return appointments than men. However, the reasons for this are not clear.

Studies that have examined gender as a factor for receiving several major diagnostic or therapeutic interventions, however, suggest that women have less access than men to these interventions.

DISPARITIES IN PROVIDING MAJOR DIAGNOSTIC AND THERAPEUTIC INTERVENTIONS

Kidney Dialysis and Transplantation. Gender has been found to correlate with the likelihood that a patient with kidney disease will receive dialysis or a kidney transplant. In one study researchers analyzed the percentage of patients in the United States with end-stage renal disease who received dialysis.[15] Of men who needed dialysis, 37.3% were given dialysis, compared with 31.1% of women. Ninety percent of the difference resulted from the fact that younger people have a greater likelihood of receiving dialysis than older people.

Disparities based on gender are more pronounced for the likelihood of receiving a kidney transplant. An analysis of patient dialysis data from 1981 through 1985 indicated that women undergoing renal dialysis were approximately 30% less likely to receive a cadaver kidney transplant than men.[16] Another study, done during the period 1979 through 1985, showed that a female dialysis patient had only three-quarters the chance of a male patient to receive a renal transplant.[17] Controlling for age did not significantly reduce gender as a factor in the likelihood of receiving a transplant. Men were more likely to receive a transplant in every age category. The discrepancy between sexes was most pronounced in the group 46 to 60 years old, with women having only half the chance of receiving a transplant as men the same age.[18]

Diagnosis of Lung Cancer. Recent autopsy studies have revealed that in as many as a quarter of patients with lung cancer, a diagnosis is not made while they are alive.[18-20] A comparison between the population in which lung cancer is diagnosed and the population in which it is not diagnosed shows that a detection bias favors the ordering of diagnostic testing for lung cancer in patients who are smokers, have a recent or chronic cough, or are male.[20]

One study compared the rates of lung cancer detected at autopsy with the way cytologic studies of sputum were ordered in a hospital setting to detect lung cancer. Men and women have relatively equal rates of previously undiagnosed lung cancer detected during autopsy. In addition, other studies have shown that women and men with similar smoking practices are at essentially equivalent risk for lung cancer.[21] However, men were twice as likely to have cytologic studies of sputum ordered as women. Once smoking status and other medical considerations were taken into account, men still had 1.6 times the chance of having a cytologic test done.[20]

Catheterization for Coronary Bypass Surgery. Men seem to have cardiac catheterizations ordered at a rate disproportionately higher than women, regardless of each gender's likelihood of having coronary artery disease. A study done in 1987 showed that in a group of 390 patients, of those with abnormal exercise radionuclide scans, 40% of the male patients were referred for cardiac catheterization, while only 4% of the female patients were referred for further testing.[22] The study showed that once researchers controlled for the variables of abnormal test results, age, types of angina, presence of symptoms, and confirmed previous myocardial infarction, men were still 6.5 times more likely to be referred for catheterization than women, although men have only three times the likelihood of having coronary heart disease than women.

Of those patients whose nuclear scan test results ultimately were abnormal, women were more than twice as likely to have their symptoms attributed to somatic, psychiatric, or other noncardiac causes as men. For patients whose test scans were normal, men and women had a relatively equal chance of having their symptoms attributed to cardiac causes.

The authors concluded that the wide difference in referral rates between men and women could not be explained by gender-based differences in the accuracy of nuclear scans. Even after abnormal test results had been established, men were referred significantly more often than women. It is unlikely that the discrepancy results from a higher likelihood of referral in some types of nuclear scan abnormalities, since men had higher referral rates in every category of abnormality. Men were also more likely to be referred regardless of the probability of their having coronary artery disease before the nuclear scan.

POSSIBLE EXPLANATIONS

BIOLOGICAL DIFFERENCES BETWEEN THE SEXES

Differences in biological needs between male and female patients probably account for a large part of the differences in the use of health care services. The kind and number[23] of illnesses that are reported differ somewhat for women and men. Possibly, women get more care because they have more illnesses or because the types of illnesses they have require more overall care. Some figures show that the generally lower socioeconomic status of women may be associated with poorer health. Also, women tend to live longer than men and individuals of older ages may have more morbidities.[8] However, real differences in morbidity and mortality between the sexes would not explain the fact that women seem to receive more care than men for the same type of complaint or illness.[8]

Real biological differences also cannot account for the gender disparities in rates of cardiac catheterization, kidney transplantation, or lung cancer diagnoses. For instance, the discrepancy in dialysis rates might be explained by the existence of coexisting diseases in women that lessen the potential effectiveness of dialysis. However, the Health Care Financing Administration reports that female patients receiving dialysis have a slightly better survival pattern than male patients.[24]

Also, biological differences between the sexes, such as the level of cytotoxic antibodies, number of complications after transplantation, or differences in the type of renal disease between men and women did not explain the disparity in the likelihood of receiving a kidney transplant.[17] It is unlikely that the difference reflects either patient or physician preference; successful transplantation is generally considered superior to lifetime dialysis by both patients and physicians.[16,17]

The difference in sputum cytologic findings between male and female patients may reflect the historical association between male sex and cigarette smoking. Traditionally, more men than women have been smokers.[21] In fact, past demographic data showed that men were more likely to have lung cancer than women. Physicians, in turn, may view smoking and being male as independent risk factors for lung cancer and therefore tend to suspect cancer more readily in patients who either smoked or were men even though gender is not an independent risk factor.[21]

Differences in disease prevalence between men and women have been cited to explain the disparity in cardiac catheterization rates.[25] However, the difference in disease prevalence between men and women is 3:1, whereas the difference in catheterization rates was almost 7:1.[22,26] Additionally, the similarities in use of antianginal drug treatment indicates that the patients were clinically comparable.[22]

Other evidence also suggests that women may be disadvantaged by inadequate attention to the manifestations of cardiovascular disease in women. There is some evidence that cardiovascular disease is not diagnosed or treated early enough in women. Studies show that women have a higher operative mortality rate for coronary bypass surgery[27,28] and a higher mortality rate at the time of an initial myocardial infarction.[29–31] The higher mortality rates reflect the fact that cardiovascular disease is further advanced in women than men at both the time of surgery and the time of an initial heart attack.[29]

The lack of research done specifically on women may have resulted in a failure to develop diagnostic criteria and treatments that are appropriate for cardiovascular disease in women. Cardiovascular disease in women differs from the disease in men in several significant ways. One study showed that diabetes is a greater risk factor in women for morbidity and mortality from coronary heart disease than in men.[32] The same study also showed that the level of high-density lipoprotein cholesterol is a stronger predictor of heart disease in women than in men.[32] These differences between the sexes in the manifestation of cardiovascular disease may affect diagnostic and treatment indications for women. Yet, research on cardiovascular disease has concentrated almost entirely on men[3] despite the fact that cardiovascular disease is the leading cause of death in women in the United States.[2,29] Also, tests traditionally used to detect cardiovascular disease in men, such as treadmill testing, are not as sensitive or specific for detecting cardiovascular disease in women as for men.[28]

Data that suggest that a patient's gender plays an inappropriate role in medical decision making raise the question of possible gender bias in clinical decision making. Gender bias may not necessarily manifest itself as overt discrimination based on sex. Rather, social attitudes, including stereotypes, prejudices and other evaluations based on gender roles may play themselves out in a variety of subtle ways.

For instance, some evidence suggests that physicians are more likely to attribute women's health complaints to emotional rather than physical causes.[33–35] Women's concerns about their health and their greater use of health care services have been perceived to be due to "overanxiousness" about their health.[35] However, characterizing women's use patterns as a result of emotional excess or overuse risks providing inadequate care for women. For example, in the study of catheterization rates, attributing a disproportionate percentage of women's abnormal nuclear scan results to psychiatric or noncardiac causes for their symptoms may have compromised their care.[22]

Perceiving men's use practices as normal and attributing *over*anxiousness to women's concerns about their health may be doing a disservice to both sexes. One study concluded that "women's greater interest in and concern with health matters and their greater attentiveness to bodily changes may be part of a set of behaviors that do contribute to women's lower mortality rates."[12] Men may tend to be "*under*anxious" about their health or to ignore symptoms or illnesses and, consequently, underuse health care. Statistics that show that men tend to have a lesser number but more severe types of health problems may reflect men's resistance to seeking care until a health problem has become acute.

Societal value judgments placed on gender or gender roles may also put women at a disadvantage in the context of receiving certain major diagnostic and therapeutic interventions, such as kidney transplantation and cardiac catheterization. A general perception that men's social role obligations or of their contributions to society are greater than women's may fuel these disparities.[9] For instance, altering one's work schedule to accommodate health concerns may be viewed as more difficult for men than women. Overall, men's financial contribution to the family may be considered more critical than women's. A kidney transplant is much less cumbersome than dialysis. Coronary bypass surgery, for which catheterization is a prerequisite, is a more efficient and immediate solution to the problem of coronary artery disease than continuous antianginal drug therapy. However, judgments based on evaluations of social worth or preconceptions about the probable roles of men and women are clearly inexcusable in the context of medical decision making.

ROLE OF THE MEDICAL PROFESSION IN EXAMINING GENDER DISPARITIES AND ELIMINATING BIASES

Available data do not conclusively demonstrate a connection between gender bias and gender disparities in the provision of health care. Designing a study that can control for the myriad social, economic, and cultural factors that might influence decision making in a clinical context has proved extraordinarily difficult.

Historically, societal perceptions regarding women's health status have often disadvantaged women. Throughout the mid-19th and well into the 20th century, women's perceived disposition toward both physical and mental illness was used as a rationale for keeping them from worldly spheres such as politics, science, medicine, and law. For women, behavior that violated expected gender-role norms was frequently attributed to various physical or mental illnesses[36,37] and in turn often was treated in a variety of ways, including gynecological surgeries, such as hysterectomies and, occasionally, clitoridectomies.[38] Society and medicine have addressed and are working to remedy sex stereotypes and biases. Yet, many social and cultural attitudes that endorse sex-stereotyped roles for men and women remain in our society.

The medical community cannot tolerate any discrepancy in the provision of care that is not based on appropriate biological or medical indications. The US Public Health Service's Task Force on Women's Health Issues concluded that "[b]ecause health care is a legitimate concern of all people, the health professions are obligated to seek ways of ensuring that clinical decisions are based on science that adequately pertains to all people."[6] Insufficient research on women is not only discriminatory but may be dangerous; medical care or drug treatments that prove effective in men may not always be safely generalizable to women.[4] The influence that social attitudes and perceptions have had on health care in the past suggest that some biases could remain and affect modern medical care. Such attitudes and perceptions may disadvantage both women and men by reinforcing gen-

der-based stereotypes or inhibiting access to care. Current evidence of possible discrepancies indicates a need for further scrutiny.

SUMMARY OF RECOMMENDATIONS

Physicians should examine their practices and attitudes for the influence of social or cultural biases that could affect medical care. Physicians must ensure that gender is not used inappropriately as a consideration in clinical decision making. Assessments of need based on presumptions about the relative worth of certain social roles must be avoided. Procedures and techniques that preclude or minimize the possibility of gender bias should be developed and implemented. A gender-neutral determination for kidney transplant eligibility should be used.

More medical research on women's health and women's health problems should be pursued. Results of medical testing done solely on men should not be generalized to women without evidence that results can be applied safely and effectively to both sexes. Research on health problems that affect both sexes should include male and female subjects. Sound medical and scientific reasons should be required for excluding women from medical tests and studies, such as that the proposed research does not or would not affect the health of women. An obvious example would be research on prostatic cancer. Also, further research into the possible causes of gender disparities should be conducted. The extent to which physician-patient interactions may be influenced by cultural and social conceptions of gender should be ascertained.

Finally, awareness of and responsiveness to sociocultural factors that could lead to gender disparities may be enhanced by increasing the number of female physicians in leadership roles and other positions of authority in teaching, research, and the practice of medicine.

REFERENCES

1. US Public Health Service. *Women's Health: Report of the Public Health Service Task Force on Women's Health Issues.* Washington, DC: US Dept of Health and Human Services; 1985;2.

2. Cotton P. Is there still too much extrapolation from data on middle-aged white men? *JAMA.* 1990;263:1049–1050.

3. Cotton P. Examples abound of gaps in medical knowledge because of groups excluded from scientific study. *JAMA.* 1990;263:1051–1052.

4. *Hearings Before the House Energy and Commerce Subcommittee on Health and the Environment,* 101st Congr, 1st Sess

(1990) (testimony of Mark V. Nadel, associate director, US General Accounting Office).

5. Hamilton J, Parry B. Sex-related differences in clinical drug response: implications for women's health. *J Am Med Wom Assoc.* 1983;38:126–132.

6. Hamilton JA. Guidelines for avoiding methodological and policy-making biases in gender-related health research in Public Health Service. *Women's Health: Report of the Public Health Service Task Force on Women's Health Issues.* Washington, DC: US Department of Health and Human Services; 1985;2.

7. Raskin A. Age-sex differences in response to antidepressant drugs. *J Nerv Ment Dis.* 1974;159:120–130.

8. Verbrugge LM, Steiner RP. Physician treatment of men and women patients: sex bias or appropriate care? *Med Care.* 1981;19:609–632.

9. Marcus AC, Suman TE. Sex differences in reports of illness and disability: A preliminary test of the 'fixed role' hypothesis. *J Health Soc Behav.* 1981;22:174–182.

10. Gove WR, Hughes M. Possible causes of the apparent sex differences in physical health: an empirical investigation. *Am Social Rev.* 1979;44:126–146.

11. Cleary PD, Mechanic D, Greenley JR. Sex differences in medical care utilization: an empirical investigation. *J Health Soc Behav.* 1982;23:106–119.

12. Hibbard JH, Pope CR. Another look at sex differences in the use of medical care; illness orientation and the type of morbidities for which services are used. *Women Health.* 1986; 11:21–36.

13. Armitage KJ, Schneiderman LF, Bass RA. Response of physicians to medical complaints in men and women. *JAMA.* 1979;241:2186.

14. Natanson CA. Illness and the feminine role: a theoretical review. *Soc Sci Med.* 1975;9:57–63.

15. Kjellstrand CM, Logan GM. Racial, sexual and age inequalities in chronic dialysis. *Nephron.* 1987;45:257–263.

16. Held PJ, Pauly MV, Bovbjerg RR, et al. Access to kidney transplantation. *Arch Intern Med.* 1988;148:2594–2600.

17. Kjellstrand CM. Age, sex, and race inequality in renal transplantation. *Arch Intern Med.* 1988;148:1305–1309.

18. McFarlane MJ, Feinstein AR, Wells CK. The 'epidemiologic necropsy': unexpected detections, demographic selections, and the changing rates of lung cancer. *JAMA.* 1987;258:331–338.

19. McFarlane MJ, Feinstein AR, Wells CK. Necropsy evidence of detection bias in the diagnosis of lung cancer. *Arch Intern Med.* 1986; 146:1695–1698.

20. Wells CK, Feinstein AR. Detection bias in the diagnostic pursuit of lung cancer. *Am J Epidemiol.* 1988;128:1016–1026.

21. Schoenberg JB, Wilcox HB, Mason TJ, et al. Variation in smoking-related lung cancer risk among New Jersey women. *Am J Epidemiol.* 1989;130:688–695.

22. Tobin JN, Wassertheil-Smoller S, Wexler JP, et al. Sex bias in considering coronary bypass surgery. *Ann Intern Med.* 1987;107:19–25.

23. Verbrugge LM. Sex differentials in health. *Prevention.* 1982;97:417–437.

24. Eggers PW, Connerton R, McMullan M. The Medicare experience with end-stage renal disease: trends in incidence, prevalence, and survival. *Health Care Fin Rev.* 1984;5:69–88.

25. Karlin BG. Sex bias and coronary bypass surgery. *Ann Intern Med.* 1988;108:149.

26. Tobin JN, Wassertheil-Smoller S, Wexler JP, et al. Sex bias in considering coronary bypass surgery. *Ann Intern Med.* 1987; 107:19–25.

27. Khan SS, Nessim S, Gray R, Czer LS, Chaux A, Matloff J. Increased mortality of women in coronary artery bypass surgery: Evidence for referral bias. *Ann Intern Med.* 1990;112:561–567.

28. Wenger NK. Gender, coronary artery disease, and coronary bypass surgery. *Ann Intern Med.* 1990;112:557–558.

29. Wenger NK. Coronary disease in women. *Ann Rev Med.* 1985;36:285–294.

30. Fiebach NH, Viscoli CM, Horwitz RI. Differences between women and men in survival after myocardial infarction. *JAMA.* 1990;263:1092–1096.

31. Dittrich H, Gilpin E, Nicod P, Cali G, Henning H, Ross J. Acute myocardial infarction in women: influence of gender on mortality and prognosis variables. *Am J Cardiol.* 1988;62:1–7.

32. Lerner DJ, Kannel WB. Patterns of coronary heart disease morbidity and mortality in the sexes: a 26-year follow-up of the Framingham population. *Am Heart J.* 1986;111:383–390.

33. Bernstein B, Kane R. Physicians' attitudes toward female patients. *Med Care.* 1981;19:600–608.

34. Colameco S, Becker L, Simpson M. Sex bias in the assessment of patient complaints. *J Fam Pract.* 1983;16:1117–1121.

35. Savage WD, Tate P. Medical students' attitudes towards women: a sex-linked variable? *Med Educ.* 1983;17:159–164.

36. Waisberg J, Page P. Gender role nonconformity and perception of mental illness. *Women Health.* 1988;14:3–16.

37. Broverman IK, Broverman DM, Clarkson FE, et al. Sex-role stereotypes and clinical judgments of mental health. *J Consult Clin Psychol.* 1970;34:1–7.

38. Barker-Benfield B. 'The spermatic economy.' In: Gordon M, ed. *The American Family in Sociohistorical Perspective.* New York, NY: St Martin's Press; 1973.

CHRISTINE K. CASSEL AND BERNICE L. NEUGARTEN

The Goals of Medicine in an Aging Society

The unprecedented aging of our society has recently set off a vigorous debate about the appropriate use of expensive and extensive medical care for elderly persons. This debate involves very complex issues, which are too often and too easily oversimplified both in the media and in the professional literature. Some argue that because the increases in longevity in the past two decades are largely the result of advances in medical technology, we can and should continue, by means of research and the implementation of new technologies, to push back the age barriers that presently create limits to good health and to length of life (e.g., Schneider, 1989). Others argue that there must be a natural end to the human life span, that old age is a reasonable and acceptable indicator of proximity to death, and that it is both unseemly and wasteful to keep augmenting medical technology in a struggle against the inevitability of death (e.g., Callahan, 1987).

In this [essay] we will examine the goals of medicine in light of the dramatic demographic and epidemiologic changes in our society. We do this in the hope of developing a framework within which the complex questions about appropriate medical care for patients of advanced age can be addressed most rationally, most effectively, and most humanely.

THE "STATE" OF MODERN MEDICINE

The decade of the 1970s saw the beginning of a reexamination of modern medicine. Many different and often conflicting voices were heard, as is true to the present day. Critics included John Knowles (1977),

Reprinted with permission of the publisher from Robert H. Binstock and Stephen G. Post, eds., *Too Old for Health Care? Controversies in Medicine, Law, Economics, and Ethics* (Baltimore: Johns Hopkins University Press, 1991), pp. 75–91.

who edited an issue of the journal *Daedalus* entitled *Doing Better and Feeling Worse*. The title referred to the apparent difference between objective indicators of health, which showed improvement, and subjective reports from patients, which indicated increases in health-related complaints as well as growing dissatisfaction with physicians and hospitals.

Carlson's book *The End of Medicine* (1975) also was an indication of the introspection going on in the medical profession and the public examination of the practice of medicine and its role in our society. The title of the book suggested both a critique of the end(s), or the goal(s), of medicine, and a prediction that an oversized technocracy that has outgrown its human roots must inevitably decline and come to an end. Similar apocalyptic visions were popularized by Ivan Illich in his book *Medical Nemesis* (1976), which put forward the view of modern medicine as too narrowly focused on reductionist technical approaches to problems that would be better approached through social reforms or preventive practices. Howard Waitzkin, in *The Second Sickness* (1983), argued that perverse financial incentives were responsible for the imbalances described by Illich, Carlson, and others.

This reexamination of the goals of medicine and the proper place of medicine in society continued through the 1980s, but the themes became more focused. In the 1970s attention was concentrated on the role that unbridled technology has played in diminishing the humanism of medicine. In the 1980s, it was focused on the costs of that technology and on the ways to stem the steadily increasing expenditures (see Hiatt, 1987).

Today, increasing costs are often described as being closely linked to the increase in life expectancy, because older people use far greater amounts of medical care than do younger people. The increasing life expectancy of Americans is, at least in part, due to advances in medical care. Moreover, because today people seldom die prematurely, they need more medical care to help cope with the chronic diseases of senescence. The special interplay between advanced medical technologies and increasing life expectancy has led to even greater questioning of the goals of medicine. The issues of cost containment and the risks of dehumanized technology are often invoked to argue for setting limits on the use of medical interventions, especially for aged persons (e.g., Callahan 1987; Callahan, 1990).

The goals of medicine in today's society must be examined in the context of medical technology and the rising costs of health care. Also, however, they must be reconsidered in light of the increasing longevity of the population, and the moral and ethical issues that underlie the practice of medicine.

THE INCREASE IN LIFE EXPECTANCY

Longevity has increased dramatically in this century, with average life expectancy almost doubling in the period from 1900 to 1965. During that period, two basic assumptions were made. The first was that most of the decline in mortality was due to advances in social conditions rather than to advances in medical treatment. Better sanitation, nutrition, education, and working conditions were largely responsible for the drop in premature deaths that occurred, historically, long before the advent of any specific life-saving medical discoveries, such as insulin or antibiotics.

The second assumption was that the genetically determined life span of the human species is probably about 75 years. It was recognized that a gap exists between maximum life span and average length of life. By the mid-1960s, however, as average life expectancy began to approach 70 years, it was assumed that the gap had been narrowed about as much as possible: that, in short, we had come close to maximizing life expectancy in this country.

Within a decade, however, the latter assumption was proved wrong, and the great demographic transition of the 1980s had begun. Life expectancy, after remaining stable for two decades, began to increase again. This transition has been described in extraordinary detail by demographers, epidemiologists, and health policy specialists (e.g., Olshansky and Ault, 1986).

The increase in longevity has not yet reached a plateau, nor has it ended. In fact, it is continuing at an unprecedented and unanticipated rate. Average life expectancy is now nearly 80 years for women and nearly 74 years for men, and mortality rates are declining most rapidly among the persons who are over 85. The latter group presently constitutes about 1 percent of the population, but it is projected to be over 2 percent in the next 20 years (U.S. Senate, Special Committee on Aging, et al., 1987). While still a small percentage, the numbers of people in this age group, now some 5 million, will increase to as many as 20 million in two decades. A sense of how dramatic this phenomenon has been can be seen in the U.S. Bureau of the Census publication *The Centenarians* (1988), which describes the growth in the number of persons over the age of 100, a number that jumped from 15,000 in 1980 to 25,000 only five years later, in 1985. At that rate, it is predicted that the number will reach 110,000 by the year 2000 and will perhaps be tripled 30 years later, in 2030.

The recent sharp increase in life expectancy is probably due much more to advances in medical treatment than was the increase seen before the mid-1960s. It is difficult to explain the latest gains as the reflection of new social advances, and even more difficult to imagine that a genetic or other biological change has occurred in the human species that would account for such a dramatic demographic transition in a period of only two decades. Instead, the single major factor often described is the decline in mortality from cardiovascular disease which has occurred in the past 20 years. There is some evidence to support the idea that preventive health measures, combined with advanced medical treatment, are probably responsible for the fact that the onset of severe or potentially fatal coronary disease now occurs at a much later age than it did 10 to 15 years ago. Clearly enough, more research is needed to identify the factors contributing to the drop in mortality rates.

ADDED LONGEVITY: GOOD OR BAD?

The gain in longevity among Americans has been a remarkable phenomenon, and it is probably the mark of an advanced industrialized civilization, for it has also appeared in other industrialized countries of the world. But is it a good thing? Are we to be pleased that people are living so much longer than we ever thought they would? How we answer such questions has a great deal to do with our understanding of society's response to the demographic transition, and it relates directly to the basic issue of the goals of medicine in an aging society.

One way of looking at the issue is by asking, as people reach such advanced old age, how healthy and happy are they? Today, the majority of persons over 65 report at least one chronic illness. Reported illness and impairment, however, do not necessarily result in disability. It is the number and the severity of functional disabilities that are the preferred measures of health status. Persons consider themselves in ill health primarily when an illness or impairment interferes with their activities of daily living, usually defined as the tasks related to personal care and to maintenance of the home environment. As might be anticipated, such health-related difficulties increase with advancing age, yet it is noteworthy that of persons aged 65 to 74, the most recent data show that more than 80 percent report no limitations in carrying out these daily activities. Of those aged 75 to 84, more than 70 percent report no such limitations, and even of those over age 85, half report no limitations (U.S. Senate, Special Committee on Aging, et al., 1987).

This is not to underestimate the problems of those persons who are significantly burdened by ill health or those who are dependent on others for their day-to-day care. It is instead to point out that only a minority of older persons, even at advanced older ages, are ill or disabled. National surveys have also found repeatedly that older people report high levels of life satisfaction, as high as or sometimes higher than the levels reported by younger people (Campbell et al., 1976; Harris et al., 1975; Harris et al., 1981).

Not only are old people as a group faring well, but of at least equal importance in the present context is the fact that, as individuals, people grow old in very different ways, and they become increasingly different from one another with the passage of years. Women age differently from men, and there are differences among racial, ethnic, and particularly socioeconomic groups. Added to this are the idiosyncratic sequences of events that accumulate over lifetimes to create increasing individual variation. The result is that older people are a very diverse group.

Although the prevalence of illness and disability increases with age in the second half of life, the association between age and health is far from perfect. Age is a good predictor of health status in statistical terms, but for any given individual, age is a poor predictor of physical, mental, or social competence. This finding has emerged repeatedly in systematic studies of performance in which a wide range of physiologic and psychological variables has been examined (Shock et al., 1984) and has come to be called a "superfact" in gerontological research (Maddox, 1986). . . .

The most optimistic analysts, exemplified by Fries (1980), predict that the overall health status of the elderly population will continue to improve, leading to a "compression of morbidity" in the last period of life. Others, exemplified by Brody and Schneider (1983), argue that an increase in life expectancy will lead to an increase in the average period of morbidity and dependency before death.

Recent studies that examine "active life expectancy" (e.g., Katz et al., 1983) attempt to forecast patterns of morbidity and disability, as well as length of life. In these studies, it appears that with advancing age, an increasing percentage of the remaining years of life is likely to be spent in a dependent or disabled state. For example, for persons who reach age 65, an average of 16.5 years of life remain. The forecast is that this period of 16-plus years will include, on average, 6 years (or 40 percent) spent in a state of disability and dependency. For persons who reach 85, it is projected that 7.5 years of life remain, a period that includes more than 4.5 years (or 60 percent) in a disabled state. These data support the prediction that the added years of life will be characterized by disability and dependency, and contradict the optimistic view that, as Fries predicts, most persons will stay healthy until about age 85, then die quickly.

It is the specter of disability, particularly mental impairment from chronic dementing diseases such as Alzheimer's disease, that is most frightening for older people and their families. Disability also creates the greatest need for long-term care, either in institutional or home settings. Alzheimer's disease, hip fracture, and other disorders that result in major loss of function increase exponentially after approximately age 75 to 80 (see Hing, 1987; Kane and Kane, 1990; Manton, 1990). This would suggest to some observers that it may be inappropriate to provide life-extending medical care to individuals in their late seventies or older if the life that is extended is simply a life of disability and dependency. These averages, however, do not adequately describe the tremendous physiologic, psychological, and social variability among members of any age cohort, as mentioned above.

HEALTH CARE COSTS AND THE APPROPRIATENESS OF TREATMENT

Many factors are contributing to the rise in health care costs, including general inflation, the rapid escalation of physicians' fees, and the mushrooming costs of hospital care, as well as the increase in the number of old people, with their needs for health care. . . . In this connection, it is important to note that a small proportion of older people, about 17 percent, account for over 60 percent of Medicare payments. This statistic confirms the fact that it is only a small fraction of older persons in any one year who are responsible [for] the high usage of medical services. It also is consistent with the observation that most old people are not very sick until the last year of their lives. One study showed that the 6 percent of Medicare beneficiaries who died during the year 1978 accounted for 28 percent of Medicare reimbursements in that year (Lubitz and Prihoda, 1984). Other studies of high-cost Medicare patients have shown that a considerable fraction of hospital costs are attributable to patients who die during their hospitalization or shortly after discharge (Scitovsky, 1984).

Such data have led to overly simplistic exhortations that old people, instead of irresponsibly consuming all these medical resources, should accept death and thus allow more resources to be used for the young (Callahan, 1987; Callahan, 1990; Lamm, 1987). Some commentators argue that investment in acute health care yields more potential years of life in the young than in the old, and thus it is a more prudential investment plan for society's health care dollars (Daniels, 1988).

Such statements raise fundamental moral questions about the value of human life. They also make misleading generalizations about the goals of most medical treatment, describing it as "life extension" rather than as providing comfort to the patient or enhancing the patient's functional status and quality of life. Just as it is difficult to generalize about the health status of "the elderly," it is equally difficult to generalize about the appropriate use of "medical technology." When the specific uses of the resources spent on patients in their last year of life are examined, it becomes clear that most such patients were functioning at a high level prior to their last illness. Furthermore, the large

expenditures in the last year of life are much more likely to be for persons aged 65 to 80 than for persons aged 80 and over (Scitovsky, 1984).

In addition, physicians cannot predict at the onset of hospitalization which patients are likely to survive. As studies have suggested, half of the high-cost patients survive at reasonable levels of functional status for a year or more (Scitovsky, 1984). In other words, the high-cost Medicare patient has a 50:50 chance of meaningful survival. It would be difficult, on grounds of morality, to argue that for reasons of economy, not for medical reasons, all such patients should be allowed to die.

A basic question about the goals of medicine arises here. Persons in danger of dying are, by definition, persons who are extremely ill and are therefore likely to need extensive and expensive hospital care. It is not enough to look simply at the expenditures incurred for them; it may be quite appropriate to provide extensive hospital care for a person with a serious illness, especially if there is a reasonable likelihood of a successful outcome and if such care is consistent with the patient's values or expressed preferences.

The number of dollars spent does not necessarily reflect the appropriateness of any given medical intervention selected by the patient's physician. There is no doubt that life-extending technologies are sometimes used in treating elderly patients, as well as in treating some younger patients, where the prognosis does not warrant aggressive medical intervention and where the patients, if able to express their wishes, would probably refuse such treatment.

Physicians have learned a great deal from the new and emerging field of medical ethics about becoming aware of patients' preferences, which they elicit by encouraging the use of verbal or written "advance directives," or by holding discussions with family members who can report attitudes and values of the patient that might be relevant to making a decision to allow death to occur. Advance directives include legal instruments such as "living wills" and "durable powers of attorney for health care" (Kapp, 1989). They can also include conversations between the physician and the patient regarding the use or nonuse of life-sustaining treatments in the event of critical illness; in this case the patient's preferences are written down and become part of the medical record.

More and more physicians and hospitals are accepting the patient's right to die with dignity. More and more hospitals have explicit policies for do-not-resuscitate orders (Miles and Cranford, 1982). More and more physicians and hospitals are accepting the concept of hospice care for patients who are not likely to regain any meaningful level of existence. More and more state supreme courts, in cases of hopeless illness, have decided in favor of the patient's or the family's petition for the withdrawal of life-sustaining medical treatment (Wanzer et al., 1989).

There is still room for progress in this area, however, for many physicians and other personnel in hospitals and nursing homes are still unduly worried about their legal liability in such situations. They may continue to use medically unwarranted and morally unacceptable medical treatment because of their fear of legal repercussions if treatment is discontinued. Such fear is largely unwarranted, for there are few instances of successful lawsuits brought against physicians for withholding or withdrawing life-sustaining measures when the patient and the family have been involved in the decision, and when the treatment adheres to stated institutional protocols (Miles and Gomez, 1989).

Nonetheless, in the litigious environment of the United States the physician or the medical institution can never be entirely immune from lawsuits. Physicians need to reassert their moral courage to advocate the course of treatment most consistent with caring medical practice and respect for the patient's wishes. Malpractice reform and increasing attention to statutes that encourage the use of advance directives would enhance the physician's likelihood of making sensible decisions regarding the care of hopelessly ill patients. It is most important that such decisions should continue to be based on the individual case, not on some sweeping policy or regulation, especially not on a policy that uses age as the decisive criterion for withholding intensive medical treatment.

For example, some families would want the physician to administer antibiotics to treat pneumonia in a parent with advanced Alzheimer's disease, even though the quality of that parent's life may be very low when assessed by others. The family may find simple physical caregiving to be meaningful to both the aged parent and the caretakers, and may not regard it as too burdensome, even in the home setting. At the same time, treatments such as cardiopulmonary resuscitation or mechanical ventilation, which are ordinarily used only in comparatively severe life-threatening episodes, may not be indicated for the same patient because the burdens of treatment for that patient would not be justified by the chances of success. In most such instances, the situation is seen by everyone

concerned as offering no chance of the patient's recovery, and no disagreement arises. In other instances, families and physicians together come to such decisions. The decision reached depends on the patient's condition, the views of the patient and the family, and their relationship with the physician.

Decisions to withhold medical treatment are never easy, nor should they be. Struggling through the management of such cases should help physicians to become more sensitive to the needs of hopelessly ill patients, to the subtleties of clinical treatment decisions for the most frail elderly patients, and to the skills needed for communication with families who are under the stress of caring for a severely impaired relative.

WHAT ARE THE BASIC VALUES OF MEDICINE?

Concerns about health care expenditures have raised some fundamental questions about the goals of medicine. What is medical care for? Is it for prolonging the lives of the disabled, or is it only for prolonging the lives of those who can be functioning members of society? Is a person's functioning to be measured in terms of economic productivity, and is economic productivity the predominant value by which to judge human life? Should the criteria for medical treatment be different for patients who are financially covered by publicly funded programs such as Medicare and Medicaid than for patients who are privately insured and those who can pay out-of-pocket?

These issues arise not only in regard to elderly persons but also in regard to expenditures for the long-term care of disabled children and young adults. Such questions are now being raised increasingly often, especially with regard to intensive care for infants with severe birth defects. New developments in the care of AIDS patients, treatments that promise longer life expectancy but not complete recovery, will probably raise similar concerns.

In spite of these conflicting values—cost containment and patients' right to medical care—the basic values of medicine remain the same as before: the preservation of life, the relief of suffering, and respect for patients. Advances in medical technology have made the implementation of these values more complex, for in addition to problems of cost containment, the striving to save life often creates great emotional burdens for patients and families, and sometimes seems to conflict with a humanistic approach to patient care. The latter problem needs clarification if we are to understand the goals of modern medicine in an aging society.

It is useful to realize that policy controversies about the costs of medical care and about setting limits to medical interventions for old people center around two different models of medicine. Although these models are not necessarily mutually exclusive, and although, for some patients, the models may lead to identical modes of care, their primary goals are nevertheless clearly distinguishable.

THE "HEROIC" MODEL OF MEDICINE

The overriding goal of the heroic model of medicine is the extension of life. In this model, life itself is of irreducible value; and the goal for the medical researcher, as well as for the practicing physician, is to postpone death, regardless of the patient's quality of life and regardless of the cost of treatment. In its most simplistic form, the heroic model of medicine does not ask whether a death is premature, appropriate, or acceptable, but asks only how death, the enemy, can be held at bay. The physician experiences the death of a patient as a personal failure, and perhaps also as an unwelcome reminder of his or her own mortality.

The intoxicating successes of medical technology—such as routine cardiac monitoring and defibrillation, mechanical ventilation, and kidney dialysis—that appeared during the 1960s probably created a receptive environment for the growth and acceptance of this heroic model. Certainly this model did not exist in earlier periods of history, when the physician's role was as much to "abide with" families during the illness of a patient as to dramatically rescue the patient from death.

Perceptions of the inhumanity of highly technical medical care, especially in cases of terminal disease, have led to public expressions of frustration with the heroic model of medicine, especially by those who demand a right to "die with dignity." Researchers in thanatology (the study of death and dying) have examined why some physicians are unable to accept their own mortality and why other physicians can deal patiently and compassionately with their patients' deaths. Accordingly, thanatologists have suggested a range of educational and institutional changes to enable society to deal better with death and dying. One result has been the development of hospice care

for patients with terminal illness. Another is the increased discussion of death and dying in the medical curriculum.

The heroic model of medicine has brought with it, of course, an emphasis on medical research, as symbolized by the growth of the U.S. National Institutes of Health, by the "wars" on cancer and on heart disease, and by the enthusiastic search for "cures." In medical training, however, this model has resulted in much less emphasis being placed on the management of chronic disease and on the treatment of the more common but not life-threatening problems that patients present, and more emphasis being placed on the diagnosis and treatment of less common but potentially curable disorders.

The heroic model has indeed won many heroic victories, and it is a glamorous and exciting model both for health care professionals and for the public at large. It is undeniable that the goal of a longer life and the fantasy of being rescued from death are attractive to most people. However, the heroic model cannot deal with uncertainty, with decline, or with death. It cannot encompass the wide range of clinical experience or the humility and compassion that are necessary for medical care in a society characterized by increasing longevity and increasing chronic illness.

THE HUMANISTIC MODEL OF MEDICINE

In the second model of medicine, the one called the "humanistic" model, the primary goal is the improvement of the quality of life. In this model, the physician is much more likely to accept the patient on the patient's own terms and to establish goals of treatment which improve or maintain that person's level of functioning and quality of life. The prolongation of the patient's life is not necessarily what the physician strives for if that is not the patient's goal.

One example of this humanistic model is seen in the palliative approach of hospice care, in which the aim is to control the patient's symptoms and to make the patient comfortable. The application of this model is fairly straightforward in the care of a patient who is suffering from a clearly terminal illness and whose life expectancy is measured in days or weeks. However, in the great majority of elderly patients, multiple chronic diseases are the rule. The distinction between treatment aimed at improving the quality of life for these persons and treatment aimed at life prolongation is not so clear. This is particularly true in patients of advanced old age.

The humanistic approach must extend to psychological, social, and other issues, and it often requires a multidisciplinary team approach. This is especially true in treating older people, because the health problems that cause them distress often cannot be dealt with simply by prescriptions or surgery. The old patient may require economic, psychological, and social support, possibly including improved transportation, suitable housing, education about nutrition, and more.

In the humanistic model, the physician seeks medical interventions that place a low burden on the patient and have a high likelihood of benefit. The physician is unlikely to subject a patient to a procedure or treatment that involves a great deal of pain, as, for example, in resuscitating a frail elderly patient where there is only a small likelihood of improvement in that patient's life after the treatment ends.

In many of the interventions that improve the quality of life, particularly in a very old person, the prolongation of life may be an inevitable side effect. A good example is when a physician recently prescribed a pacemaker for a 99-year-old woman who was experiencing attacks of fainting caused by cardiac arrhythmia. While it may be agreed that extraordinary efforts to prolong the patient's life would be unseemly, "contraindicated," or perhaps even rejected by the patient herself, nonetheless the implantation of a pacemaker will prevent her from continually fainting, and thus falling and risking a broken hip, with its likelihood of protracted disability. The goal of such treatment is palliative — to prevent falling and potential fracture — but the salutary effect that the pacemaker will have on her heart rhythm will undoubtedly extend her life.

The observation that treatments that improve life and those that extend life are often indistinguishable applies to almost any palliative measure, ranging from the administration of insulin to persons with diabetes and the administration of oxygen to persons who suffer from shortness of breath, to modern, technology-intensive treatments for heart failure or symptomatic malignancies.

A MODEL OF MEDICINE FOR THE AGING SOCIETY

Why is it that we are seeking a principle by which to limit medical treatment? Is it not obvious to the clinician when a certain treatment is or is not indicated? Clearly, physicians themselves often feel at sea, particularly in the care of very old patients. Old people are a new population to be served, and how best to serve them is a question that has only recently been receiving attention in medical research and training (Cassel, 1987). The guidelines are not clear, and they become especially problematic in a society in which physicians are pressured to be the gatekeepers of society's wealth and to prevent the wasteful use of dollars on people who will not "benefit."

Who is to decide what it means for the patient to benefit? Must the patient's life also be of present benefit to society? One assumption often made in this discourse is that if we could identify the best-functioning elderly person, or perhaps the best-functioning person of any age, we could then produce proper guidelines and would then know to whom medical care should best be offered.

OPTIMAL CARE ONLY FOR THOSE WHO FUNCTION WELL?

Various indexes of functioning have been explored by investigators who believe that when the patient's quality of life is very low, it is appropriate to limit medical care, particularly life-extending medical care. Those who are arguing for the rationing of medical care for old people advocate such decisions in treating all older patients, even those who are not extremely ill or terminally ill, and the establishment of a general policy of this kind.

This would mean that over time medical care would be provided more often to old persons whose quality of life is relatively high — those who are often described as "aging successfully" — than to persons whose quality of life is low.

One problem is that, for many observers, the quality of life is defined in reductionist terms, as the level of functioning. In one notable instance, it has been defined in even more reductionist terms, as the level of physiologic functioning; in that instance, old persons who score high on tests of half a dozen physiologic functions are termed the "successful agers" (Rowe and Kahn, 1987).

If the level of functioning were to become, for policy makers, the criterion for determining the type of medical care to be provided, the outcome would be to give more medical care to those who are physically and mentally able, and less to those who are disabled. Not only would such a policy increase inequities in the allocation of health care, but it also raises other underlying ethical questions. Except for the most extremely ill patients, about whom disagreements are rare, how and by whom shall the patient's quality of life be determined? At what point is any given type of medical care no longer warranted? Is it acceptable, on ethical grounds, to make such distinctions and then to act on them, in the interest of cost containment?

If such a policy mandating old-age-based rationing of medical care were to be implemented, it would represent a major departure from the prevailing goal of medicine in our society. Perhaps more importantly, however, for most persons in the society it would represent, on ethical grounds, too high a price for the society to pay.

OPTIMAL CARE FOR ALL PERSONS?

The goal of medicine our society has been pursuing to date is to provide medical care that enhances not only the level of functioning but also the quality of life for all persons. Today that goal focuses more sharply than before on the expectation that over time a larger and larger proportion of the population will age "successfully." However, to produce a population most of whose members are at high levels of functioning may not necessarily be the optimum, or even the preferred, goal for a society like our own.

We have been experiencing a tidal wave of improvement in health, which is most clearly shown by the dramatic rise in average life expectancy. Although not all subgroups in the population are experiencing the same rapid gains, still there is no disagreement that the population as a whole has benefited enormously. There is a price to be paid for this, however: the one implied by the metaphor "The rising tide lifts all boats equally." That is, the frail as well as the sturdy are being lifted. Although most people who survive to an advanced old age remain quite vigorous and independent, we shall never be without a certain number who, while they too are now surviving, do so with significant disability and with great need for both medical and social support.

In light of all the advantages of an increase in life expectancy, is the task of caring for those who are aging less than successfully too great a price for our society to pay? A related question is the one already suggested above, namely, whether our measures of success are too narrow. We have learned the sobering lessons of eugenics from a recent society in which only those persons who were regarded as the most highly functioning were allowed to survive. Equally sobering, in the present context, is the fact that the genocide practiced by the Nazis began with physician-supported "mercy killing" of persons who were retarded, mentally ill, or aged and infirm.

Whether or not our own society would move along the same downward path is debatable, but our medical successes have led some of us to view chronic disability and dependence, no matter what the cause, as simply undesirable, as a drain on our resources, or as our failure. These attitudes could lead to a harsh and unforgiving society, one that values only the healthy or only those who can pay their own way. It would be a regressive society, rather than one that reflects the successes of modern civilization. The civilized society allocates resources, both financial and emotional, for including in the life of the community those of its members who are less fortunate, and for providing care to them.

EMBRACING THE AGING SOCIETY

Some observers believe that caring for disabled elderly persons will be an unbearable burden on society and will enervate and destroy us. Perhaps, to the contrary, society will benefit if it is challenged by the need to care for the vulnerable and the frail. Society's vitality and productivity may be improved if it learns how to sustain the lessons of compassion and how best to care for those who need care—in so doing, developing attributes such as loyalty and trust—as well as how to increase community cohesion.

Caring for the disabled may lead, also, to the creation of institutions of medicine and health care which reflect the needs of the modern society—to provide more home care and long-term care, and to be more prudent in the use of expensive medical commodities of unproven value (Brook and Lohr, 1986). We might learn to cut costs by using governmental power to limit the profits generated by entrepreneurial pharmaceutical and medical equipment companies, and to discourage their marketing practices that lead to wasteful overutilization of high-priced therapeutic and diagnostic procedures. We might learn instead how to create policies and methods for the strict assessment of technological procedures. Modern technology is not an evil in itself, but its indiscriminate use is medically inappropriate and wasteful, for it often diverts resources that could be used for long-term or preventive care (see Hiatt, 1987, especially pp. 13–33).

The appropriateness of any technology or treatment must be decided separately for each individual patient. The physician's role is to understand the potential efficacy or lack of efficacy of a given treatment, and to recommend treatment consistent with the patient's condition and the patient's values, regardless of the patient's age, sex, skin color, or income level.

Medicine in today's world needs to embrace the changing society in which people are living so much longer, and to create a humane model of medical care that fits the new social realities. It should focus not on setting age limits for medical care but, rather, on adding opportunities for a continuing sense of the value of life, especially for the very old. In this approach one is neither nihilistic nor fatalistic about the chances of helping old as well as young people.

The complexity of modern medicine requires an integration of the heroic and the humanistic, the technologic and the psychosocial approaches to health. The welfare of the individual patient is the measure by which any medical intervention must be assessed. The aging of our society, and the critique of modern medicine it has engendered, can lead to a medical practice that is better for all patients, and therefore for the society at large. At the same time, it requires a careful examination of the complexities involved. Otherwise it could lead to discrimination against sick and disabled persons and to the dehumanization of our society.

REFERENCES

Brody, J.A., and Schneider, E.L. (1983). Aging, natural death, and the compression of morbidity: another view. *New England Journal of Medicine, 309*, 854–856.

Brook, R.H., and Lohr, K.N. (1986). Will we need to ration effective health care? *Issues in Science and Technology, 3*(1), 68–77.

Callahan, D. (1987). *Setting limits: medical goals in an aging society*. New York: Simon & Schuster.

Callahan, D. (1990). *What kind of life: the limits of medical progress*. New York: Simon & Schuster.

Campbell, A., Converse, P., and Rodgers, W. (1976). *The quality of American life*. New York: Russell Sage Foundation.

Carlson, R.J. (1975). *The end of medicine*. New York: John Wiley & Sons.

Cassel, C.K. (1987). Certification: another step for geriatric medicine. *Journal of the American Medical Association, 258*, 1518–1519.

Daniels, N. (1988). *Am I my parents' keeper? An essay on justice between the young and the old*. New York: Oxford University Press.

Fries, J.F. (1980). Aging, natural death, and the compression of morbidity. *New England Journal of Medicine, 303*, 130–135.

Harris, L., and Associates (1975). *The myth and reality of aging in America*. Washington, D.C.: National Council on the Aging.

Harris, L., and Associates (1981). *Aging in the eighties*. Washington, D.C.: National Council on the Aging.

Hiatt, H.H. (1987). *America's health in the balance*. New York: Harper & Row.

Hing, E. (1987). *Use of nursing homes by the elderly: preliminary data from the 1985 National Nursing Home Survey, Advance Data No. 135*. Hyattsville, Md: National Center for Health Statistics, May 14.

Illich, I. (1976). *Medical nemesis: the expropriation of health*. New York: Pantheon Books.

Kane, R.L., and Kane, R.A. (1990). Health care for older people: organizational and policy issues. In R.H. Binstock and L.K. George, eds, *Handbook of aging and the social sciences* (3rd ed.), pp. 415–437. San Diego: Academic Press.

Kapp, M. (1989). Medical treatments and the physician's legal duties. In C.K. Cassel and D. Reisenberg, eds., *Geriatric medicine* (2nd ed.), pp. 623–639. New York: Springer-Verlag.

Katz, S., Branch, L.G., Branson, M.H., Papsidero, J.A., Beck, J.C., and Greer, D.S. (1983). Active life expectancy. *New England Journal of Medicine, 309*, 1218–1224.

Knowles, J.H., ed. (1977). Doing better and feeling worse: health in the United States. *Daedalus: Journal of the American Academy of Arts and Sciences, 106*(1).

Lamm, R.D. (1987). Ethical health care for the elderly: are we cheating our children? In T.M. Smeeding, ed., *Should medical care be rationed by age?*, pp. xi–xv. Totowa, N.J.: Rowman & Littlefield.

Lubitz, J., and Prihoda, R. (1984). The uses and costs of Medicare services in the last two years of life. *Health Care Financing Review, 5*(3), 117–131.

Maddox, G. (1986). Dynamics of population aging: a changing, changeable profile. In *America's aging workforce: a Traveler's symposium*, pp. 30–37. Hartford, Conn.: Traveler's Insurance Co.

Manton, K.G. (1990). Mortality and morbidity. In R.H. Binstock and L.K. George, eds., *Handbook of aging and the social sciences* (3rd ed.), pp. 64–90. San Diego: Academic Press.

Miles, S.H., and Cranford, R. (1982). The do-not-resuscitate order in a teaching hospital. *Annals of Internal Medicine, 96*, 660–664.

Miles, S.H., and Gomez, C.F. (1989). *Protocols for elective use of life-sustaining treatments*. New York: Springer Publishing Co.

Olshansky, S.J., and Ault, B.A. (1986). The fourth stage of the epidemiologic transition: the age of delayed degenerative diseases. *Milbank Memorial Fund Quarterly/Health and Society, 64*, 355–391.

Rowe, J.W., and Kahn, R.L. (1987). Human aging: usual and successful. *Science, 237*, 143–149.

Schneider, E.L. (1989). Options to control the rising health care costs of older Americans. *Journal of the American Medical Association, 261*, 907.

Scitovsky, A.A. (1984). The high cost of dying: what do the data show? *Milbank Memorial Fund Quarterly/Health and Society, 62*, 591–608.

Shock, N.W., Greulich, R., Andres, R., Arenberg, D., Costa, P., Jr., Lakatta, E., and Tobin, J. (1984). *Normal human aging: the Baltimore longitudinal study of aging*. Washington, D.C.: U.S. Government Printing Office.

U.S. Bureau of the Census, Office of the Actuary (1988). *The centenarians*. Washington, D.C.: U.S. Government Printing Office.

U.S. Senate, Special Committee on Aging, in conjunction with the American Association of Retired Persons, the Federal Council on the Aging, and the U.S. Administration on Aging (1987). *Aging America: trends and projections*. Washington, D.C.: U.S. Government Printing Office.

Waitzkin, H. (1983). *The second sickness: contradictions of capitalist health care*. New York: Free Press.

Wanzer, S., Federman, D., Adelstein, S.J., Cassel, C., Cassem, E., Cranford, R., Hook, E., Lo, B., Mortel, C., Safar, P., Stone, A., and van Eys, J. (1989). The physician's responsibility toward hopelessly ill patients: a second look. *New England Journal of Medicine, 320*, 844–849.

PAUL CHODOFF

The Case for Involuntary Hospitalization of the Mentally Ill

I will begin this paper with a series of vignettes designed to illustrate graphically the question that is my focus: under what conditions, if any, does society have the right to apply coercion to an individual to hospitalize him against his will, by reason of mental illness?

Case 1. A woman in her mid 50s, with no previous overt behavioral difficulties, comes to believe that she is worthless and insignificant. She is completely preoccupied with her guilt and is increasingly unavailable for the ordinary demands of life. She eats very little because of her conviction that the food should go to others whose need is greater than hers, and her physical condition progressively deteriorates. Although she will talk to others about herself, she insists that she is not sick, only bad. She refuses medication, and when hospitalization is suggested she also refuses that on the grounds that she would be taking up space that otherwise could be occupied by those who merit treatment more than she.

Case 2. For the past 6 years the behavior of a 42-year-old woman has been disturbed for periods of 3 months or longer. After recovery from her most recent episode she has been at home, functioning at a borderline level. A month ago she again started to withdraw

Reprinted from *American Journal of Psychiatry,* 133, 496–501, 1976. Copyright 1976, the American Psychiatric Association. Reprinted by permission.

from her environment. She pays increasingly less attention to her bodily needs, talks very little, and does not respond to questions or attention from those about her. She lapses into a mute state and lies in her bed in a totally passive fashion. She does not respond to other people, does not eat, and does not void. When her arm is raised from the bed it remains for several minutes in the position in which it is left. Her medical history and a physical examination reveal no evidence of primary physical illness.

Case 3. A man with a history of alcoholism has been on a binge for several weeks. He remains at home doing little else than drinking. He eats very little. He becomes tremulous and misinterprets spots on the wall as animals about to attack him, and he complains of "creeping" sensations in his body, which he attributes to infestation by insects. He does not seek help voluntarily, insists there is nothing wrong with him, and despite his wife's entreaties he continues to drink.

Case 4. Passersby and station personnel observe that a young woman has been spending several days at Union Station in Washington, D.C. Her behavior appears strange to others. She is finally befriended by a newspaper reporter who becomes aware that her perception of her situation is profoundly unrealistic and that she is, in fact, delusional. He persuades her to accompany him to St. Elizabeths Hospital, where she is examined by a psychiatrist who recommends admission. She refuses hospitalization and the psychiatrist allows her to leave. She returns to Union Station. A few days later she is found dead, murdered, on one of the surrounding streets.

Case 5. A government attorney in his late 30s begins to display pressured speech and hyperactivity. He is too busy to sleep and eats very little. He talks rapidly, becomes irritable when interrupted, and makes phone calls all over the country in furtherance of his political ambitions, which are to begin a campaign for the presidency of the United States. He makes many purchases, some very expensive, thus running through a great deal of money. He is rude and tactless to his friends, who are offended by his behavior, and his job is in jeopardy. In spite of his wife's pleas he insists that he does not have the time to seek or accept treatment, and he refuses hospitalization. This is not the first such disturbance for this individual; in fact, very similar episodes have been occurring at roughly 2-year intervals since he was 18 years old.

Case 6. Passersby in a campus area observe two young women standing together, staring at each other, for over an hour. Their behavior attracts attention, and eventually the police take the pair to a nearby precinct station for questioning. They refuse to answer questions and sit mutely, staring into space. The police request some type of psychiatric examination but are informed by the city attorney's office that state law (Michigan) allows persons to be held for observation only if they appear obviously dangerous to themselves or others. In this case, since the women do not seem homicidal or suicidal, they do not qualify for observation and are released.

Less than 30 hours later the two women are found on the floor of their campus apartment, screaming and writhing in pain with their clothes ablaze from a self-made pyre. One woman recovers; the other dies. There is no conclusive evidence that drugs were involved.[1]

Most, if not all, people would agree that the behavior described in these vignettes deviates significantly from even elastic definitions of normality. However, it is clear that there would not be a similar consensus on how to react to this kind of behavior and that there is a considerable and increasing ferment about what attitude the organized elements of our society should take toward such individuals. Everyone has a stake in this important issue, but the debate about it takes place principally among psychiatrists, lawyers, the courts, and law enforcement agencies.

Points of view about the question of involuntary hospitalization fall into the following three principal groups: the "abolitionists," medical model psychiatrists, and civil liberties lawyers.

THE ABOLITIONISTS

Those holding this position would assert that in none of the cases I have described should involuntary hospitalization be a viable option because, quite simply, it should never be resorted to under any circumstances. As Szasz[2] has put it, "we should value liberty more highly than mental health no matter how defined" and "no one should be deprived of his freedom for the sake of his mental health." Ennis[3] has said that the goal "is nothing less than the abolition of involuntary hospitalization."

Prominent among the abolitionists are the "anti-psychiatrists," who, somewhat surprisingly, count in their ranks a number of well-known psychiatrists. For them mental illness simply does not exist in the field of psychiatry.[4] They reject entirely the medical model of mental illness and insist that acceptance of it relies on a fiction accepted jointly by the state and by psychiatrists as a device for exerting social control over annoying or unconventional people. The anti-psychiatrists hold that these people ought to be afforded the dignity of being held responsible for their behavior and required to accept its consequences. In addition, some members of this group believe that the phenomena of "mental illness" often represent essentially a tortured protest against the insanities of an irrational society.[5] They maintain that society should not be encouraged in its oppressive course by affixing a pejorative label to its victims.

Among the abolitionists are some civil liberties lawyers who both assert their passionate support of the magisterial importance of individual liberty and react with repugnance and impatience to what they see as the abuses of psychiatric practice in this field — the commitment of some individuals for flimsy and possibly self-serving reasons and their inhuman warehousing in penal institutions wrongly called "hospitals."

The abolitionists do not oppose psychiatric treatment when it is conducted with the agreement of those being treated. I have no doubt that they would try to gain the consent of the individuals described earlier to undergo treatment, including hospitalization. The psychiatrists in this group would be very likely to confine their treatment methods to psychotherapeutic efforts to influence the aberrant behavior. They would be unlikely to use drugs and would certainly eschew such somatic therapies as ECT [electroconvulsive therapy]. If efforts to enlist voluntary compliance with treatment failed, the abolitionists would not employ any means of coercion. Instead, they would step aside and allow social, legal, and community sanctions to take their course. If a human being should be jailed or a human life lost as a result of this attitude, they would accept it as a necessary evil to be tolerated in order to avoid the greater evil of unjustified loss of liberty for others.[6]

THE MEDICAL MODEL PSYCHIATRISTS

I use this admittedly awkward and not entirely accurate label to designate the position of a substantial number of psychiatrists. They believe that mental illness is a meaningful concept and that under certain conditions its existence justifies the state's exercise, under the doctrine of *parens patriae*, of its right and obligation to arrange for the hospitalization of the sick individual even though coercion is involved and he is deprived of his liberty. I believe that these psychiatrists would recommend involuntary hospitalization for all six of the patients described earlier.

THE MEDICAL MODEL

There was a time, before they were considered to be ill, when individuals who displayed the kind of behavior I described earlier were put in 'ships of fools" to wander the seas or were left to the mercies, sometimes tender but often savage, of uncomprehending communities that regarded them as either possessed or bad. During the Enlightenment and the early nineteenth century, however, these individuals gradually came to be regarded as sick people to be included under the humane and caring umbrella of the Judeo-Christian attitude toward illness. This attitude, which may have reached its height during the era of moral treatment in the early nineteenth century, has had unexpected and ambiguous consequences. It became overextended and partially perverted, and these excesses led to the reaction that is so strong a current in today's attitude toward mental illness.

However, reaction itself can go too far, and I believe that this is already happening. Witness the disastrous consequences of the precipitate dehospitalization that is occurring all over the country. To remove the protective mantle of illness from these disturbed people is to expose them, their families, and their communities to consequences that are certainly maladaptive and possibly irreparable. Are we really acting in accordance with their best interests when we allow them to "die with their rights on"[1] or when we condemn them to a "preservation of liberty which is actually so destructive as to constitute another form of imprisonment"?[7] Will they not suffer "if [a] liberty they cannot enjoy is made superior to a health that must sometimes be forced on them"?[8]

Many of those who reject the medical model out of hand as inapplicable to so-called "mental illness" have tended to oversimplify its meaning and have, in fact, equated it almost entirely with organic disease. It is necessary to recognize that it is a complex concept and that there is a lack of agreement about its meaning. Sophisticated definitions of the medical model do not require only the demonstration of unequivocal organic pathology. A broader formulation, put forward by sociologists and deriving largely from Talcott Parsons' description of the sick role,[9] extends the domain of illness to encompass certain forms of social deviance as well as biological disorders. According to this definition, the medical model is characterized not only by organicity but also by being negatively valued by society, by "non-voluntariness," thus exempting its exemplars from blame, and by the understanding that physicians are the technically competent experts to deal with its effects.[10]

Except for the question of organic disease, the patients I described earlier conform well to this broader conception of the medical model. They are all suffering both emotionally and physically, they are incapable by an effort of will of stopping or changing their destructive behavior, and those around them consider them to be in an undesirable sick state and to require medical attention.

Categorizing the behavior of these patients as involuntary may be criticized as evidence of an intolerably paternalistic and antitherapeutic attitude that fosters the very failure to take responsibility for their lives and behavior that the therapist should uncover rather than encourage. However, it must also be acknowledged that these severely ill people are not capable at a conscious level of deciding what is best for themselves and that in order to help them examine their behavior and motivation, it is necessary that they be alive and available for treatment. Their verbal message that they will not accept treatment may at the same time be conveying other more covert messages—that they are desperate and want help even though they cannot ask for it.[11]

Although organic pathology may not be the only determinant of the medical model, it is of course an important one and it should not be avoided in any discussion of mental illness. There would be no question that the previously described patient with delirium tremens is suffering from a toxic form of brain disease. There are a significant number of other patients who require involuntary hospitalization because of organic brain syndrome due to various causes. Among those who are not overtly organically ill, most of the candidates for involuntary hospitalization suffer from schizophrenia or one of the major affective disorders. A growing and increasingly impressive body of evidence points to the presence of an important genetic-biological factor in these conditions; thus, many of them qualify on these grounds as illnesses.

Despite the revisionist efforts of the anti-psychiatrists, mental illness *does* exist. It does not by any means include all of the people being treated by psychiatrists (or by nonpsychiatrist physicians), but it does encompass those few desperately sick people for whom involuntary commitment must be considered. In the words of a recent article, "The problem is that mental illness is not a myth. It is not some palpable falsehood propagated among the populace by power-mad psychiatrists, but a cruel and bitter reality that has been with the human race since antiquity."[12]

CRITERIA FOR INVOLUNTARY HOSPITALIZATION

Procedures for involuntary hospitalization should be instituted for individuals who require care and treatment because of diagnosable mental illness that produces symptoms, including marked impairment in judgment, that disrupt their intrapsychic and interpersonal functioning. All three of these criteria must be met before involuntary hospitalization can be instituted.

1. Mental Illness. This concept has already been discussed, but it should be repeated that only a belief in the existence of illness justifies involuntary commitment. It is a fundamental assumption that makes aberrant behavior a medical matter and its care the concern of physicians.

2. Disruption of Functioning. This involves combinations of serious and often obvious disturbances that are both intrapsychic (for example, the suffering of severe depression) and interpersonal (for example, withdrawal from others because of depression). It does not include minor peccadilloes or eccentricities. Furthermore, the behavior in question must represent symptoms of the mental illness from which the patient is suffering. Among these symptoms are actions that are imminently or potentially dangerous in a physical sense to self or others, as well as other manifestations of mental illness such as those in the cases I have described. This is not to ignore dangerousness as a criterion for commitment but rather to put it in its proper place as one of a number of symptoms of the illness. A further manifestation of the illness, and indeed, the one that makes involuntary rather than voluntary hospitalization necessary, is impairment of the patient's judgment to such a degree that he is unable to consider his condition and make decisions about it in his own interests.

3. Need for Care and Treatment. The goal of physicians is to treat and cure their patients; however, sometimes they can only ameliorate the suffering of their patients and sometimes all they can offer is care. It is not possible to predict whether someone will respond to treatment; nevertheless, the need for treatment and the availability of facilities to carry it out constitute essential preconditions that must be met to justify requiring anyone to give up his freedom. If mental hospital patients have a right to treatment, then psychiatrists have a right to ask for treatability as a front-door as well as a back-door criterion for commitment.[7] All of the six individuals I described earlier could have been treated with a reasonable expectation of return to a more normal state of functioning.

I believe that the objections to this formulation can be summarized as follows:

1. The whole structure founders for those who maintain that mental illness is a fiction.

2. These criteria are also untenable to those who hold liberty to be such a supreme value that the presence of mental illness per se does not constitute justification for depriving an individual of his freedom; only when such illness is manifested by clearly dangerous behavior may commitment be considered. For reasons to be discussed later, I agree with those psy-

chiatrists[13,14] who do not believe that dangerousness should be elevated to primacy above other manifestations of mental illness as a *sine qua non* for involuntary hospitalization.

3. The medical model criteria are "soft" and subjective and depend on the fallible judgment of psychiatrists. This is a valid objection. There is no reliable blood test for schizophrenia and no method for injecting grey cells into psychiatrists. A relatively small number of cases will always fall within a grey area that will be difficult to judge. In those extreme cases in which the question of commitment arises, competent and ethical psychiatrists should be able to use these criteria without doing violence to individual liberties and with the expectation of good results. Furthermore, the possible "fuzziness" of some aspects of the medical model approach is certainly no greater than that of the supposedly "objective" criteria for dangerousness, and there is little reason to believe that lawyers and judges are any less fallible than psychiatrists.

4. Commitment procedures in the hands of psychiatrists are subject to intolerable abuses. Here, as Peszke said, "It is imperative that we differentiate between the principle of the process of civil commitment and the practice itself."[13] Abuses can contaminate both the medical and the dangerousness approaches, and I believe that the abuses stemming from the abolitionist view of no commitment at all are even greater. Measures to abate abuses of the medical approach include judicial review and the abandonment of indeterminate commitment. In the course of commitment proceedings and thereafter, patients should have access to competent and compassionate legal counsel. However, this latter safeguard may itself be subject to abuse if the legal counsel acts solely in the adversary tradition and undertakes to carry out the patient's wishes even when they may be destructive.

COMMENT

The criteria and procedures outlined will apply most appropriately to initial episodes and recurrent attacks of mental illness. To put it simply, it is necessary to find a way to satisfy legal and humanitarian considerations and yet allow psychiatrists access to initially or acutely ill patients in order to do the best they can for them. However, there are some involuntary patients who have received adequate and active treatment but have not responded satisfactorily. An irreducible minimum of such cases, principally among those with brain disorders and process schizophrenia, will not improve sufficiently to be able to adapt to even a tolerant society.

The decision of what to do at this point is not an easy one, and it should certainly not be in the hands of psychiatrists alone. With some justification they can state that they have been given the thankless job of caring, often with inadequate facilities, for badly damaged people and that they are now being subjected to criticism for keeping these patients locked up. No one really knows what to do with these patients. It may be that when treatment has failed they exchange their sick role for what has been called the impaired role,[15] which implies a permanent negative evaluation of them coupled with a somewhat less benign societal attitude. At this point, perhaps a case can be made for giving greater importance to the criteria for dangerousness and releasing such patients if they do not pose a threat to others. However, I do not believe that the release into the community of these severely malfunctioning individuals will serve their interests even though it may satisfy formal notions of right and wrong.

It should be emphasized that the number of individuals for whom involuntary commitment must be considered is small (although, under the influence of current pressures, it may be smaller than it should be). Even severe mental illness can often be handled by securing the cooperation of the patient, and certainly one of the favorable effects of the current ferment has been to encourage such efforts. However, the distinction between voluntary and involuntary hospitalization is sometimes more formal than meaningful. How "voluntary" are the actions of an individual who is being buffeted by the threats, entreaties, and tears of his family?

I believe, however, that we are at a point (at least in some jurisdictions) where, having rebounded from an era in which involuntary commitment was too easy and employed too often, we are now entering one in which it is becoming very difficult to commit anyone, even in urgent cases. Faced with the moral obloquy that has come to pervade the atmosphere in which the decision to involuntarily hospitalize is considered, some psychiatrists, especially younger ones, have become, as Stone[16] put it, "soft as grapes" when faced with the prospect of committing anyone under any circumstances.

I use this admittedly inexact label to designate those members of the legal profession who do not in principle reject the necessity for involuntary hospitalization but who do reject or wish to diminish the importance of medical model criteria in the hands of psychiatrists. Accordingly, the civil liberties lawyers, in dealing with the problem of involuntary hospitalization, have enlisted themselves under the standard of dangerousness, which they hold to be more objective and capable of being dealt with in a sounder evidentiary manner than the medical model criteria. For them the question is not whether mental illness, even of disabling degree, is present, but only whether it has resulted in the probability of behavior dangerous to others or to self. Thus they would scrutinize the cases previously described for evidence of such dangerousness and would make the decision about involuntary hospitalization accordingly. They would probably feel that commitment is not indicated in most of these cases, since they were selected as illustrative of severe mental illness in which outstanding evidence of physical dangerousness was not present.

The dangerousness standard is being used increasingly not only to supplement criteria for mental illness but, in fact, to replace them entirely. The recent Supreme Court decision in *O'Connor v. Donaldson*[17] is certainly a long step in this direction. In addition, "dangerousness" is increasingly being understood to refer to the probability that the individual will inflict harm on himself or others in a specific physical manner rather than in other ways. This tendency has perhaps been carried to its ultimate in the *Lessard v. Schmidt* case[18] in Wisconsin, which restricted suitability for commitment to the "extreme likelihood that if the person is not confined, he will do immediate harm to himself or others." (This decision was set aside by the U.S. Supreme Court in 1974.) In a recent Washington, D.C., Superior Court case[19] the instructions to the jury stated that the government must prove that the defendant was likely to cause "substantial physical harm to himself or others in the reasonably foreseeable future."

For the following reasons, the dangerousness standard is an inappropriate and dangerous indicator to use in judging the conditions under which someone should be involuntarily hospitalized. Dangerousness is being taken out of its proper context as one among other symptoms of the presence of severe mental illness that should be the determining factor.

1. To concentrate on dangerousness (especially to others) as the sole criterion for involuntary hospitalization deprives many mentally ill persons of the protection and treatment that they urgently require. A psychiatrist under the constraints of the dangerousness rule, faced with an out-of-control manic individual whose frantic behavior the psychiatrist truly believes to be a disguised call for help, would have to say, "Sorry, I would like to help you but I can't because you haven't threatened anybody and you are not suicidal." Since psychiatrists are admittedly not very good at accurately predicting dangerousness to others, the evidentiary standards for commitment will be very stringent. This will result in mental hospitals becoming prisons for a small population of volatile, highly assaultive, and untreatable patients.[14]

2. The attempt to differentiate rigidly (especially in regard to danger to self) between physical and other kinds of self-destructive behavior is artificial, unrealistic, and unworkable. It will tend to confront psychiatrists who want to help their patients with the same kind of dilemma they were faced with when justification for therapeutic abortion on psychiatric grounds depended on evidence of suicidal intent. The advocates of the dangerousness standard seem to be more comfortable with and pay more attention to the factor of dangerousness to others even though it is a much less frequent and much less significant consequence of mental illness than is danger to self.

3. The emphasis on dangerousness (again, especially to others) is a real obstacle to the right-to-treatment movement since it prevents the hospitalization and therefore the treatment of the population most amenable to various kinds of therapy.

4. Emphasis on the criterion of dangerousness to others moves involuntary commitment from a civil to a criminal procedure, thus, as Stone[14] put it, imposing the procedures of one terrible system on another. Involuntary commitment on these grounds becomes a form of preventive detention and makes the psychiatrist a kind of glorified policeman.

5. Emphasis on dangerousness rather than mental disability and helplessness will hasten the process of deinstitutionalization. Recent reports[20,21] have shown that these patients are not being rehabilitated and reintegrated into the community, but rather, that the burden of custodialism has been shifted from the hospital to the community.

6. As previously mentioned, emphasis on the dangerousness criterion may be a tactic of some of the abolitionists among the civil liberties lawyers[22] to end involuntary hospitalization by reducing it to an unworkable absurdity.

DISCUSSION

It is obvious that it is good to be at liberty and that it is good to be free from the consequences of disabling and dehumanizing illness. Sometimes these two values are incompatible, and in the heat of the passions that are often aroused by opposing views of right and wrong, the partisans of each view may tend to minimize the importance of the other. Both sides can present their horror stories—the psychiatrists, their dead victims of the failure of the involuntary hospitalization process, and the lawyers, their Donaldsons. There is a real danger that instead of acknowledging the difficulty of the problem, the two camps will become polarized, with a consequent rush toward extreme and untenable solutions rather than working toward reasonable ones.

The path taken by those whom I have labeled the abolitionists is an example of the barren results that ensue when an absolute solution is imposed on a complex problem. There are human beings who will suffer greatly if the abolitionists succeed in elevating an abstract principle into an unbreakable law with no exceptions. I find myself oppressed and repelled by their position, which seems to stem from an ideological rigidity which ignores that element of the contingent immanent in the structure of human existence. It is devoid of compassion.

The positions of those who espouse the medical model and the dangerousness approaches to commitment are, one hopes, not completely irreconcilable. To some extent these differences are a result of the vantage points from which lawyers and psychiatrists view mental illness and commitment. The lawyers see and are concerned with the failures and abuses of the process. Furthermore, as a result of their training, they tend to apply principles to classes of people rather than to take each instance as unique. The psychiatrists, on the other hand, are required to deal practically with the singular needs of individuals. They approach the problem from a clinical rather than a deductive stance. As physicians, they want to be in a position to take care of and to help suffering people whom they regard as sick patients. They sometimes become impatient with the rules that prevent them from doing this.

I believe we are now witnessing a pendular swing in which the rights of the mentally ill to be treated and protected are being set aside in the rush to give them their freedom at whatever cost. But is freedom defined only by the absence of external constraints? Internal physiological or psychological processes can contribute to a throttling of the spirit that is as painful as any applied from the outside. The "wild" manic individual without his lithium, the panicky hallucinator without his injection of fluphenazine hydrochloride and the understanding support of a concerned staff, the sodden alcoholic—are they free? Sometimes, as Woody Guthrie said, "Freedom means no place to go."

Today the civil liberties lawyers are in the ascendancy and the psychiatrists on the defensive to a degree that is harmful to individual needs and the public welfare. Redress and a more balanced position will not come from further extension of the dangerousness doctrine. I favor a return to the use of medical criteria by psychiatrists—psychiatrists, however, who have been chastened by the buffeting they have received and are quite willing to go along with even strict legal safeguards as long as they are constructive and not tyrannical.

NOTES

1. Treffert, D. A.: "The practical limits of patients' rights." *Psychiatric Annals* 5(4):91–96, 1971.

2. Szasz, T.: *Law, Liberty and Psychiatry*. New York, Macmillan Co., 1963.

3. Ennis, B.: *Prisoners of Psychiatry*. New York, Harcourt Brace Jovanovich, 1972.

4. Szasz, T.: *The Myth of Mental Illness*. New York, Harper & Row, 1961.

5. Laing, R.: *The Politics of Experience*. New York, Ballantine Books, 1967.

6. Ennis, B.: "Ennis on 'Donaldson.'" *Psychiatric News*, Dec. 3, 1975, pp. 4, 19, 37.

7. Peele, R., Chodoff, P., Taub, N.: "Involuntary hospitalization and treatability. Observations from the DC experience." *Catholic University Law Review* 23:744–753, 1974.

8. Michels, R.: "The right to refuse psychotropic drugs." *Hastings Center Report*, 3(3):10–11, 1973.

9. Parsons, T.: *The Social System*. New York, Free Press, 1951.

10. Veatch, R. M.: "The medical model: its nature and problems." *Hastings Center Studies* 1(3):59–76, 1973.

11. Katz, J.: "The right to treatment—an enchanting legal fiction?" *University of Chicago Law Review* 36:755–783, 1969.

12. Moore, M. S.: "Some myths about mental illness." *Arch Gen Psychiatry* 32:1483–1497, 1975.

13. Peszke, M. A.: "Is dangerousness an issue for physicians in emergency commitment?" *Am J Psychiatry* 132:825–828, 1975.

14. Stone, A. A.: "Comment on Peszke, M. A.: Is dangerousness an issue for physicians in emergency commitment?" *Ibid.*, 829–831.

15. Siegler, M., Osmond, H.: *Models of Madness, Models of Medicine.* New York, Macmillan Co., 1974.

16. Stone, A.: Lecture for course on The Law, Litigation, and Mental Health Services. Adelphi, Md., Mental Health Study Center, September 1974.

17. O'Connor v Donaldson, 43 USLW 4929 (1975).

18. Lessard v Schmidt, 349 F Supp 1078, 1092 (ED Wis 1972).

19. In re Johnnie Hargrove. Washington, D.C., Superior Court Mental Health number 506–575, 1975.

20. Rachlin, S., Pam, A., Milton, J.: "Civil liberties versus involuntary hospitalization." *Am J Psychiatry* 132:189–191, 1975.

21. Kirk, S. A., Therrien, M. E.: "Community mental health myths and the fate of former hospitalized patients." *Psychiatry* 38:209–217, 1975.

22. Dershowitz, A. A.: "Dangerousness as a criterion for confinement." *Bulletin of the American Academy of Psychiatry and the Law* 2:172–179, 1974.

Moral Quandaries of Professionals

DAN W. BROCK AND STEVEN A. WARTMAN

When Competent Patients Make Irrational Choices

[handwritten: overview of shared decision making]

In recent years, physicians and patients have tended to move toward shared decision making. Although it sounds reasonable on the surface that patients and physicians should collaborate in making decisions about medical care, surprisingly little attention has been given to the complex and troubling issues that can arise. In particular, what does shared decision making imply for a physician's responsibilities when an apparently competent patient's choice appears to be irrational? A discussion of this issue requires a taxonomy of the different sources and forms of irrational decision making. We believe such a taxonomy should include the bias toward the present and near future, the belief that "it won't happen to me," the fear of pain or the medical experience, patients' values or wants that make no sense, framing effects, and conflicts between individual and social rationality. Our main aim here is to develop this taxonomy and thus to bring out some of the theoretical and practical obstacles involved in distinguishing between a patient's irrational choices, which the physician may seek to change, and merely unusual choices that should be respected. To avoid any misunderstanding, we emphasize at the outset that even the irrational choices of a competent patient must be respected if the patient cannot be persuaded to change them.

SHARED DECISION MAKING BETWEEN PHYSICIAN AND PATIENT

Historically, the professional ideal of the physician–patient relationship held that the physician directed care and made decisions about treatment; the patient's principal role was to comply with "doctor's orders."

From *New England Journal of Medicine* 322 (1990), 1595–1599. Reprinted by permission of the *New England Journal of Medicine*.

Although this paternalistic approach often took account of the patient's general preferences and attitudes toward treatment, it gave the patient only a minimal role in making decisions. When faced with what appeared to be a patient's irrational choices or preferences, physicians were encouraged by this approach to overlook or override them as not being in the patient's true interests.

Challenged by a number of forces within and outside the medical profession during the past two or three decades, the paternalistic approach has generally been replaced by the concept of shared decision making, in which both physicians and patients make active and essential contributions.[1] Physicians bring their medical training, knowledge, and expertise—including an understanding of the available treatment alternatives—to the diagnosis and management of patients' conditions. Patients bring a knowledge of their own subjective aims and values, through which the risks and benefits of various treatment options can be evaluated. With this approach, selecting the best treatment for a particular patient requires the contributions of both parties.[2]

This description of the division of labor oversimplifies the complexities of the roles and contributions of physicians and patients when real decisions about treatment are made, but it does highlight the patient's new, active part in that process. Some have concluded that in shared decision making, proper respect for patient autonomy and self-determination means accepting the patient's treatment preferences however they are arrived at. We believe that such a conclusion is unwarranted, because it fails to recognize the trade-off between the sometimes conflicting values that underlie shared decision making and that are involved in respecting or seeking to change patients' choices. The first value is the well-being of patients, which can require the physician to attempt to protect them from the harmful consequences of their choices when their judgment is irrational. The second value is respecting the right of patients to make decisions about their own lives when they are able. Whenever competent patients appear to be making irrational choices about treatment that are contrary to their own well-being, the two values will be in conflict.

Distinguishing choices that are truly irrational from those that are merely unusual often requires complex, difficult, and controversial judgments. When the physician properly judges a patient's treatment choice to be irrational, attempts to change that choice through persuasion are common and proper. Noncoercive and nonmanipulative attempts to persuade patients of the irrational and harmful nature of their choices do not violate their right of self-determination. Instead, they reflect an appropriate responsibility and concern for the patients' well-being.

Sometimes, however, attempts to persuade will fail. Physicians lack both ethical and legal authority to override patients' treatment choices unilaterally. Nevertheless, in a few cases an irrational choice that cannot be changed by persuasion may reflect a sufficiently serious impairment in decision making—and the consequences of that choice may be sufficiently harmful to the patient—to call the patient's competence into question. In such cases, the physician may begin an investigation of the patient's competence that can ultimately involve recourse to the courts. Since the vast majority of irrational decisions are made by apparently competent patients, we shall not address the determination of incompetence here.[3] Our concern is with the more usual cases, in which the patient's competence does not come into question. The responsibility to try to change their competent patients' irrational choices requires that physicians gain a better understanding of the different forms of irrational treatment choices and of the theoretical and practical difficulties involved in distinguishing truly irrational from merely unusual choices.

THE STANDARD OF RATIONAL DECISION MAKING

Utilitarian model
3rd view
subjective

Any discussion of irrational decision making must rely on a description of rational decision making.[4] We believe it will be helpful to make that description explicit, if only in brief outline. Specifically, what is the norm of rationality that underlies the ideal of shared decision making between patients and physicians? Essentially, shared decision making entitles patients (or their surrogates if they are incompetent) to weigh the benefits and risks of alternative treatments, including the alternative of no treatment, according to their own values and to select the alternative that best promotes those values. In the language of decision theory, each patient's values will determine his or her utility function, and the rational choice will be the one that maximizes expected utility. Since treatment decisions always involve some degree of uncertainty about the beneficial and harmful effects of alternative treatments, these effects should be discounted by their probabilities (to the extent that they are known) in calculating the expected utility of various treatment alternatives. If the probabilities are not known, each patient's attitude toward risk will determine the weight given to uncertain beneficial or adverse effects.

Shared decision making requires that physicians ensure that their patients are well informed.[5] Thus, another aspect of rational decision making is that each patient has and uses correct information about relevant alternatives. This sketch of rational decision making relies ultimately on the patient's own aims and values, unless they are irrationally distorted in the ways discussed below, as the ends that guide decision making. An irrational choice is one that satisfies those aims and values less completely than another available choice.

There is a second notion of irrational decision making that deems a patient's choice irrational if it fails to promote a set of basic aims and values that belong to the physician or to standard guidelines of medical practice. Physicians who criticize a patient's choice as irrational in this sense are disagreeing with the basic aims and values by which the patient defines his or her own good, rather than arguing that the patient's choice will fail to promote those aims and values best. Since this second notion ignores the patient's own aims and values and thus fails to respect the right of self-determination, we rely here on the first account of rational and irrational choices.

FORMS OF IRRATIONAL DECISION MAKING

We now turn to common forms of irrational decision making by patients or their surrogates (and sometimes by physicians). In many treatment decisions, more than one form of irrationality affects a single choice, but we separate them here for analytical clarity.

BIAS TOWARD THE PRESENT AND NEAR FUTURE

The ideal of rational decision making gives equal weight to a beneficial or harmful effect whenever it occurs in a person's life, with differences determined only by the size and probability of the effect. In the case of money it is rational to apply a discount rate, because a dollar received today can earn interest and is thus worth more than a dollar received 10 years from now. Some effects of health care are similar: it is rational to prefer a restoration of function now rather than later and to prefer that a loss of function occur as far in the future as possible, so as to minimize the pe-

riod of disability. Similarly, it is rational to prefer that the loss of one's life be postponed for as long as possible, at least while it remains a life worth living. For other effects of medical care—especially pain and suffering—rational choice would seem to require indifference to their timing. In particular, it is irrational to refuse to undergo a painful experience now, if by undergoing it one can avoid a much worse experience in the future. Such a refusal would amount to preferring more rather than less pain or suffering in one's life.

Yet, as doctors know, medical practice is replete with such irrational choices by patients. Some patients who continue to smoke or drink heavily or who fail to follow relatively simple steps to control moderate hypertension may not be irrational, but are simply willing to gamble that they will beat the odds. Others, however, have given inadequate weight in their present decision making to the harm they are likely to suffer in the relatively distant future. We call this a bias to the present and near future, because people commonly give disproportionate weight to securing benefits and avoiding harm in the present and near future as opposed to the more distant future.[6] The physician's task in such cases is to help the patient fully appreciate the size and seriousness of the more distant harm or benefit, so that it can play an appropriate part in the patient's decision making.

"IT WON'T HAPPEN TO ME"

Patients may view the nature of the risk or harm of not following medical advice differently. This is especially true for events that have a low probability of occurring.[7] However, what constitutes low probability may vary considerably from patient to patient. Furthermore, since some patients are more willing to take risks than others, it is often difficult to determine whether a patient is more of a risk taker than most or whether the patient has simply failed to give adequate weight to a low probability or a distant event. This situation is complicated by the difficulty of distinguishing among patients who, for example, ignore a risk (that is, acknowledge the risk but decide to accept it), irrationally deny the possibility that an untoward event could happen to them, have "magical" or illusory beliefs about their vulnerability to harm, or simply have a different way of viewing the medical problem.[8] Adolescents, for example, are commonly subject to feelings of invulnerability to certain harms disproportionate to the real risk of those harms.

Physicians often need to gain some understanding of their patients' general attitudes toward risk and the extent to which they are risk averse, perhaps as evidenced by their past behavior. Physicians should attempt to distinguish among the possibilities noted above. Sometimes a physician can help a patient appreciate a risk more vividly and relate it to the patient's life. However, for patients who deny a risk or have magical beliefs, a more detailed medical and scientific explanation is not likely to be helpful. In these cases, formal counseling or psychiatric evaluation may be more fruitful.

FEAR OF PAIN OR THE MEDICAL EXPERIENCE

Many patients delay or will not even consider a particular treatment for fear of the perceived nature of the experience, although they may acknowledge that the treatment is clearly in their best interests. Sometimes their decision is coupled with some form of rationalization—"there's no need to do it yet," or "I'm too busy now with other things," for example. In other cases, when a dreaded experience draws near, a patient may be almost paralyzed with fear. Sometimes the fear may be focused not on pain or suffering but on other dreaded experiences, such as being "cut open" or being "put to sleep" in surgery. In still other cases, the fear of a disease such as cancer or the acquired immunodeficiency syndrome can prevent a person from making informed decisions about its treatment.

Determining when this form of irrational decision making is present is considerably complicated by the fact that no single, correct weight can be given to pain or a particular medical experience as measured against the beneficial outcomes for which the experience may be necessary. Patients differ, for example, in the degree to which they are prepared to tolerate painful treatments or conditions for the sake of other ends,[9] but these reasonable differences are difficult to distinguish from the undue weight some patients give to certain aspects of treatment because of irrational fear. Physicians may have seen patients who in the end were grateful that they had been pressured or even forced to undergo painful or dreaded treatments. The responsibility of the physician in these cases is a difficult one—to respect the different weights people give to avoiding pain and suffering, while helping patients overcome the irrational fear that prevents them from pursuing promising treatment plans. The physician's tasks will often involve helping patients to distinguish whether they are experiencing a fear that they want to overcome or whether they have made a choice with which they are comfortable.

WHAT THE PATIENT WANTS DOES NOT MAKE SENSE

When competent patients decline a recommended course of treatment because of an obvious and understandable, albeit unusual, belief—Jehovah's Witnesses, for example, who refuse blood transfusions—physicians (and the courts) commonly yield to that belief. When patients request treatment that physicians believe to be ineffective—Asian patients who request "coining," for example—physicians are not obliged to provide it, but they may respect the patients' right to pursue it when medically acceptable treatment is also provided. Special difficulties arise when a seemingly competent patient wants something that does not make sense and is not attributable to a clearly recognizable religious belief or cultural preference. It can be extremely difficult in these situations for the physician to determine the basis of the patient's preference. However unusual, the more the preference seems to reflect a deeply held, enduring value that is important in the patient's life, the stronger the case for respecting it, as long as it does not require that the physician participate in useless or medically unacceptable treatment.

In other cases, what the patient does not care about makes no sense. For example, patients may state that they understand but simply do not care that death or serious disability will result from a refusal of treatment. It may be difficult to determine whether this is an authentic, although unusual, choice, or the result of a distortion of values caused by a treatable condition such as depression.

FRAMING EFFECTS

It is well known that the way choices are formulated and presented, or framed, can have major effects on decisions.[10] A simple example is the presentation of a surgical treatment as "substantially extending the lives of 70 percent of the patients who select it" or as "potentially killing on the operating table 30 percent of the patients who select it." Both characterizations may be true, but which is used, or emphasized, may have a substantial effect on the rate of selection of the surgery. There is a variety of different and more subtle framing effects, one of which we illustrate below.

Studies in the psychology of choice show that losses tend to loom larger than gains in most people's decision making. Of course, whether a particular outcome is viewed as a gain or loss depends on the reference point against which the outcome is compared. Many choices in medicine can be framed in either way. For example, lowering moderate hypertension can be presented as adding months to the patient's expected life span or as a way to avoid shortening the life span because of untreated hypertension. Neither framing of the choice before the patient is wrong; each simply relies on different characterizations of the patient's present situation. Tversky and Kahneman[10] have compared the framing effects in decision making to changes in perspective in visual judgments. Which of two mountains appears to be higher, for example, depends on the position from which one views them. There is, of course, an objective standard by which the height of the mountains can be determined, but there appears to be no objectively correct way to frame many medical choices, such as that facing the patient with moderate hypertension. There are simply two different but correct ways to frame the choice, and the one that is used will influence whether some patients choose treatment. Sometimes, the best that physicians can do is present the choice in alternative ways in the hope of minimizing framing effects.

INDIVIDUAL VERSUS SOCIAL RATIONALITY

The Irrational Use of Resources. The circumstances that make individual choices rational can sometimes make the outcome of those choices irrational when viewed from a different perspective.[11] One factor fueling the intense pressure to control rapidly rising health care costs is the perception that resources are often used in circumstances in which their expected benefits do not justify their true costs. An insured patient has little or no economic incentive to weigh the true costs of medical care against its expected benefits. When patients have no out-of-pocket costs, it is rational for them to choose all the care that has any expected medical benefit, no matter how small or costly. If physicians accept the common professional norm that their obligation is to do whatever may benefit their patients, without regard to cost, then it is also rational for them to ignore the cost of care in making recommendations and decisions about treatment. The result will be the overuse of health care as compared with other goods and services whose benefits are weighed against their true costs. From the perspective of those who pay the insurance premiums (employers or the government, for example), the result is an irrational overallocation of resources to health care.

The issues raised by this form of irrational social choice involving the use of resources are very different from those involved in the forms of irrational patient choice previously discussed. It would be a mistake for physicians to seek to persuade insured patients that choosing care that is not cost effective is irrational. On the contrary, an insured patient's choice of such care is rational, but it leads to an irrational overallocation of resources to health care. Since the irrationality is not at the level of the insured patient's choice of treatment, the principal response to it cannot be at that level. A physician's failure to respect an insured patient's choice of such care on the grounds that it is irrational is not justifiable. Instead, the irrationality must be addressed where it exists—in the social and economic system of health care financing.

Public Health versus Individual Benefit. Often, physicians are concerned about the public health benefits of medical interventions, whereas their patients are not. For example, national campaigns to reduce serum cholesterol levels will clearly benefit the health of the country as a whole. However, the chance of a substantial benefit in a given patient may be very small. Consequently, some people may rationally decide that for them the benefits of the intervention do not outweigh its burdens. This distinction between community-wide and individual benefits has been called the "prevention paradox"; in it, a treatment that brings large benefits to the community may not seem worth the trouble to individual participants.[12] There is no true paradox, however. The existence of a society-wide benefit constitutes no reason to view as irrational an individual's choice to decline an intervention.

For some infectious diseases, preventing infection through the vaccination of one person (or shortening the period of transmissibility through treatment) lessens the risk of disease for others. A patient's or parent's refusal to accept immunization may be rational if the patient or parent is not concerned about the risks for others or believes that because enough of the population is immunized, the threat of the disease is minimal and the risks of immunization outweigh the benefits. In this case, for the protection of others, society may adopt mandatory immunization programs or physicians may seek to change the patient's mind. Patients do not have an unqualified right to make even rational individual choices that risk serious harm to others.

WHAT SHOULD PHYSICIANS DO?

Shared decision making respects the patient's right of self-determination but does not require that the patient's preferences be simply accepted when they are irrational. In most cases, it is appropriate for physicians to attempt to persuade competent patients to reconsider their irrational choices. However, distinguishing irrational preferences from those that simply express different attitudes, values, and beliefs can be difficult in both theory and practice. Physicians need to be sensitive to the complexity of these judgments in helping patients to make sound treatment choices. They must also bear in mind that even truly irrational choices are not sufficient to establish a patient's incompetence and to justify overriding them. The taxonomy of irrational treatment choices we have presented here (and expand on elsewhere[13]) is meant to be a beginning guide for further consideration of the issue. More research is needed on the frequency of irrational treatment choices and their different forms, as well as on how physicians and patients can work together to overcome them.

REFERENCES

1. President's Commission for the Study of Ethical Problems in Medicine and Biomedical and Behavioral Research. Making health care decisions: the ethical and legal implications of informed consent in the patient-practitioner relationship. Vol. 1. Washington, D.C.: Government Printing Office, 1982.

2. Forrow L., Wartman SA, Brock DW. Science, ethics, and the making of clinical decisions. JAMA 1988: 259:3161–7.

3. Buchanan AE, Brock DW. Deciding for others: the ethics of surrogate decisionmaking. Cambridge: Cambridge University Press, 1989.

4. Pauker SG, Kassirer JP. Decision analysis. N Engl J Med 1987: 316:250–8.

5. Katz J. Why doctors don't disclose uncertainty. Hastings Cent Rep 1984; 14(1):35–44.

6. Parfit D. Reasons and persons. Oxford: Oxford University Press, 1984.

7. Tversky A, Kahneman D. Judgment under uncertainty: heuristics and biases. Science 1974; 185:1124–31.

8. Gillick MR. Talking with patients about risk. J Gen Intern Med 1988; 3:166–70.

9. Cassel EJ. The relief of suffering. Arch Intern Med 1983; 143:522–3.

10. Tversky A, Kahneman D. The framing of decisions and the psychology of choice. Science 1981; 211:453–8.

11. Menzel PT. Medical costs, moral choices: a philosophy of health care economics in America. New Haven, Conn.: Yale University Press, 1983.

12. Rose G. Strategy of prevention: lessons from cardiovascular disease. BMJ 1981; 282:1847–51.

13. Kassirer JP, ed. Current therapy in internal medicine. 3rd ed. Philadelphia: B.C. Decker, 1990.

LYNN M. PETERSON AND TROYEN A. BRENNAN

Medical Ethics and Medical Injuries: Taking Our Duties Seriously

INTRODUCTION

Unintentional injuries are an uncommon, but inevitable, product of the best medical care. Even the best physicians, practicing under optimal conditions, inadvertently injure patients. Approximately 1.5 million such injuries occur in the US each year.[1] Besides exerting "due care" in each individual encounter, how should a concerned, "ethical" physician respond to these injuries?

Some physicians have developed ways to cope psychologically with the anguish produced by human fallibility and malpractice trials. Depression, frustration, and anxiety are inevitable products of these events. Physician support is important and can be obtained from psychologists, peer groups,[2] and the catharsis of public presentations.[3]

But what about the injured patient? Have physicians paid enough attention to the victims of medical injury? What can a physician do when he or she inadvertently injures a patient? Is psychological rehabilitation enough?

If physicians take an ethical view seriously, one which is neither elitist nor self-serving but still based on what it means to be a physician, then the answer to these questions is "no." Such an ethical view has been developed by authors like Leon Kass,[4] Edmund Pellegrino,[5] and Lawrence Churchill,[6] based on the distinctive features of medical practice and the roles and duties of physicians. This distinctive ethics gives a physician *qua* physician grounds to respond to the question, "What should I do, as a physician, about the problem of medical injuries?"

This paper begins with a case example of what might be defined as an avoidable, but non-negligent, medical injury. Ethical responses to these injuries have two components: restitution (connecting the medical goal of restoration with the social manifestation of compensation) and prevention. Carefully analyzing and appreciating the magnitude of medical injuries should lead doctors, on the basis of their distinctive ethics, to become more actively involved in devising schemes for compensation and in modifying medical practices to reduce risks.

THE CASE OF THE INJURED URETER

Mrs. Jones, a sixty-three-year-old secretary, had an obstructing tumor of her colon. At the time of her operation, the tumor was adherent to the uterus and ovary. In order to adequately remove the tumor, the uterus and ovary also had to be removed. The surgeon prepared the uterus and ovary for removal first. The left ureter was carefully identified in its lower portion. Next, the surgeon worked on another portion of the colon in order to prepare it for transection. As its mesentery was divided, the left ureter was inadvertently transected. Because the bowel had been chronically distended, it was hard to maneuver and the obstructed, distended bowel was much closer to the ureter than usual. The accidental transection was recognized and the ureter was repaired. A tube was placed in the ureter and brought out through the bladder.

Postoperatively, the patient developed a fistula between the ureter and the colon that required a second operation and a temporary colostomy. She was hospitalized for nearly three weeks. Eight weeks later, she was readmitted to the hospital for closure of the colostomy. The second operation necessitated an additional six days in the hospital.

From *Journal of Clinical Ethics* 1 (1990), 207–211. Copyright 1990, The Journal of Clinical Ethics. Used with permission of the Journal of Clinical Ethics.

Mrs. Jones's husband had taken an early retirement because of chronic respiratory disease. The Joneses relied on her income as a secretary for daily expenses and repayment of debts. She missed ten weeks of work altogether and had only two weeks of available sick leave. Their savings had been depleted by Mr. Jones's chronic illness. When she was ready to return to work, her employer had hired someone else in her place, and she lost her job. Due to her age, she was unable to readily find other employment.

The surgeon, a certified, competent, and leading professional, had done many similar operations. He was not suffering from a cognitive or manual impairment. He thought he had exerted "due care" and had followed a usual practice of identifying the ureter in a specific location. He was not influenced by irrelevant factors and the procedure had been done skillfully.

But, and this is important, there was an alternative. If the surgeon had traced the ureter further, he would have discovered its abnormal location and avoided the injury. Another surgeon in the same situation might have dissected the ureter more completely and avoided the adverse outcome. Thus, there is a sense in which, because the adverse outcome was avoidable, the surgeon bears some fault.

The determination of fault relies heavily on the standard of care. If the surgeon followed the "standard" then he was not liable for the adverse outcome. It was out of his control, the result of chance, and not something for which he could be held accountable. Establishing the standard in a case like this requires the opinion of experts, and here one expects some degree of variability. Almost everyone would agree that this surgeon followed a generally acceptable standard for identifying ureters. But some would believe that the standard for a case like this would involve more extensive dissection.[7] Surgical training focuses on avoiding ureteral transection; unintentionally dividing the ureter is, *prima facie*, a mistake.

SOURCES OF VARIABILITY

This leaves us with two major sources of variability: variations in the standard and variations in judgment. Standards vary slightly depending on the case or situation. They also vary with time. An optimal standard for a case like this might be to identify the ureter high in the retroperitoneum whenever there is significant displacement and compression by a large tumor mass. But following that standard for every case of colon cancer would lengthen the operation, risk injuring the ureteral blood supply or the ureter itself, and would usually not be necessary. Another standard might be to "identify the ureter at the pelvic brim and avoid injuring it"; this is a more general standard for cases of colon surgery. Standards are set to prevent common and serious mistakes. They are not set to avoid rare complications since that would lead to a worse outcome overall. Excessive caution can be just as harmful as carelessness. Courageously removing Mrs. Jones's large tumor and the attached organs improved her chances for cure but jeopardized her ureter. Not resecting the tumor would have preserved the ureter but would have condemned the patient to death from cancer. The standard of care, therefore, reflects a choice between possible mistakes rather than mistake versus no mistake.

The other source of variation involves judgment: knowing what standard to apply in a particular instance. Should the standard of complete exposure of the ureter with its attendant risks be applied? Or the standard of limited exposure? In retrospect, one can often see the right alternative and others, given the description of the situation, may have even seen it clearly at the time. But the crucial judgment has to be made on the spot. It depends on perception and insight, and this may be very difficult. Two equally competent and expert individuals might easily disagree. Furthermore, it is hard to see how another expert, viewing the situation from a distant place and time, can reliably assess the standard to be applied in a given situation.

Therefore, Mrs. Jones's divided ureter might be characterized as an example of non-negligent, but avoidable, medical failure. The physician followed a standard of care, yet the injury was avoidable and surgeons generally expect to take extra care in avoiding it. Perhaps one might say there was a minimal or mild degree of negligence. But the fact of an adverse outcome often exaggerates a slight deficiency in the care process, especially when there was an alternative.

For the purpose of further discussion, we assume that Mrs. Jones's injury was a rare occurrence for this surgeon. But this kind of injury is not uncommon. Figures from our recent study of medical practice in the state of New York indicate that approximately 1.5 million such injuries occur in the US each year.[8] Furthermore, the approximately 200,000 annual deaths produced by medical injury are considerably greater than the 140,000 deaths caused by trauma.[9] Therefore, while this may be an uncommon problem for an individual physician, it is not an uncommon problem for the medical profession as a whole.

Mrs. Jones's injury occupies a central or midpoint between two extremes of severe or obvious negligence and unavoidable injury. The extremes are handled fairly at the present time. On the one hand, the tort system deals with obvious negligence by awarding injured victims compensation upon proof (more likely than not) of fault. The tort system, however, has two goals: deterrence and compensation,[10] dual objectives leading to compromises.[11] On the other extreme, unavoidable injuries are no more compensable than other adversities dealt by the "natural lottery," such as short stature, lack of athletic prowess, or average intelligence.[12]

But the cases in between, like Mrs. Jones's, are different. In these cases, the likelihood of proving negligence is small. A court ruling would depend on such factors as Mrs. Jones's appearance, the surgeon's manner, the attorney's skill, and the attitude of the jury. Mrs. Jones might even have trouble finding an attorney to take her case because her losses might not be sufficient enough to provide a contingency fee covering the legal expense. Without seeking a substantial reward for things like "pain and suffering" or "loss of consortium," modest losses, like Mrs. Jones's, make litigation economically unfeasible.[13] This is despite the fact that for Mrs. Jones, the loss is substantial; compensating her for additional medical expenses and loss of income would make an enormous difference.

THE PHYSICIAN'S ETHICAL RESPONSE

The first step of an ethical response requires that the surgeon tell Mrs. Jones exactly what happened: the ureter was injured and repaired, and the subsequent urine leakage led to the need for her second and third operations. The surgeon could also honestly say the injury might have been avoided, but that the large tumor and involvement by the other organs made avoidance difficult.

Secondly, an ethical response requires an apology. An apology arises naturally because of the sense of regret felt by someone unintentionally injuring another person. This sense of regret is a basic feature of responsible action.[14] Connected to the reactive attitude of regret is a sense of needing to "right the wrong." An apology is the minimal response. Another more complete response involves restitution. Restitution occurs on both a technical and a moral or humane level.

Technical correction arises from the professional's striving to do things in the best possible manner. The good surgeon, partly due to character and partly due to surgical training, wants to avoid technical mistakes. Charles Bosk found that surgeons and surgical training pay a great deal of attention to dealing with mistakes.[15]

On the humane level, restitution rests on the sense of sympathy, compassion, or imaginative identification with the victim. Humane versions of morality emphasize feeling or sympathy, but even Kant, who eschewed feeling as a basis for morality, thought there was a contradiction of the "will" in acting on the basis of a principle of unconcern for others. Rather, a truly universal law of nature (morality) must be based on "love and sympathy" for others.[16] Thus it would be a contradiction of the will in Kantian terms, and hence immoral, for the surgeon not to seek to do something for his injured patient.

Because the surgeon is in a unique position vis-à-vis Mrs. Jones, his compassion and "will" are important. As an objective witness to the impact of the injury on the patient as a person, he has the opportunity to appreciate how, and to determine the extent to which Mrs. Jones's life has been affected. He sees her reactive depression, excessive weakness, additional weight loss, emotional strain and discomfort; furthermore, the physician knows that Mrs. Jones's lost income means that she has to forego important plans and commitments. By knowing what a normal recovery entails, the surgeon realizes that this particular patient's recovery is excessive. He knows more than anyone else the disability that can result from the injury.

Should the surgeon be concerned that Mrs. Jones's life is now significantly worse off than she would have been had the ureteral injury not occurred? Other than feeling sympathetic does he have a duty to improve Mrs. Jones's welfare? Kass and Pellegrino believe that physicians are responsible for more than the technical elements of medical care.[17] Both derive the extent and limits of the physician's responsibility from the meaning, purpose, and value of medicine.

Kass believes that the physician's moral obligation follows from the end of medicine, seeking the natural norm of health for patients.[18] Health, according to Kass, involves the "well-working" of both the body and the mind. Hope and aspiration are as important as nausea and vomiting. This means that doctors should help patients improve their capacity for friendship and learning, just as they should help to relieve pain and shortness of breath. Kass believes that physicians perform an ethical act when they "profess," and this entails devotion to a special calling of healing and comforting. Thus, the physician should be concerned about Mrs. Jones's situation, even though the cancer had been removed and her body returned to normal, because her welfare was sharply curtailed.

Pellegrino has a somewhat different perspective.[19] He believes that the physician's obligation arises out of the nature of illness, a promise to help, and the power gained from professional skill and knowledge. Like Kass, Pellegrino also contends that the physician's moral obligation is intrinsically *greater* than that of others. The physician, *qua* physician, must be more altruistic and less self-interested. Physicians must be concerned with restoring sick persons to a state of wholeness, a state in which patients are unimpaired. The focus is on persons, conscious selves in lived bodies. The physician must be concerned with the meaning of illness to Mrs. Jones, with her experience, and with her whole biography.

Taking the medical duty propounded by Kass and Pellegrino seriously means that the responsible physician should recognize at least a *prima facie* duty toward restoring patients like Mrs. Jones to a state of "well-working" and to limiting medical injuries. We need to spell out how physicians can be involved in the tasks of restitution and prevention based on their distinctive ethics.

RESTITUTION

Physicians cannot be responsible for providing resources for every patient with limited welfare. Therefore, a distinction is needed between patients like Mrs. Jones, sustaining an avoidable injury, [and] others suffering the unavoidable consequences of illness. Patients like Mrs. Jones need to be compared with people injured at work, victims of crime and automobile accidents, and coal miners with black lung disease. These people are compensated by insurance plans designed to diminish losses incurred as a result of injury.

Frank Zimring traces how these insurance schemes developed.[20] They were created when the following conditions prevailed: the losses were substantial, the victim was not to blame, society identified with the victim, a consensus existed regarding the cause of the injury, and tort law failed to achieve the desired compensation results. Once these conditions exist, then political pressure brings about mechanisms for compensation. Therefore people who appreciate the impact of these injuries should work to modify existing social programs.

The legal and social history of the treatment of injury is extremely relevant in this regard. G. L. Priest describes the transformation of modern tort law from a system with obstacles to recovery by injured individuals, to a system increasingly determined to provide compensation, spreading the losses associated with industry and technology.[21] In order to make compensation feasible, the legal doctrines of contributory negligence, assumption of risk, and the fellow-servant rule have changed. Thus, a physician aware of these changes would realize that evolving legal theory strongly favors constructing insurance schemes to compensate for injuries.

Tort reforms, often advocated by physicians,[22] are usually designed to restrict the number of claims and to prevent excessive awards. Indeed, abolishing frivolous claims is ethically important since unjustified legal action psychologically traumatizes practitioners, aggravates defensive medical practices, leads to extra administrative costs, and produces an added burden in terms of time and effort on patients. However, making litigation more difficult also reduces access to compensation for patients who sustain medical injury. Therefore, tort reform alone threatens to compromise the central issue for the ethical physician: the patient's welfare.

Medical injuries indicate the work that needs to be done in order to put into practice the distinctive medical ethics of physicians. Since medicine is important and valuable, physicians must be responsible for more than technical proficiency. Physicians should help develop schemes to distinguish between avoidable and unavoidable medical injury. No system of justice requires compensating all forms of misfortune, but misfortunes that are unfair are compensable. Injuries occurring as a result of medical care, from the point of view of the physician's distinctive ethics, fall into this category.

LEGAL VERSUS MEDICAL PERSPECTIVE ON RISK MANAGEMENT

The ethical doctor needs to be concerned with measures minimizing medical injury. Risk management programs, as they presently exist, often have ulterior or external motives, different from those of providing good medical care. For instance, in the example of the ureteral injury, risk managers would condemn the use of the word "inadvertent" in describing the event in the operating room. Use of this word exposes the physician, the hospital, and the insurance company to financial losses through legal action. In court, the word "inadvertent" can be seen as implying that the physician acted without "due care." The defense lawyer, or risk manager, would prefer that the action be seen as intentional, something not inadvertent. If the action is intentional, then it was required, and had to be done in order to successfully carry out the procedure. But the surgeon uses "inadvertent" naturally in truthfully describing what took place. The ureter was not carefully identified and transected; it was unexpectedly discovered after it had been cut. This difference might be important in the patient's future medical care. Since the chances of complications are greater following accidental injury, it would be more prudent to follow or monitor renal function and the integrity of the ureteral repair more closely. It would seem, therefore, that good medical practice requires records to be accurate and truthful; material left out for the purpose of concealment, deception, or obfuscation, regardless of the legal benefit, potentially thwarts the aim of good medical practice.

Another area where risk management programs, as they currently exist, conflict with the goals of good medical practice concerns the doctor-patient relationship. Risk management programs encourage doctors to develop good relations *in order to* prevent a lawsuit.[23] Plaintiff surveys have demonstrated that claims are often brought because a physician was seen as unfriendly, dishonest, [or] unsympathetic, or [because] he only provided perfunctory explanations.[24] On the other hand, patients who sustain significant injuries often do not seek legal sanction because their doctor seemed kindly, concerned, and took extra time for explanation. Thus, risk management promotes the idea that physicians should encourage trust and be open and warm in order to avoid legal action. However, an ethical view like that voiced by Kass and Pellegrino asserts that trust and the physician-patient relationship are an intrinsic good—they are part of the fabric of good medicine. To develop trust only to avoid legal sanction gives the wrong message and demeans the value of medicine. Indeed, the legal perspective on risk management entails a potential unethical act of manipulating people for someone else's good: a problem of "one-thought-too-many."[25]

Another area where risk management threatens good medical practice concerns its potential for infringing on a patient's liberty.[26] Competent patients may be forcibly restrained because of a minimal risk of falling, or emergency room patients may be forced against their wishes to undergo testing for reasons of legal liability without any likely medical benefit. Overzealous protection threatens human dignity and freedom.

While risk management and the law are essential and beneficial in improving safety and protecting patients, they run the risk of compelling doctors to commit acts inimical to good medical practice. Good practice requires that records be truthful, that physicians avoid manipulating patients except for the patient's benefit, and that patients have the freedom to choose their medical care. In light of their distinctive ethical duty, physicians, therefore, should not simply accept current risk management programs, but they should actively participate in vigorous criticism and revision of these programs.

In summary, the physician should move from feeling regret to appreciating the need for restitution in the case of medically caused injury. Taking medical duty seriously means appreciating the impact of the outcome on Mrs. Jones as a person, not just on her physical well-being. Recognizing this duty as well as the social goal of compensating unfair injuries means that physicians should seek to devise a mechanism for compensating injured patients. Medical ethics thereby moves from a profession-oriented ethics to one of social application. The ethical physician also must take a strong positive role in promoting risk management. She or he should not accept an imperative of good business practice or courtroom defense in keeping medical records, in establishing human relationships, or in zealously overprotecting competent patients from minimal risks. Caring for patients is complex, important, and extensive; compensating injured patients and safe medical practices are essential ingredients.

NOTES

1. *Patients, Doctors and Lawyers: Medical Injury, Malpractice Litigation, and Patient Compensation in New York* (Boston: The Harvard Medical Practice Study [for] the State of New York, 1990), 11–1.

2. W. Levinson and P. Dunn, "Coping with Fallibility," *Journal of the American Medical Association* 261 (1989): 2252.

3. H.C. Snider, *Jury of My Peers* (Greenwood, FL: Penkevill, 1989).

4. L.R. Kass, *Toward a More Natural Science* (New York: Free Press, 1985), 157–246.

5. E.D. Pellegrino, "The Healing Relationship: The Architectonics of Clinical Medicine," in *The Clinical Encounter,* ed. E. Shelp (Dordrecht, Holland: D. Reidel, 1983), 153–72; E. Pellegrino and D.C. Thomasma, *For the Patient's Good* (New York: Oxford University Press, 1988), 127–36.

6. L.R. Churchill, "Revising a Distinctive Medical Ethic," *Hastings Center Report* 19, no. 3 (1989): 28–34.

7. L. Orkin, "The Surgical Legal Aspect of Ureteral Injury," *The Ureter,* ed. H. Bergamann (New York: Springer-Verlag, 1981), 467–82.

8. *Patients, Doctors, and Lawyers,* 11–1.

9. "Interview with U.S. Representative Henry A. Waxman," *Bulletin of the American College of Surgeons* (June 1988): 8.

10. G.L. Priest, "Modern Tort Law and Its Reform," *Valparaiso University Law Review* 22, no. 1 (1987): 1–38.

11. D. Harris, "Medical Malpractice: Incidence, Prevention and Litigation," presented at the Second International Conference on Health Law and Ethics, London, 17 July 1989.

12. H.T. Engelhardt, *The Foundations of Bioethics* (New York: Oxford University Press, 1986), 339–41.

13. *Patients, Doctors and Lawyers*, 1–8.

14. P.F. Strawson, "Freedom and Resentment," *Studies on the Philosophy of Thought and Action* (London: Oxford University Press, 1968), 71–96.

15. C.L. Bosk, *Forgive and Remember* (Chicago: University of Chicago Press, 1979), 171.

16. I. Kant, *Foundations of the Metaphysics of Morals,* trans. L.W. Beck (Indianapolis: Bobbs-Merrill, 1969), 47.

17. Kass, *Natural Science,* 157–246; and Pellegrino, "Healing Relationship," 153–72.

18. Kass, *Natural Science.*

19. Pellegrino, "Healing Relationship."

20. F.E. Zimring, "Some Social Bases of Compensation Schemes," in *Medical Innovation and Bad Outcomes,* ed. M. Siegler, S. Toulmin, F.E. Zimring, and K. Schaffner (Ann Arbor: Health Administration Press, 1987), 241–50.

21. G.L. Priest, "The Invention of Enterprise Liability: A Critical History of the Intellectual Foundations of Modern Tort Law," *Journal of Legal Studies* 14 (December 1985): 461–527.

22. O.R. Bowen, "Congressional Testimony on Senate Bill S. 1984," *Journal of the American Medical Association* 257 (1987): 816–19.

23. J. Holzer, "The Process of Informed Consent," *Bulletin of American College of Surgeons* 74, no. 9 (1989): 10–14.

24. R.S. Shapiro, D.E. Simpson, S.L. Lawrence, *et al.*, "A Survey of Sued and Nonsued Physicians and Suing Patients," *Archives of Internal Medicine* 149 (1989): 2190–96.

25. B. Williams's discussion of integrity forcefully underlines the problems of giving up commitments for consequentialist reasons. J.J.C. Smart and B. Williams, *Utilitarianism: For and Against* (Cambridge: Cambridge University Press, 1973), 108–18.

26. J. Francis, "Using Restraints in the Elderly Because of the Fear of Litigation," *New England Journal of Medicine* 320 (1989): 870.

SUGGESTED READINGS

GENERAL ISSUES

Ackerman, Terrence F., and Strong, Carson. *A Casebook of Medical Ethics.* New York: Oxford University Press, 1989.

Annas, George J. *The Rights of Patients: The Basic ACLU Guide to Patient Rights.* 2nd ed. Totowa, NJ: Humana Press, 1992.

Annas, George J. *Standard of Care: The Law of American Bioethics.* New York: Oxford University Press, 1993.

Bandman, Elsie L., and Bandman, Bertram. *Nursing Ethics Through the Life Span.* 2nd ed. Norwalk, CT: Appleton and Lange, 1990.

Beauchamp, Tom L., and Childress, James F. *Principles of Biomedical Ethics.* 4th ed. New York: Oxford University Press, 1994.

Benjamin, Martin. "Nursing Ethics." In Becker, Lawrence C., and Becker, Charlotte B., eds. *Encyclopedia of Ethics.* New York: Garland, 1992, 915–17.

Benjamin, Martin, and Curtis, Joy. *Ethics in Nursing.* 3rd ed. New York: Oxford University Press, 1992.

Brody, Baruch. *Life and Death Decision Making.* New York: Oxford University Press, 1988.

Brody, Howard. *The Healer's Power.* New Haven, CT: Yale University Press, 1992.

Culver, Charles M., ed. *Ethics at the Bedside.* Hanover, NH: Dartmouth College, published by University Press of New England, 1990.

Davis, Anne J., and Aroskar, Mila A. *Ethical Dilemmas and Nursing Practice.* 3rd ed. Norwalk, CT: Appleton and Lange, 1991.

Dubler, Nancy Neveloff, and Nimmons, David. *Ethics on Call: A Medical Ethicist Shows How to Take Charge of Life-and-Death Choices.* New York: Harmony Books, 1992.

Emanuel, Ezekiel J. *The Ends of Human Life: Medical Ethics in a Liberal Polity.* Cambridge, MA: Harvard University Press, 1991.

Engelhardt, H. Tristram, Jr. *The Foundations of Bioethics.* New York: Oxford University Press, 1986.

Flack, Harley E., and Pellegrino, Edmund D., eds. *African-American Perspectives on Biomedical Ethics.* Washington, DC: Georgetown University Press, 1992.

Fry, Sara T., ed. "Nursing Ethics." *Journal of Medicine and Philosophy* 16 (1991), 231–359. Thematic issue.

Gillon, Ranaan. *Philosophical Medical Ethics.* New York: Wiley, 1986.

Gorovitz, Samuel. "Bioethics." In Becker, Lawrence C., and Becker, Charlotte B., eds. *Encyclopedia of Ethics.* New York: Garland, 1992, 89–91.

Gorovitz, Samuel. *Drawing the Line: Life, Death, and Ethical Choices in an American Hospital.* New York: Oxford University Press, 1991.

Hanna, Kathi E., ed. *Biomedical Politics.* Washington, DC: National Academy Press, 1991.

Jonsen, Albert R. *The New Medicine and the Old Ethics.* Cambridge, MA: Harvard University Press, 1990.

Jonsen, Albert R., Siegler, Mark, and Winslade, William J. *Clinical Ethics: A Practical Approach to Ethical Decisions in Clinical Medicine.* 3rd ed. New York: McGraw-Hill, 1992.

Kass, Leon R. *Toward a More Natural Science: Biology and Human Affairs*. New York: Free Press, 1985.

Kennedy, Ian. *Treat Me Right: Essays in Medical Law and Ethics*. New York: Oxford University Press, 1988.

Macklin, Ruth. *Enemies of Patients*. New York: Oxford University Press, 1993.

Macklin, Ruth. *Mortal Choices: Bioethics in Today's World*. New York: Pantheon Books, 1987.

McCormick, Richard A. *How Brave a New World?* Expanded ed. Washington, DC: Georgetown University Press, 1985.

Pence, Gregory E. *Classic Cases in Medical Ethics*. New York: McGraw-Hill, 1990.

Pence, Terry, and Cantrall, Janice, comps. *Ethics in Nursing: An Anthology*. New York: National League for Nursing, 1990.

Rothman, David J. *Strangers at the Bedside: A History of How Law and Bioethics Transformed Medical Decision Making*. New York: Basic Books, 1991.

Ruddick, William. "Medical Ethics." In Becker, Lawrence C., and Becker, Charlotte B., eds. *Encyclopedia of Ethics*. New York: Garland, 1992, 778–781.

Sherwin, Susan. "Feminist and Medical Ethics: Two Different Approaches to Contextual Ethics." *Hypatia* 4 (1989), 57–72.

Silva, Mary Cipriano. *Ethical Decision Making in Nursing Administration*. Norwalk, CT: Appleton and Lange, 1990.

Starr, Paul. *The Social Transformation of American Medicine*. New York: Basic Books, 1982.

Veatch, Robert M. *A Theory of Medical Ethics*. New York: Basic Books, 1981.

Veatch, Robert M., ed. *Medical Ethics*. Boston: Jones and Bartlett, 1989.

Veatch, Robert M., and Fry, Sara T. *Case Studies in Nursing Ethics*. Philadelphia: Lippincott, 1987.

Warren, Virginia L. "Feminist Directions in Medical Ethics." *Hypatia* 4 (1989), 73–87.

PROFESSIONAL CODES

American College of Physicians, Ethics Committee. *Ethics Manual*. Philadelphia: The College, 1989.

American Medical Association, Council on Ethical and Judicial Affairs. *Current Opinions of the Council on Ethical and Judicial Affairs*. Chicago: American Medical Association, 1992.

American Nurses Association. *Code for Nurses with Interpretive Statements*. Kansas City, MO: American Nurses Association, 1985.

Annas, George J., and Grodin, Michael A., eds. *The Nazi Doctors and the Nuremberg Code: Human Rights in Human Experimentation*. New York: Oxford University Press, 1992.

Baylis, Françoise, and Downie, Jocelyn. *Codes of Ethics: Ethics Codes, Standards, and Guidelines for Professionals Working in a Health Care Setting in Canada*. Toronto: Department of Bioethics, Hospital for Sick Children, 1992.

British Medical Association. *Philosophy and Practice of Medical Ethics*. Revised ed. London: The Association, 1988.

Canadian Medical Association. *The Canadian Medical Association Code of Ethics*. Ottawa: The Association, April 1990.

Gorlin, Rena A. *Codes of Professional Responsibility*. Washington, DC: Bureau of National Affairs, 1990.

THE VIRTUES AND OBLIGATIONS OF PROFESSIONALS

Agich, George J. "Medicine as Business and Profession." *Theoretical Medicine* 11 (1990), 311–324.

Beauchamp, Tom L., and Childress, James F. *Principles of Biomedical Ethics*. 4th ed. New York: Oxford University Press, 1994. Chapter 8.

Bernal, Ellen W. "The Nurse as Patient Advocate." *Hastings Center Report* 22 (July–August 1992), 18–23.

Brennan, Troyen A. *Just Doctoring: Medical Ethics in the Liberal State*. Berkeley: University of California Press, 1991.

Caplan, Arthur L., ed. *When Medicine Went Mad: Bioethics and the Holocaust*. Totowa, NJ: Humana Press, 1992.

Carse, Alisa L. "The 'Voice of Care': Implications for Bioethical Education." *Journal of Medicine and Philosophy* 16 (1991), 5–28.

Cassell, Eric J. *The Nature of Suffering and the Goals of Medicine*. New York: Oxford University Press, 1991.

Churchill, Larry R. "Reviving a Distinctive Medical Ethic." *Hastings Center Report* 21 (January–February 1991), 25–31.

Daniels, Norman. "Why Saying No to Patients in the United States Is So Hard." *New England Journal of Medicine* 314 (1986), 1380–1383.

Danis, Marion, and Churchill, Larry R. "Autonomy and the Common Weal." *Hastings Center Report* 21 (January–February 1991), 25–31.

Emmanuel, Ezekiel J., and Ezekiel, Linda L. "Four Models of the Physician–Patient Relationship." *Journal of the American Medical Association* 267 (1992), 2221–2226.

Green, Ronald M. "Medical Joint-Venturing: An Ethical Perspective." *Hastings Center Report* 20 (July–August 1990), 22–26.

Jecker, Nancy S. "Integrating Medical Ethics with Normative Theory: Patient Advocacy and Social Responsibility." *Theoretical Medicine* 11 (1990), 125–139.

Johnson, G. Timothy. "Restoring Trust between Doctor and Patient." *New England Journal of Medicine* 322 (1990), 195–197.

Katz, Jay, with the assistance of Alexander Morgan Capron and Eleanor Swift Glass. *Experimentation with Human Beings*. New York: Russell Sage Foundation, 1972.

May, William F. *The Physician's Covenant: Images of the Healer in Medical Ethics*. Philadelphia: Westminster Press, 1983.

Pellegrino, Edmund, and Thomasma, David. *For the Patient's Good: The Restoration of Beneficence in Health Care*. New York: Oxford University Press, 1988.

Pellegrino, Edmund D., Veatch, Robert M., and Langan, John P., eds. *Ethics, Trust, and the Professions: Philosophical and Cultural Aspects*. Washington, DC: Georgetown University Press, 1991.

Ramsey, Paul. *The Patient as Person*. New Haven, CT: Yale University Press, 1970.

Shelp, Earl E., ed. *Virtue and Medicine: Explorations in the Character of Medicine*. Philosophy and Medicine Series, No. 17. Boston: Kluwer Academic Publishers, 1985.

Winslow, Betty J., and Winslow, Gerald R. "Integrity and Compromise in Nursing Ethics." *Journal of Medicine and Philosophy* 16 (1991), 307–323.

PROFESSIONALS AND SPECIFIC PATIENT POPULATIONS

American Medical Association, Council on Ethical and Judicial Affairs. "Sexual Misconduct in the Practice of Medicine." *Journal of the American Medical Association* 266 (1991), 2741–2745.

Binstock, Robert H., and Post, Stephen G., eds. *Too Old for Health Care? Controversies in Medicine, Law, Economics, and Ethics*. Baltimore: Johns Hopkins University Press, 1991.

Jecker, Nancy S., ed. *Aging and Ethics: Philosophical Problems in Gerontology*. Clifton, NJ: Humana Press, 1991.

Jecker, Nancy S., and Self, Donnie J. "Medical Ethics in the 21st Century: Respect for Autonomy in Care of the Elderly Patient." *Journal of Critical Care* 6 (1991), 46–51.

Lynn, Joanne. "Ethical Issues in Caring for Elderly Residents of Nursing Homes." *Primary Care* 13 (1986), 295–306.

McCullough, Laurence B., and Chervenak, Frank A. *Ethics in Obstetrics and Gynecology*. New York: Oxford University Press, 1994.

Mahowald, Mary Briody. *Women and Children in Health Care: An Unequal Majority*. New York: Oxford University Press, 1993.

Miles, Steven H. "What Are We Teaching about Indigent Patients?" *Journal of the American Medical Association* 268 (1992), 2561–2562.

Kopelman, Loretta M., and Moskop, John C., eds. *Children and Health Care: Moral and Social Issues*. Boston: Kluwer Academic Publishers, 1989.

May, William F. *The Patient's Ordeal*. Bloomington: Indiana University Press, 1991.

See also the suggested readings for Chapters 4 and 8.

JOURNALS

American Journal of Law and Medicine

Bioethics

Cambridge Quarterly of Healthcare Ethics

Hastings Center Report

International Journal of Bioethics

Journal of Clinical Ethics

Journal of Health Politics, Policy and Law

Journal of Medical Ethics

Journal of Medicine and Philosophy

Kennedy Institute of Ethics Journal

Law, Medicine, and Health Care

Theoretical Medicine

BIBLIOGRAPHIES AND ENCYCLOPEDIAS
WITH BIBLIOGRAPHIES

Coutts, Mary Carrington. "Basic Resources in Bioethics." Scope Note 15. Washington, DC: Kennedy Institute of Ethics, Georgetown University, September 1991.

Goldstein, Doris Mueller. *Bioethics: A Guide to Information Sources*. Detroit: Gale Research Company, 1982. See under "Bioethics," "Codes of Ethics," and "Professional–Patient Relationship."

Goldstein, Doris Mueller. "Nursing Ethics: A Selected Bibliography, 1987 to Present." Scope Note 19. Washington, DC: Kennedy Institute of Ethics, Georgetown University, June 1992.

Lineback, Richard H., ed. *Philosopher's Index*. Vols. 1-27. Bowling Green, OH: Philosophy Documentation Center, Bowling Green State University. Issued quarterly. See under "Bioethics," "Medical Ethics," "Medicine," "Nursing," and "Therapy."

Reich, Warren T., ed. *Encyclopedia of Bioethics*. 2nd ed. New York: Macmillan, 1994.

Walters, LeRoy, and Kahn, Tamar Joy, eds. *Bibliography of Bioethics*. Vols. 1-19. Washington, DC: Kennedy Institute of Ethics, Georgetown University. Issued annually. See under "Medical Ethics," "Nursing Ethics," "Patient Care," "Patients' Rights," "Professional Ethics," and "Professional Patient Relationship." (The information contained in the annual *Bibliography* can also be retrieved from BIOETHICSLINE, an online database of the National Library of Medicine, and from *BIOETHICSLINE Plus*, a CD-ROM disc distributed by Silver-Platter.)

3.
The Management of Medical Information

INTRODUCTION

In Chapter 2 we examined professional obligations and patients' rights. In this chapter we extend this discussion to the presentation, communication, and confidentiality of information. The primary problems are (1) how to determine the conditions under which patients and related parties should have control over information about the patient's health status and (2) how professionals should manage and protect information in the medical setting.

Several pioneers in the history of medical ethics have explored issues of justifiable non-disclosure and confidentiality. These figures include writers of classic historical documents such as the Hippocratic writings (fifth to fourth century B.C.), Thomas Percival's *Medical Ethics* (1803), and the authors of the first *Code of Ethics* (1847) of the American Medical Association. In these traditional codes and writings, moral concerns for the *autonomy* of patients are uncommon. By contrast, a major feature of the contemporary discussion is whether respect for autonomy requires *more* disclosure, consultation, mutual decision making, and protection of confidential information than traditionally has been required.

TRUTH TELLING AND THE MANAGEMENT OF BAD NEWS

In modern medicine the nature and quality of the physician-patient relationship varies with prior contact, the mental or physical state of the patient, the manner in which the physician relates to the family, and problems with respect to patient-family interaction. The patient's right to know the truth and the physician's obligation to tell it are contingent on these and other factors in the relationship. Physician Timothy Quill and Nurse Penelope Townsend express this point eloquently in the first selection in this chapter.

Few medical ethics writers regard truth telling as an absolute obligation, and many of them believe that when information itself carries risks for patients departures from the general principle of truth telling are justified. As Quill and Townsend discuss, this thesis seems especially plausible in cases in which bad news must be delivered to fragile patients or to strangers. Roger Higgs also argues that there are major differences between telling truths under crisis conditions and telling them under ordinary circumstances. Nevertheless, almost all authorities now agree that there is a strong duty of veracity in medicine because of respect for autonomous patients. Can these views about justified disclosure and justified nondisclosure be rendered consistent?

Many physicians and philosophers — represented by Quill, Townsend, and Higgs in this chapter — view truthfulness as limited by the Hippocratic principle that they should do no harm to patients in difficult circumstances by revealing upsetting conditions. If disclosure of a diagnosis of cancer, for example, would cause the patient anxiety or lead to an act of self-destruction, medical ethics requires that the physician carefully monitor and, at times, withhold the information that could cause additional harm. A common thesis is that in cases in which risks of harm from nondisclosure are low and benefits of nondisclosure to the patient are substantial, a physician may legitimately deceive or underdisclose the truth, and sometimes lie.

Deception is often believed to be easier to justify than blatant lying, because deception does not necessarily threaten the relationship of trust. Furthermore, underdisclosure and nondisclosure are thought to be more easily justified than blatant lying in many contexts. Those who share this perspective argue that it is important not to conflate duties not to lie, not to deceive, and to disclose as if they were a single duty of veracity.

A contrasting view is that (with the exception of patients who do not want to know the truth) all intentional suppression of pertinent information violates a patient's autonomy rights and violates the fundamental duties of the health profession. Here the duty of veracity is derived from obligations of respect for persons. A less severe thesis is that lying is prima facie wrong, but sometimes permissible, and even morally right. The question then becomes, "What are the limits of justified deception and nondisclosure?"

INFORMED CONSENT

It is now widely believed that the physician has a moral obligation not only to tell patients the truth but also to help them decide important matters that affect their health. This ability to "make an educated decision" is dependent upon the availability of truthful information and the patient's capacity to handle the information. Hence, it is often said that before a physician performs a medical procedure on a competent patient, he or she has an obligation to obtain the patient's informed consent and to engage in mutual decision making with the patient.

The practice of obtaining informed consent has its history predominantly in medicine and medical research, where the disclosure and the withholding of information are daily events. But the history of informed consent is not ancient. The term "informed consent" never appeared in any literature until 1957, and discussions of the concept as it is used today began only around 1972. As the idea of informed consent evolved, discussion of appropriate guidelines increasingly moved from a narrow focus on the physician's obligation to disclose information to the quality of a patient's or subject's understanding of information and right to authorize or refuse a biomedical intervention.

Prior to the late 1950s, there was no firm ground in which a commitment to informed consent could take root. This is not to say, however, that there is no relevant history of the physician's management of medical information in the encounter with patients. The major writings of prominent figures in ancient, medieval, and modern medicine contain a storehouse of information about commitments to disclosure and discussion in medical practice. But it is a disappointing history from the perspective of informed consent. Medical ethics developed with the profession of medicine. With few exceptions, no serious consideration was given to issues of either consent or self-determination by patients and research subjects. Proper principles, practices, and virtues of "truthfulness" in disclosure were occasionally discussed, but the perspective was largely one of maximizing medical benefits through the careful management of medical information. The central concern was how to make disclosures without harming patients by revealing their condition too abruptly and starkly. Withholding of information and even outright deception were regularly justified as morally appropriate means of avoiding such harm.

Because of the considerable vagueness around the term "informed consent," some writers have been interested in tightening the concept so that its meaning is as clear as possible. They note that many interactions between a physician and a patient or an investigator and a subject that have been called informed consents have only been so labeled because they rest on underdemanding criteria; they are inappropriately referred to as informed consents. Jay Katz has been at the forefront of this effort to analyze the concept of informed consent. He argues that "informed consent" and "shared decision making" should be treated as virtually synonymous terms. By contrast, Ruth Faden and Tom Beauchamp argue that although there is a historical relationship between shared decision making and informed consent, it is confusing to treat them as *synonymous*. They argue that decision making should be distinguished from a subject's or patient's act of knowledgeably *authorizing* the intervention, that is, giving an informed consent.

Informed consent has been widely analyzed in terms of the following elements: (1) disclosure, (2) comprehension, (3) voluntariness, (4) competence, and (5) consent. The idea is that one gives an informed consent to an intervention if and only if: one receives a thorough disclosure about it; one comprehends the disclosure; one acts voluntarily; one is competent to act; and one consents to the intervention. But the widespread agreement that these conditions are necessary for an informed consent hides a considerable disagreement about how to explicate each one of these five conditions. In this chapter Katz and also Faden and Beauchamp concentrate on (1), (2), and (5).

One of the crucial questions addressed in the readings on informed consent is whether a valid informed consent can be given if a patient or subject does *not* autonomously authorize an intervention. All four articles in this chapter answer "No" to this question. Yet most of the "consents" obtained in health care institutions at the present time likely do not constitute autonomous authorizations, in the sense of autonomy discussed in Chapter 1. That is, it is doubtful that a patient substantially understands the circumstances, makes a decision absent coercion, and intentionally authorizes a professional to proceed with a medical or research intervention. This opens up a range of questions about the validity of the practices of consent currently at work in contemporary medicine and research.

Another problem addressed in these articles concerns adequate standards of disclosure in informed consent contexts. Legal history reveals an evolving legal doctrine of informed consent from a 1767 case to the 1972 *Canterbury* v. *Spence* case (and its aftermath). *Canterbury* was the first and most influential of the recent landmark informed consent cases. In *Canterbury* surgery on the patient's back and a subsequent accident in the hospital led to further injuries and unexpected paralysis, the possibility of which had not yet been disclosed. Judge Spottswood Robinson's opinion focuses on the needs of the reasonable person and the right to self-determination. As for sufficiency of information, the court holds: "The patient's right of self-decision shapes the boundaries of the duty to reveal. That right can be effectively exercised only if the patient possesses enough information to enable an intelligent choice." Katz delivers a blistering attack on the development of these standards in the precedent legal cases, especially the *Canterbury* case.

Many have challenged whether any legal standard is adequate for clinical ethics (as distinct from a standard in law). Katz argues that no broad duty of disclosure follows from any legal standard as now envisaged. If one takes this view, the alternative would seem to be a subjective standard that pays attention to how individual information needs can differ and the extent to which physicians must anticipate individual needs for information and counseling. Katz adopts this perspective as appropriate for ethics. However, critics of this view have objected that it is too onerous on the health care professional. They hold that the worthy ideal of informed consent is unrealistic under this standard, requiring much more discussion and disclosure than the medical system can afford or meaningfully provide.

In recent years the focus on informed consent has turned more toward the quality of consent. Much has been made of Katz's claim that the key to effective communication is to invite participation by patients or subjects in an exchange of information and dialogue. Asking questions, eliciting the concerns and interests of the patient or subject, and establishing a climate that encourages the patient or subject to ask questions seems to be more important for medical ethics than the full body of requirements of disclosed information in law.

PATIENT SELF-DETERMINATION AND ADVANCE DIRECTIVES

On December 1, 1991, the Patient Self-Determination Act—a federal law known as PSDA—went into effect in the United States. It was the first federal legislation regarding life-sustaining treatments and advance directives. (On types of *advance directives*, see also pp. 381–412 in this volume.)

PSDA is linked in a direct line to the history of informed consent and its cousin, informed refusal. PSDA stresses the importance of patient and surrogate decision making about life-sustaining treatments and writing advance directives. The law requires health care facilities certified by Medicare or Medicaid to notify competent adult patients of the right to accept or refuse medical treatment and their right to execute an advance directive, under applicable state law. Five forms of action by institutions are required under this law:

1. Provide information to patients upon admission about rights under state law so that they may make decisions and formulate advance directives.
2. Document in patients' records whether an advance directive exists.
3. Maintain written policies, procedures, and records regarding advance directives and institutional obligations under law.
4. Comply with state laws regarding advance directives and various forms of education.
5. Be sure patients are not discriminated against because they have or have not created an advance directive.

The law fails to set forth provisions about the quality of disclosure and understanding in the patient. By requiring only notification, the law follows the long-standing federal bias toward basic disclosure. The intent of the law is to allow patients to take control of their medical fate, on the grounds that their interests will ultimately be best served by making their own decisions, rather than having the decisions made for them. The right to refuse as well as the right to consent have become the core values that frame the provisions of this statute. These values, of course, are intimately tied to moral values of respect for autonomy and to the legal values of self-determination in the common law that we have already examined.

Like the law of informed consent, the PSDA grows out of the conviction that there is more than the *physician's* conception of what is standard or good practice; there is also the patient's conception of what makes for a good life and a good death. This is especially important when choices are about the end of life, and even more important when those choices are made by one party for another.

The spirit of PSDA acknowledges that most people are unaware of their rights to make decisions in health care at the present time and that few know how to make arrangements or decisions should they become incompetent. However, it is difficult to capture this spirit in the letter of the law without creating major difficulties for health care institutions. Susan Wolf and her coauthors, as well as Margot White and John Fletcher, consider the strengths and weaknesses of the PSDA in this chapter.

The PSDA is now challenging hospitals and other facilities to clarify for patients what their rights are, but also to clarify what the institutions' approaches should be regarding matters such as the withdrawal of treatment, what happens in the event of no advance directive, when parents' wishes regarding their children will and will not be acted upon, and the like.

MANAGING INFORMATION IN RANDOMIZED CLINICAL TRIALS

Biomedical research involving human subjects also faces problems of the management of information. Two main types of research can be identified: (1) *clinical research*, which aims at discovering better methods of treating an illness or condition from which patients are suffering; and (2) *nonclinical biomedical research*, which is research that is not specifically designed to provide a therapeutic benefit, including to human subjects of the research, if any. Research of both types is a worthy social undertaking, but it is also morally perilous and in need of justification when human subjects are exposed to some level of risk for the advancement of science.

Clinical trials, an important type of clinical research, make use of "control groups." A "control group" is composed of members who do not receive the experimental intervention, but who instead receive either no treatment, a standard therapy, or a placebo (a procedure or substance, such as a sugar pill, that the investigator believes is inactive for the patient's condition). The aim is to determine whether an experimental therapy is safer and more effective than the standard therapy or than nothing at all.

The research design assigns group members *randomly* to avoid bias in the assignment of members of both the control and experimental groups. Such a randomized clinical trial (RCT) is designed to keep extraneous variables from distorting study results. RCTs are generally preferred to observational or retrospective studies because their results tend to have a higher degree of validity. The RCTs are structured to confirm that an observed effect, such as reduced mortality from a particular disease, is the result of a particular intervention rather than the result of an unknown variable in the patient population. The intent of the trials is to protect current and future patients from medical enthusiasm and speculation, and to replace them with knowledge.

Blinding certain persons from some information about the RCT provides an additional protection against bias by eliminating subjective responses to a treatment by patients as well as investigators' interpretations of the data. RCTs may be single-blind (the subject does now know whether he or she is in the control group or the experimental group), double-blind (neither the subject nor the investigator knows), or unblinded (all parties know). Blinding the physician-investigator, according to some interpretations, also serves an ethical function, because it obviates any conflict of interest that might occur in both providing therapy and performing research.

RCTs are generally sound ways to generate knowledge, but they present several moral problems. First, the informed consent process is more complicated when the patient, and in many cases the professional, does not know the treatment. It is difficult to explain the full set of methods, treatments, whether or not and how placebos will be used, the known risks and benefits of the alternatives, and the situation's uncertainties. Some researchers are reluctant even to disclose the fact of randomization. Placebos pose an informed consent problem because if subjects are told they are receiving a placebo, the very purpose of using the placebo is undermined. All of the aforementioned factors raise the question: Can potential subjects who are being kept partially ignorant about a particular intervention or research project give an informed consent?

Failure to disclose the method of randomization and the rationale for its use seems simply to be a failure to obtain informed consent. However, if this information is provided, potential subjects should then have an adequate informational base. Adequate disclosure need not be full disclosure, and subjects can be informed that they cannot be told the purpose of the investigation without damaging the research. Placebos present one variant of this problem because if subjects are informed that they are receiving a placebo, the strategy in using the placebo is undercut. But the solution again may be to disclose that the research uses a placebo whose identity and pattern of distribution must remain undisclosed.

Second, monitoring of data from the trial, the disclosure to patients and investigators of interim data, and the appropriate criteria for prematurely terminating a trial present additional problems. Should there be periodic disclosures to subjects of new information generated during the research that may be relevant to their decision to remain in the study or seek alternative therapies? Omission of periodic, updated information seems a breach of investigator's obligations unless the subject has agreed specifically to have this information withheld. But is it fair to ask a subject to agree to waive his or her right to such pertinent information for the benefit of improving science and for the benefit of other patients?

Third, the dual role of physician and scientist presents competing obligations to the patient and to science. It is inconsistent with serving the patient's best interests to select a treatment randomly and to promote social goals of increasing scientific knowledge that could benefit future patients. A patient does not expect a *physician* to endorse a random procedure, although it is perfectly understandable that a *scientist* would favor this procedure.

Proponents of RCTs—as the readings in this chapter note—argue that RCTs do not violate moral obligations to patients because they are only used when physicians genuinely doubt the merits of existing, standard, or new therapies. Prior to conducting the research, no one knows whether it is more advantageous to be in the control group or the experimental group (this is sometimes called the "null hypothesis"). Reasonable physicians are, therefore, in a circumstance called "clinical equipoise"; that is, available evidence indicates that the relevant expert medical community is undecided about the relative merits of and finds equally acceptable any one of the treatment strategies to be tested in the randomized clinical trial. No patient, under this conception, receives a treatment believed to be less safe or more effective than an alternative, and therefore no person is asked to make a sacrifice. Indeed, patients may actually benefit from sound results achieved through the research. These trials therefore do not seem unjustifiable for current patients and are strongly supported by their promise for future patients.

Equipoise—the major topic in the essay by Benjamin Freedman—is now widely agreed to be essential for justified clinical research. A shift in belief that disturbs equipoise destroys the rationale for using the patients involved because a preferred treatment has emerged. A trend that eliminates equipoise also eliminates the justification for using the patients involved. Such equipoise is no less necessary for all justified clinical research, not merely in the conduct of randomized clinical trials.

As Samuel and Deborah Hellman note in their essay, these moral problems about RCTs express the tension between utilitarian and Kantian theories, as well as theories oriented toward individual rights that we have been tracking across medical ethics since Chapter 1. Utilitarianism supports the commitment of the research scientist to eliminate inferior and dangerous therapies and to prove bona fide or risk-reduced therapies for both present and future generations. This goal of proving therapies rather than operating with a patchwork of hunches or guesswork is a noble goal worthy of society's support. Nonetheless, Kantians and those concerned about individual rights fear that the nature of the scientific commitment is such that patients will be treated as means to the ends of scientists, without due regard for their rights and interests. The concern is that the worthy goal of proven therapies will inescapably lead to gaps of disclosure, compromises in physician concern for patients, and inadequate monitoring of therapeutic benefit. These problems lead the Hellmans to question whether these trials, in the end, sacrifice the interests of present patients for the sake of the interests of future generations of patients.

THE MANAGEMENT OF CONFIDENTIAL INFORMATION

Unlike relatively *recent* notions such as informed consent and clinical equipoise, confidentiality has played a significant role since *ancient* codes of professional ethics, including the Hippocratic Oath. Here the physician vows: "What I may see or hear in the course of treatment or even outside of the treatment in regard to the life of men, . . . I will keep to myself." Rules of confidentiality today are still understood as a means of controlling access to sensitive information.

But despite a venerable history and status in health care, Mark Siegler questions whether confidentiality is now a "decrepit" concept of more symbolic than real value. Siegler maintains that traditional medical confidentiality is a relic of the past that has been systematically compromised in the course of modern bureaucratic health care and data storage systems. He and other critics argue that infringements of confidentiality have become routine parts of medical practice — the rule rather than the exception. Medical confidentiality, they say, lacks credibility and needs to be reconstructed into a more viable form if it is to be anything more than a myth. Andrew Markus and Michael Lockwood then ask whether it is permissible to edit medical records. This raises a different set of questions about whether doctors and patients should be able to edit medical records prior to their being passed on to third parties such as insurance companies, consulting physicians, and future physicians. They consider whether the patient's right of confidentiality includes a power to control information, including a veto over information in their medical record.

In assessing these problems, we need to ask why we care so much about confidentiality and what would justify a practice of maintaining confidentiality in a profession where access to vital information may mean the difference between life and death. Two general types of justifications have been proposed for the confidentiality principle in health care relationships. The first type of justification appeals to the principle of respect for autonomy. This argument is that the health professional does not show proper respect for the patient's autonomy and privacy if he or she does not uphold the confidentiality of the professional-patient relationship. A variant of this approach asserts that there is an implied promise of confidentiality inherent in the professional-patient relationship, whether the professional explicitly recognizes the promise or not. In the absence of an explicit acknowledgment that confidentiality does *not* hold, the patient would always be entitled to assume that it does hold.

A second justification is that violations of confidentiality make patients unwilling to reveal sensitive information to health professionals; this unwillingness renders diagnosis and cure more difficult and, in the long run, is detrimental to the health of patients. The assumption of the argument is that the physician-patient relationship rests on a basis of trust that would be imperiled if physicians were not under an obligation to maintain confidence.

This second justification appeals to the positive *consequences* of confidentiality, whereas the first looks to a moral violation that would be wrong irrespective of the kinds of consequences envisaged in the second. That is, the first set of arguments maintains that breaches of trust, broken promises, and failures to keep contractual obligations are themselves wrong, whereas the second argument looks not at what is intrinsically wrong but instead at whether the balance of the consequences supports maintaining confidentiality. As we might expect, criticisms have been made of both arguments. Both have been challenged, for example, by the argument that there is a duty to warn those who might be harmed if confidentiality were maintained.

Whatever its justification, if one holds that the rule of medical confidentiality expresses a duty, there remains the question of whether it states an absolute duty. If not, there is an additional question as to the conditions under which it is permissible to reveal otherwise confidential information. Many who support a *firm* rule of confidentiality do not support an *absolute* rule, because they recognize a range of exceptions under which disclosure of clearly confidential information is permitted. One example of this problem is found in the contemporary discussion of the conditions under which confidential information about AIDS patients may be disclosed, especially when the disclosure constitutes a warning to others of imminent danger. (This is the primary subject of an essay in another chapter by Richard L. North and Karen H. Rothenberg.)

A classic case of conflict between the obligation of confidentiality and the obligation to protect others from harm occurred in *Tarasoff* v. *Regents of the University of California*. In this case a patient confided to his psychologist that he intended to kill a third party. The psychologist then faced the choice of preserving the confidentiality of the patient or of infringing his right of confidentiality to warn a young woman that her life might be in danger. The court finds that health care professionals must weigh a peril to the public that a patient discloses in confidence against the disvalue of infringing confidentiality. However, this court and the courts generally have left open precisely *which duties* legitimately override obligations of confidentiality. Whatever the regional variations, almost every jurisdiction has recognized a core set of justified infringements of confidentiality. These requirements include the reporting of contagious diseases, child abuse, gunshot wounds, epilepsy (to a motor vehicle department), and the like.

Not all examples of the problem of confidentiality are so dramatic or socially significant. More troublesome and pervasive problems concern questions such as how much of a patient's medical record can be fed into a widely accessed "public" data bank, how much information about a patient's genetic makeup may be revealed to a sexual partner if there is a substantial likelihood of the couple's producing genetically handicapped children, how information about an irresponsible and publicly dangerous AIDS patient is to be handled, what information employers and insurance companies should and should not receive, and to whom in a family the full range of test results in genetic screening should be disclosed.

T. L. B.

TIMOTHY E. QUILL AND PENELOPE TOWNSEND

Bad News: Delivery, Dialogue, and Dilemmas

A 37-year-old man who used intravenous drugs was diagnosed as having human immunodeficiency virus (HIV). He and his wife were estranged and had not had sexual relations in 3 years. His wife was an independent, family-oriented, devoutly Christian woman with three children who worked as a nurse's aide. She had a prolactin-secreting pituitary adenoma for which she had reluctantly accepted medical treatment (bromocriptine) in the past. She preferred to use her faith in God, taking the medication only when her prolactin level became markedly elevated. She and I (T.E.Q.) had known each other for 6 years, and our recurrent complex discussions resulted in a close relationship where each of our perspectives was understood and respected by the other. When her husband was diagnosed with HIV, she came to see me to discuss the situation and assess her risk. We discussed the test, and the difference between HIV and AIDS. She understood the distinction, but continued to call any infection AIDS. She decided she wanted to be tested, but when asked what she would do if her test were positive, she responded "I don't know, but I don't think God would do this to me." This left me unsettled, but we went ahead with the test and planned a follow-up visit where the results would be discussed.

The results showed she was HIV infected, leaving me feeling sad both for her as a person and for the realization that the epidemic is truly reaching all walks of life. I also began to dread the meeting where I would deliver the news. I was uncertain how she would respond, and I feared this could shake the foundations of her faith (one of her major strengths) and her sense of who she was. What follows is an unedited transcript of the first minutes of our meeting.

PATIENT: Is it AIDS?

DR QUILL: I'm afraid it is.

PATIENT: Oh no, Dr. Quill. Oh my God!

DR QUILL: I was shocked too.

PATIENT: Oh God. Oh Lord have mercy. Oh God, don't tell me that. Oh Lord have mercy. Oh my God. Oh my God, no., Dr. Quill. Oh God. Oh no. Please don't do it again. Please don't tell me that. Oh my God. Oh my children. Oh Lord have mercy. Oh God, why did He do this to me? Why did He do this to me? Why did He do this to me, Dr. Quill? Oh Lord have mercy. Oh my God, Jesus.

DR QUILL: You're still alright at this point, okay.

PATIENT: You don't know how long I've had it, Dr. Quill?

DR QUILL: I don't know.

PATIENT: I can't sit. [She walks around room.]

DR QUILL: It's okay.

PATIENT: Why did he do this to me? Why? What have I done to him? Why does he do this to me? Why? Why? Why? Oh Lord. What am I going to do with all of my children? I won't be able to see my grandchildren. I just had another grandbaby. I won't ever be able to see . . . I won't live to see the baby. I won't be able to get up off my chair. Oh, Dr. Quill, I

Reprinted with permission from Timothy E. Quill and Penelope Townsend, "Bad News: Delivery, Dialogue, and Dilemmas," *Archives of Internal Medicine* 151 (March 1991), pp. 463–68. ©1991 The American Medical Association.

don't know what to do. Oh God, I don't know what to do. My son-in-law is not going to let the kids come over.

DR QUILL: First thing we have to do is learn as much as we can about it, because right now you are okay.

PATIENT: I don't even have a future. Everything I know is that you gonna die anytime. What is there to do? What if I'm a walking time bomb? People will be scared to even touch me or say anything to me.

DR QUILL: No, that's not so.

PATIENT: Yes they will, 'cause I feel that way about people. You don't know what to say to them and what to do. Oh God.

DR QUILL: What we have to do is to learn some things about it . . . even though it's scary it may not be as scary as you think. Okay?

PATIENT: Oh my God. Oh my God. I hate him. I hate him. I hate the ground he walks on. I hate him, Dr. Quill. I hate him. He gave this to me. I hate him. He took my life away from me. I have been robbed. I feel as if I have been robbed of a future. I don't have nothing.

DR QUILL: There is a future for you.

PATIENT: They don't even have a cure for me.

DR QUILL: There's a lot of work going on right now, and you can have the infection for a long time before you get sick. There is a lot of research going on.

PATIENT: I read about it. I have a friend with it. I went over to the university . . . Since you told him he had AIDS, he has been at my house and I feel so sorry for him. I was being nice to him. Oh my God, my God. It just doesn't pay to be nice. It doesn't. What do you get out of it?

DR QUILL: Neither you nor he knew that there was a risk back then.

PATIENT: Another cross to bear.

DR QUILL: You never did anything wrong.

PATIENT: What am I going to tell my children when they are old enough to tell them?

DR QUILL: Before you tell them anything, you are going to learn a lot about this.

PATIENT: I can't go home. I can't even stay here. I'm so scared. Oh my God. I knew that you were going to tell me this. I always liked you. I didn't want you to tell me this. Oh God. I don't know if I can deal with this. I don't know, Dr. Quill, if I can deal with this.

DR QUILL: You've worked through this before. It's going to be hard, but it may not be as bad as you think. Okay? I think what you have to do . . .

PATIENT: I got my church, Dr. Quill. I can't let them see me like that. I can't do it. I would rather . . . because I can't let our church see me like this. They mean a lot to me. Oh, Dr. Quill, and my daughter. Oh, I won't see my daughter and my baby.

DR QUILL: You are still the same person. Okay?

PATIENT: Why is He doing this to me?

DR QUILL: I don't know. You are still the same person. What we have to do is eventually learn as much as you can about this. The odds are that you are going to stay healthy for a long time. Okay? You are still very healthy right now.

PATIENT: What you telling me? I still have a chance to beat it? Can I beat it?

DR QUILL: I think that is possible.

PATIENT: How can you be sure when you don't even know what the cure is for it?

DR QUILL: A couple of things, okay? We don't think you've had this very long; a couple of years at the most. Alright. A lot of people believe that the virus can stay around for many years before it produces many problems. Sometimes 6 or 8 years. There is a lot of research going on now to try to find ways to treat it.

PATIENT: Oh God, Lord Jesus.

DR QUILL: You may have a lot of time before we have to deal with this. I think the first thing we have to do is probably get some further blood tests. We should because it's such a surprise for you and for me that you have it, even though we think we know how you got it. We maybe should repeat it to be 100%, 1000% sure, even though they repeat it once. I think that's wise to do because the only way that you could have gotten it is from your husband. I think we ought to repeat it even though we know that it is probably true.

PATIENT: I don't know if I can live with myself . . . in my bed right now. I don't like him, Dr. Quill. I don't even want to stand by him. I won't even stay with him. I don't. Why must I pay for his sins? Why?

DR QUILL: There's nothing fair about it.

PATIENT: My children.

DR QUILL: It's very scary. Also, there are a lot of things we can do.

PATIENT: Oh Lord have mercy. Then I have the pituitary thing.

DR QUILL: Like your pituitary tumor, it has been there for years. It doesn't . . .

DR QUILL: No, it's not the same thing. If the tumor gets worse, we know what the treatment is.

PATIENT: It's not the same. It can't be cured. You talking about something they never came up with, never came up with a cure for. I've got nothing. All they can do is just treat whatever comes along, like a cold, or pneumonia, stuff like that—that's all.

DR QUILL: That's right. But right now there are millions and millions of dollars being poured into research and that's what we have to hope for.

PATIENT: It doesn't make me feel good.

DR QUILL: I wish I had something more clear to tell you, but I think there are a lot of folks who are in the same shoes that you're in and they are all hoping. They are figuring out ways to cope. That's what we have to figure out.

PATIENT: Dr. Quill, will you still be my doctor?

DR QUILL: Absolutely, I will.

PATIENT: You promise?

DR QUILL: Absolutely. We'll meet very regularly so we know what's going on.

PATIENT: Okay, alright. I'm so scared. I don't want to die. I don't want to die, Dr. Quill, not yet. I know I got to die, but I don't want to die.

DR QUILL: We've got to think about a couple of things. . . .

We both felt overwhelmed by the news and the encounter. With great difficulty, I allowed her rage and terror to be expressed, yet also to find some boundaries. I was concerned for her, and needed to be reassured before she left that there was a basic plan. Through the intense emotional expression, she raised several basic questions that needed to be addressed: (1) Will you still be my doctor? (Will I be alone?) (2) How contagious (repulsive) am I? (3) Am I still the same person? (4) When am I going to die? (5) How can I tell my family, friends, and church? Though these questions were by no means simple, struggling to answer them began to give some definition to her problem.

My struggle to respond adequately caused me to reflect on the process of delivering bad news. . . .

ADVANCE PREPARATION

Advance knowledge about the patient's strengths, weaknesses, and coping style can be invaluable in deciding how to present bad news. This patient's spiritual beliefs, family support from her children, and fierce independence were clear strengths to be called on and reconciled. Her previous fearful, ambivalent feelings and use of denial about medical diagnosis and treatment with her pituitary adenoma were potential sources of concern. Our advance discussions concerning her knowledge and beliefs about HIV allowed her to begin anticipatory grief work. They also allowed her physician to begin to understand the potential meaning of the news. Her thought about what she would do if infected ("I don't know, but I don't think God would do this to me") was potentially ominous and might have been explored further in advance. . . .

TIMING

Bad news should be delivered in a face-to-face encounter in a private setting with time set aside to allow the patient and family to respond and ask questions. It is not a task to be delegated or to be done in an indirect way, such as over the phone. Though this patient did not want to come in to hear the news, she was strongly encouraged to make an appointment. Advance agreements about how and when to share the results are helpful, as are advance considerations of how directly or indirectly to involve significant others. This patient clearly wanted to receive the news alone and then consider the difficult process of involving her family only if the test were positive.

Often questions are raised by physicians or families about whether the patient is medically or psychologically strong enough to handle bad news.[4,5] Though there may be exceptional circumstances where delivering the bad news directly to the patient should be delayed or avoided, this requires careful analysis of who is really being protected. If the patient is competent, some advance assessment of the patient's wish to be informed should be made. A patient's direct request for information creates an obligation to inform that takes precedence over a family member's or a physician's fear of doing the patient harm unless the evidence suggesting harm is very clear. It is not the physician's role to protect a patient from the truth about his or her condition or from the ensuing grief. Exploring the family's fears and concerns, and also informing the family about the necessity for responding to the patient's questions, may allow the family to grieve and prepare for the patient's being told. If this short delay is not likely to harm the patient, then it may be justified in the interest of overall patient and family well-being.

DELIVERING THE NEWS

An initial assessment of the patient's readiness to hear the news is the first step. This patient requested the results as I walked into the room ("Is it AIDS?") and could read the answer on my face. Direct requests for information should be responded to clearly and simply in language that is easily comprehensible to the patient. Hopefully, the language selected was explored in advance when the purpose of the test was being considered. The complex meanings that any person may have for words such as *tumor, cancer, malignancy, HIV infection*, or *AIDS* means that common understanding cannot be ensured without joint exploration.

Other patients do not want to hear the news right away or perhaps would rather not hear it at all. With these patients, time initially spent exploring how they are feeling, how the time has been since the test was taken, and what thoughts and feelings they have had about the test and about getting the results is extremely important. First, it allows the patient to control the flow of information and to have time to settle and brace himself or herself before hearing the news. Second, it helps the physician understand more about the patient's coping style and about the potential impact of the news once delivered. Unless the patient specifically requests not to hear the news (a request that needs in-depth exploration and understanding), the physician eventually should deliver the news in a clear, sensitive manner.

If the news to be delivered has complex ramifications, the physician should avoid the temptation to deliver too much information all at once. Each piece of news, from the reality of the diagnosis to each of its implications, may or may not have a profound impact on the patient, so the patient should be given time and opportunity to respond. This is particularly true initially, when the patient's self-image and world view may be severely threatened.[1,7] Though the patient's beliefs about the disease and previous reactions to stressful situations may help predict his or her response, the prediction is not always reliable, particularly if the news is perceived by the patient as overwhelming.

INITIAL PATIENT RESPONSE

Patients will respond to their perception of the threat, which may or may not be congruent with the medical reality.[2,3,7-10] These discrepancies, if not recognized and sensitively worked through, can create profound barriers between physician and patient.[11] This woman's perception of her HIV diagnosis as a death sentence and as a disease that could transform her into a pariah were overwhelming: "I don't even have a future. Everything I know is that you gonna die anytime. What is there to do? What if I'm a walking time bomb? People will be scared to even touch me or say anything to me."

Each perception had some truth and some distortion. The challenge for the clinician is to respond empathically to the devastating feelings and perceptions, while simultaneously beginning to correct distortions so that the loss has some boundaries and coping can begin. In this patient, emotions flowed freely, whereas in others emotions may be too shameful[12] or threatening to be expressed. In the latter circumstances, the physician might ask, "What is the most frightening part?" in an effort to understand the patient's hidden experience.

When the threat of the diagnosis is severe, basic coping responses are elicited that fall into three categories:[2,3,7-10] (1) basic psychophysiologic, (2) cognitive, and (3) affective. The two basic psychophysiologic mechanisms are the fight-flight response and the conservation-withdrawal response,[13] which correspond to activation of the sympathetic and parasympathetic nervous systems, respectively. This patient wanted to flee and began pacing around the small examination room, unable to sit still. I wanted to give her room to pace, but I was also fearful that if she fled she might harm herself or find herself completely alone without any direction when the high-energy state wore off. By being allowed to pace and freely express herself, she was eventually able to accept some personal contact[24] and information to help put her losses in perspective, and we were able to make a basic plan for follow-up.

An example of the conservation-withdrawal response would be a patient who became withdrawn and silent on hearing the news. Cognitive processes in this state are very limited, so patients often report feeling numb and having little recollection of the content of discussions beyond the initial news. In other species, this response may have considerable survival value when the creature is severely threatened ("playing possum"). Expectations in terms of information exchange need to be scaled down considerably once a patient enters a conservation-withdrawal state. In the extreme, a patient could become hypotensive from vasovagal syncope, attesting to the strong physiologic concomitants.

There are five basic cognitive coping strategies: denial, blame, intellectualization, disbelief, and acceptance. This patient used denial as a cognitive coping strategy with her pituitary adenoma, allowing her to lead a very full, untroubled life without treatment in spite of substantial galactorrhea.[15,16] When confronted with her HIV diagnosis, her initial cognitive responses were somewhat disorganized but dominated by blame of her husband and God. She did not overtly feel guilt but openly wondered how this could happen to her after leading such a good Christian life. The cognitive response that physicians are most comfortable with is intellectualization.[6] Many patients (often to the relief of their physician) will seek information to control the emotional impact of the diagnosis. Though the physician should respond to requests for information, he or she should be aware that complex information may not be retained,[17] in part because of the patient's affective state and consequent cognitive disorganization created by the initial news. If the patient's questions and quest for information become overly aggressive, they may represent an indirect expression of anger or blame that may need more direct exploration.

Affective responses will be present when anyone receives bad news. These may include anger (rage), fear (terror), anxiety, helplessness, hopelessness, shame, relief, or guilt. For this patient, the overwhelming affects were overtly expressed, whereas for others they may be hidden to the patient, the physician, or both. Her initial affects were consistent with the fight-flight response, a mixture of rage, terror, and fear. The feelings flowed, giving tremendous power to her cognitive responses and a frightening reality to having one's world and self-image under siege: "Oh my God. Oh my God. I hate him. I hate him. I hate the ground he walks on. I hate him, Dr. Quill. I hate him. He gave this to me. I hate him. He took my life away from me. I have been robbed. I feel as if I have been robbed of a future. I don't have nothing."

Other patients may become acutely anxious or may be dominated by feelings of helplessness ("There is nothing I can do") or hopelessness ("There is nothing anyone can do"). This patient's powerful affect was unmistakable, but in others it may be more subtle or covert. If strong affects are present but persistently unaddressed, they may limit a patient's ability to cope effectively with his or her illness.

. . . To understand and respond to the patient's initial responses and distortions, the physician must listen, acknowledge, legitimize, explore, and empathize; these communication skills are described in detail elsewhere.[18–20] Exploring, tolerating, and listening to a patient's response to bad news are perhaps the most vital steps. To begin to relieve a patient's suffering, the physician must have thoroughly explored the patient's unique experience of pain and the meaning of the loss.[1] This is particularly difficult when part of the response is anger and some of the blame is focused directly or indirectly on the physician. Feelings of hopelessness and despair may also be hard for physicians to tolerate, particularly when the patient has a condition where there are severe limits on the effectiveness of biomedical intervention. By hearing and attempting to understand and empathize with a patient's pain and struggle, the physician can help the patient feel less alone and therefore less overwhelmed, hopefully creating the foundation on which the patient can begin to face the problems ahead.

Not all patients will respond initially with cognitive distortions or strong affective responses. Some will simply want to know the medical facts and readily make decisions. An occasional patient who has been suffering with an undefined illness may actually feel relieved by bad news, which at least clarifies the problem. By exploring the meaning that the news has for the patient, the physician can better understand whether an affectively neutral exchange of information represents a coping style (intellectualization) that helps control and limit affect, or if in fact the news has little meaning for the patient. Other patients will go elsewhere to work through the emotional side of their responses (family, friends, other health professionals), preferring to keep the physician-patient relationship a more traditional biomedical exchange.

INFORMATIONAL NEEDS

Patients retrospectively report wanting information about the disease (prognosis, further tests, treatment options), the physicians' availability, and the impact of the disease on themselves, their families, and their careers.[21–26] Whereas information in all of these domains is important, it must be tailored initially to the patient's perception of the problem, to direct patient requests, and to the patient's major cognitive distortions. Reconciling discrepancies between perception (HIV as an immediate death sentence) and the medical reality (likelihood of a significant latency period) is a vital early informing task. Since the patient's initial ability to integrate information may be markedly limited, the physician should give simple, focused bits of information, using language that the patient can understand. Both verbal and nonverbal responses to each piece of information should be observed, and the amount of information should depend on the patient's continued active engagement. Information-laden physician soliloquies unfortunately can alienate, distance, and control the patient without truly educating.

Some of the information this patient needed at this initial visit included that (1) I would be her doctor and available to her; (2) the infection usually has a long latency period, and there are medical interventions to help control it (there is hope); (3) she is only contagious through blood or sexual contact; (4) she needs to tell her closest, most trusted supporting people, in this case her children; and (5) I would want to see her and any family she might choose in a few days. More complex information about HIV infection, unless specifically requested, would probably not have been retained at this initial visit. . . .

REFERENCES

1. Cassell EJ. The nature of suffering and the goals of medicine. *N Engl J Med.* 1982;306:639–645.

2. Meyers BA. The informing interview: enabling parents to 'hear and cope' with bad news. *AJDC.* 1983;137:572–577.

3. Hoy AM. Breaking bad news to patients. *Br J Hosp Med.* 1985;34:96–99.

4. Goldie L. The ethics of telling the patient. *J Med Ethics.* 1982;3:128–133.

5. Reiser SJ. Words as scalpels: transmitting evidence in the clinical dialogue. *Ann Intern Med.* 1980;92:837–842.

6. Zinn WM. Doctors have feelings too. *JAMA.* 1988;259: 3296–3298.

7. Jewett LS, Greenberg LW, Champion LA, et al. The teaching of crisis counseling to pediatric residents: a one-year study. *Pediatrics.* 1982;70:907–911.

8. Lindemann E. Symptomatology and management of acute grief. *Am J Psychiatry.* 1944;101:141–148.

9. Mason JW. A historical view of the stress field. *Hum Stress.* 1975;1:6–12, 22–36.

10. Lazarus RS. *Psychological Stress and Coping Process.* New York, NY: McGraw-Hill International Book Co; 1966.

11. Baldwin BA. Crisis intervention: an overview of theory and practice. *Counseling Psychol.* 1979;8:43–52.

12. Quill TE. Recognizing and adjusting to barriers in doctor-patient communication. *Ann Intern Med.* 1989;111:51–57.

13. Lazare A. Shame and humiliation in the medical encounter. *Arch Intern Med.* 1981;94:492–498.

14. Schmale AH. Giving up as a final common pathway to changes in health. *Adv Psychosom Med.* 1972;8:20–40.

15. Suchman AL, Mathews D. What makes the patient-doctor relationship therapeutic? exploring the connectional dimension of medical care. *Ann Intern Med.* 1988;108:125–130.

16. Watson M, Greer S, Blake S, Shrapnell K. Reaction to a diagnosis of breast cancer: relationship between denial, delay and rates of psychological morbidity. *Cancer.* 1984;53:2008–2012.

17. Hackett TP, Casseum NH. Development of a quantitative rating scale to assess denial. *J Psychosom Res.* 1974;18:93–100.

18. Cassileth BR, Zupkis RB, Sutton-Smith K, March V. Informed consent: why are its goals imperfectly realized? *N Engl J Med.* 1980;302:896–900.

19. Cohen-Cole SA, Bird J. Interviewing the cardiac patient, II: a practical guide for helping patients cope with their emotions. In: Wenger N, ed. *Quality of Life and Cardiovascular Care.* New York, NY: LeJacq Publishers; 1986:53–63.

20. Lazare A, Lipkin M, Putnam SM. The functions of the medical interview. In: Lipkin M, Putnam SM, Lazare A, eds. *The Medical Interview.* New York, NY:Springer-Verlag NY Inc. In press.

21. Novack DH. Therapeutic aspects of the clinical encounter. *J Gen Intern Med.* 1987;2:346–355.

22. Gath A. The impact of an abnormal child upon the parents. *Br J Psychiatry.* 1977;130:405–410.

23. Derdiarian AK. Information needs of recently diagnosed cancer patients. *Nurs Res.* 1986;35:276–281.

24. Feldman FL. *Work and Cancer Health Histories: A Study of the Experiences of Recovered Patients.* San Francisco, Calif: American Cancer Society; 1978:36–52.

25. Greenleigh Associates. *The Social, Economic and Psychological Needs of Cancer Patients in California: Major Findings and Implications.* San Francisco, Calif.: American Cancer Society; 1979:40–116.

26. Weisman AL, Worden WJ. Coping and vulnerability in cancer patients. In: *Report of Project Omega.* Boston, Mass: Department of Psychiatry, Harvard Medical School, Massachusetts General Hospital; 1980.

ROGER HIGGS

On Telling Patients the Truth

That honesty should be an important issue for debate in medical circles may seem bizarre. Nurses and doctors are usually thought of as model citizens. Outside the immediate field of health care, when a passport is to be signed, a reference given, or a special allowance made by a government welfare agency, a nurse's or doctor's signature is considered a good warrant, and false certification treated as a serious breach of professional conduct. Yet at the focus of medical activity or skill, at the bedside or in the clinic, when patient meets professional there is often doubt. Is the truth being told?

. . . Although openness is increasingly practised, there is still uncertainty in the minds of many doctors or nurses faced with communicating bad news; as for instance when a test shows up an unexpected and probably incurable cancer, or when meeting the gaze of a severely ill child, or answering the questions of a mother in mid-pregnancy whose unborn child is discovered to be badly handicapped. What should be said? There can be few who have not, on occasions such as these, told less than the truth. Certainly the issue is a regular preoccupation of nurses and doctors in training. Why destroy hope? Why create anxiety, or something worse? Isn't it 'First, do no harm'?

The concerns of the patient are very different. For many, fear of the unknown is the worst disease of all, and yet direct information seems so hard to obtain. The ward round goes past quickly, unintelligible words are muttered—was I supposed to hear and understand? In the surgery the general practitioner signs his prescription pad and clearly it's time to be gone. Everybody is too busy saving lives to give explana-tions. It may come as a shock to learn that it is policy, not just pressure of work, that prevents a patient learn-ing the truth about himself. If truth is the first casualty, trust must be the second. 'Of course they wouldn't say, especially if things were bad,' said the elderly woman just back from out-patients, 'they've got that Oath, haven't they?' She had learned to expect from doctors, at the best, silence; at the worst, deception. It was part of the system, an essential ingredient, as old as Hippocrates. However honest a citizen, it was somehow part of the doctor's job not to tell the truth to his patient.

These reactions, from both patient and doctor, are most commonly encountered when there is news to communicate of a relatively insidious and life-threatening disease like cancer. . . .

However harrowing these occasions, it is easier to decide what to do when the ultimate outcome is clear. It may be much more difficult to know what to say when the future is less certain, such as in the first episode of what is probably multiple sclerosis, or when a patient is about to undergo a mutilating opera-tion. But even in work outside hospital, where such dramatic problems arise less commonly, whether to tell the truth and how much to tell can still be a regu-lar issue. How much should this patient know about the side effects of his drugs? An elderly man sits weeping in an old people's home, and the healthy but exhausted daughter wants the doctor to tell her father that she's medically unfit to have him back. The single mother wants a certificate to say that she is unwell so that she can stay at home to look after her sick child. A colleague is often drunk on duty, and is making mistakes. A husband with venereal disease wants his wife to be treated without her knowledge. An out-raged father demands to know if his teenage daughter has been put on the pill. A mother comes in with a

Reprinted from Roger Higgs, "On Telling Patients the Truth," in Michael Lockwood, ed., *Moral Dilemmas in Modern Medicine*, 1985, by permission of Oxford University Press, pp. 187ff.

child to have a boil lanced. 'Please tell him it won't hurt.' A former student writes from abroad needing to complete his professional experience and asks for a reference for a job he didn't do. Whether the issue is large or small, the truth is at stake. What should the response be?

Discussion of the apparently more dramatic situations may provide a good starting point. Recently a small group of medical students, new to clinical experience, were hotly debating what a patient with cancer should be told. One student maintained strongly that the less said to the patient the better. Others disagreed. When asked whether there was any group of patients they could agree should never be told the truth about a life-threatening illness, the students chose children, and agreed that they would not speak openly to children under six. When asked to try to remember what life was like when they were six, one student replied that he remembered how his mother had died when he was that age. Suddenly the student who had advocated non-disclosure became animated. 'That's extraordinary. My mother died when I was six too. My father said she'd gone away for a time, but would come back soon. One day he said she was coming home again. My younger sister and I were very excited. We waited at the window upstairs until we saw his car drive up. He got out and helped a woman out of the car. Then we saw. It wasn't mum. I suppose I never forgave him — or her, really.'

It is hard to know with whom to sympathize in this sad tale. But its stark simplicity serves to highlight some essential points. First, somehow more clearly than in the examples involving patients, not telling the truth is seen for what it really is. It is, of course, quite possible, and very common in clinical practice, for doctors (or nurses) to engage in deliberate deceit without actually *saying* anything they believe to be false. But, given the special responsibilities of the doctor, and the relationship of trust that exists between him and his patient, one could hardly argue that this was morally any different from telling outright lies. Surely it is the *intention* that is all important. We may be silent, tactful, or reserved, but if we intend to deceive, what we are doing is tantamount to lying. The debate in ward or surgery is suddenly stood on its head. The question is no longer 'Should we tell the truth?' but 'What justification is there for telling a lie?' This relates to the second important point, that medical ethics are part of general morality, and not a separate field of

their own with their own rules. Unless there are special justifications, healthcare professionals are working within the same moral constraints as lay people. A lie is a lie wherever told and whoever tells it.

But do doctors have a special dispensation from the usual principles that guide the conduct of our society? It is widely felt that on occasion they do, and such a dispensation is as necessary to all doctors as freedom from the charge of assault is to a surgeon. But if it is impossible to look after ill patients and always be open and truthful, how can we balance this against the clear need for truthfulness on all other occasions? If deception is like a medicine to be given in certain doses in certain cases, what guidance exists about its administration?

My elderly patient reflected the widely held view that truth-telling, or perhaps withholding, was part of the tradition of medicine enshrined in its oaths and codes. Although the writer of the 'Decorum' in the Hippocratic corpus advises physicians of the danger of telling patients about the nature of their illness '. . . for many patients through this cause have taken a turn for the worse',[1] the Oath itself is completely silent on this issue. This extraordinary omission is continued through all the more modern codes and declarations. The first mention of veracity as a principle is to be found in the American Medical Association's 'Principles of Ethics' of 1980, which states that the physician should 'deal honestly with patients and colleagues and strive to expose those physicians deficient in character or competence, or who engage in fraud and deception'.[2] Despite the difficulties of the latter injunction, which seems in some way to divert attention from the basic need for honest communication with the patient, here at last is a clear statement. This declaration signally fails, however, to provide the guidance that we might perhaps have expected for the professional facing his or her individual dilemma.

The reticence of these earlier codes is shared, with some important exceptions, by medical writing elsewhere. Until recently most of what had been usefully said could be summed up by the articles of medical writers such as Thomas Percival, Worthington Hooker, Richard Cabot, and Joseph Collins, which show a wide scatter of viewpoints but do at least confront the problems directly. There is, however, one widely quoted statement by Lawrence Henderson, writing in the *New England Journal of Medicine* in 1955.[3] 'It is meaningless to speak of telling the truth, the whole truth and nothing but the truth to a patient . . . because it is . . . a sheer impossibility . . .

Since telling the truth is impossible, there can be no sharp distinction between what is true and what is false.' Unfortunately, Henderson's analysis embodies a major and important error. . . .

We must not allow ourselves to be confused, as Henderson was, and as so many others have been, by a failure to distinguish between truth, the abstract concept, of which we shall always have an imperfect grasp, and *telling* the truth, where the intention is all important. Whether or not we can ever fully grasp or express the whole picture, whether we know ultimately what the truth really is, we must speak truthfully, and intend to convey what we understand, or we shall lie. In Sissela Bok's words 'The moral question of whether you are lying or not is not *settled* by establishing the truth or falsity of what you say. In order to settle the question, we must know whether you *intend your statement to mislead*.'[4] . . .

Plato was among the first to suggest that falsehood should be available to physicians as 'medicine' for the good of patients (but not to lawyers who should have no part in it!). Sidgwick followed him in arguing that lies to invalids and children could sometimes be justified as being in the best interests of those deceived. But by and large, most early philosophers have looked to truthfulness as fundamental to trust between men. There is a division of opinion between those who, with Kant, see no circumstances in which the duty to be truthful can be abrogated, 'whatever the disadvantages accruing',[5] and those who believe deception can be justifiably undertaken at times. . . .

Most modern thinkers in the field of medical ethics would hold that truthfulness is indeed a central principle of conduct, but that it is capable of coming into conflict with other principles, to which it must occasionally give way. On the other hand, the principle of veracity often receives support from other principles. For instance, it is hard to see how a patient can have autonomy, can make a free choice about matters concerning himself, without some measure of understanding of the facts as they influence the case; and that implies, under normal circumstances, some open, honest discussion with his advisers.[6] Equally, consent is a nonsense if it is not in some sense informed. The doctor's perspective, related to the patient's perceived needs and interests, is becoming less dominant over the patient's perspective, often expressed in terms of 'rights'. . . .

Once the central position of honesty has been established, we still need to examine whether doctors and nurses really do have, as has been suggested, special exemption from being truthful because of the nature of their work, and if so under what circumstances. The analogy with the discussion of the use of force may be helpful. Few would take the absolutist view here, and most would feel that some members of society, such as the police, have at times exemption from the usual prohibition against the use of physical force. The analogy reminds us, however, that the circumstances need to be carefully examined, and there is no blanket permission. The analogy is also helpful in that we can see that there may be circumstances at either end of the scale of importance when the issues, for most people, are clear cut. In a crisis, when there is absolutely no other alternative, we condone the use of force. At the other end of the scale, there may be occasions, such as controlling a good-natured crowd, in which the use of force is accepted by all for the smooth running of society, and that the 'offence', in the sense of breaking the prohibition on the use of force against a person's will, is trivial — although the physical force required may be anything but! Similarly, there are arguments for lying at either end of the scale of importance. It may finally be decided that in a crisis there is no acceptable alternative, as when life is ebbing and truthfulness would bring certain disaster. Alternatively, the moral issue may appear so trivial as not to be worth considering (as, for example, when a doctor is called out at night by a patient who apologizes by saying, 'I hope you don't mind me calling you at this time, doctor', and the doctor replies, 'No, not at all.'). However, the force analogy alerts us to the fact that occasions of these two types are few, fewer than those in which deliberate deceit would generally be regarded as acceptable in current medical practice, and should regularly be debated 'in public' if abuses are to be avoided.[7] To this end it is necessary now to examine critically the arguments commonly used to defend lying to patients.

First comes the argument that it is enormously difficult to put across a technical subject to those with little technical knowledge and understanding, in a situation where so little is predictable. A patient has bowel cancer. With surgery it might be cured, or it might recur. Can the patient understand the effects of treatment? The symptom she is now getting might be due to cancer, there might be secondaries, and they in turn might be suppressible for a long time, or not at all. What future symptoms might occur, how long will she live, how will she die — all these are desperately important questions for the patient, but even for her doctor the answers can only be informed guesses, in an area where uncertainty is so hard to bear.

Yet to say we do not know anything is a lie. As doctors we know a great deal, and *can* make informed guesses or offer likelihoods. The whole truth may be impossible to attain, but truthfulness is not. 'I do not know' can be a major piece of honesty. To deprive the patient of honest communication because we cannot know everything is, as we have seen, not only confused thinking but immoral. Thus deprived, the patient cannot plan, he cannot choose. . . .

The second argument for telling lies to patients is that no patient likes hearing depressing or frightening news. That is certainly true. There must be few who do. But in other walks of life no professional would normally consider it his or her duty to suppress information simply in order to preserve happiness. No accountant, foreseeing bankruptcy in his client's affairs, would chat cheerfully about the Budget or a temporarily reassuring credit account. Yet such suppression of information occurs daily in wards or surgeries throughout the country. Is this what patients themselves want?

In order to find out, a number of studies have been conducted over the past thirty years.[8] In most studies there is a significant minority of patients, perhaps about a fifth, who, if given information, deny having been told. Sometimes this must be pure forgetfulness, sometimes it relates to the lack of skill of the informer, but sometimes with bad or unwelcome news there is an element of what is (perhaps not quite correctly) called 'denial'. The observer feels that at one level the news has been taken in, but at another its validity or reality has not been accepted. This process has been recognized as a buffer for the mind against the shock of unacceptable news, and often seems to be part of a process leading to its ultimate acceptance. But once this group has been allowed for, most surveys find that, of those who have had or who could have had a diagnosis made of, say, cancer, between two-thirds and three-quarters of those questioned were either glad to have been told, or declared that they would wish to know. Indeed, surveys reveal that most *doctors* would themselves wish to be told the truth, even though (according to earlier studies at least) most of those same doctors said they would not speak openly to their patients—a curious double standard! Thus these surveys have unearthed, at least for the

present, a common misunderstanding between doctors and patients, a general preference for openness among patients, and a significant but small group whose wish not to be informed must surely be respected. We return once more to the skill needed to detect such differences in the individual case, and the need for training in such skills.

Why doctors have for so long misunderstood their patients' wishes is perhaps related to the task itself. Doctors don't want to give bad news, just as patients don't want it in abstract, but doctors have the choice of withholding the information, and in so doing protecting themselves from the pain of telling, and from the blame of being the bearer of bad news. . . .

Paternalism may be justifiable in the short term, and to 'kid' someone, to treat him as a child because he is ill, and perhaps dying, may be very tempting. Yet true respect for that person (adult or child) can only be shown by allowing him allowable choices, by granting him whatever control is left, as weakness gradually undermines his hold on life. If respect is important then at the very least there must be no acceptable or effective alternative to lying in a particular situation if the lie is to be justified.

Staying with the assessment of consequences, however, a third argument for lying can be advanced, namely, that truthfulness can actually do harm. 'What you don't know can't hurt you' is a phrase in common parlance (though it hardly fits with concepts of presymptomatic screening for preventable disease!). However, it is undeniable that blunt and unfeeling communication of unpleasant truths can cause acute distress, and sometimes long-term disability. The fear that professionals often have of upsetting people, of causing a scene, of making fools of themselves by letting unpleasant emotions flourish, seems to have elevated this argument beyond its natural limits. It is not unusual to find that the fear of creating harm will deter a surgical team from discussing a diagnosis gently with a patient, but not deter it from performing radical and mutilating surgery. Harm is a very personal concept. Most medical schools have, circulating in the refectory, a story about a patient who was informed that he had cancer and then leapt to his death. The intended moral for the medical student is, keep your mouth shut and do no harm. But that may not be the correct lesson to be learned from such cases (which I believe, in any case, to be less numerous than is commonly supposed). The style of telling could have been brutal, with no follow-up or support. It may have been the suggested treatment, not the basic illness, that led the patient to resort to such a desperate measure. Suicide in illness is remarkably rare, but, though tragic, could be seen as a logical response to an overwhelming challenge. No mention is usually made of suicide rates in other circumstances, or the isolation felt by ill and warded patients, or the feelings of anger uncovered when someone takes such precipitate and forbidden action against himself. What these cases do, surely, is argue, not for no telling, but for better telling, for sensitivity and care in determining how much the patient wants to know, explaining carefully in ways the patient can understand, and providing full support and 'after-care' as in other treatments.

But even if it is accepted that the short-term effect of telling the truth may sometimes be considerable psychological disturbance, in the long term the balance seems definitely to swing the other way. The effects of lying are dramatically illustrated in 'A Case of Obstructed Death?'[9] False information prevented a woman from returning to healthy living after a cancer operation, and robbed her of six months of active life. Also, the long-term effect of lies on the family and, perhaps most importantly, on society, is incalculable. If trust is gradually corroded, if the 'wells are poisoned', progress is hard. Mistrust creates lack of communication and increased fear, and this generation has seen just such a fearful myth created around cancer.[10] Just how much harm has been done by this 'demonizing' of cancer, preventing people coming to their doctors, or alternatively creating unnecessary attendances on doctors, will probably never be known.

There are doubtless many other reasons why doctors lie to their patients; but these can hardly be used to justify lies, even if we should acknowledge them in passing. Knowledge is power, and certainly doctors, though usually probably for reasons of work-load rather than anything more sinister, like to remain 'in control'. Health professionals may, like others, wish to protect themselves from confrontation, and may find it easier to coerce or manipulate than to gain permission. There may be a desire to avoid any pressure for change. And there is the constant problem of lack of time. But in any assessment, the key issues remain. Not telling the truth normally involves telling lies, and doctors and nurses have no 'carte blanche' to lie. To do so requires a justification and this justification must be strong enough to overcome the negative moral weight of the lie itself. How can we set about this assessment in practical terms? . . .

There still seems to be a need to tell lies, [but] we must be able to justify them. That the person is a child, or 'not very bright', will not do. Given the two ends of the spectrum of crisis and triviality, the vast middle range of communication requires honesty, so that autonomy and choice can be maintained. If lies are to be told, there really must be no acceptable alternative. The analogy with force may again be helpful here: perhaps using the same style of thinking as is used in the Mental Health Act, to test whether we are justified in removing someone's liberty against their will, may help us to see the gravity of what we are doing when we consider deception. It also suggests that the decision should be shared, in confidence, and be subject to debate, so that any alternative which may not initially have been seen may be considered. And it does not end there. If we break an important moral principle, that principle still retains its force, and its 'shadow' has to be acknowledged. As professionals we shall have to ensure that we follow up, that we work through the broken trust or the disillusionment that the lie will bring to the patient, just as we would follow up and work through bad news, a major operation, or a psychiatric 'sectioning'. This follow-up may also be called for in our relationship with our colleagues if there has been major disagreement about what should be done.

In summary, there are *some* circumstances in which the health professions are probably exempted from society's general requirement for truthfulness. But not telling the truth is usually the same as telling a lie, and a lie requires strong justification. Lying must be a last resort, and we should act as if we were to be called upon to defend the decision in public debate, even if our duty of confidentiality does not allow this in practice. We should always aim to respect the other important principles governing interactions with patients, especially the preservation of the patient's autonomy. When all is said and done, many arguments for individual cases of lying do not hold water. Whether or not knowing the truth is essential to the patient's health, telling the truth is essential to the health of the doctor–patient relationship.

NOTES

1. Quoted in Reiser, Dyck, and Curran (eds), *Ethics in Medicine, Historical Perspectives and Contemporary Concerns* (Cambridge, Mass.: MIT Press, 1977).

2. American Medical Association, 'Text of the American Medical Association New Principles of Medical Ethics' *American Medical News* (August 1–8 1980), 9.

3. Lawrence Henderson, 'Physician and Patient as a Social System', *New England Journal of Medicine,* 212 (1935).

4. Sissela Bok, *Lying: Moral Choice in Public and Private Life* (London: Quartet, 1980).

5. Immanuel Kant, 'On a Supposed Right to Lie from Benevolent Motives', translated by T. K. Abbott, in Kant's *Critique of Practical Reason and other works on the Theory of Ethics* (London: Longmans, 1909).

6. Alastair Campbell and Roger Higgs, *In That Case* (London: Darton, Longman and Todd, 1982).

7. John Rawls, *A Theory of Justice* (Cambridge, Mass.: Harvard University Press, Belknap Press, 1971).

8. Summarized well in Robert Veatch, 'Truth-telling I' in *Encyclopaedia of Bioethics,* op. cit.

9. Roger Higgs, 'Truth at the last—A Case of Obstructed Death?', *Journal of Medical Ethics,* 8 (1982), 48–50, and Roger Higgs, 'Obstructed Death Revisited', *Journal of Medical Ethics,* 8 (1982), pp. 154–6.

10. Susan Sontag, *Illness as Metaphor* (New York: Farrar, Straus and Giroux, 1978).

Informed Consent

UNITED STATES COURT OF APPEALS

Canterbury v. Spence

SPOTTSWOOD W. ROBINSON, III,
Circuit Judge

Suits charging failure by a physician adequately to disclose the risks and alternatives of proposed treatment are not innovations in American law. They date back a good half-century, and in the last decade they have multiplied rapidly. There is, nonetheless, disagreement among the courts and the commentators on many major questions, and there is no precedent of our own directly in point. For the tools enabling resolution of the issues on this appeal, we are forced to begin at first principles.

The root premise is the concept, fundamental in American jurisprudence, that "[e]very human being of adult years and sound mind has a right to determine what shall be done with his own body. . . ." True consent to what happens to one's self is the informed exercise of a choice, and that entails an opportunity to evaluate knowledgeably the options available and the risks attendant upon each. The average patient has little or no understanding of the medical arts, and ordinarily has only his physician to whom he can look for enlightenment with which to reach an intelligent decision. From these almost axiomatic considerations springs the need, and in turn the requirement, of a reasonable divulgence by physician to patient to make such a decision possible.

• • •

Once the circumstances give rise to a duty on the physician's part to inform his patient, the next inquiry is the scope of the disclosure the physician is legally obliged to make. The courts have frequently confronted this problem, but no uniform standard defining the adequacy of the divulgence emerges from the decisions. Some have said "full" disclosure,[1] a norm we are unwilling to adopt literally. It seems obviously prohibitive and unrealistic to expect physicians to discuss with their patients every risk of proposed treatment—no matter how small or remote—and gener-

No. 22099, U.S. Court of Appeals, District of Columbia Circuit, May 19, 1972. 464 Federal Reporter, 2nd Series, 772.

ally unnecessary from the patient's viewpoint as well. Indeed, the cases speaking in terms of "full" disclosure appear to envision something less than total disclosure,[2] leaving unanswered the question of just how much.

The larger number of courts, as might be expected, have applied tests framed with reference to prevailing fashion within the medical profession. Some have measured the disclosure by "good medical practice," others by what a reasonable practitioner would have bared under the circumstances, and still others by what medical custom in the community would demand. We have explored this rather considerable body of law but are unprepared to follow it. The duty to disclose, we have reasoned, arises from phenomena apart from medical custom and practice. The latter, we think, should no more establish the scope of the duty than its existence. Any definition of scope in terms purely of a professional standard is at odds with the patient's prerogative to decide on projected therapy himself. That prerogative, we have said, is at the very foundation of the duty to disclose, and both the patient's right to know and the physician's correlative obligation to tell him are diluted to the extent that its compass is dictated by the medical profession.

In our view, the patient's right of self-decision shapes the boundaries of the duty to reveal. That right can be effectively exercised only if the patient possesses enough information to enable an intelligent choice. The scope of the physician's communications to the patient, then, must be measured by the patient's need, and that need is the information material to the decision. Thus the test for determining whether a particular peril must be divulged is its materiality to the patient's decision: all risks potentially affecting the decision must be unmasked. And to safeguard the patient's interest in achieving his own determination on treatment, the law must itself set the standard for adequate disclosure.

Optimally for the patient, exposure of a risk would be mandatory whenever the patient would deem it significant to his decision, either singly or in combination with other risks. Such a requirement, however, would summon the physician to second-guess the patient, whose ideas on materiality could hardly be known to the physician. That would make an undue demand upon medical practitioners, whose conduct, like that of others, is to be measured in terms of reasonableness. Consonantly with orthodox negligence doctrine, the physician's liability for nondisclosure is to be de-

termined on the basis of foresight, not hindsight; no less than any other aspect of negligence, the issue of nondisclosure must be approached from the viewpoint of the reasonableness of the physician's divulgence in terms of what he knows or should know to be the patient's informational needs. If, but only if, the factfinder can say that the physician's communication was unreasonably inadequate is an imposition of liability legally or morally justified.

Of necessity, the content of the disclosure rests in the first instance with the physician. Ordinarily it is only he who is in a position to identify particular dangers; always he must make a judgment, in terms of materiality, as to whether and to what extent revelation to the patient is called for. He cannot know with complete exactitude what the patient would consider important to his decision, but on the basis of his medical training and experience he can sense how the average, reasonable patient expectably would react. Indeed, with knowledge of, or ability to learn, his patient's background and current condition, he is in a position superior to that of most others—attorneys, for example—who are called upon to make judgments on pain of liability in damages for unreasonable miscalculation.

From these considerations we derive the breadth of the disclosure of risks legally to be required. The scope of the standard is not subjective as to either the physician or the patient; it remains objective with due regard for the patient's informational needs and with suitable leeway for the physician's situation. In broad outline, we agreed that "[a] risk is thus material when a reasonable person, in what the physician knows or should know to be the patient's position, would be likely to attach significance to the risk or cluster of risks in deciding whether or not to forgo the proposed therapy."[3]

The topics importantly demanding a communication of information are the inherent and potential hazards of the proposed treatment, the alternatives to that treatment, if any, and the results likely if the patient remains untreated. The factors contributing significance to the dangerousness of a medical technique are, of course, the incidence of injury and the degree of the harm threatened. A very small chance of death or serious disablement may well be significant; a potential disability which dramatically outweighs the potential benefit of the therapy or the detriments of the existing malady may summon discussion with the patient.

There is no bright line separating the significant from the insignificant; the answer in any case must abide a rule of reason. Some dangers—infection, for example—are inherent in any operation; there is no obligation to communicate those of which persons of average sophistication are aware. Even more clearly, the physician bears no responsibility for discussion of hazards the patient has already discovered, or those having no apparent materiality to patients' decision on therapy. The disclosure doctrine, like others marking lines between permissible and impermissible behavior in medical practice, is in essence a requirement of conduct prudent under the circumstances. Whenever nondisclosure of particular risk information is open to debate by reasonable-minded men, the issue is for the finder of the facts.

Two exceptions to the general rule of disclosure have been noted by the courts. Each is in the nature of a physician's privilege not to disclose, and the reasoning underlying them is appealing. Each, indeed, is but a recognition that, as important as is the patient's right to know, it is greatly outweighed by the magnitudinous circumstances giving rise to the privilege. The first comes into play when the patient is unconscious or otherwise incapable of consenting, and harm from a failure to treat is imminent and outweighs any harm threatened by the proposed treatment. When a genuine emergency of that sort arises, it is settled that the impracticality of conferring with the patient dispenses with need for it. Even in situations of that character the physician should, as current law requires, attempt to secure a relative's consent if possible. But if time is too short to accommodate discussion obviously the physician should proceed with the treatment.

The second exception obtains when risk-disclosure poses such a threat of detriment to the patient as to become unfeasible or contraindicated from a medical point of view. It is recognized that patients occasionally become so ill or emotionally distraught on disclosure as to foreclose a rational decision, or complicate or hinder the treatment, or perhaps even pose psychological damage to the patient. Where that is so, the cases have generally held that the physician is armed with a privilege to keep the information from the patient, and we think it clear that portents of that type may justify the physician in action he deems medically warranted. The critical inquiry is whether the physician responded to a sound medical judgment that communication of the risk information would present a threat to the patient's well-being.

The physician's privilege to withhold information for therapeutic reasons must be carefully circumscribed, however, for otherwise it might devour the disclosure rule itself. The privilege does not accept the paternalistic notion that the physician may remain silent simply because divulgence might prompt the patient to forgo therapy the physician feels the patient really needs. That attitude presumes instability or perversity for even the normal patient, and runs counter to the foundation principle that the patient should and ordinarily can make the choice for himself. Nor does the privilege contemplate operation save where the patient's reaction to risk information, as reasonably foreseen by the physician, is menacing. And even in a situation of that kind, disclosure to a close relative with a view to securing consent to the proposed treatment may be the only alternative open to the physician.

NOTES

1. *E.g.*, Salgo v. Leland Stanford Jr. Univ. Bd. of Trustees, 154 Cal. App. 2d 560, 317 P.2d 170, 181 (1975); Woods v. Brumlop, *supra* note 13 [in original text], 377 P.2d at 524–525.

2. See, Comment, Informed Consent in Medical Malpractice, 55 Calif. L. Rv. 1396, 1402–03 (1967).

3. Waltz and Scheuneman, Informed Consent to Therapy, 64, Nw. U.L. Rev. 628, 640 (1970).

JAY KATZ

Physicians and Patients:
A History of Silence

beneficence

Disclosure and consent, except in the most rudimentary fashion, are obligations alien to medical thinking and practice. Disclosure in medicine has served the function of getting patients to "consent" to what physicians wanted them to agree to in the first place. "Good" patients follow doctor's orders without question. Therefore, disclosure becomes relevant only with recalcitrant patients. Since they are "bad" and "ungrateful," one does not need to bother much with them. Hippocrates once said, "Life is short, the Art long, Opportunity fleeting, Experiment treacherous, Judgment difficult. The physician must be ready, not only to do his duty himself, but also to secure the cooperation of the patient, of the attendants and of externals." These were, and still are, the lonely obligations of physicians: to wrestle as best they can with life, art, opportunity, experiment and judgment. Sharing with patients the vagaries of available opportunities, however perilous or safe, or the rationale underlying judgments, however difficult or easy, is not part of the Hippocratic task. For doing that, the Art is too long and Life too short.

Physicians have always maintained that patients are only in need of caring custody. Doctors felt that in order to accomplish that objective they were obligated to attend to their patients' physical and emotional needs and to do so on their own authority, without consulting with their patients about the decisions that needed to be made. Indeed, doctors intuitively believed that such consultations were inimical to good patient care. The idea that patients may also be entitled to liberty, to sharing the burdens of decision with their doctors, was never part of the ethos of medicine.

Reprinted by permission of the author.

Being unaware of the idea of patient liberty, physicians did not address the possible conflict between notions of custody and liberty. When, however, in recent decades courts were confronted with allegations that professionals had deprived citizen-patients of freedom of choice, the conflict did emerge. Anglo-American law has, at least in theory, a long-standing tradition of preferring liberty over custody; and however much judges tried to sidestep law's preferences and to side with physicians' traditional beliefs, the conflict remained and has ever since begged for a resolution. . . .

The legal doctrine remained limited in scope, in part, because judges believed or wished to believe that their pronouncements on informed consent gave legal force to what good physicians customarily did; therefore they felt that they could defer to the disclosure practices of "reasonable medical practitioners." Judges did not appreciate how deeply rooted the tradition of silence was and thus did not recognize the revolutionary, alien implications of their appeal for patient "self-determination." In fact, precisely because of the appeal's strange and bewildering novelty, physicians misinterpreted it as being more far-reaching than courts intended it to be.

Physicians did not realize how much their opposition to informed consent was influenced by suddenly encountering obligations divorced from their history, their clinical experience, or medical education. Had they appreciated that even the doctrine's modest appeal to patient self-determination represented a radical break with medical practices, as transmitted from teacher to student during more than two thousand years of recorded medical history, they might have been less embarrassed by standing so unpreparedly, so nakedly before this new obligation. They might then perhaps have realized that their silence had been until most recently a historical necessity, dictated not only by the inadequacy of medical knowledge but also by physicians' incapacity to discriminate between therapeutic effectiveness based on their actual physical interventions and benefits that must be ascribed to other causes. They might also have argued that the practice of silence was part of a long and venerable tradition that deserved not to be dismissed lightly. . . .

When I speak of silence I do not mean to suggest that physicians have not talked to their patients at all. Of course, they have conversed with patients about all kinds of matters, but they have not, except inadvertently, employed words to invite patients' participation in sharing the burden of making joint decisions. . . .

Judges have made impassioned pleas for patient self-determination, and then have undercut them by giving physicians considerable latitude to practice according to their own lights, exhorting them only to treat each patient with the utmost care. Judges could readily advance this more limited plea because generally doctors do treat their patients with solicitude. The affirmation of physicians' commitment to patients' physical needs, however, has failed to address physicians' lack of commitment to patients' decision making needs. These tensions have led judges to fashion a doctrine of informed consent that has secured for patients the right to better custody but not to liberty — the right to choose how to be treated. . . .

CANTERBURY V. SPENCE (1972)

Judge Robinson, of the D.C. Court of Appeals, who authored the . . . last landmark informed consent decision, also had good intentions. . . . The lesson to be learned from a study of Canterbury [is that]: The strong commitment to self-determination at the beginning of the opinion gets weaker as the opinion moves from jurisprudential theory to the realities of hospital and courtroom life. By the end, the opinion has only obscured the issue it intended to address: the nature of the relationship between the court's doctrine of informed consent, as ultimately construed, and its root premise of self-determination. . . .

Respect for the patient's right of self-determination on particular therapy demands a standard set by law for physicians rather than one which physicians may or may not impose upon themselves.

For this apparently bold move, Canterbury has been widely celebrated, as well as followed in many jurisdictions.

The new rule of law laid down in Canterbury, however, is far from clear. Judge Robinson, returning to basic principles of expert testimony, simply said that there is "no basis for operation of the special medical standard where the physician's activity does not bring his medical knowledge and skills peculiarly into play," and that ordinarily disclosure is not such a situation. But he left room for such situations by adding: "When medical judgment enters the picture and for that reason the special standard controls, prevailing medical practice must be given its just due." He did not spell out the meaning of "just due."

Both standards tend to confuse the need for medical knowledge to elucidate the risks of and alternatives to a proposed procedure in the light of professional experience with the need for medical judgment to establish the limits of appropriate disclosure to patients. The difference is crucial to the clarification of the law of informed consent. In Natanson and many subsequent cases, judges lumped the two together uncritically, relying solely on current medical practice to resolve the question of reasonableness of disclosure. In Canterbury, the distinction was formally recognized. The plaintiff was required to present expert evidence of the applicable medical knowledge, while the defendant had to raise the issue of medical judgment to limit disclosure in defense. But even Canterbury did not undertake a detailed judicial analysis of the nature of medical judgment required, precisely because judges were hesitant to make rules in an area that doctors strongly believed was solely the province of medicine.

In Canterbury, Dr. Spence claimed that "communication of that risk (paralysis) to the patient is not good medical practice because it might deter patients from undergoing needed surgery and might produce adverse psychological reactions which could preclude the success of the operation." Such claims will almost invariably be raised by physicians since they are derived from deeply held tenets of medical practice. Judge Robinson's enigmatic phrase of "just due" certainly suggests that the medical professional standard would be applicable in such a case, raising profound questions about the extent to which the novel legal standard has been swallowed up by the traditional and venerable medical standard.

In fact, medical judgment was given its "just due" twice. It could also be invoked under the "therapeutic privilege" not to disclose, which Judge Robinson retained as a defense to disclosure:

It is recognized that patients occasionally become so ill or emotionally distraught on disclosure as to foreclose a rational decision, or complicate or hinder the treatment, or perhaps even pose psychological damage to the patient. . . . The critical inquiry is whether the physician responded to a sound medical judgment that communication of the risk information would present a threat to the patient's well-being.

The therapeutic privilege not to disclose is merely a procedurally different way of invoking the professional standard of care. . . .

Since the court wished to depart from medical custom as the standard, it had to give some indication as to the information it expected physicians to disclose. The court said that "the test for determining whether a particular peril must be divulged is its materiality to the patient's decision: all risks potentially affecting the decision must be unmasked." It added that physicians must similarly disclose alternatives to the proposed treatment and the "results likely if the patient remains untreated."

But then the court chose to adopt an "objective" test for disclosure of risks and alternatives—what a [reasonable] *prudent* person in the patient's position would have decided if suitably informed"—and rejected a "subjective" test of materiality—"what an *individual* patient would have considered a significant risk." In opting for an "objective" standard, self-determination was given unnecessarily short shrift. The whole point of the inquiry was to safeguard the right of *individual* choice, even where it may appear idiosyncratic. Although law generally does not protect a person's right to be unreasonable and requires reasonably prudent conduct where injury to another may occur, it remains ambiguous about the extent to which prudence can be legally enforced where the potential injury is largely confined to the individual decision maker. For example, courts have split on the question of whether society may require the wearing of motorcycle helmets and whether an adult patient may be compelled to undergo unwanted blood transfusions.

The "objective" standard for disclosure contradicts the right of each individual to decide what will be done with his or her body. The belief that there is one "reasonable" or "prudent" response to every situation inviting medical intervention is nonsense, from the point of view of both the physician and the patient. The most cursory examination of medical practices demonstrates that what is reasonable to the internist

may appear unreasonable to the surgeon or even to other internists and, more significantly, that the value preferences of physicians may not coincide with those of their patients. For example, doctors generally place a higher value on physical longevity than their patients do. But physical longevity is not the only touchstone of prudence. Why should not informed consent law countenance a wide range of potentially reasonable responses by patients to their medical condition based on other value preferences? . . .

Ascertaining patients' informational needs is difficult. Answers do not lie in guessing or "sensing" patients' particular concerns or in obliterating the "subjective" person in an "objective" mass of persons. The "objective" test of materiality only tempts doctors to introduce their own unwarranted subjectivity into the disclosure process. It would have been far better if the court had not committed itself prematurely to the labels "objective" and "subjective." Instead it should have considered more the patients' plight and required physicians to learn new skills: how to inquire openly about their patients' *individual* informational needs and patients' concerns, doubts, and misconceptions about treatment—its risks, benefits, and alternatives. Safeguarding self-determination requires assessing whether patients' informational needs have been satisfied by asking them whether they understand what has been explained to them. Physicians should not try to "second-guess" patients or "sense" how they will react. Instead, they need to explore what questions require further explanation. Taking such unaccustomed obligations seriously is not easy. . . .

SUMMING UP

The legal life of "informed consent," if quality of human life is measured not merely by improvements in physical custody but also by advancement of liberty, was over almost as soon as it was born. Except for the . . . law promulgated in a handful of jurisdictions and the more generally espoused dicta about "self-determination" and "freedom of choice," this is substantially true. Judges toyed briefly with the idea of patients' right to self-determination and largely cast it aside. . . .

Treatment decisions are extremely complex and require a more sustained dialogue, one in which patients are viewed as participants in medical decisions affecting their lives. This is not the view of most physicians, who believe instead that patients are too ignorant to make decisions on their own behalf, that disclosure increases patients' fears and reinforces "foolish" decisions, and that informing them about the uncertainties of medical interventions in many instances seriously undermines faith so essential to the success of therapy. Therefore, physicians asserted that they must be the ultimate decision makers. Judges did not probe these contentions in depth but were persuaded to refrain from interfering significantly with traditional medical practices.

I have not modified my earlier assessment of law's informed consent vision:

> [T]he law of informed consent is substantially mythic and fairy tale-like as far as advancing patients' rights to self-decisionmaking is concerned. It conveys in its dicta about such rights a fairy tale-like optimism about human capacities for "intelligent" choice and for being respectful of other persons' choices; yet in its implementation of dicta, it conveys a mythic pessimism of human capacities to be choice-makers. The resulting tensions have had a significant impact on the law of informed consent which only has made a bow toward a commitment to patients' self-determination, perhaps in an attempt to resolve these tensions by a belief that it is "less important that this commitment be total than that we believe it to be there."

Whether fairy tale and myth can and should be reconciled more satisfactorily with reality remains to be seen. If judges contemplate such a reconciliation, they must acquire first a more profound understanding and appreciation of medicine's vision of patients and professional practice, of the capacities of physicians and patients for autonomous choice, and of the limits of professional knowledge. Such understanding cannot readily be acquired in courts of law, during disputes in which inquiry is generally constrained by claims and counter-claims that seek to assure victory for one side.

The call to liberty, embedded in the doctrine of informed consent, has only created an atmosphere in which freedom has the potential to survive and grow. The doctrine has not as yet provided a meaningful blueprint for implementing patient self-determination. The message . . . is this: Those committed to greater patient self-determination can, if they look hard enough, find inspiration in the common law of informed consent, and so can those, and more easily, who seek to perpetuate medical paternalism. Those who look for evidence of committed implementation will be sadly disappointed. The legal vision of informed consent, based on *self-determination*, is still largely a mirage. Yet a mirage, since it not only deceives but also can sustain hope, is better than no vision at all. . . .

RUTH R. FADEN AND TOM L. BEAUCHAMP

The Concept of Informed Consent

From *A History and Theory of Informed Consent* by Ruth R. Faden and Tom L. Beauchamp. Copyright © 1986 by Oxford University Press, Inc. Reprinted by permission.

What is an informed consent? Answering this question is complicated because there are two common, entrenched, and starkly different meanings of "informed consent." That is, the term is analyzable in two profoundly different ways—not because of mere subtle differences of connotation that appear in different contexts, but because two different *conceptions* of informed consent have emerged from its history and are still at work, however unnoticed, in literature on the subject.

In one sense, which we label *sense₁*, "informed consent" is analyzable as a particular kind of action by individual patients and subjects: an autonomous authorization. In the second sense, *sense₂*, informed consent is analyzable in terms of the web of cultural and policy rules and requirements of consent that collectively form the social practice of informed consent in institutional contexts where *groups* of patients and subjects must be treated in accordance with rules, policies, and standard practices. Here, informed consents are not always *autonomous* acts, nor are they always in any meaningful respect *authorizations*.

SENSE₁: INFORMED CONSENT AS AUTONOMOUS AUTHORIZATION

The idea of an informed consent suggests that a patient or subject does more than express agreement with, acquiesce in, yield to, or comply with an arrangement or a proposal. He or she actively *authorizes* the proposal in the act of consent. John may *assent* to a treatment plan without authorizing it. The assent may be a mere submission to the doctor's authoritative order, in which case John does not call on his *own* authority in order to give permission, and thus does not authorize the plan. Instead, he acts like a child who submits, yields, or assents to the school principal's spanking and in no way gives permission for or authorizes the spanking. Just as the child merely submits to an authority in a system where the lines of authority are quite clear, so often do patients.

Accordingly, an informed consent in sense₁ should be defined as follows: An informed consent is an autonomous action by a subject or a patient that authorizes a professional either to involve the subject in research or to initiate a medical plan for the patient (or both). We can whittle down this definition by saying that an informed consent in sense₁ is given if a patient or subject with (1) substantial understanding and (2) in substantial absence of control by others (3) intentionally (4) authorizes a professional (to do intervention I).

All substantially autonomous acts satisfy conditions 1–3; but it does not follow from that analysis alone that all such acts satisfy 4. The fourth condition is what distinguishes informed consent as one *kind* of autonomous action. (Note also that the definition restricts the kinds of authorization to medical and research contexts.) A person whose act satisfies conditions 1–3 but who refuses an intervention gives an *informed refusal*.

The Problem of Shared Decisionmaking. This analysis of informed consent in sense₁ is deliberately silent on the question of how the authorizer and agent(s) being authorized *arrive at an agreement* about the performance of "I." Recent commentators on informed consent in clinical medicine, notably Jay Katz and the President's Commission, have tended to equate the idea of informed consent with a model of "shared decisionmaking" between doctor and patient. The President's Commission titles the first chapter of its report on informed consent in the patient-practitioner relationship "Informed Consent as Active, Shared Decision Making," while in Katz's work "the idea of informed consent" and "mutual decisionmaking" are treated as virtually synonymous terms.[1]

There is of course an historical relationship in clinical medicine between medical decisionmaking and informed consent. The emergence of the legal doctrine of informed consent was instrumental in drawing attention to issues of decisionmaking as well as authority in the doctor-patient relationship. Nevertheless, it is a confusion to treat informed consent and shared decisionmaking as anything like *synonymous*. For one thing, informed consent is not restricted to clinical medicine. It is a term that applies equally to biomedical and behavioral research contexts where a model of shared decisionmaking is frequently inappropriate. Even in clinical contexts, the social and psychological dynamics involved in selecting medical interventions should be distinguished from the patient's *authorization*.

We endorse Katz's view that effective communication between professional and patient or subject is often instrumental in obtaining informed consents (sense₁), but we resist his conviction that the idea of informed consent entails that the patient and physician "share decisionmaking," or "reason together," or reach a consensus about what is in the patient's best interest. This is a manipulation of the concept from a too singular and defined moral perspective on the practice of medicine that is in effect a moral program for changing the practice. Although the patient and physician *may* reach a decision together, they need not. It is the essence of informed consent in sense₁ only that the patient or subject *authorizes autonomously*; it is a matter of indifference where or how the proposal being authorized originates.

For example, one might advocate a model of shared decisionmaking for the doctor-patient relationship without simultaneously advocating that every medical procedure requires the consent of patients. Even relationships characterized by an ample slice of shared decisionmaking, mutual trust, and respect would and should permit many decisions about routine and low-risk aspects of the patient's medical treatment to remain the exclusive province of the physician, and thus some decisions are likely always to remain subject exclusively to the physician's authorization. Moreover, in the uncommon situation, a patient could autonomously authorize the physician to make *all* decisions about medical treatment, thus giving his or her informed consent to an arrangement that scarcely resembles the sharing of decisionmaking between doctor and patient.

Authorization. In authorizing, one both assumes responsibility for what one has authorized and transfers to another one's authority to implement it. There is no informed consent unless one *understands* these features of the act and *intends* to perform that act. That is, one must understand that one is assuming responsibility and warranting another to proceed.

To say that one assumes responsibility does not quite locate the essence of the matter, however, because a *transfer* of responsibility as well as of authority also occurs. The crucial element in an authorization is that the person who authorizes uses whatever right, power, or control he or she possesses in the situation to endow another with the right to act. In so doing, the authorizer assumes some responsibility for the actions taken by the other person. Here one could either authorize *broadly* so that a person can act in accordance with general guidelines, or *narrowly* so as to authorize only a particular, carefully circumscribed procedure.

SENSE₂: INFORMED CONSENT AS EFFECTIVE CONSENT

By contrast to sense₁, sense₂, or *effective* consent, is a policy-oriented sense whose conditions are not derivable solely from analyses of autonomy and authorization, or even from broad notions of respect for autonomy. "Informed consent" in this second sense does not refer to *autonomous* authorization, but to a legally or institutionally *effective* (sometimes misleadingly called *valid*) authorization from a patient or a subject. Such an authorization is "effective" because it has been obtained through procedures that satisfy the rules and requirements defining a specific institutional practice in health care or in research.

The social and legal practice of requiring professionals to obtain informed consent emerged in institutional contexts, where conformity to operative rules was and still is the sole necessary and sufficient condition of informed consent. Any consent is an informed consent in sense₂ if it satisfies whatever operative rules apply to the practice of informed consent. Sense₂ requirements for informed consent typically do not focus on the autonomy of the act of giving consent (as sense₁ does), but rather on regulating the behavior of the *consent-seeker* and on establishing *procedures and rules* for the context of consent. Such requirements of professional behavior and procedure are obviously more readily monitored and enforced by institutions.

However, because formal institutional rules such as federal regulations and hospital policies govern whether an act of authorizing is effective, a patient or subject can autonomously authorize an intervention, and so give an informed consent in sense₁, and yet *not effectively authorize* that intervention in sense₂.

Consider the following example. Carol and Martie are nineteen-year-old, identical twins attending the same university. Martie was born with multiple birth defects, and has only one kidney. When both sisters are involved in an automobile accident, Carol is not badly hurt, but her sister is seriously injured. It is quickly determined that Martie desperately needs a kidney transplant. After detailed discussions with the transplant team and with friends, Carol consents to be the donor. There is no question that Carol's authorization of the transplant surgery is substantially autonomous. She is well informed and has long anticipated being in just such a circumstance. She has had ample opportunity over the years to consider what she would do were she faced with such a decision. Unfortunately, Carol's parents, who were in Nepal at the time of the accident, do not approve of her decision. Furious that they were not consulted, they decide to sue the transplant team and the hospital for having performed an unauthorized surgery on their minor daughter. (In this state the legal age to consent to surgical procedures is twenty-one.)

According to our analysis, Carol gave her informed consent in sense₁ to the surgery, but she did not give her informed consent in sense₂. That is, she autonomously authorized the transplant and thereby gave an informed consent in sense₁ but did not give a consent that was effective under the operative legal and institutional policy, which in this case required that the person consenting be a legally authorized agent. Examples of other policies that can define sense₂ informed consent (but not sense₁) include rules that consent be witnessed by an auditor or that there be a one-day waiting period between solicitation of consent and implementation of the intervention in order for the person's authorization to be effective. Such rules can and do vary, both within the United States by jurisdiction and institution, and across the countries of the world.

Medical and research codes, as well as case law and federal regulations, have developed models of informed consent that are delineated entirely in a sense$_2$ format, although they have sometimes attempted to justify the rules by appeal to something like sense$_1$. For example, disclosure conditions for informed consent are central to the history of "informed consent" in sense$_2$, because disclosure has traditionally been a *necessary* condition of effective informed consent (and sometimes a *sufficient* condition!). The legal doctrine of informed consent is primarily a law of disclosure; satisfaction of disclosure rules virtually consumes "informed consent" in law. This should come as no surprise, because the legal system needs a generally applicable informed consent mechanism by which injury and responsibility can be readily and fairly assessed in court. These disclosure requirements in the legal and regulatory contexts are not conditions of "informed consent" in sense$_1$; indeed disclosure may be entirely irrelevant to giving an informed consent in sense$_1$. If a person has an adequate *understanding* of relevant information without benefit of a disclosure, then it makes no difference whether someone *discloses* that information.

Other sense$_2$ rules besides those of disclosure have been enforced. These include rules requiring evidence of adequate comprehension of information and the aforementioned rules requiring the presence of auditor witnesses and mandatory waiting periods. Sense$_2$ informed consent requirements generally take the form of rules focusing on disclosure, comprehension, the minimization of potentially controlling influences, and competence. These requirements express the present-day mainstream conception in the federal government of the United States. They are also typical of international documents and state regulations, which all reflect a sense$_2$ orientation.

THE RELATIONSHIP BETWEEN SENSE$_1$ AND SENSE$_2$

A sense$_1$ "informed consent" can fail to be an informed consent in sense$_2$ by a lack of conformity to applicable rules and requirements. Similarly, an informed consent in sense$_2$ may not be an informed con-

sent in sense$_1$. The rules and requirements that determine sense$_2$ consents need not result in autonomous authorizations at all in order to qualify as informed consents.

Such peculiarities in informed consent law have led Jay Katz to argue that the legal doctrine of "informed consent" bears a "name" that "promises much more than its construction in case law has delivered." He has argued insightfully that the courts have, in effect, imposed a mere duty to warn on physicians, an obligation confined to risk disclosures and statements of proposed interventions. He maintains that "This judicially imposed obligation must be distinguished from the *idea* of informed consent, namely, that patients have a decisive role to play in the medical decision-making process. The idea of informed consent, though alluded to also in case law, cannot be implemented, as courts have attempted, by only expanding the disclosure requirements." By their actions and declarations, Katz believes, the courts have made informed consent a "cruel hoax" and have allowed "the idea of informed consent . . . to wither on the vine."[2]

The most plausible interpretation of Katz's contentions is through the sense$_1$/sense$_2$ distinction. If a physician obtains a consent under the courts' criteria, then an informed consent (sense$_2$) has been obtained. But it does not follow that the courts are using the *right* standards, or *sufficiently rigorous* standards in light of a stricter autonomy-based model — or "idea" as Katz puts it — of informed consent (sense$_1$).[3] If Katz is correct that the courts have made a mockery of informed consent and of its moral justification in respect for autonomy, then of course his criticisms are thoroughly justified. At the same time, it should be recognized that people can proffer legally or institutionally effective authorizations under prevailing rules even if they fall far short of the standards implicit in sense$_1$.

Despite the differences between sense$_1$ and sense$_2$, a definition of informed consent need not fall into one or the other class of definitions. It may conform to both. Many definitions of informed consent in policy contexts reflect at least a strong and definite reliance on informed consent in sense$_1$. Although the conditions of sense$_1$ are not logically necessary conditions for sense$_2$, we take it as morally axiomatic that they *ought* to serve — and in fact have served — as the benchmark or model against which the moral adequacy of a definition framed for sense$_2$ purposes is to be evaluated. This position is, roughly speaking, Katz's position.

A defense of the moral viewpoint that policies governing informed consent in sense$_2$ *should* be formulated to conform to the standards of informed consent in sense$_1$ is not hard to express. The goal of informed consent in medical care and in research—that is, the purpose behind the obligation to obtain informed consent—is to enable potential subjects and patients to make autonomous decisions about whether to grant or refuse authorization for medical and research interventions. Accordingly, embedded in the reason for having the social institution of informed consent is the idea that institutional requirements for informed consent in sense$_2$ *should* be intended to maximize the likelihood that the conditions of informed consent in sense$_1$ will be satisfied.

A major problem at the policy level, where rules and requirements must be developed and applied in the aggregate, is the following: The obligations imposed to enable patients and subjects to make authorization decisions must be evaluated not only in terms of the demands of a set of abstract conditions of "true" or sense$_1$ informed consent, but also in terms of the impact of imposing such obligations or requirements on various institutions with their concrete concerns and priorities. One must take account of what is fair and reasonable to require of health care professionals and researchers, the effect of alternative consent requirements on efficiency and effectiveness in the delivery of health care and the advancement of science, and—particularly in medical care—the effect of requirements on the welfare of patients. Also relevant are considerations peculiar to the particular social context, such as proof, precedent, or liability theory in case law, or regulatory authority and due process in the development of federal regulations and IRB consent policies.

Moreover, at the sense$_2$ level, one must resolve not only which requirements will define effective consent; one must also settle on the rules stipulating the conditions under which effective consents must be obtained. In some cases, hard decisions must be made about whether requirements of informed consent (in sense$_2$) should be imposed at all, even though informed consent (in sense$_1$) *could* realistically and meaningfully be obtained in the circumstances and could serve as a model for institutional rules. For example, should there be any consent requirements in the cases of minimal risk medical procedures and research activities?

This need to balance is not a problem for informed consent in sense$_1$, which is not policy oriented. Thus, it is possible to have a *morally acceptable* set of requirements for informed consent in sense$_2$ that deviates considerably from the conditions of informed consent in sense$_1$. However, the burden of moral proof rests with those who defend such deviations since the primary moral justification of the obligation to obtain informed consent is respect for autonomous action.

NOTES

1. President's Commission, *Making Health Care Decisions*, Vol. 1, 15 and Jay Katz, *The Silent World of Doctor and Patient* (New York: The Free Press, 1984), 87 and "The Regulation of Human Research—Reflections and Proposals," *Clinical Research* 21 (1973): 758–91. Katz does not provide a sustained analysis of joint or shared decisionmaking, and it is unclear precisely how he would relate this notion to informed consent.

2. Jay Katz, "Disclosure and Consent," in A. Milunsky and G. Annas, eds., *Genetics and the Law II* (New York: Plenum Press, 1980), 122, 128.

3. We have already noted that Katz's "idea" of informed consent—as the active involvement of patients in the medical decisionmaking process—is different from our sense$_1$.

SUSAN M. WOLF, ET AL.

Sources of Concern About the Patient Self-Determination Act

On December 1, 1991, the Patient Self-Determination Act of 1990 (PSDA)[1] went into effect. This is the first federal statute to focus on advance directives and the rights of adults to refuse life-sustaining treatment. The law applies to all health care institutions receiving Medicare or Medicaid funds, including hospitals, skilled-nursing facilities, hospices, home health and personal care agencies, and health maintenance organizations (HMOs).

The statute requires that the institution provide written information to each adult patient on admission (in the case of hospitals or skilled-nursing facilities), enrollment (HMOs), first receipt of care (hospices), or before the patient comes under an agency's care (home health or personal care agencies). The information provided must describe the person's legal rights in that state to make decisions concerning medical care, to refuse treatment, and to formulate advance directives, plus the relevant written policies of the institution. In addition, the institution must document advance directives in the person's medical record, ensure compliance with state law regarding advance directives, and avoid making care conditional on whether or not patients have directives or otherwise discriminating against them on that basis. Finally, institutions must maintain pertinent written policies and procedures and must provide staff and community education on advance directives. The states must help by preparing descriptions of the relevant law, and the Secretary of Health and Human Services must assist with the development of materials and conduct a public-education campaign. The Health Care Financing Administration has authority to issue regulations.

Reprinted by permission of the publisher from Susan M. Wolf, et al., "Sources of Concern about the Patient Self-Determination Act," *New England Journal of Medicine* 325, No. 23, December 5, 1991.

A goal of the statute is to encourage but not require adults to fill out advance directives—treatment directives (documents such as a living will stating the person's treatment preferences in the event of future incompetence), proxy appointments (documents such as a durable power of attorney appointing a proxy decision maker), or both. There is widespread agreement that directives can have many benefits.[2-5] These include improved communication between doctor and patient, increased clarity about the patient's wishes, and ultimately greater assurance that treatment accords with the patient's values and preferences. Yet few Americans have executed advance directives. Estimates range from 4 to 24 percent[6-8] (and Knox RA: personal communication).

A second goal of the PSDA is to prompt health professionals and institutions to honor advance directives. The U.S. Supreme Court's *Cruzan* decision suggests that advance directives are protected by the federal constitution.[9] The great majority of states and the District of Columbia also have specific statutes or judicial decisions recognizing treatment directives.[10] In addition, all states have general durable-power-of-attorney statutes, and most states further specify how this or another format can be used to appoint a proxy for health care decisions.[10] Patients thus have a right to use directives that are based in constitutional, statutory, and common law, and others must honor the recorded choices.[11] There is evidence, however, that advance directives are ignored or overridden one fourth of the time.[12]

Efforts to educate patients about directives and to educate health care professionals about their obligation to honor them thus seem warranted. But the PSDA has caused concern.[6,13,14] Implementation may result in drowning patients in written materials on admission, insensitive and ill-timed inquiry into patients' preferences, and untrained bureaucrats attempting a job that should be performed by physicians. Indeed, one can favor directives yet oppose the PSDA because of these dangers. The question is how to accomplish the statute's positive underlying goals while minimizing the potential adverse effects.

The key to avoiding an insensitive and bureaucratic process is to ensure that physicians integrate discussions of directives into their ongoing dialogue with patients about current health status and future care. Many have urged that doctors do this.[4,6,15] Yet the literature shows that physicians still have reservations about advance directives,[6,12,13,16-19] and some remain reluctant to initiate discussion.[7,15,20,21] Only by forthrightly addressing these reservations can we successfully make directives part of practice, realize the potential benefits for all involved, and avoid implementing the PSDA in a destructive way.

Our multidisciplinary group—including physicians, a nurse, philosophers, and lawyers—convened to address those reservations in order to dispel doubts when appropriate and delineate continuing controversy where it exists.

RESERVATIONS ABOUT TREATMENT DIRECTIVES

Patients do not really want to discuss future incompetence and death, and so would rather not discuss advance directives. Future incompetence, serious illness, and death are not easy topics to discuss for either patients or physicians. Yet studies indicate that most patients want to discuss their preferences for future treatment[4,7,18,22] and that such discussion usually evokes positive reactions and an enhanced sense of control.[18,23]

Misconceptions nonetheless remain and may produce anxiety in some patients. Some people wrongly assume that treatment directives are used only to refuse treatments and thus shorten life.[24] But people use directives to request treatments as well.[4,25] Such a demand for treatment can raise important ethical problems later if the physician becomes concerned that the treatment may be medically inappropriate or futile for that patient. These problems are currently being debated.[26-29] Yet they are not peculiar to advance directives; they can arise whenever a patient or surrogate demands arguably inappropriate treatment. The point is that treatment directives are a way to express the

patient's preferences for treatment, whatever they may be.

There are substantial advantages to both patients and doctors in discussing and formulating treatment directives. A discussion of future medical scenarios can reduce the uncertainty of patients and physicians, strengthen rapport, and facilitate decision making in the future.[16,23,30] Beyond their clinical advantages, directives are one way to fulfill the legal requirement in some states that there be "clear and convincing evidence" of the patient's wishes before life-sustaining treatment is withdrawn.[31,32] The state statutes on treatment directives also generally give physicians a guarantee of civil and criminal immunity when they withhold or withdraw life-sustaining treatment relying in good faith on a patient's directive.

Some debate remains, however, about when directives should first be discussed and with which patients.[4,21,33] The PSDA requires giving information to all adults when they first enter a relevant institution or receive care. This will involve some healthy patients and patients who are expected to return to good health after treatment for a reversible problem. Yet even healthy persons and young people wish to engage in advance planning with their physicians.[4]

Concern nonetheless persists about whether the time of admission or initial receipt of treatment is an appropriate moment to broach the topic of directives. Ideally, initial discussion should take place in the outpatient setting, before the patient experiences the dislocation that often attends inpatient admission. Many patients, however, will reach admission without the benefit of such discussion. If the discussion on admission is handled sensitively and as the first of many opportunities to discuss these matters with the physician and other care givers, admission is an acceptable time to begin the process. For patients who already have directives, admission is a logical time to check the directives in the light of their changed medical circumstances.

Discussion of advance directives takes too much time and requires special training and competence. The discussion of advance directives is an important part of the dialogue between doctor and patient about the patient's condition, prognosis, and future options. But the physician need not discharge this function alone. Others in the health care institution may play an important part in answering questions, providing information, or assisting with documents. The PSDA helpfully makes health care institutions and organizations responsible for the necessary staff education.

However, because patients considering treatment directives need to understand their health status and treatment options, physicians have a central role.

Physicians may nonetheless harbor understandable concern about the amount of time that will be required to counsel each patient. An initial discussion of directives structured by a document describing alternative medical scenarios can be accomplished in 15 minutes,[4] but some will undoubtedly find that the initial discussion takes longer, and further discussion is also necessary in any case. Institutions may want to acquire brochures, videotapes, and other materials to help educate patients, and may enlist other personnel in coordinated efforts to assist patients. In addition, the PSDA requires institutions and organizations to engage in community education, which may reach patients before they are admitted. All these efforts promise to facilitate the discussion between doctor and patient.

Treatment directives are not useful, because patients cannot really anticipate what their preferences will be in a future medical situation and because patients know too little about life-support systems and other treatment options. The first part of this objection challenges the very idea of making decisions about medical situations that have not yet developed. Patients who make such decisions will indeed often be making decisions that are less fully informed than those of patients facing a current health problem.[6] Yet the decisions recorded in directives, even if imperfect, give at least an indication of what the patient would want. If the goal is to guide later treatment decisions by the patient's preferences, some indication is better than none.

The question, then, is not whether the decisions embodied in directives are just as informed as those made contemporaneously by a competent patient. It is instead whether the recorded decisions accurately indicate the patient's preferences as best he or she could know them when competent. The answer to that question depends largely on how skillful physicians are in explaining possible medical scenarios and the attendant treatment options. There are many spheres in which we ask people to anticipate the future and state their wishes — wills governing property and most contracts are examples. But in each case the quality of their decisions depends a good deal on the quality of the counseling they receive. It is incumbent on physicians to develop their skills in this regard. Several instruments have been described in the literature to help them communicate successfully with patients.[19,34,35] In addition, the patient's designation of a proxy can provide a person to work with the physician as the medical situation unfolds.

Good counseling by physicians is the best remedy for patients' ignorance about life-support systems, too. Patients need to understand these treatments in order to judge whether the expected burdens will outweigh the benefits in future medical circumstances. Yet a patient choosing in advance will usually have a less detailed understanding than a patient facing an immediate and specific decision, who may even try the treatment for a time to gain more information.[3] This too supports the wisdom of designating a proxy to work with the medical team.

Treatment-directive forms are too vague and open to divergent interpretations to be useful guides to treatment decisions later. Some forms do contain outmoded language. Terms such as "extraordinary" treatment and "heroic" care have been widely discredited as being overly vague[3,36] (even though "extraordinary" is used in some state laws[37]), and patients should be discouraged from using such generalities. Instead, patients who wish to use treatment directives should be encouraged to specify which treatments they wish to request or refuse, and the medical circumstances under which they want those wishes to go into effect. Although such specification has been challenged,[17] it is a more effective way for patients to communicate their wishes than a general refusal of life-sustaining treatment. The desire for a particular treatment may well vary according to diagnosis and prognosis[4,38] — for instance, artificial nutrition may be desired if the patient is conscious and has a reversible condition, but unwanted if the patient is in a persistent vegetative state. Another way to communicate wishes is for patients to state their preferred goals of treatment, depending on diagnosis[39] — for example, in case of terminal illness, provide comfort care only.

It is nonetheless almost impossible to write a directive that leaves no room for interpretation. Whatever language the patient uses, the goal is to try to determine the patient's intent. Often family members or other intimates can help. Even a vague directive will usually provide some guidance. Some patients will choose to avoid problems of interpretation and application by appointing a proxy and writing no treatment directive. The proxy can then work with the physician as circumstances unfold. Yet the proxy must still strive to choose as the patient would. If the patient has left a treatment directive or other statement of preferences, it will fall to the proxy to determine what the patient intended.

The incompetent patient's best interests should take precedence over even the most thoughtful choices of a patient while competent. Some people argue that the choices stated in a directive are sometimes less relevant than the current experience of the now incompetent patient.[40,41] In the vast majority of cases, this problem does not arise, because the patient's earlier decisions do not conflict with his or her best interests when incompetent. Yet some demented patients, in particular, may seem to derive continued enjoyment from life, although they have a directive refusing life-sustaining treatment. The argument for discounting the directive is that these patients are now such different people that they should not be bound by the choices of their earlier selves, they may no longer hold the values embodied in the directive, and they may appear to accept a quality of life they formerly deemed unacceptable.

Our group did not reach agreement on this argument for overriding some directives. Members who rejected it argued that it is essential that competent patients who record their wishes know those wishes will be followed later, a person's values and choices should govern even after loss of competence because he or she remains essentially the same person, and to recognize the proposed exception would invite widespread disregard of treatment directives. Although we did not resolve this controversy, we did agree on certain procedural safeguards. A treatment directive should not be overridden lightly. In cases in which this controversy arises, only the patient's appointed proxy, a court, or a court-appointed decision maker should be able to consider overriding the directive. Finally, physicians should specifically discuss with patients what the patients' preferences are in the event of dementia.

Even if a directive is valid in all other respects, it is not a reliable guide to treatment because patients may change their minds. Patients may indeed change their minds as their circumstances change. Physicians should therefore reexamine directives periodically with their patients. Data suggest, however, that there is considerable stability in patients' preferences concerning life-sustaining treatment.[16,42-44] In one study of hospitalized patients, 65 to 85 percent of choices did not change during a one-month period, the percentage depending on the illness scenario presented (kappa = 0.35 to 0.70, where 0 represents random and 1 perfect agreement).[42] In another study there was 58 and 81 percent stability in patients' decisions over a six-month period when they were presented with two scenarios (kappa = 0.23 and 0.31).[43] Further research is necessary, but in any case, patients are always free to change or revoke earlier directives. Once a patient has lost competence and the physician can no longer check with the patient about treatment preferences, a directive becomes the most reliable guide to what the patient would want. Physicians cannot justifiably disregard directives because the patient might hypothetically have changed his or her mind.

RESERVATIONS ABOUT PROXY APPOINTMENTS

Patients may appoint a proxy to make treatment decisions in the event of incompetence, using a durable power of attorney or other document. Some patients both appoint a proxy and execute a treatment directive. Proxy appointments raise some different sources of concern than treatment directives.

The appointed proxy may later seem to be the wrong surrogate decision maker. This concern may arise for one of several reasons. The proxy may have had no involvement in the patient's health planning and may not even realize that the patient has chosen him or her as proxy. To avoid this problem the physician should encourage the patient both to secure the proxy's acceptance of the appointment and to consider involving the proxy in the process of making decisions about future care. The proxy will then be prepared to discharge the function and will have some knowledge of the patient's wishes. The physician should also encourage the patient to tell family members and other intimates who the chosen proxy is, especially since some patients will prefer to designate a proxy from outside their families. This will reduce the chance of surprise and disagreement later.

Physicians may nonetheless encounter appointed proxies with little previous involvement in the patient's planning process and daily life. Yet a patient's designation of a proxy is an exercise in self-determination. The physician is bound to contact that person if the patient loses competence and the appointment goes into effect, rather than ignore the appointment and simply turn to someone else. There may be no further problems, because everyone may agree anyway on what course of treatment the patient would wish. But uncertainty or disagreement about the right choice of treatment may force the resolution of questions about who the most appropriate proxy is. If the medical team or the patient's relatives or other intimates have serious doubts about whether the designated proxy can fulfill the required functions, it is their responsibility to address these doubts through discussion. If the problem cannot be resolved in this way, they may need to seek judicial resolution and the appointment of an alternate.

Sometimes the designated proxy seems inappropriate not because the person is too remote but because the person is so involved that his or her own wishes and interests seem to govern, rather than the patient's. Family members and other intimates almost always have to deal with their own emotional and financial issues in serving as a proxy decision maker, and the mere existence of such issues does not disqualify them. Physicians and other members of the medical team have a responsibility to work with proxies, helping them to identify their own matters of concern, to separate those from the patient's, and to focus on the patient's wishes and interests in making decisions about treatment. Occasionally, the medical team will encounter a proxy who simply cannot do this. If efforts among the involved parties to remedy the problem fail, then care givers may have to seek judicial scrutiny and the appointment of another proxy.

Even a diligent proxy cannot tell what the patient wanted without an explicit treatment directive, so a proxy's choice should carry no particular weight. Family members, other intimates, and physicians often fail to select the same treatment the patient chooses when asked.[45–49] In one study there was 59 to 88 percent agreement, depending on the illness scenario the researchers posed (kappa ≤ 0.3 in all cases)[45]; in another study, agreement was 52 to 90 percent (kappa ≤ 0.4 in all cases).[49] Advising the proxy to choose as the patient would, rather than simply asking for a recommendation, seems to act as a partial corrective.[46]

These data should come as no surprise. Even a person's relatives and other intimates are not clairvoyant and may not share identical values. Moreover, proxies are not always adequately informed that their choices for the patient must be based on the patient's wishes and interests, even when those do not accord with the proxy's. Yet there is often no one better informed about the patient's past values and preferences than the proxy, and the patient in any case has manifested trust by appointing that person. Physicians should encourage patients not only to appoint a proxy, but also

to provide instructions to guide the proxy. Physicians should also explicitly clarify for the proxy the primacy of the patient's wishes and interests.

The proxy may make a treatment choice contrary to the patient's treatment directive, claiming that the proxy appointment takes precedence over the directive. Some patients will appoint a proxy and leave no treatment directive or other instructions to limit the proxy's authority. Others will guide their proxy by writing a treatment directive or other record of preferences.[5] Problems may then arise if the proxy tries to override the preferences. The law in individual states often directly addresses the relation between proxy appointments and treatment directives.[50–53] In general, the proxy is ethically and legally bound to effectuate the patient's treatment choices. When the patient has failed to make explicit treatment choices, either in a treatment directive or orally, the proxy is bound to extrapolate from what is known of the patient's values and preferences to determine as best he or she can what the patient would want; this is typically labeled an exercise in "substituted judgment." If not enough is known of the patient's values and preferences to ground such a judgment, the proxy is bound to decide in the patient's best interests. A proxy's authority is thus governed by certain decision-making standards, and the proxy is obligated to honor the patient's wishes, whether stated in a treatment directive or elsewhere. One caveat has been noted: there is some disagreement over whether a proxy can override a treatment directive that seriously threatens an incompetent but conscious patient's best interests.

The proxy may make a decision with which the physician or institution disagrees. This is not a problem peculiar to appointed proxies or advance directives. Disagreement surfaces with some frequency between physicians and patients, families, other intimates, and proxies. As always, it is crucial for the physician to discuss the disagreement with the relevant decision maker, attempting to understand the source and resolve the matter. If resolution is elusive, others within the institution can sometimes assist. Judicial resolution is available if all else fails.

One source of disagreement deserves special mention. The proxy (or for that matter, the treatment directive itself) may state a treatment choice that the individual physician believes he or she cannot carry out as a matter of conscience or that violates the commitments and mission of the institution. There has been scholarly discussion[54,55] and some adjudication[56] of the circumstances under which institutions and physicians or other care givers can exempt themselves from carrying out treatment choices. Care givers and institutions are not free to impose unwanted treatment. The PSDA recognizes, however, that a number of states (such as New York) allow providers to assert objections of conscience.[57] Before a patient is admitted, institutions should give notice of any limitation on their willingness to implement treatment choices. Similarly, an individual physician should give as much notice as possible and should assist in the orderly transfer of the patient to a physician who can carry out those choices.

CONCLUSION

Advance directives have provoked a number of reservations. As the PSDA goes into effect, requiring discussion and implementation of directives, it will be essential to address physicians' further reservations as they arise.

Yet that necessary step will not be sufficient to ensure that the PSDA produces more benefit than harm. There is a risk that written advance directives may wrongly come to be viewed as the only way to make treatment decisions for the future. Physicians and other care givers may improperly begin to require an advance directive before treatment may be forgone for incompetent patients. To avoid this, staff education must include discussion of the various ways to decide about life-sustaining treatment and plan future care. Even under the PSDA, not all patients will use advance directives.

There is a further risk of confusion about the procedures and materials to use in implementing the PSDA. All personnel in the relevant institutions will need clarification of the step-by-step process to be followed with patients, the written materials to use, and how to resolve specific questions. The information conveyed to patients must be understandable, accurate in summarizing the patients' rights, and sensitively communicated. All staff members who are involved must be trained. Institutions must design appropriate protocols.

Finally, there is a risk that the PSDA will reduce the discussion of treatment options and directives to a bureaucratic process dominated by brochures and forms. To avoid this, the discussion of advance directives must be part of an ongoing dialogue between physician and patient about the patient's health status and future. Doctors must accept responsibility for initiating these discussions and conducting them skillfully. Such discussions should begin early in the patient's relationship with the doctor, and the content of directives should be reviewed periodically. Institutions and organizations should set up complementary systems to support this effort. The PSDA's requirements must become not a ceiling but a floor — a catalyst for broader innovation to integrate directives into good patient care.

Susan M. Wolf, J.D.
Philip Boyle, Ph.D.
Daniel Callahan, Ph.D.
Joseph J. Fins, M.D.
Bruce Jennings, M.A.
James Lindemann Nelson, Ph.D.
Jeremiah A. Barondess, M.D.
Dan W. Brock, Ph.D.
Rebecca Dresser, J.D.
Linda Emanuel, M.D., Ph.D.
Sandra Johnson, J.D.
John Lantos, M.D.
DaCosta R. Mason, J.D.
Mathy Mezey, Ed.D., R.N.
David Orentlicher, M.D., J.D.
Fenella Rouse, J.D.

REFERENCES

1. Omnibus Budget Reconciliation Act of 1990. Pub. L. No. 101–508 §§ 4206, 4751 (codified in scattered sections of 42 U.S.C., especially §§ 1395cc, 1396a (West Supp. 1991)).

2. President's Commission for the Study of Ethical Problems in Medicine and Biomedical and Behavioral Research. Making health care decisions: the ethical and legal implications of informed consent in the patient-practitioner relationship. Vol. 1. Report. Washington, D.C.: Government Printing Office, 1982.

3. Guidelines on the termination of life-sustaining treatment and the care of the dying. Bloomington, Ind.: Indiana University Press and the Hastings Center, 1987.

4. Emanuel LL, Barry MJ, Stoeckle JD, Ettelson LM, Emanuel EJ. Advance directives for medical care — a case for greater use. N Engl J Med 1991; 324:889–95.

5. Annas GJ. The health care proxy and the living will. N Engl J Med 1991;324:1210–3.

6. La Puma J, Orentlicher D, Moss RJ. Advance directives on admission: clinical implications and analysis of the Patient Self-Determination Act of 1990. JAMA 1991;266:402–5.

7. Gamble ER, McDonald PJ, Lichstein PR. Knowledge, attitudes, and behavior of elderly persons regarding living wills. Arch Intern Med 1991;151:277–80.

8. Knox RA. Poll: Americans favor mercy killing. Boston Globe, November 3, 1991:1, 22.

9. Cruzan v. Director, Mo. Dep't of Health, 110 S. Ct. 2841 (1990).

10. Society for the Right to Die. Refusal of treatment legislation: a state by state compilation of enacted and model statutes. New York: Society for the Right to Die, 1991.

11. Meisel A. The right to die. New York: John Wiley, 1989.

12. Danis M, Southerland LI, Garrett JM, et al. A prospective study of advance directives for life-sustaining care. N Engl J Med 1991;324:882–8.

13. White ML, Fletcher JC. The Patient Self-Determination Act: on balance, more help than hindrance. JAMA 1991;266:410–2.

14. Greco PJ, Schulman KA, Lavizzo-Mourey R, Hansen-Flaschen J. The Patient Self-Determination Act and the future of advance directives. Ann Intern Med 1991;115:639–43.

15. Teno J, Fleishman J, Brock DW, Mor V. The use of formal prior directives among patients with HIV-related diseases. J Gen Intern Med 1990;5:490–4.

16. Davidson KW, Hackler C, Caradine DR, McCord RS. Physicians' attitudes on advance directives. JAMA 1989;262:2415–9.

17. Brett AS. Limitations of listing specific medical interventions in advance directives. JAMA 1991;266:825–8.

18. Lo B, McLeod GA, Saika G. Patient attitudes to discussing life-sustaining treatment. Arch Intern Med 1986;146:1613–5.

19. Emanuel LL, Emanuel EJ. The medical directive: a new comprehensive advance care document. JAMA 1989;261:3288–93.

20. Kohn M, Menon G. Life prolongation: views of elderly outpatients and health care professionals. J Am Geriatr Soc 1988;36: 840–4.

21. McCrary SV, Botkin JR. Hospital policy on advance directives: do institutions ask patients about living wills? JAMA 1989;262:2411–4.

22. Shmerling RH, Bedell SE, Lilienfeld A, Delbanco TL. Discussing cardiopulmonary resuscitation: a study of elderly outpatients. J Gen Intern Med 1988;3:317–21.

23. Finucane TE, Shumway JM, Powers RL, D'Alessandri RM. Planning with elderly outpatients for contingencies of severe illness: a survey and clinical trial. J Gen Intern Med 1988;3:322–5.

24. Ackerman F. Not everybody wants to sign a living will. New York Times. October 13, 1989:A32.

25. Molloy DW, Guyatt GH. A comprehensive health care directive in a home for the aged. Can Med Assoc J 1991;145:307–11.

26. Callahan D. Medical futility, medical necessity: the problem-without-a-name. Hastings Cent Rep 1991;21(4):30–5.

27. Youngner SJ. Futility in context. JAMA 1990;264:1295–6.

28. Idem. Who defines futility? JAMA 1988;260:2094–5.

29. Lantos JD, Singer PA, Walker RM, et al. The illusion of futility in clinical practice. Am J Med 1989;87:81–4.

30. Emanuel LL. Does the DNR order need life-sustaining intervention? Time for comprehensive advance directives. Am J Med 1989;86:87–90.

31. Orentlicher D. The right to die after Cruzan. JAMA 1990;264:2444–6.

32. Weir RF, Gostin L. Decisions to abate life-sustaining treatment for non-autonomous patients: ethical standards and legal liability for physicians after Cruzan. JAMA 1990;264:1846–53.

33. Hardin SB, Welch HG, Fisher ES. Should advance directives be obtained in the hospital? A review of patient competence during hospitalizations prior to death. Clin Res 1991;39:626A. abstract.

34. Doukas DJ, McCullough LB. The values history: the evaluation of the patient's values and advance directives. J Fam Pract 1991;32:145–53.

35. Gibson JM. National values history project. Generations 1990;14:Suppl:51–64.

36. Eisendrath SJ, Jonsen AR. The living will: help or hindrance? JAMA 1983;249:2054–8.

37. North Carolina Gen. Stat. § 90–321(a)(2) (1991).

38. Forrow L, Gogel E, Thomas E. Advance directives for medical care. N Engl J Med 1991;325:1255.

39. Emanuel L. The health care directive: learning how to draft advance care documents. J Am Geriatr Soc 1991;39:1221–8.

40. Dresser RS. Advance directives, self-determination, and personal identity. In: Hackler C, Moseley R, Vawter DE, eds. Advance directives in medicine. New York: Praeger Publishers, 1989:155–70.

41. Buchanan AE, Brock DW. Deciding for others: the ethics of surrogate decision making. New York: Cambridge University Press, 1989:152–89.

42. Everhart, MA, Pearlman RA. Stability of patient preferences regarding life-sustaining treatments. Chest 1990;97:159–64.

43. Silverstein MD, Stocking CB, Antel JP, Beckwith J, Roos RP, Siegler M. Amyotrophic lateral sclerosis and life-sustaining therapy: patients' desires for information, participation in decision making, and life-sustaining therapy. May Clin Proc 1991;66:906–13.

44. Emanuel LL, Barry MJ, Stoeckle JD, Emanuel EJ. A detailed advance care directive: practicality and durability. Clin Res 1990;38:738A. abstract.

45. Seckler AB, Meier DE, Mulvihill M, Paris BEC. Substituted judgement: how accurate are proxy predictions? Ann Intern Med 1991;115:92–8.

46. Tomlinson T, Howe K, Notman M, Rossmiller D. An empirical study of proxy consent for elderly persons. Gerontologist 1990;30:54–64.

47. Zweibel NR, Cassel CK. Treatment choices at the end of life: a comparison of decisions by older patients and their physician-selected proxies. Gerontologist 1989;29:615–21.

48. Ouslander JG, Tymchuk AJ, Rahbar B. Health care decisions among elderly long-term care residents and their potential proxies. Arch Intern Med 1989; 149:1367–72.

49. Uhlmann RF, Pearlman RA, Cain KC. Physicians' and spouses' predictions of elderly patients' resuscitation preferences. J Gerontol 1988;43:M115–M121.

50. Kansas Stat. Ann. § 58–629 (Supp. 1990).

51. Vermont Stat. Ann. tit. 14, §§ 3453, 3463 (Supp. 1991).

52. West Virginia Code § 16–30A–4 (Supp. 1991).

53. Wisconsin Stat. Ann. § 155.20 (1989–90).

54. Annas GJ. Transferring the ethical hot potato. Hastings Cent Rep 1987;17(1):20–1.

55. Miles SH, Singer PA, Siegler M. Conflicts between patients' wishes to forgo treatment and the policies of health care facilities. N Engl J Med 1989;321:48–50.

56. In re Jobes, 529 A.2d 434 (N.J. 1987).

57. New York Pub. Health Law § 2984 (McKinney Supp. 1991).

MARGOT L. WHITE AND JOHN C. FLETCHER

The Patient Self-Determination Act: On Balance, More Help Than Hindrance

The Patient Self-Determination Act (hereafter, the Act), which took effect on December 1, 1991, creates no new rights for patients or for citizens generally. The law requires Medicare/Medicaid-receiving health care providers to inform patients of their existing rights under state law to refuse treatment and prepare advance directives. By doing so, it merely affirms principles that have their roots in both common law and constitutional law dating back to the late 19th century. ("[N]o right is held more sacred, or is more carefully guarded, by the common law, than the right of every individual to the possession and control of his person, free from all restraint or interference of others, unless by clear and unquestionable authority of law."[1]) Legal and ethical principles that govern decision making about medical treatment, familiar to most clinicians as the doctrine of informed consent, have played a significant role in clinical decision making for decades and are the cornerstone of modern clinical ethics. State courts since 1914 have repeatedly affirmed the right of competent adults to determine for themselves the kind of health care they wish to receive or refuse. ("Every human being of adult years and sound mind has a right to determine what shall be done with his own body; and a surgeon who performs an operation without his patient's consent commits an assault, for which he is liable in damages."[2]) This common law right of self-determination was recently

declared a federal constitutional "liberty interest" guaranteed by the 14th Amendment.[3]

The so-called advance directive, whereby competent individuals may indicate their consent to or refusal of health care under conditions that have yet to materialize, is a more recent development. Advance directives may take the form of instructional directives for end-of-life care ("living wills") or the appointment of a proxy decision maker to serve in the event of the patient's incapacity (known variously as health care proxy, medical power of attorney, durable power of attorney for health care, living will designee), or both. Since the first "Natural Death Act" was enacted in California in 1976, more than 40 states have provided a statutory basis for the use of advance directives, and many state courts have recognized their validity even where there is no statutory basis. The federal constitutional guarantee means that the exercise of the right to self-determination in health care is independent of the state in which the patient is located.

The reasons to welcome the provisions of the Act are not legal but medical and ethical: by and large, advance directives will greatly assist clinicians, patients and family members, and other surrogates with increasingly complex health care decision making. Advance directives, however, are not without significant flaws, as the article . . . by La Puma et al[4] points out. Most of these flaws, though, are inherent in clinical decision making itself and are not attributes of advance directives per se. Prognostic uncertainty, for example, has been cited as a factor that may increase the difficulty of implementing a living will.[5] Diagnostic

Reprinted by permission of the publisher from Margot L. White and John Fletcher, "The Patient Self-Determination Act: On Balance, More Help than Hindrance," *JAMA* 266, No. 3, July 17, 1991, pp. 410–12. ©1991 the American Medical Association.

and prognostic uncertainties are not cause by living wills, but decision making may become more problematic when the patient's preferences must be factored into an already complex equation.

The fact that a patient's written living will is subject to interpretation and may be vague and often difficult to apply to the circumstances at hand is a valid criticism. However, vagueness and imprecision are certainly no less present in anecdotal evidence, fragments of recollected conversations, or other forms of verbal "hearsay" on which clinical decisions, including terminal care decisions, are most often based. The very nature of advance directives is that they are anticipatory; they cannot be as precise as an informed decision made by a competent patient at the time of treatment. The health care proxy is the patient's "stand-in" during periods of incapacity; he or she is likely to have had relevant discussions with the patient and so can be an invaluable help in interpreting and applying the intent of the patient's written instructions.[5,6]

The Act neither requires nor assumes that all, or even most, patients will complete living wills or formally appoint health care proxies. Rather, it is intended simply to provide those patients who wish to do so with the choice of using this method of health care planning. The law explicitly prohibits differential treatment of patients on the basis of the presence or absence of an advance directive, or requiring patients to complete one. Advance directives are unnecessary for many people, particularly those with close and intact families. Indeed, some cultures and religions would find this method of personal decision making highly repugnant. Many elderly individuals may be more comfortable with established patterns of deference to their physicians.

One purpose of advance directives is to avoid recourse to the courts to resolve difficulties associated with decision making for incapacitated patients.[7] Two common sources of physician anxiety in decisions to withdraw life-sustaining treatment are uncertainty regarding the identity of the appropriate decision maker and uncertainty about the range or scope of his or her authority. Granting legal authority to patient-selected proxies does not mean that whatever the proxy decides is legally enforceable. Hospital attorneys whose area of expertise is corporate law and whose client is the hospital and not the patient may provide misleading or inaccurate information about state laws relating to withdrawal of treatment. Hospital attorneys and

risk managers should be included in educational efforts undertaken in compliance with the Act.

Fears of liability for refusing to comply with patients' or their surrogates' demands for medically inappropriate, useless, or harmful treatments, tests, or procedures are utterly baseless. Legal advice to the contrary is simply wrong. Whether from an attorney, a risk manager, a senior clinician, or the patient's proxy, advice to initiate or continue treatment believed to be unwanted by the now-incapacitated patient but insisted on by the proxy should be carefully reviewed by an institutional mechanism such as an ethics committee or ethics consultation service. In these circumstances, such internal review is preferable to judicial review and is usually sufficient to resolve the difficulty and arrive at an appropriate decision. Advance directives cannot in themselves entirely safeguard patients from questionable motives, conflicts of interest, or unreasonable requests on the part of their surrogate decision makers. However, the careful prior designation of the proxy by the patient, combined with written or oral evidence of his or her treatment preferences, concern, and requests, increases the likelihood that, in the event problems do arise, they can be resolved in the clinical setting rather than in a judicial one.

La Puma et al raise the valid concern that cost containment rather than patient well-being may have been a primary motive for passage of the legislation. It is probably safe to say that in recent years a good many of the health care regulations that have come from federal sources have had cost containment as their major, if not primary, goal. The ethical concern is certainly not cost containment per se, but the danger that institutional financial considerations will constitute some form of "undue influence" or subtle coercion applied to patients or their families to limit care inappropriately. This concern is well founded and strongly suggests that internal procedural review mechanisms, ethics committees, or bedside ethics consultants may be helpful in protecting patients from such occurrences.

At the same time, concerns about the cost-containment motives of Congress or the dangers of pressuring patients into refusing expensive treatments should perhaps be placed in historical perspective. Specifically, it is important to keep in mind that nearly all of the more than 50 "right to die" decisions that have emanated from our state courts since the landmark *Quinlan* decision in 1976 were initiated by patients and/or families on behalf of patients. Clearly, the impetus for the use of advance directives has come from patients, not from providers or insurance companies. Patients may well choose to avoid marginally beneficial or nearly futile procedures toward the end of life in part because of the financial drain on their surviving family members. Certainly, cost containment is not an unethical motive in and of itself: the issue is rather who decides what costs are contained and when. The crucial ethical responsibility is to ensure that the patient, and not the institution, the third-party payers, or even the patient's (interested) relatives, make this decision. It would seem to us that decisions to limit treatment would ethically "belong" to the health care provider only when the treatment requested is inappropriate or medically useless.

We emphatically agree with La Puma et al that acute-care hospitals and nursing homes are not optimal settings for first discussions of advance directives. We have stated elsewhere[8] that the Act offers an opportunity for institutionally based health care providers to choose between a minimalist position, in which legalistic, written information is distributed mechanically by uninformed hospital admissions clerks (the "medical *Miranda*" approach) and an ethically optimal approach in which an institutional ethics program educates staff, patients, and community in the issues that led to the Act in the first place.

The fact that hospital admission is not the best time to initiate discussions about advance directives is not an argument against advance directives themselves. Rather, it is an indication that patients need to be able to discuss with someone knowledgeable the role of an advance directive in their care. It indicates also that physicians need to pay more, not less, attention to enhancing the patient's ability to articulate personal values and preferences in all clinical encounters, at all stages of life, so that the patient's pattern of choice is clearly documented over time.

Ideally, discussions of living wills should begin in the primary care setting, not in an attorney's office, as part of patients' ongoing participation in their own health management. Studies show that both patients and physicians believe that discussions about treatment preferences should take place and both would prefer that they occur prior to a critical or terminal phase of illness, when patients are well and during a routine office visit.[9] Yet, as La Puma et al point out, the same studies indicate that such discussions are not taking place in a routine, ongoing, deliberate fashion. It appears that patients and physicians each wait for the other to raise this sensitive subject. Communication is usually postponed until the patient is no longer capable of participating in the decision-making process.

We agree wholeheartedly with the caution that these discussions and deliberations must be part of a *clinical* process, and not an administrative—or legalistic—one. We also believe, though, that if the clinical process is not developing, an administrative nudge such as the Act may prove a helpful stimulus. Contrary to La Puma et al, we would urge that hospitals distribute advance directives to patients along with other admission or preadmission materials, provided that patients are assured of an opportunity to talk about these matters in the hospital with the health professionals involved in their care.

Hospitals and schools of medicine and nursing may use the educational mandate of the Act as an opportunity to develop new methods of staff and student education. For example, in one program already under way, 20 first-year residents in internal medicine use advance directives to improve their communication skills with patients.[10] This program, although unrelated to the Act, illustrates an innovative and effective approach to increasing the likelihood that physicians will more readily initiate discussions with patients about treatment preferences prior to the onset of incapacity or terminal illness.

As La Puma et al point out, the reasons for the relatively low incidence of written advance directives among the population in general from 1976 to the present are not well understood. However, it is difficult to know the value and the utility of these instruments for the patient population as a whole so long as there is no mechanism for broadly based, consistent, and deliberate educational efforts about advance directives. The Patient Self-Determination Act mandates such efforts, not only for patients, but also for clinical staff and for communities. We would, therefore, go beyond the recommendation of La Puma et al that the Secretary of Health and Human Services provide research funds to study the limited use of written directives; we would urge that such funds be directed toward research to identify and remove the barriers to effective and timely communication between patients and physicians about treatment choices.

1. *Union Pacific R Co v Botsford,* 141 US 250 (1891).

2. *Schloendorff v Society of New York Hosp,* 211 NY, 125, 105 NE 92 (1914).

3. *Cruzan v Director, Missouri Dept of Health,* 110 S Ct 2841, 1990.

4. La Puma J, Orentlicher D, Moss RJ. Advance directives on admission: clinical implications and analysis of the Patient Self-Determination Act of 1990. *JAMA.* 1991;266:402–405.

5. Eisendrath, SJ, Jonsen AR. The living will: help or hindrance? *JAMA.* 1983;249:2054–2058.

6. Annas GJ. The health care proxy and the living will. *N Engl J Med.* 1991;324:1210–1213.

7. Meisel A. *The Right to Die.* New York, NY: John Wiley & Sons Inc; 1989.

8. Fletcher JC, White ML. Patient Self-Determination Act to become law: how should institutions prepare? *Biolaw.* 1991; 2(46–47):S509–S514.

9. Gamble ER, McDonald PJ, Lichstein PR. Knowledge, attitudes and behavior of elderly persons regarding living wills. *Arch Intern Med.* 1991;151:277–280.

10. Gordon CH, Tolle SW. Discussing life-sustaining treatment: A teaching program for residents. *Arch Intern Med.* 1991; 151:567–570.

Managing Information in Randomized Clinical Trials

SAMUEL HELLMAN AND DEBORAH S. HELLMAN

Of Mice but Not Men: Problems of the Randomized Clinical Trial

As medicine has become increasingly scientific and less accepting of unsupported opinion or proof by anecdote, the randomized controlled clinical trial has become the standard technique for changing diagnostic or therapeutic methods. The use of this technique creates an ethical dilemma.[1,2] Researchers participating in such studies are required to modify their ethical commitments to individual patients and do serious damage to the concept of the physician as a practicing, empathetic professional who is primarily concerned with each patient as an individual. Researchers using a randomized clinical trial can be described as physician-scientists, a term that expresses the tension between the two roles. The physician, by entering into a relationship with an individual patient, assumes certain obligations, including the commitment always to act in the patient's best interests. As Leon Kass has rightly maintained, "the physician must produce unswervingly the virtues of loyalty and fidelity to his patient."[3] Though the ethical requirements of this relationship have been modified by legal obligations to report wounds of a suspicious nature and certain infectious diseases, these obligations in no way conflict with the central ethical obligation to act in the best interests of the patient medically. Instead, certain nonmedical interests of the patient are preempted by other social concerns.

The role of the scientist is quite different. The clinical scientist is concerned with answering questions—

Reprinted by permission of the publisher from Samuel Hellman and Deborah S. Hellman, "Of Mice but Not Men: Problems of the Randomized Clinical Trial," *New England Journal of Medicine* 324, No. 22, May 30, 1991 ,pp. 1585–89.

i.e., determining the validity of formally constructed hypotheses. Such scientific information, it is presumed, will benefit humanity in general. The clinical scientist's role has been well described by Dr. Anthony Fauci, director of the National Institute of Allergy and Infectious Diseases, who states the goals of the randomized clinical trial in these words: "It's not to delivery therapy. It's to answer a scientific question so that the drug can be available for everybody once you've established safety and efficacy."[4] The demands of such a study can conflict in a number of ways with the physician's duty to minister to patients. The study may create a false dichotomy in the physician's opinions: according to the premise of the randomized clinical trial, the physician may only know or not know whether a proposed course of treatment represents an improvement; no middle position is permitted. What the physician thinks, suspects, believes, or has a hunch about is assigned to the "not knowing" category, because knowing is defined on the basis of an arbitrary but accepted statistical test performed in a randomized clinical trial. Thus, little credence is given to information gained beforehand in other ways or to information accrued during the trial but without the required statistical degree of assurance that a difference is not due to chance. The randomized clinical trial also prevents the treatment technique from being modified on the basis of the growing knowledge of the physicians during their participation in the trial. Moreover, it limits access to the data as they are collected until specific milestones are achieved. This prevents physicians from profiting not only from their individual experience, but also from the collective experience of the other participants.

The randomized clinical trial requires doctors to act simultaneously as physicians and as scientists. This puts them in a difficult and sometimes untenable ethical position. The conflicting moral demands arising from the use of the randomized clinical trial reflect the classic conflict between rights-based moral theories and utilitarian ones. The first of these, which depend on the moral theory of Immanuel Kant (and seen more recently in neo-Kantian philosophers, such as John Rawls[5]), asserts that human beings, by virtue of their unique capacity for rational thought, are bearers of dignity. As such, they ought not to be treated merely as means to an end; rather, they must always be treated as ends in themselves. Utilitarianism, by contrast, defines what is right as the greatest good for the greatest number—that is, as social utility. This view, articulated by Jeremy Bentham and John Stuart Mill, requires that pleasures (understood broadly, to include such pleasures as health and well-being) and pains be added together. The morally correct act is the act that produces the most pleasure and the least pain overall.

A classic objection to the utilitarian position is that according to that theory, the distribution of pleasures and pains is of no moral consequence. This element of the theory severely restricts physicians from being utilitarians, or at least from following the theory's dictates. Physicians must care very deeply about the distribution of pain and pleasure, for they have entered into a relationship with one or a number of individual patients. They cannot be indifferent to whether it is these patients or others that suffer for the general benefit of society. Even though society might gain from the suffering of a few, and even though the doctor might believe that such a benefit is worth a given patient's suffering (i.e., that utilitarianism is right in the particular case), the ethical obligation created by the covenant between doctor and patient requires the doctor to see the interests of the individual patient as primary and compelling. In essence, the doctor–patient relationship requires doctors to see their patients as bearers of rights who cannot be merely used for the greater good of humanity.

As Fauci has suggested,[4] the randomized clinical trial routinely asks physicians to sacrifice the interests of their particular patients for the sake of the study and that of the information that it will make available for the benefit of society. This practice is ethically problematic. Consider first the initial formulation of a trial. In particular, consider the case of a disease for which there is no satisfactory therapy—for example, advanced cancer or the acquired immunodeficiency syndrome (AIDS). A new agent that promises more effectiveness is the subject of the study. The control group must be given either an unsatisfactory treatment or a placebo. Even though the therapeutic value of the new agent is unproved, if physicians think that it has promise, are they acting in the best interests of their patients in allowing them to be randomly assigned to the control group? Is persisting in such an assignment consistent with the specific commitments taken on in the doctor–patient relationship? As a result of interactions with patients with AIDS and their advocates, Merigan[6] recently suggested modifications in the design of clinical trials that attempt to deal with the unsatisfactory treatment given to the control group. The view of such activists has been expressed by Rebecca Pringle Smith of Community Research Initiative in New York: "Even if you have a supply of compliant martyrs, trials must have some ethical validity."[4]

If the physician has no opinion about whether the new treatment is acceptable, then random assignment is ethically acceptable, but such lack of enthusiasm for the new treatment does not augur well for either the patient or the study. Alternatively, the treatment may show promise of beneficial results but also present a risk of undesirable complications. When the physician believes that the severity and likelihood of harm and good are evenly balanced, randomization may be ethically acceptable. If the physician has no preference for either treatment (is in a state of equipoise),[7,8] then randomization is acceptable. If, however, he or she believes that the new treatment may be either more or less successful or more or less toxic, the use of randomization is not consistent with fidelity to the patient.

The argument usually used to justify randomization is that it provides, in essence, a critique of the usefulness of the physician's beliefs and opinions, those that have not yet been validated by a randomized clinical trial. As the argument goes, these not-yet-validated beliefs are as likely to be wrong as right. Although physicians are ethically required to provide their patients with the best available treatment, there simply is no best treatment yet known.

The reply to this argument takes two forms. First, and most important, even if this view of the reliability of a physician's opinions is accurate, the ethical constraints of an individual doctor's relationship with a particular patient require the doctor to provide individual care. Although physicians must take pains to make clear the speculative nature of their views, they cannot withhold these views from the patient. The patient asks from the doctor both knowledge and judgment. The relationship established between them rightfully allows patients to ask for the judgment of their particular physicians, not merely that of the medical profession in general. Second, it may not be true, in fact, that the not-yet-validated beliefs of physicians are as likely to be wrong as right. The greater certainty obtained with a randomized clinical trial is beneficial, but that does not mean that a lesser degree of certainty is without value. Physicians can acquire knowledge through methods other than the randomized clinical trial. Such knowledge, acquired over time and less formally than is required in a randomized clinical trial, may be of great value to a patient.

Even if it is ethically acceptable to begin a study, one often forms an opinion during its course—especially in studies that are impossible to conduct in a truly double-blinded fashion—that makes it ethically problematic to continue. The inability to remain blinded usually occurs in studies of cancer or AIDS, for example, because the therapy is associated by nature with serious side effects. Trials attempt to restrict the physician's access to the data in order to prevent such unblinding. Such restrictions should make physicians eschew the trial, since their ability to act in the patient's best interests will be limited. Even supporters of randomized clinical trials, such as Merigan, agree that interim findings should be presented to patients to ensure that no one receives what seems an inferior treatment.[6] Once physicians have formed a view about the new treatment, can they continue randomization? If random assignment is stopped, the study may be lost and the participation of the previous patients wasted. However, if physicians continue the randomization when they have a definite opinion about the efficacy of the experimental drug, they are not acting in accordance with the requirements of the doctor–patient relationship. Furthermore, as their opinion becomes more firm, stopping the randomization may not be enough. Physicians may be ethically required to treat the patients formerly placed in the control group with the therapy that now seems probably effective. To do so would be faithful to the obligations created by the doctor–patient relationship, but it would destroy the study.

To resolve this dilemma, one might suggest that the patient has abrogated the rights implicit in a doctor–patient relationship by signing an informed-consent form. We argue that such rights cannot be waived or abrogated. They are inalienable. The right to be treated as an individual deserving the physician's best judgment and care, rather than to be used as a means to determine the best treatment for others, is inherent in every person. This right, based on the concept of dignity, cannot be waived. What of altruism, then? Is it not the patient's right to make a sacrifice for the general good? This question must be considered from both positions—that of the patient and that of the physician. Although patients may decide to waive this right, it is not consistent with the role of a physician to ask that they do so. In asking, the doctor acts as a scientist instead. The physician's role here is to propose what he or she believes is best medically for the specific patient, not to suggest participation in a study from which the patient cannot gain. Because the opportunity to help future patients is of potential value to a patient, some would say physicians should not deny it. Although this point has merit, it offers so many opportunities for abuse that we are extremely uncomfortable about accepting it. The responsibilities of physicians are much clearer; they are to minister to the current patient.

Moreover, even if patients could waive this right, it is questionable whether those with terminal illness would be truly able to give voluntary informed consent. Such patients are extremely dependent on both their physicians and the health care system. Aware of this dependence, physicians must not ask for consent, for in such cases the very asking breaches the doctor–patient relationship. Anxious to please their physicians, patients may have difficulty refusing to participate in the trial the physicians describe. The patients may perceive their refusal as damaging to the relationship, whether or not it is so. Such perceptions of coercion affect the decision. Informed-consent forms are difficult to understand, especially for patients under the stress of serious illness for which there is no satisfactory treatment. The forms are usually lengthy, somewhat legalistic, complicated, and confusing, and they hardly bespeak the compassion expected of the medical profession. It is important to remember that those who have studied the doctor–patient relationship have emphasized its empathetic nature.

[The] relationship between doctor and patient partakes of a peculiar intimacy. It presupposes on the part of the physician not only knowledge of his fellow men but sympathy. . . . This aspect of the practice of medicine has been designated as the art; yet I wonder whether it should not, most properly, be called the essence.[9]

How is such a view of the relationship consonant with random assignment and informed consent? The Physician's Oath of the World Medical Association affirms the primacy of the deontologic view of patients' rights: "Concern for the interests of the subject must always prevail over the interests of science and society."[10]

Furthermore, a single study is often not considered sufficient. Before a new form of therapy is generally accepted, confirmatory trials must be conducted. How can one conduct such trials ethically unless one is convinced that the first trial was in error? The ethical problems we have discussed are only exacerbated when a completed randomized clinical trial indicates that a given treatment is preferable. Even if the physician believes the initial trial was in error, the physician must indicate to the patient the full results of that trial.

The most common reply to the ethical arguments has been that the alternative is to return to the physician's intuition, to anecdotes, or to both as the basis of medical opinion. We all accept the dangers of such a practice. The argument states that we must therefore accept randomized, controlled clinical trials regardless of their ethical problems because of the great social benefit they make possible, and we salve our conscience with the knowledge that informed consent has been given. This returns us to the conflict between patients' rights and social utility. Some would argue that this tension can be resolved by placing a relative value on each. If the patient's right that is being compromised is not a fundamental right and the social gain is very great, then the study might be justified. When the right is fundamental, however, no amount of social gain, or almost none, will justify its sacrifice. Consider, for example, the experiments on humans done by physicians under the Nazi regime. All would agree that these are unacceptable regardless of the value of the scientific information gained. Some people go so far as to say that no use should be made of the results of those experiments because of the clearly unethical manner in which the data were collected. This extreme example may not seem relevant, but we believe that in its hyperbole it clarifies the fallacy of a utilitarian approach to the physician's relationship with the patient. To consider the utilitarian gain is consistent neither with the physician's role nor with the patient's rights.

It is fallacious to suggest that only the randomized clinical trial can provide valid information or that all information acquired by this technique is valid. Such experimental methods are intended to reduce error and bias and therefore reduce the uncertainty of the result. Uncertainty cannot be eliminated, however. The scientific method is based on increasing probabilities and increasingly refined approximations of truth.[11] Although the randomized clinical trial contributes to these ends, it is neither unique nor perfect. Other techniques may also be useful.[12]

Randomized trials often place physicians in the ethically intolerable position of choosing between the good of the patient and that of society. We urge that such situations be avoided and that other techniques of acquiring clinical information be adopted. For example, concerning trials of treatments for AIDS, Byar et al.[13] have said that "some traditional approaches to the clinical-trials process may be unnecessarily rigid and unsuitable for this disease." In this case, AIDS is not what is so different; rather, the difference is in the presence of AIDS activists, articulate spokespersons for the ethical problems created by the application of the randomized clinical trial to terminal illnesses. Such arguments are equally applicable to advanced cancer and other serious illnesses. Byar et al. agree that there are even circumstances in which uncontrolled clinical trials may be justified: when there is no effective treatment to use as a control, when the prognosis is uniformly poor, and when there is a reasonable expectation of benefit without excessive toxicity. These conditions are usually found in clinical trials of advanced cancer.

The purpose of the randomized clinical trial is to avoid the problems of observer bias and patient selection. It seems to us that techniques might be developed to deal with these issues in other ways. Randomized clinical trials deal with them in a cumbersome and heavy-handed manner, by requiring large numbers of patients in the hope that random assignment will balance the heterogeneous distribution of patients into the different groups. By observing known characteristics of patients, such as age and sex, and distributing them equally between groups, it is thought that unknown factors important in determining outcomes will also be distributed equally. Surely, other techniques can be developed to deal with both observer bias and patient selection. Prospective studies without randomization, but with the evaluation of patients by uninvolved third parties, should remove observer bias. Similar methods have been suggested by Royall.[12] Prospective matched-pair analysis, in which patients are treated in a manner consistent with their physician's views, ought to help ensure equivalence between the groups and thus mitigate the effect of patient selection, at least with regard to known covariates. With regard to unknown covariates, the security

would rest, as in randomized trials, in the enrollment of large numbers of patients and in confirmatory studies. This method would not pose ethical difficulties, since patients would receive the treatment recommended by their physician. They would be included in the study by independent observers matching patients with respect to known characteristics, a process that would not affect patient care and that could be performed independently any number of times.

This brief discussion of alternatives to randomized clinical trials is sketchy and incomplete. We wish only to point out that there may be satisfactory alternatives, not to describe and evaluate them completely. Even if randomized clinical trials were much better than any alternative, however, the ethical dilemmas they present may put their use at variance with the primary obligations of the physician. In this regard, Angell cautions, "If this commitment to the patient is attenuated, even for so good a cause as benefits to future patients, the implicit assumptions of the doctor–patient relationship are violated."[14] The risk of such attenuation by the randomized trial is great. The AIDS activists have brought this dramatically to the attention of the academic medical community. Techniques appropriate to the laboratory may not be applicable to humans. We must develop and use alternative methods for acquiring clinical knowledge.

REFERENCES

1. Hellman S. Randomized clinical trials and the doctor–patient relationship: an ethical dilemma. Cancer Clin Trials 1979; 2:189–93.

2. *Idem.* A doctor's dilemma: the doctor–patient relationship in clinical investigation. In: Proceedings of the Fourth National Conference on Human Values and Cancer, New York, March 15–17, 1984. New York: American Cancer Society, 1984:144–6.

3. Kass LR. Toward a more natural science: biology and human affairs. New York: Free Press, 1985:196.

4. Palca J. AIDS drug trials enter new age. Science 1989; 246:19–21.

5. Rawls J. A theory of justice. Cambridge, Mass.: Belknap Press of Harvard University Press, 1971:183–92, 446–52.

6. Merigan TC. You *can* teach an old dog new tricks — how AIDS trials are pioneering new strategies. N Engl J Med 1990; 323:1341–3.

7. Freedman B. Equipoise and the ethics of clinical research. N Engl J Med 1987; 317:141–5.

8. Singer PA. Lantos JD, Whitington PF, Broelsch CE, Siegler M. Equipoise and the ethics of segmental liver transplantation. Clin Res 1988; 36:539–45.

9. Longcope WT. Methods and medicine. Bull Johns Hopkins Hosp 1932; 50:4–20.

10. Report on medical ethics. World Med Assoc Bull 1949; 1:109, 111.

11. Popper K. The problem of induction. In: Miller D, ed. Popper selections. Princeton, N.J.: Princeton University Press, 1985: 101–17.

12. Royall RM. Ethics and statistics in randomized clinical trials. Stat Sci 1991; 6(1):52–63.

13. Byar DP, Schoenfeld DA, Green SB, et al. Design considerations for AIDS trials. N Engl J Med 1990; 323:1343–8.

14. Angell M. Patients' preferences in randomized clinical trials. N Engl J Med 1984; 310:1385–7.

BENJAMIN FREEDMAN

Equipoise and the Ethics of Clinical Research

There is widespread agreement that ethics requires that each clinical trial begin with an honest null hypothesis.[1,2] In the simplest model, testing a new treatment B on a defined patient population P for which the current accepted treatment is A, it is necessary that the clinical investigator be in a state of genuine uncertainty regarding the comparative merits of treatments A and B for population P. If a physician knows that these treatments are not equivalent, ethics requires that the superior treatment be recommended. Following Fried, I call this state of uncertainty about the relative merits of A and B "equipoise."[3]

Equipoise is an ethically necessary condition in all cases of clinical research. In trials with several arms, equipoise must exist between all arms of the trial; otherwise the trial design should be modified to exclude the inferior treatment. If equipoise is disturbed during the course of a trial, the trial may need to be terminated and all subjects previously enrolled (as well as other patients within the relevant population) may have to be offered the superior treatment. It has been rigorously argued that a trial with a placebo is ethical only in investigating conditions for which there is no known treatment[2]; this argument reflects a special application of the requirement for equipoise. Although equipoise has commonly been discussed in the special context of the ethics of randomized clinical trials,[4,5] it is important to recognize it as an ethical condition of all controlled clinical trials, whether or not they are randomized, placebo-controlled, or blinded.

The recent increase in attention to the ethics of research with human subjects has highlighted problems associated with equipoise. Yet, as I shall attempt to show, contemporary literature, if anything, minimizes those difficulties. Moreover, there is evidence that concern on the part of investigators about failure to satisfy the requirements for equipoise can doom a trial as a result of the consequent failure to enroll a sufficient number of subjects.

The solutions that have been offered to date fail to resolve these problems in a way that would permit clinical trials to proceed. This paper argues that these problems are predicated on a faulty concept of equipoise itself. An alternative understanding of equipoise as an ethical requirement of clinical trials is proposed, and its implications are explored.

Many of the problems raised by the requirement for equipoise are familiar. Shaw and Chalmers have written that a clinician who "knows, or has a good reason to believe," that one arm of the trial is superior may not ethically participate.[6] But the reasoning or preliminary results that prompt the trial (and that may themselves be ethically mandatory)[7] may jolt the investigator (if not his or her colleagues) out of equipoise before the trial begins. Even if the investigator is undecided between A and B in terms of gross measures such as mortality and morbidity, equipoise may be disturbed because evident differences in the

Reprinted by permission of the publisher from Benjamin Freedman, "Equipoise and the Ethics of Clinical Research," *New England Journal of Medicine* 317, No. 3, July 16, 1987, pp. 141–45.

quality of life (as in the case of two surgical approaches) tip the balance.[3-5,8] In either case, in saying "we do not know" whether A or B is better, the investigator may create a false impression in prospective subjects, who hear him or her as saying "no evidence leans either way," when the investigator means "no controlled study has yet had results that reach statistical significance."

Late in the study—when P values are between 0.05 and 0.06—the moral issue of equipoise is most readily apparent,[9,10] but the same problem arises when the earliest comparative results are analyzed.[11] Within the closed statistical universe of the clinical trial, each result that demonstrates a difference between the arms of the trial contributes exactly as much to the statistical conclusion that a difference exists as does any other. The contribution of the last pair of cases in the trial is no greater than that of the first. If, therefore, equipoise is a condition that reflects equivalent evidence for alternative hypotheses, it is jeopardized by the first pair of cases as much as by the last. The investigator who is concerned about the ethics of recruitment after the penultimate pair must logically be concerned after the first pair as well.

Finally, these issues are more than a philosopher's nightmare. Considerable interest has been generated by a paper in which Taylor et al.[12] describe the termination of a trial of alternative treatments for breast cancer. The trial foundered on the problem of patient recruitment, and the investigators trace much of the difficulty in enrolling patients to the fact that the investigators were not in a state of equipoise regarding the arms of the trial. With the increase in concern about the ethics of research and with the increasing presence of this topic in the curricula of medical and graduate schools, instances of the type that Taylor and her colleagues describe are likely to become more common. The requirement for equipoise thus poses a practical threat to clinical research.

RESPONSES TO THE PROBLEMS OF EQUIPOISE

The problems described above apply to a broad class of clinical trials, at all stages of their development. Their resolution will need to be similarly comprehensive. However, the solutions that have so far been proposed address a portion of the difficulties, at best, and cannot be considered fully satisfactory.

Chalmers' approach to problems at the onset of a trial is to recommend that randomization begin with the very first subject.[11] If there are no preliminary, uncontrolled data in support of the experimental treatment B, equipoise regarding treatments A and B for the patient population P is not disturbed. There are several difficulties with this approach. Practically speaking, it is often necessary to establish details of administration, dosage, and so on, before a controlled trial begins, by means of uncontrolled trials in human subjects. In addition, as I have argued above, equipoise from the investigator's point of view is likely to be disturbed when the hypothesis is being formulated and a protocol is being prepared. It is then, before any subjects have been enrolled, that the information that the investigator has assembled makes the experimental treatment appear to be a reasonable gamble. Apart from these problems, initial randomization will not, as Chalmers recognizes, address disturbances of equipoise that occur in the course of a trial.

Data-monitoring committees have been proposed as a solution to problems arising in the course of the trial.[13] Such committees, operating independently of the investigators, are the only bodies with information concerning the trial's ongoing results. Since this knowledge is not available to the investigators, their equipoise is not disturbed. Although committees are useful in keeping the conduct of a trial free of bias, they cannot resolve the investigators' ethical difficulties. A clinician is not merely obliged to treat a patient on the basis of the information that he or she currently has, but is also required to discover information that would be relevant to treatment decisions. If interim results would disturb equipoise, the investigators are obliged to gather and use that information. Their agreement to remain in ignorance of preliminary results would, by definition, be an unethical agreement, just as a failure to call up the laboratory to find out a patient's test results is unethical. Moreover, the use of a monitoring committee does not solve problems of equipoise that arise before and at the beginning of a trial.

Recognizing the broad problems with equipoise, three authors have proposed radical solutions. All three think that there is an irresolvable conflict between the requirement that a patient be offered the best treatment known (the principle underlying requirement for equipoise) and the conduct of clinical trials; they therefore suggest that the "best treatment" requirement be weakened.

Schafer has argued that the concept of equipoise, and the associated notion of the best medical treatment, depends on the judgment of patients rather than of clinical investigators.[14] Although the equipoise of an investigator may be disturbed if he or she favors B over A, the ultimate choice of treatment is the patient's. Because the patient's values may restore equipoise, Schafer argues, it is ethical for the investigator to proceed with a trial when the patient consents. Schafer's strategy is directed toward trials that test treatments with known and divergent side effects and will probably not be useful in trials conducted to test efficacy or unknown side effects. This approach, moreover, confuses the ethics of competent medical practice with those of consent. If we assume that the investigator is a competent clinician, by saying that the investigator is out of equipoise, we have by Schafer's account said that in the investigator's professional judgment one treatment is therapeutically inferior — for that patient, in that condition, given the quality of life that can be achieved. Even if a patient would consent to an inferior treatment, it seems to me a violation of competent medical practice, and hence of ethics, to make the offer. Of course, complex issues may arise when a patient refuses what the physician considers the best treatment and demands instead an inferior treatment. Without settling that problem, however, we can reject Schafer's position. For Schafer claims that in order to continue to conduct clinical trials, it is ethical for the physician to offer (not merely accede to) inferior treatment.

Meier suggests that "most of us would be quite willing to forego a modest expected gain in the general interest of learning something of value."[15] He argues that we accept risks in everyday life to achieve a variety of benefits, including convenience and economy. In the same way, Meier states, it is acceptable to enroll subjects in clinical trials even though they may not receive the best treatment throughout the course of the trial. Schafer suggests an essentially similar approach.[5,14] According to this view, continued progress in medical knowledge through clinical trials requires an explicit abandonment of the doctor's fully patient-centered ethic.

These proposals seem to be frank counsels of desperation. They resolve the ethical problems of equipoise by abandoning the need for equipoise. In any event, would their approach allow clinical trials to be conducted? I think this may fairly be doubted. Although many people are presumably altruistic enough to forgo the best medical treatment in the interest of the progress of science, many are not. The numbers and proportions required to sustain the statistical validity of trial results suggest that in the absence of overwhelming altruism, the enrollment of satisfactory numbers of patients will not be possible. In particular, very ill patients, toward whom many of the most important clinical trials are directed, may be disinclined to be altruistic. Finally, as the study by Taylor et al.[12] reminds us, the problems of equipoise trouble investigators as well as patients. Even if patients are prepared to dispense with the best treatment, their physicians, for reasons of ethics and professionalism, may well not be willing to do so.

Marquis has suggested a third approach. "Perhaps what is needed is an ethics that will justify the conscription of subjects for medical research," he has written. "Nothing less seems to justify present practice."[4] Yet, although conscription might enable us to continue present practice, it would scarcely justify it. Moreover, the conscription of physician investigators, as well as subjects, would be necessary, because, as has been repeatedly argued, the problems of equipoise are as disturbing to clinicians as they are to subjects. Is any less radical and more plausible approach possible?

THEORETICAL EQUIPOISE VERSUS CLINICAL EQUIPOISE

The problems of equipoise examined above arise from a particular understanding of that concept, which I will term "theoretical equipoise." It is an understanding that is both conceptually odd and ethically irrelevant. Theoretical equipoise exists when, overall, the evidence on behalf of two alternative treatment regimens is exactly balanced. This evidence may be derived from a variety of sources, including data from the literature, uncontrolled experience, considerations of basic science and fundamental physiologic processes, and perhaps a "gut feeling" or "instinct" resulting from (or superimposed on) other considerations. The problems examined above arise from the principle that if theoretical equipoise is disturbed, the physician has, in Schafer's words, a "treatment preference" — let us say, favoring experimental treatment B. A trial testing A against B requires that some patients be enrolled in violation of this treatment preference.

Theoretical equipoise is overwhelmingly fragile; that is, it is disturbed by a slight accretion of evidence favoring one arm of the trial. In Chalmers' view, equipoise is disturbed when the odds that A will be more successful than B are anything other than 50 percent. It is therefore necessary to randomize treatment assignments beginning with the very first patient, lest equipoise be disturbed. We may say that theoretical equipoise is balanced on a knife's edge.

Theoretical equipoise is most appropriate to one-dimensional hypotheses and causes us to think in those terms. The null hypothesis must be sufficiently simple and "clean" to be finely balanced: Will A or B be superior in reducing mortality or shrinking tumors or lowering fevers in population P? Clinical choice is commonly more complex. The choice of A or B depends on some combination of effectiveness, consistency, minimal or relievable side effects, and other factors. On close examination, for example, it sometimes appears that even trials that purport to test a single hypothesis in fact involve a more complicated, portmanteau measure — e.g., the "therapeutic index" of A versus B. The formulation of the conditions of theoretical equipoise for such complex, multidimensional clinical hypotheses is tantamount to the formulation of a rigorous calculus of apples and oranges.

Theoretical equipoise is also highly sensitive to the vagaries of the investigator's attention and perception. Because of its fragility, theoretical equipoise is disturbed as soon as the investigator perceives a difference between the alternatives — whether or not any genuine difference exists. Prescott writes, for example, "It will be common at some stage in most trials for the survival curves to show visually different survivals," short of significance but "sufficient to raise ethical difficulties for the participants."[16] A visual difference, however, is purely an artifact of the research methods employed: when and by what means data are assembled and analyzed and what scale is adopted for the graphic presentation of data. Similarly, it is common for researchers to employ interval scales for phenomena that are recognized to be continuous by nature — e.g., five-point scales of pain or stages of tumor progression. These interval scales, which represent an arbitrary distortion of the available evidence to simplify research, may magnify the differences actually found, with a resulting disturbance of theoretical equipoise.

Finally, as described by several authors, theoretical equipoise is personal and idiosyncratic. It is disturbed when the clinician has, in Schafer's words, what "might even be labeled a bias or a hunch," a prefer-

ence of a "merely intuitive nature."[14] The investigator who ignores such a hunch, by failing to advise the patient that because of it the investigator prefers B to A or by recommending A (or a chance of random assignment to A) to the patient, has violated the requirement for equipoise and its companion requirement to recommend the best medical treatment.

The problems with this concept of equipoise should be evident. To understand the alternative, preferable interpretation of equipoise, we need to recall the basic reason for conducting clinical trials: there is a current or imminent conflict in the clinical community over what treatment is preferred for patients in a defined population P. The standard treatment is A, but some evidence suggests that B will be superior (because of its effectiveness or its reduction of undesirable side effects, or for some other reason). (In the rare case when the first evidence of a novel therapy's superiority would be entirely convincing to the clinical community, equipoise is already disturbed.) Or there is a split in the clinical community, with some clinicians favoring A and others favoring B. Each side recognizes that the opposing side has evidence to support its position, yet each still thinks that overall its own view is correct. There exists (or, in the case of a novel therapy, there may soon exist) an honest, professional disagreement among expert clinicians about the preferred treatment. A clinical trial is instituted with the aim of resolving this dispute.

At this point, a state of "clinical equipoise" exists. There is no consensus within the expert clinical community about the comparative merits of the alternatives to be tested. We may state the formal conditions under which such a trial would be ethical as follows: at the start of the trial, there must be a state of clinical equipoise regarding the merits of the regimens to be tested, and the trial must be designed in such a way as to make it reasonable to expect that, if it is successfully concluded, clinical equipoise will be disturbed. In other words, the results of a successful clinical trial should be convincing enough to resolve the dispute among clinicians.

A state of clinical equipoise is consistent with a decided treatment preference on the part of the investigators. They must simply recognize that their less-favored treatment is preferred by colleagues whom they consider to be responsible and competent. Even if the interim results favor the preference of the

MEDICAL INFORMATION

172

investigators, treatment B, clinical equipoise persists as long as those results are too weak to influence the judgment of the community of clinicians, because of limited sample size, unresolved possibilities of side effects, or other factors. (This judgment can necessarily be made only by those who know the interim results—whether a data-monitoring committee or the investigators.)

At the point when the accumulated evidence in favor of B is so strong that the committee or investigators believe no open-minded clinician informed of the results would still favor A, clinical equipoise has been disturbed. This may occur well short of the original schedule for the termination of the trial, for unexpected reasons. (Therapeutic effects or side effects may be much stronger than anticipated, for example, or a definable subgroup within population P may be recognized for which the results demonstrably disturb clinical equipoise.) Because of the arbitrary character of human judgment and persuasion, some ethical problems regarding the termination of a trial will remain. Clinical equipoise will confine these problems to unusual or extreme cases, however, and will allow us to cast persistent problems in the proper terms. For example, in the face of a strong established trend, must we continue the trial because of others' blind fealty to an arbitrary statistical benchmark?

Clearly, clinical equipoise is a far weaker—and more common—condition than theoretical equipoise. Is it ethical to conduct a trial on the basis of clinical equipoise, when theoretical equipoise is disturbed? Or, as Schafer and others have argued, is doing so a violation of the physician's obligation to provide patients with the best medical treatment?[4,5,14] Let us assume that the investigators have a decided preference for B but wish to conduct a trial on the grounds that clinical (not theoretical) equipoise exists. The ethics committee asks the investigators whether, if they or members of their families were within population P, they would not want to be treated with their preference, B? An affirmative answer is often thought to be fatal to the prospects for such a trial, yet the investigators answer in the affirmative. Would a trial satisfying this weaker form of equipoise be ethical?

I believe that it clearly is ethical. As Fried has emphasized,[3] competent (hence, ethical) medicine is social rather than individual in nature. Progress in medicine relies on progressive consensus within the medical and research communities. The ethics of medical practice grants no ethical or normative meaning to a treatment preference, however powerful, that is based on a hunch or on anything less than evidence publicly presented and convincing to the clinical community. Persons are licensed as physicians after they demonstrate the acquisition of this professionally validated knowledge, not after they reveal a superior capacity for guessing. Normative judgments of their behavior—e.g., malpractice actions—rely on a comparison with what is done by the community of medical practitioners. Failure to follow a "treatment preference" not shared by this community and not based on information that would convince it could not be the basis for an allegation of legal or ethical malpractice. As Fried states: "[T]he conception of what is good medicine is the product of a professional consensus." By definition, in a state of clinical equipoise, "good medicine" finds the choice between A and B indifferent.

In contrast to theoretical equipoise, clinical equipoise is robust. The ethical difficulties at the beginning and end of a trial are therefore largely alleviated. There remain difficulties about consent, but these too may be diminished. Instead of emphasizing the lack of evidence favoring one arm over another that is required by theoretical equipoise, clinical equipoise places the emphasis in informing the patient on the honest disagreement among expert clinicians. The fact that the investigator has a "treatment preference," if he or she does, could be disclosed; indeed, if the preference is a decided one, and based on something more than a hunch, it could be ethically mandatory to disclose it. At the same time, it would be emphasized that this preference is not shared by others. It is likely to be a matter of chance that the patient is being seen by a clinician with a preference for B over A, rather than by an equally competent clinician with the opposite preference.

Clinical equipoise does not depend on concealing relevant information from researchers and subjects, as does the use of independent data-monitoring committees. Rather, it allows investigators, in informing subjects, to distinguish appropriately among validated knowledge accepted by the clinical community, data on treatments that are promising but are not (or, for novel therapies, would not be) generally convincing, and mere hunches. Should informed patients decline to participate because they have chosen a specific clinician and trust his or her judgment—over and above the consensus in the professional community — that is no more than the patients' right. We do not conscript patients to serve as subjects in clinical trials.

THE IMPLICATIONS OF CLINICAL EQUIPOISE

The theory of clinical equipoise has been formulated as an alternative to some current views on the ethics of human research. At the same time, it corresponds closely to a preanalytic concept held by many in the research and regulatory communities. Clinical equipoise serves, then, as a rational formulation of the approach of many toward research ethics; it does not so much change things as explain why they are the way they are.

Nevertheless, the precision afforded by the theory of clinical equipoise does help to clarify or reformulate some aspects of research ethics; I will mention only two.

First, there is a recurrent debate about the ethical propriety of conducting clinical trials of discredited treatments, such as Laetrile.[17] Often, substantial political pressure to conduct such tests is brought to bear by adherents of quack therapies. The theory of clinical equipoise suggests that when there is no support for a treatment regimen within the expert clinical community, the first ethical requirement of a trial — clinical equipoise — is lacking; it would therefore be unethical to conduct such a trial.

Second, Feinstein has criticized the tendency of clinical investigators to narrow excessively the conditions and hypotheses of a trial in order to ensure the validity of its results.[18] This "fastidious" approach purchases scientific manageability at the expense of an inability to apply the results to the "messy" conditions of clinical practice. The theory of clinical equipoise adds some strength to this criticism. Overly "fastidious" trials, designed to resolve some theoretical question, fail to satisfy the second ethical requirement of clinical research, since the special conditions of the trial will render it useless for influencing clinical decisions, even if it is successfully completed.

The most important result of the concept of clinical equipoise, however, might be to relieve the current crisis of confidence in the ethics of clinical trials.

Equipoise, properly understood, remains an ethical condition for clinical trials. It is consistent with much current practice. Clinicians and philosophers alike have been premature in calling for desperate measures to resolve problems of equipoise.

REFERENCES

1. Levine RJ. Ethics and regulation of clinical research. 2nd ed. Baltimore: Urban & Schwarzenberg, 1986.

2. *Idem.* The use of placebos in randomized clinical trials. IRB: Rev Hum Subj Res 1985; 7(2):1–4.

3. Fried C. Medical experimentation: personal integrity and social policy. Amsterdam: North-Holland Publishing, 1974.

4. Marquis D. Leaving therapy to chance. Hastings Cent Rep 1983; 13(4):40–7.

5. Schafer A. The ethics of the randomized clinical trial. N Engl J Med 1982; 307:719–24.

6. Shaw LW, Chalmers TC. Ethics in cooperative clinical trials. Ann NY Acad Sci 1970; 169:487–95.

7. Hollenberg NK, Dzau VJ, Williams GH. Are uncontrolled clinical studies ever justified? N Engl J Med 1980; 303:1067.

8. Levine RJ, Lebacqz K. Some ethical considerations in clinical trials. Clin Pharmacol Ther 1979; 25:728–41.

9. Klimt CR, Canner PL. Terminating a long-term clinical trial. Clin Pharmacol Ther 1979; 25:641–6.

10. Veatch RM. Longitudinal studies, sequential designs and grant renewals: what to do with preliminary data. IRB: Rev Hum Subj Res 1979; 1(4):1–3.

11. Chalmers T. The ethics of randomization as a decision-making technique and the problem of informed consent. In: Beauchamp TL, Walters L, eds. Contemporary issues in bioethics. Encino, Calif.: Dickenson, 1978:426–9.

12. Taylor KM, Margolese RG, Soskolne CL. Physicians' reasons for not entering eligible patients in a randomized clinical trial of surgery for breast cancer. N Engl J Med 1984; 310:1363–7.

13. Chalmers TC. Invited remarks. Clin Pharmacol Ther 1979; 25:649–50.

14. Schafer A. The randomized clinical trial: for whose benefit? IRB: Rev Hum Subj Res 1985; 7(2):4–6.

15. Meier P. Terminating a trial — the ethical problem. Clin Pharmacol Ther 1979; 25:633–40.

16. Prescott RJ. Feedback of data to participants during clinical trials. In: Tagnon HJ, Staquet MJ, eds. Controversies in cancer: design of trials and treatment. New York: Masson Publishing, 1979:55–61.

17. Cowan DH. The ethics of clinical trials of ineffective therapy. IRB: Rev Hum Subj Res 1981; 3(5):10–1.

18. Feinstein AR. An additional basic science for clinical medicine. II. The limitations of randomized trials. Ann Intern Med 1983; 99:544–50.

CALIFORNIA SUPREME COURT

Tarasoff v. Regents of the University of California

TOBRINER, Justice

On October 27, 1969, Prosenjit Poddar killed Tatiana Tarasoff. Plaintiffs, Tatiana's parents, allege that two months earlier Poddar confided his intention to kill Tatiana to Dr. Lawrence Moore, a psychologist employed by the Cowell Memorial Hospital at the University of California at Berkeley. They allege that on Moore's request, the campus police briefly detained Poddar, but released him when he appeared rational. They further claim that Dr. Harvey Powelson, Moore's superior, then directed that no further action be taken to detain Poddar. No one warned plaintiffs of Tatiana's peril. . . .

We shall explain that defendant therapists cannot escape liability merely because Tatiana herself was not their patient. When a therapist determines, or pursuant to the standards of his profession should determine, that his patient presents a serious danger of violence to another, he incurs an obligation to use reasonable care to protect the intended victim against such danger. The discharge of this duty may require the therapist to take one or more of various steps, depending upon the nature of the case. Thus it may call for him to warn the intended victim or others likely to apprise the victim of the danger, to notify the police, or to take whatever other steps are reasonably necessary under the circumstances. . . .

1. PLAINTIFFS' COMPLAINTS

Plaintiffs, Tatiana's mother and father, filed separate but virtually identical second amended complaints.

131 California Reporter 14. Decided July 1, 1976. All footnotes and numerous references in the text of the decision and a dissent have been omitted.

The issue before us on this appeal is whether those complaints now state, or can be amended to state, causes of action against defendants. We therefore begin by setting forth the pertinent allegations of the complaints.

Plaintiffs' first cause of action, entitled "Failure to Detain a Dangerous Patient," alleges that on August 20, 1969, Poddar was a voluntary outpatient receiving therapy at Cowell Memorial Hospital. Poddar informed Moore, his therapist, that he was going to kill an unnamed girl, readily identifiable as Tatiana, when she returned home from spending the summer in Brazil. Moore, with the concurrence of Dr. Gold, who had initially examined Poddar, and Dr. Yandell, assistant to the director of the department of psychiatry, decided that Poddar should be committed for observation in a mental hospital. Moore orally notified Officers Atkinson and Teel of the campus police that he would request commitment. He then sent a letter to Police Chief William Beall requesting the assistance of the police department in securing Poddar's confinement.

Officers Atkinson, Brownrigg, and Halleran took Poddar into custody, but, satisfied that Poddar was rational, released him on his promise to stay away from Tatiana. Powelson, director of the department of psychiatry at Cowell Memorial Hospital, then asked the police to return Moore's letter, directed that all copies of the letter and notes that Moore had taken as therapist be destroyed, and "ordered no action to place Prosenjit Poddar in 72-hour treatment and evaluation facility."

Plaintiffs' second cause of action, entitled "Failure to Warn On a Dangerous Patient," incorporates the allegations of the first cause of action, but adds the assertion that defendants negligently permitted Poddar to be released from police custody without "notifying the parents of Tatiana Tarasoff that their daughter was in grave danger from Prosenjit Poddar." Poddar persuaded Tatiana's brother to share an apartment with him near Tatiana's residence; shortly after her return from Brazil, Poddar went to her residence and killed her. . . .

2. PLAINTIFFS CAN STATE A CAUSE OF ACTION AGAINST DEFENDANT THERAPISTS FOR NEGLIGENT FAILURE TO PROTECT TATIANA

The second cause of action can be amended to allege that Tatiana's death proximately resulted from defendants' negligent failure to warn Tatiana or others likely to apprise her of her danger. Plaintiffs contend that as amended, such allegations of negligence and proximate causation, with resulting damages, establish a cause of action. Defendants, however, contend that in the circumstances of the present case they owed no duty of care to Tatiana or her parents and that, in the absence of such duty, they were free to act in careless disregard of Tatiana's life and safety. . . .

In the landmark case of *Rowland v. Christian* (1968), Justice Peters recognized that liability should be imposed "for an injury occasioned to another by his want of ordinary care or skill" as expressed in section 1714 of the Civil Code. Thus, Justice Peters, quoting from *Heaven v. Pender* (1883) stated: "'whenever one person is by circumstances placed in such a position with regard to another . . . that if he did not use ordinary care and skill in his own conduct . . . he would cause danger of injury to the person or property of the other, a duty arises to use ordinary care and skill to avoid such danger.'"

We depart from "this fundamental principle" only upon the "balancing of a number of considerations"; major ones "are the foreseeability of harm to the plaintiff, the degree of certainty that the plaintiff suffered injury, the closeness of the connection between the defendant's conduct and the injury suffered, the moral blame attached to the defendant's conduct, the policy of preventing future harm, the extent of the burden to the defendant and consequences to the community of imposing a duty to exercise care with resulting liability for breach, and the availability, cost and prevalence of insurance for the risk involved."

The most important of these considerations in establishing duty is foreseeability. As a general principle, a "defendant owes a duty of care to all persons who are foreseeably endangered by his conduct, with respect to all risks which make the conduct unreasonably dangerous."

As we shall explain, however, when the avoidance of foreseeable harm requires a defendant to control the conduct of another person, or to warn of such conduct, the common law has traditionally imposed liability only if the defendant bears some special relationship to the dangerous person or to the potential victim. Since the relationship between a therapist and his patient satisfies this requirement, we need not here decide whether foreseeability alone is sufficient to create a duty to exercise reasonable care to protect a potential victim of another's conduct. . . .

A relationship of defendant therapists to either Tatiana or Poddar will suffice to establish a duty of care; as explained in section 315 of the Restatement Second of Torts, a duty of care may arise from either "(a) a special relation . . . between the actor and the third person which imposes a duty upon the actor to control the third person's conduct, or (b) a special relation . . . between the actor and the other which gives to the other a right of protection." . . .

The courts hold that a doctor is liable to persons infected by his patient if he negligently fails to diagnose a contagious disease, or, having diagnosed the illness, fails to warn members of the patient's family.

Since it involved a dangerous mental patient, the decision in *Merchants Nat. Bank & Trust Co. of Fargo v. United States* (1967) comes closer to the issue. The Veterans Administration arranged for the patient to work on a local farm, but did not inform the farmer of the man's background. The farmer consequently permitted the patient to come and go freely during nonworking hours; the patient borrowed a car, drove to his wife's residence and killed her. Notwithstanding the lack of any "special relationship" between the Veterans Administration and the wife, the court found the Veterans Administration liable for the wrongful death of the wife.

In their summary of the relevant rulings Fleming and Maximov conclude that the "case law should dispel any notion that to impose on the therapists a duty to take precautions for the safety of persons threatened by a patient, where due care so requires, is in any way opposed to contemporary ground rules on the duty relationship. On the contrary, there now seems to be sufficient authority to support the conclusion that by entering into a doctor-patient relationship the therapist becomes sufficiently involved to assume some responsibility for the safety, not only of the patient himself, but also of any third person whom the doctor knows to be threatened by the patient." (Fleming & Maximov, *The Patient or His Victim: The Therapist's Dilemma* [1974] 62 Cal.L.Rev. 1025, 1030.)

Defendants contend, however, that imposition of a duty to exercise reasonable care to protect third persons is unworkable because therapists cannot accurately predict whether or not a patient will resort to violence. In support of this argument amicus representing the American Psychiatric Association and other professional societies cites numerous articles which indicate that therapists, in the present state of the art, are unable reliably to predict violent acts; their forecasts, amicus claims, tend consistently to overpredict violence, and indeed are more often wrong than right. Since predictions of violence are often erroneous, amicus concludes, the courts should not render rulings that predicate the liability of therapists upon the validity of such predictions. . . .

We recognize the difficulty that a therapist encounters in attempting to forecast whether a patient presents a serious danger of violence. Obviously we do not require that the therapist, in making that determination, render a perfect performance; the therapist need only exercise "that reasonable degree of skill, knowledge, and care ordinarily possessed and exercised by members of [that professional specialty] under similar circumstances." Within the broad range of reasonable practice and treatment in which professional opinion and judgment may differ, the therapist is free to exercise his or her own best judgment without liability; proof, aided by hindsight, that he or she judged wrongly is insufficient to establish negligence.

In the instant case, however, the pleadings do not raise any question as to failure of defendant therapists to predict that Poddar presented a serious danger of violence. On the contrary, the present complaints allege that defendant therapists did in fact predict that Poddar would kill, but were negligent in failing to warn.

Amicus contends, however, that even when a therapist does in fact predict that a patient poses a serious danger of violence to others, the therapist should be absolved of any responsibility for failing to act to protect the potential victim. In our view, however, once a therapist does in fact determine, or under applicable

professional standards reasonably should have determined, that a patient poses a serious danger of violence to others, he bears a duty to exercise reasonable care to protect the foreseeable victim of that danger. While the discharge of this duty of due care will necessarily vary with the facts of each case, in each instance the adequacy of the therapist's conduct must be measured against the traditional negligence standard of the rendition of reasonable care under the circumstances. As explained in Fleming and Maximov, *The Patient or His Victim: The Therapist's Dilemma* (1974) 62 Cal.L.Rev. 1025, 1967: ". . . the ultimate question of resolving the tension between the conflicting interests of patient and potential victim is one of social policy, not professional expertise. . . . In sum, the therapist owes a legal duty not only to his patient, but also to his patient's would-be victim and is subject in both respects to scrutiny by judge and jury." . . .

The risk that unnecessary warning may be given is a reasonable price to pay for the lives of possible victims that may be saved. We could hesitate to hold that the therapist who is aware that his patient expects to attempt to assassinate the President of the United States would not be obligated to warn the authorities because the therapist cannot predict with accuracy that his patient will commit the crime.

Defendants further argue that free and open communication is essential to psychotherapy, that "Unless a patient . . . is assured that . . . information [revealed to him] can and will be held in utmost confidence, he will be reluctant to make the full disclosure upon which diagnosis and treatment . . . depends." The giving of a warning, defendants contend, constitutes a breach of trust which entails the revelation of confidential communications.

We recognize the public interest in supporting effective treatment of mental illness and in protecting the rights of patients to privacy, and the consequent public importance of safeguarding the confidential character of psychotherapeutic communication. Against this interest, however, we must weigh the public interest in safety from violent assault. . . .

We realize that the open and confidential character of psychotherapeutic dialogue encourages patients to express threats of violence, few of which are ever executed. Certainly a therapist should not be encouraged routinely to reveal such threats; such disclosures could seriously disrupt the patient's relationship with his therapist and with the persons threatened. To the contrary, the therapist's obligations to his patient require that he not disclose a confidence unless such disclosure is necessary to avert danger to others, and even then that he do so discretely, and in a fashion that would preserve the privacy of his patient to the fullest extent compatible with the prevention of the threatened danger.

The revelation of a communication under the above circumstances is not a breach of trust or a violation of professional ethics; as stated in the Principles of Medical Ethics of the American Medical Association (1957), section 9: "A physician may not reveal the confidence entrusted to him in the course of medical attendance . . . *unless he is required to do so by law or unless it becomes necessary in order to protect the welfare of the individual or of the community.*" (Emphasis added.) We conclude that the public policy favoring protection of the confidential character of patient-psychotherapist communications must yield to the extent to which disclosure is essential to avert danger to others. The protective privilege ends where the public peril begins. . . .

For the foregoing reasons, we find that plaintiffs' complaints can be amended to state a cause of action against defendants Moore, Powelson, Gold, and Yandell and against the Regents as their employer, for breach of a duty to exercise reasonable care to protect Tatiana.

• • •

CLARK, Justice (dissenting).

Until today's majority opinion, both legal and medical authorities have agreed that confidentiality is essential to effectively treat the mentally ill, and that imposing a duty on doctors to disclose patient threats to potential victims would greatly impair treatment. Further, recognizing that effective treatment and society's safety are necessarily intertwined, the Legislature has already decided effective and confidential treatment is preferred over imposition of a duty to warn.

The issue of whether effective treatment for the mentally ill should be sacrificed to a system of warnings is, in my opinion, properly one for the Legislature, and we are bound by its judgment. Moreover, even in the absence of clear legislative direction, we must reach the same conclusion because imposing the majority's new duty is certain to result in a net increase in violence. . . .

Overwhelming policy considerations weigh against imposing a duty on psychotherapists to warn a potential victim against harm. While offering virtually no benefit to society, such a duty will frustrate psychiatric treatment, invade fundamental patient rights and increase violence.

The importance of psychiatric treatment and its need for confidentiality have been recognized by this court. "It is clearly recognized that the very practice of psychiatry vitally depends upon the reputation in the community that the psychiatrist will not tell." (Slovenko, *Psychiatry and a Second Look at the Medical Privilege* (1960) 6 Wayne L.Rev. 175, 188.)

Assurance of confidentiality is important for three reasons.

DETERRENCE FROM TREATMENT

First, without substantial assurance of confidentiality, those requiring treatment will be deterred from seeking assistance. It remains an unfortunate fact in our society that people seeking psychiatric guidance tend to become stigmatized. Apprehension of such stigma—apparently increased by the propensity of people considering treatment to see themselves in the worst possible light—creates a well-recognized reluctance to seek aid. This reluctance is alleviated by the psychiatrist's assurance of confidentiality.

FULL DISCLOSURE

Second, the guarantee of confidentiality is essential in eliciting the full disclosure necessary for effective treatment. The psychiatric patient approaches treatment with conscious and unconscious inhibitions against revealing his innermost thoughts. "Every person, however well-motivated, has to overcome resistances to therapeutic exploration. These resistances seek support from every possible source and the possibility of disclosure would easily be employed in the service of resistance." (Goldstein & Katz, 36 Conn. Bar J. 175, 179.) Until a patient can trust his psychiatrist not to violate their confidential relationship, "the unconscious psychological control mechanism of repression will prevent the recall of past experiences." (Butler, *Psychotherapy and Griswold: Is Confidentiality a Privilege or a Right?* (1971) 3 Conn.L.Rev. 599, 604.)

SUCCESSFUL TREATMENT

Third, even if the patient fully discloses his thoughts, assurance that the confidential relationship will not be breached is necessary to maintain his trust in his psychiatrist—the very means by which treatment is effected. "[T]he essence of much psychotherapy is the contribution of trust in the external world and ultimately in the self, modelled upon the trusting relationship established during therapy." (Dawidoff, *The Malpractice of Psychiatrists*, 1966 Duke L.J. 696, 704.) Patients will be helped only if they can form a trusting relationship with the psychiatrist. All authorities appear to agree that if the trust relationship cannot be developed because of collusive communication between the psychiatrist and others, treatment will be frustrated.

Given the importance of confidentiality to the practice of psychiatry, it becomes clear the duty to warn imposed by the majority will cripple the use and effectiveness of psychiatry. Many people, potentially violent—yet susceptible to treatment—will be deterred from seeking it; those seeking it will be inhibited from making revelations necessary to effective treatment; and, forcing the psychiatrist to violate the patient's trust will destroy the interpersonal relationship by which treatment is effected.

VIOLENCE AND CIVIL COMMITMENT

By imposing a duty to warn, the majority contributes to the danger to society of violence by the mentally ill and greatly increases the risk of civil commitment—the total deprivation of liberty—of those who should not be confined. The impairment of treatment and risk of improper commitment resulting from the new duty to warn will not be limited to a few patients but will extend to a large number of the mentally ill. Although under existing psychiatric procedures only a relatively few receiving treatment will ever present a risk of violence, the number making threats is huge, and it is the latter group—not just the former—whose treatment will be impaired and whose risk of commitment will be increased.

Both the legal and psychiatric communities recognize that the process of determining potential violence in a patient is far from exact, being fraught with complexity and uncertainty. In fact precision has not even been attained in predicting who of those having already committed violent acts will again become violent, a task recognized to be of much simpler proportions.

This predictive uncertainty means that the number of disclosures will necessarily be large. As noted above, psychiatric patients are encouraged to discuss all thoughts of violence, and they often express such thoughts. However, unlike this court, the psychiatrist does not enjoy the benefit of overwhelming hindsight in seeing which few, if any, of his patients will ultimately become violent. Now, confronted by the majority's new duty, the psychiatrist must instantaneously calculate potential violence from each patient on each visit. The difficulties researchers have encountered in accurately predicting violence will be heightened for the practicing psychiatrist dealing for brief periods in his office with heretofore nonviolent patients. And, given the decision not to warn or commit must always be made at the psychiatrist's civil peril, one can expect most doubts will be resolved in favor of the psychiatrist protecting himself.

MARK SIEGLER

Confidentiality in Medicine — A Decrepit Concept

Medical confidentiality, as it has traditionally been understood by patients and doctors, no longer exists. This ancient medical principle, which has been included in every physician's oath and code of ethics since Hippocratic times, has become old, worn-out, and useless; it is a decrepit concept. Efforts to preserve it appear doomed to failure and often give rise to more problems than solutions. Psychiatrists have tacitly acknowledged the impossibility of ensuring the confidentiality of medical records by choosing to establish a separate, more secret record. The following case illustrates how the confidentiality principle is compromised systematically in the course of routine medical care.

A patient of mine with mild chronic obstructive pulmonary disease was transferred from the surgical intensive-care unit to a surgical nursing floor two days after an elective cholecystectomy. On the day of transfer, the patient saw a respiratory therapist writing in his medical chart (the therapist was recording the results of an arterial blood gas analysis) and became concerned about the confidentiality of his hospital records. The patient threatened to leave the hospital prematurely unless I could guarantee that the confidentiality of his hospital record would be respected.

This patient's complaint prompted me to enumerate the number of persons who had both access to his hospital record and a reason to examine it. I was amazed to learn that at least 25 and possibly as many as 100 health professionals and administrative personnel at our university hospital had access to the patient's record and that all of them had a legitimate need, indeed a professional responsibility, to open and

use that chart. These persons included 6 attending physicians (the primary physician, the surgeon, the pulmonary consultant, and others); 12 house officers (medical, surgical, intensive-care unit, and "covering" house staff); 20 nursing personnel (on three shifts); 6 respiratory therapists, 3 nutritionists; 2 clinical pharmacists; 15 students (from medicine, nursing, respiratory therapy, and clinical pharmacy); 4 unit secretaries; 4 hospital financial officers; and 4 chart reviewers (utilization review, quality assurance review, tissue review, and insurance auditor). It is of interest that this patient's problem was straightforward, and he therefore did not require many other technical and support services that the modern hospital provides. For example, he did not need multiple consultants and fellows, such specialized procedures as dialysis, or social workers, chaplains, physical therapists, occupational therapists, and the like.

Upon completing my survey I reported to the patient that I estimated that at least 75 health professionals and hospital personnel had access to his medical record. I suggested to the patient that these people were all involved in providing or supporting his health care services. They were, I assured him, working for him. Despite my reassurances the patient was obviously distressed and retorted, "I always believed that medical confidentiality was part of a doctor's code of ethics. Perhaps you should tell me just what you people mean by 'confidentiality'!"

TWO ASPECTS OF MEDICAL CONFIDENTIALITY

CONFIDENTIALITY AND THIRD-PARTY INTERESTS

Previous discussions of medical confidentiality usually have focused on the tension between a physician's

Reprinted by permission of *New England Journal of Medicine*, Vol. 307. © 1982 Massachusetts Medical Society.

responsibility to keep information divulged by patients secret and a physician's legal and moral duty, on occasion, to reveal such confidences to third parties, such as families, employers, public-health authorities, or police authorities. In all these instances, the central question relates to the stringency of the physician's obligation to maintain patient confidentiality when the health, well-being, and safety of identifiable others or of society in general would be threatened by a failure to reveal information about the patient. The tension in such cases is between the good of the patient and the good of others.

CONFIDENTIALITY AND THE PATIENT'S INTEREST

As the example above illustrates, further challenges to confidentiality arise because the patient's personal interest in maintaining confidentiality comes into conflict with his personal interest in receiving the best possible health care. Modern high-technology health care is available principally in hospitals (often, teaching hospitals), requires many trained and specialized workers (a "health-care team"), and is very costly. The existence of such teams means that information that previously had been held in confidence by an individual physician will now necessarily be disseminated to many members of the team. Furthermore, since health-care teams are expensive and few patients can afford to pay such costs directly, it becomes essential to grant access to the patient's medical record to persons who are responsible for obtaining third-party payment. These persons include chart reviewers, financial officers, insurance auditors, and quality-of-care assessors. Finally, as medicine expands from a narrow, disease-based model to a model that encompasses psychological, social, and economic problems, not only will the size of the health-care team and medical costs increase, but more sensitive information (such as one's personal habits and financial condition) will now be included in the medical record and will no longer be confidential.

The point I wish to establish is that hospital medicine, the rise of health-care teams, the existence of third-party insurance programs, and the expanding limits of medicine will appear to be responses to the wishes of people for better and more comprehensive medical care. But each of these developments necessarily modifies our traditional understanding of medical confidentiality.

THE ROLE OF CONFIDENTIALITY IN MEDICINE

Confidentiality serves a dual purpose in medicine. In the first place, it acknowledges respect for the patient's sense of individuality and privacy. The patient's most personal physical and psychological secrets are kept confidential in order to decrease a sense of shame and vulnerability. Secondly, confidentiality is important in improving the patient's health care—a basic goal of medicine. The promise of confidentiality permits people to trust (i.e., have confidence) that information revealed to a physician in the course of a medical encounter will not be disseminated further. In this way patients are encouraged to communicate honestly and forthrightly with their doctors. This bond of trust between patient and doctor is vitally important both in the diagnostic process (which relies on an accurate history) and subsequently in the treatment phase, which often depends as much on the patient's trust in the physician as it does on medications and surgery. These two important functions of confidentiality are as important now as they were in the past. They will not be supplanted entirely either by improvements in medical technology or by recent changes in relations between some patients and doctors toward a rights-based, consumerist model.

POSSIBLE SOLUTIONS TO THE CONFIDENTIALITY PROBLEM

First of all, in all nonbureaucratic, noninstitutional medical encounters—that is, in the millions of doctor–patient encounters that take place in physician's offices, where more privacy can be preserved—meticulous care should be taken to guarantee that patients' medical and personal information will be kept confidential.

Secondly, in such settings as hospitals or large-scale group practices, where many persons have opportunities to examine the medical record, we should aim to provide access only to those who have "a need to know." This could be accomplished through such administrative changes as dividing the entire record into several sections—for example, a medical and financial section—and permitting only health professionals access to the medical information.

The approach favored by many psychiatrists—that of keeping a psychiatric record separate from the general medical record—is an understandable strategy but one that is not entirely satisfactory and that should not be generalized. The keeping of separate psychiatric records implies that psychiatry and medicine are different undertakings and thus drives deeper the wedge between them and between physical and psychological illness. Furthermore, it is often vitally important for internists or surgeons to know that a partient is being seen by a psychiatrist or is taking a particular medication. When separate records are kept, this information may not be available. Finally, if generalized, the practice of keeping a separate psychiatric record could lead to the unacceptable consequence of having a separate record for each type of medical problem.

Patients should be informed about what is meant by "medical confidentiality." We should establish the distinction between information about the patient that generally will be kept confidential regardless of the interest of third parties and information that will be exchanged among members of the health-care team in order to provide care for the patient. Patients should be made aware of the large number of persons in the modern hospital who require access to the medical record in order to serve the patient's medical and financial interests.

Finally, at some point most patients should have an opportunity to review their medical record and to make informed choices about whether their entire record is to be available to everyone or whether certain portions of the record are privileged and should be accessible only to their principal physician or to others designated explicitly by the patient. This approach would rely on traditional informed-consent procedural standards and might permit the patient to balance the personal value of medical confidentiality against the personal value of high-technology, team health care. There is no reason that the same procedure should not be used with psychiatric records instead of the arbitrary system now employed, in which everything related to psychiatry is kept secret.

AFTERTHOUGHT:
CONFIDENTIALITY AND INDISCRETION

There is one additional aspect of confidentiality that is rarely included in discussions of the subject. I am referring here to the wanton, often inadvertent, but avoidable exchanges of confidential information that occur frequently in hospital rooms, elevators, cafeterias, doctors' offices, and at cocktail parties. Of course, as more people have access to medical information about the patient the potential for this irresponsible abuse of confidentiality increases geometrically.

Such mundane breaches of confidentiality are probably of greater concern to most patients than the broader issues of whether their medical records may be entered into a computerized data bank or whether a respiratory therapist is reviewing the results of an arterial blood gas determination. Somehow, privacy is violated and a sense of shame is heightened when intimate secrets are revealed to people one knows or is close to—friends, neighbors, acquaintances, or hospital roommates—rather than when they are disclosed to an anonymous bureaucrat sitting at a computer terminal in a distant city or to a health professional who is acting in an official capacity.

I suspect that the principles of medical confidentiality, particularly those reflected in most medical codes of ethics, were designed principally to prevent just this sort of embarrassing personal indiscretion rather than to maintain (for social, political, or economic reasons) the absolute secrecy of doctor–patient communications. In this regard, it is worth noting that Percival's Code of Medical Ethics (1803) includes the following admonition: "Patients should be interrogated concerning their complaint in a tone of voice which cannot be overheard."* We in the medical profession frequently neglect these simple courtesies.

CONCLUSION

The principle of medical confidentiality described in medical codes of ethics and still believed in by patients no longer exists. In this respect, it is a decrepit concept. Rather than perpetuate the myth of confidentiality and invest energy vainly to preserve it, the public and the profession would be better served if they devoted their attention to determining which aspects of the original principle of confidentiality are worth retaining. Efforts could then be directed to salvaging those.

*Leake CD, ed. Percival's medical ethics. Baltimore: Williams & Wilkins, 1927.

ANDREW MARKUS
AND MICHAEL LOCKWOOD

Is It Permissible to Edit Medical Records?

Whatever, in connection with my professional practice, or not in connection with it, I see or hear, in the life of men, which ought not to be spoken of abroad, I will not divulge, as reckoning that all such should be kept secret.

Thus the Hippocratic Oath—by which members of the medical profession, at least in the West, still consider themselves bound—states the principle of confidentiality. As it stands, however, the Hippocratic statement is essentially empty. It binds doctors not to divulge what "ought not to be spoken of abroad" on the strength of the tautology that what ought not to be spoken of abroad "should be kept secret." But it offers no guidance as to what sort of information a doctor is or is not obliged to keep secret, under what circumstances, and from whom. Nor does it tell us who is entitled to decide, in any specific case, whether or not a given item of information can be divulged to a third party, including another doctor or health care worker, and in particular (and of special relevance to the topic of this paper) when the patient should be given power of veto over any such disclosure. The General Medical Council has listed a number of exceptions to the rule of confidentiality, mainly situations in which doctors are permitted to break the rule without the patient's consent.[1]

We shall be better placed to consider the issue of whether it is acceptable to edit medical records when we have first briefly explored the moral basis of confidentiality in medicine.

Two distinct values seem to be at the heart of the principle of confidentiality, one specific to the medical

context and the other not. The value not specific to medicine is that of respect for people's privacy. It is generally accepted that there are certain aspects of people's lives which are their own business, and not the business of others (save, perhaps, for a few to whom they have close personal or professional ties). The ability to choose (within certain limits) what others know about us—especially in regard to more intimate personal details—is of importance to us all because it is one of the things that enables us to maintain control over our own lives, and in particular over our relationships with others. That is not to deny that in a close relationship one person may need to know many personal details of the other for trust to be established. Privacy is thus a value closely related to, and perhaps ultimately grounded on, the value of personal autonomy. To take this value of privacy seriously is to subscribe to a number of familiar precepts. It means that we should be reluctant to pry, that we should respect personal confidences, and that when we enter into relationships with others that render us privy to sensitive or intimate personal information we should be chary about passing this information on, even in the absence of any specific request not to do so. (A promise to keep some personal matter secret often serves merely to reinforce an independently existing obligation.) Here, then, is a general principle that applies to everyone—but with particular force to doctors: firstly, because the doctor is especially likely to become aware of sensitive information and, secondly, because the doctor–patient relationship is, par excellence, one based upon trust. These considerations alone would constitute grounds enough for placing doctors under a specific obligation of confidentiality in their professional dealings.

Reprinted by permission of the publisher from Andrew Markus and Michael Lockood, "Is It Permissible to Edit Medical Records?" British Medical Journal 303, No. 6798, 10 August 1991, pp. 349–51.

That, however, is only half the story. The other value underlying the principle of confidentiality in medicine is that of the furthering of effective care. A doctor's ability to help a patient is likely to be directly related to the amount the doctor knows about the patient. So the more a patient can rely upon the doctor to treat personal disclosures as confidential, the more open that patient is likely to be, and the better able the doctor may be to provide effective treatment. By the same token, a patient is more likely to consult the doctor in the first place—and thereby receive effective treatment—if he or she can rely on the doctor's discretion in disclosing to third parties sensitive information that emerges in the consultation. These considerations constitute the second main reason for imposing on doctors a specific duty of confidentiality.

Many of the practical difficulties surrounding medical confidentiality in the modern world have to do with the fact that today's doctor is no longer the independent agent that the Hippocratic corpus presumably had in mind. The general practitioner of the 1990s is often a member of a group practice, and his or her patients will sometimes need to be referred to colleagues or admitted to hospital. The patient's records, if he or she is an NHS patient, do not even belong to the patient's family doctor, or indeed to any doctor. They are government property, under the ultimate control of the secretary of state. Some 40 people other than the doctors, all with good reason, have access to records in the health centre where one of us (AM) works—reception staff, nurses, health visitors, social workers, clinical psychologists, visiting consultants, medical students, and sometimes others involved in "bona fide" research.

This brings us to the central problem that we are here concerned to address. It seems to us that patients generally give information to their doctors on the understanding that this is to enable that specific doctor to treat them at that particular time. One is not entitled to assume that patients would wish such knowledge to be freely available to any other doctor who might treat them in the future (and perhaps much less to social workers, health visitors, receptionists, medical researchers, and the like). Once such information has been entered into a patient's records, however (quite apart from its becoming immediately accessible, as we have seen, to a number of different people), it will automatically be passed on, by way of the family health services authority, to the patient's next general practitioner, should the patient change doctors.

There can be no doubt that this is sometimes contrary to the patient's own wishes. A case known to one of us (AM) concerned a 21 year old university student who had suffered a psychotic breakdown during her Oxford career but had nevertheless successfully completed her course. She came to see her doctor after getting her degree to say goodbye and to ask that all mention of the episode should be removed from her records, including hospital letters. She did not want future doctors to label or prejudge her. Another instance was that of a 27 year old male student who was HIV positive and who asked his doctor (AM) to remove all mention of this fact from his records when he was due to leave college. "I gave *you* that information," he insisted, "not every Tom, Dick, and Harry." A third, hypothetical case (put to ML by a retired general practitioner), is that of a woman whose husband's "sexual shenanigans" are referred to in this woman's records as a possible explanation of symptoms that her doctor was inclined to regard as psychosomatic. It would be only natural for the woman to be concerned, when she moved, that not only her own but her husband's personal affairs would become known to her new general practitioner. It seems to us that in each of these situations a case may be argued for acceding to the patient's wishes.

There are two principles at stake here. The first is that respect for the patient's privacy and autonomy requires that the doctor's disclosure of personal information be sensitive to the intentions and legitimate expectations of the patient. These intentions and expectations will extend both to who is to receive the information and to what it is to be used for. (Thus, it clearly raises ethical problems when a doctor, in connection with an insurance application, is asked to give information that is possibly detrimental to the patient and that was disclosed by the patient for the sole purpose of assisting treatment or diagnosis.)

The second principle is that the patient should not be deprived of the ability to control his or her new doctor's access to personal information that may adversely affect the patient's relationship with that doctor. This goes back to what we identified at the outset as one key rationale of the value of privacy. That the patient who had suffered a psychotic episode be able to start her relationship with her new doctor with a clean slate is surely an entirely reasonable desire and one that demands respect. (It demands respect even if some principle of reciprocity would suggest that a patient has a certain obligation, other things being equal, to cooperate with the doctor to the extent of providing such information as is likely materially to assist diagnosis or treatment, if and when it is needed.)

The case of the HIV patient is more problematic because the new doctor might be argued to have a legitimate interest in the information, relating to his or her own safety. But on the other hand it is recommended practice nowadays that all doctors should behave on the assumption that their patients may be HIV positive.

If the foregoing line of thought is correct then the present situation is profoundly unsatisfactory, for as things now stand it is considered by the General Medical Council to be a disciplinary offence to remove information from records without "adequate justification"; indeed, it would probably constitute falsification of records. This raises the question of what *is* adequate justification, but it is doubtful whether the mere fact that the patient wants some item of information removed would be regarded by the GMC as such justification. (Where there is a factual error it is of course perfectly permissible to cross out the offending passage, provided it remains legible and the reason for the emendation is made plain.)

At present the general practitioner has no power to prevent the records being passed on to the new doctor. There are moves afoot to allow patients access to their own records, which if realised will probably deter doctors from writing things in the records to which the patient is particularly liable to take exception (though the plan also raises problems of its own). Although no current proposal would seem really to address the problem that concerns us here, access to records might be a first step towards a system in which a certain amount of periodic editing was permitted, on the basis of negotiation between the doctor and the patient. Some set of guidelines would then be needed as to what sorts of requests from patients for deletions in the records should generally be accepted. A more radical proposal would be to follow the practice adopted in some countries, whereby patients have the right to keep their own records and presumably can exercise their own discretion as to how much information is passed on to any new doctor. (It would always be possible to keep duplicates somewhere else in case of loss, and access to these, except perhaps in emergencies, would be allowed only with the patient's express permission.)

Some will no doubt argue that it is in patients' best interests that their new doctor is not deprived of information contained in their previous records, inasmuch as it would not have been recorded by their previous general practitioner had it not been of relevance to their health care. To that, however, there are three answers. In the first place, much of what is recorded is in fact extremely unlikely to be of any future value. Secondly, even under the present system, no doctor is entitled to assume that any records are complete, or even fully accurate: information may be lacking simply because a doctor has never got around to putting it in the notes, or the patient may not have given all relevant facts. This consideration has a bearing, too, on the GMC's view that deletion of relevant information might constitute falsification of records, as also on the argument that such deletions could put doctors themselves at risk. The real moral here is that a doctor should never assume that what is not stated in the records is not, in fact, the case.

But, thirdly, shouldn't it in any case be for the patient ultimately to decide? After all, it is up to the patient what he or she tells the doctor in the first place. If through exercising this choice the patient deprives the new doctor of information that can be of therapeutic or diagnostic value then that, it might be considered, is the patient's own lookout. This view, that in general autonomy should take precedence over what others think might be best for the patient (beneficence), is widely held. It reflects the status of the patient as an adult capable of weighing up the implications of his or her own decisions. Moreover, we think a case can be made out that the patient, in a moral sense, retains a proprietary interest in such personal information as is revealed to the doctor in the course of a consultation. It remains his or her secret, and it should remain for the patient to have the ultimate say as to what use that information is put to and to whom it is revealed — always assuming, of course, that no one else's welfare is at stake here. Even if the records, as physical objects, are government property it does not follow that this is true also of the information that they contain. Personal information disclosed in a consultation should perhaps be seen as effectively "on trust" to the doctor for the period of treatment, or for the period in which that doctor continues to have the person as a patient. (The whole issue of ownership of information is one that would merit more attention from moral philosophers.)

Other arguments of a more pragmatic character will no doubt be advanced in favour of maintaining the status quo. One should be reluctant, it may be said, to advocate any new system that would add to the administrative burden under which hard pressed general practitioners and the NHS generally, currently labour. Some sacrifice of patient autonomy may be justified on the basis that it is a relatively small price to pay in return for the very great benefits of the present system, which allows the use of information collected over a long time to be used whenever required in a consultation. But even in therapeutic terms there could be much to be gained by a system that gave patients greater control over their own records; it might well serve to encourage greater openness, enhanced trust, and a greater spirit of cooperation between doctor and patient. We find it difficult to believe that a system more respectful of confidentiality and of the patient's wishes could not be made to work successfully if there was a sufficient will so to do.

NOTE

1. General Medical Council. *Professional conduct and discipline: fitness to practice*. London: GMC, 1987; sections 79–88.

SUGGESTED READINGS

TRUTH TELLING AND THE MANAGEMENT OF BAD NEWS

Bok, Sissela. *Lying: Moral Choice in Public and Private Life*. New York: Pantheon Books, 1978.

Burnum, John F. "Secrets about Patients." *New England Journal of Medicine* 324 (April 18, 1991), 1130–1133.

Cabot, Richard C. "The Use of Truth and Falsehood in Medicine," as edited by Jay Katz from the 1909 version. *Connecticut Medicine* 42 (1978), 189–194.

Hattori, Hiroyuki, et al. "The Patient's Right to Information in Japan—Legal Rules and Doctors' Opinions." *Social Science and Medicine* 32 (1991), 1007–1016.

Jackson, Jennifer. "Telling the Truth." *Journal of Medical Ethics* 17 (1991), 5–9.

Novack, Dennis, Barbara J. Detering, Robert Arnold, et al. "Physicians' Attitudes Toward Using Deception to Resolve Difficult Ethical Problems." *Journal of the American Medical Association* 261 (May 26, 1989), 2980–2985.

Schöne-Seifert, Bettina, and Childress, James F. "How Much Should the Patient Know and Decide?" *CA—A Cancer Journal for Clinicians* 36 (1986), 85–94.

Siminoff, L. A., Fetting, J. H., and Abeloff, M. D. "Doctor–Patient Communication about Breast Cancer Adjuvant Therapy." *Journal of Clinical Oncology* 7 (1989), 1192–1200.

VanDeVeer, Donald. "The Contractual Argument for Withholding Medical Information." *Philosophy & Public Affairs* 9 (1980), 198–205.

Veatch, Robert M. *Case Studies in Medical Ethics*. Cambridge, MA: Harvard University Press, 1977. Chaps. 6 and 12.

Weir, Robert. "Truthtelling in Medicine." *Perspectives in Biology and Medicine* 24 (Autumn 1980), 95–112.

INFORMED CONSENT

Appelbaum, Paul, and Grisso, Thomas. "Assessing Patients' Capacities to Consent to Treatment." *New England Journal of Medicine* 319 (December 22, 1988), 1635–1638.

Appelbaum, Paul S., Lidz, Charles W., and Meisel, Alan. *Informed Consent: Legal Theory and Clinical Practice*. New York: Oxford University Press, 1987.

Beauchamp, Tom L., and Childress, James F. *Principles of Biomedical Ethics*. 4th ed. New York: Oxford University Press, 1994. Chap. 3.

Bok, Sissela. "Informed Consent in Tests of Patient Reliability." *Journal of the American Medical Association* 267 (February 26, 1992), 1118–1119.

Buchanan, Allen E., and Brock, Dan W. *Deciding for Others: The Ethics of Surrogate Decision Making*. Cambridge: Cambridge University Press, 1989.

Curran, William J. "Informed Consent in Malpractice Cases: A Turn Toward Reality." *New England Journal of Medicine* 314 (February 13, 1986), 429–431.

Faden, Ruth R., and Beauchamp, Tom L. *A History and Theory of Informed Consent*. New York: Oxford University Press, 1986.

Gunderson, Martin. "Justifying a Principle of Informed Consent: A Case Study in Autonomy-based Ethics." *Public Affairs Quarterly* 4 (1990), 249–265.

Katz, Jay. "Informed Consent—A Fairy Tale? Law's Vision." *University of Pittsburgh Law Review* 39 (1977), 137–174.

_____. *The Silent World of Doctor and Patient*. New York: Free Press, 1984.

Levine, Robert J. *Ethics and Regulation of Clinical Research*. 2d ed. New Haven: Yale University Press, 1988.

Lidz, Charles W., et al. *Informed Consent: A Study of Decisionmaking in Psychiatry*. New York: Guilford Press, 1984.

Merz, Jon F., and Fischoff, Baruch. "Informed Consent Does Not Mean Rational Consent." *Journal of Legal Medicine* 11 (1990), 321–350.

President's Commission for the Study of Ethical Problems in Medicine and Biomedical and Behavioral Research. *Making Health Care Decisions*. Washington: Government Printing Office, 1982. Vols. 1–3.

Swartz, Martha, "AIDS Testing and Informed Consent." *Journal of Health Politics, Policy, and Law* 13 (1988), 607–621.

Veatch, Robert M. *The Patient as Partner: A Theory of Human-Experimentation Ethics*. Bloomington, IN: Indiana University Press, 1987. Chaps. 3 and 12.

Weisbard, Alan J. "Informed Consent: The Law's Uneasy Compromise with Ethical Theory." *Nebraska Law Review* 65 (1986), 749–767.

PATIENT SELF-DETERMINATION AND ADVANCE DIRECTIVES

Advance Directives Seminar Group. "Advance Directives: Are They an Advance?" *Canadian Medical Association Journal* 146 (January 15, 1992), 127–134.

Brock, Dan. "Trumping Advance Directives." *Hastings Center Report* 21 (Sept./Oct. 1991).

Eisendrath, Stuart, and Jonsen, Albert R. "The Living Will." *Journal of the American Medical Association* 249 (April 15, 1983), 2054–2058.

Gamble, E. R., et al. "Knowledge, Attitudes, and Behavior of Elderly Persons Regarding Living Wills." *Archives of Internal Medicine* 151 (1991), 277–280.

King, Nancy. *Making Sense of Advance Directives.* Dordrecht: Kluwer Academic Publishers, 1991.

Olick, Robert. "Approximating Informed Consent and Fostering Communication: The Anatomy of an Advance Directive." *Journal of Clinical Ethics* 2 (1991), 181–195.

Sehgal, A., et al. "How Strictly Do Dialysis Patients Want Their Advance Directives Followed?" *Journal of the American Medical Association* 267 (January 1, 1992), 59–63.

Omnibus Budget Reconciliation Act of 1990. Public Law 101–508 (Nov. 5, 1990), §§ 4206, 4751. See 42 USC, scattered sections.

MANAGING INFORMATION
IN RANDOMIZED CLINICAL TRIALS

Angell, Marcia. "Patient Preferences in Randomized Clinical Trials." *New England Journal of Medicine* 310 (May 24, 1984), 1385–1387.

Capron. "Human Experimentation." In Veatch, Robert M., ed. *Medical Ethics.* Boston: Jones and Bartlett, 1989. Chap. 6.

Freedman, Benjamin. "Equipoise and the Ethics of Clinical Research." *New England Journal of Medicine* 317 (July 16, 1987), 141–145.

Fried, Charles. *Medical Experimentation: Personal Integrity and Social Policy.* New York: American Elsevier, 1974.

Journal of Medicine and Philosophy 11 (1986). Special issue on "Ethical Issues in the Use of Clinical Controls."

Lantos, John D., and Frader, Joel. "Extracorporeal Membrane Oxygenation and the Ethics of Clinical Research in Pediatrics." *New England Journal of Medicine* 326 (August 9, 1990), 409–413.

Levine, Robert J. *Ethics and Regulation of Clinical Research.* 2d ed. New Haven: Yale University Press, 1988.

Marquis, Donald. "An Argument that All Prerandomized Clinical Trials Are Unethical." *Journal of Medicine and Philosophy* 11 (1986).

Miller, Bruce. "Experimentation on Human Subjects: The Ethics of Random Clinical Trials." In VanDeVeer, Donald, and Regan, Tom, eds. *Health Care Ethics.* Philadelphia: Temple University Press, 1987.

Passamani, Eugene. "Clinical Trials — Are they Ethical?" *New England Journal of Medicine* 324 (May 30, 1991), 1590–1591.

Veatch, Robert. *The Patient as Partner: A Theory of Human Experimentation Ethics.* Bloomington, IN: Indiana University Press, 1987.

THE MANAGEMENT OF CONFIDENTIAL INFORMATION

Allen, Anita. *Uneasy Access: Privacy for Women in a Free Society.* Totowa, N.J.: Rowman and Allanheld, 1987.

American Psychiatric Association, Board of Trustees. "AIDS Policy: Confidentiality and Disclosure." *American Journal of Psychiatry* 145 (1988), 541. See also APA. "Guidelines on Confidentiality." *American Journal of Psychiatry* 144 (1987), 1522–1526.

Appelbaum, Paul S., et al. "Researchers' Access to Patient Records: An Analysis of the Ethical Problems." *Clinical Research* 32 (1984), 399–403.

Bayer, Ronald, and Toomey, Kathleen E. "HIV Prevention and the Two Faces of Partner Notification." *American Journal of Public Health* 82 (August 1992), 1158–1164.

Beauchamp, Tom L., and Childress, James F. *Principles of Biomedical Ethics.* 4th ed. New York: Oxford University Press, 1994. Chaps. 3 and 7.

Beck, James C., ed. *Confidentiality Versus the Duty to Protect: Foreseeable Harm in the Practice of Psychiatry.* Washington, D.C.: American Psychiatry Press, Inc., 1990.

Bok, Sissela. *Secrets: On the Ethics of Concealment and Revelation.* New York: Pantheon Books, 1983.

Dick, Richard, and Steen, Elaine, eds. *The Computer-Based Patient Record.* Washington: National Academy of Science, Institute of Medicine, 1991.

Gillon, Raanan. "Confidentiality." *British Medical Journal* 291 (December 7, 1985), 1634–1636.

Gordis, Leon, and Gold, Ellen. "Privacy, Confidentiality, and the Use of Medical Records in Research." *Science* 207 (January 11, 1980), 153–156.

Havard, John. "Medical Confidence." *Journal of Medical Ethics* 11 (1985), 8–11.

Kelsey, Jennifer L. "Privacy and Confidentiality in Epidemiological Research Involving Patients." *IRB: A Review of Human Subjects Research* 3 (1981), 1–4.

Kottow, Michael H. "Medical Confidentiality: an Intransigent and Absolute Obligation." *Journal of Medical Ethics* 12 (1986), 117–122.

Schoeman, Ferdinand D., ed. *Philosophical Dimensions of Privacy: An Anthology.* New York: Cambridge University Press, 1984.

Turkington, Richard C., Trubow, George B., and Allen, Anita L., eds. *Privacy: Cases and Materials.* Houston: John Marshall Publishing Co., 1992.

United Hospital Fund of New York. *The Tuberculosis Revival: Individual Rights and Societal Obligation in a Time of AIDS: A Special Report.* New York: United Hospital Fund, 1992.

U.S. Congress. House Committee on the Judiciary, Subcommittee on Civil and Constitutional Rights. *Unauthorized Access to Individual Medical Records.* Washington, D.C.: Government Printing Office, 1986.

Weiss, Barry D. "Confidentiality Expectations of Patients, Physicians, and Medical Students." *Journal of the American Medical Association* 247 (1982), 2695–2697.

BIBLIOGRAPHIES AND ENCYCLOPEDIAS
WITH BIBLIOGRAPHIES

Bioethicsline: Computer Retrieval Service.

Encyclopedia of Bioethics. ed. Warren Reich. New York: Macmillan, 1994.

Lineback, Richard H., ed. *Philosopher's Index.* Vols. 1–27. Bowling Green, Ohio: Philosophy Documentation Center, Bowling Green State University.

Living Wills and Durable Powers of Attorney: Advance Directive Legislation and Issues (1990). Bibliography available from the National Reference Center for Bioethics Literature, Kennedy Institute of Ethics, Georgetown University, Washington, D.C. 20057.

Walters, LeRoy, and Kahn, Tamar Joy, ed. *Bibliography of Bioethics.* Vols. 1–19. New York: Free Press. Issued annually.

Part III

4.

Reproductive Technologies
and Surrogate Parenting Arrangements

INTRODUCTION

This chapter considers the moral quandaries faced by individuals or couples contemplating the conception, gestation, birth, and rearing of a child or multiple children. In the idealized traditional model, the members of a heterosexual couple make a rational decision about whether to have a child, or another child. If their decision is positive, they proceed to conceive a child by means of sexual intercourse. It is always understood, of course, that the process of rational decision making may occur after the unintended initiation of a pregnancy.

The idealized traditional model is not always realized in practice. In the latter part of the twentieth century, health professionals and couples alike have made the general public increasingly aware of the problem of involuntary infertility. As a response to this problem, both older and newer technologies of assisted reproduction have been developed and increasingly employed. At the same time, novel social arrangements for the bearing, begetting, and rearing of children are becoming more prevalent. In turn, these new arrangements and technologies have called into question the previously settled notions of "family," "parent," "mother," and "father."

PARENTING AND THE FAMILY

In the first section of this chapter, Ruth Macklin and Barbara Katz Rothman explore the implications of assisted reproductive techniques for the notions of family and motherhood. Macklin notes that there are four major determinants of what is meant by the term "family": biological connection, law, custom, and subjective intentions. On this view, a homosexual couple, a single woman and child, or a commissioning couple and surrogate mother could each be viewed as a family from a certain perspective. Macklin cautions against seeking a "single, univocal concept of the family." In contrast, Katz Rothman proposes a revisionary and univocal definition of motherhood. She argues that men have imposed a seed-based notion of parenthood on women, in part because men are biologically incapable of gestation, giving birth, and breast-feeding a child. These unique and intimate relationships of nurturance are, in her view, much more important than the genetic contribution of a sperm or egg cell could ever be. Katz Rothman's thesis has clear implications for the question of who the real mother is in cases where a surrogate carries and delivers a child to whom she has not made a genetic contribution.

In the final selection of this section the Ethics Committee of the American Fertility Society provides an overview of ethical questions raised by the new (and old) reproductive technologies. Some of these questions are reminiscent of venerable themes that have been discussed for centuries by philosophers and theologians alike. For example, what is the moral status of an eight-cell human preimplantation embryo, which can be divided into viable identical "twins," subjected to genetic testing through the removal of one or two cells, or frozen and stored indefinitely? This selection also raises questions about what is natural and unnatural. According to one view, what is natural is what human beings share in common with nonhuman animals or what human beings have traditionally done. On another view, it is natural for human beings to create technologies or social arrangements that radically alter traditional practices. A final question anticipates issues discussed at length in Chapter 10, namely, whether government should play a role in providing publicly supported access to the technologies of assisted reproduction.

THE PROBLEM OF INFERTILITY

The best statistics suggest that approximately one U.S. married couple in seven faces the problem of involuntary infertility at some point in life. The causes of infertility vary from couple to couple but seem to include lower fertility rates among couples who defer having children until the spouses are in their thirties and the deleterious effects on fertility of sexually transmitted diseases like gonorrhea. The excerpt from a 1988 report of the Office of Technology Assessment provides an overview of the demography of infertility.

But how should the problem of infertility be viewed, philosophically and ethically? Some critics of the new reproductive technologies have argued that infertility is not a disease and that medical intervention to alleviate infertility amounts to nothing more than doctoring the desires of patients.[1] The two remaining selections in this section adopt a different approach. The first, an excerpt from the Warnock Committee report in the United Kingdom, argues that even if infertility is not a disease in the strict sense, it is a bodily "malfunction" that health professionals can and should help to remedy. In her essay, Barbara Katz Rothman employs a different metaphor, suggesting that involuntary infertility should be regarded as a disability. While accepting the view that women should be totally free to choose whether or not to become parents, the author presents a nuanced approach to the problems faced by couples, and especially women, who are surprised to discover that they cannot easily bear children. With the aid of the disability metaphor, Katz Rothman notes that infertility can sometimes be prevented, sometimes cured. In other cases, the disabled person must simply find ways to compensate for the disability. Whatever path is chosen, the author argues, it is the person herself and not a successful reproductive outcome that should remain the central focus of attention.

IN VITRO FERTILIZATION

The birth of Louise Brown in Lancashire, England, in 1978 inaugurated a new era in the history of the reproductive technologies. Louise had not been conceived inside her mother's body but in a petri dish, where eggs removed from her mother had been mixed with sperm from her father, and where fertilization had taken place.

In vitro fertilization (literally, "fertilization in glass") is most often proposed as a technique for overcoming infertility in married couples. The simplest case involves the use of semen from the husband and eggs from the wife. No reproductive cells are donated to the couple, and no "surplus" embryos are produced. All embryos that result from in vitro fertilizations (IVF) contain the parents' genes, and all are transferred to the uterus of the wife in the hope that at least one pregnancy will be achieved. In addition, the simplest case involves no freezing and storage of early human embryos.

There are, of course, variations on this simplest case. Either the sperm cells or the egg cells or the early embryo may be derived from sources other than the husband and the wife (donors or vendors). Even if the sperm and egg cells are provided by the husband and wife, there are numerous options. The developing embryos may be tested for genetic or chromosomal abnormalities, frozen and stored, donated to other couples, provided for research, or allowed to die. Thus, multiple procedures that previously had been possible only with semen or prenatally (that is, after implantation) are now able to be performed after fertilization and before implantation.

Since 1978, the use of IVF as a means for overcoming infertility has steadily increased in most industrialized countries. By the early 1990s IVF had achieved the status of a standard and accepted therapy for certain types of infertility. In part because IVF is more technically complicated and expensive than artificial insemination by donor (AID), IVF is less widely used and produces fewer children than AID. Thus, a privately funded registry that captures most IVF births in the United States and Canada recorded the delivery of 3,215 infants in 1991.[2] For Australia and New Zealand, the official registry for calendar year 1990 noted 1,110 live births following IVF.[3]

As the essays on IVF in this chapter indicate, this relatively new reproductive technique raises a series of interesting metaphysical and ethical problems. Arthur Caplan's essay provides an overview of ethical and public policy issues surrounding the practice of IVF, with special emphasis on questions of justice. Susan Sherwin notes several issues treated by moral philosophers and theologians in their discussions of IVF, then proceeds to identify a series of feminist themes that have been neglected in traditional analyses. Among these themes are discriminatory criteria for selecting among candidates for IVF, unexamined assumptions about women's natural roles as mothers, and an undue emphasis on the importance of a genetic connection between parents and the children they rear.

SURROGATE PARENTING ARRANGEMENTS

In contrast to the new technology of IVF, surrogate parenting involves the combination of a relatively old technology, artificial insemination, with a new social arrangement. The first documented attempt to establish a fee-for-service surrogate motherhood arrangement in the United States occurred in 1976 under the direction of Michigan attorney Noel Keane.[4] According to the terms of such arrangements, which are usually spelled out in written contracts, a woman agrees to become pregnant on behalf of a couple and to deliver the resulting infant to the couple, in exchange for the couple's payment of a fee to the surrogate. In the early years of this new social practice, the technique of artificial insemination donor (AID) was generally employed, using sperm provided by the husband of the future social mother. Thus, the child in the usual or "full" surrogate motherhood arrangement contains genes from the egg of the surrogate mother and the sperm of the would-be social father. However, in 1985 the first instance of surrogate motherhood assisted by IVF occurred. The future social mother was able to produce fertilizable eggs but was medically unable to carry a pregnancy. Her eggs were therefore fertilized in vitro with sperm from her husband, and the resulting embryos were transferred to the uterus of a surrogate mother. In this arrangement, which is sometimes called "partial" surrogacy, the surrogate mother can also be designated a "surrogate carrier" because she makes no genetic contribution to the embryo or infant. (Note that genetic, gestational, and social motherhood can be distinguished in surrogate motherhood arrangements.)

The most celebrated early case of surrogate motherhood involved Noel Keane as attorney and arranger, Mary Beth Whitehead as surrogate mother, William Stern as semen donor and intended social father, and an infant, "Baby M," who became the object of an intense and protracted custody dispute. This case eventually came before the New Jersey Supreme Court, which announced its decision in early 1988. First, the court noted, surrogate motherhood contracts are unenforceable in New Jersey, both because they contradict existing statutes and because they are against "the public policies of this state."[5] Second, the court awarded custody of the child to Stern and his wife because, in the court's judgment, the stable environment of the Sterns' home would be a better setting for the child's rearing than the rather turbulent household of the Whiteheads. Third, the court directed that the trial court award visitation rights to Whitehead, the genetic and gestational mother of Baby M.

Paid, or commercial, surrogacy is not a prevalent method of reproduction in the United States or any other country. The best estimates are that by the beginning of 1988 only about 600 children had been born through surrogate parenting arrangements.[6] However, the ethical and legal issues raised by this reproductive alternative are so sweeping and so profound that surrogate parenting has spawned a substantial bioethics literature. The final section of Chapter 4 provides a cross section of the major viewpoints on this most contentious topic.

The first two essays in this section present diametrically opposed perspectives on the ethical acceptability of surrogacy. According to Elizabeth Anderson, paid surrogate parenting arrangements transform the work of "bringing forth children into the world" into a commodity. In her view, commercial norms are inherently manipulative when applied to "the sphere of parental love." In contrast, Laura Purdy argues that, if reasonably regulated, the practice of surrogacy can "empower women and increase their status in society." In many cases, this option will be less risky to women's health than alternative occupations. Purdy does acknowledge, however, that oppressive stipulations in surrogate parenting contracts can render this otherwise permissible practice wrong in certain cases.

In the final two essays reprinted in this section three lawyers present opposing viewpoints on the appropriate legal perspective from which to view, and therefore to regulate, surrogacy. Richard Posner argues that the law of contracts within commercial law is perfectly adequate for the practice of surrogate parenting. Indeed, according to Posner, enforceable surrogacy contracts produce a situation in which the members of the commissioning couple and the surrogate mother are all better off than before they entered the contractual relationship. The commissioning parents know that they can rely on the surrogate's agreement to surrender her parental rights to the child that she bears for them, and the surrogate can rely on the commissioning parents' agreement to pay her for carrying the pregnancy and giving birth to the child, as well as for her surrender of parental rights. However, Alexander Capron and Margaret Jane Radin reply that adoption is the closest existing analogy to surrogate parenting arrangements and that family law, not commercial law, provides the best model for society's attempts to regulate the practice of surrogate parenting. Specifically, Capron and Radin argue that the gestational mother (and therefore birth mother) of a child should be regarded as the legal mother unless and until she relinquishes the child for adoption. Further, laws against the selling of infants should be enforced against any surrogate mother who attempts to collect a fee in exchange for her surrender of parental rights.

L.W.

NOTES

1. See, for example, Leon R. Kass, "Making Babies: The New Biology and the 'Old' Morality," *Public Interest,* No. 26 (1972), 18–56.

2. "Assisted Reproductive Technology in the United States and Canada: 1991 Results from the Society for Assisted Reproductive Technology Generated from the American Fertility Society Registry," *Fertility and Sterility* 59 (1993), 956–962.

3. Fertility Society of Australia, AIHW Perinatal Statistics Unit, *Assisted Conception, Australia and New Zealand: 1990* (Sydney: AIHW National Perinatal Statistics Unit, 1992), p. 2.

4. Noel P. Keane and Dennis L. Breo, *The Surrogate Mother* (New York: Dodd, Mead, 1981).

5. New Jersey Supreme Court, *In the Matter of Baby M, Atlantic Reporter*, 537 A.2d 1227 (1988), Pt. II.

6. United States, Congress, Office of Technology Assessment, *Infertility: Medical and Social Choices* (Washington, DC: U.S. Government Printing Office, May 1988), p. 267.

Parenting and the Family

RUTH MACKLIN

Artificial Means of Reproduction and Our Understanding of the Family

It is an obvious truth that scientific and technologic innovations produce changes in our traditional way of perceiving the world around us. We have only to think of the telescope, the microscope, and space travel to recall that heretofore unimagined perceptions of the macrocosm and the microcosm have become commonplace. Yet it is not only perceptions, but also conceptions of the familiar that become altered by advances in science and technology. As a beginning student of philosophy, I first encountered problems in epistemology generated by scientific knowledge: If physical objects are really composed of molecules in motion, how is it that we perceive them as solid? Why is it that objects placed on a table don't slip through the empty spaces between the molecules? If the mind is nothing but electrical processes occurring in the brain, how can we explain Einstein's ability to create the special theory of relativity or Bach's ability to compose the Brandenburg Concertos?

Now questions are being raised about how a variety of modes of artificial means of reproduction might alter our conception of the family. George Annas has observed:

> Dependable birth control made sex without reproduction possible. . . . Now medicine is closing the circle . . . by offering methods of reproduction without sex, including artificial insemination by donor (AID), in vitro fertilization (IVF), and surrogate embryo transfer (SET). As with birth control, artificial reproduction is defended as life-affirming and loving by its proponents, and denounced as unnatural by its detractors.[1]

Opponents of artificial reproduction have expressed concerns about its effects on the family. This concern has centered largely but not entirely on surrogacy arrangements. Among the objections to surrogacy made by the Roman Catholic Church is the charge that "the practice of surrogate motherhood is a threat to the stability of the family."[2] But before the consequences for the family of surrogacy arrangements or other new reproductive practices can be assessed, we need to inquire into our understanding of the family. Is there a single, incontrovertible conception of the family? And who are the "we" presupposed in the phrase, "our understanding"? . . .

From *Hastings Center Report* 21 (January–February 1991), 5–11. Reprinted by permission of The Hastings Center.

THE BIOLOGICAL CONCEPT OF FAMILY

It is possible, of course, to settle these conceptual matters simply and objectively by adopting a biological criterion for determining what counts as a family. According to this criterion, people who are genetically related to one another would constitute a family, with the type and degree of relatedness described in the manner of a family tree. This sense of *family* is important and interesting for many purposes, but it does not and cannot encompass everything that is actually meant by *family*, nor does it reflect the broader cultural customs and kinship systems that also define family ties. . . .

Newly developed artificial means of reproduction have rendered the term *biological* inadequate for making some critical conceptual distinctions, along with consequent moral decisions. The capability of separating the process of producing eggs from the act of gestation renders obsolete the use of the word *biological* to modify the word *mother*. The techniques of egg retrieval, in vitro fertilization (IVF), and gamete intrafallopian transfer (GIFT) now make it possible for two different women to make a biological contribution to the creation of a new life. It would be a prescriptive rather than a descriptive definition to maintain that the egg donor should properly be called the biological mother. The woman who contributes her womb during gestation—whether she is acting as a surrogate or is the intended rearing mother—is also a biological mother. We have only to reflect on the many ways that the intrauterine environment and maternal behavior during pregnancy can influence fetal and later child development to acknowledge that a gestating woman is also a biological mother. I will return to this issue later in considering how much genetic contributions should count in disputed surrogacy arrangements.

ADDITIONAL DETERMINANTS OF THE MEANING OF *FAMILY*

In addition to the biological meaning, there appear to be three chief determinants of what is meant by *family*. These are law, custom, and what I shall call subjective intentions. All three contribute to our understanding of the family. The effect of artificial means of reproduction on our understanding of the family will vary, depending on which of these three determinants is chosen to have priority. There is no way to assign a priori precedence to any one of the three. Let me illustrate each briefly.

LAW AS A DETERMINANT OF FAMILY

Legal scholars can elaborate with precision and detail the categories and provisions of family law. This area of law encompasses legal rules governing adoption, artificial insemination by donor, foster placement, custody arrangements, and removal of children from a home in which they have been abused or neglected. For present purposes, it will suffice to summarize the relevant areas in which legal definitions or decisions have determined what is to count as a family.

Laws governing adoption and donor insemination stipulate what counts as a family. In the case of adoption, a person or couple genetically unrelated to a child is deemed that child's legal parent or parents. By this legal rule, a new family is created. The biological parent or parents of the child never cease to be genetically related, of course. But by virtue of law, custom, and usually emotional ties, the adoptive parents become the child's family.

The Uniform Parentage Act holds that a husband who consents to artificial insemination by donor (AID) of his wife by a physician is the legal father of the child. Many states have enacted laws in conformity with this legal rule. I am not aware of any laws that have been enacted making an analogous stipulation in the case of egg donation, but it is reasonable to assume that there will be symmetry of reasoning and legislation.

Commenting on the bearing of family law on the practice of surrogacy, Alexander M. Capron and Margaret J. Radin contend that the "legal rules of greatest immediate relevance" to surrogacy are those on adoption. These authors identify a number of provisions of state laws on adoption that should apply in the case of surrogacy. The provisions include allowing time for a "change of heart" period after the agreement to release a child, and prohibition of agreements to relinquish parental rights prior to the child's birth.[3]

Capron and Radin observe that in the context of adoption, "permitting the birth mother to reclaim a child manifests society's traditional respect for biological ties."[4] But how does this observation bear on artificial reproduction where the biological tie can be either genetic or gestational?

Consider first the case of the gestational surrogate who is genetically unrelated to the child. Does society's traditional respect for biological ties give her or the genetic mother the right to "reclaim" (or claim in the first place) the child? Society's traditional respect is more likely a concern for genetic inheritance than a recognition of the depth of the bond a woman may feel toward a child she has given birth to.

Secondly, consider the case of egg donation and embryo transfer to the wife of the man whose sperm was used in IVF. If the sperm donor and egg recipient were known to the egg donor, could the donor base her claim to the child on "society's traditional respect for biological ties"? As I surmised earlier, it seems reasonable to assume that any laws enacted for egg donation will be similar to those now in place for donor insemination. In the latter context, society's traditional respect for biological ties gave way to other considerations arising out of the desire of couples to have a child who is genetically related to at least one of the parents.

CUSTOM AS A DETERMINANT OF FAMILY

The most telling examples of custom as a determinant of family are drawn from cultural anthropology. Kinship systems and incest taboos dictated by folkways and mores differ so radically that few generalizations are possible.

Ruth Benedict writes: "No known people regard all women as possible mates. This is not in an effort, as is so often supposed, to prevent inbreeding in our sense, for over great parts of the world it is an own cousin, often the daughter of one's mother's brother, who is the predestined spouse."[5] In contrast, Benedict notes, some incest taboos are

extended by a social fiction to include vast numbers of individuals who have no traceable ancestors in common. . . . This social fiction receives unequivocal expression in the terms of relationship which are used. Instead of distinguishing lineal from collateral kin as we do in the distinction between father and uncle, brother and cousin, one term means literally "man of my father's group (relationship, locality, etc.) or his generation." . . . Certain tribes of eastern Australia use an extreme form of this so-called classificatory kinship system. Those whom they call brothers and sisters are all those of their generation with whom they recognize any relationship.[6]

One anthropologist notes that "the family in all societies is distinguished by a stability that arises out of the fact that it is based on marriage, that is to say, on socially sanctioned mating entered into with the assumption of permanency."[7] If we extend the notion of socially sanctioned mating to embrace socially sanctioned procreation, it is evident that the new artificial means of reproduction call for careful thought about what should be socially sanctioned before policy decisions are made.

SUBJECTIVE INTENTION AS A DETERMINANT OF FAMILY

This category is most heterogeneous and amorphous. It includes a variety of ways in which individuals — singly, in pairs, or as a group — consider themselves a family even if their arrangement is not recognized by law or custom. Without an accompanying analysis, I list here an array of examples, based on real people and their situations.

- A homosexual couple decides to solidify their relationship by taking matrimonial vows. Despite the fact that their marriage is not recognized by civil law, they find an ordained minister who is willing to perform the marriage ceremony. Later they apply to be foster parents of children with AIDS whose biological parents have died or abandoned them. The foster agency accepts the couple. Two children are placed in foster care with them. They are now a family.

- A variation on this case: A lesbian couple has a long-term monogamous relationship. They decide they want to rear a child. Using "turkey-baster" technology, one of the women is inseminated, conceives, and gives birth to a baby. The three are now a family, with one parent genetically related to the child.

- Pat Anthony, a forty-seven-year-old grandmother in South Africa, agreed to serve as gestational surrogate for her own daughter. The daughter had had her uterus removed, but could still produce eggs and wanted more children. The daughter's eggs were inseminated with her husband's sperm, and the resulting embryos implanted in her own mother. Mrs. Anthony gave birth to triplets when she was forty-eight. She was the gestational mother and the genetic grandmother of the triplets.

- Linda Kirkman was the gestational mother of a baby conceived with a sister's egg and destined to live with the infertile sister and her husband. Linda Kirkman said, "I always considered myself her aunt." Carol Chan donated eggs so that her sister Susie could bear and raise a child. Carol Chan said: "I could never regard the twins as anything but my nephews." The two births occurred in Melbourne within weeks of each other.[8]

My point in elucidating this category of heterogeneous examples is to suggest that there may be entirely subjective yet valid elements that contribute to our understanding of the family, family membership, or family relationships. I believe it would be arbitrary and narrow to rule out all such examples by fiat. The open texture of our language leaves room for conceptions of family not recognized by law or preexisting custom.

Posing the question, Who counts as family? Carol Levine replies: "The answer to this apparently simple question is by no means easy. It depends on why the question is being asked and who is giving the answer."[9] Levine's observation, made in the context of AIDS, applies equally well to the context of artificial means of reproduction.

THE GESTATIONAL VERSUS THE GENETIC MOTHER

One critical notion rendered problematic by the new technological capabilities of artificial reproduction is the once-simple concept of a mother. The traditional concept is complicated by the possibility that a woman can gestate a fetus genetically unrelated to her. This prospect has implications both for public policy and our understanding of the family. The central policy question is, How much should genetic relatedness count in disputed surrogacy arrangements?

A MATTER OF DISCOVERY OR DECISION?

Which criterion—genetic or gestational—should be used to determine who is the "real" mother? I contend that this question is poorly formulated. Referring to the "real" mother implies that it is a matter of discovery, rather than one calling for a decision. To speak of "the real x" is to assume that there is an underlying metaphysical structure to be probed by philosophical inquiry. But now that medical technology has separated the two biological contributions to motherhood, in place of the single conjoint role provided by nature, some decisions will have to be made.

One decision is conceptual, and a second is moral. The conceptual question is: Should a woman whose contribution is solely gestational be termed a mother of the baby? We may assume, by analogy with our concept of paternity, that the woman who makes the genetic contribution in a surrogacy arrangement can properly be termed a mother of the baby. So it must be decided whether there can be only one mother, conceptually speaking, or whether this technological advance calls for new terminology.

Conceptual decisions often have implications beyond mere terminology. A decision not to use the term *mother* (even when modified by the adjective *gestational*) to refer to a woman who acts in this capacity can have important consequences for ethics and public policy. As a case in point, the Wayne County Circuit Court in Michigan issued an interim order declaring a gamete donor couple to be the biological parents of a fetus being carried to term by a woman hired to be the gestational mother. Upon birth, the court entered an order that the names of the ovum and sperm donors be listed on the birth certificate, rather than that of the woman who gave birth, who was termed by the court a "human incubator."[10]

The ethical question posed by the separation of biological motherhood into genetic and gestational components is, Which role should entitle a woman to a greater claim on the baby, in case of dispute? Since the answer to this question cannot be reached by discovery, but is, like the prior conceptual question, a matter for decision, we need to determine which factors are morally relevant and which have the greatest moral weight. To avoid begging any ethical questions by a choice of terminology, I use the terms *genetic mother* and *gestational mother* to refer to the women who make those respective contributions. And instead of speaking of the "real" mother, I'll use the phrase *primary mother* when referring to the woman presumed to have a greater claim on the child.

MORALLY RELEVANT FACTORS

The possibilities outlined below are premised on the notion that surrogacy contracts are voidable. I take this to mean that no legal presumption is set up by the fact that there has been a prior contract between the surrogate and the intended rearing parents. From an ethical perspective, that premise must be argued for independently, and convincing arguments have been advanced by a number of authors.[11] If we accept the premise that a contractual provision to relinquish a child born of a surrogacy agreement has no legal force, the question then becomes, Is there a morally relevant distinction between the two forms of surrogacy with respect to a claim on the child? Who has the weightiest moral claim when a surrogate is unwilling to give the baby up after its birth? Where should the moral presumption lie? The question may be answered in one of three ways.

1. Gestation. According to this position, whether a woman is merely the gestational surrogate, or also contributes her genetic material, makes no difference in determining moral priorities. In either case, the surrogate is the primary mother because the criterion is gestation.

The gestational position is adopted by George Annas and others who have argued that the gestational mother should be legally presumed to have the right and responsibility to rear the child. One reason given in support of this presumption is "the greater biological and psychological investment of the gestational mother in the child."[12] This is referred to as "sweat equity." A related yet distinct reason is "the biological reality that the mother at this point has contributed more to the child's development, and that she will of necessity be present at birth and immediately thereafter to care for the child.[13]

The first reason focuses on what the gestational mother deserves, based on her investment in the child, while the second reason, though mentioning her contribution, also focuses on the interests of the child during and immediately after birth. Annas adds that "to designate the gestational mother, rather than the genetic mother, the legal or 'natural mother' would be protective of children."[14]

2. Genetics. In surrogacy arrangements, it is the inseminating male who is seen as the father, not the husband of the woman who acts as a surrogate. This is because the genetic contribution is viewed as determinative for fatherhood. By analogy, the woman who makes the genetic contribution is the primary mother. This position sharply distinguishes between the claim to the child made by the two different types of surrogate. It makes the surrogate who contributes her egg as well as her womb the primary (or sole) mother. But now recall the fact that in AID, the law recognizes the husband of the inseminated woman as the father — proof that laws can be made to go either way.

This position was supported by the court in Smith & Smith v. Jones & Jones, on grounds of the analogy with paternity. The court said: "The donor of the ovum, the biological mother, is to be deemed, in fact, the natural mother of this infant, as is the biological father to be deemed the natural father of this child."[15]

Legal precedents aside, is there a moral reason that could be invoked in support of this position? One possibility is "ownership" of one's genetic products. Since each individual has a unique set of genes, people might be said to have a claim on what develops from their own genes, unless they have explicitly relinquished any such claims. This may be a metaphorical sense of ownership, but it reflects the felt desire to have genetically related children — the primary motivation behind all forms of assisted reproduction.

Another possible reason for assigning greater weight to the genetic contribution is the child-centered position. Here it is argued that it is in children's best interest to be reared by parents to whom they are genetically related. Something like this position is taken by Sidney Callahan. She writes:

The most serious ethical problems in using third-party donors in alternative reproduction concern the well-being of the potential child. . . . A child who has donor(s) intruded into its parentage will be cut off from its genetic heritage and part of its kinship relations in new ways. Even if there is no danger of transmitting unknown genetic disease or causing physiological harm to the child, the psychological relationship of the child to its parents is endangered — with or without the practice of deception and secrecy about its origins.[16]

Additional considerations lending plausibility to this view derive from data concerning adopted children who have conducted searches for their biological parents, and similar experiences of children whose birth was a result of donor insemination and who have sought out their biological fathers. In the case of gestational surrogacy, the child is genetically related to both of the intended rearing parents. However, there [are] no data to suggest whether children born of gestational mothers might someday begin to seek out those women in a quest for their "natural" or "real" mothers.

3. Gestation and genetics. According to this position, the surrogate who contributes both egg and womb has more of a claim to being the primary mother than does the surrogate who contributes only her womb. Since the first type of surrogate makes both a genetic and a gestational contribution, in case

of a dispute she gets to keep the baby instead of the biological father, who has made only one contribution. But this does not yet settle the question of who has a greater moral claim to the infant in cases where the merely gestational surrogate does not wish to give up the baby to the genetic parents. To determine that, greater weight must be given either to the gestational component or the genetic component.

SUBSIDIARY VIEWS

One may reject the notion that the only morally relevant considerations are the respective contributions of each type of surrogate. Another possible criterion draws on the biological conception of family, and thus takes into account the contribution of the genetic father. According to this position, two genetic contributions count more than none. This leads to three subsidiary views, in addition to the three main positions outlined above.

4. Gestational surrogates have less of a moral claim to the infant than the intended parents, both of whom have made a genetic contribution. This is because two (genetic) contributions count more than one (gestational) contribution. This view, derived from "society's traditional respect for biological ties," gives greatest weight to the concept of family based on genetic inheritance.

5. A woman who contributes both egg and womb has a claim equal to that of the biological father, since both have made genetic contributions. If genetic contribution is what determines both "true" motherhood and fatherhood, the policy implications of this view are that each case in which a surrogate who is both genetic and gestational mother wishes to keep the baby would have to go to court and be settled in the manner of custody disputes.

As a practical suggestion, this model is of little value. It throws every case of this type of surrogacy — the more common variety — open to this possibility, which is to move backwards in public policy regarding surrogacy.

6. However, if genetic and gestational contributions are given equal weight, but it is simply the number of contributions that counts, the artificially inseminated surrogate has the greater moral claim since she has made two contributions — genetic and gestational — while the father has made only one, the genetic contribution.

What can we conclude from all this about the effects of artificial means of reproduction on the family and on our conception of the family? Several conclusions emerge, although each requires a more extended elaboration and defense than will be given here.

A broad definition of *family* is preferable to a narrow one. A good candidate is the working definition proposed by Carol Levine: "Family members are individuals who by birth, adoption, marriage, or declared commitment share deep personal connections and are mutually entitled to receive and obligated to provide support of various kinds to the extent possible, especially in times of need."[17]

Some of the effects of the new reproductive technologies on the family call for the development of public policy, while others remain private, personal matters to be decided within a given family. An example of the former is the determination of where the presumptions should lie in disputed surrogacy arrangements, whose rights and interests are paramount, and what procedures should be followed to safeguard those rights and interests. An example of the latter is disclosure to a child of the facts surrounding genetic paternity or maternity in cases of donor insemination or egg donation, including the identity of the donor when that is known. These are profound moral decisions, about which many people have strong feelings, but they are not issues to be addressed by public policy.

It is not at all clear that artificial modes of reproduction threaten to produce greater emotional difficulties for family members affected, or pose more serious ethical problems, than those already arising out of long-standing practices such as adoption and artificial insemination. The analogy is often made between the impact on women who serve as surrogates and those who have lost their biological offspring in other ways.

Warning of the dangers of surrogacy, defenders of birth mothers have related the profound emotional trauma and lasting consequences for women who have given their babies up for adoption. One such defender is Phyllis Chesler, a psychologist who has written about the mother-infant bond and about custody battles in which mothers have lost their children to fathers. Dr. Chesler reports that many women never get over having given up their child for adoption. Their decision "leads to thirty to forty years of being haunted."[18] Chesler contends that the trauma to women who have given up their babies for adoption is far greater than that of incest, and greater than that felt by mothers who have lost custody battles for their children.

Additional evidence of the undesirable consequences for birth mothers of adoption is provided by Alison Ward, a woman who serves as an adoption reform advocate. Having given up her own daughter for adoption in 1967, she found and was reunited with her in 1980. Ms. Ward said to an audience assembled to hear testimony on surrogacy:

I think that you lack the personal experience I have: that of knowing what it is like to terminate your parental rights and go for years not knowing if your child is dead or alive. All the intellectual and philosophical knowledge in the world cannot begin to touch having to live your life as a birthparent. Last Sunday was Mother's Day. It seems ironic, as our country gives such lip service to the values of motherhood and the sanctity of the bond between mother and child, that we even consider legalizing a process [surrogacy] which would destroy all that.[19]

The effects of these practices on children are alleged to be equally profound and damaging. Scholarly studies conducted in recent years have sought to evaluate the adjustment of children to adoption. One expert notes that "the pattern emerging from the more recent clinical and nonclinical studies that have sampled widely and used appropriate controls, generally supports the view that, on the average, adopted children are more likely to manifest psychological problems than nonadopted children."[20] The additional fact that numerous adopted children have sought to find their biological parents, despite their being in a loving family setting, suggests that psychological forces can intrude on the dictates of law or custom regarding what counts as a family. Although it is easier to keep secret from a child the circumstances surrounding artificial insemination and egg donation, such secrets have sometimes been revealed with terrible emotional consequences for everyone involved.

Alison Ward compares the impact of surrogacy on children to both situations:

There will always be pain for these children. Just as adoptive parents have learned that they cannot love the pain of their adopted children away, couples who raise children obtained through surrogacy will have to deal with a special set of problems. Donor offspring . . . rarely find out the truth of their origins. But, some of them do, and we must listen to them when they speak of their anguish, of not knowing who fathered them; we must listen when they tell us how destructive it is to their self-esteem to find out their father sold the essence of his lineage for $40 or so, without ever intending to love or take responsibility for them. For children born of surrogacy contracts, it will be even worse: their own mothers did this to them.[21]

Phyllis Chesler paints a similarly bleak picture of the effect on children of being adopted away from their birth mothers. She contends that this has "dramatic, extreme psychological consequences." She cites evidence indicating that adopted children seem more prone to mental and emotional disorders than other children, and concludes that "children need to know their natural origins."[22]

These accounts present only one side, and there is surely another, more positive picture of parents and children flourishing in happy, healthy families that would not have existed but for adoption or artificial insemination. Yet the question remains, What follows in any case from such evidence? Is it reasonable to conclude that the negative consequences of these practices, which have altered traditional conceptions of the family, are reasons for abolishing them? Or for judging that it was wrong to institute them in the first place, since for all practical purposes they cannot be reversed? A great deal more evidence, on a much larger scale, would be needed before a sound conclusion could be reached that adoption and artificial insemination have had such negative consequences for the family that they ought never to have been socially sanctioned practices.

Similarly, there is no simple answer to the question of how artificial means of reproduction affect our understanding of the family. We need to reflect on the variety of answers, paying special attention to what follows from answering the question one way rather than another. Since there is no single, univocal concept of the family, it is a matter for moral and social decision just which determinants of "family" should be given priority.

REFERENCES

1. George J. Annas, "Redefining Parenthood and Protecting Embryos," in *Judging Medicine* (Clifton, N.J.: Humana Press, 1988), p. 59. Reprinted from the *Hastings Center Report* 14, no. 5 (1984).

2. William F. Bolan, Jr., Executive Director, New Jersey Catholic Conference, "Statement of New Jersey Catholic Conference in Connection with Public Hearing on Surrogate Mothering," Commission on Legal and Ethical Problems in the Delivery of Health Care, Newark, N.J.:, 11 May 1988.

3. Alexander M. Capron and Margaret J. Radin, "Choosing Family Law over Contract Law as a Paradigm for Surrogate Motherhood," *Law, Medicine & Health Care* 16 (Spring–Summer 1988): 35.

4. Capron and Radin, "Choosing Family Law over Contract Law," p. 35.

5. Ruth Benedict, *Patterns of Culture* (New York: Mentor Books, 1934), p. 29.

6. Benedict, *Patterns of Culture*, p. 30.

7. Melville J. Herskovits, *Cultural Anthropology* (New York: Alfred A. Knopf, 1955), p. 171.

8. R. Alta Charo, "Legislative Approaches to Surrogate Motherhood," *Law, Medicine & Health Care* 16 (Spring–Summer 1988): 104

9. Levine, "AIDS and Changing Concepts of Family," *Milbank Quarterly* 68, supp. 1 (1990): 35.

10. O.T.A. report, "Infertility: Medical and Social Choices," p. 284; case cited *Smith & Smith v. Jones & Jones*, 85-532014 DZ, Detroit, MI, 3rd Dist. (15 March 1986), as reported in *BioLaw*, ed. James F. Childress, Patricia King, Karen H. Rothenberg, et al. (Frederick, Md.: University Publishers of America, 1986). See also George J. Annas, "The Baby Broker Boom," *Hastings Center Report* 16, no. 3 (1986): 30–31.

11. See, e.g., George J. Annas, "Death without Dignity for Commercial Surrogacy: The Case of Baby M," *Hastings Center Re-*

port, 18, no. 2 (1988): 21–24; and Bonnie Steinbock, "Surrogate Motherhood as Prenatal Adoption," in *Surrogate Motherhood: Politics and Privacy,* ed. Larry Gostin (Bloomington: Indiana University Press, 1990), pp. 123–135.

12. Sherman Elias and George J. Annas, "Noncoital Reproduction," *JAMA* 255 (3 January 1986): 67.

13. Annas, "Death without Dignity," p. 23.

14. Annas, "Death without Dignity," p. 24.

15. Annas, "The Baby Broker Boom," p. 31.

16. "The Ethical Challenge of the New Reproductive Technology," presentation before the Task Force on New Reproductive Practices; published in John F. Monagle and David C. Thomasma, eds., *Medical Ethics: A Guide for Health Care Professionals* (Frederick, Md.: Aspen Publishers, 1987).

17. Levine, "AIDS and Changing Concepts of Family," p. 36.

18. This statement and subsequent ones attributed to Phyllis Chesler are taken from her unpublished remarks made at a public hearing on surrogacy conducted by the New Jersey Bioethics Commission, Newark, N.J., 11 May 1988, in which the author was a participant.

19. Written testimony, presented orally at the New Jersey Bioethics Commission's public hearing on surrogacy, 11 May 1988.

20. David M. Brodzinsky, "Adjustment to Adoption: A Psychosocial Perspective," *Clinical Psychology Review* 7 (1987): 29.

21. Ward, written testimony from New Jersey public hearing.

22. Chesler, oral testimony at New Jersey public hearing.

BARBARA KATZ ROTHMAN

Motherhood: Beyond Patriarchy*

INTRODUCTION

Law works by precedent and by analogy. While that has shown extraordinary advantages in maintaining an orderly system and avoiding capriciousness, it has its limitations. The law has a hard time confronting something new. New things can be incorporated only by stressing their points of similarity to old things, to concepts already embedded in the law.

The "something new" to which I refer here is not so much surrogacy arrangements and new reproductive technology per se, as it is the issues and concerns,

the *interests*, of women where those are not the same as, or analogous to, those of men.

American law has, since the time of the constitution, continually if haltingly expanded the definition of citizen, of individual entitled to full legal rights. The rights and privileges of the white men framers of the constitution have thus been extended to men of color, to native American men, and eventually to women. In the areas of employment, housing, education—all of the areas of what we think of as the "public sphere"—this has been an effective technique to achieve a more just society.

As new concerns arise around family and procreation—the areas we think of in America as "private life"—the limitations of the workings of the law become apparent. It is these limitations which I address here.

From *Nova Law Review* 13 (1989), 481–486. ©1989 by *Nova Law Review*. Reprinted by permission of the publisher.

*Parts of this article are drawn from the author's book, *Recreating Motherhood: Ideology and Technology in a Patriarchal Society* (W. W. Norton & Co. 1989).

Legal definitions of the family are reflections not of biological relationships, but rather of cultural values and ideology. The law reifies the values and beliefs of the law-makers. American family law has its roots in patriarchy, and in men's view of family relationships.

The term "patriarchy" is often used loosely as a synonym for "sexism," or to refer to any social system where men rule. The term has a more specific, technical meaning, however: the rule of fathers. It is in that specific sense that I am using it here.

Patriarchal kinship is the core of what is meant by patriarchy: the idea that paternity is the definitive social relationship. A very clear statement of patriarchal kinship is found in the book of Genesis, in the "begats." Each man, from Adam onward, is described as having begot a son in his likeness, after his image. After the birth of this firstborn son, the men are described as having lived so many years, and having begot sons and daughters. The text then turns to that firstborn son, and in turn his firstborn son after him. Women appear as "the daughters of men who bore them offspring." In a patriarchal kinship system, children are reckoned as being born to men, out of women. Women, in this system of patriarchy, bear the children of men.

The central concept here is the "seed," that part of men that grows into children of their likeness within the bodies of women. Such a system is inevitably male dominated, but it is a particular kind of male domination. Men control women as daughters, much as they control their sons, but they also control women as the mothers of men's children. It is women's motherhood that men must control to maintain patriarchy. In a patriarchy, because what is valued is the relationship of a man to his sons, women are a vulnerability that men have: to beget these sons, men must pass their seed through the body of a woman.

While all societies appear to be male dominated to some degree, not all societies are patriarchal. In some, the line of descent is not from father to son, but along the lines of the women. These are called "matrilineal" societies: it is a shared woman that makes for shared lineage of the family group. Men still rule in these groups, but they do not rule as fathers. They rule the women and children who are related to them through their mother's line. In such a system, people are not men's children coming through the bodies of women, but the children of women.

Our society developed out of a patriarchal system, in which paternity was the fundamentally important relationship. Some of our social customs and traditions, as well as such laws as those defining "illegitimacy," reflected men's concern for maintaining paternity. But the modern American society's kinship system is not classically patriarchal. It is what anthropologists call a bilateral system, in that individuals are considered to be equally related to both their mother's and their father's "sides" of the family.

We carry our history with us, though. Out of the patriarchal focus on the seed as the source of being, on the male production of children from men's seed, has grown our current thinking about procreation.

Modern procreative technology has been forced to go beyond the sperm as seed, to recognize the egg as seed also. But the central concept of patriarchy, the importance of the seed, was retained by extending the concept to women. Women too have seed, and women too can be said to have their "own" children, just as men do. In this modified system based on the older ideology of patriarchy, women's "rights" to their children are not based on the unique relationship of pregnancy, the long months of gestation and nurturance, the intimate connections of birth and suckling, but on women's status as producers of seed. Women gain their control over their children not as mothers, but as father-equivalents. Thus the rights and privileges of men are extended to women. But there are costs, as we are increasingly coming to see.

REDEFINING MOTHERHOOD AND FATHERHOOD

When biological paternity could only be assumed and never proved, the legal relationship between men and women in marriage gave men control over the children of women: any child of a man's wife was legally a child of the man. Motherhood was obvious; and fatherhood was reckoned by the relationship of the man to the mother.

Now that biological paternity can be brought under the control of science, with doctors both controlling paternity by moving insemination from the bed to the operating table or petri dish, and by proving paternity with newly definitive paternity testing, the legal relationship between men, women and their children has begun to shift.

A man's paternity need no longer be reckoned through his legal relationship with the mother of the child, but can now be ascertained directly. In consequence, we occasionally find ourselves reckoning maternity through a woman's legal relationship with the father. Consider here the newly available technology which permits a woman to carry to term a fetus not conceived of her ovum. There is nothing in *in vitro* technology that requires the fertilized ovum to be placed in the uterus of the same woman from whom the ovum was originally retrieved. We have, to put it simply, a technology that takes Susan's egg and puts it in Mary's body. And so who, we ask, is the mother? Is Mary substituting for Susan's body, growing Susan's baby for Susan? Or is Susan's egg substituting for Mary's, growing into Mary's baby in Mary's body?

The way American society has been answering that question depends on which woman is married to the baby's father. If Mary's husband is the father, then Mary is the mother, and Susan considered an "ovum donor," comparable to a sperm donor, with no recognized claim to the child. But if Susan's husband is the father, then Susan is the mother, and Mary the surrogate, the hired uterus, the incubator. There exist now in the U.S., birth certificates that list as the mother the ovum donor, and the name of the woman who carried the pregnancy and birthed the baby is nowhere on the birth certificate. Just as there exist birth certificates that list as the mother the woman who carried the baby, and not the name of the woman who donated the egg. Legal motherhood is being determined by the relationship of the woman to the father.

Thus, while we have moved beyond traditional patriarchal definitions, we have not moved beyond the focus on seeds and genetics, and sperm and paternity specifically. This focus on the genetic connection between parents and their children is not a simple reflection of biological reality. The parent-child relationship is invested with social and legal rights and claims that are not recognized, in this society, in any other genetic relationship. And that is not because it is a uniquely close relationship. If an individual carries a certain gene, the chances that a sibling will carry the same gene are fifty-fifty, the same as the parent-child relationship. Genetically, "there is nothing special about the parent-offspring relationship except its close degree and a certain fundamental asymmetry. The full-sib relationship is just as close."[1]

The significance we claim for the parent-child relationship is rooted in our social heritage of patriarchy: that genetic connection was the basis for men's control over the children of women. The contemporary

modification of traditional patriarchy has been to recognize the genetic parenthood of women as being equivalent to the genetic parenthood of men. Genetic parenthood is the only parenthood men could have biologically; and thus in our legal system, the only parenthood that is recognized for women. The significance of gestation, having no analogy to the experience of men's parenthood, is dismissed.

SURROGACY: BEYOND BABY M

It is in this context, in which genetic parenthood is acknowledged and pregnancy ignored, that the marketing of mothering services, commercial surrogacy, has developed.

Surrogacy, some people tell us, is not new; it is as old as the bible, as old as the story of Abraham, Sarah and Hagar. But Hagar was not a surrogate mother for Ishmael. She was unquestionably the mother of that child. Sarah was not Ishmael's adoptive, foster, rearing, or social mother. She was Abraham's wife, and Hagar was the mother of the child, *his* child, the child of Abraham. If Hagar served as a surrogate, it was as a surrogate wife, bearing a child for Abraham, the child of his seed, in her body.

Abraham and Hagar were living in a true patriarchy; William Stern and Mary Beth Whitehead do not. Our society, recognizing the genetic tie between mother and child, understood Baby M to be "half his, half hers." But the child might just as well have grown in the backyard. The unique relationship of pregnancy, the motherhood experience, received no recognition. Even without a legal contract for a surrogacy arrangement, Stern had as much right to the child, in our modified patriarchy, as did Whitehead. Abraham claimed his child but acknowledged the mother. Stern claimed his child but recognized no mother, only a rented uterus, a human incubator. The court ultimately rejected his argument, but only to the extent of recognizing Whitehead's *genetic* tie to the child, not the significance of her mothering of that child through pregnancy and birth.

The "Baby M" case simply highlighted what is true for all mothers in this system: we are only recognized as half owners of the children of our bodies. Women have gained recognition of our genetic ties to our children, but we have lost recognition of our nurturance, our motherhood. In a sense, we have gained paternity rights at the cost of maternity rights.

And now that women's genetic parenthood can be split off from gestational parenthood, the costs of equating our parenthood with that of men comes clear. If parenthood is understood as a genetic relationship, divided equally between sperm and ovum donors, then where is the place for pregnancy?

The new reproductive technology permits the development of surrogacy arrangements quite different from that of the Baby M situation. What will happen as the new technology allows brokers to hire women who are not related genetically to the babies that are to be sold? Like the poor and non-white women who are hired to do other kinds of nurturing and caretaking tasks, these mothers can be paid very little, with few benefits, and no long-term commitment. The same women who are pushing white babies in strollers, white old folks in wheelchairs, can be carrying white babies in their bellies. Poor, uneducated, third world women and women of color from the United States and elsewhere, with fewer economic alternatives, can be hired more cheaply. They can also be controlled more tightly. With a legally supported surrogate motherhood contract, and with new technology, the marketing possibilities are enormous—and terrifying. Just as Perdue and Holly Farms advertise their chickens based on superior breeding and feeding, the baby brokers could begin to advertise their babies: brand-name, state-of-the-art babies, produced from the "finest" of genetic materials and an all-natural, vitamin-enriched diet.

IN SUM: BEYOND PATERNITY

We cannot allow the law to inch along, extending to women some of the privileges of patriarchy, but understanding the experiences of women only as they are analogous to those of men. What is needed is to move beyond the principles of patriarchy and beyond its modifications, to an explicit recognition of *motherhood*. Women are not, and must not be thought of as, incubators, bearing the children of others—not the children of men, and not the children of other women. Every woman is the mother of the child she bears, regardless of the source of the sperm, and regardless of the source of the egg. The law must come to such an explicit recognition of the maternity relationship.

NOTE

1. Hamilton, "The Genetic Evolution of Social Behavior," in *The Sociobiology Debate: Readings on Ethical and Scientific Issues* 191 (A. Caplan, ed. 1978).

AMERICAN FERTILITY SOCIETY, ETHICS COMMITTEE

Ethics and the New Reproductive Technologies

Many ethical questions have been raised about specific cases involving the new reproductive technologies. This [essay] seeks to survey some of the generic issues under discussion and to examine the ethical principles and theories that inform the current debate.

From the Ethics Committee of The American Fertility Society, "Ethics and the New Reproductive Technologies," *Fertility and Sterility* 53 (Supplement 2; 1990), 17S–21S. Reproduced with permission of the publisher, The American Fertility Society.

ISSUES

THE NATURALNESS OR ARTIFICIALITY OF THE NEW TECHNOLOGIES

If one believes that nothing artificial should intrude into the sexual relations between human beings, that belief will have profound implications for one's attitude toward contraceptive techniques and the new reproductive technologies. One critic of these technologies has formulated his objection as follows:

Is there possibly some wisdom in that mystery of nature which joins the pleasure of sex, the communication of love, and the desire for children in the very activity by which we continue the chain of human existence? . . . My point is simply this: there are more and less human ways of bringing a child into the world. I am arguing that the laboratory production of human beings is no longer *human* procreation, that making babies in laboratories—even "perfect" babies—means a degradation of parenthood (Kass, 1972).

Diametrically opposed to this antitechnologic viewpoint is the perspective of those who regard the rational control of nature as one of the major achievements of human beings. According to this view, liberation from some of the unpredictable aspects of human reproduction is a major boon to the human species.

Should we leave the fruits of human reproduction to take shape at random, keeping our children dependent upon the accidents of romance and genetic endowment, of (the) sexual lottery, or what one physician calls 'the meiotic roulette of his parents' chromosomes'? Or should we be responsible about this, that is, exercise our rational and human choice, no longer submissively trusting to the blind worship of raw nature? (Fletcher, 1974).

A third position tends to mediate between these radically divergent views. In agreement with the first, this third position accepts reproduction without technologic assistance as natural and good. However, this position also argues that the development and use of new methods of contraception or reproduction can be morally justifiable, depending on the circumstances and on the reasons adduced. According to this view, it is natural for human beings to create a social structure in an effort to cope with the uncertainties and inconveniences of the "natural" world; technology is an important part of that structure (Callahan, 1972). The Committee accepts this third position. . . .

THE MORAL STATUS OF THE HUMAN PREEMBRYO

To speak of the moral status of anything is to use a shorthand expression for more complex formulations, such as "What are our moral obligations to X?" or "What moral rights does X possess?" Analogously, one can speak of the legal status of an adult, a newborn infant, or a human preembryo.

There are three principal viewpoints on the moral status of the human preembryo. The first viewpoint asserts that human preembryos are entitled to protection as human beings from the time of fertilization forward. According to this view, any research or other manipulation, such as freezing, that may damage a preembryo or interfere with its prospects for transfer to a uterus and its subsequent development is ethically unacceptable. This perspective on preembryonic status cites two kinds of factual evidence. First, a new genotype is established during fertilization. Second, given the appropriate environment, some preembryos have the potential to become full-term fetuses, children, and adults.

A second viewpoint denies that human preembryos have any moral status. According to this viewpoint, we have no moral obligations to human preembryos. This position also appeals to scientific evidence, especially the fact that only 30% to 40% of preembryos produced through human sexual intercourse develop to maturity in utero and are delivered as live infants (Leridon, 1973). It also notes that the biologic individuality of the preembryo is assured only toward the end of the first 14 days of development; before that time, one preembryo can divide into twins; or, experimentally, multiple preembryos with different genotypes can be combined into a single preembryo. Finally, this position argues that an undifferentiated entity like the preembryo—which has no organs, limbs, or sentience—cannot have moral status.

Again on this issue there is an intermediate position. This viewpoint accords some moral status to the preembryo on grounds both of its unique genotype and its potential. The potential to become an adult differentiates the preembryo from nonembryonic human tissues or cells. However, this third viewpoint acknowledges that our prima facie moral obligations to human preembryos can be outweighed by other moral duties, for example, the duty to develop new and better methods of providing care to infertile couples or pregnant women. . . . [The Committee accepts this intermediate position.]

THE ROLE OF FAMILY OR GENETIC LINEAGE

The modern techniques of artificial insemination (AID, AIH), in vitro fertilization (IVF), and—to a lesser extent—uterine lavage have made the notion of "parenthood" more complex. In some contexts of medically assisted reproduction, one must distinguish among the genetic, gestational, and rearing mothers and between the genetic and rearing fathers. Table 1 illustrates the major ways in which third parties can become participants in the reproductive process (Walters, 1985).

Table 1 Alternate Reproductive Methods[a, b]

| | Source of gametes | | Site of | Site of | |
	Male	Female	fertilization	pregnancy	Notes
1	H	W	W	W	Customary, AIH, GIFT, TPET
2	S	W	W	W	AID
3	H	W	L	W	IVF
4	S	W	L	W	IVF with donated sperm
5	H	S	L	W	IVF with donated egg
6	S	S	L	W	IVF with both gametes donated (or donated embryo)
7	H	S	S	W	AIH with donor woman plus uterine lavage (semidonated embryo)
8	S	S	S	W	AID with donor woman plus uterine lavage (donated embryo)
9	H	W	W	S	⎫
10	S	W	W	S	
11	H	W	L	S	
12	S	W	L	S	⎬ Surrogate motherhood
13	H	S	L	S	
14	S	S	L	S	
15	H	S	S	S	
16[c]	S	S	S	S	⎭

[a]Chart developed by William B. Weil, Jr., and LeRoy Walters.
[b]H, husband; W, wife; S, third-party substitute, or surrogate; and L, laboratory.
[c]Planned procreation for placement; traditional adoption is not part of the schematic.

The practice of donating gametes or preembryos has occasioned debate among commentators on the new reproductive technologies. One view is that these technologies should be employed only within the family unit. Proponents of this view conclude that if the couple cannot conceive a child by means of their own gametes, even with medical assistance, they should accept their infertility and explore alternatives such as adoption. According to this viewpoint, adoption is qualitatively different from the deliberate and premeditated introduction of "foreign" gametes or preembryos into the family unit, because adopting parents rescue an already existing child from a situation of homelessness. . . .

The opposing viewpoint on gamete and preembryo donation is that these practices are morally justified when employed by a couple for good reasons, such as untreatable infertility or the presence of a genetic defect in one or both partners. The use of the new reproductive technologies is therefore seen as a useful adjunct that allows couples to approximate, as closely as possible, the usual experience of reproduction.

In [later] chapters . . . the Committee discusses various types of gamete or preembryo donation. The conclusion of the Committee in most of the donation scenarios is that the alleviation of infertility or the prevention of the transmission of known genetic defects provides a sufficient rationale for donation. On the other hand, the Committee finds that the use of donation for nonmedical reasons, such as the desire to produce a "superbaby," is ethically unacceptable.

A second controversial issue is the meaning of the term *family*. The traditional understanding of family was that it included a husband, a wife, and one or more children. This traditional understanding has been challenged not primarily by the new reproductive technologies but rather by several social developments of the 20th century, especially divorce rates approaching 50% in the United States and the increasing number of children born to single women. The general debate about the meaning of family, however, will be carried over into discussions of the new reproductive technologies as members of nontraditional families—unmarried heterosexual couples, homosexual couples, single men or women — request technical assistance in reproduction.

The Committee considers parenthood by a heterosexual couple to be the most appropriate arrangement, other things being equal. However, the Committee discusses . . . the moral right to reproduce in terms that allow a role for other patterns of parenthood. The Committee is opposed to the legal prohibition of medically assisted reproduction by nontraditional families.*

A third controversial issue is whether or not the donors of gametes or preembryos should be known to members of the rearing family. In other words, should donors be regarded as part of an extended family? If donations are made by relatives or close friends, they will automatically be known to the recipient couple. In other donation situations, practice has varied, with artificial insemination — donor (AID) usually remaining anonymous; surrogate mothers, however, are often known to the rearing couple. The Committee viewpoint is that practice in this area should be governed by the results of careful empiric research on the effects of the arrangements on the participants, which includes the children, and by the wishes of the principals involved. However, the Committee considers it an ethical obligation of the health professionals involved to retain some means for recontacting donors and providing medical follow-up. . . . This information link with donors becomes especially critical if offspring are born with genetic defects.

THE MORAL LEGITIMACY OF PAYMENTS TO GAMETE PROVIDERS AND SURROGATES

The providers of semen or oocytes, the genetic parents of preembryos, and surrogate mothers may receive compensation for their participation in the new reproductive technologies and arrangements. In cases where gametes or preembryos are involved, the compensation is quite modest. In cases involving surrogate parenting arrangements, where the intensity and duration of the woman's involvement are greater, the payments can be much more substantial.

*The statement is excessively broad. There are certain types of persons who would fall within the term "nontraditional families," but who might very appropriately be prohibited by law from having access to reproductive technologies; for example, teenagers, drug dependents. Similarly, further experience with surrogacy may well indicate the need for some form of prohibitive legislation (Richard A. McCormick).

There are six major policy approaches to this question. The first cites the analogy of whole-blood donation and argues that semen and oocyte providers, at least, should be genuine *donors;* that is, they should be encouraged to provide their gametes to infertile couples as a public service, without compensation even for their time and expenses. The French government has sought to embody this charitable approach in a regional network of sperm banks, and the Warnock Committee report of 1984 advocates that the United Kingdom adopt a similar policy (United Kingdom, 1984).

A second policy advocates that gamete providers or surrogates be reimbursed for actual out-of-pocket expenses, such as transportation costs and medical fees, but that no payment be made for the time of the participant or for the "product" of the donation process, whether that product is a cell or an infant.

A third possible policy is similar to the second but would allow, in addition, reasonable payment for the time of the gamete provider or surrogate, or for his/her pain, risk, and inconvenience. In the case of gamete providers, this policy would involve, at most, a specified number of hours or days. Further, there would be a clear differential between semen and oocyte providers, because the latter must undergo a surgical procedure and may receive prior hormonal stimulation as well. In the case of surrogate mothers, this policy would allow monetary compensation for pre- and postpartum leave from a job and could include the entire period from the woman's first involvement with the commissioning couple to the end of postpartum leave.

Three other policy options would allow payment for specific "products" of third-party involvement in the reproductive process. The first of these, and the fourth option of the six, would permit payment for gametes but not for preembryos or infants. The second would accept payment for both gametes and preembryos, but not for infants. The third would permit payment for infants as well.

In accord with deeply-rooted and well-founded moral sentiments in our society, the Committee rejects the buying and selling of infants as demeaning to all parties involved. While recognizing the clear difference between infants and preembryos, the Committee is also opposed to payments for preembryos because it views such commercial transactions as incompatible with the respect due to preembryos. . . . The Committee has grave reservations about the sale and purchase of gametes because of the dehumanization that such practices might entail. In particular, the Committee is concerned that the advertising and marketing of human gametes might cause these important cells to be viewed as mere commodities. In the Committee's view, the same kind of noncommercial environment which surrounds the transfer of solid organs in our society would be appropriate for the provision and receipt of human sperm and oocytes.

. . . [T]he Committee's position most closely approximates the third policy approach enumerated above, allowing payment for time, risk, and inconvenience to gamete providers and surrogates. . . . This policy respects the autonomous choices of adults who agree to become involved in reproduction, while at the same time attempting to avoid inappropriate commercialization and to protect the welfare of children who may result from the new reproductive technologies and arrangements.

THE POSSIBLE ROLE OF SEX PRESELECTION

If safe and reliable methods of distinguishing X- and Y-bearing sperm or XX and XY embryos become available, couples employing the new reproductive technologies will have the option of choosing, with a high degree of probability, the gender of their future children. The best available empirical data indicate that approximately two-thirds of women in the United States have a gender preference for their first child and that approximately two-thirds of women who have a preference would want to have a male child first (Pebley and Westoff 1982).

Most couples who seek medical assistance for infertility are interested primarily in having children, not in having children of a particular gender. However, if couples who make use of the new reproductive technologies shared the beliefs of the women surveyed and if most couples employed sex preselection techniques, they would produce an excess of male children. Given the substantial number of infertile couples in the United States, the private choices of those couples could eventually have a public impact on the sex ratio.

In the Committee's view, this arena is one in which moral suasion rather than government intervention is the most appropriate policy. Specifically, couples employing the new reproductive technologies should be *encouraged* to allow the gender of their children to be determined by chance rather than by preselection, unless a sex-linked genetic condition renders this decision imprudent. The Committee regards this moral advice as a natural outgrowth of its commitment to nondiscrimination on the basis of gender.

THE APPROPRIATE ROLE OF GOVERNMENT

To philosophers like Plato, the classical Western view of the proper role of government was that it should promote virtue in its citizens, who were viewed as parts of an organic whole, the state. In modern times, this view has been rejected by most Western political philosophers. The closest modern parallel to the Platonic viewpoint is that a government should ensure that its citizens act in accordance with the principles of morality. According to this view, governments are justified in intervening to prevent even private immoral behavior, such as illicit sexual activity, because in the long run such behavior undermines the public good (Devlin, 1965).

A second viewpoint sees the primary role of government as protecting individual liberties and preventing persons from inflicting harm on others. This view often includes the "clear and present danger" test, namely, that only serious, imminent harms are of sufficient importance to warrant government intrusion (Feinberg, 1973). According to this view, government would not normally intervene in the private sexual activities or reproductive efforts of consenting adults except perhaps to prevent tangible, highly probable physical harm to potential offspring.

A third view limits individual liberty, not only to protect citizens from harm, but also to ensure that every citizen enjoys at least a certain minimum of welfare—income, food, clothing, shelter, and health care (Rawls, 1971; Daniels, 1985). Applied to the new reproductive technologies, this view of government might include infertility treatment within the scope of guaranteed minimum health services.

The Committee is aware that the general role of government in the delivery of health care services differs among the countries that have devoted the most detailed discussion to the new reproductive technologies. The Committee clearly subscribes to the view that government should intervene to prevent substantial harm to offspring, for example, by requiring donor screening if such screening is not voluntarily practiced by sperm banks or health practitioners involved in the donation process. . . .

REFERENCES

Callahan D: New beginnings in life: a philosopher's response. In The New Genetics and the Future of Man, Edited by M Hamilton. Grand Rapids, MI, Eerdmans, 1972, p. 100.

Daniels N: Just Health Care. New York, Cambridge University Press, 1985.

Devlin P: The Enforcement of Morals. New York, Oxford University Press, 1965.

Feinberg J: Social Philosophy. Englewood Cliffs, NJ, Prentice-Hall, 1973, p. 36.

Fletcher J: The Ethics of Genetic Control. Garden City, NY, Anchor Books, 1974, p. 36.

Kass LR: Making babies—the new biology and the 'old' morality. Public Interest 26:49, 1972.

Leridon H: Démographie des échers de la reproduction. In Les Accidents Chromosomiques de la Reproduction, Edited by A Boué, C Thibault. Paris, Centre International de l'Enfance, 1973, p. 13.

Pebley AR, Westoff CF: Women's sex preferences in the United States: 1970 to 1975. Demography 19:177, 1982.

Rawls, J: A Theory of Justice. Boston, Belknap Press, 1971, p. 302.

United Kingdom: Dept of Health and Social Security: Report of the Committee of Inquiry into Human Fertilisation and Embryology, Edited by M Warnock. London, Her Majesty's Stationery Office, 1984, pp. 27, 63.

Walters L: Editor's introduction. J Med Philos 10:210, 1985.

The Problem of Infertility

UNITED STATES CONGRESS, OFFICE OF TECHNOLOGY ASSESSMENT

The Demography of Infertility

Epidemiological studies of infertility attempt to define variations in reproductive impairments for men and women of different ages, races, and parities (the number of children born to a woman), to illuminate historical trends, and to identify possible contributory factors. Three national demographic surveys—the 1965 National Fertility Study (NFS); the 1976 National Survey of Family Growth (NSFG), Cycle II; and the 1982 National Survey of Family Growth, Cycle III—provide data on infertility in the United States. All three surveys describe couples with married women in their childbearing years (defined as age 15 to 44) in the continental United States; the 1982 survey also contains information on never-married women of the same ages. . . .

NSFG DATA

In 1982, the NSFG surveyed a sample of 7,969 women of reproductive age, of whom 3,551 were married. The data for each woman are multiplied by the number of women she represents in the population, so the 7,969 women interviewed represent the 54 million women aged 15 to 44 in the United States. Thus, the data in this [excerpt] represent national estimates (15).

The questions were addressed only to women, so in married couples the wife spoke for herself and her husband. Data from the surveys thus measure infertility of the couple. They do not distinguish male and female factors related to infertility. This [excerpt] refers

From *Infertility: Medical and Social Choices* (Washington, DC: U.S. Government Printing Office, May 1988), pp. 49–52, 57.

to the "couple" instead of the "wife" when presenting the data. Similar data for men do not exist, as the Government collects little information on the reproductive health of men.

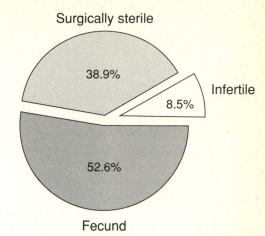

Figure 1. Infertility Status—1982. (Married couples, wives aged 15 to 44)

DEFINITIONS

A couple's reproductive ability is categorized in three ways by demographers: surgically sterile (impossible to have a baby, whether by choice or not); impaired fecundity (nonsurgically sterile or difficult or dangerous to have a baby); and fecund (no known physical problem). Many couples classified as fecund actually have unknown fecundity—those using contraception, for example.

Fecundity refers to the potential of a couple to reproduce. The medical profession prefers the term fertility, which refers to actual conception rates. Infertility is a medical term indicating 12 months of unprotected intercourse without conception. . . . Thus, infertility does not indicate sterility but instead highlights a population that has trouble conceiving and may need medical assistance.

For this report, the term infertility rather than impaired fecundity is used. The percentage of infertile couples is slightly less than the percentage with impaired fecundity, as the latter category includes couples for whom it is difficult or dangerous for the woman to maintain a pregnancy (a category that includes miscarriage). Infertility refers only to couples who have tried to conceive and failed, not to couples who choose not to attempt conception (whether for medical or social reasons).

SURVEY RESULTS

In 1982, 8.5 percent (2.4 million) of married couples were infertile, 38.9 percent (11.0 million) were surgically sterile, and 52.6 percent (14.8 million) were fecund (see figure 1). *The number of infertile couples declined from 3.0 million in 1965 to 2.4 million in 1982. More importantly, primary infertility (childlessness) doubled, from 500,000 in 1965 to 1 million in 1982, while secondary infertility (in which couples have at least one biological child) declined, from 2.5 million in 1965 to 1.4 million in 1982 (see table 1)* (13).

This increase in primary infertility can be explained partly by the fact that more couples are attempting to have children, as members of the baby-boom generation reach their childbearing years and try to have their first baby. The decrease in secondary infertility can be explained by the increase in voluntary surgical sterilization (from 15.8 percent in 1965 to 38.9 percent in 1982). This increase was due solely to the increase in sterilization for contraceptive purposes; the change in noncontraceptive sterilization was slight (13,16). Contraceptive sterilization masks a number of women who might otherwise discover that they were infertile, especially at ages 30 and older (16).

Although the percentage of couples infertile appears to have decreased over the past two decades (from 11.2 percent in 1965 to 8.5 percent in 1982), this drop is entirely due to the rise in surgical sterilization. *Excluding the surgically sterile, the percentage of couples infertile has changed only slightly, rising from 13.3 to 13.9 percent* (13).

Black couples are more likely than white couples to be infertile; in 1982, the risk of infertility for black couples was 1.5 times that for white couples (19). Many possible explanations for these higher rates have been presented, although no data exist on the subject:

- the higher incidence of sexually transmitted diseases (STDs), as STDs account for an estimated 30 percent of infertility in some high-risk populations in the United States (19) and may account for up to 20 percent of infertility overall (3) (the difference in rates of STD between blacks and whites reflects the difference in other relevant demographic characteristics, such as urban dwelling, rather than actual racial differences) (4).

Table 1. Infertile Couples, 1965 and 1982

Couples	All		Excluding surgically sterile	
	1965	1982	1965	1982
Number of couples (millions)[a]				
Total	26.5	28.2	22.3	17.2
Childless	3.5	5.1	3.2	4.6
1 or more children	23.0	23.1	19.1	12.6
Number infertile (millions)				
Total	3.0	2.4	3.0	2.4
Childless	0.5	1.0	0.5	1.0
1 or more children	2.5	1.4	2.5	1.4
Percent infertile				
Total	11.2	8.5	13.3	13.9
Childless	14.5	19.6	15.6	21.8
1 or more children	10.9	6.1	13.1	11.1

[a]Wives 15 to 44 years old.
SOURCE: Adapted from W.D. Mosher, "Infertility: Why Business is Booming," *American Demographics* 9:42-43, 1987.

- the greater use of intrauterine devices (which can increase the likelihood of pelvic inflammatory disease);
- environmental factors, such as occupational hazards affecting reproduction (21) and
- complications or infections following childbirth or abortion (18).

Couples with wives having less than a high school education were also more likely to be infertile (1, 11).

Within age groups, the only significant change over time occurred in those 20 to 24 years old. In 1965, 4 percent of this group were infertile; by 1982, 11 percent were infertile (12,19). This increase may be linked to the tripled gonorrhea rate of this age group between 1960 and 1977 (13) as well as to the factors mentioned previously regarding the higher rates of infertility in black couples. This particular group is important, as one in three births in the United States occurs to women 20 to 24 (16).

Data from the NSFG indicate that infertility increases with age: *Excluding the surgically sterile, 14 percent of married couples with wives aged 30 to 34 are infertile, while 25 percent of couples with wives aged 35 to 39 are infertile* (see table 2) (13). To date, the influence of age on female fertility has been examined more closely than has its influence on male fertility. Although viable sperm production does decline with age in humans (8), the effect of this on fertility has not been determined (17).

In recent years there has been controversy in the scientific and popular literature over the rate at which a woman's fertility decreases with age (2,5,6,9,10,20). Studies have attempted to control for variables such as frequency of intercourse (which is known to decrease as the length of marriage increases) and to examine societies that have little evidence of deliberate fertility control. The results are varied and widely debated, but all seem to indicate that *female fertility does decrease somewhat before age 35 and significantly more after age 35*. The disagreement focuses primarily on the extent of the decrease when a woman reaches age 30. Most of the available statistics are more useful for indicating the number and

Table 2. Infertility and Age, 1965 and 1982 (percent)[a]

Age of wife	1965	1982
15 to 19	0.6	2.1
20 to 24	3.6	10.6
25 to 29	7.2	8.7
30 to 34	14.0	13.6
35 to 39	18.4	24.6
40 to 44	27.7	27.2
Total, 15 to 44	13.3	13.9

[a]Percent of married couples excluding those surgically sterilized. Data are based on samples. The only statistically significant change between 1965 and 1982 is the increase at age 20 to 24.
SOURCE: W.D. Mosher, "Infertility: Why Business is Booming," *American Demographics* 9:42-43, 1987.

types of women who are likely to need and use infertility services than for estimating a woman's decreased fertility with age and the effects of delayed childbearing (10).

SURVEY LIMITATIONS

Available survey data may misrepresent the true numbers of infertile couples. First, the boundary of 1 year for the definition of infertility is somewhat arbitrary; many couples classified as infertile after 1 year will conceive later without medical assistance (10). In an unrandomized observational study of 1,145 infertile couples, 41 percent of those whose infertility problems were treated later conceived, while 35 percent of those untreated also became pregnant (2). However, the 1-year limit has both a practical and a theoretical justification. Practically, the NFS and NSFG are the only national surveys to examine infertility status, and they use the 1-year definition. Most physicians use this definition as well (14). Furthermore, if an average woman with no infertility problems has an approximate monthly probability of conception of 20 percent (0.2 as a proportion), 93 percent of all women would theoretically conceive after 1 year of unprotected intercourse (7).

Second, the surveys did not directly ask whether the respondent had ever tried to become pregnant (16), meaning that women who have always used contraception, never had intercourse, or never tried to become pregnant were assumed to be fertile. A number of potentially infertile couples may be hidden in the groups of surgically sterilized couples and couples using contraception. The authors corrected for one problem by excluding the surgically sterile from some data and thus removing the effects of the sharp rise in surgical sterilization between 1965 and 1982. However, couples using contraception who have not been proved fertile are included in the category "fecund," which may lead to an underestimation of the extent of infertility.

Third, the surveys refer to married couples with wives aged 15 to 44. As a result, unmarried men and women are not included in these figures (except in the 1982 data, when unmarried women were also surveyed). Excluding unmarried couples may have resulted in an underestimate of the absolute number of infertile couples. Finally, the data only permit a guess at the populations at increased risk for infertility.

REFERENCES

1. Aral, S.O., and Cates, W., "The Increasing Concern With Infertility: Why Now?" *Journal of the American Medical Association* 250:2327–2331, 1983.

2. Bongaarts, J., "Infertility After Age 30: A False Alarm," *New England Journal of Medicine* 14:75–78, 1982.

3. Cates, W., Jr., Director, Division of Sexually Transmitted Diseases, Centers for Disease Control, Atlanta, GA, personal communication, Apr. 28, 1987.

4. Cooper, G.S., Research Associate, Uniformed Services University of the Health Sciences, Bethesda, MD, personal communication, Aug. 28, 1987.

5. DeCherney, A.H., and Berkowitz, G.S., "Female Fecundity and Age," *New England Journal of Medicine* 306:424–425, 1982.

6. Hendershot, G.E., Mosher, W.D., and Pratt, W.F., "Infertility and Age: An Unresolved Issue," *Family Planning Perspectives* 14:287–289, 1982.

7. Jansen, R., "The Clinical Impact of In Vitro Fertilization: I. Results and Limitations of Conventional Reproductive Medicine," based on the 1985 Sheddon Adam Memorial Lecture, delivered at the Royal Brisbane Hospital, June 1985.

8. Johnson, L., Petty, C.S., and Neaves, W.B. "Influence of Age on Sperm Production and Testicular Weights in Men," *Journal of Reproductive Fertility* 70:211–218, 1984.

9. Menken, J., "Age and Fertility: How Late Can You Wait?" *Demography* 22:469–483, 1985.

10. Menken, J., Trussell, J., and Larsen, U., "Age and Infertility," *Science* 233:1389–1394, 1986.

11. Mosher, W.D., "Infertility Trends Among U.S. Couples, 1965–1976," *Family Planning Perspectives* 14:22–30, 1982.

12. Mosher, W.D., "Infertility in the United States, 1965-1982," paper presented at the 3rd International Congress of Andrology Post Graduate Course, Boston, MA, Apr. 28, 1985.

13. Mosher, W.D., "Infertility: Why Business is Booming," *American Demographics* 9:42–43, 1987.

14. Mosher, W.D., Statistician, Family Growth Survey Branch, Division of Vital Statistics, National Center for Health Statistics, Hyattsville, MD, personal communication, Aug. 18, 1987.

15. Mosher, W.D., "Fecundity and Infertility in the United States," *American Journal of Pubic Health* 78:181–182, 1988.

16. Mosher, W.D., and Pratt, W.F., "Fecundity and Infertility in the United States, 1965–82," *NCHS: Advancedata* 104:1–8, 1985.

17. Nieschlag, E., Lammers, U., Freischem, C.W., et al., "Reproductive Functions in Young Fathers and Grandfathers," *Journal of Clinical Endocrinology and Metabolism* 55:676–681, 1982.

18. Pratt, W.F., Mosher, W.D., Bachrach, C.A., et al., "Understanding U.S. Fertility: Findings From the National Survey of Family Growth, Cycle III," *Population Bulletin* 39:5, 1984.

19. Pratt, W.F., Mosher, W.D., Bachrach, C.A., et al., "Infertility—United States, 1982," *Morbidity and Mortality Weekly Report* 34:197–199, 1985.

20. Schwartz, D., and Mayaux, M.J. (Federation CECOS), "Female Fecundity as a Function of Age: Results of Artificial Insemination in 2193 Nulliparous Women With Azoospermic Husbands," *New England Journal of Medicine* 306:404–406, 1982.

21. U.S. Congress, Office of Technology Assessment, *Reproductive Health Hazards in the Workplace,* OTA-BA-266 (Washington, DC: U.S. Government Printing Office, 1985).

WARNOCK COMMITTEE

Infertility

In the past, there was considerable public ignorance of the causes and extent of infertility, as well as ignorance of possible remedies. At one time, if a couple were childless, there was very little they could do about it. Generally the cause of infertility was thought to be something in the woman which made her childless; only occasionally was it thought that there might be something wrong with the man. Even today, there is very little factual information about the prevalence of infertility. A commonly quoted figure is that one couple in ten is childless, but accurate statistics are not available, nor is it known what proportion of this figure relates to couples who choose not to have children. In certain religious and cultural traditions, infertility was, and still is, considered sufficient grounds for divorce. In our own society childless couples used to be advised to adopt a child. Now, as a result of improved contraception, the wider availability of legal abortion and changed attitudes toward the single mother, far fewer babies are placed for adoption.

Childlessness can be a source of stress even to those who have deliberately chosen it. Family and friends often expect a couple to start a family, and express their expectations, either openly or by implication. The family is a valued institution within our present society: within it the human infant receives nurture and protection during its prolonged period of dependence. It is also the place where social behaviour is learnt and where the child develops its own identity and feeling of self-value. Parents likewise feel their identity in society enhanced and confirmed by their role in the family unit. For those who long for

children, the realisation that they are unable to found a family can be shattering. It can disrupt their picture of the whole of their future lives. They may feel that they will be unable to fulfil their own and other people's expectations. They may feel themselves excluded from a whole range of human activity and particularly the activities of their child-rearing contemporaries. In addition to social pressures to have children there is, for many, a powerful urge to perpetuate their genes through a new generation. This desire cannot be assuaged by adoption.

Arguments have been put to us both for and against the treatment of infertility. First, we have encountered the view that in an over-populated world it is wrong to take active steps to create more human beings who will consume finite resources. However strongly a couple may wish to have children, such a wish is ultimately selfish. It has been said that if they cannot have children without intervention, they should not be helped to do so. Secondly, there is a body of opinion which holds that it is wrong to interfere with nature, or with what is perceived to be the will of God. Thirdly, it has been argued that the desire to have children is no more than a wish; it cannot be said to constitute a need. Other people have genuine needs which must be satisfied if they are to survive. Thus services designed to meet these needs must have priority for scarce resources.

In answer to the first point, it is never easy to counter an argument based on the situation of the world as a whole with an argument relying on the desires of individuals. We saw it as our function to concentrate on individuals rather than on the world at large. Questions about the distribution of resources within the world as a whole lie far outside our terms of reference. In any event, the number of children born as a result of techniques to assist in the treatment

From United Kingdom, Department of Health and Social Security, *Report on the Committee of Inquiry into Human Fertilisation and Embryology* (London: Her Majesty's Stationery Office, July 1984), pp. 8–10. Reproduced with permission of the Controller of Her Britannic Majesty's Stationery Office.

of infertility will always be insignificant in comparison with the naturally increasing world population. On the second point, the argument that to offer treatment to the infertile is contrary to nature fails to convince in view of the ambiguity of the concepts "natural" and "unnatural". We took the view that actions taken with the intention of overcoming infertility can, as a rule, be regarded as acceptable substitutes for natural fertilisation. Thirdly, the argument that the desire to have children is only a wish, not a need, and therefore should not be satisfied at the expense of other more urgent demands on resources can be answered in several ways. There are many other treatments not designed to satisfy absolute needs (in the sense that the patient would die without them) which are readily available within the NHS [National Health Service]. Medicine is no longer exclusively concerned with the preservation of life, but with remedying the malfunctions of the human body. On this analysis, an inability to have children is a malfunction and should be considered in exactly the same way as any other. Furthermore infertility may be the result of some disorder which in itself needs treatment for the benefit of the patient's health. Infertility is not something mysterious, nor a cause of shame, nor necessarily something that has to be endured without attempted cure. In addition, the psychological distress that may be caused by infertility in those who want children may precipitate a mental disorder warranting treatment. It is, in our view, better to treat the primary cause of such distress than to alleviate the symptoms. In summary, we conclude that infertility is a condition meriting treatment.

B A R B A R A   K A T Z   R O T H M A N

Infertility as Disability

The treatment of infertility needs to be recognized as an issue of self-determination. It is as important an issue for women as access to contraception and abortion, and freedom from forced sterilization. There is no contradiction in assuring access to both infertility services and abortion services for all women who would choose them. Not only do different women have different needs, but the same women have different needs at different points in their lives. A woman who had an unwanted pregnancy and abortion at eighteen may very well need, for unrelated reasons, treatment for infertility at twenty-eight. Being infertile at twenty-eight, or thirty-eight, does not necessarily make a woman regret abortions she may have had at eighteen—what the woman wants is to have a child now, not to have spent the past decade of her life raising a child she didn't want then.[1] And a woman who needed to have medical treatment for infertility at one point in her life may very well have an accidental, unwanted pregnancy at some later point, and want an abortion. The issue is not getting more women pregnant or fewer: the concern is women having as much control as they can over entry into motherhood.

Of course the issue of individual control is inherently complicated. It raises the basic questions of free will, individual choice in any social structure, and our limitations as embodied beings whose bodies do not always accede to our will.

Feminists have been struggling with all of these questions in one area or another. In regard to motherhood, we have become particularly sensitive to the loss of individual choice in a pro-natalist system. There is no question but that women have been forced into motherhood, and into repeated motherhood, when that is not what they themselves wanted. And it is also true that social systems create our wants as surely as they create the ways in which we meet them. Women have been carefully trained to want motherhood, to experience themselves and their womanhood, their very purpose in life, through motherhood. And that is wrong.

And yet. Wanting children, and wanting our children to want children, is not such an awful thing. I am frankly at a loss as to how I could possibly raise my own children in a way that was not pro-natalist. I love them, I love having them in my life, my children bring me joy—and I share that with them. I love friendships, and long talks—and I share that with them, too. And it delights me when I see them developing their own friendships, learning the pleasures of conversations with friends. How can it delight me less to see them develop their own interest in children? I love it when someone brings a baby around, and my son is eager for his turn to hold and play with it. I love to watch him teaching his sister and her friend how mirrors work, or helping them work a problem through. I look at him and I think, He's going to be a great father. It's not that I insist on this for them, or insist that they experience children in the same way I do, as a parent, but I want them to have the pleasures life can bring, and to me children are one such pleasure.

Certainly a world in which nobody much cared whether or not they had children would be a sad place. So pro-natalism, in a general, joyous, but not coercive way, is a good thing.

Like all the things we teach our children, some lessons are learned more powerfully by some children than by others. Some of our children will learn from us the joys of having children to raise, and will want that for themselves very much, and some won't. How much a person wants to have children, how well they learned that lesson, is not connected to the condition of their tubes, their exposure to infection, or to any other cause of infertility.

In this sense, infertility is just like any other adult-onset disability. I have a good friend who ultimately had to have a leg amputated. He fought it as hard as it could be fought, for years. He endured great pain, repeated prolonged hospitalizations, the loss of a business he had developed, risks to his health from drugs, and repeated surgery. I thought he was crazy. It's only a leg—use crutches. Other people thought *I*

was crazy to suggest such a thing. It's his *leg,* they'd say, how can he not fight to save his leg?

I watch women go through painful, dangerous, expensive, life-encompassing infertility treatments, and hear the same kinds of discussions among their friends and family. Some say, "So she won't have children, what's the big deal. She can join 'Big Sister,' take her nephews to the circus. It's nice to have children in your life, but it's not worth risking all this." And other say, "If there's a chance, the slightest chance that she could get pregnant, how can she not take it?"

If we are to recognize and respect choice, we have to respect these choices as well: the choice to accept infertility and the choice to fight it.

Thinking about infertility as a disability does gives us a particularly useful model for developing social policy.

We begin with the "simple idea that society defines, implicitly, a population of 'normal' people; that is, people tend to think of the 'standard human model' as able-bodied, having what are considered typical functional abilities."[2] Disability then can be understood only in the context of normal abilities, and is inherently a *social* and not a *medical* concept. The relevant medical concept is impairment, defined as "the expression of a physiological, anatomical or mental loss or abnormality. . . . an impairment can be the result of accident, disease or congenital condition."[3] Examples of impairment which result in infertility include scarred fallopian tubes, congenital malformations of the uterus, testicular damage done by mumps, and so on.

Disability is most often based on an impairment, and is a "'dis' (lack of) 'ability' to perform certain functions. . . . Disabilities apply to generic or basic human functions: walking, speaking, grasping, hearing, excreting and so on."[4] Procreation—sperm production and ejaculation in the male, the ability to ovulate, conceive, and gestate in the female—can certainly be considered a basic human function, and the loss of ability to perform such functions a disability.

The third level of analysis, beyond impairment and disability, is handicap, defined as a "socially, environmentally and personally specified limitation. Aspirations or life goals must be taken into account when defining or identifying a handicap."[5] In the case of infertility, a person who does not want (any or any more) children is not handicapped by an impairment in procreative capacity—surgical sterilization is in fact the purposeful creation of such an impairment.

But for a person who does want a child, the same impairment constitutes the basis for a handicap.

Even under these circumstances, the handicapping effects of any given impairment vary, depending on the social environment. For me, a very sedentary person, a below-the-knee amputation of one leg would not be particularly handicapping—I don't think it would change my life dramatically, provided I had an adequate prosthesis, good banisters to hand when I needed them, cars with hand controls, etc. For my friend, the loss of a leg was experienced as handicapping. For a professional athlete or dancer, it would be even more profoundly handicapping.

Similarly, an infertile person who can adopt a baby, and so enter into the social role of parent, may not be handicapped by infertility. The handicap depends on how goals are defined (having a baby rather than having a pregnancy) and the societal resources (babies available for adoption) to which the person has access. For a man who is infertile, the availability of a sperm donation, enabling his mate to become pregnant, can offset the handicapping effects of his impairment and resulting disability.

An advantage of thinking about infertility as a disability is that we can see the proper place for medical treatment. Some treatments can cure the cause of the impairment: blocked tubes can be unblocked, ending an impairment, whether it's a fallopian tube and the impairment caused infertility, or the eustachian tube and the impairment caused hearing loss. Other treatments can bypass the impairment and prevent the disability: in vitro fertilization offsets the disabling effects of tubal impairment. But there are equally important, non-medical ways of managing disability, ways that address the handicapping effects of the disability—like learning sign language, having wheelchair ramps, adopting babies.

This analysis leaves two unresolved issues, however. One is deciding which ways of overcoming the handicap are socially acceptable. Kidnapping newborns would also ameliorate the handicap of disability—and was the story in the film *Raising Arizona*. That is quite obviously not an acceptable solution, any more than buying a human slave to carry around a person without a leg or purchasing corneas from starving people to cure blindness would be acceptable. So while the principle of providing services to overcome a handicap is not unique to infertility, there remains with all handicaps the problem of deciding which services, medical or other, are socially acceptable.

Second, we have to remember that not all ways of solving the handicap are equally acceptable to the *individual*. Returning to the example of the leg amputation, a wheelchair, crutches, and various levels of sophistication in prosthetic devices will all help overcome the handicap. But some (technologically sophisticated replacement leg) may be better than others (crutches). With infertility, as with other disabilities, ways of overcoming the handicap that most closely approximate normal functioning are usually the most acceptable: donor insemination or in vitro fertilization rather than adoption, for example. But these are individual decisions: some people with an amputated leg might find adjustment to a prosthetic too difficult, painful, or aesthetically unappealing, and prefer crutches. And some infertile couples might prefer adoption to the risks and discomforts of infertility treatments, especially those of in vitro fertilization.

For now, while there are babies needing homes, adoption is the preferred solution of many infertile couples. But adoption is problematic. . . . As a long-range feminist social policy, we cannot rely on adoption, but are going to have to address directly the prevention and treatment of the impairments that cause infertility.

As a rule, prevention generally makes more sense than treatment when designing social policy. On an individual, clinical level, we certainly have to respond to a crisis with appropriate treatment, but as a plan, we can put our efforts into avoiding crises.

Much infertility is avoidable, though no one knows quite how much. We need more basic research on the causes of infertility, with particular attention paid to the neglected areas of environmental and iatrogenic causes. Infertility is approximately one and a half times as common among women of color as among white women[6]—access to good nutrition, a generally higher standard of living, and better medical care, high priorities in any feminist agenda, would prevent some infertility.

But a focus on prevention has its negative side as well, in that it may lead to a "victim-blaming" stance, individuals being held accountable for their own infertility. Consider the attention paid in recent years to the infertility problems of the so-called delayed-childbearing women, the women who "put off" motherhood until their thirties, or sometimes even forties. One reason their infertility gets so much attention is that precisely because they are older, and put off child-bearing to develop careers, they are the ones who can now afford the high-tech, high-cost treatments. But their infertility is often blamed on their own choice, as if they're now paying the piper for their carefree years in graduate school or the years establishing jobs, businesses, and careers rather than making babies.

Besides its unkindness, there are at least two problems with holding women accountable for their own infertility. In the first place, the data are not all that clear on just how much fertility is actually lost as originally fertile women enter their mid to late thirties. While common sense tells us that infertility must increase with age, simply because each year of life presents that many more opportunities for damage to fertility, it is very difficult to get an accurate measure of the extent of this loss.

Until recently, fertility data were collected on married women only. Particularly prior to the legalization of abortion, a period which covers the early reproductive years of today's "delayed-childbearing" women, many of the most fertile women became wives and mothers. Many highly fertile young women were the pregnant brides of twenty years ago, pushed into marriage and motherhood by fertility. On the other hand, among those who avoided early motherhood and early marriage were those women who were markedly less fertile. Simply put, young married women have been likely to be fertile—it's one of the reasons they've married young. Older women who have never had children are likely to have higher rates of infertility— it's one of the reasons they were able to avoid having had children. It is not altogether clear what percentage of women discovering infertility at say, thirty-seven were any more fertile at twenty-two.

Second, and I think even more important, this blaming of the women themselves ignores the context in which women have "chosen" to delay childbearing: a lack of maternity leave, of child care, of shared parenting by men, and so on. Shall we blame the woman for putting off childbearing while she became a lawyer, art historian, physician, set designer, or engineer? Or shall we blame the system that makes it so very difficult for young lawyers, art historians, physicians, set designers, and engineers to have children without having wives to care for them? Men did not have to delay entry into parenthood for nearly as many years in the pursuit of their careers as women now do.

It is easier to blame the individual woman than to understand the political and economic context in which she must act, but it does not make for good social policy. If we want to decrease infertility in part by having women concentrate childbearing in their twenties and early thirties, we have to make that possible for them.

Unfortunately, we have no reason to think that we can prevent all infertility: even if everyone had excellent health care, a safe working environment, good nutrition, and tried to get pregnant at twenty-four, we'd still have some people experiencing infertility. If prevention won't solve it, and adoption should not be relied on as a long-range solution, they we're left with medical management.

One school of thought among feminists has been to do away with high-technology infertility treatments. For all of the reasons I have outlined, I don't think that is acceptable policy.

But neither is business as usual. Infertility treatment embodies all that is bad in our medical care: it is available only to the well-to-do, it is male dominated, and it is offered in a way that is totally divorced from the context of one's life. And worse, it doesn't work. In vitro fertilization (IVF) fails 90 percent of the women who try it.

Much has been written about the skewed reporting of IVF clinics. Some of it is like the psychological self-protection in which many medical workers engage. Calling a "chemical pregnancy" (a positive pregnancy test even if the woman "miscarries" in time for a normal period) a success is a way of shifting blame for the failure to achieve a baby from the clinic staff (*we* got you pregnant) to the woman (*you* lost it). Blaming the patient for failing when the treatment was "successful" is a fairly common medical practice.

Some of the reporting, I think, is deliberately misleading. Some clinics cite the best success rates available for IVF even if they themselves have never achieved a baby. Half of the IVF clinics in the United States have not, in fact, ever gotten a baby born. There are more subtle misleading reports, too: dividing the number of babies by the number of women; for example, as if two sets of twins and one set of triplets among twenty women was the same as seven out of twenty women having babies. I've only seen one IVF clinic, but I'd be willing to bet that its wall of baby photos near the intake area is a near-universal feature. A few minutes of study and I realized that the same babies were pictured repeatedly—here at birth, there dressed for "First Christmas," over in the top corner showing off a new tooth. Innocent enough — grateful parents send photos, pleased staff puts them up — but the image is one of lots and lots of babies, a misleading image of lots and lots of "successes."

IVF clinics are having more success these days, getting more women pregnant and more babies born. But I fear it has as much to do with a change in admissions as anything else. Where the original candidates had no other chance of a pregnancy — no tubes at all, for example — today IVF and the related procedure GIFT (gamete intra-fallopian transfer) are being used with less and less indication, earlier and earlier in the infertility workup. That is, IVF and GIFT are now being used with women of greater fertility, women who might very well have conceived on their own in another few months. There are now women who do get pregnant while on the waiting list for IVF treatment.

The most significant shift in IVF use, however, is that it is now being used to treat male infertility. A man with a very low sperm count, or with other fertility problems, can use IVF to have his sperm fertilize an ovum. This means that fertile women, women who could get pregnant readily with another man, or with insemination with donor sperm, are being subjected to IVF treatment, including hormonal stimulation, sonograms, and surgery, to maintain their husband's genetic paternity.

The medical community likes to talk about infertility as a problem "of the couple." Since fertility level is a continuum (some of us get pregnant very readily, some less so; some men have higher sperm counts, some lower) this often makes sense. Two people of lower fertility will have more trouble conceiving with each other than either would with a highly fertile partner.

But if a man has a high sperm count the infertility problem is treated entirely as the woman's, whereas if the man has a low sperm count, the problem is *still* treated largely as the woman's. Further, Judith Lorber reports that most women who are undergoing IVF or GIFT for male infertility are told about "some little thing wrong" in themselves as well.[7] Which of course is probably quite true. Even very fertile people aren't perfectly fertile, and nobody seems to get pregnant at every possible opportunity.

This inclusion of "some little problem" of the woman's in the treatment makes the treatment of the woman as the patient for male infertility "more acceptable medically to the couple and to the staff."[8] All of this is particularly problematic when "sexual dys-

function" seems to be a common reason why couples present themselves for infertility treatment, and why there are so many 'waiting list pregnancies.' It may also be the reason why the husband's inability to masturbate to ejaculation on demand is a perennial problem in IVF clinics the world over."[9]

A couple may be a social unit, but it is not a physiological unit. If a man cares deeply enough about an impairment which prevents him from producing adequate sperm, that impairment should be treated. We do therefore need more research on *male* treatment of *male* infertility, an area now neglected in favor of female treatment of male infertility. But if a man is more concerned about simply overcoming the handicapping effects of his impairment, insemination with donor sperm should be encouraged.

Many men do care less about the infertility per se than they care about what it is doing to their lives and to their wives.[10] Women have been very protective of men, and ultimately of themselves and their potential children, concerned that the man may not feel he is the social father to a child if he is not the genetic father. Doctors have colluded with women to protect genetic paternity, at the cost of women's safety and health. I think that a focus on men's nurturing capacities is more than appropriate, and that many more men would in fact accept the use of insemination with donor sperm (that is, accept the loss of their own genetic paternity) if it were recommended by infertility specialists as a relatively inexpensive, quick, and safe way to achieve a pregnancy and, as so many infertile men and women have expressed with longing, "get on with their lives." The more we learn to think of fathering as a social, emotional, nurturing, loving relationship, the less important genetic paternity will be.

In sum, I think we as a society need to think about infertility as we need to think about any other disability, We need to see it as a multifaceted problem. Some of it can be prevented, some can be cured, and some needs to be lived with. Part of the solution to any disability problem is a change in societal attitudes; part is a change in societal services. Disability is not doom, life is not over, and one does learn to cope. But recognizing that blind people can live wonderful and full lives neither excuses us from preventing and treating that blindness which is preventable and treatable nor gives us cause to deny the sadness in loss of sight.

We can recognize and acknowledge and fully appreciate the depth of grief that may accompany infertility, just as such grief may accompany the loss of a leg or of sight. To say that women are more than just mothers, that we are persons in our own right, does not mean that we have to deny the sadness of loss of motherhood.

NOTES

1. Joan Leibmann-Smith, 1988, "Delayed Childbearing and Infertility: Social Antecedents and Consequences," dissertation in progress, City University of New York.

2. Office of Technology Assessment (OTA) of the U.S. Congress, 1982, *Technology and Handicapped People,* p. 19.

3. Ibid.

4. Ibid., p. 20.

5. Ibid.

6. OTA, 1988, *Infertility: Medical and Social Choices,* p. 51.

7. Judith Lorber, 1988, "Whose Problem, Whose Decision: The Use of In Vitro Fertilization in Male Infertility," unpublished paper presented to the Eastern Sociological Society, Philadelphia.

8. Ibid.

9. Ibid.

10. Arthur L. Greil, Thomas A. Leitko, and Karen L. Porter, 1988, "Infertility: His and Hers," *Gender & Society,* Vol. 2; No. 2, in press.

In Vitro Fertilization

ARTHUR L. CAPLAN

The Ethics of In Vitro Fertilization

ASSISTED REPRODUCTION — A CORNUCOPIA OF MORAL MUDDLES

There has been an explosion in recent years in the demand for and resources devoted to the treatment of infertility in the United States. Many parents have benefited from the availability of new techniques such as artificial insemination, microsurgery, fertility drugs, and the various forms of what is generically known as "in vitro fertilization." At the same time, increases in the demand for and allocation of resources to the medical treatment of infertility raise profoundly disturbing and complex moral issues.

The scientific status of the current generation of infertility interventions remains unclear. Some commentators assert that it is obvious that artificial reproduction is still in its infancy. Others, usually more directly involved in providing the technology to patients, avow that the level of success is so high that many forms of artificial reproduction can be viewed only as therapies. The issue of whether medicine is capable of treating infertility is important not only for scientific reasons but also because basic moral issues concerning informed consent, liability for untoward results, and public policies concerning reimbursement pivot around the answer. Where should artificial reproduction be placed on the experiment/therapy continuum?

Little consensus exists either within the medical profession or among the general public as to the moral status of the entities that are the objects of a great deal of medical manipulation in any attempt to treat infertility: ova, sperm, and embryos. The ethics of manipulating, storing, or destroying reproductive materials raise basic questions about the moral status of possible and potential human beings.

It is not even clear whether infertility is or ought to be viewed as a disease requiring or meriting medical

From *Primary Care* 13 (1986), 241–253. © 1986 W. B. Saunders Co. Reprinted by permission of the author and publisher.

intervention. Many of the causes of infertility and many of the possible remedies are as much a function of social, cultural, and economic factors as they are physiologic or biologic abnormalities. Attitudes about conception, child rearing, and the nature of the family are greatly influenced by social and ethical beliefs concerning individual rights, the duties of marriage, and the desirability of passing on a particular set of genetic information into the next generation.

The treatment of infertility also raises basic questions concerning equity and justice. These fall roughly into two broad categories: questions of social justice and questions of individual justice.

QUESTIONS OF SOCIAL JUSTICE

At the social level, increasing amounts of scarce medical resources are being invested in the provision of services for those suffering from impaired fertility. It is estimated conservatively that the United States is now spending more than 200 million dollars annually on medical interventions intended to correct infertility. In the years from 1981 to 1983, more than 2 million visits were made to physicians in private practice by those seeking assistance regarding procreation.

Not only are many persons seeking help, but also an increasing proportion of medical resources are being devoted to this problem. The number of programs offering in vitro fertilization doubled in 1984 alone from 60 to 120. Private clinics whose sole interest is the provision of services to treat infertility have opened in many areas of the country.[9]

Increases in both the supply and demand for medical services to treat infertility can be expected to continue. The number of persons seeking medical assistance is still far below the number of persons in the general population estimated to have serious impairments of fertility.

The expenditure of scarce funds for health resources is not the only social issue raised by technologic progress with respect to reproduction. It is not uncommon for fertility services to be located in the same building, if not on the same floor, as services devoted to the termination of pregnancies. If this situation were not ironic enough in itself, it is surely odd to contemplate increases in the resources devoted to the alleviation of infertility at a time when millions of children in the United States and around the world lack parents as well as the basic necessities of life.

In the United States itself, there are still thousands of children who cannot be placed with either foster families or adoptive parents. This situation raises obvious issues of social justice and individual rights, particularly when many of the children requiring adoption have special physical, cognitive, and emotional needs.

Issues regarding the priority that should be given to the development of fertility-enhancing services are made all the more pressing at a time when both federal and state governments have been moving rapidly to institute cost-containment measures such as prospective payment and reimbursement by diagnosis related groups (DRGs). These efforts are likely to curtail sharply access to proven therapeutic services for the elderly, the disabled, and the poor, who depend on public expenditures for their care.

QUESTIONS OF INDIVIDUAL JUSTICE

At an individual or familial level, access to infertility services frequently is limited to those who can pay for them, either out of pocket or, in some cases, through private insurance. Access to services also is constrained by patient awareness of the existence of medical options, geography, and the ability to bear the often onerous financial, psychosocial, and time commitments associated with many of the available forms of assisted reproduction.

The proper role of the law and of the state in influencing or controlling individual decisions concerning reproduction is also a matter of much disagreement and dispute. Traditionally, American courts have been loathe to countenance any interference with matters pertaining to the family and individual decisions concerning procreation. As one philosopher has observed, parental decisions concerning children have been seen as "a right against all the rest of society to be indulged within wide limits, . . . immune from the scrutiny of and direction of others."[15]

However, in recent years, federal and state law has begun to acknowledge a powerful state interest in the welfare of children, particularly newborns. Child abuse statutes in many states have recently been revised and strengthened. The federal government has expressed its wish that children born with handicaps or congenital defects receive access to the same opportunities for medical assistance and treatment as would be available to other children. The traditional assumption in American law and morality that privacy provides an inviolate shield against intervention by other parties or the state has weakened somewhat in the face of increasing concern about protecting the interests of especially vulnerable human beings such as newborns and children and assuring that no one is subject to invidious discrimination on the basis of handicap, race, sex, or ethnic origin.[12]

THE GROWING DEMAND FOR MEDICAL ASSISTANCE IN PROCREATION

Infertility is a major problem in the United States. Almost one in six couples who have tried to conceive a child for one year fail to do so. Although the overall incidence of infertility appears to be relatively stable, the demand for infertility services is increasing rapidly.

The increase in demand for medical assistance in conceiving children is due to a variety of factors. Many couples have chosen to delay conception, thereby exposing themselves to the increased risks of infertility associated with aging. There appears to be some increase in the number of women encountering iatrogenic fertility problems as a result of difficulties associated with various forms of birth control, such as intrauterine devices (IUDs). More women have entered the work force and, as a result, have been exposed to reproductive hazards and pollutants that may adversely affect fertility. Increases in the incidence of sexually transmitted diseases, especially pelvic inflammatory disease, have also produced a higher incidence of infertility among some subgroups within the general population.

The causes of increased demand for fertility services are not confined to physiologic factors. Couples who might have considered adoption in earlier decades are now turning in increasing numbers to the medical profession for assistance with respect to conception. Moreover, there has been a dramatic increase in the availability of infertility services in the United States. Advances in diagnostic techniques such as laparoscopy and hormonal and genetic analysis also allow health care professionals to identify with increasing reliability those suffering from impairments in fertility.[8]

Attitudes toward human variability, the desirability of marriage and family, and the importance of biologic kinship between parent and child also play a powerful role in influencing the demand for medical assistance with respect to infertility. There is some evidence that parental expectations concerning pregnancy and reproduction have changed drastically during the past decade.

Lawsuits against and malpractice rates among those engaged in obstetrics have increased dramatically in recent years. Our society has come, whether wisely or not, to expect physicians to facilitate the conception of optimally healthy children at the conclusion of every pregnancy.

The power of medical intervention to influence procreation and reproduction challenges social norms concerning human differences and variability that are, at best, poorly understood by social scientists and moral philosophers. A growing emphasis on perfection in procreation and child rearing contributes to a situation in which those who are disabled, dysfunctional, or merely different from the norm may encounter increasing difficulties in securing social acceptance and material security. The availability of technologic methods for detecting and eliminating disease and disorder early in pregnancy as well as technologic methods for facilitating procreation in those for whom this would not have been an option in earlier times means that personal autonomy and individual choice are enhanced. However, it may also mean that such gains are purchased at the cost of lowering public tolerance for differences and diversity among individual human beings and about decisions concerning childbearing, child rearing, childlessness, and disability.[12]

IN VITRO FERTILIZATION: A CASE STUDY

Perhaps the most controversial and provocative of all the new forms of medically assisted reproduction available today is in vitro fertilization. Although it has been common practice for decades in the United States as well as in other nations to utilize sperm donated by either spouses or strangers for the purpose of facilitating procreation, it is only in the past 10 years that efforts have been made to utilize donated ova by various means in order to facilitate reproduction.

It is not merely the novelty of in vitro fertilization that makes it worthy of special comment and ethical reflection. The fact that in vitro fertilization is a technology that severs the traditional link between gestation and maternal identity raises serious and novel issues for both the law and morality. The prevailing ideology of equality, at least with respect to opportunity, in the United States makes it easy to overlook the fact that one of our society's most basic and fundamental beliefs about reproduction and the family is that the mothers of children are undeniably that, the mothers. Although it is true that artificial insemination by donor (AID) raises questions about paternal identity, the fact is that paternal identity, whether men like to admit it or not, has always been subject to a certain degree of uncertainty—with or without artificial insemination by donor.

Prior to the appearance of in vitro fertilization, there has never been any doubt, much less any empiric reason for doubting, that the woman who bore a child bore a direct familial relationship to that child. It is difficult to know exactly what the social reverberations of a technology capable of severing the tie between genetic relationship and gestation will be. However, the fact that this new technology can change a previously basic and undeniable reality of the human condition makes this particular technology worthy of serious and special moral consideration.

STANDARD IN VITRO FERTILIZATION

In vitro fertilization actually refers to a family of procedures that all involve the fertilization of an ovum outside of the human body. In the most commonly utilized technique, which might be termed "standard in vitro fertilization," one or more eggs are removed from the ovaries using a syringe known as a laparoscope. Egg cells are exceedingly small, so that the process of retrieval requires considerable skill and experience.

In many but not in all centers in which standard in vitro fertilization is practiced, the ovaries are stimulated artificially by hormones administered to the donor to produce more than one egg in the menstrual cycle. The eggs that are removed are subjected to microscopic inspection to determine which appears to be structurally most sound. One or more of the eggs is then fertilized in vitro using the husband's or a donor's sperm. The egg or eggs are then observed until they have grown to the eight-cell stage in an artificial medium. A decision is then made as to which of the developing embryos will be reimplanted into the prospective mother's womb.[3,18]

Reimplantation or, as it is often termed, "embryo transfer," also requires careful monitoring of the prospective mother in order to ascertain the optimal time for reimplanting the egg back into the uterus. Timing is critical to the success of reimplantation.

In some centers, some of the embryos that are produced are frozen for later use should the initial attempt at reimplantation fail. Techniques for freezing fertilized eggs at very low temperatures are well developed. The decision to freeze a fertilized egg allows for further efforts at reimplantation, but it also raises questions about the disposition of unused embryos.

The first successful use of standard in vitro fertilization took place in Britain in 1978. Since that time, nearly 1000 infants have been born utilizing this technique in the United States, Australia, the Netherlands, and a number of other countries. The procedure generally costs between $3000 and $5000 per attempt. Several attempts are often required in order to achieve pregnancy. One recent report stated that out of 24,037 oocytes collected, 7722 resulted in fertilized embryos that were reimplanted in the mother's uterus. From this group, 590 children were born, among which were 56 twins, 7 triplets, and 1 set of quadruplets. These multiple births were a result of the simultaneous reimplantation of more than one embryo in order to increase the likelihood of a successful implantation and birth.[10]

These data indicate that the pregnancy rate achieved is about 25 per cent, although the number of pregnancies resulting in a liveborn child is less than 10 per cent. These figures are low, but it should be noted that they do not differ all that much from the rates of pregnancy and birth associated with sexual intercourse between fertile parents.[14]

NONSTANDARD IN VITRO FERTILIZATION

The techniques utilized in standard in vitro fertilization allow for a startling number of permutations and combinations with respect to the donors of sperm and eggs, the choice of a recipient to receive the embryos that result, and the choice of individuals to parent the children who are born as a result of these techniques. Donors of sperm or eggs may or may not be persons who are married. Women who cannot produce viable eggs or who for some reason are unwilling or unable to undergo the procedures necessary to perform laparoscopy may ask another woman to supply eggs for the in vitro fertilization.

It is also possible to utilize women other than the biologic donor to serve as the "gestational mother" for a fertilized egg. These women may carry an embryo to term and then either keep the resulting child or turn it over to another party—either the biologic donor or yet another person or persons. Because it is possible to freeze embryos, it is also possible to utilize in vitro fertilization techniques to produce a child after the death of the biologic donors or without the knowledge and consent of the biologic donors.

Nonstandard in vitro fertilization techniques allow for a division of the roles of mother and parent that was, quite simply, impossible before the appearance of these techniques. It is now possible to produce a child who has one set of biologic parents who may be either alive or dead and who provide eggs and sperm, another person or persons who are involved in pregnancy and gestation, and still a third person or persons who serve as the actual or social parent(s) of the child![20]

The fact that it is now possible to separate the biologic, gestational, and social aspects of mothering and parenting introduces a range of further novel possibilities concerning fertilization, reproduction, and birth. For example, frozen embryos not utilized for in vitro fertilization are available for research directly related to in vitro fertilization techniques or other medical purposes involving therapies not related to procreation (for example, the development of embryos in order to produce and harvest useful organic materials). Nonstandard in virtro fertilization techniques raise the possibility of remuneration of women for their services as either egg donors or gestational mothers, or, as the role is often termed, surrogates. The availability of standard and nonstandard in vitro fertilization techniques may facilitate the application of genetic engineering either for therapeutic purposes, aesthetic reasons, or even eugenic goals.

MAJOR POLICY ISSUES RAISED BY IN VITRO FERTILIZATION

The development of in vitro fertilization techniques of various types poses a direct and pressing challenge to public policy. At present, in vitro fertilization is still a relatively new medical modality, and as such, there are many aspects of the techniques utilized, including hormonal induction of ovulation, the freezing and storage of embryos, and the development of optimal media for embryo growth, in which further research is necessary. Little is known about the long-term psychosocial impacts of in vitro fertilization on children born by these methods or on the families who raise children produced by either standard or nonstandard in vitro fertilization techniques.[18]

Little formal supervision and regulation has been exercised to date by local, state, and federal authorities in the United States over the provision of in vitro fertilization as a therapy. At present, the only form of control over those who provide in vitro fertilization exists in the form of peer regulation through professional societies and individual collegial review. Few

courts have ruled on matters pertaining to in vitro fertilization, and there are few legislative statutes that govern either research or therapy in this area.[2]

In 1975, a federal law required the creation of an Ethics Advisory Board (EAB) with the Department of Health, Education and Welfare (now Health and Human Services). In June 1979, the EAB issued a report on the scientific, ethical, legal, and social aspects of in vitro fertilization that concluded that the conduct of research pertaining to in vitro fertilization was ethically acceptable and worthy of monetary support by the federal government.[7] However, those who have served as the secretary of the Department of Health and Human Services have chosen not to respond to the report or to extend the life of the EAB. The EAB was disbanded at the end of 1979. Because its approval is necessary for any research protocols to receive federal funding, to date, no American research or clinical trials on in vitro fertilization have received any federal dollars. A key recommendation of the EAB was that a model statute be drafted to clarify the rights of in vitro fertilization donors, offspring, parents, and medical professionals. No subsequent efforts have been made to draft such a statute.

It is interesting to note that 23 states have enacted laws prohibiting "fetal research or embryo research." Some states also prohibit the performance of autopsies or research procedures on abortuses, miscarried fetuses, or stillborn fetuses. No state has enacted legislation or regulation governing the conduct of medical facilities identifying themselves as in vitro fertilization clinics or fertility clinics. Minimal standards for in vitro fertilization programs have been developed by the American Fertility Society,[1] but these standards have not yet received explicit legal or legislative recognition.

Other nations have established commissions or committees at the national level to examine in vitro fertilization. In England, the Department of Health and Social Security established a commission under the leadership of Dame Mary Warnock to conduct an inquiry into human fertilization and embryology. This commission issued a detailed report in July 1984.[18] This report addressed such topics as artificial insemination, in vitro fertilization, surrogacy, the freezing and storage of reproductive materials, and the use of embryos for research.

The Warnock commission issued a list of more than 60 recommendations concerning artificial techniques for assisting human reproduction. Among these were a call for the creation of a new licensing authority to regulate both research and therapy pertaining to artificial insemination by donor and both standard and nonstandard forms of in vitro fertilization, a 14-day limit on the use of frozen embryos for either research or therapeutic purposes, the need to obtain consent from the donor for any interventions pertaining to . . . embryos, and, perhaps most controversially, the criminalization of surrogacy. Similar studies reaching somewhat different conclusions have been issued recently by committees in the Netherlands, Canada, and Australia.[17]

Perhaps the most glaring public policy question arising in the United States today is whether there is any need for legal, legislative, or regulatory action at the federal, state, or local level with respect to in vitro fertilization and its associated technologies. These regulatory interventions might take the form of bans or moratoriums on various forms of in vitro fertilization research or therapy, modifications of existing state laws to clarify the legal status of in vitro fertilization, or statutes intended to recognize and spur the development of research and therapy regarding in vitro fertilization.

The heated and critical reaction that greeted the appearance of the Warnock commission's report in the United Kingdom should give pause to those in the United States who believe that the time has come to initiate any form of regulation or legislation with respect to in vitro fertilization. The Warnock report has been strongly criticized by various members of Parliament in the United Kingdom who believe that its recommendations are too permissive, by prominent scientists and scientific societies who worry that it is too restrictive in its recommendations concerning research, and by a number of legal authorities concerning its stance on such matters as surrogacy and the commercialization of in vitro fertilization.[14,19]

Although there is certainly a need for both federal and state bodies to encourage and solicit further study of the many moral and legal issues raised by in vitro fertilization, there would not yet appear to exist the empiric or valuational foundation for establishing regulatory policies that could command consent and compliance from health care professionals, researchers, or those who wish to avail themselves of in vitro fertilization for various reasons. Such forums as the Congressional Office of Technology Assessment, the newly formed Committee on Life and the Law in New York state, or a reconstituted President's Commission for the Study of Ethical Problems in Medicine and Biomedical and Behavioral Research, whose mandate expired at the end of 1983, would appear to be ideal forums for attempting to attain the consensus requisite for the implementation of rules and regulations governing the application of medical knowledge and skills to as sensitive and as fundamental an arena of human experience as human reproduction. These bodies could attempt to grapple with some of the basic ethical issues that still have not received sufficient public deliberation and reflection.

MAJOR ETHICAL ISSUES RAISED BY IN VITRO FERTILIZATION

There is a tendency in the existing literature on in vitro fertilization to move directly to arguments about the moral implications of the nonstandard forms of the technique.[13,16] In many ways, this is understandable, because as noted earlier, the permutations and combinations of nonstandard in vitro fertilization techniques do allow for the separation of biologic, gestational, and parental functions, especially with respect to women, that pose enormous challenges to the legal system.

However, although issues pertaining to the moral acceptability of surrogacy, the desirability or undesirability of commercial relationships in nonstandard and standard forms of in vitro fertilization, and the policies that should be followed with regard to matters such as inheritance where in vitro fertilization embryos and children are concerned raise obvious moral and legal conundrums, it is not clear that these issues are actually the pivotal ones raised by advances in in vitro fertilization techniques. I suspect that moral matters regarding in vitro fertilization in terms of both research and therapy will actually hinge on the answers that are given to the following questions:

1. Is infertility a disease?
2. What counts as fair and equitable access to in vitro fertilization?
3. What is the moral status of a human embryo?

IS INFERTILITY A DISEASE?

One common definition of disease often found in medical literature is that disease represents any deviation from the existing norms that prevail for human functioning.[4] Certainly, infertility, although not uncommon, is uncommon enough to qualify as abnormal or deviant relative to the average capacities and abilities of the human population.

Nonetheless, defining disease as abnormality has its own significant problems, not the least of which is that such a definition makes any physical or mental state at the tail ends of normal distributions a disease by definition. Thus, the state of being very tall, very smart, very dark-skinned, or very strong all qualify as diseases according to the abnormality criterion.

One way of avoiding including too much in the disease category is to restrict the definition of disease to those states that represent biologic dysfunction. According to this view, infertility would qualify as a disease because the relevant organ systems are not functioning as they presumably were designed to do.

However, again, a strictly biologic definition of disease flounders on empiric grounds. Not all dysfunctional bodily states constitute sources of symptoms or even problems for those who possess them. One can be afflicted with any number of dysfunctional states and attributes over the course of a normal life span without either knowing or caring very much about them one way or another. It seems odd to argue that a person who does not want children and who also has a low sperm count should be labeled as diseased.

Perhaps the most satisfying way to handle the problem of defining disease is to attempt a definition that captures both physiologic and patient perspectives. Disease would appear to refer to those dysfunctional states that a person recognizes or, if left untreated, will eventually come to recognize as dysfunctional either due to impairments in abilities or capacities or as a result of noxious symptoms.[5]

Using a definition that recognizes both the biologic and psychosocial aspects of disease, it would appear defensible to argue that infertility is a disease that falls reasonably within medicine's purview. Although not all persons afflicted with fertility problems find this state distressing or limiting, many certainly do. Furthermore, although it is true that fertility and the ability to have children is a desire that is strongly mediated by social and cultural values, it is also true that this desire comes as close as can be to constituting a universal desire that can be found among every human society.

Indeed, it is the pervasiveness of the importance assigned to the ability to have offspring that provides one of the empiric warrants not only for labeling infertility as a disease but also for assigning its care and treatment a relatively high priority with respect to other disease states. If it is reasonable to include the capacity to bear children among those abilities and skills that constitute basic human goods, such as cognition, locomotion, and perception, infertility not only is a disease but also is one that should receive special attention and concern from physicians and those concerned with health policy.

WHAT COUNTS AS FAIR AND EQUITABLE ACCESS TO IN VITRO FERTILIZATION?

If it is true that infertility is a disease that adversely affects a basic and important human capacity, it would seem important to assure access to efficacious and safe diagnostic, therapeutic, and palliative health care services that may contribute to the enhancement of this capacity. Indeed, infertility would appear to constitute so severe an impairment of a basic human capacity that, other things being equal, access to such services should not be contingent upon the individual patient's or family's ability to pay.

However, the major issue requiring resolution with respect to justice and equity in the allocation of resources for the diagnosis and treatment of infertility is not how much to spend or who should foot the bill, but rather whether the diagnostic and therapeutic techniques now in existence are safe and efficacious. Until the requisite empiric information for analyzing this issue has been obtained, it would be unethical to divert resources from other medical interventions already known to be safe and efficacious.

Moreover, although high priority should be accorded to the treatment of infertility, it should not be assumed that in vitro fertilization and other techniques are the only techniques that can be utilized to cope with the dysfunctional consequences of infertility or that the demonstration of a need for services thereby entails that any and all health care practitioners who wish to engage in treatment are thereby entitled to do so. Equity and fairness demand that those afflicted with the disease of infertility be aware of all options available to them, including adoption and foster parenting, and that public policy facilitate the utilization of these options. Equity and fairness also require that the resources devoted to in vitro fertilization and other techniques be used in the most efficient manner possible. This may require that diagnostic and therapeutic services be regionalized and that funding be restricted to those centers that can demonstrate a high level of safety and efficacy with regard to in vitro fertilization techniques.[11]

One of the most perplexing issues raised by the evolution of in vitro fertilization is the need to examine the moral standing that should be accorded to an embryo. Arguments about research on embryos and about the storage and disposition of embryos will ultimately pivot upon the moral status that should be accorded to these entities.

In general, the scientific and medical communities have tried to shy away from the suggestion that science has anything much to say about the questions of when life begins or what counts as a human being. Recent Congressional hearings on the question of the definition of life produced a barrage of disclaimers, dodges, and apologies from those scientists called upon to testify.

The unwillingness of many members of the scientific and medical communities to address squarely the issue of when life begins and what counts as a human being is perhaps not surprising. After all, the definition of human life raises theologic and psychologic issues that are difficult and disturbing to contemplate.

However, it is important to note that members of the scientific and medical communities have not been reticent about an analogous issue — when does human life end. The existence of brain death statutes in most states is evidence of the fact that the biomedical community has been willing to offer its expert opinion as to both the definition of death and the criteria that should be followed to assess whether a particular person meets this definition.[6]

The issues of when life begins and what entities count as human beings demand similar degrees of courage and attention from the biomedical community. Although biomedical scientists may not be able to formulate definitions of life and personhood among themselves that can command societal assent, they surely have a role to play in participating in the formulation of definitions and criteria that society will have to establish in order to cope with the existence of in vitro fertilization.

Two lessons should be learned from other attempts to define life and personhood in such arenas as the debates about abortion and animal experimentation. First, no single property is likely to serve as a distinct boundary for establishing the existence of personhood or even life. The criteria used in a definition are more likely to constitute a family or cluster of concepts.

Second, the definition of life and the criteria used to assess its presence do not end moral matters.

Knowing when life begins and when personhood or humanity can be attributed to a particular entity provides only the starting point for arguments about what to do with embryos. It is still necessary to consider the rights, duties, and obligations of donors, prospective parents, and health care professionals in deciding what is to be done with and to embryos. However, it will not do for the biomedical community to continue to adopt an ostrich-like posture and proclaim that it has nothing whatsoever to contribute in the way of empiric information that might facilitate the formulation of an answer to the question of what moral status should be accorded to human embryos.

CONCLUSION

The evolution of medicine's capacity to assist those afflicted with impairments of fertility is an exciting and commendable prospect. However, enthusiasm for the techniques and for the benefit they can bring to those afflicted with a disease that impairs a fundamental and universally valued human capacity should not blind us to the fact that these techniques are still new, relatively poorly understood, and surrounded with uncertainty as to their efficacy and safety.

In vitro fertilization is not only a scientific and financial challenge to society but also a moral challenge. The possibility of separating the functions of biologic, gestational, and social parenting raises dilemmas of policy, law, and regulation that have never before faced humankind. However, insufficient attention has been given to some of the basic moral issues that underlie much of the current fascination with and fear of in vitro fertilization. Given the implications of this technique for basic social institutions such as the family, kinship, and parenting, it is imperative that our regulatory, legal, and legislative responses to it be wise. We as a society must look much more carefully before we take a leap in any particular regulatory or legal direction.

REFERENCES

1. American Fertility Society: Minimal standards for programs of in vitro fertilization. Fertil. Steril., *41*:12–13, 1984.

2. Annas, G., and Elias, S.: In vitro fertilization and embryo transfer: Medicolegal aspects of a new technique to create a family. Family Law Quarterly, *17*:199–223, 1983.

3. Blank, R.: Making babies: The state of the art. The Futurist, *19*:1–17, 1985.

4. Caplan, A., and Engelhardt, H. T. (eds.): Concepts of Health and Disease. Reading, Massachusetts, Addison-Wesley, 1981.

5. Caplan, A.: Is aging a disease? *In* Spicker, S., and Ingman, S. (eds.): Vitalizing Long-Term Care. New York, Springer-Verlag, 1984, pp. 14–28.

6. Culver, C., and Gert, B.: Philosophy in Medicine, New York, Oxford University Press, 1982.

7. Department of Health, Education and Welfare: Protection of Human Subjects: HEW Support of Human In Vitro Fertilization and Embryo Transfer. Washington, D.C., Government Printing Office, 1979.

8. Grobstein, C., Flower, M., and Mendeloff, J.: External human fertilization: An evaluation of policy. Science, *222*:127–133, 1983.

9. Henahan, J.: Fertilization: Embryo transfer procedures raise many questions. J.A.M.A., *252*:877–882, 1984.

10. Hodgen, G.: The Need for Infertility Treatment. Testimony in Hearings on Human Embryo Transfer, Subcommittee on Investigations and Oversight, Committee on Science and Technology, U.S. House of Representatives, August 8, 1984.

11. Institute of Medicine: Assessing Medical Technologies. Washington, D.C., National Academy Press, 1985.

12. Murray, T., and Caplan, A. (eds.): Which Babies Shall Live? Clifton, New Jersey, Humana, 1985.

13. Robertson, J. A.: Procreative liberty and the control of conception, pregnancy and childbirth. Virginia Law Review, *69:* 20–80, 1983.

14. Sattaur, O.: New conception threatened by old morality. New Scientist, *103:*12–17, 1984.

15. Schoeman, F.: Rights of children, rights of parents and the moral basis of the family. Ethics, *91:*6–19, 1980.

16. Wadlington, W.: Artificial conception: The challenge for family law. Virginia Law Review, *69:*126–174, 1983.

17. Waller, L., et al.: Report on the Disposition of Embryos Produced by In Vitro Fertilization. Victoria, Australia, Committee to Consider the Social, Ethical and Legal Issues Arising from In Vitro Fertilization, August 1984.

18. Warnock, M.: Report of the Committee of Inquiry into Human Fertilization and Embryology: London, HMSO, 1984.

19. Warnock Proposals in trouble. Nature, *313:*417, 1985.

20. Working Party, Council for Science and Society: Human Procreation: Ethical Aspects of the New Techniques. Oxford, Oxford University Press, 1984.

SUSAN SHERWIN

Feminist Ethics and In Vitro Fertilization[1]

New technology in human reproduction has provoked wide ranging arguments about the desirability and moral justifiability of many of these efforts. Authors of biomedical ethics have ventured into the field to offer the insight of moral theory to these complex moral problems of contemporary life. I believe, however, that the moral theories most widely endorsed today are problematic and that a new approach to ethics is necessary if we are to address the concerns and perspectives identified by feminist theorists in our considerations of such topics. Hence, I propose to look at one particular technique in the growing repertoire of new reproductive technologies, in vitro fertilization (IVF), in order to consider the insight which the mainstream approaches to moral theory have offered to this debate, and to see the difference made by a feminist approach to ethics.

From Marsha Hanen and Kai Nielsen, eds., *Science, Morality and Feminist Theory* (Calgary, Alberta: University of Calgary Press, 1987), pp. 265–284. Reprinted by permission of the author and the University of Calgary Press.

I have argued elsewhere that the most widely accepted moral theories of our time are inadequate for addressing many of the moral issues we encounter in our lives, since they focus entirely on such abstract qualities of moral agents as autonomy or quantities of happiness, and they are addressed to agents who are conceived of as independent, non-tuistic individuals. In contrast, I claimed, we need a theory which places the locus of ethical concerns in a complex social network of interrelated persons who are involved in special sorts of relations with one another. Such a theory, as I envision it, would be influenced by the insights and concerns of feminist theory, and hence, I have called it feminist ethics.[2]

In this [essay], I propose to explore the differences between a feminist approach to ethics and other, more traditional approaches in examining the propriety of developing and implementing in vitro fertilization and related technologies. This is a complicated task, since each sort of ethical theory admits of a variety of interpretations and hence of a variety of conclusions on concrete ethical issues. Nonetheless, certain themes and trends can be seen to emerge. Feminist thinking is also ambivalent in application, for feminists are quite torn about their response to this sort of technology. It is my hope that a systematic theoretic evaluation of IVF from the point of view of a feminist ethical theory will help feminists like myself sort through our uncertainty on these matters.

Let me begin with a quick description of IVF for the uninitiated. In vitro fertilization is the technology responsible for what the media likes to call 'test tube babies.' It circumvents, rather than cures, a variety of barriers to conception, primarily those of blocked fallopian tubes and low sperm counts. In vitro fertilization involves removing ova from the woman's body, collecting sperm from the man's, combining them to achieve conception in the laboratory, and, a few days later, implanting some number of the newly fertilized eggs directly into the woman's womb with the hope that pregnancy will continue normally from this point on. This process requires that a variety of hormones be administered to the woman — which involve profound emotional and physical changes — that her blood and urine be monitored daily, and then at 3 hour intervals, [and] that ultrasound be used to determine when ovulation occurs. In some clinics, implantation requires that she remain immobile for 48 hours (including 24 hours in the head down position). IVF is successful in about 10–15% of the cases selected as suitable, and commonly involves multiple efforts at implantation.

Let us turn now to the responses that philosophers working within the traditional approaches to ethics have offered on this subject. A review of the literature in bioethics identifies a variety of concerns with this technology. Philosophers who adopt a theological perspective tend to object that such technology is wrong because it is not 'natural' and undermines God's plan for the family. Paul Ramsey, for instance, is concerned about the artificiality of IVF and other sorts of reproductive technology with which it is potentially associated, e.g. embryo transfer, ova as well as sperm donation or sale, increased eugenic control, etc.:

But there is as yet no discernable evidence that we are recovering a sense for man [sic] as a natural object . . . toward whom a . . . form of "natural piety" is appropriate . . . parenthood is certainly one of those "courses of action" natural to man, which cannot without violation be disassembled and put together again.[3]

Leon Kass argues a similar line in '"Making Babies" Revisited.'[4] He worries that our conception of

humanness will not survive the technological permutations before us, and that we will treat these new artificially conceived embryos more as objects than as subjects; he also fears that we will be unable to track traditional human categories of parenthood and lineage, and that this loss would cause us to lose track of important aspects of our identity. The recent position paper of the Catholic Church on reproductive technology reflects related concerns:

It is through the secure and recognized relationship to his [sic] own parents that the child can discover his own identity and achieve his own proper human development . . .

Heterologous artificial fertilization violates the rights of the child; it deprives him of his filial relationship with his parental origins and can hinder the maturing of his personal identity.[5]

Philosophers partial to utilitarianism prefer a more scientific approach; they treat these sorts of concerns as sheer superstition. They carefully explain to their theological colleagues that there is no clear sense of 'natural' and certainly no sense that demands special moral status. All medical activity, and perhaps all human activity, can be seen in some sense as being 'interference with nature,' but that is hardly grounds for avoiding such action. 'Humanness,' too, is a concept that admits of many interpretations; generally, it does not provide satisfactory grounds for moral distinctions. Further, it is no longer thought appropriate to focus too strictly on questions of lineage and strict biological parentage, and, they note, most theories of personal identity do not rely on such matters.

Where some theologians object that 'fertilization achieved outside the bodies of the couple remains by this very fact deprived of the meanings of the values which are expressed in the language of the body and the union of human persons,'[6] utilitarians quickly dismiss the objection against reproduction without sexuality in a properly sanctified marriage. See, for instance, Michael Bayles in *Reproductive Ethics*: '. . . even if reproduction should occur only within a context of marital love, the point of that requirement is the nurturance of offspring. Such nurturance does not depend on the sexual act itself. The argument confuses the biological act with the familial context.'[7]

Another area of disagreement between theological ethicists and their philosophical critics is the significance of the wedge argument to the debate about IVF. IVF is already a complex technology involving research on superovulation, 'harvesting' of ova, fertilization, and embryo implants. It is readily adaptable to technology involving the transfer of ova and embryos, and hence their donation or sale, as well as to the 'rental of womb space'; it also contributes to an increasing ability to foster fetal growth outside of the womb and, potentially, to the development of artificial wombs covering the whole period of gestation. It is already sometimes combined with artificial insemination and is frequently used to produce surplus fertilized eggs to be frozen for later use. Theological ethicists worry that such activity, and further reproductive developments we can anticipate (such as human cloning), violate God's plan for human reproduction. They worry about the cultural shift involved in viewing reproduction as a scientific enterprise, rather than the 'miracle of love' which religious proponents prefer: '[He] cannot be desired or conceived as the product of an intervention of medical or biological techniques; that would be equivalent to reducing him to an object of scientific technology.'[8] And, worse, they note, we cannot anticipate the ultimate outcome of this rapidly expanding technology.

The where-will-it-all-end hand-wringing that comes with this sort of religious futurology is rejected by most analytical philosophers; they urge us to realize that few slopes are as slippery as the pessimists would have us believe, that scientists are moral people and quite capable of evaluating each new form of technology on its own merits, and that IVF must be judged by its own consequences and not the possible result of some future technology with which it may be linked. Samuel Gorovitz is typical:

It is not enough to show that disaster awaits if the process is not controlled. A man walking East in Omaha will drown in the Atlantic—if he does not stop. The argument must also rest on the evidence about the likelihood that judgment and control will be exercised responsibly . . . Collectively we have significant capacity to exercise judgment and control . . . our record has been rather good in regard to medical treatment and research.[9]

The question of the moral status of the fertilized eggs is more controversial. Since the superovulation involved in producing eggs for collection tends to produce several at once, and the process of collecting eggs is so difficult, and since the odds against conception on any given attempt are so slim, several eggs are usually collected and fertilized at once. A number of these fertilized eggs will be introduced to the womb with the hope that at least one will implant and gestation will begin, but there are frequently some 'extras.' Moral problems arise as to what should be done with these surplus eggs. They can be frozen for future use (since odds are against the first attempt 'taking'), or they can be used as research material, or simply discarded. Canadian clinics get around the awkwardness of their ambivalence on the moral status of these cells by putting them all into the woman's womb. This poses the devastating threat of six or eight 'successfully' implanting, and a woman being put into the position of carrying a litter; something, we might note, her body is not constructed to do.

Those who take a hard line against abortion and argue that the embryo is a person from the moment of conception object to all these procedures, and, hence, they argue, there is no morally acceptable means of conducting IVF. To this line, utilitarians offer the standard responses. Personhood involves moral, not biological categories. A being neither sentient nor conscious is not a person in any meaningful sense. For example, Gorovitz argues, 'Surely the concept of person involves in some fundamental way the capacity for sentience, or an awareness of sensations at the very least.'[10] Bayles says, 'For fetuses to have moral status they must be capable of good or bad in their lives . . . What happens to them must make a difference to them. Consequently some form of awareness is necessary for moral status.'[11] (Apparently, clinicians in the field have been trying to avoid this whole issue by coining a new term in the hopes of identifying a new ontological category, that of the 'pre-embryo.')[12]

Many bioethicists have agreed here, as they have in the abortion debate, that the principal moral question of IVF is the moral status and rights of the embryo. Once they resolve that question, they can, like Engelhardt, conclude that since fetuses are not persons, and since reproductive processes occurring outside a human body pose no special moral problems, 'there will be no sustainable moral arguments in principle . . . against in vitro fertilization.'[13] He argues,

in vitro fertilization and techniques that will allow us to study and control human reproduction are morally neutral instruments for the realization of profoundly important human goals, which are bound up with the realization of the good of others: children for infertile parents and greater health for the children that will be born.[14]

Moral theorists also express worries about the safety of the process, and by that they tend to mean the safety to fetuses that may result from this technique. Those fears have largely been put to rest in the years since the first IVF baby was born in 1978, for the couple of thousand infants reportedly produced by this technique to date seem no more prone to apparent birth defects than the population at large, and, in fact, there seems to be evidence that birth defects may be less common in this group—presumably because of better monitoring and pre and post natal care. (There is concern expressed, however, in some circles outside of the bioethical literature about the longterm effect of some of the hormones involved, in light of our belated discoveries of the effect of DES usage on offspring. This concern is aggravated by the chemical similarity of clomid, one of the hormones used in IVF, to DES.)[15]

Most of the literature tends to omit comment on the uncertainties associated with the effect of drugs inducing superovulation in the woman concerned, or with the dangers posed by the general anaesthetic required for the laparoscopy procedure; the emotional costs associated with this therapy are also overlooked, even though there is evidence that it is extremely stressful in the 85–90% of the attempts that fail, and that those who succeed have difficulty in dealing with common parental feelings of anger and frustration with a child they tried so hard to get. Nonetheless, utilitarian theory could readily accommodate such concerns, should the philosophers involved think to look for them. In principle, no new moral theory is yet called for, although a widening of perspective (to include the effects on the women involved) would certainly be appropriate.

The easiest solution to the IVF question seems to be available to ethicists of a deontological orientation who are keen on autonomy and rights and free of religious prejudice. For them, IVF is simply a private matter, to be decided by the couple concerned together with a medical specialist. The desire to have and raise children is a very common one and generally thought to be a paradigm case of a purely private matter. Couples seeking this technology face medical complications that require the assistance of a third party, and it is thought, 'it would be unfair to make infertile couples pass up the joys of rearing infants or suffer the burdens of rearing handicapped children.'[16] Certainly, meeting individuals' desires/needs is the most widely accepted argument in favour of the use of this technology.

What is left, then, in the more traditional ethical discussions, is usually some hand waving about costs.

This is an extremely expensive procedure; estimates range from $1500 to $6000 per attempt. Gorovitz says, for instance, 'there is the question of the distribution of costs, a question that has heightened impact if we consider the use of public funds to pay for medical treatment.'[17] Debate tends to end here in the mystery of how to balance soaring medical costs of various sorts and a comment that no new ethical problems are posed.

Feminists share many of these concerns, but they find many other moral issues involved in the development and use of such technology and note the silence of the standard moral approaches in addressing these matters. Further, feminism does not identify the issues just cited as the primary areas of moral concern. Nonetheless, IVF is a difficult issue for feminists.

On the one hand, most feminists share the concern for autonomy held by most moral theorists, and they are interested in allowing women freedom of choice in reproductive matters. This freedom is most widely discussed in connection with access to safe and effective contraception and, when necessary, to abortion services. For women who are unable to conceive because of blocked fallopian tubes, or certain fertility problems of their partners, IVF provides the technology to permit pregnancy which is otherwise impossible. Certainly most of the women seeking IVF perceive it to be technology that increases their reproductive freedom of choice. So, it would seem that feminists should support this sort of technology as part of our general concern to foster the degree of reproductive control women may have over their own bodies. Some feminists have chosen this route. But feminists must also note that IVF as practiced does not altogether satisfy the motivation of fostering individual autonomy.

It is, after all, the sort of technology that requires medical intervention, and hence it is not really controlled by the women seeking it, but rather by the medical staff providing this 'service.' IVF is not available to every woman who is medically suitable, but only to those who are judged to be worthy by the medical specialists concerned. To be a candidate for this procedure, a woman must have a husband and an apparently stable marriage. She must satisfy those specialists that she and her husband have appropriate resources to support any children produced by this arrangement (in addition, of course, to the funds required to purchase the treatment in the first place), and that they generally 'deserve' this support. IVF is not available to single women, lesbian women, or women not securely placed in the middle class or beyond. Nor is it available to women whom the controlling medical practitioners judge to be deviant with respect to their norms of who makes a good mother. The supposed freedom of choice, then, is provided only to selected women who have been screened by the personal values of those administering the technology.

Further, even for these women, the record on their degree of choice is unclear. Consider, for instance, that this treatment has always been very experimental: it was introduced without the prior primate studies which are required for most new forms of medical technology, and it continues to be carried out under constantly shifting protocols, with little empirical testing, as clinics try to raise their very poor success rates. Moreover, consent forms are perceived by patients to be quite restrictive procedures and women seeking this technology are not in a particularly strong position to bargain to revise the terms; there is no alternate clinic down the street to choose if a women dislikes her treatment at some clinic, but there are usually many other women waiting for access to her place in the clinic should she choose to withdraw.

Some recent studies indicate that few of the women participating in current programs really know how low the success rates are.[18] And it is not apparent that participants are encouraged to ponder the medical unknowns associated with various aspects of the technique, such as the long term consequences of superovulation and the use of hormones chemically similar to DES. Nor is it the case that the consent procedure involves consultation on how to handle the disposal of 'surplus' zygotes. It is doubtful that the women concerned have much real choice about which procedure is followed with the eggs they will not need. These policy decisions are usually made at the level of the clinic. It should be noted here that at least one feminist argues that neither the woman, nor the doctors have the right to choose to destroy these embryos: '. . . because no one, not even its parents, owns the embryo/fetus, no one has the *right* to destroy it, even at a very early development stage . . . to destroy an embryo is not an automatic entitlement held by anyone, including its genetic parents.'[19]

Moreover, some participants reflect deep seated ambivalence on the part of many women about the procedure—they indicate that their marriage and status depends on a determination to do 'whatever is possible' in pursuit of their 'natural' childbearing function—and they are not helped to work through the seeming imponderables associated with their long term well-being. Thus, IVF as practiced involves significant limits on the degree of autonomy deontologists insist on in other medical contexts, though the non-feminist literature is insensitive to this anomaly.

From the perspective of consequentialism, feminists take a long view and try to see IVF in the context of the burgeoning range of techniques in the area of human reproductive technology. While some of this technology seems to hold the potential of benefitting women generally—by leading to better understanding of conception and contraception, for instance—there is a wary suspicion that this research will help foster new techniques and products such as human cloning and the development of artificial wombs which can, in principle, make the majority of women superfluous. (This is not a wholly paranoid fear in a woman-hating culture: we can anticipate that there will be great pressure for such techniques in subsequent generations, since one of the 'successes' of reproductive technology to date has been to allow parents to control the sex of their offspring; the 'choice' now made possible clearly threatens to result in significant imbalances in the ratio of boy to girl infants. Thus, it appears, there will likely be significant shortages of women to bear children in the future, and we can anticipate pressures for further technological solutions to the 'new' problem of reproduction that will follow.)

Many authors from all traditions consider it necessary to ask why it is that some couples seek this technology so desperately. Why is it so important to so many people to produce their 'own' child? On this question, theorists in the analytic tradition seem to shift to previously rejected ground and suggest that this is a natural, or at least a proper, desire. Engelhardt, for example, says 'The use of technology in the fashioning of children is integral to the goal of rendering the world congenial to persons.'[20] Bayles more cautiously observes that 'A desire to beget for its own sake . . . is probably irrational'; nonetheless, he immediately concludes, 'these techniques for fulfilling that desire have been found ethically permissible.'[21] R. G. Edwards and David Sharpe state the case most strongly: 'the desire to have children must be among the most basic of human instincts, and denying it can lead to considerable psychological and social difficulties.'[22] Interestingly, although the recent pronouncement of the Catholic Church assumes that 'the desire for a child is natural,'[23] it denies that a couple has a right to a child: 'The child is not an object to which one has a right.'[24]

Here, I believe, it becomes clear why we need a deeper sort of feminist analysis. We must look at the sort of social arrangements and cultural values that underlie the drive to assume such risks for the sake of biological parenthood. We find that the capitalism, racism, sexism, and elitism of our culture have combined to create a set of attitudes which views children as commodities whose value is derived from their possession of parental chromosomes. Children are valued as privatized commodities, reflecting the virility and heredity of their parents. They are also viewed as the responsibility of their parents and are not seen as the social treasure and burden that they are. Parents must tend their needs on pain of prosecution, and, in return, they get to keep complete control over them. Other adults are inhibited from having warm, stable interactions with the children of others—it is as suspect to try to hug and talk regularly with a child who is not one's own as it is to fondle and hang longingly about a car or a bicycle which belongs to someone else—so those who wish to know children well often find they must have their own.

Women are persuaded that their most important purpose in life is to bear and raise children; they are told repeatedly that their life is incomplete, that they are lacking in fulfillment if they do not have children. And, in fact, many women do face a barren existence without children. Few women have access to meaningful, satisfying jobs. Most do not find themselves in the centre of the romantic personal relationships which the culture pretends is the norm for heterosexual couples. And they have been socialized to be fearful of close friendships with others—they are taught to distrust other women, and to avoid the danger of friendship with men other than their husbands. Children remain the one hope for real intimacy and for the sense of accomplishment which comes from doing work one judges to be valuable.

To be sure, children can provide that sense of self worth, although for many women (and probably for all mothers at some times) motherhood is not the romanticized satisfaction they are led to expect. But there is something very wrong with a culture where childrearing is the only outlet available to most women in which to pursue fulfillment. Moreover, there is something wrong with the ownership theory of children that keeps other adults at a distance from

children. There ought to be a variety of close relationships possible between children and adults so that we all recognize that we have a stake in the well-being of the young, and we all benefit from contact with their view of the world.

In such a world, it would not be necessary to spend the huge sums on designer children which IVF requires while millions of other children starve to death each year. Adults who enjoyed children could be involved in caring for them whether or not they produced them biologically. And, if the institution of marriage survives, women and men would marry because they wished to share their lives together, not because the men needed someone to produce heirs for them and women needed financial support for their children. That would be a world in which we might have reproductive freedom of choice. The world we now live in has so limited women's options and self-esteem, it is legitimate to question the freedom behind women's demand for this technology, for it may well be largely a reflection of constraining social perspectives.

Nonetheless, I must acknowledge that some couples today genuinely mourn their incapacity to produce children without IVF, and there are very significant and unique joys which can be found in producing and raising one's own children which are not accessible to persons in infertile relationships. We must sympathize with these people. None of us shall live to see the implementation of the ideal cultural values outlined above which would make the demand for IVF less severe. It is with real concern that some feminists suggest that the personal wishes of couples with fertility difficulties may not be compatible with the overall interests of women and children.

Feminist thought, then, helps us to focus on different dimensions of the problem than do other sorts of approaches. But, with this perspective, we still have difficulty in reaching a final conclusion on whether to encourage, tolerate, modify, or restrict this sort of reproductive technology. I suggest that we turn to the developing theories of feminist ethics for guidance in resolving this question.[25]

In my view, a feminist ethics is a moral theory that focuses on relations among persons as well as on individuals. It has as a model an inter-connected social fabric, rather than the familiar one of isolated, independent atoms; and it gives primacy to bonds among people rather than to rights to independence. It is a theory that focuses on concrete situations and persons and not on free-floating abstract actions.[26] Although many details have yet to be worked out, we can see some of its implications in particular problem areas such as this.

It is a theory that is explicitly conscious of the social, political, and economic relations that exist among persons; in particular, as a feminist theory, it attends to the implications of actions or policies on the status of women. Hence, it is necessary to ask questions from the perspective of feminist ethics in addition to those which are normally asked from the perspective of mainstream ethical theories. We must view issues such as this one in the context of the social and political realities in which they arise, and resist the attempt to evaluate actions or practices in isolation (as traditional responses in biomedical ethics often do). Thus, we cannot just address the question of IVF per se without asking how IVF contributes to general patterns of women's oppression. As Kathryn Payne Addleson has argued about abortion,[27] a feminist perspective raises questions that are inadmissible within the traditional ethical frameworks, and yet, for women in a patriarchal society, they are value questions of greater urgency. In particular, a feminist ethics, in contrast to other approaches in biomedical ethics, would take seriously the concerns just reviewed which are part of the debate in the feminist literature.

A feminist ethics would also include components of theories that have been developed as 'feminine ethics,' as sketched out by the empirical work of Carol Gilligan.[28] (The best example of such a theory is the work of Nel Noddings in her influential book *Caring*.)[29] In other words, it would be a theory that gives primacy to interpersonal relationships and woman-centered values such as nurturing, empathy, and cooperation. Hence, in the case of IVF, we must care for the women and men who are so despairing about their infertility as to want to spend the vast sums and risk the associated physical and emotional costs of the treatment, in pursuit of 'their own children.' That is, we should, in Noddings' terms, see their reality as our own and address their very real sense of loss. In so doing, however, we must also consider the implications of this sort of solution to their difficulty. While meeting the perceived desires of some women—desires which are problematic in themselves, since they are so compatible with the values of a culture deeply oppressive to women—this technology threatens to

further entrench those values which are responsible for that oppression. A larger vision suggests that the technology offered may, in reality, reduce women's freedom and, if so, it should be avoided.

A feminist ethics will not support a wholly negative response, however, for that would not address our obligation to care for those suffering from infertility; it is the responsibility of those who oppose further implementation of this technology to work towards the changes in the social arrangements that will lead to a reduction of the sense of need for this sort of solution. On the medical front, research and treatment ought to be stepped up to reduce the rates of peral sepsis and gonorrhea which often result in tubal blockage, more attention should be directed at the causes and possible cures for male infertility, and we should pursue techniques that will permit safe reversible sterilization providing women with better alternatives to tubal ligation as a means of fertility control; these sorts of technology would increase the control of many women over their own fertility and would be compatible with feminist objectives. On the social front, we must continue the social pressure to change the status of women and children in our society from that of breeder and possession respectively; hence, we must develop a vision of society as community where all participants are valued members, regardless of age or gender. And we must challenge the notion that having one's wife produce a child with his own genes is sufficient cause for the wives of men with low sperm counts to be expected to undergo the physical and emotional assault such technology involves.

Further, a feminist ethics will attend to the nature of the relationships among those concerned. Annette Baier has eloquently argued for the importance of developing an ethics of trust,[30] and I believe a feminist ethics must address the question of the degree of trust appropriate to the relationships involved. Feminists have noted that women have little reason to trust the medical specialists who offer to respond to their reproductive desires, for commonly women's interests have not come first from the medical point of view.[31] In fact, it is accurate to perceive feminist attacks on reproductive technology as expressions of the lack of trust feminists have in those who control the technology. Few feminists object to reproductive technology per se; rather they express concern about who controls it and how it can be used to further exploit women. The problem with reproductive technology is that it concentrates power in reproductive matters in the hands of those who are not directly involved in the actual bearing and rearing of the child; i.e., in men who relate to their clients in a technical, professional, authoritarian manner. It is a further step in the medicalization of pregnancy and birth which, in North America, is marked by relationships between pregnant women and their doctors which are very different from the traditional relationships between pregnant women and midwives. The latter relationships fostered an atmosphere of mutual trust which is impossible to replicate in hospital deliveries today. In fact, current approaches to pregnancy, labour, and birth tend to view the mother as a threat to the fetus who must be coerced to comply with medical procedures designed to ensure delivery of healthy babies at whatever cost necessary to the mother. Frequently, the fetus-mother relationship is medically characterized as adversarial and the physicians choose to foster a sense of alienation and passivity in the role they permit the mother. However well IVF may serve the interests of the few women with access to it, it more clearly serves the interests (be they commercial, professional, scholarly, or purely patriarchal) of those who control it.

Questions such as these are a puzzle to those engaged in the traditional approaches to ethics, for they always urge us to separate the question of evaluating the morality of various forms of reproductive technology in themselves, from questions about particular uses of that technology. From the perspective of a feminist ethics, however, no such distinction can be meaningfully made. Reproductive technology is not an abstract activity; it is an activity done in particular contexts and it is those contexts which must be addressed.

Feminist concerns cited earlier made clear the difficulties we have with some of our traditional ethical concepts; hence, feminist ethics directs us to rethink our basic ethical notions. Autonomy, or freedom of choice, is not a matter to be determined in isolated instances, as is commonly assumed in many approaches to applied ethics. Rather it is a matter that involves reflection on one's whole life situation. The freedom of choice feminists appeal to in the abortion situation is freedom to define one's status as a childbearer, given the social, economic, and political significance of reproduction for women. A feminist perspective permits us to understand that reproductive freedom includes control of one's sexuality, protection against coerced sterilization (or iatrogenic sterilization, e.g. as caused by the Dalkon Shield), and the existence of a social and economic network of support for the children we may choose to bear. It is the freedom to redefine our roles in society according to our concerns and needs as women.

In contrast, the consumer freedom to purchase technology, allowed only to a few couples of the privileged classes (in traditionally approved relationships), seems to entrench further the patriarchal notions of woman's role as childbearer and of heterosexual monogamy as the only acceptable intimate relationship. In other words, this sort of choice does not seem to foster autonomy for women on the broad scale. IVF is a practice which seems to reinforce sexist, classist, and often racist assumptions of our culture; therefore, on our revised understanding of freedom, the contribution of this technology to the general autonomy of women is largely negative.

We can now see the advantage of a feminist ethics over mainstream ethical theories, for a feminist analysis explicitly accepts the need for a political component to our understanding of ethical issues. In this, it differs from traditional ethical theories and it also differs from a simply feminine ethics approach, such as the one Noddings offers, for Noddings seems to rely on individual relations exclusively and is deeply suspicious of political alliances as potential threats to the pure relation of caring. Yet, a full understanding of both the threat of IVF, and the alternative action necessary should we decide to reject IVF, is possible only if it includes a political dimension reflecting on the role of women in society.

From the point of view of feminist ethics, the primary question to consider is whether this and other forms of reproductive technology threaten to reinforce the lack of autonomy which women now experience in our culture—even as they appear, in the short run, to be increasing freedom. We must recognize that the interconnections among the social forces oppressive to women underlie feminists' mistrust of this technology which advertises itself as increasing women's autonomy.[32] The political perspective which directs us to look at how this technology fits in with general patterns of treatment for women is not readily accessible to traditional moral theories, for it involves categories of concern not accounted for in those theories—e.g., the complexity of issues which makes it inappropriate to study them in isolation from one another, the role of oppression in shaping individual desires, and potential differences in moral status which are connected with differences in treatment.

It is the set of connections constituting women's continued oppression in our society which inspires feminists to resurrect the old slippery slope arguments to warn against IVF. We must recognize that women's existing lack of control in reproductive matters begins the debate on a pretty steep incline. Technology with the potential to further remove control of reproduction from women makes the slope very slippery indeed. This new technology, though offered under the guise of increasing reproductive freedom, threatens to result, in fact, in a significant decrease in freedom, especially since it is a technology that will always include the active involvement of designated specialists and will not ever be a private matter for the couple or women concerned.

Ethics ought not to direct us to evaluate individual cases without also looking at the implications of our decisions from a wide perspective. My argument is that a theory of feminist ethics provides that wider perspective, for its different sort of methodology is sensitive to both the personal and the social dimensions of issues. For that reason, I believe it is the only ethical perspective suitable for evaluating issues of this sort.

NOTES

1. I appreciate the helpful criticism I have received from colleagues in the Dalhousie Department of Philosophy, the Canadian Society for Women in Philosophy, and the Women's Studies program of the University of Alberta where earlier versions of this paper were read. I am particularly grateful for the careful criticism it has received from Linda Williams and Christine Overall.

2. Susan Sherwin, 'A Feminist Approach to Ethics,' *Dalhousie Review* 64, 4 (Winter 1984–85) 704–13.

3. Paul Ramsey, 'Shall We Reproduce?' *Journal of the American Medical Association* 220 (June 12, 1972), 1484.

4. Leon Kass, '"Making Babies" Revisited,' *The Public Interest* 54 (Winter 1979), 32–60.

5. Joseph Cardinal Ratzinger and Alberto Bovone, 'Instruction on Respect for Human Life in its Origin and on the Dignity of Procreation: Replies to Certain Questions of the Day' (Vatican City: Vatican Polyglot Press 1987), 23–4.

6. Ibid., 28.

7. Michael Bayles, *Reproductive Ethics* (Englewood Cliffs, NJ: Prentice-Hall 1984), 15.

8. Ratzinger and Bovone, 28.

9. Samuel Gorovitz, *Doctors' Dilemmas: Moral Conflict and Medical Care* (New York: Oxford University Press 1982), 168.

10. Ibid., 173.

11. Bayles, 66.

12. I owe this observation to Linda Williams.

13. H. Tristram Engelhardt, *The Foundations of Bioethics* (Oxford: Oxford University Press 1986), 237.

14. Ibid., 241.

15. Anita Direcks, 'Has the Lesson Been Learned?' *DES Action Voice* 28 (Spring 1986), 1–4; and Nikita A. Crook, 'Clomid,' DES Action/Toronto Factsheet #442 (available from 60 Grosvenor St., Toronto, M5S 1B6).

16. Bayles, 32. Though Bayles is not a deontologist, he does concisely express a deontological concern here.

17. Gorovitz, 177.

18. Michael Soules, 'The In Vitro Fertilization Pregnancy Rate: Let's Be Honest with One Another,' *Fertility and Sterility* 43, 4 (1985) 511–13.

19. Christine Overall, *Ethics and Human Reproduction: A Feminist Analysis* (Allen and Unwin, forthcoming), 104 ms.

20. Engelhardt, 239.

21. Bayles, 31.

22. Robert G. Edwards and David J. Sharpe, 'Social Values and Research in Human Embryology,' *Nature* 231 (May 14, 1971), 87.

23. Ratzinger and Bovone, 33.

24. Ibid., 34.

25. Many authors are now working on an understanding of what feminist ethics entail. Among the Canadian papers I am familiar with, are Kathryn Morgan's 'Women and Moral Madness,' Sheila Mullet's 'Only Connect: The Place of Self-Knowledge in Ethics,' [in Marsha Hanen and Kai Nielsen, eds., *Science, Monthly, and Feminist Theory* (Calgary, Alberta: University of Calgary Press, 1987)], and Leslie Wilson's 'Is a Feminine Ethics Enough?' *Atlantis* (forthcoming).

26. Sherwin, 'A Feminist Approach to Ethics.'

27. Kathryn Payne Addelson, 'Moral Revolution,' in Marilyn Pearsall, ed., *Women and Values* (Belmont, CA: Wadsworth 1986), 291–309.

28. Carol Gilligan, *In a Different Voice* (Cambridge, MA: Harvard University Press 1982).

29. Nel Noddings, *Caring* (Berkeley: University of California Press 1984).

30. Annette Baier, 'What Do Women Want in a Moral Theory?' *Nous* 19 (March 1985), 53–64, and 'Trust and Antitrust,' *Ethics* 96 (January 1986), 231–60.

31. Linda Williams presents this position particularly clearly in her invaluable work 'But What Will They Mean for Women? Feminist Concerns About the New Reproductive Technologies,' No. 6 in the *Feminist Perspectives* Series, CRIAW.

32. Marilyn Frye vividly describes the phenomenon of interrelatedness which supports sexist oppression by appeal to the metaphor of a bird cage composed of thin wires, each relatively harmless in itself, but, collectively, the wires constitute an overwhelming barrier to the inhabitant of the cage. Marilyn Frye, *The Politics of Reality: Essays in Feminist Theory* (Trumansburg, NY: The Crossing Press 1983), 4–7.

ELIZABETH S. ANDERSON

Is Women's Labor a Commodity?

In the past few years the practice of commercial surrogate motherhood has gained notoriety as a method for acquiring children. A commercial surrogate mother is anyone who is paid money to bear a child for other people and terminate her parental rights, so that the others may raise the child as exclusively their own. The growth of commercial surrogacy has raised with new urgency a class of concerns regarding the proper scope of the market. Some critics have objected to commercial surrogacy on the ground that it improperly treats children and women's reproductive capacities as commodities.[1] The prospect of reducing children to consumer durables and women to baby factories surely inspires revulsion. But are there good reasons behind the revulsion? And is this an accurate description of what commercial surrogacy implies? This article offers a theory about what things are properly regarded as commodities which support the claim that commercial surrogacy constitutes an unconscionable commodification of children and of women's reproductive capacities.

WHAT IS A COMMODITY?

The modern market can be characterized in terms of the legal and social norms by which it governs the production, exchange, and enjoyment of commodities. To say that something is properly regarded as a com-

modity is to claim that the norms of the market are appropriate for regulating its production, exchange, and enjoyment. To the extent that moral principles or ethical ideals preclude the application of market norms to a good, we may say that the good is not a (proper) commodity.

Why should we object to the application of a market norm to the production or distribution of a good? One reason may be that to produce or distribute the good in accordance with the norm is to *fail to value it in an appropriate way*. Consider, for example, a standard Kantian argument against slavery, or the commodification of persons. Slaves are treated in accordance with the market norm that owners may use commodities to satisfy their own interests without regard for the interests of the commodities themselves. To treat a person without regard for her interests is to fail to respect her. But slaves are persons who may not be merely used in this fashion, since as rational beings they possess a dignity which commands respect. In Kantian theory, the problem with slavery is that it treats beings worthy of *respect* as if they were worthy merely of *use*. "Respect" and "use" in this context denote what we may call different *modes of valuation*. We value things and persons in other ways than by respecting and using them. For example, love, admiration, honor, and appreciation constitute distinct modes of valuation. To value a thing or person in a distinctive way involves treating it in accordance with a particular set of norms. For example, courtesy expresses a mode of valuation we may call "civil respect," which differs from Kantian respect in that it calls for obedience to the rules of etiquette rather than to the categorical imperative.

The author thanks David Anderson, Steven Darwall, Ezekiel Emanuel, Daniel Hausman, Don Herzog, Robert Nozick, Richard Pildes, John Rawls, Michael Sandel, Thomas Scanlon, and Howard Wial for helpful comments and criticisms.

Any ideal of human life includes a conception of how different things and persons should be valued. Let us reserve the term "use" to refer to the mode of valuation proper to commodities, which follows the market norm of treating things solely in accordance with the owner's nonmoral preferences. Then the Kantian argument against commodifying persons can be generalized to apply to many other cases. It can be argued that many objects which are worthy of a higher mode of valuation than use are not properly regarded as mere commodities.[2] Some current arguments against the colorization of classic black-and-white films take this form. Such films have been colorized by their owners in an attempt to enhance their market value by attracting audiences unused to black-and-white cinematography. But some opponents of the practice object that such treatment of the film classics fails to appreciate their aesthetic and historical value. True appreciation of these films would preclude this kind of crass commercial exploitation, which debases their aesthetic qualities in the name of profits. Here the argument rests on the claim that the goods in question are worthy of appreciation, not merely of use.

The ideals which specify how one should value certain things are supported by a conception of human flourishing. Our lives are enriched and elevated by cultivating and exercising the capacity to appreciate art. To fail to do so reflects poorly on ourselves. To fail to value things appropriately is to embody in one's life an inferior conception of human flourishing.[3]

These considerations support a general account of the sorts of things which are appropriately regarded as commodities. Commodities are those things which are properly treated in accordance with the norms of the modern market. We can question the application of market norms to the production, distribution, and enjoyment of a good by appealing to ethical ideals which support arguments that the good should be valued in some other way than use. Arguments of the latter sort claim that to allow certain market norms to govern our treatment of a thing expresses a mode of valuation not worthy of it. If the thing is to be valued appropriately, its production, exchange, and enjoyment must be removed from market norms and embedded in a different set of social relationships.

THE CASE OF COMMERCIAL SURROGACY

Let us now consider the practice of commercial surrogate motherhood in the light of this theory of com-

modities. Surrogate motherhood as a commercial enterprise is based upon contracts involving three parties: the intended father, the broker, and the surrogate mother. The intended father agrees to pay a lawyer to find a suitable surrogate mother and make the requisite medical and legal arrangements for the conception and birth of the child, and for the transfer of legal custody to himself.[4] The surrogate mother agrees to become impregnated with the intended father's sperm, to carry the resulting child to term, and to relinquish her parental rights to it, transferring custody to the father in return for a fee and medical expenses. Both she and her husband (if she has one) agree not to form a parent-child bond with her child and to do everything necessary to effect the transfer of the child to the intended father. At current market prices, the lawyer arranging the contract can expect to gross $15,000 from the contract, while the surrogate mother can expect a $10,000 fee.[5]

The practice of commercial surrogacy has been defended on four main grounds. First, given the shortage of children available for adoption and the difficulty of qualifying as adoptive parents, it may represent the only hope for some people to be able to raise a family. Commercial surrogacy should be accepted as an effective means for realizing this highly significant good. Second, two fundamental human rights support commercial surrogacy: the right to procreate and freedom of contract. Fully informed autonomous adults should have the right to make whatever arrangements they wish for the use of their bodies and the reproduction of children, so long as the children themselves are not harmed. Third, the labor of the surrogate mother is said to be a labor of love. Her altruistic acts should be permitted and encouraged.[6] Finally, it is argued that commercial surrogacy is no different in its ethical implications from many already accepted practices which separate genetic, gestational, and social parenting, such as artificial insemination by donor, adoption, wet-nursing, and day care. Consistency demands that society accept this new practice as well.[7]

In opposition to these claims, I shall argue that commercial surrogacy does raise new ethical issues, since it represents an invasion of the market into a new sphere of conduct, that of specifically women's labor—that is, the labor of carrying children to term in pregnancy. When women's labor is treated as a commodity, the women who perform it are degraded. Furthermore, commercial surrogacy degrades children by reducing their status to that of commodities. Let us consider each of the goods of concern in surrogate motherhood—the child, and women's reproductive labor—to see how the commercialization of parenthood affects people's regard for them.

CHILDREN AS COMMODITIES

The most fundamental calling of parents to their children is to love them. Children are to be loved and cherished by their parents, not to be used or manipulated by them for merely personal advantage. Parental love can be understood as a passionate, unconditional commitment to nurture one's child, providing it with the care, affection, and guidance it needs to develop its capacities to maturity. This understanding of the way parents should value their children informs our interpretation of parental rights over their children. Parents' rights over their children are trusts, which they must always exercise for the sake of the child. This is not to deny that parents have their own aspirations in raising children. But the child's interests beyond subsistence are not definable independently of the flourishing of the family, which is the object of specifically parental aspirations. The proper exercise of parental rights includes those acts which promote their shared life as a family, which realize the shared interests of the parents and the child.

The norms of parental love carry implications for the ways other people should treat the relationship between parents and their children. If children are to be loved by their parents, then others should not attempt to compromise the integrity of parental love or work to suppress the emotions supporting the bond between parents and their children. If the rights to children should be understood as trusts, then if those rights are lost or relinquished, the duty of those in charge of transferring custody to others is to consult the best interests of the child.

Commercial surrogacy substitutes market norms for some of the norms of parental love. Most importantly, it requires us to understand parental rights no longer as trusts but as things more like property rights—that is, rights of use and disposal over the things owned. For in this practice the natural mother deliberately conceives a child with the intention of giving it up for material advantage. Her renunciation of parental responsibilities is not done for the child's sake, nor for the sake of fulfilling an interest she shares with the child, but typically for her own sake (and possibly, if "altruism" is a motive, for the intended parents' sakes). She and the couple who pay her to give up her parental rights over her child thus treat her rights as a kind of property right. They

thereby treat the child itself as a kind of commodity, which may be properly bought and sold.

Commercial surrogacy insinuates the norms of commerce into the parental relationship in other ways. Whereas parental love is not supposed to be conditioned upon the child having particular characteristics, consumer demand is properly responsive to the characteristics of commodities. So the surrogate industry provides opportunities to adoptive couples to specify the height, I.Q., race, and other attributes of the surrogate mother, in the expectation that these traits will be passed on to the child.[8] Since no industry assigns agents to look after the "interests" of its commodities, no one represents the child's interests in the surrogate industry. The surrogate agency promotes the adoptive parents' interests and not the child's interests where matters of custody are concerned. Finally, as the agent of the adoptive parents, the broker has the task of policing the surrogate (natural) mother's relationship to her child, using persuasion, money, and the threat of a lawsuit to weaken and destroy whatever parental love she may develop for her child.[9]

All of these substitutions of market norms for parental norms represent ways of treating children as commodities which are degrading to them. Degradation occurs when something is treated in accordance with a lower mode of valuation than is proper to it. We value things not just "more" or "less," but in qualitatively higher and lower ways. To love or respect someone is to value her in a higher way than one would if one merely used her. Children are properly loved by their parents and respected by others. Since children are valued as mere use-objects by the mother and the surrogate agency when they are sold to others, and by the adoptive parents when they seek to conform the child's genetic makeup to their own wishes, commercial surrogacy degrades children insofar as it treats them as commodities.[10]

One might argue that since the child is most likely to enter a loving home, no harm comes to it from permitting the natural mother to treat it as property. So the purchase and sale of infants is unobjectionable, at least from the point of view of children's interests.[11] But the sale of an infant has an expressive significance which this argument fails to recognize. By engaging in the transfer of children by sale, all of the parties to the surrogate contract express a set of attitudes toward children which undermine the norms of parental love. They all agree in treating the ties between a natural mother and her children as properly loosened by a monetary incentive. Would it be any wonder if a child born of a surrogacy agreement feared resale by parents who have such an attitude? And a child who knew how anxious her parents were that she have the "right" genetic makeup might fear that her parent's love was contingent upon her expression of these characteristics.[12]

The unsold children of surrogate mothers are also harmed by commercial surrogacy. The children of some surrogate mothers have reported their fears that they may be sold like their half-brother or half-sister, and express a sense of loss at being deprived of a sibling.[13] Furthermore, the widespread acceptance of commercial surrogacy would psychologically threaten all children. For it would change the way children are valued by people (parents and surrogate brokers)— from being loved by their parents and respected by others, to being sometimes used as objects of commercial profit-making.[14]

Proponents of commercial surrogacy have denied that the surrogate industry engages in the sale of children. For it is impossible to sell to someone what is already his own, and the child is already the father's own natural offspring. The payment to the surrogate mother is not for her child, but for her services in carrying it to term.[15] The claim that the parties to the surrogate contract treat children as commodities, however, is based on the way they treat the *mother's* rights over her child. It is irrelevant that the natural father also has some rights over the child; what he pays for is exclusive rights to it. He would not pay her for the "service" of carrying the child to term if she refused to relinquish her parental rights to it. That the mother regards only her labor and not her child as requiring compensation is also irrelevant. No one would argue that the baker does not treat his bread as property just because he sees the income from its sale as compensation for his labor and expenses and not for the bread itself, which he doesn't care to keep.[16]

Defenders of commercial surrogacy have also claimed that it does not differ substantially from other already accepted parental practices. In the institutions of adoption and artificial insemination by donor (AID), it is claimed, we already grant parents the right to dispose of their children.[17] But these practices differ in significant respects from commercial surrogacy. The purpose of adoption is to provide a means for placing children in families when their parents cannot

or will not discharge their parental responsibilities. It is not a sphere for the existence of a supposed parental right to dispose of one's children for profit. Even AID does not sanction the sale of fully formed human beings. The semen donor sells only a product of his body, not his child, and does not initiate the act of conception.

Two developments might seem to undermine the claim that commercial surrogacy constitutes a degrading commerce in children. The first is technological: the prospect of transplanting a human embryo into the womb of a genetically unrelated woman. If commercial surrogacy used women only as gestational mothers and not as genetic mothers, and if it was thought that only genetic and not gestational parents could properly claim that a child was "theirs," then the child born of a surrogate mother would not be hers to sell in the first place. The second is a legal development: the establishment of the proposed "consent-intent" definition of parenthood.[18] This would declare the legal parents of a child to be whoever consented to a procedure which leads to its birth, with the intent of assuming parental responsibilities for it. This rule would define away the problem of commerce in children by depriving the surrogate mother of any legal claim to her child at all, even if it were hers both genetically and gestationally.[19]

There are good reasons, however, not to undermine the place of genetic and gestational ties in these ways. Consider first the place of genetic ties. By upholding a system of involuntary (genetic) ties of obligation among people, even when the adults among them prefer to divide their rights and obligations in other ways, we help to secure children's interests in having an assured place in the world, which is more firm than the wills of their parents. Unlike the consent-intent rule, the principle of respecting genetic ties does not make the obligation to care for those whom one has created (intentionally or not) contingent upon an arbitrary desire to do so. It thus provides children with a set of preexisting social sanctions which give them a more secure place in the world. The genetic principle also places children in a far wider network of associations and obligations than the consent-intent rule sanctions. It supports the roles of grandparents and other relatives in the nurturing of children, and provides children with a possible focus of stability and an additional source of claims to care if their parents cannot sustain a well-functioning household.

In the next section I will defend the claims of gestational ties to children. To deny these claims, as commercial surrogacy does, is to deny the significance of reproductive labor to the mother who undergoes it and thereby to dehumanize and degrade the mother herself. Commercial surrogacy would be a corrupt practice even if it did not involve commerce in children.

WOMEN'S LABOR AS A COMMODITY

Commercial surrogacy attempts to transform what is specifically women's labor—the work of bringing forth children into the world—into a commodity. It does so by replacing the parental norms which usually govern the practice of gestating children with the economic norms which govern ordinary production processes. The application of commercial norms to women's labor reduces the surrogate mothers from persons worthy of respect and consideration to objects of mere use.

Respect and consideration are two distinct modes of valuation whose norms are violated by the practices of the surrogate industry. To respect a person is to treat her in accordance with principles she rationally accepts—principles consistent with the protection of her autonomy and her rational interests. To treat a person with consideration is to respond with sensitivity to her and to her emotional relations with others, refraining from manipulating or denigrating these for one's own purposes. Given the understanding of respect as a dispassionate, impersonal regard for people's interests, a different ethical concept—consideration—is needed to capture the engaged and sensitive regard we should have for people's emotional relationships. The failure of consideration on the part of the other parties to the surrogacy contract explains the judgment that the contract is not simply disrespectful of the surrogate mother, but callous as well.[20]

The application of economic norms to the sphere of women's labor violates women's claims to respect and consideration in three ways. First, by requiring the surrogate mother to repress whatever parental love she feels for the child, these norms convert women's labor into a form of alienated labor. Second, by manipulating and denying legitimacy to the surrogate mother's evolving perspective on her own pregnancy, the norms of the market degrade her. Third, by taking advantage of the surrogate mother's noncommercial motivations without offering anything but what the norms of commerce demand in return, these norms leave her open to exploitation. The fact that these problems arise in the attempt to commercialize the labor of bearing children shows that women's labor is not properly regarded as a commodity.

The key to understanding these problems is the normal role of the emotions in noncommercialized pregnancies. Pregnancy is not simply a biological process but also a social practice. Many social expectations and considerations surround women's gestational labor, marking it off as an occasion for the parents to prepare themselves to welcome a new life into their family. For example, obstetricians use ultrasound not simply for diagnostic purposes but also to encourage material bonding with the fetus.[21] We can all recognize that it is good, although by no means inevitable, for loving bonds to be established between the mother and her child during this period.

In contrast with these practices, the surrogate industry follows the putting-out system of manufacturing. It provides some of the raw materials of production (the father's sperm) to the surrogate mother, who then engages in production of the child. Although her labor is subject to periodic supervision by her doctors and by the surrogate agency, the agency does not have physical control over the product of her labor as firms using the factory system do. Hence, as in all putting-out systems, the surrogate industry faces the problem of extracting the final product from the mother. This problem is exacerbated by the fact that the social norms surrounding pregnancy are designed to encourage parental love for the child. The surrogate industry addresses this problem by requiring the mother to engage in a form of emotional labor.[22] In the surrogate contract, she agrees not to form or attempt to form a parent-child relationship with her offspring.[23] Her labor is alienated, because she must divert it from the end which the social practices of pregnancy rightly promote—an emotional bond with her child. The surrogate contract thus replaces a norm of parenthood, that during pregnancy one create a loving attachment to one's child, with a norm of commercial production, that the producer shall not form any special emotional ties to her product.

The demand to deliberately alienate oneself from one's love for one's own child is a demand which can reasonably and decently be made of no one. Unless we were to remake pregnancy into a form of drudgery which is only performed for a wage, there is every reason to expect that many women who do sign a surrogate contract will, despite this fact, form a loving attachment to the child they bear. For this is what the social practices surrounding pregnancy encourage. Treating women's labor as just another kind of commercial production process violates the precious emotional ties which the mother might rightly and properly establish with her "product," the child, and thereby violates her claims to consideration.[24]

Commercial surrogacy is also a degrading practice. The surrogate mother, like all persons, has an independent evaluative perspective on her activities and relationships. The realization of her dignity demands that the other parties to the contract acknowledge rather than evade the claims which her independent perspective makes upon them. But the surrogate industry has an interest in suppressing, manipulating, and trivializing her perspective, for there is an ever-present danger that she will see her involvement in her pregnancy from the perspective of a parent rather than from the perspective of a contract laborer.

How does this suppression and trivialization take place? The commercial promoters of surrogacy commonly describe the surrogate mothers as inanimate objects: mere "hatcheries," "plumbing," or "rented property"—things without emotions which could make claims on others.[25] They also refuse to acknowledge any responsibility for the consequences of the mother's emotional labor. Should she suffer psychologically from being forced to give up her child, the father is not liable to pay for therapy after her pregnancy, although he is liable for all other medical expenses following her pregnancy.[26]

The treatment and interpretation of surrogate mothers' grief raises the deepest problems of degradation. Most surrogate mothers experience grief upon giving up their children—in 10 percent of cases, seriously enough to require therapy.[27] Their grief is not compensated by the $10,000 fee they receive. Grief is not an intelligible response to a successful deal, but rather reflects the subject's judgment that she has suffered a grave and personal loss. Since not all cases of grief resolve themselves into cases of regret, it may be that some surrogate mothers do not regard their grief, in retrospect, as reflecting an authentic judgment on their part. But in the circumstances of emotional manipulation which pervade the surrogate industry, it is difficult to determine which interpretation of her grief more truly reflects the perspective of the surrogate mother. By insinuating a trivializing interpretation of her emotional responses to the prospect of losing her child, the surrogate agency may be able to manipulate her into accepting her fate without too much fuss, and may even succeed in substituting its interpretation of her emotions for her own. Since she has already signed a contract to perform emotional labor—to express or repress emotions which are dictated by the interests of the surrogate industry—this might not be a difficult task.[28] A considerate treatment of the mothers' grief, on the other hand, would take the evaluative basis of their grief seriously.

Some defenders of commercial surrogacy demand that the provision for terminating the surrogate mother's parental rights in her child be legally enforceable, so that peace of mind for the adoptive parents can be secured.[29] But the surrogate industry makes no corresponding provision for securing the peace of mind of the surrogate. She is expected to assume the risk of a transformation of her ethical and emotional perspective on herself and her child with the same impersonal detachment with which a futures trader assumes the risk of a fluctuation in the price of pork bellies. By applying the market norms of enforcing contracts to the surrogate mother's case, commercial surrogacy treats a moral transformation as if it were merely an economic change.[30]

The manipulation of the surrogate mother's emotions which is inherent in the surrogate parenting contract also leaves women open to grave forms of exploitation. A kind of exploitation occurs when one party to a transaction is oriented toward the exchange of "gift" values, while the other party operates in accordance with the norms of the market exchange of commodities. Gift values, which include love, gratitude, and appreciation of others, cannot be bought or obtained through piecemeal calculations of individual advantage. Their exchange requires a repudiation of a self-interested attitude, a willingness to give gifts to others without demanding some specific equivalent good in return each time one gives. The surrogate mother often operates according to the norms of gift relationships. The surrogate agency, on the other hand, follows market norms. Its job is to get the best deal for its clients and itself, while leaving the surrogate mother to look after her own interests as best as she can. This situation puts the surrogate agencies in a position to manipulate the surrogate mothers' emotions to gain favorable terms for themselves. For example, agencies screen prospective surrogate mothers for submissiveness, and emphasize to them the importance of the motives of generosity and love. When applicants question some of the terms of the contract, the broker sometimes intimidates them by questioning their character and morality: if they were really generous and loving they would not be so solicitous about their own interests.[31]

Some evidence supports the claim that most surrogate mothers are motivated by emotional needs and vulnerabilities which lead them to view their labor as a form of gift and not a purely commercial exchange. Only 1 percent of applicants to surrogate agencies would become surrogate mothers for money alone; the others have emotional as well as financial reasons for applying. One psychiatrist believes that most, if not all, of the 35 percent of applicants who had had a previous abortion or given up a child for adoption wanted to become surrogate mothers in order to resolve their guilty feelings or deal with their unresolved loss by going through a process of losing a child again.[32] Women who feel that giving up another child is an effective way to punish themselves for past abortions, or a form of therapy for their emotional problems, are not likely to resist manipulation by surrogate brokers.

Many surrogate mothers see pregnancy as a way to feel "adequate," "appreciated," or "special." In other words, these women feel inadequate, unappreciated, or unadmired when they are not pregnant.[33] Lacking the power to achieve some worthwhile status in their own right, they must subordinate themselves to others' definitions of their proper place (as baby factories) in order to get from them the appreciation they need to attain a sense of self-worth. But the sense of self-worth one can attain under such circumstances is precarious and ultimately self-defeating. For example, those who seek gratitude on the part of the adoptive parents and some opportunity to share the joys of seeing their children grow discover all too often that the adoptive parents want nothing to do with them.[34] For while the surrogate mother sees in the arrangement some basis for establishing the personal ties she needs to sustain her emotionally, the adoptive couple sees it as an impersonal commercial contract, one of whose main advantages to them is that all ties between them and the surrogate are ended once the terms of the contract are fulfilled.[35] To them, her presence is a threat to marital unity and a competing object for the child's affections.

These considerations should lead us to question the model of altruism which is held up to women by the surrogacy industry. It is a strange form of altruism which demands such radical self-effacement, alienation from those whom one benefits, and the subordination of one's body, health, and emotional life to the independently defined interests of others.[36] Why

should this model of "altruism" be held up to *women*? True altruism does not involve such subordination, but rather the autonomous and self-confident exercise of skill, talent, and judgment. (Consider the dedicated doctor.) The kind of altruism we see admired in surrogate mothers involves a lack of self-confidence, a feeling that one can be truly worthy only through self-effacement. This model of altruism, far from affirming the freedom and dignity of women, seems all too conveniently designed to keep their sense of self-worth hostage to the interests of a more privileged class.[37]

The primary distortions which arise from treating women's labor as a commodity — the surrogate mother's alienation from loved ones, her degradation, and her exploitation — stem from a common source. This is the failure to acknowledge and treat appropriately the surrogate mother's emotional engagement with her labor. Her labor is alienated, because she must suppress her emotional ties with her own child, and may be manipulated into reinterpreting these ties in a trivializing way. She is degraded, because her independent ethical perspective is denied, or demoted to the status of a cash sum. She is exploited, because her emotional needs and vulnerabilities are not treated as characteristics which call for consideration, but as factors which may be manipulated to encourage her to make a grave self-sacrifice to the broker's and adoptive couple's advantage. These considerations provide strong grounds for sustaining the claims of women's labor to its "product," the child. The attempt to redefine parenthood so as to strip women of parental claims to the children they bear does violence to their emotional engagement with the project of bringing children into the world.

COMMERCIAL SURROGACY, FREEDOM, AND THE LAW

In the light of these ethical objections to commercial surrogacy, what position should the law take on the practice? At the very least, surrogate contracts should not be enforceable. Surrogate mothers should not be forced to relinquish their children if they have formed emotional bonds with them. Any other treatment of women's ties to the children they bear is degrading.

But I think these arguments support the stronger conclusion that commercial surrogate contracts should be illegal, and that surrogate agencies who arrange such contracts should be subject to criminal penalties.[38] Commercial surrogacy constitutes a degrading and harmful traffic in children, violates the dignity of women, and subjects both children and women to a serious risk of exploitation. But are these problems inherent in the practice of commercial surrogacy? Defenders of the practice have suggested three reforms intended to eliminate these problems: (1) give the surrogate mother the option of keeping her child after birth; (2) impose stringent regulations on private surrogate agencies; (3) replace private surrogate agencies with a state-run monopoly on surrogate arrangements. Let us consider each of these options in turn.

Some defenders of commercial surrogacy suggest that the problem of respecting the surrogate mother's potential attachment to her child can be solved by granting the surrogate mother the option to reserve her parental rights after birth.[39] But such an option would not significantly change the conditions of the surrogate mother's labor. Indeed, such a provision would pressure the agency to demean the mother's self-regard more than ever. Since it could not rely on the law to enforce the adoptive parents' wishes regardless of the surrogate's feelings, it would have to make sure that she assumed the perspective which it and its clients have of her: as "rented plumbing."

Could such dangers be avoided by careful regulation of the surrogate industry? Some have suggested that exploitation of women could be avoided by such measures as properly screening surrogates, setting low fixed fees (to avoid tempting women in financial duress), and requiring independent counsel for the surrogate mother.[40] But no one knows how to predict who will suffer grave psychological damage from surrogacy, and the main forms of duress encountered in the industry are emotional rather than financial. Furthermore, there is little hope that regulation would check the exploitation of surrogate mothers. The most significant encounters between the mothers and the surrogate agencies take place behind closed doors. It is impossible to regulate the multifarious ways in which brokers can subtly manipulate the emotions of the vulnerable to their own advantage. Advocates of commercial surrogacy claim that their failure rate is extremely low, since only five out of the first five hundred cases were legally contested by surrogate mothers. But we do not know how many surrogate mothers were browbeaten into relinquishing their children, feel violated by their treatment, or would feel violated had their perspectives not been manipulated by the other

parties to the contract. The dangers of exploiting women through commercial surrogacy are too great to ignore, and too deep to effectively regulate.

Could a state-run monopoly on surrogate arrangements eliminate the risk of degrading and exploiting surrogate mothers?[41] A nonprofit state agency would arguably have no incentive to exploit surrogates, and it would screen the adoptive parents for the sake of the best interests of the child. Nevertheless, as long as the surrogate mother is paid money to bear a child and terminate her parental rights, the commercial norms leading to her degradation still apply. For these norms are constitutive of our understanding of what the surrogate contract is for. Once such an arrangement becomes socially legitimized, these norms will govern the understandings of participants in the practice and of society at large, or at least compete powerfully with the rival parental norms. And what judgment do these norms make of a mother who, out of love for her child, decides that she cannot relinquish it? They blame her for commercial irresponsibility and flighty emotions. Her transformation of moral and emotional perspective, which she experiences as real but painful growth, looks like a capricious and selfish exercise of will from the standpoint of the market, which does not distinguish the deep commitments of love from arbitrary matters of taste.[42]

The fundamental problem with commercial surrogacy is that commercial norms are inherently manipulative when they are applied to the sphere of parental love. Manipulation occurs whenever norms are deployed to psychologically coerce others into a position where they cannot defend their own interests or articulate their own perspective without being charged with irresponsibility or immorality for doing so. A surrogate contract is inherently manipulative, since the very form of the contract invokes commercial norms which, whether upheld by the law or by social custom only, imply that the mother should feel guilty and irresponsible for loving her own child.

But hasn't the surrogate mother decided in advance that she is not interested in viewing her relationship to her child in this way? Regardless of her initial state of mind, once she enters the contract, she is not free to develop an autonomous perspective on her relationship with her child. She is contractually bound to manipulate her emotions to agree with the interests of the adoptive parents. Few things reach deeper into the self than a parent's evolving relationship with her own child. To lay claim to the course of this relationship in virtue of a cash payment constitutes a severe violation of the mother's personhood and a denial of the mother's autonomy.

Two final objections stand in the way of criminalizing commercial surrogacy. Prohibiting the practice might be thought to infringe two rights: the right of procreation, and the right to freedom of contract. Judge Harvey Sorkow, in upholding the legality and enforceability of commercial surrogate parenting contracts, based much of his argument on an interpretation of the freedom to procreate. He argued that the protection of the right to procreate requires the protection of noncoital means of procreation, including commercial surrogacy. The interests upheld by the creation of the family are the same, regardless of the means used to bring the family into existence.[43]

Sorkow asserts a blanket right to procreate, without carefully examining the specific human interests protected by such a right. The interest protected by the right to procreate is that of being able to create and sustain a family life with some integrity. But the enforcement of surrogate contracts against the will of the mother destroys one family just as surely as it creates another. And the same interest which generates the right to procreate also generates an obligation to uphold the integrity of family life which constrains the exercise of this right.[44] To recognize the legality of commercial surrogate contracts would undermine the integrity of families by giving public sanction to a practice which expresses contempt for the moral and emotional ties which bind a mother to her children, legitimates the view that these ties are merely the product of arbitrary will, properly loosened by the offering of a monetary incentive, and fails to respect the claims of genetic and gestational ties to children which provide children with a more secure place in the world than commerce can supply.

The freedom of contract provides weaker grounds for supporting commercial surrogacy. This freedom is already constrained, notably in preventing the purchase and sale of human beings. Yet one might object that prohibiting surrogate contracts could undermine the status of women by implying that they do not have the competence to enter into and rationally discharge the obligations of commercial contracts. Insofar as the justification for prohibiting commercial surrogacy depends upon giving special regard to women's emotional ties to their children, it might be thought to suggest that women as a group are too emotional to subject themselves to the dispassionate discipline

of the market. Then prohibiting surrogate contracts would be seen as an offensive, paternalistic interference with the autonomy of the surrogate mothers.

We have seen, however, that the content of the surrogate contract itself compromises the autonomy of surrogate mothers. It uses the norms of commerce in a manipulative way and commands the surrogate mothers to conform their emotions to the interests of the other parties to the contract. The surrogate industry fails to acknowledge the surrogate mothers as possessing an independent perspective worthy of consideration. And it takes advantage of motivations—such as self-effacing "altruism"—which women have formed under social conditions inconsistent with genuine autonomy. Hence the surrogate industry itself, far from expanding the realm of autonomy for women, actually undermines the external and internal conditions required for fully autonomous choice by women.

If commercial surrogate contracts were prohibited, this would be no cause for infertile couples to lose hope for raising a family. The option of adoption is still available, and every attempt should be made to open up opportunities for adoption to couples who do not meet standard requirements—for example, because of age. While there is a shortage of healthy white infants available for adoption, there is no shortage of children of other races, mixed-race children, and older and handicapped children who desperately need to be adopted. Leaders of the surrogate industry have proclaimed that commercial surrogacy may replace adoption as the method of choice for infertile couples who wish to raise families. But we should be wary of the racist and eugenic motivations which make some people rally to the surrogate industry at the expense of children who already exist and need homes.

The case of commercial surrogacy raises deep questions about the proper scope of the market in modern industrial societies. I have argued that there are principled grounds for rejecting the substitution of market norms for parental norms to govern the ways women bring children into the world. Such substitutions express ways of valuing mothers and children which reflect an inferior conception of human flourishing. When market norms are applied to the ways we allocate and understand parental rights and responsibilities, children are reduced from subjects of love to objects of use. When market norms are applied to the ways we treat and understand women's reproductive labor, women are reduced from subjects of respect and consideration to objects of use. If we are to retain the capacity to value children and women in ways consistent with a rich conception of human flourishing, we must resist the encroachment of the market upon the sphere of reproductive labor. Women's labor is *not* a commodity.

NOTES

1. See, for example, Gena Corea, *The Mother Machine* (New York: Harper and Row, 1985), pp. 216, 219; Angela Holder, "Surrogate Motherhood: Babies for Fun and Profit," *Case and Comment* 90 (1985): 3–11; and Margaret Jane Radin, "Market Inalienability," *Harvard Law Review* 100 (June 1987): 1849–1937.

2. The notion of valuing something more highly than another can be understood as follows. Some preferences are neither obligatory nor admirable. To value a thing as a mere use-object is to treat it solely in accordance with such nonethical preferences. To value a thing or person more highly than as a mere use-object is to recognize it as having some special intrinsic worth, in virtue of which we form preferences about how to treat the thing which we regard as obligatory or admirable. The person who truly appreciates art does not conceive of art merely as a thing which she can use as she pleases, but as something which commands appreciation. It would be contemptible to willfully destroy the aesthetic qualities of a work of art simply to satisfy some of one's nonethical preferences, and it is a mark of a cultivated and hence admirable person that she has preferences for appreciating art. This account of higher and lower modes of valuation is indebted to Charles Taylor's account of higher and lower values. See Charles Taylor, "The Diversity of Goods," in *Utilitarianism and Beyond*, ed. Amartya Sen and Bernard Williams (Cambridge: Cambridge University Press, 1982), pp. 129–44.

3. This kind of argument shows why treating something as a commodity may be deplorable. Of course, more has to be said to justify prohibiting the commodification of a thing. I shall argue below that the considerations against the commodification of children and of women's labor are strong enough to justify prohibiting the practice of commercial surrogacy.

4. State laws against selling babies prevent the intended father's wife (if he has one) from being a party to the contract.

5. See Katie Marie Brophy, "A Surrogate Mother Contract to Bear a Child," *Journal of Family Law* 20 (1981–82): 263–91, and Noel Keane, "The Surrogate Parenting Contract," *Adelphia Law Journal* 2 (1983): 45–53, for examples and explanations of surrogate parenting contracts.

6. Mary Warnock, *A Question of Life* (Oxford: Blackwell, 1985), p. 45. This book reprints the Warnock Report on Human Fertilization and Embryology, which was commissioned by the British government for the purpose of recommending legislation concerning surrogacy and other issues. Although the Warnock Report mentions the promotion of altruism as one defense of surrogacy, it strongly condemns the practice overall.

7. John Robertson, "Surrogate Mothers: Not So Novel after All," *Hastings Center Report*, October 1983, pp. 28–34; John Harris, *The Value of Life* (Boston: Routledge and Kegan Paul, 1985).

8. See "No Other Hope for Having a Child," *Time*, 19 January 1987, pp. 50–51. Radin argues that women's traits are also commodified in this practice. See "Market Inalienability," pp. 1932–35.

9. Here I discuss the surrogate industry as it actually exists today. I will consider possible modifications of commercial surrogacy in the final section below.

10. Robert Nozick has objected that my claims about parental love appear to be culture-bound. Do not parents in the Third World, who rely on children to provide for the family subsistence, regard their children as economic goods? In promoting the livelihood of their families, however, such children need not be treated in accordance with market norms—that is, as commodities. In particular, such children usually remain a part of their families, and hence can still be loved by their parents. But insofar as children are treated according to the norms of modern capitalist markets, this treatment is deplorable wherever it takes place.

11. See Elizabeth Landes and Richard Posner, "The Economics of the Baby Shortage," *Journal of Legal Studies* 7 (1978): 323–48, and Richard Posner, "The Regulation of the Market in Adoptions," *Boston University Law Review* 67 (1987): 59–72.

12. Of course, where children are concerned, it is irrelevant whether these fears are reasonable. One of the greatest fears of children is separation from their parents. Adopted children are already known to suffer from separation anxiety more acutely than children who remain with their natural mothers, for they feel that their original mothers did not love them. In adoption, the fact that the child would be even worse off if the mother did not give it up justifies her severing of ties and can help to rationalize this event to the child. But in the case of commercial surrogacy, the severing of ties is done not for the child's sake, but for the parents' sakes. In the adoption case there are explanations for the mother's action which may quell the child's doubts about being loved which are unavailable in the case of surrogacy.

13. Kay Longcope, "Surrogacy: Two Professionals on Each Side of Issue Give Their Arguments for Prohibition and Regulation," *Boston Globe*, 23 March 1987, pp. 18–19; and Iver Peterson, "Baby M Case: Surrogate Mothers Vent Feelings," *New York Times*, 2 March 1987, pp. B1, B4.

14. Herbert Krimmel, "The Case against Surrogate Parenting," *Hastings Center Report*, October 1983, pp. 35–37.

15. Judge Sorkow made this argument in ruling on the famous case of Baby M. See *In Re Baby M*, 217 N.J. Super 313. Reprinted in *Family Law Reporter* 13 (1987): 2001–30. Chief Justice Wilentz of the New Jersey Supreme Court overruled Sorkow's judgment. See *In the Matter of Baby M*, 109 N.J. 396, 537 A:2d 1227 (1988).

16. Sallyann Payton has observed that the law does not permit the sale of parental rights, only their relinquishment or forced termination by the state, and these acts are subject to court review for the sake of the child's best interests. But this legal technicality does not change the moral implications of the analogy with baby-selling. The mother is still paid to do what she can to relinquish her parental rights and to transfer custody of the child to the father. Whether or not the courts occasionally prevent this from happening, the actions of the parties express a commercial orientation to children which is degrading and harmful to them. The New Jersey Supreme Court ruled that surrogacy contracts are void precisely because they assign custody without regard to the child's best interests. See *In the Matter of Baby M*, p. 1246.

17. Robertson, "Surrogate Mothers: Not So Novel after All," p. 32; Harris, *The Value of Life*, p. 144–45.

18. See Philip Parker, "Surrogate Motherhood: The Interaction of Litigation, Legislation and Psychiatry," *International Journal of Law and Psychiatry* 5 (1982): 341–54.

19. The consent-intent rule would not, however, change the fact that commercial surrogacy replaces parental norms with market norms. For the rule itself embodies the market norm which acknowledges only voluntary, contractual relations among people as having moral force. Whereas familial love invites children into a

network of unwilled relationships broader than those they have with their parents, the willed contract creates an exclusive relationship between the parents and the child only.

20. I thank Steven Darwall and David Anderson for clarifying my thoughts on this point.

21. I am indebted to Dr. Ezekiel Emanuel for this point.

22. One engages in emotional labor when one is paid to express or repress certain emotions. On the concept of emotional labor and its consequences for workers, see Arlie Hochschild, *The Managed Heart* (Berkeley and Los Angeles: University of California Press, 1983).

23. Noel Keane and Dennis Breo, *The Surrogate Mother* (New York: Everest House, 1981), p. 291; Brophy, "A Surrogate Mother Contract," p. 267. The surrogate's husband is also required to agree to this clause of the contract.

24. One might ask why this argument does not extend to all cases in which one might form an emotional attachment to an object one has contracted to sell. If I sign a contract with you to sell my car to you, can I back out if I decide I am too emotionally attached to it? My argument is based upon the distinctive characteristics of parental love—a mode of valuation which should not be confused with less profound modes of valuation which generate sentimental attachments to things. The degree to which other modes of valuation generate claims to consideration which tell against market norms remains an open question.

25. Corea, *The Mother Machine*, p. 222.

26. Keane and Breo, *The Surrogate Mother*, p. 292.

27. Kay Longcope, "Standing Up for Mary Beth," *Boston Globe*, 5 March 1987, p. 83; Daniel Goleman, "Motivations of Surrogate Mothers," *New York Times*, 20 January 1987, p. C1; Robertson, "Surrogate Mothers: Not So Novel after All," pp. 30, 34 n. 8. Neither the surrogate mothers themselves nor psychiatrists have been able to predict which women will experience such grief.

28. See Hochschild, *The Managed Heart*, for an important empirical study of the dynamics of commercialized emotional labor.

29. Keane and Breo, *The Surrogate Mother*, pp. 236–37.

30. For one account of how a surrogate mother who came to regret her decision viewed her own moral transformation, see Elizabeth Kane: *Birth Mother: The Story of America's First Legal Surrogate Mother* (San Diego: Harcourt Brace Jovanovich, 1988). I argue below that the implications of commodifying women's labor are not significantly changed even if the contract is unenforceable.

31. Susan Ince, "Inside the Surrogate Industry," in *Test-Tube Women*, ed. Rita Arditti, Renate Duelli Klein, and Shelley Minden (Boston: Pandora Press, 1984), p. 110.

32. Philip Parker, "Motivation of Surrogate Mothers: Initial Findings," *American Journal of Psychiatry* 140 (1983): 117–18.

33. The surrogate broker Noel Keane is remarkably open about reporting the desperate emotional insecurities which shape the lives of so many surrogate mothers, while displaying little sensitivity to the implications of his taking advantage of these motivations to make his business a financial success. See especially Keane and Breo, *The Surrogate Mother*, pp. 247ff.

34. See, for example, the story of the surrogate mother Nancy Barrass in Anne Fleming, "Our Fascination with Baby M," *New York Times Magazine*, 29 March 1987, p. 38.

35. For evidence of these disparate perspectives, see Peterson, "Baby M Case: Surrogate Mothers Vent Feelings," p. B4.

36. The surrogate mother is required to obey all doctor's orders made in the interests of the child's health. (See Brophy, "A Surrogate Mother Contract"; Keane, "The Surrogate Parenting Contract"; and Ince, "Inside the Surrogate Industry.") These orders could include forcing her to give up her job, travel plans, and recreational activities. The doctor could confine her to bed, and order her to submit to surgery and take drugs. One can hardly exercise an autonomous choice over one's health if one could be held in breach of contract and liable for $35,000 damages for making a decision contrary to the wishes of one's doctor.

37. See Corea, *The Mother Machine*, pp. 227–33, and Christine Overall, *Ethics and Human Reproduction* (Boston: Allen and Unwin, 1987), pp. 122–28. Both emphasize the social conditions which undermine the claim that women choose to be surrogate mothers under conditions of autonomy.

38. Both of these conclusions follow the Warnock commission's recommendations. See Warnock, *A Question of Life*, pp. 43–44, 46–47. Since the surrogate mother is a victim of commercial surrogacy arrangements, she should not be prosecuted for entering into them. And my arguments are directed only against surrogacy as a commercial enterprise.

39. Barbara Cohen, "Surrogate Mothers: Whose Baby Is It?" *American Journal of Law and Medicine* 10 (1984): 282; Peter Singer and Deane Wells, *Making Babies* (New York: Scribner, 1985), pp. 106–7, 111.

40. Harris, *The Value of Life*, pp. 143–44, 156.

41. Singer and Wells support this recommendation in *Making Babies*, pp. 110–11. See also the dissenting opinion of the Warnock commission, *A Question of Life*, pp. 87–89.

42. See Fleming, "Our Fascination with Baby M," for a sensitive discussion of Americans' conflicting attitudes toward surrogate mothers who find they cannot give up their children.

43. *In Re Baby M*, p. 2022. See also Robertson, "Surrogate Mothers: Not So Novel after All," p. 32.

44. The Catholic Church makes this principle the fundamental basis for its own criticism of surrogate motherhood. See Congregation for the Doctrine of the Faith, "Instruction on Respect for Human Life In Its Origin and on the Dignity of Procreation: Replies to Certain Questions of the Day," reproduced in *New York Times*, 11 March 1987, pp. A14–A17.

L A U R A   M .   P U R D Y

Surrogate Mothering: Exploitation or Empowerment?

INTRODUCTION

'Pregnancy is barbaric'[1] proclaimed Shulamith Firestone in the first heady days of the new women's
movement; she looked forward to the time when technology would free women from the oppression of biological reproduction. Yet as reproductive options multiply, some feminists are making common cause with
conservatives for a ban on innovations. What is going on?

Firestone argued that nature oppresses women by
leaving them holding the reproductive bag, while men
are free of such burden; so long as this biological inequality holds, women will never be free. (Firestone,
198–200) It is now commonplace to point out the
naivety of her claim: it is not the biological difference,
per se, that oppresses women, but its social significance. So we need not change biology, only attitudes
and institutions.

This insight has helped us to see how to achieve a
better life for women, but I wonder if it is the whole
story. Has Firestone's brave claim no lesson at all
for us?

Her point was that being with child is uncomfortable and dangerous, and it can limit women's lives.
We have become more sensitive to the ways in which
social arrangements can determine how much these
difficulties affect us. However, even in feminist
utopias, where sex or gender are considered morally
irrelevant except where they may entail special needs,
a few difficulties would remain. Infertility, for instance, would exist, as would the desire for a child
in circumstances where pregnancy is impossible or
undesirable.

From *Bioethics* 3 (1989), 18–34. © 1989 by Basil Blackwell, Ltd.
Reprinted by permission of Basil Blackwell, Ltd., and the author.

At present, the problem of infertility is generating a
whole series of responses and solutions. Among them
are high-tech procedures like IVF, and social arrangements like surrogate motherhood. Both these techniques are also provoking a storm of concern and
protest. As each raises a distinctive set of issues, they
need to be dealt with separately, and I shall here consider only surrogate motherhood.

One might argue that no feminist paradise would
need any practice such as this. As Susan Sherwin argues, it could not countenance 'the capitalism, racism,
sexism, and elitism of our culture [that] have combined to create a set of attitudes which views children
as commodities whose value is derived from their
possession of parental chromosomes.'[2] Nor will society define women's fulfilment as only in terms of their
relationship to genetically related children. No longer
will children be needed as men's heirs or women's
livelihood.

We will, on the contrary, desire relationships with
children for the right reasons: the urge to nurture,
teach and be close to them. No longer will we be driven by narcissistic wishes for clones or immortality to
seek genetic offspring no matter what the cost. Indeed,
we will have recognized that children are the promise
and responsibility of the whole human community.
And childrearing practices will reflect these facts, including at least a more diffuse family life that allows
children to have significant relationships with others.
Perhaps childbearing will be communal.

This radically different world is hard to picture realistically, even by those like myself who — I think —
most ardently wish for it. The doubts I feel are fanned
by the visions of so-called 'cultural feminists' who
glorify traditionally feminine values. Family life can
be suffocating, distorting, even deadly.[3] Yet there is a

special closeness that arises from being a child's primary caretaker, just as there can be a special thrill in witnessing the unfolding of biologically driven traits in that child. These pleasures justify risking neither the health of the child[4] nor that of the mother; nobody's general well-being should be sacrificed to them, nor do they warrant huge social investments. However, they are things that, other things being equal, it would be desirable to preserve so long as people continue to have anything like their current values. If this is so, then evaluating the morality of practices that open up new ways of creating children is worthwhile.[5]

MORAL OR IMMORAL?

What is surrogate mothering exactly? Physically, its essential features are as follows: a woman is inseminated with the sperm of a man to whom she is not married. When the baby is born she relinquishes her claim to it in favour of another, usually the man from whom the sperm was obtained. As currently practiced, she provides the egg, so her biological input is at least equal to that of the man. 'Surrogate' mothering may not therefore be the best term for what she is doing.[6]

By doing these things she also acts socially—to take on the burden and risk of pregnancy for another, and to separate sex and reproduction, reproduction and childrearing, and reproduction and marriage. If she takes money for the transaction (apart from payment of medical bills), she may even be considered to be selling a baby.

The bare physical facts would not warrant the welter of accusation and counter-accusation that surrounds the practice.[7] It is the social aspects that have engendered the acrimony about exploitation, destruction of the family, and baby-selling. So far we have reached no consensus about the practice's effect on women or its overall morality.

I believe that the appropriate moral framework for addressing questions about the social aspects of contracted pregnancy is consequentialist.[8] This framework requires us to attempt to separate those consequences that invariably accompany a given act from those that accompany it only in particular circumstances. Doing this compels us to consider whether a practice's necessary features lead to unavoidable overridingly bad consequences. It also demands that we look at how different circumstances are likely to affect the outcome. Thus a practice which is moral in a feminist society may well be immoral in a sexist one. This distinction allows us to tailor morality to different conditions for optimum results without thereby incurring the charge of malignant relativism.

Before examining arguments against the practice of contracted pregnancy, let us take note of why people might favour it. First, as noted before, alleviating infertility can create much happiness. Secondly, there are often good reasons to consider transferring burden and risk from one individual to another. Pregnancy may be a serious burden or risk for one woman, whereas it is much less so for another. Some women love being pregnant, others hate it; pregnancy interferes with work for some, not for others; pregnancy also poses much higher levels of risk to health (or even life) for some than for others. Reducing burden and risk is a benefit not only for the woman involved, but also for the resulting child. High-risk pregnancies create, among other things, serious risk of prematurity, one of the major sources of handicap in babies. Furthermore, we could prevent serious genetic diseases by allowing carriers to avoid pregnancy. A third benefit of 'surrogate mothering' is that it makes possible the creation of non-traditional families. This can be a significant source of happiness to single women and gay couples.

All of the above presuppose that there is some advantage in making possible at least partially genetically based relationships between parents and offspring. Although, as I have argued above, we might be better off without this desire, I doubt that we will soon be free of it. Therefore, if we can satisfy it at little cost, we should try to do so.

IS SURROGATE MOTHERING
ALWAYS WRONG?

Despite the foregoing advantages, some feminists argue that the practice is *necessarily* wrong: it is wrong because it must betray women's and society's basic interests.[9]

What, if anything is wrong with the practice? Let us consider the first three acts I described earlier: transferring burden and risk, separating sex and reproduction, and separating reproduction and childrearing. Separation of reproduction and marriage will not be dealt with here.

Is it wrong to take on the burden of pregnancy for another? Doing this is certainly supererogatory, for pregnancy can threaten comfort, health, even life. One might argue that women should not be allowed to take these risks, but that would be paternalistic. We do not forbid mountain-climbing or riding a motorcycle on these grounds. How could we then forbid a woman to undertake this particular risk?

Perhaps the central issue is the transfer of burden from one woman to another. However, we frequently do just that—much more often than we recognize. Anyone who has her house cleaned, her hair done, or her clothes dry-cleaned is engaging in this procedure;[10] so is anyone who depends on agriculture or public works such as bridges.[11] To the objection that in this case the bargain includes the risk to life and limb, as well as use of time and skills, the answer is that the other activities just cited entail surprisingly elevated risk rates from exposure to toxic chemicals or dangerous machinery.[12]

Furthermore, it is not even true that contracted pregnancy merely shifts the health burden and risks associated with pregnancy from one woman to another. In some cases (infertility, for example) it makes the impossible possible; in others (for women with potentially high-risk pregnancies) the net risk is lowered.[13] As we saw, babies benefit, too, from better health and fewer handicaps. Better health and fewer handicaps in both babies and women also means that scarce resources can be made available for other needs, thus benefiting society in general.

I do think that there is, in addition, something suspect about all this new emphasis on risk. Awareness of risks inherent in even normal pregnancy constitutes progress: women have always been expected to forge ahead with childbearing oblivious to risk. Furthermore, childbearing has been thought to be something women owed to men or to society at large, regardless of their own feelings about a given—or any—pregnancy. When women had little say about these matters, we never heard about risk.[14] Why are we hearing about risk only now, now that women finally have some choices, some prospect of remuneration?[15] For that matter, why is our attention not drawn to the fact that surrogacy is one of the least risky approaches to non-traditional reproduction?[16]

Perhaps what is wrong about this kind of transfer is that it necessarily involves exploitation. Such exploitation may take the form of exploitation of women by men and exploitation of the rich by the poor. This possibility deserves serious consideration, and will be dealt with shortly.

Is there anything wrong with the proposed separation of sex and reproduction? Historically, this separation—in the form of contraception—has been beneficial to women and to society as a whole. Although there are those who judge the practice immoral, I do not think we need belabour the issue here.

It may be argued that not all types of separation are morally on a par. Contraception is permissible, because it spares women's health, promotes autonomy, strengthens family life, and helps make population growth manageable. But separation of sex and reproduction apart from contraception is quite another kettle of fish: it exploits women, weakens family life, and may increase population. Are these claims true and relevant?

Starting with the last first, if we face a population problem, it would make sense to rethink overall population policy, not exploit the problems of the infertile.[17] If family strengthening is a major justification for contraception, we might point out that contracted pregnancy will in some cases do the same. Whether or not having children can save a failing marriage, it will certainly prevent a man who wants children from leaving a woman incapable of providing them. We may bewail his priorities, but if his wife is sufficiently eager for the relationship to continue it would again be paternalistic for us to forbid 'surrogacy' in such circumstances. That 'surrogacy' reduces rather than promotes women's autonomy may be true under some circumstances, but there are good grounds for thinking that it can also enhance autonomy. It also remains to be shown that the practice systematically burdens women, or one class of women. In principle, the availability of new choices can be expected to nourish rather than stunt women's lives, so long as they retain control over their bodies and lives. The claim that contracted pregnancy destroys women's individuality and constitutes alienated labour, as Christine Overall argues, depends not only on a problematic Marxist analysis, but on the assumption that other jobs available to women are seriously less alienating.[18]

Perhaps what is wrong here is that contracted pregnancy seems to be the other side of the coin of prostitution. Prostitution is sex without reproduction; 'surrogacy' is reproduction without sex. But it is difficult to form a persuasive argument that goes beyond mere guilt by association. Strictly speaking, contracted pregnancy is not prostitution; a broad-based Marxist definition would include it, but also traditional marriage. I think that in the absence of further argument, the force of this accusation is primarily emotional.

Perhaps the dread feature contracted pregnancy shares with prostitution is that it is a lazy person's way of exploiting their own 'natural resources'. But I suspect that this idea reveals a touchingly naive view of what it takes to be a successful prostitute, not to mention the effort involved in running an optimum pregnancy. Overall takes up this point by asserting that it

is not and cannot be merely one career choice among others. It is not a real alternative. It is implausible to suppose that fond parents would want it for their daughters. We are unlikely to set up training courses for surrogate mothers. Schools holding 'career days' for their future graduates will surely not invite surrogate mothers to address the class on advantages of 'vocation'. And surrogate motherhood does not seem to be the kind of thing one would put on one's curriculum vitae. (p. 126)

But this seems to me to be a blatant *ad populum* argument.

Such an objection ought, in any case, to entail general condemnation of apparently effortless ways of life that involved any utilization of our distinctive characteristics.

We surely exploit our personal 'natural resources' whenever we work. Ditchdiggers use their bodies, professors use their minds. Overall seems particularly to object to some types of 'work': contracted pregnancy 'is no more a real job option than selling one's blood or one's gametes or one's bodily organs can be real job options.' (p. 126) But her discussion makes clear that her denial that such enterprises are 'real' jobs is not based on any social arrangements that preclude earning a living wage doing these things, but rather on the moral judgement that they are wrong. They are wrong because they constitute serious 'personal and bodily alienation'. Yet her arguments for such alienation are weak. She contends that women who work as 'surrogates' are deprived of any expression of individuality (p. 126), are interchangeable (p. 127), and they have no choice about whose sperm to harbor (p. 128). It is true that, given a reasonable environment (partly provided by the woman herself), bodies create babies without conscious effort. This fact, it seems to me, has no particular moral significance: many tasks can be accomplished in similar ways yet are not thought valueless.[19]

It is also usually true that women involved in contracted pregnancy are, in some sense, interchangeable. But the same is true, quite possibly necessarily so, of most jobs. No one who has graded mounds of logic exams or introductory ethics essays could reasonably withhold their assent to this claim, even though college teaching is one of the most autonomous careers available. Even those of us lucky enough to teach upper level courses that involve more expression of individual expertise and choice can be slotted into standardized job descriptions. Finally, it is just false that a woman can have no say about whose sperm she accepts: this could be guaranteed by proper regulation.

I wonder whether there is not some subtle devaluing of the physical by Overall. If so, then we are falling into the trap set by years of elitist equations of women, nature and inferiority.

What I think is really at issue here is the disposition of the fruit of contracted pregnancy: babies. However, it seems to be generally permissible to dispose of or barter what we produce with both our minds and our bodies — except for that which is created by our reproductive organs. So the position we are considering may just be a version of the claim that it is wrong to separate reproduction and childrearing.

Why? It is true that women normally expect to become especially attached to the product of this particular kind of labour, and we generally regard such attachment as desirable. It seems to be essential for successfully rearing babies the usual way. But if they are to be reared by others who are able to form the appropriate attachment, then what is wrong if a surrogate mother fails to form it? It seems to me that the central question here is whether this 'maternal instinct' really exists, and, if it does, whether suppressing it is always harmful.

Underlying these questions is the assumption that bonding with babies is 'natural' and therefore 'good'. Perhaps so: the evolutionary advantage of such a tendency would be clear. It would be simpleminded, however, to assume that our habits are biologically determined: our culture is permeated with pronatalist bias.[20] 'Natural' or not, whether a tendency to such attachment is desirable could reasonably be judged to depend on circumstance. When infant mortality is high[21] or responsibility for childrearing is shared by the community, it could do more harm than good. Beware the naturalistic fallacy![22]

But surely there is something special about gestating a baby. That is, after all, the assumption behind the judgement that Mary Beth Whitehead, not William Stern, had a stronger claim to Baby M. The moral

scoreboard seems clear: they both had the same genetic input, but she gestated the baby, and therefore
has a better case for social parenthood.[23]

We need to be very careful here. Special rights
have a way of being accompanied by special responsibilities: women's unique gestational relationship with
babies may be taken as reason to confine them once
more to the nursery. Furthermore, positing special
rights entailed directly by biology flirts again with the
naturalistic fallacy and undermines our capacity to
adapt to changing situations and forge our destiny.[24]

Furthermore, we already except many varieties of
such separation. We routinely engage in sending children to boarding school, foster parenting, daycare, and
so forth; in the appropriate circumstances, these practices are clearly beneficial. Hence, any blanket condemnation of separating reproduction and childrearing
will not wash; additional argument is needed for particular classes of cases.

John Robertson points out that the arguments
against separating reproduction and childrearing used
against contracted pregnancy are equally valid — but
unused — with respect to adoption.[25] Others, such as
Herbert Krimmel, reject this view by arguing that
there is a big moral difference between giving away
an already existing baby and deliberately creating one
to give away. This remains to be shown, I think. It is
also argued that as adoption outcomes are rather negative, we should be wary of extending any practice that
shares its essential features. In fact, there seems to be
amazingly little hard information about adoption outcomes. I wonder if the idea that they are bad results
from media reports of offspring seeking their biological forbears. There is, in any case, reason to think that
there are differences between the two practices such
that the latter is likely to be more successful than the
former.[26]

None of the social descriptions of surrogacy thus
seem to clearly justify the outcry against the practice.
I suspect that the remaining central issue is the crucial
one: surrogacy is baby-selling and participating in this
practice exploits and taints women.

IS SURROGACY BABY-SELLING?

In the foregoing, I deliberately left vague the question
of payment in contracted pregnancy. It is clear that
there is a recognizable form of the practice that does
not include payment; however, it also seems clear that

controversy is focusing on the commercial form. The
charge is that it is baby-selling and that this is wrong.

Is paid 'surrogacy' baby-selling? Proponents deny
that it is, arguing that women are merely making
available their biological services. Opponents retort
that as women are paid little or nothing if they fail to
hand over a live, healthy child, they are indeed selling
a baby. If they are merely selling their services they
would get full pay, even if the child were born dead.

It is true [that] women who agree to contracts relieving clients of responsibility in this case are being
exploited. They, after all, have done their part, risked
their risks, and should be paid — just like the physicians involved. Normal childbearing provides no
guarantee of a live, healthy child — why should contracted pregnancy?

There are further reasons for believing that women
are selling their services, not babies. Firstly, we do not
consider children property. Therefore, as we cannot
sell what we do not own, we cannot be selling babies.
What creates confusion here is that we do think we
own sperm and ova. (Otherwise, how could men sell
their sperm?) Yet we do not own what they become,
persons. At what point, then, does the relationship
cease to be describable as 'ownership'?

Resolution of this question is not necessary to the
current discussion. If we can own babies, there seems
to be nothing problematic about selling them. If ownership ceases at some time before birth (and could
thus be argued to be unconnected with personhood),
then it is not selling of babies that is going on.

Although this response deals with the letter of the
objection about babyselling, it fails to heed its spirit,
which is that we are trafficking in persons, and that
such trafficking is wrong. Even if we are not 'selling',
something nasty is happening.

The most common analogy, with slavery, is weak.
Slavery is wrong according to any decent moral theory: the institution allows people to be treated badly.
Their desires and interests, whose satisfaction is held
to be essential for a good life, are held in contempt.
Particularly egregious is the callous disregard of emotional ties to family and self-determination generally.
But the institution of surrogate mothering deprives babies of neither.[27] In short, as Robertson contends, 'the
purchasers do not buy the right to treat the child . . . as
a commodity or property. Child abuse and neglect
laws still apply' (p. 655).

If 'selling babies' is not the right description of
what is occurring, then how are we to explain what

happens when the birth mother hands the child over to others? One plausible suggestion is that she is giving up her parental right to have a relationship with the child.[28] That it is wrong to do this for pay remains to be shown. Although it would be egoistic and immoral to 'sell' an ongoing, friendly relationship (doing so would raise questions about whether it was friendship at all), the immorality of selling a relationship with an organism your body has created but with which you do not yet have a unique social bond, is a great deal less clear.[29]

People seem to feel much less strongly about the wrongness of such acts when motivated by altruism; refusing compensation is the only acceptable proof of such altruism. The act is, in any case, socially valuable. Why then must it be motivated by altruistic considerations? We do not frown upon those who provide other socially valuable services even when they do not have the 'right' motive. Nor do we require them to be unpaid. For instance, no one expects physicians, no matter what their motivation, to work for beans. They provide an important service; their motivation is important only to the extent that it affects quality.

In general, workers are required to have appropriate skills, not particular motivations.[30] Once again, it seems that there is a different standard for women and for men.

One worry is that women cannot be involved in contracted pregnancy without harming themselves, as it is difficult to let go of a child without lingering concern. So far, despite the heavily publicized Baby M case, this appears not to be necessarily true.[31]

Another worry is that the practice will harm children. Children's welfare is, of course, important. Children deserve the same consideration as other persons, and no society that fails to meet their basic needs is morally satisfactory. Yet I am suspicious of the objections raised on their behalf in these discussions: recourse to children's alleged well-being is once again being used as a trump card against women's autonomy.

First, we hear only about possible risks, never possible benefits, which, as I have been arguing, could be substantial.[32] Second, the main objection raised is the worry about how children will take the knowledge that their genetic mother conceived on behalf of another. We do not know how children will feel about having had such 'surrogate' mothers. But as it is not a completely new phenomenon we might start our inquiry about this topic with historical evidence, not

pessimistic speculation. In any case, if the practice is dealt with in an honest and commonsense way, particularly if it becomes quite common (and therefore 'normal'), there is likely to be no problem. We are also hearing about the worries of existing children of women who are involved in the practice: there are reports that they fear their mother will give them away, too. But surely we can make clear to children the kinds of distinctions that distinguish the practice from slavery or baby-selling in the first place.

Although we must try to foresee what might harm children, I cannot help but wonder about the double standards implied by this speculation. The first double standard occurs when those who oppose surrogacy (and reproductive technologies generally) also oppose attempts to reduce the number of handicapped babies born.[33] In the latter context, it is argued that despite their problems handicapped persons are often glad to be alive. Hence it would be paternalistic to attempt to prevent their birth.

Why then do we not hear the same argument here? Instead, the possible disturbance of children born of surrogacy is taken as a reason to prevent their birth. Yet this potential problem is both more remote and most likely involves less suffering than such ailments as spina bifida, Huntington's Disease or cystic fibrosis, which some do not take to be reasons to refrain from childbearing.[34]

Considering the sorts of reasons why parents have children, it is hard to see why the idea that one was conceived in order to provide a desperately wanted child to another is thought to be problematic. One might well prefer that to the idea that one was an 'accident', adopted, born because contraception or abortion were not available, conceived to cement a failing marriage, to continue a family line, to qualify for welfare aid, to sex-balance a family, or as an experiment in childrearing. Surely what matters for a child's well-being in the end is whether it is being raised in a loving, intelligent environment.

The second double standard involves a disparity between the interests of women and children. Arguing that surrogacy is wrong because it may upset children suggests a disturbing conception of the moral order. Women should receive consideration at least equal to that accorded children. Conflicts of interest between the two should be resolved according to the same rules we use for any other moral subjects. Those rules should never prescribe sacrificing one individual's basic interest at the mere hint of harm to another.

In sum, there seems to be no reason to think that there is anything necessarily wrong with 'surrogate mothering', even the paid variety. Furthermore, some objections to it depend on values and assumptions that have been the chief building blocks of women's inequality. Why are some feminists asserting them? Is it because 'surrogacy' as currently practiced often exploits women?

IS 'SURROGATE MOTHERING' WRONG IN CERTAIN SITUATIONS?

Even if 'surrogate mothering' is not necessarily immoral, circumstances can render it so. For instance, it is obviously wrong to coerce women to engage in the practice. Also, certain conditions are unacceptable. Among them are clauses in a contract that subordinate a woman's reasonable desires and judgements to the will of another contracting party,[35] clauses legitimating inadequate pay for the risks and discomforts involved, and clauses that penalize her for the birth of a handicapped or dead baby through no fault of her own. Such contracts are now common.[36]

One popular solution to the problem of such immoral contracts is a law forbidding all surrogacy agreements; their terms would then be unenforceable. But I believe that women will continue to engage in surrogate mothering, even if it is unregulated, and this approach leaves them vulnerable to those who change their mind, or will not pay. Fair and reasonable regulations are essential to prevent exploitation of women. Although surrogate mothering may seem risky and uncomfortable to middle-class persons safely ensconced in healthy, interesting, relatively well-paid jobs, with adequate regulation it becomes an attractive option for some women. That these women are more likely than not to be poor is no reason to prohibit the activity.

As I suggested earlier, poor women now face substantial risks in the workplace. Even a superficial survey of hazards in occupations available to poor women would give pause to those who would prohibit surrogacy on the grounds of risk.[37]

Particularly shocking is the list of harmful substances and conditions to which working women are routinely exposed. For instance, cosmeticians and hairdressers, dry cleaners and dental technicians are all exposed to carcinogens in their daily work. (Stellman, Appendixes 1 and 2) Most low-level jobs also have high rates of exposure to toxic chemicals and dangerous machinery, and women take such jobs in disproportionate numbers. It is therefore unsurprising that poor women sicken and die more often than other members of society.[38]

This is not an argument in favour of adding yet another dangerous option to those already facing such women. Nor does it follow that the burdens they already bear justify the new ones. On the contrary, it is imperative to clean up dangerous workplaces. However, it would be utopian to think that this will occur in the near future. We must therefore attempt to improve women's lot under existing conditions. Under these circumstances it would be irrational to prohibit surrogacy on the grounds of risk when women would instead have to engage in still riskier pursuits.

Overall's emphatic assertion that contracted pregnancy is not a 'real choice' for women is unconvincing. Her major argument, as I suggested earlier, is that it is an immoral, alienating option. But she also believes that such apparently expanded choices simply mask an underlying contraction of choice (p. 124). She also fears that by 'endorsing an uncritical freedom of reproductive choice, we may also be implicitly endorsing all conceivable alternatives that an individual might adopt; we thereby abandon the responsibility for evaluating substantive actions in favour of advocating merely formal freedom of choice' (p. 125). Both worries are, as they stand, unpersuasive.

As I argued before, there is something troubling here about the new and one-sided emphasis on risk. If nothing else, we need to remember that contracted pregnancy constitutes a low-tech approach to a social problem, one which would slow the impetus toward expensive and dangerous high-tech solutions.[39]

A desire for children on the part of those who normally could not have them is not likely to disappear anytime soon. We could discount it, as many participants in debate about new reproductive technologies do. After all, nobody promised a rose garden to infertile couples, much less to homosexuals or to single women. Nor is it desirable to propagate the idea that having children is essential for human fulfilment.

But appealing to the sacrosancity of traditional marriage or of blood ties to prohibit otherwise acceptable practices that would satisfy people's desires hardly makes sense, especially when those practices may provide other benefits. Not only might contracted pregnancy be less risky and more enjoyable than other jobs women are forced to take, but there are other advantages as well. Since being pregnant is not usually a full-time occupation, 'surrogate mothering' could buy time for women to significantly improve their lot; students, aspiring writers, and social activists could make real progress toward their goals.

Women have until now done this reproductive labour for free.[40] Paying women to bear children should force us all to recognize this process as the socially useful enterprise that it is, and children as socially valuable creatures whose upbringing and welfare are critically important.

In short, 'surrogate mothering' has the potential to empower women and increase their status in society. The darker side of the story is that it also has frightening potential for deepening their exploitation. The outcome of the current warfare over control of new reproductive possibilities will determine which of these alternatives comes to pass.

NOTES

1. Shulamith Firestone, *The Dialectic of Sex* (New York: Bantam Books, 1970), p. 198. A version of this paper was given at the Eastern SWIP meeting, 26 March 1988. I would like especially to thank Helen B. Holmes and Sara Ann Ketchum for their useful comments on this paper; they are, of course, in no way responsible for its perverse position! Thanks also to the editors and referees of *Bioethics* for their helpful criticisms.

2. Susan Sherwin, 'Feminist Ethics and In Vitro Fertilization,' *Science, Morality and Feminist Theory*, ed. Marsha Hanen and Kai Nielsen, *The Canadian Journal of Philosophy* supplementary volume 13, 1987, p. 277.

3. Consider the many accounts of the devastating things parents have done to children, in particular.

4. See L. M. Purdy 'Genetic Diseases: Can Having Children be Immoral?' *Moral Problems in Medicine*, ed. Samuel Gorovitz, (N.J.: Prentice-Hall, 1983), 377–84.

5. Another critical issue is that no feminist utopia will have a supply of 'problem' children whom no one wants. Thus the proposal often heard nowadays that people should just adopt all those handicapped, non-white kids will not do. (Nor does it 'do' now.)

6. I share with Sara Ann Ketchum the sense that this term is not adequate, although I am not altogether happy with her suggestions that we call it 'contracted motherhood' ('New Reproductive Technologies and the Definition of Parenthood: A Feminist Perspective', paper given at the 1987 *Feminism and Legal Theory Conference*, at the University of Wisconsin at Madison, summer 1987, p. 44ff.) It would be better, I think, to reserve terms like 'mother' for the social act of nurturing. I shall therefore substitute the terms 'contracted pregnancy' and 'surrogacy' (in scare quotes).

7. This is not to say that no one would take the same view as I: the Catholic Church, for instance, objects to the masturbatory act required for surrogacy to proceed.

8. The difficulty in choosing the 'right' moral theory to back up judgments in applied ethics, given that none are fully satisfactory continues to be vexing. I would like to reassure those who lose interest at the mere sight of consequentialist — let alone utilitarian — judgment, that there are good reasons for considering justice an integral part of moral reasoning, as it quite obviously has utility.

A different issue is raised by the burgeoning literature on feminist ethics. I strongly suspect that utilitarianism could serve feminists well, if properly applied. (For a defence of this position, see my paper 'Do Feminists Need a New Moral Theory', to be given at the University of Minnesota, Duluth, at the conference *Explorations in Feminist Ethics: Theory and Practice*, 8–9 October 1988.)

9. See for example Gena Corea, *The Mother Machine*, and Christine Overall, *Ethics and Human Reproduction* (Winchester, Mass.: Allen and Unwin, 1987).

10. These are just a couple of examples in the sort of risky service that we tend to take for granted.

11. Modern agricultural products are brought to us at some risk by farm workers. Any large construction project will also result in some morbidity and mortality.

12. Even something so mundane as postal service involves serious risk on the part of workers.

13. The benefit to both high-risk women, and to society is clear. Women need not risk serious deterioration of health or abnormally high death rates.

14. See Laura Purdy, 'The Morality of New Reproductive Technologies', *The Journal of Social Philosophy* (Winter 1987), pp. 38–48.

15. For elaboration of this view, consider Jane Ollenburger and John Hamlin, '"All Birthing Should Be Paid Labor"—A Marxist Analysis of the Commodification of Motherhood', *On the Problem of Surrogate Parenthood: Analyzing the Baby M Case*, ed. Herbert Richardson (Lewistong, N.Y.: The Edwin Mellen Press, 1987).

16. Compare the physicial risk with that of certain contraceptive technologies, and high-tech fertility treatments like IVF.

17. Infertility is often a result of social arrangements. This process would therefore be especially unfair to those who already have been exposed to more than their share of toxic chemicals or other harmful conditions.

18. Christine Overall, *Ethics and Human Reproduction* (Winchester, Mass.: Allen & Unwin, 1987), ch. 6. Particularly problematic are her comments about women's loss of individuality, as I will be arguing shortly.

19. Men have been getting handsome pay for sperm donation for years; by comparison with childbearing, such donation is a lark. Yet there has been no outcry about its immorality. Another double standard?

20. See Ellen Peck and Judith Senderowitz, *Pronatalism: The Myth of Mom and Apple Pie* (New York: Thomas Y. Crowell Co., 1974).

21. As it has been at some periods in the past: see for example information about family relationships in Philippe Ariès, *Centuries of Childhood: A Social History of Family Life*, trans. Robert Baldick (New York, 1982), and Lloyd DeMause's work.

22. Consider the arguments in chapter 8 of *Women's Work*, by Ann Oakley (New York: Vintage Books, 1974).

23. One of the interesting things about the practice of contracted pregnancy is that it can be argued to both strengthen and weaken the social recognition of biological relationships. On the one hand, the pregnant woman's biological relationship is judged irrelevant beyond a certain point; on the other, the reason for not valuing it is to enhance that of the sperm donor. This might be interpreted as yet another case where men's interests are allowed to overrule women's. But it might also be interpreted as a salutary step toward awareness that biological ties can and sometimes should be subordinated to social ones. Deciding which interpretation is correct will depend on the facts of particular cases, and the arguments taken to justify the practice in the first place.

24. Science fiction, most notably John Wyndham's *The Midwich Cuckoos*, provides us with thought-provoking material.

25. John Robertson, 'Surrogate Mothers: Not So Novel After All', *Hastings Center Report*, vol. 13, no. 5 (October 1983). This article is reprinted in *Bioethics*, ed. Rem B. Edwards and Glen C. Graber, San Diego, California: Harcourt, Brace Jovanovich, 1988). Krimmel's article ('The Case Against Surrogate Parenting') was also originally published in the *Hastings Center Report* and is reprinted in *Bioethics*. References here are to the latter.

26. One major difference between adoption and contracted pregnancy is that the baby is handed over virtually at birth, thus ensuring that the trauma sometimes experienced by older adoptees is not experienced. Although children of contracted pregnancy might well be curious to know about their biological mother, I do not see this as a serious obstacle to the practice, since we could change our policy about this. There is also reason to believe that carefully screened women undertaking a properly regulated contracted pregnancy are less likely to experience lingering pain of separation. First, they have deliberately chosen to go through pregnancy, knowing that they will give the baby up. The resulting sense of control is probably critical to both their short- and long-term well-being. Second, their pregnancy is not the result of trauma. See also Monica B. Morris, 'Reproductive Technology and Restraints', *Transaction/SOCIETY*, March/April 1988, pp. 16–22, especially p. 18.

27. There may be a problem for the woman who gives birth, as the Baby M case has demonstrated. There is probably a case for a waiting period after the birth during which the woman can change her mind.

28. Heidi Malm suggested this position in her comment on Sara Ann Ketchum's paper 'Selling Babies and Selling Bodies: Surrogate Motherhood and the Problem of Commodification', at the Eastern Division *APA* meetings, 30 December 1987.

29. Mary Anne Warren suggests, alternatively, that this objection could be obviated by women and children retaining some rights and responsibilities toward each other in contracted pregnancy. Maintaining a relationship of sorts might also, she suggests, help forestall and alleviate whatever negative feelings children might have about such transfers. I agree that such openness is probably a good idea in any case. (Referee's comment.)

30. Perhaps lurking behind the objections of surrogacy is some feeling that it is wrong to earn money by letting your body work, without active effort on your part. But this would rule out sperm selling, as well as using women's beauty to sell products and services.

31. See, for example, James Rachels 'A Report from America: The Baby M Case', *Bioethics*, vol. 1, n. 4 (October 1987), p. 365. He reports that there have been over six hundred successful cases; see also the above note on adoption.

32. Among them the above mentioned one of being born healthier.

33. To avoid the difficulties about abortion added by the assumption that we are talking about existing foetuses, let us consider here only the issue of whether certain couples should risk pregnancy.

34. There is an interesting link here between these two aspects of reproduction, as the promise of healthier children is, I think, one of the strongest arguments for contracted pregnancy.

35. What this may consist of naturally requires much additional elucidation.

36. See Susan Ince, 'Inside the Surrogate Industry', *Test-Tube Women*, ed. Rita Arditti, Renate Duelli Klein, and Shelley Minden (London: Pandora Press, 1984).

37. See, for example, Jeanne Mager Stellman, *Women's Work, Women's Health* (New York: Pantheon 1977).

38. See George L. Waldbott, *Health Effects of Environmental Pollutants* (St. Louis: The C.V. Mosby Co., 1973); Nicholas Ashford, *Crisis in the Workplace: Occupational Disease and Injury* (Cambridge: MIT Press, 1976); *Cancer and the Worker* (The New York Academy of Science, 1977); *Environmental Problems in Medicine*, ed. William D. McKee (Springfield, Ill.: Charles C. Thomas, 1977).

39. These are the ones most likely to put women in the clutches of the paternalistic medical establishment. Exploitation by commercial operations such as that of Noel Keane could be avoided by tight regulation or prohibition altogether of for-profit enterprises.

40. The implications of this fact remain to be fully understood; I suspect that they are detrimental to women and children, but that this is a topic for another paper.

RICHARD A. POSNER*

The Ethics and Economics
of Enforcing Contracts of Surrogate Motherhood

My topic is surrogate motherhood, and specifically the issue — the central issue in the controversy over surrogacy — whether contracts of surrogate motherhood, that is contracts whereby a woman agrees, in exchange for money, to become impregnated through artificial insemination and to give up the newly born child to the father, should be legally enforceable, whether by damages or specific performance. I shall not consider whether such contracts *are* enforceable under existing law, nor the intricate legal questions that such contracts even when enforceable could be expected to raise,[1] but whether they *should* be enforceable. To this question of policy, issues of economics and ethics are central, and are the focus of this [essay].

My interest in the question stems from a longstanding interest in the law and economics of the family and adoption, an interest that has resulted in false charges that I advocate "baby-selling."[2] For any readers who may wonder at the sources of that interest, let me make clear that it is purely professional. I am not an adopted child, my children are not adopted, I have never tried to adopt a child, no one in my family has ever been involved in adoption, surrogacy, *in vitro* fertilization, or any other atypical familial arrangements.

My interest in surrogate motherhood is at least a disinterested one.

The question of the enforceability of contracts of surrogate motherhood became front-page news with the *Baby M* case. . . . The case and the controversy it aroused are a byproduct of the increasing frequency of contracts of surrogate motherhood. Although statistics are hard to come by, it appears that by the end of 1986 at least 500 surrogate contracts had been made;[3] the number may be much greater today, despite efforts in a number of states to make such contracts unenforceable, and the resulting uncertainty that surrounds the practice of surrogate motherhood.

I conjecture that three factors are key in explaining the growing popularity of the practice. The first is scientific advances in the field of reproduction, which make infertile couples less prone to resign themselves to their infertility. The second (and I think related) factor is the decline in conventional attitudes toward sex and the family. The third, and perhaps most important factor is the acute shortage of babies for adoption. (I mean of healthy, white infants — there is no shortage of black, or handicapped, or older children for adoption, but this is because there is, unfortunately, very little demand for such children.) The extent, character, and causes of the shortage of babies for adoption are the subject of my writings on the gray and black markets in adoption, in other words, on "baby-selling", a practice that, contrary to the impression fostered by the media and others, I have not advocated but have merely tried to explain.[4] The irony is that those who attack surrogate motherhood out of a general hostility to free markets do not realize that surrogate motherhood is itself a product, in part, of the interference with a market — the market in adoption.

*Judge, United States Court of Appeals for the Seventh Circuit; Senior Lecturer, University of Chicago Law School. This article is the lightly revised text of the Brendan Brown Lecture delivered at The Catholic University of America, The Columbus School of Law, on November 17, 1988. I realize that the term "surrogate motherhood" might be thought to belittle the surrogate mother, who is, after all, the biological mother — not just a stand-in or incubator. But I shall stick with what has become the accepted term.

From *Journal of Contemporary Health Law and Policy* 5 (1989), 21–29. © 1989 by Catholic University of America. Reprinted by permission of the publisher.

Yet even if there were no shortage of babies for adoption, there would be a demand for surrogate motherhood. People (a biologist would say their genes) desire genetic continuity, and surrogacy enables the man (although not his wife) to satisfy this desire.

The case for allowing people to make legally enforceable contracts of surrogate motherhood is straightforward. Such contracts would not be made unless the parties to them believed that surrogacy would be mutually beneficial. Suppose the contract requires the father and his wife to pay the surrogate mother $10,000 (apparently this is the most common price in contracts of surrogate motherhood[5]). The father and wife must believe that they will derive a benefit from having the baby that is greater than $10,000, or else they would not sign the contract. The surrogate must believe that she will derive a benefit from the $10,000 (more precisely, from what she will use the money for) that is greater than the cost to her of being pregnant and giving birth and then surrendering the baby. So *ex ante*, as an economist would say (*i.e.*, before the fact), all the parties to the contract are made better off. The mutual benefits, moreover, depend critically on the contract's being enforceable. If it is unenforceable, the father and his wife will have no assurance that they will actually obtain a baby as a result of the contract even if the surrogate becomes pregnant. For if the surrogate, having become pregnant and given birth, changes her mind about giving up the baby, the father and wife will have lost almost a year in their quest for a baby (the period necessary for the surrogate to become pregnant plus the period of gestation); they will also be intensely disappointed. Because surrogacy is so much less attractive to the father and wife when it is not enforceable, they will not be willing to pay nearly as much as they would if it were enforceable — so the surrogate is hurt. After all, the surrogate always has the option of offering to accept a lower price in return for retaining the right to keep the baby if she wants. If she surrenders that right in exchange for a higher price, it is, at least presumptively, because she prefers the extra money to the extra freedom of choice. Her preference is thwarted if the contract is unenforceable.

There are various objections to this simple economic analysis. The one that fits the framework of economic theory most comfortably is that the analysis fails to consider that a contract of surrogate motherhood has effects on nonparties, in particular on the baby that the surrogate gives birth to. The presence of an affected but nonconsenting third party makes it difficult to say that the transaction is Pareto superior (*i.e.*, that at least one person is made better off by the transaction and no one is made worse off) — the strongest normative concept of efficiency. In fact, however, it is very likely that the baby is made better off by the contract of surrogate motherhood, and certainly not worse off. For without the contract the baby probably wouldn't be born at all. With the contract, he (or she) becomes a member of a family consisting of the biological father and his wife. The baby's position is much like that of a baby whose mother dies during the baby's infancy and whose father then remarries. If there is any evidence that such babies, when they become adults, decide they'd rather not have been born, I am not aware of it. The surrogate baby's position is also much like that of a baby whose mother was inseminated artificially with the sperm of a man other than her husband, because he was infertile. Do such babies grow up to be miserable? So miserable that they derive a net disutility from life — would rather never have been born? Again, I am not aware of any evidence they do, and it seems unlikely that they do. Although there is some evidence that adopted children are occasionally maladjusted, the best evidence seems to be that, on average, adopted children are no more unhappy or unstable than natural children.[6] And the child of a surrogate mother is only half-adopted. He is the natural son of his father, and, in effect, the adopted son of his mother (that is, the father's wife).

The remaining possibility is that knowledge that surrogate mothers are paid will blight the child's life. The child will know that his natural mother gave him up for money. But this knowledge will surely be less wrenching than knowledge that one's mother had *sold* one (as in baby selling). For the mother had agreed from the outset to bear the child for the father and the father's wife. Are children conceived after artificial insemination with sperm obtained from a sperm donor devastated to learn that their parents had *bought* the sperm? Are children embarrassed or distressed to discover that they are the product of *in vitro* fertilization which may have cost their parents thousands of dollars? The world is changing, and practices that seem weird and unnatural to members of the current adult generation will seem much less so, I predict, to the next generation.

A subtler third-party effect of surrogacy is on those unfortunate children who are available for adoption but whom very few people want to adopt. If surrogacy were unavailable, the comfortable white middle-class couple that turns to surrogacy because there are so few healthy white infants available for adoption might turn back to the adoption market and adopt a black or handicapped or older child. This is not likely to happen very often; an alternative of course is that the husband will abandon his wife for a woman who is fertile. Even if forbidding the enforcement of surrogacy contracts would drive a few couples into the market for adopting unwanted children (and no doubt it would), one could well question the appropriateness of placing what amounts to a heavy tax on the infertile to correct a social problem — that of unwanted children — that is emphatically not of their creation. Are the *infertile* to be blamed for a glut of unwanted children? If not, should they be taxed disproportionately in order to alleviate the glut?

The most frequent argument one hears against contracts of surrogate motherhood is that they are not truly voluntary, because the surrogate mother doesn't know what she is getting into and would not sign such a contract unless she was desperate. The first point has a more secure foundation in economics than the second. Information costs provide a traditional reason for doubting whether a particular contract is actually value-maximizing *ex ante*. If women who agree to make surrogate contracts don't know how distressed they will be when it comes time to surrender the baby, then the contracts may not result in a net increase in welfare. To put this differently, the tendency in economics to evaluate welfare on an *ex ante* rather than *ex post* basis depends on an assumption that expectations are not systematically biased. Contracts cannot be depended on to maximize welfare if parties signing them don't know what they're committing themselves to.

However, there is no persuasive evidence or convincing reason to believe that, on average, women who agree to become surrogate mothers underestimate the distress they will feel at having to give up the baby. Granted, Mrs. Whitehead, the surrogate mother in the *Baby M* case, underestimated that distress. But we must be wary of generalizing from a single case. There is no indication that Mrs. Whitehead's experience is typical of surrogate mothers. Hundreds of babies have been born to surrogate mothers, and since very few of these arrangements have been drawn into litigation one's guess is that most surrogate mothers do *not* balk when it comes time to surrender the baby. Newspaper and magazine interviews with surrogate mothers confirm this impression. Oblique but important corroborative evidence is that most surrogate mothers already have children and that few are under 20 years of age.[7] A mature woman who has borne children should be able to estimate the psychic cost to her of giving up her next baby. Finally, the enormous publicity that the *Baby M* case has received should provide additional warning of the perils of surrogacy, if any is needed, to women contemplating it.

Are these *desperate* women — women who value $10,000 more than a baby only because society has failed to spread a safety net under them? Even if they were, this might not justify a ban on the enforcement of surrogate contracts. To someone who is desperately in need of $10,000, a court's refusal to allow her to obtain it will seem a hypocritical token of concern for her plight, especially since the court has no power to alleviate that plight in some other way. At all events, there is no evidence that surrogate mothers are drawn from the ranks of the desperately poor, and it seems unlikely they would be. Mrs. Whitehead was not poor. A couple would be unlikely to want the baby of a *desperately* poor woman; they would be concerned about her health, and therefore the baby's. Interviews with surrogate mothers indicate not only that they are not poor, but that they have made a careful tradeoff between the use they can make of $10,000 (or whatever the contract price is) and the costs (including regret) of bearing a child for another couple.[8] When asked what they plan to do with the $10,000, they give standard middle-class answers (home improvement, a new car, a better education for their children). For many surrogate mothers, moreover, regret at giving up the child is balanced by empathy for the father's infertile wife. This is particularly likely where the surrogate mother has already had children — but that is, as I have noted, usually the case with surrogate arrangements.

There is, in short, no persuasive evidence that contracts of surrogate motherhood are less likely to maximize value than the classes of contracts that the law routinely enforces. However, other arguments are also made against the enforcement of surrogacy contracts. One is that such enforcement is inequitable because only middle-class couples can afford the price of a surrogate contract and because invariably the surrogate mother comes from a lower income class than the father and his wife. But society does not forbid contracts for luxury goods or contracts that involve the purchase of services from persons lower on the income ladder. Only wealthy people employ butlers, and butlers are invariably less well off than their employers. Nevertheless employment contracts with butlers are enforceable. Moreover, while probably no truly poor person could afford the price of a surrogate contract, it is hardly the case that only wealthy people can pay $10,000 for a good or service. Most Americans can afford a new car, and most new cars cost more than $10,000. In any event, unless envy is very intense and widespread, it is very difficult to see how people who can't afford to pay for surrogate arrangements are helped by a law that forbids those who can afford to pay to enter into enforceable contracts of surrogacy.

Next it is argued—and not only by Marxists as one might have expected—that to enforce surrogacy contracts is to endorse the "commodification" of motherhood. It is true that our society does not permit every good or service to be bought and sold, even where there are no palpable or demonstrable third-party effects. People are not permitted to make contracts of self-enslavement, to enter into suicide pacts, to agree to enter gladiatorial contests (or even to box without gloves), or to sign loan agreements enforceable by breaking the borrower's knees in the event of default. And some forms of "commodification" that are permitted, such as the sale of blood to blood banks, are heavily criticized. Apart from objections, based on a variety of grounds unrelated to surrogate motherhood, to specific forms of "commodification," there is a widespread aversion, particularly but not only among intellectuals, to placing all relations and interactions in society on a strictly pecuniary basis. It is feared that pervasive reliance on the "cash nexus" would extinguish altruism and foster anomie, anxious privatism, and other alleged ills of a capitalist system.

I am skeptical. People are what they are, and what they are is the result of millions of years of evolution rather than of such minor cultural details as the precise scope of the market principle in a particular society. I don't think we would be more selfish than we are if the market sector in this country were larger than it is, or less selfish if it were smaller. People in countries that have less "commodification" than we— countries ranging from Sweden to Ethiopia—do not appear to be less selfish than Americans. Anyway, allowing the enforcement of contracts of surrogate motherhood isn't going to have any significant effect on underlying norms and attitudes in our society. Very

few fertile couples will be interested in surrogate motherhood; most couples are fertile; and the fraction of infertile couples is bound to decline with continued advances in medical technology, even as women marry later (fertility problems increase with age).

The last ethical argument that I will consider against the enforcement of surrogacy contracts is mounted by feminists. They argue that surrogacy is akin to prostitution in that it also involves the sale of female sexuality; and just as prostitution is widely regarded as exploitive of women, so surrogacy is (these feminists argue) inevitably exploitive of the deluded women who agree to market their reproductive capacity. Moreover, there is a small but irreducible risk of death or serious illness to the surrogate mother.

The argument is unconvincing. It overlooks, to begin with, the fact that the surrogates are not the only women in the picture. There are also the infertile wives to be considered. Not only are they hurt if their ability to obtain a baby (necessarily not borne by them) is impeded by a ban on the enforcement of contracts of surrogate motherhood, but their already weak bargaining position in a marriage to a fertile husband is further weakened, for under modern permissive divorce law he is always free to "walk," and seek a fertile woman to marry.[9] Beyond this, the idea that women who "sell" (really, rent) their reproductive capacity, like women who sell sexual favors, are "exploited" patronizes women. Few would argue that a gigolo or a sperm donor or a man who marries for money or a male prostitute is "exploited." These men might not be admirable, but they are not victims. The idea that women are particularly prone to be exploited in the marketplace hearkens back to the time (not so long ago) when married women were deemed legally incompetent to make enforceable contracts. I am surprised that feminists—not all of them, however[10]— should want to resurrect the idea in the surrogacy context. It is only worse when the argument is bolstered by pointing out that hormonal changes incident to pregnancy may induce a regret at parting with the baby that the surrogate mother could not have foreseen when she signed the contract. The idea that women are peculiarly dominated by their hormones (and not men by their testosterone?) is a traditional rationalization for limiting women's access to responsible employment.

The feminist criticisms of surrogacy are inconsistent with mainstream feminist thought. They reinforce the anti-feminist stereotype summed up in the slogan, "biology is destiny." The unintended implication of the feminist position on surrogate motherhood (but I emphasize that this is the position of some, not all, feminists) is, if you're infertile, you shouldn't have a baby; and if you are fertile, and have a baby, you should keep it. A main thrust of modern feminism has been to deny that biology is destiny, that it is woman's predestined lot to be a bearer and raiser of children. Some women don't want to have children; some want to have children but not in the traditional setting of heterosexual marriage; some want to have but not bear children and some, finally, want to bear but not have children (or more children)— they are the surrogate mothers. Feminism seeks to expand the opportunities of women beyond the traditional role, felt as stifling by many, of being a housewife and mother who makes a career of bearing and raising children. The opportunity to hire a surrogate mother and the opportunity to be a surrogate mother are two unconventional opportunities now open to women. It is curious that feminists, of all people, should want to close the door on these opportunities.

The last and least argument against surrogate motherhood is that it is just another form of "baby selling." This is argumentation by epithet. The surrogate mother no more "owns" the baby than the father does. What she sells is not the baby but her parental rights, and in this respect she is no different from a woman who agrees in a divorce proceeding to surrender her claim to custody of the children of the marriage in exchange for some other concession from her husband—or from a sperm donor who receives cash, but no parental rights, in exchange for his donation.

I have reviewed the arguments pro and con for the enforceability of surrogate contracts and have made no secret of how I believe the balance inclines. But in a matter that has aroused such strong emotions, argumentation *a priori* will not provide a fully convincing resolution. Evidence is more important than argument. I have mentioned evidence that surrogacy is not exploitive in the sense of making the surrogate mothers worse off, but the evidence is casual and anecdotal and a more systematic study is necessary and indeed urgent. Efforts should be made by scholars to identify and randomly sample surrogate mothers for purposes of determining the demographic and other relevant characteristics of the parties to the contracts and the experience with surrogate contracts. Are the surrogates responsible adults making apparently rational decisions? Are parties to surrogacy contracts generally satisfied? Do the contracts contain adequate safeguards of the surrogate mother's interests? What is the average price and the range of prices? How many surrogate mothers experience profound distress at giving up the baby? How many balk and have to be dragged into court? Are the children healthy and happy? These questions are answerable. Until they are answered, with greater confidence than is possible at present, the public policy issue examined in this [essay] will not be resolved. It would, though, be a tragedy if the states or Congress sought to extirpate the practice before a rational judgment of its pros and cons could be made. . . .

NOTES

1. *See, e.g.,* Smith, *The Razor's Edge of Human Bonding: Artificial Fathers and Surrogate Mothers,* 5 W. New Eng. L. Rev. 639, 652–64 (1983).

2. *See* Posner, *The Regulation of the Market in Adoptions,* 67 B.U.L. Rev. 59 nn. 1–2 (1987).

3. *See* M. Field, Surrogate Motherhood 5 (1988).

4. *See* Posner, *supra* note 2; Landes & Posner, *The Economics of the Baby Shortage,* 7 J. Legal Stud. 323 (1978); R. Posner, Economic Analysis of Law § 5.4 at 139–43 (3d ed. 1986).

5. *See* Field, *supra* note 3, at 25–26.

6. *See, e.g.,* Andrews, *Surrogate Motherhood: The Challenge for Feminists,* 16 Law, Med. & Health Care 72, 77 (1988).

7. *See* Field, *supra* note 3, at 6.

8. *See, e.g.,* Chapman, *Surrogacy Successes Make New Laws All the More Ill-Advised,* Chi. Trib., July 31, 1988 at 3, col. 1.

9. I realize that not all wives who want to hire surrogate mothers are infertile. Some may be fertile but endangered by pregnancy; others may simply not want to take time off from work to bear a child. The latter reason will strike many as frivolous; it is in any event rare.

10. Andrews, *supra* note 6, presents a powerful feminist defense of surrogate motherhood.

ALEXANDER MORGAN CAPRON AND MARGARET JANE RADIN

Choosing Family Law over Contract Law as a Paradigm for Surrogate Motherhood

Among the many new forms of human reproduction,[1] none raises more problems of public policy and of law than the practice of what is known, rather inaccurately, as "surrogate motherhood" or "surrogacy."[2] The central policy issue is settling on the paradigm that should govern surrogate motherhood, a model of family relations (adoption) or of contractual relations (sale of a product or service). And the central legal issue is whether any restrictions on personal choice that follow from the policy selected—and especially from a rejection of the contractual model with its implication of free choice—are constitutionally permissible.

We conclude that surrogate mother arrangements should be handled from the perspective of adoption. As recent judicial decisions have demonstrated, existing law on parents and children is largely adequate, and the emergence of surrogacy as a social practice does not require major "law reform" efforts. Furthermore, neither these rulings nor legislation proposed in many jurisdictions to ban commercialized surrogacy intrude impermissibly on the range of choices about reproduction protected by the Constitution of the United States. Although we conclude that commercialized surrogacy may be prohibited, we think the weight of any legal sanctions should be concentrated against those who arrange such transactions for profit rather than against the parties (parents and would-be parents) themselves. And we believe that unpaid surrogacy should be permitted.

From *Law, Medicine, and Health Care* 16 (1988), 34–43. Reprinted with permission of the authors and the American Society of Law, Medicine, and Ethics.

THE FAMILY LAW MODEL

EXISTING POLICIES AND THE VALUES ON WHICH THEY REST

Families in our society take many forms and may take even more as single people or couples who are not legally married, including gays and lesbians, assume the role of parents in increasing numbers. Under existing family law, a great deal of latitude is allowed in "private ordering" without state interference, and we believe that it is beneficial for society to take a liberal view of "the family" when framing family law, especially rules governing adoption and reproduction.

Certain core values are recognized, however, as matters of legitimate concern for the state. Among these are the protection of children's welfare and interests (especially through encouraging responsible behavior by parents), the maintenance of accurate records of vital statistics and family status, the promotion of human well-being, and the prevention of human exploitation. In light of concern for these values, the states have adopted laws about parentage, usually through provisions in the codes on civil law and evidence.

Presumptions of Parentage. California's laws are typical. The evidentiary laws provide that the woman who gives birth to a child—its natural mother—and that woman's husband are presumed to be the parents of that child.[3] In the case of artificial insemination by donor (AID), California follows the Uniform Parentage Act and holds that a husband who consents to AID of his wife by a physician is the legal father of the child.[4] Although such rules are often analyzed from the vantage point of the adults involved—"What rights do I have over this child?"—it is also essential to be alert to their beneficial effects for children, especially newborns.[5] In most cases, the persons identified and regarded by society as the parents of a child can be expected to provide care for the child and otherwise to behave responsibly toward it. Indeed, there are many means in society—cultural and social as well as official—to assist, to encourage, and if necessary even to force them to do so.

These legal rules serve children's interest in having clearly identified people recognized from the moment of birth as their legal parents, with all the obligations and expectations consequent to this role. If the status of adult parties in relation to a newborn child is dependent on any contracts or other agreements they may have reached, then this status—and the rights and responsibilities that flow from it—may be thrown into doubt when contractual terms are unclear or when the contract is disavowed due to alleged breaches or other disagreements.[6]

The interests of society, as well as those of parents and children, are also served by the laws on parentage. The state's interest in achieving certainty on this subject arises primarily from its parens patriae role as protector of minors and others who are unable to defend their own interests. The state also has interests in the certainty and reliability of records and in simplicity and economy in making determinations. These interests are well served by the existing law, which presumes the birth mother and her husband (if she is married) to be the parents. The resulting designations are seldom subject to dispute or litigation.

Adoptions and Foster Placement. Of course, the state has had to recognize that children also need protection when their parents die or are unable or unwilling to fulfill the parental role. All states have responded by creating procedures for transferring custody and control (either to temporary custodians or permanently to adopting parents) of children who are orphaned, abused, neglected, abandoned, or relinquished voluntarily for adoption.

The legal rules of greatest immediate relevance to the present topic are those on adoption. In many states, agreements to relinquish parental rights are not permitted prior to the child's birth.[7] Further, the statutes typically provide for a "change of heart" period after the agreement to release a child, although the standards for revoking one's choice vary.[8] Such

provisions aim to balance several interests. On the one hand, the child needs unqualified acceptance and stability in its surroundings. This need is fostered by ensuring the people who are serving as caregivers and who intend to adopt the child that they will be able to keep it. On the other hand, permitting the birth mother to reclaim a child manifests society's traditional respect for biological ties. It also recognizes that circumstances may propel some women to make a decision before or immediately after the birth of a child that does not reflect their true wishes and the depth of the bond they feel to the child. Consequently, for some (usually brief) period, a parent who has consented to transfer custody and permit adoption of a child may reverse this choice, after which time an affirmative showing of unsuitability in the child's new home is usually necessary to reverse the choice.

The standards applicable to this area of the law seem—perhaps inevitably—vague and imprecise. In many cases—including those in which the parents' rights and responsibilities are suspended or revoked involuntarily, on grounds of abuse or neglect of the child—a child protective services agency or other state officer assumes responsibility for a child, subject to supervision by the family court or comparable judicial body. Regrettably, such agencies are woefully underfunded and the rules and standards they apply often seem arbitrary, especially in cases of temporary suspensions of parental rights and placement of children in foster homes. Such problems have badly tarnished the "best interests" standard applied by these agencies and the judicial officers who have ultimate control in such cases.

Although many adoptions are handled by agencies operated or licensed by the government, "private adoptions" are also permitted and are especially sought when the supply of children that couples want to adopt falls below the demand, causing lengthy delays and much frustration. Even when an adoption is privately arranged (by a family member, physician, lawyer, or the like), the official step of transferring parental rights and obligations is subject to state supervision. This will typically involve a social worker or comparable person inquiring into the background of the prospective parents and the suitability of their home. The results of such inquiries are then evaluated by a judge to ascertain that the placement is in the child's best interests.

Laws Against a Market in Children. Many states have forbidden "baby selling"—specifically, the paying or receiving of any money or other valuable consideration in connection with the placement of a child for adoption. The prohibition applies both to the transfer of already existing children and to the commissioning of pregnancy specifically for the release of the child for adoption (commissioned adoption). Moreover, it extends to those who arrange the adoption as well as to the natural and adoptive parents, except that reasonable medical expenses may be paid for the delivery and care of the child. Since such laws usually except the payment of the administrative fees of a state-approved adoption agency,[9] it is apparent that they are aimed especially at payments for privately arranged adoptions.

The prohibition on payments may be understood as protecting several important values. First, it may protect women—especially poor, single women—from being exploited.[10] Plainly, the concern that women not become paid "breeding stock," like farm animals, attaches at all points in reproduction. The view that women's reproductive capacities should not be placed into a market context is at least as offended by the choice of a woman who seeks to become pregnant in order to produce a salable product as it is by a much less free choice made by a woman who, after a birth, concludes that she should give up her child because she is unable to raise it.

The role of paid breeder is incompatible with a society in which individuals are valued for themselves and are aided in achieving a full sense of human well-being and potentiality. The fact that there are other impediments to human flourishing in contemporary society is no reason why the state cannot act—as it has in restricting payment for adoptions—to protect people from the dehumanizing pressures that would arise were reproductive capabilities removed from a private, and uniquely personal, sphere and turned into items of commerce. One such dehumanizing pressure on women—especially poor women—would be social pressure either to relinquish children for paid adoption or to create children for others for a price, in order to support their families.

The prohibition on paid adoptions serves the value of human personhood from another vantage point as well. It not merely restricts the freedom of women (and men) to sell their reproductive capabilities, but it also restricts the creation of a market in the products

of those capabilities. Society has a legitimate interest in these goals, not the least because a market in reproductive services and babies would have adverse effects on all persons, not simply on those who choose to enter that market. All personal attributes of ourselves as well as our children (sex, eye color, predicted IQ and athletic ability, and so forth) would be given a dollar value by the market, whether or not we wanted to regard ourselves and our progeny in these terms.

What is probably most remarkable about the debate over surrogate motherhood is that it has necessitated defending a claim that was previously taken as self-evident: namely, that society has an interest in people being regarded as intrinsically valuable, not as monetized units in a marketplace. It oversimplifies matters to think of monetization as enslavement. In the adoption context, some of the rationale in support of the Thirteenth Amendment—that it is wrong for one group of people to treat another as chattel whom they are free to exploit (to the point of death)—is inapposite. The fact that adopting parents have paid for a child does not mean they will fail to incorporate it as a full family member. To worry that paying for babies will have the effect of "commodifying" them is not to suggest that parents will treat the children of paid, commissioned adoptions or commercial surrogacy as trivial objects to be discarded at will, like a magazine or a blouse. Many material objects, after all, are treated with respect and kept for a long time; but they are objects nevertheless.[11]

Moreover, even if a child once incorporated into a family is never again thought of as something acquired in an expensive transaction, the fact remains that during the *process* of the transaction the child was a thing. People had a transferable ownership interest[12] in it and bargained over it in a market in which other "products" were also for sale and in which other potential buyers may also have been bidding. In the townhouse outside Detroit where Michigan lawyer Noel Keane conducts his commercial surrogacy business, couples circulate among the rooms where surrogates wait their scrutiny. After each interview, the couple is encouraged to make its selection before the surrogate is snatched up by someone else.[13] Likewise, during the *process* of commissioning a pregnancy, the woman becomes a breeder to be bargained over in a market that will place a specific dollar value on personal traits that she may pass on to her offspring.

To demonstrate the unacceptability of commercial reproduction and transactions in children, one need only imagine the market carried to its natural conclusion (that is, to the point at which it would display its greatest strengths): an open, structured process of offering children of all ages to the highest qualified bidders (even markets may have entrance requirements).[14] In such a setting, advertising would play a large role. Buyers would seek protection in implied warranties of merchantability and in express warranties based on any claims of special attributes. And, to ensure market liquidity and responsiveness, participants would have to be free to resell what they had bought, either depreciated (like a used car) or appreciated on account of changes in the market or improvements made in the product since it was purchased (like real estate).

Transfers associated with the marketplace are simply very different both in their subjective connotations (that all things can be given a dollar value) and in their legal expectations (that people have special rights regarding things that they have purchased) from gifts and other nonmarket transfers. Thus, the intuition that baby-selling is simply wrong and ought to be prohibited reflects the view that the market model inherently misdescribes the reason that we value people[15] and wrongly suggests that they are fungible goods. Moreover, by undermining the relationship between personhood and social context, a market in babies would interfere with individuation and self-development and hence would detract from the ideal of human flourishing that society should seek to foster.[16]

APPLYING EXISTING RULES TO NEW REPRODUCTIVE METHODS

We believe that the interests of the children and adults involved, as well as collective interests, mandate applying the same rules to surrogacy as to other arrangements involving the transfer of parental rights and responsibilities.

Enforcement of the anti–baby selling law will not prevent surrogacy, merely paid surrogacy. To further discourage paid contracts, and to remove the most distasteful aspects of a "market in babies," it is necessary to go a step beyond the United Kingdom's Surrogacy Arrangements Act 1985. The act prohibits individuals and organizations from engaging on a commercial basis in such activities as making lists of potential surrogates or negotiating or advertising surrogacy arrangements. However, it permits the parties to a surrogacy arrangement to agree on, pay, and receive money or other valuable consideration. The proposed 1986

amendments would have prohibited all paid surrogacy while continuing to allow unpaid surrogacy. Because the dangers of commodification are posed more imminently by those who organize and implement a market in babies than by parents and would-be parents themselves, [any] statute should be designed so that the weight of legal sanctions is brought to bear on those who attempt to create such a market (for example, lawyers who act as commercial brokers).

To protect both the children in surrogate arrangements and the women who bear them, the law should not differentiate women who are impregnated pursuant to surrogate mother contracts from those who bear babies under other circumstances. Thus, the normal rules of adoption would apply to the transfer of parental status to the woman who will raise the child that is biologically her husband's (though legally probably the child of the surrogate's husband, if the surrogate is married). Any element of uncertainty created by restricting specific performance and allowing "change of heart" by the natural mother will merely serve to underline the need for caution by all parties involved.[17]

Moreover, because there is no relevant distinction between a surrogacy contract and an ordinary commissioned adoption, the laws against baby-selling should be enforced when a "surrogate mother" (and her mate, if any) relinquish a child for adoption by its biological father (and his mate, if any). The claim that the payment to the "surrogate" is merely for "gestational services" is plainly just a pretense, since payment is made "upon surrender of custody" of the child and for "carrying out . . . obligations" under the agreement. These obligations include taking all steps necessary to establish the biological father's paternity[18] and to transfer all parental rights to the biological father and his mate.

Although language isn't everything (and an ingenious lawyer might find a subtler way to disguise the truth), the pretense of the contract-for-services can be seen in the Baby M case. The contract signed by William Stern, the biological father, and by Mary Beth Whitehead, the biological mother, and her husband, Richard, provided in part:

$10,000 shall be paid to MARY BETH WHITEHEAD, surrogate, upon surrender of custody to WILLIAM STERN, the natural and biological father of the child born pursuant to the provisions of this Agreement for surrogate services and expenses in carrying out her obligations under this Agreement; . . .

. . . MARY BETH WHITEHEAD, surrogate, and RICHARD WHITEHEAD, her husband, agree to surrender custody of the child to WILLIAM STERN, Natural Father, immediately upon birth, acknowledging that it is the intent of this Agreement in the best interests of the child to do so; as well as institute and cooperate in proceedings to terminate their respective parental rights to said child, and sign any and all necessary affidavits, documents, and the like, in order to further the intent and purposes of this Agreement . . . .

. . . MARY BETH WHITEHEAD and RICHARD WHITEHEAD agree to sign all necessary affidavits prior to and after the birth of the child and voluntarily participate in any paternity proceedings necessary to have WILLIAM STERN'S name entered on said child's birth certificate as the natural or biological father.

Bringing surrogacy arrangements within the usual rules of adoption will also mean that the state — through social workers and eventually through the court that approves the adoption — will be involved in the process, in order to ensure that the transfer will be in the child's best interests. The mere fact that a couple is willing to pay a good deal of money to obtain a child does not vouchsafe that they will be suitable parents; the mere fact that a child is born to a "surrogate mother," rather than to a woman who wishes to give the child up to a man who is not its father and to that man's wife, does not diminish the state's obligations toward that child. In the United Kingdom, where surrogacy is recognized as falling within existing family law expectations, local authorities have been reminded that when they know

that a baby has been, or is about to be, born in its area as a result of a surrogacy arrangement it will wish to make enquiries . . . so as to be satisfied that the baby is not, or will not be, at risk as a result of the arrangement.[19]

Beyond reiterating the conclusion that "surrogate mother" arrangements are governed by the usual provisions of the parentage and adoption laws, the state should also regularize the process of record-keeping in such arrangements and in AID generally. As in adoption, this would preserve confidential records with accurate information about a child's biological origins, should such information later be needed for medical (especially genetic and diagnostic) reasons.[20]

The noncommercial treatment of surrogacy that we have in mind is illustrated by the judgment of Latey, J., in *In Re Adoption Application (Payment for Adoption)*,[21] handed down in the Royal Courts of Justice in London on March 11, 1987. In that case, the court approved an adoption by the child's father and his wife, Mr. and Ms. A., of a girl (then aged two years and four months) who had been conceived through sexual intercourse of the father and Ms. B., with whom Mr. and Ms. A had made "a surrogacy arrangement," as the court termed it. Initially, the parties had agreed that Ms. B would receive £10,000 to cover her expenses and loss of earnings during the pregnancy. In the end, the couple paid £5,000 and the surrogate refused to accept the balance.[22]

The question for the court was whether the adoption could be approved in light of statutes against baby-selling. Justice Latey accepted Ms. B's position that "I did not go into the arrangement for commercial reasons." Identifying commercial activities with profit-seeking, he concluded, "[T]here was nothing commercial in what happened." Although monetization and commodification can exist even without profit-seeking, adoption statutes do permit the payment of expenses in supervised settings. More important, the court was at pains to emphasize that what was involved was not commercial in the sense of involving a contract but was merely an arrangement. "There was no written contract or agreement; no lawyers were consulted until after the baby was born. The arrangement was one of trust which was fully honoured on both sides."

CONSTITUTIONAL IMPLICATIONS

We believe that policies on surrogate motherhood should — and can — be properly framed as issues of social policy, not constitutional law. Nevertheless, some commentators have attempted to "constitutionalize" the debate about the appropriate regulation of reproduction and adoption.[23] We will here reply briefly to the assertion that the states are constitutionally required to give effect both to commercial surrogacy contracts and to unpaid arrangements. Stated conversely, does a public policy that disfavors surrogacy unconstitutionally burden the rights of people[24] to establish a family by the use of methods — such as contracts that *are* worked out by lawyers and then honored by courts — to provide themselves with stronger assurance of a favorable outcome when trust breaks down and an arrangement to transfer a child is *not* "fully honoured on both sides"? We believe that limitations on surrogacy that arise from applying the family law model rather than the contracts model do not unconstitutionally burden any rights under present or ideal interpretations of the three doctrines of primary relevance — equal protection of the laws, substantive due process, and the right to privacy in family and reproductive choices.

EQUAL PROTECTION

Equal protection claims rest on an assertion that a particular group has been disadvantaged by the law as compared with other groups. With whom should those who wish to use surrogacy — typically couples with female infertility — be compared? Were the comparison made with people generally, it would suggest that not just infertility but *any* barriers to founding a family, such as those caused by advanced age, low intelligence, poverty, and so forth, would be legally suspect — a dubious conclusion. Consequently, the comparison for surrogacy is usually framed in terms of the rules that govern AID, the principal procedure designed to overcome infertility.

So long as AID is legal — and, indeed, is facilitated by laws that make a consenting husband the legal father of the child and remove any parental rights or responsibilities from the man from whom the semen came — must surrogate motherhood contracts also be legally protected, lest couples with male infertility be favored over couples with female infertility? More specifically, if payments to semen "donors" are permitted, is commercial surrogacy — rather than just unpaid surrogacy (which we would allow) — constitutionally protected on equal protection grounds? An initial response is that the law does not differentiate the reasons people have for using one form of "assisted reproduction" or another. Indeed, surrogacy itself typically involves AID, except that the source of the semen does not view himself as a "donor" but as a "lender" or "beneficiary" who is making use of the services of a woman to produce a child whom he will then claim. On a formal basis, then, the laws adopted for AID can, and should, be applied to surrogacy. The woman who bears a child, and her mate, if any, are presumed to be the parents of the child, until the presumption is overcome or until they give up their parental rights and responsibilities to the biological father and his mate, if any. Thus, legal acceptance of AID is facially neutral among couples with different types of infertility.

Of course, the argument is then made that taken as a whole, AID (in which the child will stay with the woman who bore it) and surrogacy (in which the child will go to its genetic father) are different procedures, regardless of the use of artificial insemination in the latter. Yet even assuming that the equal protection clause would require that two procedures affecting somewhat different infertile populations must be treated symmetrically, AID and surrogate motherhood are simply not equivalent. First, the biological parallel fails: the female procedure that is comparable to (though more complex than) AID is egg or embryo donation. Second, the biological difference matters: the physical risk and labor of surrogacy, to say nothing of the emotional attachment of a surrogate mother to the child she carries and bears, is incomparably greater than the risk, labor, and attachment of a semen donor to the child or children who may be produced by inseminations with his ejaculate.[25]

Furthermore, the assumption of formal symmetry in the law as applied to men and women is itself questionable. Equal protection arguments turn on what counts as equal treatment of different groups, a much debated issue especially for feminist legal theorists. Some writers define equality between women and men as symmetrical treatment, whereas others argue that equality requires asymmetrical treatment because of the power imbalance that flows from gender bias and hierarchy.[26] It would be wrong to claim that equal protection rigidly requires that men and women be treated with formal symmetry in matters involving reproduction.[27]

A possible example of legitimate asymmetry can be found in the present custom of paying a small amount ($25–$50 in most cases) to semen "donors" (actually, vendors). Even if the law continues to permit women to pay for sperm for AID, it does not follow that it would be a denial of equal protection to prohibit men from paying surrogates to bear and turn over children to them. Paying women to deliver children to genetic fathers may pose a greater risk of commodifying women than paying men for sperm poses of commodifying men because, given the current gender structure, these payments may have different social significance. The desire to carry on the male line through the use of surrogates is more likely to render women fungible than is the desire to carry on the female line through the use of sperm donors likely to render men fungible.

Nevertheless, for the reasons already advanced, market transactions in human beings are troublesome.

To the extent that semen partakes of humanness—especially because the semen may be valued differentially for the genetic traits it is believed to transmit[28]—then its sale for amounts more than that which is appropriate payment for the costs of "harvesting," testing, storing, and distributing should be discouraged or perhaps even prohibited. Of course, the same policy should be applied to the female equivalent of AID—obtaining eggs and embryos from women.

As stated earlier, we reach such conclusions on policy, not constitutional, grounds. But an equal-protection argument against banning paid surrogacy because it discriminates against men should fail, because, at least in the current context of gender hierarchy, the state has a stronger interest in protecting women against exploitation. In other words, in the view of some feminists, the major issue of inequality associated with surrogate motherhood is the preference it seems to display for enabling men to continue their genetic lineage through an oppressive use of women as breeders, deprived of any involvement with the offspring they have produced on contract.

Yet if, as some feminists also urge, men should share equally in parenting—on the psychological and spiritual levels as well as on the material—then social policy should not devalue a man's desire to rear a child. Nor should it disparage his desire to have (if possible) a genetic as well as a social link with the child, even if the ideal of human flourishing would suggest that a genetic connection should not be the basis for psychological and spiritual interrelationships with one's children. Thus, although the *preference* for the male connection to the child manifested in the trial court opinion in the Baby M case[29] is improper, the law probably ought not to make it more difficult for a man without a fertile female partner to create a child of whom he is the biological parent than it is for a woman without a fertile male partner[30]—provided, in all cases, that one person's fulfillment of her or his wishes does not come at the expense of another person's rights (whether defined symmetrically or asymmetrically).

SUBSTANTIVE DUE PROCESS, PRIVACY, AND REPRODUCTIVE FREEDOM

Rather than making the equality argument that paid surrogacy must be permitted in a social context in which AID is permitted, some would argue that there is an absolute right to paid surrogacy. Such an argument would be based upon a claim of substantive due process, [or] more plausibly upon its modern reincarnation in the constitutional right to privacy.

The claim that the government infringes liberty if it denies people the right to make enforceable contracts of exchange about anything they wish, children included, rests on a discredited view of the due process clause.[31] If the government has good reasons for declaring something off-limits to the market, there is no absolute right to market-liberty that can trump regulation.[32] In the context of commissioned adoption and paid surrogacy, the good reason for enforced noncommodification is to protect the fundamental rights of women and children to be treated as unique persons not subject to monetization.

The more powerful claim under modern constitutional doctrine is that a ban on paid surrogacy violates the right to privacy (in certain reproductive and family matters) fashioned by the Court in recent years. It has been suggested that the failure of a state to enforce surrogacy contracts, or laws that restrict any agreements people desire to make to enable themselves to obtain children, would violate the right of privacy recognized in the contraception and abortion cases.[33] We think this claim fails because it rests on the misinterpretation of the rationale and effect of the privacy decisions.

The heart of the privacy doctrine developed by the Supreme Court has been to shelter individuals from governmental intrusion into the choices they make about selected intimate matters including abortion, contraception, and family living. As the Court stated in *Eisenstadt v. Baird*, the doctrine is particularly relevant to decisions about offspring:

If the right of privacy means anything, it is the right of the *individual*, married or single, to be free from unwarranted governmental intrusion into matters so fundamentally affecting a person as the decision whether to bear or beget a child.[34]

The right to be *free from* interference is what Sir Isaiah Berlin terms a negative liberty,[35] rather than a positive liberty. In this instance it would amount to an obligation on the part of the state to ensure that individuals have the *freedom to* achieve the family they desire. How does the family law-oriented analysis for which we have argued here relate to either type of liberty, negative or positive?

Freedom from. The right of privacy gives wide scope for liberty of the former type — that is, freedom from undue governmental interference with decisions about reproduction — but it certainly does not preclude all types of state regulation. Requirements for accurate record-keeping, for example, are accepted without legal challenge. Their application to surrogacy (such as by requiring adoption procedures that result in confidential court records) are not an undue or discriminatory burden here. Furthermore, such rules and procedures are justified by state interests that are not merely legitimate but that may even be "compelling" to the extent that such records are necessary to protect the health and well-being of the children produced.

Indeed, regulations that go well beyond record-keeping requirements could be legitimate even if they precluded total freedom in reproductive choices. The interests of the state in protecting the health of the public would justify many forms of regulation of third parties who offer reproduction-related services. Sperm banks or in vitro clinics, for example, could be regulated to ensure compliance with at least minimum standards of safety and efficacy, as well as truthful advertising of services.

Freedom from governmental interference is itself subject to limitation on constitutional grounds. As one civil liberties group has concluded, the exercise of a person's fundamental right to have a family "[d]oes not embrace any right, nor permit any person, to treat a child as property."[36] The claim that the right to privacy protects surrogacy may be more plausible for noncommercial than for commercial surrogacy; even if the Constitution should be understood as including a right to bear a child for someone else, it should not be interpreted as including a right to be paid for it.

Because there is no substantive constitutional guarantee for people's choices to commodify reproductive capacities or children, there can be no constitutional objection to a state's choosing to prohibit commercial surrogacy agencies or other commercial reproductive brokerage. Moreover, despite the Supreme Court's recent propensity to treat commercial speech in the same fashion as noncommercial speech for First Amendment purposes, there is no objection on free speech grounds to prohibiting advertising by commercial surrogacy agencies or other brokers, as an aid to prohibitions on baby-selling.

Freedom to The thrust of our argument, however, has not been toward prohibiting all surrogacy. Rather,

we have urged only that paid surrogacy be prohibited and that other surrogacy arrangements not be regarded as legally binding. Arrangements made by individuals that are carried out voluntarily could continue to be accepted, provided that they accord with the usual rules on adoption (e.g., no payment, no agreement before a child's birth to give up custody, opportunity for the birth mother to change her mind, and protection against custody or adoption that is not in a child's best interests). People are thus free to choose unpaid surrogacy but cannot expect the state to enforce completion of the arrangement if disagreements arise.

Proponents of "procreative liberty" may claim that this result is unacceptable because the state is required by the constitutional right of privacy at least to enforce unpaid surrogacy arrangements. According to settled contract-law doctrines, however, promises without consideration are unenforceable. Moreover, the argument fails to distinguish negative from positive freedom. In finding a broad (albeit not unlimited) freedom from state interference in personal choices, the Supreme Court has declined to recognize a corresponding right to state aid in effectuating those choices.[37]

Moreover, declining to order specific performance of a surrogacy arrangement seems, in the language of *Eisenstadt*, less an "unwarranted governmental intrusion" into the would-be parents' reproductive liberty than the intrusion into the surrogate mother's rights that would occur were the state to enforce the arrangement.[38] The Court has been very specific in restricting state regulation of the reproductive choices of women and their *physicians*,[39] but it has never suggested a comparable obligation of the state to enhance the "contractual rights" of couples and their *lawyers* (or other *brokers* of children).

One need not agree with the current Court's emphasis on negative liberty to conclude that the protection of bodily integrity and consequently of the reproductive process encompassed within the right of privacy simply does not generate an affirmative duty on the part of the state to enforce all arrangements through which people seek to form a family. To hold otherwise would lead to the conclusion that all means by which people decide to obtain children are allowable, including paying money for any adoption (not just adoptions involving surrogates). In light of the strong connotations of commodifying all human beings, were buying and selling permitted in our social context, this is an untenable proposition, and one that is clearly not compelled by the Court's decisions on the right of privacy.

In the end, we believe that whether or not the state must—or, indeed, may permissibly—provide enforcement machinery for arrangements regarding reproduction and children must be considered separately for each type of arrangement. For so-called surrogate motherhood, the weight of protected "procreative liberty" rests with the biological mother who changes her mind and decides to keep her child. Hence, arguments about procreative liberty cannot support constitutionalizing a requirement that states provide laws and mechanisms to enforce such arrangements. Indeed, we have argued in favor of a public policy that denies that states may permissibly maintain such legal rules and procedures.

REFERENCES

This article is adapted from testimony presented at a "Hearing on Surrogate Parenting" before the Senate Committee on Health and Human Services of the California Legislature on December 11, 1987.

1. See, gen., Alexander Morgan Capron, "Alternative Birth Technologies: Legal Challenges," *U.C. Davis Law Review,* 20 (1987): 679.

2. The term "surrogate mother" is inaccurate because in ordinary parlance one would say that a surrogate is someone who raises another's offspring, not a child's birth mother who then releases it to the wife of its biological father. The better term would be "surrogate wife" or "breeding mother." If the pregnancy results from an ovum that has come from the woman who plans to raise the child, the appropriate term might be "surrogate womb."

The use of the term "surrogacy" as shorthand for the practice adds further confusion, since the term has established legal connotations associated both with decisionmakers who are legally authorized to act on behalf of incompetents and with the courts that are responsible for the welfare of incompetents. Similarly, in the bioethics literature, much attention has been paid in recent years to the use of surrogate decisionmakers for those who are incapable of making medical decisions for themselves and particularly to the advantages for competent patients of executing a durable power of attorney to name a surrogate to make decisions if and when the patient becomes incapacitated. See, e.g., U.S. President's Commission for the Study of Ethical Problems in Medicine and Biomedical and Behavioral Research, *Making Health Care Decisions* (Washington, D.C.: U.S. Gov't Printing Office, 1982): 158–60.

3. Cal. Evid. Code §621 (West 1966). See also Cal. Civ. Code §7004 (West 1983), which extends the presumption in certain special circumstances (death, annulment, or divorce within 300 days of a child's birth; attempted but invalid marriages; subsequent marriage; holding out as natural child; etc.).

4. Cal. Civ. Code §7005 (West 1983).

5. See Capron, supra note 1, at 690–94.

6. As, for example, in the Malahoff–Stiver "case" that was worked out on the "Phil Donahue Show" in 1983, or the dispute over an early attempt at in vitro fertilization at Columbia University that was litigated in Del Zio v. Presbyterian Hosp., 74 N.Y. Civ. Ct. (S.D.N.Y. Nov. 14, 1978) (memorandum decision).

7. See, e.g., N.Y. Dom. Rel. Law §11–1 (c) (McKinney 1977); Lori Andrews, *New Conceptions: A Consumer's Guide to the Newest Infertility Treatments,* rev. ed. (New York: St. Martin's, 1985), 207; S. Green and J. Long, *Marriage and Family Law Agreements* (1984), 311 n. 693.

8. The standards vary from revocation at will to requiring proof of fraud or duress. Susan M. Wolf, "Enforcing Surrogate Motherhood Agreements: The Trouble with Specific Performance," *New York Law School Human Rights Annual,* 4 (Spring 1987): 375, 382–83.

9. See, e.g., N.J.S.A. 9:3–54b (West Supp. 1984–85) (exempts stepparents).

10. We recognize that poor women themselves may, under some circumstances, think themselves not exploited but, rather, empowered by an entitlement to sell babies. But poor women are caught in a double bind: it may be disempowering either to allow or to disallow "commodification" of children. If sales are disallowed, poor women remain in circumstances they perceive to be worse than becoming paid baby-producers; but if sales are allowed, poor women and their children are in danger of degrading their personhood by becoming fungible objects of exchange. See Margaret Jane Radin, "Market-Inalienability," *Harvard Law Review,* 100 (June 1987): 1849, 1915–36.

Sometimes an "incomplete commodification" may be the best pragmatic solution to this kind of dilemma. For example, prostitution (commodification of sexuality) may be best handled by criminalizing pimping or other forms of brokering of sexual services, while allowing prostitutes themselves to receive money for their services as long as they do not seek state enforcement of broken promises to pay. See id.: 1921–25. On balance, however, we do not think an analogous "incomplete commodification" would be appropriate for surrogacy, at least while other forms of commissioned adoption are treated as prohibited baby-selling. See id.: 1928–30.

11. See Margaret Jane Radin, "Justice and the Market Domain," in John W. Chapman, ed., *Markets and Justice* (NOMOS XXXI) (New York: New York University Press, forthcoming). Whether or not babies could be priced and yet not be inappropriately commodified depends on how risky allowing buying and selling would be, given the degree to which people in our society conceive of things that are purchased as fungible commodities. Even though there can be nonmarket aspects to much of what we buy and sell (for example, the personal care and concern we hope for between physician and patient), in our nonideal world, the mere fact that money changes hands might be rightly treated as having bad implications, or at least bad possibilities, for an especially sensitive case like the sale of babies, in which complete commodification would deeply undermine personhood as we conceive it.

12. The notion of an ownership interest was strongly expressed in the trial court opinion in In re Baby M, 217 N.J. Super 313, 372, 525 A.2d 1128, 1157 (1987), in which Judge Sorkow ruled the anti-baby-selling provisions of the adoption law inapplicable because Mr. Stern "cannot purchase what is already his." It is also notable that in the trial court's view, the property right apparently resides with the biological father.

13. Anne Taylor Fleming, "Our Fascination with Baby M," *New York Times Magazine,* March 29, 1987, p. 32.

14. But see William Landes and Richard Posner, "The Economics of the Baby Shortage," *Journal of Legal Studies,* 7 (1978): 323 (speculating on the possibility of a thriving market in infants).

15. Of course, sometimes—for reasons of deterrence as well as of compensation—the legal system places a "dollar value" on human life. Yet in doing so—even when factors such as the emotional loss to survivors or the "loss of life's pleasures" by the de-

ceased enter the calculation of damages—the tort system acknowledges that the money is no substitute for the person. In a social system in which families are dependent on their members' earning power to obtain a decent standard of living, some compensation for the loss of earning power of a family member is just. The existence of tort remedies is of more dubious value in deterrence terms, however. While the threat of liability may deter individuals from unduly risky behavior, the existence of the system—in which the loss of human life is "compensated" by the payment of money—may encourage more life-risking activities than would occur were such losses to lie beyond the scope of the tort system, in the realm of individual revenge or societal disruption and disharmony.

16. See Radin, supra note 10, at 1903–21.

17. The child's interests would, however, be protected because when a surrogacy agreement is held invalid or is "breached" (by a mother's refusal to turn over the child), *both* natural parents are bound by "the statutory rights and obligations [that] exist in the absence of contract," including custodial disposition based on the child's best interests. Surrogate Parenting v. Com. ex rel. Armstrong, 704 S.W.2d 209, 213 (Ky. 1986). The New Jersey Supreme Court likewise concluded that determining Baby M's custody on the basis of her best interests rather than automatically returning her to her mother would not embolden people to use surrogacy because its holding that surrogate mother arrangements are "unenforceable and illegal is sufficient to deter such agreements." In re Baby M, 537 A.2d 1227, 1257 (N.J. 1988). The court also held for the future that, pending a court determination of the child's best interests, a woman who decides not to go through with a surrogate arrangement should be allowed to keep her child, absent proof that she is an unfit mother.

18. For example, Cal. Civ. Code §7006 (West 1983) provides that actions to establish a father and child relationship may only be commenced by the child, its natural mother, or the man presumed to be the child's father.

19. U.K. Department of Health and Social Security, "Responsibility of Local Authority Social Service Departments in Surrogacy Cases," *Local Authority Circular* (85)12 (3 May 1985).

20. U.S. President's Commission for the Study of Ethical Problems in Medicine and Biomedical and Behavioral Research, *Screening and Counseling for Genetic Conditions* (Washington, D.C.: U.S. Gov't Printing Office, 1983): 45–47, 68–70.

21. [1987] Fam. 81, [1987] All ER 826, [1987] 3 WLR 31.

22. The court states that the refusal came from the fact that Ms. B and a professional writer co-authored a book telling her story, from which she made money.

23. See, e.g., Ethics Committee of the American Fertility Society, "Ethical Considerations of the New Reproductive Technologies," *Fertility & Sterility,* 46 (Supp. 1) (1986): 2S–6S; John Robertson, "Procreative Liberty and the Control of Conception, Pregnancy and Childbirth," *Virginia Law Review,* 69 (1983): 405.

24. Although the people who seek surrogate arrangements are today typically married couples, single persons—especially single men—might also seek to make such contracts. If "reproductive rights" apply here, that which is permitted to couples may apply to singles as well because the Supreme Court has made clear in other contexts that many privacy rights regarding reproductive decisions protect the unmarried equally with the married. See, e.g., Eisenstadt v. Baird, 405 U.S. 438 (1972). See also Note, "Reproductive Technology and the Procreative Rights of the Unmarried," *Harvard Law Review,* 98 (1985): 669, 684–85.

25. See Capron, supra note 1, at 699–700.

26. See Christine Littleton, "Reconstructing Sexual Equality," *California Law Review,* 75 (1987): 1279.

27. Cf. Laurence Tribe, *American Constitutional Law,* 2d ed. (Mineola, N.Y.: Foundation Press, 1988), 1582: "[A]n approach to the equal protection clause that is dominated by formal comparisons between classes of people thought to be similarly situated is inadequate to the task of ferreting out inequality when a court confronts laws dealing with reproductive biology, since such laws, by definition, identify ways in which women and men are definitely *not* similarly situated." The Supreme Court's attempts to deal with such problems have been seen by many commentators as unsatisfactory, whether its approach has been symmetrical or asymmetrical. See, e.g., Geduldig v. Aiello, 417 U.S. 484 (1974) (California's failure to cover pregnancy and childbirth in its disability insurance system did not violate equal protection, because it covered all "nonpregnant persons," both male and female); Michael M. v. Superior Court, 450 U.S. 464 (1981) (California's statutory rape law providing for criminal sanctions only upon the male participant in underage, nonmarital sex did not violate equal protection, because only women bear the risk of becoming pregnant). Recently the Court adopted an asymmetrical approach, albeit in a statutory context, in California Federal Savings & Loan Ass'n v. Guerra, 107 S.Ct. 683 (1987) (California statute requiring unpaid leave with guaranteed job reinstatement for pregnancy, but not for disabilities unrelated to pregnancy, is not preempted by Title VII of the Civil Rights Act of 1964, as amended by the Pregnancy Discrimination Act to require that employers treat pregnancy the same as any other disability, because the statute makes it possible for female as well as male workers to keep their jobs and also become parents). For a discussion of the debate on this issue within the community of feminist legal scholars, see Littleton, supra note 26.

28. Although the "Nobel Sperm Bank" plainly hoped to attract suitable female clients because of the perception that its sperm samples were genetically superior, it did not operate on a market basis. Yet it still serves as an illustration of the risk that the men from whom sperm are obtained could be treated like commodities were a true "sperm market" permitted to operate.

29. See *Baby M,* supra note 12.

30. The same argument applies when reasons other than infertility (such as genetic risk) preclude a person from being a biological parent.

31. Since the downfall of *Lochner v. New York* (198 U.S. 45 [1905])—which invalidated a state law setting a ten-hour daily maximum and sixty-hour weekly maximum for employment by bankers—there is no constitutional right to treat anything and everything as commodities in a laissez-faire marketplace. Tribe, supra note 27, summarizes this era in American legal history in Chapter 8, entitled "The Model of Implied Limitations on Government: The Rise and Fall of Contractual Liberty."

32. Substantive due process notions do still occasionally emerge in decisions in which the Supreme Court limits governmental restrictions of individual choices about some fundamental matters. See, e.g., Moore v. City of East Cleveland, 431 U.S. 494 (1977) (plurality opinion voids city's attempt to zone for nuclear family residence).

33. See, e.g., John Robertson, "Embryos, Families, and Procreative Liberty: The Legal Structure of the New Reproduction," *Southern California Law Review,* 59 (1986): 939.

34. 405 U.S. 438, 453 (1972).

35. Isaiah Berlin, *Four Essays on Liberty* (Oxford: Clarendon Press, 1969).

36. American Civil Liberties Union of Southern California, *Policy #262a (Surrogate Parenting)* §C(1)(b) (adopted March 18, 1987). The policy states that a child is being treated as property "if (a) her/his custody is conditioned on payment of consideration or vice versa or (b) consideration or custody is conditioned upon the child surviving for any fixed period of time, or upon the child's

meeting specifications concerning fitness, health, race, gender, color, genetic identification, or other such criteria." Id.: §B(1).

37. In Maher v. Roe, 432 U.S. 464 (1977), for example, the Court denied the claim that a woman had a right to public funding of an abortion, even though the choice to abort is for the Court a cardinal instance of the right of privacy. Although *Maher* is thus a formidable doctrinal obstacle for those who would claim some positive right to enforcement of surrogacy contracts, we do not mean to endorse its rationale. Because state denial of freedom to choose abortion is, in the context of the current gender bias in economic and social power, a denial of equal opportunity to women, we think the right to choose abortion would be better analyzed as an equality right than as a privacy right.

38. As the ACLU of Southern California concludes, people may not exercise their right to form a family in a manner "that would compel the waiver or alienation of the fundamental rights of [a] surrogate." See ACLU, *Surrogate Parenting*, supra note 36, at §C(1)(a). In the *Baby M* decision, the New Jersey Supreme Court identified the surrogate's right to the companionship of her child as "a recognized fundamental interest protected by the Constitution" (subject, it said, to state regulation). In re Baby M, 537 A.2d 1227, 1255 (N.J. 1988). In contrast, it noted that the father's asserted right to procreate "very simply is the right to have natural children whether through sexual intercourse or artificial insemination." Id.: 1253. William Stern had a right to father Baby M but not to insist that she be turned over to him to raise or that the Whiteheads be forced to fulfill their promise to relinquish their parental rights to the Sterns.

39. For example, in *Roe v. Wade* the Court held that through the first trimester of pregnancy, "the attending physician, in consultation with his patient, is free to determine, without regulation by the State, that, in his medical judgment the patient's pregnancy should be terminated." 410 U.S. 113, 147 (1973).

SUGGESTED READINGS FOR CHAPTER 4

GENERAL ISSUES

Alpern, Kenneth D. *The Ethics of Reproductive Technology.* New York: Oxford University Press, 1992.

American Fertility Society, Ethics Committee. "Ethical Considerations of the New Reproductive Technologies." *Fertility and Sterility* 53 (Supplement 2; 1990), 1S–109S.

Andrews, Lori B. "Control and Compensation: Laws Governing Extracorporeal Generative Materials." *Journal of Medicine and Philosophy* 14 (1989), 541–560.

Andrews, Lori B. *New Conceptions: A Consumer's Guide to the Newest Infertility Treatments.* Revised ed. New York: St. Martin's, 1985.

Annas, George J. "Predicting the Future of Privacy in Pregnancy: How Medical Technology Affects the Legal Rights of Pregnant Women." *Nova Law Review* 13 (1989), 329–353.

Bartels, Diane M., et al., eds. *Beyond Baby M: Ethical Issues in New Reproductive Techniques.* Clifton, NJ: Humana Press, 1990.

Blank, Robert H. *Regulating Reproduction.* New York: Columbia University Press, 1990.

Cahill, Lisa Sowle. "Moral Traditions, Ethical Language, and Reproductive Technologies." *Journal of Medicine and Philosophy* 14 (1989), 497–522.

Canada, Law Reform Commission. *Medically Assisted Procreation.* Working Paper 65. Ottawa: Minister of Supply and Services, 1992.

Capron, Alexander M. "Surrogate Motherhood: Legal Issues Raised by the New Reproductive Alternatives." In Evans, Mark I., et al., eds. *Fetal Diagnosis and Therapy: Science, Ethics, and the Law.* Philadelphia: J. B. Lippincott, 1989, 372–386.

Corea, Gena. *Man-Made Women: How New Reproductive Technologies Affect Women.* Bloomington: Indiana University Press, 1987.

Corea, Gena. *The Mother Machine: Reproductive Technologies from Artificial Insemination to Artificial Wombs.* New York: Harper & Row, 1985.

Glover, Jonathan, et al. *Ethics of New Reproductive Technologies: The Glover Report to the European Commission.* DeKalb: Northern Illinois University Press, 1989.

Holmes, Helen Bequaert. "Reproductive Technologies." In Becker, Lawrence C., and Becker, Charlotte B., eds. *Encyclopedia of Ethics.* New York: Garland, 1992, pp. 1083–1089.

Hull, Richard T., ed. *Ethical Issues in the New Reproductive Technologies.* Belmont, CA: Wadsworth, 1990.

Knoppers, Bartha M., LeBris, Sonia. "Recent Advances in Medically Assisted Conception: Legal, Ethical and Social Issues." *American Journal of Law and Medicine* 17 (1991), 329–361.

McCullough, Laurence B., and Chervenak, Frank A. *Ethics in Obstetrics and Gynecology.* New York: Oxford University Press, 1994.

Overall, Christine. *Ethics and Human Reproduction: A Feminist Analysis.* Boston: Allen & Unwin, 1987.

Overall, Christine, ed. *The Future of Human Reproduction.* Toronto: The Women's Press, 1989.

Pellegrino, Edmund D., Harvey, John Collins, and Langan, John P., eds. *Gift of Life: Catholic Scholars Respond to the Vatican Instruction.* Washington, DC: Georgetown University Press, 1990.

Robertson, John A. *Autonomy and Ambivalence: Reproductive Technology and the Limits of Procreative Liberty.* Princeton: Princeton University Press, 1994.

Rothman, Barbara Katz. *Recreating Motherhood: Ideology and Technology in a Patriarchal Society.* New York: W. W. Norton, 1989.

Rowland, Robyn. *Living Laboratories: Women and Reproductive Technology.* Bloomington: Indiana University Press, 1992.

Ryan, Maura A. "The Argument for Unlimited Procreative Liberty: A Feminist Critique." *Hastings Center Report* 20 (July–August 1990), 6–12.

Singer, Peter, and Wells, Deane. *Making Babies: The New Science and Ethics of Conception.* New York: Scribner's Sons, 1985.

Steinbock, Bonnie. *Life Before Birth: The Moral and Legal Status of Embryos and Fetuses.* New York: Oxford University Press, 1992.

United States, Congress, Office of Technology Assessment, *Infertility: Medical and Social Choices.* Washington, DC: U.S. Government Printing Office, May 1988.

Walters, LeRoy, "Ethics and New Reproductive Technologies: An International Review of Committee Statements." *Hastings Center Report* 17 (June 1987; Supplement), 3–9.

Warnock, Mary, and United Kingdom, Department of Health and Social Security, Committee of Inquiry into Human Fertilisation and Embryology. *A Question of Life: The Warnock Report on Human Fertilisation and Embryology.* New York: Basil Blackwell, 1985.

Annas, George J. "Crazy Making: Embryos and Gestational Mothers." *Hastings Center Report* 21 (January–February 1991), 35–38.

Bonnicksen, Andrea L. *In Vitro Fertilization: Building Policy from Laboratories to Legislatures.* New York: Columbia University Press, 1989.

Capron, Alexander M. "Parenthood and Frozen Embryos: More Than Property and Privacy." *Hastings Center Report* 22 (September–October 1992), 32–33.

Dawson, Karen, and Singer, Peter. "Should Fertile People Have Access to In Vitro Fertilization?" *British Medical Journal* 300 (1990), 167–170.

Fleischer, Eva. "Ready for Any Sacrifice? Women in IVF Programmes." *Issues in Reproductive and Genetic Engineering* 3 (1990), 1–11.

Klein, Renate D. "IVF Research: A Question of Feminist Ethics." *Issues in Reproductive and Genetic Engineering* 3 (1990), 243–251.

Rothman, Barbara Katz. "Not All That Glitters Is Gold." *Hastings Center Report* 22 (July–August 1992; Supplement), S11–S15.

Singer, Peter, et al. *Embryo Experimentation.* New York: Cambridge University Press, 1990.

Tennessee, Supreme Court. Davis v. Davis. *Southwestern Reporter,* SW.2d 842, 588–604 (1992).

SURROGATE PARENTING ARRANGEMENTS

Allen, Anita L. "Surrogacy, Slavery, and the Ownership of Life." *Harvard Journal of Law and Public Policy* 13 (1990), 139–149.

American College of Obstetricians and Gynecologists, Committee on Ethics. "Ethical Issues in Surrogate Motherhood." *Women's Health Issues* 1 (1991), 129–134. See also pp. 135–160.

Annas, George J. "Crazy Making: Embryos and Gestational Mothers." *Hastings Center Report* 21 (January–February 1991), 35–38.

Annas, George J. "Using Genes to Define Motherhood—the California Solution." *New England Journal of Medicine* 326 (1992), 417–420.

Arneson, Richard J. "Commodification and Commercial Surrogacy." *Philosophy and Public Affairs* 21 (1992), 132–164.

California, Court of Appeal, Fourth District, Division 3. Anna J. v. Mark C. *California Reporter* 286 Cal. Rptr. 369 (1991).

California Supreme Court. Anna Johnson v. Mark Calvert. *Pacific Reporter,* 2d Series, 851. P 2d 776–801 (1993).

Capron, Alexander M. "Whose Child Is This?" *Hastings Center Report* 21 (November–December 1991), 37–38.

Field, Martha A. *Surrogate Motherhood.* Cambridge, MA: Harvard University Press, 1988.

Gostin, Larry O., ed. *Surrogate Motherhood: Politics and Privacy.* Bloomington: Indiana University Press, 1990.

New Jersey, Supreme Court. *In the Matter of Baby M. Atlantic Reporter* 537 A.2d 1227 (1988).

Rothenberg, Karen H. "Gestational Surrogacy and the Health Care Provider: Put Part of the 'IVF Genie' Back in the Bottle." *Law, Medicine and Health Care* 18 (1990), 345–352.

Satz, Debra. "Markets in Women's Reproductive Labor." *Philosophy and Public Affairs* 21 (1992), 107–131.

New Jersey, Commission on Legal and Ethical Problems in the Delivery of Health Care. *After Baby M: The Legal, Ethical and Social Dimensions of Surrogacy.* Trenton, NJ: The Commission, September 1992.

Wadlington, Walter J. "Baby M: Catalyst for Family Law Reform?" *Journal of Contemporary Health Law and Policy* 5 (1989), 1–20.

BIBLIOGRAPHIES

Coutts, Mary Carrington. "Ethical Issues in In Vitro Fertilization." Scope Note 10. Washington, DC: Kennedy Institute of Ethics, Georgetown University, December 1988.

Goldstein, Doris Mueller. *Bioethics: A Guide to Information Sources.* Detroit: Gale Research Company, 1982. See under "Reproductive Technologies."

Lineback, Richard H., ed. *Philosopher's Index.* Vols. 1–27. Bowling Green, OH: Philosophy Documentation Center, Bowling Green State University. Issued quarterly. See under "Artificial Insemination," "In Vitro Fertilization," and "Surrogates."

Meinke, Sue A. "Surrogate Motherhood: Ethical and Legal Issues." Scope Note 6. Washington, DC: Kennedy Institute of Ethics, Georgetown University, January 1988.

Musgrove, Michèle, comp. *Artificial Insemination Bibliography.* Ottawa: Royal Commission on New Reproductive Technologies, 1992.

Reich, Warren T., ed. *Encyclopedia of Bioethics.* Second ed. New York: Macmillan, 1994.

Walters, LeRoy, and Kahn, Tamar Joy, eds. Bibliography of Bioethics. Vols. 1–19. Washington, DC: Kennedy Institute of Ethics, Georgetown University. Issued annually. See under "Artificial Insemination," "In Vitro Fertilization," "Reproduction," "Reproductive Technologies," and "Surrogate Mothers." (The information contained in the annual Bibliography can also be retrieved from BIOETHICSLINE, an online database of the National Library of Medicine, and from BIOETHICSLINE Plus, a CD-ROM disc distributed by SilverPlatter.)

5.
Abortion and Maternal–Fetal Relations

INTRODUCTION

Despite the legality of abortion in many Western nations, questions of its ethical and legal acceptability continue to be widely debated. Many high government officials are morally opposed to the law of their land. At the same time, the adequacy of court decisions that have declared antiabortion laws unconstitutional is also debated. In this chapter these and other contemporary ethical and legal issues about abortion will be examined.

THE PROBLEM OF MORAL JUSTIFICATION

An abortion might be desired for many reasons: cardiac complications, a suicidal state of mind, psychological trauma, pregnancy caused by rape, the inadvertent use of fetus-deforming drugs, genetic predisposition to disease, prenatally diagnosed birth defects, and many personal and family reasons, such as the financial burden or intrusiveness of a child. These reasons explain why an abortion is often viewed as a desirable way to extricate a woman or a family from an undesired circumstance. But explanations of this sort do not answer the problem of *justification:* What reasons, if any, are sufficient to justify the act of aborting a human fetus?

Some contend that abortion is never acceptable or, at most, is permissible only if necessary to save the pregnant woman's life. This view is commonly called the conservative theory of abortion because it emphasizes conserving life. Traditionally, Roman Catholics have been exponents of the conservative approach, but they are by no means its only advocates. The case for this point of view is presented in this chapter by John Noonan. The other extreme holds that abortion is always permissible, whatever the state of fetal development. This view is commonly termed the liberal theory of abortion because it emphasizes freedom of choice and the right of a woman to make decisions that affect her body. Mary Anne Warren defends this approach in this chapter.

Finally, many defend intermediate theories, according to which abortion is ethically permissible up to a specified stage of fetal development or for some limited set of moral reasons that are believed to be sufficient to warrant abortions under special circumstances. Baruch Brody discusses possible intermediate theories leaning toward conservatism, while Judith Thomson's essay suggests an intermediate theory that leans toward liberalism. However, it is worth noting that the traditional terminology of "liberal" and "conservative" can be both distracting and inaccurate. The issues before us are not directly linked to *political* liberalism and conservatism.

THE ONTOLOGICAL STATUS OF THE FETUS

Recent controversies about abortion focus on ethical problems of our obligations to fetuses and on what rights, if any, fetuses possess. A more basic issue, some say, concerns the *kind of entities* fetuses are. Following current usage, we can refer to this as the problem of *ontological status*. In law, "status" or "standing" is "one's place in the community in the estimation of others; one's relative position in social, commercial, or moral relations; one's repute, grade, or rank" *(Black's Law Dictionary)*. An account of the kind of entities fetuses are will determine their status and will have important implications for the issues of our obligations to fetuses and their rights.

Several layers of questions may be distinguished about ontological status: (1) Is the fetus *an individual organism?* (2) Is the fetus *biologically a human being?* (3) Is the fetus *psychologically a human being?* and (4) Is the fetus a *person?* Some who write on problems of ontological status attempt to develop a theory that specifies the conditions under which the fetus can be said to be independent and alive. Others focus on the conditions, if any, under which the fetus is human. Still others are concerned with explaining the conditions, if any, under which the fetus is a person. It is widely agreed that one attributes a more significant status to the fetus by granting that it is fully a human being (biologically and psychologically), rather than merely saying that it is an individual organism, and that one enhances its status still further by attributing personhood to the fetus.

Many are willing to concede that an individual life begins at fertilization but will not concede that there is a human being or a person at fertilization. Others claim that the fetus is human at fertilization but not a person. Still others grant full personhood at fertilization. Those who espouse these views sometimes differ because they define one or the other of these terms differently. Many differences, however, derive from theoretical disagreements about what constitutes life or humanity or personhood.

THE CONCEPT OF HUMANITY

The concept of human life has long been at the center of the abortion discussion. It is a confusing concept, because "human life" can take two very different meanings. On the one hand, it can mean *biological human life,* that group of biological characteristics that set the human species apart from nonhuman species. On the other hand, "human life" can be used to mean *life that is distinctively human*—that is, a life characterized by psychological rather than biological properties. For example, the ability to use symbols, to imagine, to love, and to perform higher intellectual skills are among the most distinctive human properties. Having these properties implies that one is a human being.

A simple example will illustrate the differences between these two senses. Some infants with extreme disabilities die shortly after birth. They are born of human parents, and they are biologically human. However, they never exhibit any distinctively human psychological traits, and (in many cases) have no potential to do so. For these individuals it is not possible to make human life in the biological sense human in the psychological sense. We do not differentiate these two aspects of life in discourse about any other animal species. We do not, for example, speak of making feline life more distinctively feline. But we do meaningfully speak of making human life more human, and this usage makes sense because of the dual meaning just discussed.

In discussions of abortion, it is important to be clear about which meaning is being employed when using the expression "the taking of human life." Many proponents of abortion, and some opponents as well, would agree that while biological human life is taken by abortions, human life in the second or psychological sense is not taken.

THE CONCEPT OF PERSONHOOD

The concept of personhood may or may not be different from either the biological sense or the psychological sense of "human life." That is, one might claim that what it means to be a person is simply to have some properties that make an organism human in one or both of these senses. But other writers have suggested a list of more demanding criteria for being a person. A list of conditions for being a person, similar to the following, is advanced by Warren and several other recent writers:

1. Self-consciousness
2. Freedom to act and the capacity to engage in purposeful sequences of actions
3. Having reasons for actions and the ability to appreciate reasons for acting
4. Ability to communicate with other persons using a language
5. Capacity to make moral judgments
6. Rationality.

Sometimes it is said by those who propose such a list that in order to be a person, an individual need only satisfy one of the aforementioned criteria—for example, bona fide linguistic behavior (4)—but need not also satisfy the other conditions (2–3, 5–6). Others say that all of these conditions (and perhaps others as well) must be satisfied. Despite this dispute about which properties are jointly necessary and sufficient for personhood, there is now a widespread consensus that more than one of the above criteria is necessary to qualify as a person. It allegedly follows that fetuses, newborns, profoundly brain-damaged persons, and most if not all animals fail the cognitive criteria, and so do not have the moral standing conferred by the category of person. These creatures might gain moral protections in some other way, but no metaphysical, biological, or status-conferring category provides them with moral protection on this account. But the dominant and prior question is whether any list approximating (1)–(6) is acceptable. Noonan, Brody, and Thomson tend not to view the core problems of abortion as turning on the acceptance or rejection of such a list.

The problem of ontological status is further complicated by a factor related to the biological development of the fetus. It is important to state *at what point of development* an entity achieves the status of a human or a person. Locating the crucial point of development is the central task in Brody's essay and also in the opinions in *Roe* v. *Wade* and *Planned Parenthood* v. *Carey* of the U.S. Supreme Court.

One polar position (sometimes called the extreme liberal position) is that the fetus never satisfies any of the criteria mentioned above and therefore has *no ontological status* of any importance. Warren defends this view. The opposite position (sometimes said to be the extreme conservative position) is that the fetus always has *full ontological status* in regard to all of the significant measures of status. Noonan supports this view. He and others claim that the line is drawn at conception, so that the fetus is *always* an individual human person. Obviously, there are many intermediate positions, which draw the line somewhere between the extremes of conception and birth. For example, the line may be drawn at quickening or viability, or when brain waves are first present, as Brody argues.

THE MORAL STATUS OF THE FETUS

The notion of "moral status" has been explicated in several ways. In a weak sense, "status" here refers to a standing, grade, or rank of moral importance or of moral value. In a stronger sense, "status" means to have rights, or the functional equivalent of rights, in the form of having protected interests, and the like. In either sense, having moral status is to qualify under, or be ranked under, some range of moral protections.

If, for example, fetuses have *full moral status,* then many maintain that they possess all the same rights as those who have been born. Brody holds this thesis for at least some periods of fetal development, and Noonan holds it for all periods. By contrast, at least some hold that fetuses have only a *partial moral status* and therefore only a partial set of rights. Many liberals maintain that fetuses possess *no moral status* and therefore no rights, as

Warren maintains. If this liberal account is accepted, then fetuses and animals have no more right to life than a body cell or a tumor, and an abortion is no more morally objectionable than surgery to remove the tumor. But if the conservative view is accepted, fetuses possess all the rights possessed by human beings, and an abortion is as objectionable as any common killing of an innocent person.

Theories of moral status are often directly connected with prior theories of ontological status. A typical conservative thesis is that because the line between the human and the nonhuman is properly drawn at conception, the fetus has full ontological status and, *therefore,* full moral status. A typical liberal claim is that the line between the human and the nonhuman must be drawn at birth; the fetus has no significant ontological status and, *therefore,* no moral status. Some liberals argue that even though the fetus is biologically human, it nonetheless is not human in a morally significant sense and hence has no significant moral status. This claim is usually accompanied by the thesis that only persons constitute the moral community, and because fetuses are not persons they do not have a moral status (see Warren).

Moderates use a diverse mixture of arguments, which sometimes do and sometimes do not combine an ontological account with a moral one. Typical of moderate views is the claim that the line between the human and the nonhuman or the line between persons and nonpersons should be drawn at some point between conception and birth. Therefore, the fetus has no significant moral status during some stages of growth but does have significant moral status beginning at some later stage. In many recent accounts, viability has been an especially popular point at which to draw the line, with the result that the fetus is given either full moral status or partial moral status at viability. Some legal strategies adopted to protect the rights of the pregnant woman in the opinions in U.S. Supreme Court cases involve a similar although not identical premise about the place of viability.

THE PROBLEM OF CONFLICTING RIGHTS

If either the liberal or the conservative view of the moral status of the fetus is adopted, the problem of morally justifying abortion at first seems uncomplicated. If one accepts that a fetus should not enjoy treatment as a human being, it can then be argued that abortions are not morally reprehensible and are prudentially justified just as other surgical procedures are. In contrast, if one accepts that a fetus at any stage of development is a human life with full moral status, and is possibly a person, then the equation "abortion is murder" is plausible. By this reasoning abortion is never justified under any conditions, or at least it can be permitted only if it is an instance of "justified homicide."

However, establishing a position on abortion is not this straightforward. Even on a conservative theory there may be cases of justified abortion. For example, it has been argued by many conservatives that a pregnant woman may legitimately abort the fetus in "self-defense" if both will die unless the life of the fetus is terminated. In order to claim that abortion is *always* wrong, one must justify maintaining the position that the fetus's "right to life" *always* overrides (or at least is equal to) all the pregnant woman's rights, including her rights to both life and liberty.

Even if the conservative theory is construed so that it entails that human fetuses have equal rights because of their moral status, nothing in the theory requires that these moral rights *always override* all other moral rights. Here a proponent of this theory bluntly confronts the problem of conflicting rights: The unborn possess some rights (including a right to life) and pregnant women also possess rights (including a right to life). Those who possess the rights have a *(prima facie)* moral claim to be treated in accordance with their rights. But what happens when these rights conflict?

This problem is as problematic for those who hold a moderate theory of the moral status of the fetus. These theories provide moral grounds against arbitrary termination of fetal life (the fetus has some claim to protection against the actions of others), yet do not grant to the fetus (at least in some stages) the same rights to life possessed by living persons. Accordingly, advocates of these theories are faced with the problem of specifying which rights should take precedence. Does the woman's right to decide what happens to her body justify abortion? Does pregnancy resulting from rape justify abortion? Does self-defense justify abortion? Does psychological damage justify abortion? Does knowledge of a grossly deformed fetus justify abortion? And further, does the fetus have a right to a "minimum quality of life," that is, to protection against wrongful life? Some of these issues of conflicting rights are raised by Thomson, who is then criticized by both Brody and Warren.

LEGAL ISSUES OF ABORTION

The 1973 U.S. Supreme Court case of *Roe* v. *Wade* addressed the social problem of how abortion legislation may and may not be formulated in the attempt to protect the fetus against abortion. In the opinion of the court, the majority held that the right to privacy implicit in the Fourteenth Amendment is broad enough to encompass a woman's decision to have an abortion. This right overrides all other concerns until the fetus reaches the point of viability. After that point, the Court finds that states may have an interest in protecting the life of the fetus, even if offering that protection directly competes with the woman's interest in liberty (but not if the protection interferes with maternal health).

In addition to the viability criterion, the Court correspondingly divides pregnancy into three periods, called trimesters. Because the fetus becomes viable in roughly the third trimester, the Court protects the fetus in this period. The Court's conception of a solution to the social problem of abortion has increasingly come under attack, both from external critics and internally from Supreme Court justices who have filed dissenting opinions. O'Connor represents an early version of these justices' views in the *Akron* case in this chapter. O'Connor's attack on the trimester framework criticizes arguments used in the Court majority in *Roe*. She maintains that the Court's reasoning is not sufficient to justify its fundamental analytical framework of "stages" of pregnancy. She accuses the Court of inconsistency both in handling abortion cases and in processing cases involving fundamental rights in other areas.

She also argues that the state's compelling interests in maternal and fetal health must change as medical technology changes. O'Connor envisions the following possibility: If the woman's right to privacy overrides the state's interest in protecting fetal health only up to the point of viability, then as the point of viability is pushed back by technological advancement, the point at which abortion is legally allowed must also be pushed back. O'Connor argues that as medical practices improve, the need to protect maternal health will also be reduced. These two considerations taken together lead her to argue that *Roe* necessitates continuous, ongoing medical review by the Court. She concludes that the *Roe* framework is unworkable and "on a collision course with itself."

In *Planned Parenthood* v. *Casey,* O'Connor and two other justices join hands in reaffirming the essential holding in *Roe* that a woman has a legal right to seek an abortion prior to fetal viability, but they strip *Roe* of what they consider its untenable parts, especially the trimester conception. They argue that an undue burden test should be used rather than the trimester framework in evaluating any legal restrictions placed on access to abortion prior to viability. They then defend certain restrictions as not constituting undue burdens, including requirements of informed consent, parental notification and consent, and a twenty-four-hour waiting period. However, they argue that a spousal notification provision does place an undue burden on a woman, and they therefore declare it legally invalid.

MATERNAL—FETAL RELATIONSHIPS AND RIGHTS

We earlier encountered the problem of conflicting rights—the fetus's rights and the pregnant woman's rights. Under the assumption that both have rights, we discussed whose rights should prevail if the woman seeks an abortion. Now we extend this discussion beyond abortion to forms of maternal—fetal conflict that arise not from the desire to end pregnancy, but from the condition of pregnancy itself.

In order to protect the fetus, various laws and court decisions have attempted to restrict or otherwise control the behavior of pregnant women and, in some cases, women who may become pregnant. In a number of historic law cases, U.S. courts held that women cannot legitimately be excluded from employment while pregnant merely *because* they are pregnant. Far more untested in the courts are circumstances in which corporations, municipalities, states, and institutions such as hospitals have adopted laws and policies that involve the coercion, detention, or incarceration of pregnant women for alcohol and drug abuse during pregnancy. In a few widely discussed cases, physicians or courts have imposed or attempted to impose surgical and other medical interventions on women who do not consent to the procedures. Remedies in some cases include forced surgical procedures such as cesarean sections, forced medication such as penicillin, and incarceration to reduce the threat of harm. In some cases the motives are paternalistic—to protect the women—but in virtually all cases there is a motive to protect the fetus.

No one doubts that women have moral obligations to protect the fetus from harm, but do others gain a right to limit their liberty when they fail to live up to this obligation? Two areas of controversy have centered on (1) what constitutes a risk of harm to the fetus that is sufficiently grave to justify limitation of the woman's liberty, and (2) what constitutes a legitimate reason for the woman not to take appropriate steps to prevent harm. Regarding the first question, in some cases the possibility of harm is remote, whereas in other cases it is virtually certain that harm will occur. Regarding the second question, women often have reasons for their actions that are elsewhere recognized as valid grounds for refusing treatment, such as religious beliefs that lead to refusing a surgical intervention requiring blood transfusions.

These two problems can be situated as parts of the larger question, "What constitutes a sufficient reason for legal coercion of pregnant women?" Many believe that it is fundamentally wrong to transform any *moral* obligation to prevent harm to or promote the health of the fetus into a *legal* obligation that allows institutions and courts to coerce pregnant women. Several reasons have been offered in support of this view. One is the right of all competent persons to refuse medical interventions, and another is that we usually make an action a legal violation only if one person has *actually* caused harm to another, not because there is merely a risk that harm may be caused. These reasons are often conjoined with arguments about negative consequences that will occur if laws restrict a pregnant woman's liberty. For example, some argue (1) that women who are most likely to harm a fetus by their behavior will be the first to stay away from prenatal care (where their abuse must by law be reported), thereby increasing rather than decreasing risk to the fetus; (2) that women will become skeptical and distrustful of their physicians; and (3) that society and the fetus will be worse off rather than better off by placing pregnant women in correctional facilities, which typically offer poor health care. Here the argument is that the negative consequences of these policies outweigh the positive consequences.

However, persons who defend rights of fetuses are typically unpersuaded by utilitarian arguments that weigh the social consequences of public policies. They regard the fetus no less than the woman as a patient to be helped, and they see fetal abuse as both a violation of rights and a cause of avoidable deaths and serious birth defects. These violations, they argue, are wrong irrespective of the consequences, and should be declared legal as well as moral wrongs. From their perspective, to prosecute a woman who abuses a fetus or to remove a child at birth from the woman's care is the least society can do to protect the fetus and the newborn from harm. Here we see again a conflict of rights, because defenders of pregnant women regard the control of women to protect fetuses as a denial of the woman's most fundamental civil rights.

The opening selection dealing with these issues — the U.S. Supreme Court opinion in *Automobile Workers* v. *Johnson Controls, Inc.*—illustrates one facet of these problems, and the one that has been most decisively handled in the courts. The problem in this case emerged in the 1980s, when it was reported in leading newspapers that fertile women workers were, in increasing numbers, electing to undergo voluntary sterilization rather than give up high-paying jobs involving exposure to chemicals that are potentially harmful to a developing fetus. This disclosure precipitated discussion of a new civil rights issue regarding whether a company is unjustifiably discriminating against a woman in order to protect her unborn child.

In *Johnson Controls*, a corporation's Fetal Protection Program held that women must be excluded unless they can prove sterility and that women of childbearing capacity would not be hired for positions that exposed them to unacceptable lead contamination or for positions from which they could transfer to such jobs. The reasons for corporate policies excluding women from hazardous workplaces is straightforward: Of the thousands of toxic substances listed by the National Institute of Occupational Safety and Health (NIOSH), over fifty are animal mutagens (that is, they cause chromosomal damage to either the ova or the sperm cells), and roughly five hundred are animal teratogens (that is, they can cause deformations in a developing fetus). Corporations sought to protect the fetus against these effects of chemicals in the workplace by banning pregnant and potentially pregnant women from jobs that used known mutagens and teratogens.

However, the Supreme Court found that employers cannot legally adopt "fetal protection policies" that exclude women of childbearing age from a hazardous workplace, because such policies involve illegal sex discrimination. Because of this decision most U.S. corporations no longer have policies to protect fetuses that involve the actual exclusion of women, although prior to 1990 policies of exclusion had been the industry standard. Instead, corporations now simply notify employees of potential harm. Many believe that these policies are inadequate to protect the fetus.

In a second, distinct legal opinion reprinted in this chapter, *Johnson* v. *State of Florida*, the District Court of Appeal, Fifth District, held that a young mother, Jennifer Johnson, was guilty of delivering cocaine to minors, because she gave birth to children whose blood contained cocaine. The court found that Johnson voluntarily took cocaine, knowing its dangers to the fetus.

The next two articles involve the most common and most publicized area of maternal—fetal conflict: forced cesarean sections. In the case of *In re A.C.*, a twenty-eight-year-old, terminally ill woman named Angela Carder was forced under court order to undergo a cesarean section in a failed attempt to save her twenty-six-and-a-half-week-old fetus. Her premature infant was born, but died within three hours. The patient had agreed to a cesarean at twenty-eight weeks, but not at twenty-six-and-a-half. The family wanted her to be allowed to die in peace, but the hospital had requested legal intervention, and a court allowed an emergency cesarean to be performed. Angela had expressly, but perhaps incompetently, refused to consent to the intervention. At the critical time of the decision in the case, testimony indicated that Angela was too heavily medicated to be able to respond to questions, and that the medication could not be reduced without threatening to reduce her survival time.

However, on April 26, 1990—in the opinion reprinted in this chapter—the District of Columbia Court of Appeals held the trial judge in error in authorizing the cesarean. The appellate court vacated the decision of the lower court, holding that there had been an incorrect weighing of Angela's interests against the state's interests in her fetus, and also an error in attempting to determine if Angela was competent. *In re A.C.* has been viewed as especially important because it breaks with a strong judicial trend of ordering women to submit to cesarean sections at the request of physicians. However, the court left unaddressed many questions about a woman's rights in pregnancy when her behavior presents substantial risk to the fetus.

In the final two selections in this section, Nancy Rhoden and Patricia King discuss various moral and legal problems of maternal—fetal relations. Rhoden takes the view that courts should not order cesarean deliveries against a woman's will even if the woman is acting in a morally improper way and there will be tragic consequences to the fetus. Patricia King intentionally avoids attempting to state and resolve these controversies in terms of whose *rights* should prevail. She chooses the categories of appropriate *relationships* and *obligations* instead, and then attempts to sidestep analysis in terms of conflict and legal constraints. She looks for essential moral obligations that a pregnant woman has to a fetus. But she also argues that recognition of these moral obligations does not warrant corresponding legal requirements that constrain the woman's choice.

These maternal—fetal conflicts present difficult choices for health care centers and clinicians. If both the woman and the fetus are patients, clinicians will have to decide in difficult circumstances who the primary patient is, and therefore whose rights have priority. "When does the fetus become a significant patient?" is a question that looks very much like the question "When does the fetus gain significant status?" Problems of ontological and moral status, then, underlie moral problems of maternal—fetal conflict no less than moral problems of abortion.

T. L. B.

JOHN T. NOONAN, JR.

An Almost Absolute Value in History

The most fundamental question involved in the long history of thought on abortion is: How do you determine the humanity of a being? To phrase the question that way is to put in comprehensive humanistic terms what the theologians either dealt with as an explicitly theological question under the heading of "ensoulment" or dealt with implicitly in their treatment of abortion. The Christian position as it originated did not depend on a narrow theological or philosophical concept. It had no relation to theories of infant baptism.[1] It appealed to no special theory of instantaneous ensoulment. It took the world's view on ensoulment as that view changed from Aristotle to Zacchia. There was, indeed, theological influence affecting the theory of ensoulment finally adopted, and, of course, ensoulment itself was a theological concept, so that the position was always explained in theological terms. But the theological notion of ensoulment could easily be translated into humanistic language by substituting "human" for "rational soul"; the problem of knowing when a man is a man is common to theology and humanism.

If one steps outside the specific categories used by the theologians, the answer they gave can be analyzed as a refusal to discriminate among human beings on the basis of their varying potentialities. Once conceived, the being was recognized as man because he had man's potential. The criterion for humanity, thus, was simple and all-embracing: if you are conceived by human parents, you are human.

The strength of this position may be tested by a review of some of the other distinctions offered in the contemporary controversy over legalizing abortion. Perhaps the most popular distinction is in terms of viability. Before an age of so many months, the fetus is not viable, that is, it cannot be removed from the mother's womb and live apart from her. To that extent, the life of the fetus is absolutely dependent on the life of the mother. This dependence is made the basis of denying recognition to its humanity.

There are difficulties with this distinction. One is that the perfection of artificial incubation may make the fetus viable at any time: it may be removed and artificially sustained. Experiments with animals already show that such a procedure is possible. This hypothetical extreme case relates to an actual difficulty: there is considerable elasticity to the idea of viability. Mere length of life is not an exact measure. The viability of the fetus depends on the extent of its anatomical and functional development. The weight and length of the fetus are better guides to the state of its development than age, but weight and length vary. Moreover, different racial groups have different ages at which their fetuses are viable. Some evidence, for example, suggests that Negro fetuses mature more quickly than white fetuses. If viability is the norm, the standard would vary with race and with many individual circumstances.

The most important objection to this approach is that dependence is not ended by viability. The fetus is still absolutely dependent on someone's care in order to continue existence; indeed a child of one or three or even five years of age is absolutely dependent on another's care for existence; uncared for, the older fetus

Reprinted by permission of the publishers from John T. Noonan, Jr., editor, *The Morality of Abortion: Legal and Historical Perspectives* (Cambridge, Mass.: Harvard University Press. Copyright ©1970 by the President and Fellows of Harvard College), pp. 51–59.

or the younger child will die as surely as the early fetus detached from the mother. The unsubstantial lessening in dependence at viability does not seem to signify any special acquisition of humanity.

A second distinction has been attempted in terms of experience. A being who has had experience, has lived and suffered, who possesses memories, is more human than one who has not. Humanity depends on formation by experience. The fetus is thus "unformed" in the most basic human sense.

This distinction is not serviceable for the embryo which is already experiencing and reacting. The embryo is responsive to touch after eight weeks and at least at that point is experiencing. At an earlier stage the zygote is certainly alive and responding to its environment. The distinction may also be challenged by the rare case where aphasia has erased adult memory: has it erased humanity? More fundamentally, this distinction leaves even the older fetus or the younger child to be treated as an unformed inhuman thing. Finally, it is not clear why experience as such confers humanity. It could be argued that certain central experiences such as loving or learning are necessary to make a man human. But then human beings who have failed to love or to learn might be excluded from the class called man.

A third distinction is made by appeal to the sentiments of adults. If a fetus dies, the grief of the parents is not the grief they would have for a living child. The fetus is an unnamed "it" till birth, and is not perceived as personality until at least the fourth month of existence when movements in the womb manifest a vigorous presence demanding joyful recognition by the parents.

Yet feeling is notoriously an unsure guide to the humanity of others. Many groups of humans have had difficulty in feeling that persons of another tongue, color, religion, sex, are as human as they. Apart from reactions to alien groups, we mourn the loss of a ten-year-old boy more than the loss of his one-day-old brother or his 90-year-old grandfather. The difference felt and the grief expressed vary with the potentialities extinguished, or the experience wiped out; they do not seem to point to any substantial difference in the humanity of baby, boy, or grandfather.

Distinctions are also made in terms of sensation by the parents. The embryo is felt within the womb only after about the fourth month. The embryo is seen only at birth. What can be neither seen nor felt is different from what is tangible. If the fetus cannot be seen or touched at all, it cannot be perceived as man.

Yet experience shows that sight is even more untrustworthy than feeling in determining humanity. By sight, color became an appropriate index for saying who was a man, and the evil of racial discrimination was given foundation. Nor can touch provide the test; a being confined by sickness, "out of touch" with others, does not thereby seem to lose his humanity. To the extent that touch still has appeal as a criterion, it appears to be a survival of the old English idea of "quickening"—a possible mistranslation of the Latin *animatus* used in the canon law. To that extent touch as a criterion seems to be dependent on the Aristotelian notion of ensoulment, and to fall when this notion is discarded.

Finally, a distinction is sought in social visibility. The fetus is not socially perceived as human. It cannot communicate with others. Thus, both subjectively and objectively, it is not a member of society. As moral rules are rules for the behavior of members of society to each other, they cannot be made for behavior toward what is not yet a member. Excluded from the society of men, the fetus is excluded from the humanity of men.[2]

By force of the argument from the consequences, this distinction is to be rejected. It is more subtle than that founded on an appeal to physical sensation, but it is equally dangerous in its implications. If humanity depends on social recognition, individuals or whole groups may be dehumanized by being denied any status in their society. Such a fate is fictionally portrayed in *1984* and has actually been the lot of many men in many societies. In the Roman empire, for example, condemnation to slavery meant the practical denial of most human rights; in the Chinese Communist world, landlords have been classified as enemies of the people and so treated as nonpersons by the state. Humanity does not depend on social recognition, though often the failure of society to recognize the prisoner, the alien, the heterodox as human has led to the destruction of human beings. Anyone conceived by a man and a woman is human. Recognition of this condition by society follows a real event in the objective order, however imperfect and halting the recognition. Any attempt to limit humanity to exclude some group runs the risk of furnishing authority and precedent for excluding other groups in the name of the consciousness or perception of the controlling group in the society.

A philosopher may reject the appeal to the humanity of the fetus because he views "humanity" as a secular view of the soul and because he doubts the existence of anything real and objective which can be identified as humanity. One answer to such a philosopher is to ask how he reasons about moral questions without supposing that there is a sense in which he and the others of whom he speaks are human. Whatever group is taken as the society which determines who may be killed is thereby taken as human. A second answer is to ask if he does not believe that there is a right and wrong way of deciding moral questions. If there is such a difference, experience may be appealed to: to decide who is human on the basis of the sentiment of a given society has led to consequences which rational men would characterize as monstrous.

The rejection of the attempted distinctions based on viability and visibility, experience and feeling, may be buttressed by the following considerations: Moral judgments often rest on distinctions, but if the distinctions are not to appear arbitrary *fiat*, they should relate to some real difference in probabilities. There is a kind of continuity in all life, but the earlier stages of the elements of human life possess tiny probabilities of development. Consider, for example, the spermatozoa in any normal ejaculate: There are about 200,000,000 in any single ejaculate, of which one has a chance of developing into a zygote. Consider the oocytes which may become ova: there are 100,000 to 1,000,000 oocytes in a female infant, of which a maximum of 390 are ovulated. But once spermatozoon and ovum meet and the conceptus is formed, such studies as have been made show that roughly in only 20 percent of the cases will spontaneous abortion occur. In other words, the chances are about 4 out of 5 that this new being will develop. At this stage in the life of the being there is a sharp shift in probabilities, an immense jump in potentialities. To make a distinction between the rights of spermatozoa and the rights of the fertilized ovum is to respond to an enormous shift in possibilities. For about twenty days after conception the egg may split to form twins or combine with another egg to form a chimera, but the probability of either event happening is very small.

It may be asked, What does a change in biological probabilities have to do with establishing humanity? The argument from probabilities is not aimed at establishing humanity but at establishing an objective discontinuity which may be taken into account in moral discourse. As life itself is a matter of probabilities, as most moral reasoning is an estimate of probabilities, so it seems in accord with the structure of reality and the nature of moral thought to found a moral judgment on the change in probabilities at conception. The appeal to probabilities is the most commonsensical of arguments; to a greater or smaller degree all of us base our actions on probabilities, and in morals, as in law, prudence and negligence are often measured by the account one has taken of the probabilities. If the chance is 200,000,000 to 1 that the movement in the bushes into which you shoot is a man's, I doubt if many persons would hold you careless in shooting; but if the chances are 4 out of 5 that the movement is a human being's, few would acquit you of blame. Would the argument be different if only one out of ten children conceived came to term? Of course this argument would be different. This argument is an appeal to probabilities that actually exist, not to any and all states of affairs which may be imagined.

The probabilities as they do exist do not show the humanity of the embryo in the sense of a demonstration in logic any more than the probabilities of the movement in the bush being a man demonstrate beyond all doubt that the being is a man. The appeal is a "buttressing" consideration, showing the plausibility of the standard adopted. The argument focuses on the decisional factor in any moral judgment and assumes that part of the business of a moralist is drawing lines. One evidence of the nonarbitrary character of the line drawn is the difference of probabilities on either side of it. If a spermatozoon is destroyed, one destroys a being which had a chance of far less than 1 in 200 million of developing into a reasoning being, possessed of the genetic code, a heart and other organs, and capable of pain. If a fetus is destroyed, one destroys a being already possessed of the genetic code, organs, and sensitivity to pain, and one which had an 80 percent chance of developing further into a baby outside the womb who, in time, would reason.

The positive argument for conception as the decisive moment of humanization is that at conception the new being receives the genetic code. It is this genetic information which determines his characteristics, which is the biological carrier of the possibility of human wisdom, which makes him a self-evolving being. A being with a human genetic code is man.

This review of current controversy over the humanity of the fetus emphasizes what a fundamental question the theologians resolved in asserting the inviolability of the fetus. To regard the fetus as possessed of equal rights with other humans was not, however, to decide every case where abortion might be employed. It did decide the case where the argument was that the fetus should be aborted for its own good. To say a being was human was to say it had a destiny to decide for itself which could not be taken from it by another man's decision. But human beings with equal rights often come in conflict with each other, and some decision must be made as to whose claims are to prevail. Cases of conflict involving the fetus are different only in two respects: the total inability of the fetus to speak for itself and the fact that the right of the fetus regularly at stake is the right to life itself.

The approach taken by the theologians to these conflicts was articulated in terms of "direct" and "indirect." Again, to look at what they were doing from outside their categories, they may be said to have been drawing lines or "balancing values." "Direct" and "indirect" are spatial metaphors; "line-drawing" is another. "To weigh" or "to balance" values is a metaphor of a more complicated mathematical sort hinting at the process which goes on in moral judgments. All the metaphors suggest that, in the moral judgments made, comparisons were necessary that no value completely controlled. The principle of double effect was no doctrine fallen from heaven, but a method of analysis appropriate where two relative values were being compared. In Catholic moral theology, as it developed, life even of the innocent was not taken as an absolute. Judgments on acts affecting life issued from a process of weighing. In the weighing, the fetus was always given a value greater than zero, always a value separate and independent from its parents. The valuation was crucial and fundamental in all Christian thought on the subject and marked it off from any approach which considered that only the parents' interests needed to be considered.

Even with the fetus weighed as human, one interest could be weighed as equal or superior: that of the mother in her own life. The casuists between 1450 and 1895 were willing to weigh this interest as superior. Since 1895, that interest was given decisive weight only in the two special cases of the cancerous uterus and the ectopic pregnancy. In both of these cases the fetus itself had little chance of survival even if the abortion were not performed. As the balance was once struck in favor of the mother whenever her life was endangered, it could be so struck again. The balance reached between 1895 and 1930 attempted prudentially and pastorally to forestall a multitude of exceptions for interests less than life.

The perception of the humanity of the fetus and the weighing of fetal rights against other human rights constituted the work of the moral analysts. But what spirit animated their abstract judgments? For the Christian community it was the injunction of Scripture to love your neighbor as yourself. The fetus as human was a neighbor; his life had parity with one's own. The commandment gave life to what otherwise would have been only rational calculation.

The commandment could be put in humanistic as well as theological terms: Do not injure your fellow man without reason. In these terms, once the humanity of the fetus is perceived, abortion is never right except in self-defense. When life must be taken to save life, reason alone cannot say that a mother must prefer a child's life to her own. With this exception, now of great rarity, abortion violates the rational humanist tenet of the equality of human lives.

For Christians the commandment to love had received a special imprint in that the exemplar proposed of love was the love of the Lord for his disciples. In the light given by this example, self-sacrifice carried to the point of death seemed in the extreme situations not without meaning. In the less extreme cases, preference for one's own interests to the life of another seemed to express cruelty or selfishness irreconcilable with the demands of love.

NOTES

1. According to Glanville Williams (*The Sanctity of Human Life supra* n. 169, at 193), "The historical reason for the Catholic objection to abortion is the same as for the Christian Church's historical opposition to infanticide: the horror of bringing about the death of an unbaptized child." This statement is made without any citation of evidence. As has been seen, desire to administer baptism could, in the Middle Ages, even be urged as a reason for procuring an abortion. It is highly regrettable that the American Law Institute was apparently misled by Williams' account and repeated after him the same baseless statement. See American Law Institute, *Model Penal Code: Tentative Draft No. 9* (1959), p. 148, n. 12.

2. . . . Thomas Aquinas gave an analogous reason against baptizing a fetus in the womb: "As long as it exists in the womb of the mother, it cannot be subject to the operation of the ministers of the Church as it is not known to men" (*In sententias Petri Lombardi* 4.6 1.1.2).

JUDITH JARVIS THOMSON

A Defense of Abortion[1]

Most opposition to abortion relies on the premise that the fetus is a human being, a person, from the moment of conception. The premise is argued for, but, as I think, not well. Take, for example, the most common argument. We are asked to notice that the development of a human being from conception through birth into childhood is continuous; then it is said that to draw a line, to choose a point in this development and say "before this point the thing is not a person, after this point it is a person" is to make an arbitrary choice, a choice for which in the nature of things no good reason can be given. It is concluded that the fetus is, or anyway that we had better say it is, a person from the moment of conception. But this conclusion does not follow. Similar things might be said about the development of an acorn into an oak tree, and it does not follow that acorns are oak trees, or that we had better say they are. Arguments of this form are sometimes called "slippery slope arguments"—the phrase is perhaps self-explanatory—and it is dismaying that opponents of abortion rely on them so heavily and uncritically.

I am inclined to agree, however, that the prospects for "drawing a line" in the development of the fetus look dim. I am inclined to think also that we shall probably have to agree that the fetus has already become a human person well before birth. Indeed, it comes as a surprise when one first learns how early in its life it begins to acquire human characteristics. By the tenth week, for example, it already has a face, arms and legs, fingers and toes; it has internal organs, and brain activity is detectable.[2] On the other hand, I think that the premise is false, that the fetus is not a person from the moment of conception. A newly fer-

tilized ovum, a newly implanted clump of cells, is no more a person than an acorn is an oak tree. But I shall not discuss any of this. For it seems to me to be of great interest to ask what happens if, for the sake of argument, we allow the premise. How, precisely, are we supposed to get from there to the conclusion that abortion is morally impermissible? Opponents of abortion commonly spend most of their time establishing that the fetus is a person, and hardly any time explaining the step from there to the impermissibility of abortion. Perhaps they think the step too simple and obvious to require much comment. Or perhaps instead they are simply being economical in argument. Many of those who defend abortion rely on the premise that the fetus is not a person, but only a bit of tissue that will become a person at birth; and why pay out more arguments than you have to? Whatever the explanation, I suggest that the step they take is neither easy nor obvious, that it calls for closer examination than it is commonly given, and that when we do give it this closer examination we shall feel inclined to reject it.

I propose, then, that we grant that the fetus is a person from the moment of conception. How does the argument go from here? Something like this, I take it. Every person has a right to life. So the fetus has a right to life. No doubt the mother has a right to decide what shall happen in and to her body; everyone would grant that. But surely a person's right to life is stronger and more stringent than the mother's right to decide what happens in and to her body, and so outweighs it. So the fetus may not be killed; an abortion may not be performed.

It sounds plausible. But now let me ask you to imagine this. You wake up in the morning and find yourself back to back in bed with an unconscious violinist. A famous unconscious violinist. He has been found to have a fatal kidney ailment, and the Society

Reprinted with permission of the publisher from *Philosophy and Public Affairs*, Vol. 1, No. 1 (1971), pp. 47–66. Copyright © 1971 by Princeton University Press.

of Music Lovers has canvassed all the available medical records and found that you alone have the right blood type to help. They have therefore kidnapped you, and last night the violinist's circulatory system was plugged into yours, so that your kidneys can be used to extract poisons from his blood as well as your own. The director of the hospital now tells you, "Look, we're sorry the Society of Music Lovers did this to you—we would never have permitted it if we had known. But still, they did it, and the violinist now is plugged into you. To unplug you would be to kill him. But never mind, it's only for nine months. By then he will have recovered from his ailment, and can safely be unplugged from you." Is it morally incumbent on you to accede to this situation? No doubt it would be very nice of you if you did, a great kindness. But do you *have* to accede to it? What if it were not nine months, but nine years? Or longer still? What if the director of the hospital says, "Tough luck, I agree, but you've now got to stay in bed, with the violinist plugged into you, for the rest of your life. Because remember this. All persons have a right to life, and violinists are persons. Granted you have a right to decide what happens in and to your body, but a person's right to life outweighs your right to decide what happens in and to your body. So you cannot ever be unplugged from him." I imagine you would regard this as outrageous, which suggests that something really is wrong with that plausible-sounding argument I mentioned a moment ago.

In this case, of course, you were kidnapped; you didn't volunteer for the operation that plugged the violinist into your kidneys. Can those who oppose abortion on the ground I mentioned make an exception for a pregnancy due to rape? Certainly. They can say that persons have a right to life only if they didn't come into existence because of rape; or they can say that all persons have a right to life, but that some have less of a right to life than others, in particular, that those who came into existence because of rape have less. But these statements have a rather unpleasant sound. Surely the question of whether you have a right to life at all, or how much of it you have, shouldn't turn on the question of whether or not you are the product of a rape. And in fact the people who oppose abortion on the ground I mentioned do not make this distinction, and hence do not make an exception in case of rape.

Nor do they make an exception for a case in which the mother has to spend the nine months of her pregnancy in bed. They would agree that would be a great pity, and hard on the mother; but all the same, all persons have a right to life, the fetus is a person, and so on. I suspect, in fact, that they would not make an exception for a case in which, miraculously enough, the pregnancy went on for nine years, or even the rest of the mother's life.

Some won't even make an exception for a case in which continuation of the pregnancy is likely to shorten the mother's life; they regard abortion as impermissible even to save the mother's life. Such cases are nowadays very rare, and many opponents of abortion do not accept this extreme view. All the same, it is a good place to begin: a number of points of interest come out in respect to it.

1. Let us call the view that abortion is impermissible even to save the mother's life "the extreme view." I want to suggest first that it does not issue from the argument I mentioned earlier without the addition of some fairly powerful premises. Suppose a woman has become pregnant, and now learns that she has a cardiac condition such that she will die if she carries the baby to term. What may be done for her? The fetus, being a person, has a right to life, but as the mother is a person too, so has she a right to life. Presumably they have an equal right to life. How is it supposed to come out that an abortion may not be performed? If mother and child have an equal right to life, shouldn't we perhaps flip a coin? Or should we add to the mother's right to life her right to decide what happens in and to her body, which everybody seems to be ready to grant—the sum of her rights now outweighing the fetus's right to life?

The most familiar argument here is the following. We are told that performing the abortion would be directly killing[3] the child, whereas doing nothing would not be killing the mother, but only letting her die. Moreover, in killing the child, one would be killing an innocent person, for the child has committed no crime, and is not aiming at his mother's death. And then there are a variety of ways in which this might be continued. (a) But as directly killing an innocent person is always and absolutely impermissible, an abortion may not be performed. Or, (b) as directly killing an innocent person is murder, and murder is always and absolutely impermissible, an abortion may not be performed.[4] Or, (c) as one's duty to refrain from directly killing an innocent person is more stringent than one's duty to keep a person from dying, an abortion may not be performed. Or, (d) if one's only options are directly killing an innocent person or letting a person die, one must prefer letting the person die, and thus an abortion may not be performed.[5]

Some people seem to have thought that these are not further premises which must be added if the conclusion is to be reached, but that they follow from the very fact that an innocent person has a right to life.[6] But this seems to me to be a mistake, and perhaps the simplest way to show this is to bring out that while we must certainly grant that innocent persons have a right to life, the theses in (a) through (d) are all false. Take (b), for example. If directly killing an innocent person is murder, and thus is impermissible, then the mother's directly killing the innocent person inside her is murder, and thus is impermissible. But it cannot seriously be thought to be murder if the mother performs an abortion on herself to save her life. It cannot seriously be said that she *must* refrain, that she *must* sit passively by and wait for her death. Let us look again at the case of you and the violinist. There you are, in bed with the violinist, and the director of the hospital says to you, "It's all most distressing, and I deeply sympathize, but you see this is putting an additional strain on your kidneys, and you'll be dead within the month. But you *have* to stay where you are all the same. Because unplugging you would be directly killing an innocent violinist, and that's murder, and that's impermissible." If anything in the world is true, it is that you do not commit murder, you do not do what is impermissible, if you reach around to your back and unplug yourself from that violinist to save your life.

The main focus of attention in writings on abortion has been on what a third party may or may not do in answer to a request from a woman for an abortion. This is in a way understandable. Things being as they are, there isn't much a woman can safely do to abort herself. So the question asked is what a third party may do, and what the mother may do, if it is mentioned at all, is deduced, almost as an afterthought, from what it is concluded that third parties may do. But it seems to me that to treat the matter in this way is to refuse to grant to the mother that very status of person which is so firmly insisted on for the fetus. For we cannot simply read off what a person may do from what a third party may do. Suppose you find yourself trapped in a tiny house with a growing child. I mean a very tiny house, and a rapidly growing child — you are already up against the wall of the house and in a few minutes you'll be crushed to death. The child on the other hand won't be crushed to death; if nothing is done to stop him from growing he'll be hurt, but in the end he'll simply burst open the house and walk out a free man. Now I could well understand it if a bystander were to say, "There's nothing we can do for you. We cannot choose between your life and his, we cannot be the ones to decide who is to live, we cannot intervene." But it cannot be concluded that you too can do nothing, that you cannot attack it to save your life. However innocent the child may be, you do not have to wait passively while it crushes you to death. Perhaps a pregnant woman is vaguely felt to have the status of house, to which we don't allow the right of self-defense. But if the woman houses the child, it should be remembered that she is a person who houses it.

I should perhaps stop to say explicitly that I am not claiming that people have a right to do anything whatever to save their lives. I think, rather, that there are drastic limits to the right of self-defense. If someone threatens you with death unless you torture someone else to death, I think you have not the right, even to save your life, to do so. But the case under consideration here is very different. In our case there are only two people involved, one whose life is threatened, and one who threatens it. Both are innocent: the one who is threatened is not threatened because of any fault, the one who threatens does not threaten because of any fault. For this reason we may feel that we bystanders cannot intervene. But the person threatened can.

In sum, a woman surely can defend her life against the threat to it posed by the unborn child, even if doing so involves its death. And this shows not merely that the theses in (a) through (d) are false; it shows also that the extreme view of abortion is false, and so we need not canvass any other possible ways of arriving at it from the argument I mentioned at the outset.

2. The extreme view could of course be weakened to say that while abortion is permissible to save the mother's life, it may not be performed by a third party, but only by the mother herself. But this cannot be right either. For what we have to keep in mind is that the mother and the unborn child are not like two tenants in a small house which has, by an unfortunate mistake, been rented to both: the mother *owns* the house. The fact that she does adds to the offensiveness of deducing that the mother can do nothing from the supposition that third parties can do nothing. But it does more than this: it casts a bright light on the supposition that third parties can do nothing. Certainly it

lets us see that a third party who says "I cannot choose between you" is fooling himself if he thinks this is impartiality. If Jones has found and fastened on a certain coat, which he needs to keep him from freezing, but which Smith also needs to keep him from freezing, then it is not impartiality that says "I cannot choose between you" when Smith owns the coat. Women have said again and again "This body is *my* body!" and they have reason to feel angry, reason to feel that it has been like shouting into the wind. Smith, after all, is hardly likely to bless us if we say to him, "Of course it's your coat, anybody would grant that it is. But no one may choose between you and Jones who is to have it."

We should really ask what it is that says "no one may choose" in the face of the fact that the body that houses the child is the mother's body. It may be simply a failure to appreciate this fact. But it may be something more interesting, namely, the sense that one has a right to refuse to lay hands on people, even where it would be just and fair to do so, even where justice seems to require that somebody do so. Thus justice might call for somebody to get Smith's coat back from Jones, and yet you have a right to refuse to be the one to lay hands on Jones, a right to refuse to do physical violence to him. This, I think, must be granted. But then what should be said is not "no one may choose," but only "*I* cannot choose," and indeed not even this, but "*I* will not *act*," leaving it open that somebody else can or should, and in particular that anyone in a position of authority, with the job of securing people's rights, both can and should. So this is no difficulty. I have not been arguing that any given third party must accede to the mother's request that he perform an abortion to save her life, but only that he may.

I suppose that in some views of human life the mother's body is only on loan to her, the loan not being one which gives her any prior claim to it. One who held this view might well think it impartiality to say "I cannot choose." But I shall simply ignore this possibility. My own view is that if a human being has any just, prior claim to anything at all, he has a just, prior claim to his own body. And perhaps this needn't be argued for here anyway, since, as I mentioned, the arguments against abortion we are looking at do grant that the woman has a right to decide what happens in and to her body.

But although they do grant it, I have tried to show that they do not take seriously what is done in granting it. I suggest the same thing will reappear even more clearly when we turn away from cases in which the mother's life is at stake, and attend, as I propose we now do, to the vastly more common cases in which a woman wants an abortion for some less weighty reason than preserving her own life.

3. Where the mother's life is not at stake, the argument I mentioned at the outset seems to have a much stronger pull. "Everyone has a right to life, so the unborn person has a right to life." And isn't the child's right to life weightier than anything other than the mother's own right to life, which she might put forward as ground for an abortion?

This argument treats the right to life as if it were unproblematic. It is not, and this seems to me to be precisely the source of the mistake.

For we should now, at long last, ask what it comes to, to have a right to life. In some views having a right to life includes having a right to be given at least the bare minimum one needs for continued life. But suppose that what in fact *is* the bare minimum a man needs for continued life is something he has no right at all to be given. If I am sick unto death, and the only thing that will save my life is the touch of Henry Fonda's cool hand on my fevered brow, then all the same, I have no right to be given the touch of Henry Fonda's cool hand on my fevered brow. It would be frightfully nice of him to fly in from the West Coast to provide it. It would be less nice, though no doubt well meant, if my friends flew out to the West Coast and carried Henry Fonda back with them. But I have no right at all against anybody that he should do this for me. Or again, to return to the story I told earlier, the fact that for continued life that violinist needs the continued use of your kidneys does not establish that he has a right to be given the continued use of your kidneys. He certainly has no right against you that *you* should give him continued use of your kidneys. For nobody has any right to use your kidneys unless you give him such a right; and nobody has the right against you that you shall give him this right—if you do allow him to go on using your kidneys, this is a kindness on your part, and not something he can claim from you as his due. Nor has he any right against anybody else that *they* should give him continued use of your kidneys. Certainly he had no right against the Society of Music Lovers that they should plug him into you in the first place. And if you now start to unplug yourself, having learned that you will otherwise have to spend nine years in bed with him, there is nobody in the world who must try to prevent you, in order to see to it that he is given something he has a right to be given.

Some people are rather stricter about the right to life. In their view, it does not include the right to be given anything, but amounts to, and only to, the right not to be killed by anybody. But here a related difficulty arises. If everybody is to refrain from killing that violinist, then everybody must refrain from doing a great many different sorts of things. Everybody must refrain from slitting his throat, everybody must refrain from shooting him—and everybody must refrain from unplugging you from him. But does he have a right against everybody that they shall refrain from unplugging you from him? To refrain from doing this is to allow him to continue to use your kidneys. It could be argued that he has a right against us that *we* should allow him to continue to use your kidneys. That is, while he had no right against us that we should give him the use of your kidneys, it might be argued that he anyway has a right against us that we shall not now intervene and deprive him of the use of your kidneys. I shall come back to third-party interventions later. But certainly the violinist has no right against you that *you* shall allow him to continue to use your kidneys. As I said, if you do allow him to use them, it is a kindness on your part, and not something you owe him.

The difficulty I point to here is not peculiar to the right to life. It reappears in connection with all the other natural rights; and it is something which an adequate account of rights must deal with. For present purposes it is enough just to draw attention to it. But I would stress that I am not arguing that people do not have a right to life—quite to the contrary, it seems to me that the primary control we must place on the acceptability of an account of rights is that it should turn out in that account to be a truth that all persons have a right to life. I am arguing only that having a right to life does not guarantee having either a right to be given the use of or a right to be allowed continued use of another person's body—even if one needs it for life itself. So the right to life will not serve the opponents of abortion in the very simple and clear way in which they seem to have thought it would.

4. There is another way to bring out the difficulty. In the most ordinary sort of case, to deprive someone of what he has a right to is to treat him unjustly. Sup-

pose a boy and his small brother are jointly given a box of chocolates for Christmas. If the older boy takes the box and refuses to give his brother any of the chocolates, he is unjust to him, for the brother has been given a right to half of them. But suppose that, having learned that otherwise it means nine years in bed with that violinist, you unplug yourself from him. You surely are not being unjust to him for you gave him no right to use your kidneys, and no one else can have given him any such right. But we have to notice that in unplugging yourself, you are killing him; and violinists, like everybody else, have a right to life, and thus in the view we were considering just now, the right not to be killed. So here you do what he supposedly has a right you shall not do, but you do not act unjustly to him in doing it.

The emendation which may be made at this point is this: the right to life consists not in the right not to be killed, but rather in the right not to be killed unjustly. This runs a risk of circularity, but never mind: it would enable us to square the fact that the violinist has a right to life with the fact that you do not act unjustly toward him in unplugging yourself, thereby killing him. For if you do not kill him unjustly, you do not violate his right to life, and so it is no wonder you do him no injustice.

But if this emendation is accepted, the gap in the argument against abortion stares us plainly in the face: It is by no means enough to show that the fetus is a person, and to remind us that all persons have a right to life—we need to be shown also that killing the fetus violates its right to life, i.e., that abortion is unjust killing. And is it?

I suppose we may take it as a datum that in a case of pregnancy due to rape the mother has not given the unborn person a right to the use of her body for food and shelter. Indeed, in what pregnancy could it be supposed that the mother has given the unborn person such a right? It is not as if there were unborn persons drifting about the world, to whom a woman who wants a child says "I invite you in."

But it might be argued that there are other ways one can have acquired a right to the use of another person's body than by having been invited to use it by that person. Suppose a woman voluntarily indulges in intercourse, knowing of the chance it will issue in pregnancy, and then she does become pregnant; is she not in part responsible for the presence, in fact the very existence, of the unborn person inside her? No doubt she did not invite it in. But doesn't her partial responsibility for its being there itself give it a right to the use of her body?[7] If so, then her aborting it would be more like the boy's taking away the chocolates, and less like your unplugging yourself from the violinist—doing so would be depriving it of what it does have a right to, and thus would be doing it an injustice.

And then, too, it might be asked whether or not she can kill it even to save her own life: If she voluntarily called it into existence, how can she now kill it, even in self-defense?

The first thing to be said about this is that it is something new. Opponents of abortion have been so concerned to make out the independence of the fetus, in order to establish that it has a right to life, just as its mother does, that they have tended to overlook the possible support they might gain from making out that the fetus is *dependent* on the mother, in order to establish that she has a special kind of responsibility for it, a responsibility that gives it rights against her which are not possessed by any independent person—such as an ailing violinist who is a stranger to her.

On the other hand, this argument would give the unborn person a right to its mother's body only if her pregnancy resulted from a voluntary act, undertaken in full knowledge of the chance a pregnancy might result from it. It would leave out entirely the unborn person whose existence is due to rape. Pending the availability of some further argument, then, we would be left with the conclusion that unborn persons whose existence is due to rape have no right to the use of their mothers' bodies, and thus that aborting them is not depriving them of anything they have a right to and hence is not unjust killing.

And we should also notice that it is not at all plain that this argument really does go even as far as it purports to. For there are cases and cases, and the details make a difference. If the room is stuffy, and I therefore open a window to air it, and a burglar climbs in, it would be absurd to say, "Ah, now he can stay, she's given him a right to the use of her house—for she is partially responsible for his presence there, having voluntarily done what enabled him to get in, in full knowledge that there are such things as burglars, and that burglars burgle." It would be still more absurd to say this if I had had bars installed outside my windows, precisely to prevent burglars from getting in, and a burglar got in only because of a defect in the bars. It remains equally absurd if we imagine it is not a burglar who climbs in, but an innocent person who blunders or falls in. Again, suppose it were like this: people-seeds drift about in the air like pollen, and if you open your windows, one may drift in and take root in your carpets or upholstery. You don't want children, so you fix up your windows with fine mesh screens, the very best you can buy. As can happen, however, and on very, very rare occasions does happen, one of the screens is defective; and a seed drifts in and takes root. Does the person-plant who now develops have a right to the use of your house? Surely not—despite the fact that you voluntarily opened your windows, you knowingly kept carpets and upholstered furniture, and you knew that screens were sometimes defective. Someone may argue that you are responsible for its rooting, that it does have a right to your house, because after all you *could* have lived out your life with bare floors and furniture, or with sealed windows and doors. But this won't do—for by the same token anyone can avoid a pregnancy due to rape by having a hysterectomy, or anyway by never leaving home without a (reliable!) army.

It seems to me that the argument we were looking at can establish at most that there are *some* cases in which the unborn person has a right to the use of its mother's body, and therefore *some* cases in which abortion is unjust killing. There is room for much discussion and argument as to precisely which, if any. But I think we should sidestep this issue and leave it open, for at any rate the argument certainly does not establish that all abortion is unjust killing.

5. There is room for yet another argument here, however. We surely must all grant that there may be cases in which it would be morally indecent to detach a person from your body at the cost of his life. Suppose you learn that what the violinist needs is not nine years of your life, but only one hour. All you need do to save his life is to spend one hour in that bed with him. Suppose also that letting him use your kidneys for that one hour would not affect your health in the slightest. Admittedly you were kidnapped. Admittedly you did not give anyone permission to plug him into you. Nevertheless it seems to me plain you *ought* to allow him to use your kidneys for that hour—it would be indecent to refuse.

Again, suppose pregnancy lasted only an hour, and constituted no threat to life or health. And suppose that a woman becomes pregnant as a result of rape. Admittedly she did not voluntarily do anything to bring about the existence of a child. Admittedly she did nothing at all which would give the unborn person a right to the use of her body. All the same it might well be said, as in the newly emended violinist story, that she *ought* to allow it to remain for that hour— that it would be indecent in her to refuse.

Now some people are inclined to use the term "right" in such a way that it follows from the fact that you ought to allow a person to use your body for the hour he needs, that he has a right to use your body for the hour he needs, even though he has not been given that right by any person or act. They may say that it follows also that if you refuse, you act unjustly toward him. This use of the term is perhaps so common that it cannot be called wrong; nevertheless it seems to me to be an unfortunate loosening of what we would do better to keep a tight rein on. Suppose that box of chocolates I mentioned earlier had not been given to both boys jointly, but was given only to the older boy. There he sits, stolidly eating his way through the box, his small brother watching enviously. Here we are likely to say "You ought not to be so mean. You ought to give your brother some of those chocolates." My own view is that it just does not follow from the truth of this that the brother has any right to any of the chocolates. If the boy refuses to give his brother any, he is greedy, stingy, callous—but not unjust. I suppose that the people I have in mind will say it does follow that the brother has a right to some of the chocolates, and thus that the boy does act unjustly if he refuses to give his brother any. But the effect of saying this is to obscure what we should keep distinct, namely the difference between the boy's refusal in this case and the boy's refusal in the earlier case, in which the box was given to both boys jointly, and in which the small brother thus had what was from any point of view clear title to half.

A further objection to so using the term "right" that from the fact that A ought to do a thing for B, it follows that B has a right against A that A do it for him, is that it is going to make the question of whether or not a man has a right to a thing turn on how easy it is to provide him with it; and this seems not merely unfortunate, but morally unacceptable. Take the case of Henry Fonda again. I said earlier that I had no right to the touch of his cool hand on my fevered brow, even though I needed it to save my life. I said it would be frightfully nice of him to fly in from the West Coast to provide me with it, but that I had no right against him that he should do so. But suppose he isn't on the West Coast. Suppose he has only to walk across the room, place a hand briefly on my brow—and lo, my life is saved. Then surely he ought to do it, it would be indecent to refuse. Is it to be said "Ah well, it follows that in this case she has a right to the touch of his hand on her brow, and so it would be an injustice in him to refuse"? So that I have a right to it when it is easy for him to provide it, though no right when it's hard? It's rather a shocking idea that anyone's right should fade away and disappear as it gets harder and harder to accord them to him.

So my own view is that even though you ought to let the violinist use your kidneys for the one hour he needs, we should not conclude that he has a right to do so—we would say that if you refuse, you are, like the boy who owns all the chocolates and will give none away, self-centered and callous, indecent in fact, but not unjust. And similarly, that even supposing a case in which a woman pregnant due to rape ought to allow the unborn person to use her body for the hour he needs, we should not conclude that he has a right to do so; we should conclude that she is self-centered, callous, indecent, but not unjust, if she refuses. The complaints are no less grave; they are just different. However, there is no need to insist on this point. If anyone does wish to deduce "he has a right" from "you ought," then all the same he must surely grant that there are cases in which it is not morally required of you that you allow that violinist to use your kidneys, and in which he does not have a right to use them, and in which you do not do him an injustice if you refuse. And so also for mother and unborn child. Except in such cases as the unborn person has a right to demand it—and we were leaving open the possibility that there may be such cases—nobody is morally *required* to make large sacrifices, of health, of all other interests and concerns, of all other duties and commitments, for nine years, or even for nine months, in order to keep another person alive.

6. We have in fact to distinguish between two kinds of Samaritan: the Good Samaritan and what we might call the Minimally Decent Samaritan. The story of the Good Samaritan, you will remember, goes like this:

A certain man went down from Jerusalem to Jericho, and fell among thieves, which stripped him of his raiment, and wounded him, and departed, leaving him half dead.

And by chance there came down a certain priest that way; and when he saw him, he passed by on the other side.

And likewise a Levite, when he was at the place, came and looked on him, and passed by on the other side.

But a certain Samaritan, as he journeyed, came where he was; and when he saw him he had compassion on him.

And went to him, and bound up his wounds, pouring in oil and wine, and set him on his own beast, and brought him to an inn, and took care of him.

And on the morrow, when he departed, he took out two pence, and gave them to the host, and said unto him, "Take care of him; and whatsoever thou spendest more, when I come again, I will repay thee."

(Luke 10:30–35)

The Good Samaritan went out of his way, at some cost to himself, to help one in need of it. We are not told what the options were, that is, whether or not the priest and the Levite could have helped by doing less than the Good Samaritan did, but assuming they could have, then the fact they did nothing at all shows they were not even Minimally Decent Samaritans, not because they were not Samaritans, but because they were not even minimally decent.

These things are a matter of degree, of course, but there is a difference, and it comes out perhaps most clearly in the story of Kitty Genovese, who, as you will remember, was murdered while thirty-eight people watched or listened, and did nothing at all to help her. A Good Samaritan would have rushed out to give direct assistance against the murderer. Or perhaps we had better allow that it would have been a Splendid Samaritan who did this, on the ground that it would have involved a risk of death for himself. But the thirty-eight not only did not do this, they did not even trouble to pick up a phone to call the police. Minimally Decent Samaritanism would call for doing at least that, and their not having done it was monstrous.

After telling the story of the Good Samaritan, Jesus said, "Go, and do thou likewise." Perhaps he meant that we are morally required to act as the Good Samaritan did. Perhaps he was urging people to do more than is morally required of them. At all events it seems plain that it was not morally required of any of the thirty-eight that he rush out to give direct assistance at the risk of his own life, and that it is not morally required of anyone that he give long stretches of his life—nine years or nine months—to sustaining the life of a person who has no special right (we were leaving open the possibility of this) to demand it.

Indeed, with one rather striking class of exceptions, no one in any country in the world is *legally* required to do anywhere near as much as this for anyone else. The class of exceptions is obvious. My main concern here is not the state of the law in respect to abortion, but it is worth drawing attention to the fact that in no state in this country is any man compelled by law to be even a Minimally Decent Samaritan to any person; there is no law under which charges could be brought against the thirty-eight who stood by while Kitty Genovese died. By contrast, in most states in this country women are compelled by law to be not merely Minimally Decent Samaritans, but Good Samaritans to unborn persons inside them. This doesn't by itself settle anything one way or the other, because it may well be argued that there should be laws in this country—as there are in many European countries—compelling at least Minimally Decent Samaritanism.[8] But it does show that there is a gross injustice in the existing state of the law. And it shows also that the groups currently working against liberalization of abortion laws, in fact working toward having it declared unconstitutional for a state to permit abortion, had better start working for the adoption of Good Samaritan laws generally, or earn the charge that they are acting in bad faith.

I should think, myself, that Minimally Decent Samaritan laws would be one thing, Good Samaritan laws quite another, and in fact highly improper. But we are not here concerned with the law. What we should ask is not whether anybody should be compelled by law to be a Good Samaritan, but whether we must accede to a situation in which somebody is being compelled—by nature, perhaps—to be a Good Samaritan. We have, in other words, to look now at third-party interventions. I have been arguing that no person is morally required to make large sacrifices to sustain the life of another who has no right to demand them, and this even where the sacrifices do not include life itself; we are not morally required to be Good Samaritans or anyway Very Good Samaritans to one another. But what if a man cannot extricate himself from such a situation? What if he appeals to us to extricate him? It seems to me plain that there are cases in which we can, cases in which a Good Samaritan would extricate him. There you are, you were kidnapped, and nine years in bed with that violinist lie ahead of you. You have your own life to lead. You are sorry, but you simply cannot see giving up so much of your life to the sustaining of his. You cannot extricate yourself, and ask us to do so. I should have thought that—in light of his having no right to the use of your body—it was obvious that we do not have to accede to your being forced to give up so much. We can do what you ask. There is no injustice to the violinist in our doing so.

7. Following the lead of the opponents of abortion, I have throughout been speaking of the fetus merely as a person, and what I have been asking is whether or not the argument we began with, which proceeds only from the fetus's being a person, really does establish its conclusion. I have argued that it does not.

But of course there are arguments and arguments, and it may be said that I have simply fastened on the wrong one. It may be said that what is important is not merely the fact that the fetus is a person, but that it is a person for whom the woman has a special kind of responsibility issuing from the fact that she is its mother. And it might be argued that all my analogies are therefore irrelevant—for you do not have that special kind of responsibility for that violinist, Henry Fonda does not have that special kind of responsibility for me. And our attention might be drawn to the fact that men and women both *are* compelled by law to provide support for their children.

I have in effect dealt (briefly) with this argument in section 4 above; but a (still briefer) recapitulation now may be in order. Surely we do not have any such "special responsibility" for a person unless we have assumed it, explicitly or implicitly. If a set of parents do not try to prevent pregnancy, do not obtain an abortion, and then at the time of birth of the child do not put it out for adoption, but rather take it home with them, then they have assumed responsibility for it, they have given it rights, and they cannot *now* withdraw support from it at the cost of its life because they now find it difficult to go on providing for it. But if they have taken all reasonable precautions against having a child, they do not simply by virtue of their biological relationship to the child who comes into existence have a special responsiblity for it. They may wish to assume responsibility for it, or they may not wish to. And I am suggesting that if assuming responsibility for it would require large sacrifices, then they may refuse. A good Samaritan would not refuse—or anyway, a Splendid Samaritan, if the sacrifices that had to be made were enormous. But then so would a Good Samaritan assume responsibility for that violinist; so would Henry Fonda, if he is a Good Samaritan, fly in from the West Coast and assume responsibility for me.

8. My argument will be found unsatisfactory on two counts by many of those who want to regard abortion as morally permissible. First, while I do argue that abortion is not impermissible, I do not argue that it is always permissible. There may well be cases in which carrying the child to term requires only Min-imally Decent Samaritanism of the mother, and this is a standard we must not fall below. I am inclined to think it a merit of my account precisely that it does *not* give a general yes or a general no. It allows for and supports our sense that, for example, a sick and desperately frightened fourteen-year-old schoolgirl, pregnant due to rape, may *of course* choose abortion, and that any law which rules this out is an insane law. And it also allows for and supports our sense that in other cases resort to abortion is even positively indecent. It would be indecent in the woman to request an abortion, and indecent in a doctor to perform it, if she is in her seventh month and wants the abortion just to avoid the nuisance of postponing a trip abroad. The very fact that the arguments I have been drawing attention to treat all cases of abortion, or even all cases of abortion in which the mother's life is not at stake, as morally on a par ought to have made them suspect at the outset.

Secondly, while I am arguing for the permissibility of abortion in some cases, I am not arguing for the right to secure the death of the unborn child. It is easy to confuse these two things in that up to a certain point in the life of the fetus it is not able to survive outside the mother's body; hence removing it from her body guarantees its death. But they are importantly different. I have argued that you are not morally required to spend nine months in bed, sustaining the life of that violinist; but to say this is by no means to say that if, when you unplug yourself, there is a miracle and he survives, you then have a right to turn around and slit his throat. You may detach yourself even if this costs him his life; you have no right to be guaranteed his death, by some other means, if unplugging yourself does not kill him. There are some people who will feel dissatisfied by this feature of my argument. A woman may be utterly devastated by the thought of a child, a bit of herself, put out for adoption and never seen or heard of again. She may therefore want not merely that the child be detached from her, but more, that it die. Some opponents of abortion are inclined to regard this as beneath contempt—thereby showing insensitivity to what is surely a powerful source of despair. All the same, I agree that the desire for the child's death is not one which anybody may gratify, should it turn out to be possible to detach the child alive.

At this place, however, it should be remembered that we have only been pretending throughout that the fetus is a human being from the moment of conception. A very early abortion is surely not the killing of a person, and so is not dealt with by anything I have said here.

NOTES

1. I am very much indebted to James Thomson for discussion, criticism, and many helpful suggestions.

2. Daniel Callahan, *Abortion: Law, Choice and Morality* (New York, 1970), p. 373. This book gives a fascinating survey of the available information on abortion. The Jewish tradition is surveyed in David M. Feldman, *Birth Control in Jewish Law* (New York, 1968), Part 5; the Catholic tradition in John T. Noonan, Jr., "An Almost Absolute Value in History," in *The Morality of Abortion,* ed. John T. Noonan, Jr. (Cambridge, Mass., 1970).

3. The term "direct" in the arguments I refer to is a technical one. Roughly, what is meant by "direct killing" is either killing as an end in itself, or killing as a means to some end, for example, the end of saving someone else's life. See note 6, below, for an example of its use.

4. Cf. *Encyclical Letter of Pope Pius XI on Christian Marriage,* St. Paul Editions (Boston, n.d.), p. 32: "however much we may pity the mother whose health and even life is gravely imperiled in the performance of the duty allotted to her by nature, nevertheless what could ever be a sufficient reason for excusing in any way the direct murder of the innocent? This is precisely what we are dealing with here." Noonan (*The Morality of Abortion,* p. 43) reads this as follows: "What cause can ever avail to excuse in any way the direct killing of the innocent? For it is a question of that."

5. The thesis in (d) is in an interesting way weaker than those in (a), (b), and they rule out abortion even in cases in which both mother *and* child will die if the abortion is not performed. By contrast, one who held the view expressed in (d) could consistently say that one needn't prefer letting two persons die to killing one.

6. Cf. the following passage from Pius XII, *Address to the Italian Catholic Society of Midwives:* "The baby in the maternal breast has the right to life immediately from God. — Hence there is no man, no human authority, no science, no medical eugenic, social, economic or moral 'indication' which can establish or grant a valid juridical ground for a direct deliberate disposition of an innocent human life, that is a disposition which looks to its destruction either as an end or as a means to another end perhaps in itself not illicit. — The baby, still not born, is a man in the same degree and for the same reason as the mother" (quoted in Noonan, *The Morality of Abortion,* p. 45).

7. The need for a discussion of this argument was brought home to me by members of the Society for Ethical and Legal Philosophy, to whom this paper was originally presented.

8. For a discussion of the difficulties involved, and a survey of the European experience with such laws, see *The Good Samaritan and the Law,* ed. James M. Ratcliffe (New York, 1966).

BARUCH BRODY

The Morality of Abortion

THE WOMAN'S RIGHT TO HER BODY

It is a common claim that a woman ought to be in control of what happens to her body to the greatest extent possible, that she ought to be able to use her body in ways that she wants to and refrain from using it in ways that she does not want to. This right is particularly pressed where certain uses of her body have deep and lasting effects upon the character of her life, personal, social, and economic. Therefore, it is argued, a

From *Abortion and the Sanctity of Human Life: A Philosophical View* (Cambridge, Mass.: MIT Press, 1975), pp. 26–32, 37–39, 44–47, 123–129, 131, and "Fetal Humanity and the Theory of Essentialism," in *Philosophy and Sex,* Robert Baker and Frederick Elliston, eds. (Buffalo, N.Y.: Prometheus Books, 1975), pp. 348–352. (Some parts of these essays were later revised by Professor Brody.) Reprinted by permission.

woman should be free either to carry her fetus to term, thereby using her body to support it, or to abort the fetus, thereby not using her body for that purpose.

In some contexts in which this argument is advanced, it is clear that it is not addressed to the issue of the morality of abortion at all. Rather, it is made in opposition to laws against abortion on the ground that the choice to abort or not is a moral decision that should belong only to the mother. But that specific direction of the argument is irrelevant to our present purposes; I will consider it [later] when I deal with the issues raised by laws prohibiting abortions. For the moment, I am concerned solely with the use of this principle as a putative ground tending to show the permissibility of abortion, with the claim that because it is the woman's body that carries the fetus and upon which the fetus depends, she has certain rights to abort the fetus that no one else may have.

We may begin by remarking that it is obviously correct that, as carrier of the fetus, the mother has it within her power to choose whether or not to abort the fetus. And, as an autonomous and responsible agent, she must make this choice. But let us notice that this in no way entails either that whatever choice she makes is morally right or that no one else has the right to evaluate the decision that she makes.

● ● ●

At first glance, it would seem that this argument cannot be used by anyone who supposes, as we do for the moment, that there is a point in fetal development from which time on the fetus is a human being. After all, people do not have the right to do anything whatsoever that may be necessary for them to retain control over the uses of their bodies. In particular, it would seem wrong for them to kill another human being in order to do so.

In a recent article,[1] Professor Judith Thomson has, in effect, argued that this simple view is mistaken. How does Professor Thomson defend her claim that the mother has a right to abort the fetus, even if it is a human being, whether or not her life is threatened and whether or not she has consented to the act of intercourse in which the fetus is conceived? At one point,[2] discussing just the case in which the mother's life is threatened, she makes the following suggestion:

In [abortion], there are only two people involved, one whose life is threatened and one who threatens it. Both are innocent: the one who is threatened is not threatened because of any fault, the one who threatens does not threaten because of any fault. For this reason, we may feel that we bystanders cannot intervene. But the person threatened can.

But surely this description is equally applicable to the following case: A and B are adrift on a lifeboat, B has a disease that he can survive, but A, if he contracts it, will die, and the only way that A can avoid that is by killing B and pushing him overboard. Surely, A has no right to do this. So there must be some special reason why the mother has, if she does, the right to abort the fetus.

There is, to be sure, an important difference between our lifeboat case and abortion, one that leads us to the heart of Professor Thomson's argument. In the case that we envisaged, both A and B have equal rights to be in the lifeboat, but the mother's body is hers and not the fetus's and she has first rights to its use. The primacy of these rights allows an abortion whether or not her life is threatened. Professor Thomson summarizes this argument in the following way:[3]

I am arguing only that having a right to life does not guarantee having either a right to be given the use of, or a right to be allowed continued use of, another person's body—even if one needs it for life itself.

One part of this claim is clearly correct. I have no duty to X to save X's life by giving him the use of my body (or my life savings, or the only home I have, and so on), and X has no right, even to save his life, to any of those things. Thus, the fetus conceived in the laboratory that will perish unless it is implanted into a woman's body has in fact no right to any woman's body. But this portion of the claim is irrelevant to the abortion issue, for in abortion of the fetus that is a human being the mother must kill X to get back the sole use of her body, and that is an entirely different matter.

This point can also be put as follows: . . . we must distinguish the taking of X's life from the saving of X's life, even if we assume that one has a duty not to do the former and to do the latter. Now that latter duty, if it exists at all, is much weaker than the first duty; many circumstances may relieve us from the latter duty that will not relieve us from the former one. Thus, I am certainly relieved from my duty to save X's life by the fact that fulfilling it means the loss of my life savings. It may be noble for me to save X's life at the cost of everything I have, but I certainly have no duty to do that. And the same observation may be made about cases in which I can save X's life by giving him the use of my body for an extended period of time. However, I am not relieved of my duty not to take X's life by the fact that fulfilling it means the loss of everything I have and not even by the fact that fulfilling it means the loss of my life. . . .

At one point in her paper, Professor Thomson does consider this objection. She has previously imagined the following case: a famous violinist, who is dying from a kidney ailment, has been, without your consent, plugged into you for a period of time so that his body can use your kidneys:

Some people are rather stricter about the right to life. In their view, it does not include the right to be given anything, but amounts to, and only to, the right not to be killed by anybody. But here a related difficulty arises. If everybody is to refrain from killing that violinist, then everybody must refrain from doing a great many different sorts of things . . . everybody must refrain from unplugging you from him. But does he have a right against everybody that they shall refrain from unplugging you from him? To refrain from doing this is to allow him to continue to use your kidneys . . . certainly the violinist has no right against you that you shall allow him to continue to use your kidneys.

Applying this argument to the case of abortion, we can see that Professor Thomson's argument would run as follows:

a. Assume that the fetus's right to life includes the right not to be killed by the woman carrying him.
b. But to refrain from killing the fetus is to allow him the continued use of the woman's body.
c. So our first assumption entails that the fetus's right to life includes the right to the continued use of the woman's body.
d. But we all grant that the fetus does not have the right to the continued use of the woman's body.
e. Therefore, the fetus's right to life cannot include the right not to be killed by the woman in question.

And it is also now clear what is wrong with this argument. When we granted that the fetus has no right to the continued use of the woman's body, all that we meant was that he does not have this right merely because the continued use saves his life. But, of course, there may be other reasons why he has this right. One would be that the only way to take the use of the woman's body away from the fetus is by killing him, and that is something that neither she nor we have the right to do. So, I submit, the way in which Assumption d is true is irrelevant, and cannot be used by Professor Thomson, for Assumption d is true only in cases where the saving of the life of the fetus is at stake and not in cases where the taking of his life is at stake.

I conclude therefore that Professor Thomson has not established the truth of her claims about abortion, primarily because she has not sufficiently attended to the distinction between our duty to save X's life and our duty not to take it. Once one attends to that distinction, it would seem that the mother, in order to regain control over her body, has no right to abort the fetus from the point at which it becomes a human being.

It may also be useful to say a few words about the larger and less rigorous context of the argument that the woman has a right to her own body. It is surely true that one way in which women have been oppressed is by their being denied authority over their own bodies. But it seems to me that, as the struggle is carried on for meaningful amelioration of such oppression, it ought not to be carried so far that it violates the steady responsibilities all people have to one another. Parents may not desert their children, one class may not oppress another, one race or nation may not exploit another. For parents, powerful groups in society, races or nations in ascendancy, there are penalties for refraining from these wrong actions, but those penalties can in no way be taken as the justification for such wrong actions. Similarly, if the fetus is a human being, the penalty of carrying it cannot, I believe, be used as the justification for destroying it.

• • •

THE MODEL PENAL CODE CASES

All of the arguments that we have looked at so far are attempts to show that there is something special about abortion that justifies its being treated differently from other cases of the taking of human life. We shall now consider claims that are confined to certain special cases of abortion: the case in which the mother has been raped, the case in which bearing the child would be harmful to her health, and the case in which having the child may cause a problem for the rest of her family (the latter case is a particular case of the societal argument). In addressing these issues, we shall see whether there is any point to the permissibility of abortions in some of the cases covered by the Model Penal Code[4] proposals.

When the expectant mother has conceived after being raped, there are two different sorts of considerations that might support the claim that she has the right to take the life of the fetus. They are the following: (A) the woman in question has already suffered immensely from the act of rape and the physical and/or psychological aftereffects of that act. It would be particularly unjust, the argument runs, for her to have to live through an unwanted pregnancy owing to that act of rape. Therefore, even if we are at a stage at which the fetus is a human being, the mother has the right to abort it; (B) the fetus in question has no right to be in that woman. It was put there as a result of an act of aggression upon her by the rapist, and its continued presence is an act of aggression against the mother. She has a right to repel that aggression by aborting the fetus.

The first argument is very compelling. We can all agree that a terrible injustice has been committed on the woman who is raped. The question that we have to consider, however, is whether it follows that it is morally permissible for her to abort the fetus. We must make that consideration reflecting that, however unjust the act of rape, it was not the fetus who committed or commissioned it. The injustice of the act, then, should in no way impinge upon the rights of the fetus, for it is innocent. What remains is the initial misfortune of the mother (and the injustice of her having to pass through the pregnancy, and, further, to assume responsibility of at least giving the child over for adoption or assuming the burden of its care). However unfortunate that circumstance, however unjust, the misfortune and the injustice are not sufficient cause to justify the taking of the life of an innocent human being as a means of mitigation.

It is at this point that Argument B comes in, for its whole point is that the fetus, by its mere presence in the mother, is committing an act of aggression against her, one over and above the one committed by the rapist, and one that the mother has a right to repel by abortion. But . . . (1) the fetus is certainly innocent (in the sense of not responsible) for any act of aggression against the mother and . . . (2) the mere presence of the fetus in the mother, no matter how unfortunate for her, does not constitute an act of aggression by the fetus against the mother. Argument B fails then at just that point at which Argument A needs its support, and we can therefore conclude that the fact that pregnancy

is the result of rape does not give the mother the right to abort the fetus.

We turn next to the case in which the continued existence of the fetus would threaten the mental and/or physical health but not necessarily the life of the mother. Again, . . . the fact that the fetus's continued existence poses a threat to the life of the mother does not justify her aborting it.* It would seem to be true, a fortiori, that the fact that the fetus's continued existence poses a threat to the mental and/or physical health of the mother does not justify her aborting it either.

We come finally to those cases in which the continuation of the pregnancy would cause serious problems for the rest of the family. There are a variety of cases that we have to consider here together. Perhaps the health of the mother will be affected in such a way that she cannot function effectively as a wife and mother during, or even after, the pregnancy. Or perhaps the expenses incurred as a result of the pregnancy would be utterly beyond the financial resources of the family. The important point is that the continuation of the pregnancy raises a serious problem for other innocent people involved besides the mother and the fetus, and it may be argued that the mother has the right to abort the fetus to avoid that problem.

By now, the difficulties with this argument should be apparent. We have seen earlier that the mere fact that the continued existence of the fetus threatens to harm the mother does not, by itself, justify the aborting of the fetus. Why should anything be changed by the fact that the threatened harm will accrue to the other members of the family and not to the mother? Of course, it would be different if the fetus were committing an act of aggression against the other members of the family. But, once more, this is certainly not the case.

We conclude, therefore, that none of these special circumstances justifies an abortion from that point at which the fetus is a human being.

• • •

FETAL HUMANITY AND BRAIN FUNCTION

The question which we must now consider is the question of fetal humanity. Some have argued that the fetus is a human being with a right to life (or, for convenience, just a human being) from the moment of conception. Others have argued that the fetus

*Ed. note: Professor Brody provided a lengthy argument to this effect in a chapter not here excerpted. His summary of that argument is as follows: "Is it permissible, as an act of killing a pursuer, to abort the fetus in order to save the mother? The first thing that we should note is that Pope Pius's objection to aborting the fetus as a permissible act of killing a pursuer is mistaken. His objection is that the fetus shows no knowledge or intention in his attempt to take the life of the mother, that the fetus is, in a word, innocent. But that only means that the condition of guilt is not satisfied, and we have seen that its satisfaction is not necessary.

"Is, then, the aborting of the fetus, when necessary to save the life of the mother, a permissible act of killing a pursuer? It is true that in such cases the fetus is a danger to the mother. But it is also clear that the condition of attempt is not satisfied. The fetus has neither the beliefs nor the intention to which we have referred. Furthermore, there is on the part of the fetus no action that threatens the life of the mother. So not even the condition of action is satisfied. It seems to follow, therefore, that aborting the fetus could not be a permissible act of killing a pursuer."

only becomes a human being at the moment of birth. Many positions in between these two extremes have also been suggested. How are we to decide which is correct?

The analysis which we will propose here rests upon certain metaphysical assumptions which I have defended elsewhere. These assumptions are: (a) the question is when has the fetus acquired all the properties essential (necessary) for being a human being, for when it has, it is a human being; (b) these properties are such that the loss of any one of them means that the human being in question has gone out of existence and not merely stopped being a human being; (c) human beings go out of existence when they die. It follows from these assumptions that the fetus becomes a human being when it acquires all those characteristics which are such that the loss of any one of them would result in the fetus's being dead. We must, therefore, turn to the analysis of death.

• • •

We will first consider the question of what properties are essential to being human if we suppose that death and the passing out of existence occur only if there has been an irreparable cessation of brain function (keeping in mind that that condition itself, as we have noted, is a matter of medical judgment). We shall then consider the same question on the supposition that [Paul] Ramsey's more complicated theory of death (the modified traditional view) is correct.

According to what is called the brain-death theory, as long as there has not been an irreparable cessation of brain function the person in question continues to exist, no matter what else has happened to him. If so, it seems to follow that there is only one property—leaving aside those entailed by this one property—that is essential to humanity, namely, the possession of a brain that has not suffered an irreparable cessation of function.

Several consequences follow immediately from this conclusion. We can see that a variety of often advanced claims about the essence of humanity are false. For example, the claim that movement, or perhaps just the ability to move, is essential for being human is false. A human being who has stopped moving, and even one who has lost the ability to move, has not therefore stopped existing. Being able to move, and a fortiori moving, are not essential properties of human beings and therefore are not essential to

being human. Similarly, the claim that being perceivable by other human beings is essential for being human is also false. A human being who has stopped being perceivable by other humans (for example, someone isolated on the other side of the moon, out of reach even of radio communication) has not stopped existing. Being perceivable by other human beings is not an essential property of human beings and is not essential to being human. And the same point can be made about the claims that viability is essential for being human, that independent existence is essential for being human, and that actual interaction with other human beings is essential for being human. The loss of any of these properties would not mean that the human being in question had gone out of existence, so none of them can be essential to that human being and none of them can be essential for being human.

Let us now look at the following argument: (1) A functioning brain (or at least, a brain that, if not functioning, is susceptible of function) is a property that every human being must have because it is essential for being human. (2) By the time an entity acquires that property, it has all the other properties that are essential for being human. Therefore, when the fetus acquires that property it becomes a human being. It is clear that the property in question is, according to the brain-death theory, one that is had essentially by all human beings. The question that we have to consider is whether the second premise is true. It might appear that its truth does follow from the brain-death theory. After all, we did see that the theory entails that only one property (together with those entailed by it) is essential for being human. Nevertheless, rather than relying solely on my earlier argument, I shall adopt an alternative approach to strengthen the conviction that this second premise is true: I shall note the important ways in which the fetus resembles and differs from an ordinary human being by the time it definitely has a functioning brain (about the end of the sixth week of development). It shall then be evident, in light of our theory of essentialism, that none of these differences involves the lack of some property in the fetus that is essential for its being human.

Structurally, there are few features of the human being that are not fully present by the end of the sixth week. Not only are the familiar external features and all the internal organs present, but the contours of the body are nicely rounded. More important, the body is functioning. Not only is the brain functioning, but the heart is beating sturdily (the fetus by this time has its own completely developed vascular system), the stomach is producing digestive juices, the liver is manufacturing blood cells, the kidney is extracting uric acid from the blood, and the nerves and muscles are operating in concert, so that reflex reactions can begin.

What are the properties that a fetus acquires after the sixth week of its development? Certain structures do appear later. These include the fingernails (which appear in the third month), the completed vocal chords (which also appear then), taste buds and salivary glands (again, in the third month), and hair and eyelashes (in the fifth month). In addition, certain functions begin later than the sixth week. The fetus begins to urinate (in the third month), to move spontaneously (in the third month), to respond to external stimuli (at least in the fifth month), and to breathe (in the sixth month). Moreover, there is a constant growth in size. And finally, at the time of birth the fetus ceases to receive its oxygen and food through the placenta and starts receiving them through the mouth and nose.

I will not examine each of these properties (structures and functions) to show that they are not essential for being human. The procedure would be essentially the one used previously to show that various essentialist claims are in error. We might, therefore, conclude, on the supposition that the brain-death theory is correct, that the fetus becomes a human being about the end of the sixth week after its development.

There is, however, one complication that should be noted here. There are, after all, progressive stages in the physical development and in the functioning of the brain. For example, the fetal brain (and nervous system) does not develop sufficiently to support spontaneous motion until some time in the third month after conception. There is, of course, no doubt that that stage of development is sufficient for the fetus to be human. No one would be likely to maintain that a spontaneously moving human being has died; and similarly, a spontaneously moving fetus would seem to have become human. One might, however, want to claim that the fetus does not become a human being until the point of spontaneous movement. So then, on the supposition that the brain-death theory of death is correct, one ought to conclude that the fetus becomes a human being at some time between the sixth and twelfth week after its conception.

But what if we reject the brain-death theory, and replace it with its equally plausible contender, Ramsey's theory of death? According to that theory— which we can call the brain, heart, and lung theory of

death—the human being does not die, does not go out of existence, until such time as the brain, heart and lungs have irreparably ceased functioning naturally. What are the essential features of being human according to this theory?

Actually, the adoption of Ramsey's theory requires no major modifications. According to that theory, what is essential to being human, what each human being must retain if he is to continue to exist, is the possession of a functioning (actually or potentially) heart, lung, or brain. It is only when a human being possesses none of these that he dies and goes out of existence; and the fetus comes into humanity, so to speak, when he acquires one of these.

On Ramsey's theory, the argument would now run as follows: (1) The property of having a functioning brain, heart, or lungs (or at least organs of the kind that, if not functioning, are susceptible of function) is one that every human being must have because it is essential for being human. (2) By the time that an entity acquires that property it has all the other properties that are essential for being human. Therefore, when the fetus acquires that property it becomes a human being. There remains, once more, the problem of the second premise. Since the fetal heart starts operating rather early, it is not clear that the second premise is correct. Many systems are not yet operating, and many structures are not yet present. Still, following our theory of essentialism, we should conclude that the fetus becomes a human being when it acquires a functioning heart (the first of the organs to function in the fetus).

There is, however, a further complication here, and it is analogous to the one encountered if we adopt the brain-death theory: When may we properly say that the fetal heart begins to function? At two weeks, when occasional contractions of the primitive fetal heart are present? In the fourth to fifth week, when the heart, although incomplete, is beating regularly and pumping blood cells through a closed vascular system, and when the tracings obtained by an ECG exhibit the classical elements of an adult tracing? Or after the end of the seventh week, when the fetal heart is functionally complete and "normal"?

We have not reached a precise conclusion in our study of the question of when the fetus becomes a human being. We do know that it does so some time between the end of the second week and the end of the third month. But it surely is not a human being at the moment of conception and it surely is one by the end of the third month. Though we have not come to a final answer to our question, we have narrowed the range of acceptable answers considerably.

[In summary] we have argued that the fetus becomes a human being with a right to life some time between the second and twelfth week after conception. We have also argued that abortions are morally impermissible after that point except in rather unusual circumstances. What is crucial to note is that neither of these arguments appeal to any theological considerations. We conclude, therefore, that there is a human-rights basis for moral opposition to abortions.

. . .

LAW AND SOCIETY IN A DEMOCRACY

Before turning to such considerations, however, we must first examine several important assertions about law and society that, if true, would justify the joint assertion of the principles that abortion is murder but nevertheless should be or remain legal. The first is the assertion that citizens of a pluralistic society must forgo the use of the law as a method of enforcing what are their private moralities. It might well be argued that in our pluralistic society, in which there are serious disagreements about the status of the fetus and about the rightness and wrongness of abortion in consequence, it would be wrong (or inappropriate) to legislate against abortion.

Such assertions about a pluralistic society are difficult to evaluate because of their imprecision. So let us first try to formulate some version of them more carefully. Consider the following general principle: Principle [1]. When the citizens of a society strongly disagree about the rightness and wrongness of a given action, and a considerable number think that such an action is right (or, at least, permissible), then it is wrong (or inappropriate) for that society to prohibit that action by law, even if the majority of citizens believe such an action to be wrong.

There are a variety of arguments that can be offered in support of the principle. One appeals to the right of the minority to follow its own conscience rather than being compelled to follow the conscience of the majority. That right has a theoretical political justification, but it also is practically implicit in the inappropriateness in the members of the majority imposing this kind of enforcement upon the minority that would be opposed were they the minority and were the enforcement being imposed upon them. Another argument appeals to the detrimental consequences to a society of the sense on the part of a significant minority that the law is being used by the majority to coerce. Such considerations make it seem that a principle like [1] is true.

If Principle [1] is true, it is easy to offer a defense of the joint assertion of the principles that abortion is murder but nevertheless should be or remain legal. All we need are the additional obvious assumptions that the citizens of our society strongly disagree about the morality of abortion and that at least a significant minority of individuals believe that there are many cases in which abortion is permissible. From these assumptions and Principle [1] it follows that abortions should be or remain legal even if they are murders.

The trouble with this argument is that it depends upon Principle [1]. I agree that, because of the considerations mentioned already, something like Principle [1] must be true. But Principle [1] as formulated is much too broad to be defensible. Consider, after all, a society in which a significant number of citizens think that it is morally permissible, and perhaps even obligatory, to kill Blacks or Jews, for example, because they are seen as being something less than fully human. It would seem to follow from Principle [1] that the law should not prohibit such actions. Surely this consequence of Principle [1] is wrong. Even if a pluralistic society should forgo passing many laws out of deference to the views of those who think that the actions that would thereby be prevented are not wrong, there remain some cases in which the force of the law should be applied because of the evil of the actions it is intended to prevent. If such actions produce very harmful results and infringe upon the rights of a sufficiently large number of individuals, then the possible benefits that may be derived from passing and enforcing a law preventing those actions may well override the rights of the minority (or even of the majority) to follow its conscience.

Principle [1] must therefore be modified as follows: Principle [2]. When the citizens of a society strongly disagree about the rightness and wrongness of a given action, and a considerable number think that such an action is right (or, at least, permissible), then it is wrong (or inappropriate) for that society to prohibit that action by law, even if the majority of citizens believe such an action to be wrong, unless the action in question is so evil that the desirability of legal prohibition outweighs the desirability of granting to the minority the right to follow its own conscience.

Principle [2] is, of course, rather vague. In particular, its last clause needs further clarification. But Principle [2] is clear enough for us to see that it cannot be used to justify the joint assertibility of the principles that abortion is murder but should nevertheless be or remain legal. Principle [2], conjoined with the obvious truths that the citizens of our society strongly disagree about the rightness and wrongness of abortion and that a significant number of citizens believe that, in certain circumstances, the right (or, at least, a permissible) thing to do is to have an abortion, does not yield the conclusion that abortion should be or remain legal if abortion is murder. After all, if abortion is murder, then the action in question is the unjustifiable taking of a human life and may well fall under the last clause of Principle [2]. The destruction of a fetus may not be unlike the killing of a Black or Jew. They may all be cases of the unjust taking of a human life.

• • •

THE DECISION IN *ROE* V. *WADE*

Two decisions were announced by the [United States Supreme] Court on January 22 [1973]. The first (*Roe v. Wade*) involved a challenge to a Texas law prohibiting all abortions not necessary to save the life of the mother. The second (*Doe v. Bolton*) tested a Georgia law incorporating many of the recommendations of the Model Penal Code as to the circumstances under which abortion should be allowed (in the case of rape and of a defective fetus, as well as when the pregnancy threatens the life or health of the mother), together with provisions regulating the place where abortions can be performed, the number of doctors that must concur, and other factors.

Of these two decisions, the more fundamental was *Roe v. Wade*. It was in this case that the Court came to grips with the central legal issue, namely, the extent to which it is legitimate for the state to prohibit or regulate abortion. In *Doe v. Bolton*, the Court was more concerned with subsidiary issues involving the legitimacy of particular types of regulations.

The Court summarized its decision in *Roe v. Wade* as follows:[5]

(a) For the stage prior to approximately the end of the first trimester/three months the abortion decision and its effectuation must be left to the medical judgment of the pregnant woman's attending physician.

(b) For the stage subsequent to approximately the end of the first trimester, the state, in promoting its interest in the health of the mother, may, if it chooses, regulate the abortion procedure in ways that are reasonably related to maternal health.

(c) For the stage subsequent to viability, the state, in promoting its interest in the potentiality of human life, may, if it chooses, regulate, and even proscribe, abortion except where it is necessary, in appropriate medical judgment, for the preservation of the life or health of the mother.

In short, the Court ruled that abortion can be prohibited only after viability and then only if the life or health of the mother is not threatened. Before viability, abortions cannot be prohibited, but they can be regulated after the first trimester if the regulations are reasonably related to maternal health. This last clause is taken very seriously by the Court. In *Doe v. Bolton*, instances of regulation in the Georgia code were found unconstitutional on the ground that they were not reasonably related to maternal health.

How did the Court arrive at this decision? In Sections V and VII of the decision, it set out the claims on both sides. Jane Roe's argument was summarized in these words:[6]

The principal thrust of appellant's attack on the Texas statutes is that they improperly invade a right, said to be possessed by the pregnant woman, to choose to determine her pregnancy.

On the other hand, the Court saw as possible legitimate interests of the state the regulation of abortion, like other medical procedures, so as to ensure maximum safety for the patient and the protection of prenatal life. At this point in the decision, the Court added the following very significant remark:[7]

Logically, of course, a legitimate state interest in this area need not stand or fall on acceptance of the belief that life begins at conception or at some other point prior to live birth. In assessing the state's interest, recognition may be given to the less rigid claim that as long as at least potential life is involved, the state may assert interests beyond the protection of the pregnant woman alone.

In Sections VIII to X, the Court stated its conclusion. It viewed this case as one presenting a conflict of interests, and it saw itself as weighing these interests. It began by agreeing that the woman's right to privacy did encompass her right to decide whether or not to terminate her pregnancy. But it argued that this right is not absolute, since the state's interests must also be considered:[8]

We therefore conclude that the right of personal privacy includes the abortion decision, but that this right is not unqualified and must be considered against important state interests in regulation.

The Court had no hesitation in ruling that the woman's right can be limited after the first trimester because of the state's interest in preserving and protecting maternal health. But the Court was less prepared to agree that the woman's right can be limited because of the state's interest in protecting prenatal life. Indeed, the Court rejected Texas's strong claim that life begins at conception, and that the state therefore has a right to protect such life by prohibiting abortion. The first reason advanced for rejecting that claim was phrased in this way:[9]

We need not resolve the difficult question of when life begins. When those trained in the respective disciplines of medicine, philosophy, and theology are unable to arrive at any consensus, the judiciary, at this point in the development of man's knowledge, is not in a position to speculate as to the answer.

Its second reason was that[10]

In areas other than criminal abortion, the law has been reluctant to endorse any theory that life, as we recognize it, begins before live birth or to accord legal rights to the unborn except in narrowly defined situations and except when the rights are contingent upon live birth.

The Court accepted the weaker claim that the state has an interest in protecting the potential of life. But when does that interest become compelling enough to enable the state to prohibit abortion? The Court said:[11]

. . . the compelling point is at viability. This is so because the fetus then has the capacity of meaningful life outside the mother's womb. State regulation protective of fetal life after viability thus has both logical and biological justifications. If the state is interested in protecting fetal life after viability, it may go so far as to proscribe abortion during that period except where it is necessary to preserve the life or health of the mother.

THE COURT ON POTENTIAL LIFE

I want to begin by considering that part of the Court's decision that allows Texas to proscribe abortions after viability so as to protect its interest in potential life. I note that it is difficult to evaluate that important part of the decision because the Court had little to say in defense of it other than the paragraph just quoted.

There are three very dubious elements of this ruling:

1. Why is the state prohibited from proscribing abortions when the life or health of the mother is threatened? Perhaps the following argument may be offered in the case of threat to maternal life: the mother is actually alive but the fetus is only potentially alive, and the protection of actual life takes precedence over the protection of potential life. Even if we grant this argument, why is the state prevented from prohibiting abortion when only maternal health is threatened? What is the argument against the claim that protecting potential life takes precedence in that case?

2. Why does the interest in potential life become compelling only when the stage of viability is reached? The Court's whole argument for this claim is[12]

This is so because the fetus then presumably has the capacity of meaningful life outside the mother's womb.

There is, no doubt, an important type of potential for life, the capacity of meaningful life outside the mother's womb, that the fetus acquires only at the time of viability. But there are other types of potential for life that it acquires earlier. At conception, for example, the fertilized cell has the potential for life in the sense that it will, in the normal course of events, develop into a human being. A six-week-old fetus has the potential for life in the stronger sense that all of the major organs it needs for life are already functioning. Why then does the state's interest in protecting potential life become compelling only at the point of viability? The Court failed to answer that question.

3. It can fairly be said that those trained in the respective disciplines of medicine, philosophy, and theology are unlikely to be able to arrive at any consensus on the question of when the fetus becomes potentially alive and when the state's interest in protecting this potential life becomes compelling enough to outweigh the rights of the mother. Why then did not the Court conclude, as it did when it considered the question of fetal humanity, that the judiciary cannot rule on such a question?

In pursuit of this last point, we approach the Court's more fundamental arguments against prohibiting abortion before viability.

THE COURT ON ACTUAL LIFE

The crucial claim in the Court's decision is that laws prohibiting abortion cannot be justified on the ground that the state has an interest in protecting the life of the fetus who is a human being. The Court offered two reasons for this claim: that the law has never yet accorded the fetus this status, and that the matter of fetal humanity is not one about which it is appropriate for the courts to speculate.

The first of the Court's reasons is not particularly strong. Whatever force we want to ascribe to precedent in the law, the Court has in the past modified its previous decisions in light of newer information and insights. In a matter as important as the conflict between the fetus's right to life and the rights of the mother, it would have seemed particularly necessary to deal with the issues rather than relying upon precedent.

In its second argument, the Court did deal with those issues by adopting the following principle:

1. It is inappropriate for the Court to speculate about the answer to questions about which relevant professional specialists cannot arrive at a consensus. This principle seems irrelevant. The issue before the Court was whether the Texas legislature could make a determination in light of the best available evidence and legislate on the basis of it. Justice White, in his dissent, raised this point:[13]

The upshot is that the people and legislatures of the fifty states are constitutionally disentitled to weigh the relative importance of the continued existence and development of the fetus on the one hand against the spectrum of possible impacts on the mother on the other hand.

This objection could be met, however, if we modified the Court's principle in the following way:

2. It is inappropriate for a legislature to write law upon the basis of its best belief when the relevant professional specialists cannot agree that that belief is correct.

On the basis of such a principle, the Court could argue that Texas had no right to protect by law the right of the fetus to life, thereby acknowledging it to be a human being with such a right, because the relevant specialists do not agree that the fetus has that right. As it stands, however, Principle 2 is questionable. In a large number of areas, legislatures regularly do (and must) act upon issues upon which there is a wide diversity of opinion among professional specialists. So Principle 2 has to be modified to deal with only certain cases, and the obvious suggestion is:

3. It is inappropriate for the legislature, on the ground of belief, to write law in such a way as to violate the basic rights of some individuals, when professional specialists do not agree that that belief is correct.

This principle could be used to defend the Court's decision. But is there any reason to accept it as true? Two arguments for this principle immediately suggest themselves: (a) If the relevant professional specialists do not agree, then there cannot be any proof that the answer in question is the correct one. But a legislature should not infringe the rights of people on the basis of unproved belief. (b) When the professional specialists do not agree, there must be legitimate and reasonable alternatives of belief, and we ought to respect the rights of believers in each of these alternatives to act on their own judgments.

• • •

We have already discussed . . . the principles that lie behind these arguments. We saw . . . that neither of these arguments, as applied to abortion, is acceptable if the fetus is a human being. To employ these arguments correctly, the Court must presuppose that the fetus is not a human being. And that, of course, it cannot do, since the aim of its logic is the view that courts and legislatures, at least at this juncture, should remain neutral on the issue of fetal humanity.

There is a second point that should be noted about Principles 1 to 3. There are cases in which, by failing to deal with an issue, an implicit, inevitable decision is in fact reached. We have before us such a case. The Court was considering Texas's claim that it had the right to prohibit abortion in order to protect the fetus. The Court conceded that if the fetus had a protectable right to life, Texas could prohibit abortions. But when the Court concluded that it (and, by implication, Texas) could not decide whether the fetus is a human being with the right to life, Texas was compelled to act as if the fetus had no such right that Texas could protect. Why should Principles like 1 to 3 be accepted if the result is the effective endorsement of one disputed claim over another?[14]

There is an alternative to the Court's approach. It is that each of the legislatures should consider the vexing problems surrounding abortions, weigh all of the relevant factors, and write law on the basis of its conclusions. The legislature would, undoubtedly, have to consider the question of fetal humanity, but, I submit, the Court is wrong in supposing that there is a way in which that question can be avoided.

• • •

CONCLUSION

The Supreme Court has ruled, and the principal legal issues in this country are, at least for now, resolved. I have tried to show, however, that the Court's ruling was in error, that it failed to grapple with the crucial issues surrounding the laws prohibiting abortion. The serious public debate about abortion must, and certainly will, continue.

NOTES

1. J. Thomson, "A Defense of Abortion," *Philosophy and Public Affairs,* Vol. 1 (1971), pp. 47–66.

2. *Ibid.,* p. 53.

3. *Ibid.,* p. 56.

4. On the Model Penal Code provisions, see American Law Institute, *Model Penal Code:* Tentative Draft No. 9 (1959).

5. *Roe v. Wade,* 41 *LW* 4229.

6. *Roe,* 41 *LW* 4218.

7. *Roe,* 41 *LW* 4224.

8. *Roe,* 41 *LW* 4226.

9. *Roe,* 41 *LW* 4227.

10. *Roe,* 41 *LW* 4228.

11. *Roe,* 41 *LW* 4228–4229.

12. *Ibid.*

13. *Roe,* 41 *LW* 4246.

14. This argument is derived from one used (for very different purposes) by William James in *The Will to Believe,* reprinted in William James, *The Will to Believe and Other Essays on Popular Philosophy* (New York: Dover, 1956), pp. 1–31.

M A R Y   A N N E   W A R R E N

On the Moral and Legal Status of Abortion

We will be concerned with both the moral status of abortion, which for our purposes we may define as the act which a woman performs in voluntarily terminating, or allowing another person to terminate, her pregnancy, and the legal status which is appropriate for this act. I will argue that, while it is not possible to produce a satisfactory defense of a woman's right to obtain an abortion without showing that a fetus is not a human being, in the morally relevant sense of that term, we ought not to conclude that the difficulties involved in determining whether or not a fetus is human make it impossible to produce any satisfactory solution to the problem of the moral status of abortion. For it is possible to show that, on the basis of intuitions which

we may expect even the opponents of abortion to share, a fetus is not a person, and hence not the sort of entity to which it is proper to ascribe full moral rights.

Of course, while some philosophers would deny the possibility of any such proof,[1] others will deny that there is any need for it, since the moral permissibility of abortion appears to them to be too obvious to require proof. But the inadequacy of this attitude should be evident from the fact that both the friends and the foes of abortion consider their position to be morally self-evident. Because proabortionists have never adequately come to grips with the conceptual issues surrounding abortion, most, if not all, of the arguments which they advance in opposition to laws restricting access to abortion fail to refute or even weaken the traditional antiabortion argument, i.e., that a fetus is a human being, and therefore abortion is murder.

Reprinted from *The Monist,* Vol. 57, No. 1 (January 1973) with the permission of the publisher. Copyright © 1973, *The Monist.*

These arguments are typically of one of two sorts. Either they point to the terrible side effects of the restrictive laws, e.g., the deaths due to illegal abortions, and the fact that it is poor women who suffer the most as a result of these laws, or else they state that to deny a woman access to abortion is to deprive her of her right to control her own body. Unfortunately, however, the fact that restricting access to abortion has tragic side effects does not, in itself, show that the restrictions are unjustified, since murder is wrong regardless of the consequences of prohibiting it; and the appeal to the right to control one's body, which is generally construed as a property right, is at best a rather feeble argument for the permissibility of abortion. Mere ownership does not give me the right to kill innocent people whom I find on my property, and indeed I am apt to be held responsible if such people injure themselves while on my property. It is equally unclear that I have any moral right to expel an innocent person from my property when I know that doing so will result in his death.

Furthermore, it is probably inappropriate to describe a woman's body as her property, since it seems natural to hold that a person is something distinct from her property, but not from her body. Even those who would object to the identification of a person with his body, or with the conjunction of his body and his mind, must admit that it would be very odd to describe, say, breaking a leg, as damaging one's property, and much more appropriate to describe it as injuring one*self*. Thus it is probably a mistake to argue that the right to obtain an abortion is in any way derived from the right to own and regulate property.

But however we wish to construe the right to abortion, we cannot hope to convince those who consider abortion a form of murder of the existence of any such right unless we are able to produce a clear and convincing refutation of the traditional antiabortion argument, and this has not, to my knowledge, been done. With respect to the two most vital issues which that argument involves, i.e., the humanity of the fetus and its implication for the moral status of abortion, confusion has prevailed on both sides of the dispute.

Thus, both proabortionists and antiabortionists have tended to abstract the question of whether abortion is wrong to that of whether it is wrong to destroy a fetus, just as though the rights of another person were not necessarily involved. This mistaken abstraction has led to the almost universal assumption that if a fetus is a human being, with a right to life, then it follows immediately that abortion is wrong (except

perhaps when necessary to save the woman's life), and that it ought to be prohibited. It has also been generally assumed that unless the question about the status of the fetus is answered, the moral status of abortion cannot possibly be determined.

Two recent papers, one by B. A. Brody,[2] and one by Judith Thomson,[3] have attempted to settle the question of whether abortion ought to be prohibited apart from the question of whether or not the fetus is human. Brody examines the possibility that the following two statements are compatible: (1) that abortion is the taking of innocent human life, and therefore wrong; and (2) that nevertheless it ought not to be prohibited by law, at least under the present circumstances.[4] Not surprisingly, Brody finds it impossible to reconcile these two statements since, as he rightly argues, none of the unfortunate side effects of the prohibition of abortion is bad enough to justify legalizing the *wrongful* taking of human life. He is mistaken, however, in concluding that the incompatibility of (1) and (2), in itself, shows that "the legal problem about abortion cannot be resolved independently of the status of the fetus problem" (p. 369).

What Brody fails to realize is that (1) embodies the questionable assumption that if a fetus is a human being, then of course abortion is morally wrong, and that an attack on *this* assumption is more promising, as a way of reconciling the humanity of the fetus with the claim that laws prohibiting abortion are unjustified, than is an attack on the assumption that if abortion is the wrongful killing of innocent human beings then it ought to be prohibited. He thus overlooks the possibility that a fetus may have a right to life and abortion still be morally permissible, in that the right of a woman to terminate an unwanted pregnancy might override the right of the fetus to be kept alive. The immorality of abortion is no more demonstrated by the humanity of the fetus, in itself, than the immorality of killing in self-defense is demonstrated by the fact that the assailant is a human being. Neither is it demonstrated by the *innocence* of the fetus, since there may be situations in which the killing of innocent human beings is justified.

It is perhaps not surprising that Brody fails to spot this assumption, since it has been accepted with little or no argument by nearly everyone who has written on the morality of abortion. John Noonan is correct in saying that "the fundamental question in the long history of abortion is, How do you determine the humanity of a being?"[5] He summarizes his own antiabortion argument, which is a version of the official position of the Catholic Church, as follows:

... it is wrong to kill humans, however poor, weak, defenseless, and lacking in opportunity to develop their potential they may be. It is therefore morally wrong to kill Biafrans. Similarly, it is morally wrong to kill embryos.[6]

Noonan bases his claim that fetuses are human upon what he calls the theologians' criterion of humanity: that whoever is conceived of human beings is human. But although he argues at length for the appropriateness of this criterion, he never questions the assumption that if a fetus is human then abortion is wrong for exactly the same reason that murder is wrong.

Judith Thomson is, in fact, the only writer I am aware of who has seriously questioned this assumption; she has argued that, even if we grant the antiabortionist his claim that a fetus is a human being, with the same right to life as any other human being, we can still demonstrate that, in at least some and perhaps most cases, a woman is under no moral obligation to complete an unwanted pregnancy.[7] Her argument is worth examining, since if it holds up it may enable us to establish the moral permissibility of abortion without becoming involved in problems about what entitles an entity to be considered human, and accorded full moral rights. To be able to do this would be a great gain in the power and simplicity of the proabortion position, since, although I will argue that these problems can be solved at least as decisively as can any other moral problem, we should certainly be pleased to be able to avoid having to solve them as part of the justification of abortion.

On the other hand, even if Thomson's argument does not hold up, her insight, i.e., that it requires *argument* to show that if fetuses are human then abortion is properly classified as murder, is an extremely valuable one. The assumption she attacks is particularly invidious, for it amounts to the decision that it is appropriate, in deciding the moral status of abortion, to leave the rights of the pregnant woman out of consideration entirely, except possibly when her life is threatened. Obviously, this will not do; determining what moral rights, if any, a fetus possesses is only the first step in determining the moral status of abortion. Step two, which is at least equally essential, is finding a just solution to the conflict between whatever rights the fetus may have, and the rights of the woman who is unwillingly pregnant. While the historical error has been to pay far too little attention to the second step, Ms. Thomson's suggestion is that if we look at the second step first we may find that a woman has a right to obtain an abortion *regardless* of what rights the fetus has.

Our own inquiry will also have two stages. In Section I, we will consider whether or not it is possible to establish that abortion is morally permissible even on the assumption that a fetus is an entity with a full-fledged right to life. I will argue that in fact this cannot be established, at least not with the conclusiveness which is essential to our hopes of convincing those who are skeptical about the morality of abortion, and that we therefore cannot avoid dealing with the question of whether or not a fetus really does have the same right to life as a (more fully developed) human being.

In Section II, I will propose an answer to this question, namely, that a fetus cannot be considered a member of the moral community, the set of beings with full and equal moral rights, for the simple reason that it is not a person, and that it is personhood, and not genetic humanity, i.e., humanity as defined by Noonan, which is the basis for membership in this community. I will argue that a fetus, whatever its stage of development, satisfies none of the basic criteria of personhood, and is not even enough *like* a person to be accorded even some of the same rights on the basis of this resemblance. Nor, as we will see, is a fetus's *potential* personhood a threat to the morality of abortion, since, whatever the rights of potential people may be, they are invariably overridden in any conflict with the moral rights of actual people.

I

We turn now to Professor Thomson's case for the claim that even if a fetus has full moral rights, abortion is still morally permissible, at least sometimes, and for some reasons other than to save the woman's life. Her argument is based upon a clever, but I think faulty, analogy. She asks us to picture ourselves waking up one day, in bed with a famous violinist. Imagine that you have been kidnapped, and your bloodstream hooked up to that of the violinist, who happens to have an ailment which will certainly kill him unless he is permitted to share your kidneys for a period of nine months. No one else can save him, since you alone have the right type of blood. He will be unconscious all that time, and you will have to stay in bed with him, but after the nine months are over he may be unplugged, completely cured, that is, provided that you have cooperated.

Now then, she continues, what are your obligations in this situation? The antiabortionist, if he is consistent, will have to say that you are obligated to stay in bed with the violinist: for all people have a right to life, and violinists are people, and therefore it would be murder for you to disconnect yourself from him and let him die (p. 49). But this is outrageous, and so there must be something wrong with the same argument when it is applied to abortion. It would certainly be commendable of you to agree to save the violinist, but it is absurd to suggest that your refusal to do so would be murder. His right to life does not obligate you to do whatever is required to keep him alive; nor does it justify anyone else in forcing you to do so. A law which required you to stay in bed with the violinist would clearly be an unjust law, since it is no proper function of the law to force unwilling people to make huge sacrifices for the sake of other people toward whom they have no such prior obligation.

Thomson concludes that, if this analogy is an apt one, then we can grant the antiabortionist his claim that a fetus is a human being, and still hold that it is at least sometimes the case that a pregnant woman has the right to refuse to be a Good Samaritan towards the fetus, i.e., to obtain an abortion. For there is a great gap between the claim that x has a right to life, and the claim that y is obligated to do whatever is necessary to keep x alive, let alone that he ought to be forced to do so. It is y's duty to keep x alive only if he has somehow contracted a *special* obligation to do so; and a woman who is unwillingly pregnant, e.g., who was raped, has done nothing which obligates her to make the enormous sacrifice which is necessary to preserve the conceptus.

This argument is initially quite plausible, and in the extreme case of pregnancy due to rape it is probably conclusive. Difficulties arise, however, when we try to specify more exactly the range of cases in which abortion is clearly justifiable even on the assumption that the fetus is human. Professor Thomson considers it a virtue of her argument that it does not enable us to conclude that abortion is *always* permissible. It would, she says, be "indecent" for a woman in her seventh month to obtain an abortion just to avoid having to postpone a trip to Europe. On the other hand, her argument enables us to see that "a sick and desperately frightened schoolgirl pregnant due to rape may *of course* choose abortion, and that any law which rules

this out is an insane law" (p. 65). So far, so good; but what are we to say about the woman who becomes pregnant not through rape but as a result of her own carelessness, or because of contraceptive failure, or who gets pregnant intentionally and then changes her mind about wanting a child? With respect to such cases, the violinist analogy is of much less use to the defender of the woman's right to obtain an abortion.

Indeed, the choice of a pregnancy due to rape, as an example of a case in which abortion is permissible even if a fetus is considered a human being, is extremely significant; for it is only in the case of pregnancy due to rape that the woman's situation is adequately analogous to the violinist case for our intuitions about the latter to transfer convincingly. The crucial difference between a pregnancy due to rape and the *normal* case of an unwanted pregnancy is that in the normal case we cannot claim that the woman is in no way responsible for her predicament; she could have remained chaste, or taken her pills more faithfully, or abstained on dangerous days, and so on. If on the other hand, you are kidnapped by strangers, and hooked up to a strange violinist, then you are free of any shred of responsibility for the situation, on the basis of which it would be argued that you are obligated to keep the violinist alive. Only when her pregnancy is due to rape is a woman clearly just as nonresponsible.[8]

Consequently, there is room for the antiabortionist to argue that in the normal case of unwanted pregnancy a woman has, by her own actions, assumed responsibility for the fetus. For if x behaves in a way which he could have avoided, and which he knows involves, let us say, a 1 percent chance of bringing into existence a human being, with a right to life, and does so knowing that if this should happen then that human being will perish unless x does certain things to keep him alive, then it is by no means clear that when it does happen x is free of any obligation to what he knew in advance would be required to keep that human being alive.

The plausibility of such an argument is enough to show that the Thomson analogy can provide a clear and persuasive defense of a woman's right to obtain an abortion only with respect to those cases in which the woman is in no way responsible for her pregnancy, e.g., where it is due to rape. In all other cases, we would almost certainly conclude that it was necessary to look carefully at the particular circumstances in order to determine the extent of the woman's responsibility, and hence the extent of her obligation. This is an extremely unsatisfactory outcome, from the viewpoint of the opponents of restrictive abortion laws, most of whom are convinced that a woman has a right to obtain an abortion regardless of how and why she got pregnant.

Of course a supporter of the violinist analogy might point out that it is absurd to suggest that forgetting her pill one day might be sufficient to obligate a woman to complete an unwanted pregnancy. And indeed it *is* absurd to suggest this. As we shall see, the moral right to obtain an abortion is not in the least dependent upon the extent to which the woman is responsible for her pregnancy. But unfortunately, once we allow the assumption that a fetus has full moral rights, we cannot avoid taking this absurd suggestion seriously. Perhaps we can make this point more clear by altering the violinist story just enough to make it more analogous to a normal unwanted pregnancy and less to a pregnancy due to rape, and then seeing whether it is still obvious that you are not obligated to stay in bed with the fellow.

Suppose, then, that violinists are peculiarly prone to the sort of illness the only cure for which is the use of someone else's bloodstream for nine months, and that because of this there has been formed a society of music lovers who agree that whenever a violinist is stricken they will draw lots and the loser will, by some means, be made the one and only person capable of saving him. Now then, would you be obligated to cooperate in curing the violinist if you had voluntarily joined this society, knowing the possible consequences, and then your name had been drawn and you had been kidnapped? Admittedly, you did not promise ahead of time that you would, but you did deliberately place yourself in a position in which it might happen that a human life would be lost if you did not. Surely this is at least a prima facie reason for supposing that you have an obligation to stay in bed with the violinist. Suppose that you had gotten your name drawn deliberately; surely *that* would be quite a strong reason for thinking that you had such an obligation.

It might be suggested that there is one important disanalogy between the modified violinist case and the case of an unwanted pregnancy, which makes the woman's responsibility significantly less, namely, the fact that the fetus *comes into existence* as the result of the woman's actions. This fact might give her a right to refuse to keep it alive, whereas she would not have had this right had it existed previously, independently, and then as a result of her actions become dependent upon her for its survival.

My own intuition, however, is that x has no more right to bring into existence, either deliberately or as a foreseeable result of actions he could have avoided, a being with full moral rights (y), and then refuse to do what he knew beforehand would be required to keep that being alive, than he has to enter into an agreement with an existing person, whereby he may be called upon to save that person's life, and then refuse to do so when so called upon. Thus, x's responsibility for y's existence does not seem to lessen his obligation to keep y alive, if he is also responsible for y's being in a situation in which only he can save him.

Whether or not this intuition is entirely correct, it brings us back once again to the conclusion that once we allow the assumption that a fetus has full moral rights it becomes an extremely complex and difficult question whether and when abortion is justifiable. Thus the Thomson analogy cannot help us produce a clear and persuasive proof of the moral permissibility of abortion. Nor will the opponents of the restrictive laws thank us for anything less; for their conviction (for the most part) is that abortion is obviously *not* a morally serious and extremely unfortunate, even though sometimes justified act, comparable to killing in self-defense or to letting the violinist die, but rather is closer to being a morally neutral act, like cutting one's hair.

The basis of this conviction, I believe, is the realization that a fetus is not a person, and thus does not have a full-fledged right to life. Perhaps the reason why this claim has been so inadequately defended is that it seems self-evident to those who accept it. And so it is, insofar as it follows from what I take to be perfectly obvious claims about the nature of personhood, and about the proper grounds for ascribing moral rights, claims which ought, indeed, to be obvious to both the friends and foes of abortion. Nevertheless, it is worth examining these claims, and showing how they demonstrate the moral innocuousness of abortion, since this apparently has not been adequately done before.

II

The question which we must answer in order to produce a satisfactory solution to the problem of the moral status of abortion is this: How are we to define the moral community, the set of beings with full and

equal moral rights, such that we can decide whether a
human fetus is a member of this community or not? What sort of entity, exactly, has the inalienable rights to life, liberty, and the pursuit of happiness? Jefferson attributed these rights to all *men*, and it may or may not be fair to suggest that he intended to attribute them *only* to men. Perhaps he ought to have attributed them to all human beings. If so, then we arrive, first, at Noonan's problem of defining what makes a being human, and second, at the equally vital question which Noonan does not consider, namely, What reason is there for identifying the moral community with the set of all human beings, in whatever way we have chosen to define that term?

ON THE DEFINITION OF "HUMAN"

One reason why this vital second question is so frequently overlooked in the debate over the moral status of abortion is that the term "human" has two distinct, but not often distinguished, senses. This fact results in a slide of meaning, which serves to conceal the fallaciousness of the traditional argument that since (1) it is wrong to kill innocent human beings, and (2) fetuses are innocent human beings, then (3) it is wrong to kill fetuses. For if "human" is used in the same sense in both (1) and (2) then, whichever of the two senses is meant, one of these premises is question-begging. And if it is used in two different senses, then of course the conclusion doesn't follow.

Thus, (1) is a self-evident moral truth,[9] and avoids begging the question about abortion, only if "human being" is used to mean something like "a full-fledged member of the moral community." (It may or may not also be meant to refer exclusively to members of the species *Homo sapiens*.) We may call this the *moral* sense of "human." It is not to be confused with what we will call the *genetic* sense, i.e., the sense in which *any* member of the species is a human being, and no member of any other species could be. If (1) is acceptable only if the moral sense is intended, (2) is non-question-begging only if what is intended is the genetic sense.

In "Deciding Who Is Human," Noonan argues for the classification of fetuses with human beings by pointing to the presence of the full genetic code, and the potential capacity for rational thought (p. 135). It is clear that what he needs to show, for his version of the traditional argument to be valid, is that fetuses are human in the moral sense, the sense in which it is analytically true that all human beings have full moral rights. But, in the absence of any argument showing

that whatever is genetically human is also morally human, and he gives none, nothing more than genetic humanity can be demonstrated by the presence of the human genetic code. And, as we will see, the *potential* capacity for rational thought can at most show that an entity has the potential for *becoming* human in the moral sense.

DEFINING THE MORAL COMMUNITY

Can it be established that genetic humanity is sufficient for moral humanity? I think that there are very good reasons for not defining the moral community in this way. I would like to suggest an alternative way of defining the moral community, which I will argue for only to the extent of explaining why it is, or should be, self-evident. The suggestion is simply that the moral community consists of all and only *people*, rather than all and only human beings;[10] and probably the best way of demonstrating its self-evidence is by considering the concept of personhood, to see what sorts of entity are and are not persons, and what the decision that a being is or is not a person implies about its moral rights.

What moral characteristics entitle an entity to be considered a person? This is obviously not the place to attempt a complete analysis of the concept of personhood, but we do not need such a fully adequate analysis just to determine whether and why a fetus is or isn't a person. All we need is a rough and approximate list of the most basic criteria of personhood, and some idea of which, or how many, of these an entity must satisfy in order to properly be considered a person.

In searching for such criteria, it is useful to look beyond the set of people with whom we are acquainted, and ask how we would decide whether a totally alien being was a person or not. (For we have no right to assume that genetic humanity is necessary for personhood.) Imagine a space traveler who lands on an unknown planet and encounters a race of beings utterly unlike any he has ever seen or heard of. If he wants to be sure of behaving morally toward these beings, he has to somehow decide whether they are people, and hence have full moral rights, or whether they are the sort of thing which he need not feel guilty about treating as, for example, a source of food.

How should he go about making this decision? If he has some anthropological background he might look for such things as religion, art, and the manufacturing of tools, weapons, or shelters, since these factors have been used to distinguish our human from our prehuman ancestors, in what seems to be closer to the moral than the genetic sense of "human." And no doubt he would be right to consider the presence of such factors as good evidence that the alien beings were people, and morally human. It would, however, be overly anthropocentric of him to take the absence of these things as adequate evidence that they were not, since we can imagine people who have progressed beyond, or evolved without ever developing, these cultural characteristics.

I suggest that the traits which are most central to the concept of personhood, or humanity in the moral sense, are, very roughly, the following:

1. Consciousness (of objects and events external and/or internal to the being), and in particular the capacity to feel pain;
2. Reasoning (the *developed* capacity to solve new and relatively complex problems);
3. Self-motivated activity (activity which is relatively independent of either genetic or direct external control);
4. The capacity to communicate, by whatever means, messages of an indefinite variety of types, that is, not just with an indefinite number of possible contents, but on indefinitely many possible topics;
5. The presence of self-concepts, and self-awareness, either individual or racial, or both.

Admittedly, there are apt to be a great many problems involved in formulating precise definitions of these criteria, let alone in developing universally valid behavioral criteria for deciding when they apply. But I will assume that both we and our explorer know approximately what (1)–(5) mean, and that he is also able to determine whether or not they apply. How, then, should he use his findings to decide whether or not the alien beings are people? We needn't suppose that an entity must have *all* of these attributes to be properly considered a person; (1) and (2) alone may well be sufficient for personhood, and quite probably (1)–(3) are sufficient. Neither do we need to insist that any one of these criteria is *necessary* for personhood, although once again (1) and (2) look like fairly good candidates for necessary conditions, as does (3), if "activity" is construed so as to include the activity of reasoning.

All we need to claim, to demonstrate that a fetus is not a person, is that any being which satisfies *none* of (1)–(5) is certainly not a person. I consider this claim to be so obvious that I think anyone who denied it, and claimed that a being which satisfied none of (1)–(5) was a person all the same, would thereby demonstrate that he had no notion at all of what a person is—perhaps because he had confused the concept of a person with that of genetic humanity. If the opponents of abortion were to deny the appropriateness of these five criteria, I do not know what further arguments would convince them. We would probably have to admit that our conceptual schemes were indeed irreconcilably different, and that our dispute could not be settled objectively.

I do not expect this to happen, however, since I think that the concept of a person is one which is very nearly universal (to people), and that it is common to both proabortionists and antiabortionists, even though neither group has fully realized the relevance of this concept to the resolution of their dispute. Furthermore, I think that on reflection even the antiabortionists ought to agree not only that (1)–(5) are central to the concept of personhood, but also that it is a part of this concept that all and only people have full moral rights. The concept of a person is in part a moral concept; once we have admitted that *x* is a person we have recognized, even if we have not agreed to respect, *x*'s right to be treated as a member of the moral community. It is true that the claim that *x* is a *human being* is more commonly voiced as part of an appeal to treat *x* decently than is the claim that *x* is a person, but this is either because "human being" is here used in the sense which implies personhood, or because the genetic and moral senses of "human" have been confused.

Now if (1)–(5) are indeed the primary criteria of personhood, then it is clear that genetic humanity is neither necessary nor sufficient for establishing that an entity is a person. Some human beings are not people, and there may well be people who are not human beings. A man or woman whose consciousness has been permanently obliterated but who remains alive is a human being which is no longer a person; defective human beings, with no appreciable mental capacity, are not and presumably never will be people; and a fetus is a human being which is not yet a person, and which therefore cannot coherently be said to have full moral rights. Citizens of the next century should be prepared to recognize highly advanced, self-aware robots or computers, should such be developed, and intelligent inhabitants of other worlds, should such be found, as people in the fullest sense, and to respect their moral rights. But to ascribe full moral rights to an entity which is not a person is as absurd as to ascribe moral obligations and responsibilities to such an entity.

FETAL DEVELOPMENT AND THE RIGHT TO LIFE

Two problems arise in the application of these suggestions for the definition of the moral community to the determination of the precise moral status of a human fetus. Given that the paradigm example of a person is a normal adult being, then (1) How like this paradigm, in particular how far advanced since conception, does a human being need to be before it begins to have a right to life by virtue, not of being fully a person as of yet, but of being *like* a person? and (2) To what extent, if any, does the fact that a fetus has the *potential* for becoming a person endow it with some of the same rights? Each of these questions requires some comment.

In answering the first question, we need not attempt a detailed consideration of the moral rights of organisms which are not developed enough, aware enough, intelligent enough, etc., to be considered people, but which resemble people in some respects. It does seem reasonable to suggest that the more like a person, in the relevant aspects, a being is, the stronger is the case for regarding it as having a right to life, and indeed the stronger its right to life is. Thus we ought to take seriously the suggestion that, insofar as "the human individual develops biologically in a continuous fashion . . . the rights of a human person might develop in the same way."[11] But we must keep in mind that the attributes which are relevant in determining whether or not an entity is enough like a person to be regarded as having some of the same moral rights are no different from those which are relevant to determining whether or not it is fully a person—i.e., are not different from (1)–(5)—and that being genetically human, or having recognizably human facial and other physical features, or detectable brain activity, or the capacity to survive outside the uterus, are simply not among these relevant attributes.

Thus it is clear that even though a seven- or eight-month fetus has features which make it apt to arouse in us almost the same powerful protective instinct as is commonly aroused by a small infant, nevertheless it is not significantly more personlike than is a very small embryo. It is *somewhat* more personlike; it can apparently feel and respond to pain, and it may even have a rudimentary form of consciousness, insofar as its brain is quite active. Nevertheless, it seems safe to say that it is not fully conscious, in the way that an infant of a few months is, and that it cannot reason, or communicate messages of indefinitely many sorts, does not engage in self-motivated activity, and has no self-awareness. Thus, in the *relevant* respects, a fetus, even a fully developed one, is considerably less personlike than is the average mature mammal, indeed the average fish. And I think that a rational person must conclude that if the right to life of a fetus is to be based upon its resemblance to a person, then it cannot be said to have any more right to life than, let us say, a newborn guppy (which also seems to be capable of feeling pain), and that a right of that magnitude could never override a woman's right to obtain an abortion, at any stage of her pregnancy.

There may, of course, be other arguments in favor of placing legal limits upon the stage of pregnancy in which an abortion may be performed. Given the relative safety of the new techniques of artificially inducing labor during the third trimester, the danger to the woman's life or health is no longer such an argument. Neither is the fact that people tend to respond to the thought of abortion in the later stages of pregnancy with emotional repulsion, since mere emotional responses cannot take the place of moral reasoning in determining what ought to be permitted. Nor, finally, is the frequently heard argument that legalizing abortion, especially late in the pregnancy, may erode the level of respect for human life, leading, perhaps to an increase in unjustified euthanasia and other crimes. For this threat, if it is a threat, can be better met by educating people to the kinds of moral distinctions which we are making here than by limiting access to abortion (which limitation may, in its disregard for the rights of women, be just as damaging to the level of respect for human rights).

Thus, since the fact that even a fully developed fetus is not personlike enough to have any significant right to life on the basis of its person-likeness shows that no legal restrictions upon the stage of pregnancy in which an abortion may be performed can be justified on the grounds that we should protect the rights of the older fetus; and since there is no other apparent justification for such restrictions, we may conclude that they are entirely unjustified. Whether or not it would be *indecent* (whatever that means) for a woman in her seventh month to obtain an abortion just to avoid having to postpone a trip to Europe, it would not, in itself, be *immoral*, and therefore it ought to be permitted.

POTENTIAL PERSONHOOD AND THE RIGHT TO LIFE

We have seen that a fetus does not resemble a person in any way which can support the claim that it has even some of the same rights. But what about its *potential*, the fact that if nurtured and allowed to develop naturally it will very probably become a person? Doesn't that alone give it at least some right to life? It is hard to deny that the fact that an entity is a potential person is a strong prima facie reason for not destroying it; but we need not conclude from this that a potential person has a right to life, by virtue of that potential. It may be that our feeling that it is better, other things being equal, not to destroy a potential person is better explained by the fact that potential people are still (felt to be) an invaluable resource, not to be lightly squandered. Surely, if every speck of dust were a potential person, we would be much less apt to conclude that every potential person has a right to become actual.

Still, we do not need to insist that a potential person has no right to life whatever. There may well be something immoral, and not just imprudent, about wantonly destroying potential people, when doing so isn't necessary to protect anyone's rights. But even if a potential person does have some prima facie right to life, such a right could not possibly outweigh the right of a woman to obtain an abortion, since the rights of any actual person invariably outweigh those of any potential person, whenever the two conflict. Since this may not be immediately obvious in the case of a human fetus, let us look at another case.

Suppose that our space explorer falls into the hands of an alien culture, whose scientists decide to create a few hundred thousand or more human beings, by breaking his body into its component cells, and using these to create fully developed human beings, with, of course, his genetic code. We may imagine that each of these newly created men will have all of the original man's abilities, skills, knowledge, and so on, and also have an individual self-concept, in short that each of them will be a bona fide (though hardly unique) person. Imagine that the whole project will take only seconds, and that its chances of success are extremely high, and that our explorer knows all of this, and also knows that these people will be treated fairly. I maintain that in such a situation he would have every right

to escape if he could, and thus to deprive all of these potential people of their potential lives; for his right to life outweighs all of theirs together, in spite of the fact that they are all genetically human, all innocent, and all have a very high probability of becoming people very soon, if only he refrains from action.

Indeed, I think he would have a right to escape even if it were not his life which the alien scientists planned to take, but only a year of his freedom, or, indeed, only a day. Nor would be he obligated to stay if he had gotten captured (thus bringing all these people-potentials into existence) because of his own carelessness, or even if he had done so deliberately, knowing the consequences. Regardless of how he got captured, he is not morally obligated to remain in captivity for *any* period of time for the sake of permitting any number of potential people to come into actuality, so great is the margin by which one actual person's right to liberty outweighs whatever rights to life even a hundred thousand potential people have. And it seems reasonable to conclude that the rights of a woman will outweigh by a similar margin whatever right to life a fetus may have by virtue of its potential personhood.

Thus, neither a fetus's resemblance to a person, nor its potential for becoming a person provides any basis whatever for the claim that it has any significant right to life. Consequently, a woman's right to protect her health, happiness, freedom, and even her life,[12] by terminating an unwanted pregnancy will always override whatever right to life it may be appropriate to ascribe to a fetus, even a fully developed one. And thus, in the absence of any overwhelming social need for every possible child, the laws which restrict the right to an abortion, or limit the period of pregnancy during which an abortion may be performed, are a wholly unjustified violation of a woman's most basic moral and constitutional rights.[13]

POSTSCRIPT ON INFANTICIDE

Since the publication of this [essay], many people have written to point out that my argument appears to justify not only abortion, but infanticide as well. For a new-born infant is not significantly more person-like than an advanced fetus, and consequently it would seem that if the destruction of the latter is permissible so too must be that of the former. Inasmuch as most people, regardless of how they feel about the morality of abortion, consider infanticide a form of murder, this might appear to represent a serious flaw in my argument.

Now, if I am right in holding that it is only people who have a full-fledged right to life, and who can be murdered, and if the criteria of personhood are as I have described them, then it obviously follows that killing a new-born infant isn't murder. It does *not* follow, however, that infanticide is permissible, for two reasons. In the first place, it would be wrong, at least in this country and in this period of history, and other things being equal, to kill a new-born infant, because even if its parents do not want it and would not suffer from its destruction, there are other people who would like to have it, and would, in all probability, be deprived of a great deal of pleasure by its destruction. Thus, infanticide is wrong for reasons analogous to those which make it wrong to wantonly destroy natural resources, or great works of art.

Secondly, most people, at least in this country, value infants and would much prefer that they be preserved, even if foster parents are not immediately available. Most of us would rather be taxed to support orphanages than allow unwanted infants to be destroyed. So long as there are people who want an infant preserved, and who are willing and able to provide the means of caring for it, under reasonably humane conditions, it is, *certeris paribus*, wrong to destroy it.

But, it might be replied, if this argument shows that infanticide is wrong, at least at this time and in this country, doesn't it also show that abortion is wrong? After all, many people value fetuses, are disturbed by their destruction, and would much prefer that they be preserved, even at some cost to themselves. Furthermore, as a potential source of pleasure to some foster family, a fetus is just as valuable as an infant. There is, however, a crucial difference between the two cases: so long as the fetus is unborn, its preservation, contrary to the wishes of the pregnant woman, violates her rights to freedom, happiness, and self-determination. Her rights override the rights of those who would like the fetus preserved, just as if someone's life or limb is threatened by a wild animal, his right to protect himself by destroying the animal overrides the rights of those who would prefer that the animal not be harmed.

The minute the infant is born, however, its preservation no longer violates any of its mother's rights, even if she wants it destroyed, because she is free to put it up for adoption. Consequently, while the moment of birth does not mark any sharp discontinuity in the degree to which an infant possesses the right to life, it does mark the end of its mother's right to determine its fate. Indeed, if abortion could be performed without killing the fetus, she would never possess the right to have the fetus destroyed, for the same reasons that she has no right to have an infant destroyed.

On the other hand, it follows from my argument that when an unwanted or defective infant is born into a society which cannot afford and/or is not willing to care for it, then its destruction is permissible. This conclusion will, no doubt, strike many people as heartless and immoral; but remember that the very existence of people who feel this way, and who are willing and able to provide care for unwanted infants, is reason enough to conclude that they should be preserved.

NOTES

1. For example, Roger Wertheimer, who in "Understanding the Abortion Argument" (*Philosophy and Public Affairs*, 1, No. 1 [Fall, 1971], 67–95), argues that the problem of the moral status of abortion is insoluble, in that the dispute over the status of the fetus is not a question of fact at all, but only a question of how one responds to the facts.

2. B. A. Brody, "Abortion and the Law," *The Journal of Philosophy*, 68, No. 12 (June 17, 1971), 357–69.

3. Judith Thomson, "A Defense of Abortion," *Philosophy and Public Affairs*, 1, No. 1 (Fall, 1971), 47–66.

4. I have abbreviated these statements somewhat, but not in a way which affects the argument.

5. John Noonan, "Abortion and the Catholic Church: A Summary History," *Natural Law Forum*, 12 (1967), 125.

6. John Noonan, "Deciding Who Is Human," *Natural Law Forum*, 13 (1968), 134.

7. "A Defense of Abortion."

8. We may safely ignore the fact that she might have avoided getting raped, e.g., by carrying a gun, since by similar means you might likewise have avoided getting kidnapped, and in neither case does the victim's failure to take all possible precautions against a highly unlikely event (as opposed to reasonable precautions against a rather likely event) mean that he is morally responsible for what happens.

9. Of course, the principle that it is (always) wrong to kill innocent human beings is in need of many other modifications, e.g., that it may be permissible to do so to save a greater number of other innocent human beings, but we may safely ignore these complications here.

10. From here on, we will use "human" to mean genetically human, since the moral sense seems closely connected to, and perhaps derived from, the assumption that genetic humanity is sufficient for membership in the moral community.

11. Thomas L. Hayes, "A Biological View," *Commonweal*, 85 (March 17, 1967), 677–78; quoted by Daniel Callahan, in *Abortion, Law, Choice, and Morality* (London: Macmillan & Co., 1970).

12. That is, insofar as the death rate, for the woman, is higher for childbirth than for early abortion.

13. My thanks to the following people, who were kind enough to read and criticize an earlier version of this paper: Herbert Gold, Gene Glass, Anne Lauterbach, Judith Thomson, Mary Mothersill, and Timothy Binkley.

UNITED STATES SUPREME COURT

Roe v. Wade: Majority Opinion and Dissent

[Mr. Justice Blackmun delivered the opinion of the Court.]

It is . . . apparent that at common law, at the time of the adoption of our Constitution, and throughout the major portion of the nineteenth century, abortion was viewed with less disfavor than under most American statutes currently in effect. Phrasing it another way, a woman enjoyed a substantially broader right to terminate a pregnancy than she does in most states today. At least with respect to the early stage of pregnancy, and very possibly without such a limitation, the opportunity to make this choice was present in this country well into the nineteenth century. Even later, the law continued for some time to treat less punitively an abortion procured in early pregnancy. . . .

Three reasons have been advanced to explain historically the enactment of criminal abortion laws in the nineteenth century and to justify their continued existence.

It has been argued occasionally that these laws were the product of a Victorian social concern to discourage illicit sexual conduct. Texas, however, does not advance this justification in the present case, and it appears that no court or commentator has taken the argument seriously. . . .

A second reason is concerned with abortion as a medical procedure. When most criminal abortion laws were first enacted, the procedure was a hazardous one for the woman. This was particularly true prior to the development of antisepsis. Antiseptic techniques, of course, were based on discoveries by Lister, Pasteur, and others first announced in 1867, but were not generally accepted and employed until about the turn of the century. Abortion mortality was high. Even after 1900, and perhaps until as late as the development of antibiotics in the 1940s, standard modern techniques such as dilation and curettage were not nearly so safe as they are today. Thus it has been argued that a state's real concern in enacting a criminal abortion law was to protect the pregnant woman, that is, to restrain her from submitting to a procedure that placed her life in serious jeopardy.

Modern medical techniques have altered this situation. Appellants and various *amici* refer to medical data indicating that abortion in early pregnancy, that is, prior to the end of first trimester, although not without its risk, is now relatively safe. Mortality rates for women undergoing early abortions, where the procedure is legal, appear to be as low as or lower than the rates for normal childbirth. Consequently, any interest of the state in protecting the woman from an inherently hazardous procedure, except when it would be equally dangerous for her to forgo it, has largely disappeared. Of course, important state interests in the area of health and medical standards do remain. The state has a legitimate interest in seeing to it that abortion like any other medical procedure, is performed under circumstances that insure maximum safety for the patient. This interest obviously extends at least to the performing physician and his staff, to the facilities involved, to the availability of after-care, and to adequate provision for any complication or emergency

Reprinted from 410 *United States Reports* 113; decided January 22, 1973.

that might arise. The prevalence of high mortality rates at illegal "abortion mills" strengthens, rather than weakens, the state's interest in regulating the conditions under which abortions are performed. Moreover, the risk to the woman increases as her pregnancy continues. Thus the state retains a definite interest in protecting the woman's own health and safety when an abortion is performed at a late stage of pregnancy.

The third reason is the state's interest — some phrase it in terms of duty — in protecting prenatal life. Some of the argument for this justification rests on the theory that a new human life is present from the moment of conception. The state's interest and general obligation to protect life then extends, it is argued, to prenatal life. Only when the life of the pregnant mother herself is at stake, balanced against the life she carries within her, should the interest of the embryo or fetus not prevail. Logically, of course, a legitimate state interest in this area need not stand or fall on acceptance of the belief that life begins at conception or at some other point prior to live birth. In assessing the state's interest, recognition may be given to the less rigid claim that as long as at least *potential* life is involved, the state may assert interests beyond the protection of the pregnant woman alone.

Parties challenging state abortion laws have sharply disputed in some courts the contention that a purpose of these laws, when enacted, was to protect prenatal life. Pointing to the absence of legislative history to support the contention, they claim that most state laws were designed solely to protect the woman. Because medical advances have lessened this concern, at least with respect to abortion in early pregnancy, they argue that with respect to such abortions the laws can no longer be justified by any state interest. There is some scholarly support for this view of original purpose. The few states courts called upon to interpret their laws in the late nineteenth and early twentieth centuries did focus on the state's interest in protecting the woman's health rather than in preserving the embryo and fetus. . . .

The Constitution does not explicitly mention any right of privacy. In a line of decisions, however, going back perhaps as far as *Union Pacific R. Co. v. Botsford* (1891), the Court has recognized that a right of personal privacy, or a guarantee of certain areas or zones of privacy, does exist under the Constitution. In varying contexts the Court or individual Justices have indeed found at least the roots of that right in the First Amendment, . . . in the Fourth and Fifth Amendments,

. . . in the penumbras of the Bill of Rights, . . . in the Ninth Amendment, . . . or in the concept of liberty guaranteed by the first section of the Fourteenth Amendment. . . . These decisions make it clear that only personal rights that can be deemed "fundamental" or "implicit in the concept of ordered liberty" . . . are included in this guarantee of personal privacy. They also make it clear that the right has some extension to activities relating to marriage, . . . procreation, . . . contraception, . . . family relationships, . . . and child rearing and education. . . .

This right of privacy, whether it be founded in the Fourteenth Amendment's concept of personal liberty and restrictions upon state action, as we feel it is, or, as the District Court determined, in the Ninth Amendment's reservation of rights to the people, is broad enough to encompass a woman's decision whether or not to terminate her pregnancy. . . .

Appellants and some *amici* argue that the woman's right is absolute and that she is entitled to terminate her pregnancy at whatever time, in whatever way, and for whatever reason she alone chooses. With this we do not agree. Appellants' arguments that Texas either has no valid interest at all in regulating the abortion decision, or no interest strong enough to support any limitation upon the woman's sole determination, is unpersuasive. The Court's decisions recognizing a right of privacy also acknowledge that some state regulation in areas protected by that right is appropriate. As noted above, a state may properly assert important interests in safeguarding health, in maintaining medical standards, and in protecting potential life. At some point in pregnancy, these respective interests become sufficiently compelling to sustain regulation of the factors that govern the abortion decision. The privacy rights involved, therefore, cannot be said to be absolute. . . .

We therefore conclude that the right of personal privacy includes the abortion decision, but that this right is not unqualified and must be considered against important state interests in regulation.

We note that those federal and state courts that have recently considered abortion law challenges have reached the same conclusion. . . .

Although the results are divided, most of these courts have agreed that the right of privacy, however based, is broad enough to cover the abortion decision; that the right, nonetheless, is not absolute and is subject to some limitations; and that at some point the state interests as to protection of health, medical standards, and prenatal life, become dominant. We agree with this approach. . . .

The appellee and certain *amici* argue that the fetus is a "person" within the language and meaning of the Fourteenth Amendment. In support of this they outline at length and in detail the well-known facts of fetal development. If this suggestion of personhood is established, the appellant's case, of course, collapses, for the fetus's right to life is then guaranteed specifically by the Amendment. The appellant conceded as much on reargument. On the other hand, the appellee conceded on reargument that no case could be cited that holds that a fetus is a person within the meaning of the Fourteenth Amendment. . . .

All this, together with our observation, *supra*, that throughout the major portion of the nineteenth century prevailing legal abortion practices were far freer than they are today, persuades us that the word "person," as used in the Fourteenth Amendment, does not include the unborn. . . . Indeed, our decision in *United States v. Vuitch* (1971), inferentially is to the same effect, for we there would not have indulged in statutory interpretation favorable to abortion in specified circumstances if the necessary consequence was the termination of life entitled to Fourteenth Amendment protection.

. . . As we have intimated above, it is reasonable and appropriate for a state to decide that at some point in time another interest, that of health of the mother or that of potential human life, becomes significantly involved. The woman's privacy is no longer sole and any right of privacy she possesses must be measured accordingly.

Texas urges that, apart from the Fourteenth Amendment, life begins at conception and is present throughout pregnancy, and that, therefore, the state has a compelling interest in protecting that life from and after conception. We need not resolve the difficult question of when life begins. When those trained in the respective disciplines of medicine, philosophy, and theology are unable to arrive at any consensus, the judiciary, at this point in the development of man's knowledge, is not in a position to speculate as to the answer.

It should be sufficient to note briefly the wide divergence of thinking on this most sensitive and difficult question. There has always been strong support for the view that life does not begin until live birth. This was the belief of the Stoics. It appears to be the predominant, though not the unanimous, attitude of the Jewish faith. It may be taken to represent also the position of a large segment of the Protestant community, insofar as that can be ascertained; organized groups that have taken a formal position on the abortion issue have generally regarded abortion as a matter for the conscience of the individual and her family. As we have noted, the common law found greater significance in quickening. Physicians and their scientific colleagues have regarded that event with less interest and have tended to focus either upon conception or upon live birth or upon the interim point at which the fetus becomes "viable," that is, potentially able to live outside the mother's womb, albeit with artificial aid. Viability is usually placed at about seven months (28 weeks) but may occur earlier, even at 24 weeks. . . .

In areas other than criminal abortion the law has been reluctant to endorse any theory that life, as we recognize it, begins before live birth or to accord legal rights to the unborn except in narrowly defined situations and except when the rights are contingent upon live birth. . . . In short, the unborn have never been recognized in the law as persons in the whole sense.

In view of all this, we do not agree that, by adopting one theory of life, Texas may override the rights of the pregnant woman that are at stake. We repeat, however, that the state does have an important and legitimate interest in preserving and protecting the health of the pregnant woman, whether she be a resident of the state or a nonresident who seeks medical consultation and treatment there, and that it has still *another* important and legitimate interest in protecting the potentiality of human life. These interests are separate and distinct. Each grows in substantiality as the woman approaches term and, at a point during pregnancy, each becomes "compelling."

With respect to the state's important and legitimate interest in the health of the mother, the "compelling" point, in the light of present medical knowledge, is at approximately the end of the first trimester. This is so because of the now established medical fact . . . that until the end of the first trimester mortality in abortion is less than mortality in normal childbirth. It follows that, from and after this point, a state may regulate the abortion procedure to the extent that the regulation reasonably relates to the preservation and protection of maternal health. Examples of permissible state regulation in this area are requirements as to the qualifications of the person who is to perform the abortion; as to the licensure of that person; as to the facility in which the procedure is to be performed, that is, whether it must be a hospital or may be a clinic or some other place of less-than-hospital status; as to the licensing of the facility; and the like.

This means, on the other hand, that, for the period of pregnancy prior to this "compelling" point, the attending physician, in consultation with his patient, is free to determine, without regulation by the state, that in his medical judgment the patient's pregnancy should be terminated. If that decision is reached, the judgment may be effectuated by an abortion free of interference by the state.

With respect to the state's important and legitimate interest in potential life, the "compelling" point is at viability. This is so because the fetus then presumably has the capability of meaningful life outside the mother's womb. State regulation protective of fetal life after viability thus has both logical and biological justifications. If the state is interested in protecting fetal life after viability, it may go so far as to proscribe abortion during that period except when it is necessary to preserve the life or health of the mother. . . .

To summarize and repeat:

1. A state criminal abortion statute of the current Texas type, that excepts from criminality only a *life-saving* procedure on behalf of the mother, without regard to pregnancy stage and without recognition of the other interests involved, is violative of the Due Process Clause of the Fourteenth Amendment.

(a) For the stage prior to approximately the end of the first trimester, the abortion decision and its effectuation must be left to the medical judgment of the pregnant woman's attending physician.

(b) For the stage subsequent to approximately the end of the first trimester, the state, in promoting its interest in the health of the mother, may, if it chooses, regulate the abortion procedure in ways that are reasonably related to maternal health.

(c) For the stage subsequent to viability the state, in promoting its interest in the potentiality of human life, may, if it chooses, regulate, and even proscribe, abortion except where it is necessary, in appropriate medical judgment, for the preservation of the life or health of the mother.

2. The state may define the term "physician" . . . to mean only a physician currently licensed by the state, and may proscribe any abortion by a person who is not a physician as so defined.

. . . The decision leaves the state free to place increasing restrictions on abortion as the period of pregnancy lengthens, so long as those restrictions are tailored to the recognized state interests. The decision vindicates the right of the physician to administer medical treatment according to his professional judgment up to the points where important state interests provide compelling justifications for intervention. Up to those points the abortion decision in all its aspects is inherently, and primarily, a medical decision, and basic responsibility for it must rest with the physician. If an individual practitioner abuses the privilege of exercising proper medical judgment, the usual remedies, judicial and intraprofessional, are available. . . .

[Mr. Justice White, with whom Mr. Justice Rehnquist joins, dissenting.]

At the heart of the controversy in these cases are those recurring pregnancies that pose no danger whatsoever to the life or health of the mother but are, nevertheless, unwanted for any one or more of a variety of reasons—convenience, family planning, economics, dislike of children, the embarrassment of illegitimacy, etc. The common claim before us is that for any one of such reasons, or for no reason at all, and without asserting or claiming any threat to life or health, any woman is entitled to an abortion at her request if she is able to find a medical advisor willing to undertake the procedure.

The Court for the most part sustains this position: During the period prior to the time the fetus becomes viable, the Constitution of the United States values the convenience, whim, or caprice of the putative mother more than the life or potential life of the fetus; the Constitution, therefore, guarantees the right to an abortion as against any state law or policy seeking to protect the fetus from an abortion not prompted by more compelling reasons of the mother.

With all due respect, I dissent. I find nothing in the language or history of the Constitution to support the Court's judgment. The Court simply fashions and announces a new constitutional right for pregnant mothers and, with scarcely any reason or authority for its action, invests that right with sufficient substance to override most existing state abortion statutes. The upshot is that the people and the legislatures of the 50 states are constitutionally disentitled to weigh the relative importance of the continued existence and development of the fetus, on the one hand, against a spectrum of possible impacts on the mother, on the other hand. As an exercise of raw judicial power, the Court perhaps has authority to do what it does today; but in my view its judgment is an improvident and extravagant exercise of the power of judicial review that the Constitution extends to this Court.

The Court apparently values the convenience of the pregnant mother more than the continued existence and development of the life or potential life that she carries. Whether or not I might agree with that marshaling of values, I can in no event join the Court's judgment because I find no constitutional warrant for imposing such an order of priorities on the people and legislatures of the states. In a sensitive area such as this, involving as it does issues over which reasonable men may easily and heatedly differ, I cannot accept the Court's exercise of its clear power of choice by interposing a constitutional barrier to state efforts to protect human life and by investing mothers and doctors with the constitutionally protected right to exterminate it. This issue, for the most part, should be left with the people and to the political processes the people have devised to govern their affairs.

It is my view, therefore, that the Texas statute is not constitutionally infirm because it denies abortions to those who seek to serve only their convenience rather than to protect their life or health. Nor is this plaintiff, who claims no threat to her mental or physical health, entitled to assert the possible rights of those women whose pregnancy assertedly implicated their health. This, together with *United States v. Vuitch*, 402 U.S. 62 (1971), dictates reversal of the judgment of the District Court.

UNITED STATES SUPREME COURT

City of Akron v. Akron Center for Reproductive Health

[Justice O'Connor delivered this dissenting opinion.]

I

The trimester or "three-stage" approach adopted by the Court in *Roe*, and, in a modified form, employed by the Court to analyze the state regulations in these cases, cannot be supported as a legitimate or useful framework for accommodating the woman's right and the State's interests. The decision of the Court today graphically illustrates why the trimester approach is a completely unworkable method of accommodating the conflicting personal rights and compelling state interests that are involved in the abortion context.

As the Court indicates today, the State's compelling interest in maternal health changes as medical technology changes, and any health regulation must not "depart from accepted medical practice." . . . In applying this standard, the Court holds that "the safety of second-trimester abortions has increased dramatically" since 1973, when *Roe* was decided. . . .

It is not difficult to see that despite the Court's purported adherence to the trimester approach adopted in *Roe*, the lines drawn in that decision have now been "blurred" because of what the Court accepts as technological advancement in the safety of abortion procedure. The State may no longer rely on a "bright line" that separates permissible from impermissible regulation, and it is no longer free to consider the second trimester as a unit and weigh the risks posed by all abortion procedures throughout that trimester. Rather, the State must continuously and conscientiously study contemporary medical and scientific literature in order to determine whether the effect of a particular regulation is to "depart from accepted medical practice" insofar as particular procedures and particular periods within the trimester are concerned. Assuming that legislative bodies are able to engage in this exacting task,

Reprinted from 462 *United States Reports* 416; decided June 15, 1983.

it is difficult to believe that our Constitution *requires* that they do it as a prelude to protecting the health of their citizens. . . . As today's decision indicates, medical technology is changing, and this change will necessitate our continued functioning as the nation's "*ex officio* medical board with powers to approve or disapprove medical and operative practices and standards throughout the United States." [*Planned Parenthood v. Danforth*, 428 U. S. 52, 99 (1976) (White, J., concurring in part and dissenting in part).]

Just as improvements in medical technology inevitably will move *forward* the point at which the State may regulate for reasons of maternal health, different technological improvements will move *backward* the point of viability at which the State may proscribe abortions except when necessary to preserve the life and health of the mother.

In 1973, viability before 28 weeks was considered unusual. The fourteenth edition of L. Hellman & J. Pritchard, Williams Obstetrics, on which the Court relied in *Roe* for its understanding of viability, stated that "[a]ttainment of a [fetal] weight of 1,000 g [or a fetal age of approximately 28 weeks gestation] is . . . widely used as the criterion of viability." *Id.*, at 493. However, recent studies have demonstrated increasingly earlier fetal viability. It is certainly reasonable to believe that fetal viability in the first trimester of pregnancy may be possible in the not too distant future. Indeed, the Court has explicitly acknowledged that *Roe* left the point of viability "flexible for anticipated advancements in medical skill." *Colautti v. Franklin*, 439 U. S. 379, 387 (1979). "[W]e recognized in *Roe* that viability was a matter of medical judgment, skill, and technical ability, and we preserved the flexibility of the term." *Danforth, supra*, 428 U. S. at 64.

The *Roe* framework, then, is clearly on a collision course with itself. As the medical risks of various abortion procedures decrease, the point at which the State may regulate for reasons of maternal health is moved further forward to actual childbirth. As medical science becomes better able to provide for the separate existence of the fetus, the point of viability is moved further back toward conception. . . . The *Roe* framework is inherently tied to the state of medical technology that exists whenever particular litigation ensues. Although legislatures are better suited to make the necessary factual judgments in this area, the Court's framework forces legislatures, as a matter of constitutional law, to speculate about what constitutes "accepted medical practice" at any given time. Without the necessary expertise or ability, courts must then

pretend to act as science review boards and examine those legislative judgments. . . .

II

The Court in *Roe* correctly realized that the State has important interests "in the areas of health and medical standards" and that "[t]he State has a legitimate interest in seeing to it that abortion, like any other medical procedure, is performed under circumstances that insure maximum safety for the patient." . . . The Court also recognized that the State has "*another* important and legitimate interest in protecting the potentiality of human life." I agree completely that the State has these interests, but in my view, the point at which these interests become compelling does not depend on the trimester of pregnancy. Rather, these interests are present *throughout* pregnancy. . . .

The fallacy inherent in the *Roe* framework is apparent: just because the State has a compelling interest in ensuring maternal safety once an abortion may be more dangerous in childbirth, it simply does not follow that the State has *no* interest before that point that justifies state regulation to ensure that first-trimester abortions are performed as safely as possible.

The state interest in potential human life is likewise extant throughout pregnancy. In *Roe*, the Court held that although the State had an important and legitimate interest in protecting potential life, that interest could not become compelling until the point at which the fetus was viable. The difficulty with this analysis is clear: *potential* life is no less potential in the first weeks of pregnancy than it is at viability or afterward. At any stage in pregnancy, there is the *potential* for human life. Although the Court refused to "resolve the difficult question of when life begins," *id.*, at 159, the Court chose the point of viability—when the fetus is *capable* of life independent of its mother—to permit the complete proscription of abortion. The choice of viability as the point at which the state interest in *potential* life becomes compelling is no less arbitrary than choosing any point before viability or any point afterward. Accordingly, I believe that the State's interest in protecting potential human life exists throughout the pregnancy.

III

. . . The Court's reliance on increased abortion costs and decreased availability is misplaced. As the City of Arkon points out, there is no evidence in this case to show that the two Akron hospitals that performed second-trimester abortions denied an abortion to any woman, or that they would not permit abortion by the D&E procedure. In addition, there was no evidence presented that other hospitals in nearby areas did not provide second-trimester abortions. Further, almost *any* state regulation, including the licensing requirements that the Court *would* allow, inevitably and necessarily entails increased costs for *any* abortion. In *Simopoulos* v. *Virginia*, the Court upholds the State's stringent licensing requirements that will clearly involve greater cost because the State's licensing scheme "is not an unreasonable means of furthering the State's compelling interest in" preserving maternal health. Although the Court acknowledges this indisputably correct notion in *Simopoulos*, it inexplicably refuses to apply it in this case. A health regulation, such as the hospitalization requirement, simply does not rise to the level of "official interference" with the abortion decision. . . .

Section 1870.05(B) of the Akron ordinance provides that no physician shall perform an abortion on a minor under 15 years of age unless the minor gives written consent, and the physician first obtains the informed written consent of a parent or guardian, or unless the minor first obtains "an order from a court having jurisdiction over her that the abortion be performed or induced." Despite the fact that this regulation has yet to be construed in the state courts, the Court holds that the regulation is unconstitutional because it is not "reasonably susceptible of being construed to create an 'opportunity for case-by-case evaluations of the maturity of pregnant minors.'" [*Ante*, at 23 (quoting *Bellotti II, supra*, 443 U. S., at 643–644, n. 23 (plurality opinion)).] I believe that the Court should have abstained from declaring the ordinance unconstitutional.

In *Bellotti I, supra*, the Court abstained from deciding whether a state parental consent provision was unconstitutional as applied to mature minors. The Court recognized and respected the well-settled rule that abstention is proper "where an unconstrued state statute is susceptible of a construction by the state judiciary 'which might avoid in whole or in part the necessity for federal constitutional adjudication, or at least materially change the nature of the problem.'" [428 U. S., at 147 (quoting *Harrison* v. *NAACP*, 360 U. S. 167, 177, (1959)).] While acknowledging the force of the abstention doctrine, see *ante*, at 22, the Court never-

theless declines to apply it. Instead, it speculates that a state juvenile court *might* inquire into a minor's maturity and ability to decide to have an abortion in deciding whether the minor is being provided "'surgical care . . . necessary for his health, morals, or well being,'" *ante* at 23, n. 31 (quoting Ohio Rev. Code Ann. § 2151.03). The Court ultimately rejects this possible interpretation of state law, however, because filing a petition in juvenile court requires parental notification, an unconstitutional condition insofar as mature minors are concerned.

Assuming *arguendo* that the Court is correct in holding that a parental notification requirement would be unconstitutional as applied to mature minors, I see no reason to assume that the Akron ordinance and the state juvenile court statute compel state judges to notify the parents of a mature minor if such notification was contrary to the minor's best interests. Further, there is no reason to believe that the state courts would construe the consent requirement to impose any type of parental or judicial veto on the abortion decisions of mature minors. . . .

The Court invalidates the informed consent provisions of § 1870.06(B) and § 1870.06(C) of the Akron ordinance.[1] . . .

We have approved informed consent provisions in the past even though the physician was required to deliver certain information to the patient. In *Danforth, supra*, the Court upheld a state informed consent requirement because "[t]he decision to abort, indeed, is an important, and often a stressful one, and it is desirable and imperative that it be made with full knowledge of its nature and consequences." 428 U. S., at 67.[2] In *H.L.* v. *Matheson, supra*, the Court noted that the state statute in the case required that the patient "be advised at a minimum about available adoption services, about fetal development, and about forseeable complications and risks of an abortion. . . .

The remainder of § 1870.06(B), and § 1870.06(C), impose no undue burden or drastic limitation on the abortion decision. The City of Akron is merely attempting to ensure that the decision to abort is made in light of that knowledge that the City deems relevant to informed choice. As such, these regulations do not impermissibly affect any privacy right under the Fourteenth Amendment.

Section 1870.07 of the Akron ordinance requires a 24-hour waiting period between the signing of a consent form and the actual performance of the abortion, except in cases of emergency. See § 1870.12. The court below invalidated this requirement because it affected abortion decisions during the first trimester of pregnancy. The Court affirms the decision below, not on the ground that it affects early abortions, but because "Akron has failed to demonstrate that any legitimate state interest is furthered by an arbitrary and inflexible waiting period." . . .

The State's compelling interests in maternal physical and mental health and protection of fetal life clearly justify the waiting period. As we acknowledged in *Danforth, supra,* 428 U. S., at 67, the decision to abort is "a stressful one," and the waiting period reasonably relates to the State's interest in ensuring that a woman does not make this serious decision in undue haste. The decision also has grave consequences for the fetus, whose life the State has a compelling interest to protect and preserve. "No other [medical] procedure involves the purposeful termination of a potential life." [*Harris, supra,* 448 U. S., at 325.] The waiting period is surely a small cost to impose to ensure that the woman's decision is well-considered in light of its certain and irreparable consequences on fetal life, and the possible effects on her own. . . .

IV

For the reasons set forth above, I dissent from the judgment of the Court in these cases.

NOTES

1. Section 1870.06(B) requires that the attending physician orally inform the pregnant woman: (1) that she is pregnant; (2) the probable number of weeks since conception; (3) that the unborn child is a human being from the moment of conception, and has certain anatomical and physiological characteristics; (4) that the unborn child may be viable and if so, the physician has a legal responsibility to try to save the child; (5) that abortion is a major surgical procedure that can result in serious physical and psychological complications; (6) that various agencies exist that will provide the pregnant woman with information about birth control; and (7) that various agencies exist that will assist the woman through pregnancy should she decide not to undergo the abortion. Section 1870.06(C) requires the attending physician to inform the woman of risks associated with her particular pregnancy and proposed abortion technique, as well as information that the physician deems relevant "in his own medical judgment."

2. The Court in *Danforth* did not even view the informed consent requirement as having a "legally significant impact" on first-trimester abortions that would trigger the *Roe* and *Doe* proscriptions against state interference in the decision to seek a first-trimester abortion. See 428 U. S., at 81 (recordkeeping requirements).

UNITED STATES SUPREME COURT

Planned Parenthood of Southeastern Pennsylvania v. Robert P. Casey, et al., etc.

[June 29, 1992]

[Justice O'Connor, Justice Kennedy, and Justice Souter announced the judgment of the Court and delivered the opinion of the Court.]

I

Liberty finds no refuge in a jurisprudence of doubt. Yet 19 years after our holding that the Constitution

Slip Opinion, Docket No. 91–744, 29 June 1992.

protects a woman's right to terminate her pregnancy in its early stages, *Roe* v. *Wade,* 410 U. S. 113 (1973), that definition of liberty is still questioned. Joining the respondents as *amicus curiae,* the United States, as it has done in five other cases in the last decade, again asks us to overrule *Roe.* . . .

At issue in these cases are five provisions of the Pennsylvania Abortion Control Act of 1982 as amended in 1988 and 1989. . . . The Act requires that a woman seeking an abortion give her informed consent prior to the abortion procedure, and specifies that she be provided with certain information at least 24 hours before the abortion is performed. For a minor to obtain an abortion, the Act requires the informed consent of one of her parents, but provides for a judicial bypass option if the minor does not wish to or cannot obtain a parent's consent. Another provision of the Act requires that, unless certain exceptions apply, a married woman seeking an abortion must sign a statement indicating that she has notified her husband of her intended abortion. The Act exempts compliance with these three requirements in the event of a "medical emergency," which is defined in § 3203 of the Act. In addition to the above provisions regulating the performance of abortions, the Act imposes certain reporting requirements on facilities that provide abortion services. . . .

We find it imperative to review once more the principles that define the rights of the woman and the legitimate authority of the State respecting the termination of pregnancies by abortion procedures.

After considering the fundamental constitutional questions resolved by *Roe*, principles of institutional integrity, and the rule of *stare decisis*, we are led to conclude this: the essential holding of *Roe* v. *Wade* should be retained and once again reaffirmed.

It must be stated at the outset and with clarity that *Roe*'s essential holding, the holding we reaffirm, has three parts. First is a recognition of the right of the woman to choose to have an abortion before viability and to obtain it without undue interference from the State. Before viability, the State's interests are not strong enough to support a prohibition of abortion or the imposition of a substantial obstacle to the woman's effective right to elect the procedure. Second is a confirmation of the State's power to restrict abortions after fetal viability, if the law contains exceptions for pregnancies which endanger a woman's life or health. And third is the principle that the State has legitimate interests from the outset of the pregnancy in protecting the health of the woman and the life of the fetus that may become a child. These principles do not contradict one another; and we adhere to each.

II

Constitutional protection of the woman's decision to terminate her pregnancy derives from the Due Process Clause of the Fourteenth Amendment. It declares that no State shall "deprive any person of life, liberty, or property, without due process of law." The controlling word in the case before us is "liberty." . . .

It is a promise of the Constitution that there is a realm of personal liberty which the government may not enter. We have vindicated this principle before. Marriage is mentioned nowhere in the Bill of Rights and interracial marriage was illegal in most States in the 19th century, but the Court was no doubt correct in finding it to be an aspect of liberty protected against state interference by the substantive component of the Due Process Clause. . . .

In *Griswold*, we held that the Constitution does not permit a State to forbid a married couple to use contraceptives. That same freedom was later guaranteed, under the Equal Protection Clause, for unmarried couples. See *Eisenstadt* v. *Baird*, 405 U. S. 438 (1972). Constitutional protection was extended to the sale and distribution of contraceptives in *Carey* v. *Population Services International, supra*. It is settled now, as it was when the Court heard arguments in *Roe* v. *Wade*, that the Constitution places limits on a State's right to interfere with a person's most basic decisions about family and parenthood. . . .

The inescapable fact is that adjudication of substantive due process claims may call upon the Court in interpreting the Constitution to exercise that same capacity which by tradition courts always have exercised: reasoned judgment. Its boundaries are not susceptible of expression as a simple rule. That does not mean we are free to invalidate state policy choices with which we disagree; yet neither does it permit us to shrink from the duties of our office. . . .

It should be recognized, moreover, that in some critical respects the abortion decision is of the same character as the decision to use contraception, to which *Griswold* v. *Connecticut, Eisenstadt* v. *Baird*, and *Carey* v. *Population Services International*, afford constitutional protection. We have no doubt as to the correctness of those decisions. They support the reasoning in *Roe* relating to the woman's liberty because they involve personal decisions concerning not only the meaning of procreation but also human responsibility and respect for it. As with abortion, reasonable people will have differences of opinion about these matters. One view is based on such reverence for the wonder of creation that any pregnancy ought to be welcomed and carried to full term no matter how difficult it will be to provide for the child and ensure its well-being. Another is that the inability to provide for the nurture and care of the infant is a cruelty to the child and an anguish to the parent. These are intimate views with infinite variations, and their deep, personal character underlay our decisions in *Griswold*, *Eisenstadt*, and *Carey*. The same concerns are present where the woman confronts the reality that, perhaps despite her attempts to avoid it, she has become pregnant. . . .

III

. . . No evolution of legal principle has left *Roe*'s doctrinal footings weaker than they were in 1973. No development of constitutional law since the case was decided has implicitly or explicitly left *Roe* behind as a mere survivor of obsolete constitutional thinking. . . .

The *Roe* Court itself placed its holding in the succession of cases most prominently exemplified by *Griswold* v. *Connecticut*, 381 U. S. 479 (1965), see *Roe*, 410 U. S., at 152–153. When it is so seen, *Roe* is clearly in no jeopardy, since subsequent constitutional developments have neither disturbed, nor do they threaten to diminish, the scope of recognized protection accorded to the liberty relating to intimate relationships, the family, and decisions about whether or not to beget or bear a child. . . .

[However], time has overtaken some of *Roe*'s factual assumptions: advances in maternal health care allow for abortions safe to the mother later in pregnancy than was true in 1973, see *Akron I*, *supra*, at 429, n. 11, and advances in neonatal care have advanced viability to a point somewhat earlier. . . . But these facts go only to the scheme of time limits on the realization of competing interests, and the divergences from the factual premises of 1973 have no bearing on the validity of *Roe*'s central holding, that viability marks the earliest point at which the State's interest in fetal life is constitutionally adequate to justify a legislative ban on nontherapeutic abortions. The soundness or unsoundness of that constitutional judgment in no sense turns on whether viability occurs at approximately 28 weeks, as was usual at the time of *Roe*, at 23 to 24 weeks, as it sometimes does today, or at some moment even slightly earlier in pregnancy, as it may if fetal respiratory capacity can somehow be enhanced in the future. Whenever it may occur, the attainment of viability may continue to serve as the critical fact, just as it has done since *Roe* was decided; which is to say that no change in *Roe*'s factual underpinning has left its central holding obsolete, and none supports an argument for overruling it. . . .

. . . Liberty must not be extinguished for want of a line that is clear. And it falls to us to give some real substance to the woman's liberty to determine whether to carry her pregnancy to full term.

We conclude the line should be drawn at viability, so that before that time the woman has a right to choose to terminate her pregnancy. We adhere to this principle for two reasons. First . . . is the doctrine of *stare decisis*. Any judicial act of line-drawing may seem somewhat arbitrary, but *Roe* was a reasoned statement, elaborated with great care. We have twice reaffirmed it in the face of great opposition. . . .

The second reason is that the concept of viability, as we noted in *Roe*, is the time at which there is a realistic possibility of maintaining and nourishing a life outside the womb, so that the independent existence of a second life can in reason and all fairness be the object of state protection that now overrides the rights of the woman. See *Roe* v. *Wade*, 410 U. S., at 163. Consistent with other constitutional norms, legislatures may draw lines which appear arbitrary without the necessity of offering a justification. But courts may not. We must justify the lines we draw. And there is no line other than viability which is more workable. To be sure, as we have said, there may be some medical developments that affect the precise point of viability, but this is an imprecision within tolerable limits given that the medical community and all those who must apply its discoveries will continue to explore the matter. The viability line also has, as a practical matter, an element of fairness. In some broad sense it might be said that a woman who fails to act before viability has consented to the State's intervention on behalf of the developing child.

The woman's right to terminate her pregnancy before viability is the most central principle of *Roe* v. *Wade*. It is a rule of law and a component of liberty we cannot renounce.

On the other side of the equation is the interest of the State in the protection of potential life. The *Roe* Court recognized the State's "important and legitimate interest in protecting the potentiality of human life." *Roe*, *supra*, at 162. The weight to be given this state interest, not the strength of the woman's interest, was the difficult question faced in *Roe*. We do not need to say whether each of us, had we been Members of the Court when the valuation of the State interest came before it as an original matter, would have concluded, as the *Roe* Court did, that its weight is insufficient to justify a ban on abortions prior to viability even when it is subject to certain exceptions. The matter is not before us in the first instance, and coming as it does after nearly 20 years of litigation in *Roe*'s wake we are satisfied that the immediate question is not the soundness of *Roe*'s resolution of the issue, but the precedential force that must be accorded to its holding. And we have concluded that the essential holding of *Roe* should be reaffirmed.

Yet it must be remembered that *Roe v. Wade* speaks with clarity in establishing not only the woman's liberty but also the State's "important and legitimate interest in potential life." *Roe, supra*, at 163. That portion of the decision in *Roe* has been given too little acknowledgement and implementation by the Court in its subsequent cases. . . .

Roe established a trimester framework to govern abortion regulations. Under this elaborate but rigid construct, almost no regulation at all is permitted during the first trimester of pregnancy; regulations designed to protect the woman's health, but not to further the State's interest in potential life, are permitted during the second trimester; and during the third trimester, when the fetus is viable, prohibitions are permitted provided the life or health of the mother is not at stake. *Roe v. Wade, supra*, at 163–166. Most of our cases since *Roe* have involved the application of rules derived from the trimester framework. . . .

The trimester framework no doubt was erected to ensure that the woman's right to choose not become so subordinate to the State's interest in promoting fetal life that her choice exists in theory but not in fact. We do not agree, however, that the trimester approach is necessary to accomplish this objective. A framework of this rigidity was unnecessary and in its later interpretation sometimes contradicted the State's permissible exercise of its powers.

Though the woman has a right to choose to terminate or continue her pregnancy before viability, it does not at all follow that the State is prohibited from taking steps to ensure that this choice is thoughtful and informed. Even in the earliest stages of pregnancy, the State may enact rules and regulations designed to encourage her to know that there are philosophic and social arguments of great weight that can be brought to bear in favor of continuing the pregnancy to full term and that there are procedures and institutions to allow adoption of unwanted children as well as a certain degree of state assistance if the mother chooses to raise the child herself. . . .

Numerous forms of state regulation might have the incidental effect of increasing the cost or decreasing the availability of medical care, whether for abortion or any other medical procedure. The fact that a law which serves a valid purpose, one not designed to strike at the right itself, has the incidental effect of making it more difficult or more expensive to procure an abortion cannot be enough to invalidate it. Only where state regulation imposes an undue burden on a woman's ability to make this decision does the power of the State reach into the heart of the liberty protected by the Due Process Clause. . . .

These considerations of the nature of the abortion right illustrate that it is an overstatement to describe it as a right to decide whether to have an abortion "without interference from the State," *Planned Parenthood of Central Mo. v. Danforth*, 428 U. S. 52, 61 (1976). All abortion regulations interfere to some degree with a woman's ability to decide whether to terminate her pregnancy. . . .

Roe v. Wade was express in its recognition of the State's "important and legitimate interest[s] in preserving and protecting the health of the pregnant woman [and] in protecting the potentiality of human life." 410 U. S., at 162. The trimester framework, however, does not fulfill *Roe*'s own promise that the State has an interest in protecting fetal life or potential life. *Roe* began the contradiction by using the trimester framework to forbid any regulation of abortion designed to advance that interest before viability. *Id.*, at 163. Before viability, *Roe* and subsequent cases treat all governmental attempts to influence a woman's decision on behalf of the potential life within her as unwarranted. This treatment is, in our judgment, incompatible with the recognition that there is a substantial state interest in potential life throughout pregnancy. Cf. *Webster*, 492 U. S., at 519 (opinion of Rehnquist, C. J.); *Akron I, supra*, at 461 (O'Connor, J., dissenting).

The very notion that the State has a substantial interest in potential life leads to the conclusion that not all regulations must be deemed unwarranted. Not all burdens on the right to decide whether to terminate a pregnancy will be undue. In our view, the undue burden standard is the appropriate means of reconciling the State's interest with the woman's constitutionally protected liberty. . . .

A finding of an undue burden is a shorthand for the conclusion that a state regulation has the purpose or effect of placing a substantial obstacle in the path of a woman seeking an abortion of a nonviable fetus. A statute with this purpose is invalid because the means chosen by the State to further the interest in potential life must be calculated to inform the woman's free choice, not hinder it. . . . That is to be expected in the application of any legal standard which must accommodate life's complexity. We do not expect it to be otherwise with respect to the undue burden standard. We give this summary:

(a) To protect the central right recognized by *Roe v. Wade* while at the same time accommodating the State's profound interest in potential life, we will employ the undue burden analysis as explained in this opinion. An undue burden exists, and therefore a provision of law is invalid, if its purpose or effect is to place a substantial obstacle in the path of a woman seeking an abortion before the fetus attains viability.

(b) We reject the rigid trimester framework of *Roe v. Wade*. To promote the State's profound interest in potential life, throughout pregnancy the State may take measures to ensure that the woman's choice is informed, and measures designed to advance this interest will not be invalidated as long as their purpose is to persuade the woman to choose childbirth over abortion. These measures must not be an undue burden on the right.

(c) As with any medical procedure, the State may enact regulations to further the health or safety of a woman seeking an abortion. Unnecessary health regulations that have the purpose or effect of presenting a substantial obstacle to a woman seeking an abortion impose an undue burden on the right.

(d) Our adoption of the undue burden analysis does not disturb the central holding of *Roe v. Wade*, and we reaffirm that holding. Regardless of whether exceptions are made for particular circumstances, a State may not prohibit any woman from making the ultimate decision to terminate her pregnancy before viability.

(e) We also reaffirm *Roe*'s holding that "subsequent to viability, the State in promoting its interest in the potentiality of human life may, if it chooses, regulate, and even proscribe, abortion except where it is necessary, in appropriate medical judgment, for the preservation of the life or health of the mother." *Roe v. Wade*, 410 U. S., at 164–165.

These principles control our assessment of the Pennsylvania statute, and we now turn to the issue of the validity of its challenged provisions.

V

The Court of Appeals applied what it believed to be the undue burden standard and upheld each of the provisions except for the husband notification requirement. We agree generally with this conclusion, but refine the undue burden analysis in accordance with the principles articulated above. . . .

B

We next consider the informed consent requirement. 18 Pa. Cons. Stat. Ann. § 3205. Except in a medical emergency, the statute requires that at least 24 hours before performing an abortion a physician inform the woman of the nature of the procedure, the health risks of the abortion and of childbirth, and the "probable gestational age of the unborn child." The physician or a qualified nonphysician must inform the woman of the availability of printed materials published by the State describing the fetus and providing information about medical assistance for childbirth, information about child support from the father, and a list of agencies which provide adoption and other services as alternatives to abortion. An abortion may not be performed unless the woman certifies in writing that she has been informed of the availability of these printed materials and has been provided them if she chooses to view them.

Our prior decisions establish that as with any medical procedure, the State may require a woman to give her written informed consent to an abortion. . . .

In *Akron I*, 462 U. S. 416 (1983), we invalidated an ordinance which required that a woman seeking an abortion be provided by her physician with specific information "designed to influence the woman's informed choice between abortion or childbirth." *Id.*, at 444. As we later described the *Akron I* holding in *Thornburgh v. American College of Obstetricians and Gynecologists*, 476 U. S., at 762, there were two purported flaws in the Akron ordinance: the information was designed to dissuade the woman from having an abortion and the ordinance imposed "a rigid requirement that a specific body of information be given in all cases, irrespective of the particular needs of the patient. . . ." *Ibid.* . . .

In attempting to ensure that a woman apprehend the full consequences of her decision, the State furthers the legitimate purpose of reducing the risk that a woman may elect an abortion, only to discover later, with devastating psychological consequences, that her decision was not fully informed. If the information the State requires to be made available to the woman is truthful and not misleading, the requirement may be permissible.

We also see no reason why the State may not require doctors to inform a woman seeking an abortion of the availability of materials relating to the consequences to the fetus, even when those consequences have no direct relation to her health. An example illustrates the point. We would think it constitutional for the State to require that in order for there to be informed consent to a kidney transplant operation the recipient must be supplied with information about risks to the donor as well as risks to himself or herself. . . .

Whether the mandatory 24-hour waiting period is nonetheless invalid because in practice it is a substantial obstacle to a woman's choice to terminate her pregnancy is a closer question. The findings of fact by the District Court indicate that because of the distances many women must travel to reach an abortion provider, the practical effect will often be a delay of much more than a day because the waiting period requires that a woman seeking an abortion make at least two visits to the doctor. The District Court also found that in many instances this will increase the exposure of women seeking abortions to "the harassment and hostility of anti-abortion protestors demonstrating outside a clinic." 744 F. Supp., at 1351. As a result, the District Court found that for those women who have the fewest financial resources, those who must travel long distances, and those who have difficulty explaining their whereabouts to husbands, employers, or others, the 24-hour waiting period will be "particularly burdensome." . . .

We are left with the argument that the various aspects of the informed consent requirement are unconstitutional because they place barriers in the way of abortion on demand. Even the broadest reading of *Roe*, however, has not suggested that there is a constitutional right to abortion on demand. See, *e.g., Doe* v. *Bolton*, 410 U. S., at 189. Rather, the right protected by *Roe* is a right to decide to terminate a pregnancy free of undue interference by the State. Because the informed consent requirement facilitates the wise exercise of that right it cannot be classified as an interference with the right *Roe* protects. The informed consent requirement is not an undue burden on that right.

Section 3209 of Pennsylvania's abortion law provides, except in cases of medical emergency, that no physician shall perform an abortion on a married woman without receiving a signed statement from the woman that she has notified her spouse that she is about to undergo an abortion. The woman has the option of providing an alternative signed statement certifying that her husband is not the man who impregnated her; that her husband could not be located; that the pregnancy is the result of spousal sexual assault which she has reported; or that the woman believes that notifying her husband will cause him or someone else to inflict bodily injury upon her. A physician who performs an abortion on a married woman without receiving the appropriate signed statement will have his or her license revoked, and is liable to the husband for damages. . . .

The American Medical Association (AMA) has published a summary of the recent research in this field, which indicates that in an average 12-month period in this country, approximately two million women are the victims of severe assaults by their male partners. In a 1985 survey, women reported that nearly one of every eight husbands had assaulted their wives during the past year. The AMA views these figures as "marked underestimates," because the nature of these incidents discourages women from reporting them, and because surveys typically exclude the very poor, those who do not speak English well, and women who are homeless or in institutions or hospitals when the survey is conducted. According to the AMA, "[r]esearchers on family violence agree that the true incidence of partner violence is probably *double* the above estimates; or four million severely assaulted women per year. Studies suggest that from one-fifth to one-third of all women will be physically assaulted by a partner or ex-partner during their lifetime." AMA Council on Scientific Affairs, Violence Against Women 7 (1991) (emphasis in original). Thus on an average day in the United States, nearly 11,000 women are severely assaulted by their male partners. Many of these incidents involve sexual assault. . . . In families where wife-beating takes place, moreover, child abuse is often present as well. . . .

In well-functioning marriages, spouses discuss important intimate decisions such as whether to bear a child. But there are millions of women in this country who are the victims of regular physical and psychological abuse at the hands of their husbands. Should these women become pregnant, they may have very good reasons for not wishing to inform their husbands of their decision to obtain an abortion. Many may have justifiable fears of physical abuse, but may be no less fearful of the consequences of reporting prior abuse to the Commonwealth of Pennsylvania. Many may have a reasonable fear that notifying their husbands will provoke further instances of child abuse; these women are not exempt from § 3209's notification requirement. . . . If anything in this field is certain, it is that victims of spousal sexual assault are extremely reluctant to report the abuse to the government; hence, a great many spousal rape victims will not be exempt from the notification requirement imposed by § 3209.

The spousal notification requirement is thus likely to prevent a significant number of women from obtaining an abortion. It does not merely make abortions a little more difficult or expensive to obtain; for many women, it will impose a substantial obstacle. We must not blind ourselves to the fact that the significant number of women who fear for their safety and the safety of their children are likely to be deterred from procuring an abortion as surely as if the Commonwealth had outlawed abortion in all cases. . . .

This conclusion is in no way inconsistent with our decisions upholding parental notification or consent requirements. See, *e.g., Akron II*. Those enactments, and our judgment that they are constitutional, are based on the quite reasonable assumption that minors will benefit from consultation with their parents and that children will often not realize that their parents

have their best interests at heart. We cannot adopt a parallel assumption about adult women. . . .

Our cases establish, and we reaffirm today, that a State may require a minor seeking an abortion to obtain the consent of a parent or guardian, provided that there is an adequate judicial bypass procedure. See, *e.g., Akron II*. Under these precedents, in our view, the one-parent consent requirement and judicial bypass procedure are constitutional. . . .

VI

Our Constitution is a covenant running from the first generation of Americans to us and then to future generations. It is a coherent succession. Each generation must learn anew that the Constitution's written terms embody ideas and aspirations that must survive more ages than one. We accept our responsibility not to retreat from interpreting the full meaning of the covenant in light of all of our precedents. We invoke it once again to define the freedom guaranteed by the Constitution's own promise, the promise of liberty.

• • •

The judgment in No. 91–902 is affirmed. The judgment in No. 91–744 is affirmed in part and reversed in part, and the case is remanded for proceedings consistent with this opinion, including consideration of the question of severability.

It is so ordered.

UNITED STATES SUPREME COURT

Automobile Workers v. Johnson Controls, Inc.

[March 20, 1991]

Justice Blackmun delivered the opinion of the Court.

In this case we are concerned with an employer's gender-based fetal-protection policy. May an employer exclude a fertile female employee from certain jobs because of its concern for the health of the fetus the woman might conceive?

I

Respondent Johnson Controls, Inc., manufactures batteries. In the manufacturing process, the element lead is a primary ingredient. Occupational exposure to lead entails health risks, including the risk of harm to any fetus carried by a female employee.

Before the Civil Rights Act of 1964, 78 Stat. 241, became law, Johnson Controls did not employ any woman in a battery-manufacturing job. In June 1977, however, it announced its first official policy concerning its employment of women in lead-exposure work. . . .

Johnson Controls "stopped short of excluding women capable of bearing children from lead exposure," *id.*, at 138, but emphasized that a woman who expected to have a child should not choose a job in which she would have such exposure. The company also required a woman who wished to be considered for employment to sign a statement that she had been advised of the risk of having a child while she was exposed to lead. . . .

Supreme Court Reporter 111, 1196–1217. March 20, 1991.

Five years later, in 1982, Johnson Controls shifted from a policy of warning to a policy of exclusion. Between 1979 and 1983, eight employees became pregnant while maintaining blood lead levels in excess of 30 micrograms per deciliter. Tr. of Oral Arg. 25, 34. This appeared to be the critical level noted by the Occupational Health and Safety Administration (OSHA) for a worker who was planning to have a family. See 29 CFR § 1910.1025 (1989). The company responded by announcing a broad exclusion of women from jobs that exposed them to lead:

". . . [I]t is [Johnson Controls'] policy that women who are pregnant or who are capable of bearing children will not be placed into jobs involving lead exposure or which could expose them to lead through the exercise of job bidding, bumping, transfer or promotion rights." App. 85–86.

The policy defined "women . . . capable of bearing children" as "[a]ll women except those whose inability to bear children is medically documented." *Id.*, at 81. It further stated that an unacceptable work station was one where, "over the past year," an employee had recorded a blood lead level of more than 30 micrograms per deciliter or the work site had yielded an air sample containing a lead level in excess of 30 micrograms per cubic meter. *Ibid.*

II

In April 1984, petitioners filed in the United States District Court for the Eastern District of Wisconsin a class action challenging Johnson Controls' fetal-protection policy as sex discrimination that violated Title

VII of the Civil Rights Act of 1964, as amended, 42 U. S. C. § 2000e *et seq.* Among the individual plaintiffs were petitioners Mary Craig, who had chosen to be sterilized in order to avoid losing her job. . . .

III

The bias in Johnson Controls' policy is obvious. Fertile men, but not fertile women, are given a choice as to whether they wish to risk their reproductive health for a particular job. Section 703(a) of the Civil Rights Act of 1964, 78 Stat. 255, as amended, 42 U. S. C. § 2000e-2(a), prohibits sex-based classifications in terms and conditions of employment, in hiring and discharging decisions, and in other employment decisions that adversely affect an employee's status. Respondent's fetal-protection policy explicitly discriminates against women on the basis of their sex. The policy excludes women with childbearing capacity from lead-exposed jobs and so creates a facial classification based on gender. Respondent assumes as much in its brief before this Court. Brief for Respondent 17, n. 24.

Nevertheless, the Court of Appeals assumed, as did the two appellate courts who already had confronted the issue, that sex-specific fetal-protection policies do not involve facial discrimination. . . .

. . . The court assumed that because the asserted reason for the sex-based exclusion (protecting women's unconceived offspring) was ostensibly benign, the policy was not sex-based discrimination. That assumption, however, was incorrect.

First, Johnson Controls' policy classifies on the basis of gender and childbearing capacity, rather than fertility alone. Respondent does not seek to protect the unconceived children of all its employees. Despite evidence in the record about the debilitating effect of lead exposure on the male reproductive system, Johnson Controls is concerned only with the harms that may befall the unborn offspring of its female employees. . . . Johnson Controls' policy is facially discriminatory because it requires only a female employee to produce proof that she is not capable of reproducing.

Our conclusion is bolstered by the Pregnancy Discrimination Act of 1978 (PDA), 92 Stat. 2076, 42 U. S. C. § 2000e(k), in which Congress explicitly provided that, for purposes of Title VII, discrimination "on the basis of sex" includes discrimination "because of or on the basis of pregnancy, childbirth, or related medical conditions." "The Pregnancy Discrimination Act has now made clear that, for all Title VII pur-

poses, discrimination based on a woman's pregnancy is, on its face, discrimination because of her sex." *Newport News Shipbuilding & Dry Dock Co.* v. *EEOC*, 462 U. S. 669, 684 (1983). In its use of the words "capable of bearing children" in the 1982 policy statement as the criterion for exclusion, Johnson Controls explicitly classifies on the basis of potential for pregnancy. Under the PDA, such a classification must be regarded, for Title VII purposes, in the same light as explicit sex discrimination. Respondent has chosen to treat all its female employees as potentially pregnant; that choice evinces discrimination on the basis of sex. . . .

The beneficence of an employer's purpose does not undermine the conclusion that an explicit gender-based policy is sex discrimination under § 703(a) and thus may be defended only as a BFOQ [bona fide occupational qualification].

The enforcement policy of the Equal Employment Opportunity Commission accords with this conclusion. On January 24, 1990, the EEOC issued a Policy Guidance in the light of the Seventh Circuit's decision in the present case. . . .

In sum, Johnson Controls' policy "does not pass the simple test of whether the evidence shows 'treatment of a person in a manner which but for that person's sex would be different.'" . . .

IV

Under § 703(e)(1) of Title VII, an employer may discriminate on the basis of "religion, sex, or national origin in those certain instances where religion, sex, or national origin is a bona fide occupational qualification reasonably necessary to the normal operation of that particular business or enterprise." 42 U. S. C. § 2000e-2(e)(1). We therefore turn to the question whether Johnson Controls' fetal-protection policy is one of those "certain instances" that come within the BFOQ exception. . . .

The PDA's amendment to Title VII contains a BFOQ standard of its own: unless pregnant employees differ from others "in their ability or inability to work," they must be "treated the same" as other employees "for all employment-related purposes." 42 U. S. C. § 2000e(k). This language clearly sets forth Congress' remedy for discrimination on the basis of pregnancy and potential pregnancy. Women who are either pregnant or potentially pregnant must be treated like others "similar in their ability . . . to work." *Ibid*. In other words, women as capable of doing their jobs as their male counterparts may not be forced to choose between having a child and having a job. . . .

V

We have no difficulty concluding that Johnson Controls cannot establish a BFOQ. Fertile women, as far as appears in the record, participate in the manufacture of batteries as efficiently as anyone else. Johnson Controls' professed moral and ethical concerns about the welfare of the next generation do not suffice to establish a BFOQ of female sterility. Decisions about the welfare of future children must be left to the parents who conceive, bear, support, and raise them rather than to the employers who hire those parents. Congress has mandated this choice through Title VII, as amended by the Pregnancy Discrimination Act. Johnson Controls has attempted to exclude women because of their reproductive capacity. Title VII and the PDA simply do not allow a woman's dismissal because of her failure to submit to sterilization.

Nor can concerns about the welfare of the next generation be considered a part of the "essence" of Johnson Controls' business. . . .

Johnson Controls argues that it must exclude all fertile women because it is impossible to tell which women will become pregnant while working with lead. This argument is somewhat academic in light of our conclusion that the company may not exclude fertile women at all; it perhaps is worth noting, however, that Johnson Controls has shown no "factual basis for believing that all or substantially all women would be unable to perform safely and efficiently the duties of the job involved." *Weeks* v. *Southern Bell Tel. & Tel. Co.*, 408 F. 2d 228, 235 (CA5 1969), quoted with approval in *Dothard*, 433 U. S., at 333. Even on this sparse record, it is apparent that Johnson Controls is concerned about only a small minority of women. Of the eight pregnancies reported among the female employees, it has not been shown that any of the babies have birth defects or other abnormalities. The record does not reveal the birth rate for Johnson Controls' female workers but national statistics show that approximately nine percent of all fertile women become pregnant each year. The birthrate drops to two percent for blue collar workers over age 30. See Becker, 53 U. Chi. L. Rev., at 1233. Johnson Controls' fear of prenatal injury, no matter how sincere, does not begin to show that substantially all of its fertile women employees are incapable of doing their jobs. . . .

It is no more appropriate for the courts than it is for individual employers to decide whether a woman's reproductive role is more important to herself and her family than her economic role. Congress has left this choice to the woman as hers to make.

The judgment of the Court of Appeals is reversed and the case is remanded for further proceedings consistent with this opinion.

It is so ordered.

DISTRICT COURT OF APPEAL OF THE STATE OF FLORIDA

Johnson v. State of Florida

[Opinion filed April 18, 1991]

Dauksch, J.

This is an appeal from two convictions for delivery of a controlled substance to minors.

It was established by the evidence that appellant consumed cocaine knowing that the cocaine would pass to her soon-to-be-born fetus. Upon the birth of her children it was medically determined that each of them had received some of the cocaine into their bodies. A qualified witness testified that some of the cocaine left the mother and was received by the child after birth but before the umbilical cord was cut. Under Florida law a person comes into being upon birth. . . .

Section 893.13(1)(c), Florida Statutes (1989) says:

(c) Except as authorized by this chapter, it is unlawful for any person 18 years of age or older to deliver any controlled substance to a person under the age of 18 years, or to use or hire a person under the age of 18 years as an agent or employee in the sale or delivery of such a substance, or to use such person to assist in avoiding detection or apprehension for a violation of this chapter.

The question is whether the acts of appellant violate the statute. Logic leads us to say that appellant violated the statute.

Appellant voluntarily took cocaine into her body, knowing it would pass to her fetus and knowing (or should have known) that birth was imminent. She is deemed to know that an infant at birth is a person, and a minor, and that delivery of cocaine to the infant is illegal. We can reach no other conclusion logically. . . .

Appeal from the Circuit Court for Seminole County, case 89-1765. Opinion filed April 18, 1991.

This appellant on two occasions took cocaine into her pregnant body and caused the passage of that cocaine to each of her children through the umbilical cord after birth of the child, then an infant person. The statute was twice violated.

We certify to the Supreme Court of Florida that the question resolved by this opinion is of great public importance and suggest that court answer:

Whether the ingestion of a controlled substance by a mother who knows the substance will pass to her child after birth is a violation of Florida law?

Convictions affirmed.
Cobb, J., concurs specially with opinion.
Sharp, W., J., dissents with opinion.

Cobb, J., concurring specially.

. . . Under the instant factual evidence, there can be no doubt that cocaine was delivered from one person to another person, both in 1987 and 1989. The fact that the legislature has elected not to criminalize the transmission of cocaine to a fetus cannot alter the fact that it has criminalized transmission to a person, and the recipients of the cocaine in the instant case, beyond any legal disputation, were persons as defined by the law of Florida. . . .

If the Florida Legislature wishes to exempt the transmission of cocaine through the umbilical cord from the operation of section 893.13 for the public policy reasons set forth in the dissent, that is its prerogative. But it has not done so, and the setting of public policy, however tempting, is not a court function. In all candor, I do not know whether it is the better public policy to prosecute the mothers of cocaine babies. I do know that the resolution of the problem should be determined by the legislature and not the judiciary. Our job, as Justice Holmes once riposted to Judge Hand, is not to do justice (as we may see it) but to apply the law.

Sharp, W., J., dissenting.

. . . The record in this case establishes the following facts. On October 3, 1987, Johnson delivered a son. The birth was normal with no complications. There was no evidence of fetal distress either within the womb or during the delivery. About one and one-half minutes elapsed from the time the son's head emerged from his mother's birth canal to the time he was placed on her stomach and the cord was clamped.

The obstetrician who delivered Johnson's son testified he presumed that the umbilical cord was functioning normally and that it was delivering blood to the baby after he emerged from the birth canal and before the cord was clamped. Johnson admitted to the baby's pediatrician that she used cocaine the night before she delivered. A basic toxicology test performed on Johnson and her son was positive for benzoylecgonine, a metabolite or "breakdown" product of cocaine.

In December 1988, Johnson, while pregnant with a daughter, suffered a crack overdose. Johnson told paramedics that she had taken $200 of crack cocaine earlier that evening and that she was concerned about the effects of the drug on her unborn child. Johnson was then taken to the hospital for observation.

Johnson was hospitalized again on January 23, 1989, when she was in labor. Johnson told Dr. Tompkins, an obstetrician, that she had used rock cocaine that morning while she was in labor. With the exception of finding meconium stain fluid in the amniotic sack, there were no other complications with the birth of Johnson's baby daughter. Approximately sixty-to-ninety seconds elapsed from the time the child's head emerged from her mother's birth canal until her umbilical cord was clamped.

The following day, the Department of Health and Rehabilitative Services investigated an abuse report of a cocaine baby concerning Johnson's daughter. Johnson told the investigator that she had smoked pot and crack cocaine three to four times every other day throughout the duration of her pregnancy with her daughter. Johnson's mother acknowledged that Johnson had been using cocaine for at least three years during the time her daughter and son were born.

At Johnson's trial, Dr. Tompkins testified that a mother's blood passes nutrients, oxygen and chemicals to an unborn child by a diffusion exchange at the capillary level from the womb to the placenta. The umbilical cord then circulates the baby's blood (including the exchange from its mother) between the placenta and the child. Metabolized cocaine derivatives in the mother's blood thus diffuse from the womb to the placenta, and then reach the baby through its umbilical cord. Although the blood flow is somewhat restricted during the birthing process, a measurable amount of blood is transferred from the placenta to the baby through the umbilical cord during delivery and after birth.

Dr. Shashi Gore, a pathologist and toxicologist, testified that cocaine has a half life of about one hour. This means that half of the amount of the drug remains in a person's blood stream for about one hour. The remainder gradually decreases over a period of forty-eight to seventy-two hours. The liver metabolizes the cocaine into benzoylecgonine which travels through the kidneys and into the urine until it is voided.

When Dr. Gore was asked whether a woman who had smoked cocaine at 10:00 p.m. and again between 6:00 and 7:00 a.m. the following morning and delivered a child at 1:00 p.m. that afternoon would still have cocaine or benzoylecgonine present in her blood stream at the time of delivery, the response was yes. When asked whether a woman who had smoked cocaine sometime the night before delivering a child at 8:00 in the morning would still have cocaine or benzoylecgonine in her system at the time of the child's birth, the response again was yes.

Dr. Stephen Kandall, a neonatologist, testified for the defense that it was impossible to tell whether the cocaine derivatives which appeared in these children's urine shortly after birth were the result of the exchange from the mother to her children before or after they were born because most of it took place from womb to the placenta before the birth process was complete.

He also testified that blood flow to the infant from the placenta through the umbilical cord to the child is restricted during contractions. Cocaine also constricts the passage of blood dramatically but benzoylecgonine does not. Dr. Kandall admitted that it is theoretically possible that cocaine or other substances can pass between a mother and her baby during the thirty-to-sixty-second period after the child is born and before the umbilical cord is cut, but that the amount would be tiny.

I submit there was no medical testimony adequate to support the trial court's finding that a "delivery" occurred here during the birthing process, even if the criminal statute is applicable. The expert witnesses all testified about blood flow from the umbilical cord to child. But that blood flow is the child's and the placenta through which it flows, is *not* part of the mother's body. No witness testified in this case that any cocaine derivatives passed from the mother's womb to the placenta during the sixty-to-ninety seconds after the child was expelled from the birth canal. That is when any "delivery" would have to have taken place under this statute, from one "person" to another "person."

Further, there was no evidence that Johnson timed her dosage of cocaine so as to be able to transmit some small amount after her child's birth. Predicting the day or hour of a child's birth is difficult to impossible even for experts. Had Johnson given birth one or two days later, the cocaine would have been completely eliminated, and no "crime" would have occurred. But since she went into labor which progressed to birth after taking cocaine when she did, the only way Johnson could have prevented the "delivery" would have been to have severed the cord before the child was born which, of course, would probably have killed both herself and her child. This illustrates the absurdity of applying the delivery-of-a-drug statute to this scenario.

However, in my view, the primary question in this case is whether section 893.13(1)(c)1. was intended by the Legislature to apply to the birthing process. Before Johnson can be prosecuted under this statute, it must be clear that the Legislature intended for it to apply to the delivery of cocaine derivatives to a newborn during a sixty-to-ninety second interval, before severance of the umbilical cord. I can find no case where "delivery" of a drug was based on an involuntary act such as diffusion and blood flow. . . .

From . . . legislative history, it is clear that the Legislature *considered* and *rejected* a specific statutory provision authorizing criminal penalties against mothers for delivering drug-affected children who received transfer of an illegal drug derivative metabolized by the mother's body, *in utero*. In light of this express legislative statement, I conclude that the Legislature never intended for the general drug delivery statute to authorize prosecutions of those mothers who take

illegal drugs close enough in time to childbirth that a doctor could testify that a tiny amount passed from mother to child in the few seconds before the umbilical cord was cut. Criminal prosecution of mothers like Johnson will undermine Florida's express policy of "keeping families intact" and could destroy the family by incarcerating the child's mother when alternative measures could protect the child and stabilize the family. . . .

It is well established that the effects of cocaine use by a pregnant woman on her fetus and later on her newborn can be severe. . . . Florida could possibly have elected to make *in utero* transfers criminal. But it chose to deal with this problem in other ways. One way is to allow evidence of drug use by women as a ground for removal of the child to the custody of protective services, as was done in this case. Some states have responded to this crisis by charging women with child abuse and neglect. . . .

However, prosecuting women for using drugs and "delivering" them to their newborns appears to be the least effective response to this crisis. Rather than face the possibility of prosecution, pregnant women who are substance abusers may simply avoid prenatal or medical care for fear of being detected. Yet the newborns of these women are, as a group, the most fragile and sick, and most in need of hospital neonatal care. A decision to deliver these babies "at home" will have tragic and serious consequences. . . . Prosecution of pregnant women for engaging in activities harmful to their fetuses or newborns may also unwittingly increase the incidence of abortion.

Such considerations have led the American Medical Association Board of Trustees to oppose criminal sanctions for harmful behavior by a pregnant woman toward her fetus and to advocate that pregnant substance abusers be provided with rehabilitative treatment appropriate to their specific psychological and physiological needs. 264 JAMA at 2670. Likewise, the American Public Health Association has adopted the view that the use of illegal drugs by pregnant women is a public health problem. It also recommends that no punitive measures be taken against pregnant women who are users of illicit drugs when no other illegal acts, including drug-related offenses, have been committed. *See* 1990 Policy Statement.

In summary, I would hold that section 893.13 (1)(c)1. does not encompass "delivery" of an illegal drug derivative from womb to placenta to umbilical cord to newborn after a child's birth. If that is the intent of the Legislature, then this statute should be redrafted to clearly address the basic problem of passing illegal substances from mother to child *in utero*, not just in the birthing process. Since the majority opinion is a case of first impression in this state, and necessarily will have a tremendous impact on law enforcement, as well as (I fear) an adverse impact on the health and welfare of addicted pregnant women and their unborn children, I think we should certify this case to the Florida Supreme Court as one involving a question of great public importance.

DISTRICT OF COLUMBIA COURT OF APPEALS

In Re A.C.

On Hearing en Banc
Terry, Associate Judge:

This case comes before the court for the second time. In *In re A. C.*, 533 A.2d 611 (D.C.1987), a three-judge motions division denied a motion to stay an order of the trial court which had authorized a hospital to perform a caesarean section on a dying woman in an effort to save the life of her unborn child. The operation was performed, but both the mother and the child died. A few months later, the court ordered the case heard en banc and vacated the opinion of the motions division. *In re A. C.*, 539 A.2d 203 (D.C.1988). Although the motions division recognized that, as a practical matter, it "decided the entire matter when [it] denied the stay," 533 A.2d at 613, the en banc court has nevertheless heard the full case on the merits.

We are confronted here with two profoundly difficult and complex issues. First, we must determine who has the right to decide the course of medical treatment for a patient who, although near death, is pregnant with a viable fetus. Second, we must establish how that decision should be made if the patient cannot make it for herself—more specifically, how a court should proceed when faced with a pregnant patient, *in extremis*, who is apparently incapable of making an informed decision regarding medical care for herself and her fetus. We hold that in virtually all cases the question of what is to be done is to be decided by the patient—the pregnant woman—on behalf of herself and the fetus. If the patient is incompetent or otherwise unable to give an informed consent to a proposed course of medical treatment, then her decision must be ascertained through the procedure known as substituted judgment. Because the trial court did not follow that procedure, we vacate its order and remand the case for further proceedings.

This case came before the trial court when George Washington University Hospital petitioned the emergency judge in chambers for declaratory relief as to how it should treat its patient, A.C., who was close to death from cancer and was twenty-six and one-half weeks pregnant with a viable fetus. After a hearing lasting approximately three hours, which was held at the hospital (though not in A.C.'s room), the court ordered that a caesarean section be performed on A.C. to deliver the fetus. Counsel for A.C. immediately sought a stay in this court, which was unanimously denied by a hastily assembled division of three judges. *In re A. C.*, 533 A.2d 611 (D.C.1987). The caesarean was performed, and a baby girl, L.M.C., was delivered. Tragically, the child died within two and one-half hours, and the mother died two days later.

District of Columbia Court of Appeals. 573 A.2d 1235 (D.C. App. 1990).

Counsel for A.C. now maintain that A.C. was competent and that she made an informed choice not to have the caesarean performed. Given this view of the facts, they argue that it was error for the trial court to weigh the state's interest in preserving the potential life of a viable fetus against A.C.'s interest in having her decision respected. They argue further that, even if the substituted judgment procedure had been followed, the evidence would necessarily show that A.C. would not have wanted the caesarean section. . . .

A.C. was first diagnosed as suffering from cancer at the age of thirteen. In the ensuing years she underwent major surgery several times, together with multiple radiation treatments and chemotherapy. A.C. married when she was twenty-seven, during a period of remission, and soon thereafter she became pregnant. . . .

On Tuesday, June 9, 1987, when A.C. was approximately twenty-five weeks pregnant, she went to the hospital for a scheduled check-up. Because she was experiencing pain in her back and shortness of breath, an x-ray was taken, revealing an apparently inoperable tumor which nearly filled her right lung. On Thursday, June 11, A.C. was admitted to the hospital as a patient. By Friday her condition had temporarily improved, and when asked if she really wanted to have her baby, she replied that she did.

Over the weekend A.C.'s condition worsened considerably. Accordingly, on Monday, June 15, members of the medical staff treating A.C. assembled, along with her family, in A.C.'s room. The doctors then informed her that her illness was terminal, and A.C. agreed to palliative treatment designed to extend her life until at least her twenty-eighth week of pregnancy. The "potential outcome [for] the fetus," according to the doctors, would be much better at twenty-eight weeks than at twenty-six weeks if it were necessary to "intervene." A.C. knew that the palliative treatment she had chosen presented some increased risk to the fetus, but she opted for this course both to prolong her life for at least another two weeks and to maintain her own comfort. When asked if she still wanted to have the baby, A.C. was somewhat equivocal, saying "something to the effect of 'I don't know, I think so.'" As the day moved toward evening, A.C.'s condition grew still worse, and at about 7:00 or 8:00 p.m. she consented to intubation to facilitate her breathing.

The next morning, June 16, the trial court convened a hearing at the hospital . . . and the District of Columbia was permitted to intervene for the fetus as *parens patriae*. The court heard testimony . . . that the chances of survival for a twenty-six-week fetus delivered at the hospital might be as high as eighty percent, but that this particular fetus, because of the mother's medical history, had only a fifty to sixty percent chance of survival. . . .

Regarding A.C.'s ability to respond to questioning and her prognosis, Dr. Louis Hamner, another treating obstetrician, testified that A.C. would probably die within twenty-four hours "if absolutely nothing else is done. . . . As far as her ability to interact, she has been heavily sedated in order to maintain her ventilatory function. She will open her eyes sometimes when you are in the room, but as far as her being able to . . . carry on a meaningful-type conversation . . . at this point, I don't think that is reasonable.". . .

There was no evidence before the court showing that A.C. consented to, or even contemplated, a caesarean section before her twenty-eighth week of pregnancy. There was, in fact, considerable dispute as to whether she would have consented to an immediate caesarean delivery at the time the hearing was held. A.C.'s mother opposed surgical intervention, testifying that A.C. wanted "to live long enough to hold that baby" and that she expected to do so, "even though she knew she was terminal." Dr. Hamner testified that, given A.C.'s medical problems, he did not think she would have chosen to deliver a child with a substantial degree of impairment. . . .

After hearing this testimony and the arguments of counsel, the trial court made oral findings of fact. It found, first, that A.C. would probably die, according to uncontroverted medical testimony, "within the next twenty-four to forty-eight hours"; second, that A.C. was "pregnant with a twenty-six and a half week viable fetus who, based upon uncontroverted medical testimony, has approximately a fifty to sixty percent chance to survive if a caesarean section is performed as soon as possible"; third, that because the fetus was viable, "the state has [an] important and legitimate interest in protecting the potentiality of human life"; and fourth, that there had been some testimony that the operation "may very well hasten the death of [A.C.]," but that there had also been testimony that delay would greatly increase the risk to the fetus and that "the prognosis is not great for the fetus to be delivered post-mortem. . . ." Most significantly, the court found:

The court is of the view that it does not clearly know what [A.C.'s] present views are with respect to the issue of whether or not the child should live or die. . . .

Having made these findings of fact and conclusions of law, the court ordered that a caesarean section be performed to deliver A.C.'s child.

The court's decision was then relayed to A.C., who had regained consciousness. When the hearing reconvened later in the day, Dr. Hamner told the court:

I explained to her essentially what was going on. . . . I said it's been deemed we should intervene on behalf of the baby by caesarean section and it would give it the only possible chance of it living. Would you agree to this procedure? *She said yes.* I said, do you realize that you may not survive the surgical procedure? *She said yes.* And I repeated the two questions to her again [and] asked her did she understand. *She said yes.* [Emphasis added.]

When the court suggested moving the hearing to A.C.'s bedside, Dr. Hamner discouraged the court from doing so, but he and Dr. Weingold, together with A.C.'s mother and husband, went to A.C.'s room to confirm her consent to the procedure. . . .

[A.C.] then seemed to pause for a few moments and then very clearly mouthed words several times, *I don't want it done. I don't want it done.*

[Dr. Weingold testified:]

I would obviously state the obvious and that is this is an environment in which, from my perspective as a physician, this would not be an informed consent one way or the other. She's under tremendous stress with the family on both sides, but I'm satisfied that I heard clearly what she said. . . .

Dr. Weingold later qualified his opinion as to A.C.'s ability to give an informed consent, stating that he thought the environment for an informed consent was non-existent because A.C. was in intensive care, flanked by a weeping husband and mother. . . .

After hearing this new evidence, the court found that it was "still not clear what her intent is" and again ordered that a caesarean section be performed. A.C.'s counsel sought a stay in this court, which was denied. *In re A. C.*, 533 A.2d 611, 613 (D.C.1987). The operation took place, but the baby lived for only a few hours, and A.C. succumbed to cancer two days later. . . .

It has been suggested that fetal cases are different [from other duty-to-aid cases] because a woman who "has chosen to lend her body to bring [a] child into the world" has an enhanced duty to assure the welfare of the fetus, sufficient even to require her to undergo caesarean surgery. Robertson, *Procreative Liberty*, 69 Va.L.Rev. at 456. Surely, however, a fetus cannot have rights in this respect superior to those of a person who has already been born. . . .

This court has recognized as well that, above and beyond common law protections, the right to accept or forego medical treatment is of constitutional magnitude. . . .

What we distill from the [precedent] cases is that every person has the right, under the common law and the Constitution, to accept or refuse medical treatment. This right of bodily integrity belongs equally to persons who are competent and persons who are not. Further, it matters not what the quality of a patient's life may be; the right of bodily integrity is not extinguished simply because someone is ill, or even at death's door. To protect that right against intrusion by others — family members, doctors, hospitals, or anyone else, however well-intentioned — we hold that a court must determine the patient's wishes by any means available, and must abide by those wishes unless there are truly extraordinary or compelling reasons to override them. . . .

From the record before us, we simply cannot tell whether A.C. was ever competent, after being sedated, to make an informed decision one way or the other regarding the proposed caesarean section. The trial court never made any finding about A.C.'s competency to decide. Undoubtedly, during most of the proceedings below, A.C. was incompetent to make a treatment decision; that is, she was unable to give an informed consent based on her assessment of the risks and benefits of the contemplated surgery. . . .

We have no reason to believe that, if competent, A.C. would or would not have refused consent to a caesarean. We hold, however, that without a competent refusal from A.C. to go forward with the surgery, and without a finding through substituted judgment that A.C. would not have consented to the surgery, it was error for the trial court to proceed to a balancing analysis, weighing the rights of A.C. against the interests of the state. . . .

The court should also consider previous decisions of the patient concerning medical treatment, especially when there may be a discernibly consistent pattern of conduct or of thought. . . . Thus in a case such as this it would be highly relevant that A.C. had consented to intrusive and dangerous surgeries in the past, and that she chose to become pregnant and to protect her pregnancy by seeking treatment at the hospital's high-risk pregnancy clinic. It would also be relevant that she accepted a plan of treatment which contemplated caesarean intervention at the twenty-eighth week of pregnancy, even though the possibility of a caesarean during the twenty-sixth week was apparently unforeseen. On the other hand, A.C. agreed to a plan of palliative treatment which posed a greater danger to the fetus than would have been necessary if she were unconcerned about her own continuing care. Further, when A.C. was informed of the fatal nature of her illness, she was equivocal about her desire to have the baby.

Courts in substituted judgment cases have also acknowledged the importance of probing the patient's value system as an aid in discerning what the patient would choose. We agree with this approach. . . . Most people do not foresee what calamities may befall them; much less do they consider, or even think about, treatment alternatives in varying situations. The court in a substituted judgment case, therefore, should pay special attention to the known values and goals of the incapacitated patient, and should strive, if possible, to extrapolate from those values and goals what the patient's decision would be. . . .

After reviewing the transcript of the hearing and the court's oral findings, it is clear to us that the trial court did not follow the substituted judgment procedure. . . .

The court did not go on, as it should have done, to make a finding as to what A.C. would have chosen to do if she were competent. Instead, the court undertook to balance the state's and L.M.C.'s interests in surgical intervention against A.C.'s perceived interest in not having the caesarean performed.

After A.C. was informed of the court's decision, she consented to the caesarean; moments later, however, she withdrew her consent. The trial court did not then make a finding as to whether A.C. was competent to make the medical decision or whether she had made an informed decision one way or the other. Nor did the court then make a substituted judgment for A.C. Instead, the court said that it was "still not clear what her intent is" and again ordered the caesarean.

It is that order which we must now set aside. What a trial court must do in a case such as this is to determine, if possible, whether the patient is capable of making an informed decision about the course of her medical treatment. If she is, and if she makes such a decision, her wishes will control in virtually all cases. . . .

Accordingly, we vacate the order of the trial court and remand the case for such further proceedings as may be appropriate. We note, in doing so, that the trial court's order allowing the hospital to perform the caesarean section was presumptively valid from the date it was entered until today. What the legal effect of that order may have been during its lifetime is a matter on which we express no opinion here.

Vacated and remanded.

Belson, Associate Judge, concurring in part and dissenting in part:

I agree with much of the majority opinion, but I disagree with its ultimate ruling that the trial court's order must be set aside, and with the narrow view it takes of the state's interest in preserving life and the unborn child's interest in life. . . .

The state's interest in preserving human life and the viable unborn child's interest in survival are entitled, I think, to more weight than I find them assigned by the majority when it states that "in virtually all cases the decision of the patient . . . will control." Majority opinion at 1252. I would hold that in those instances, fortunately rare, in which the viable unborn child's interest in living and the state's parallel interest in protecting human life come into conflict with the mother's decision to forgo a procedure such as a caesarean section, a balancing should be struck in which the unborn child's and the state's interests are entitled to substantial weight.

It was acknowledged in *Roe v. Wade*, 410 U.S. 113, 93 S.Ct. 705, 35 L.Ed.2d 147 (1973), that the state's interest in potential human life becomes compelling at the point of viability. Even before viability, the state has an "important and legitimate interest in protecting the potentiality of human life." . . .

We are dealing with the situation that exists when a woman has carried an unborn child to viability. When the unborn child reaches the state of viability, the child becomes a party whose interests must be considered. . . .

[In] *Bonbrest v. Kotz,* 65 F.Supp. 138 (D.D.C. 1946) . . . the court . . . stated:

It has, if viable, its own bodily form and members, manifests all the anatomical characteristics of individuality, possesses its own circulatory, vascular and excretory systems and is capable *now* of being ushered into the visible world.

Id. at 141 (footnote omitted).

Bonbrest proved to be a landmark case. In *Greater Southeast Hospital v. Williams,* 482 A.2d 394 (D.C. 1984), this court noted that "every jurisdiction in the United States has followed *Bonbrest* in recognizing a cause of action for prenatal injury, at least when the injury is to a viable infant later born alive." *Id.* at 396. We went on to hold in *Greater Southeast Hospital* that a viable unborn child *is a person* within the coverage of the wrongful death statute, D.C.Code § 16-2701 (1981):

Inherent in our adoption of *Bonbrest* is the recognition that a viable fetus is an independent person with the right to be free of prenatal injury. The liability for prenatal injury recognized in *Bonbrest* arises at the time of the injury. If a viable fetus is a "person injured" at the time of the injury, then perforce the fetus is a "person" when he dies of those injuries, and it can make no difference in liability under the wrongful death and survival statutes whether the fetus dies of the injuries just prior to or just after birth. . . .

A viable unborn child is a *person* at common law who has legal rights that are entitled to the protection of the courts. In a case like the one before us, the unborn child is a patient of both the hospital and any treating physician, and the hospital or physician may be liable to the child for the child's prenatal injury or death if caused by their negligence. . . .

The balancing test should be applied in instances in which women become pregnant and carry an unborn child to the point of viability. This is not an unreasonable classification because, I submit, a woman who carries a child to viability is in fact a member of a unique category of persons. Her circumstances differ fundamentally from those of other potential patients for medical procedures that will aid another person, for example, a potential donor of bone marrow for transplant. This is so because she has undertaken to bear another human being, and has carried an unborn child to viability. Another unique feature of the situation we address arises from the singular nature of the dependency of the unborn child upon the mother. A woman carrying a viable unborn child is not in the same category as a relative, friend, or stranger called upon to donate bone marrow or an organ for transplant. Rather, the expectant mother has placed herself in a special class of persons who are bringing another person into existence, and upon whom that other person's life is totally dependent. Also, uniquely, the vi-

able unborn child is literally captive within the mother's body. No other potential beneficiary of a surgical procedure on another is in that position.

For all of these reasons, a balancing becomes appropriate in those few cases where the interests we are discussing come into conflict. To so state is in no sense to fail to recognize the extremely strong interest of each individual person, including of course the expectant mother, in her bodily integrity, her privacy, and, where involved, her religious beliefs.

Thus, I cannot agree with the conclusion of the majority opinion that while we "do not quite foreclose the possibility that a conflicting state interest may be so compelling that the patient's wishes must yield . . . we anticipate that such cases will be extremely rare and truly exceptional." Majority opinion at 1252. While it is, fortunately, true that such cases will be rare in the sense that such conflicts between mother and viable unborn child are rare, I cannot agree that in cases where a viable unborn child is in the picture, it would be extremely rare, within that universe, to require that the mother accede to the vital needs of the viable unborn child. . . .

I next address the sensitive question of how to balance the competing rights and interests of the viable unborn child and the state against those of the rare expectant mother who elects not to have a caesarean section necessary to save the life of her child. The indisputable view that a woman carrying a viable child has an extremely strong interest in her own life, health, bodily integrity, privacy, and religious beliefs necessarily requires that her election be given correspondingly great weight in the balancing process. In a case, however, where the court in an exercise of a substituted judgment has concluded that the patient would probably opt against a caesarean section, the court should vary the weight to be given this factor in proportion to the confidence the court has in the accuracy of its conclusion. Thus, in a case where the indicia of the incompetent patient's judgment are equivocal, the court should accord this factor correspondingly less weight. The appropriate weight to be given other factors will have to be worked out by the development of law in this area, and cannot be prescribed in a single court opinion. Some considerations obviously merit special attention in the balancing process. One such consideration is any danger to the mother's life or health, physical or mental, including the relatively small but still significant danger that necessarily inheres in any caesarean delivery, and including especially any danger that exceeds that level. The mother's religious beliefs as they relate to the operation would appear to deserve inclusion in the balancing process.

On the other side of the analysis, it is appropriate to look to the relative likelihood of the unborn child's survival. . . . The child's interest in being born with as little impairment as possible should also be considered. This may weigh in favor of a delivery sooner rather than later. The most important factor on this side of the scale, however, is life itself, because the viable unborn child that dies because of the mother's refusal to have a caesarean delivery is deprived, entirely and irrevocably, of the life on which the child was about to embark.

. . . Also to be considered in the balance was the rather minimal, but nevertheless undisputable, additional risk that caesarean delivery presented for the mother.

Turning to the interest of the unborn child in living and the parallel interest of the state in protecting that life, the evidence indicated that the child had a fifty to sixty percent chance of survival and a less than twenty percent chance of entering life with a serious handicap such as cerebral palsy or mental retardation. The evidence also showed that a delay in delivering the child would have increased the likelihood of a handicap. In view of the record before Judge Sullivan, and on the basis that there had been no plain error in not applying the sort of substituted judgment analysis that we for the first time mandate in today's ruling, I think it cannot be said that he abused his discretion in the way he struck the balance between the considerations that favored the procedure and those that went against it.

For the reasons stated above, I would affirm.

N A N C Y K. R H O D E N

Cesareans and Samaritans

Until recently, if one asked the proverbial person on the street to list maternal–fetal conflicts, he or she would have mentioned abortion and, when pressed to continue, looked at the questioner blankly. Now, however, the populace is becoming aware of a host of maternal–fetal conflicts. Indeed, mother-and-child, long a somewhat romanticized unity, are increasingly being treated by physicians, courts, and the media as potential adversaries, locked in battle on the rather inconvenient battleground of the woman's belly.

Some of these newly publicized conflicts — pregnant women abusing drugs or alcohol, or continuing to work in occupations hazardous to fetal health — are not all that new: the hazards of various substances have been known for years. Other of the conflicts are new, inasmuch as doctors could not recommend Cesareans or other procedures for the fetus' benefit until

they could detect fetal problems during or before labor. But probably what is most unprecedented is that now, suddenly, physicians are seeking court intervention to protect these imperiled fetuses — intervention that, inevitably, constitutes a significant intrusion into the woman's conduct during pregnancy or birth.

This essay will discuss just one of the proliferating array of maternal–fetal conflicts — the question whether courts should have the power to authorize doctors to perform Cesarean deliveries against the woman's will. Doctors typically seek these orders when they believe, based on diagnostic techniques, that vaginal delivery risks death or neurological damage to the fetus. (In some cases, vaginal delivery is a risk for the woman as well.) Women who refuse most commonly do so based on religious beliefs opposed to surgery, though they may refuse because they fear surgery, do not believe the doctor's prognoses, or whatever. . . .

Law, Medicine & Health Care 15(3) Fall, 1987, pp. 118–125. Reprinted by permission of the publisher.

The position I will defend is that courts should not order competent women to have Cesareans, despite the potentially tragic consequences to the fetus. This is neither an easy position nor a fully satisfactory one. Indeed, it is the sort of hard-line civil libertarian position that I ordinarily find oversimplified in bioethics issues. Yet I believe that it is the morally and legally correct position—albeit merely the "least worst" one—because these orders (1) impose an unparalleled intrusion upon pregnant women; (2) undermine the teachings of the informed consent doctrine that only the individual being subjected to a procedure can assess its risks and benefits; and (3) contain within them the seeds of widespread and pernicious usurpation of women's choices during obstetrical care.

JUSTIFICATIONS FOR NONCONSENSUAL CESAREANS

ABORTION LAW

In the cases of which I am aware, every judge but one who has ruled on an application for nonconsensual Cesarean delivery has granted the request. Interestingly, *Roe v. Wade,*[1] which has stood firmly for a woman's right to privacy and right to make her own decisions about pregnancy, is the case most commonly invoked by courts to justify these orders.[2] Under *Roe,* women must be allowed to choose abortion prior to fetal viability (subject to state regulation to protect the mother's health in the second trimester). But once a fetus is capable of independent life outside the womb, albeit with artificial aid, the state's interest in potential life becomes compelling.[3] Then the state can prohibit abortion, unless it is necessary to protect the woman's life or health. Courts invoking *Roe* to support nonconsensual Cesarean delivery reason that since states can prohibit the intentional termination of fetal life after viability, they can likewise protect viable fetuses by preventing vaginal delivery when it will have the same effect as abortion.[4]

At first glance this analysis appears attractive. Attempting a vaginal delivery when responsible medical opinion says that surgical delivery is necessary for the fetus may cause a stillbirth or, perhaps worse, profound neurological damage to the child. These consequences are clearly ones that states have an interest in preventing. But the fact that states have an interest in preventing certain consequences does not mean that any and all action to prevent such consequences is

constitutional. For example, states have an interest in preventing use of illicit drugs, and they can make such conduct criminal. But this doesn't mean that they can take any and all other steps to prevent drug use, such as ordering random strip searches at airports (though the way things are going, we may soon see random urine samples). Similarly, the Court in *Roe* said that in the third trimester, the state can even "go so far as to proscribe abortion,"[5] unless the woman's health is at stake. That the state can go this far, prohibiting intentional fetal destruction, doesn't necessarily mean that it can go even farther, and mandate major surgery to protect and preserve the fetus' life. There is a quantum leap in logic between prohibiting destruction and requiring surgical preservation that courts and commentators relying on abortion law have ignored.

In fact, if one reads *Roe* and its progeny more closely, it becomes apparent that court-ordered Cesareans violate *Roe*'s constitutional schema. *Roe* emphasizes that even after the fetus is viable, the woman's life and health come first. If her health is threatened by her pregnancy even after the fetus is viable, she must be allowed to abort.[6] In *Colautti v. Franklin,*[7] the Supreme Court discussed the primacy of maternal health even more specifically. It invalidated a statute that required doctors performing post-viability abortions to use the technique least harmful to the fetus, unless another technique was necessary for the woman's health. Among other infirmities, this statute impermissibly implied that the more hazardous technique had to be *indispensable* to the woman's health, and suggested that doctors could be required to make trade-offs between her health and additional percentage points of the fetus' survival.[8] Abortion law makes clear that such trade-offs cannot be required.

Thus a state could not, under *Colautti,* require that all abortions after viability be done by hysterotomy, a surgical technique that is basically a mini-Cesarean, on the grounds that this is safest for the fetus. A state could not require this because such a technique is less safe for the woman. It may not be immediately apparent that this proscription of compulsory maternal–fetal trade-offs in late abortion applies to the Cesarean dilemma. Yet this becomes quite clear when one realizes that after a fetus is viable, the methods of abortion and of premature delivery simply merge. Although the Supreme Court in *Roe* and subsequent cases has spoken of post-viability abortion, doctors have historically thought of late terminations necessitated by a health problem on the woman's part as premature deliveries—deliveries that may put the fetus at great risk but that are not specifically intended to destroy it. In other words, post-viability terminations of pregnancy are simply inductions of labor, just as might be done at full term.

Once we recognize this, we see that what the Court says about third-trimester abortion should apply to delivery methods as well. When that yardstick is applied, it yields the conclusion that a state clearly could not enact a statute requiring Cesarean over vaginal delivery to protect the fetus. Inasmuch as surgical delivery involves approximately four times the maternal mortality rate of vaginal delivery, such a statute would impermissibly mandate trade-offs between maternal and fetal health. The state could not statutorily mandate surgical delivery even in those cases where the fetus' health was seriously threatened by vaginal delivery, because the mother's health will still almost always be somewhat threatened by surgical delivery. Likewise, it violates the Constitution for courts to authorize nonconsensual Cesarean delivery in individual cases, since it seems clear that courts should not issue orders in individual cases that, if generalized in the form of a statute, would be unconstitutional.

THE CHILD NEGLECT/FETAL NEGLECT ANALOGY

Despite the strong argument that nonconsensual Cesareans are at odds with the teachings of *Roe* and other Supreme Court abortion cases, it may be objected that in rejecting maternal–fetal trade-offs, the Supreme Court was thinking only about abortions, not about full-term deliveries. Given the state's strong interest in preservation of life, why, one might ask, must doctors stand by while a baby who could be fine if delivered surgically dies or suffers irreversible brain damage? Whatever abortion law says, should women really have a right to make this potentially lethal choice, when the risk to them is quite minimal?

Courts and commentators have frequently relied on the law of child neglect to argue that harmful choices such as these are not the woman's to make.[9] Parents, of course, cannot refuse needed medical care for their children, even if the provision of such care violates their most cherished religious beliefs. Likewise, it is often argued, pregnant women cannot refuse care necessary for their fetus' well-being. To do so is the prenatal equivalent of child neglect (and, according to this theory, taking substances such as heroin while one is pregnant is the prenatal equivalent of child abuse).

There's a simple charm to this notion that if parents cannot deny care to a child, neither can a pregnant woman deny it to a fetus, at least to a fetus that is fully formed and clearly viable. When analyzed, however, this notion is far from charming. It has far-reaching and very alarming implications, and it is far less simple than it appears. Child neglect is, of course, the failure to perform one's legal duties to one's children. The term "fetal neglect" implies that there are legally enforceable duties to fetuses. But while parents have historically owed a whole panoply of duties to their children, women have not heretofore been held to have legally enforceable duties to fetuses. . . .

Obviously, "fetal neglect" proponents recognize the *fact* of the fetus' internal location. They then draw the analogy with child neglect by stating that this difference in location is the only difference between a fetus and a child. True, it is (at least for very late-term fetuses). But in terms of what a state must do to end "fetal neglect" as opposed to ending child neglect, this "slight disanalogy" is like the difference between night and day. Children can simply be treated, in opposition to parental demands. But "fetal neglect" cannot be remedied without, as it were, "breaching the maternal barrier"—restraining and physically invading the woman. . . .

THE STATE'S INTEREST IN
THE WELL-BEING OF THIRD PARTIES

Competent persons can refuse medical treatment, even when it means their death. Their rights to privacy and bodily integrity are increasingly respected, even though the state has interests, such as in preserving life, that are arrayed against virtually all treatment refusals. In other words, while the state's interests are neither negligible nor forgotten, the patients' privacy rights trump them. But most refusals do not have a direct and devastating effect upon third parties. How do we weigh the individual's right to refuse in these cases against the state's interest in preserving a third party's life—an interest that puts these cases in a class by themselves?

Courts have not taken the interests of third parties lightly, even when the goal was to preserve their emotional welfare rather than to protect them from physical harm. Some courts have overridden treatment refusals by parents of dependent children (usually Jehovah's Witnesses refusing blood transfusions), on the grounds that the parent should not be allowed to orphan his or her child.[10] It can readily be argued that if a parent's privacy right can be overridden to spare his child emotional or financial loss, surely it can be overridden to prevent a stillbirth or a birth injury that may cause profound impairment. The only problem with this argument is that these cases are, in my opinion, clearly wrong. Although the practice is frowned upon, parents can abandon their children by putting them in foster care or even up for adoption; some parents de facto abandon their children by, for example, divorcing and leaving the jurisdiction; and parents take health risks, such as hang gliding, sky diving, or joining the U.S. army, that could potentially result in their children being orphaned. Why, in the one sphere of medical treatment, should they be required to violate their faith and adhere to medical orthodoxy? I see no good reason why here, but not elsewhere, parenthood should obliterate personal autonomy. . . .

Having recognized that the true analogue to imposed Cesareans is nonconsensual surgery sought to benefit a third party, we now confront a significant dearth of caselaw. One reason is that there are few fact patterns in which a medical procedure performed on A will save B. Another reason is that compelling A to undergo risks so as to save B has always been considered beyond the reaches of state authority. . . .

In this country there is no general duty to rescue. There are exceptions, which include a special relationship between the parties such as that of innkeeper and guest, common carrier and passenger, and, most importantly, parent and child.[11] But even when a special relationship gives rise to a duty to rescue, there is still no duty to undertake *risky* rescues.[12] Nor is there such a duty in countries where there is a general duty to rescue.[13] It is easy to see that a demand for someone's kidney falls under the law of rescue (Samaritan law) and goes far beyond what is ever required of potential rescuers. In the one case on point, *McFall v. Shimp*,[14] a man dying of aplastic anemia asked the court to mandate that his cousin donate bone marrow to save him. The court called the relative's refusal to donate morally reprehensible, but held that for the law to "sink its teeth into the jugular vein or neck of one of its members and suck from it sustenance for *another* member, is revolting to our hard-wrought concepts of jurisprudence. Such would raise the spectre of the swastika and the Inquisition, reminiscent of the horrors this portends."[15] Although there are no *McFall*-type cases involving parent–child donation, I think we can say with a fair degree of certainty that the outcome would and should be the same. Parents have a duty to rescue their children—i.e., to be basic Good

Samaritans—but they have no duty to be "Splendid Samaritans,"[16] embarking upon rescues that risk their life or health.

THE ILLEGITIMACY OF INTERPERSONAL RISK–BENEFIT COMPARISONS

If what a court does in mandating a Cesarean is no different from mandating a bone marrow transfusion to save a dying relative, it clearly exceeds the state's legitimate authority. While the two seem equivalent to me, they certainly haven't seemed so to most of the courts that have considered requests for nonconsensual Cesareans. For various reasons, court-ordered Cesareans strike many people as legitimate, while court-ordered bone marrow transfusions or kidney donations (a more equivalent intrusion), even from parent to child, seem outrageous. These reasons are important and cannot be ignored—they are what makes this situation so agonizing. However, I will try to show that while these reasons go to the woman's conduct, the appropriate question concerns the nature of the *state's* conduct. When we look to it, all nonconsensual risks imposed on one person to save another are equally illegitimate.

The Cesarean cases unquestionably *feel* different from cases or hypotheticals involving forced intrusions on parents to save children. For one thing, the woman is going to give birth anyway, and if she just does it surgically instead of vaginally the baby will probably be fine. Cesareans are common and relatively safe, and the potential harm from delivering the baby vaginally is very serious. Moreover, it seems to some that women who choose not to abort thereby assume certain obligations to their fetuses, a by no means unreasonable suggestion. Finally, pregnancy simply is a unique situation. A dying relative, even a child, is a separate, independent person. However dire his need, he is not a tiny, helpless, totally dependent creature.

Emotional responses should certainly not be disregarded in bioethics. But neither should they necessarily rule. Physicians understandably become very uncomfortable when a woman appears ready to risk her fetus' life and health for the sake of her religious faith, and they feel even stronger when her reasons appear less weighty. Indeed, trivial reasons for running this risk may justify our casting moral aspersions on the woman's conduct. Despite the uniqueness of pregnancy, however, and despite the strength or weakness of the woman's reason for refusal (assuming she is competent), what the *state* does when it orders a compulsory Cesarean is no different from what it does when it orders compulsory bone marrow or kidney "donation," and what the state does is wrong.

The most significant feature of decisions ordering Cesareans is that the court, explicitly or implicitly, finds that the potential harm to the fetus overrides the woman's rights to privacy, autonomy, and bodily integrity, and justifies imposing a physical harm upon her (because surgery is a harm even if it has no untoward consequences). The court, in other words, takes two people, looks at the potential consequences of a bad situation, and says that the probably severe harm to X warrants imposing a lesser physical harm on Y. The legitimacy of this argument depends upon the assumption that a third party can step in and weigh the risks of surgery for someone who has competently chosen to forego them, and can then order that these risks be run. This is an assumption that has always been rejected in American jurisprudence, and that, if accepted, has far-reaching and extraordinarily frightening implications.

There is something special about the body. In theory, we can all recognize that everyone's body is equally special. But in practice, somehow our own seems far more special than anyone else's. It is very easy for us to say, as objective third parties, that a patient really should have needed surgery, because its risks are minute—perhaps only 1 in 10,000. But when we are thinking about that same surgery for ourselves, the minuteness of that chance may somehow seem less pertinent than the ghastly thought that we might be that one. This different attitude toward low statistical risks when run by a group of strangers and when run by oneself explains the old saying, "Minor surgery is surgery performed on somebody else." Perhaps this difference also explains why even countries with general duties to rescue never require risky rescues. While cowardice may not be admired, it is too human a quality to be formally punished by law.

Needless to say, a court can contemplate surgery for a pregnant woman only as a third-party bystander, albeit a careful and concerned bystander. It can assess the objective risks of surgery to the woman and the corresponding benefits to the fetus. But its ability truly to understand the situation is radically limited. . . .

In ordering surgery, the court is thus rendering objective a determination that cannot rightfully be anything but subjective. Although it is doing so for the best of reasons, its action nonetheless denies to a disturbing extent the woman's uniqueness and individuality. It denies her special fears or her special spiritual reasons for rejecting surgery and "leaving things in the hands of God." When it subjugates her views about having her body invaded (or about interfering with Providence) to its assessment of the "right" action based on potential consequences, it is making an interpersonal risk–benefit comparison and holding that she must run the risk to prevent the greater risk to the baby. Objectively, this may well be the proper assessment. But decisions about major surgery on unconsenting adults simply are not delegated to third parties, and delegating this one is no different from delegating a decision about bone marrow extraction or kidney transplant. I can think of no other instance where a state feels it has the authority to compare the risks faced by one individual to those faced by the other. The court compromises its integrity in making these orders, because whether it realizes it or not, it is treating the woman as a means—a vehicle for rescuing an imperiled fetus—and not as an end in herself.

Two disturbing potential scenarios will help illustrate why a nonconsensual Cesarean is inevitably a wrong against the woman. First, imagine surgery has been authorized, and the woman struggles to try to avoid it. In the case at North Central Bronx, doctors repeatedly asked what they should do if this occurred. Should they hold her down and anesthetize her? Some proponents of intervention would characterize this as merely a practical problem in enforcement—some injunctions being easier to enforce than others. Yet this is much more than a mere enforcement issue. It illustrates the violence lurking here, whether or not it is ever actually committed. The court is at one remove from the violence, because its role is limited to issuing the order. Nonetheless, the court has authorized an act of violence against the woman, even if the violence is obscured by her cowed compliance in the face of judicial power.

Second, imagine that the highly unexpected happens, and the woman is killed or injured by the surgery. Although this is exceedingly unlikely, its possibility raises an interesting moral issue. The court cannot, of course, be held legally responsible for this harm, nor can the doctors, assuming they were not negligent. Yet the court would be, it seems, morally responsible, because it chose to subject the woman to this risk. There is no comparison between the state's responsibility under this scenario and its responsibility if the woman's refusal is upheld and the baby is harmed. If the baby suffers, the woman is causally responsible (assuming surgery would have prevented the harm) and in some cases, at least, will be morally to blame. But the state won't be implicated, because the state does not normally intervene in a person's medical decisions. In other words, a private wrong will have occurred. But if the state has the hubris to intervene in what is ordinarily a private (albeit potentially tragic) choice, it takes on the moral responsibility for the outcome as well. Although the chances of maternal injury are low, the moral risk is great, and this possibility should make courts think twice before mandating surgery.

SOME ADDITIONAL SOCIAL CONCERNS

For purposes of analyzing nonconsensual Cesareans, I have been assuming that the physicians' predictions of harm to the infant are correct. In any individual case, of course, the doctor's alarm is most likely warranted—although it is interesting to note that in *Jefferson, Headley,* and *Jeffries,* the women delivered vaginally and the infants were fine. But when we think of mandatory Cesareans not simply as individual cases but as a social policy, we must recognize that some of the operations will be unnecessary. This is because the tools upon which doctors rely to diagnose problems during pregnancy or labor detect abnormally high risks, but do not necessarily distinguish cases in which the risks will materialize from those in which they will not.

Some tools and diagnoses are better than others. For example, ultrasonography is highly reliable in detecting placenta previa, and diagnosis of complete placenta previa reliably dictates Cesarean delivery. But even here prediction is not 100-percent accurate: both Ms. Jefferson and Ms. Jeffries, who were diagnosed as having complete placenta previa, delivered vaginally. Other tools are as likely to be wrong as right. . . .

Physicians should be risk-averse and reluctant to gamble with the lives of babies, and fears of legal liability naturally enhance these traits. However, technological limitations combined with a cautious, risk-averse approach virtually ensure that some of the Cesareans doctors recommend will turn out not to have been required. While the vast majority of women would far rather risk an unnecessary operation than an impaired infant, it is not so clear that, given the technological limitations, it is irrational or immoral to take

a different approach to risk. At any rate, mandatory Cesareans will mean that the judicial system requires this risk-averse approach, and forces pregnant women as a group to run some unnecessary risks to ensure healthy babies.

Although it might be suggested that courts can distinguish truly risky situations from only somewhat risky ones, this suggestion unfortunately puts more faith in the judicial system than it deserves, at least in these types of cases. The doctors bringing them will undoubtedly believe that surgery is necessary. The courts will have little choice but to accept the doctor's assessment—especially since in the typical Cesarean case the woman is either not present at all (and of course not represented by counsel) or represented by an attorney appointed only hours or days before and patently incapable of presenting contrary medical evidence even if it could be obtained. These cases have thus far been very one-sided, and given the time constraints will almost surely continue to be so. This may account in part for the fact that most courts have issued the orders. It is interesting to note that in the Pamela Rae Stewart case, where Ms. Stewart was criminally prosecuted for prenatal conduct that allegedly caused her child to be born with brain damage and then to die, there was for once a two-sided debate. Here the American Civil Liberties Union came to Ms. Stewart's defense, and all charges against her were dismissed.[17]

Another social consequence of mandatory Cesareans might well be harm to the babies themselves. When the court authorized nonconsensual surgery for Ms. Jeffries, she went into hiding and could not be found even by a police search. When the court authorized the surgery for Ms. Headley, she avoided the hospital by having a home birth with a lay midwife. If women with unorthodox religious beliefs know that their beliefs will not be honored, they may avoid physicians during delivery or even during their entire pregnancy, thus placing their babies at greatly increased risk. Presumably the informed consent doctrine would dictate that physicians tell women, early on in prenatal care, that they will not honor their religious beliefs if their fetus is endangered. This disclosure, however, will only serve to make such women avoid prenatal care (much as the reporting of drug abuse will make pregnant drug users avoid doctors and hospitals). Hence as a general social policy, mandatory fetal protection will have questionable success in protecting fetuses.

Emotionally compelling cases often make bad law. It is very hard for physicians and judges to resist the urge to save fetuses threatened by what appears to be the irrational conduct of the mother. The benevolence they feel is deeply rooted and deserves our respect. Unfortunately, mandatory rescue of the fetus requires an imposition upon the mother that goes far beyond what our society has imposed, or should impose, on others. Our historical restraint regarding such impositions has strong constitutional and ethical bases. Technology threatens this restraint, by making mandatory intervention possible. But technology cannot change the ethical principles that make mandatory intervention wrong.

REFERENCES

1. 410 U.S. 113 (1973).

2. Jefferson v. Griffin Spalding County Hospital Authority, 274 S.E.2d 457 (Ga. 1981); North Central Bronx Hospital Authority v. Headley, No. 1992-85 (N.Y. Sup. Ct. Jan. 6, 1986), slip op. at 5; In re Unborn Baby Kenner, No. 79-JN-83 (Colo. Juv. Ct. Mar. 6, 1979), slip op. at 6–9.

3. 410 U.S. at 163–64.

4. North Central Bronx Hospital Authority v. Headley, No. 1992-85 (N.Y. Sup. Ct. Jan. 6, 1986); In re Unborn Baby Kenner, No. 79-JN-83 (Colo. Juv. Ct. Mar. 6, 1979).

5. 410 U.S. at 163–64.

6. Id.

7. 439 U.S. 379 (1979).

8. Id. at 400.

9. See, e.g., Jefferson v. Griffin Spalding County Hospital Authority, 274 S.E.2d 457 (Ga. 1981).

10. See In re President and Directors of Georgetown College, Inc., 331 F.2d 1000, 1008 (D.C. Cir.), reh. denied en banc, 331 F.2d 1010, cert. denied 377 U.S. 978 (1964); Powell v. Columbian [sic] Presbyterian Medical Center, 267 N.Y.S.2d 450 (Misc. 2d 1965). Cf. In re Osborne, 294 A.2d 372 (D.C. 1972).

11. Prosser W, Keeton W, The law of torts, 5th ed., St. Paul: West Publishing Co., 1984, §56, 376–377.

12. See, e.g., Vt. Stat. Ann. tit.12, §519(a) (1973); Minn. Stat. Ann. §604.05.01 (West Supp. 1986).

13. European countries, which generally do require rescue, exempt physically hazardous rescues. See, e.g., Code Penal, art. 63 (Fr.).

14. 10 Pa. D. & C.3d 90 (1978).

15. Id. at 92 (emphasis in original).

16. This terminology is from Judith Jarvis Thomson's famous article defending abortion on the grounds that requiring a woman to continue a pregnancy is requiring her to be a "Splendid Samaritan," a requirement not imposed on anyone else in society. See Thomson JJ, A defense of abortion, Philosophy & Public Affairs 1971, 1(1): 47–66, 48–52.

17. People v. Stewart, No. M508197 (San Diego Mun. Ct. Feb. 26, 1987).

P A T R I C I A   K I N G

Should Mom Be Constrained in the Best Interests of the Fetus?

I. INTRODUCTION

There is a growing judicial conundrum. Should pregnant women be compelled to act in the best interests of their fetuses? Judges are undoubtedly familiar with the issue of whether a woman should be compelled to deliver by cesarean section if the procedure is considered to be in the best interest of her fetus, but conflicts between maternal and fetal interests also arise in other settings. Two recent cases from my own jurisdiction, the District of Columbia, illustrate these conflicts.

In re A.C. involved a dying pregnant woman, Angela Carder, and her twenty-six and one half week old fetus. . . . [see pp. 332–337 above]

On February 5, 1988, Brenda Vaughan was arrested on charges of uttering after forging a check against her employer who had previously paid for a private drug rehabilitation program to help her overcome her addiction. She pled guilty to a lesser charge of second

Nova Law Review 13 (2), 1989, pp. 393–404. Reprinted by permission of the publisher.

degree theft. Despite a prosecutor's recommendation of probation, she was sentenced to jail for one hundred and eighty days because she tested positive for cocaine, and she was pregnant. Her sentence was subject to a motion to reduce the time to be served after the baby's birth. . . .

Most commentators, particularly legal commentators, tend to approach the subject of conflict between fetal and maternal interests as a question of rights. Some commentators conclude that the mother's rights should prevail in all circumstances. Others conclude that fetal rights should have priority. A few have argued that an effort should be made to balance the interests of mother and fetus according to a prescribed set of factors, to be applied case by case.[1]

I start at a slightly different point and focus not on the rights of the parties involved but rather on the connections between prospective parents and the fetus, between the pregnant woman and the fetus in particular. By focusing on the relationship, I am able to consider what obligations, if any, prospective parents owe the fetus. It seems to me that the decision to have a child puts the decisionmaker into a parentlike relationship. Moreover, at least one prospective parent and the fetus are physically and emotionally linked. I prefer this approach because the interests of prospective parents and the fetus are not posed as being distinct and possibly conflicting. By focusing on roles and relationships between prospective parents and fetuses, we capture the complexity of the interaction rather than concentrating our attention on individuals only.

I begin, therefore, with an examination of the moral duties a parent, specifically a pregnant woman, might owe to the fetus. I next ask, if we conclude that the pregnant women has a moral obligation to the fetus, does it follow that she ought to have a legal obligation as well? I conclude that both mothers and fetuses have interests that are important and should be respected, but that *other* societal values are decisive in deciding that *law* should not constrain women to act in the best interests of their fetus contrary to their preferences in matters of medical treatment and lifestyle.

II. WHAT MORAL OBLIGATION, IF ANY, DOES A PREGNANT WOMAN OWE HER FETUS?

It seems that mothering has long been celebrated as the paradigm benevolent relationship between human beings. Even though we think of mothering in such a special way, it is surprising to find that we really have spent very little time considering the nature and scope of the mother-fetal relationship except in the context of abortion.

In part, we have not spent a great deal of time talking about the maternal-fetal relationship because of the inaccessible nature of the fetus and our lack of data about fetal development. New scientific and technical developments have produced, however, a wealth of information about how a woman and the acts that she takes or omits to take, can affect the fetus. If one were to peruse some of the literature about fetal development and therapies to ameliorate or avoid disabilities in fetuses, one would get a list that looks a little bit like the following:

Eat a balanced diet.

Take vitamins.

Obtain prenatal care. Do not smoke and avoid spending time in a room with somebody who does smoke.

Do not drink alcohol.

Avoid all over the counter drugs and all prescription drugs.

Do not use abusive substances of any kind.

If necessary, as in the case of mothers who have phenylketonuria, return to a highly restrictive and very unpleasant diet.

Avoid unnecessary exercise.

Avoid certain workplaces, as an example, where X-rays are used.

Avoid sexual intercourse with her spouse or lover, if recommended by her physician.

Do not travel late in pregnancy.

Stay in bed for the duration if need be.

Agree to surgery if it is in the interest of the fetus.

Agree to cesarean delivery, if recommended.

Agree to stay hooked to life support, in the case of brain death, in the interests of the fetus.

Decline to terminate lifesaving procedures, if terminally ill.

This list does not begin to exhaust all the things that a pregnant woman might do or not do in order to benefit her fetus.

In considering whether a pregnant woman has obligations to her fetus, there are several things to note about this list, in addition to its length. First, the list implicates everything a pregnant woman does, from the time she gets up in the morning until the time she goes to bed at night. Second, it touches on the most private kinds of behavior, including the sexual relationship with her spouse or lover, not just what she does in public or at work, but also what she eats and how, or whether, she moves. Third, this list leaves little room for a mother's own needs and normal desires and preferences. She may not attend to the needs of her spouse, her other children or her parents. We might [and indeed we do] admire a pregnant woman who follows the "ideal" list, but it is equally likely that we would find fault or blame if her dedication to her developing fetus led her entirely to disregard her other obligations to family and co-workers.

Fourth, to comply with the mandate would be asking too much of any pregnant woman. We would be asking her to be a saint. If she chose to be a saint, that would be commendable. Requiring her to be a saint is something else. The possibility of being a saint is not something that is peculiar to pregnant women. We could all be saints. Yet, we do not require sainthood of ourselves. And, we could all do more. We could save the life of one child per year by providing food, or save the life of one homeless person by providing shelter. Even if we saved one life, with greater effort we could save two. Most of us do not believe that we are required to do that much. Impositions on a pregnant woman's time, liberty of action, economic resources and her own needs could well approach the level we would not require of ourselves.

The fact that a pregnant woman might not be required to do everything on the list does not mean that we cannot require of her some of the things on the list. But how to distinguish among the items? There is a range of conduct that we might try to distinguish. Requiring that harm or evil not be inflicted is different from requiring that harm or evil be removed. The proposition that we have a greater obligation to refrain from causing harm than to promote good finds support in common notions of morality as well as law. In thinking about what is required, we might take account of several factors. We might consider the degree of risk that we would require of a pregnant woman and the degree of risk to the fetus if action were not taken. We might take into account requirements based upon actions or omissions to act. We might compare what we would require of pregnant women with what we do require of parents with respect to their children. With respect to this latter consideration, it is worth noting that we have no consensus on the nature and extent of obligations of parents to existing children. For example, would we require that a parent donate a

kidney to his/her child if that were the only hope for the child? Finally, we might take account of the obligations a pregnant woman owes to others and herself when considering the obligations owed to her fetus. . . .

In summary then, we might agree that pregnant women have moral obligations to the fetuses that they carry. We could probably all agree that she should not be required to be a saint. But we would have difficulty in defining with precision what the scope of that obligation should be in part because we have not yet worked out an adequate account of what parental obligations should be. We turn then to ask, in view of our conclusions about a pregnant woman's moral obligations and their scope, what, if anything, law should require of pregnant women.

III. WHAT OUGHT LAW TO REQUIRE OF PREGNANT WOMEN?

If one takes the position that a woman has some moral obligation to act in the best interests of her fetus, does it follow that law, both judge-made and legislative statutory law, ought to require a woman to do or fulfill her moral obligation? A way of thinking about this is to say, why of course, the law ought to follow morality. Making moral obligations legal obligations, is a good and useful way for courts in our society, to coerce the least willing members of the community to conform to a moral norm. Moreover, the relationship between a pregnant woman and fetus is analogous to the relationship between parent and child where the law does indeed impose legal obligations. Perhaps the need for legal intervention is even stronger in the case of a fetus that is particularly vulnerable and dependent and in a position where no other person other than the pregnant woman can supply needed assistance. It is, in short, not difficult to understand why judges, faced with the conflict between a pregnant woman and her fetus, all too often have decided that the pregnant woman and her interests should be constrained in the best interests of her fetus.

Let me suggest that the matter is more complicated. There are other, and perhaps even compelling, reasons for not constraining a pregnant woman's interests.

I suggest that there are two categories of considerations that deserve our attention. For the sake of simplicity I designate these categories as equity concerns and privacy concerns. In privacy considerations, I group together the autonomy and privacy concerns of the pregnant woman and the distinct privacy concerns of the family of which the pregnant woman is a part.

A. EQUITY CONCERNS

I believe that we should not examine the interests of the pregnant woman in isolation from our treatment of analogous interests of other members of society. We should be concerned that the pregnant woman is not singled out or treated in a *sui generis* fashion. Historically, when the pregnant woman or women in general have been treated in some isolated way, the treatment has all too often turned out to be in fact discriminatory and limiting. First, we should not ask more of pregnant women than we are willing to ask of parents in general. Since the fetus is not as developmentally advanced as is the newborn, society should be reluctant to ask of the pregnant woman more than it would ask of parents. For example, some courts have required that the pregnant woman have a cesarean operation— a procedure that is risky and physically invasive. Yet, we have not been willing to require of parents that they be required to donate kidneys to children who might otherwise die in the absence of a kidney transplant. I realize that children are not physically linked to their parents in the way that a fetus is linked to the pregnant woman. But there will not always be someone else around to provide an organ, and we should not lose sight of the fact that a fetus does not have the legal, and for many, the moral status of a child.

The second equity concern is that we should not single out pregnant women for special attention. What about the prospective father? Many of the cases that have involved women objecting to medical treatment have been cases in which the woman was married. In some of these cases husbands, too, have objected to compelled medical treatment. Perhaps more to the point, all too often we have ignored the fact that prospective fathers have responsibilities too. In some instances they have perhaps contributed to fetal harm. In the Pamela Rae Stewart Monson case in California, where a woman was unsuccessfully criminally prosecuted after the birth of an injured child, the prosecutor alleged that she had endangered her fetus by engaging in intercourse with her husband.[2] The last time that I examined the issue, the act of intercourse required two people. Yet, her husband was not criminally indicted. But the problem is more serious. What of the prospective father who possibly harms the fetus by supplying illicit drugs to the pregnant woman or who is a heavy smoker or who abuses the pregnant woman? To focus only on the pregnant woman is to ignore the fact that, if we are serious about children and serious about fetuses, then we have to be equally serious about examining the responsibilities of both men and women.

The third equity concern is that we should be careful about creating legal obligations for the pregnant woman that are out of line with those that we impose on members of society in general. In our society there is no general obligation to be a good samaritan. Indeed, the ruling of one court underscores this point. In the case of *McFall v. Shimp,*[3] one man suffered from leukemia. He needed a bone marrow transplantation and his cousin was an appropriate match. The cousin, however, who had previously agreed to take the test to determine whether he was an appropriate match, refused to donate bone marrow. McFall went to court to see if he could compel his cousin to provide bone marrow. Keep in mind that bone marrow is something that persons regenerate, so the cousin was not going to lose the bone marrow forever. Also keep in mind that, while bone marrow transplantation is uncomfortable and inconvenient, it surely does not carry with it some of the risks that cesareans do. Nevertheless, the court held that the cousin had no obligation to provide bone marrow even if it meant that the proposed transplantation procedure offered the only hope of saving a human life.

My final equity concern is that if you look at cases of coerced medical treatment in the United States, two characteristics stand out. Almost all of these pregnant women were members of a minority group and/or poor. In one study of women forced to accept treatment, 81% were minority, 44% were unmarried, and 24% did not have English as a primary language. They were all in teaching hospitals since the study itself was conducted in teaching hospitals, but more importantly, they were all on public assistance.[4] Moreover, these women will already be disadvantaged by inadequate education and access to prenatal care. So, one of my primary worries in discussing imposition of legal obligations on pregnant women is that some women will be more heavily burdened than others.

B. PRIVACY CONCERNS

As I mentioned previously, privacy concerns include those concerns of the pregnant woman herself and the distinct concerns of her family. I will first address the pregnant woman's pregnancy concerns. . . .

Imagine, if you can, the prospect of tying a pregnant woman to an operating table so that we can perform surgery over her objection. Or consider the prospect of force-feeding a special diet to a woman suffering from phenylketonuria. I picked two particularly horrible examples to underscore that one of the reasons we recognize and respect autonomy is that we appreciate the importance of having voluntary cooperation in treatment decisions, not to mention our interest in the value of preserving bodily integrity.

Moreover, physicians do make mistakes. For example, in at least one reported case, the diagnosis of risk to the fetus was inaccurate. In light of the problems of medical uncertainty, it is preferable that patients rather than physicians make health care decisions. It is patients who will bear the burden of inaccurate diagnosis and prognosis.

Finally, the fact that a competent patient places priority on her own needs ought not disqualify her as a decisionmaker. The fact that many women would and indeed do place fetal interests ahead of their own interests should not be a reason for forcing all women to do so. The positions that women find themselves in vary enormously. Women are in the best position to take account of the many constraints that operate on them.

A second reason for respecting a pregnant woman's autonomy is that to do otherwise would severely burden the doctor-patient relationship. Pregnant women would have to worry that if they disagreed with their physicians' advice that they would be at risk of court intervention. Pregnant women would not be able to trust their physicians. This issue is obviously a bigger problem for women who use publicly provided medical services rather than privately provided medical services, but it would be a problem for private care as well. If we are not careful, we might actually encourage women to avoid prenatal care. This is particularly a problem in a country that does not provide adequate prenatal care to its women to begin with. The prospect of penalizing women for seeking prenatal treatment when we do not make it generally available, at least for those who cannot afford it, is surely unacceptable.

In addition to the privacy and autonomy interests of the pregnant woman herself, interests of the family are implicated by any thought of imposing legal obligations on the pregnant woman. There is a doctrine in family law that the State ordinarily should not intervene in the ongoing family or in the decisionmaking of the ongoing family. The assumption has been that the family can ordinarily be expected to reach decisions that are in the best interest of the family and its

members. The doctrine respects the pluralism that is a hallmark of this society. If a pregnant woman's husband supports the decision not to permit intervention in the interest of the fetus, but the state nonetheless intervenes, in a very real way, the family's interests have been as ignored as those of the pregnant woman.

Moreover, state intervention to override family decisionmaking has the effect of the state working in conjunction with physicians to reallocate decisionmaking with respect to the pregnant women's health care to the physician. Judges do not have medical expertise. They are dependent upon the expertise of physicians in deciding whether to constrain pregnant women. Often physicians who act in knowledgeable, assured and confident ways can only really offer educated guesses about the prognosis of any particular case. This is particularly true of obstetrics, where what we know with respect to treatment of fetuses—and newborns as well—is rapidly undergoing change. You should not be surprised to learn that in some of the cases where coerced treatment was sought it turned out that the physicians were wrong and indeed the women delivered naturally without injury to themselves or to the fetus. Medical uncertainty is, thus, a major factor not only in considering the woman's privacy concerns but in considering the family's interests as well. Medical decisionmaking strategy, which has been described in an article by Professor Nancy Rhoden, is even more disturbing. She documents that what physicians really do in the face of uncertainty, especially where there is a fetus involved, is adopt a maximum treatment strategy or last hope strategy.[5] In the emergency situation—and most of the cases that I am discussing arise in an emergency context—with no information about current law or current medicine, no time to get it, and often no time to appoint counsel for all the parties involved, the likelihood of the judge in effect reallocating decisionmaking to the physician is even greater. The judge often must travel to the hospital to hold a hearing. And it takes a mighty courageous judge to disagree with the doctors because judges, like the rest of us, are intimidated when we are outside of our own setting and in the setting of other professionals.

IV. CONCLUSION

The hardest kind of case that a judge or anyone else faces is a situation where moral considerations seem to require or permit a particular result but, social considerations seem to dictate an opposite conclusion. Let me give you an example. I have had lots of reasons to think recently about active euthanasia for very ill, elderly persons in a great deal of pain and suffering. I can justify in [my] own mind that in some instances a lethal injection for a competent elderly person who is asking not to have to survive additional painful weeks or months is ethically acceptable. However, I am not prepared to argue that as a matter of public policy, we should permit the use of a lethal injection for that one elderly person or in general. It seems to me that there are social considerations involved in this issue that go beyond the needs of a particular individual. Similarly, it is possible and just as tough to say that society should not coerce women to act in the best interests of their fetuses even if they have a moral obligation to act. Equity and privacy concerns deserve consideration and perhaps greater priority than the fact that, in a particular case, the pregnant woman *seems* to be doing the morally wrong thing.

NOTES

1. *See, e.g.,* Rhoden, *The Judge in the Delivery Room: The Emergence of Court-Ordered Caesareans,* 74 Cal. L. Rev. 1951 (1986); Nelson & Milliken, *Compelled Medical Treatment of Pregnant Women,* 260 J.A.M.A. 32 (1988); Robertson, *Procreational Liberty and the Control of Conception, Pregnancy and Childbirth,* 69 Va. L. Rev. 405 (1983); Shaw, *Conditional Prospective Rights of the Fetus,* 5 J. Legal Med 63 (March 1984).

2. Chambers, *Dead Baby's Mother Faces Criminal Charges on Acts in Pregnancy,* N.Y. Times, October 9, 1986 at A22, col. 1.

3. No. 78-17711 In equity (C.P. Allegheny County, Penn., July 26, 1978. *See* Meisel & Roth, *Must a Man Be His Cousin's Keeper?* 8 Hastings Center Rep. 5 (Oct. 1978).

4. Kolder, Gallagher, & Parsons, *Court-Ordered Obstetrical Interventions,* 316 New Eng. J. Med. 1192 (1987).

5. Rhoden, *Informed Consent in Obstetrics: Some Special Problems,* 23 New Eng. L. Rev. 67 (1987).

SUGGESTED READINGS

American Academy of Pediatrics. Committee on Bioethics. *Fetal Therapy: Ethical Considerations. Pediatrics* 81 (June 1988), 898–899.

American College of Obstetricians and Gynecologists. Committee on Ethics. *Patient Choice: Maternal-Fetal Conflict.* Committee Opinion No. 55. October 1987.

American Medical Association. Board of Trustees. "Legal Interventions During Pregnancy: Court-Ordered Medical Treatments and Legal Penalties for Potentially Harmful Behavior by Pregnant Women." *Journal of the American Medical Association* 264 (November, 1990), 2663–2670.

Brandt, Richard B. "The Morality of Abortion." *The Monist* 36 (1972), 503–526.

Brock, Dan W. "Taking Human Life." *Ethics* 95 (1985), 851–865.

Brody, Baruch A. "Abortion and the Sanctity of Human Life." *American Philosophical Quarterly* 10 (1973), 133–140.

Callahan, Daniel. *Abortion: Law, Choice and Morality.* New York: Macmillan, 1970.

Callahan, Daniel, and Callahan, Sidney, eds. *Abortion: Understanding Differences.* New York: Plenum Press, 1984.

Chervenak, Frank, et al. "When Is Termination of Pregnancy During the Third Trimester Morally Justifiable?" *New England Journal of Medicine* 310 (February 23, 1984), 501–504.

Chervenak, Frank A., and McCullough, Laurence B. "Inadequacies with the ACOG and AAP Statements on Managing Ethical Conflict During the Intrapartum Period." *Journal of Clinical Ethics* 2 (Spring, 1991), 23–24.

Clinics in Perinatology 14 (1987), 329–343. Special issue on "Maternal-Fetal Relations." See essays by Strong, Carson, and Murray, Thomas H.

Connery, John R. *Abortion: The Development of the Roman Catholic Perspective.* Chicago: Loyola University Press, 1977.

Cooper, Phillip J. "Rusty Pipes: The Rust Decision and the Supreme Court's Free Flow Theory of the First Amendment." *Notre Dame Journal of Law, Ethics and Public Policy* 6 (1992), 359–392.

Cudd, Ann E. "Sensationalized Philosophy: A Reply to Marquis's 'Why Abortion Is Immoral.'" *Journal of Philosophy* 87 (1990), 262–264.

Davis, Michael. "Fetuses, Famous Violinists, and the Right to Continued Aid." *Philosophical Quarterly* 33 (1983), 259–278.

Davis, Nancy. "Abortion and Self-Defense." *Philosophy & Public Affairs* 13 (1984), 175–207.

Devine, Philip E. *The Ethics of Homicide.* Ithaca, N.Y.: Cornell University Press, 1978.

Dickens, Bernard M. "Abortion and Distortion of Justice in the Law." *Law, Medicine and Health Care* 17 (1989), 395–406.

Dore, Clement. "Abortion, Some Slippery Slope Arguments and Identity over Time." *Philosophical Studies* 55 (1989), 279–291.

Ely, John Hart. "The Wages of Crying Wolf: A Comment on *Roe v. Wade.*" *Yale Law Journal* 82 (1973), 920–949.

Engelhardt, H. Tristram. *The Foundations of Bioethics.* New York: Oxford University Press, 1986. Chap. 6.

English, Jane. "Abortion and the Concept of a Person." *Canadian Journal of Philosophy* 5 (1975), 233–243.

Feinberg, Joel, ed. *The Problem of Abortion.* 2d ed. Belmont, CA: Wadsworth, 1984.

Finnis, John. "The Rights and Wrongs of Abortion: A Reply to Judith Thomson." *Philosophy & Public Affairs* 2 (1973), 117–145.

Fletcher, John C. "Abortion Politics, Science, and Research Ethics: Take Down the Wall of Separation." *Journal of Contemporary Health Law & Policy* 8 (1992), 95–121.

Fleming, Lorette. "The Moral Status of the Fetus: A Reappraisal." *Bioethics* 1 (1987), 15–34.

Foot, Philippa. "The Problem of Abortion and the Doctrine of Double Effect." *The Oxford Review* 5 (1967), 59–70.

Goldberg, Susan. "Medical Choices During Pregnancy: Whose Decision Is It, Anyway?" *Rutgers Law Review* 41 (1989), 591–623.

Hare, R. M. "Abortion and the Golden Rule." *Philosophy & Public Affairs* 4 (1975), 201–222.

Hursthouse, Rosalind. "Virtue Theory and Abortion." *Philosophy & Public Affairs* 20 (1991), 223–246.

Johnsen, Dawn. "A New Threat To Pregnant Women's Autonomy." *Hastings Center Report* 17 (August 1987), 33–40.

Jordan, James M. "Incubating for the State: The Precarious Autonomy of Persistently Vegetative and Brain-Dead Pregnant Women." *Georgia Law Review* 22 (1988), 1103–65.

King, Patricia A. "The Juridical Status of the Fetus: A Proposal for Legal Protection of the Unborn." *Michigan Law Review* 77 (1979), 1647–1687.

Kluge, Eike-Henner W. "When Cesarean Section Operations Imposed by a Court Are Justified." *Journal of Medical Ethics* 14 (1988), 206–211.

Loewy, Arnold H. "Why *Roe v. Wade* Should Be Overruled." *North Carolina Law Review* 67 (1989), 939–948.

Macklin, Ruth. "Antiprogestin Drugs: Ethical Issues." *Law, Medicine and Health Care* (1992), 215–219.

Mahowald, Mary B. "Is There Life After *Roe v. Wade?*" *Hastings Center Report* 19 (1989), 22–29.

Marquis, Donald. "Why Abortion Is Immoral." *Journal of Philosophy* 86 (1989), 183–202.

Mathieu, Deborah. *Preventing Prenatal Harm: Should the State Intervene?* Boston: Kluwer Academic, 1991.

Nicholson, Susan Teft. *Abortion and the Roman Catholic Church.* Knoxville, TN: *Journal of Religious Ethics* Monographs (1978).

Noonan, John T., Jr., ed. *The Morality of Abortion: Legal and Historical Perspectives.* Cambridge, MA: Harvard University Press, 1970.

———. "The Supreme Court and Abortion: Upholding Constitutional Principles." *Hastings Center Report* 10 (December 1980), 14–16.

Overall, Christine. "Mother/Fetus/State Conflicts." *Health Law in Canada* 9 (1989), 101–103, 122.

Pence, Gregory. *Classic Cases in Medical Ethics.* New York: McGraw-Hill, 1990.

Purdy, Laura M. "Are Pregnant Women Fetal Containers?" *Bioethics* 4 (1990), 273–291.

Quinn, Warren. "Abortion: Identity and Loss." *Philosophy & Public Affairs* 13 (1984), 24–54.

Regan, Tom, ed. *Matters of Life and Death.* 3d ed. New York: Random House, 1992.

Rhoden, Nancy K. "A Compromise on Abortion." *Hastings Center Report* 19 (1989), 32–37.

———. "The Judge in the Delivery Room: The Emergence of Court-Ordered Cesareans." *California Law Review* 74 (1986), 1951–2030.

Royal College of Physicians and Surgeons of Canada. Biomedical Ethics Committee. "Reflections on the Physician's Responsibility to Mother and Fetus." Ottawa, Canada, 1990.

Ryan, Kenneth J. "Abortion or Motherhood, Suicide and Madness." *American Journal of Obstetrics and Gynecology* 166 (1992), 1029–1036.

Solomon, Renee I. "Future Fear: Prenatal Duties Imposed by Private Parties." *American Journal of Law and Medicine* 17 (1991), 411–434.

Stein, Ellen J. "Maternal–Fetal Conflict: Reformulating the Equation." In Grubb, Andrew, ed. *Challenges in Medical Care.* New York: Wiley, 1992, 91–108.

Strong, Carson. "Fetal Tissue Transplantation: Can It Be Morally Insulated from Abortion?" *Journal of Medical Ethics* 17 (1991), 70–76.

Sugarman, Jeremy, and Powers, Madison. "How the Doctor Got Gagged: The Disintegrating Right of Privacy in the Physician–Patient Relationship." *Journal of the American Medical Association* 266 (1991), 3323–3327.

Sumner, L. W. *Abortion and Moral Theory.* Princeton, N.J.: Princeton University Press, 1981.

Thompson, Elizabeth. "Criminalization of Maternal Conduct During Pregnancy: Decisionmaking Model for Lawmakers." *Indiana Law Journal* 64 (1988–89), 357–374.

Thomson, Judith Jarvis. "Rights and Deaths." *Philosophy & Public Affairs* 2 (1973), 146–155.

Tooley, Michael. *Abortion and Infanticide.* Oxford, Oxford University Press, 1983.

Tribe, Laurence H. *Abortion: The Clash of Absolutes.* New York: Norton, 1990.

Veatch, Robert M. *Case Studies in Medical Ethics.* Cambridge, MA: Harvard University Press, 1977. Chap. 7.

Warren, Mary Anne. "Abortion." In Singer, Peter, ed. *A Companion to Ethics.* Cambridge, MA: Blackwell Reference, 1991, 303–314.

Wing, Kenneth R. "Speech, Privacy, and the Power of the Purse: Lessons from the Abortion 'Gag Rule' Case." *Journal of Health Politics, Policy and Law* 17 (1992), 163–175.

Winston, M.E. "Abortion and Parental Responsibility." *Journal of Medical Humanities and Bioethics* 7 (1986), 33–56.

Women's Health Issues 1 (1990 Fall). Special issue on "Maternal–Fetal Relations." See essays by Ryan, Kenneth J., Macklin, Ruth, Grodin, Michael A., Evans, Mark I. (et al.), Elkins, Thomas E., and Allen, Ann E.

Zaitchik, Alan. "Viability and the Morality of Abortion." *Philosophy & Public Affairs* 10 (1981), 18–26.

BIBLIOGRAPHIES AND ENCYCLOPEDIAS WITH BIBLIOGRAPHIES

Bioethicsline: Computer Retrieval Service.

Encyclopedia of Bioethics, ed. Warren Reich. New York: Macmillan, 1994.

Encyclopedia of Ethics, ed. Lawrence Becker and Charlotte Becker, New York: Garland Publishing Inc., 1992.

Lineback, Richard H., ed. *Philosopher's Index.* Vols. 1–27. Bowling Green, Ohio: Philosophy Documentation Center, Bowling Green State University. Issued quarterly.

Maternal–Fetal Conflict: Legal and Ethical Issues (1990). Bibliography available from the National Reference Center for Bioethics Literature, Kennedy Institute of Ethics, Georgetown University, Washington, D.C. 20057.

Walters, LeRoy, and Kahn, Tamar Joy, ed. *Bibliography of Bioethics.* Vols. 1–19. New York: Free Press.

Part IV

DECISIONS ABOUT THE
END OF LIFE

6.

The Right to Die

INTRODUCTION

The present chapter is the first of two dealing with questions of life and death after birth. In Chapter 6 the central issue is the kinds of medical treatments that are appropriate or inappropriate when a patient is seriously or terminally ill. Chapter 7 discusses the moral relevance of the distinction between killing and allowing to die and inquires whether the active killing of patients, at their request and with their consent, is ever morally justifiable.

The subject of Chapter 6 is often debated in terms of "forgoing" or "withholding or withdrawing" life-sustaining treatment. From the standpoint of a competent patient, or a competent person thinking ahead to future patient status, this question is most naturally phrased as follows: "What kinds of treatment should I accept, and what kinds of treatment should I refuse in particular circumstances?" For third parties—whether family members, friends, or health care providers—the question is usually formulated in the following terms: "What types of treatment should be started (or continued), and what kinds of treatment should be withheld (or withdrawn) for the sake of this patient on whose behalf I am deciding or making recommendations about treatment?"

The interventions referred to simply as "treatment" in the preceding questions include several powerful biomedical technologies that have been available only in the latter half of the twentieth century. In the 1960s and 1970s the respirator (or ventilator) and the kidney dialysis machine were the major foci of ethical debate. In the late 1980s and early 1990s new modes of providing long-term nutrition and hydration to unconscious patients provoked intense discussion in hospitals and nursing homes, in academic circles, and in the courts. In addition, since about 1960 randomized clinical trials have validated the effectiveness of multiple new treatment options—some of them quite expensive, others relatively cheap, some of them quite toxic, others relatively benign in their side effects. Think, for example, of the treatment alternatives now presented to patients diagnosed as having heart disease or a particular type of cancer.

The three sections of this chapter move from the simplest paradigm case to the most complex. We begin with the situation in which a presumably competent person expresses preferences about the kinds of treatment he or she wishes to have or declines to have. Somewhat more complicated is the situation in which treatment decisions must be made on behalf of a formerly competent patient who is now incompetent. If the now-incompetent person left a clear written statement of his or her wishes, the decision-making process is simplified. Even if the formerly competent patient left no such statement, the patient's general approach to life while competent may provide important clues for life-and-death decisions. Still more difficult are situations involving the never-competent. This third group of patients is represented in the present chapter by infants. Decision makers on behalf of the never-competent have no guidance from the patient him- or herself and must therefore reach judgments on some other basis.

DECISIONS BY COMPETENT ADULTS

Advance directives or "living wills" have been a central emphasis of the right-to-die movement in the United States since the early 1970s. The first state to give explicit legal recognition to such patient directives was California, with its Natural Death Act of 1976. By the early 1990s a majority of states had enacted laws that enable patients to express their wishes about terminal care. In addition, the 1990 federal Patient Self-Determination Act requires all hospitals and nursing homes that receive any federal funds to inform patients of their legal right to prepare advance directives (see Chapter 3).

The two sample advance directives reprinted in this chapter represent mature forms of the genre. In the earliest living wills, distributed by the Euthanasia Educational Council in 1974, three paragraphs of text were provided that expressed the wish to be "allowed to die and not [to] be kept alive by artificial means or 'heroic measures.'" An early variation of living wills allowed the signers to supplement the prepared text with their own instructions for care. The next generation of advance directives provided for the signer's designation of a surrogate decision maker who is entrusted with the responsibility of making decisions on behalf of the signer if he or she becomes incompetent.

The Medical Directive prepared by Linda and Ezekiel Emanuel goes beyond even the most complete earlier forms in several respects. It provides six scenarios, or illness situations, and asks the person filling out the form to choose among treatment options and to state a general goal of treatment in each hypothetical situation. The authors also provide separate sections of the directive for the signer's personal statement, a choice among settings for terminal care, a decision about organ donation, and designation of a proxy. The Values History constructed by David Doukas and Laurence McCullough complements the Medical Directive in several interesting ways. The history encourages the patient to summarize his or her primary goals in life and in approaching medical treatment decisions. In the light of these goals, the patient is then asked specific questions about preferred modes of treatment and their duration. Of note is the fact that three different methods of nutrition and hydration are distinguished: the intravenous approach, total parenteral nutrition (delivered through a large vein in the chest), and tube feeding into the stomach (either through a tube inserted through the nose and esophagus or through a tube introduced by means of a surgical incision in the abdomen).

In the final essay of this section, Leon Kass raises questions about both the coherence and the consequences of the frequently asserted right to die. Noting that the language of rights was introduced into political discourse by Hobbes and Locke, Kass argues that the right to die betrays the excessive individualism of its intellectual forebears. Kass questions whether the right-to-die notion applies equally well to contexts in which treatment is refused with uncertain consequences and to situations in which treatment is refused in order to achieve the result of the patient's death. The author also suspects that the right to die is at times cynically asserted on behalf of others by bright, healthy, beautiful people who fervently hope that the unproductive, the incurable, and the repulsive will die sooner rather than later.

DECISIONS ON BEHALF OF THE FORMERLY COMPETENT

The initial essay in this section is a set of guidelines for life-and-death decisions that was developed by a Hastings Center study group. In the case of a patient who lacks decision-making capacity, the guidelines distinguish two principal standards for deciding. The first standard, often called the "substituted judgment" standard, relies either on the patient's explicit directives or on the patient's own preferences and values. The alternative standard, sometimes called the "best interests" standard, requires attempting to discern what a reasonable person in the patient's circumstances would want to have done.

The remaining selections of this section focus on the case of Nancy Cruzan, a young woman from Missouri who at the age of twenty-five was involved in a near-fatal automobile accident. Ms. Cruzan was resuscitated by paramedics, who found her face-down in a ditch, without perceptible respiratory or cardiac function. When Ms. Cruzan did not recover consciousness after several weeks, a gastrostomy tube was introduced into her stomach to facilitate nutrition and hydration. After their daughter had remained in this persistent vegetative state for more than three years, her parents petitioned a county probate judge for permission to remove the feeding tube, so that their daughter could die. The controversy surrounding this request eventually reached the United States Supreme Court, and the *Cruzan* decision handed down by the court in June 1990 is arguably the most important U.S. judicial decision on the right to withdraw life-sustaining treatment from incompetent patients.

The majority opinion in the *Cruzan* case argues that a state may constitutionally require "clear and convincing evidence" when third parties claim that they are representing the wishes of a patient regarding life-sustaining treatment. Part of the rationale for this high threshold is that family members may wish to see a patient's life end for reasons that have nothing to do with the patient's welfare. The majority also asserted that this strict evidentiary requirement reflects an appropriate judgment by society that it is better to make an error that preserves life in a vegetative state, with all its limitations, than to make an error that leads automatically to death.

The concurring and dissenting opinions in the *Cruzan* case provide additional insight into the reasoning of the court. In her concurring opinion, Justice O'Connor makes two points that reveal limits to the scope of her support for the majority decision: Artificial modes of nutrition and hydration cannot readily be distinguished from other types of medical intervention; and the court's decision in this case, where no surrogate decision maker had been designated by Ms. Cruzan, would not necessarily apply to a case in which a "patient's duly appointed surrogate" were requesting the discontinuation of life-sustaining treatment. The dissenting justices seem almost incredulous in their response to the majority opinion. Justice Brennan, joined by Justices Marshall and Blackmun, asserts that "Nancy Cruzan has a fundamental right to be free of unwanted artificial nutrition and hydration, which right is not outweighed by any interests of the State." Justice Stevens adds that the majority erred in giving greater weight to legislative abstractions than to the wishes of concerned family members: "The meaning and completion of [Ms. Cruzan's] life should be controlled by persons who have her best interests at heart—not by a state legislature concerned only with the 'preservation of human life.'"

As the newspaper account of Nancy Cruzan's death indicates, the U.S. Supreme Court decision was followed by a second hearing before the Jasper County probate judge. At the hearing three acquaintances of Ms. Cruzan provided additional evidence that she had expressed the wish not to live "like a vegetable" connected to machines. In the light of this new evidence, the judge accepted the parents' request to remove the feeding tube from the stomach of their daughter. Thirteen days later, after surviving for almost eight years in a coma, Nancy Cruzan died.

The essay by John Arras responds both to the Cruzan case and the *Cruzan* decision. In the concluding essay of this section, Arras argues for a new approach to decision making in cases involving formerly competent patients like Nancy Cruzan. According to Arras, the families of such patients should be presumed to represent the prior wishes or best interests of such patients unless and until there is clear evidence to the contrary.

DECISIONS ABOUT INFANTS

Infants are by definition never-competent individuals. Thus, decisions about their care must of necessity be made by others. Two questions immediately arise: Who should make such decisions? On the basis of what substantive criteria should such decisions be made?

Three general answers to the second question can be identified. The first is that every infant with a life-threatening condition should receive whatever treatments are required to save the infant's life, if such salvage seems medically possible. On this view, allowing an infant to die is always morally wrong. The primary justifications for this position are, negatively, that no one should be authorized to make life-and-death decisions on behalf of (at least) never-competent individuals and, positively, that every patient, regardless of his or her physical or mental condition, has an overriding right to life. A second general answer is that life-and-death decisions should be made on the basis of the patient's best interests alone. This answer would generally be implemented with the aid of a proxy's judgment about the quality of life that the patient is likely to experience as balanced against the suffering that the patient is likely to endure.

A third answer would allow decisions concerning the treatment of infants to be determined, or at least strongly influenced, by familial and broader social considerations. According to this view, if an infant patient's continued existence would be likely to undermine a marriage, adversely affect other family members, or claim an undue share of society's resources, then a decision to allow the patient to die would be morally justifiable. A benefit-harm calculus is involved in the implementation of this answer, as it was in the case of the second. However, factors other than patient benefit are also included in the calculus.

Who should select among these answers and apply them in specific cases? The parents of an infant are generally regarded as the principal protectors of the infant's interests, unless they disqualify themselves through neglectful or abusive behavior. Health professionals, including physicians, nurses, and perhaps other groups as well, possess information that is clearly relevant to such decisions and often devote enormous effort to preserving the lives and promoting the health of infants. Other possible participants in decisions about life-sustaining treatment for infants include hospital administrators, hospital ethics committees (sometimes called, in these cases, "infant bioethics committees"), attorneys, and public officials acting to protect what they perceive to be the interests of society.

The "Johns Hopkins case" in the excerpt from James Gustafson's essay was an early example of the moral dilemmas surrounding infant care. This case, which involved an infant with Down's syndrome, became the focus of national and international debate when in 1971 it was made the subject of a film entitled *Who Shall Live?* by the Joseph P. Kennedy, Jr. Foundation. During the early years of the Reagan administration, a similar "Baby Doe" case in Indiana led to intense efforts by the United States federal government to protect handicapped infants from abuse and neglect. The final version of the new federal rules on "Child Abuse and Neglect Prevention and Treatment," published in April 1985, seemed to require the administration of "appropriate nutrition, hydration, and medication" to virtually all infants.[1] Only if treatment would be "futile" or "virtually futile" in promoting the infant's survival, or if the infant were "chronically and irreversibly comatose," could life-prolonging interventions be withheld.

The essays by Robert Weir and Nancy Rhoden were both written after the promulgation of at least the early versions of the federal rules on infant care. Weir attempts to classify into three categories the handicapping conditions with which infants are sometimes born. According to the author, infants afflicted with the conditions in the first two categories should not be treated, either because the condition itself is untreatable or because life with the condition is judged to be worse than death. Note that Down's syndrome falls into Weir's third category, for which he recommends treatment to prolong and enhance life. Nancy Rhoden's essay surveys the differing strategies of newborn care practiced in Sweden, the United Kingdom, and the United States. The author herself opts for a middle way that is highly individualized and requires frequent reassessment of the infant patient's medical status.

L.W.

NOTE

1. United States, Department of Health and Human Services, Office of Human Development Services, "Child Abuse and Neglect Prevention and Treatment," *Federal Register* 50 (April 15, 1985), pp. 14887–14888.

Decisions by Competent Adults

LINDA L. EMANUEL AND EZEKIEL J. EMANUEL

The Medical Directive*

INTRODUCTION

As part of a person's right to self-determination, every adult may accept or refuse any recommended medical treatment. This is relatively easy when people are well

*An earlier version of this form was originally published as part of an article by Linda L. Emanuel and Ezekiel J. Emanuel, "The Medical Directive: A New Comprehensive Advance Care Document," *Journal of the American Medical Association* 261: 3288–3293, June 9, 1989. It does not reflect the official policy of the American Medical Association.

From Fred H. Cate and Barbara A. Gill, *The Patient Self-Determination Act: Implementation Issues and Opportunities* (Washington, D.C.: The Annenberg Washington Program in Communications Policy Studies of Northwestern University, 1991), pp. 58–64. © 1991, Linda L. Emanuel and Ezekiel J. Emanuel. Reprinted by permission of the authors and publisher.

and can speak. Unfortunately, during serious illness they are often unconscious or otherwise unable to communicate their wishes—at the very time when many critical decisions need to be made.

The Medical Directive allows you to record your wishes regarding various types of medical treatment in several representative situations so that your desires can be respected. It also lets you appoint someone to make medical decisions for you if you should become unable to make them on your own.

The Medical Directive comes into effect only if you become incompetent (unable to make decisions or to express your wishes), and you can change it at any time until then. As long as you are competent, you should discuss your care directly with your physician.

MY MEDICAL DIRECTIVE

This Medical Directive expresses, and shall stand for, my wishes regarding medical treatments in the event that illness should make me unable to communicate them directly. I make this Directive, being 18 years or more of age, of sound mind, and appreciating the consequences of my decisions.

SITUATION A

If I am in a coma or a persistent vegetative state and, in the opinion of my physician and two consultants, have no known hope of regaining awareness and higher mental functions no matter what is done, then my wishes — if medically reasonable — for this and any additional illness would be:

	I want	I want treatment tried. If no clear improvement, stop.	I am undecided	I do not want
1. Cardiopulmonary resuscitation (chest compressions, drugs, electric shocks, and artificial breathing aimed at reviving a person who is on the point of dying), or major surgery (for example, removing the gall bladder or part of the colon)		Not applicable		
2. Mechanical breathing (respiration by machine, through a tube in the throat), or dialysis (cleaning the blood by machine or by fluid passed through the belly)				
3. Blood transfusions or blood products		Not applicable		
4. Artificial nutrition and hydration (given through a tube in a vein or in the stomach)				
5. Simple diagnostic tests (for example, blood tests or x-rays), or antibiotics (drugs to fight infection)		Not applicable		
6. Pain medications, even if they dull consciousness and indirectly shorten my life		Not applicable		

THE GOAL OF MEDICAL CARE SHOULD BE
(check one):

___ prolong life; treat everything
___ choose quality of life over longevity
___ provide comfort care only
___ other (*please specifiy*): _____
_____

SITUATION B

If I am in a coma and, in the opinion of my physician and two consultants, have a small but uncertain chance of regaining higher mental functions, a somewhat greater chance of surviving with permanent brain damage, and a much greater chance of not recovering at all, then my wishes — if medically reasonable — for this and any additional illness would be:

I want	I want treatment tried. If no clear improvement, stop.	I am undecided	I do not want
	Not applicable		
	Not applicable		
	Not applicable		
	Not applicable		

____ prolong life; treat everything
____ attempt to cure, but reevaluate often
____ choose quality of life over longevity
____ provide comfort care only
____ other (*please specifiy*): _____

SITUATION C

If I have brain damage or some brain disease that in the opinion of my physician and two consultants cannot be reversed and that makes me unable to recognize people, to speak meaningfully to them, or to live independently, *and I also have a terminal illness,* then my wishes — if medically reasonable — for this and any additional illness would be:

I want	I want treatment tried. If no clear improvement, stop.	I am undecided	I do not want
	Not applicable		
	Not applicable		
	Not applicable		
	Not applicable		
	Not applicable		

____ prolong life; treat everything
____ attempt to cure, but reevaluate often
____ choose quality of life over longevity
____ provide comfort care only
____ other (*please specifiy*): _____

MY MEDICAL DIRECTIVE (continued)

SITUATION D

If I have brain damage or some brain disease that in the opinion of my physician and two consultants cannot be reversed and that makes me unable to recognize people, to speak meaningfully to them, or to live independently, *but I have no terminal illness,* then my wishes — if medically reasonable — for this and any additional illness would be:

	I want	I want treatment tried. If no clear improvement, stop.	I am undecided	I do not want
1. Cardiopulmonary resuscitation (chest compressions, drugs, electric shocks, and artificial breathing aimed at reviving a person who is on the point of dying), **or major surgery** (for example, removing the gall bladder or part of the colon)		Not applicable		
2. Mechanical breathing (respiration by machine, through a tube in the throat), **or dialysis** (cleaning the blood by machine or by fluid passed through the belly)				
3. Blood transfusions or blood products		Not applicable		
4. Artificial nutrition and hydration (given through a tube in a vein or in the stomach)				
5. Simple diagnostic tests (for example, blood tests or x-rays), **or antibiotics** (drugs to fight infection)		Not applicable		
6. Pain medications, even if they dull consciousness and indirectly shorten my life		Not applicable		

THE GOAL OF MEDICAL CARE SHOULD BE (*check one*):

____ prolong life; treat everything
____ attempt to cure, but reevaluate often
____ choose quality of life over longevity
____ provide comfort care only
____ other (*please specifiy*): _____
_____

SITUATION E

If, in the opinion of my physician and two consultants, I have an incurable chronic illness that involves mental disability or physical suffering and ultimately causes death, and in addition I have an illness that is immediately life threatening but reversible, and I am temporarily unable to make decisions, then my wishes — if medically reasonable — would be:

I want	I want treatment tried. If no clear improvement, stop.	I am undecided	I do not want
	Not applicable		
	Not applicable		
	Not applicable		
	Not applicable		

____ prolong life; treat everything
____ attempt to cure, but reevaluate often
____ choose quality of life over longevity
____ provide comfort care only
____ other (*please specifiy*): _____
_____

SITUATION F

If I am in my current state of health (*describe briefly*):
_____
_____

and then have an illness that, in the opinion of my physician and two consultants, is life threatening but reversible, and I am temporarily unable to make decisions, then my wishes — if medically reasonable — would be:

I want	I want treatment tried. If no clear improvement, stop.	I am undecided	I do not want
	Not applicable		
	Not applicable		
	Not applicable		
	Not applicable		

____ prolong life; treat everything
____ attempt to cure, but reevaluate often
____ choose quality of life over longevity
____ provide comfort care only
____ other (*please specifiy*): _____
_____

COMPLETING THE FORM

You should, if possible, complete the form in the context of a discussion with your physician. Ideally, this should occur in the presence of your proxy. This lets your physician and your proxy know how you think about these decisions, and it provides you and your physician with the opportunity to give or clarify relevant personal or medical information. You may wish to discuss the issues with your family, friends, or religious mentor.

The Medical Directive contains six illness situations that include incompetence. For each one, you consider possible interventions and goals of medical care. Situations A and B involve coma; C and D, dementia; E, chronic disability; E and F, temporary inability to make decisions.

The interventions are divided into six groups: (1) cardiopulmonary resuscitation or major surgery; (2) mechanical breathing or dialysis; (3) blood transfusions or blood products; (4) artificial nutrition and hydration; (5) simple diagnostic tests or antibiotics; and (6) pain medications, even if they dull consciousness and indirectly shorten life. Most of these treatments are described briefly. If you have further questions, consult your physician.

Your wishes for treatment options (I want this treatment; I want this treatment tried, but stopped if there is no clear improvement; I am undecided; I do not want this treatment) should be indicated. If you choose a trial of treatment, you should understand that this indicates you want the treatment *withdrawn* if your physician and proxy believe you would have agreed that it has become futile.

The Personal Statement section allows you to mention anything that you consider important to tell those who may make decisions for you concerning the limits of your life and the goals of intervention. For example, your description of insufferable disability in the Personal Statement will aid your health-care team in understanding exactly when to avoid interventions you may have declined in situation E. Or if, in situation B, you wish to define "uncertain chance" with numerical probability, you may do so here.

Next you may express your preferences concerning organ donation. Do you wish to donate your body or some or all of your organs after your death? If so, for what purposes(s) and to which physician or institute? If not, this should also be indicated in the appropriate box.

In the final section you may designate one or more proxy decision-makers, who would be asked to make choices under circumstances in which your wishes are unclear. You can indicate whether the decisions of the proxy should override, or be overridden by, your wishes if there are differences. And, should you name more than one proxy, you can state who is to have the final say if there is disagreement. Your proxy must understand that this role usually involves making judgments that you would have made for yourself, had you been able — and making them by the criteria you have outlined. Proxy decisions should ideally be made in discussion with your family, friends, and physician.

WHAT TO DO WITH THE FORM

Once you have completed the form, you and two adult witnesses (other than your proxy) who have no interest in your estate need to sign and date it.

Many states have legislation covering documents of this sort. To determine the laws in your state, you should call the office of its attorney general or consult a lawyer. If your state has a statutory document, you may wish to use the Medical Directive and append it to this form.

You should give a copy of the completed document to your physician. His or her signature is desirable but not mandatory. The Directive should be placed in your medical records and flagged so that anyone who might be involved in your care can be aware of its presence. Your proxy, a family member, and/or a friend should also have a copy. In addition, you may want to carry a wallet card noting that you have such a document and where it can be found.

MY PERSONAL STATEMENT
(*use another page if necessary*)

Please mention anything that would be important for your physician and your proxy to know. In particular, try to answer the following questions: (1) What medical conditions, if any, would make living so unpleasant that you would want life-sustaining treatment *withheld*? (Intractable pain? Irreversible mental damage? Inability to share love? Dependence on others? Another condition you would regard as intolerable?) (2) Under what medical circumstances would you want to *stop* interventions that might already have been started?

Should there be any difference between my preferences detailed in the illness situations and those understood from my goals or from my personal statement, I wish my treatment selections / my goals / my personal statement (*please delete as appropriate*) to be given greater weight.

When I am dying, I would like — if my proxy and my health-care team think it is reasonable — to be cared for:

- ☐ at home or in a hospice
- ☐ in a nursing home
- ☐ in a hospital
- ☐ other (*please specify*): _____

ORGAN DONATION
(*please check boxes and fill in blanks where appropriate*)

—I hereby make this anatomical gift, to take effect after my death:

I give
- ☐ my body
- ☐ any needed organs or parts
- ☐ the following parts: _____

to
- ☐ the following person or institution: _____
- ☐ the physician in attendance at my death
- ☐ the hospital in which I die
- ☐ the following physician, hospital storage bank, or other medical institution: _____

for
- ☐ any purpose authorized by law
- ☐ therapy of another person
- ☐ medical education
- ☐ transplantation
- ☐ research

—I do not wish to make any anatomical gift from my body.

DURABLE POWER OF ATTORNEY FOR HEALTH CARE

I appoint as my proxy decision-maker(s):

_____
Name and Address

and (*optional*)

_____
Name and Address

I direct my proxy to make health-care decisions based on his/her assessment of my personal wishes. If my personal desires are unknown, my proxy is to make health-care decisions based on his/her best guess as to my wishes. My proxy shall have the authority to make all health-care decisions for me, including decisions about life-sustaining treatment, if I am unable to make them myself. My proxy's authority becomes effective if my attending physician determines in writing that I lack the capacity to make or to communicate health-care decisions. My proxy is then to have the same authority to make health-care decisions as I would if I had the capacity to make them, EXCEPT (*list the limitations, if any, you wish to place on your proxy's authority*):

Should there be any disagreement between the wishes I have indicated in this document and the decisions favored by my above-named proxy, I wish my proxy to have authority over my written statements / I wish my written statements to bind my proxy. (*Please delete as necessary.*) If I have appointed more than one proxy and there is disagreement between their wishes, _____
shall have final authority.

Signed: _____
Signature   Printed Name

_____
Address   Date

Witness: _____
Signature   Printed Name

_____
Address   Date

Witness: _____
Signature   Printed Name

_____
Address   Date

Physician (*optional*):

I am _____'s physician. I have seen this advance care document and have had an opportunity to discuss his/her preferences regarding medical interventions at the end of life. If _____ becomes incompetent, I understand that it is my duty to interpret and implement the preferences contained in this document in order to fulfill his/her wishes.

_____
Signature   Printed Name

_____
Address   Date

DAVID J. DOUKAS AND LAURENCE B. McCULLOUGH

The Values History

Complex ethical dilemmas in the care of debilitated patients in hospitals and long-term care facilities happen with increasing frequency. One response has been the development and use of advance directives as a means of respecting the autonomy of those patients who may later become incompetent.[1-4] Legal instruments, primarily the living will and the durable power of attorney, have been developed to direct physicians and institutions to discontinue life supports.[5] These legal instruments, however, focus little attention on the patient's underlying values and beliefs regarding such directives. To remedy this shortcoming, the authors propose a more systematic evaluation of advance health care decision making by the competent patient: the "Values History."

The validity of the Values History is based on a basic ethical consideration: the Values History enhances the autonomy of the patient in a way that present advance directives do not, by clarifying for the health care team the patient's expressed values underlying decisions to be carried out when decision making by the patient is no longer possible. One possible benefit of such an evaluation is to help physicians and institutions manage more reliably the uncertainties that surround advance directives.

FUNDAMENTAL ADVANCE DIRECTIVES

THE LIVING WILL

Living wills are intended to document in advance patients' preferences concerning the administration of mechanical or artificial means of life support in the event of a terminal illness or condition. Typical statutes authorizing these directives, now in effect in 41 states and the District of Columbia, provide that a living will becomes effective when the patient has no reasonable hope of recovery and is unable to participate in decisions regarding his or her care. Until that time, the patient can revoke or change the living will at any time.[1] Executed in accordance with statutory requirements, a living will is binding on health care providers.

A major shortcoming of living wills is that they only vaguely define which medical procedures the patient has rejected.[6] Their language is general and imprecise, leaving them open to subjective interpretation. In some states they must be reexecuted periodically.[7] Most important, they do not obligate the physician and the patient to work together prospectively, in anticipation of possible hospitalization or admission to a critical care unit, to identify the patient's beliefs and values concerning terminal care, quality of life, aggressive treatment to sustain life, interests of family members, and other issues. An equally important process of this physician-patient collaboration would be the imparting of information by the physician, permitting the patient to make informed choices among the various possible treatment options.

THE DURABLE POWER OF ATTORNEY

The durable power of attorney is the legal empowerment of a person other than the patient to make decisions for the patient when the patient is incompetent. The word *durable* is important, because a (simple) power of attorney becomes ineffective immediately upon the patient's incapacity. The durable power of attorney allows the assignment of a legally enforceable surrogate decision maker for the incompetent patient.

David J. Doukas and Laurence B. McCullough, "The Values History," *Journal of Family Practice* 32 (1991), 145–153. © 1991, Appleton & Lange, Inc. Reprinted by permission of Appleton & Lange, Inc., and the authors.

All states as well as the District of Columbia have durable power of attorney statutes, and several of them (including DC) specifically define this authority for health-related decisions. The responsibility of the person holding durable power of attorney is to consider the medical choices available to the incompetent patient and choose the option that most closely adheres to the earlier spoken or written wishes and values of the patient. If no living will has been signed, the durable power of attorney permits transferral of the patient's decisional authority to his or her agent. The complete responsibility for treatment decision making will not rest as heavily on the shoulders of the agent if the patient has signed a living will or prior discussions on medical directives between patient and agent have taken place. Yet the durable power of attorney alone may constitute a better approach than a living will alone because it provides the greater flexibility of the two documents.

The main drawback to the durable power of attorney concept is the limit to which one person can fully understand the health care preferences of another unless there have been comprehensive discussions between them.[8] It is questionable whether a surrogate decision maker can foresee the patient's responses in all circumstances when critical decisions must be made. Indeed, there is evidence that communication between the competent patient and the patient's appointed agent has not always taken place,[9] with the possibility that the person holding the durable power of attorney may fail to follow precisely the patient's prior autonomous directives.

In summary, while living wills and durable powers of attorney protect decision-making authority (either directly or indirectly), they do not always enhance autonomy. The enhancement of autonomy is more than mere decision-making authority; it is the exercise of such authority in the particular, concrete context of a patient's values and beliefs. The Values History supplements advance directives by protecting and promoting patient autonomy. Advance directives also tend to take an "either-or" approach to intervention, a view that overlooks the clinical reality that severely ill patients could possibly benefit from a trial intervention,[10] which may be needed only temporarily and can be withdrawn, returning the patient to a preintervention status. Whether mechanical ventilation or administration of antibiotics can benefit a particular patient

often cannot be reliably determined in advance. If the patient so chooses, a trial of intervention could be stopped either after a specific time has elapsed or when reasonable medical judgment shows that the intervention will not be beneficial, ie, it will only prolong the patient's dying process. This more nuanced approach reflects the emerging concept of levels of intervention as an important concern of critical care, replacing the now fading all-or-nothing approach.[11]

THE VALUES HISTORY

The Values History has two parts: (1) an explicit identification of values, and (2) the articulation of advance directives based on the patient's values. Almost all jurisdictions allow specific directives to be appended to the living will if the intent is in concordance with the living will statute. The Values History can therefore address the vagueness of "withholding heroic means" by allowing the patient to detail those health care measures that are wanted (and to what degree) and those that are not wanted. The Values History is proposed as an ethically justified, clinically applicable supplement to the living will for acute and chronic medical care.

The first section of the Values History invites the patient to identify those values and beliefs associated with terminal care that are most important to him or her. This section offers an advantage over the "medical directive" that was proposed by the Emanuels in 1989 in that it asks the patient to focus fully on clarifying his or her values-related reasons for specific treatment choices. The goal is not to assess the validity of the patient's values and beliefs according to the perspective of the physician, other health care professionals, or institutions. To judge the validity of another person's values is a gross and wholly unacceptable form of medical paternalism.[12] On the other hand, the physician may be valuable to the patient in facilitating the exposition of the patient's values.[13] As the patient articulates his or her values, the physician can enhance the patient's autonomy by assisting in the removal of "physical, cognitive, psychological, and social constraints" that could impede the informed consent process.[13] The goal of this process is twofold: (1) to help the patient to become clear about what he or she wants and does not want and why, and (2) to help health care professionals and institutions to understand, respect, and implement the cluster of value-based decisions that result from using the Values History in the clinical setting. As a result, doubts about health decisions at risk for being too vague, too general, or only loosely connected to the patient's values are reduced. Further, such values clarification would be valuable in enhancing physician-patient communication during the discussion concerning terminal care when compared with the Emanuels' medical directive.

The second section of the Values History begins with acute care designations: consent for or refusal of cardiopulmonary resuscitation, use of a respirator, and placement of an endotracheal tube. The chronic care designations then follow and include decisions for administering intravenous fluids, enteral [involving the intestines] feeding tubes, and total parenteral [not involving the intestines; for example, intravenous] nutrition for nutritional support, use of medication, and use of dialysis. For directives 2 through 8, the patient is afforded these options: intervention, trial of intervention (limited by time or medical judgment), or nonintervention. This section of the Values History also offers directives not found in living wills or the Emanuels' document, such as admission to the hospital but without specific services (eg, admission to general medical floor only, forbidding admission to critical care), and "Do not call 911" for patients in long-term care facilities.[14] The Values History concludes with the assignment designations, and the assignment or exclusion of a named decision maker for the patient, consent for autopsy, and consent for organ donation. The Values History in a format updated from earlier versions,[1,2,15] can be seen in the Appendix to this article.

In summary, after the patient has signed a living will, the patient would discuss his or her values and advance directives of the Values History with the physician. First, the physician would engage the patient in discussion(s) on perspectives on the quality of life vs. length of life (i.e., the Values Section of the Values History). When the values section is completed, the physician would begin the patient education and disclosure process that would lead to discussion and possible signing of the Directives Section of the Values History.

In our judgment, a Values History can be completed on a patient within five visits or 1 year. The patient should be encouraged to share the Values History with family members of the patient's choice and with the person, if any, chosen to hold the durable power of attorney. The physician can serve as a facilitator of this process if that is the patient's preference. Early involvement of the family in discussing the patient's values and advance directives on terminal care helps avoid the difficulties of substitute decision making when the patient becomes incompetent. Also, this exchange within the family helps clarify the patient's health care goals so that relatives with conflicting health care goals will better understand and respect the patient's reasoning. Hence, the purpose of this exchange is to enhance patient autonomy through the informed consent to health care decisions (as discussed with the family), and to negate future attempts of family members to interfere with physician compliance with the patient's preferences. The completed Values History should be reviewed with the patient periodically, especially if there is a significant deterioration in the patient's health status.

THE VALUES SECTION

The first choice in the Values Section of the Values History is basic: the question of length of life vs. quality of life. Next, the patient is asked to identify which values relevant to terminal care (eg, based on dignity, comfort, or personal philosophy) are important. These values-based statements have been found in pilot testing with patients to be those that express commonly held values in patient health care decision making. Obviously these values may be supplemented to reflect the values of an individual patient. Alternatively, the patient may add other value-based statements to the list. The list provided is a useful starting point.

THE DIRECTIVES SECTION

The first three directives in this section, dealing with acute care situations, are crucial to do-not-resuscitate order decision making. An early and direct approach to cardiopulmonary resuscitation is necessary to reduce ambiguity. To detail explicitly that the patient has autonomously decided against cardiopulmonary resuscitation would help more precisely to clarify the code status of the patient.

The directives that follow include the choice of trial of intervention. The patient can choose either a predetermined time to attempt an intervention that, if fruitless, should be discontinued, or can have this attempt continued as long as there appears to be, in the physician's best judgment, medical benefit for the patient. The former choice is structurally more concrete by mandating termination at a specific time and is more explicit about the patient's autonomous preferences by setting definitive boundaries. The latter choice allows some variation when to discontinue the therapy only if no benefit is evident, but does not easily allow paternalistic intervention because it does not condone therapy that will prolong the dying process. The choice of time vs. benefit trials more accurately reflects the needs of patients when consenting to trials of intervention than do those solely based on medical benefit as in the Emanuels' document. The utility of including the trial-of-intervention options becomes apparent with the following directives. The next acute care directive, the option of consenting to respirator acceptance, is important, especially for patients with chronic pulmonary disease. Endotracheal tube placement is integral to the implementation of the first two directives and may help clarify the first two directives.

The chronic care designations cover those directives that might apply to long-term patient care. The directives begin with total parenteral nutrition. The patient should be fully informed about how total parenteral nutrition is used and how it differs from intravenous fluids. Intravenous hydration and medication also need to be discussed as directives in the context of long-term care. Further, a separate directive should explore the medications necessary for the treatment of illness by other routes (eg, by mouth or by intramuscular injection). The patient should be assured that the administration of intravenous medicines and fluids would never be withheld if requested by the patient for comfort care or pain relief. Directives addressing enteral feeding tubes and dialysis should be undertaken in the context of long-term recuperative or vegetative care.

The assignment designations are the last part of the Directives Section, which is composed of several directives detailing autopsy, paramedic or intensive care unit care, proxy negation, organ donation, and appointment of a durable power of attorney. The patient's directive regarding autopsy can be a highly charged personal decision.

The next directives allow the patient to decide on admission to an intensive care unit or to receive paramedic care. Following these directives is an option to add consent, refusal, or trials of intervention to other specific directives not otherwise addressed (eg, specific types of surgery).

All the above 10 directives are initialed by the patient and dated as they are decided over time. Each of these directives requests that the patient explain the reasons for his or her decision in terms of the values earlier identified. The importance of this information is to understand the patient's motivations, to examine and discuss possible inconsistent values, and to expose and reverse possible psychological factors that may hinder the patient from participating in the informed consent process.

Throughout this consent process, the operating assumption is that the patient is competent to make these decisions unless reliably shown to be incompetent to do so. The burden of proof is upon the clinician to establish and thoroughly document in the chart a clinical judgment regarding the patient's competence. If the patient possesses questionable ability to evidence a health care choice, understand information relevant to making that decision, or appreciate the importance or risks and benefits of the decision, then the physician needs to reevaluate the patient's informed consent capabilities.[16] When disclosure attempts have been repeated exhaustively, rendering informed consent untenable, the physician must attempt to reverse those treatable processes so that the patient can make his or her own health care decisions.[16] Failing such measures, the physician would turn to identify alternative substitute decision makers.

The proxy negation directive allows the patient to name a person or persons to be excluded from decision making if the patient should become incompetent, thereby preventing later ethical crises regarding the standing of these individuals to make decisions for the patient. This directive may be useful to exclude a family member with a differing philosophy toward life and medical care, or if the patient suspects some conflict of interest or ill will.

The organ donation directive is the Uniform Donor Card in the form permitted by the patient's state to allow the advance designation for the use of organs in transplantation, medical therapy, medical research, or education.

The last major directive is durable power of attorney, again as allowed by the local jurisdiction, preferably in the form of a durable power of attorney for health care. The limits of the durable power of attorney for health care can then be framed to reflect the preferences of the patient as voiced in the Values and Directives sections. Further, the person holding durable power of attorney can serve as the patient's agent to decide on any treatment measures not specified in the Directives Section. It should be understood, however, that the patient should make his or her own decisions, rather than leave a relative or friend to identify, perhaps mistakenly, the patient's wishes.

BARRIERS TO THE USE OF THE VALUES HISTORY

The physician, the patient, the patient's family, and the law can all act as barriers to the successful use of the Values History. The physician may have difficulty with accepting the concept of spending time in the outpatient setting discussing advance directives, much less values, with their patients. Educational efforts (in the medical and lay literature) directed at both physicians and patients could enhance the interchange necessary to elicit the Values History. Particular appeal could be made to physicians that such an intervention would obviate the far more difficult crisis management needed when the patient becomes critically ill. The benefits of such "prophylactic bioethics" measures more than offset the burden of time invested.

The physician may perceive that discussing the possibility of death with the patient is a harmful act, contrary to the physician's beneficence-based role. The physician could also feel constrained by discomfort in disclosing the eventuality of death or by a paternalistic desire to wait until the "right time." If the physician is not the health provider who elicited the Values History, when the patient becomes hospitalized the physician may refuse to honor it and insist on transferring the patient's care. These examples illustrate how paternalistic desires to protect or benefit the patient could be used to overrule autonomy claims of the patient. Such attempts to strip patient decision-making capabilities are, therefore, ethically suspect.

The patient's condition, especially an incompetent mental status, can be a barrier to implementing the Values History.[17] No autonomous advance directives can be obtained if the patient lacks comprehension or decision-making capabilities. Certain barriers to competence may be reversible; such barriers should be evaluated, and when possible, treated. An indecisive, competent patient or a patient who refuses to discuss the prospect of dying can also impair efforts to elicit a Values History. In both circumstances, sensitive educational efforts should be the first response. If these efforts fail, the physician should consider recommending that the patient choose a durable power of attorney who is knowledgeable about the patient's values and previously stated preferences.

The family of the patient may also act as a barrier to the implementation of the Values History. A family member may try to ignore the patient's advance directives to withhold or withdraw certain therapies, challenging the patient's decisions and the physician's duty to carry them out. Educating such a family member on the patient's right to refuse specific interventions can help here. Discussing the patient's Values History when it is completed (with the patient's permission) can help prevent the family from becoming a barrier to its implementation.

Finally, the possibility of legal barriers to the Values History must be considered. While most states now have living will statutes, nine states do not. Lack of the living will statute would not eliminate the usefulness of both instruments, however, since both would help the medical team by clarifying the patient's prior competent values and preferences. Within the Values History, the durable power of attorney and organ donation statutes vary by jurisdiction; therefore, the wording specified by statute should be used for that section of the Values History. The durable power of attorney is commonly available from hospital counsel and health care attorneys, while the organ donor card is readily available from local departments of motor vehicles.

Explicit advance instructions within the living will may create another legal barrier to the Values History. Although permissible in most living wills, such instructions are not addressed in some.[7] The listing of directives can be complicated when living will statutes prohibit withholding certain medical therapies (eg, intravenous hydration and nutrition).[18] If there exists such a prohibition, patients could be informed that although withholding these therapies is not condoned by state statute, these statutes have been successfully challenged in the past.[19] In such cases, consult hospital or office legal counsel about adding to the living will directives that are not condoned in the legislation. Alternatively, specific directives could be deleted from the Values History if the patient so consents. Despite such differences, it is hoped that the clinician will strive to implement the Values History by reconciling its ethical foundation with the legal stipulations of the jurisdiction involved.

CONCLUSIONS

The Values History is proposed as an ethically justified clinical tool intended to be used as an adjunct to legal advance directives. Although changes in sections 14 and 15 are necessary by jurisdiction, such alterations are easily adapted to this document. The durable power of attorney and organ donor legislation of the physician's jurisdiction should be inserted or substituted before using the Values History. By customizing the Values History in this way, the clinician will have a tool of considerable precision with which the value-based advance directives of patients can be clarified. We propose that the use of the Values History will enhance patient autonomy significantly by allowing the patient to identify health care decisions prospectively, to discuss them with family members, and to have the physician implement them.

REFERENCES

1.   Doukas D, McCullough L. Assessing the values history of the elderly patient regarding critical and chronic care. In: Gallo J, Reichel W, Anderson L, eds. Handbook of geriatric assessment. Rockville, Md: Aspen, 1988:111–24.

2.   Doukas D, Lipson S, McCullough L. Value history. In: Reichel W, ed. Clinical aspects of aging. 3rd ed. Baltimore, Williams & Wilkins, 1989:615–6.

3.   Wanzer S, Federman D, Adelstein SJ, et al. The physician's responsibility toward hopelessly ill patients—a second look. N Engl J Med 1989; 320:844–9.

4.   Emanuel L, Emanuel E. The medical directive; a new comprehensive advance care document. JAMA 1989; 261:3288–93.

5.   Kapp M, Pies H, Doudera A, eds. Legal and ethical aspects of health care for the elderly. Ann Arbor, Mich, Health Administration Press, 1985.

6.   Eisendrath S, Jonsen A. The living will—help or hindrance? JAMA 1983; 249:2054–8.

7.   President's Commission for the Study of Ethical Problems in Medicine and Biomedical and Behavioral Research: Deciding to forego life-sustaining treatment. Washington, DC, Government Printing Office, 1983:310–2.

8.   Wanzer S, Adelstein J, Cranford R, et al. The physician's responsibility toward hopelessly ill patients. N Engl J Med 1984; 310:955–9.

9.   Evans A, Brody B. The do-not-resuscitate order in teaching hospitals. JAMA 1985; 253:2236–9.

10. Wear S. Anticipatory ethical decision-making: the role of the primary care physician. HMO Pract, Mar-Apr 1989; 3:41–6.

11. Civetta J, Taylor R, Kirby R, eds. Critical care. Philadelphia, JB Lippincott, 1988.

12. McCullough L, Lipson S. A framework for geriatric ethics. In Reichel W, ed. Clinical aspects of aging. 3rd ed. Baltimore, Williams & Wilkins, 1989:577–86.

13. Ackerman T. Why doctors should intervene. Hastings Cent Rep August 1982:14–7.

14. Stollerman G. Decisions to leave home [editorial]. J Am Geriatr Soc 1988; 36:375–6.

15. Doukas D, McCullough L. Truthtelling and confidentiality in the aged patient. In Reichel W, ed. Clinical aspects of aging. 3rd ed. Baltimore, Williams & Wilkins, 1989:608–15.

16. Appelbaum P, Grisso T. Assessing patients' capacities to consent to treatment. New Engl J Med 1988; 319:25, 1635–8.

17. McCullough L, Lipson S. Informed consent. In Reichel W, ed: Clinical aspects of aging, 3rd ed. Baltimore, Williams & Wilkins, 1989:587–96.

18. Society for the Right to Die. The physician and the hopelessly ill patient: legal, medical, and ethical guidelines. New York, Society for the Right to Die, 1985:32–3.

19. *Corbett v D'Allesandro*, 487, So2d 368 (Fla App), *rev denied*, 492 So2d 1331 (Fla 1986).

Appendix
The Values History

Patient Name _____

This Values History serves as a set of my specific value-based directives for various medical interventions. It is to be used in health care circumstances when I may be unable to voice my preferences. These directives shall be made a part of the medical record and used as supplementary to my Living Will.

VALUES SECTION

There are several values important in decisions about terminal treatment and care. This section of the Values History invites you to identify your most important values.

BASIC LIFE VALUES

Perhaps the most basic values in this context concern length of life versus quality of life. Which of the following two statements is the most important to you?

__1. I want to live as long as possible, regardless of the quality of life that I experience.

__2. I want to preserve a good quality of life, even if this means that I may not live as long.

QUALITY OF LIFE VALUES

Many values help to define the quality of life that we want to live. The following list contains some that appear to be the most common. Review this list (and feel free to either elaborate on it or add to it) and circle those values that are important to your definition of quality of life.

1. I want to maintain my capacity to think clearly.
2. I want to feel safe and secure.
3. I want to avoid unnecessary pain and suffering.
4. I want to be treated with respect.
5. I want to be treated with dignity when I can no longer speak for myself.
6. I do not want to be an unnecessary burden on my family.
7. I want to be able to make my own decisions.
8. I want to experience a comfortable dying process.
9. I want to be with my loved ones before I die.
10. I want to leave good memories of me to my loved ones.
11. I want to be treated in accord with my religious beliefs and traditions.
12. I want respect shown for my body after I die.
13. I want to help others by making a contribution to medical education and research.
14. Other values or clarification of values above:

DIRECTIVES SECTION

Some directives involve simple yes/no decisions. Other provide for the choice of a trial of intervention.
Initials/Date

_____ 1. I want to undergo cardiopulmonary resuscitation.
 _____ Yes
 _____ No
 Why?

_____ 2. I want to be placed on a ventilator.
 _____ Yes
 _____ TRIAL for the period of _____
 _____ TRIAL to determine effectiveness using reasonable medical judgment.
 _____ No
 Why?

_____ 3. I want to have an endotracheal tube used in order to perform items 1 and 2.
 _____ Yes
 _____ TRIAL for the period of _____
 _____ TRIAL to determine effectiveness using reasonable medical judgment.
 _____ No
 Why?

_____ 4. I want to have total parenteral nutrition administered for my nutrition.
 _____ Yes
 _____ TRIAL for the period of _____
 _____ TRIAL to determine effectiveness using reasonable medical judgment.
 _____ No
 Why?

_____ 5. I want to have intravenous medication and hydration administered; regardless of my decision, I understand that intravenous hydration to alleviate discomfort or pain medication will not be withheld from me if I so request them.

      _____ Yes

      _____ TRIAL for the period of _____

      _____ TRIAL to determine effectiveness using reasonable medical judgment.

      _____ No

Why?

_____ 6. I want to have all medications used for the treatment of my illness continued; regardless of my decision, I understand that pain medication will continue to be administered, including narcotic medications.

      _____ Yes

      _____ TRIAL for the period of _____

      _____ TRIAL to determine effectiveness using reasonable medical judgment.

      _____ No

Why?

_____ 7. I want to have nasogastric, gastrostomy, or other enteral feeding tubes introduced and administered for my nutrition.

      _____ Yes

      _____ TRIAL for the period of _____

      _____ TRIAL to determine effectiveness using reasonable medical judgment.

      _____ No

Why?

_____ 8. I want to be placed on a dialysis machine.

      _____ Yes

      _____ TRIAL for the period of _____

      _____ TRIAL to determine effectiveness using reasonable medical judgment.

      _____ No

Why?

_____ 9. I want to have an autopsy done to determine the cause(s) of my death.

      _____ Yes

      _____ No

Why?

_____ 10. I want to be admitted to the Intensive Care Unit.

      _____ Yes

      _____ No

Why?

_____ 11. [For patients in long-term care facilities who experience a life-threatening change in health status]: I want 911 called in case of a medical emergency.

      _____ Yes

      _____ No

Why?

_____ 12. *Other Directives*

I consent to these directives after receiving honest disclosure of their implications, risks, and benefits by my physician, free from constraints and being of sound mind.

Signature	Date
Witness	Date
Witness	Date

_____ 13. Proxy Negation

I request that the following persons *not* be allowed to make decisions on my behalf in the event of my disability or incapacity:

Signature	Date
Witness	Date
Witness	Date

_____ 14. Organ Donation [Specific state version inserted here]

_____ 15. Durable Power of Attorney [Specific state version inserted here]

LEON R. KASS

Is There a Right to Die?

It has been fashionable for some time now and in many aspects of American public life for people to demand what they want or need as a matter of rights. During the past few decades we have heard claims of a right to health or health care, a right to education or employment, a right to privacy (embracing also a right to abort or to enjoy pornography, or to commit suicide or sodomy), a right to clean air, a right to dance naked, a right to be born, and a right not to have been born. Most recently we have been presented with the ultimate new rights claim, a "right to die."

From *Hastings Center Report* 23 (January-February 1993), 34–40, 41–43. © 1993, Leon R. Kass. Reprinted by permission of the author.

This claim has surfaced in the context of changed circumstances and burgeoning concerns regarding the end of life. Thanks in part to the power of medicine to preserve and prolong life, many of us are fated to end our once-flourishing lives in years of debility, dependence, and disgrace. Thanks to the respirator and other powerful technologies that can, all by themselves, hold comatose and other severely debilitated patients on this side of the line between life and death, many who would be dead are alive only because of sustained mechanical intervention. Of the 2.2 million annual deaths in the United States, 80 percent occur in health care facilities; in roughly 1.5 million of these cases, death is preceded by some explicit decision about stopping or not starting medical treatment. Thus, death in America is not only medically managed, but its timing is also increasingly subject to deliberate choice. It is from this background that the claims of a right to die emerge.

I do not think that the language and approach of rights are well suited either to sound personal decision-making or to sensible public policy in this very difficult and troubling matter. In most of the heartrending end-of-life situations, it is hard enough for practical wisdom to try to figure out what is morally right and humanly good, without having to contend with intransigent and absolute demands of a legal or moral right to die. And, on both philosophical and legal grounds, I am inclined to believe that there can be no such thing as a *right* to die—that the notion is groundless and perhaps even logically incoherent. Even its proponents usually put "right to die" in quotation marks, acknowledging that it is at best a misnomer.

Nevertheless, we cannot simply dismiss this claim, for it raises important and interesting practical and philosophical questions. Practically, a right to die is increasingly asserted and gaining popular strength; increasingly, we see it in print without the quotation marks. The former Euthanasia Society of America, shedding the Nazi-tainted and easily criticized "E" word, changed its name to the more politically correct Society for the Right to Die before becoming Choice In Dying. End-of-life cases coming before the courts, nearly always making their arguments in terms of rights, have gained support for some sort of "right to die." The one case to be decided by a conservative Supreme Court, the *Cruzan* case, has advanced the cause. . . .

The voter initiatives to legalize physician-assisted suicide and euthanasia in Washington and California were narrowly defeated, in part because they were badly drafted laws; yet the proponents of such practices seem to be winning the larger social battle over principle. According to several public opinion polls, most Americans now believe that "if life is miserable, one has the right to get out, actively and with help if necessary." Though the burden of philosophical proof for establishing new rights (especially one as bizarre as a "right to die") should always fall on the proponents, the social burden of proof has shifted to those who would oppose the voluntary choice of death through assisted suicide. Thus it has become politically necessary—and at the same time exceedingly

difficult—to make principled arguments about why doctors must not kill, about why euthanasia is not the proper human response to human finitude, and about why there is no right to die, natural or constitutional. This is not a merely academic matter: our society's willingness and ability to protect vulnerable life hang in the balance.

An examination of "right to die" is even more interesting philosophically. It reveals the dangers and the limits of the liberal—that is, rights-based—political philosophy and jurisprudence to which we Americans are wedded. As the ultimate new right, grounded neither in nature nor in reason, it demonstrates the nihilistic implication of a new ("postliberal") doctrine of rights, rooted in the self-creating will. And as liberal society's response to the bittersweet victories of the medical project to conquer death, it reveals in pure form the tragic meaning of the entire modern project, both scientific and political.

The claim of a right to die is made only in Western liberal societies—not surprisingly, for only in Western liberal societies do human beings look first to the rights of individuals. Also, only here do we find the high-tech medicine capable of keeping people from dying when they might wish. Yet the claim of a right to die is also a profoundly strange claim, especially in a liberal society founded on the primacy of the right to life. We Americans hold as a self-evident truth that governments exist to secure inalienable rights, first of all, to self-preservation; now we are being encouraged to use government to secure a putative right of self-destruction. A "right to die" is surely strange and unprecedented, and hardly innocent. Accordingly, we need to consider carefully what it could possibly mean, why it is being asserted, and whether it really exists—that is, whether it can be given a principled grounding or defense.

A *RIGHT* TO DIE

Though the major ambiguity concerns the substance of the right—namely, to die—we begin by reminding ourselves of what it means, in general, to say that someone has a right to something. I depart for now from the original notion of *natural* rights, and indeed abstract altogether from the question of the source of rights. I focus instead on our contemporary usage, for it is only in contemporary usage that this current claim of a right to die can be understood.

A right, whether legal or moral, is not identical to a need or a desire or an interest or a capacity. I may have both a need and a desire for, and also an interest in, the possessions of another, and the capacity or power to take them by force or stealth—yet I can hardly be said to have a right to them. A right, to begin with, is a species of liberty. Thomas Hobbes, the first teacher of rights, held a right to be a *blameless* liberty. Not everything we are free to do, morally or legally, do we have a right to do: I may be at liberty to wear offensive perfumes or to sass my parents or to engage in unnatural sex, but it does not follow that I have a right to do so. Even the decriminalization of a once-forbidden act does not yet establish a legal right, not even if I can give reasons for doing it. Thus, the freedom to take my life—"I have inclination, means, reasons, opportunity, and you cannot stop me, and it is not against the law"—does not suffice to establish the *right* to take my life. A true right would be at least a blameless or permitted liberty, at best a praiseworthy or even rightful liberty, to do or not to do, without anyone else's interference or opposition.

Historically, the likelihood of outside interference and opposition was in fact the necessary condition for the assertion of rights. Rights were and are, to begin with, *political* creatures, the first principles of liberal politics. The rhetoric of claiming rights, which are in principle always absolute and unconditional, performs an important function of defense, but only because the sphere of life in which they are asserted is limited. Rights are asserted to protect, by deeming them blameless or rightful, certain liberties that others are denying or threatening to curtail. Rights are claimed to defend the safety and dignity of the individual against the dominion of tyrant, king, or prelate, and against those high-minded moralizers and zealous meddlers who seek to save man's soul or to preserve his honor at the cost of his life and liberty.

To these more classical, negative rights against interference with our liberties, modern thought has sought to add certain so-called welfare rights—rights that entitle us to certain opportunities or goods to which, it is argued, we have a rightful claim on others, usually government, to provide. The rhetoric of welfare rights extends the power of absolute and unqualified claims beyond the goals of defense against tyranny and beyond the limited sphere of endangered liberties; for these reasons their legitimacy as rights is often questioned. Yet even these ever-expanding lists of rights are not unlimited. I cannot be said to have a right to be loved by those who I hope will love me, or a right to become wise. There are many good things that I may rightfully possess and enjoy, but to which I have no claim if they are lacking. Most generally,

then, having a right means having a *justified* claim against others that they act in a fitting manner: either that they refrain from interfering or that they deliver what is justly owed. It goes without saying that the mere assertion of a claim or demand, or the stipulation of a right, is insufficient to establish it; making a claim and actually having a rightful claim to make are not identical. In considering an alleged right to die, we must be careful to look for a *justifiable* liberty or claim, and not merely a desire, interest, power, or demand.

Rights seem to entail obligations: one person's right, whether to noninterference or to some entitled good or service, necessarily implies another person's obligation. It will be important later to consider what obligations on others might be entailed by enshrining a right to die.

A RIGHT *TO DIE*

Taken literally, a right to die would denote merely a right to the inevitable; the certainty of death for all that lives is the touchstone of fated inevitability. Why claim a right to what is not only unavoidable, but is even, generally speaking, an evil? Is death in danger of losing its inevitability? Are we in danger of bodily immortality? Has death, for us, become a good to be claimed rather than an evil to be shunned or conquered?

Not exactly and not yet, though these questions posed by the literal reading of "right to die" are surely germane. They hint at our growing disenchantment with the biomedical project, which seeks, in principle, to prolong life indefinitely. It is the already available means to sustain life for prolonged periods—not indefinitely, but far longer than is in many cases reasonable or desirable—that has made death so untimely late as to seem less than inevitable, that has made death, when it finally does occur, appear to be a blessing.

For we now have medical "treatments" (that is, interventions) that do not treat (that is, cure or ameliorate) specific diseases, but do nothing more than keep people alive by sustaining vital functions. The most notorious such device is the respirator. Others include simple yet still artificial devices for supplying food and water and the kidney dialysis machine for removing wastes. And, in the future, we shall have the artificial heart. These devices, backed by aggressive institutional policies favoring their use, are capable of keeping people alive, even when comatose, often for decades. The "right to die," in today's discourse, often refers to—and certainly is meant to embrace—a right to refuse such life-sustaining medical treatment.

But the "right to die" usually embraces also something more. The ambiguity of the term blurs over the difference in content and intention between the already well-established common-law right to refuse surgery or other unwanted medical treatments and hospitalization and the newly alleged "right to die." The former permits the refusal of therapy, even a respirator, even if it means accepting an increased risk of death. The latter permits the refusal of therapy, such as renal dialysis or the feeding tube, *so that* death *will* occur. The former seems more concerned with choosing how to live while dying; the latter seems mainly concerned with a choice *for death*. In this sense the claimed "right to die" is not a misnomer.

Still less is it a misnomer when we consider that some people who are claiming it demand not merely the discontinuance of treatment but positive assistance in bringing about their deaths. Here the right to die embraces the (welfare!) right to a lethal injection or an overdose of pills administered by oneself, by one's physician, or by someone else. This "right to die" would better be called a right to assisted suicide or a right to be mercifully killed—in short, a right *to become dead*, by assistance if necessary.

This, of course, looks a lot like a claim to a right to commit suicide, which need not have any connection to the problems of dying or medical technology. Some people in fact argue that the "right to die" through euthanasia or medically assisted suicide grows not from a right to refuse medical treatment but rather from this putative right to commit suicide (suicide is now decriminalized in most states). There does seem to be a world of moral difference between submitting to death (when the time has come) and killing yourself (in or out of season), or between permitting to die and causing death. But the boundary becomes fuzzy with the alleged right to refuse food and water, artificially delivered. Though few proponents of a right to die want the taint of a general defense of suicide (which though decriminalized remains in bad odor), they in fact presuppose its permissibility and go well beyond it. They claim not only a right to attempt suicide but a right to succeed, and this means, in practice, a *right to the deadly assistance of others*. It is thus certainly proper

to understand the "right to die" in its most radical sense, namely, as a right to become or to be made dead, by whatever means.

This way of putting the matter will not sit well with those who see the right to die less as a matter of life and death, more as a matter of autonomy or dignity. For them the right to die means the right to continue, despite disability, to exercise control over one's own destiny. It means, in one formulation, not the right to become dead, but the right to choose the manner, the timing, and the circumstances of one's death, or the right to choose what one regards as the most humane or dignified way to finish out one's life. Here the right to die means either the right to self-command or the right to death with dignity—claims that would oblige others, at a minimum, to stop interfering, but also, quite commonly, to "assist self-command" or to "provide dignity" by participating in bringing one's life to an end, according to plan. In the end, these proper and high-minded demands for autonomy and dignity turn out in most cases to embrace also a right to become dead, with assistance if necessary.

This analysis of current usage shows why one might be properly confused about the meaning of the term "right to die." In public discourse today, it merges all the aforementioned meanings: right to refuse treatment even if, or so that, death may occur; right to be killed or to become dead; right to control one's own dying; right to die with dignity; right to assistance in death. Some of this confusion inheres in the term; some of it is deliberately fostered by proponents of all these "rights," who hope thereby to gain assent to the more extreme claims by merging them with the more modest ones. Partly for this reason, however, we do well to regard the "right to die" at its most radical—and I will do so in this essay—as a right to become dead, by active means and if necessary with the assistance of others. In this way we take seriously and do justice to the novelty and boldness of the claim, a claim that intends to go beyond both the existing common-law right to refuse unwanted medical treatment and the so-called right to commit suicide all by oneself. (The first right is indisputable, the second, while debatable, will not be contested in this essay. What concerns us here is those aspects of the "right to die" that go beyond a right to attempt suicide and a right to refuse treatment.)

Having sought to clarify the meaning of "right to die," we face next the even greater confusion about who it is that allegedly has such a right. Is it only those who are "certifiably" terminally ill and irreversibly dying, with or without medical treatment? Also those who are incurably ill and severely incapacitated, although definitely not dying? Everyone, mentally competent or not? Does a senile person have a "right to die" if he is incapable of claiming it for himself? Do I need to be able to claim *and act* on such a right in order to have it, or can proxies be designated to exercise my right to die on my behalf? If the right to die is essentially an expression of my autonomy, how can anyone else exercise it for me?

Equally puzzling is the question, Against whom or what is a right to die being asserted? Is it a liberty right mainly against those officious meddlers who keep me from dying—against those doctors, nurses, hospitals, right-to-life groups, and district attorneys who interfere either with my ability to die (by machinery and hospitalization) or with my ability to gain help in ending my life (by criminal sanctions against assisting suicide)? If it is a right to become dead, is it not also a welfare right claimed against those who do not yet assist—a right demanding also the provision of the poison that I have permission to take? (Compare the liberty right to seek an abortion with the welfare right to obtain one.) Or is it, at bottom, a demand asserted also *against nature*, which has dealt me a bad hand by keeping me alive, beyond my wishes and beneath my dignity, and alas without terminal illness, too senile or enfeebled to make matters right?

The most radical formulations, whether in the form of "a right to become dead" or "a right to control my destiny" or "a right to dignity," are, I am convinced, the complaint of human pride against what our tyrannical tendencies lead us to experience as "cosmic injustice, directed against me." Here the ill-fated demand a right not to be ill-fated; those who want to die, but cannot, claim a right to die, which becomes, as Harvey Mansfield has put it, a tort claim against nature. It thus becomes the business of the well-fated to correct nature's mistreatment of the ill-fated *by making them dead*. Thus would the same act that was only yesterday declared a crime against humanity become a mandated act, not only of compassionate charity but of compensatory justice!

WHY ASSERT A RIGHT TO DIE?

Before proceeding to the more challenging question of the existence and ground of a "right to die," it would be useful briefly to consider why such a right is being asserted, and by whom. Some of the reasons have already been noted in passing:

- fear of prolongation of dying due to medical intervention; hence, a right to refuse treatment or hospitalization, even if death occurs as a result;
- fear of living too long, without fatal illness to carry one off; hence, a right to assisted suicide;
- fear of the degradations of senility and dependence; hence, a right to death with dignity;
- fear of loss of control; hence, a right to choose the time and manner of one's death.

Equally important for many people is the fear of becoming a burden to others—financial, psychic, social. Few parents, however eager or willing they might be to stay alive, are pleased by the prospect that they might thereby destroy their children's and grandchildren's opportunities for happiness. Indeed, my own greatest weakening on the subject of euthanasia is precisely this: I would confess a strong temptation to remove myself from life to spare my children the anguish of years of attending my demented self and the horrible likelihood that they will come, hatefully to themselves, to resent my continued existence. Such reasons in favor of death might even lead me to think I had a *duty* to die—they do not, however, establish for me any right to become dead.[1]

But the advocates of a "right to die" are not always so generous. On the contrary, much dishonesty and mischief are afoot. Many people have seen the advantage of using the language of individual rights, implying voluntary action, to shift the national attitudes regarding life and death, to prepare the way for the practice of terminating "useless" lives.[2]

Many who argue for a right to die mean for people not merely to have it but to exercise it with dispatch, so as to decrease the mounting socioeconomic costs of caring for the irreversibly ill and dying. In fact, most of the people now agitating for a "right to die" are themselves neither ill nor dying. Children looking at parents who are not dying fast enough, hospital administrators and health economists concerned about cost-cutting and waste, doctors disgusted with caring for incurables, people with eugenic or aesthetic interests who are repelled by the prospect of a society in which the young and vigorous expend enormous energy to keep alive the virtually dead—all these want to change our hard-won ethic in favor of life.

But they are either too ashamed or too shrewd to state their true intentions. Much better to trumpet a right to die, and encourage people to exercise it. These advocates understand all too well that the present American climate requires one to talk of rights if one wishes to have one's way in such moral matters. Consider the analogous use of arguments for abortion rights by organizations which hope thereby to get women — especially the poor, the unmarried, and the nonwhite — to exercise their "right to choose," to do their supposed duty toward limiting population growth and the size of the underclass.

This is not to say that all reasons for promoting a "right to die" are suspect. Nor do I mean to suggest that it would never be right or good for someone to elect to die. But it might be dangerous folly to circumvent the grave need for prudence in these matters by substituting the confused yet absolutized principle of a "right to die," especially given the mixed motives and dangerous purposes of some of its proponents.

Truth to tell, public discourse about moral matters in the United States is much impoverished by our eagerness to transform questions of the right and the good into questions about individual rights. Partly, this is a legacy of modern liberalism, the political philosophy on which the genius of the American republic mainly rests. But it is augmented by American self-assertion and individualism, increasingly so in an age when family and other mediating institutions are in decline and the naked individual is left face to face with the bureaucratic state.

But the language of rights gained a tremendous boost from the moral absolutism of the 1960s, with the discovery that the nonnegotiable and absolutized character of all rights claims provides the most durable battering ram against the status quo. Never mind that it fuels resentments and breeds hatreds, that it ignores the consequences to society, or that it short-circuits a political process that is more amenable to working out a balanced view of the common good. Never mind all that: go to court and demand your rights. And the courts have been all too willing to oblige, finding or inventing new rights in the process.

These sociocultural changes, having nothing to do with death and dying, surely are part of the reason we are now confronted with vociferous claims of a right to die. These changes are also part of the reason why, despite its notorious difficulties, a right to die is the leading moral concept advanced to address these most complicated and delicate human matters at the end of life. Yet the reasons for the assertion, even if suspect, do not settle the question of truth, to which, at long last, we finally turn. Let us examine whether philosophically . . . we can truly speak of a right to die.

IS THERE A RIGHT TO DIE?

Philosophically speaking, it makes sense to take our bearings from those great thinkers of modernity who are the originators and most thoughtful exponents of our rights-based thinking. They above all are likely to have understood the purpose, character, grounds, and limits for the assertion of rights. If a newly asserted right, such as the right to die, cannot be established on the natural or rational ground for rights offered by these thinkers, the burden of proof must fall on the proponents of novel rights, to provide a new yet equally solid ground in support of their novel claims.

If we start at the beginning, with the great philosophical teachers of natural rights, the very notion of a right to die would be nonsensical. As we learn from Hobbes and from John Locke, all the rights of man, given by nature, presuppose our self-interested attachment to our own lives. All natural rights trace home to the primary right to life, or better, the right to self-preservation — itself rooted in the powerful, self-loving impulses and passions that seek our own continuance, and asserted first against deadly, oppressive policies or against those who might insist that morality requires me to turn the other cheek when my life is threatened. Mansfield summarizes the classical position elegantly:

Rights are given to men by nature, but they are needed because men are also subject to nature's improvidence. Since life is in danger, men's equal rights would be to life, to the liberty that protects life, and to the pursuit of the happiness with which life, or a tenuous life, is occupied.

In practice, the pursuit of happiness will be the pursuit of property, for even though property is less valuable than life or liberty, it serves as guard for them. Quite apart from the pleasures of being rich, having secure property shows that one has liberty secure from invasion either by the government or by others; and secure liberty is the best sign of a secure life.[3]

Because death, my extinction, is the evil whose avoidance is the condition of the possibility of my having any and all of my goods, my right to secure my life against death — that is, my rightful liberty to self-preservative conduct — is the bedrock of all other rights and of all politically relevant morality. Even

Hans Jonas, writing to defend "the right to die," acknowledges that it stands alone, and concedes that "every other right ever argued, claimed, granted, or denied can be viewed as an extension of this primary right [to life], since every particular right concerns the exercise of some faculty of life, the access to some necessity of life, the satisfaction of some aspiration of life."[4] It is obvious that one cannot found on this rock any right to die or right to become dead. Life loves to live, and it needs all the help it can get.

This is not to say that these early modern thinkers were unaware that men might tire of life or might come to find existence burdensome. But the decline in the will to live did not for them drive out or nullify the right to life, much less lead to a trumping new right, a right to die. For the right to life is a matter of nature, not will. Locke addresses and rejects a natural right to suicide, in his discussion of the state of nature:

But though this be a state of liberty, yet it is not a state of license; though man in that state has an uncontrollable liberty to dispose of his person or possessions, yet he has not liberty to destroy himself, or so much as any creature in his possession, but where some nobler use than its bare preservation calls for it. The state of nature has a law of nature to govern it, which obliges everyone; and reason, which is that law, teaches all mankind who will but consult it, that, being all equal and independent, no one ought to harm another in his life, health, liberty, or possessions.[5]

Admittedly, the argument here turns explicitly theological — we are said to be our wise Maker's property. But the argument against a man's willful "quitting of his station" seems, for Locke, to be a corollary of the natural inclination and right of self-preservation.

Some try to argue, wrongly in my view, that Locke's teaching on property rests on a principle of self-ownership, which can then be used to justify self-destruction: since I own my body and my life, I may do with them as I please. As this argument has much currency, it is worth examining in greater detail. Locke does indeed say something that seems at first glance to suggest self-ownership:

Though the earth and all inferior creatures be common to all men, yet every man has a property in his own person; this nobody has a right to but himself. The labor of his body and the work of his hands we may say are properly his.[6]

But the context defines and constricts the claim. Unlike the property rights in the fruits of his labor, the property a man has in his own person is inalienable: a man cannot transfer title to himself by selling himself into slavery. The "property in his own person" is less a metaphysical statement declaring self-ownership, more a political statement denying ownership by another. This right removes each and every human being from the commons available to all human beings for appropriation and use. My body and my life are my property *only in the limited sense* that they are *not yours*. They are different from my alienable property — my house, my car, my shoes. My body and my life, while mine to use, are not mine to dispose of. In the deepest sense, my body is nobody's body, not even mine.[7]

Even if one continues, against reason, to hold to strict self-ownership and self-disposability, there is a further argument, one that is decisive. Self-ownership might enable one at most to justify *attempting* suicide; it cannot justify a right to succeed or, more important, a right to the assistance of others. The designated potential assistant-in-death has neither a natural duty nor a natural right to become an actual assistant-in-death, and the liberal state, instituted above all to protect life, can never countenance such a right to kill, even on request. A right to become dead or to be made dead cannot be sustained on classical liberal grounds.

Later thinkers in the liberal tradition, including those who prized freedom above preservation, also make no room for a "right to die." Jean-Jacques Rousseau's complaints about the ills of civil society centered especially and most powerfully on the threats to life and limb from a social order whose main purpose should have been to protect them.[8] And Immanuel Kant, for whom rights are founded not in nature but in reason, holds that the self-willed act of self-destruction is simply self-contradictory.

It seems absurd that a man can injure himself (*volenti non fit injuria* [Injury cannot happen to one who is willing]). The Stoic therefore considered it a prerogative of his personality as a wise man to walk out of his life with an undisturbed mind whenever he liked (as out of a smoke-filled room), not because he was afflicted by actual or anticipated ills, but simply because he could make use of nothing more in this life. And yet this very courage, this strength of mind — of not fearing death and of knowing of something which man can prize more highly than his life — ought to have been an ever so much greater motive for him not to destroy himself, a being having such authoritative superiority over the strongest sensible incentives; consequently, it ought to have been a motive for him not to deprive himself of life.

Man cannot deprive himself of his personhood so long as one speaks of duties, thus so long as he lives. That man ought to have the authorization to withdraw himself from all obligation, i.e., to be free to act as if no authorization at all were required for this withdrawal, involves a contradiction. To destroy the subject of morality in his own person is tantamount to obliterating from the world, as far as he can, the very existence of morality itself; but morality is, nevertheless, an end in itself. Accordingly, to dispose of oneself as a mere means to some end of one's own liking is to degrade the humanity in one's person (*homo noumenon*), which, after all, was entrusted to man (*homo phænomenon*) to preserve.[9]

It is a heavy irony that it should be autonomy, the moral notion that the world owes mainly to Kant, that is now invoked as the justifying ground of a right to die. For Kant, autonomy, which literally means self-legislation, requires acting in accordance with one's true self—that is, with one's rational will determined by a universalizable, that is, rational, maxim. Being autonomous means not being a slave to instinct, impulse, or whim, but rather doing as one ought, as a rational being. But autonomy has now come to mean "doing as you please," compatible no less with self-indulgence than with self-control. Herewith one sees clearly the triumph of the Nietzschean self, who finds reason just as enslaving as blind instinct and who finds his true "self" rather in unconditioned acts of pure creative will.

Yet even in its willful modern meaning, "autonomy" cannot ground a right to die. First, one cannot establish on this basis a right to have *someone else's* assistance in committing suicide—a right, by the way, that would impose an obligation on someone else and thereby restrict *his* autonomy. Second, even if my choice for death were "reasonable" and my chosen assistant freely willing, my autonomy cannot ground *his right* to kill me, and, hence, it cannot ground my right to become dead. Third, a liberty right to an assisted death (that is, a right against interference) can at most approve assisted suicide or euthanasia for the mentally competent and alert—a restriction that would prohibit effecting the deaths of the mentally incompetent or comatose patients who have not left explicit instructions regarding their treatment. It is, by the way, a long philosophical question whether all such instructions must be obeyed, for the person who gave them long ago may no longer be "the same person" when they become relevant. Can my fifty-three-year-old self

truly prescribe today the best interests for my seventy-five-year-old and senile self?

In contrast to arguments presented in recent court cases, it is self-contradictory to assert that a proxy not chosen by the patient can exercise the patient's rights of autonomy. Can a citizen have a right to vote that would be irrevocably exercised "on his behalf," and in the name of his autonomy, by the government?[10] Finally, if autonomy and dignity lie in the free exercise of will and choice, it is at least paradoxical to say that our autonomy licenses an act that puts our autonomy permanently out of business.

It is precisely this paradox that appeals to the Nietzschean creative self, the bearer of so many of this century's "new rights." As Mansfield brilliantly shows, the creative ones are not bound by normality or good sense:

Creative beings are open-ended. They are open-ended in fact and not merely in their formal potentialities. Such beings do not have interests; for who can say what is in the interest of a being that is becoming something unknown? Thus the society of new rights is characterized by a loss of predictability and normality: no one knows what to expect, even from his closest companions.[11]

The most authentic self-creative self revels in the unpredictable, the extreme, the perverse. He does not even flinch before self-contradiction; indeed, he can display the triumph of his will most especially in self-negation. And though it may revolt us, who are we to deny him this form of self-expression? Supremely tolerant of the rights of others to their own eccentricities, we avert our glance and turn the other moral cheek. Here at last is the only possible philosophical ground for a right to die: arbitrary will, backed by moral relativism. Which is to say, no ground at all.

• • •

THE TRAGIC MEANING OF "RIGHT TO DIE"

The claim of a "right to die," asserted especially against physicians bent on prolonging life, clearly exposes certain deep difficulties in the foundations of modern society. Modern liberal, technological society rests especially upon two philosophical pillars raised first in the seventeenth century, at the beginning of the modern era: the preeminence of the human individual, embodied in the doctrine of natural rights as espoused first by Hobbes and Locke; and the idea of mastery of nature, attained through a radically new science of nature as proposed by Francis Bacon and René Descartes.

Both ideas were responses to the perceived partial inhospitality of nature to human need. Both encouraged man's opposition to nature, the first through the flight from the state of nature into civil society for the purpose of safeguarding the precarious rights to life and liberty; the second through the subduing of nature for the purpose of making life longer, healthier, and more commodious. One might even say that it is especially an opposition to death that grounds these twin responses. Politically, the fear of violent death at the hands of warring men requires law and legitimate authority to secure natural rights, especially life. Technologically, the fear of death as such at the hands of unfriendly nature inspires a bolder approach, namely, a scientific medicine to wage war against disease and even against death itself, ultimately with a promise of bodily immortality.

Drunk on its political and scientific successes, modern thought and practice have abandoned the modest and moderate beginnings of political modernity. In civil society the natural rights of self-preservation, secured through active but moderate self-assertion, have given way to the non-natural rights of self-creation and self-expression; the new rights have no connection to nature or to reason, but appear as the rights of the untrammeled will. The "self" that here asserts itself is not a natural self, with the predictable interests given it by a universal human nature with its bodily needs, but a uniquely individuated and self-made self. Its authentic selfhood is demonstrated by its ability to say no to the needs of the body, the rules of society, and the dictates of reason. For such a self, self-negation through suicide and the right to die can be the ultimate form of self-assertion.

In medical science, the unlimited battle against death has found nature unwilling to roll over and play dead. The successes of medicine so far are partial at best and the victory incomplete, to say the least. The welcome triumphs against disease have been purchased at the price of the medicalized dehumanization of the end of life: to put it starkly, once we lick cancer and stroke, we can all live long enough to get Alzheimer's disease. And if the insurance holds out, we can die in the intensive care unit, suitably intubated. Fear of the very medical power we engaged to do battle against death now leads us to demand that it give us poison.

Finally, both the triumph of individualism and our reliance on technology (not only in medicine) and on government to satisfy our new wants-demanded-as-rights have weakened our more natural human associations—especially the family, on which we all need to rely when our pretense to autonomy and mastery is eventually exposed by unavoidable decline. Old age and death have been taken out of the bosom of family life and turned over to state-supported nursing homes and hospitals. Not the clergyman but the doctor (in truth, the nurse) presides over the end of life, in sterile surroundings that make no concessions to our finitude. Both the autonomous will and the will's partner in pride, the death-denying doctor, ignore the unavoidable limits on will and technique that nature insists on. Failure to recognize these limits now threatens the entire venture, for rebellion against the project through a "right to die" will only radicalize its difficulties. Vulnerable life will no longer be protected by the state, medicine will become a death-dealing profession, and isolated individuals will be technically dispatched to avoid the troubles of finding human ways to keep company with them in their time of ultimate need.

• • •

Nothing I have said should be taken to mean that I believe life should be extended under all circumstances and at all costs. Far from it. I continue, with fear and trembling, to defend the practice of allowing to die while opposing the practice of deliberately killing—despite the blurring of this morally bright line implicit in the artificial food and water cases, and despite the slide toward the retailing of death that continues on the sled of a right to refuse treatment. I welcome efforts to give patients as much choice as possible in how they are to live out the end of their lives. I continue to applaud those courageous patients and family members and those conscientious physicians who try prudently to discern, in each case, just what form of treatment or nontreatment is truly good for the patient, even if it embraces an increased likelihood of death. But I continue to insist that we cannot serve the patient's good by deliberately eliminating the patient. And if we have no right to do this to another, we have no right to have others do this to ourselves. There is, when all is said and done, no defensible right to die.

A CODA: ABOUT RIGHTS

The rhetoric of rights still performs today the noble, time-honored function of protecting individual life and liberty, a function now perhaps even more necessary than the originators of such rhetoric could have imagined, given the tyrannical possibilities of the modern bureaucratic and technologically competent state. But with the claim of a "right to die," as with so many of the novel rights being asserted in recent years, we face an extension of this rhetoric into areas where it no longer relates to that protective function, and beyond the limited area of life in which rights claims are clearly appropriate and indeed crucial. As a result, we face a number of serious and potentially dangerous distortions in our thought and in our practice. We distort our understanding of rights and weaken their respectability in their proper sphere by allowing them to be invented—without ground in nature or in reason—in response to moral questions that lie outside the limited domain of rights. We distort our understanding of moral deliberation and the moral life by reducing all complicated questions of right and good to questions of individual rights. We subvert the primacy and necessity of prudence by pretending that the assertion of rights will produce the best—and most moral—results. In trying to batter our way through the human condition with the bludgeon of personal rights, we allow ourselves to be deceived about the most fundamental matters: about death and dying, about our unavoidable finitude, and about the sustaining interdependencies of our lives.

Let us, by all means, continue to deliberate about whether and when and why it might make sense for someone to give up on his life, or even actively to choose death. But let us call a halt to all this dangerous thoughtlessness about rights. Let us refuse to talk any longer about a "right to die."

NOTES

1. For my "generosity" to succeed, I would, of course, have to commit suicide without assistance and without anyone's discovering it—i.e., well before I were demented. I would not want my children to believe that I suspected them of being incapable of loving me through my inevitable decline. There is another still more powerful reason for resisting this temptation: is it not unreasonably paternalistic of me to try to order the world so as to free my children from the usual intergenerational experiences, ties, obligations, and burdens? What principle of family life am I enacting and endorsing with my "altruistic suicide"?

2. Here is a recent example from a professor of sociology who objected to my condemnation of Derek Humphry's *Final Exit:*

Is Mr. Kass absolutely opposed to suicide? Would he have dissuaded Hitler? Would he disapprove of suicide by Pol Pot? . . . If we would welcome suicide by certain figures on limited occasions, should we prolong the lives of people who lived useless, degrading or dehumanized lives; who inflicted these indignities upon others; or who led vital lives but were reduced to uselessness and degradation by incurable disease? (*Commentary,* May 1992, p. 12).

3. Harvey C. Mansfield, Jr., "The Old Rights and the New: Responsibility vs. Self-Expression," in *Old Rights and New,* ed. Robert A. Licht (Washington: American Enterprise Institute, 1993), in press.

4. Hans Jonas, "The Right to Die," *Hastings Center Report* 8, no. 4 (1978): 31–36, at 31.

5. John Locke, *Second Treatise on Civil Government,* ch. 2, "Of the State of Nature," para. 6.

6. Locke, *Second Treatise,* ch. 5, "Of Property," para. 27. Emphasis added.

7. Later, in discussing the extent of legislative power, Locke denies to the legislative, though it be the supreme power in every commonwealth, arbitrary power over the individual and, in particular, power to destroy his life. "For nobody can transfer to another more power than he has in himself; and nobody has an absolute arbitrary power over himself or over any other to destroy his own life, or take away the life or property of another." *Second Treatise,* ch. 9, "Of the Extent of the Legislative Power," para. 135. Because the state's power derives from the people's power, the person's lack of arbitrary power over himself is the ground for restricting the state's power to kill him.

8. See, for example, Rousseau, *Discourse on the Origin and Foundations of Inequality among Men,* note 9, especially paragraphs four and five.

9. Immanuel Kant, *The Metaphysical Principles of Virtue,* trans. James Ellington (Indianapolis: Bobbs-Merrill, 1964), pp. 83–84. My purpose in citing Kant here is not to defend Kantian morality—and I am not myself a Kantian—but simply to show that the thinker who thought most deeply about rights in relation to *reason* and *autonomy* would have found the idea of a "right to die" utterly indefensible on these grounds.

10. The attempt to ground a right to die in the so-called right to privacy fails for the same reasons. A right to make independent judgments regarding one's body in one's private sphere, free of governmental inference, cannot be the basis of the right of someone else, appointed by or protected by government, to put an end to one's bodily life.

11. Mansfield, "The Old Rights and the New." This permanent instability of "the self" defeats the main benefit of a rights-based politics, which knows how to respect individual rights precisely because they are understood to be rooted in a common human nature, with reliable common interests, both natural and rational. The self-determining self, because it is variable, also turns out to be an embarrassment for attempts to respect prior acts of self-determination, as in the case of living wills. For if the "self" is truly constantly being re-created, there is no reason to honor today "its" prescriptions of yesterday, for the two selves are not the same.

Decisions on Behalf of the Formerly Competent

THE HASTINGS CENTER

Guidelines on the Termination of Life-Sustaining Treatment and the Care of the Dying

[1] MAKING THE DECISION

(a) The patient with decisionmaking capacity. If the patient has decisionmaking capacity, then the patient is the ultimate judge of the benefits and burdens of a life-sustaining treatment, and whether the burdens outweigh the benefits. Individuals differ in what they see as a burden and a benefit, and in how they weigh the two against each other. To most people burdens include pain or suffering, hardships imposed on their loved ones, and financial cost. Most regard as benefits improved functioning, the relief of pain or suffering, the opportunity to live longer, and the chance to engage in satisfying activities.

Patients will usually find that life-sustaining treatment offers more benefits than burdens. In those cases, the treatment should be used. Some patients—particularly if they are terminally ill or suffering from an illness or disabling condition that is severe and irreversible—may decide that the burdens of a particular treatment outweigh the benefits, and choose to forgo that treatment. That choice should be honored. The responsible health care professional, however, should first discuss with the patient why he or she prefers to forgo treatment. Exploring the decision together is an important part of the process. If the patient is experiencing pain or suffering that can be ameliorated, the professional should discuss the possi-

bility of amelioration to then see whether the patient still prefers to forgo treatment. The professional should make sure that the patient has not decided to forgo life-sustaining treatment in order to obtain relief from pain or suffering that can be alleviated without forgoing life-sustaining treatment. . . .

(b) The patient whose capacity is fluctuating or uncertain. Some patients neither clearly possess nor clearly lack decisionmaking capacity; their capacity is fluctuating or uncertain. If the patient, responsible health care professional, and likely surrogate agree on the treatment decision, then there is no need to clarify the patient's capacity. When they do not agree or when no likely surrogate is on hand, and it is possible to adjust conditions or to delay the decision until the patient has decisionmaking capacity, that is the optimal course; the Guidelines above for patients with capacity then apply. If that is not possible, the Guidelines below for patients without decisionmaking capacity should apply instead.

(c) The patient who lacks decisionmaking capacity. When a patient lacks the capacity to make the treatment decision, so that a surrogate decisionmaker has decisionmaking authority instead, the surrogate should seek to choose as the patient would if he or she were able. Because the strength of the evidence of the patient's preferences will vary, the surrogate should apply one of the three different standards listed below. Whenever a surrogate can come to no clear view as to whether to forgo treatment, treatment should be administered; using the treatment on a trial basis with reevaluation after a set interval should be considered. (See Section [2] (a), [below].)

From *Guidelines on the Termination of Life-Sustaining Treatment and the Care of the Dying* (Briarcliff Manor, NY: The Hastings Center, 1987), pp. 26–29, 30–31. © 1988, Indiana University Press. Reprinted by permission of Indiana University Press.

1. *Follow the patient's explicit directives.** Where a patient who had decisionmaking capacity at the time, has left written directions in an advance directive . . . or another form, or clear oral directions, and these directions seem intended to cover the situation presented, the surrogate should follow the directions.
2. *Or apply the patient's preferences and values.** If the patient has left no directions about the treatment in question, the surrogate should apply what is known about the patient's preferences and values, trying to choose as the patient would have wanted.
3. *Or choose as a reasonable person in the patient's circumstances would.*** If there is not enough known about the patient's directions, preferences, and values to make an individualized decision, the surrogate should choose so as to promote the patient's interests as they would probably be conceived by a reasonable person in the patient's circumstances, selecting from within the range of choices that reasonable people would make. In order to flesh out this standard, we suggest below the major considerations involved in applying it to some important categories of patients:

(i) *The patient who is terminally ill.* In applying the "reasonable person" standard to the terminally ill patient without decisionmaking capacity, the major considerations are usually whether forgoing treatment will allow the patient to avoid the burden of prolonged dying with pain or suffering, and whether the patient has the potential benefit of achieving some satisfaction if he or she survives longer.

(ii) *The patient who has an illness or disabling condition that is severe and irreversible.* In applying the "reasonable person" standard to the patient with an illness or disabling condition that is severe and irreversible and who lacks decisionmaking capacity, the major consideration is the following: Would a reasonable person in the patient's circumstance probably prefer the termination of treatment because the patient's life is largely devoid of

opportunities to achieve satisfaction, or full of pain or suffering with no corresponding benefits?

(iii) *The patient with irreversible loss of consciousness.* For the patient who has suffered an irreversible loss of consciousness, the major considerations in applying the "reasonable person" standard are somewhat different. Patients who are permanently unconscious are unaware of benefits or burdens. The only possible benefit to them of life-sustaining treatment is the possibility that the diagnosis of irreversible unconsciousness is wrong and they will regain consciousness. Accordingly, the major considerations are whether a reasonable person in the patient's circumstance would find that this benefit, as well as the benefits to the patient's family and concerned friends (such as satisfaction in caring for the patient and the meaningfulness of the patient's continued survival) are outweighed by the burdens on those loved ones (such as financial cost or emotional suffering).

(The above list in no way suggests that treatment should be forgone just because a person falls into one of these categories; nor does it mean that treatment may not be terminated for other patients.) . . .

[2] IMPLEMENTING THE DECISION

(a) Time-limited trials. When possible, the responsible health care professional should present to the patient or surrogate the option of starting or continuing a particular life-sustaining treatment on a trial basis, with reevaluation after a specific time. Having a trial period may make it easier to evaluate a life-sustaining treatment if the effectiveness, benefits, or burdens are difficult to assess in advance. It is ethically preferable to try a treatment and to withdraw it if it fails, than not to try it at all. A trial period may reduce the patient's fears of losing control of a treatment and being "stuck on machines." It may also reduce emotional distress if a decision is later made to forgo the treatment. Time-limited trials will be impossible, however, in the case of some treatments. . . .

(b) Supportive care. When a life-sustaining treatment is forgone, and whenever a patient is dying, the treatment team has an obligation to provide supportive care, to make the patient as comfortable as possible, and to assure the patient that adequate symptom con-

*These are sometimes called a "substituted judgment" standard.
**This is sometimes called a "best interests" standard.

trol and support will be provided. Health care institutions and financers also have a responsibility for seeing that this occurs. Such care may include a wide variety of measures to provide symptomatic relief, sedation and pain control, skin care, and turning and positioning. If relieving the patient's pain or suffering requires sedation to the point of unconsciousness, it is ethically acceptable to do so with the patient's or surrogate's consent. . . .

(c) Maximal therapeutic care. A decision to forgo one kind of life-sustaining treatment does not imply that the patient is forgoing any other forms of treatment. Forgoing one life-sustaining treatment is compatible with maximal therapeutic care of other types. . . .

(d) Stress and communication. Health care professionals may sometimes find it stressful to care for dying or seriously ill patients, particularly when a life-sustaining treatment is forgone. There is a need for continual communication among the treatment team, patient, surrogate if any, and others who are involved. Any or all of these persons may need support; assistance from relevant professionals (including clergy) should be sought as required.

. . . [N]urses and physicians have independent ethical duties to patients, but decisions to forgo life-sus-

taining treatment may place special burdens on nurses. Nursing care (such as bathing, feeding, and toileting) is highly personal and involves intimate contact with the patient. Nurses may experience difficulty in implementing decisions to forgo treatment when they have formed a close attachment to the patient. Yet nurses usually play an important role in implementation, because forgoing life-sustaining treatment often demands particularly attentive nursing care. Nurses therefore need ways to discuss the consequences that such decisions have for their practice. Health care institutions should ensure that such ways exist. . . .

[3] CHANGING THE DECISION

A patient with decisionmaking capacity may change his or her decision concerning a life-sustaining treatment at any time. The surrogate for a patient without decisionmaking capacity may at any time change the decision concerning a life-sustaining treatment, provided that the change is in keeping with the Guidelines in Section [1] (c) above. . . . The change, and the reasons for it, should be documented in the patient's medical records.

UNITED STATES SUPREME COURT

Cruzan v. Director, Missouri Department of Health

ARGUED DECEMBER 6, 1989.
DECIDED JUNE 25, 1990.

OPINION OF THE COURT
Chief Justice **Rehnquist** delivered the opinion of the Court.

From *United States [Supreme Court] Reports* 497 (1990), 261–357 (excerpts). Some footnotes and references omitted.

Petitioner Nancy Beth Cruzan was rendered incompetent as a result of severe injuries sustained during an automobile accident. Co-petitioners Lester and Joyce Cruzan, Nancy's parents and co-guardians, sought a court order directing the withdrawal of their daughter's artificial feeding and hydration equipment after it became apparent that she had virtually no chance of recovering her cognitive faculties. The Supreme Court of Missouri held that because there was no clear and convincing evidence of Nancy's desire to have life-sustaining treatment withdrawn under such circumstances, her parents lacked authority to effectuate such a request. We granted certiorari, 106 L Ed 2d 587 (1989), and now affirm.

On the night of January 11, 1983, Nancy Cruzan lost control of her car as she traveled down Elm Road in Jasper County, Missouri. The vehicle overturned, and Cruzan was discovered lying face down in a ditch without detectable respiratory or cardiac function. Paramedics were able to restore her breathing and heartbeat at the accident site, and she was transported to a hospital in an unconscious state. An attending neurosurgeon diagnosed her as having sustained probable cerebral contusions compounded by significant anoxia (lack of oxygen). The Missouri trial court in this case found that permanent brain damage generally results after 6 minutes in an anoxic state; it was estimated that Cruzan was deprived of oxygen from 12 to 14 minutes. She remained in a coma for approximately three weeks and then progressed to an unconscious state in which she was able to orally ingest some nutrition. In order to ease feeding and further the recovery, surgeons implanted a gastrostomy feeding and hydration tube in Cruzan with the consent of her then husband. Subsequent rehabilitative efforts proved unavailing. She now lies in a Missouri state hospital in what is commonly referred to as a persistent vegetative state: generally, a condition in which a person exhibits motor reflexes but evinces no indications of significant cognitive function.[1] The State of Missouri is bearing the cost of her care.

After it had become apparent that Nancy Cruzan had virtually no chance of regaining her mental facilities her parents asked hospital employees to terminate the artificial nutrition and hydration procedures. All agree that such a removal would cause her death. The employees refused to honor the request without court approval. The parents then sought and received authorization from the state trial court for termination. The court found that a person in Nancy's condition had a fundamental right under the State and Federal Constitutions to refuse or direct the withdrawal of "death prolonging procedures." App to Pet for Cert A99. The court also found that Nancy's "expressed thoughts at age twenty-five in somewhat serious conversation with a housemate friend that if sick or injured she would not wish to continue her life unless she could live at least halfway normally suggest that given her present condition she would not wish to continue with her nutrition and hydration." Id., at A97-A98.

The Supreme Court of Missouri reversed by a divided vote. The court recognized a right to refuse treatment embodied in the common-law doctrine of informed consent, but expressed skepticism about the application of that doctrine in the circumstances of this case. Cruzan v Harmon, 760 SW2d 408, 416-417 (Mo 1988) (en banc). The court also declined to read a broad right of privacy into the State Constitution which would "support the right of a person to refuse medical treatment in every circumstance," and expressed doubt as to whether such a right existed under the United States Constitution. Id., at 417-418. It then decided that the Missouri Living Will statute, Mo Rev Stat § 459.010 et seq. (1986), embodied a state policy strongly favoring the preservation of life. 760 SW2d, at 419-420. The court found that Cruzan's statements to her roommate regarding her desire to live or die under certain conditions were "unreliable for the purpose of determining her intent," id., at 424, "and thus insufficient to support the co-guardians claim to exercise substituted judgment on Nancy's behalf." Id., at 426. It rejected the argument that Cruzan's parents were entitled to order the termination of her medical treatment, concluding that "no person can assume that choice for an incompetent in the absence of the formalities required under Missouri's Living Will statutes or the clear and convincing, inherently reliable evidence absent here." Id., at 425. The court also expressed its view that "[b]road policy questions bearing on life and death are more properly addressed by representative assemblies" than judicial bodies. Id., at 426.

We granted certiorari to consider the question of whether Cruzan has a right under the United States Constitution which would require the hospital to withdraw life-sustaining treatment from her under these circumstances.

At common law, even the touching of one person by another without consent and without legal justification was a battery. See W. Keeton, D. Dobbs, R. Keeton, & D. Owen, Prosser and Keeton on Law of Torts § 9, pp. 39–42 (5th ed 1984). Before the turn of the century, this Court observed that "[n]o right is held more sacred, or is more carefully guarded, by the common law, than the right of every individual to the possession and control of his own person, free from all restraint or interference of others, unless by clear and unquestionable authority of law." Union Pacific R. Co. v Botsford, 141 US 250, 251 (1891). This notion of bodily integrity has been embodied in the requirement that informed consent is generally required for medical treatment. Justice Cardozo, while on the Court of Appeals of New York, aptly described this doctrine: "Every human being of adult years and sound mind has a right to determine what shall be done with his own body; and a surgeon who performs an operation without his patient's consent commits an assault, for which he is liable in damages." Schloendorff v Society of New York Hospital, 211 NY 125, 129-30, 105 NE 92, 93 (1914). The informed consent doctrine has become firmly entrenched in American tort law. See Dobbs, Keeton, & Owen, supra, § 32, pp 189–192; F. Rozovsky, Consent to Treatment, A Practical Guide 1–98 (2d ed 1990).

The logical corollary of the doctrine of informed consent is that the patient generally possesses the right not to consent, that is, to refuse treatment. Until about 15 years ago and the seminal decision in In re Quinlan, 70 NJ 10, 355 A2d 647, cert denied sub nom., Garger v New Jersey, 429 US 922 (1976), the number of right-to-refuse-treatment decisions were relatively few.[2] Most of the earlier cases involved patients who refused medical treatment forbidden by their religious beliefs, thus implicating First Amendment rights as well as common law rights of self-determination.[3] More recently, however, with the advance of medical technology capable of sustaining life well past the point where natural forces would have brought certain death in earlier times, cases involving the right to refuse life-sustaining treatment have burgeoned. See 760 SW2d, at 412, n 4 (collecting 54 reported decisions from 1976–1988).

In the Quinlan case, young Karen Quinlan suffered severe brain damage as the result of anoxia, and entered a persistent vegetative state. Karen's father sought judicial approval to disconnect his daughter's respirator. The New Jersey Supreme Court granted the relief, holding that Karen had a right of privacy grounded in the Federal Constitution to terminate treatment. In re Quinlan, 70 NJ, at 38–42, 355 A2d at 662–664. Recognizing that this right was not absolute, however, the court balanced it against asserted state interests. Noting that the State's interest "weakens and the individual's right to privacy grows as the degree of bodily invasion increases and the prognosis dims," the court concluded that the state interests had to give way in that case. Id., at 41, 355 A2d, at 664. The court also concluded that the "only practical way" to prevent the loss of Karen's privacy right due to her incompetence was to allow her guardian and family to decide "whether she would exercise it in these circumstances." Ibid.

After Quinlan, however, most courts have based a right to refuse treatment either solely on the common law right to informed consent or on both the common law right and a constitutional privacy right. See L. Tribe, American Constitutional Law § 15–11, p. 1365 (2d ed 1988). In Superintendent of Belchertown State School v Saikewicz, 373 Mass 728, 370 NE2d 417 (1977), the Supreme Judicial Court of Massachusetts relied on both the right of privacy and the right of informed consent to permit the withholding of chemotherapy from a profoundly-retarded 67-year-old man suffering from leukemia. Id., at 737–738, 370 NE2d, at 424. Reasoning that an incompetent person retains the same rights as a competent individual "because the value of human dignity extends to both," the court adopted a "substituted judgment" standard whereby courts were to determine what an incompetent individual's decision would have been under the circumstances. Id., at 745, 752–753, 757–758, 370 NE2d, at 427, 431, 434. Distilling certain state interests from prior case law—the preservation of life, the protection of the interests of innocent third parties, the prevention of suicide, and the maintenance of the ethical integrity of the medical profession—the court recognized the first interest as paramount and noted it was greatest when an affliction was curable, "as opposed to the State interest where, as here, the issue is not whether, but when, for how long, and at what cost to the individual [a] life may be briefly extended." Id., at 742, 370 NE2d, at 426.

In In re Storar 52 NY2d 363, 420 NE2d 64, cert denied, 454 US 858 (1981), the New York Court of Appeals declined to base a right to refuse treatment on a constitutional privacy right. Instead, it found such a right "adequately supported" by the informed consent doctrine. Id., at 376–377, 420 NE2d, at 70. In In re Eichner (decided with In re Storar, supra) an 83-year-old man who had suffered brain damage from anoxia entered a vegetative state and was thus incompetent to consent to the removal of his respirator. The court, however, found it unnecessary to reach the question of whether his rights could be exercised by others since it found the evidence clear and convincing from statements made by the patient when competent that he "did not want to be maintained in a vegetative coma by use of a respirator." Id., at 380, 420 NE2d, at 72. In the companion Storar case, a 52-year-old man suffering from bladder cancer had been profoundly re-tarded during most of his life. Implicitly rejecting the approach taken in Saikewicz, supra, the court reasoned that due to such life-long incompetency, "it is unrealistic to attempt to determine whether he would want to continue potentially life prolonging treatment if he were competent." 52 NY2d, at 380, 420 NE2d, at 72. As the evidence showed that the patient's required blood transfusions did not involve excessive pain and without them his mental and physical abilities would deteriorate, the court concluded that it should not "allow an incompetent patient to bleed to death because someone, even someone as close as a parent or sibling, feels that this is best for one with an incurable disease." Id., at 382, 420 NE2d, at 73.

Many of the later cases build on the principles established in Quinlan, Saikewicz and Storar/Eichner. For instance, in In re Conroy, 98 NJ 321, 486 A2d 1209 (1985), the same court that decided Quinlan considered whether a nasogastric feeding tube could be removed from an 84-year-old incompetent nursing-home resident suffering irreversible mental and physical ailments. While recognizing that a federal right of privacy might apply in the case, the court, contrary to its approach in Quinlan, decided to base its decision on the common-law right to self-determination and informed consent. 98 NJ, at 348, 486 A2d, at 1223. "On balance, the right to self-determination ordinarily outweighs any countervailing state interests, and competent persons generally are permitted to refuse medical treatment, even at the risk of death. Most of the cases that have held otherwise, unless they involved the interest in protecting innocent third parties, have concerned the patient's competency to make a rational and considered choice." Id., at 353–354, 486 A2d, at 1225.

Reasoning that the right of self-determination should not be lost merely because an individual is unable to sense a violation of it, the court held that incompetent individuals retain a right to refuse treatment. It also held that such a right could be exercised by a surrogate decisionmaker using a "subjective" standard when there was clear evidence that the incompetent person would have exercised it. Where such evidence was lacking, the court held that an individual's right could still be invoked in certain circumstances under objective "best interest" standards. Id., at 361–368, 486 A2d, at 1229–1233. Thus, if some

trustworthy evidence existed that the individual would have wanted to terminate treatment, but not enough to clearly establish a person's wishes for purposes of the subjective standard, and the burden of a prolonged life from the experience of pain and suffering markedly outweighed its satisfactions, treatment could be terminated under a "limited-objective" standard. Where no trustworthy evidence existed, and a person's suffering would make the administration of life-sustaining treatment inhumane, a "pure-objective" standard could be used to terminate treatment. If none of these conditions obtained, the court held it was best to err in favor of preserving life. Id., at 364–368, 486 A2d, at 1231–1233.

The court also rejected certain categorical distinctions that had been drawn in prior refusal-of-treatment cases as lacking substance for decision purposes: the distinction between actively hastening death by terminating treatment and passively allowing a person to die of a disease; between treating individuals as an initial matter versus withdrawing treatment afterwards; between ordinary versus extraordinary treatment; and between treatment by artificial feeding versus other forms of life-sustaining medical procedures. Id., at 369–374, 486 NE2d, at 1233–1237. As to the last item, the court acknowledged the "emotional significance" of food, but noted that feeding by implanted tubes is a "medical procedur[e] with inherent risks and possible side effects, instituted by skilled health care providers to compensate for impaired physical functioning" which analytically was equivalent to artificial breathing using a respirator. Id., at 373, 486 A2d, at 1236.[4]

• • •

In contrast to Conroy, the Court of Appeals of New York recently refused to accept less than the clearly expressed wishes of a patient before permitting the exercise of her right to refuse treatment by a surrogate decisionmaker. In re Westchester County Medical Center on behalf of O'Connor, 531 NE2d 607 (1988) (O'Connor). There, the court, over the objection of the patient's family members, granted an order to insert a feeding tube into a 77-year-old woman rendered incompetent as a result of several strokes. While continuing to recognize a common-law right to refuse treatment, the court rejected the substituted judgment approach for asserting it "because it is inconsistent with our fundamental commitment to the notion that no person or court should substitute its judgment as to what would be an acceptable quality of life for another. Consequently, we adhere to the view that, despite its pitfalls and inevitable uncertainties, the inquiry must always be narrowed to the patient's expressed intent, with every effort made to minimize the opportunity for error." Id., at 530, 531 NE2d, at 613 (citation omitted). The court held that the record lacked the requisite clear and convincing evidence of the patient's expressed intent to withhold life-sustaining treatment. Id., at 531–534, 531 NE2d, at 613–615.

• • •

As these cases demonstrate, the common-law doctrine of informed consent is viewed as generally encompassing the right of a competent individual to refuse medical treatment. Beyond that, these decisions demonstrate both similarity and diversity in their approach to decision of what all agree is a perplexing question with unusual strong moral and ethical overtones. State courts have available to them for decision a number of sources—state constitutions, statutes, and common law—which are not available to us. In this Court, the question is simply and starkly whether the United States Constitution prohibits Missouri from choosing the rule of decision which it did. This is the first case in which we have been squarely presented with the issue of whether the United States Constitution grants what is in common parlance referred to as a "right to die." We follow the judicious counsel of our decision in Twin City Bank v Nebeker, 167 US 196, 202 (1897), where we said that in deciding "a question of such magnitude and importance . . . it is the [better] part of wisdom not to attempt, by any general statement, to cover every possible phase of the subject."

The Fourteenth Amendment provides that no State shall "deprive any person of life, liberty, or property, without due process of law." The principle that a competent person has a constitutionally protected liberty interest in refusing unwanted medical treatment may be inferred from our prior decisions. In Jacobson v Massachusetts, 197 US 11, 24–30 (1905), for instance, the Court balanced an individual's liberty interest in declining an unwanted smallpox vaccine against the State's interest in preventing disease. Decisions prior to the incorporation of the Fourth Amendment into the Fourteenth Amendment analyzed searches and seizures involving the body under the Due Process Clause and were thought to implicate

substantial liberty interests. See, e.g., Breithaupt v Abrams, 352 US 432, 439 (1957) ("As against the right of an individual that his person be held inviolable . . . must be set the interests of society . . .").

Just this Term, in the course of holding that a State's procedures for administering antipsychotic medication to prisoners were sufficient to satisfy due process concerns, we recognized that prisoners possess "a significant liberty interest in avoiding the unwanted administration of antipsychotic drugs under the Due Process Clause of the Fourteenth Amendment." Washington v Harper, 108 L Ed 2d 178, (1990); see also id., at 108 L Ed2d 178 ("The forcible injection of medication into a nonconsenting person's body represents a substantial interference with that person's liberty"). Still other cases support the recognition of a general liberty interest in refusing medical treatment. Vitek v Jones, 445 US 480, 494 (1980) (transfer to mental hospital coupled with mandatory behavior modification treatment implicated liberty interests); Parham v J. R., 442 US 584, 600 (1979) ("a child, in common with adults, has a substantial liberty interest in not being confined unnecessarily for medical treatment").

But determining that a person has a "liberty interest" under the Due Process Clause does not end the inquiry;[5] "whether respondent's constitutional rights have been violated must be determined by balancing his liberty interests against the relevant state interests." Youngberg v Romeo, 457 US 307, 321 (1982). See also Mills v Rogers, 457 US 291, 299 (1982).

Petitioners insist that under the general holdings of our cases, the forced administration of life-sustaining medical treatment, and even of artificially-delivered food and water essential to life, would implicate a competent person's liberty interest. Although we think the logic of the cases discussed above would embrace such a liberty interest, the dramatic consequences involved in refusal of such treatment would inform the inquiry as to whether the deprivation of the interest is constitutionally permissible. But for purposes of this case, we assume that the United States Constitution would grant a competent person a constitutionally protected right to refuse lifesaving hydration and nutrition.

Petitioners go on to assert that an incompetent person should possess the same right in this respect as is possessed by a competent person. They rely primarily on our decisions in Parham v J. R., supra, and Young-berg v Romeo, 457 US 307 (1982). In Parham, we held that a mentally disturbed minor child had a liberty interest in "not being confined unnecessarily for medical treatment," 442 US, at 600, but we certainly did not intimate that such a minor child, after commitment, would have a liberty interest in refusing treatment. In Youngberg, we held that a seriously retarded adult had a liberty interest in safety and freedom from bodily restraint, 457 US, at 320. Youngberg, however, did not deal with decisions to administer or withhold medical treatment.

The difficulty with petitioners' claim is that in a sense it begs the question: an incompetent person is not able to make an informed and voluntary choice to exercise a hypothetical right to refuse treatment or any other right. Such a "right" must be exercised for her, if at all, by some sort of surrogate. Here, Missouri has in effect recognized that under certain circumstances a surrogate may act for the patient in electing to have hydration and nutrition withdrawn in such a way as to cause death, but it has established a procedural safeguard to assure that the action of the surrogate conforms as best it may to the wishes expressed by the patient while competent. Missouri requires that evidence of the incompetent's wishes as to the withdrawal of treatment be proved by clear and convincing evidence. The question, then, is whether the United States Constitution forbids the establishment of this procedural requirement by the State. We hold that it does not.

Whether or not Missouri's clear and convincing evidence requirement comports with the United States Constitution depends in part on what interests the State may properly seek to protect in this situation. Missouri relies on its interest in the protection and preservation of human life, and there can be no gainsaying this interest. As a general matter, the States—indeed, all civilized nations—demonstrate their commitment to life by treating homicide as serious crime. Moreover, the majority of States in this country have laws imposing criminal penalties on one who assists another to commit suicide.[6] We do not think a State is required to remain neutral in the face of an informed and voluntary decision by a physically-able adult to starve to death.

But in the context presented here, a State has more particular interests at stake. The choice between life and death is a deeply personal decision of obvious and overwhelming finality. We believe Missouri may legitimately seek to safeguard the personal element of this choice through the imposition of heightened evidentiary requirements. It cannot be disputed that the Due Process Clause protects an interest in life as well as an interest in refusing life-sustaining medical treatment. Not all incompetent patients will have loved ones available to serve as surrogate decisionmakers. And even where family members are present "[t]here will, of course, be some unfortunate situations in which family members will not act to protect a patient." In re Jobes, 108 NJ 394, 419, 529 A2d 434, 477 (1987). A State is entitled to guard against potential abuses in such situations. Similarly, a State is entitled to consider that a judicial proceeding to make a determination regarding an incompetent's wishes may very well not be an adversarial one, with the added guarantee of accurate factfinding that the adversary process brings with it. See Ohio v Akron Center for Reproductive Health, 111 L Ed 2d 405 (1990). Finally, we think a State may properly decline to make judgments about the "quality" of life that a particular individual may enjoy, and simply assert an unqualified interest in the preservation of human life to be weighed against the constitutionally protected interests of the individual.

In our view, Missouri has permissibly sought to advance these interests through the adoption of a "clear and convincing" standard of proof to govern such proceedings. "The function of a standard of proof, as that concept is embodied in the Due Process Clause and in the realm of factfinding, is to 'instruct the factfinder concerning the degree of confidence our society thinks he should have in the correctness of factual conclusions for a particular type of adjudication.'" Addington v Texas, 441 US 418, 423 (quoting In re Winship, 397 US 358, 370 (1970) (Harlan, J., concurring)). "This Court has mandated an intermediate standard of proof—'clear and convincing evidence'—when the individual interests at stake in a state proceeding are both 'particularly important' and 'more substantial than mere loss of money.'" Santosky v Kramer, 455 US 745, 756 (1982) (quoting Addington, supra, at 424. Thus, such a standard has been required in deportation proceedings, Woodby v INS, 385 US 276 (1966), in denaturalization proceedings, Schneiderman v United States, 320 US 118 (1943), in civil commitment proceedings, Addington, supra, and in proceedings for the termination of parental rights. Santosky, supra. Further, this level of proof, "or an even higher one, has traditionally been imposed in cases involving allegations of civil fraud, and in a variety of other kinds of civil cases involving such issues as . . . lost wills, oral contracts to make bequests, and the like." Woodby, supra, at 285, n 18.

We think it self-evident that the interests at stake in the instant proceedings are more substantial, both on an individual and societal level, than those involved in a run-of-the-mill civil dispute. But not only does the standard of proof reflect the importance of a particular adjudication, it also serves as "a societal judgment about how the risk of error should be distributed between the litigants." Santosky, supra, 455 US at 755; Addington, supra, at 423. The more stringent the burden of proof a party must bear, the more that party bears the risk of an erroneous decision. We believe that Missouri may permissibly place an increased risk of an erroneous decision on those seeking to terminate an incompetent individual's life-sustaining treatment. An erroneous decision not to terminate results in a maintenance of the status quo; the possibility of subsequent developments such as advancements in medical science, the discovery of new evidence regarding the patient's intent, changes in the law, or simply the unexpected death of the patient despite the administration of life-sustaining treatment, at least create the potential that a wrong decision will eventually be corrected or its impact mitigated. An erroneous decision to withdraw life-sustaining treatment, however, is not susceptible of correction. In Santosky, one of the factors which led the Court to require proof by clear and convincing evidence in a proceeding to terminate parental rights was that a decision in such a case was final and irrevocable. Santosky, supra, at 759. The same must surely be said of the decision to discontinue hydration and nutrition of a patient such as Nancy Cruzan, which all agree will result in her death.

It is also worth noting that most, if not all, States simply forbid oral testimony entirely in determining the wishes of parties in transactions which, while important, simply do not have the consequences that a decision to terminate a person's life does. At common law and by statute in most States, the parole evidence rule prevents the variations of the terms of a written contract by oral testimony. The statute of frauds makes unenforceable oral contracts to leave property by will, and statutes regulating the making of wills universally require that those instruments be in writing. See 2 A. Corbin, Contracts § 398, pp 360–361 (1950); 2 W. Page, Law of Wills §§ 19.3–19.5, pp 61–71 (1960). There is no doubt that statutes requiring wills to be in writing, and statutes of frauds which require that a contract to make a will be in writing, on occasion frustrate the effectuation of the intent of a particular decedent, just as Missouri's requirement of proof in this case may have frustrated the effectuation of the not-fully-expressed desires of Nancy Cruzan. But the Constitution does not require general rules to work faultlessly; no general rule can.

In sum, we conclude that a State may apply a clear and convincing evidence standard in proceedings where a guardian seeks to discontinue nutrition and hydration of a person diagnosed to be in a persistent vegetative state. We note that many courts which have adopted some sort of substituted judgment procedure in situations like this, whether they limit consideration of evidence to the prior expressed wishes of the incompetent individual, or whether they allow more general proof of what the individual's decision would have been, require a clear and convincing standard of proof for such evidence. . . .

The Supreme Court of Missouri held that in this case the testimony adduced at trial did not amount to clear and convincing proof of the patient's desire to have hydration and nutrition withdrawn. In so doing, it reversed a decision of the Missouri trial court which had found that the evidence "suggest[ed]" Nancy Cruzan would not have desired to continue such measures, App to Pet for Cert A98, but which had not adopted the standard of "clear and convincing evidence" enunciated by the Supreme Court. The testimony adduced at trial consisted primarily of Nancy Cruzan's statements made to a housemate about a year before her accident that she would not want to live should she face life as a "vegetable," and other observations to the same effect. The observations did not deal in terms with withdrawal of medical treatment or of hydration and nutrition. We cannot say that the Supreme Court of Missouri committed constitutional error in reaching the conclusion that it did.

Petitioners alternatively contend that Missouri must accept the "substituted judgment" of close family members even in the absence of substantial proof that their views reflect the views of the patient. They rely primarily upon our decisions in Michael H. v Gerald D., 105 L Ed 2d 91 (1989), and Parham v J. R., 442 US 584, 61 (1979). But we do not think these cases support their claim. In Michael H., we *upheld* the constitutionality of California's favored treatment of traditional family relationships; such a holding may not be turned around into a constitutional requirement that a State must recognize the primacy of those relationships in a situation like this. And in Parham, where the patient was a minor, we also *upheld* the constitutionality of a state scheme in which parents made certain decisions for mentally ill minors. Here again petitioners would seek to turn a decision which allowed a State to rely on family decisionmaking into a constitutional requirement that the State recognize such decisionmaking. But constitutional law does not work that way.

No doubt is engendered by anything in this record but that Nancy Cruzan's mother and father are loving and caring parents. If the States were required by the United States Constitution to repose a right of "substituted judgment" with anyone, the Cruzans would surely qualify. But we do not think the Due Process Clause requires the State to repose judgment on these matters with anyone but the patient herself. Close family members may have a strong feeling—a feeling not at all ignoble or unworthy, but not entirely disinterested, either—that they do not wish to witness the continuation of the life of a loved one which they regard as hopeless, meaningless, and even degrading. But there is no automatic assurance that the view of close family members will necessarily be the same as the patient's would have been had she been confronted with the prospect of her situation while competent. All of the reasons previously discussed for allowing Missouri to require clear and convincing evidence of the patient's wishes lead us to conclude that the State may choose to defer only to those wishes, rather than confide the decision to close family members.[7]

The judgment of the Supreme Court of Missouri is affirmed.

NOTES

1. The State Supreme Court, adopting much of the trial court's findings, described Nancy Cruzan's medical condition as follows:

". . . (1) [H]er respiration and circulation are not artificially maintained and are within the normal limits of a thirty-year-old female; (2) she is oblivious to her environment except for reflexive responses to sound and perhaps painful stimuli; (3) she suffered anoxia of the brain resulting in a massive enlargement of the ventricles filling with cerebrospinal fluid in the area where the brain has degenerated and [her] cerebral cortical atrophy is irreversible, permanent, progressive and ongoing; (4) her highest cognitive brain function is exhibited by her grimacing perhaps in recognition of ordinarily painful stimuli, indicating the experience of pain and apparent response to sound; (5) she is a spastic quadriplegic; (6) her four extremities are contracted with irreversible muscular and tendon damage to all extremities; (7) she has no cognitive or reflexive ability to swallow food or water to maintain her daily essential needs and . . . she will never recover her ability to swallow sufficient [sic] to satisfy her needs. In sum, Nancy is diagnosed as in a persistent vegetative state. She is not dead. She is not terminally ill. Medical experts testified that she could live another thirty years." Cruzan v Harmon, 760 SW2d 408, 411 (Mo 1989) (en banc) (quotations omitted; footnote omitted).

In observing that Cruzan was not dead, the court referred to the following Missouri statute:

"For all legal purposes, the occurrence of human death shall be determined in accordance with the usual and customary standards of medical practice, provided that death shall not be determined to have occurred unless the following minimal conditions have been met:

"(1) When respiration and circulation are not artificially maintained, there is an irreversible cessation of spontaneous respiration and circulation; or

"(2) When respiration and circulation are artificially maintained, and there is total and irreversible cessation of all brain function, including the brain stem and that such determination is made by a licensed physician." Mo Rev Stat § 194.005 (1986).

Since Cruzan's respiration and circulation were not being artificially maintained, she obviously fit within the first proviso of the statute.

Dr. Fred Plum, the creator of the term "persistent vegetative state" and a renowned expert on the subject, has described the "vegetative state" in the following terms:

"'Vegetative state describes a body which is functioning entirely in terms of its internal controls. It maintains temperature. It maintains heart beat and pulmonary ventilation. It maintains digestive activity. It maintains reflex activity of muscles and nerves for low level conditioned responses. But there is no behavioral evidence of either self-awareness or awareness of the surroundings in a learned manner.'" In re Jobes, 108 NJ 394, 403, 529 A2d 434, 438 (1987).

See also Brief for American Medical Association et al., as Amici Curiae, 6 ("The persistent vegetative state can best be understood as one of the conditions in which patients have suffered a loss of consciousness").

2. See generally Karnezis, Patient's Right to Refuse Treatment Allegedly Necessary to Sustain Life, 93 ALR3d 67 (1979) (collecting cases); Cantor, A Patient's Decision to Decline Life-Saving Medical Treatment: Bodily Integrity Versus the Preservation of Life, 26 Rutgers L Rev 228, 229, and n 5 (1973) (noting paucity of cases).

3. See Chapman, The Uniform Rights of the Terminally Ill Act: Too Little, Too Late?, 42 Ark L Rev 319, 324, n 15 (1989); see also F. Rozovsky, Consent to Treatment, A Practical Guide 415–423 (2d ed 1984).

4. In a later trilogy of cases, the New Jersey Supreme Court stressed that the analytic framework adopted in Conroy was limited to elderly, incompetent patients with shortened life expectancies, and established alternative approaches to deal with a different set of situations. See In re Farrell, 108 NJ 335, 529 A2d 404 (1987) (37-year-old competent mother with terminal illness had right to removal of respirator based on common law and constitutional principles which overrode competing state interests); In re Peter, 108 NJ 365, 529 A2d 419 (1987) (65-year-old woman in persistent vegetative state had right to removal of nasogastric feeding tube—under Conroy subjective test, power of attorney and hearsay testimony constituted clear and convincing proof of patient's intent to have treatment withdrawn); In re Jobes, 108 NJ 394, 529 A2d 434 (1987) (31-year-old woman in persistent vegetative state entitled to removal of jejunostomy feeding tube—even though hearsay testimony regarding patient's intent insufficient to meet clear and convincing standard of proof, under Quinlan, family or close friends entitled to make a substituted judgment for patient).

5. Although many state courts have held that a right to refuse treatment is encompassed by a generalized constitutional right of privacy, we have never so held. We believe this issue is more properly analyzed in terms of a Fourteenth Amendment liberty interest. See Bowers v Hardwick, 478 US 186, 194–195, 92 L Ed 2d 140, 106 S Ct 2841 (1986).

6. See Smith, All's Well That Ends Well: Toward a Policy of Assisted Rational Suicide or Merely Enlightened Self-Determination?, 22 UC Davis L Rev 275, 290–291, n 106 (1989) (compiling statutes).

7. We are not faced in this case with the question of whether a State might be required to defer to the decision of a surrogate if competent and probative evidence established that the patient herself had expressed a desire that the decision to terminate life-sustaining treatment be made for her by that individual. . . .

SEPARATE OPINIONS

Justice **O'Connor,** concurring.

I agree that a protected liberty interest in refusing unwanted medical treatment may be inferred from our prior decisions . . . and that the refusal of artificially delivered food and water is encompassed within that liberty interest. . . . I write separately to clarify why I believe this to be so.

As the Court notes, the liberty interest in refusing medical treatment flows from decisions involving the State's invasions into the body. . . . Because our notions of liberty are inextricably entwined with our idea of physical freedom and self-determination, the Court has often deemed state incursions into the body repugnant to the interests protected by the Due Process Clause. . . . The State's imposition of medical treatment on an unwilling competent adult necessarily involves some form of restraint and intrusion. A seriously ill or dying patient whose wishes are not honored may feel a captive of the machinery required for life-sustaining measures or other medical interventions. Such forced treatment may burden that individual's liberty interests as much as any state coercion. See, e.g., Washington v Harper, 108 L Ed 2d 178 (1990); Parham v J. R. 442 US 584, 600, 61 (1979) ("It is not disputed that a child in common with adults, has a substantial liberty interest in not being confined unnecessarily for medical treatment").

The State's artificial provision of nutrition and hydration implicates identical concerns. Artificial feeding cannot readily be distinguished from other forms of medical treatment. See, e.g., Council on Ethical and Judicial Affairs, American Medical Association, AMA Ethical Opinion 2.20, Withholding or Withdrawing Life-Prolonging Medical Treatment, Current Opinions 13 (1989); The Hastings Center, Guidelines on the Termination of Life-Sustaining Treatment and the Care of the Dying 59 (1987). Whether or not the techniques used to pass food and water into the patient's alimentary tract are termed "medical treatment," it is clear they all involve some degree of intrusion and restraint. Feeding a patient by means of a nasogastric tube requires a physician to pass a long flexible tube through the patient's nose, throat and esophagus and into the stomach. Because of the discomfort such a tube causes, "[m]any patients need to be restrained forcibly and their hands put into large mittens to prevent them from removing the tube." Major, The Medical Procedures for Providing Food and Water: Indications and Effects, in By No Extraordinary Means: The Choice to Forgo Life-Sustaining Food and Water 25 (J. Lynn ed 1986). A gastrostomy tube (as was used to provide food and water to Nancy Cruzan, see [above] or jejunostomy tube must be surgically implanted into the stomach or small intestine. Office of Technology Assessment Task Force, Life-Sustaining Technologies and the Elderly 282 (1988). Requiring a competent adult to endure such procedures against her will burdens the patient's liberty, dignity, and freedom to determine the course of her own treatment. Accordingly, the liberty guaranteed by the Due Process Clause must protect, if it protects anything, an individual's deeply personal decision to reject medical treatment, including the artificial delivery of food and water.

I also write separately to emphasize that the Court does not today decide the issue whether a State must also give effect to the decisions of a surrogate decisionmaker. . . . In my view, such a duty may well be constitutionally required to protect the patient's liberty interest in refusing medical treatment. Few individuals provide explicit oral or written instructions regarding their intent to refuse medical treatment should they become incompetent.[1] States which decline to consider any evidence other than such instructions may frequently fail to honor a patient's intent. Such failures might be avoided if the State considered an equally probative source of evidence: the patient's appointment of a proxy to make health care decisions on her behalf. Delegating the authority to make medical decisions to a family member or friend is becoming a common method of planning for the future. See, e.g., Areen, The Legal Status of Consent Obtained from Families of Adult Patients to Withhold or Withdraw Treatment, 258 JAMA 229, 230 (1987). Several States have recognized the practical wisdom of such a procedure by enacting durable power of attorney statutes that specifically authorize an individual to appoint a surrogate to make medical treatment decisions.[2] Some state courts have suggested that an agent appointed pursuant to a general durable power of attorney statute would also be empowered to make health care decisions on behalf of the patient.[3] See, e.g., In re Peter, 108 NJ 365, 378–379, 529 A2d 419, 426 (1987); see also 73 Op Md Atty Gen No. 88–046 (1988) (interpreting Md Est & Trusts Code Ann §§ 13–601 to 13–602 (1974), as authorizing a delegatee to make health care decisions). Other States allow an individual to designate a proxy to carry out the intent of a living will.[4] These procedures for surrogate decision-making, which appear to be rapidly gaining in acceptance, may be a valuable additional safeguard of the patient's interest in directing his medical care. Moreover, as patients are likely to select a family member as a surrogate, see 2 President's Commission for the Study of Ethical Problems in Medicine and Biomedical and Behavioral Research, Making Health Care Decisions 240 (1982), giving effect to a proxy's decisions may also protect the "freedom of personal choice in matters of . . . family life." Cleveland Board of Education v LaFleur, 414 US 632, 639 (1974).

Today's decision, holding only that the Constitution permits a State to require clear and convincing evidence of Nancy Cruzan's desire to have artificial hydration and nutrition withdrawn, does not preclude a future determination that the Constitution requires the States to implement the decisions of a patient's duly appointed surrogate. Nor does it prevent States from developing other approaches for protecting an incompetent individual's liberty interest in refusing medical treatment. As is evident from the Court's survey of state court decisions, see [above], no national consensus has yet emerged on the best solution for this difficult and sensitive problem. Today we decide only that one State's practice does not violate the Constitution; the more challenging task of crafting appropriate procedures for safeguarding incompetents' liberty interests is entrusted to the "laboratory" of the States, New State Ice Co. v Liebmann, 285 US 262, 311 (1932) (Brandeis, J., dissenting), in the first instance.

NOTES

1. See 2 President's Commission for the Study of Ethical Problems in Medicine and Biomedical and Behavioral Research, Making Health Care Decisions 241–242 (1982) (36% of those surveyed gave instructions regarding how they would like to be treated if they ever became too sick to make decisions; 23% put those instructions in writing) (Lou Harris Poll, September 1982); American Medical Association Surveys of Physician and Public Opinion on Health Care Issues 29–30 (1988) (56% of those surveyed had told family members their wishes concerning the use of life-sustaining treatment if they entered an irreversible coma; 15% had filled out a living will specifying those wishes).

2. At least 13 states and the District of Columbia have durable power of attorney statutes expressly authorizing the appointment of proxies for making health care decisions. . . .

3. All 50 states and the District of Columbia have general durable power of attorney statutes. . . .

4. Thirteen states have living will statutes authorizing the appointment of healthcare proxies. . . .

[For excerpts of Justice Scalia's concurring opinion see Chapter 7 pp. 459–461.]

Justice **Brennan**, with whom Justice **Marshall** and Justice **Blackmun** join, dissenting.

"Medical technology has effectively created a twilight zone of suspended animation where death commences while life, in some form, continues. Some patients, however, want no part of a life sustained only by medical technology. Instead, they prefer a plan of medical treatment that allows nature to take its course and permits them to die with dignity."[1]

Nancy Cruzan has dwelt in that twilight zone for six years. She is oblivious to her surroundings and will remain so. Cruzan v Harmon, 760 SW2d 408, 411 (Mo 1988). Her body twitches only reflexively, without consciousness. Ibid. The areas of her brain that once thought, felt, and experienced sensations have degenerated badly and are continuing to do so. The cavities remaining are filling with cerebrospinal fluid. The "'cerebral cortical atrophy is irreversible, permanent, progressive and ongoing.'" Ibid. "Nancy will never interact meaningfully with her environment again. She will remain in a persistent vegetative state until her death." Id., at 422.[2] Because she cannot swallow, her nutrition and hydration are delivered through a tube surgically implanted in her stomach.

A grown woman at the time of the accident, Nancy had previously expressed her wish to forgo continuing medical care under circumstances such as these. Her family and her friends are convinced that this is what she would want. See n [19], infra. A guardian ad litem appointed by the trial court is also convinced that this is what Nancy would want. See 760 SW2d, at 444 (Higgins, J., dissenting from denial of rehearing). Yet the Missouri Supreme Court, alone among state courts deciding such a question, has determined that an irreversibly vegetative patient will remain a passive prisoner of medical technology—for Nancy, perhaps for the next 30 years. See id., at 424, 427.

Today the Court, while tentatively accepting that there is some degree of constitutionally protected liberty interest in avoiding unwanted medical treatment, including life-sustaining medical treatment such as artificial nutrition and hydration, affirms the decision of the Missouri Supreme Court. The majority opinion, as I read it, would affirm that decision on the ground that a State may require "clear and convincing" evidence of Nancy Cruzan's prior decision to forgo life-sustaining treatment under circumstances such as hers in order to ensure that her actual wishes are honored. See ante, [above]. Because I believe that Nancy Cruzan has a fundamental right to be free of unwanted artificial nutrition and hydration, which right is not outweighed by any interests of the State, and because I find that the improperly biased procedural obstacles imposed by the Missouri Supreme Court impermissibly burden that right, I respectfully dissent. Nancy Cruzan is entitled to choose to die with dignity.

I

A

"[T]he timing of death — once a matter of fate — is now a matter of human choice." Office of Technology Assessment Task Force, Life Sustaining Technologies and the Elderly 41 (1988). Of the approximately two million people who die each year, 80% die in hospitals and long-term care institutions,[3] and perhaps 70% of those after a decision to forgo life-sustaining treatment has been made.[4] Nearly every death involves a decision whether to undertake some medical procedure that could prolong the process of dying. Such decisions are difficult and personal. They must be made on the basis of individual values, informed by medical realities, yet within a framework governed by law. The role of the courts is confined to defining that framework, delineating the ways in which government may and may not participate in such decisions.

The question before this Court is a relatively narrow one: whether the Due Process Clause allows Missouri to require a now-incompetent patient in an irreversible persistent vegetative state to remain on life-support absent rigorously clear and convincing evidence that avoiding the treatment represents the patient's prior, express choice. . . . If a fundamental right is at issue, Missouri's rule of decision must be scrutinized under the standards this Court has always applied in such circumstances. As we said in Zablocki v Redhail, 434 US 374, 388 (1978), if a requirement imposed by a State "significantly interferes with the ex-

ercise of a fundamental right, it cannot be upheld unless it is supported by sufficiently important state interests and is closely tailored to effectuate only those interests." The Constitution imposes on this Court the obligation to "examine carefully . . . the extent to which [the legitimate government interests advanced] are served by the challenged regulation." Moore v East Cleveland, 431 US 494, 499 (1977). See also Carey v Population Services International, 431 US 678, 690 (1977) (invalidating a requirement that bore "no relation to the State's interest"). An evidentiary rule, just as a substantive prohibition, must meet these standards if it significantly burdens a fundamental liberty interest. Fundamental rights "are protected not only against heavy-handed frontal attack, but also from being stifled by more subtle governmental interference." Bates v Little Rock, 361 US 516, 523 (1960).

B

The starting point for our legal analysis must be whether a competent person has a constitutional right to avoid unwanted medical care. Earlier this Term, this Court held that the Due Process Clause of the Fourteenth Amendment confers a significant liberty interest in avoiding unwanted medical treatment. Washington v Harper, 108 L Ed 2d 178 (1990). Today, the Court concedes that our prior decisions "support the recognition of a general liberty interest in refusing medical treatment." See [above]. The Court, however, avoids discussing either the measure of that liberty interest or its application by assuming, for purposes of this case only, that a competent person has a constitutionally protected liberty interest in being free of unwanted artificial nutrition and hydration. . . . Justice O'Connor's opinion is less parsimonious. She openly affirms that "the Court has often deemed state incursions into the body repugnant to the interests protected by the Due Process Clause," that there is a liberty interest in avoiding unwanted medical treatment and that it encompasses the right to be free of "artificially delivered food and water." . . .

But if a competent person has a liberty interest to be free of unwanted medical treatment, as both the majority and Justice O'Connor concede, it must be fundamental. "We are dealing here with [a decision] which involves one of the basic civil rights of man." Skinner v Oklahoma ex rel. Williamson, 316 US 535, 541 (1942) (invalidating a statute authorizing sterilization of certain felons). Whatever other liberties protected by the Due Process Clause are fundamental, "those liberties that are 'deeply rooted in this Nation's history and tradition'" are among them. Bowers v Hardwick, 478 US 186, 192 (1986) (quoting Moore v East Cleveland, supra, at 503 (plurality opinion). "Such a tradition commands respect in part because the Constitution carries the gloss of history." Richmond Newspapers, Inc. v Virginia, 448 US 555, 589 (1980) (Brennan, J., concurring in judgment).

The right to be free from medical attention without consent, to determine what shall be done with one's own body, *is* deeply rooted in this Nation's traditions, as the majority acknowledges. . . . This right has long been "firmly entrenched in American tort law" and is securely grounded in the earliest common law. Ibid. See also Mills v Rogers, 457 US 291, 294, n 4 (1982) ("the right to refuse any medical treatment emerged from the doctrines of trespass and battery, which were applied to unauthorized touchings by a physician"). "'Anglo-American law starts with the premise of thoroughgoing self determination. It follows that each man is considered to be master of his own body, and he may, if he be of sound mind, expressly prohibit the performance of lifesaving surgery, or other medical treatment.'" Natanson v Kline, 186 Kan 393, 406–407, 350 P2d 1093, 1104 (1960). "The inviolability of the person" has been held as "sacred" and "carefully guarded" as any common law right. Union Pacific R. Co. v Botsford, 141 US 250, 251–252 (1891). Thus, freedom from unwanted medical attention is unquestionably among those principles "so rooted in the traditions and conscience of our people as to be ranked as fundamental." Snyder v Massachusetts, 291 US 97, 105 (1934).[5]

That there may be serious consequences involved in refusal of the medical treatment at issue here does not vitiate the right under our common law tradition of medical self-determination. It is "a well-established rule of general law . . . that it is the patient, not the physician, who ultimately decides if treatment—any treatment—is to be given at all. . . . The rule has never been qualified in its application by either the nature or purpose of the treatment, or the gravity of the consequences of acceding to or foregoing it." Tune v Walter Reed Army Medical Hospital, 602 F Supp 1452, 1455 (DC 1985). See also Downer v Veilleux, 322 A2d 82, 91 (Me 1974) ("The rationale of this rule lies in the fact that every competent adult has the right to forego

treatment, or even cure, if it entails what for him are intolerable consequences or risks, however unwise his sense of values may be to others").[6]

No material distinction can be drawn between the treatment to which Nancy Cruzan continues to be subject—artificial nutrition and hydration—and any other medical treatment. See [above] (O'Connor, J., concurring). The artificial delivery of nutrition and hydration is undoubtedly medical treatment. The technique to which Nancy Cruzan is subject—artificial feeding through a gastrostomy tube—involves a tube implanted surgically into her stomach through incisions in her abdominal wall. It may obstruct the intestinal tract, erode and pierce the stomach wall or cause leakage of the stomach's contents into the abdominal cavity. See Page, Andrassy, & Sandler, Techniques in Delivery of Liquid Diets, in Nutrition in Clinical Surgery 66–67 (M. Deitel 2d ed 1985). The tube can cause pneumonia from reflux of the stomach's contents into the lung. See Bernard & Forlaw, Complications and Their Prevention, in Enteral and Tube Feeding 553 (J. Rombeau & M. Caldwell eds 1984). Typically, and in this case (see Tr 377), commercially prepared formulas are used, rather than fresh food. See Matarese, Enteral Alimentation, in Surgical Nutrition 726 (J. Fischer ed 1983). The type of formula and method of administration must be experimented with to avoid gastrointestinal problems. Id., at 748. The patient must be monitored daily by medical personnel as to weight, fluid intake and fluid output; blood tests must be done weekly. Id., at 749, 751.

Artificial delivery of food and water is regarded as medical treatment by the medical profession and the Federal Government.[7] According to the American Academy of Neurology, "[t]he artificial provision of nutrition and hydration is a form of medical treatment . . . analogous to other forms of life-sustaining treatment, such as the use of the respirator. When a patient is unconscious, both a respirator and an artificial feeding device serve to support or replace normal bodily functions that are compromised as a result of the patient's illness." Position of the American Academy of Neurology on Certain Aspects of the Care and Management of the Persistent Vegetative State Patient, 39 Neurology 125 (Jan. 1989). See also Council on Ethical and Judicial Affairs of the American Medical Association, Current Opinions, Opinion 2.20 (1989) ("Life-prolonging medical treatment includes medication and artificially or technologically supplied respiration, nutrition or hydration"); President's Commission 88 (life-sustaining treatment includes respirators, kidney dialysis machines, special feeding procedures). The Federal Government permits the cost of the medical devices and formulas used in enteral [through a gastric or nasogastric tube] feeding to be reimbursed under Medicare. . . .

Nor does the fact that Nancy Cruzan is now incompetent deprive her of her fundamental rights. See Youngberg v Romeo, 457 US 307, 315–316, 319 (1982) (holding that severely retarded man's liberty interests in safety, freedom from bodily restraint and reasonable training survive involuntary commitment); Parham v J. R., 442 US 584, 600 (1979) (recognizing a child's substantial liberty interest in not being confined unnecessarily for medical treatment); Jackson v Indiana, 406 US 715, 730, 738 (1972) (holding that Indiana could not violate the due process and equal protection rights of a mentally retarded deaf mute by committing him for an indefinite amount of time simply because he was incompetent to stand trial on the criminal charges filed against him). As the majority recognizes, . . . the question is not whether an incompetent has constitutional rights, but how such rights may be exercised. As we explained in Thompson v Oklahoma, 487 US 815 (1988), "[t]he law must often adjust the manner in which it affords rights to those whose status renders them unable to exercise choice freely and rationally. Children, the insane, and *those who are irreversibly ill with loss of brain function, for instance, all retain 'rights,'* to be sure, but often such rights are only meaningful as they are exercised by agents acting with the best interests of their principals in mind." Id., at 825, n 23 (emphasis added). "To deny [its] exercise because the patient is unconscious or incompetent would be to deny the right." Foody v Manchester Memorial Hospital, 40 Conn Super 127, 133, 482 A2d 713, 718 (1984).

II

A

The right to be free from unwanted medical attention is a right to evaluate the potential benefit of treatment and its possible consequences according to one's own values and to make a personal decision whether to subject oneself to the intrusion. For a patient like Nancy Cruzan, the sole benefit of medical treatment is being kept metabolically alive. Neither artificial nutrition nor any other form of medical treatment available today can cure or in any way ameliorate her condition.[8] Irreversibly vegetative patients are devoid of thought, emotion and sensation; they are permanently and completely unconscious. See n 2, supra.[9] As the President's Commission concluded in approving the withdrawal of life support equipment from irreversibly vegetative patients:

"[T]reatment ordinarily aims to benefit a patient through preserving life, relieving pain and suffering, protecting against disability, and returning maximally effective functioning. If a prognosis of permanent unconsciousness is correct, however, continued treatment cannot confer such benefits. Pain and suffering are absent, as are joy, satisfaction, and pleasure. Disability is total and no return to an even minimal level of social or human functioning is possible." President's Commission 181–182.

There are also affirmative reasons why someone like Nancy might choose to forgo artificial nutrition and hydration under these circumstances. Dying is personal. And it is profound. For many, the thought of an ignoble end, steeped in decay, is abhorrent. A quiet, proud death, bodily integrity intact, is a matter of extreme consequence. "In certain, thankfully rare, circumstances the burden of maintaining the corporeal existence degrades the very humanity it was meant to serve." Brophy v New England Sinai Hospital, Inc. 398 Mass 417, 434, 497 NE2d 626, 635–636 (1986) (finding the subject of the proceeding "in a condition which [he] has indicated he would consider to be degrading and without human dignity" and holding that "[t]he duty of the State to preserve life must encompass a recognition of an individual's right to avoid circumstances in which the individual himself would feel that efforts to sustain life demean or degrade his humanity"). Another court, hearing a similar case, noted:

"It is apparent from the testimony that what was on [the patient's] mind was not only the invasiveness of life-sustaining systems, such as the [nasogastric] tube, upon the integrity of his body. It was also the utter helplessness of the permanently comatose person, the wasting of a once strong body, and the submission of the most private bodily functions to the attention of others." In re Gardner, 534 A2d 947, 953 (Me 1987).

Such conditions are, for many, humiliating to contemplate,[10] as is visiting a prolonged and anguished vigil on one's parents, spouse, and children. A long, drawn-out death can have a debilitating effect on family members. See Carnwath & Johnson, Psychiatric Morbidity Among Spouses of Patients With Stroke, 294 Brit Med J 409 (1987); Livingston, Families Who

Care, 291 Brit Med J 919 (1985). For some, the idea of being remembered in their persistent vegetative states rather than as they were before their illness or accident may be very disturbing.[11]

B

Although the right to be free of unwanted medical intervention, like other constitutionally protected interests, may not be absolute,[12] no State interest could outweigh the rights of an individual in Nancy Cruzan's position. Whatever a State's possible interests in mandating life-support treatment under other circumstances, there is no good to be obtained here by Missouri's insistence that Nancy Cruzan remain on life-support systems if it is indeed her wish not to do so. Missouri does not claim, nor could it, that society as a whole will be benefited by Nancy's receiving medical treatment. No third party's situation will be improved and no harm to others will be averted. Cf. nn 6 and 8, supra.[13]

The only state interest asserted here is a general interest in the preservation of life.[14] But the State has no legitimate general interest in someone's life, completely abstracted from the interest of the person living that life, that could outweigh the person's choice to avoid medical treatment. "[T]he regulation of constitutionally protected decisions . . . must be predicated on legitimate state concerns *other than* disagreement with the choice the individual has made. . . . Otherwise, the interest in liberty protected by the Due Process Clause would be a nullity." Hodgson v Minnesota, 111 L Ed 2d 344 (1990) (Opinion of Stevens, J.) (emphasis added). Thus, the State's general interest in life must accede to Nancy Cruzan's particularized and intense interest in self-determination in her choice of medical treatment. There is simply nothing legitimately within the State's purview to be gained by superseding her decision.

Moreover, there may be considerable danger that Missouri's rule of decision would impair rather than serve any interest the State does have in sustaining life. Current medical practice recommends use of heroic measures if there is a scintilla of a chance that the patient will recover, on the assumption that the measures will be discontinued should the patient improve. When the President's Commission in 1982 approved the withdrawal of life support equipment from irreversibly vegetative patients, it explained that "[a]n even more troubling wrong occurs when a treatment that might save life or improve health is not started because the health care personnel are afraid that they will find it very difficult to stop the treatment if, as is fairly likely, it proves to be of little benefit and greatly burdens the patient." President's Commission 75. A New Jersey court recognized that families as well as doctors might be discouraged by an inability to stop life-support measures from "even attempting certain types of care [which] could thereby force them into hasty and premature decisions to allow a patient to die." In re Conroy, 98 NJ 321, 370, 486 A2d 1209, 1234 (1985). See also Brief for American Academy of Neurology as Amicus Curiae 9 (expressing same concern.)[15]

III

This is not to say that the State has no legitimate interests to assert here. As the majority recognizes, . . . Missouri has a parens patriae interest in providing Nancy Cruzan, now incompetent, with as accurate as possible a determination of how she would exercise her rights under these circumstances. Second, if and when it is determined that Nancy Cruzan would want to continue treatment, the State may legitimately assert an interest in providing that treatment. But *until* Nancy's wishes have been determined, the only state interest that may be asserted is an interest in safeguarding the accuracy of that determination.

Accuracy, therefore, must be our touchstone. Missouri may constitutionally impose only those procedural requirements that serve to enhance the accuracy of a determination of Nancy Cruzan's wishes or are at least consistent with an accurate determination. The Missouri "safeguard" that the Court upholds today does not meet that standard. The determination needed in this context is whether the incompetent person would choose to live in a persistent vegetative state on life-support or to avoid this medical treatment. Missouri's rule of decision imposes a markedly asymmetrical evidentiary burden. Only evidence of specific statements of treatment choice made by the patient when competent is admissible to support a finding that the patient, now in a persistent vegetative state, would wish to avoid further medical treatment. Moreover, this evidence must be clear and convincing. No proof is required to support a finding that the incompetent person would wish to continue treatment.

• • •

The majority claims that the allocation of the risk of error [in favor of a decision to extend treatment] is justified because it is more important not to terminate life-support for someone who would wish it continued than to honor the wishes of someone who would not. An erroneous decision to terminate life-support is irrevocable, says the majority, while an erroneous decision not to terminate "results in a maintenance of the status quo." See [above, p.389].[16] But, from the point of view of the patient, an erroneous decision in either direction is irrevocable. An erroneous decision to terminate artificial nutrition and hydration, to be sure, will lead to failure of that last remnant of physiological life, the brain stem, and result in complete brain death. An erroneous decision not to terminate life-support, however, robs a patient of the very qualities protected by the right to avoid unwanted medical treatment. His own degraded existence is perpetuated; his family's suffering is protracted; the memory he leaves behind becomes more and more distorted.

Even a later decision to grant him his wish cannot undo the intervening harm. But a later decision is unlikely in any event. "[T]he discovery of new evidence," to which the majority refers, ibid., is more hypothetical than plausible. The majority also misconceives the relevance of the possibility of "advancements in medical science," ibid., by treating it as a reason to force someone to continue medical treatment against his will. The possibility of a medical miracle is indeed part of the calculus, but it is a part of the *patient's* calculus. If current research suggests that some hope for cure or even moderate improvement is possible within the life-span projected, this is a factor that should be and would be accorded significant weight in assessing what the patient himself would choose.[17]

B

Even more than its heightened evidentiary standard, the Missouri court's categorical exclusion of relevant evidence dispenses with any semblance of accurate factfinding. The court adverted to no evidence supporting its decision, but held that no clear and convincing, inherently reliable evidence had been presented to show that Nancy would want to avoid further treatment. In doing so, the court failed to consider statements Nancy had made to family members and a close friend.[18] The court also failed to consider testimony from Nancy's mother and sister that they

were certain that Nancy would want to discontinue artificial nutrition and hydration,[19] even after the court found that Nancy's family was loving and without malignant motive. See 760 SW2d, at 412. The court also failed to consider the conclusions of the guardian ad litem, appointed by the trial court, that there was clear and convincing evidence that Nancy would want to discontinue medical treatment and that this was in her best interests. Id., at 444 (Higgins, J., dissenting from denial of rehearing); Brief for Respondent Guardian Ad Litem 2–3. The court did not specifically define what kind of evidence it would consider clear and convincing, but its general discussion suggests that only a living will or equivalently formal directive from the patient when competent would meet this standard. See 760 SW2d, at 424–425.

Too few people execute living wills or equivalently formal directives for such an evidentiary rule to ensure adequately that the wishes of incompetent persons will be honored.[20] While it might be a wise social policy to encourage people to furnish such instructions, no general conclusion about a patient's choice can be drawn from the absence of formalities. The probability of becoming irreversibly vegetative is so low that many people may not feel an urgency to marshal formal evidence of their preferences. Some may not wish to dwell on their own physical deterioration and mortality. Even someone with a resolute determination to avoid life-support under circumstances such as Nancy's would still need to know that such things as living wills exist and how to execute one. Often legal help would be necessary, especially given the majority's apparent willingness to permit States to insist that a person's wishes are not truly known unless the particular medical treatment is specified. . . .

As a California appellate court observed: "The lack of generalized public awareness of the statutory scheme and the typically human characteristics of procrastination and reluctance to contemplate the need for such arrangements however makes this a tool which will all too often go unused by those who might desire it." Barber v Superior Court, 147 Cal App 3d 1006, 1015, 194 Cal Rptr 484, 489 (1983). When a person tells family or close friends that she does not want her life sustained artificially, she is "express[ing] her wishes in the only terms familiar to her, and . . . as clearly as a lay person should be asked to express them. To require more is unrealistic, and for

all practical purposes, it precludes the rights of patients to forego life-sustaining treatment." In re
O'Connor, 72 NY2d 517, 551, 531 NE2d 607, 626
(1988) (Simons, J., dissenting).[21] When Missouri enacted a living will statute, it specifically provided that
the absence of a living will does not warrant a presumption that a patient wishes continued medical
treatment. . . . Thus, apparently not even Missouri's
own legislature believes that a person who does not
execute a living will fails to do so because he wishes
continuous medical treatment under all circumstances.

The testimony of close friends and family members, on the other hand, may often be the best evidence available of what the patient's choice would be.
It is they with whom the patient most likely will have
discussed such questions and they who know the patient best. "Family members have a unique knowledge
of the patient which is vital to any decision on his or
her behalf." Newman, Treatment Refusals for the
Critically and Terminally Ill: Proposed Rules for the
Family, the Physician, and the State, 3 NYLS Human
Rights Annual 35, 46 (1985). The Missouri court's decision to ignore this whole category of testimony is
also at odds with the practices of other States. See,
e.g., In re Peter, 108 NJ 365, 529 A2d 419 (1987),
Brophy v New England Sinai Hospital, Inc. 398 Mass
417, 497 NE2d 626 (1986); In re Severns, 425 A2d
156 (Del Ch 1980).

The Missouri court's disdain for Nancy's statements in serious conversations not long before her accident, for the opinions of Nancy's family and friends
as to her values, beliefs and certain choice, and even
for the opinion of an outside objective factfinder appointed by the State evinces a disdain for Nancy
Cruzan's own right to choose. The rules by which an
incompetent person's wishes are determined must represent every effort to determine those wishes. The rule
that the Missouri court adopted and that this Court upholds, however, skews the result away from a determination that as accurately as possible reflects the individual's own preferences and beliefs. It is a rule that
transforms human beings into passive subjects of
medical technology.

"[M]edical care decisions must be guided by the individual patient's interests and values. Allowing persons to determine their own medical treatment is an important way in
which society respects persons as individuals. Moreover, the
respect due to persons as individuals does not diminish sim-

ply because they have become incapable of participating in
treatment decisions. . . . [I]t is still possible for others to
make a decision that reflects [the patient's] interests more
closely than would a purely technological decision to do
whatever is possible. Lacking the ability to decide, [a pa-
tient] has a right to a decision that takes his interests into account." In re Drabick, 200 Cal App 3d 185, 208; 245 Cal
Rptr 840, 854–855 (1988).

C

I do not suggest that States must sit by helplessly if
the choices of incompetent patients are in danger of
being ignored. . . .

There are various approaches to determining an incompetent patient's treatment choice in use by the
several States today and there may be advantages and
disadvantages to each and other approaches not yet
envisioned. The choice, in largest part, is and should
be left to the States, so long as each State is seeking,
in a reliable manner, to discover what the patient
would want. But with such momentous interests in the
balance, States must avoid procedures that will prejudice the decision. "To err either way—to keep a person alive under circumstances under which he would
rather have been allowed to die, or to allow that person to die when he would have chosen to cling to
life—would be deeply unfortunate." In re Conroy, 98
NJ, at 343, 486 A2d, at 1220.

D

Finally, I cannot agree with the majority that where it
is not possible to determine what choice an incompetent patient would make, a State's role as parens patriae permits the State automatically to make that
choice itself. . . . A State's legitimate interest in safeguarding a patient's choice cannot be furthered by
simply appropriating it.

The majority justifies its position by arguing that,
while close family members may have a strong feeling about the question, "there is no automatic assurance that the view of close family members will necessarily be the same as the patient's would have been
had she been confronted with the prospect of her situation while competent." Ibid. I cannot quarrel with
this observation. But it leads only to another question:
Is there any reason to suppose that a State is *more*
likely to make the choice that the patient would
have made than someone who knew the patient intimately? To ask this is to answer it. As the New Jersey
Supreme Court observed: "Family members are best
qualified to make substituted judgments for incompe-

tent patients not only because of their peculiar grasp of the patient's approach to life, but also because of their special bonds with him or her. . . . It is . . . they who treat the patient as a person, rather than a symbol of a cause." In re Jobes, 108 NJ 394, 416, 529 A2d 434, 445 (1987). The State, in contrast, is a stranger to the patient.

A State's inability to discern an incompetent patient's choice still need not mean that a State is rendered powerless to protect that choice. But I would find that the Due Process Clause prohibits a State from doing more than that. A State may ensure that the person who makes the decision on the patient's behalf is the one whom the patient himself would have selected to make that choice for him. And a State may exclude from consideration anyone having improper motives. But a State generally must either repose the choice with the person whom the patient himself would most likely have chosen as proxy or leave the decision to the patient's family.[22]

IV

As many as 10,000 patients are being maintained in persistent vegetative states in the United States, and the number is expected to increase significantly in the near future. See Cranford, supra n 2, at 27, 31. Medical technology, developed over the past 20 or so years, is often capable of resuscitating people after they have stopped breathing or their hearts have stopped beating. Some of those people are brought fully back to life. Two decades ago, those who were not and could not swallow and digest food, died. Intravenous solutions could not provide sufficient calories to maintain people for more than a short time. Today, various forms of artificial feeding have been developed that are able to keep people metabolically alive for years, even decades. See Spencer & Palmisano, Specialized Nutritional Support of Patients—A Hospital's Legal Duty? 11 Quality Rev Bull 160, 160–161 (1985). In addition, in this century, chronic or degenerative ailments have replaced communicable diseases as the primary causes of death. See R. Weir, Abating Treatment with Critically Ill Patients 12–13 (1989); President's Commission 15–16. The 80% of Americans who die in hospitals are "likely to meet their end . . . 'in a sedated or comatose state; betubed nasally, abdominally and intravenously; and far more like manipulated objects than like moral subjects.'"[23] A fifth of all adults surviving to age 80 will suffer a progressive dementing disorder prior to

death. See Cohen & Eisdorfer, Dementing Disorders, in The Practice of Geriatrics 194 (E. Calkins, P. Davis, & A. Ford eds 1986).

"[L]aw, equity and justice must not themselves quail and be helpless in the face of modern technological marvels presenting questions hitherto unthought of." In re Quinlan, 70 NJ 10, 44, 355 A2d 647, 665, cert denied, 429 US 922 (1976). The new medical technology can reclaim those who would have been irretrievably lost a few decades ago and restore them to active lives. For Nancy Cruzan, it failed, and for others with wasting incurable disease it may be doomed to failure. In these unfortunate situations, the bodies and preferences and memories of the victims do not escheat to the State; nor does our Constitution permit the State or any other government to commandeer them. No singularity of feeling exists upon which such a government might confidently rely as parens patriae. The President's Commission, after years of research, concluded:

"In few areas of health care are people's evaluations of their experiences so varied and uniquely personal as in their assessments of the nature and value of the processes associated with dying. For some, every moment of life is of inestimable value; for others, life without some desired level of mental or physical ability is worthless or burdensome. A moderate degree of suffering may be an important means of personal growth and religious experience to one person, but only frightening or despicable to another." President's Commission 276.

Yet Missouri and this Court have displaced Nancy's own assessment of the processes associated with dying. They have discarded evidence of her will, ignored her values, and deprived her of the right to a decision as closely approximating her own choice as humanly possible. They have done so disingenuously in her name, and openly in Missouri's own. That Missouri and this Court may truly be motivated only by concern for incompetent patients makes no matter. As one of our most prominent jurists warned us decades ago: "Experience should teach us to be most on our guard to protect liberty when the government's purposes are beneficient. . . . The greatest dangers to liberty lurk in insidious encroachment by men of zeal, well meaning but without understanding." Olmstead v United States, 277 US 438, 479 (1928) (Brandeis, J., dissenting).

I respectfully dissent.

NOTES

1. Rasmussen v Fleming, 154 Ariz 207, 211, 741 P2d 674, 678 (1987) (en banc).

2. Vegetative state patients may *react reflexively* to sounds, movements and normally painful stimuli, but they do not *feel* any pain or *sense* anybody or anything. Vegetative state patients may appear awake but are completely unaware. See Cranford, The Persistent Vegetative State: The Medical Reality, 18 Hastings Ctr Rep 27, 28, 31 (1988).

3. See President's Commission for the Study of Ethical Problems in Medicine and Biomedical and Behavioral Research, Deciding to Forego Life Sustaining Treatment 15, n 1, and 17–18 (1983) (hereafter President's Commission).

4. See Lipton, Do-Not-Resuscitate Decisions in a Community Hospital: Incidence, Implications and Outcomes, 256 JAMA 1164, 1168 (1986).

5. See, e.g., Canterbury v Spence, 150 US App DC 263, 271, 464 F2d 772, 780, cert denied, 409 US 1064 (1972) ("The root premise" of informed consent "is the concept, fundamental in American jurisprudence, that '[e]very human being of adult years and sound mind has a right to determine what shall be done with his own body'") (quoting Schloendorff v Society of New York Hospital, 211 NY 125, 129–130, 105 NE 92, 93 (1914) (Cardozo, J.)). See generally Washington v Harper, 108 L Ed 2d 178 (1990) (Stevens, J., dissenting) ("There is no doubt . . . that a competent individual's right to refuse [psychotropic] medication is a fundamental liberty interest deserving the highest order of protection").

6. Under traditional tort law, exceptions have been found only to protect dependent children. See Cruzan v Harmon, 760 SW2d 408, 422, n 17 (Mo 1988) (citing cases where Missouri courts have ordered blood transfusions for children over the religious objection of parents); see also Winthrop University Hospital v Hess, 128 Misc 2d 804, 490 NYS2d 996 (Sup Ct Nassau Co 1985) (court ordered blood transfusion for religious objector because she was the mother of an infant and had explained that her objection was to the signing of the consent, not the transfusion itself); Application of President & Directors of Georgetown College, Inc. 118 US App DC 80, 88, 331 F2d 1000, 1008, cert denied, 377 US 978 (1964) (blood transfusion ordered for mother of infant). Cf. In re Estate of Brooks, 32 Ill 2d 361, 373, 205 NE2d 435, 441–442 (1965) (finding that lower court erred in ordering a blood transfusion for a woman—whose children were grown—and concluding: "Even though we may consider appellant's beliefs unwise, foolish or ridiculous, in the absence of an overriding danger to society we may not permit interference therewith in the form of a conservatorship established in the waning hours of her life for the sole purpose of compelling her to accept medical treatment forbidden by her religious principles, and previously refused by her with full knowledge of the probable consequences").

7. The Missouri court appears to be alone among state courts to suggest otherwise, 760 SW2d, at 419 and 423, although the court did not rely on a distinction between artificial feeding and other forms of medical treatment. Id., at 423. See, e.g., Delio v Westchester County Medical Center, 129 App Div 2d 1, 19, 516 NYS2d 677, 689 (1987) ("review of the decisions in other jurisdictions . . . failed to uncover a single case in which a court confronted with an application to discontinue feeding by artificial means has evaluated medical procedures to provide nutrition and hydration differently from other types of life-sustaining procedures").

8. While brain stem cells can survive 15 to 20 minutes without oxygen, cells in the cerebral hemispheres are destroyed if they are deprived of oxygen for as few as 4 to 6 minutes. See Cranford & Smith, Some Critical Distinctions Between Brain Death and the Persistent Vegetative State, 6 Ethics Sci & Med 199, 203 (1979). It is estimated that Nancy's brain was deprived of oxygen from 12 to 14 minutes. . . . Out of the 100,000 patients who, like Nancy, have fallen into persistive vegetative states in the past 20 years due to loss of oxygen to the brain, there have been only three even partial recoveries documented in the medical literature. Brief for American Medical Association et al. as Amici Curiae 11-12. The longest any person has ever been in a persistent vegetative state and recovered was 22 months. See Snyder, Cranford, Rubens, Bundlie, & Rockswold, Delayed Recovery from Postanoxic Persistent Vegetative State, 14 Annals Neurol 156 (1983). Nancy has been in this state for seven years.

9. The American Academy of Neurology offers three independent bases on which the medical profession rests these neurological conclusions:

"First, direct clinical experience with these patients demonstrates that there is no behavioral indication of any awareness of pain or suffering.

"Second, in all persistent vegetative state patients studied to date, postmortem examination reveals overwhelming bilateral damage to the cerebral hemispheres to a degree incompatible with consciousness. . . .

"Third, recent data utilizing positron emission tomography indicates that the metabolic rate for glucose in the cerebral cortex is greatly reduced in persistent vegetative state patients, to a degree incompatible with consciousness." Position of the American Academy of Neurology on Certain Aspects of the Care and Management of the Persistent Vegetative State Patient, 39 Neurology 125 (Jan. 1989).

10. Nancy Cruzan, for instance, is totally and permanently disabled. All four of her limbs are severely contracted; her fingernails cut into her wrists. App to Pet for Cert A93. She is incontinent of bowel and bladder. The most intimate aspects of her existence are exposed to and controlled by strangers. Brief for Respondent Guardian Ad Litem 2. Her family is convinced that Nancy would find this state degrading. See n [19], infra.

11. What general information exists about what most people would choose or would prefer to have chosen for them under these circumstances also indicates the importance of ensuring a means for now-incompetent patients to exercise their right to avoid unwanted medical treatment. A 1988 poll conducted by the American Medical Association found that 80% of those surveyed favored withdrawal of life support systems from hopelessly ill or irreversibly comatose patients if they or their families requested it. New York Times, June 5, 1988, p 14, col 4 (citing American Medical News, June 3, 1988, p 9, col 1). Another 1988 poll conducted by the Colorado University Graduate School of Public Affairs showed that 85% of those questioned would not want to have their own lives maintained with artificial nutrition and hydration if they became permanently unconscious. The Coloradoan, Sept. 29, 1988, p 1.

Such attitudes have been translated into considerable political action. Since 1976, 40 States and the District of Columbia have enacted natural death acts, expressly providing for self-determination under some or all of these situations. See Brief for Society for the Right to Die, Inc. as Amicus Curiae 8; Weiner, Privacy, Family, and Medical Decision Making for Persistent Vegetative Patients, 11 Cardozo L Rev 713, 720 (1990). Thirteen States and the District of Columbia have enacted statutes authorizing the appointment of proxies for making health care decisions. . . .

12. See Jacobson v Massachusetts, 197 US 11, 26–27, 49 L Ed 643, 25 S Ct 358 (1905) (upholding a Massachusetts law imposing fines or imprisonment on those refusing to be vaccinated as "of paramount necessity" to that State's fight against a smallpox epidemic).

13. Were such interests at stake, however, I would find that the Due Process Clause places limits on what invasive medical procedures could be forced on an unwilling comatose patient in pursuit of the interests of a third party. If Missouri were correct that its interests outweigh Nancy's interest in avoiding medical procedures as

long as she is free of pain and physical discomfort, see 760 SW2d, at 424, it is not apparent why a State could not choose to remove one of her kidneys without consent on the ground that society would be better off if the recipient of that kidney were saved from renal poisoning. Nancy cannot feel surgical pain. See n 2, supra. Nor would removal of one kidney be expected to shorten her life expectancy. See The American Medical Association Family Medical Guide 506 (J. Kunz ed 1982). Patches of her skin could also be removed to provide grafts for burn victims, and scrapings of bone marrow to provide grafts for someone with leukemia. Perhaps the State could lawfully remove more vital organs for transplanting into others who would then be cured of their ailments, provided the State placed Nancy on some other life-support equipment to replace the lost function. Indeed, why could the State not perform medical experiments on her body, experiments that might save countless lives, and would cause her no greater burden than she already bears by being fed through the gastrostomy tube? This would be too brave a new world for me and, I submit, for our Constitution.

14. The Missouri Supreme Court reviewed the state interests that had been identified by other courts as potentially relevant—prevention of homicide and suicide, protection of interests of innocent third parties, maintenance of the ethical integrity of the medical profession, and preservation of life—and concluded that: "In this case, only the state's interest in the preservation of life is implicated." 760 SW2d, at 419.

15. In any event, the State interest identified by the Missouri Supreme Court—a comprehensive and "unqualified" interest in preserving life, id., at 420, 424—is not even well supported by that State's own enactments. In the first place, Missouri has no law requiring every person to procure any needed medical care nor a state health insurance program to underwrite such care. Id., at 429 (Blackmar, J., dissenting). Second, as the state court admitted, Missouri has a living will statute which specifically "allows and encourages the pre-planned termination of life." Ibid.; see Mo Rev Stat § 459.015(1) (1986). The fact that Missouri actively provides for its citizens to choose a natural death under certain circumstances suggests that the State's interest in life is not so unqualified as the court below suggests. It is true that this particular statute does not apply to nonterminal patients and does not include artificial nutrition and hydration as one of the measures that may be declined. Nonetheless, Missouri has also not chosen to require court review of every decision to withhold or withdraw life-support made on behalf of an incompetent patient. Such decisions are made every day, without state participation. See 760 SW2d, at 428 (Blackmar, J., dissenting). . . .

16. The majority's definition of the "status quo," of course, begs the question. Artificial delivery of nutrition and hydration represents the "status quo" only if the State has chosen to permit doctors and hospitals to keep a patient on life-support systems over the protests of his family or guardian. The "status quo" absent that state interference would be the natural result of his accident or illness (and the family's decision). The majority's definition of status quo, however, is "to a large extent a predictable, yet accidental confluence of technology, psyche, and inertia. The general citizenry . . . never said that it favored the creation of coma wards where permanently unconscious patients would be tended for years and years. Nor did the populace as a whole authorize the preeminence of doctors over families in making treatment decisions for incompetent patients." Rhoden, Litigating Life and Death, 102 Harv L Rev 375, 433–434 (1988).

17. For Nancy Cruzan, no such cure or improvement is in view. So much of her brain has deteriorated and been replaced by fluid, see App to Pet for Cert A94, that apparently the only medical advance that could restore consciousness to her body would be a brain transplant. Cf. n [21], infra.

18. The trial court had relied on the testimony of Athena Comer, a longtime friend, co-worker and a housemate for several months, as sufficient to show that Nancy Cruzan would wish to be free of medical treatment under her present circumstances. App to Pet for Cert A94. Ms. Comer described a conversation she and Nancy had while living together, concerning Ms. Comer's sister who had become ill suddenly and died during the night. The Comer family had been told that if she had lived through the night, she would have been in a vegetative state. Nancy had lost a grandmother a few months before. Ms. Comer testified that: "Nancy said she would never want to live [as a vegetative state] because if she couldn't be normal or even, you know, like half way, and do things for yourself, because Nancy always did, that she didn't want to live . . . and we talked about it a lot." Tr 388–389. She said "several times" that "she wouldn't want to live that way because if she was going to live, she wanted to be able to live, not to just lay in a bed and not be able to move because you can't do anything for yourself." Id., at 390, 396. "[S]he said that she hoped that [all the] people in her family knew that she wouldn't want to live [as a vegetable] because she knew it was usually up to the family whether you lived that way or not." Id., at 399.

The conversation took place approximately a year before Nancy's accident and was described by Ms. Comer as a "very serious" conversation that continued for approximately half an hour without interruption. Id., at 390. The Missouri Supreme Court dismissed Nancy's statement as "unreliable" on the ground that it was an informally expressed reaction to other people's medical conditions. 760 SW2d, at 424.

The Missouri Supreme Court did not refer to other evidence of Nancy's wishes or explain why it was rejected. Nancy's sister Christy, to whom she was very close, testified that she and Nancy had had two very serious conversations about a year and a half before the accident. A day or two after their niece was stillborn (but would have been badly damaged if she had lived), Nancy had said that maybe it was part of a "greater plan" that the baby had been stillborn and did not have to face "the possible life of mere existence." Tr 537. A month later, after their grandmother had died after a long battle with heart problems, Nancy said that "it was better for my grandmother not to be kind of brought back and forth [by] medical [treatment], brought back from a critical near point of death. . . . Id., at 541.

19. Nancy's sister Christy, Nancy's mother, and another of Nancy's friends testified that Nancy would want to discontinue the hydration and nutrition. Christy said that "Nancy would be horrified at the state she is in." Id., at 535. She would also "want to take that burden away from [her family]." Id., at 544. Based on "a lifetime of experience [I know Nancy's wishes] are to discontinue the hydration and the nutrition." Id., at 542. Nancy's mother testified: "Nancy would not want to be like she is now. [I]f it were me up there or Christy or any of us, she would be doing for us what we are trying to do for her. I know she would, . . . as her mother." Id., at 526.

20. Surveys show that the overwhelming majority of Americans have not executed such written instructions. See Emmanuel & Emmanuel, The Medical Directive: A New Comprehensive Advance Care Document, 261 JAMA 3288 (1989) (only 9% of Americans execute advance directives about how they would wish treatment decisions to be handled if they become incompetent); American Medical Association Surveys of Physician and Public Opinion on Health Care Issues 29–30 (1988) (only 15% of those surveyed had executed living wills); 2 President's Commission for the Study of Ethical Problems in Medicine and Biomedical and Behavioral Research, Making Health Care Decisions 241–242 (1982) (23% of those surveyed said that they had put treatment instructions in writing).

21. New York is the only State besides Missouri to deny a request to terminate life support on the ground that clear and convincing evidence of prior, expressed intent was absent, although New

York did so in the context of very different situations. Mrs. O'Connor, the subject of In re O'Connor, had several times expressed her desire not to be placed on life-support if she were not going to be able to care for herself. However, both of her daughters testified that they did not know whether their mother would want to decline artificial nutrition and hydration under her present circumstances . . . . Moreover, despite damage from several strokes, Mrs. O'Connor was conscious and capable of responding to simple questions and requests and the medical testimony suggested she might improve to some extent. . . . The New York Court of Appeals also denied permission to terminate blood transfusions for a severely retarded man with terminal cancer because there was no evidence of a treatment choice made by the man when competent, as he had never been competent. See In re Storar, 52 NY2d 363, 420 NE2d 64, cert denied, 454 US 858 (1981). Again, the court relied on evidence that the man was conscious, functioning in the way he always had, and that the transfusions did not cause him substantial pain (although it was clear he did not like them).

22. Only in the exceedingly rare case where the State cannot find any family member or friend who can be trusted to endeavor genuinely to make the treatment choice the patient would have made does the State become the legitimate surrogate decisionmaker.

23. Fadiman, The Liberation of Lolly and Gronky, Life Magazine, Dec. 1986, p 72 (quoting medical ethicist Joseph Fletcher).

Justice **Stevens**, dissenting.

Our Constitution is born of the proposition that all legitimate governments must secure the equal right of every person to "Life, Liberty, and the pursuit of Happiness."[1] In the ordinary case we quite naturally assume that these three ends are compatible, mutually enhancing, and perhaps even coincident.

The Court would make an exception here. It permits the State's abstract, undifferentiated interest in the preservation of life to overwhelm the best interests of Nancy Beth Cruzan, interests which would, according to an undisputed finding, be served by allowing her guardians to exercise her constitutional right to discontinue medical treatment. Ironically, the court reaches this conclusion despite endorsing three significant propositions which should save it from any such dilemma. First, a competent individual's decision to refuse life-sustaining medical procedures is an aspect of liberty protected by the Due Process Clause of the Fourteenth Amendment. . . . Second, upon a proper evidentiary showing, a qualified guardian may make that decision on behalf of an incompetent ward. . . . Third, in answering the important question presented by this tragic case, it is wise "not to attempt by any general statement, to cover every possible phase of the subject." . . . Together, these considerations suggest that Nancy Cruzan's liberty to be free from medical treatment must be understood in light of the facts and circumstances particular to her.

I would so hold: in my view, the Constitution requires the State to care for Nancy Cruzan's life in a way that gives appropriate respect to her own best interests.

. . .

In this case, as is no doubt true in many others, the predicament confronted by the healthy members of the Cruzan family merely adds emphasis to the best interests finding made by the trial judge. Each of us has an interest in the kind of memories that will survive after death. To that end, individual decisions are often motivated by their impact on others. A member of the kind of family identified in the trial court's findings in this case would likely have not only a normal interest in minimizing the burden that her own illness imposes on others, but also an interest in having their memories of her filled predominantly with thoughts about her past vitality rather than her current condition. The meaning and completion of her life should be controlled by persons who have her best interests at heart—not by a state legislature concerned only with the "preservation of human life."

The Cruzan family's continuing concern provides a concrete reminder that Nancy Cruzan's interests did not disappear with her vitality or her consciousness. However commendable may be the State's interest in human life, it cannot pursue that interest by appropriating Nancy Cruzan's life as a symbol for its own purposes. Lives do not exist in abstraction from persons, and to pretend otherwise is not to honor but to desecrate the State's responsibility for protecting life. A State that seeks to demonstrate its commitment to life may do so by aiding those who are actively struggling for life and health. In this endeavor, unfortunately, no State can lack for opportunities: there can be no need to make an example of tragic cases like that of Nancy Cruzan.

I respectfully dissent.

NOTE

1. It is stated in the Declaration of Independence that:

"We hold these truths to be self-evident, that all men are created equal, that they are endowed by their Creator with certain unalienable Rights, that among these are Life, Liberty and the pursuit of Happiness.—That to secure these rights, Governments are instituted among Men, deriving their just powers from the consent of the governed,—That whenever any Form of Government becomes destructive of these ends, it is the Right of the People to alter or to abolish it, and to institute new Government, laying its foundation on such principles and organizing its powers in such form, as to them shall seem most likely to effect their Safety and Happiness."

MALCOLM GLADWELL

Woman in Right-to-Die Case Succumbs

Nancy Cruzan, who lay in a coma for eight years while a national debate over treatment of the hopelessly ill raged around her, is dead.

Cruzan's parents fought a prolonged and nationally publicized legal battle for the right to let their severely brain-damaged daughter die, arguing before two Missouri courts and ultimately the U.S. Supreme Court that she would not have wanted to live indefinitely in what doctors called "a persistent vegetative state."

Thirteen days ago, the family finally received permission from a state court to disconnect the tube that supplied their daughter with food and water; and yesterday at 3 a.m., while anti-euthanasia protesters sang carols outside the hospital, the 33-year-old woman died of dehydration.

"She remained peaceful throughout and showed no sign of discomfort or distress in any way," the Cruzan family said in a statement. "Knowing Nancy as only a family can, there remains no question that we made the choice she would want."

The Cruzan case, the first of its kind to come before the Supreme Court, brought national attention to right-to-die issues and prompted national legislation requiring that patients be informed of their right to refuse life-sustaining treatment. . . .

Cruzan sustained severe brain damage in a automobile accident Jan. 11, 1983. Although she could breathe without an oxygen tent or respirator, her body was rigid, her eye movements erratic and she was kept alive only by means of the tube to her stomach.

Her ailments included bleeding gums, vomiting, seizures and diarrhea. Her care at the public hospital where she was treated cost Missouri taxpayers $112,000 a year.

In 1987, Cruzan's parents asked a state court for permission to have the tube disconnected, arguing that their daughter would never have wanted to be kept alive when she had no consciousness and no hope of recovery. A lower court judge approved their request the following July.

That decision was reversed, however, by the Missouri Supreme Court, which held that the Cruzans had to present "clear and convincing evidence" that, under the circumstances, their daughter would have wanted to die. In a landmark ruling last June 25, the U.S. Supreme Court upheld the Missouri decision.

In November, the Cruzans returned to the Missouri court, and several of their daughter's former co-workers testified that she had told them she never wanted to live "like a vegetable." The state court ruled that this met the "clear and convincing evidence" standard, and it gave permission Dec. 14 for removal of the life-sustaining tube.

KEY EVENTS IN LANDMARK LEGAL CONTEST

- Jan. 11, 1983: Nancy Cruzan, 25, is thrown from a car in an accident on a country road southeast of Carthage, Mo. Paramedics restart her breathing, but her brain is without oxygen for so long that she never regains consciousness.
- Feb. 5, 1983: Doctors implant a feeding tube in Cruzan's stomach; she is not on any other life-support system.
- Oct. 19, 1983: Cruzan is moved to the Missouri Rehabilitation Center in Mount Vernon.
- Oct. 23, 1987: Joe and Joyce Cruzan ask Jasper County Probate Judge Charles Teel for permission to remove their daughter's feeding tube so she can die as they believe she would want.
- March 9, 1988: A three-day hearing begins on the family's request. The Cruzans say Nancy has

a common-law right to be free from unwanted medical treatment as well as state and federal constitutional rights to privacy that protect her right to refuse unwanted medical treatment.

- July 27, 1988: Teel approves the request.
- Aug. 3, 1988: Missouri Attorney General William Webster files notice that the state will appeal to the state Supreme Court.
- Nov. 16, 1988: Voting 4 to 3, the state Supreme Court overturns the lower court. The family appeals to the U.S. Supreme Court.
- Dec. 6, 1989: The U.S. Supreme Court hears arguments; it is the first time the high court has considered a right-to-die case.
- June 25, 1990: Voting 5 to 4, the Supreme Court blocks removal of the tube, saying the state can keep a patient on life support in the absence of "clear and convincing" evidence that the person wants to die.
- Aug. 30: The Cruzans ask Teel for a second hearing, saying they have new evidence that Nancy once indicated to three people that she would rather die than live in a vegetative state.

- Sept. 17: Webster, saying the state no longer has a "recognizable legal interest" in the case, asks Teel to drop the state Health Department and the director of the Missouri Rehabilitation Center from future litigation.
- Oct. 23: Teel drops the state as a defendant.
- Nov. 1: Three former co-workers tell Teel that they recall conversations with Cruzan in which she said she never would want to live "like a vegetable" on medical machines. Cruzan's physician, who had opposed removing the feeding tube, terms her life "a living hell" and testifies that she should be allowed to die.
- Dec. 5: Cruzan's court-appointed guardian recommends that the feeding tube be removed so she may die.
- Dec. 14: Teel approves.
- Dec. 18-24: State and federal courts deny various injunction requests by anti-euthanasia groups.
- Yesterday: Cruzan dies in the Missouri Rehabilitation Center.

SOURCE: [for Key Events] Associated Press.

J O H N   D.   A R R A S

Beyond *Cruzan*: Individual Rights, Family Autonomy and the Persistent Vegetative State

Twelve days after her family won the legal right to remove her from artificial life support, 6 months after the United States Supreme Court issued its landmark ruling on her case, and 8 years after the tragic automobile accident that ended her conscious life, Nancy Beth Cruzan died in a nursing home at the age of 33. The final stages of her dying process proved to be as

controversial as the nationwide debate that had accompanied her case through the courts.

After the Supreme Court rejected their plea to have Nancy removed from artificial life supports, her parents reappeared months later in probate court equipped with new testimony. Three of Nancy's former co-workers testified to the effect that Nancy had told them she would not want to live like a "vegetable." Although this new evidence appeared to be essentially the same as that previously rejected by the Missouri Supreme Court, the judge concluded that the "clear and convincing" evidence test had indeed been

Reprinted with permission of the American Geriatric Society, "Beyond *Cruzan*: Individual Rights, Family Autonomy and the Persistent Vegetative State," by John D. Arras, *Journal of the American Geriatric Society*, 39, 1018–1024, 1991.

met, and he accordingly authorized Nancy's parents to secure the removal of the tube.[1]

This essay attempts to clarify and extend the debate initiated by the tragic case of Nancy Cruzan. My purpose here is threefold; first, to deemphasize the role of rights and constitutional law in the debate over surrogate decision making; second, to argue for a presumption in favor of families to decide such cases; and third, to urge a reversal of our usual presumption in favor of continued life for patients in a persistent vegetative state (PVS). Although Nancy Cruzan was only 33 years old when she died, her case raises issues directly relevant to the care of similar patients of all ages.

THE LEGACY OF *CRUZAN*

A number of important conclusions can be drawn from the Supreme Court's decision in Cruzan.[2] First and foremost, the Court recognized for all practical purposes a constitutionally protected "liberty interest" of competent patients to refuse life-sustaining medical treatments. Although Justice Rehnquist's majority opinion did not explicitly and directly affirm such a right, apparently because this case did not involve a competent patient, he did "assume" that the Court would so rule if and when such a case arose. Secondly, the Court affirmed that this constitutional right to refuse treatment survives the loss of decision-making capacity. Even though the patient lacks capacity to decide, his or her right to refuse treatment may be exercised by a surrogate.

Third, the Court held that there is no constitutionally significant difference between artificially administered food and fluids and other medical treatments. In contrast to those who argue that the former constitute not medical treatment but ordinary care and maintenance that must be provided, the Court held that artificial food and fluids may be rejected along with all other forms of treatment ([U.S. Law Week, Vol. 50] p. 4920). Fourth, in addition to upholding the validity of living wills as proper vehicles for advancing the rights of presently incompetent patients, the *Cruzan* decision (through Justice O'Connor's concurring opinion) suggests that individuals may have a constitutionally protected right to designate another person to make decisions for them (p. 4923). Thus, the "health care proxy" may well be empowered by the constitution to make life or death decisions for the now incompetent patients who named them.

So much for the "good news." The final, highly contested holding of the *Cruzan* decision was that in-

dividual states have very wide latitude in establishing procedural safeguards for decisions on behalf of incompetent patients (p. 4921). The Court held that states may erect very strict standards of evidence of the incompetent's former wishes—as Missouri and New York[3] have done through their rules requiring "clear and convincing" evidence—without violating the constitutional rights of incompetent patients. In those states, surrogates may not remove life-supports from incompetent patients in the absence of evidence coming very close to that found in a living will. Significantly, however, the Court did not require any state to adopt such a strict evidentiary standard. States thus remain as free as they were before *Cruzan* to establish policies granting substantial discretion to families and other surrogates.

CONSTITUTIONAL RIGHTS AND STANDARDS OF EVIDENCE

What must one do in order to qualify as a holder of this newly minted constitutional right to make decisions? Where on the spectrum between the permanently mentally impaired and the holder of a detailed living will lies the threshold of individual rights? Some possible markers include the following:

1. Patient previously made an actual decision, precisely stated in a detailed living will or health care proxy.
2. Patient previously made an oral declaration of his or her precise wishes. (eg, "If I ever end up like Karen Quinlan, I don't want to be put on a respirator.)
3. Patient made an oral declaration of general wishes. (eg, "If I ever become unable to recognize my children—or if I ever become a "vegetable"—I don't want any aggressive treatments." Patient does not specify the meaning of "aggressive," which might well encompass respirators, dialysis, TPN, G-tubes, etc.)
4. Patient does not make a self-regarding statement of wishes, but does express very strong attitudes about the treatment of others in similar situations (eg, "I think it's just terrible what they do to dying cancer patients these days. All those machines and tubes. It's so sad.")
5. Patient has not made a self-regarding statement of wishes, but has certain attitudes and values upon which family or friends might base

speculative judgments of varying plausibility. (eg, "She was always such an athletic person. She would not have wanted this.")

6. Patient lacks capacity (due to age, mental deficits, etc.) to formulate and express wishes regarding life-sustaining treatment.

Although it makes good sense to say that patients in categories (1) and (2) above, having already made a definite choice, clearly have a right to have their wishes respected, it makes no sense to say the same of patients in categories (5) and (6), who for one reason or another have failed to make an actual decision. To speak breezily about the "choice" or "rights" of the latter sort of incompetent patients to "make decisions," as some judges have done, is to stretch the appropriate extension of patients' rights to the breaking point.

Categories (3) and (4) sit on the borderline of meaningful talk about rights to decide. Although there will no doubt be some cases in which the lack of precision about medical condition or treatment modalities in category (3) will give rise to genuine perplexity, and a corresponding hesitancy to invoke the language of rights, in most such cases we know perfectly well what the patient was talking about. She was saying, in effect, that if she is in the process of dying or can no longer meaningfully interact with family and friends, she doesn't want any treatments designed primarily to extend her life. This is a clear and compelling wish, and it seems an adequate basis for the ascription of rights.

Category (4) is more of a mixed bag. Although these patients have not made an explicitly self-regarding choice, the emphatic responses of some to the treatment of others—"God, I think it's terrible what they do to these poor patients"—makes them look like many of the patients in category (3). It may make sense to talk as if they had a right to refuse here. On the other hand, patients whose responses lack conviction, passion, and specificity bear more resemblance to those in category (5). We can speculate about what they might have wanted, but they did not come close to making a choice and thus have no right to have that choice respected.

Justice Rehnquist's account of the "liberty interest" in *Cruzan* appears roughly consistent with the above analysis. He notes that the constitutional right of incompetent patients is grounded in the right of competent patients to refuse medical treatment (p. 4920). He then implies that, in order to ascribe this liberty inter-

est to an incompetent patient, he or she must have expressed a wish regarding future care while competent (p. 4920). Thus, notwithstanding the tendency of many courts and commentators to speak of rights to decide in the absence of any semblance of choice or expression of wishes, Justice Rehnquist would (correctly, I think) probably restrict the ascription of genuine constitutional rights to those within the ambit of categories (1) through (4).

In order to gauge the "force" or "weight" of this constitutional right, Justice Rehnquist next engages in a judicial balancing act between the individual's right to liberty and the state's various interests. In this particular case, the state of Missouri claimed the following interests: (1) safeguarding the personal element involved in the patient's choice; (2) an "unqualified" interest in protecting and preserving human life, no matter what its quality, and (3) avoiding abusive decisions by surrogates that do not reflect the preferences or best interests of the patient (pp. 4921–4922). According to Rehnquist, state interests such as these justify the imposition of procedural safeguards, including standards of evidence of varying strictness. In *Cruzan*, Rehnquist allowed states extremely broad latitude in vindicating their various interests. Missouri could, he concluded, even go so far as to circumscribe the individual's right with an exceedingly strict "clear and convincing" evidence standard. According to this standard, only patients in categories (1) and (2), and perhaps a very small proportion from (3), would be allowed to exercise their constitutional right.

What emerges from *Cruzan*, then, is a constitutional right whose force or weight varies from state to state, depending upon the various procedural safeguards and standards of evidence in place. Thus, while all patients in categories (1)–(3), and a good number from (4), possess a constitutional right, this right will not have sufficient "effective weight" to prevail in jurisdictions like Missouri where the state's interests tend to predominate.

APPLYING THE "CLEAR AND CONVINCING EVIDENCE" TEST

In criticizing *Cruzan*, one can either argue that the Missouri high court erred in its application of the clear and convincing standard to the case of Nancy Cruzan, or one can reject that standard as an inappropriate guide to decision making in this context. I wish to do both.

First, it should be noted that the "clear and convincing" test is itself amenable to interpretations of varying strictness. What is clear and convincing in one state may be neither in Missouri, an avowedly "pro-life" state that announces an "unqualified" interest in preserving human life. As applied in Missouri, this test might be better described as a "beyond a reasonable doubt" test or a test requiring the solemn and constant announcement of precise treatment wishes under carefully articulated circumstances (eg, "If I am ever in a persistent vegetative state, I solemnly declare that I do not wish to receive artificial nutrition and hydration."). Under such a test, only patients in categories (1) and (2) would have an effective right to refuse treatment through surrogates.

Although the evidence amassed in the *Cruzan* case failed this exaggerated test, it is hard to understand how anyone could deem it either unclear or unconvincing in the common meaning of these terms. Nancy's mother, sister and two long-time friends testified, for example, that Nancy stated several times that she would never want to live in this sort of condition (p. 4932 n 20). Although her wishes regarding different treatment modalities were not specific, Nancy definitely expressed a preference for discontinuance of treatment under certain circumstances (eg, if she "couldn't live halfway normally" or were a "vegetable.") She belongs, then, in category (3) where there isn't much ambiguity about the possession of a right to refuse.

Scornfully dismissing Nancy's authentic voice on the ground that it did not specifically name the treatments she wished to forego and that it merely expressed an informal reaction to other people's medical conditions, the Missouri Supreme Court allowed its pro-life ideology to obscure entirely the undeniable "personal element" in her case. Other courts, including the probate court that eventually rendered the final judgment in this case, have reached very different conclusions on the basis of nearly identical testimony.[1,4]

BEYOND "CLEAR AND CONVINCING" EVIDENCE

Although the "clear and convincing" standard has been declared constitutional, it remains exceedingly bad law, even when interpreted in a more reasonable manner. While the court said nothing about the wisdom or desirability of such a test—which only a few states, including Missouri and New York, have seen fit to embrace—much can be said against it.

First and foremost, the "clear and convincing" test establishes an entirely unrealistic standard. Since only

a vanishingly small minority of citizens have either the requisite medical knowledge, foresight, or luck accurately to predict the precise kinds of treatments they would refuse under specified conditions, the court's new liberty interest will be unattainable in practice for individuals in categories (3), (4), and (5), most of whom have a constitutionally protected liberty interest in refusing care.

Secondly, the "clear and convincing" test methodically excludes from consideration those "reasons of the heart" that "reason does not know."[5] By insisting on such rationalistic standards of clarity and precision, this test brushes aside the most compelling kind of evidence available in such cases, i.e., the testimony of family members based on years of experience and personal (as opposed to technical) knowledge of the patient's values. Thus, the family and friends of patients from category (5)—who may have deeply sedimented values regarding medical care, but who have not made an explicit choice—are precluded from deciding for them under this standard.

Finally, the "clear and convincing" standard, because it is so hopelessly out of step with medical and social realities, encourages families and hospitals to resort to lies and deception in order to do the right thing. In jurisdictions like Missouri and New York, the families of presently incompetent patients without living wills or the equivalent have no legal right to decline life-sustaining medical treatments. Informally, however, most health care providers and administrators want to involve families and follow their reasonable wishes. In order to bring about what everyone involved sees as the most reasonable and humane result, caregivers and administrators may indirectly coach families whose personal knowledge of the patient is insufficiently clear and convincing to the bureaucratic mind.

When such families are unable to produce a living will or to remember recent conversations in which the patient solemnly and carefully declared her opposition to treatments x, y, and z under conditions a, b, and c, such providers and administrators might gently urge them to "go home and try to remember" such conversations. The family's sudden recovery of memory upon its return to the hospital is often greeted with satisfaction and relief all around. Given the high stakes for families and the patent unreasonableness of the evidentiary standard, everyone's participation in a demeaning charade seems a small price to pay.

BEYOND AN EMPHASIS
ON INDIVIDUAL RIGHTS

Just as the "clear and convincing" test tends to render a constitutional right to refuse treatment practically useless for many patients in categories (3) and (4), it is time we took note that an overweening emphasis on individual rights to refuse has an analogous impact on many patients in categories (4), (5), and (6) who are not right holders, yet who ought nevertheless to be released from the thrall of high-technology medicine.

We must recall here that the vast majority of incompetent patients, especially among the elderly, belong in categories (4) and (5), most of whom have not made a self-regarding statement of wishes and therefore do not, strictly speaking, have a right to have treatment removed. Many of these patients have, however, a more or less coherent set of values and beliefs that can be reliably interpreted by close friends and family members. Even in the absence of a discrete decision, those close to the patient can say, "Jack wasn't a very articulate guy, but knowing him the way we did, he would never want to be kept alive forever in an unconscious state."

Social policies that place exclusive emphasis upon the possession and exercise of individual rights in surrogate decision making would make it extremely difficult, if not impossible, for such surrogates to speak for their loved ones and bring such tacit knowledge to bear. Thus, when the New York Court of Appeal in *O'Connor* rules that "no person or court should substitute its judgment as to what would be an acceptable quality of life for another,"[3] it leaves the majority of incompetent patients in a high-tech limbo.

A policy based exclusively on patient's rights will likewise have nothing to say about all the patients in category (6), and a good many in category (5), who either lack altogether the capacity for rational decision making, who have left their surrogates with no clue as to their wishes, or who have no relatives or friends to act as surrogate. Obviously, any adequate social policy on surrogate decision making must address this vast population of patients who fall below the threshold of legally effective rights.

THE CASE FOR FAMILY DISCRETION

The solution to this problem, absent a personally chosen surrogate, is to lodge decision making authority squarely with the patient's family or a close personal friend. As many commentators have pointed out,[6-9] the family or close friends should have the right to make such ultimate decisions because they are most likely to have a close personal bond with the patient and are thus often in the best position to interpret the probable wishes and best interests of the incompetent patient in the light of his or her history. In addition, the special role of the family in our society reinforces the claims of family members to act as surrogates. In order to create a zone of privacy within which crucially important relationships might flourish, decision making within the family is often granted the protection of law and custom.[6]

I propose that the surrogate should control decisions on life-sustaining treatments unless and until others (eg, hospital administrators, health care providers, other family members) can show that such decisions would pose a clear threat either to the previous wishes or best interests of the patient. In other words, the present burden of proof should be reversed: instead of imposing a strict presumption of treatment requiring families to prove that they have a uniquely correct answer to the problem, we should rather presume that families and friends know best and require others to prove them wrong.[8] An approach to surrogate decision making based upon familial discretion would restore to families their rightful claim to make such personal decisions in open, honest, and dignified circumstances.

Do families then have a constitutional right to make surrogate decisions? Given the law's unrelenting focus on individuals as opposed to groups, the strictly legal case for such a family right appears rather tenuous. In explicitly denying the notion of a constitutional familial right to surrogate decision making, however, the court simultaneously affirmed the discretion of states to create such rights through legislation (p. 4922). Families and close friends should thus have a right to refuse treatment for their incompetent loved ones, but in the vast majority of cases this right will not be based upon a constitutional right belonging either to patient or family. Rather, the family's right to decide should be a legislatively created right based more on notions of sound public policy than on individual rights. The search for the optimal mix of familial discretion and patient protection, of principles and procedural safeguards, should thus revert to the "laboratory of the states," where some would say it always belonged. (The nature of these procedural safeguards and the problem of selecting the most appropriate surrogate are issues of crucial importance, but I cannot explore them here.)

DECIDING FOR THE PERSISTENTLY VEGETATIVE PATIENT

Suppose, then, that families are given discretion to decide for incompetent patients in general and for patients in persistent vegetative states in particular. How should surrogates decide for patients like Nancy Cruzan?

The standard approach to this question is to ask what the patient would most likely have wanted in such circumstances (the subjective or so-called substituted judgment approach) and then, supposing no reliable answer to this question is forthcoming, to ask what is in the patient's current "best interests" (the so-called "objective" test).[6-8] For the vast majority of patients in persistent vegetative states, either approach should give surrogates the moral authority to decide in favor of withdrawing life sustaining medical treatments, including artificially administered food and fluids.

A reasonably reformulated subjective test would require, not clear and convincing evidence of the patient's prior wishes, but rather merely the surrogate's reasonable, good-faith supposition of what the patient would want.[8,10] Although many surrogates would base their "substituted judgement" on the patient's actual statements, others could draw on the sort of personal knowledge often offered by close relatives and friends. The vast majority of such decision makers, e.g., the 85% in one poll cited by Justice Brennan (p. 4929 n.11), would no doubt decide, after the diagnosis of persistent vegetative state had become reasonably certain, to withdraw medical treatments.

The primary rationale for this decision is the widespread and well-founded belief that such an existence is an indignity to the patient and a burden to families that such patients would want to avoid. Notwithstanding Justice Rehnquist's characteristically detached observation that no great loss attends an erroneous decision to continue treatment in such cases, the continued treatment of patients like Nancy Cruzan does indeed rob them of significant interests that motivated their lives prior to incompetency. As Justice Brennan observes of such patients, "[h]is own degraded existence is perpetuated; his family's suffering is protracted; the memory he leaves behind becomes more and more distorted" (p. 4931).

What, however, of that rare patient who, in spite of the foreknowledge that a persistent vegetative state would render her completely insensate, would wish to be kept alive for as long as possible with the help of artificial nutrients and other medical treatments? What of the life-long vitalist and pro-life activist whose wishes concerning continued treatment are known to the surrogate?[11] Some have cogently argued that PVS patients should be regarded as already dead, and therefore have no right to demand from the state or insurance pools upwards of $130,000 per year for their medical treatment. While I am sympathetic with this position—it strikes me as obscene, actually, that the state of Missouri eagerly pays this much to maintain a patient who can no longer consciously experience anything while neglecting the basic health care needs of children in blighted urban areas and rural communities—it probably goes a bit too far in view of current practices and expectations. While I would propose that private insurers or the state continue to pay for the upkeep of identifiable vitalists in the absence of a systematic and comprehensive system for ranking health care priorities, I would allow such sources to give PVS patients the lowest possible priority for support within such a system.

Coming finally to the hardest cases, what should be done for PVS patients without identifiable surrogates or whose surrogates have no idea what the patient would have wanted? What, in other words, is in the "best interests" of such patients?

The answer to this question depends upon a proper appreciation of the persistent vegetative state.[12] In contrast to patients whose brain injuries still permit some conscious awareness, some interaction with other people, and some enjoyment of life, patients in PVS have completely lost the psychological capacity for consciousness, including the awareness of pleasure and pain. Patients whose cerebrum has been destroyed lack the capacity to experience the world as aware subjects; strictly speaking, they have no "point of view" and therefore no interests that an objective "best interests" test could measure. Apart from whatever interests they may have had prior to entering this state of "cognitive death", eg, interests in personal dignity or safeguarding the well-being of their families that might well survive the vegetative state, such patients have no interests and therefore can neither be benefitted nor burdened here and now by further medical treatment.[7,13]

Although patients like Nancy Cruzan have lost all distinctly "biographical life" despite the presence of "biological life,"[14] Missouri insists upon vindicating an "unqualified" interest in human life. Since the invocation of such an unqualified interest cannot provide PVS patients with any cognizable benefit—it provides them with "life," to be sure, but a life of which they remain completely unaware—it is hard to understand how a state can justify imposing this interest upon unwilling patients or surrogates.

It might be argued that such patients are somehow "especially vulnerable," and therefore deserve special protection from the state. This claim is no doubt correct for large numbers of weak and voiceless patients—the anomalous newborn, the congenitally retarded, the demented elderly—but its unthinking and ritualized extension to PVS patients is highly problematic.[15] Whereas most vulnerable patients stand to gain from being alive, and therefore from the heightened protection of the state, PVS patients can no longer experience anything and thus do not benefit from state intervention. Apart from the possibility of advancing or setting back the previously expressed interests of PVS patients, it is actually a misnomer to describe them as "vulnerable," as though they were still within the pale of our helping and hurting.

Thus, in the absence of previously expressed vitalist concerns, there is no "patient centered" reason for keeping PVS patients alive and [there are] many reasons for ending their tragic permanent exile from the human world. (The possibility of misdiagnosis of PVS is a patient-centered reason to remain alive, but this possibility shrinks down to a virtual nullity in light of an expertly conducted neurological examination and the passage of several months.) Apart from the fact that a healthy concern for personal dignity and for the well-being of their families would prompt most people to shudder at the prospect of such a fate, the burdens imposed upon others by continued treatment should also have some weight in our moral deliberations. The physical maintenance of PVS patients is very expensive either to the family, insurance companies, or the state; and, as the tormented images of the Cruzans attest, the emotional toll of years at the bedside of such patients can be devastating.

While our society and medical profession in general rightly refuse to sacrifice the best interests of patients on the altar of interpersonal comparisons of utility, steadfastly clinging to a patient-centered ethic against the encroachments of selfish relatives and bedside cost-cutters alike, this exclusion of the interests of third parties needs to be rethought in the context of PVS. We think it wrong to deprive patients of needed care and treatment merely to make life easier or less expensive for their relatives, caregivers, or the state; patients, we say, have a right to personalized care. We think such deprivation to be wrong, however, precisely because it compromises the interests of patients and robs them of benefits to which they are entitled. Now if PVS patients are truly beyond the pale of treatment and caring gestures, if there is nothing but a zero under the heading of "personal benefits" in our "benefit/burden ratio," it appears perfectly licit and reasonable for decision makers to take the interests of others into account.[16] Thus, even in the absence of any clue as to the patient's former wishes, surrogate decision makers should be allowed to forgo medical treatments for PVS patients on the ground that they can only impose great emotional and financial burdens on families and caregivers while doing the patient no earthly good at all.

PVS AND PUBLIC POLICY

I strongly suspect that the vast majority of people in our society will concur in the above ethical analysis; indeed, I take it to be nothing more than dressed up common sense. There will, however, be dissenters. Foremost among them will be those who cling steadfastly to the idea that PVS patients are, after all, still human beings who deserve decent, respectful care and treatment. While such persons might balk at the prospect of mandating so-called "extraordinary" treatments such as heart transplants or kidney dialysis, they certainly will insist upon the provision of artificial food and fluids that do not pose an "excessive burden." To do otherwise, they will insist, amounts to a form of invidious discrimination against a distinct category of human beings. Even if PVS patients aren't getting much (if anything) out of life, it is still wrong and dangerous to say that some human beings are entitled to a patient-centered "best interests" assessment while others are not.

Even though I think it clear that PVS patients cannot presently be "burdened" and that genuine respect would amount to letting them die "all the way," there is no denying that a large segment of the population will not accept my "no interests" justification for terminating treatment for PVS patients. Indeed, they will be profoundly offended by it. How, then, might these ethical arguments be appropriately channelled into public policy?

One unacceptable option would be to allow the above "minority view" to determine public policy for the vast majority of the population. Simply because some people's ideological commitments prevent them from admitting that PVS patients cannot benefit from continued medical care, and hence have no interests to which a "best interests" test could attach, they should not be allowed to impose what is almost certainly a religiously inspired, "vitalist" commitment upon the rest of the population.

The converse policy option, which would have the majority establish its own clearly defined standard of "acceptable" quality of human life over the objections of an affronted minority, poses different problems. While such a policy would not limit the liberty of the "pro-life" minority, who could continue to ask for the maintenance of their relatives and friends in PVS, it would still be highly offensive to them and would do nothing to allay their fears that the establishment of special categories of humans will lead to real abuse and neglect on the "slippery slope."

There may be good reason to heed these concerns. Although the ethical analysis provided here might be on the right track, basing public policy on an official distinction between different categories of human beings—ie, between persons and non-persons—might well yield correct results in the short run while in the long run jeopardizing the overall fabric of respect for human life.[17]

A third policy approach, then, might attempt to achieve the correct result as dictated by the above ethical analysis through a more oblique, less polarizing approach. If the minority's primary concern is to avoid the possibly bad long-term consequences of an official societal endorsement of the distinction in moral status between PVS patients and other humans, this concern might well be acknowledged and accommodated without forcing most vegetative patients to subsist indefinitely in that state.

We must recall that the vast majority of patients will have surrogates, and these surrogates should be empowered to make decisions on the basis of what the patient would have wanted. Since the vast majority of persons would, when competent, express a desire not to be maintained in a persistent vegetative state, surrogates should be able to forgo treatment for them without invoking a socially sanctioned distinction between different sorts of humans.

Even with regard to the more difficult category of patients without surrogates, or whose surrogates have no idea of their probable wishes, a similarly oblique strategy might be available. Instead of relying on some officially sanctioned version of the "no interests" principle, decision makers for such patients (e.g., surrogates, physicians, ethics committees) might be given sufficient latitude to invoke something like a "reasonable person" standard. They might be permitted to ask, for example, what the average reasonable person would want for himself or herself should such a tragic plight ever befall them. Since the vast majority of adults in our society would no doubt desire to avoid persisting in PVS, these decision makers could again opt to withdraw or withhold treatment without resorting to problematical distinctions between humans.

True enough, the reasons why most reasonable persons would reject continued maintenance in PVS may be a commonsensical version of the "no interests" argument. (e.g. "What's the point of keeping them alive if they can't experience anything?") Nevertheless, this strategy of obliqueness may be sufficiently ad hoc and localized, at least in comparison with some sort of legislative endorsement of the "no interests" argument, to satisfy the more moderate sector of the oppositional minority.

CONCLUSION

A critical reading of the facts and judicial opinions in the *Cruzan* case reveals that, at least in some jurisdictions, our most basic presumptions are misleading and harmful. The Missouri Supreme Court, as well as its New York counterpart, presumes that judges or health care providers who disagree with families should be given the discretion to make decisions for incompetent patients. I have argued in this [essay] that this presumption ought to be reversed. Except for proposed decisions that clearly threaten the best interests of incompetent patients, families should be allowed ample discretion to decide what would advance the prior wishes or best interests of their loved ones. In so doing, moreover, they should not have to measure up to the extravagant demands of the "clear and convincing evidence" test, a rule whose predominant effect in such delicate cases is to silence the voices and nullify the preferences of patients.

I have also argued that Missouri's presumption in favor of sustaining the persistent vegetative state ought to be reversed. A presumption in favor of life and against discontinuance of life-sustaining treatment may well make eminently good sense in most contexts. It makes no sense, however, to presume that most people would want to be maintained indefinitely in a persistent vegetative state. On the contrary, only a vitalist concerned not with his or her own perceptible welfare, but rather with some sort of religious duty, could see some point in being maintained for years in a completely unconscious state before finally dying. Whatever decision making apparatus our society eventually selects, whether it be through legislative will, court decisions, or local bioethics committees, the operative (but, of course, rebuttable) presumption should be that ending an expertly diagnosed persistent vegetative condition will best advance the prior wishes or best interests of patients.

ACKNOWLEDGMENTS

The author thanks Nancy Dubler, Liz Emrey, Alan Fleischman, Alice Herb, Bonnie Steinbock, and David Thomasma for helpful comments and critical readings of a previous draft of this paper.

NOTES

1. Nancy Beth Cruzan vs. David B. Mouton and Thad C. Mc-Canse. Judgment of Charles E. Teel, Jr., Circuit Court of Jasper County, Probate Division at Carthage, Missouri, December 14, 1990.

2. Cruzan v. Director, Missouri Department of Health. 58 US Law Week 4916 (1990). (Subsequent citations to *Cruzan* will be given in the text, in parentheses.)

3. In re Westchester County Medical Center. 72 NY 2nd 517, 531 NE 2d 607 (1988).

4. In re Gardner. 534 A2d 947 (Maine 1987).

5. Pascal B. Pensées. Paris: Garnier, 1964.

6. President's Commission for the Study of Ethical Problems in Medicine and Biomedical and Behavioral Research. Deciding to Forego Life-Sustaining Treatment. Washington: US Government Printing Office, 1983.

7. Buchanan A, Brock D. Deciding for Others. New York: Cambridge University Press, 1989.

8. Rhoden N. Litigating Life and Death. Harvard Law Rev 1988;102:375–446.

9. Veatch RM. Limits of guardian treatment refusal: A reasonableness standard. Am J Law & Med 1984;9:442–47.

10. In re Jobes. 108 NJ 394, 529 A 2d 434 (1987).

11. Colen BD. Fight over life: Against family wishes, a Minnesota hospital may go to court in an effort to end measures keeping a woman alive by artificial means. Newsday, January 29, 1991, p. 57.

12. Council on Scientific Affairs and Council on Ethical and Judicial Affairs, American Medical Association. Persistent vegetative state and the decision to withdraw or withhold life support. JAMA 1990;263:426–430.

13. Arras JD. The severely demented, minimally functional patient: An ethical analysis. J Am Geriatr Soc 1988;36:938–944.

14. Rachels J. The End of Life. New York: Oxford University Press; 1986.

15. Dworkin R. The right to death. NY Rev Books, Jan 31, 1991;14–17.

16. Brody BA. Life and Death Decision Making. New York: Oxford University Press 1988; pp. 170–71.

17. Burt R. The ideal of community in the work of the President's Commission. Cardozo Law Rev 1984;6:267–286.

JAMES M. GUSTAFSON

The Johns Hopkins Case

THE PROBLEM

THE FAMILY SETTING

Mother, 34 years old, hospital nurse.

Father, 35 years old, lawyer.

Two normal children in the family.

In late fall of 1963, Mr. and Mrs. _____ gave birth to a premature baby boy. Soon after birth, the child was diagnosed as a "mongoloid" (Down's syndrome) with the added complication of an intestinal blockage (duodenal atresia). The latter could be corrected with an operation of quite nominal risk. Without the operation, the child could not be fed and would die.

At the time of birth Mrs. _____ overheard the doctor express his belief that the child was a mongol. She immediately indicated she did not want the child. The next day, in consultation with a physician, she maintained this position, refusing to give permission for the corrective operation on the intestinal block. Her husband supported her in this position, saying that his wife knew more about these things (i.e., mongoloid children) than he. The reason the mother gave for her position—"It would be unfair to the other children of the household to raise them with a mongoloid."

The physician explained to the parents that the degree of mental retardation cannot be predicted at birth—running from very low mentality to borderline subnormal. As he said: "Mongolism, it should be stressed, is one of the milder forms of mental retardation. That is, mongols' IQs are generally in the 50–80

Reprinted by permission of the author and publisher, The University of Chicago Press, from"Mongolism, Parental Desires, and the Right to Life," *Perspectives in Biology and Medicine* 16 (1973), 529–531. © 1973 by the University of Chicago.

range, and sometimes a little higher. That is, they're almost always trainable. They can hold simple jobs. And they're famous for being happy children. They're perennially happy and usually a great joy." Without other complications, they can anticipate a long life.

Given the parents' decision, the hospital staff did not seek a court order to override the decision (see "Legal Setting" below). The child was put in a side room and, over an 11-day period, allowed to starve to death.

Following this episode, the parents undertook genetic counseling (chromosome studies) with regard to future possible pregnancies.

THE LEGAL SETTING

Since the possibility of a court order reversing the parents' decision naturally arose, the physician's opinion in this matter—and his decision not to seek such an order—is central. As he said: "In the situation in which the child has a known, serious mental abnormality, and would be a burden both to the parents financially and emotionally and perhaps to society, I think it's unlikely that the court would sustain an order to operate on the child against the parents' wishes." He went on to say: "I think one of the great difficulties, and I hope [this] will be part of the discussion relative to this child, is what happens in a family where a court order is used as the means of correcting a congenital abnormality. Does that child ever really become an accepted member of the family? And what are all of the feelings, particularly guilt and coercion feelings that the parents must have following that type of extraordinary force that's brought to bear upon them for making them accept a child that they did not wish to have?"

Both doctors and nursing staff were firmly convinced that it was "clearly illegal" to hasten the child's death by the use of medication.

One of the doctors raised the further issue of consent, saying: "Who has the right to decide for a child anyway? . . . The whole way we handle life and death is the reflection of the long-standing belief in this country that children don't have any rights, that they're not citizens, that their parents can decide to kill them or to let them live, as they choose."

THE HOSPITAL SETTING

When posed the question of whether the case would have been taken to court had the child had a normal IQ, with the parents refusing permission for the intestinal operation, the near unanimous opinion of the doctors: "Yes, we would have tried to override their decision." Asked why, the doctors replied: "When a retarded child presents us with the same problem, a different value system comes in; and not only does the staff acquiesce in the parent's decision to let the child die, but it's probable that the courts would also. That is, there is a different standard. . . . There is this ten-

dency to value life on the basis of intelligence. . . . [It's] a part of the American ethic."

The treatment of the child during the period of its dying was also interesting. One doctor commented on "putting the child in a side room." When asked about medication to hasten the death, he replied: "No one would ever do that. No one would ever think about it, because they feel uncomfortable about it. . . . A lot of the way we handle these things has to do with our own anxieties about death and our own desires to be separated from the decisions that we're making."

The nursing staff who had to tend to the child showed some resentment at this. One nurse said she had great difficulty just in entering the room and watching the child degenerate—she could "hardly bear to touch him." Another nurse, however, said: "I didn't mind coming to work. Because like I would rock him. And I think that kind of helped me some—to be able to sit there and hold him. And he was just a tiny little thing. He was really a very small baby. And he was cute. He had a cute little face to him, and it was easy to love him, you know?" And when the baby died, how did she feel?—"I was glad that it was over. It was an end for him."

ROBERT F. WEIR

Selective Nontreatment of Handicapped Newborns

The argument was previously advanced that selective nontreatment decisions should be governed primarily by diagnostic categories. If a newborn has an [abnormal] condition that can be effectively treated, the child should generally be given the recommended treatment. In contrast, if a newborn has a diagnostic condition that cannot be effectively treated, the child should generally be spared from efforts at life

prolongation, because such efforts will be futile and/or harmful to the child.

In addition, it was argued that selecting by diagnostic categories is consistent with the principles of nonmaleficence and justice. According to the principle of nonmaleficence, it is justifiable to withhold life-prolonging treatment from all infants who have conditions that "overmaster" them (to use the Hippocratic terminology) and that seem impervious to even the most advanced medical procedures. To persist in trying to treat such infants is to go counter to their best interests and thereby to inflict unwarranted harm on

From *Selective Treatment of Handicapped Newborns: Moral Dilemmas in Neonatal Medicine* by Robert F. Weir. Copyright © 1984 by Oxford University Press, Inc. Reprinted by permission.

them. According to an egalitarian interpretation of justice, it is morally correct to withhold treatment from all infants born with the same kind of severe anomalous condition—as long as all available means of treating the condition are judged to be counter to those infants' best interests. To take another approach by comparing infants across major diagnostic lines is to engage in unfair quality-of-life assessments, because any less-than-normal infant will lose out in such a comparison.

It is now time to be more specific about which diagnostic conditions call for selective nontreatment. Any serious effort to do this kind of ethical line-drawing must meet three interrelated requirements: indicate as clearly as possible *where* the line is to be drawn between conditions to treat and those not to treat, provide reasons as to *why* the treatment/nontreatment line is drawn where it is, and apply the proposed line-drawing to actual cases.

It is improbable that all persons reading these words will agree with my placement of all the diagnostic conditions to be discussed below, especially since there are differences of opinion in the pediatric medical community regarding some of the conditions. Nevertheless, it seems reasonable that selection by diagnostic categories should be done by placing any of the congenital anomalies in one of three groups: anomalous conditions that should not be treated because efforts to save newborns with these conditions will not succeed; anomalous conditions that should not be treated because of the consensus judgment that life-prolonging treatment is not in the best interests of these infants; and anomalous conditions that should be treated because life-prolonging treatment is in the best interests of these infants. This threefold grouping of congenital anomalies results in the placement of diagnostic conditions as follows:

1. *Withhold efforts at treatment* (desist unsuccessful rescue): anencephaly [lack of a cerebral cortex]; other untreatable neurological [involving the nervous system, especially the brain] conditions . . . ; infantile polycystic [composed of many cysts] kidney disease; untreatable types of congenital heart disease . . . , and multiple severe anomalies requiring repetitious efforts at resuscitation.
2. *Withhold or withdraw treatment* (allow to die): hydranencephaly [fluid concentrated in the ventricles of the brain]; trisomy 18 [three copies of chromosome 18 instead of the usual two]; tri-

somy 13; Lesch-Nyhan syndrome [see below]; Tay-Sachs disease [see below]; lissencephaly [a condition in which the brain has few or shallow convolutions]; cri-du-chat syndrome [see below]; and metachromatic leukodystrophy [see below].
3. *Treat to prolong and enhance life:* hydrocephalus [excessive fluid around the brain]; most cases of prematurity; esophageal atresia [blockage] with tracheo-esophageal fistula [an opening between the trachea and the esophagus; duodenal atresia [blockage in the small intestine]; most cases of congenital heart disease; most cases of intraventricular hemorrhage; trisomy 21 (Down's syndrome); hyaline membrane disease [lung disorder]; most cases of spina bifida cystica [an abnormal opening in the spine that allows soft tissue to protrude]; Apert's syndrome [peaked head, fused fingers]; diaphragmatic hernia; most cases of congenital kidney disease; abnormalities of the abdominal wall; exstrophy of the cloaca [rectum turned out]; neurofibromatosis [the disease of the "Elephant Man"]; phenylketonuria; maple syrup urine disease; homocystinuria; cystic fibrosis; congenital hypothyroidism; and others too numerous to mention.

The reasons for drawing the treatment/nontreatment line in this manner are fairly straightforward. The congenital anomalies placed in the first nontreatment group seem, on the basis of current medical evidence, to be untreatable. Most of the conditions are rapidly fatal within the first few days of life.[1] At most, aggressive efforts at treatment may salvage these neonates for a short period of time, but for questionable moral reasons. Vigorous attempts at treatment with these generally acknowledged lethal cases appear to be done for the interests (and egos) of the medical personnel involved, not for the interests of the newborns subjected to futile rescue efforts.

When combined with the anomalous conditions in the first nontreatment group, the diagnostic conditions placed in the second nontreatment group represent less than 1 percent of all neonates. Nevertheless, good reasons are required to deny treatment to the nondying newborns whose conditions place them in this nontreatment group because, in contrast to the newborns in group 1, the nontreatment of infants in group 2 is done by choice. The reasons for nontreatment, in general terms, are that when infants are accurately diagnosed as having one of the anomalous conditions in the second group, a careful prognosis indicates that the lives that can be prolonged for an indeterminate period of time will not be in the best interests of the infants and children who have to endure them. Rather than proving beneficial to these children, life-prolonging treatment will subject them to a fate worse than death.

More specifically, there are several reasons for thinking that death, not severely handicapped life, is in the best interests of infants having any of the anomalous conditions in the second nontreatment group. First, a correct diagnosis of most of these conditions leads to a prognosis of *extremely short life expectancy*. Although some infants with some of these conditions (e.g., Lesch-Nyhan, Tay-Sachs, cri-du-chat) live for a few years after birth, the odds are very high that most newborns in the second nontreatment group will die in their first year of life even if given some forms of treatment. No matter how much sustaining treatment is given, continued life is simply not likely for most of these neonates.

Second, there is *no curative or corrective* treatment for these conditions. Little can be done for these children other than marginal life prolongation, palliative care, and institutionalization in a custodial ward. For the conditions with late onset dates (Lesch-Nyhan, Tay-Sachs, and the late infantile form of metachromatic leukodystrophy), the lack of effective treatment means that infants who appear normal during their first few months of life will experience progressive neurological and physical deterioration that is simply impossible to prevent or minimize.

Third, virtually all of the infants in the second nontreatment group who manage to survive beyond their first year end up with *serious neurological deficiencies*. In most cases the neurological deficiencies are very serious. With rare exceptions, infants with these conditions develop into children with severe (below 50 I.Q.) to profound (below 25 I.Q.) mental retardation.

Fourth, there are a *multiplicity of other serious medical problems* that accompany the neurological deficiencies in these conditions. Most of the infants have some form of congenital heart disease. Most of them also have hypotonia [poor muscle tone], apnea [respiration stops], seizures, and numerous other clinical features of their particular anomalous conditions.

It may be helpful to focus on some of the conditions in the second group. Newborns who inherit the autosomal recessive condition of Tay-Sachs disease (one form of G_{M2}-gangliosidosis) appear normal for approximately six months, then have an inexorable decline toward a totally vegetative existence followed by death when they are three or four years of age. The progressive loss of contact with parents and the environment is characterized by profound mental retardation, convulsions, paralysis, blindness, inability to feed orally, and severe weight loss.[2]

Male neonates who inherit the X-linked recessive condition of Lesch-Nyhan syndrome also appear normal at birth, then at approximately six months begin a process of neurological and physiological deterioration first evidenced by athetosis (ceaseless, involuntary writhing movements). Along with severe mental deficiency, the most striking neurological feature of this condition is compulsive self-mutilation that requires placing the elbows in splints, wrapping the hands in gauze, and sometimes extracting the teeth. Even then, children with this condition often bang their heads against inanimate objects or take out their aggression on other persons.[3]

Infants (usually girls) with trisomy 18 generally do not survive the first two months of life. The 10 percent who live past the 12-month point do so with serious abnormalities of the brain, congenital heart disease, problems with apnea and cyanosis [skin turns blue because of lack of oxygen], hypertonia [extreme tension of muscles and arteries], severe gastrointestinal and renal deformities, dislocated hips, and virtually no chance to live to a second birthday.[4]

Metachromatic leukodystrophy is a rare autosomal recessive disease, with the late infantile form being the most common type of the condition. Neonates with the disease appear normal but have a serious disturbance of the white matter in the cerebral hemispheres that results in a diffuse loss of myelin in the central nervous system. Symptoms of the condition appear late in the first year of life, then progress through four clinical stages until, at the age of three or four, children with the condition are decerebrate, bedridden, quadriplegic, blind, without verbal sounds, and in need of tube feeding.[5]

Cri-du-chat syndrome (or 5p— syndrome) is a chromosomal disorder involving a deletion of the short arm of the fifth chromosome. The commonly used name for the condition is a reference to the cat-like cry of infants having the disorder. In addition to this unusual cry, the most important aspect of this syndrome is the profound retardation that affects intellectual and motor development. Other symptoms of the condition include severely slowed growth, hypertonia, microcephaly [small head], congenital heart disease, scoliosis [curved spine], and inability to speak.[6]

The severity of these conditions—and the absence of effective treatment—forces one to conclude that death is preferable to severely handicapped existence for these children. Most reasonable persons—whether parents, physicians, other proxies, or other thoughtful individuals—will agree that the combination of harmful conditions accompanying these birth defects represents a fate worse than death for these afflicted newborns.

By contrast, infants with any of the anomalous conditions listed in the third group should be given treatment to prolong and to enhance their lives. The reasons for drawing the line at this point are several. First, the majority of the conditions *do not involve mental deficiency* at all, thus indicating that these neonates are potential persons in a way that newborns in the first two groups are not. Most of the anomalies in these conditions are physiological ones of one sort or another. Furthermore, for the disorders that do involve the possibility of neurological damage (e.g., hydrocephalus, phenylketonuria, intraventricular hemorrhage) or actual mental deficiency (e.g., trisomy 21), there is either a good chance of effectively treating the condition or at least a reasonable chance that the mental handicap will be rather mild.

Second, there is *curative or corrective treatment* available for most of the mental and physical handicaps associated with these conditions. In some instances (e.g., esophageal or duodenal atresia) the treatment is curative. In other instances (e.g., hydrocephalus, diaphragmatic hernia) the treatment is usually corrective. In other instances (e.g., phenylketonuria, maple syrup urine disease, homocystinuria) the treatment involves nothing more sophisticated than a special diet to adjust an underlying error of metabolism. Even for most cases of spina bifida cystica, in which surgery can neither cure nor correct the paralysis below the lesion, there is reasonably effective treatment for most of the physical and mental problems associated with the condition.

Third, most of these conditions *do not require institutionalization* if the affected infants are given appropriate treatment sufficiently early. Of course some parents may choose to institutionalize children with more severe forms of Down's syndrome or spina bifida or some of the other conditions that present on-

going problems, but these disorders do not usually have the degree of severity (as those in the second nontreatment group do) that necessitates placement in a handicapped children's facility. In fact, most children in this third group tend to do better if given care, emotional support, and friendship outside of an institutional setting.

Fourth, as already implied, infants with conditions listed in the third group have significantly *longer life expectancy* than newborns in the second group. A number of the conditions (e.g., congenital heart disease, hyaline membrane disease) cause neonatal fatalities if not effectively treated, but on the whole the availability of effective treatment means that neonates with these conditions will live many years beyond infancy.

Fifth, *very few adolescents or adults* with any of these conditions indicate that they *wish they had never survived infancy.* Even individuals with serious, ongoing handicaps (such as those associated with the more severe cases of spina bifida) rarely indicate to researchers that they would prefer no life to the life they have had. They may covet the normalcy they see in other persons, but they do not want to give up the abnormal lives they have for the alternative of death.

Of the various diagnostic conditions in the treatment group, Down's syndrome and spina bifida stand out because of the frequency of their occurrence and the conflicting points of view regarding the merits of life-prolonging treatment. Down's syndrome is unquestionably a serious congenital anomaly that no one would choose to have, and that no prospective parents would choose as the genetic composition of any of their children. As previously mentioned, the most serious feature of this disorder is moderately severe to severe mental retardation (typically in the 25–60 I.Q. range). However, the mental deficiency is occasionally milder, with some Down's syndrome children having I.Q. scores in the 60–80 range. In addition, these children have physical abnormalities ranging from relatively minor ones (e.g., shortened fingers, slanting eyes with inner canthal folds) to much more serious ones in some cases such as congenital heart disease (in 40 percent of the cases), esophageal or duodenal atresia (in 4 percent of the cases), and increased susceptibility to infections.[7]

Likewise, spina bifida cystica is a serious congenital anomaly that adults would never choose for themselves or their as yet unconceived children. During pregnancy it is possible to screen for spina bifida cases using the combination of ultrasonography, amniocentesis, and alpha-fetoprotein assays. Once born, infants with spina bifida have a number of physical abnormalities that have been previously discussed. In addition, these children often have hydrocephalus. Whether mental deficiency becomes an acquired feature of spina bifida cases with hydrocephalus depends on the effectiveness of shunting and the medical team's ability to prevent central nervous system infections (ventriculitis and/or meningitis). As a consequence, I.Q. scores in one study of children with spina bifida range from 102 in cases without hydrocephalus, to 95 for shunted hydrocephalus, to 72 for shunted cases with a history of ventriculitis.[8]

The day may come when spina bifida cases will be prevented or drastically reduced in number by having women take multivitamin supplements before and during pregnancy, or by having mandatory screening for spina bifida cases during pregnancy by running laboratory tests on the blood serum of pregnant women. Until that time, the question remains the same for cases of Down's syndrome and cases of spina bifida: is life-prolonging treatment in the best interests of these birth-defective infants? My answer is affirmative in cases of Down's syndrome and in the great majority of spina bifida cases. Children born with either of these anomalous conditions obviously do not have normal lives ahead of them. In this respect, they lack the chance for the quality of life that most normal children enjoy. Children born with either of these conditions also do not have desirable lives—except when these lives are compared with the alternative of death. The argument that these handicapped lives (or others in the treatment group) represent a fate worse than death is neither persuasive nor

supported by studies of these children when they reach adolescence and adulthood.[9]

NOTES

1. See Donald C. Fyler and Peter Lang, "Neonatal Heart Disease," in Gordon B. Avery, ed., *Neonatology: Pathophysiology and Management of the Newborn*, 2d ed. (Philadelphia: Lippincott, 1981), pp. 438–72; and Joseph J. Volpe and Richard Koenigsberger, "Neurologic Disorders," in Avery, *Neonatology*, pp. 910–963.

2. See Edwin H. Kolodny, "Tay Sachs Disease," in R. M. Goodman and Arno Motulsky, eds., *Genetic Disease among Ashkenazi Jews* (New York: Raven Press, 1979), pp. 217–229; Michael M. Kaback, D. L. Rimoin, and J. S. O'Brien, eds., *Tay-Sachs Disease: Screening and Prevention* (New York: Alan R. Liss, 1977); and Hans Galjaard, *Genetic Metabolic Diseases* (Amsterdam, New York, and Oxford: Elsevier/North Holland Biomedical Press, 1980), pp. 266–281.

3. See William L. Nyhan, "The Lesch-Nyhan Syndrome," *Annual Review of Medicine* (1973), 24:41–60; and John B. Stanbury et al., eds., *The Metabolic Basis of Inherited Disease*, 5th ed. (New York: McGraw-Hill, 1983), pp. 1115–1138.

4. See M. E. Hodes et al., "Clinical Experience with Trisomies 18 and 13," *Journal of Medical Genetics* (1978), 15:48–60.

5. See Galjaard, *Genetic Metabolic Diseases*, pp. 215–25; and Stanbury el al., *Metabolic Basis of Inherited Disease*, pp. 881–901.

6. See William L. Nyhan and Nadia O. Sakati, *Genetic and Malformation Syndromes in Clinical Medicine* (Chicago: Year Book Medical Publishers, 1976), pp. 128–131; David W. Smith, *Recognizable Patterns of Human Malformation* (Philadelphia: Saunders, 1970), pp. 48–49, and E. Neibuhr, "The Cri-du-Chat Syndrome: Epidemiology, Cytogenetics, and Clinical Features," *Human Genetics* (1978), pp. 227–234.

7. David W. Smith and Ann Asper Wilson, *The Child with Down's Syndrome* (Philadelphia: Saunders, 1973), pp. 21–44.

8. David G. McLone et al., "Central Nervous System Infections as a Limiting Factor in the Intelligence of Children with Myelomeningocele," *Pediatrics* (September 1982), 70:338–342.

9. See Smith and Wilson, *The Child with Down's Syndrome*, pp. 91–105; Kathleen Evans, Veronica Hickman, and C. O. Carter, "Handicap and Social Status of Adults with Spina Bifida Cystica," *British Journal of Preventive and Social Medicine* (1974), 28: 85–92; S. Dorner, "Adolescents with Spina Bifida: How They See Their Situation," *Archives of Disease in Childhood* (June 1976), 51:439–44; K. M. Laurence and Ann Beresford, "Degree of Physical Handicap, Education and Occupation of 51 Adults with Spina Bifida," *British Journal of Preventive and Social Medicine* (September 1976), 30:197–202.

NANCY K. RHODEN

Treating Baby Doe:
The Ethics of Uncertainty

In recent years, public attention has focused on the so-called Baby Doe dilemma. The plight of the original Bloomington Baby Doe, who suffered from Down syndrome and an esophageal defect, has come to exemplify, for many, the nature of these dilemmas. Yet by far the most common problems in the newborn nursery involve not infants with genetic anomalies, but ones who are born too soon. Down syndrome results in retardation within a wide, but nonetheless predictable, range. Extreme prematurity, on the other hand, is characterized by enormous uncertainty. Infants born prematurely, or severely asphyxiated at birth, may die; they may live to develop normally; or they may survive but suffer from profound retardation or other severe impairments. In these cases, predictions of outcome at birth are probabilistic at best.

All Baby Doe dilemmas involve the vexing ethical questions of whether any quality-of-life judgments are justifiable, and if so, how they can be appropriately circumscribed. But medical uncertainty compounds these dilemmas enormously. In these cases, doctors do not know whether the baby can live at all, and if it does survive, they cannot predict what degree of handicap, if any, it may have. This medical uncertainty creates another level of ethical uncertainty: how to make life-or-death decisions for infants in the absence of the information necessary to predict or evaluate their future quality of life. Everyone hopes to avoid, or at least minimize, the chances of letting a baby die who could have lived normally, or aggressively treating one who will suffer horribly and die anyway, or "salvaging" one who will have devastating handicaps. Unfortunately, acting to minimize the chances of one of these outcomes may increase the chances that another will occur.

This analysis of alternative approaches to prognostic uncertainty draws on my research in the United States, Sweden, and Great Britain. It focuses on the *strategies* for decision making, rather than on the more commonly discussed issues of substantive standards and appropriate procedures for decision making. Let me note at the outset, however, that certain substantive standards are incompatible with certain strategies for decision making. For example, the principle termed "vitalism" requires sustaining life under any conditions, no matter how bleak.[1] In this country, the Department of Health and Human Services (DHHS) has promoted, through a series of federal regulations, a slightly modified vitalism that allows treatment to be withheld only if an infant is dying or permanently comatose.[2] DHHS's stringent regulations have now been invalidated by the Supreme Court.[3] Congress has passed somewhat less rigid legislation as a compromise.[4] However, this new act still prohibits (at least ostensibly) consideration of an infant's future impairments—that is, its quality of life. Because I believe that appropriately circumscribed quality-of-life judgments are, in this area, necessary and even inevitable,[5] my analysis of decision strategies under uncertainty presumes that they should not be implementing a vitalistic substantive standard that rejects all quality-of-life judgments.

THE NATIONAL DIFFERENCES

EXTREME PREMATURITY

With a few exceptions, Swedish doctors withhold artificial ventilation from the most premature infants—whose weighting less than 750 grams.[6] These infants,

From *Hastings Center Report* 16 (August 1986), 34–42. Reprinted by permission of the Hastings Center.

who are usually fewer than 26 weeks gestation, will be given "special care," which includes warmth, extra oxygen, and in some units, continuous positive airway pressure (CPAP). (CPAP assists an infant's spontaneous breathing by providing continuous gas pressure that is greater than atmospheric pressure.[7]) Most will die quickly. If an infant appears hearty but, after a few days, develops breathing difficulties, doctors may reassess the situation and put it on a respirator. Once on, an infant will seldom be removed unless it becomes brain-dead. Swedish doctors state that this policy of giving babies the "trial of life" helps ensure that only those who are in fact capable of surviving are treated aggressively.

Although it is the predominant practice to provide this lesser level of care to the most premature, this practice is not followed uniformly. Physicians at Gotenburg disapprove of providing "special care" with CPAP but not artificial ventilation for infants under 750 grams. Instead they either treat aggressively or provide only an incubator and extra oxygen and warmth. Moreover, physicians at Uppsala have been heavily influenced by American treating practices and will "go all out" for infants weighing as little as 500 to 600 grams. (This was likewise the practice at Lund until 1982, when physicians there reassessed it in light of the number of infants who became respirator-dependent or developed severe neurological deficits. They now provide intensive care to those infants below 700 grams who appear particularly hearty, but otherwise do not treat aggressively below 700 grams.) Doctors in centers that treat more aggressively remain reluctant to remove an infant who is doing very badly from a respirator, and physicians in hospitals that adhere to the 750-gram cut-off suggest that the units that have abandoned it are producing an increasing number of extremely impaired newborns.

In recent years many British hospitals have adhered to a 750-gram cut-off, and some still do.[8] However, an increasing number are moving away from a strict cut-off and toward a policy of initially doing everything for potentially viable infants (those above 500 or 600 grams), but being willing to reassess and withdraw treatment if it appears either that the infant has little chance of surviving or faces a high risk of severe brain damage. Most British doctors did not specify any particular time as appropriate for reassessment, although some mentioned one week. In general

they remain willing, throughout the course of treatment, to reevaluate and terminate treatment if very adverse clinical symptoms appear.

The difficulty, of course, is in making accurate predictions. Extremely premature infants are very susceptible to intraventricular hemorrhages—bleeding in the brain. Many British doctors said that a few years ago they would have withdrawn treatment from a baby having a Grade IV hemorrhage—the most severe level—because it is highly correlated with death or profound brain damage.[9] But recent data have shown that some infants may be only mildly impaired by even a Grade IV bleed if it is relatively localized within the brain. Many doctors stated that only a few years back there was great optimism that ultrasound and CT scanning, which can diagnose Grade IV hemorrhages, would yield sufficiently certain prognostic data to justify termination of treatment. However, it is now recognized that even a Grade IV hemorrhage is not followed invariably by profound retardation.[10] Hence in most units only a massive, bilateral Grade IV hemorrhage will, by itself, be grounds for withdrawal.

Other grounds British doctors often listed include: (1) severe necrotizing enterocolitis (a sometimes fatal intestinal inflammation); (2) severe coagulation problems; or (3) severe pulmonary hemorrhages. Some physicians also stated that infants who have been on 100 percent oxygen for a significant period have a very bad prognosis. At some point, doctors will consider such infants to be permanently respirator-dependent, and will either remove them from the respirator or withhold additional treatment if a new crisis occurs. There is still uncertainty: according to one doctor, "Someone will always say they had an infant just like this that did fine. But this is too unlikely to justify going on and on."

Although some U.S. physicians favor a cut-off of 700 or 750 grams,[11] the general tendency is to treat any potentially viable infant aggressively, that is, to provide artificial ventilation and any other needed therapies. With regard to withdrawing treatment, practices in this country are much more diverse than in Britain and Sweden, making it hard to provide more than broad generalizations. Some U.S. doctors remain willing to stop treatment if severe neurological impairment appears probable. However, a number of doctors at various hospitals said that although a few years ago they would have withdrawn treatment for such conditions as Grade IV hemorrhages, today, because of both the legal climate and the increased recognition that predictions may be inaccurate, they tend to continue.

In describing three babies with severe broncho-pulmonary dysplasia who had been in her unit from three to six months, one Texas physician said that she knew that none of them would ever leave the nursery. Nonetheless, these infants were still being treated as aggressively as possible. In her unit and, she felt, in an increasing number of U.S. hospitals, doctors will seldom withdraw treatment unless an infant is either dying or appears permanently comatose. This policy, of course, results in some survivors who do surprisingly well, as well as others who suffer from impairments such as blindness, cerebral palsy, and severe or profound retardation.

BIRTH ASPHYXIA

For birth asphyxia, the Swedes have written guidelines providing that resuscitation should stop after twenty minutes if there is no spontaneous heartbeat.[12] This is not unusual—these infants are very unlikely to live, and doctors in Britain and the United States follow a similar, though informal, policy. The more interesting policy, incorporated in the written guidelines of certain Swedish hospitals, is that if there is a heartbeat but no spontaneous respiration after forty-five minutes, resuscitative efforts should likewise cease.[13] In other words, asphyxiated infants who do not breathe spontaneously within this time are not placed on a respirator.

Since artificial ventilation is simply withheld from this group of infants—who, if they live, are most likely to suffer severe brain damage—this policy significantly decreases any subsequent need to make individualized decisions about withdrawing treatment. As with premature infants in Sweden, if these infants are placed on a respirator, the machine will seldom be removed for conditions short of brain death. Doctors in Sweden frequently stated that respirators were virtually never withdrawn and that parents should not participate in decisions to stop treatment (if there ever were such decisions) because of the guilt they would feel.

The British, like the Swedes, stop resuscitative efforts if there is no heartbeat for about twenty minutes. However, they do not withhold artificial ventilation from an infant who does not breathe spontaneously. Such an infant is put on a respirator. Subsequently the doctors reassess the situation, some at forty-eight

hours, others at seventy-two. Obviously, if the infant is brain-dead at that time, life supports are withdrawn. However, the situation often is not so clear-cut. Doctors in Britain are likewise inclined to withdraw ventilatory support if there are good clinical indications that the infant will ultimately either die or have devastating brain damage. Indications include: continuing to lack spontaneous breathing; being flaccid; being unresponsive, including having no auditory or visual responses; having an ultrasound reading that shows severe cerebral edema; having an extremely abnormal EEG; having seizures that are uncontrollable even with medication; and/or requiring peritoneal dialysis. Naturally, the extent to which infants meet these criteria varies and doctors differ as to the length of time and the amount of evidence that is sufficient to warrant withdrawal of life supports.

If terminating treatment is deemed appropriate, the parents are told that their baby will most likely die or have minimal brain function and, with parental agreement, the infant is removed from the respirator. Many British doctors emphasized the fairly short window of time during which death will in fact result from removal of life supports as a major reason for reassessing at forty-eight or seventy-two hours rather than later. Even then, a few babies gasp for a while or even breathe spontaneously and hence survive. Several British doctors stated that parents may be warned of this prognostic uncertainty.

American policy with regard to birth asphyxia is diverse. As in the other countries, if there is no heartbeat within approximately twenty minutes, doctors I spoke with will stop attempts at resuscitation. There is, however, no time limit with regard to spontaneous breathing. Any baby with a heartbeat is given ventilatory support. Doctors here too spoke of the window of time during which a severely asphyxiated infant will die if removed from a respirator, and noted that delay may yield a profoundly damaged survivor. However, more doctors here tend to postpone or avoid removing the respirator, although they may forego initiating additional therapies such as dialysis if a new crisis occurs. While some American doctors would definitely stop treating an infant who was not brain-dead, but who showed prolonged unresponsiveness, many others, citing prognostic uncertainty or legal concerns, would not. Even unresponsive infants sometimes recover and thrive, so these decisions are exceedingly difficult. The strong impression among the many Swedish and British experts who had visited or practiced in U.S. hospitals was that more asphyxiated infants remain on respirators here, resulting in decreased mortality but increased morbidity.

SOME CULTURAL SPECULATIONS

Recognizing that practices vary within each country, we can nonetheless characterize each country's typical decision strategy under conditions of uncertainty. The British gather as much information as possible about the individual infant (though with birth asphyxia there are time constraints), assess its chances of survival and expected quality of life and, if deemed appropriate, forthrightly terminate treatment. The Swedes, who express a strong aversion to stopping treatment, as opposed to withholding it at the outset, do not begin ventilatory support if statistical criteria place an infant within a category for which prognosis is generally poor. The trend in this country, though with much more diversity than in the other two, is to begin treating almost all infants and to seek a higher degree of certainty than British doctors require before terminating treatment.

Almost all doctors I spoke with, in all three countries, believed that impairments caused by prematurity or asphyxia can be so severe that death could be considered preferable (were the degree of disability known in advance). There is likewise significant agreement across cultures that aggressive treatment can appropriately be withheld from infants with genetic disorders like Trisomy 13 or 18 that have fairly certain prognoses of severe mental and physical impairments and early death. Thus, at least among medical personnel, there appears to be little support in any of the countries either for vitalism—the view that *any* life must be preserved—or the modified vitalist position that any *conscious* life must be preserved.

But if doctors in all three countries accept the substantive principle that some types of impairments can be viewed as worse than death, and treat chromosomal anomalies with fairly clear prognoses similarly, why this difference in strategies when outcome is uncertain?

I cannot suggest a full social or cultural explanation for the differences I found. But certain cultural factors at least warrant mention. The most salient difference is that U.S. physicians are subject to far more nonmedical influences than are doctors in other countries. While Swedish doctors need not fear malpractice suits (Sweden has a no-fault compensation system for medical accidents somewhat similar to our workers' compensation system) and malpractice litigation is relatively rare in Great Britain, U.S. doctors are acutely aware of the possibility of legal liability if an infant is impaired.

U.S. doctors are likewise highly conscious of DHHS's position concerning nontreatment and of the danger of being reported to child abuse agencies for withholding treatment. The U.S. doctor who described three infants with bronchopulmonary dysplasia who were, against her better judgment, still being aggressively treated, felt that it was the hospital's legal interests that were being protected, not the baby's medical ones. Swedish doctors face no such pressures; British doctors are beginning to experience some, but very few in comparison to this country.

In seeking to explain the differences, doctors themselves often invoked economics and the impact of the various countries' different health care systems. Some in each country attributed questionable motives to foreign practitioners: for example, U.S. doctors suggested that the British terminate treatment because of the greater societal willingness to ration medical care, while British physicians suggested that their U.S. counterparts prolong treatment so as to profit financially.

Such economic factors should probably not be viewed (except in the hands of the occasional unethical practitioner) as overtly influential. More likely, along with other factors, they contribute to making a certain style of medical practice seem most appropriate. But whatever the cause, although all three countries have the same sophisticated medical technology, U.S. doctors use this technology more aggressively. Professor A. G. M. Campbell, formerly at Yale-New Haven Hospital, and now head of neonatology at the University of Aberdeen, Scotland, suggests that there is more enchantment with technological achievement in the U.S.—a Mt. Everest sort of syndrome.

Cultural differences in the behavior of patients and doctors in the various countries may also influence strategy. It is often said that U.S. patients are more assertive, seek more information, place less faith in the physician, and more often invoke their right to make treatment decisions. There is certainly more emphasis on patients' legal rights and informed consent. How much difference this actually makes is unclear, especially given the other pressures on U.S. doctors. Doctors in all three countries repeatedly stated that the way they present information can almost always influence parents to follow the doctor's preference. Other cultural differences, such as those affecting the conduct of doctors, may be at least as important: several British doctors suggested that they require less prognostic certainty before withdrawing treatment than their American colleagues because their expectations about predictive abilities are more modest. As one put it, "We can't predict the weather here from day to day or even hour to hour. So we just don't expect as much certainty in life."

EVALUATION OF STRATEGIES

Putting aside the reasons that may influence doctors to adopt divergent strategies, we can assess the strategies simply as strategies. Naturally, no assessment can be value-neutral in regard to principles for making decisions. Hence I should say that I find a vitalist principle, even a modified one oversimplified and inappropriate for this ethically complex area. I do not believe that the goal should be to save *every* minimally conscious infant; rather we should strive to save those that can actively experience, at least to some extent, their lives. The problem, then, is how best to do this when prognosis is uncertain.

THE "WAIT UNTIL CERTAINTY" APPROACH

From my discussions with physicians in this country, it appears that an increasing number are feeling constrained to continue aggressive treatment until death or irreversible coma seems almost certain, and that those doctors who initiate discussions about termination of treatment earlier, or because of quality-of-life concerns, increasingly feel themselves in the minority. While one could adopt this "wait until certainty" approach in tandem with a vitalist substantive principle, it can readily stand on its own as one type of response to prognostic uncertainty.

Someone could believe that certain disabilities are worse than death, such that certainty about them justifies nontreatment, and still argue that treatment should continue if there is *any* chance that a baby can survive with an acceptable quality of life. With asphyxia or prematurity, such a proponent would hold that given four possible outcomes—(1) saving an infant whose life will be tolerable; (2) letting go one whose life will not be tolerable; (3) saving an infant who would not have been treated had doctors known the outcome; or (4) not treating an infant who would have been treated had doctors known the outcome—outcome (4) should be avoided at all costs. This position ranks the error of

letting an infant die who could have lived a tolerable life as being far worse than saving an infant who is devastatingly disabled. The "wait until certainty" strategy thus ensures that all errors are in one direction—on the side of life. It resembles the criminal law approach, which holds that it is better to acquit ninety-nine guilty defendants than to convict one innocent person.

Erring on the side of life is in general an appropriate principle, even though in individual cases some persons may see prolongation of a hopeless existence as the greater tragedy. Thus agreeing with the moral judgment that outcome (4) is a worse type of error than outcome (3) argues in favor of adopting the decision strategy that minimizes outcome (4)'s chances—treating until certainty. In the context of choice under uncertainty, one can pursue a policy that focuses upon the worst potential outcome and avoids it at all cost. This is known as a maximin strategy.[14] The strategy of always starting treatment and waiting until certainty to stop is this sort of strategy; it takes all steps necessary to avoid the outcome it deems worst—failing to save an infant who could have lived well.

Both psychologically and ethically, this maximin-type strategy has certain advantages. Because doctors will err only on the side of life, each infant's right to life is respected to the greatest possible extent. With their course set in advance, doctors will neither agonize over whether to stop treatment nor wonder afterwards whether they gave up too soon, sealing the fate of a baby who could have survived. Nor will parents be faced with the guilt that they participated in a decision to let their child die. Treatment can be terminated only where death or a terribly impaired life is inevitable—for example, with some chromosomal disorders or severe central nervous system malformations such as hydranencephaly, in which the cerebellum has been destroyed and the cranial vault is filled with fluid,[15] or complete holoprosencephaly, in which the brain fails to divide into separate hemispheres.[16] Perhaps a very few cases of prematurity or asphyxia would fall into this category as well. Thus the approach yields a comforting degree of certainty.

This strategy, however, has some drawbacks. Maximin strategies are most commonly proposed for choices made in complete ignorance of probabilities.[17] Clearly, the less that is known about an infant's prognosis, the more compelling is the reason to treat. However, after a period of treatment and observation, doctors usually have *some* basis for making predictions. Numerous doctors stated that the combination of ultrasound, CT scanning, and clinical observation gave them a very good sense as to which infants would suffer severe neurological handicaps if they survived. Of course, errors are always possible, but according to one physician, "If you have a child of 700 grams with a large hemorrhage and a massive amount of blood within the substance of the brain, we have enough data to know the likelihood of normal neurological development is essentially zero."[18]

As chances for severe impairment increase, this maximin strategy will at some point clash with the substantive principle that parents can legitimately view some outcomes as worse than death. Since this strategy will inevitably maximize the number of infants who die slowly over weeks or months, as well as the number who live, but in a hopelessly impaired condition, it seems most appropriate when knowledge about a particular infant's chances is absent, but increasingly inappropriate as the data suggest that a child's risk of profound handicap is extremely high. In other words, a drawback of this approach is that it ignores the good medical basis for predicting that severe impairment is highly probable, though not certain.

This approach likewise pays insufficient heed to the suffering that neonatal intensive care can cause. The infant's existence will often consist of painful and invasive medical procedures and innumerable crises. As prognosis dims, it becomes harder to justify forcing the child to endure this and the parents to watch.[19] Moreover, one doctor whose treatment practices are growing closer to the "wait until certainty" strategy says that the increase in profoundly handicapped survivors discourages doctors from following up on graduates of the NICU. Follow-up, once a joy, is now agonizing.

Perhaps the most significant drawback is that this strategy denies the ethical complexity. Doctors who follow it, whether because of their own inclinations or legal concerns, will increasingly be governed by technology instead of employing it as a tool. The parents' role is likewise reduced to that of onlookers, since the decisions, so long as there is any uncertainty, have been rendered medical rather than ethical. This result is particularly unfortunate, because physicians in the U.S. appear increasingly sensitive to the need to in-

volve parents in making these decisions. American physicians appear to be somewhat less paternalistic or autocratic than doctors in either Sweden or Britain. Although Swedish and British physicians tend to dispute this, it was my impression that while doctors in other countries frequently informed parents of the situation, they were somewhat less likely to encourage parents to participate in making the decisions.

THE STATISTICAL PROGNOSTIC STRATEGY

At the opposite end of the spectrum is the typical Swedish approach of withholding treatment from infants for whom prognosis is grim. This approach could be called the "statistical prognostic strategy." It does not regard the death of an individual infant who could have been saved as the worst type of error, although presumably losing a great many such babies would be undesirable. This strategy instead seeks to minimize the number of infants who die slow deaths or who live with profound handicaps, and is willing to sacrifice some potentially "good" survivors to achieve this goal. Just as a maximin or "treat until certainty" approach prevents the death of salvageable infants by maximizing the number of extremely handicapped survivors, this statistical prognostic strategy sacrifices potentially normal infants to avoid creating severely impaired survivors.

This approach, of course, is only as good as the statistical data upon which it relies. At the extreme, statistics can be very reliable, as in the case of the 530-gram infant born at week 23 or 24. For more borderline cases—such as the 680-gram, 26-week infant—the data are less compelling. In these cases, a drawback of this approach is that it is virtually impossible to extrapolate from the chances of death or disability in a given population to the chances in a particular individual. Hence some infants denied artificial ventilation could have survived intact, although there is no way to know which ones.

Having a statistical cut-off for starting treatment undoubtedly makes these decisions psychologically easier, because it is harder on doctors, nurses, and parents alike to begin treatment and then terminate it than never to begin. Since most Swedish doctors I interviewed felt that withholding treatment from the beginning is morally preferable to withdrawing it, they understandably adopt this strategy. Although many Swedish physicians stated that withdrawing treatment would violate Swedish homicide law, the law is completely silent on this issue.

Does the withholding/withdrawing distinction have ethical merit as well as emotional benefits? According to the President's Commission, it does not. Noting that prognostic information is usually better after a trial of treatment, it states:

> Ironically, if there is any call to draw a moral distinction between withholding and withdrawing, it generally cuts the opposite way from the usual formulation: greater justification ought to be required to withhold than to withdraw treatment.[20]

Since statistical data about categories of infants are seldom as good as information about a particular infant gained during a trial period of treatment, the statistical approach undoubtedly loses more salvageable survivors than is necessary or justifiable. Once we recognize that the withholding/withdrawing distinction in fact cuts the opposite way, this undermines any moral, as opposed to psychological, reason to favor this approach.

Moreover, this strategy, like the maximin one, minimizes the role of parents, since in cases where treatment is never initiated, parents may not realize there was a choice. This is not inevitable—in units that use a cut-off, parents could be informed of their baby's statistical chances of death or disability and could participate in the decision. However, the time constraints make parental involvement in the delivery room rather unlikely. Also, like the maximin strategy, this approach's definitive and rule-based character clashes with the complex, ambiguous nature of these situations. Of course, a cut-off may sometimes be appropriate, because at the extremes, statistics yield excellent predictions. A flexible or presumptive cut-off could be used in those cases, in conjunction with a willingness to start treatment in questionable cases and to stop it when this seems appropriate.[21] However, a pure statistical strategy brings with it the dual dangers of rigidity and of minimization of the ethical component.

THE INDIVIDUALIZED PROGNOSTIC STRATEGY

The typical British approach—starting treatment and then reevaluating based on clinical indications of ultimate death or severe brain damage—can be called the "individualized prognostic strategy." It can be time-limited, as with birth asphyxia, or it can be unlimited, as is more common with extreme prematurity. A time-limited approach is less than ideal from the perspective of obtaining maximum information. It is used only in situations where continuing treatment indefinitely will mean, in practice, that even the most profoundly impaired infants will survive.

Since time limitations raise the question of whether it is preferable to produce more extremely impaired survivors or to risk losing some babies that might have thrived despite their condition at forty-eight or seventy-two hours, British doctors have a strong incentive to develop early and accurate prognostic tests. Hence they are investigating the use of phosphorus nuclear magnetic resonance spectroscopy to detect, at twenty-four hours, derangements of brain biochemistry in asphyxiated infants that may predict eventual death or profound retardation.[22] Such research, however, is very preliminary; the researchers themselves warn that physicians routinely hope that a particular test will predict outcome only to learn that it will not.

The individualized prognostic strategy avoids the extremes of either treating all infants until the outcome is certain or withholding treatment because the infant is in a class whose prognosis is grim. Neither type of mistake—sacrificing a potentially "good" infant or saving a severely impaired one—is necessarily to be avoided at all costs. Doctors employing this strategy err in both directions, though they seek, through clinical observations, to minimize each type of mistake. They optimistically initiate treatment in borderline cases, to give these babies a chance. However, while there is an ethical reason to begin treatment, there is no equally compelling reason not to pull back once a child's prognosis appears poor. As Jeff Lyon puts it in *Playing God in the Nursery*, "What the hand of science sets loose, it can bring to heel."

The individualized prognostic strategy allows for a wide—perhaps too wide—variation in treatment decisions. Those doctors who rely on it, including many in this country as well as Great Britain, may differ as to *how likely* death or devastating impairment must be before withdrawal of treatment becomes a legitimate option. In fact, the real difference between typical American and British practices may be in the degree of certainty they seek. The degree of risk that justifies letting parents opt to terminate and/or the degree of uncertainty that requires overriding their wishes and pressing onward is a difficult ethical question. An individualized approach brings this question to the forefront of ethical deliberation, though it does not provide an answer. Yet raising the question is itself important. The Swedes virtually never raised this question. The British almost always did. American doctors are acutely aware of it, although many say the current legal climate has inhibited forthright confrontation of this issue.

The individualized prognostic strategy allows confusion, uncertainty, and errors. Sometimes treatment will yield an infant so devastatingly disabled that death would have seemed preferable. Likewise, doctors may withdraw treatment from a baby who possibly could have survived relatively intact. Doctors will agonize over decisions. Parents will agonize as well, since a nonrule-based approach, where treatment is started and then evaluated, has the distinct advantage of allowing far more room for parental involvement. Doctors and parents may later regret their decision or be tormented by it. This agonizing, however, is only commensurate with the tragic nature of these dilemmas. In fact, those approaches that minimize it may be inappropriate for precisely that reason. When medical uncertainty leads to moral uncertainty, it seems preferable, albeit harder, to confront these dual ambiguities than to bury them under either statistical criteria or unrelenting moral certitude.

Thus, the individualized prognostic strategy seems best. It is most consistent with a clinical practice sensitive to the parents' role and unconstrained either by an oversimplistic vitalism, excessive fear of legal liability, or an emotionally appealing but ethically untenable distinction between withholding and withdrawing treatment. This strategy both recognizes and reflects the complex nature of these dilemmas. It is not without flaws—but it is probably the best that doctors, parents, and society can do.

DECISION STRATEGIES AND SPINA BIFIDA

Although the individualized prognostic strategy appears preferable, doctors may: (1) fail to correlate prognostic criteria with a defensible substantive standard as to what sorts of impairments can warrant withholding of treatment; (2) adopt criteria that allow withholding in too many cases; (3) overly influence parents to follow the physician's recommendations; or (4) inflate the criteria's predictive value and/or neglect to revise the criteria to reflect medical advances.

British spina bifida policy illustrates several of these dangers. After many years of surgically closing the spinal lesions in all such infants, John Lorber, an influential British pediatrician, concluded that far too many survivors were severely handicapped. He therefore recommended withholding surgery from infants with large, high-level lesions, gross hydrocephalus [too much fluid around the brain], spinal deformities such as kyphosis or scoliosis [curvature of the spine], severe paralysis of the legs, or additional anomalies.[23] (The level of the lesion, degree of paralysis, and spinal deformities define the physical disability: hydrocephalus increases the risk of mental retardation.) Lorber initially reported virtually 100 percent mortality among the infants selected for nontreatment, which in his unit constituted over half of the total.[24]

Lorber's recommendations were extremely influential in Great Britain. All the British physicians I interviewed practiced selection more or less along Lorber's lines. Some used slightly different criteria or cut-offs, and physicians in several locations emphasized that this had been their practice before Lorber suggested it.

Lorber's recommendations were influential, though much less so, in the United States. Some American doctors thought the criteria were too strict: others objected that some untreated infants survived, and that withholding surgery worsened their handicaps.[25] These objections, along with advances in treatment techniques, ultimately influenced the majority of American doctors to operate on all but the worst 5 to 20 percent of spina bifida infants—those with extremely large, high lesions, or gross hydrocephalus and indications of massive brain damage, or those with an additional anomaly such as microcephaly.[26] The Swedish practice is similar.

British doctors today are acutely conscious of the problem of treating infants whose lesions are not closed. They all said that such infants will not be given antibiotics or artificial feeding. Most die of infection, but those who do not will, if necessary, be shunted for hydrocephalus, both to make nursing care easier and to prevent further brain damage. Also, if such an infant lives for several months, the lesion may heal by itself. Since the infant will no longer be especially susceptible to infection, doctors will reassess and often provide all necessary treatment. British doctors deny adamantly that unexpected survivors are harmed by withholding surgery. Because surgery merely preserves neurological function, they state that withholding it from an infant already paralyzed cannot worsen the physical handicap, and that shunting unexpected survivors prevents additional brain damage.

The British approach to spina bifida is an individualized prognostic strategy with statistical aspects. Assessing the individual infant yields excellent prognostic information about physical impairment. However, a high lesion and severe hydrocephalus correlate less clearly with retardation, and provide far less certainty than do such symptoms as prolonged unresponsiveness from asphyxia or severe tissue damage from Grade IV hemorrhages. Rather, they simply place the infant in a category that is at risk for neurological impairment. But however this strategy is classified, it clearly evaluates quality of life both in terms of physical impairment and mental handicap, because the 40 to 50 percent of spina bifida infants who are denied surgery will include a significant number with potentially normal or near-normal mental capacity. The differences between British and American (and Swedish) spina bifida policies may reflect a difference in substantive principles; the British may accept Lorber's view that physical handicaps such as paralysis and incontinence can make life unbearable even if intelligence is normal or only mildly impaired.

In discussions about substantive principles, however, British doctors stressed ability to relate to the environment or other persons far more than physical capacity. Hence their continued adherence to Lorber's selection criteria could reflect a strategic choice of sacrificing a significant number of infants whose lives would have been tolerable rather than saving additional extremely handicapped children. While no strategy for choice under uncertainty will avoid erring in one or more directions, Lorber's criteria seem too strict to be consistent with a substantive principle that emphasizes human interactions. Most likely, British spina bifida policy illustrates the dangers of inflating the predictive value of the criteria and/or failing to revise them when new studies reveal their limitations or when related medical techniques improve.

The line Lorber drew was probably far more justifiable in 1971 than it is today, because techniques for treating almost all the complications of spina bifida have substantially improved. Any individualized prognostic strategy must be continually reevaluated to ensure that it reflects a defensible substantive principle for decision making as well as any medical advances.

Finally, any strategy that potentially allows untreated survivors must incorporate safeguards to ensure that they are not harmed. This problem is not unique to spina bifida. While the Swedes claim that their practice of giving "special care" to infants weighing less than 750 grams does not harm the few babies who survive without being initially placed on a respirator, doctors in other countries (and a few in Sweden) tend to be skeptical, suggesting that halfway measures may increase the chances of brain damage. I cannot judge this on its facts; however, the temptation to downplay the disadvantages of a chosen policy is understandably great. No strategy will be perfect, but ethical analysis requires the forthright recognition of the flaws in each approach.

Baby Doe dilemmas are wrenching even when prognosis is clear. When there is prognostic uncertainty, they are doubly disturbing. As Lyon has put it: "If it is hard to justify creating blind paraplegics to obtain a number of healthy survivors, it is equally hard to explain to the ghosts of the potentially healthy that they had to die in order to avoid creating blind paraplegics."

I have argued that the strategy of waiting until certainty denies both parental discretion and the ethical component of these dilemmas. The statistical strategy, while perhaps appropriate in extreme cases, likewise minimizes moral complexity and unnecessarily sacrifices babies who could survive. The best strategy, or the "least worst" one, is the individualized prognostic approach, where doctors start treatment, gather as much data as possible, and then reassess. This strategy denies neither the ethical component of these decisions nor the need for a parental role.

As long as the medical criteria are viewed as guides rather than absolutes, and as long as they remain flexible enough to accommodate medical advances, this approach best reflects, and responds to, the indeterminacy inherent in these most difficult dilemmas. There will be ghosts, and there will be profoundly retarded, crib-bound survivors, but our society will have even more explaining to do if we blind ourselves to the tragic and complex nature of these choices in the newborn nursery.

ACKNOWLEDGMENTS

I would like to thank John Arras, Ronald Carson, Alan Fleischman, Thomas Murray, Judith Ross, and Bill Winslade for helpful comments on an earlier draft of this article, and the German Marshall Fund for making this research possible. I would also like to thank the numerous experts in Sweden, Great Britain and the United States with whom I consulted.

NOTES

1. For a discussion of vitalism, see Richard McCormick, "To Save or Let Die," *Journal of the American Medical Association,* 229 (1984), 172,174.

2. See 49 Fed Reg. 1,621 (1984).

3. United States v. University Hospital, State University of New York at Stony Brook, 575 F. Supp. 607 (E.D.N.Y. 1983), aff'd 729 F.2d 144 (2d. Cir. 1984); *Bowen v. American Hospital Association,* 54 LW 4579 (U.S. Sup. Ct., June 9, 1986), affirming American Hospital Association v. Heckler, 585 F. Supp. 541 (S.D.N.Y.), aff'd, Nos. 84–6211 and 84–6231 (2d Cir. Dec. 27, 1984).

4. Amendments to Child Abuse Prevention and Treatment Act, 98 Stat.1749 (1984) (codified as amended at 42 U.S.C.A. SS 5101–5104 (West. Supp. 1985).

5. For a critique of vitalism and an argument for a quality-of-life standard, see Nancy Rhoden and John Arras, "Withholding Treatment from Baby Doe: From Discrimination to Child Abuse," *Milbank Memorial Fund Quarterly,* 63 (1985), 18; and Nancy Rhoden, "Treatment Dilemmas for Imperiled Newborns: Why Quality of Life Counts," *Southern California Law Review,* 58 (1985), 1283.

6. This standard is recommended in an influential Swedish article. See L. Fohlin et al., "Views Concerning Level of Care When Very Immature Infants Are Cared For at the Perinatal State," *Lakartidningen* 79 (1982), 3579–3580 (recommending providing incubator care and an adequate thermal and oxygen environment only to infants born at 24 or 25 weeks). (Translated by Francis P. Walsh of Stockholm.)

7. See W. Allen Hodson & D. A. Belenky, "Management of Respiratory Problems," in *Neonatology: Pathophysiology and Management of the Newborn,* Gordon Avery, ed. (Philadelphia: Lippincott, 1975), 265, 283.

8. See Ernlé Young, "Caring for Disabled Infants," *Hastings Center Report,* 13 (August 1983), 15–16.

9. See e.g., Edward Brett, "Neurology of the Newborn," in *Pediatric Neurology,* Edward Brett, ed. (Livingstone, N.Y.: Churchill, 1983), 15, 21.

10. See James F. Schwartz, et al, "Neonatal Intracranial Hemorrhage and Hypoxia," in *Neurologic Emergencies in Infancy and Childhood,* John Pellock & Edwin Myer, eds. (Philadelphia: Lippincott, 1984), 37, 43.

11. See S. Schechner, "For the 1980's: How Small Is Too Small?" *Clinics in Perinatology,* 7 (1980), 142; See also William Kirkley, "Fetal Survival—What Price," *American Journal of Obstetrics & Gynecology,* 137 (1980), 873, (suggesting cut-off of 1000 grams if the infant is severely asphyxiated at birth). But see Carson Strong, "The Tiniest Newborns," *Hastings Center Report* 13: (February 1983), 14–19, (arguing against use of any such cutoff weight for aggressive treatment).

12. See Symposium on Neonatal Asphyxia, *Paediatricus,* 9 (March 1979), 1,22.

13. *Id.* See "On Treatment of Birth Asphyxia," Barnkliniken, Lund, January 1984.

14. See Daniel Albert, "Decision Theory in Medicine," *Milbank Memorial Fund Quarterly,* 56 (1978), 362, 384.

15. See Sheldon Korones, *High Risk Newborn Infants,* 3d ed. (St. Louis: Mosby, 1981), 165.

16. See David Smith, *Recognizable Patterns of Human Malformation,* 3d ed. (Philadelphia: Saunder, 1982), 460.

17. Albert, p. 384. See John Rawls, *A Theory of Justice* (1971), 150–61; Brian Barry, *The Liberal Theory of Justice* (1973), 88–90.

18. Dr. Joseph Volpe, pediatric neurologist, St. Louis Children's Hospital, quoted in Jeffrey Lyon, *Playing God in the Nursery* (New York: W. W. Norton, 1985), 123–24.

19. See Robert Stinson & Peggy Stinson, *The Long Dying of Baby Andrew* (Boston: Little, Brown, 1983).

20. President's Commission for the Study of Ethical Problems in Medicine and Biomedical and Behavioral Research, *Deciding to Forego Life-Sustaining Treatment,* (1983), 76.

21. See A. G. M. Campbell, "Which Infants Should Not Receive Intensive Care?" *Archives of Disease in Childhood,* 57 (1982), 569 (proposing a flexible cut-off and significant parental discretion in decision making).

22. See P. L. Hope, et al, "Cerebral Energy Metabolism Studied with Phosphorous N.M.R. Spectroscopy in Normal and Birth-Asphyxiated Infants," *The Lancet* (August 18, 1984), 366.

23. See e.g., John Lorber, "Results of Treatment of Myelomeningocele," *Developmental Medicine in Child Neurology,* 13 (1971), 279, 290; Lorber, "Ethical Problems in the Management of Myelomeningocele and Hydrocephalus," *Journal of the Royal College of Physicians* 10 (1975), 46, 53.

24. Lorber, "Early Results of Selective Treatment of Spina Bifida Cystica," *British Medical Journal,* 4 (1973), 201, 203–04.

25. John M. Freeman, "To Treat or Not to Treat: Ethical Dilemmas of Treating the Infant With a Myelomeningocele," *Clinical Neurosurgery,* 20 (1973), 134, 143–44.

26. See Anthony Gallo, "The Case of Baby Jane Doe, Spina Bifida: The State of the Art of Medical Management," *Hastings Center Report,* 14 (February 1984), 10,11. See also Jane Stein, *Making Medical Choices: Who is Responsible?* (Boston: Houghton Mifflin, 1978) 114, quoting Georgetown doctors saying that about 20 percent of spina bifida babies are so severely disabled that they are not treated surgically.

SUGGESTED READINGS

GENERAL ISSUES

American Medical Association, Council on Ethical and Judicial Affairs. "Decisions Near the End of Life." *Journal of the American Medical Association* 267 (1992), 2229–2233.

Berger, Arthur S., and Berger, Joyce, eds. *To Die or Not to Die? Cross-Disciplinary, Cultural, and Legal Perspectives on the Right to Choose Death.* New York: Praeger, 1990.

Brody, Baruch. *Life and Death Decision Making.* New York: Oxford University Press, 1988.

Callahan, Daniel. "Medical Futility, Medical Necessity: The Problem-Without-a-Name." *Hastings Center Report* 21 (July–August 1991), 30–35.

Cantor, Norman L. *Legal Frontiers of Death and Dying.* Bloomington, IN: Indiana University Press, 1987.

Cohen, Cynthia B., ed. *Casebook on the Termination of Life-Sustaining Treatment and the Care of the Dying.* Briarcliff Manor, NY: The Hastings Center, 1988. Distributed by Indiana University Press.

Feinberg, Joel. "Overlooking the Merits of the Individual Case: An Unpromising Approach to the Right to Die." *Ratio Juris* 4 (1991), 131–151.

Glick, Henry R. *The Right to Die: Policy Innovation and Its Consequences.* New York: Columbia University Press, 1992.

The Hastings Center. *Guidelines on the Termination of Life-Sustaining Treatment and the Care of the Dying*. Bloomington, IN: Indiana University Press, 1988.

Kamisar, Yale. "When Is There a Constitutional 'Right to Die'? When Is There *No* Constitutional 'Right to Live'?" *Georgia Law Review* 25 (1991), 1203–1242.

Lynn, Joanne, ed. *By No Extraordinary Means*. Bloomington, IN: Indiana University Press, 1986.

Meisel, Alan. "The Legal Consensus about Forgoing Life-Sustaining Treatment: Its Status and Its Prospects." *Kennedy Institute of Ethics Journal* 2 (1992), 309–345.

Meisel, Alan. *The Right to Die*. New York: Wiley, 1989. Cumulative Supplement published in 1992.

Meyers, David W. *The Human Body and the Law*. 2nd ed. Stanford, CA: Stanford University Press, 1990.

Momeyer, Richard W. *Confronting Death*. Bloomington, IN: Indiana University Press, 1988.

Moskop, John C., and Kopelmann, Loretta, eds. *Ethics and Critical Care Medicine*. Boston: D. Reidel, 1985.

President's Commission for the Study of Ethical Problems in Medicine and Biomedical and Behavioral Research. *Deciding to Forego Life-Sustaining Treatment*. Washington, DC: U.S. Government Printing Office, March 1983.

Ramsey, Paul. *The Patient as Person*. New Haven, CT: Yale University Press, 1970. Chapter 3.

Rhoden, Nancy K. "Litigating Life and Death." *Harvard Law Review* 102 (1988), 375–446.

Schneiderman, Lawrence J.; Jecker, Nancy S.; and Jonsen, Albert R. "Medical Futility: It's Meaning and Ethical Implications." *Annals of Internal Medicine* 112 (1990), 949–954.

Stanley, John M. Appleton International Conference 1991. "The Appleton International Conference: Developing Guidelines for Decisions to Forgo Life-Prolonging Medical Treatment." *Journal of Medical Ethics* 18 (Supplement; September 1992), S3–S22.

Truog, Robert; Brett, Allan S.; and Frader, Joel. "The Problem with Futility." *New England Journal of Medicine* 326 (1992), 1560–1564.

United States, Congress, Office of Technology Assessment. *Life-Sustaining Technologies and the Elderly*. Washington, DC: U.S. Government Printing Office, July 1987.

Veatch, Robert M. *Death, Dying and the Biological Revolution: Our Last Quest for Responsibility*. Revised ed. New Haven, CT: Yale University Press, 1989.

Veatch, Robert M., and Spicer, Carol Mason. "Medically Futile Care: The Role of the Physician in Setting Limits." *American Journal of Law and Medicine* 18 (1992), 15–36.

Weir, Robert F. *Abating Treatment with Critically Ill Patients: Ethical and Legal Limits to the Medical Prolongation of Life*. New York: Oxford University Press, 1989.

Weir, Robert F., ed. *Ethical Issues in Death and Dying*. 2nd ed. New York: Columbia University Press, 1986.

DECISIONS BY COMPETENT ADULTS

Annas, George J. "The Health Care Proxy and the Living Will." *New England Journal of Medicine* 324 (1991), 1210–1213.

Areen, Judith. "Advance Directives under State Law and Judicial Decisions." *Law, Medicine and Health Care* 19 (1991), 91–100.

Battin, Margaret Pabst. "The Least Worst Death." *Hastings Center Report* 13 (April 1983), 13–16.

Cantor, Normal L. "My Annotated Living Will." *Law, Medicine and Health Care* 18 (1990), 114–122.

Capron, Alexander Morgan. "The Patient Self-Determination Act: A Cooperative Model for Implementation." *Cambridge Quarterly of Healthcare Ethics* 1 (1992), 97–106.

Choice in Dying. *Advance Directive Protocols and the Patient Self-Determination Act: A Resource Manual for the Development of Institutional Protocols*. New York: Choice in Dying, 1991.

Colen, B. D. *The Essential Guide to a Living Will: How to Protect Your Right to Refuse Medical Treatment*. New York: Prentice-Hall, 1991.

Hackler, Chris; Moseley, Ray; and Vawter, Dorothy E., eds. *Advance Directives in Medicine*. New York: Praeger, 1989.

King, Nancy M. P. *Making Sense of Advance Directives*. Boston: Kluwer Academic Publishers, 1991.

Kliever, Lonnie D., ed. *Dax's Case: Essays in Medical Ethics and Human Meaning*. Dallas: Southern Methodist University Press, 1989.

McCloskey, Elizabeth Leibold. "The Patient Self-Determination Act." *Kennedy Institute of Ethics Journal* 1 (1991), 163–169.

Miles, Steven H.; Singer, Peter A.; and Siegler, Mark. "Conflicts Between Patients' Wishes to Forgo Treatment and the Policies of Health Care Facilities." *New England Journal of Medicine* 321 (1989), 48–50.

Orentlicher, David. "The Illusion of Patient Choice in End-of-Life Decisions." *Journal of the American Medical Association* 267 (1992), 2101–2104.

Robertson, John A. "Second Thoughts on Living Wills." *Hastings Center Report* 21 (November–December 1991), 6–9.

Singer, Peter A., et al. "Advance Directives: Are They an Advance?" *Canadian Medical Association Journal* 146 (1992), 127–134.

Society for the Right to Die. *Refusal of Treatment Legislation, 1991: A State by State Compilation of Enacted and Model Statutes*. New York: The Society, March 1991.

United States. "The Patient Self-Determination Act" (Sections 4206 and 4751 of the Omnibus Budget Reconciliation Act of 1990). *[United States] Statutes at Large*, November 5, 1990.

DECISIONS ON BEHALF OF THE FORMERLY COMPETENT

Annas, George J. "Nancy Cruzan and the Right to Die." *New England Journal of Medicine* 323 (1990), 670–673.

Annas, George J., et al. "Bioethicists' Statement on the U.S. Supreme Court's Cruzan Decision." *New England Journal of Medicine* 323 (1990), 686–687.

Brody, Baruch. "Special Ethical Issues in the Management of PVS Patients." *Law, Medicine and Health Care* 20 (1992), 104–115.

Campbell, Courtney S., et al. "Cruzan: Clear and Convincing?" *Hastings Center Report* 20 (September–October 1990), 5–11. Introduction and six responses to the decision.

Emanuel, Ezekiel J., and Emanuel, Linda L. "Proxy Decision Making for Incompetent Patients: An Ethical and Empirical Analysis." *Journal of the American Medical Association* 267 (1992), 2067–2071.

Journal of Medicine and Philosophy 17 (1992), 563–681. "Essays in the Aftermath of Cruzan."

Law, Medicine and Health Care 19 (1991), 5–104. Symposium on the *Cruzan* decision, its context, and its implications.

Lynn, Joanne. "Procedures for Making Medical Decisions for Incompetent Adults" [Editorial]. *Journal of the American Medical Association* 267 (1992), 2082–2084.

Massachusetts, Supreme Judicial Court, Norfolk. *Brophy* v. *New England Sinai Hospital, Inc. North Eastern Reporter,* 2d Series, 497 (1986), 626–646.

Miles, Steven H., and Allison, August. "Court, Gender, and the 'Right to Die'." *Law, Medicine and Health Care* 18 (1990), 85–95.

Robertson, John A. "Cruzan and the Constitutional Status of Nontreatment Decisions for Incompetent Patients." *Georgia Law Review* 25 (1991), 1139–1202.

Veatch, Robert M. "Limits to Guardian Treatment Refusal: A Reasonableness Standard." *American Journal of Law and Medicine* 9 (1984), 427–468.

Weir, Robert F., and Gostin, Larry. "Decisions to Abate Life-Sustaining Treatment for Non-Autonomous Patients: Ethical Standards and Legal Liability for Physicians after *Cruzan*." *Journal of the American Medical Association* 264 (1990), 1846–1853.

DECISIONS ABOUT INFANTS

Anspach, Renée R. *Deciding Who Lives: Fateful Choices in the Intensive-Care Nursery.* Berkeley: University of California Press, 1993.

Caplan, Arthur A.; Blank, Robert H.; and Merrick, Janna C., eds. *Compelled Compassion: Government Intervention in the Treatment of Critically Ill Newborns.* Totowa, NJ: Humana Press, 1992.

Fleischman, Alan R. "Parental Responsibility and the Infant Bioethics Committee." *Hastings Center Report* 20 (March–April 1990), 31–32.

King, Nancy M. P. "Transparency in Neonatal Intensive Care." *Hastings Center Report* 22 (May–June 1992), 18–25.

Hastings Center Research Project on the Care of Imperiled Newborns. "Imperiled Newborns: A Report." *Hastings Center Report* 17 (December 1987), 5–32.

Law, Medicine and Health Care 17 (1989), 295–346. Symposium on the Linares case.

Kuhse, Helga, and Singer, Peter. *Should the Baby Live? The Problem of Handicapped Newborns.* New York: Oxford University Press, 1985.

Murray, Thomas H., and Caplan, Arthur L., eds. *Which Babies Shall Live? Humanistic Dimensions of the Care of Imperiled Newborns.* Clifton, NJ: Humana Press, 1985.

Newman, Stephan A. "Baby Doe, Congress and the States: Challenging the Federal Treatment Standard for Impaired Infants." *American Journal of Law and Medicine* 15 (1989), 1–60.

Moskop, John C., and Saldanha, Rita L. "The Baby Doe Rule: Still a Threat." *Hastings Center Report* 16 (April 1986), 8–14.

United States, Department of Health and Human Services. "Child Abuse and Neglect Prevention and Treatment." *Federal Register* 50 (1985), 14873–14892.

Weir, Robert F. *Selective Treatment of Handicapped Newborns.* New York: Oxford University Press, 1984.

BIBLIOGRAPHIES

Goldstein, Doris Mueller. *Bioethics: A Guide to Information Sources.* Detroit: Gale Research Company, 1982. See under "Death and Dying."

Lineback, Richard H., ed. *Philosopher's Index.* Vols. 1–27. Bowling Green OH: Philosophy Documentation Center, Bowling Green State University. Issued quarterly. See under "Death," "Dying," "Euthanasia," and "Letting Die."

McCarrick, Pat Milmoe. "Living Wills and Durable Powers of Attorney: Advance Directive Legislation and Issues." *Scope Note 2.* Washington, DC: Kennedy Institute of Ethics, Georgetown University, September 1991.

McCarrick, Pat Milmoe. "Withholding or Withdrawing Nutrition or Hydration." *Scope Note 7.* Washington, DC: Kennedy Institute of Ethics, Georgetown University, March 1992.

Walters, LeRoy, and Kahn, Tamar Joy, eds. *Bibliography of Bioethics.* Vols. 1–19. Washington, DC: Kennedy Institute of Ethics, Georgetown University. Issued annually. See under "Allowing to Die," "Euthanasia," "Resuscitation Orders," and "Terminal Care." (The information contained in the annual *Bibliography* can also be retrieved from BIOETHICSLINE, an on-line database of the National Library of Medicine, and from *BIOETHICSLINE Plus*, a CD-ROM disc distributed by Silver-Platter.)

7.

Active Euthanasia and Assisted Suicide

INTRODUCTION

There is no stronger or more enduring prohibition in medicine than the rule against killing patients. Yet many arguments in the current literature on medical ethics suggest a need to reform both the law and medical practice. One modern trend is toward more flexibility in allowing persons who are seriously or terminally ill to die. In the discussion of these issues various words and phrases have been employed. They include: "death with dignity," "euthanasia," "allowing to die," "assisted suicide," and "mercy killing."

Several questions are addressed in this chapter about killing and letting die. Some are conceptual, some are normative, and some are both. The primary questions are: Is forgoing life-sustaining treatment sometimes a form of killing and, if so, is it suicide or euthanasia? What, if anything, distinguishes killing from letting die? Are there *morally relevant* differences between killing and letting die? Under what conditions, if any, is it permissible for health professionals to engage in assisted suicide or active euthanasia?

FORGOING TREATMENT, CAUSING DEATH, AND KILLING

Physicians and nurses have long worried and continue to worry that when they withdraw treatment and a patient dies, they will be accused of killing the patient and will be subject to criminal liability. A parallel concern exists that patients who withdraw or withhold treatment are killing themselves and that health professionals assist in the suicide if they acknowledge the refusal. Typical cases involve persons suffering from a terminal illness or mortal injury and who, as a consequence, refuse a therapy without which they will die, but with which their life can be extended.

In these cases, are health professionals or surrogates killing their patients by omitting treatment? In the past, physicians, lawyers, and moral philosophers have routinely construed forgoing treatment as letting die, not killing. Courts have explained why when an individual forgoes life-sustaining treatment, the cause of death should not be categorized as either suicide or homicide. The New Jersey Supreme Court and the Supreme Judicial Court of Massachusetts both argue in this chapter that, in acts of forgoing treatment, an underlying disease or injury is the cause of death. They further argue that medical technology — for example, a respirator — only delays the natural course of the disease or injury. When the technology is removed, a "natural death" occurs; natural conditions continue as though the technology had never been initiated. Because disease or injury is the cause of death, not the physician's, surrogate's, or patient's action, it is not homicide or suicide.

This legal premise helps to alleviate the fears of health professionals about moral blame and legal liability. Some critics in this chapter, however, argue that this premise is not consistent with many of our beliefs about killing. Dan Brock points out in his essay that if a man sneaks into a hospital to detach his business rival from a respirator, he does more than release natural conditions. We could not rightly say, "He didn't kill the patient; he only allowed the patient to die." By letting the patient die, he killed him. It would be preposterous in this case to protest a legal indictment by saying, "*I* did not kill him; the disease killed him. I merely allowed him to die." We would also consider the act to be *unjustified.* Yet the man's act seems to be exactly the same act that the physician typically performs (usually at a family's request) in a case of "allowing to die." What the physician does is *causally* no different than what the man off the street does: Machinery is removed and the patient dies as a result. Why, then, does the physician's act not involve killing? Can physicians rightly say "We do not kill our patients; only the underlying diseases and injuries do"?

According to both Brock and Schaffner, the withdrawal or withholding of life-sustaining treatment sometimes constitutes killing; they believe that this occurs in more cases than medicine and law now acknowledge. Generally, the motives *are* proper and there *is* both moral and legal justification for the action. But whether the motive is evil and reprehensible or noble and laudable, the act remains an intentional killing. These philosophers are joined in their opinion by the Superior Court of New Jersey, Appellate Division, which held in *In re Conroy* that removing the NG-tube (nasogastric tube) from 84-year-old Claire Conroy was not merely a matter of forgoing treatment. Because her physicians would dehydrate and starve Conroy, they thereby would cause her death. This court said the patient "would have been actively killed by independent means," which the court said amounted to euthanasia. It therefore reversed an earlier ruling (by the Chancery Division, Essex County) that held that the nasogastric tube could be removed.

However, the Supreme Court of New Jersey later overturned important aspects of the Appellate Division opinion. The Supreme Court found that any medical treatment, including artificial nutrition and hydration, may in principle be justifiably withheld or withdrawn from an incompetent patient. The court held that NG-tubes, for example, are analytically indistinguishable from other forms of life-sustaining treatments, such as respirators. It is not a civil or criminal liability to "allow to die" under legally appropriate conditions of refusal of treatment. All three of these New Jersey opinions appear in this chapter.

One reason for this divergence of opinion, which stretches well beyond New Jersey courts, is terminological. As we see in the appellate court decision, some persons use the term "killing" as a *normative* term meaning unjustified homicide. Justified acts of death, therefore, cannot be instances of killing; they can only be cases of *allowing to die*. Here, in the attempt to protect health-care professionals from charges of killing, *moral* (not *causal*) judgments distinguish "killing" and "allowing to die." From this perspective, physicians do not kill when they justifiably remove a life-sustaining treatment, and patients do not kill themselves when they forego treatment. However, if either *unjustifiably* omits treatment, they kill. "Killing" has thus taken on an intrinsically *moral* meaning; it is no longer merely a *causal* or *factual* category about the cause of death. Schaffner is particularly concerned about this trend of moralizing the cause. He points out that in many cases when physicians at the request of their patients withdraw respirator support, remove feeding tubes, terminate food and water, and the like, they *cause* the patient's death by executing the patient's request. For example, when nutrition and hydration are withheld, the cause of death is starvation, not the underlying health conditions. Anything in the accepted care of patients is not classified as a killing, whereas unusual measures that depart from standard practice may be so classified.

THE DISTINCTION BETWEEN KILLING AND LETTING DIE

We can now address the question, "Can *killing* and *letting die* be defined so that they are conceptually distinct?" Several commentators, including Daniel Callahan in this chapter, assert that a meaningful distinction can be drawn between them. Two major claims are commonly adduced in support of the distinction:

1. Ordinary language — Most English speakers without confusion classify allowing to die as "permitting death to occur," while killing is "causing harm or death."
2. Causation — If a terminally ill or seriously injured patient dies following justified nontreatment, the proximate cause of death is the patient's disease or injury, not non-treatment.

Unfortunately, "ordinary language" is a weak basis for these concepts. In its ordinary language meaning, *killing* is any form of deprivation or destruction of life, including animal and plant life. Neither in ordinary language nor in law does the word "killing" entail a wrongful act or a crime, even if *human* persons are killed (unlike the word "murder," which does entail criminal wrongfulness). Ordinary language also does not require that a killing be *intentional;* for example, it permits us to say that in automobile accidents one driver killed another accidentally.

In ordinary language, *killing* simply represents a family of ideas whose central condition is direct causation of another's death, whereas *allowing to die* represents another family of ideas whose central condition is intentional avoidance of causal intervention so that a natural death is caused by a disease or injury. This is a fuzzy, not a sharp distinction. If we are to retain this distinction there is a need to sharpen these notions by stipulating meanings that are pertinent and useful for medical ethics. For example, "killing" might be used exclusively in circumstances in which one person intentionally and unjustifiably causes the death of another human being. However, this is no longer an ordinary language definition.

Law, medicine, ethics, and ordinary language all recognize that some forms of allowing to die constitute acts of killing. As courts have many times pointed out, the killing of a human being can occur by an act, an omission, or through arrangement with a third party. The same can be said about "allowing to die." These overlaps and similarities between killing and letting die have led to skepticism that a sharp conceptual distinction can be drawn between killing and letting die.

Several readings in this chapter address this issue. James Rachels argues that the cessation of treatment in terminal cases is "the intentional termination of the life of one human being by another" and, more generally, that letting a patient die is an action, not merely an omission. He therefore questions whether any clear conceptual distinction between killing and allowing to die can be sustained. Callahan is much more optimistic about clarifying and using the distinction, whereas Tom Beauchamp argues for retaining the distinction, but in a revised form.

If a distinction between these two notions can be drawn, there is still a problem as to whether the distinction is *morally relevant*. Rachels holds that if it is morally permissible to intend that a patient die, then acting directly to terminate a patient's life is justified if it causes less suffering to the patient than simply allowing him or her to die. By contrast, Beauchamp argues that active or direct killing may not be justified in a particular case even if it causes less suffering for the patient, on grounds that seriously harmful consequences might occur if the killing/letting die distinction were generally viewed as morally irrelevant.

These views are not necessarily inconsistent: One could argue that some particular acts of terminating a patient's life are morally justified but that public policy should not legitimate such actions in the legal system. There are other measures of agreement between Rachels and Beauchamp as well. Neither accepts a simple correlation between the killing/letting die distinction and the wrong/right distinction. On Rachels's theory, killing is not, in itself, morally worse than letting die. That is, the "bare difference" between acts of killing and acts of letting die is not in itself a morally relevant difference. Rachels argues that if it is morally justified to act intentionally so that a person dies, then the morally important question is what makes the act justified, not what *type* of action it is (killing or letting die). Beauchamp agrees that nothing about either killing or allowing to die requires a judgment of wrongness or rightness. Rachels and Beauchamp further agree that whether an act of either killing or letting die can be declared justified or unjustified depends on the facts of the case at hand. For example, we must understand the actor's motive, whether the patient requested the act, and something about the consequences of the act. This claim is sharply denounced in some of the later selections in this chapter.

Rachels, Beauchamp, and the majority of contributors to this chapter agree that *certain* omissions "allowing" another to die are morally or legally blameworthy. The controversial question is whether or not a direct connection exists between killing (a patient) and moral wrongness. Rachels sternly rebukes the American Medical Association for its policy asserting that killing is necessarily wrong.[1] Beauchamp adopts an intermediate position, arguing that there are valid reasons for preserving some form of the killing/letting die distinction in the development of public policy.

VOLUNTARY ACTIVE EUTHANASIA

Conceptual Problems. Originally, *euthanasia* was derived from two Greek roots meaning "good death." In *Webster's Third New International Dictionary,* originally published in 1961, the definition of euthanasia was further specified as (1) "an easy death or means of inducing one" and (2) "the act or practice of painlessly putting to death persons suffering from incurable conditions or diseases." Both employ the language of acting rather than omitting to act, suggesting killing rather than allowing to die; and the second definition suggests that the action is performed by a party other than the patient. By contrast, a 1975 reference work, the *New Columbia Encyclopedia,* defines euthanasia as "either painlessly putting to death or failing to prevent death from natural causes in cases of terminal illness." The euthanasia entry continues:

> The term formerly referred only to the act of painlessly putting incurably ill patients to death. However, technological advances in medicine, which have made it possible to prolong the lives of patients who have no hope of recovery, have led to the use of the term *negative euthanasia,* i.e., the withdrawing of extraordinary means used to preserve life.[2]

If Webster's definition is accepted, euthanasia is the active termination of the life of a terminally ill patient by a second party. If the termination is requested by the patient, then the action is called *voluntary euthanasia* (and also *assisted suicide*). In cases where the patient is not mentally competent to make an informed request, the action is called "non-voluntary euthanasia." We can distinguish both forms from *involuntary* euthanasia, which involves a person capable of making an informed request but who has not done so. However, involuntary euthanasia is universally condemned and plays no role in current controversies.

If one accepts the definition proposed by the *New Columbia Encyclopedia,* two main subtypes of euthanasia are distinguishable, active (or positive) euthanasia and passive (or negative) euthanasia. The combination of the voluntary/nonvoluntary distinction with the *New Columbia Encyclopedia* definition of euthanasia yields four subtypes of euthanasia, which can be represented schematically as follows:

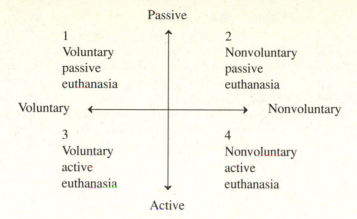

Passive

1
Voluntary
passive
euthanasia

2
Nonvoluntary
passive
euthanasia

Voluntary ← → Nonvoluntary

3
Voluntary
active
euthanasia

4
Nonvoluntary
active
euthanasia

Active

Voluntary active euthanasia is now the most frequently discussed type. Dan Brock gives a comprehensive description of its meaning and the controversies that surround it.

While four categories outline the territory of euthanasia, there still is some conceptual confusion surrounding the meaning of the term *euthanasia*. Hereafter in this introduction, a death will be described as euthanasia if and only if the following conditions are satisfied: (1) The death is intended by at least one other person who is either the cause of death or a causally relevant condition of the death; (2) the person killed is either acutely suffering or irreversibly comatose (or soon will be), and this alone is the primary reason for intending the person's death; and (3) the means chosen to produce the death must be as painless as possible, or there must be a sufficient moral justification for a more painful method.

Moral Problems. Almost all arguments favoring voluntary active euthanasia make some form of appeal to principles of beneficence and respect for autonomy, as defined in Chapter 1. Arguments from beneficence look at the consequences of an action to assess its impact on the interests and welfare of the person who will die. Supporters of voluntary active euthanasia argue that there are cases in which relief from suffering supersedes all other consequences. Here the principle of respect for autonomy obligates society to respect the decisions of autonomous persons and not to limit their liberty to end their lives. In respecting their autonomy it is not necessary to agree with their judgments, only to accord them their *right* to act upon their decisions.

The overarching moral problem about voluntary active euthanasia is usually presented by its advocates in terms of the *autonomy rights* of patients: If competent patients have a legal and moral right to refuse treatment that brings about their deaths, there would seem to be a similar right to enlist the assistance of physicians to help patients cause their deaths by an active means. If treatment refusal is justified by respect for autonomy and beneficence, can this right require physicians to prescribe barbiturates and to administer lethal injections to aid patients in killing themselves?

This question is raised in the essay by Timothy Quill, and the arguments are favorably assessed by Brock. One argument espoused by Brock, Quill, and those who defend voluntary active euthanasia is the need for both compassion and action when: (1) a condition has become overwhelmingly burdensome for a patient; (2) pain management for the patient is inadequate; and (3) only a physician seems capable of bringing relief. Increasing numbers of patients and physicians view the denial of help for these patients as an act of cruelty that violates the patient's rights as well as the fiduciary obligations of the physician.

The right to assistance in the form of voluntary active euthanasia has never been recognized in law or in codes of medical ethics (with the possible exception of the Netherlands, as noted in the final articles in this chapter). Codes of medical and research ethics from the Hippocratic corpus to today's major professional codes strictly prohibit mercy killing, even if a patient has a good reason for wanting to die. Although courts have often defended the autonomy of patients in cases of *passive* euthanasia, the courts have never allowed any form of what they judged to be voluntary active euthanasia. In opposition to active euthanasia, judicial opinions cite a principle of respect for life, according to which human life has value in itself that deserves respect. Courts say that they have a "state interest" in the protection or the preservation of life. Judicial opinions differ, however, regarding how to interpret and implement this principle. Increasingly courts look at the quality of life and the possibilities a patient has for recovery, not merely at a principle requiring respect for life.

Those who support medical traditions and are opposed to killing often appeal to either (1) professional role obligations that prohibit bringing about death and (2) the social consequences that would result from changing these traditions. The first argument is straightforward: Killing patients is inconsistent with the roles of nursing, caregiving, and healing. Edmund Pellegrino stresses this argument in his contribution in this chapter. The second argument is more complex and has come to be the centerpiece of discussion. This argument is referred to as the wedge argument or the slippery slope argument, and proceeds roughly as follows: Although particular acts of active killing are sometimes morally justified, the social consequences of sanctioning practices of killing would run serious risks of abuse and misuse and, on balance, would cause more harm than benefit. The argument is not that these negative consequences will occur immediately, but that they will grow incrementally over time. Although society might start by carefully restricting the number of patients who qualify for assistance in suicide or homicide, these restrictions would be revised and expanded over time, with an ever increasing risk of unjustified killing. Unscrupulous persons would learn how to abuse the system, just as they do with methods of tax evasion that operate on the margins of the system of legitimate tax avoidance. Pellegrino, for example, warns that the slope of the trail toward unjustified killing will be so slippery and precipitous that we ought never to get on it.

Slippery slope arguments are discussed in this chapter in the essays by Beauchamp, Brock, and Pellegrino. However, as Brock points out, the success or failure of the arguments depends on speculative predictions of a progressive erosion of moral restraints. If massively dire consequences will in fact flow from the legal legitimation of assisted suicide or voluntary active euthanasia, then the argument is a complete success and such practices should be legally prohibited. But how accurate is the evidence that such dire consequences will occur? Is there a sufficient reason to think that we cannot maintain control over public policy? Are our methods of monitoring so frail that we cannot adequately control such practices? These are among the primary questions asked in the current debate about euthanasia.

PHYSICIAN-ASSISTED SUICIDE

Physician-assisted suicide is one form of voluntary active euthanasia. Some courts and commentators have viewed acts of authorizing the withdrawal or withholding of care for patients as involving suicide or assisted suicide. Other courts see no specific intent to suicide in these cases; and some courts evade the question altogether by confining their discussion to the right to privacy, the right to choose death, and the right to refuse medical treatment.

In the *McKay* v. *Bergstedt* case reprinted in this chapter, the Supreme Court of Nevada delivers a now mainstream view in its majority opinion. The court approves quadriplegic Brian McKay's request to remove a respirator so that he can die. The court confirms his right to die, but does not consider the act suicide because the causes of death are not self-inflicted. The court finds that the state's interest in protecting life and preventing suicide are outweighed by McKay's right to refuse the treatment and die, and the court does not view the care as assisted suicide. However, in a dissenting opinion in this case, Justice Spring reaches a starkly different conclusion. He argues (1) that it is not a proper exercise of judicial authority to authorize one person to take the life of another or to sanction state-assisted suicide or medical assistance in suicide and (2) that no person has a right to be put to death by another.

CONCEPTUAL PROBLEMS ABOUT THE NATURE OF SUICIDE

In the selection from the *Cruzan* case in this chapter, Justice Scalia argues that withdrawing or withholding of treatment sometimes constitutes suicide because *any* means productive of death can be arranged to the end of killing oneself. This is so even if death is inevitable or the causes of death are natural. Pulling the plug on one's respirator is not relevantly different from plunging a knife into one's heart, if the conditions and the reason for putting an end to life are relevantly similar. There may, from this perspective, be suicidal intent in any circumstance of refusal of treatment.

What constitutes "suicidal intent"? As Brock notes, refusal of treatment cases can be identical to suicide cases, because the refusal of life-sustaining treatment is the patient's means of ending life. Exactly like typical suicides, these patients intend to end their life because of its grim prospects. In each case death *is* self-inflicted, whether by a lethal poison or by disconnecting a respirator. However, two legal decisions in this chapter take the view that refusals of treatment are *not* suicide: the New Jersey Supreme Court opinion in *Conroy* and the majority opinion in *McKay* v. *Bergstedt*. Because of the decision and circumstances of the patient, the Nevada court is particularly interesting for problems of assisted suicide. The majority opinion does *not* find suicidal intent and approves the assistance of physicians in helping McKay die. Many, including Justice Scalia and the minority opinion in *McKay,* believe that such acts *are* assisted suicides, despite the official rhetoric of many courts.

The best known of the cases about assisted suicide involves physician Quill, who reports his relationship with a leukemia patient in this chapter. Quill prescribed the barbiturates desired by a forty-five-year-old woman who had refused treatment. She had been his patient for many years, and members of her family had, as a group, come to a decision with the counsel of the physician. Many believe that Quill's actions were justified because: (1) the patient was competent and acting voluntarily; (2) there was an ongoing patient-physician relationship; (3) there was mutual and informed decisionmaking by patient and physician; (4) there was a critical and probing discussion before the decision; (5) there had been a consideration of and rejection of alternatives; (6) there was a durable death wish by the patient; (7) there was unbearable suffering from the patient's perspective; (8) and a means was used that was as painless as possible.

Nonetheless, some critics have found the action by Quill unsettling and unjustified. Quill's act violated a New York State law against assisted suicide, thereby exposing him to criminal liability. His act also opened up the possibility of misconduct charges from the New York State Health Department. (A grand jury in Rochester, New York, where the events occurred, declined to indict him, apparently because jurors sympathized with his motives and possibly his action.) In effect, Quill was acting as a civil disobedient, against established canons of physician ethics. Furthermore, in order to protect himself and the family, and to avoid a police investigation and an ambulance at the scene, he lied to the medical examiner by informing him that a hospice patient had died of acute leukemia.

The outstanding issue is whether society can legally permit certain forms of assisted suicide and, at the same time, protect life and the lives of the vulnerable. This takes us to the subject of contemporary practices of euthanasia in the Netherlands.

THE DUTCH EXPERIENCE

As the controversy over voluntary active euthanasia has heightened, increasing attention has been devoted to its practice in the Netherlands, where approximately 5 percent of deaths are acts of euthanasia. Many persons, both inside and outside the medical profession, in the Netherlands believe that physician killing in cases of seriously ill and dying patients can be morally and legally justified. The Dutch experience is now used by proponents of voluntary active euthanasia in many other countries to defend their proposals to ease rules against mercy killing and assisted suicide.

Under national legislation and somewhat loose-knit supervision, killing at the patient's informed request is allowed by state and medical authorities in the Netherlands. By policy, all cases must be reported to the Ministry of Justice, but there appear to be many unreported cases. The conditions of justified euthanasia consist of a voluntary, informed request by a patient who is suffering unbearably, physician consultation with a second physician, and careful review of the patient's condition by the physician performing the euthanasia procedure.

Significant differences emerge in this debate between North American attitudes toward euthanasia and Dutch attitudes. Whereas North American critics of Netherlands practices tend to see that country as dangerously down a slippery slope, many Dutch citizens see it the other way around. They believe that American approval of nonvoluntary passive euthanasia in which persons are allowed to die who do not request to die is a far slipperier slope than voluntary active euthanasia where the patient always makes the request. It could be, of course, that both are slippery slopes.

Dutch euthanasia practices are defended in this chapter by Dutch physician Pieter V. Admiraal, who explains why patients request euthanasia and why Dutch views about both passive and active euthanasia are starkly different from views found in other countries. The patient's autonomy rights play a strong role in Admiraal's conclusions. In opposition, Dutch cardiologist Richard Fenigsen argues that the combination of active and passive euthanasia in Holland (1) has led to a precarious slippery slope, (2) has failed to deliver on its promise to spare the sick, (3) has failed to recognize that there are painless alternatives, and (4) constitutes a serious danger to medicine.

T.L.B.

NOTES

1. In an influential statement passed in 1973 and revised in 1988 and 1991, the AMA allowed foregoing life-sustaining treatments but prohibited all "intentional termination of the life of one human being by another—mercy killing." Whether letting particular patients die is morally acceptable depends on several factors in this policy; but if the deaths involve killing—even in circumstances identical to those in which a patient is allowed to die—they are never justifiable. The AMA's 1973 statement, first distributed in reproduced typescript, is reprinted in Rachels's *The End of Life: Euthanasia and Morality* (Oxford: Oxford University Press, 1986), pp. 88, 192–93. See also American Medical Association, Council on Ethical and Judicial Affairs, *Euthanasia: Report C,* in *Proceedings of the House of Delegates* (Chicago: American Medical Association, June, 1988): 258–60 (and see *Current Opinions,* § 2.20, p. 13, 1989); "Decisions Near the End of Life," *Report B,* adopted by the House of Delegates (1991), pp. 11–15 (and see the abridged version in *Journal of the American Medical Association* 267 (April 22/29, 1992: 2229–2233)).

2. William H. Harris and Judith S. Levey, eds., *The New Columbia Encyclopedia* (New York: Columbia University Press, 1975), p. 904.

JAMES RACHELS

Active and Passive Euthanasia

The distinction between active and passive euthanasia is thought to be crucial for medical ethics. The idea is that it is permissible, at least in some cases, to withhold treatment and allow a patient to die, but it is never permissible to take any direct action designed to kill the patient. This doctrine seems to be accepted by most doctors, and it was endorsed in a statement adopted by the House of Delegates of the American Medical Association on December 4, 1973:

> The intentional termination of the life of one human being by another—mercy killing—is contrary to that for which the medical profession stands and is contrary to the policy of the American Medical Association.
>
> The cessation of the employment of extraordinary means to prolong the life of the body when there is irrefutable evidence that biological death is imminent is the decision of the patient and/or his immediate family. The advice and judgment of the physician should be freely available to the patient and/or his immediate family.

However, a strong case can be made against this doctrine. In what follows I will set out some of the relevant arguments, and urge doctors to reconsider their views on this matter.

To begin with a familiar type of situation, a patient who is dying of incurable cancer of the throat is in terrible pain, which can no longer be satisfactorily alleviated. He is certain to die within a few days, even if present treatment is continued, but he does not want to go on living for those days since the pain is unbearable. So he asks the doctor for an end to it, and his family joins in the request.

Suppose the doctor agrees to withhold treatment, as the conventional doctrine says he may. The justification for his doing so is that the patient is in terrible agony, and since he is going to die anyway, it would be wrong to prolong his suffering needlessly. But now notice this. If one simply withholds treatment, it may take the patient longer to die, and so he may suffer more than he would if more direct action were taken and a lethal injection given. This fact provides strong reason for thinking that, once the initial decision not to prolong his agony has been made, active euthanasia is actually preferable to passive euthanasia, rather than the reverse. To say otherwise is to endorse the option that leads to more suffering rather than less, and is contrary to the humanitarian impulse that prompts the decision not to prolong his life in the first place.

Part of my point is that the process of being "allowed to die" can be relatively slow and painful, whereas being given a lethal injection is relatively quick and painless. Let me give a different sort of example. In the United States about one in 600 babies is born with Down's syndrome. Most of these babies are otherwise healthy—that is, with only the usual pediatric care, they will proceed to an otherwise normal infancy. Some, however, are born with congenital defects such as intestinal obstructions that require operations if they are to live. Sometimes, the parents and the doctor will decide not to operate, and let the infant die. Anthony Shaw describes what happens then.

> When surgery is denied [the doctor] must try to keep the infant from suffering while natural forces sap the baby's life away. As a surgeon whose natural inclination is to use the scalpel to fight off death, standing by and watching a salvageable baby die is the most emotionally exhausting

Reprinted with permission from *The New England Journal of Medicine,* Vol. 292, No. 2 (January 9, 1975), pp. 78–80.

experience I know. It is easy at a conference, in a theoretical discussion, to decide that such infants should be allowed to die. It is altogether different to stand by in the nursery and watch as dehydration and infection wither a tiny being over hours and days. This is a terrible ordeal for me and the hospital staff—much more so than for the parents who never set foot in the nursery.[1]

I can understand why some people are opposed to all euthanasia, and insist that such infants must be allowed to live. I think I can also understand why other people favor destroying these babies quickly and painlessly. But why should anyone favor letting "dehydration and infection wither a tiny being over hours and days"? The doctrine that says that a baby may be allowed to dehydrate and wither, but may not be given an injection that would end its life without suffering, seems so patently cruel as to require no further refutation. The strong language is not intended to offend, but only to put the point in the clearest possible way.

My second argument is that the conventional doctrine leads to decisions concerning life and death made on irrelevant grounds.

Consider again the case of the infants with Down's syndrome who need operations for congenital defects unrelated to the syndrome to live. Sometimes there is no operation, and the baby dies, but when there is no such defect, the baby lives on. Now, an operation such as that to remove an intestinal obstruction is not prohibitively difficult. The reason why such operations are not performed in these cases is, clearly, that the child has Down's syndrome and the parents and doctor judge that because of that fact it is better for the child to die.

But notice that this situation is absurd, no matter what view one takes of the lives and potentials of such babies. If the life of such an infant is worth preserving, what does it matter if it needs a simple operation? Or, if one thinks it better that such a baby should not live on, what difference does it make that it happens to have an unobstructed intestinal tract? In either case, the matter of life and death is being decided on irrelevant grounds. It is the Down's syndrome, and not the intestines, that is the issue. The matter should be decided, if at all, on that basis, and not be allowed to depend on the essentially irrelevant question of whether the intestinal tract is blocked.

What makes this situation possible, of course, is the idea that when there is an intestinal blockage, one can "let the baby die," but when there is no such defect there is nothing that can be done, for one must not "kill" it. The fact that this idea leads to such results as deciding life or death on irrelevant grounds is another good reason why the doctrine should be rejected.

One reason why so many people think that there is an important moral difference between active and passive euthanasia is that they think killing someone is morally worse than letting someone die. But is it? Is killing, in itself, worse than letting die? To investigate this issue, two cases may be considered that are exactly alike except that one involves killing whereas the other involves letting someone die. Then, it can be asked whether this difference makes any difference to the moral assessments. It is important that the cases be exactly alike, except for this one difference, since otherwise one cannot be confident that it is this difference and not some other that accounts for any variation in the assessments of the two cases. So, let us consider this pair of cases:

In the first, Smith stands to gain a large inheritance if anything should happen to his six-year-old cousin. One evening while the child is taking his bath, Smith sneaks into the bathroom and drowns the child, and then arranges things so that it will look like an accident.

In the second, Jones also stands to gain if anything should happen to his six-year-old cousin. Like Smith, Jones sneaks in planning to drown the child in his bath. However, just as he enters the bathroom Jones sees the child slip and hit his head, and fall face down in the water. Jones is delighted; he stands by, ready to push the child's head back under if it is necessary, but it is not necessary. With only a little thrashing about, the child drowns all by himself, "accidentally," as Jones watches and does nothing.

Now Smith killed the child, whereas Jones "merely" let the child die. That is the only difference between them. Did either man behave better, from a moral point of view? If the difference between killing and letting die were in itself a morally important matter, one should say that Jones's behavior was less reprehensible than Smith's. But does one really want to say that? I think not. In the first place, both men acted from the same motive, personal gain, and both had exactly the same end in view when they acted. It may be inferred from Smith's conduct that he is a bad man, although that judgment may be withdrawn or modified if certain further facts are learned about him—for example, that he is mentally deranged. But would not the very same thing be inferred about Jones from his conduct? And would not the same further considerations also be relevant to any modification of this judgment? Moreover, suppose Jones pleaded, in his own defense, "After all, I didn't do anything except just stand there and watch the child drown. I didn't kill him; I only let him die." Again, if letting die were in itself less bad than killing, this defense should have at least some weight. But it does not. Such a "defense" can only be regarded as a grotesque perversion of moral reasoning. Morally speaking, it is no defense at all.

Now it may be pointed out, quite properly, that the cases of euthanasia with which doctors are concerned are not like this at all. They do not involve personal gain or the destruction of normal healthy children. Doctors are concerned only with cases in which the patient's life is of no further use to him, or in which the patient's life has become or will soon become a terrible burden. However, the point is the same in these cases: the bare difference between killing and letting die does not, in itself, make a moral difference. If a doctor lets a patient die, for humane reasons, he is in the same moral position as if he had given the patient a lethal injection for humane reasons. If his decision was wrong—if, for example, the patient's illness was in fact curable—the decision would be equally regrettable no matter which method was used to carry it out. And if the doctor's decision was the right one, the method used is not in itself important.

The AMA policy statement isolates the crucial issue very well; the crucial issue is "the intentional termination of the life of one human being by another." But after identifying this issue, and forbidding "mercy killing," the statement goes on to deny that the cessation of treatment is the intentional termination of a life. This is where the mistake comes in, for what is the cessation of treatment, in these circumstances, if it is not "the intentional termination of the life of one human being by another"? Of course it is exactly that, and if it were not, there would be no point to it.

Many people will find this judgment hard to accept. One reason, I think, is that it is very easy to conflate the question of whether killing is, in itself, worse than letting die, with the very different question of whether most actual cases of killing are more reprehensible than most actual cases of letting die. Most actual cases of killing are clearly terrible (think, for example, of all the murders reported in the newspapers), and one hears of such cases every day. On the other hand, one hardly ever hears of a case of letting die, except for the actions of doctors who are motivated by humanitarian reasons. So one learns to think

of killing in a much worse light than of letting die. But this does not mean that there is something about killing that makes it in itself worse than letting die, for it is not the bare difference between killing and letting die that makes the difference in these cases. Rather, the other factors—the murderer's motive of personal gain, for example, contrasted with the doctor's humanitarian motivation—account for different reactions to the different cases.

I have argued that killing is not in itself any worse than letting die; if my contention is right, it follows that active euthanasia is not any worse than passive euthanasia. What arguments can be given on the other side? The most common, I believe, is the following:

"The important difference between active and passive euthanasia is that, in passive euthanasia, the doctor does not do anything to bring about the patient's death. The doctor does nothing, and the patient dies of whatever ills already afflict him. In active euthanasia, however, the doctor does something to bring about the patient's death: he kills him. The doctor who gives the patient with cancer a lethal injection has himself caused his patient's death; whereas if he merely ceases treatment, the cancer is the cause of the death."

A number of points needs to be made here. The first is that it is not exactly correct to say that in passive euthanasia the doctor does nothing, for he does do one thing that is very important: he lets the patient die. "Letting someone die" is certainly different, in some respects, from other types of action—mainly in that it is a kind of action that one may perform by way of not performing certain other actions. For example, one may let a patient die by way of not giving medication, just as one may insult someone by way of not shaking his hand. But for any purpose of moral assessment, it is a type of action nonetheless. The decision to let a patient die is subject to moral appraisal in the same way that a decision to kill him would be subject to moral appraisal: it may be assessed as wise or unwise, compassionate or sadistic, right or wrong. If a doctor deliberately let a patient die who was suffering from a routinely curable illness, the doctor would certainly be to blame for what he had done, just as he would be to blame if he had needlessly killed the patient. Charges against him would then be appropriate. If so, it would be no defense at all for him to insist that he didn't "do anything." He would have done something very serious indeed, for he let his patient die.

Fixing the cause of death may be very important from a legal point of view, for it may determine whether criminal charges are brought against the doctor. But I do not think that this notion can be used to show a moral difference between active and passive euthanasia. The reason why it is considered bad to be the cause of someone's death is that death is regarded as a great evil—and so it is. However, if it has been decided that euthanasia—even passive euthanasia—is desirable in a given case, it has also been decided that in this instance death is no greater an evil than the patient's continued existence. And if this is true, the usual reason for not wanting to be the cause of someone's death simply does not apply.

Finally, doctors may think that all of this is only of academic interest—the sort of thing that philosophers may worry about but that has no practical bearing on their own work. After all, doctors must be concerned about the legal consequences of what they do, and active euthanasia is clearly forbidden by the law. But even so, doctors should also be concerned with the fact that the law is forcing upon them a moral doctrine that may well be indefensible, and has a considerable effect on their practices. Of course, most doctors are not now in the position of being coerced in this matter, for they do not regard themselves as merely going along with what the law requires. Rather, in statements such as the AMA policy statement that I have quoted, they are endorsing this doctrine as a central point of medical ethics. In that statement, active euthanasia is condemned not merely as illegal but as "contrary to that for which the medical profession stands," whereas passive euthanasia is approved. However, the preceding considerations suggest that there is really no moral difference between the two, considered in themselves (there may be important moral differences in some cases in their *consequences,* but, as I pointed out, these differences may make active euthanasia, and not passive euthanasia, the morally preferable option). So, whereas doctors may have to discriminate between active and passive euthanasia to satisfy the law, they should not do any more than that. In particular, they should not give the distinction any added authority and weight by writing it into official statements of medical ethics.

NOTE

1. A. Shaw, "Doctor, Do We Have a Choice?" *The New York Times Magazine,* January 30, 1972, p. 54.

T O M   L .   B E A U C H A M P

A Reply to Rachels on Active and Passive Euthanasia

James Rachels has recently argued that the distinction between active and passive euthanasia is neither appropriately used by the American Medical Association nor generally used for the resolution of moral problems of euthanasia.[1] Indeed he believes this distinction—which he equates with the killing/letting die distinction—does not in itself have any moral importance. The chief object of his attack is the following statement adopted by the House of Delegates of the American Medical Association in 1973:

The intentional termination of the life of one human being by another—mercy killing—is contrary to that for which the medical profession stands and is contrary to the policy of the American Medical Association.

The cessation of the employment of extraordinary means to prolong the life of the body when there is irrefutable evi-

From Tom L. Beauchamp and Seymour Perlin, eds., *Ethical Issues in Death and Dying* (Englewood Cliffs, N.J.: Prentice-Hall, 1978), pp. 246–258. This is a heavily revised version of an article by the same title first published in Thomas Mappes and Jane Zembaty, eds., *Social Ethics* (New York: McGraw-Hill, 1976). Reprinted by permission.

dence that biological death is imminent is the decision of the patient and/or his immediate family. The advice and judgment of the physician should be freely available to the patient and/or his immediate family.

Rachels constructs a powerful and interesting set of arguments against this statement. In this paper I attempt the following: (1) to challenge his views on the grounds that he does not appreciate the moral reasons that give weight to the active/passive distinction; (2) to provide a constructive account of the moral relevance of the active/passive distinction; and (3) to offer reasons showing that Rachels may nonetheless be correct in urging that we *ought* to abandon the active/passive distinction for purposes of moral reasoning.

I

I would concede that the active/passive distinction is *sometimes* morally irrelevant. Of this Rachels convinces me. But it does not follow that it is *always* morally irrelevant. What we need, then, is a case where the distinction is a morally relevant one and an explanation why it is so. Rachels himself uses the method of examining two cases which are exactly alike except that "one involves killing whereas the other involves letting die" (p. 440). We may profitably begin by comparing the kinds of cases governed by the AMA's doctrine with the kinds of cases adduced by Rachels in order to assess the adequacy and fairness of his cases.

The second paragraph of the AMA statement is confined to a narrowly restricted range of passive euthanasia cases, viz., those (a) where the patients are on extraordinary means, (b) where irrefutable evidence of imminent death is available, and (c) where patient or family consent is available. Rachels' two cases involve conditions notably different from these:

In the first, Smith stands to gain a large inheritance if anything should happen to his six-year-old cousin. One evening while the child is taking his bath, Smith sneaks into the bathroom and drowns the child, and then arranges things so that it will look like an accident.

In the second, Jones also stands to gain if anything should happen to his six-year-old cousin. Like Smith, Jones sneaks in planning to drown the child in his bath. However, just as he enters the bathroom Jones sees the child slip and hit his head, and fall face down in the water. Jones is delighted; he stands by, ready to push the child's head back under if it is necessary, but it is not necessary. With only a

little thrashing about, the child drowns all by himself, "accidentally," as Jones watches and does nothing.

Now Smith killed the child, whereas Jones "merely" let the child die. That is the only difference between them (p. 440).

Rachels says there is no moral difference between the cases in terms of our moral assessments of Smith and Jones' behavior. This assessment seems fair enough, but what can Rachels' cases be said to prove, as they are so markedly disanalogous to the sorts of cases envisioned by the AMA proposal? Rachels concedes important disanalogies, but thinks them irrelevant:

The point is the same in these cases: the bare difference between killing and letting die does not, in itself, make a moral difference. If a doctor lets a patient die, for humane reasons, he is in the same moral position as if he had given the patient a lethal injection for humane reasons (p. 441).

Three observations are immediately in order. First, Rachels seems to infer that from such cases we can conclude that the distinction between killing and letting die is *always* morally irrelevant. This conclusion is fallaciously derived. What the argument in fact shows, being an analogical argument, is only that in all *relevantly similar* cases the distinction does not in itself make a moral difference. Since Rachels concedes that other cases are disanalogous, he seems thereby to concede that his argument is as weak as the analogy itself. Second, Rachels' cases involve two *unjustified* actions, one of killing and the other of letting die. The AMA statement distinguishes one set of cases of unjustified killing and another of *justified* cases of allowing to die. Nowhere is it claimed by the AMA that what makes the difference in these cases is the active/passive distinction itself. It is only implied that one set of cases, the justified set, *involves* (passive) letting die while the unjustified set *involves* (active) killing. While it is said that justified euthanasia cases are passive ones and unjustified ones active, it is not said either that what makes some acts justified is the fact of their being passive or that what makes others unjustified is the fact of their being active. This fact will prove to be of vital importance.

The third point is that in both of Rachels' cases the respective moral agents—Smith and Jones—are morally responsible for the death of the child and are morally blameworthy—even though Jones is presumably not causally responsible. In the first case death is caused by the agent, while in the second it is not; yet the second agent is no less morally responsible. While the law might find only the first homicidal, morality condemns the motives in each case as equally wrong, and it holds that the duty to save life in such cases is as compelling as the duty not to take life. I suggest that it is largely because of this equal degree of moral responsibility that there is no morally relevant difference in Rachels' cases. In the cases envisioned by the AMA, however, an agent is held to be responsible for taking life by actively killing but is not held to be morally required to preserve life, and so not responsible for death, when removing the patient from extraordinary means (under conditions a–c above). I shall elaborate this latter point momentarily. My only conclusion thus far is the negative one that Rachels' arguments rest on weak foundations. His cases are not relevantly similar to euthanasia cases and do not support his apparent conclusion that the active/passive distinction is *always* morally irrelevant.

II

I wish first to consider an argument that I believe has powerful intuitive appeal and probably is widely accepted as stating the main reason for rejecting Rachels' views. I will maintain that this argument fails, and so leaves Rachels' contentions untouched.

I begin with an actual case, the celebrated Quinlan case.[2] Karen Quinlan was in a coma, and was on a mechanical respirator which artificially sustained her vital processes and which her parents wished to cease. At least some physicians believed there was irrefutable evidence that biological death was imminent and the coma irreversible. This case, under this description, closely conforms to the passive cases envisioned by the AMA. During an interview the father, Mr. Quinlan, asserted that he did not wish to kill his daughter, but only to remove her from the machines in order to see whether she would live or would die a natural death.[3] Suppose he had said—to envision now a second and hypothetical, but parallel case—that he wished only to see her die painlessly and therefore wished that the doctor could induce death by an overdose of morphine. Most of us would think the second act, which involves active killing, morally unjustified in these circumstances, while many of us would think the first act morally justified. (This is not the place to consider whether in fact it is justified, and if so under

what conditions.) What accounts for the apparent morally relevant difference?

I have considered these two cases together in order to follow Rachels' method of entertaining parallel cases where the only difference is that the one case involves killing and the other letting die. However, there is a further difference, which crops up in the euthanasia context. The difference rests in our judgments of medical fallibility and moral responsibility. Mr. Quinlan seems to think that, after all, the doctors might be wrong. There is a remote possibility that she might live without the aid of a machine. But whether or not the medical prediction of death turns out to be accurate, if she dies then no one is morally responsible for directly bringing about or causing her death, as they would be if they caused her death by killing her. Rachels finds explanations which appeal to causal conditions unsatisfactory; but perhaps this is only because he fails to see the nature of the causal link. To bring about her death is by that act to preempt the possibility of life. To "allow her to die" by removing artificial equipment is to allow for the possibility of wrong diagnosis or incorrect prediction and hence to absolve oneself of moral responsibility for the taking of life under false assumptions. There may, of course, be utterly no empirical possibility of recovery in some cases since recovery would violate a law of nature. However, judgments of empirical impossibility in medicine are notoriously problematic—the reason for emphasizing medical fallibility. And in all the hard cases we do not *know* that recovery is empirically impossible, even if good *evidence* is available.

The above reason for invoking the active/passive distinction can now be generalized: Active termination of life removes all possibility of life for the patient, while passively ceasing extraordinary means may not. This is not trivial since patients have survived in several celebrated cases where, in knowledgeable physicians' judgments, there was "irrefutable" evidence that death was imminent.[4]

One may, of course, be entirely responsible and culpable for another's death either by killing him or by letting him die. In such cases, of which Rachels' are examples, there is no morally significant difference between killing and letting die precisely because whatever one does, omits, or refrains from doing does not absolve one of responsibility. Either active or passive involvement renders one responsible for the death of another, and both involvements are equally wrong for the same principled moral reason: it is (prima facie) morally wrong to bring about the death of an innocent person capable of living whenever the causal intervention or negligence is intentional. (I use causal terms here because causal involvement need not be active, as when by one's negligence one is nonetheless causally responsible.) But not all cases of killing and letting die fall under this same moral principle. One is sometimes culpable for killing, because morally responsible as the agent for death, as when one pulls the plug on a respirator sustaining a recovering patient (a murder). But one is sometimes not culpable for letting die because one is not morally responsible as agent, as when one pulls the plug on a respirator sustaining an irreversibly comatose and unrecoverable patient (a routine procedure, where one is *merely* causally responsible).[5] Different degrees and means of involvement assess different degrees of responsibility, and our assessments of culpability can become intricately complex. The only point which now concerns us, however, is that because different moral principles may govern very similar circumstances, we are sometimes morally culpable for killing but not for letting die. And to many people it will seem that in passive cases we are not morally responsible for causing death, though we are responsible in active cases.

This argument is powerfully attractive. Although I was once inclined to accept it in virtually the identical form just developed,[6] I now think that, despite its intuitive appeal, it cannot be correct. It is true that different degrees and means of involvement entail different degrees of responsibility, but it does not follow that we are *not* responsible and therefore are absolved of possible culpability in *any* case of intentionally allowing to die. We are responsible and *perhaps* culpable in either active or passive cases. Here Rachels' argument is entirely to the point: It is not primarily a question of greater or lesser responsibility by an active or a passive means that should determine culpability. Rather, the question of culpability is decided by the moral *justification* for choosing either a passive or an active means. What the argument in the previous paragraph overlooks is that one might be unjustified in using an active means or unjustified in using a passive means, and hence be culpable in the use of either; yet one might be justified in using an active means or justified in using a passive means, and hence not be culpable in using either. Fallibility might just as well be present in a judgment to use one means as in a judgment to use another. (A judgment to allow to die is just as subject to being based on *knowledge which is fallible* as a

judgment to kill.) Moreover, in either case, it is a matter of what one knows and believes, and not a matter of a particular kind of causal connection or causal chain. If we kill the patient, then we are certainly causally responsible for his death. But, similarly, if we cease treatment, and the patient dies, the patient might have recovered if treatment had been continued. The patient might have been saved in either case, and hence there is no morally relevant difference between the two cases. It is, therefore, simply beside the point that "one is sometimes culpable for killing . . . but one is sometimes not culpable for letting die" — as the above argument concludes.

Accordingly, despite its great intuitive appeal and frequent mention, this argument from responsibility fails.

III

There may, however, be more compelling arguments against Rachels, and I wish now to provide what I believe is the most significant argument that can be adduced in defense of the active/passive distinction. I shall develop this argument by combining (1) so-called wedge or slippery slope arguments with (2) recent arguments in defense of rule utilitarianism. I shall explain each in turn and show how in combination they may be used to defend the active-passive distinction.

(1) *Wedge arguments* proceed as follows: if killing were allowed, even under the guise of a merciful extinction of life, a dangerous wedge would be introduced which places all "undesirable" or "unworthy" human life in a precarious condition. Proponents of wedge arguments believe the initial wedge places us on a slippery slope for at least one of two reasons: (i) It is said that our justifying principles leave us with no principled way to avoid the slide into saying that all sorts of killings would be justified under similar conditions. Here it is thought that once killing is allowed, a firm line between justified and unjustified killings cannot be securely drawn. It is thought best not to redraw the line in the first place, for redrawing it will inevitably lead to a downhill slide. It is then often pointed out that as a matter of historical record this is precisely what has occurred in the darker regions of human history, including the Nazi era, where euthanasia began with the best intentions for horribly ill, non-Jewish Germans and gradually spread to anyone

deemed an enemy of the people. (ii) Second, it is said that our basic principles against killing will be gradually eroded once some form of killing is legitimated. For example, it is said that permitting voluntary euthanasia will lead to permitting involuntary euthanasia, which will in turn lead to permitting euthanasia for those who are a nuisance to society (idiots, recidivist criminals, defective newborns, and the insane, e.g.). Gradually other principles which instill respect for human life will be eroded or abandoned in the process.

I am not inclined to accept the first reason (i).[7] If our justifying principles are themselves justified, then any action they warrant would be justified. Accordingly, I shall only be concerned with the second approach (ii).

(2) *Rule utilitarianism* is the position that a society ought to adopt a rule if its acceptance would have better consequences for the common good (greater social utility) than any comparable rule could have in that society. Any action is right if it conforms to a valid rule and wrong if it violates the rule. Sometimes it is said that alternative rules should be measured against one another, while it has also been suggested that whole moral *codes* (complete sets of rules) rather than individual rules should be compared. While I prefer the latter formulation (Brandt's), this internal dispute need not detain us here. The important point is that a particular rule or a particular code of rules is morally justified if and only if there is no other competing rule or moral code whose acceptance would have a higher utility value for society, and where a rule's acceptability is contingent upon the consequences which would result if the rule were made current.

Wedge arguments, when conjoined with rule utilitarian arguments, may be applied to euthanasia issues in the following way. We presently subscribe to a no-active-euthanasia rule (which the AMA suggests we retain). Imagine now that in our society we make current a restricted-active-euthanasia rule (as Rachels seems to urge). Which of these two moral rules would, if enacted, have the consequence of maximizing social utility? Clearly a restricted-active-euthanasia rule would have *some* utility value, as Rachels notes, since some intense and uncontrollable suffering would be eliminated. However, it may not have the highest utility value in the structure of our present code or in any imaginable code which could be made current, and therefore may not be a component in the

ideal code for our society. If wedge arguments raise any serious questions at all, as I think they do, they rest in this area of whether a code would be weakened or strengthened by the addition of active euthanasia principles. For the disutility of introducing legitimate killing into one's moral code (in the form of active euthanasia rules) may, in the long run, outweigh the utility of doing so, as a result of the eroding effect such a relaxation would have on rules in the code which demand respect for human life. If, for example, rules permitting active killing were introduced, it is not implausible to suppose that destroying defective newborns (a form of involuntary euthanasia) would become an accepted and common practice, that as population increases occur the aged will be even more neglectable and neglected than they now are, that capital punishment for a wide variety of crimes would be increasingly tempting, that some doctors would have appreciably reduced fears of actively injecting fatal doses whenever it seemed to them propitious to do so, and that laws of war against killing civilians would erode in efficacy even beyond their already abysmal level.

A hundred such possible consequences might easily be imagined. But these few are sufficient to make the larger point that such rules permitting killing could lead to a general reduction of respect for human life. Rules against killing in a moral code are not *isolated* moral principles; they are pieces of a web of rules against killing which forms the code. The more threads one removes, the weaker the fabric becomes. And if, as I believe, moral principles against active killing have the deep and continuously civilizing effect of promoting respect for life, and if principles which allow passively letting die (as envisioned in the AMA statement) do not themselves cut against this effect, then this seems an important reason for the maintenance of the active/passive distinction. (By the logic of the above argument, passively letting die would also have to be prohibited if a rule permitting it had the serious adverse consequence of eroding acceptance or rules protective of respect for life. While this prospect seems to me improbable, I can hardly claim to have refuted those conservatives who would claim that even rules that sanction letting die place us on a precarious slippery slope.)

A troublesome problem, however, confronts my use of utilitarian and wedge arguments. Most all of us would agree that both killing and letting die are justified under some conditions. Killings in self-defense and in "just" wars are widely accepted as justified because the conditions excuse the killing. If society can withstand these exceptions to moral rules prohibiting killing, then why is it not plausible to suppose society can accept another excusing exception in the form of justified active euthanasia? This is an important and worthy objection, but not a decisive one. The defenseless and the dying are significantly different classes of persons from aggressors who attack individuals and/or nations. In the case of aggressors, one does not confront the question whether their lives are no longer *worth living*. Rather, we reach the judgment that the aggressors' morally blameworthy actions justify counteractions. But in the case of the dying and the otherwise ill, there is no morally blameworthy action to justify our own. Here we are required to accept the judgment that their lives are no longer *worth living* in order to believe that the termination of their lives is justified. It is the latter sort of judgment which is feared by those who take the wedge argument seriously. We do not now permit and never have permitted the taking of morally blameless lives. I think this is the key to understanding why recent cases of intentionally allowing the death of defective newborns (as in the now famous case at the Johns Hopkins Hospital) have generated such protracted controversy. Even if such newborns could not have led meaningful lives (a matter of some controversy), it is the wedged foot in the door which creates the most intense worries. For if we once take a decision to allow a restricted infanticide justification or any justification at all on grounds that a life is not meaningful or not worth living, we have qualified our moral rules against killing. That this qualification is a matter of the utmost seriousness needs no argument. I mention it here only to show why the wedge argument may have moral force even though we *already* allow some very different conditions to justify intentional killing.

There is one final utilitarian reason favoring the preservation of the active/passive distinction.[8] Suppose we distinguish the following two types of cases of wrongly diagnosed patients:

1. Patients wrongly diagnosed as hopeless, and who will survive even if a treatment *is* ceased (in order to allow a natural death).
2. Patients wrongly diagnosed as hopeless, and who will survive only if the treatment is *not ceased* (in order to allow a natural death).

If a social rule permitting only passive euthanasia were in effect, then doctors and families who "allowed death" would lose only patients in class 2, not those in class 1; whereas if active euthanasia were permitted, at least some patients in class 1 would be needlessly lost. Thus, the consequence of a no-active-euthanasia rule would be to save some lives which could not be saved if both forms of euthanasia were allowed. This reason is not a *decisive* reason for favoring a policy of passive euthanasia, since these classes (1 and 2) are likely to be very small and since there might be counterbalancing reasons (extreme pain, autonomous expression of the patient, etc.) in favor of active euthanasia. But certainly it is *a* reason favoring only passive euthanasia and one which is morally relevant and ought to be considered along with other moral reasons.

IV

It may still be insisted that my case has not touched Rachels' leading claim, for I have not shown, as Rachels puts it, that it is "the bare difference between killing and letting die that makes the difference in these cases" (p. 441). True, I have not shown this and in my judgment it cannot be shown. But this concession does not require capitulation to Rachels' argument. I adduced a case which is at the center of our moral intuition that killing is morally different (in at least some cases) from letting die; and I then attempted to account for at least part of the grounds for this belief. The grounds turn out to be other than the *bare* difference, but nevertheless *make* the distinction morally relevant. The identical point can be made regarding the voluntary/involuntary distinction, as it is commonly applied to euthanasia. It is not the bare difference between voluntary euthanasia (i.e., euthanasia with patient consent) and involuntary euthanasia (i.e., without patient consent) that makes one justifiable and one not. Independent moral grounds based on, for example, respect for autonomy or beneficence, or perhaps justice will alone make the moral difference.

In order to illustrate this general claim, let us presume that it is sometimes justified to kill another person and sometimes justified to allow another to die. Suppose, for example, that one may kill in self-defense and may allow to die when a promise has been made to someone that he would be allowed to die. Here conditions of self-defense and promising justify actions. But suppose now that someone *A* promises in exactly similar circumstances to kill someone *B* at *B*'s request, and also that someone *C* allows someone *D* to die in an act of self-defense.

Surely *A* is obliged equally to kill or to let die if he promised; and surely *C* is permitted to let *D* die if it is a matter of defending *C*'s life. If this analysis is correct, then it follows that killing is sometimes right, sometimes wrong, depending on the circumstances, and the same is true of letting die. It is the justifying reasons which make the difference whether an action is right, not merely the kind of action it is.

Now, *if* letting die led to disastrous conclusions but killing did not, then letting die but not killing would be wrong. Consider, for example, a possible world in which dying would be indefinitely prolongable even if all extraordinary therapy were removed and the patient were allowed to die. Suppose that it costs over one million dollars to let each patient die, that nurses consistently commit suicide from caring for those being "allowed to die," that physicians are constantly being successfully sued for malpractice for allowing death by cruel and wrongful means, and that hospitals are uncontrollably overcrowded and their wards filled with communicable diseases which afflict only the dying. Now suppose further that killing in this possible world is quick, painless, and easily monitored. I submit that in this world we would believe that *killing is morally acceptable but that allowing to die is morally unacceptable*. The point of this example is again that it is the circumstances that make the difference, not the bare difference between killing and letting die.

It is, however, worth noticing that there is nothing in the AMA statement which says that the bare difference between killing and letting die itself and alone makes the difference in our differing moral assessments of rightness and wrongness. Rachels forces this interpretation on the statement. Some philosophers may have thought the bare difference makes the difference, but there is scant evidence that the AMA or any thoughtful ethicist *must* believe it in order to defend the relevance and importance of the active/passive distinction. When this conclusion is coupled with my earlier argument that from Rachels' paradigm cases it follows only that the active/passive distinction is sometimes, but not always, morally irrelevant, it would seem that his case against the AMA is rendered highly questionable.

V

There remains, however, the important question as to whether we *ought* to accept the distinction between active and passive euthanasia, now that we are clear about (at least one way of drawing) the moral grounds for its invocation. That is, should we employ the distinction in order to judge some acts of euthanasia justified and others not justified? Here, as the hesitant previous paragraph indicates, I am uncertain. This problem is a substantive moral issue—not merely a conceptual one—and would require at a minimum a lengthy assessment of wedge arguments and related utilitarian considerations. In important respects empirical questions are involved in this assessment. We should like to know, and yet have hardly any evidence to indicate, what the consequences would be for our society if we were to allow the use of active means to produce death. The best hope for making such an assessment has seemed to some to rest in analogies to suicide and capital punishment statutes. Here it may reasonably be asked whether recent liberalizations of laws limiting these forms of killing have served as the thin end of a wedge leading to a breakdown of principles protecting life or to widespread violations of moral principles. Nonetheless, such analogies do not seem to me promising, since they are still fairly remote from the pertinent issue of the consequences of allowing active humanitarian killing of one person by another.

It is interesting to notice the outcome of the Kamisar–Williams debate on euthanasia—which is almost exclusively cast by both writers in a consequential, utilitarian framework.[9] At one crucial point in the debate, where possible consequences of laws permitting euthanasia are under discussion, they exchange "perhaps" judgments:

I [Williams] will return Kamisar the compliment and say: "Perhaps." We are certainly in an area where no solution is going to make things quite easy and happy for everybody, and all sorts of embarrassments may be conjectured. But these embarrassments are not avoided by keeping to the present law: we suffer from them already.[10]

Because of the grave difficulties which stand in the way of making accurate predictions about the impact of liberalized euthanasia laws—especially those that would permit active killing—it is not surprising that those who debate the subject would reach a point of exchanging such "perhaps" judgments. And that is why, so it seems to me, we are uncertain whether to perpetuate or to abandon the active-passive distinction in our moral thinking about euthanasia. I think we *do* perpetuate it in medicine, law, and ethics because we are still somewhat uncertain about the conditions under which *passive* euthanasia should be permitted by law (which is one form of social *rule*). We are unsure about what the consequences will be of the California "Natural Death Act" and all those similar acts passed by other states which have followed in its path. If no untoward results occur, and the balance of the results seems favorable, then we will perhaps be less concerned about further liberalizations of euthanasia laws. If untoward results do occur (on a widespread scale), then we would be most reluctant to accept further liberalizations and might even abolish natural death acts.

In short, I have argued in this section that euthanasia in its active and its passive forms presents us with a dilemma which can be developed by using powerful consequentialist arguments on each side, yet there is little clarity concerning the proper resolution of the dilemma precisely because of our uncertainty regarding proclaimed consequences.

VI

I reach two conclusions at the end of these several arguments. First, I think Rachels is incorrect in arguing that the distinction between active and passive is (always) morally irrelevant. It may well be relevant, and for moral reasons—the reasons adduced in section III above. Second, I think nonetheless that Rachels may ultimately be shown correct in his contention that we ought to dispense with the active-passive distinction—for reasons adduced in sections IV–V. But if he is ultimately judged correct, it will be because we have come to see that some forms of active killing have generally acceptable social consequences, and not primarily because of the arguments he adduces in his paper—even though *something* may be said for each of these arguments. Of course, in one respect I have conceded a great deal to Rachels. The bare difference argument is vital to his position, and I have fully agreed to it. On the other hand, I do not see that the bare difference argument does play or need play a major role in our moral thinking—or in that of the AMA.

NOTES

1. "Active and Passive Euthanasia," *New England Journal of Medicine* 292 (January 9, 1975), 78–80. [All page references in parentheses refer to Rachels' article as reprinted in this chapter.]

2. As recorded in the Opinion of Judge Robert Muir, Jr., Docket No. C-201-75 of the Superior Court of New Jersey, Chancery Division, Morris County (November 10, 1975).

3. See Judge Muir's Opinion, p. 18—a slightly different statement but on the subject.

4. This problem of the strength of evidence also emerged in the Quinlan trial, as physicians disagreed whether the evidence was "irrefutable." Such disagreement, when added to the problems of medical fallibility and causal responsibility just outlined, provides, in the eyes of some, one important argument against the *legalization* of active euthanasia, as perhaps the AMA would agree.

5. Among the moral reasons why one is held to be responsible in the first sort of case and not responsible in the second sort are, I believe, the moral grounds for the active/passive distinction under discussion in this section.

6. In *Social Ethics,* as cited in the permission note to this essay.

7. An argument of this form, which I find unacceptable for reasons given below, is Arthur Dyck, "Beneficent Euthanasia and Benemortasia: Alternative Views of Mercy," in M. Kohl, ed., *Beneficent Euthanasia* (Buffalo: Prometheus Books, 1975), pp. 121f.

8. I owe most of this argument to James Rachels, whose comments on an earlier draft of this paper led to several significant alterations.

9. Williams bases his pro-euthanasia argument on the prevention of two consequences: (1) loss of liberty and (2) cruelty. Kamisar bases his anti-euthanasia position on three projected consequences of euthanasia laws: (1) mistaken diagnosis, (2) pressured decisions by seriously ill patients, and (3) the wedge of the laws will lead to legalized involuntary euthanasia. Kamisar admits that individual acts of euthanasia are sometimes justified. It is the rule that he opposes. He is thus clearly a rule-utilitarian, and I believe Williams is as well (cf. his views on children and the senile). Their assessments of wedge arguments are, however, radically different.

10. Glanville Williams, "Mercy-Killing Legislation—A Rejoinder," *Minnesota Law Review* 43, no. 1 (1958), 5.

When Is Forgoing Treatment Also Killing?

SUPERIOR COURT OF NEW JERSEY, CHANCERY DIVISION, ESSEX COUNTY

In the Matter of Claire C. Conroy

DECIDED Feb. 2, 1983

STANTON, J.S.C.

The question presented by this case is whether a nasogastric tube should be removed from an 84-year-old patient who is suffering from severe organic brain syndrome and a variety of serious ailments. The patient is totally dependent upon the tube for nutriment and fluids. Removal of the tube will probably result in death within a few days. I have decided that it would be wrong to prolong the life of the patient. Her guardian will be authorized to have the tube removed.

Claire Conroy was adjudicated incompetent in 1979. Her nephew, Thomas C. Whittemore, plaintiff in the present action, was appointed as her guardian. Since 1979 the patient has been a resident of Parklane Nursing Home in Bloomfield, New Jersey. In July 1982 the patient was admitted to Clara Maas Memorial Hospital, Belleville, because of a severe infection of her left foot. Her left foot was diagnosed as being gangrenous. Her physicians recommended amputation of her left leg above the knee. The physicians believed that death could occur within two weeks if the leg was not amputated. In the belief that the amputation was not in the best interests of his aunt, the guardian refused permission. The physicians declined to press the issue. The leg was not amputated, but the patient did not die. The patient was discharged from the hospital

Reprinted from 457 *Atlantic Reporter*, 2d Series. 457 A.2d 1232 (N.J. Super. Ch. 1983).

back to the nursing home on November 17, 1982. At present the lower left leg is wasted and rotted. However, the infection has been contained and the leg does not presently pose a threat to the patient's life. The leg does not now seem to be a source of major pain.

Claire Conroy suffers from severe organic brain syndrome, necrotic decubitus ulcers on her left foot, left leg and left hip, urinary tract infection, arteriosclerotic heart disease, hypertension and diabetes mellitus. Except for minor movements of her head, neck, arms and hands, she is unable to move. She does not speak. She lies in bed in a fetal position. . . All the testimony in the case and my own direct observation of the patient convince me that she has no cognitive or volitional functioning. There is no reasonable expectation that the patient's condition will ever improve.

During her recent hospitalization a nasogastric tube was inserted through the patient's nose, down her throat and into her stomach. Several times a day water, a nutrient formula, vitamins and medicine are poured through the tube. The patient is unable to swallow. Nurses would not be able to feed her by hand. Without the tube the patient would probably die of starvation and dehydration within a few days. With the tube the patient will probably be able to live for some months, perhaps even a year or more.

Claire Conroy never married. Her siblings are all dead. Her only surviving relative is plaintiff, who is her nephew and guardian. Plaintiff testifies that his aunt never saw a physician or received medical treatment at any time prior to her becoming incompetent in 1979. She scorned medicine. Her nephew believes that she would not willingly accept the tube and the treatment she is now receiving. The guardian wishes to have the tube removed and to allow his aunt to die. . . .

I think it fair to say that everyone involved in this case wishes that this poor woman would die. This wish does not flow from any lack of concern for Claire Conroy. On the contrary, it flows from a very deep sympathy for her sad plight. The disagreement among the participants involves differences in perception about what helping this patient means under the circumstances of this case.

[1] Life is our most basic possession. The will to stay alive is probably our strongest instinctive drive. As a general proposition, the protection of life is one of the law's strongest imperatives, and preservation of life is the major goal of medical practice. The interest of the State in preserving life is so great that courts have ordered medical procedures to be performed on patients even though the patients were competent and had objected to the procedure. In these cases, however, the expectation is that the patient will have a reasonably full and vibrant life after the treatment has been performed. There is a point at which a patient, or someone acting for him if he is incompetent, has the right to refuse treatment. That point is reached when intellectual functioning is permanently reduced to a very primitive level or when pain has become unbearable and unrelievable. . . .

When we deal with questions such as the ones presented in this case, a certain basic humility and a sense of one's own limitations are appropriate. We know that mankind's understanding of the ultimate meaning of life, suffering and death is (and probably always will be) flawed and limited. Many of us believe that an abiding reverence for life is perhaps our most special and most worthy human characteristic, but most of us would agree that when a person has been permanently reduced to a very primitive intellectual level or is permanently suffering from unbearable and unrelievable pain there is no valid human purpose to be served by employing active treatment designed to prolong life. Every sick human being is entitled to loving care, but there comes a time in the loving care of some patients when the proper decision is to let nature take its course, to allow the patient to die.

Even when we decide that it is proper to withhold active treatment, it would be wrong to act directly to terminate life or to withdraw nourishment, fluids,

shelter or normal supportive care such as washing and body positioning. When I say that it would be wrong to withdraw nourishment or fluids, I mean that it would be wrong to refuse to give them to the patient if she could take them herself or with the manual assistance of others. It would also be wrong to withhold medications which would reduce pain without unduly prolonging life. I conclude that these things would be wrong because I perceive a need in this area of decision making (1) to recognize the limitations of our understanding of life, suffering and death, (2) to continue a fundamental respect for life even in the most dire human circumstances and (3) to keep in place some fairly simple conceptual controls designed to give some measure of protection against ill-informed or badly motivated decisions. . . .

If the patient can be restored by treatment to some meaningful level of intellectual functioning and to some acceptable level of comfort, then the full range of medical knowledge, skill and technology which is available should be brought into action as a matter of ordinary routine. Conversely, if the clear prognosis is that the patient will never return to some meaningful level of intellectual functioning and to some acceptable level of pain, then virtually every act of treatment other than the simple care mentioned in the preceding paragraph is inappropriate and is extraordinary. The focus of inquiry should be upon whether the life of the patient has become and is likely to remain impossibly burdensome to the patient. If the patient's life has become impossibly and permanently burdensome, then we simply are not helping the patient by prolonging her life, and active treatment designed to prolong life becomes utterly pointless and probably cruel. . . .

Presently available knowledge, skills and technology (to say nothing of what the future may hold) now give us the ability to prolong some lives which ought not be prolonged. We cannot mindlessly and indiscriminately act to prolong all lives, by all means, under all circumstances. We must make some choices.

Of course, once we human beings start making choices we start making mistakes. It is inevitable that we will allow some people to die when we could have and should have prolonged their lives. But we cannot let this fear of error force us into abdicating our basic human responsibility to make choices. The fear of error should be used constructively as an incentive to make our choices carefully and soundly.

[2] I am firmly convinced by the evidence in this case that Claire Conroy's intellectual functioning has been permanently reduced to an extremely primitive level. She suffers from all of the medical problems mentioned above. The general state of her health is very poor and will remain so. Her life has become impossibly and permanently burdensome for her. Prolonging her life would not help her. It would be a wrong to her. The nasogastric tube should be removed, even though that will almost certainly lead to death by starvation and dehydration within a few days, and even though that death may be a painful one for the patient. . . .

For the reasons stated above, on this 2nd day of February, 1983, it is adjudged and ordered as follows:

1. Thomas C. Whittemore, as guardian of Claire C. Conroy, has the right to cause the removal of the nasogastric tube presently inserted in Claire C. Conroy. The actual removal is to be made by a qualified health care professional person who has no personal or professional objection to such removal.

2. Although it is expected that the removal of the tube will lead to suffering and death, the guardian and health care personnel retained by him must take reasonable steps to minimize the discomfort of Claire C. Conroy during her passage from life.

SUPERIOR COURT OF NEW JERSEY, APPELLATE DIVISION

In the Matter of Claire C. Conroy

ARGUED May 11, 1983
DECIDED July 8, 1983
The opinion of the Court was delivered by
MICHELS, P.J.A.D.

John J. DeLaney, Jr. (DeLaney), guardian *ad litem* of Claire C. Conroy (Conroy), appeals from a judgment of the Chancery Division entered following a plenary trial, which declared that Thomas C. Whittemore (Whittemore) as guardian of Claire C. Conroy had "the right to cause the removal of the nasogastric tube presently inserted in Claire C. Conroy." . . .

On July 23, 1982, after observing that Conroy was not eating, Dr. Kazemi placed her on a nasogastric tube, which is a simple flexible plastic tube that is run through the patient's nose into the stomach and through which liquid nutrients are passed. Except for a two-week period in October and November 1982,

during which time she was fed pureed food but with poor results, this tube remained in place until her death. Conroy was unable to swallow sufficient quantities of food and water to live without the help of the nasogastric tube.

Dr. Kazemi further testified at trial that Conroy was not brain dead, not comatose, and not in a chronic vegetative state. Dr. Bernard Davidoff, who testified for the guardian *ad litem* DeLaney, described Conroy's mental state as "severely demented." Severe contractions of her lower legs kept her in a semi-fetal position. Although Conroy did not respond to verbal stimuli, she followed movements with her eyes, used her hands to scratch herself, and was able to move her head, neck, arms and hands voluntarily. Catherine Rittel, an administrator-nurse at Parklane, testified that Conroy smiled when she was massaged or her hair was combed and moaned when she was fed.

Neither physician could determine whether Conroy could feel pain. They speculated that although her gangrene and ulcers did not seem to be a source of

Reprinted from 464 *Atlantic Reporter*, 2d Series. 464 A.2d (N.J. Super. A.D. 1983).

pain, the leg contractions probably were. According to the physicians' testimony, if the nasogastric tube were to have been removed, Conroy would have died of dehydration and starvation in about a week. Dr. Kazemi described this as a painful death. Moreover, the trial judge recognized that "the removal of the tube will lead to suffering and death," and ordered the guardian and health care personnel "to take reasonable steps to minimize [Conroy's] discomfort . . . during her passage from life." 188 *N.J. Super.* at 532, 457 A.2d 1232.

The physicians agreed there was no chance of an improvement in Conroy's mental condition. Dr. Davidoff observed, however, that none of Conroy's medical conditions was fatal and therefore that it could not be predicted when or from what cause Conroy would die. . . .

The basic issue before us is whether the judgment here entered represents a legally permissible application of the principles of *In re Quinlan.* . . . The decision in *Quinlan* was based upon the patient's right of privacy which was deemed, under the circumstances there, to outweigh the State's interest in the preservation of life. . . . If the State's interest in the preservation of life outweighs the patient's right of privacy, such withdrawal would be an act of euthanasia, constituting homicide. It is only if the right of privacy could be reasonably deemed to prevail that withdrawal would be legally permissible under the *Quinlan* doctrine. We reverse the judgment here entered because in our view we regard it as the authorization of euthanasia. . . .

The State's interest in preserving a patient's life is small with regard to the hopelessly ill or irreversibly comatose patient, but great with regard to the patient whose condition will substantially improve as the result of continued treatment. This distinction is borne out by the case law. . . .

Conroy's prognosis supports a significantly greater state interest in continued treatment than in the cases cited above. At the time of trial, Conroy was unable to move from a fetal position and had a severely limited ability to respond to her surroundings. However, she was not in a chronic vegetative state; she was simply very confused. Dr. Kazemi testified that because Conroy was aware of some external stimuli and responded to them, she was neither vegetative nor comatose. This testimony draws a very different picture from that drawn in the *Quinlan* case. It seems to describe a woman who, like an infant less than a year old, experienced and responded to her surroundings but lacked the intellectual capacity to understand most of them. By comparison, Karen Quinlan was unaware of her environment and had only the most reflexive reactions to outside stimuli. . . .

The distinction between an "awake" but confused patient like Conroy and an "asleep," vegetative patient like Karen Quinlan is material and is determinative in this case. The *Quinlan* court held that the State's interest in preserving a patient's life depends on whether the patient ever will return to cognitive, sapient life. 70 *N.J.* at 41, 355 A.2d 647. Thus, it is plain that *Quinlan* applies only to noncognitive, vegetative patients. . . . Conroy was sapient, but lacked the intellectual capacity to understand what she observed. Under the principles of the *Quinlan* case, the State had a substantial and overriding interest in preserving her life.

We are also troubled by the trial judge's framing of the issue as whether the patient will return "to some meaningful level of intellectual functioning." Put simply, to allow a physician or family member to discontinue life-sustaining treatment to a person solely because that person's lack of intellectual capacity precludes him from enjoying a meaningful quality of life would establish a dangerous precedent that logically could be extended far beyond the facts of the case now before us. In our view, the right to terminate life-sustaining treatment based on a guardian's substituted judgment should be limited to incurable and terminally ill patients who are brain dead, irreversibly comatose or vegetative and who would gain no medical benefit from continued treatment. *A fortiori,* there can be no justification for withholding nourishment, which is really not "treatment" at all . . . from a patient who does not meet these criteria. Any further extension of the *Quinlan* rule would place into the hands of physicians, family members and judges the determination of whose quality of life is so slight that he should not be kept alive. . . .

[T]he treatment given to Conroy differs significantly from that given Karen Quinlan. The bodily invasion necessary to treat Karen Quinlan was "very great." 70 *N.J.* at 41, 355 A.2d 647. It included 24-hour intensive nursing care, antibiotics and the assistance of a respirator, a catheter and a feeding tube. As a result, her personal dignity was taken from her and she was placed in a position of helplessness and dependence. In contrast, Conroy was in the less restrictive environment of a nursing home, was not subject to intensive nursing care, and had none of her bodily functions replaced by a machine. The nasogastric tube was no more than a simple device which was part of Conroy's routine nursing care. It was not really "medical treatment" at all. In truth, Conroy was little different from the many other ill, senile or mentally disabled persons who are bedridden and cared for in nursing homes. Consequently, the bodily invasion she suffered as the result of her treatment was small, and should not be held to outweigh the State's interest in preserving her life. . . .

If . . . the patient is not comatose and does not face imminent and inevitable death, nourishment accomplishes the substantial benefit of sustaining life until the illness takes its natural course. Under such circumstances nourishment always will be an essential element of ordinary care which physicians are ethically obligated to provide. . . .

We are further convinced that the withdrawal of the feeding tube here would also violate medical ethics. . . . Medical ethicists have long distinguished between killing and letting die. Hyland and Baime frame the distinction as one between euthanasia ("the deliberate easing into death of a patient suffering from a painful and fatal disease") and antidysthanasia ("the failure to take positive action to prolong the life of an incurable patient"). Hyland & Baime, "*In re Quinlan:* A Synthesis of Law and Medical Technology," 8 *Rut.-Cam.L.J.* 37, 52 (1976). While the latter has gained acceptance in the medical community, the former always has been considered unethical. . . .

Thus, the American Medical Association Judicial Council has recommended that the following standard be adopted by courts and legislatures faced with issues of euthanasia or terminal illness:

The intentional termination of the life of one human being by another—mercy killing or euthanasia—is contrary to public policy, medical tradition, and the most fundamental measures of human value and worth. [*Judicial Council, American Medical Association, Opinions and Reports* para. 5.17 (1979).]

Similarly, the Judicial Council's Opinion 2.11, quoted above, states, "For humane reasons, with informed consent a physician may do what is medically necessary to alleviate severe pain, *but he should not intentionally cause death*" (emphasis added).

The trial judge in the present case in effect authorized euthanasia rather than antidysthanasia. At the time of trial, Conroy, unlike the patients permitted to discontinue treatment in the other reported cases, was neither terminally ill nor critically injured and kept alive only by artificial means. She suffered from no specific life-threatening illness or injury, and she was not, apparently, suffering any pain. Her treatment consisted basically of providing the comforts of routine nursing care. If the trial judge's order had been enforced, Conroy would not have died as the result of an existing medical condition, but rather she would have died, and painfully so, as the result of a new and independent condition: dehydration and starvation. Thus, she would have been actively killed by independent means rather than allowed to die of existing illness or injury. Instead of easing her passage from life, the result of the judge's order would have been to inflict new suffering.

Such a result has frightening implications. When a patient, guardian or physician is permitted to decide that a nonterminal patient's life is worthless and should be terminated rather than merely to decide that an artificially extended life should be allowed to expire naturally, the decision necessarily involves a judgment of the patient's quality of life. Such a precedent could be applied with equal force to circumstances much different from and less compelling than those present here. Therefore, we reject the extension of *Quinlan* to the active euthanasia of a patient.

CONCLUSION

In sum, the trial judge erred in holding that a noncomatose, non-brain-dead patient not facing imminent death, not maintained by any life-support machine, and not able to speak for herself should be painfully put to death by dehydration and starvation. Accordingly, the judgment so ordering is reversed.

SUPREME COURT OF NEW JERSEY

In the Matter of Claire C. Conroy

[J. SCHREIBER]

. . . Declining life-sustaining medical treatment may not properly be viewed as an attempt to commit suicide. Refusing medical intervention merely allows the disease to take its natural course; if death were eventually to occur, it would be the result, primarily, of the underlying disease, and not the result of a self-inflicted injury. . . . In addition, people who refuse life-sustaining medical treatment may not harbor a specific intent to die, *Saikewicz, supra,* 373 *Mass.* at 743, n. 11, 370 *N.E.*2d at 426 n. 11; rather, they may fervently wish to live, but to do so free of unwanted medical technology, surgery, or drugs, and without protracted suffering. . . .

Reprinted from 486 *Atlantic Reporter,* 2d Series. 486 A.2d 1209 (N.J. 1985).

Recognizing the right of a terminally ill person to reject medical treatment respects that person's intent, not to die, but to suspend medical intervention at a point consonant with the "individual's view respecting a personally preferred manner of concluding life." . . . The difference is between self-infliction or self-destruction and self-determination. . . .

The interest in safeguarding the integrity of the medical profession . . . like the interest in preventing suicide, is not particularly threatened by permitting competent patients to refuse life-sustaining medical treatment. Medical ethics do not require medical intervention in disease at all costs. . . .

On balance, the right to self-determination ordinarily outweighs any countervailing state interests, and competent persons generally are permitted to refuse medical treatment, even at the risk of death.

SUPREME JUDICIAL COURT OF MASSACHUSETTS

Brophy v. New England Sinai Hospital

[JUSTICE LIACOS]

The right of self-determination and individual autonomy has its roots deep in our history. John Stuart Mill stated the concept succinctly: "[T]he only purpose for which power can be rightfully exercised

Reprinted from 497 Northeastern Reporter, 2d Series. 497 N.E. 2d 626 (Mass. 1986).

over any member of a civilised community, against his will, is to prevent harm to others. His own good, either physical or moral, is not a sufficient warrant. He cannot rightfully be compelled to do or forbear because it will be better for him to do so, because it will make him happier, because, in the opinion of others, to do so would be wise, or even right." . . .

It is in recognition of these fundamental principles of individual autonomy that we sought, in *Saikewicz,* to shift the emphasis away from a paternalistic view of what is "best" for a patient toward a reaffirmation that the basic question is what decision will comport with the will of the person involved, whether that person be competent or incompetent. As to the latter type of person, we concluded that the doctrine of substituted judgment, while not without its shortcomings, best served to emphasize the importance of honoring the privacy and dignity of the individual. . . .

Accepting that Brophy's substituted judgment would be to discontinue providing nutrients through the G-tube, we are left only with the question whether the Commonwealth's interests require that his judgment be overridden. It is natural to begin with the most significant interest in this case, the interest in the preservation of life. . . .

The law recognizes the individual's right to preserve his humanity, even if to preserve his humanity means to allow the natural processes of a disease or affliction to bring about a death with dignity. In stating this, we make no judgment based on our own view of the value of Brophy's life, since we do not approve of an analysis of State interest which focuses on Brophy's quality of life. . . .

The duty of the State to preserve life must encompass a recognition of an individual's right to avoid circumstances in which the individual himself would feel that efforts to sustain life demean or degrade his humanity. . . . It is antithetical to our scheme of ordered liberty and to our respect for the autonomy of the individual for the State to make decisions regarding the individual's quality of life. It is for the patient to decide such issues. Our role is limited to ensuring that a refusal of treatment does not violate legal norms. . . .

Here, Brophy is not terminally ill nor in danger of imminent death from any underlying physical illness. It is true, however, that his life expectancy has been shortened by his physical affliction. While the judge found that continued use of the G-tube is not a highly invasive or intrusive procedure and may not subject him to pain or suffering, he is left helpless and in a condition which Brophy has indicated he would consider to be degrading and without human dignity. In making this finding, it is clear that the judge failed to consider that Brophy's judgment would be that being maintained by use of the G-tube is indeed intrusive. Additionally, in our view, the maintenance of Brophy

. . . for a period of several years, is intrusive treatment as matter of law.

No case in this Commonwealth has presented such a situation. . . .

A few States have decided cases with fact patterns similar to the one at hand. The leading case is the New Jersey Supreme Court decision in *Matter of Conroy.*

Thus, we conclude that the State's interest in the preservation of life does not overcome Brophy's right to discontinue treatment. Nor do we consider his death to be against the State's interest in the prevention of suicide. He suffers an "affliction," . . . which makes him incapable of swallowing. The discontinuance of the G-tube feedings will not be the "death producing agent" set "in motion with the intent of causing his own death." "Prevention of suicide is . . . an inapplicable consideration. . . ." "A death which occurs after the removal of life sustaining systems is from natural causes, neither set in motion nor intended by the patient." *Welfare of Colyer,* [99 Wash.2d 114] . . . "[D]eclining life-sustaining medical treatment may not properly be viewed as an attempt to commit suicide. Refusing medical intervention merely allows the disease to take its natural course; if death were eventually to occur, it would be the result, primarily, of the underlying disease, and not the result of a self-inflicted injury." *Matter of Conroy,* 98 N.J. 321, 350–351, 486 A.2d 1209 (1985). . . .

Conclusion. Accordingly, we . . . set aside that portion of the judgment which enjoins the guardian from authorizing a facility to remove or clamp Brophy's G-tube. A new judgment is to be entered ordering the hospital to assist the guardian in transferring the ward to a suitable facility, or to his home, where his wishes may be effectuated, and authorizing the guardian to order such measures as she may deem necessary and appropriate in the circumstances.

So ordered.

NOLAN, JUSTICE (DISSENTING)

The court today has rendered an opinion which affronts logic, ethics, and the dignity of the human person.

As to logic, the court has built its entire case on an outrageously erroneous premise, i.e., food and liquids are medical treatment. The issue is not whether the tube should be inserted but whether food should be given through the tube. The process of feeding is simply *not* medical treatment and is not invasive, as the word is used in this context. Food and water are basic human needs. They are not medicines and feeding them to a patient is just not medical treatment. Because of this faulty premise, the court's conclusions must inevitably fall under the weight of logic.

In the forum of ethics, despite the opinion's high-blown language to the contrary, the court today has endorsed euthanasia and suicide. Suicide is direct self-destruction and is intrinsically evil. No set of circumstances can make it moral. Paul Brophy will die as a direct result of the cessation of feeding. The ethical principle of double effect is totally inapplicable here. This death by dehydration and starvation has been approved by the court. He will not die from the aneurysm which precipitated loss of consciousness, the surgery which was performed, the brain damage that followed or the insertion of the G-tube. He will die as a direct result of the refusal to feed him. He will starve to death, and the court approves this death. See Bannon, Rx: Death by Dehydration, 12 Human Life Rev., 70 (No. 3, 1986).

I pass over the glaring weakness in the evidentiary basis for the finding that Paul Brophy would decline provisions for food and water. The evidence that he knew the horrors of such a death is not present in this case, and without such evidence it can be argued persuasively that Brophy never made a judgment that food and water should be denied him.

Finally, I can think of nothing more degrading to the human person than the balance which the court struck today in favor of death and against life. It is but another triumph for the forces of secular humanism (modern paganism) which have now succeeded in imposing their anti-life principles at both ends of life's spectrum. Pro dolor.

LYNCH, JUSTICE (DISSENTING IN PART)

This case turns on a fine balancing of competing interests. I disagree with the majority and believe that that balance tips in favor of continuing to provide nutrition and hydration to Paul Brophy. . . .

My principal objection is that the State's interest in the preservation of life has not been given appropriate weight. In addition, unlike *Saikewicz,* the majority nullify, if only in part, the law against suicide.

The interest in the preservation of life consists of at least two related concerns. First, the State has an interest in preserving the life of the particular patient. Second, the State has a closely related interest in preserving the sanctity of all human life. *Matter of Conroy,* . . .

The majority recognize that the first concern is implicated in this case but fail to acknowledge significant concern for preserving the sanctity of all human life. The withdrawal of the provision of food and water is a particularly difficult, painful and gruesome death;[1] the cause of death would not be some underlying physical disability like kidney failure or the withdrawal of some highly invasive medical treatment, but the unnatural cessation of feeding and hydration which, like breathing, is part of the responsibilities we assume toward our bodies routinely. Such a process would not be very far from euthanasia, and the natural question is: Why not use more humane methods of euthanasia if that is what we endorse? The State has an interest in maintaining the public integrity of the symbols of life — apparent euthanasia, and an apparently painful and difficult method of euthanasia, is contrary to that interest.

Moreover, until this case, it was clear that the State's interest in life was to be balanced against the individual's right to privacy and bodily integrity. No case in this Commonwealth has ever construed the right to privacy and bodily integrity as more than the right to avoid invasive treatments and certain other bodily invasions under appropriate conditions. Today, however, the majority essentially equate the right to privacy-bodily integrity with a right to choose or refuse all bodily invasions. Thus, if an individual's choice would be to refuse treatment or care, it is not important that the treatment or care is minimally invasive (except to the extent that it factors into the individual's choice). The majority now go well beyond *Saikewicz* in following the New Jersey Supreme Court's pronouncement that the primary focus should be on the patient's choices and not on the type of treatment involved. . . .

Second, it appears that the majority have refused to overrule *Saikewicz* directly and to rule in favor of a constitutional right to die, so as to avoid the obvious conflict with the law against suicide. The State has an interest in the prevention of suicide. . . . We have stated that an adult's refusing medical treatment is not necessarily suicide because "(1) in refusing treatment the patient may not have the specific intent to die, and (2) even if he did, to the extent that the cause of death was from natural causes the patient did not set the death producing agent in motion with the intent of causing his own death." *Id.* Here, Brophy is not terminally ill, and death is not imminent, and the judge specifically found that Paul Brophy's decision would be to terminate his life by declining food and water. The judge also found that "Brophy's decision, if he were competent to make it, would be primarily based upon the present quality of life possible for him, and would not be based upon the burdens imposed upon him by receiving food and water through a G tube, which burdens are relatively minimal. . . ." Where treatment is burdensome and invasive, no such specific intent is normally at issue because, whether or not the patient seeks to die, the patient primarily seeks to end invasive or burdensome treatment.[2] There is no question that the intent here is to end a life that is "over." Moreover, death here would not be from natural causes, i.e., causes he or his agents did not set in motion, but instead, the death producing agent would be set in motion by a volitional act with the intent to cause death.[3]

Suicide is primarily a crime of commission, but can, and indeed must, also be conceived as an act of omission at times. See *In re Caulk,* 125 N.H. 226, 228, 231–232, 480 A.2d 93 (1984) (suicide can be committed by starvation [or dehydration]). If nutrition and hydration are terminated, it is not the illness which causes the death but the decision (and act in accordance therewith) that the illness makes life not worth living. There is no rational distinction between suicide by deprivation of hydration or nutrition in or out of a medical setting[4]—both are suicide.

The State therefore has an interest in preventing suicide in this case that is greater than that in any previous case which has been before this court. The majority are apparently willing to recognize a limited right to commit suicide when an individual chooses to forgo life sustaining nutrition and hydration in a medical setting. The law against suicide predates our Constitution, and we should not nullify it without express legislation to this effect. . . .

Here, where Paul Brophy did not specifically advert to the choice which the majority now make for him, we should not be so quick to overlook the State's interests in protecting human life and the law against suicide. After all, those interests are handed to us from a tradition which seeks to protect human autonomy. In such a close case we should be cautious, and the course of caution here lies in the direction of preserving life.

O'CONNOR, JUSTICE (CONCURRING IN PART AND DISSENTING IN PART). . . .

The court's statement of the trial judge's findings concerning the choice Brophy would have made, were he competent, "to decline the provision of food and water and to terminate his life," *ante* at 631, is critically incomplete. . . .

This case raises for the first time in this Commonwealth the question whether an individual has a legal right to choose to die, and to enlist the assistance of others to effectuate that choice on the ground that, irrespective of the nature of available life prolonging treatment, life in any event is not worth living and its continuation is intolerable. . . .

In light of the judge's findings, the precise issue in this case is whether the court shall honor the substituted judgment of a person in a persistent vegetative state that the artificial, *effective, and non-burdensome* maintenance of his nutrition and hydration be discontinued by others *in order to bring about his early death.* Suicide is the termination of one's own life by act or omission with the specific intention to do so. Euthanasia is the termination of another's life by act or omission, with the specific intention to do so, in order to eliminate suffering. The court must consider whether on the facts of this case legal rights to commit suicide and euthanasia should be recognized. Such rights should never be recognized.

Surely, if one has a right to commit suicide, others have a right to assist him in doing so. The fundamental question, then, is whether the court should recognize a right to commit suicide. This court's explicit recognition of an individual's right to be free of nonconsensual invasion of his bodily integrity in *Harnish v. Children's Hosp. Medical Center,* 387 Mass. 152, 439 N.E.2d 240 (1982), in no sense implied recognition of a right to commit suicide. . . .

The court's conclusion that Brophy's right to discontinue food and water is superior to the State's interest in preserving human life, *ante* at 638, appears, then, to be premised on the principle that everyone has an absolute right to commit suicide regardless of any assessment by the court of the quality of the life to be extinguished. If, indeed, that is a correct statement of the court's reasoning, it necessarily follows that the young as well as the old, the healthy as well as the sick, and the firm as well as the infirm, without exception, have the right to commit suicide, and that others have the right to participate in that act. Such a principle surely departs radically from the policy and tradition of this Commonwealth heretofore and should not be acceptable to a civilized society.

The court makes its own assessment of Brophy's condition as "helpless." *Ante* at 635. It may be, therefore, that the court does not rely exclusively on Brophy's own evaluation of the quality of his life, and that the court's evaluation is indeed a relevant factor. If that is the case, then the rule for the future is that the court will determine on a case by case basis whether the quality of life available to the individual who chooses to die justifies a State interest in protecting that life. Whether the court is establishing an absolute legal right to commit suicide or a right that depends on judicial measurement of the quality of the life involved, neither principle is consistent with this nation's traditional and fitting reverence for human life.

Even in cases involving severe and enduring illness, disability and "helplessness," society's focus must be on life, not death, with dignity. By its very nature, every human life, without reference to its condition, has a value that no one rightfully can deny or measure. Recognition of that truth is the cornerstone on which American law is built. Society's acceptance of that fundamental principle explains why, from time immemorial, society through law has extended its protection to all, including, especially, its weakest and most vulnerable members. The court's implicit, if not explicit, declaration that not every human life has sufficient value to be worthy of the State's protection denies the dignity of all human life, and undermines the very principle on which American law is constructed. I would affirm the judgment below.

NOTES

1. Removal of the G tube would likely create various effects from the lack of hydration and nutrition, leading ultimately to death. Brophy's mouth would dry out and become caked or coated with thick material. His lips would become parched and cracked. His tongue would swell, and might crack. His eyes would recede back into their orbits and his cheeks would become hollow. The lining of his nose might crack and cause his nose to bleed. His skin would hang loose on his body and become dry and scaly. His urine would become highly concentrated, leading to burning of the bladder. The lining of his stomach would dry out and he would experience dry heaves and vomiting. His body temperature would become very high. His brain cells would dry out, causing convulsions. His respiratory tract would dry out, and the thick secretions that would result could plug his lungs and cause death. At some point within five days to three weeks his major organs, including his lungs, heart, and brain, would give out and he would die. The judge found that death by dehydration is extremely painful and uncomfortable for a human being. The judge could not rule out the possibility that Paul Brophy could experience pain in such a scenario. Paul Brophy's attending physician described death by dehydration as cruel and violent.

2. This is not a case where a patient subject to burdensome or invasive treatment seeks to end that treatment *and* seeks to die. Ordinarily, mere knowledge that death will invariably result from the withdrawal of treatment is not sufficient to show a specific intent to die.

3. Contrast the situation of a person on a respirator or dialysis machine, whose failed respirator system or kidneys is the problem that will cause death.

4. Query: Do the majority recognize a right to die via starvation-dehydration if done at home, or elsewhere outside of a medical facility?

JUSTICE ANTONIN SCALIA (CONCURRING) IN UNITED STATES SUPREME COURT

Cruzan v. Director, Missouri Dept. of Health

The various opinions in this case portray quite clearly the difficult, indeed agonizing, questions that are presented by the constantly increasing power of science to keep the human body alive for longer than any reasonable person would want to inhabit it. . . .

Reprinted from 110 *Supreme Court Reporter*. 110 S.Ct. 2841 (1990).

While I agree with the Court's analysis today, and therefore join in its opinion, I would have preferred that we announce, clearly and promptly, that the federal courts have no business in this field; that American law has always accorded the State the power to prevent, by force if necessary, suicide — including suicide by refusing to take appropriate measures necessary to preserve one's life; that the point at which life becomes "worthless," and the point at which the means necessary to preserve it become "extraordinary" or "inappropriate," are neither set forth in the Constitution nor known to the nine Justices of this Court any better than they are known to nine people picked at random from the Kansas City telephone directory; and hence, that even when it *is* demonstrated by clear and convincing evidence that a patient no longer wishes certain measures to be taken to preserve her life, it is up to the citizens of Missouri to decide, through their elected representatives, whether that wish will be honored. It is quite impossible (because the Constitution says nothing about the matter) that those citizens will decide upon a line less lawful than the one we would choose; and it is unlikely (because we know no more about "life-and-death" than they do) that they will decide upon a line less reasonable. . . .

At common law in England, a suicide—defined as one who "deliberately puts an end to his own existence, or commits any unlawful malicious act, the consequence of which is his own death," 4 W. Blackstone, Commentaries *189—was criminally liable. *Ibid.* Although the States abolished the penalties imposed by the common law (*i.e.*, forfeiture and ignominious burial), they did so to spare the innocent family, and not to legitimize the act. Case law at the time of the Fourteenth Amendment generally held that assisting suicide was a criminal offense. . . . Thus, "there is no significant support for the claim that a right to suicide is so rooted in our tradition that it may be deemed 'fundamental' or 'implicit in the concept of ordered liberty.'" (quoting *Palko v. Connecticut,* 302 U.S. 319, 325, 58 S.Ct. 149, 152, 82 L.Ed. 288 (1937)).

Petitioners rely on three distinctions to separate Nancy Cruzan's case from ordinary suicide: (1) that she is permanently incapacited and in pain; (2) that she would bring on her death not by any affirmative act but by merely declining treatment that provides nourishment; and (3) that preventing her from effectuating her presumed wish to die requires violation of her bodily integrity. None of these suffices. Suicide was not excused even when committed "to avoid those ills which [persons] had not the fortitude to endure." 4 Blackstone, *supra,* at *189. "The life of those to whom life has become a burden—of those who are hopelessly diseased or fatally wounded—nay, even the lives of criminals condemned to death, are under the protection of the law, equally as the lives of those who are in the full tide of life's enjoyment, and anx-

ious to continue to live." *Blackburn v. State*, 23 Ohio St. 146, 163 (1873). Thus, a man who prepared a poison, and placed it within reach of his wife, "to put an end to her suffering" from a terminal illness was convicted of murder, *People v. Roberts,* 211 Mich. 187, 178 N.W. 690, 693 (1920); the "incurable suffering of the suicide, as a legal question, could hardly affect the degree of criminality. . . ." Note, 30 Yale L.J. 408, 412 (1921) (discussing *Roberts*). Nor would the imminence of the patient's death have affected liability. "The lives of all are equally under the protection of the law, and under that protection to their last moment. . . . [Assisted suicide] is declared by the law to be murder, irrespective of the wishes or the condition of the party to whom the poison is administered. . . ." *Blackburn, supra,* at 163. . . .

The second asserted distinction—suggested by the recent cases canvassed by the Court concerning the right to refuse treatment, *ante,* at 2846–2850—relies on the dichotomy between action and inaction. Suicide, it is said, consists of an affirmative act to end one's life; refusing treatment is not an affirmative act "causing" death, but merely a passive acceptance of the natural process of dying. I readily acknowledge that the distinction between action and inaction has some bearing upon the legislative judgment of what ought to be prevented as suicide—though even there it would seem to me unreasonable to draw the line precisely between action and inaction, rather than between various forms of inaction. It would not make much sense to say that one may not kill oneself by walking into the sea, but may sit on the beach until submerged by the incoming tide; or that one may not intentionally lock oneself into a cold storage locker, but may refrain from coming indoors when the temperature drops below freezing. Even as a legislative matter, in other words, the intelligent line does not fall between action and inaction but between those forms of inaction that consist of abstaining from "ordinary" care and those that consist of abstaining from "excessive" or "heroic" measures. Unlike action *vs.* inaction, that is not a line to be discerned by logic or legal analysis, and we should not pretend that it is.

But to return to the principal point for present purposes: the irrelevance of the action-inaction distinction. Starving oneself to death is no different from putting a gun to one's temple as far as the common-law definition of suicide is concerned; the cause of death in both cases is the suicide's conscious decision to "pu[t] an end to his own existence." 4 Blackstone, *supra,* at *189. . . .

The third asserted basis of distinction—that frustrating Nancy Cruzan's wish to die in the present case requires interference with her bodily integrity—is likewise inadequate, because such interference is impermissible only if one begs the question whether her refusal to undergo the treatment on her own is suicide. It has always been lawful not only for the State, but even for private citizens, to interfere with bodily integrity to prevent a felony. . . . That general rule has of course been applied to suicide. At common law, even a private person's use of force to prevent suicide was privileged. . . .

There is nothing distinctive about accepting death through the refusal of "medical treatment," as opposed to accepting it through the refusal of food, or through the failure to shut off the engine and get out of the car after parking in one's garage after work. Suppose that Nancy Cruzan were in precisely the condition she is in today, except that she would be fed and digest food and water *without* artificial assistance. How is the State's "interest" in keeping her alive thereby increased, or her interest in deciding whether she wants to continue living reduced? . . .

What I have said above is not meant to suggest that I would think it desirable, if we were sure that Nancy Cruzan wanted to die, to keep her alive by the means at issue here. I assert only that the Constitution has nothing to say about the subject. To raise up a constitutional right here we would have to create out of nothing (for it exists neither in text nor tradition) some constitutional principle whereby, although the State may insist that an individual come in out of the cold and eat food, it may not insist that he take medicine; and although it may pump his stomach empty of poison he has ingested, it may not fill his stomach with food he has failed to ingest. Are there, then, no reasonable and humane limits that ought not to be exceeded in requiring an individual to preserve his own life? There obviously are, but they are not set forth in the Due Process Clause. . . . Our salvation is the Equal Protection Clause, which requires the democratic majority to accept for themselves and their loved ones what they impose on you and me. This Court need not, and has no authority to, inject itself into every field of human activity where irrationality and oppression may theoretically occur, and if it tries to do so it will destroy itself.

DANIEL CALLAHAN

Vital Distinctions, Mortal Questions: Debating Euthanasia and Health-Care Costs

. . . Of late, the strongest challenge to the tradition [that prohibits active euthanasia] has been a denial that there is a meaningful distinction to be made between killing and allowing to die, between an act of commission and one of omission. While this challenge comes most strongly from those favoring the legalization of active euthanasia, it seems to draw at least implicit or inadvertent support from some prolife groups as well. Supporters of euthanasia argue that if

From Daniel Callahan, "Vital Distinctions, Mortal Questions," *Commonweal* 115 (July 15, 1988). Reprinted by permission of the publisher.

there is no serious distinction to be drawn between killing and allowing to die, then our present acceptance of allowing to die ought to be extended to active killing, when such killing would be more merciful. Prolife groups may acknowledge a strictly logical distinction between the two, but argue that "allowing to die" is a slogan that has come to be used as a legitimizing rationale to end the lives of those who are burdensome or judged to have lives not worth living. This simultaneous challenge from the liberals and the conservatives promises maximum confusion, making it that much harder to discuss carefully the euthanasia issue and all but impossible to consider coherently the allocation problem.

MAINTAINING THE DISTINCTION

My contention is that, properly understood, the distinction between killing and allowing to die is still perfectly valid for use, both in the euthanasia debate and in the allocation discussion. The distinction rests on the commonplace observation that lives can come to an end as the result of (a) the direct action of another who becomes the cause of death (as in shooting a person), or as the result of (b) impersonal forces where no human agent has acted (death by lightning or by disease).

The purpose of the distinction is to separate those deaths directly caused by human action, and those caused by nonhuman events. It is, as a distinction, meant to say something about human beings and their relationship to the world. It attempts to articulate the difference between those actions for which human beings can rightly be held responsible and those of which they are innocent. At the heart of the issue is a distinction between physical causality—the realm of impersonal events—and moral culpability—the realm of human responsibility.

Little imagination is required to see how the distinction between killing and allowing to die can be challenged. The standard objection encompasses two points. The first is that people can die equally by our omissions as well as our commissions: we can refrain from saving them when it is possible to do so and they will be just as dead as if we shot them. Our decision itself, and not necessarily how we effectuate that decision, is the reason for their death. That fact establishes the basis of the second point: if we *intend* a person's death, it can be brought about as well by acts we omit as those we commit; the crucial moral point is not how the person dies, but our intention. We can, then, be responsible for the death of another by intending that they die and we accomplish that end by standing aside and allowing them to die.

Despite these criticisms—resting upon ambiguities that can readily be acknowledged—the distinction between killing and allowing to die remains valid. It has not only a logical validity but, no less important, a social validity whose place must be as central in moral judgments about allocation as in individual patient decisions. As a way of elucidating the distinction, I propose that it is best understood as expressing three different, though overlapping, perspectives on nature and human action: metaphysical, moral, and medical.

METAPHYSICAL

The first and most fundamental premise of the distinction between killing and allowing to die is that there is a sharp difference between the self and the external world. Unlike the childish fantasy that the world is nothing more than a projection of the self, or the neurotic person's fear that he or she is responsible for everything that goes wrong, the distinction is meant to uphold a simple notion: there is a world external to the self that has its own, and independent, causal dynamism. A conflation of killing and allowing to die mistakenly assumes that the self has become master of everything within and outside of the self. It is as if the conceit that modern humans might ultimately control nature has been internalized: that, if the self might be able to influence nature by its actions, then the self and nature must be one.

But, of course, that is a fantasy. The fact that we can intervene in nature, and cure or control many diseases, does not erase the difference between the self and the external world. It is as "out there" as ever, even if more under our sway. But that sway, however great, is always limited. We can cure disease, but not always the chronic illness that follows the cure. We can forestall death with modern medicine, but death always wins because of the body's inherent limitations, stubbornly beyond final human control. We can distinguish between an aging body and a diseased body, but in the end they always become one and the same body. To attempt to deny the distinction between killing and allowing to die is, then, mistakenly to impute more power to human action than it actually has and to accept the conceit that nature has now fallen wholly within the realm of human control.

MORAL

At the center of the distinction between killing and allowing to die is the difference between physical causality and moral culpability. On the one hand, to bring the life of another to an end by an injection is to directly kill the other—our action is the physical cause of death. On the other hand, to allow someone to die from a disease we cannot cure (and that we did not cause) is to permit the *disease* to act as the cause of death. The notion of physical causality in both cases rests on the metaphysical distinction between human agency and the action of external nature. The ambiguity arises precisely because we can be morally culpable of killing someone (unless we have a moral right to do so, as in self-defense) and no less culpable for allowing someone to die (if we have both the possibility and the obligation of keeping that person alive). Thus there are cases where, morally speaking, it makes no difference whether we killed or allowed to die; we are equally responsible morally. In those cases, the lines of physical causality and moral culpability happen to cross. Yet the fact that they can cross *in some cases* in no way shows that they are always, or even usually, one and the same. We can usually dissect the difference in all but the most obscure cases. We should not, then, use the ambiguity of such cases to do away altogether with the distinction between killing and allowing to die. Ambiguity may obscure, but it does not erase the line between the two.

There is one group of ambiguous cases that is especially troublesome. Even if we grant the ordinary validity of the distinction between killing and allowing to die, what about those cases that combine (a) an illness that renders a patient unable to carry out an ordinary biological function (to eat or breathe unassisted, for example), and (b) our decision to turn off a respirator or remove an artificial feeding tube? On the level of physical causality, have we killed the patient or allowed the person to die? In one sense, it is our action that shortens the person's life, and yet in another sense it is the underlying disease that brings the life to an end. I believe it reasonable to say that, since this person's life was being sustained by artificial means (respirator or tube), and that was necessary because of the presence of an incapacitating disease, the disease is the ultimate reality behind the death. Were it not for the disease, there would be no need for artificial sustenance in the first place and no moral issue at all. To lose sight of the paramount reality of the disease is to lose sight of the difference between ourselves and the outer world. Our action may hasten, but does not finally cause, this death.

I quickly add, and underscore, a moral point: the person who, without good moral reason, turns off a respirator or pulls a feeding tube, can be morally culpable if there is no good reason to do so. (To cease treatment may or may not be morally acceptable.) The moral question is whether we are obliged to continue treating a life that is being artificially sustained.

There is an analogous issue of importance. Physicians frequently feel morally more responsible for stopping the use of a life-saving device than for not using it in the first place. While the psychology behind that feeling is understandable, there is no significant moral difference between withholding and withdrawing treatment. The point of this now almost universal denial is precisely that an intervention into the disease process does not erase the underlying disease. To accept the fact that a disease cannot be controlled, though an effort was made to do so, is as morally acceptable as deciding in advance that it cannot be successfully controlled.

MEDICAL

The main social purpose of the distinction between killing and allowing to die has been that of protecting the historical role of the physician as one who tries to cure or comfort patients rather than kill them. Physicians have been given special knowledge about the body, knowledge that can be used to kill or to cure. They are also given great privileges in making use of that knowledge. It is thus all the more important that their social role and power be, and be seen to be, a limited power. That power may be used only to cure or comfort, never to kill. Otherwise, it would open the way for powerful misuse and, no less important, represent an intrinsic violation of what it has traditionally meant to be a physician.

Yet if it is possible for physicians to misuse their knowledge and power in order to kill people directly, are they therefore required to use that same knowledge always to keep people alive, always to resist a disease that can kill the patient? The traditional answer has been: not necessarily. For the physician's ultimate obligation is to the welfare of the patient, and excessive treatment can be as detrimental to that welfare as inadequate treatment. Put another way, the obligation to resist the lethal power of disease is limited—it ceases when the patient is unwilling to have it resisted, or when the resistance no longer serves the patient's welfare. Behind this moral premise is the recognition that disease (of some kind) ultimately triumphs, and that death is both inevitable and not always the greatest human evil. To demand of physicians that they always struggle against disease, as if it were always in their power to conquer it, would be to fall into the same metaphysical trap mentioned above: that of assuming that no distinction can be drawn between natural and human agency.

THE ALLOCATION DEBATE

If the implications of doing away with the distinction between killing and allowing to die are momentous for the euthanasia debate and the treatment of individual patients, they are equally grave in their implications for the allocation debate. It is hard, in fact, to see how we can have a reasonable allocation debate without making the distinction central to that debate. Without it, we face a number of stark alternatives. If we cannot morally distinguish between killing and allowing to die, then every allocation decision can be construed as directly killing those who lose out in the process. A refusal to provide life-saving coverage under an entitlement program will be seen as a means of active *involuntary* euthanasia. To allocate money, say, to education rather than to health care could be seen as a decision to kill people for the sake of education (more specifically, to kill the sick to help children).

Given that understanding, health needs would ordinarily trump all other social claims (unless they could be justified also on health grounds); any other choice would be seen as direct killing. I do not invoke here a hypothetical worry. Even now, those who have tried to limit health allocations have been accused by some of using financial arguments as a covert way of ridding society of people unwanted on other grounds, or simply thought too burdensomely expensive to be worth support. Others have been no less quick to complain: for a society to deny health resources to the needy, or to want to limit an entitlement program, is a murderous course, a selfish way to keep for oneself resources that would save the lives of others.

I believe that way of thinking, whether from right or left, is misleading and harmful. To deny the distinction between killing and allowing to die, and then to use that denial as a way of circumventing a necessary debate or decision about allocations, only adds a social error to a metaphysical one. To say this is not to deny that allocation decisions have important life-and-death implications, or that some allocation decisions could be used to mask abominable moral attitudes or practices; or that, in practice, some allocation decisions can be wrong or unfair. I am only trying to say that issues of this kind must be decided on their merits and not dealt with by ignoring or confusing the distinction between killing and allowing to die. That helps nothing.

How, then, can we make difficult allocation decisions in ways that avoid any suggestion that they are being used as a way of wrongly killing people? Or of making them in ways that properly allow us to let disease shorten, or end, life? This problem is all the more complicated for affluent nations. For nations that have nothing, there are only "lifeboat" choices, that is, giving only to one because there is not enough for both. For affluent countries the decision is more complex. We could in this country always spend more on health care. But when would it become unreasonable to do so?

It is not easy to find a moral foothold for making such judgments. They must certainly meet some reasonable tests of justice and fairness, both substantively and procedurally. They ought also to reflect some coherent vision of a good society. I will not take up those important questions here.

KENNETH F. SCHAFFNER

Recognizing the Tragic Choice:
Food, Water, and the Right to Assisted Suicide

In 1978, Dr. Guttentag (9) wrote that the common underlying foundation of medicine was to provide an effective response to the patient's overt or hidden request: "Help me in the care of *my* health." The appropriate response is *usually* to save the patient's life and cure his or her disease—the primary topic of this conference. Frequently, the best response is to provide only "comfort care" and an "easy death." Dr. Miller's presentation focused on the ethical problems associated with cutting-edge research in resuscitation medicine. In this presentation, I will examine the *other* side of health care delivery, and discuss recent developments, chiefly in the United States, associated with comfort care of the terminally ill and the legitimacy of various means of hastening the dying process.

Before I get to the specifics of some of the court decisions, and also to some controversies they have generated, I want to take a few moments to delineate the ethical, and very general, legal principles on which these decisions are, in my view, founded.

The decisions involving a legally sanctioned right to die all begin with a recognition of a fundamental right to self-determination. This is a right that many courts have found, based on the common law tradition, in cases involving the right to determine what shall be done to one's body. The courts have also cited both federal and state constitutional grounds for such decisions, typically appealing to a "right to privacy."

This general right to self-determination extends to legitimate refusal of health care. Such a right of refusal is implemented by attempting to ascertain what the patient truly wants or what the patient *would have wanted* if he or she had been asked. The latter notion, which attempts to respect the individuality of a patient's wishes, is called in legal parlance a standard of "substituted judgment." If no trustworthy evidence about what a patient would have wanted is available either from a written record or from relatives or close friends, then the courts tend to fall back on what a "reasonable person" would want. This notion is often referred to as the "best interests" standard. It does not necessarily respect a patient's individuality, but it does attempt to safeguard the patient's interests, such as freedom from a prolonged, painful death in the event recovery is virtually nil.

I mention these ideas because they are important background to a growing number of decisions that are having literally fatal consequences for patients. They, and the refinements which I will now discuss in the context of some specific cases, are increasingly entering into the management of terminally ill or persistently vegetative-state patients nationwide.

I will begin by reviewing briefly three recent court cases associated with the treatment-nontreatment issue, the 1983 *Barber/Nedjl* case and the 1986 cases of *Brophy* and *Bouvia* (1, 2, 4).

The *Barber/Nedjl* case began in 1981 when Mr. Clarence Herbert, a 53-year-old security guard, entered Kaiser-Permanente Hospital in Los Angeles for routine surgery. His surgery was uneventful, but he apparently suffered a heart attack in the recovery room, and he was determined to have severe brain damage secondary to anoxia. Respirator support was withdrawn with Mr. Herbert's wife's permission, but the patient began to breathe on his own. Dr. Barber, the attending internist, discontinued all iv feedings and antibiotics, and soon afterward Dr. Nedjl, the surgeon, ordered removal of the patient's NG tube. Mr. Herbert died about a week later from pneumonia and

From Kenneth F. Schaffner, "Recognizing the Tragic Choice: Food, Water, and the Right to Assisted Suicide," *Critical Care Medicine*, Vol. 16, No. 10, October 1988, pp. 1063–1068. ©1988. Reprinted by permission of Williams and Wilkins.

dehydration. The two physicians, Drs. Nedjl and Barber, were prosecuted for murder by the Los Angeles District Attorney, apparently on the basis of a complaint from the nursing staff who strongly disagreed with the management of Mr. Herbert's situation. The California trial court decided that the cessation of life-support measures "is not an affirmative act but rather a withdrawal or omission of further treatment." The court (1) also wrote that:

Medical procedures to provide nutrition and hydration are more similar to other medical procedures than to typical human ways of providing nutrition and hydration. Their benefits and burdens ought to be evaluated in the same manner as any other medical procedure.

The physicians were acquitted, but the District Attorney appealed. The California Court of Appeals affirmed the original trial court's decision.

In *Brophy,* the patient was a 45-year-old fireman who, in 1983, sustained a cerebral aneurysm and became totally comatose after surgery that attempted to restore brain function. He was fed via a gastrostomy tube placed in December 1983. Early in 1985, his family requested that the hospital cease all treatment including artificial nourishment. The hospital refused, and the patient's wife sought a court order. A lower court permitted termination of all treatment except nutrition and hydration, but the Massachusetts Supreme Judicial Court determined, on September 11, 1986, that the feeding tube could be removed and the patient be allowed to die (4).

In *Bouvia,* the patient, Elizabeth Bouvia, is a woman in her late 20s who has been quadriplegic since birth and who now suffers severe pain from degenerative arthritis. In 1983, she requested assistance from Riverside Hospital in California to starve herself to death. The hospital refused, and the patient asked for court assistance, which was denied on December 16, 1983. Subsequently, when a patient in High Desert Hospital, in California, Ms. Bouvia petitioned the Superior Court of California to have her feeding tube removed (she claimed that she was then able to take adequate amounts of food by mouth), but permission was denied. She then appealed to the California Court of Appeals, which granted authorization for removal of the feeding tube on April 16, 1986.

I cite these cases principally to provide the background to several quotations from the *Barber/Nedjl*

decision as well as two of the (partially) dissenting opinions in *Brophy* and a concurring opinion in *Bouvia.* In *Brophy,* Justice Lynch felt that on the balance, nutrition and hydration for the patient should have been continued. Lynch expressed concern that the state's interest in the preservation of life had not been given sufficient weight, and noted that none of the courts in either California, New Jersey, or Massachusetts has "been willing to take the final step and rule directly that the right to privacy and bodily integrity entails a (limited) right to die . . . but now, in essence [Massachusetts law] . . . does" (4). Lynch wrote further that "There is no question that the intent here is to end a life that is over. Moreover, death here would not be from natural causes, i.e., causes he or his agents did not set in motion, but instead the death-producing agent would be set in motion by a volitional act with the intent to cause death"[a] (4). Lynch adds that such an act is tantamount to suicide and that "there is no rational distinction between suicide by deprivation of hydration or nutrition in or out of a medical setting—both are suicide" (4).

Justice Lynch was not alone in his objections; Justice O'Connor also added in a partial dissent that ". . . this case raises for the first time in this Commonwealth the question whether an individual has the legal right to choose to die, and to enlist the assistance of others to effectuate that choice on the ground that, irrespective of the nature of available life-prolonging treatment, life in any event is not worth living and its continuation is intolerable" (4).

Interestingly, one of the concurring opinions in the *Bouvia* case recognizes the same set of issues, but *affirms* the existence of a right to die with assistance. Associate Justice Compton (2) wrote in *Bouvia* that:

I have no doubt that Elizabeth Bouvia wants to die. . . . Elizabeth apparently has made a conscious and informed choice that she prefers death to continued existence in her helpless and, to her, intolerable condition. I believe that she has an absolute right to effectuate that decision. This state and the medical profession instead of frustrating her desire should be attempting to relieve her suffering by permitting and in fact assisting her to die with ease and dignity. The fact that she is forced to suffer the ordeal of self-starvation to achieve her objective is in itself inhumane.

The right to die is an integral part of our right to control our own destinies so long as the rights of others are not af-

---

[a]Justice Lynch, in an interesting footnote to this remark, says: "Contrast the situation of a person on a respirator or dialysis machine, whose failed respiratory system or kidneys is the problem that will cause death."

fected. That right should, in my opinion, include the ability to enlist assistance from others, including the medical profession, in making death as painless and quick as possible.

That ability should not be hampered by the state's threat to impose penal sanctions on those who might be disposed to lend assistance.

PHILOSOPHICAL AND LEGAL DISTINCTIONS

To those who have not been following the fairly rapid developments in both the ethical and the legal arenas concerning cessation of nourishment in terminally ill and irreversibly comatose patients, it may seem surprising that the withdrawal decisions in the *Barber/Nedjl, Brophy,* and *Bouvia* cases have prevailed. The determination that food and water can be suspended in such patients, however, is actually the result of a penetrating analysis of some traditional distinctions such as the contrast between killing and letting die and the difference between ordinary and extraordinary forms of medical treatment, and a realization that the *moral* significance of such distinctions supports these court decisions. Let me first explain the nature of this analysis, but then go on to question whether the ethical analysis has in fact gone far enough.

KILLING VS. LETTING DIE

For some time now, medical ethics has recognized the difference between *active killing,* such as administering a lethal injection of morphine to a patient, and *passive "letting die,"* for example, deciding not to treat aggressively a pneumonia in a terminally ill cancer patient. The former type of activity, sometimes referred to as "active euthanasia," is still generally recognized legally as murder; the latter practice of "passive euthanasia" is accepted by professional societies, most religious groups, and the law.[b] I shall touch on the distinction between *active* and *passive* maneuvers again later; suffice it for now to add that this distinction between killing and letting die is almost always considered in concert with another distinction, that between ordinary and extraordinary means of treatment.

ORDINARY VS. EXTRAORDINARY MEASURES

This distinction had its origin in Roman Catholic theology, but by the 1970s had entered the ethics of professional societies such as the American Medical As-

[b]Very recently, a widely publicized case described in "It's Over, Debbie," *JAMA* 1988; 259:2142, has provoked extensive debate on this distinction. See Lundberg (11) for overview and references.

KENNETH F. SCHAFFNER   467

sociation as well as figuring in court decisions such as the Quinlan case. In their inquiry, the President's Commission for the Study of Ethical Problems in Medicine noted that several different meanings have been attributed to this distinction, such as (a) common vs. uncommon, (b) simple vs. complex (roughly low-tech vs. high-tech), (c) and useful vs. burdensome (15). It is only the latter meaning that has been viewed as having *moral* significance. This interpretation has been elaborated by medical ethicists Lynn and Childress (12) as follows:

What matters . . . in determining whether to provide a treatment . . . is not a prior determination that this treatment is "ordinary" per se, but rather a determination that this treatment is likely to provide this patient benefits that are sufficient to make it worthwhile to endure the burdens that accompany the treatment.

It is this balancing of the benefits and burdens that the courts have seized upon in determining that nutrition and hydration are more like a respirator than not, and thus are contraindicated if they will not ameliorate a patient's condition. The *Barber/Nedjl* case discussed earlier provides an example of this type of reasoning (1):

Medical nutrition and hydration may not always provide net benefits to patients. Medical procedures to provide nutrition and hydration are more similar to other medical procedures than to typical human ways of providing nutrition and hydration. Their benefits and burdens ought to be evaluated in the same manner as any other medical procedure.

This assignment of food and water to the category of "extraordinary measures," even if restricted to certain patients in specific circumstances, has not been greeted with uniform acceptance in either the legal or the medical ethical communities. Daniel Callahan, the Director of the Hastings Center, physician Mark Siegler, and lawyer Alan Weisbard all have urged considerable caution in moving in this direction (5, 18). I will return to some of their reservations later.

CAUSATION OF DEATH: AN INQUIRY

At this point I want to reconsider the arguments made earlier by Justices Lynch and O'Connor in the *Brophy* case to the effect that a decision to cease nutrition and hydration was tantamount to acknowledging a legal right to medically assisted suicide.

I think that there is no question about the *intent* to end the life of the patient in the *Brophy* case; clearly, Mrs. Brophy felt that her husband and family had suffered sufficiently and that the prospect for recovery was virtually nil. There is, however, the question of whether withdrawal of nutrition and hydration is appropriately viewed as the *cause* of the patient's death, or whether some other factor, such as an underlying disease, is not the cause. The question is an important one. For if it be acknowledged that ceasing food and water is the *cause* of Brophy's death, forgoing life-sustaining food and water may be morally and legally unacceptable because such a maneuver is viewed as the determinative active factor in the patient's death. Such a concern has been noted by ethicist Dan Brock in his recent essay (3):

One source of resistance to extending this acceptance of a general right to forgo life-sustaining (medical) treatment to the case of food and water has explicitly philosophical origins: for a physician to withhold food and water might seem not merely to allow the patient to die, but to kill the patient, and therefore wrong. A closely related moral worry is that for physicians to withhold food and water would be to make them the direct cause of their patients' deaths, which also would be wrong.

Brock's answer to the first question, whether withholding food and water is killing, is not one that I can fully address in this paper. Suffice it to say that Brock (3) contends that:

. . . whenever a disease process attacks a patient's normal ability to eat and drink, and artificial means of providing nutrition are required, then feeding by artificial means *can be seen as* a form of life-sustaining treatment. . . . Forgoing feeding . . . (in such circumstances) is then . . . to allow the patient to die from a disease that has impaired his normal ability to eat and drink.

What is at issue here then are *two* processes that can bring about the death of the patient, and what Brock has done in his argument is to select one, the disease, as the *responsible* agent in bringing about the death of the patient.

This matter of selecting the cause from two or more causes that may operate to result in a patient's death is revisited in a later section of Brock's paper, which more explicitly addresses the issue of the "cause of death." Here, Brock notes that "questions of causality are exceedingly difficult and complex," but he attempts, in a quite lucid manner, to bring some order into this conceptual morass. To indicate briefly his position, Brock introduces what lawyers have termed the "but for" analysis of causation: "but for the banana peel on the sidewalk, I would not have slipped, fallen, and harmed myself."

As Brock adds, there are many "but for" conditions that cooperate to bring about a typical effect, and identifying which one (or more) of the many conditions is responsible for an effect is "in part an empirical or factual inquiry. . . , but it is shaped as well by normative concerns; these are legal concerns when it is a legal inquiry, moral concerns when it is a moral inquiry" (3). This being the case, Brock's answer to the question whether the physician's withholding of food and water is the *cause* of the patient's death falls back on the issue as to whether it is morally (or legally) permissible to withhold food and water that in conjunction with other factors brings about the patient's death. Brock (3) writes: "it will be the legal and moral permissibility helping determine what or who is *the* cause of death, not whether the physician is the cause being the determinant of legal and moral permissibility."

This is an appropriate and clever move, but I believe that it unfortunately *masks* rather than clarifies the moral and legal issue involved. As Brock points out, selecting *the* cause from a set of necessary (or contributory) factors in human situations typically involves a number of complex considerations. Just how complex the matter can become is evident to readers of Hart and Honoré's classic book *Causation in the Law* (10). There are, however, several other approaches that can be taken to elucidate which factor is best characterized as *the* cause in a complex situation. In the following section, I consider one such alternative approach and also examine what implications it has for our moral inquiry.[c]

CAUSATION AND MULTIPLE DETERMINATION

In those situations in which there are complex multiple causes in operation, one technique that may help to clarify the analysis is to construct (at least concep-

[c]Readers are encouraged to consult Mackie's book (13), which discusses some of the difficulties with complex causation. Mackie's notion of an INUS condition (an *I*nsufficient *N*onredundant part of an *U*nnecessary but *S*ufficient condition) is generally viewed as one of the most careful and sophisticated means of identifying a cause in what Salmon (16) has termed the "sufficiency/necessity view" of causal analysis.

tually) alternative causal sequences. In so doing, we bring to bear on the case at hand our extensive background knowledge, which permits us with a reasonable degree of confidence to formulate alternative scenarios with different causal factors operational at different times.

In the current case types, such as analytical exercise will indicate that the patients' death is brought about by the withholding of food and water, but that this fatal consequence is predicated on the individual's being sufficiently ill that he or she cannot take nourishment and hydration in the "normal" way. However, a patient with a good prognosis who was too ill to take food and water normally would not have such sustenance removed: it is the conscious decision that this patient's life is not worth prolonging that motivates the removal of the sustenance. Thus, it is the *perception and interpretation* of the illness by others that is controlling, not the illness per se.

Moreover, though the patient's illness may well result in the death of the patient, given sufficient time, it is the process(es) generated by the withholding of food and water, perhaps assisted by the underlying illness, that results in the patient's death *at this time*. Furthermore, such death is certain and predictable within a range of error, solely on the basis of withholding of nourishment and hydration. In cases like *Brophy,* withholding food and water thus controls or dominates and may well completely override other contributing causes in the causal explanation.[d] To construe the situation otherwise may be a convenient legal (and possibly moral) fiction, but I believe such a construal engenders significant other problems, some to be addressed below.

A brief and somewhat more technical elaboration of the above consideration involving an appeal to Mill's method of agreement for determining causation may help make the argument clearer.[e] Consider the

following way of representing the causal factors involved in the death of two patients, one *permanently* comatose and the second *temporarily* comatose.

Case 1:

Permanent coma →Inability to take food/water by mouth
and   Death
Physician's decision →Suspension of artificial food/water

Case 2:

Temporary coma →Inability to take food/water by mouth
and   Death
Physician's decision →Suspension of artificial food/water

I believe what a comparison of these cases suggests is that, by the method of agreement, the cause of death is the suspension of the artificial food/water, and that, in turn, the cause of that suspension is the decision of the physician. Such a decision is, as noted in the discussion above, always made with concurrence from the patient/family/courts. Here the cause is a "necessary condition." In the following case, however, it would also be "sufficient."

Case 3:

Absence of coma but
patient is terminal   →Ability to take food/water by mouth
and   Death
Physician's decision   → Suspension of *ALL* food/water

Here the physician's action clearly *overrides* any disease cause of death.

Now this case appears to have significantly changed the physician's action, since we have moved from "artificial" food and water to denying *all* nourishment and hydration. However, recall that such a change is only *morally* relevant if it affects the burdens and benefits involved in the patient's situation. As noted above, the courts have been following this burdens-benefits approach as well, so the change is *legally* relevant only if the benefits and burdens change. I see this as a *tu quoque* to those who argue that suspension of artificial nutrition and hydration is not the cause of death, since by their own general position it is clearly necessary (in the circumstances) and may be a sufficient cause of death.

For readers still skeptical of the use of this notion that we might not clearly be able to identify the relevant causal factor in a situation by analytical means, let me offer an example not involving food and water.

Consider a class of patients who are weaned from respirators, but we do not know whether these patients will continue to respire unaided. They are known to have or are suspected of having an underlying disease

---

[d]To be fully precise, a *ceteris paribus* or "all other things being equal" qualifier should be added to this sentence. We exclude such interfering causes as the explosion of the hospital and death of the patient due to a gas leak. More difficult to characterize is a new factor such as a pneumonia, which causes death which is substantially assisted by the debilitated state of the patient which follows from suspension of food and water. The law has not been able to develop any simple formula for such situations. See Hart and Honoré (10) and also Schaffner (17).

[e]John Stuart Mill, the great 19th century philosopher, stated his method of agreement as follows: "If two or more instances of the phenomenon under investigation have only one circumstance in common, the circumstance in which alone all the instances agree is the cause (or effect) of the given phenomenon." The method is best viewed as providing suggestive evidence. See Refs. 6 and 13.

which compromises their respiratory abilities. Add to this situation an individual who, in addition to withdrawing the patient from the respirator, also arranges hermetically to seal the patient's room. After a certain amount of time, the patient will not be able to respire and will die. The sealing of the room is controlling over any respiratory failure due to the removal of the respirator in the typical case; it *overrides* any causal role of the illness as in case 3 above. (There could, of course, be exceptions in which respiratory failure ensues before the disappearance of ambient oxygen in the sealed room.) For those who view hermetically sealing the room as in some sense more "active" than clamping a gastrostomy tube, imagine that all patients' rooms in this modern medical center are sealed hermetically, that air is delivered by forced ventilation to each room, and that the patient's forced air switch is simply turned off.

ARGUMENT TO LEGITIMIZE
ASSISTED SUICIDE

If we accept the above account of causation of death, what implications does such a view hold for the moral and legal permissibility of forgoing nutrition and hydration in a medical setting?

I believe that such a position forces us to the conclusions which Justices Lynch and O'Connor drew in the *Brophy* case, but one which can be appropriately tempered by Justice Compton's opinion in the *Bouvia* case. In my view, in the kind of case we have been discussing the withdrawal of food and water from a patient is the cause of death. Since this is permitted in the law only with the patient's agreement (or by the patient's substituted judgment), this amounts to voluntary active euthanasia and is morally equivalent to suicide. Not all suicide, however, is irrational; in fact, the deliberations surrounding the cases discussed in this article and additional ones discussed in the burgeoning literature on withholding food and water point the way to a proper consideration of factors and values which should be followed in developing a moral policy on rational suicide. It should be honestly recognized by all participants that the withholding of food and water is generally a surrogate for rational assisted suicide. To not recognize this tragic choice can lead to inefficient deliberations over nongermane issues, and to sliding down the slippery slope which commentators such as Callahan, Siegler, and Weisbard have discerned, but primarily because of inattention to the ac-

tual issues involved. (I do want to add a caveat here, however. Suicide is not a crime under the statutes of any state in the United States, nor is attempting suicide a crime. However, in 22 states and three United States territories, *assisting* suicide is a crime (7). Careful attention obviously needs to be paid to this distinction. Engelhardt and Malloy (8) have reviewed this issue, and a recent note in the *Columbia University Law Review* (7) outlines a model statute which permits an affirmative defense for the individual assisting in the suicide if the suicidal individual was "a competent adult who was suffering from permanent physical incapacitation.")

SUMMARY AND CONCLUSIONS:
RELUCTANCE TO RECOGNIZE
THE TRAGIC CHOICE

Might not such commentators as Callahan and Siegler be correct, then, in suggesting that we proceed very cautiously in those situations in which patients' nutrition and hydration are suspended? I think the answer is yes, but I hold a somewhat different perspective than do the dissenters to such policies. Callahan is concerned both about what he has termed the "klutz" factor and the "scandal" factor. The klutz factor comes into play in those situations in which practices are "taken out of the hands of the first pioneers, who act carefully and thoughtfully after due deliberation, and are put in the hands of very large numbers of people who may not approach them with the same care." The scandal factor can come into play because of sensationalizing media who misrepresent events. Callahan provides as an example a newspaper headline describing a black patient who had food and water withdrawn after careful and conscientious deliberation as "BLACK MAN STARVED TO DEATH IN HOSPITAL" (5).

Similar abuses have arisen in the not-too-distant past in association with research on human subjects. The remedy, which appears to have worked quite well, was for the political process to respond with proper regulations that were to be implemented by responsible Institutional Review Boards (IRBs) with due attention to appropriate public participation on such IRBs. I see no reason why a similar solution, perhaps with the help of hospital ethics committees or prognosis committees, cannot be developed in principle. Clearly, adequate safeguards to protect the helpless and the handicapped must be an essential part of any deliberative process. Different safeguards have been proposed in different jurisdictions, but this is a rapidly evolving area and it would be beyond the scope of this paper to comment on them. Suffice it to say that after appropriate safeguards are in place, and it may be wisest to allow these to mature through the judicial rather than the legislative process at this point in time, it would seem to be both humane and just to permit the forgoing of life-sustaining food and water for appropriately selected terminal and permanently comatose patients. "Appropriate selection" here means that such patients are protected by the safeguards, which I would assume will include a requirement that reasonably clear patient value preferences have been obtained from the patients or have been reconstructable from interviews with family and/or friends. I also believe that it would be salutary to acknowledge that granting such patients the right to forgo life-sustaining food and water is the first step toward recognizing a right to medically assisted, rational suicide, and that the implications and ramifications of such a policy need extensive further debate and analysis.

REFERENCES

1. *Barber v. Superior Court:* 195 Cal. Rptr. 484, 147 Cal. App. 3d 1006, 1983.

2. *Bouvia v. Superior Court (Glenchur):* 225 Cal. Rptr. 297, Cal. App. 2 Dist., 1986.

3. Brock D: Forgoing life-sustaining food and water: Is it killing? *In:* By No Extraordinary Means: The Choice to Forgo Life-Sustaining Food and Water. Lynn J (Ed). Bloomington, IN, University Press, 1986, pp 117–131.

4. *Brophy, PE. v. New England Sinai Hospital, Inc.* 497 N.E.2d 626 Mass. 1986.

5. Callahan D: Public policy and the cessation of nutrition. *In:* By No Extraordinary Means: The Choice to Forgo Life-Sustaining Food and Water. Lynn J (Ed). Bloomington, IN, University Press, 1986, pp 61–66.

6. Cohen MR, Nagel E: An Introduction to Logic and the Scientific Method. London, Routledge & Kegan Paul, 1934, pp 251–256.

7. Criminal Liability for Assisting Suicide. *Columbia University Law Review 86* 1986; p 348.

8. Engelhardt HT, Malloy M: Suicide and assisting suicide: A critique of legal sanctions. *Southwestern Law Journal* 1982; 36:1003.

9. Guttentag O: Care of the healthy and the sick from the attending physician's perspective: Envisioned and actual. *In:* Organism, Medicine, and Metaphysics. Spicker SF (Ed). Dordrecht, Reidel, 1978, pp 41–56.

10. Hart HLA, Honoré AM: Causation in the Law. Second Edition. New York, Oxford University Press, 1986.

11. Lundberg GD: "It's Over Debbie" and the euthanasia debate. *JAMA* 1988; 259:2142.

12. Lynn J, Childress J: Must patients always be given food and water? *In:* By No Extraordinary Means: The Choice to Forgo Life-Sustaining Food and Water. Lynn J (Ed). Bloomington, IN, Indiana University Press, 1986, p 54.

13. Mackie J: The Cement of the Universe. Oxford, Oxford University Press, 1974.

14. Mill JS: A System of Logic. London, Longmans, 1959, p 255.

15. President's Commission for the Study of Ethical Problems in Medicine: Deciding to Forego Life-Sustaining Treatment. Washington, DC, US Govt Printing Office, 1982, pp 82–89.

16. Salmon WC: Scientific Explanation and the Causal Structure of the World. Princeton, Princeton University Press, 1984.

17. Schaffner K: Causation in Medicine and the Law. *In:* Medical Innovation and Bad Outcomes. Siegler M, Toulmin S, Zimring F, et al (Eds). Ann Arbor, Health Administration Press, 1987, pp 71–99.

18. Weisbard A, Siegler M: On killing patients with kindness: An appeal to caution. *In:* By No Extraordinary Means: The Choice to Forgo Life-Sustaining Food and Water. Lynn J (Ed). Bloomington, IN, Indiana University Press, 1986.

Physician-Assisted Suicide and Voluntary Active Euthanasia

SUPREME COURT OF NEVADA

McKay v. Bergstedt

NOVEMBER 30, 1990

STEFFEN, JUSTICE

Kenneth Bergstedt was a thirty-one-year-old mentally competent quadriplegic who sought to vindicate on appeal the lower court's decision confirming his right to die. Convinced that Kenneth's position has merit, we affirm. . . .

FACTUAL BACKGROUND

At the tender age of ten, Kenneth suffered the fate of a quadriplegic as the result of a swimming accident. Twenty-one years later, faced with what appeared to be the imminent death of his ill father, Kenneth decided that he wanted to be released from a life of paralysis held intact by the life-sustaining properties of a respirator. Although Kenneth was able to read, watch television, orally operate a computer, and occasionally receive limited enjoyment from wheelchair ambulation, he despaired over the prospect of life without the attentive care, companionship and love of his devoted father.

The limited record before us reflects substantial evidence of facts relevant to the proceedings below and material to the framework upon which the resolution of this appeal is constructed. First, a board-certified neurosurgeon determined that Kenneth's quadriplegia was irreversible. Second, a psychiatrist examined Kenneth and found him to be competent and able to understand the nature and consequences of his decision. Third, Kenneth arrived at his decision after substantial deliberation. Fourth, Kenneth's trusted and devoted father understood the basis for his son's

Reprinted from 801 Pacific Reporter, 2d Series. 801 P.2d 617 (Nev. 1990).

decision and reluctantly approved. Fifth, although Kenneth's quadriplegia was irreversible, his affliction was non-terminal so long as he received artificial respiration.

Kenneth thus petitioned the district court as a non-terminal, competent, adult quadriplegic for an order permitting the removal of his respirator by one who could also administer a sedative and thereby relieve the pain that would otherwise precede his demise. Kenneth also sought an order of immunity from civil or criminal liability for anyone providing the requested assistance. Additionally, he petitioned the court for a declaration absolving him of suicide in the removal of his life-support system.

In ruling, the district court determined that Kenneth was a mentally competent adult fully capable of deciding to forego continued life connected to a respirator. The court also found that he understood that the removal of his life support system would shortly prove fatal.

In concluding that Kenneth had a constitutional privacy right to discontinue further medical treatment, the court also ruled that given Kenneth's condition, judicial recognition of the primacy of his individual rights posed no threat to the State's interest in preserving life, adversely affected no third parties, and presented no threat to the integrity of the medical profession. The district court thus concluded that Kenneth was entitled to the relief sought.

DISCUSSION

Our research revealed five cases involving decisions by competent adults to discontinue the use of life-support systems. Two of the five cases were brought by petitioners who were terminally ill. The other three actions, like the instant case, involved non-terminal, competent adults who were dependent upon artificial life support systems. Relief was granted in each of the five cases, albeit posthumously in two of the cases where petitioners had died before their appeals were decided. . . .

Courts agree that the State has several interests of significance that must be weighed in determining whether the rights of the individual should prevail. Those interests have generally been defined as: (1) the interest of the State in preserving the sanctity of all life, including that of the particular patient involved in a given action; (2) the interest of the State in preventing suicide; (3) the interest of the State in protecting innocent third persons who may be adversely affected by the death of the party seeking relief; and (4) the State's interest in preserving the integrity of the medical profession. We add to the list of State interests, a fifth concern which is the interest of the State in encouraging the charitable and humane care of those whose lives may be artificially extended under conditions which have the prospect of providing at least a modicum of quality living. . . .

The State's attenuated interest does not evince a lesser appreciation for the value of life as the physical being deteriorates, but rather a recognition of the fact that all human life must eventually succumb to the aging process or to intervening events or conditions impacting the health of an individual. Moreover, an interest in the preservation of life "at all costs" is demeaning to death as a natural concomitant of life. Despite its frightening aspects, death has important values of its own. It may come as welcome relief to prolonged suffering. It may end the indignities associated with life bereft of self-determination and cognitive activity. In the mind of some, it may satisfy longings for loved ones preceding them in death. In short, death is a natural aspect of life that is not without value and dignity.

Courts have recognized that persons may reach a condition in life where the individual preference for a natural death may have greater primacy than the State's interest in preserving life through artificial support systems. Although we would have stated it differently, the court in *Matter of Conroy*, 98 N.J. 321, 486 A.2d 1209 (1985), declared that "[i]n cases that do not involve the protection of the actual or potential life of someone other than the decision-maker, the state's indirect and abstract interest in preserving the life of the competent patient generally gives way to the patient's much stronger personal interest in directing the course of his own life." *Id.* at 1223. . . .

In both *Bouvia* [225 Cal.Rptr. 297] and *Bartling* [209 Cal.Rptr. 220] the adult patients were, as here, non-terminal and competent. The *Bartling* court disposed of the right to die issue with little comment other than to recognize the preeminence of the patient's constitutional privacy right. We therefore do not regard *Bartling* as persuasive authority. *Bouvia,* however, discusses in some detail its justification for recognizing the petitioner's right to decide over the state's interest in preserving life. In pertinent part, the *Bouvia* court stated: . . .

If her [Bouvia's] right to choose may not be exercised because there remains to her, in the opinion of a court, a physician or some committee, a certain arbitrary number of years, months, or days, her right will have lost its value and meaning.

Who shall say what the minimum amount of available life must be? Does it matter if it be 15 to 20 years, 15 to 20 months, or 15 to 20 days, if such life has been physically destroyed and its quality, dignity and purpose gone? As in all matters lines must be drawn at some point, somewhere, but that decision must ultimately belong to the one whose life is in issue.

Here Elizabeth Bouvia's decision to forego medical treatment or life-support through a mechanical means belongs to her. It is not a medical decision for her physicians to make. Neither is it a legal question whose soundness is to be resolved by lawyers or judges. It is not a conditional right subject to approval by ethics committees or courts of law. It is a moral and philosophical decision that, being a competent adult, is her's [sic] alone. . . .

We do not believe it is the policy of this State that all and every life must be preserved against the will of the sufferer. It is incongruous, if not monstrous, for medical practitioners to assert their right to preserve a life that someone else must live, or, more accurately, endure, for "15 to 20 years." We cannot conceive it to be the policy of this State to inflict such an ordeal upon anyone.

Bouvia, 179 Cal.App.3d at 1142–44, 225 Cal.Rptr. 297.

Although we may have a difference of opinion over some of the statements quoted above from *Bouvia,* we do believe that at some point in the life of a competent adult patient, the present or prospective quality of life may be so dismal that the right of the individual to refuse treatment or elect a discontinuance of artificial life support must prevail over the interest of the State in preserving life. In instances where the prospects for a life of quality are smothered by physical pain and suffering, only the sufferer can determine the value of continuing mortality. We therefore conclude that in situations involving adults who are: (1) competent; (2) irreversibly sustained or subject to being sustained by artificial life support systems or some form of heroic, radical medical treatment; and (3) enduring physical and mental pain and suffering, the individual's right to decide will generally outweigh the State's interest in preserving life.

On the assumption that Kenneth would survive the issuance of this opinion, we reviewed his record carefully in an effort to sensitively analyze the circumstances under which he lived and the reasons that prompted him to seek a judicial imprimatur of his decision to disconnect his respirator. It appeared that Kenneth's suffering resulted more from his fear of the unknown than any source of physical pain. After more than two decades of life as a quadriplegic under the loving care of parents, Kenneth understandably feared for the quality of his life after the death of his father, who was his only surviving parent. . . .

It thus appears, and the record so reflects, that Kenneth was preoccupied with fear over the quality of his life after the death of his father. He feared that some mishap would occur to his ventilator without anyone being present to correct it, and that he would suffer an agonizing death as a result. In contemplating his future under the care of strangers, Kenneth stated that he had no encouraging expectations from life, did not enjoy life, and was tired of suffering. Fear of the unknown is a common travail even among those of us who are not imprisoned by paralysis and a total dependency upon others. There is no doubt that Kenneth was plagued by a sense of foreboding concerning the quality of his life without his father.

Someone has suggested that there are few greater sources of fear in life than fear itself. In Kenneth's situation it is not difficult to understand why fear had such an overriding grasp on his view of the quality of his future life. Given the circumstances under which he labored to survive, we could not substitute our own judgment for Kenneth's when assessing the quality of his life. We therefore conclude that Kenneth's liberty interest in controlling the extent to which medical measures were used to continue to sustain his life and forestall his death outweighed the State's interest in preserving his life. As a competent adult beset by conditions noted above, Kenneth also enjoyed a preeminent right under the common law to withdraw his consent to a continued medical regimen involving his attachment to a respirator. In so ruling, we attach great significance to the quality of Kenneth's life as he perceived it under the particular circumstances that were afflicting him. . . .

The interest of the State in preventing suicide. Controversy continues to rage over this semantics-laden issue. Opponents of Kenneth's position describe it in terms of a state-sponsored suicide. Our research reveals no court declaring it so. We nevertheless recognize the controversy as a healthy concern for the value of an individual life.

The dictionary definition of suicide is "the act or an instance of taking one's own life voluntarily and intentionally; the deliberate and intentional destruction of his own life by a person of years of discretion and of sound mind; one that commits or attempts self-murder." Webster's Third New International Dictionary (1968). As we will attempt to show, Kenneth harbored no intent to take his own life, voluntarily or otherwise. He did not seek his own destruction and he most certainly eschewed self-murder, a fact made evident by his petition to the district court for an order declaring that the exercise of his right to decide would not amount to an act of suicide.

It is beyond cavil in one sense, that Kenneth was taking affirmative measures to hasten his own death. It is equally clear that if Kenneth had enjoyed sound physical health, but had viewed life as unbearably miserable because of his mental state, his liberty interest would provide no basis for asserting a right to terminate his life with or without the assistance of other persons. Our societal regard for the value of an individual life, as reflected in our Federal and State constitutions, would never countenance an assertion of liberty over life under such circumstances.

It must nevertheless be conceded, as noted above, that death is a natural end of living. There are times when its beckoning is sweet and benevolent. Most would consider it unthinkable to force one who is wracked with advanced, terminal, painful cancer to require a therapy regimen that would merely prolong the agony of dying for a brief season. In allowing such a patient to refuse therapy could it seriously be argued that he or she is committing an act of suicide? . . .

The primary factors that distinguish Kenneth's type of case from that of a person desiring suicide are attitude, physical condition and prognosis. Unlike a person bent on suicide, Kenneth sought no affirmative measures to terminate his life; he desired only to eliminate the artificial barriers standing between him and the natural processes of life and death that would otherwise ensue with someone in his physical condition. Kenneth survived artificially within a paralytic prison from which there was no hope of release other than death. But he asked no one to shorten the term of his natural life free of the respirator. He sought no fatal potions to end life or hurry death. In other words, Kenneth desired the right to die a natural death unimpeded by scientific contrivances.

Justice Scalia's concurring opinion in *Cruzan* suggests that "insofar as balancing the relative interests of the State and the individual is concerned, there is nothing distinctive about accepting death through the refusal of 'medical treatment,' as opposed to accepting it through the refusal of food, or through the failure to shut off the engine and get out of the car after parking in one's garage after work." *Cruzan,* 110 S.Ct. at 2862. We respectfully disagree with the learned justice. The distinction between refusing medical treatment and the other scenarios presented by Justice Scalia is the difference between choosing a natural death summoned by an uninvited illness or calamity and deliberately seeking to terminate one's life by resorting to death-inducing measures unrelated to the natural process of dying.

Impliedly, Justice Scalia's last two hypotheticals involved persons who were ambulatory and able to survive without artificial intervention. If they were physically healthy, society's respect for human life demanded that the State prevent, if possible, their deaths by suicide. There was no need to present either person with life-extending medical options, and both enjoyed the prospect of mental rehabilitation that might restore the will to live. There is a significant distinction between an individual faced with artificial survival resulting from heroic medical intervention and an individual, otherwise healthy or capable of sustaining life without artificial support who simply desires to end his or her life. The former adult, if competent, exercises a judgment based upon an assessment of the quality of an artificially maintained life vis-a-vis the quality of a natural death. Conversely, the latter acts from a potentially reversible pessimism or mental attitude concerning only the quality of life.

We are not deciding competing interests between a nonexistent right to choose suicide and the interest of the State in preserving life. The State's interest in the preservation of life relates to meaningful life. Insofar as this State's interest is concerned, the State has no overriding interest in interfering with the natural processes of dying among citizens whose lives are irreparably devastated by injury or illness to the point where life may be sustained only by contrivance or radical intervention. In situations such as Kenneth's, only the competent adult patient can determine the extent to which his or her artificially extended life has meaning and value in excess of the death value. . . .

Part of the complex of circumstances to be considered relates to the attitude or motive of the patient. To a large extent, a patient's attitude or motive may be judged from such factors as severity of physical condition, diagnosis, prognosis, and quality of life. If a competent adult is beset with an irreversible condition such as quadriplegia, where life must be sustained artificially and under circumstances of total dependence, the adult's attitude or motive may be presumed not to be suicidal. In our view, there is a substantial difference between the attitude of a person desiring non-interference with the natural consequences of his or her condition and the individual who desires to terminate his or her life by some deadly means either self-inflicted or through the agency of another.

As medical science continues to develop methods of prolonging life, it is not inconceivable that a person could be faced with any number of alternatives that would delay death and consign him or her to a living hell in which there is hopelessness, total dependence, a complete lack of dignity, and an ongoing cost that would impoverish loved ones. The State's interest in preserving life and preventing what some may erroneously refer to as suicide does not extend so far.

Kenneth did not wish to commit suicide. He desired only to live for as long as the state of his health would permit without artificial augmentation and support. Society had no right to force upon him the obligation to remain alive under conditions that he considered to be anathema. To rule otherwise would place an unwarranted premium on survival at the expense of human dignity, quality of life, and the value that comes from allowing death a natural and timely entrance. . . .

Despite the medical profession's healing objectives, there are increasing numbers of people who fall in the category of those who may never be healed but whose lives may be extended by heroic measures. Unfortunately, there are times when such efforts will do little or nothing more than delay death in a bodily environment essentially bereft of quality. Under such conditions or the reasonably likely prospect thereof, the medical profession is not threatened by a competent adult's refusal of life-extending treatment. . . .

476 EUTHANASIA AND SUICIDE

We are of the opinion that Kenneth's request to be relieved of his connection to a respirator did not present an ethical threat to the medical profession. Because a competent adult would have enjoyed a qualified constitutional and common law right to refuse a life-sustaining attachment to a respirator in the first instance, there is no reason why such an adult could not assert the same rights to reject a continuation of respirator-dependency that has proven too burdensome to endure. . . .

Kenneth was not without a meaningful life. His ability to give expression to his intellect by means of an orally operated computer, to learn, to enjoy reading and watching videos and television all reflected the possibility of a life imbued with a potential for significant quality and accomplishment. He nevertheless feared life in the care of strangers after the demise of an attentive and caring father. It appeared to us that Kenneth needed some type of assurance that society would not cast him adrift in a sea of indifference after his father's passing. . . .

SPRINGER, JUSTICE, DISSENTING

I dissent on two grounds. The first ground is that there was no real case or controversy before the district court. Therefore, it had no judicial power to decide that Kenneth Bergstedt could lawfully take his own life or that another person could lawfully assist him in taking his life. The second ground is that even if this had been a true case instead of a show case, it would not be a proper exercise of judicial power for a court to authorize one person to take the life of another person.

I

ABSENCE OF JUDICIAL POWER

. . . This is an agonizingly difficult case and a unique one, a case desperately in need of a two-sided debate. If there had been a life-side versus a death-side to this case, surely the life-side would at least have raised the point that the plaintiff's case must fail because it sought court approval of a "killing act," an act which knowingly caused the immediate death of a human being. As I indicate below, this would have been a strong argument to be made under the circumstances of this case. I know of no court that has adopted a rule which sanctions suicide[1] by a conscious, competent and alert human being who was not dying and who

was expressing a frank desire for immediate self-destruction.[2] There are a number of novel and perplexing questions to be answered in this case. I certainly would have had an easier time in dealing with these questions if they had been properly and adversarily litigated in the court below.

The trial court did not have the constitutional power to decide a "noncontroversy" and then to take the action that it did; but even if this had been a real case, I maintain that the trial court had no power to sanction or facilitate by court decree Kenneth Bergstedt's announced plan to take his own life by means of the mortal killing act of taking away his breathing apparatus. The Nevada Supreme Court's affirmance of the district court's decree "may make it law, but it does not make it true."[3]

II

STATE-ASSISTED SUICIDE:
OUR "CLOUDED ABILITY TO ASSESS THE SUICIDAL BASIS
OF MR. BERGSTEDT'S REQUEST TO DIE"

[V]alue judgments . . . about the worth of Mr. Bergstedt's life have clouded [the] ability to properly assess the suicidal basis for Mr. Bergstedt's request to die. . . .[4]

As I have already suggested, having the benefit of arguments on only one side of any controversy is a severe limitation upon decision-makers' ability to arrive at an informed and just decision. This limitation has in no small measure "clouded" the truth and the ability of almost everyone to "assess the suicidal basis of Mr. Bergstedt's request to die." Added to the "one-sidedness" of this case are other "clouding" factors that I think may well have affected its outcome: the extremely dramatic and sympathetic nature of Mr. Bergstedt's plea for mercy; faulty reliance on "right-to-die" cases which deal with the comatose and the terminally ill and have no application here; and, cloudiest of all, the flawed impression that persons whose lives depend on life-sustaining devices may kill themselves at will, merely by calling removal of essential-to-life machines a refusal to accept unwanted "medical treatment" or by calling their users' immediate and directly resultant demise a "natural death."

I see Kenneth Bergstedt's breathing device as being more than "medicine." It is true that the machine was introduced during a medical emergency by medical personnel. It is true also that medical and mechanical monitoring of the device must be continued and that medical personnel or paramedical personnel are required to fulfill the daily needs of persons in this kind of condition. Notwithstanding all of this, I cannot escape the conclusion that, after twenty-three years of living and breathing in this machine-aided manner, the whole process becomes something quite more than mere medical *treatment*. The mechanical breather becomes a new way of life for its user, and life cannot go on without it. Mr. Bergstedt lived at home. The "treatment" in any real sense is over; and just as heart pacemakers, artificial venous or arterial shunts, a variety of prosthetic devices and other such medically sponsored and introduced artifacts may *begin* as a medical treatment modality, the ventilator begins as a form of medical treatment but ends up as an integral part of its dependent user. Even if it is insisted that these things continue indefinitely to be considered as "treatment," they indeed become far, far more than just treatment after years and years of dependency on them.

When Kenneth Bergstedt asked the court to give legal sanction to the death-inducing act of disconnecting his breathing apparatus, he was not to my mind merely exercising his "right to be let alone,"[5] and his right to refuse unwanted medical treatment. Withdrawal of medicine or so-called "life support" may be a humane way of letting nature take its course in the lives of the near-dead or irreversibly comatose, but it is a different matter when withdrawal of these items is admitted to be the immediate and proximate cause of the death of a person who concededly is seeking to take his own life.

Use of the term "natural death" in this case is only a natural and understandable way of averting the excruciating truth. Bergstedt's explicit and express desire and intention was that of putting an immediate end to his own life. That is not what one would call a "natural death." There was nothing natural about Mr. Bergstedt's death; he killed himself. Masking this unpleasant but inescapable fact has the unfortunate result of masking the really hard question presented by this case, and that is this: If, when and how should a person in Kenneth Bergstedt's condition (or perhaps other comparable conditions) be given legal permission to have outside assistance in taking his own life, without the incurrence of civil or criminal liability by anyone involved in the process? By avoiding the question, we avoid the answer; and by avoiding the answer, we invite future agonies suffered by persons like Mr. Bergstedt, who, in my view, was not given an acceptable solution to his plight. . . .

Mr. Bergstedt was not dying, except in the sense that we are all dying, and he was not in the least danger of imminent death. He had been living steadily for over twenty-three years, breathing with the aid of a ventilator, until he reached a time in his life when he decided to die because, like most other suicides, life had become, temporarily at least, intolerable for him. The means by which he chose to take his own life was to have someone remove his breathing device during a time that he was sedated for the calculated purpose of bringing his life to a painless end. The result of the ventilator's removal, known to him and to everyone concerned, was immediate death. Withholding the ventilator was for this man not a withholding of medical treatment, it was the withholding of life itself.

If we reflect for a moment on the nature and use of this ventilator, it does not take long to see that the machine had become an integral part of Mr. Bergstedt's person and was not mere "treatment." . . .

Kenneth Bergstedt did not want to die a "natural" death; he wanted to die an immediate death. He sought an immediate death by means of disconnecting the "extension of his person" that had enabled him to live and breath for the preceding twenty-three years. Construing the ventilator in this case as a "form of extraordinary support" that can be removed at will is a terrible and terrifying rationalization and, as well, a prejudicial treatment of Mr. Bergstedt because his assisted suicide was sanctioned and facilitated only because of his disabled condition.

It is crucial that the court not put its judicial stamp of approval on negative stereotypes about disability. This would result if it were to allow the state to assist an individual to die only because he or she has a disability. Judicial decisions which are based upon societal prejudices merely reinforce those prejudices, making them even more difficult to eradicate.[6]

I register now my strong disapproval of our courts' putting their "judicial stamp of approval" on allowing "the state to assist an individual to die only because he . . . has a disability." What other conditions, physical or mental, I ask myself, will be brought to the courts as grounds for judicially approved and assisted self-destruction? We now have a growing population of people who are alive but throughout history would have been dead. Some live under conditions under which many if not most of us would probably not want to survive; yet there are those who do survive and who continue to survive under the most trying of circumstances. The distinguishing aspect of the described persons is that, unlike most of us, they do not have, because of their paralytic condition, the power to bring their lives to an end, however intolerable their lives might become. They are trapped. Life is thrust upon them—*forced* upon them. If a person like Mr. Bergstedt comes to the courts saying, "I have come to the end of my rope; I cannot stand it any more; you must give me the means to end my own life in peace and in dignity"; it is difficult indeed to say "no." Unfortunately it does not belong to the judicial realm to say "yes." The judicial department of government is not the proper agency to address the novel and perplexing question presented here, namely, the question of under what, if any, circumstances should a right to state-assisted suicide be granted. Although not called upon to do so by the writing of this dissent, I have some more to say on the subject.

III

A "RIGHT" TO STATE-ASSISTED SUICIDE?

I know of no judicially created or other legal "right" to commit suicide or to have court-ordered assistance in carrying out one's self-destruction. Although suicide is not a crime in Nevada or in any other state, there is certainly a strong enough public policy against suicide to preclude the courts from assisting in its enactment. Further, it is most certainly a crime to conspire to commit suicide or to aid and abet a suicide. Our law of crimes is legislative, and no statutory crime should be abolished or absolved without legislative enactment or repeal.

The issues presented here, though unique in many respects, are only part of a whole array of social, ethical, theological and legal problems that have come to us through the advancements of medical science. Until very recently in our history this kind of predicament was, necessarily, not a matter that was subject to being dealt with by our law. We have here a man whose consciousness was entombed in a body immobile. Unlike most of the readers of this opinion, Mr. Bergstedt did not have the power to end his life by himself, no matter how tortured his life became. . . .

This is a matter for our democratically-elected representatives in the legislature. They are the ones who must answer these questions and particularly the pressing and specific question: What are we going to do about a totally paralyzed person who is undergoing the unbearable suffering that continued consciousness brings, and who wants desperately to bring his life to an end but does not have the physical capability of doing it?

IV

CONCLUSION

It is not death, it is the dying that alarms me.

Montaigne

I want to be sure that the reader of this dissent does not get this case mixed up with the "right-to-die" cases in which there is present either imminent death or permanent unconsciousness. We are not dealing here with "overtreatment" or unwanted prolongation of the dying process. Kenneth Bergstedt was severely paralyzed and ventilator-dependent and suffered from what neurologists self-descriptively call the "locked-in syndrome"; but his consciousness was intact, and he had a life-expectancy of indefinite duration. It is unclear, however, whether his decision to take his own life was completely rational or possibly a product of some kind of clinically identifiable depression. . . .

I have agonized over this case. At one moment I am haunted by the picture of a hopeless, wretched and tortured person who has no desire except to end his suffering by ending his life. As we know, however, he did not have it within his capacity to end his life, so that he must live on, "locked" into a condition which at the time of his death Mr. Bergstedt probably saw as one of intolerable and unrelenting misery. How can any one who can help him possibly turn down his plaint? But, then, we are not even sure of the exact nature of his mental and emotional condition, or that his depression was not a temporary one. . . .

As I have said, I know in our jurisprudence of no right to commit suicide or to be mercifully put away by the medics, "as quick[ly] and painless[ly] as possible."[7] There is no natural, constitutional, statutory or court-created right that would permit a person to have the assistance of another person in deliberately taking his own life. I am sure that no one would contend that Mr. Bergstedt had a right to suicidal assistance if he had not been incapable of doing the deed himself. So this brings us to the point, discussed above, that Mr. Bergstedt has been given the court-decreed right to assisted suicide only because he was disabled to the extent described. Such a decree should not have been entered.

I would reverse the judgment of the trial court; first, on the ground that the district court was without jurisdiction to decide an uncontested, one-sided test case and thereafter enter the subject decree; and second, on the ground that, there being no *right* vested in anyone to be put to death by another, the district court had no power to disregard the law of homicide and decree the legality of assisted suicide in this "case."

NOTES

1. "Suicide" may at first seem like a harsh word to be using under these circumstances, but it is a necessary word and a word that cannot be avoided. The majority defines suicide as the "taking of one's own life voluntarily and intentionally." Mr. Bergstedt breathed for twenty-three years with mechanical assistance. Taking away the ventilator was taking away his life—a life that would have gone on indefinitely had he not made the conscious decision to *take* it away.

2. The *Bouvia* case cited in the majority opinion came very close to outright judicial approval of suicide by a suffering but non-terminal, bedridden patient. One of the three justices of the California Court of Appeal who decided the *Bouvia* case candidly took the position that some undefined types of persons should be granted by the courts the right to commit suicide, abetted by the kind help of medical personnel who would kill the person in a manner that was as "quick and painless as possible." But what about the state's criminal law forbidding the aiding and abetting of suicide? This law was, according to Justice Compton, "archaic and inhumane," and apparently, to be ignored by the court. Although I disagree with Justice Compton's position (I think it is the legislature's business to change the statutory law of homicide if it is going to be changed), I think the justice was correct in pointing out in *Bouvia* that in permitting a suffering paralytic to be starved to death at her own request, the majority justices did not come to grips with the suicidal nature of Elizabeth Bouvia's quite understandable death wish. As Justice Compton correctly declared: "Even the majority opinion here must necessarily 'dance' around the issue [of suicide]." I respectfully suggest that the majority is dancing around the issue in this case.

3. *New York v. Harris,*—U.S.—, 110 S.Ct. 1640, 1649, 109 L.Ed.2d 13 (1990) (Marshall, J., dissenting).

4. This quote is taken from the *amicus curiae* brief written by Thomas J. Marzen, general counsel for the National Legal Center for the Medically Dependent and Disabled. Although his brief was rejected by the court because of its late filing, I refer to it in this dissent because it is the only argument to be found in this case that favors life instead of death. Mr. Marzen represents "a national organization of disabled individuals, with some 3000 active members," some of whom "depend on ventilators to breathe."

5. *Olmstead v. United States,* 277 U.S. 438, 48 S.Ct. 564, 72 L.Ed. 944 (1928) (Brandeis, J.).

6. Stradley, *Elizabeth Bouvia v. Riverside Hospital; Suicide, Euthanasia, Murder: The Line Blurs,* 15 Golden Gate Univ.L.Rev. 407, 424 (1985).

7. *See* footnote 2, *supra.*

TIMOTHY E. QUILL

Death and Dignity: A Case of Individualized Decision Making

Diane was feeling tired and had a rash. A common scenario, though there was something subliminally worrisome that prompted me to check her blood count. Her hematocrit was 22, and the white-cell count was 4.3 with some metamyelocytes and unusual white cells. I wanted it to be viral, trying to deny what was staring me in the face. Perhaps in a repeated count it would disappear. I called Diane and told her it might be more serious than I had initially thought—that the test needed to be repeated and that if she felt worse, we might have to move quickly. When she pressed for the possibilities, I reluctantly opened the door to leukemia. Hearing the word seemed to make it exist. "Oh, shit!" she said. "Don't tell me that." Oh, shit! I thought, I wish I didn't have to.

Diane was no ordinary person (although no one I have ever come to know has been really ordinary). She was raised in an alcoholic family and had felt alone for much of her life. She had vaginal cancer as a young woman. Through much of her adult life, she had struggled with depression and her own alcoholism. I had come to know, respect, and admire her over the previous eight years as she confronted these problems and gradually overcame them. She was an incredibly clear, at times brutally honest, thinker and communicator. As she took control of her life, she developed a strong sense of independence and confidence. In the previous 3-1/2 years, her hard work had paid off. She was completely abstinent from alcohol,

Reprinted by permission of the publisher from Timothy E. Quill, "Death and Dignity: A Case of Individualized Decision Making," *New England Journal of Medicine* 324, No. 10 (March 7, 1991), pp. 691–94.

she had established much deeper connections with her husband, college-age son, and several friends, and her business and her artistic work were blossoming. She felt she was really living fully for the first time.

Not surprisingly, the repeated blood count was abnormal, and detailed examination of the peripheral-blood smear showed myelocytes. I advised her to come into the hospital, explaining that we needed to do a bone marrow biopsy and make some decisions relatively rapidly. She came to the hospital knowing what we would find. She was terrified, angry, and sad. Although we knew the odds, we both clung to the thread of possibility that it might be something else.

The bone marrow confirmed the worst: acute myelomonocytic leukemia. In the face of this tragedy, we looked for signs of hope. This is an area of medicine in which technological intervention has been successful, with cures 25 percent of the time — long-term cures. As I probed the costs of these cures, I heard about induction chemotherapy (three weeks in the hospital, prolonged neutropenia, probable infectious complications, and hair loss; 75 percent of patients respond, 25 percent do not). For the survivors, this is followed by consolidation chemotherapy (with similar side effects; another 25 percent die, for a net survival of 50 percent). Those still alive, to have a reasonable chance of long-term survival, then need bone marrow transplantation (hospitalization for two months and whole-body irradiation, with complete killing of the bone marrow, infectious complications, and the possibility for graft-versus-host disease — with a survival of approximately 50 percent, or 25 percent of the original group). Though hematologists may argue over the exact percentages, they don't argue about the outcome of no treatment — certain death in days, weeks, or at most a few months.

Believing that delay was dangerous, our oncologist broke the news to Diane and began making plans to insert a Hickman catheter and begin induction chemotherapy that afternoon. When I saw her shortly thereafter, she was enraged at his presumption that she would want treatment, and devastated by the finality of the diagnosis. All she wanted to do was go home and be with her family. She had no further questions about treatment and in fact had decided that she wanted none. Together we lamented her tragedy and the unfairness of life. Before she left, I felt the need to be sure that she and her husband understood that there was some risk in delay, that the problem was not going to go away, and that we needed to keep considering the options over the next several days. We agreed to meet in two days.

She returned in two days with her husband and son. They had talked extensively about the problem and the options. She remained very clear about her wish not to undergo chemotherapy and to live whatever time she had left outside the hospital. As we explored her thinking further, it became clear that she was convinced she would die during the period of treatment and would suffer unspeakably in the process (from hospitalization, from lack of control over her body, from the side effects of chemotherapy, and from pain and anguish). Although I could offer support and my best effort to minimize her suffering if she chose treatment, there was no way I could say any of this would not occur. In fact, the last four patients with acute leukemia at our hospital had died very painful deaths in the hospital during various stages of treatment (a fact I did not share with her). Her family wished she would choose treatment but sadly accepted her decision. She articulated very clearly that it was she who would be experiencing all the side effects of treatment and that odds of 25 percent were not good enough for her to undergo so toxic a course of therapy, given her expectations of chemotherapy and hospitalization and the absence of a closely matched bone marrow donor. I had her repeat her understanding of the treatment, the odds, and what to expect if there were no treatment. I clarified a few misunderstandings, but she had a remarkable grasp of the options and implications.

I have been a longtime advocate of active, informed patient choice of treatment or nontreatment, and of a patient's right to die with as much control and dignity as possible. Yet there was something about her giving up a 25 percent chance of long-term survival in favor of almost certain death that disturbed me. I had seen Diane fight and use her considerable inner resources to overcome alcoholism and depression, and I half expected her to change her mind over the next week. Since the window of time in which effective treatment can be initiated is rather narrow, we met several times that week. We obtained a second hematology consultation and talked at length about the meaning and implications of treatment and nontreatment. She talked to a psychologist she had seen in the past. I gradually understood the decision from her perspective and became convinced that it was the right decision for her. We arranged for home hospice care (although at that time Diane felt reasonably well, was active, and looked healthy), left the door open for her to change her mind, and tried to anticipate how to keep her comfortable in the time she had left.

Just as I was adjusting to her decision, she opened up another area that would stretch me profoundly. It was extraordinarily important to Diane to maintain control of herself and her own dignity during the time remaining to her. When this was no longer possible, she clearly wanted to die. As a former director of a hospice program, I know how to use pain medicines to keep patients comfortable and lessen suffering. I explained the philosophy of comfort care, which I strongly believe in. Although Diane understood and appreciated this, she had known of people lingering in what was called relative comfort, and she wanted no part of it. When the time came, she wanted to take her life in the least painful way possible. Knowing of her desire for independence and her decision to stay in control, I thought this request made perfect sense. I acknowledged and explored this wish but also thought that it was out of the realm of currently accepted medical practice and that it was more than I could offer or promise. In our discussion, it became clear that preoccupation with her fear of a lingering death would interfere with Diane's getting the most out of the time she had left until she found a safe way to ensure her death. I feared the effects of a violent death on her family, the consequences of an ineffective suicide that would leave her lingering in precisely the state she dreaded so much, and the possibility that a family member would be forced to assist her, with all the legal and personal repercussions that would follow. She discussed this at length with her family. They believed that they should respect her choice. With this in mind, I told Diane that information was available from the Hemlock Society that might be helpful to her.

A week later she phoned me with a request for barbiturates for sleep. Since I knew that this was an essential ingredient in a Hemlock Society suicide, I asked her to come to the office to talk things over. She was more than willing to protect me by participating in a superficial conversation about her insomnia, but it was important to me to know how she planned to use the drugs and to be sure that she was not in despair or overwhelmed in a way that might color her judgment. In our discussion, it was apparent that she was having trouble sleeping, but it was also evident that the security of having enough barbiturates available to commit suicide when and if the time came would leave her secure enough to live fully and concentrate on the present. It was clear that she was not despondent and that

in fact she was making deep, personal connections with her family and close friends. I made sure that she knew how to use the barbiturates for sleep, and also that she knew the amount needed to commit suicide. We agreed to meet regularly, and she promised to meet with me before taking her life, to ensure that all other avenues had been exhausted. I wrote the prescription with an uneasy feeling about the boundaries I was exploring—spiritual, legal, professional, and personal. Yet I also felt strongly that I was setting her free to get the most out of the time she had left, and to maintain dignity and control on her own terms until her death.

The next several months were very intense and important for Diane. Her son stayed home from college, and they were able to be with one another and say much that had not been said earlier. Her husband did his work at home so that he and Diane could spend more time together. She spent time with her closest friends. I had her come into the hospital for a conference with our residents, at which she illustrated in a most profound and personal way the importance of informed decision making, the right to refuse treatment, and the extraordinarily personal effects of illness and interaction with the medical system. There were emotional and physical hardships as well. She had periods of intense sadness and anger. Several times she became very weak, but she received transfusions as an outpatient and responded with marked improvement of symptoms. She had two serious infections that responded surprisingly well to empirical courses of oral antibiotics. After three tumultuous months, there were two weeks of relative calm and well-being, and fantasies of a miracle began to surface.

Unfortunately, we had no miracle. Bone pain, weakness, fatigue, and fevers began to dominate her life. Although the hospice workers, family members, and I tried our best to minimize the suffering and promote comfort, it was clear that the end was approaching. Diane's immediate future held what she feared the most—increasing discomfort, dependence, and hard choices between pain and sedation. She called up her closest friends and asked them to come over to say goodbye, telling them that she would be leaving soon. As we had agreed, she let me know as well. When we met, it was clear that she knew what she was doing, that she was sad and frightened to be leaving, but that she would be even more terrified to stay and suffer. In our tearful goodbye, she promised a reunion in the future at her favorite spot on the edge of Lake Geneva, with dragons swimming in the sunset.

Two days later her husband called to say that Diane had died. She had said her final goodbyes to her husband and son that morning, and asked them to leave her alone for an hour. After an hour, which must have seemed an eternity, they found her on the couch, lying very still and covered by her favorite shawl. There was no sign of struggle. She seemed to be at peace. They called me for advice about how to proceed. When I arrived at their house, Diane indeed seemed peaceful. Her husband and son were quiet. We talked about what a remarkable person she had been. They seemed to have no doubts about the course she had chosen or about their cooperation, although the unfairness of her illness and the finality of her death were overwhelming to us all.

I called the medical examiner to inform him that a hospice patient had died. When asked about the cause of death, I said, "acute leukemia." He said that was fine and that we should call a funeral director. Although acute leukemia was the truth, it was not the whole story. Yet any mention of suicide would have given rise to a police investigation and probably brought the arrival of an ambulance crew for resuscitation. Diane would have become a "coroner's case," and the decision to perform an autopsy would have been made at the discretion of the medical examiner. The family or I could have been subject to criminal prosecution, and I to professional review, for our roles in support of Diane's choices. Although I truly believe that the family and I gave her the best care possible, allowing her to define her limits and directions as much as possible, I am not sure the law, society, or the medical profession would agree. So I said "acute leukemia" to protect all of us, to protect Diane from an invasion into her past and her body, and to continue to shield society from the knowledge of the degree of suffering that people often undergo in the process of dying. Suffering can be lessened to some extent, but in no way eliminated or made benign, by the careful intervention of a competent, caring physician, given current social constraints.

Diane taught me about the range of help I can provide if I know people well and if I allow them to say what they really want. She taught me about life, death, and honesty and about taking charge and facing tragedy squarely when it strikes. She taught me that I can take small risks for people that I really know and care about. Although I did not assist in her suicide directly, I helped indirectly to make it possible, successful, and relatively painless. Although I know we have measures to help control pain and lessen suffering, to think that people do not suffer in the process of dying is an illusion. Prolonged dying can occasionally be peaceful, but more often the role of the physician and family is limited to lessening but not eliminating severe suffering.

I wonder how many families and physicians secretly help patients over the edge into death in the face of such severe suffering. I wonder how many severely ill or dying patients secretly take their lives, dying alone in despair. I wonder whether the image of Diane's final aloneness will persist in the minds of her family, or if they will remember more the intense, meaningful months they had together before she died. I wonder whether Diane struggled in that last hour, and whether the Hemlock Society's way of death by suicide is the most benign. I wonder why Diane, who gave so much to so many of us, had to be alone for the last hour of her life. I wonder whether I will see Diane again, on the shore of Lake Geneva at sunset, with dragons swimming on the horizon.

EDMUND D. PELLEGRINO

Euthanasia as a Distortion of the Healing Relationship

. . . Medicine is a healing relationship. Its long term range goal is restoration or cultivation of health; its more proximate goal is healing and helping a particular patient in a particular clinical situation. Medicine restores health when this is possible, and enables the patient to cope with disability and death when cure is not possible. The aims of medicine are positive, even when death is inevitable. Healing can occur even when cure is impossible. The patient can become "whole" again if the health care professional helps him to live with a disability, to face dying, and to live as human a life as circumstances will allow.

Medicine is also ineradicably grounded in trust. The physician invokes trust when she offers to help. The patient is forced to trust because he or she is vulnerable and lacks the power to cure himself without help. The patient is dependent upon the physician's good will and character. The physician, to be faithful to the trust built into the relationship with the patient, must seek to heal, not to remove the need for healing by killing the patient. When euthanasia is a possible option, this trust relationship is seriously distorted. Healing now includes killing. The already awesome powers of the doctor are expanded enormously. When cure is impossible, healing is displaced by killing. How can patients trust that the doctor will pursue every effective and beneficent measure when she can relieve herself of a difficult challenge by influencing the patient to choose death?

Uncertainty and mistrust are already too much a part of the healing relationship. Euthanasia magnifies these ordinary and natural anxieties. How will the patient know whether the physician is trying to heal or relinquishing the effort to cure or contain illness because she favors euthanasia, devalues the quality of the patient's life or wants to conserve society's resources? The physician can easily divert attention from a "good" death by subtly leading the patient to believe that euthanasia is the *only* good or gentle death.

This is not a blanket indictment of the character of physicians. But the doctor is an ordinary human being called to extraordinary tasks. Her character is rarely faultless. We cannot simply say the "good" doctor would never abuse the privilege of euthanasia. Whose agent is the doctor when treatment becomes marginal and costs escalate? Will the physician's notion of benevolence to society become malevolent for the older patient? How can the aged be secure in the hands of younger physicians whose notion of a "quality" life may not include the gentler pleasures of aging Cicero praised in the *De Senectute?* Can patients trust physicians when physicians arrogate to themselves the role of rationers of society's resources or are made to assume this role by societal policy? We already hear much talk of the social burdens imposed by chronically ill, handicapped, terminal adults and children and the necessity of rationing with physicians as the gatekeeper.

Moreover, there are clinical imponderables which can undermine the physician's judgment. To define a pain as intolerable, to distinguish gradations of suffering and to prognosticate accurately are difficult enough in themselves. These difficulties are easily compounded when the patient pleads for release or the physician is frustrated, emotionally spent, or inclined to impose his or her values on the patient. When the proscription against killing is eroded, trust in the doctor cannot survive. This is already apparent in Holland, that great social laboratory for euthanasia. According to some observers, older and handicapped people are fearful of entering Dutch hospitals and nursing homes.[1] Older Dutch physicians have confided to some of us their own personal fear of being admitted to their own hospitals. There is anecdotal evidence of physicians falsifying data to justify euthanasia, making egregious mistakes in diagnosis, and prognosis, or entering into collusion with families, ordering involuntary euthanasia, etc.[2] These anecdotal impressions must be better documented. Further study of the Dutch experience is therefore crucial for any society contemplating euthanasia as public policy. Present evidence indicates that the "slippery slope"—conceptual and actual—is no ethical myth but a reality in Holland.[3] When the physician who traditionally had only the power to heal and to help can now also kill, the medical–fiduciary relationship, one of the oldest in human history, cannot survive.

There is also the serious effect of premeditated socially sanctioned killing on the physician's psyche. Physicians are desensitized to loss of life to some degree by their experiences of the anatomy lab, autopsy, and operating room and the performance of painful procedures. To carry out their duties, doctors must steel themselves to suffering and death or they would be emotionally paralyzed. Euthanasia re-enforces this objectification of death and dying and further desensitizes to killing. A "gentle" death, as Van der Meer wants to call it, is still a premeditated, efficiently executed death of a living human being.[4]

At this point proponents of euthanasia may point out correctly that historically the prohibition against euthanasia was respected only by one group of physicians, the Hippocratics. Other physicians approved the practice of euthanasia as some physicians overtly and covertly do today. Carrick makes clear that in antiquity doctors were inconstant in their respect for the Hippocratic Oath.[5] This fact does not in any way weaken the argument I have been making based in the nature of the healing relationship. Medical codes are not self-justifying. They have only recently become the subject of critical examination. I would contend, for reasons stated briefly above, that a critical examination of the moral basis for medical practice must proscribe euthanasia because it contravenes the primary healing purposes of medical activity. Moreover the argument that since some physicians in the past and some in the present practice euthanasia, it should be legalized is capricious. An immoral act does not become moral because it is common practice. Morality must have deeper roots than mere medical custom.

Medicine is a moral community. Its members have a collective moral responsibility to patients and society. For this reason, the whole profession must oppose the legalization of euthanasia as detrimental to the welfare of patients and the integrity of society. Individual physicians cannot abstain on grounds that they oppose euthanasia but believe in free choice. The social nature of the acts of dying and of killing do not permit anyone to choose such a socially destructive option. This is why the American Medical Association and British Medical Association have recently reaffirmed the proscription against doctors killing patients under any circumstance.[6]

THE SOCIAL IMPACT OF EUTHANASIA

Much as libertarians would like to see euthanasia as an individual decision protected by an absolute privacy right, it is an event fraught with social significance. A society that sanctions killing must abandon the long standing tradition of "state's interest" in human life. This devalues all life but especially the lives of certain citizens—the chronically ill, the aged, and the handicapped. Those who do not take the exit route society offers become selfish over-consumers of their neighbor's resources. The vaunted autonomy of the choice for euthanasia withers in the face of the subtle coercion of a social policy that suggests the incurably ill are a social, economic, and emotional burden. Few of us would not feel the pressure to do the "noble" thing and ask for euthanasia.

The social sanction of euthanasia presumes a responsibility to monitor the killing process to keep it within agreed upon constraints. Killing then becomes bureaucratized and standardized. But even with standardization of criteria, it is impossible to contain euthanasia within specified boundaries. Laws will not prevent abuses despite the hopes of those who favor legalization in the U.S.

NOTES

1. R. Fenigson, "A Case Against Dutch Euthanasia," *Hastings Center Report* 19 (1) (1989): 522–530. R. Fenigson, "Euthanasia in the Netherlands," *Issues in Law and Medicine* 6 (3) (Winter 1990): 229–245.

2. Henk Ten Have, "Euthanasia in the Netherlands: The Legal Context and the Cases," *HEC Forum* 1 (1989): 41–45.

3. I. Van der Sluis, "The Practice of Euthanasia in the Netherlands," *Issues in Law and Medicine,* 4 (4) (1989): 455–465. Barry Bostrom, "Euthanasia in the Netherlands, A Model for the United States?" *Issues in Law and Medicine,* 4 (4) (1989): 467–486.

4. Van der Meer, op. cit.

5. Paul Carrick, *Medical Ethics in Antiquity* (Boston: Dordrecht, 1985), pp. 127–150.

6. *Euthanasia: Report—Council on Ethical and Judicial Affairs of the American Medical Association* (Chicago: AMA, 1989). *Euthanasia: Report—Working Part to Review the British Medical Association Guidance in Euthanasia* (London: British Medical Association, May 1988): 69.

DANIEL CALLAHAN

When Self-Determination Runs Amok

The euthanasia debate is not just another moral debate, one in a long list of arguments in our pluralistic society. It is profoundly emblematic of three important turning points in Western thought. The first is that of the legitimate conditions under which one person can kill another. The acceptance of voluntary active euthanasia would morally sanction what can only be called "consenting adult killing." By that term I mean the killing of one person by another in the name of their mutual right to be killer and killed if they freely agree to play those roles. This turn flies in the face of a long-standing effort to limit the circumstances under which one person can take the life of another, from efforts to control the free flow of guns and arms, to abolish capital punishment, and to more tightly control warfare. Euthanasia would add a whole new category of killing to a society that already has too many excuses to indulge itself in that way.

The second turning point lies in the meaning and limits of self-determination. The acceptance of euthanasia would sanction a view of autonomy holding that individuals may, in the name of their own private, idiosyncratic view of the good life, call upon others, including such institutions as medicine, to help them pursue that life, even at the risk of harm to the common good. This works against the idea that the meaning and scope of our own right to lead our own lives must be conditioned by, and be compatible with, the good of the community, which is more than an aggregate of self-directing individuals.

The third turning point is to be found in the claim being made upon medicine: it should be prepared to make its skills available to individuals to help them

From David Callahan, "When Self-Determination Runs Amok," *Hastings Center Report* 22, No. 2 (March/April 1992), pp. 52-55. Reprinted by permission of the publisher.

achieve their private vision of the good life. This puts medicine in the business of promoting the individualistic pursuit of general human happiness and well-being. It would overturn the traditional belief that medicine should limit its domain to promoting and preserving human health, redirecting it instead to the relief of that suffering which stems from life itself, not merely from a sick body.

I believe that, at each of these three turning points, proponents of euthanasia push us in the wrong direction. Arguments in favor of euthanasia fall into four general categories, which I will take up in turn: (1) the moral claim of individual self-determination and well-being; (2) the moral irrelevance of the difference between killing and allowing to die; (3) the supposed paucity of evidence to show likely harmful consequences of legalized euthanasia; and (4) the compatibility of euthanasia and medical practice.

SELF-DETERMINATION

Central to most arguments for euthanasia is the principle of self-determination. People are presumed to have an interest in deciding for themselves, according to their own beliefs about what makes life good, how they will conduct their lives. That is an important value, but the question in the euthanasia context is, What does it mean and how far should it extend? If it were a question of suicide, where a person takes her own life without assistance from another, that principle might be pertinent, at least for debate. But euthanasia is not that limited a matter. The self-determination in that case can only be effected by the moral and physical assistance of another. Euthanasia is thus no longer a matter only of self-determination, but of a mutual, social decision between two people, the one to be killed and the other to do the killing.

How are we to make the moral move from my right of self-determination to some doctor's right to kill me — from *my* right to *his* right? Where does the doctor's moral warrant to kill come from? Ought doctors to be able to kill anyone they want as long as permission is given by competent persons? Is our right to life just like a piece of property, to be given away or alienated if the price (happiness, relief of suffering) is right? And then to be destroyed with our permission once alienated?

In answer to all those questions, I will say this: I have yet to hear a plausible argument why it should be permissible for us to put this kind of power in the hands of another, whether a doctor or anyone else. The idea that we can waive our right to life, and then give to another the power to take that life, requires a justification yet to be provided by anyone.

Slavery was long ago outlawed on the ground that one person should not have the right to own another, even with the other's permission. Why? Because it is a fundamental moral wrong for one person to give over his life and fate to another, whatever the good consequences, and no less a wrong for another person to have that kind of total, final power. Like slavery, dueling was long ago banned on similar grounds: even free, competent individuals should not have the power to kill each other, whatever their motives, whatever the circumstances. Consenting adult killing, like consenting adult slavery or degradation, is a strange route to human dignity.

There is another problem as well. If doctors, once sanctioned to carry out euthanasia, are to be themselves responsible moral agents — not simply hired hands with lethal injections at the ready — then they must have their own *independent* moral grounds to kill those who request such services. What do I mean? As those who favor euthanasia are quick to point out, some people want it because their life has become so burdensome it no longer seems worth living.

The doctor will have a difficulty at this point. The degree and intensity to which people suffer from their diseases and their dying, and whether they find life more of a burden than a benefit, has very little directly to do with the nature or extent of their actual physical condition. Three people can have the same condition, but only one will find the suffering unbearable. People suffer, but suffering is as much a function of the values of individuals as it is of the physical causes of that suffering. Inevitably in that circumstance, the doctor will in effect be treating the patient's values. To be responsible, the doctor would have to share those values. The doctor would have to decide, on her own, whether the patient's life was "no longer worth living."

But how could a doctor possibly know that or make such a judgment? Just because the patient said so? I raise this question because, while in Holland at [a] euthanasia conference . . . the doctors present agreed that there is no objective way of measuring or judging the claims of patients that their suffering is unbearable. And if it is difficult to measure suffering, how much more difficult to determine the value of a patient's statement that her life is not worth living?

However one might want to answer such questions, the very need to ask them, to inquire into the physician's responsibility and grounds for medical and moral judgment, points out the social nature of the decision. Euthanasia is not a private matter of self-determination. It is an act that requires two people to make it possible, and a complicit society to make it acceptable.

KILLING AND ALLOWING TO DIE

Against common opinion, the argument is sometimes made that there is no moral difference between stopping life-sustaining treatment and more active forms of killing, such as lethal injection. Instead I would contend that the notion that there is no morally significant difference between omission and commission is just wrong. Consider in its broad implications what the eradication of the distinction implies: that death from disease has been banished, leaving only the actions of physicians in terminating treatment as the cause of death. Biology, which used to bring about death, has apparently been displaced by human agency. Doctors have finally, I suppose, thus genuinely become gods, now doing what nature and the deities once did.

What is the mistake here? It lies in confusing causality and culpability, and in failing to note the way in which human societies have overlaid natural causes with moral rules and interpretations. Causality (by which I mean the direct physical causes of death) and culpability (by which I mean our attribution of moral responsibility to human actions) are confused under three circumstances.

They are confused, first, when the action of a physician in stopping treatment of a patient with an underlying lethal disease is construed as *causing* death. On the contrary, the physician's omission can only bring about death on the condition that the patient's disease will kill him in the absence of treatment. We may hold the physician morally responsible for the death, if we have morally judged such actions wrongful omissions. But it confuses reality and moral judgment to see an omitted action as having the same causal status as one that directly kills. A lethal injection will kill both a healthy person and a sick person. A physician's omitted treatment will have no effect on a healthy person. Turn off the machine on me, a healthy person, and nothing will happen. It will only, in contrast, bring the life of a sick person to an end because of an underlying fatal disease.

Causality and culpability are confused, second, when we fail to note that judgments of moral responsibility and culpability are human constructs. By that I mean that we human beings, after moral reflection, have decided to call some actions right or wrong, and to devise moral rules to deal with them. When physicians could do nothing to stop death, they were not held responsible for it. When, with medical progress, they began to have some power over death—but only its timing and circumstances, not its ultimate inevitability—moral rules were devised to set forth their obligations. Natural causes of death were not thereby banished. They were, instead, overlaid with a medical ethics designed to determine moral culpability in deploying medical power.

To confuse the judgments of this ethics with the physical causes of death—which is the connotation of the word *kill*—is to confuse nature and human action. People will, one way or another, die of some disease; death will have dominion over all of us. To say that a doctor "kills" a patient by allowing this to happen should only be understood as a moral judgment about the licitness of his omission, nothing more. We can, as a fashion of speech only, talk about a doctor *killing* a patient by omitting treatment he should have provided. It is a fashion of speech precisely because it is the underlying disease that brings death when treatment is omitted; that is its cause, not the physician's omission. It is a misuse of the word *killing* to use it when a doctor stops a treatment he believes will no longer benefit the patient—when, that is, he steps aside to allow an eventually inevitable death to occur now rather than later. The only deaths that human beings invented are those that come from direct killing—when, with a lethal injection, we both cause death and are morally responsible for it. In the case of omissions, we do not cause death even if we may be judged morally responsible for it.

This difference between causality and culpability also helps us see why a doctor who has omitted a treatment he should have provided has "killed" that patient while another doctor—performing precisely the same act of omission on another patient in different circumstances—does not kill her, but only allows her to die. The difference is that we have come, by moral convention and conviction, to classify unauthorized or illegitimate omissions as acts of "killing." We call them "killing" in the expanded sense of the term: a culpable action that permits the real cause of death, the underlying disease, to proceed to its lethal conclusion. By contrast, the doctor who, at the patient's request, omits or terminates unwanted treatment does not kill at all. Her underlying disease, not his action, is the physical cause of death; and we have agreed to consider actions of that kind to be morally licit. He thus can truly be said to have "allowed" her to die.

If we fail to maintain the distinction between killing and allowing to die, moreover, there are some disturbing possibilities. The first would be to confirm many physicians in their already too-powerful belief that, when patients die or when physicians stop treatment because of the futility of continuing it, they are somehow both morally and physically responsible for the deaths that follow. That notion needs to be abolished, not strengthened. It needlessly and wrongly burdens the physician, to whom should not be attributed the powers of the gods. The second possibility would be that, in every case where a doctor judges medical treatment no longer effective in prolonging life, a quick and direct killing of the patient would be seen as the next, most reasonable step, on grounds of both humaneness and economics. I do not see how that logic could easily be rejected.

CALCULATING THE CONSEQUENCES

When concerns about the adverse social consequences of permitting euthanasia are raised, its advocates tend to dismiss them as unfounded and overly speculative. On the contrary, recent data about the Dutch experience suggests that such concerns are right on target. From my own discussions in Holland, and from the articles on that subject . . . , I believe we can now fully see most of the *likely* consequences of legal euthanasia.

Three consequences seem almost certain, in this or any other country: the inevitability of some abuse of the law; the difficulty of precisely writing, and then enforcing, the law; and the inherent slipperiness of the moral reasons for legalizing euthanasia in the first place.

Why is abuse inevitable? One reason is that almost all laws on delicate, controversial matters are to some extent abused. This happens because not everyone will agree with the law as written and will bend it, or ignore it, if they can get away with it. From explicit admissions to me by Dutch proponents of euthanasia, and from the corroborating information provided by the Remmelink Report and the outside studies of Carlos Gomez and John Keown, I am convinced that in the Netherlands there are a substantial number of cases of nonvoluntary euthanasia, that is, euthanasia undertaken without the explicit permission of the person being killed. The other reason abuse is inevitable is that the law is likely to have a low enforcement priority in the criminal justice system. Like other laws of similar status, unless there is an unrelenting and harsh willingness to pursue abuse, violations will ordinarily be tolerated. The worst thing to me about my experience in Holland was the casual, seemingly indifferent attitude toward abuse. I think that would happen everywhere.

Why would it be hard to precisely write, and then enforce, the law? The Dutch speak about the requirement of "unbearable" suffering, but admit that such a term is just about indefinable, a highly subjective matter admitting of no objective standards. A requirement for outside opinion is nice, but it is easy to find complaisant colleagues. A requirement that a medical condition be "terminal" will run aground on the notorious difficulties of knowing when an illness is actually terminal.

Apart from those technical problems there is a more profound worry. I see no way, even in principle, to write or enforce a meaningful law that can guarantee effective procedural safeguards. The reason is obvious yet almost always overlooked. The euthanasia transaction will ordinarily take place within the boundaries of the private and confidential doctor-patient relationship. No one can possibly know what takes place in that context unless the doctor chooses to reveal it. In Holland, less than 10 percent of the physicians report their acts of euthanasia and do so with almost complete legal impunity. There is no reason why the situation should be any better elsewhere. Doctors will have their own reasons for keeping euthanasia secret, and some patients will have no less a motive for wanting it concealed.

I would mention, finally, that the moral logic of the motives for euthanasia contain within them the ingredients of abuse. The two standard motives for euthanasia and assisted suicide are said to be our right of self-determination, and our claim upon the mercy of others, especially doctors, to relieve our suffering. These two motives are typically spliced together and presented as a single justification. Yet if they are considered independently—and there is no inherent reason why they must be linked—they reveal serious problems. It is said that a competent, adult person should have a right to euthanasia for the relief of suffering. But why must the person be suffering? Does not that stipulation already compromise the principle of self-determination? How can self-determination have any limits? Whatever the person's motives may be, why are they not sufficient?

Consider next the person who is suffering but not competent, who is perhaps demented or mentally retarded. The standard argument would deny euthanasia to that person. But why? If a person is suffering but not competent, then it would seem grossly unfair to deny relief solely on the grounds of incompetence. Are the incompetent less entitled to relief from suffering than the competent? Will it only be affluent, middle-class people, mentally fit and savvy about working the medical system, who can qualify? Do the incompetent suffer less because of their incompetence?

Considered from these angles, there are no good moral reasons to limit euthanasia once the principle of taking life for that purpose has been legitimated. If we really believe in self-determination, then any competent person should have a right to be killed by a doctor for any reason that suits him. If we believe in the relief of suffering, then it seems cruel and capricious to deny it to the incompetent. There is, in short, no reasonable or logical stopping point once the turn has been made down the road to euthanasia, which could soon turn into a convenient and commodious expressway.

EUTHANASIA AND MEDICAL PRACTICE

A fourth kind of argument one often hears both in the Netherlands and in this country is that euthanasia and assisted suicide are perfectly compatible with the aims of medicine. I would note at the very outset that a physician who participates in another person's suicide already abuses medicine. Apart from depression (the main statistical cause of suicide), people commit suicide because they find life empty, oppressive, or meaningless. Their judgment is a judgment about the value of continued life, not only about health (even if they are sick). Are doctors now to be given the right to make judgments about the kinds of life worth living and to give their blessing to suicide for those they judge wanting? What conceivable competence, technical or moral, could doctors claim to play such a role? Are we to medicalize suicide, turning judgments about its worth and value into one more clinical issue? Yes, those are rhetorical questions.

Yet they bring us to the core of the problem of euthanasia and medicine. The great temptation of modern medicine, not always resisted, is to move beyond the promotion and preservation of health into the boundless realm of general human happiness and well-being. The root problem of illness and mortality is both medical and philosophical or religious. "Why must I die?" can be asked as a technical, biological question or as a question about the meaning of life. When medicine tries to respond to the latter, which it is always under pressure to do, it moves beyond its proper role.

It is not medicine's place to lift from us the burden of that suffering which turns on the meaning we assign to the decay of the body and its eventual death. It is not medicine's place to determine when lives are not worth living or when the burden of life is too great to be borne. Doctors have no conceivable way of evaluating such claims on the part of patients, and they should have no right to act in response to them. Medicine should try to relieve human suffering, but only that suffering which is brought on by illness and dying as biological phenomena, not that suffering which comes from anguish or despair at the human condition.

Doctors ought to relieve those forms of suffering that medically accompany serious illness and the threat of death. They should relieve pain, do what they can to allay anxiety and uncertainty, and be a comforting presence. As sensitive human beings, doctors should be prepared to respond to patients who ask why they must die, or die in pain. But here the doctor and the patient are at the same level. The doctor may have no better an answer to those old questions than anyone else; and certainly no special insight from his training as a physician. It would be terrible for physicians to forget this, and to think that in a swift, lethal injection, medicine has found its own answer to the riddle of life. It would be a false answer, given by the wrong people. It would be no less a false answer for patients. They should neither ask medicine to put its own vocation at risk to serve their private interests, nor think that the answer to suffering is to be killed by another. The problem is precisely that, too often in human history, killing has seemed the quick, efficient way to put aside that which burdens us. It rarely helps, and too often simply adds to one evil still another. That is what I believe euthanasia would accomplish. It is self-determination run amok.

DAN W. BROCK

Voluntary Active Euthanasia

. . . In the recent bioethics literature some have endorsed physician-assisted suicide but not euthanasia. Are they sufficiently different that the moral arguments for one often do not apply to the other? A paradigm case of physician-assisted suicide is a patient's ending his or her life with a lethal dose of a medication requested of and provided by a physician for that purpose. A paradigm case of voluntary active euthanasia is a physician's administering the lethal dose, often because the patient is unable to do so. The only difference that need exist between the two is the person who actually administers the lethal dose — the physician or the patient. In each, the physician plays an active and necessary causal role.

In physician-assisted suicide the patient acts last (for example, Janet Adkins herself pushed the button after Dr. Kevorkian hooked her up to his suicide machine), whereas in euthanasia the physician acts last by performing the physical equivalent of pushing the button. In both cases, however, the choice rests fully with the patient. In both the patient acts last in the sense of retaining the right to change his or her mind until the point at which the lethal process becomes irreversible. How could there be a substantial moral difference between the two based only on this small difference in the part played by the physician in the causal process resulting in death? Of course, it might be held that the moral difference is clear and important — in euthanasia the physician kills the patient whereas in physician-assisted suicide the patient kills him- or herself. But this is misleading at best. In assisted suicide the physician and patient together kill the patient. To see this, suppose a physician supplied a lethal dose to a patient with the knowledge and intent that the patient will wrongfully administer it to another. We would have no difficulty in morality or the law recognizing this as a case of joint action to kill for which both are responsible.

If there is no significant, intrinsic moral difference between the two, it is also difficult to see why public or legal policy should permit one but not the other; worries about abuse or about giving anyone dominion over the lives of others apply equally to either. As a result, I will take the arguments evaluated below to apply to both and will focus on euthanasia.

My concern here will be with *voluntary* euthanasia only — that is, with the case in which a clearly competent patient makes a fully voluntary and persistent request for aid in dying. Involuntary euthanasia, in which a competent patient explicitly refuses or opposes receiving euthanasia, and nonvoluntary euthanasia, in which a patient is incompetent and unable to express his or her wishes about euthanasia, will be considered here only as potential unwanted side-effects of permitting voluntary euthanasia. I emphasize as well that I am concerned with *active* euthanasia, not withholding or withdrawing life-sustaining treatment, which some commentators characterize as "passive euthanasia." . . .

THE CENTRAL ETHICAL ARGUMENT FOR VOLUNTARY ACTIVE EUTHANASIA

The central ethical argument for euthanasia is familiar. It is that the very same two fundamental ethical values supporting the consensus on patient's rights to decide about life-sustaining treatment also support the ethical permissibility of euthanasia. These values are individual self-determination or autonomy and individual well-being. By self-determination as it bears on euthanasia, I mean people's interest in making important decisions about their lives for themselves according to their own values or conceptions of a good life, and in

From "Voluntary Active Euthanasia," *Hastings Center Report* 22, No. 2 (March/April 1992), pp. 10–22 (edited). Reprinted by permission of the publisher.

being left free to act on those decisions. Self-determination is valuable because it permits people to form and live in accordance with their own conception of a good life, at least within the bounds of justice and consistent with others doing so as well. In exercising self-determination people take responsibility for their lives and for the kinds of persons they become. A central aspect of human dignity lies in people's capacity to direct their lives in this way. The value of exercising self-determination presupposes some minimum of decisionmaking capacities or competence, which thus limits the scope of euthanasia supported by self-determination; it cannot justifiably be administered, for example, in cases of serious dementia or treatable clinical depression.

Does the value of individual self-determination extend to the time and manner of one's death? Most people are very concerned about the nature of the last stage of their lives. This reflects not just a fear of experiencing substantial suffering when dying, but also a desire to retain dignity and control during this last period of life. Death is today increasingly preceded by a long period of significant physical and mental decline, due in part to the technological interventions of modern medicine. Many people adjust to these disabilities and find meaning and value in new activities and ways. Others find the impairments and burdens in the last stage of their lives at some point sufficiently great to make life no longer worth living. For many patients near death, maintaining the quality of one's life, avoiding great suffering, maintaining one's dignity, and insuring that others remember us as we wish them to become of paramount importance and outweigh merely extending one's life. But there is no single, objectively correct answer for everyone as to when, if at all, one's life becomes all things considered a burden and unwanted. If self-determination is a fundamental value, then the great variability among people on this question makes it especially important that individuals control the manner, circumstances, and timing of their dying and death.

The other main value that supports euthanasia is individual well-being. It might seem that individual well-being conflicts with a person's self-determination when the person requests euthanasia. Life itself is commonly taken to be a central good for persons, often valued for its own sake, as well as necessary for pursuit of all other goods within a life. But when a competent patient decides to forgo all further life-sustaining treatment then the patient, either explicitly or implicitly, commonly decides that the best life possible for him or her with treatment is of sufficiently poor quality that it is worse than no further life at all. Life is no longer considered a benefit by the patient, but has now become a burden. The same judgment underlies a request for euthanasia: continued life is seen by the patient as no longer a benefit, but now a burden. Especially in the often severely compromised and debilitated states of many critically ill or dying patients, there is no objective standard, but only the competent patient's judgment of whether continued life is no longer a benefit. . . .

Most opponents do not deny that there are some cases in which the values of patient self-determination and well-being support euthanasia. Instead, they commonly offer two kinds of arguments against it that on their view outweigh or override this support. The first kind of argument is that in any individual case where considerations of the patient's self-determination and well-being do support euthanasia, it is nevertheless always ethically wrong or impermissible. The second kind of argument grants that in some individual cases euthanasia may *not* be ethically wrong, but maintains nonetheless that public and legal policy should never permit it. The first kind of argument focuses on features of any individual case of euthanasia, while the second kind focuses on social or legal policy. In the next section I consider the first kind of argument.

EUTHANASIA IS THE DELIBERATE KILLING OF AN INNOCENT PERSON

The claim that any individual instance of euthanasia is a case of deliberate killing of an innocent person is, with only minor qualifications, correct. Unlike forgoing life-sustaining treatment, commonly understood as allowing to die, euthanasia is clearly killing, defined as depriving of life or causing the death of a living being. While providing morphine for pain relief at doses where the risk of respiratory depression and an earlier death may be a foreseen but unintended side effect of treating the patient's pain, in a case of euthanasia the patient's death is deliberate or intended even if in both the physician's ultimate end may be respecting the patient's wishes. If the deliberate killing of an innocent person is wrong, euthanasia would be nearly always impermissible.

In the context of medicine, the ethical prohibition against deliberately killing the innocent derives some of its plausibility from the belief that nothing in the currently accepted practice of medicine is deliberate killing. Thus, in commenting on the "It's Over, Debbie" case, four prominent physicians and bioethicists could entitle their paper "Doctors Must Not Kill."[1] The belief that doctors do not in fact kill requires the corollary belief that forgoing life-sustaining treatment, whether by not starting or by stopping treatment, is allowing to die, not killing. Common though this view is, I shall argue that it is confused and mistaken.

Why is the common view mistaken? Consider the case of a patient terminally ill with ALS disease. She is completely respirator dependent with no hope of ever being weaned. She is unquestionably competent but finds her condition intolerable and persistently requests to be removed from the respirator and allowed to die. Most people and physicians would agree that the patient's physician should respect the patient's wishes and remove her from the respirator, though this will certainly cause the patient's death. The common understanding is that the physician thereby allows the patient to die. But is that correct?

Suppose the patient has a greedy and hostile son who mistakenly believes that his mother will never decide to stop her life-sustaining treatment and that even if she did her physician would not remove her from the respirator. Afraid that his inheritance will be dissipated by a long and expensive hospitalization, he enters his mother's room while she is sedated, extubates her, and she dies. Shortly thereafter the medical staff discovers what he has done and confronts the son. He replies, "I didn't kill her, I merely allowed her to die. It was her ALS disease that caused her death." I think this would rightly be dismissed as transparent sophistry—the son went into his mother's room and deliberately killed her. But, of course, the son performed just the same physical actions, did just the same thing, that the physician would have done. If that is so, then doesn't the physician also kill the patient when he extubates her? . . .

I have argued elsewhere that this alternative account is deeply problematic, in part because it commits us to accepting that what the greedy son does is to allow to die, not kill. Here, I want to note two other reasons why the conclusion that stopping life support is killing is resisted.

The first reason is that killing is often understood, especially within medicine, as unjustified causing of death; in medicine it is thought to be done only accidentally or negligently. It is also increasingly widely accepted that a physician is ethically justified in stopping life support in a case like that of the ALS patient. But if these two beliefs are correct, then what the physician does cannot be killing, and so must be allowing to die. Killing patients is not, to put it flippantly, understood to be part of physicians' job description. What is mistaken in this line of reasoning is the assumption that all killings are *unjustified* causings of death. Instead, some killings are ethically justified, including many instances of stopping life support.

Another reason for resisting the conclusion that stopping life support is often killing is that it is psychologically uncomfortable. Suppose the physician had stopped the ALS patient's respirator and had made the son's claim, "I didn't kill her, I merely allowed her to die. It was her ALS disease that caused her death." The clue to the psychological role here is how naturally the "merely" modifies "allowed her to die." The characterization as allowing to die is meant to shift felt responsibility away from the agent—the physician—and to the lethal disease process. Other language common in death and dying contexts plays a similar role; "letting nature take its course" or "stopping prolonging the dying process" both seem to shift responsibility from the physician who stops life support to the fatal disease process. However psychologically helpful these conceptualizations may be in making the difficult responsibility of a physician's role in the patient's death bearable, they nevertheless are confusions. Both physicians and family members can instead be helped to understand that it is the patient's decision and consent to stopping treatment that limits their responsibility for the patient's death and that shifts that responsibility to the patient. . . .

Suppose both my arguments are mistaken. Suppose that killing is worse than allowing to die and that withdrawing life support is not killing, although euthanasia is. Euthanasia still need not for that reason be morally wrong. To see this, we need to determine the basic principle for the moral evaluation of killing persons. What is it that makes paradigm cases of wrongful killing wrongful? One very plausible answer is that killing denies the victim something that he or she values greatly—continued life or a future. Moreover, since continued life is necessary for pursuing any of a person's plans and purposes, killing brings the frustration of all of these plans and desires as well. In a nutshell, wrongful killing deprives a person of a valued future, and of all the person wanted and planned to do in that future.

A natural expression of this account of the wrongness of killing is that people have a moral right not to be killed. But in this account of the wrongness of killing, the right not to be killed, like other rights, should be waivable when the person makes a competent decision that continued life is no longer wanted or a good, but is instead worse than no further life at all. In this view, euthanasia is properly understood as a case of a person having waived his or her right not to be killed.

This rights view of the wrongness of killing is not, of course, universally shared. Many people's moral views about killing have their origins in religious views that human life comes from God and cannot be justifiably destroyed or taken away, either by the person whose life it is or by another. But in a pluralistic society like our own with a strong commitment to freedom of religion, public policy should not be grounded in religious beliefs which many in that society reject. I turn now to the general evaluation of public policy on euthanasia.

WOULD THE BAD CONSEQUENCES OF EUTHANASIA OUTWEIGH THE GOOD?

The argument against euthanasia at the policy level is stronger than at the level of individual cases, though even here I believe the case is ultimately unpersuasive, or at best indecisive. The policy level is the place where the main issues lie, however, and where moral considerations that might override arguments in favor of euthanasia will be found, if they are found anywhere. It is important to note two kinds of disagreement about the consequences for public policy of permitting euthanasia. First, there is empirical or factual disagreement about what the consequences would be. This disagreement is greatly exacerbated by the lack of firm data on the issue. Second, since on any reasonable assessment there would be both good and bad consequences, there are moral disagreements about the relative importance of different effects. In addition to these two sources of disagreement, there is also no single, well-specified policy proposal for legalizing euthanasia on which policy assessments can focus. But without such specification, and especially without explicit procedures for protecting against well-intentioned misuse and ill-intentioned abuse, the consequences for policy are largely speculative. Despite these difficulties, a preliminary account of the main likely good and bad consequences is possible. This should help clarify where better data or more moral analysis and argument are needed, as well as where policy safeguards must be developed.

POTENTIAL GOOD CONSEQUENCES OF PERMITTING EUTHANASIA

What are the likely good consequences? First, if euthanasia were permitted it would be possible to respect the self-determination of competent patients who want it, but now cannot get it because of its illegality. We simply do not know how many such patients and people there are. In the Netherlands, with a population of about 14.5 million (in 1987), estimates in a recent study were that about 1,900 cases of voluntary active euthanasia or physician-assisted suicide occur annually. No straightforward extrapolation to the United States is possible for many reasons, among them, that we do not know how many people here who want euthanasia now get it, despite its illegality. Even with better data on the number of persons who want euthanasia but cannot get it, significant moral disagreement would remain about how much weight should be given to any instance of failure to respect a person's self-determination in this way.

One important factor substantially affecting the number of persons who would seek euthanasia is the extent to which an alternative is available. The widespread acceptance in the law, social policy, and medical practice of the right of a competent patient to forgo life-sustaining treatment suggests that the number of competent persons in the United States who would want euthanasia if it were permitted is probably relatively small.

A second good consequence of making euthanasia legally permissible benefits a much larger group. Polls have shown that a majority of the American public believes that people should have a right to obtain euthanasia if they want it.[2] No doubt the vast majority of those who support this right to euthanasia will never in fact come to want euthanasia for themselves. Nevertheless, making it legally permissible would reassure many people that if they ever do want euthanasia they would be able to obtain it. This reassurance would supplement the broader control over the process of dying given by the right to decide about life-sustaining treatment. Having fire insurance on one's house benefits all who have it, not just those whose houses actually burn down, by reassuring them that in the unlikely event of their house burning down, they will receive the money needed to rebuild it. Likewise, the legalization of euthanasia can be thought of as a kind of insurance policy against being forced to endure a protracted dying process that one has come to find burdensome and unwanted, especially when there is no life-sustaining treatment to forgo. The strong concern about losing control of their care expressed by many people who face serious illness likely to end in death suggests that they give substantial importance to the legalization of euthanasia as a means of maintaining this control.

A third good consequence of the legalization of euthanasia concerns patients whose dying is filled with severe and unrelievable pain or suffering. When there is a life-sustaining treatment that, if forgone, will lead relatively quickly to death, then doing so can bring an end to these patients' suffering without recourse to euthanasia. For patients receiving no such treatment, however, euthanasia may be the only release from their otherwise prolonged suffering and agony. This argument from mercy has always been the strongest argument for euthanasia in those cases to which it applies.[3]

The importance of relieving pain and suffering is less controversial than is the frequency with which patients are forced to undergo untreatable agony that only euthanasia could relieve. If we focus first on suffering caused by physical pain, it is crucial to distinguish pain that *could* be adequately relieved with modern methods of pain control, though it in fact is not, from pain that is relievable only by death.[4] For a variety of reasons, including some physicians' fear of hastening the patient's death, as well as the lack of a publicly accessible means for assessing the amount of the patient's pain, many patients suffer pain that could be, but is not, relieved.

Specialists in pain control, as for example the pain of terminally ill cancer patients, argue that there are very few patients whose pain could not be adequately controlled, though sometimes at the cost of so sedating them that they are effectively unable to interact with other people or their environment. Thus, the argument from mercy in cases of physical pain can probably be met in a large majority of cases by providing adequate measures of pain relief. This should be a high priority, whatever our legal policy on euthanasia—the relief of pain and suffering has long been, quite properly, one of the central goals of medi-

cinc. Those cases in which pain could be effectively relieved, but in fact is not, should only count significantly in favor of legalizing euthanasia if all reasonable efforts to change pain management techniques have been tried and have failed.

Dying patients often undergo substantial psychological suffering that is not fully or even principally the result of physical pain.[5] The knowledge about how to relieve this suffering is much more limited than in the case of relieving pain, and efforts to do so are probably more often unsuccessful. If the argument from mercy is extended to patients experiencing great and unrelievable psychological suffering, the numbers of patients to which it applies are much greater.

One last good consequence of legalizing euthanasia is that once death has been accepted, it is often more humane to end life quickly and peacefully, when that is what the patient wants. Such a death will often be seen as better than a more prolonged one. People who suffer a sudden and unexpected death, for example by dying quickly or in their sleep from a heart attack or stroke, are often considered lucky to have died in this way. We care about how we die in part because we care about how others remember us, and we hope they will remember us as we were, in "good times" with them and not as we might be when disease has robbed us of our dignity as human beings. As with much in the treatment and care of the dying, people's concerns differ in this respect, but for at least some people, euthanasia will be a more humane death than what they have often experienced with other loved ones and might otherwise expect for themselves.

Some opponents of euthanasia challenge how much importance should be given to any of these good consequences of permitting it, or even whether some would be good consequences at all. But more frequently, opponents cite a number of bad consequences that permitting euthanasia would or could produce, and it is to their assessment that I now turn.

POTENTIAL BAD CONSEQUENCES
OF PERMITTING EUTHANASIA

Some of the arguments against permitting euthanasia are aimed specifically against physicians, while others are aimed against anyone being permitted to perform it. I shall first consider one argument of the former sort. Permitting physicians to perform euthanasia, it is said, would be incompatible with their fundamental moral and professional commitment as healers to care for patients and to protect life. Moreover, if euthanasia by physicians became common, patients would come to fear that a medication was intended not to treat or care, but instead to kill, and would thus lose trust in their physicians. This position was forcefully stated in a paper by Willard Gaylin and his colleagues:

The very soul of medicine is on trial . . . This issue touches medicine at its moral center; if this moral center collapses, if physicians become killers or are even licensed to kill, the profession — and, therewith, each physician — will never again be worthy of trust and respect as healer and comforter and protector of life in all its frailty.

These authors go on to make clear that, while they oppose permitting anyone to perform euthanasia, their special concern is with physicians doing so:

We call on fellow physicians to say that they will not deliberately kill. We must also say to each of our fellow physicians that we will not tolerate killing of patients and that we shall take disciplinary action against doctors who kill. And we must say to the broader community that if it insists on tolerating or legalizing active euthanasia, it will have to find nonphysicians to do its killing.[6]

If permitting physicians to kill would undermine the very "moral center" of medicine, then almost certainly physicians should not be permitted to perform euthanasia. But how persuasive is this claim? Patients should not fear, as a consequence of permitting *voluntary* active euthanasia, that their physicians will substitute a lethal injection for what patients want and believe is part of their care. If active euthanasia is restricted to cases in which it is truly voluntary, then no patient should fear getting it unless she or he has voluntarily requested it. (The fear that we might in time also come to accept nonvoluntary, or even involuntary, active euthanasia is a slippery slope worry I address below.) Patients' trust of their physicians could be increased, not eroded, by knowledge that physicians will provide aid in dying when patients seek it.

Might Gaylin and his colleagues nevertheless be correct in their claim that the moral center of medicine would collapse if physicians were to become killers? This question raises what at the deepest level should be the guiding aims of medicine, a question that obviously cannot be fully explored here. But I do want to say enough to indicate the direction that I believe an appropriate response to this challenge should take. In spelling out above what I called the positive argument for voluntary active euthanasia, I suggested that two principal values — respecting patients' self-determination and promoting their well-being — underlie the consensus that competent patients, or the surrogates of incompetent patients, are entitled to refuse any life-sustaining treatment and to choose from among available alternative treatments. It is the commitment to these two values in guiding physicians' actions as healers, comforters, and protectors of their patients' lives that should be at the "moral center" of medicine, and these two values support physicians' administering euthanasia when their patients make competent requests for it.

What should not be at that moral center is a commitment to preserving patients' lives as such, without regard to whether those patients want their lives preserved or judge their preservation a benefit to them. Vitalism has been rejected by most physicians, and despite some statements that suggest it, is almost certainly not what Gaylin and colleagues intended. . . .

A second bad consequence that some foresee is that permitting euthanasia would weaken society's commitment to provide optimal care for dying patients. We live at a time in which the control of health care costs has become, and is likely to continue to be, the dominant focus of health care policy. If euthanasia is seen as a cheaper alternative to adequate care and treatment, then we might become less scrupulous about providing sometimes costly support and other services to dying patients. Particularly if our society comes to embrace deeper and more explicit rationing of health care, frail, elderly, and dying patients will need to be strong and effective advocates for their own health care and other needs, although they are hardly in a position to do this. We should do nothing to weaken their ability to obtain adequate care and services.

This second worry is difficult to assess because there is little firm evidence about the likelihood of the feared erosion in the care of dying patients. There are at least two reasons, however, for skepticism about this argument. The first is that the same worry could have been directed at recognizing patients' or surrogates' rights to forgo life-sustaining treatment, yet there is no persuasive evidence that recognizing the right to refuse treatment has caused a serious erosion in the quality of care of dying patients. The second reason for skepticism about this worry is that only a very small proportion of deaths would occur from euthanasia if it were permitted. In the Netherlands, where euthanasia under specified circumstances is permitted by the courts, though not authorized by statute, the best estimate of the proportion of overall deaths that result from it is about 2 percent.[7] Thus, the vast majority of critically ill and dying patients will not request it, and so will still have to be cared for by physicians, families, and others. Permitting euthanasia should not diminish people's commitment and concern to maintain and improve the care of these patients.

A third possible bad consequence of permitting euthanasia (or even a public discourse in which strong support for euthanasia is evident) is to threaten the progress made in securing the rights of patients or their surrogates to decide about and to refuse life-sustaining treatment.[8] This progress has been made against the backdrop of a clear and firm legal prohibition of euthanasia, which has provided a relatively bright line limiting the dominion of others over patients' lives. It has therefore been an important reassurance to concerns about how the authority to take steps ending life might be misused, abused, or wrongly extended.

Many supporters of the right of patients or their surrogates to refuse treatment strongly oppose euthanasia, and if forced to choose might well withdraw their support of the right to refuse treatment rather than accept euthanasia. Public policy in the last fifteen years has generally let life-sustaining treatment decisions be made in health care settings between physicians and patients or their surrogates, and without the involvement of the courts. However, if euthanasia is made legally permissible greater involvement of the courts is likely, which could in turn extend to a greater court involvement in life-sustaining treatment decisions. Most agree, however, that increased involvement of the courts in these decisions would be undesirable, as it would make sound decisionmaking more cumbersome and difficult without sufficient compensating benefits.

As with the second potential bad consequence of permitting euthanasia, this third consideration too is speculative and difficult to assess. The feared erosion of patients' or surrogates' rights to decide about life-sustaining treatment, together with greater court involvement in those decisions, are both possible. However, I believe there is reason to discount this general worry. The legal rights of competent patients and, to a lesser degree, surrogates of incompetent patients to decide about treatment are very firmly embedded in a long line of informed consent and life-sustaining treatment cases, and are not likely to be eroded by a debate over, or even acceptance of, euthanasia. It will not be accepted without safeguards that reassure the public about abuse, and if that debate shows the need for similar safeguards for some life-sustaining treatment decisions they should be adopted there as well. In neither case are the only possible safeguards greater court involvement, as the recent growth of institutional ethics committees shows.

The fourth potential bad consequence of permitting euthanasia has been developed by David Velleman and turns on the subtle point that making a new option or choice available to people can sometimes make them worse off, even if once they have the choice they go on to choose what is best for them.[9] Ordinarily, people's continued existence is viewed by them as given, a fixed condition with which they must cope. Making euthanasia available to people as an option denies them the alternative of staying alive by default. If people are offered the option of euthanasia, their continued existence is now a choice for which they can be held responsible and which they can be asked by others to justify. We care, and are right to care, about being able to justify ourselves to others. To the extent that our society is unsympathetic to justifying a severely dependent or impaired existence, a heavy psychological burden of proof may be placed on patients who think their terminal illness or chronic infirmity is not a sufficient reason for dying. Even if they otherwise view their life as worth living, the opinion of others around them that it is not can threaten their reason for living and make euthanasia a rational choice. Thus the existence of the option becomes a subtle pressure to request it.

This argument correctly identifies the reason why offering some patients the option of euthanasia would not benefit them. Velleman takes it not as a reason for opposing all euthanasia, but for restricting it to circumstances where there are "unmistakable and overpowering reasons for persons to want the option of euthanasia," and for denying the option in all other cases. But there are at least three reasons why such restriction may not be warranted. First, polls and other evidence support that most Americans believe euthanasia should be permitted (though the recent defeat of the referendum to permit it in the state of Washington raises some doubt about this support). Thus, many more people seem to want the choice than would be made worse off by getting it. Second, if giving people the option of ending their life really makes them worse off, then we should not only prohibit euthanasia, but also take back from people the right they now have to decide about life-sustaining treatment. The feared harmful effect should already have occurred from securing people's right to refuse life-sustaining treatment, yet there is no evidence of any such widespread harm or any broad public desire to rescind that right. Third, since there is a wide range of conditions in which reasonable people can and do disagree about whether they would want continued life, it is not possible to restrict the permissibility of euthanasia as narrowly as Velleman suggests without thereby denying it to most persons who would want it; to permit it only in cases in which virtually everyone would want it would be to deny it to most who would want it.

A fifth potential bad consequence of making euthanasia legally permissible is that it might weaken the general legal prohibition of homicide. This prohibition is so fundamental to civilized society, it is argued, that we should do nothing that erodes it. If most cases of stopping life support are killing, as I have already argued, then the court cases permitting such killing have already in effect weakened this prohibition. However, neither the courts nor most people have seen these cases as killing and so as challenging the prohibition of homicide. The courts have usually grounded patients' or their surrogates' rights to refuse life-sustaining treatment in rights to privacy, liberty, self-determination, or bodily integrity, not in exceptions to homicide laws.

Legal permission for physicians or others to perform euthanasia could not be grounded in patients' rights to decide about medical treatment. Permitting euthanasia would require qualifying, at least in effect, the legal prohibition against homicide, a prohibition that in general does not allow the consent of the victim to justify or excuse the act. Nevertheless, the very same fundamental basis of the right to decide about life-sustaining treatment—respecting a person's self-determination—does support euthanasia as well. Individual self-determination has long been a well-entrenched and fundamental value in the law, and so extending it to euthanasia would not require appeal to novel legal values or principles. That suicide or attempted suicide is no longer a criminal offense in virtually all states indicates an acceptance of individual self-determination in the taking of one's own life analogous to that required for voluntary active euthanasia.

The legal prohibition (in most states) of assisting in suicide and the refusal in the law to accept the consent of the victim as a possible justification of homicide are both arguably a result of difficulties in the legal process of establishing the consent of the victim after the fact. If procedures can be designed that clearly establish the voluntariness of the person's request for euthanasia, it would under those procedures represent a carefully circumscribed qualification on the legal prohibition of homicide. Nevertheless, some remaining worries about this weakening can be captured in the final potential bad consequence, to which I will now turn.

This final potential bad consequence is the central concern of many opponents of euthanasia and, I believe, is the most serious objection to a legal policy permitting it. According to this "slippery slope" worry, although active euthanasia may be morally permissible in cases in which it is unequivocally voluntary and the patient finds his or her condition unbearable, a legal policy permitting euthanasia would inevitably lead to active euthanasia being performed in many other cases in which it would be morally wrong. To prevent those other wrongful cases of euthanasia we should not permit even morally justified performance of it.

Slippery slope arguments of this form are problematic and difficult to evaluate.[10] From one perspective, they are the last refuge of conservative defenders of the status quo. When all the opponent's objections to the wrongness of euthanasia itself have been met, the opponent then shifts ground and acknowledges both that it is not in itself wrong and that a legal policy which resulted only in its being performed would not be bad. Nevertheless, the opponent maintains, it should still not be permitted because doing so would result in its being performed in other cases in which it is not voluntary and would be wrong. In this argument's most extreme form, permitting euthanasia is the first and fateful step down the slippery slope to Nazism. Once on the slope we will be unable to get off.

Now it cannot be denied that it is *possible* that permitting euthanasia could have these fateful consequences, but that cannot be enough to warrant prohibiting it if it is otherwise justified. A similar *possible* slippery slope worry could have been raised to securing competent patients' rights to decide about life support, but recent history shows such a worry would have been unfounded. It must be relevant how likely it is that we will end with horrendous consequences and an unjustified practice of euthanasia. How *likely* and *widespread* would the abuses and unwarranted extensions of permitting it be? By abuses, I mean the performance of euthanasia that fails to satisfy the conditions required for voluntary active euthanasia, for example, if the patient has been subtly pressured to accept it. By unwarranted extensions of policy, I mean later changes in legal policy to permit not just voluntary euthanasia, but also euthanasia in cases in which, for example, it need not be fully voluntary. Opponents of voluntary euthanasia on slippery slope grounds have not provided the data or evidence necessary to turn their speculative concerns into well-grounded likelihoods.

It is at least clear, however, that both the character and likelihood of abuses of a legal policy permitting euthanasia depend in significant part on the procedures put in place to protect against them. I will not try to detail fully what such procedures might be, but will just give some examples of what they might include:

1. The patient should be provided with all relevant information about his or her medical condition, current prognosis, available alternative treatments, and the prognosis of each.
2. Procedures should ensure that the patient's request for euthanasia is stable or enduring (a brief waiting period could be required) and fully voluntary (an advocate for the patient might be appointed to ensure this).
3. All reasonable alternatives must have been explored for improving the patient's quality of life and relieving any pain or suffering.
4. A psychiatric evaluation should ensure that the patient's request is not the result of a treatable psychological impairment such as depression.[11]

These examples of procedural safeguards are all designed to ensure that the patient's choice is fully informed, voluntary, and competent, and so a true exercise of self-determination. Other proposals for euthanasia would restrict its permissibility further—for example, to the terminally ill—a restriction that cannot be supported by self-determination. Such additional restrictions might, however, be justified by concern for limiting potential harms from abuse. At the same time, it is important not to impose procedural or substantive safeguards so restrictive as to make euthanasia impermissible or practically infeasible in a wide range of justified cases.

These examples of procedural safeguards make clear that it is possible to substantially reduce, though not to eliminate, the potential for abuse of a policy permitting voluntary active euthanasia. Any legalization of the practice should be accompanied by a well-considered set of procedural safeguards together with an ongoing evaluation of its use. Introducing euthanasia into only a few states could be a form of carefully limited and controlled social experiment that would give us evidence about the benefits and harms of the practice. Even then firm and uncontroversial data may remain elusive, as the continuing controversy over what has taken place in the Netherlands in recent years indicates.[12]

THE SLIP INTO NONVOLUNTARY ACTIVE EUTHANASIA

While I believe slippery slope worries can largely be limited by making necessary distinctions both in principle and in practice, one slippery slope concern is legitimate. There is reason to expect that legalization of voluntary active euthanasia might soon be followed by strong pressure to legalize some nonvoluntary euthanasia of incompetent patients unable to express their own wishes. Respecting a person's self-determination and recognizing that continued life is not always of value to a person can support not only voluntary active euthanasia, but some nonvoluntary euthanasia as well. These are the same values that ground competent patients' right to refuse life-sustaining treatment. Recent history here is instructive. In the medical ethics literature, in the courts since Quinlan, and in norms of medical practice, that right has been extended to incompetent patients and exercised by a surrogate who is to decide as the patient would have decided in the circumstances if competent.[13] It has been held unreasonable to continue life-sustaining treatment that the patient would not have wanted just because the patient now lacks the capacity to tell us that. Life-sustaining treatment for incompetent patients is today frequently forgone on the basis of a surrogate's decision, or less frequently on the basis of an advance directive executed by the patient while still competent. The very same logic that has extended the right to refuse life-sustaining treatment from a competent patient to the surrogate of an incompetent patient (acting with or without a formal advance directive from the patient) may well extend the scope of active euthanasia. The argument will be, Why continue to force unwanted life on patients just because they have now lost the capacity to request euthanasia from us? . . .

Even if voluntary active euthanasia should slip into nonvoluntary active euthanasia, with surrogates acting for incompetent patients, the ethical evaluation is more complex than many opponents of euthanasia allow. Just as in the case of surrogates' decisions to forgo life-sustaining treatment for incompetent patients, so also surrogates' decisions to request euthanasia for incompetent persons would often accurately reflect what the incompetent person would have wanted and would deny the person nothing that he or she would have considered worth having. Making nonvoluntary active euthanasia legally permissible, however, would greatly enlarge the number of patients on whom it might be performed and substantially enlarge the potential for misuse and abuse. As noted above, frail and debilitated elderly people, often demented or otherwise incompetent and thereby unable to defend and assert their own interests, may be especially vulnerable to unwanted euthanasia.

For some people, this risk is more than sufficient reason to oppose the legalization of voluntary euthanasia. But while we should in general be cautious about inferring much from the experience in the Netherlands to what our own experience in the United States might be, there may be one important lesson that we can learn from them. One commentator has noted that in the Netherlands families of incompetent patients have less authority than do families in the United States to act as surrogates for incompetent patients in making decisions to forgo life-sustaining treatment.[14] From the Dutch perspective, it may be we in the United States who are *already* on the slippery slope in having given surrogates broad authority to forgo life-sustaining treatment for incompetent persons. In this view, the more important moral divide, and the more important with regard to potential for abuse, is not between forgoing life-sustaining treatment and euthanasia, but instead between voluntary and nonvoluntary performance of either. If this is correct, then the more important issue is ensuring the appropriate principles and procedural safeguards for the exercise of decisionmaking authority by surrogates for incompetent persons in *all* decisions at the end of life. This may be the correct response to slippery slope worries about euthanasia. . . .

REFERENCES

1. Willard Gaylin, Leon R. Kass, Edmund D. Pellegrino, and Mark Siegler, "Doctors Must Not Kill," *JAMA* 259 (1988): 2139–40.

2. P. Painton and E. Taylor, "Love or Let Die," *Time,* 19 March 1990, pp. 62–71; *Boston Globe*/Harvard University Poll, *Boston Globe,* 3 November 1991.

3. James Rachels, *The End of Life* (Oxford: Oxford University Press, 1986).

4. Marcia Angell, "The Quality of Mercy," *NEJM* 306 (1982): 98–99; M. Donovan, P. Dillon, and L. Mcguire, "Incidence and Characteristics of Pain in a Sample of Medical-Surgical Inpatients," *Pain* 30 (1987): 69–78.

5. Eric Cassell, *The Nature of Suffering and the Goals of Medicine* (New York: Oxford University Press, 1991).

6. Gaylin et al., "Doctors Must Not Kill."

7. Paul J. Van der Maas et al., "Euthanasia and Other Medical Decisions Concerning the End of Life," *Lancet* 338 (1991): 669–674.

8. Susan M. Wolf, "Holding the Line on Euthanasia," Special Supplement, *Hastings Center Report* 19, no. 1 (1989): 13–15.

9. My formulation of this argument derives from David Velleman's statement of it in his commentary on an earlier version of this paper delivered at the American Philosophical Association Central Division meetings; a similar point was made to me by Elisha Milgram in discussion on another occasion.

10. Frederick Schauer, "Slippery Slopes," *Harvard Law Review* 99 (1985): 361–83; Wibren van der Burg, "The Slippery Slope Argument," *Ethics* 102 (October 1991): 42–65.

11. There is evidence that physicians commonly fail to diagnose depression. See Robert I. Misbin, "Physicians Aid in Dying," *NEJM* 325 (1991): 1304–7.

12. Richard Fenigsen, "A Case against Dutch Euthanasia," Special Supplement, *Hastings Center Report* 19, no. 1 (1989): 22–30.

13. Allen E. Buchanan and Dan W. Brock, *Deciding for Others: The Ethics of Surrogate Decisionmaking* (Cambridge: Cambridge University Press, 1989).

14. Margaret P. Battin, "Seven Caveats Concerning the Discussion of Euthanasia in Holland," *American Philosophical Association Newsletter on Philosophy and Medicine* 89, no. 2 (1990).

The Netherlands Experience

RICHARD FENIGSEN

A Case Against Dutch Euthanasia

Dutch general practitioners perform voluntary active euthanasia on an estimated 5,000 patients a year; the larger figure cited of 6,000 to 10,000 patients probably also includes hospital patients. However, figures as high as 18,000 or 20,000 cases a year have been mentioned. . . . Eighty-one percent of Dutch general practitioners have performed active euthanasia at some time during their professional careers; 28 percent perform active euthanasia on two patients yearly, and 14 percent on three to five patients every year. In Holland, the causes of death of people suffering from AIDS are different from those of patients with AIDS in other countries as 11.2 percent of Dutch AIDS patients die by active euthanasia.

Many people in The Netherlands carry a will requiring active euthanasia to be performed on them "in case of bodily injury or mental disturbance of which no recovery to reasonable and dignified existence is to be expected." Recently, the paper wills have begun to be replaced by small, handy plastic cards nicknamed "credit cards for easy death" by the Dutch press. In 1981 the number of people carrying such cards was reported to be 30,000, but is supposedly much higher now.

The law that would legalize euthanasia is a major issue in Dutch politics. Of the eleven political parties in Holland, ten have included the issue of euthanasia

in their electoral platforms. Government coalitions rise and fall because of agreement, or disagreement, concerning euthanasia. . . .

Acceptance of "voluntary" active euthanasia by the Dutch people is growing. According to two consecutive polls, 70 percent of the Dutch people accepted active euthanasia in 1985, and 76 percent in 1986. This is interpreted by the media as a vote for human freedom (including the freedom of the individual to decide upon his or her life or death), but the reality is more complex. An analysis of public opinion reveals other, and quite different attitudes, in particular, views that oppose the individual's freedom of choice and support society's right to cut short a person's life. Thus, there is considerable public acceptance of the view that life-saving treatment should be denied to the severely handicapped, the elderly, and perhaps to persons without families. Further, opinion polls show that a majority of the same public that proclaims support for voluntary euthanasia, freedom of choice, and the right to die, also accepts involuntary active euthanasia — that is, denial of free choice and of the right to live. . . .

EUTHANASIA IN THE COURTS

Of the 5,000 to 20,000 cases of active euthanasia occurring every year, an average of eleven prompt inquiries to be made by the offices of public prosecutors. The prosecutors act under a regulation issued by the Ministry of Justice which states that an inquiry should be launched only when it is suspected that the

From Richard Fenigsen, "A Case Against Dutch Euthanasia," *Hastings Center Report,* Special Supplement (January/February 1989), pp. 22–30 (edited). Reprinted by permission of the publisher.

doctor performing euthanasia did not act in a careful manner. The legal authorities encourage doctors performing euthanasia to state active euthanasia as the cause of death to avoid their making false statements. In some cases, the doctors inform the public prosecutor beforehand that euthanasia is to be performed. The sentence passed by the court in Leeuwaarden in 1972 (one week of suspended arrest for a doctor who killed her mother) initiated the judicial trend now followed by all the courts, higher appellate courts, the Supreme Court, public prosecutors, and the Ministry of Justice. In the few cases of "voluntary" euthanasia brought to trial, the court declares the doctor guilty but does not impose punishment, whereupon the higher court overturns the "guilty" verdict on the grounds that the doctor acted out of higher necessity. The latter ruling is now being applied in every such case.

When a perpetrator of involuntary euthanasia is brought to trial, as in the case of the doctor who secretly committed the killings in *De Terp* nursing home in The Hague, punishment is imposed but abolished on a technicality by a higher court. . . .

WHY HOLLAND?

. . . The media have been virtually monopolized by the euthanasia proponents, and a whole generation of Dutch people has been raised without ever hearing any serious opposition to it.

Several features of Dutch public life seem to have enhanced the rapid expansion of the pro-euthanasia movement. First, Holland is a very democratic, liberated, and permissive society that highly values unlimited freedom of thought and expression, and encourages the rejecting of dogmas and the overthrowing of taboos. This has facilitated open discussion of euthanasia and the questioning of the "taboo" upholding the sacredness of human life. One peculiar feature (or side-effect) of the advanced democratization and liberalism of Dutch society is popular antimedical feeling, which runs much higher here than in other European countries. There is great resentment against doctors who wield so much power without being elected, and who are seen as selfish, much too self-assured, devoid of common sense, and ignorant of people's needs. There is a strong link between this antimedical public mood, nurtured by propaganda in the Dutch media, and the rush to euthanasia. Some people would rather die soon than be left to the mercy of doctors "and their machines."

In The Netherlands, where Catholicism and Protestantism coexist, issues easily acquire religious connotations. As a result, the principle of the sacredness of human life has been unduly identified with, and confined to, the religious commandment. This has weakened the cause of opponents of euthanasia, as it is clear to all that the country belongs to believers and nonbelievers alike and no purely religious concept should be imposed as a general rule or made the law of the land. Secular reasons—moral, rational, and medical—for rejecting euthanasia are still unknown to the Dutch people.

Also, peoples speaking languages of the Germanic group have historically proved able to build particularly strong social structures. To maintain them requires the far-reaching subordination of the interests of the individual to those of the society. Important business, including the destinies of individuals, may and should be decided upon by public assembly, by consensus, or according to the tribe's laws and rules. It can be argued that these attitudes have determined the acceptance of involuntary aspects of euthanasia by the Dutch public. . . .

"VOLUNTARY" EUTHANASIA

It is the concept of "voluntary" euthanasia, evoking the themes of the right to self-determination and freedom of choice, that is being used to influence the public, the medical profession, and legislators to open the way to the legalization of euthanasia. However, there are, and always have been, compelling reasons for which "voluntary" euthanasia was rejected by Western civilization in the past, and should be rejected now and in the future.

"Voluntary" euthanasia should be rejected *because its voluntariness is often counterfeit and always questionable.* In Holland, doctors have tried to coerce patients, and wives have coerced husbands and husbands wives to undergo "voluntary" euthanasia. But it is not these flagrant incidents that matter, it is all the others. For twenty years the population of Holland has been subjected to all-intrusive propaganda in favor of death. The highest terms of praise have been applied to the request to die: this act is "brave," "wise," and "progressive." All efforts are made to convince people that this is what they ought to do, what society expects of them, what is best for themselves and their families. The result is, as Attorney General T.M. Schalken stated in 1984, that "elderly people begin to consider themselves a burden to the society, and feel under an obligation to start conversations on euthanasia, or even to request it." Recently, the Dutch Patients' Association warned Parliament of reports showing how strongly a sick person's decision to request euthanasia is influenced by pressure from the family and the physician. It is striking that doctors who practice euthanasia have killed so many patients "at the latter's own request" (one doctor gives a figure of seventeen), while other, more traditional practitioners have yet to hear such a request from a patient. When evaluating the thousands of "voluntary" requests for euthanasia submitted every year in Holland, one should take into account the influence of propaganda and of the physician-provocateur.

"TAÏGETIAN" MEDICINE AND CRYPTHANASIA

"Voluntary" euthanasia must also be rejected because, contrary to the beliefs of some of its supporters, *it is inseparable from, and inherently linked to overtly involuntary forms of euthanasia.* . . .

There is now ample evidence that "voluntary" euthanasia is accompanied by the practice of crypthanasia (active euthanasia on sick people without their knowledge). Gunning was the first to report attempts to kill off elderly patients instead of admitting them to the hospital. In 1983, extensive information on crypthanasia became available with the publication of H.W.A. Hilhorst's well-researched book, *Euthanasia in the Hospital* (in Dutch), based on the results of a study conducted in eight hospitals. In this publication (sponsored by the Royal Dutch Academy of Science and the University of Utrecht) the author analyzed the practice of involuntary euthanasia and described cases of involuntary active euthanasia on adults and children. There followed, in 1985, reports on mass secret killings in the *De Terp* senior citizens' home in The Hague; my report about practices of crypthanasia at the internal department of a hospital in Rotterdam; estimates by Dessaur, Gunning, Dessaur and Rutenfrans, and van der Sluis that more people die in this country by involuntary than by voluntary euthanasia; and, in 1987, the discovery of serial killings of comatose patients by four nurses in the department of neurosurgery at the Free University Hospital in Amsterdam. . . .

[The] four nurses at the neurosurgery department of the Free University Hospital in Amsterdam, who admitted to having secretly killed several unconscious patients, received support from the hospital's Employ-

ees' Council *(Ondernemingsraad),* which demanded their immediate release and reinstatement. The Council raised the question of the responsibility of the doctors working in the hospital, suggesting that by unduly delaying euthanasia these doctors may have forced the nurses to act. When releasing the nurses from custody, the Amsterdam court held that their actions had been prompted by humane considerations. The victims' parents, who only after the arrests of the nurses learned how their sons and daughters had died, thanked the nurses at an emotionally charged, televised ceremony. Thus crypthanasia is not an "abuse" of the practice of voluntary euthanasia; it is widely accepted, openly supported, and praised as a charitable deed.

The country's highest authorities show leniency toward doctors who practice crypthanasia: Prof. Ch. J. Enschede, advisor to the Dutch government on the juridical aspects of euthanasia, informed me that "the government and the Council of State decided to keep just these cases out of the reach of the criminal code." . . .

Thus in Holland, "voluntary" and involuntary euthanasia are advocated by the same people and the same institutions, supported by the same public, practiced alongside each other and closely linked in the public mind. Both are manifestations of the same basic attitude, that is, the now widely shared conviction that people's lives may be cut short whenever there are good reasons for doing so. Those who contend that it is possible to accept and practice "voluntary" euthanasia and not allow involuntary totally disregard the Dutch reality.

SOCIAL IMPLICATIONS

"Voluntary" euthanasia should also be rejected *because of the ominous change it brings about in the society.* Instead of the message a humane society sends to its members — "Everybody has the right to be around, we want to keep you with us, every one of you" — the society that embraces euthanasia, even the "mildest" and most "voluntary" forms of it, tells people: "We wouldn't mind getting rid of you." This message reaches not only the elderly and the sick, but all the weak and dependent. Attorney General T. M. Schalken found that Dutch society has already undergone this transformation. As a consequence, some groups live in fear and uncertainty. The Dutch Patients' Association stated in 1985 that "in recent months the fear of euthanasia among people has considerably increased." A group of severely handicapped adults from Amersfoort stated in their letter to the Parliamentary Committees for Health Care and Justice:

> We feel our lives threatened . . . We realize that we cost the community a lot . . . Many people think we are useless . . . often we notice that we are being talked into desiring death . . . We will find it extremely dangerous and frightening if the new medical legislation includes euthanasia.

In their fears, people do not distinguish "voluntary" from involuntary euthanasia.

A study conducted among hospital patients showed that many fear their own families because these are people who could decide upon euthanasia or pressure them to request death. Out of fear of euthanasia some elderly people refuse to be placed in old-age or nursing homes, refuse to be hospitalized or to see doctors or take medicines. A study of the attitudes of the elderly showed that 47 percent of those living in their own homes, and 93 percent of those living in homes for senior citizens reject any active euthanasia "because later on, when they won't be in command of the situation any more, their lives, against their will, will be put to an end by others." Pathetic attempts are made to escape imposed medical death. The "Sanctuary Association" *(Schuilplaats)* printed "declarations of the will to live." This card "which anyone can carry on his person, states that the signer does not wish euthanasia performed on him." . . .

More change must be expected if the pro-euthanasia movement, having attained the legalization of "voluntary" euthanasia, is to achieve the rest of its proclaimed goals. Proposals calling for euthanasia of handicapped newborns mean that doctors acting, as they do everywhere, under state supervision, will issue some newborn citizens permits to live and destroy others. To exist, a human being will have to be approved by the government—a reversal of the democratic principle that governments, to exist, have to be approved by people. Such parts of the program as compulsory euthanasia for the demented elderly and limiting the lifespan of people by denying medical help to those above a certain age, as, in general, any measures to eliminate from society large numbers of citizens, voters, life-long taxpayers, living people, are incompatible with our present system of government. This does not mean that these programs will not be put into effect, but it does mean that the implementation of euthanasia programs will involve an essential change in the system of government now prevailing in Western nations.

FALSE PROMISE

"Voluntary" euthanasia should further be rejected *because its promise is false*. Euthanasia is supposed to spare the sick person the agony that precedes death or the sufferings of a prolonged illness. But this is not the case. When Wibo van den Linden filmed one patient's preparation for "voluntary" euthanasia, about a million Dutch television viewers watched the unfortunate lady's anguish and despair as the fixed day of execution approached. Millions die a human death, in uncertainty, fear, and hope, as cherished members of their family, of the human community, surrounded by those who won't let them go. But euthanasia causes extreme psychological suffering—the excommunication, the exclusion of a person from the community of the living while he is still alive. . . .

FALLIBILITY AND IRREVERSIBILITY

Voluntary euthanasia must also be rejected because of the *fundamental discrepancy between the uncertainty of human (and medical) judgments,* which are fallible, *and the deadly certainty of the act.*

Clinicians have traditionally rejected euthanasia because they realized that we all make mistakes, that diagnoses are uncertain and prognoses notoriously unreliable. Erroneous diagnosis of fatal disease remains a very real possibility.

In their efforts to improve a patient's condition or save his life, doctors often have to rely on a diagnosis that is only probable. This course of action is unavoidable and justifiable intellectually. Yet, to perform euthanasia on the grounds of a diagnosis that might prove incorrect is as evil as it is mindless. We don't know how often this happens in The Netherlands because those who advocate euthanasia and the doctors who practice it never agreed to F. L. Meijler's demand that reasons for euthanasia be verified in every case by a post-mortem examination.

Moreover, plain mistakes occur in medicine as they do in every other human activity. A doctor's mistake is always deplorable but forgivable if he made it while doing his best to improve the patient's health. The damage can sometimes be repaired. The mistake of a doctor practicing euthanasia (and they do make mistakes, and even more than other doctors) is unforgivable and also irreparable: the patient is dead. . . .

"The patient's own request" is not necessarily the firm grounds for "voluntary" euthanasia it is purported to be. Anybody may in a moment of distress express wishes that he disavows the next day. The only patient ever to ask me for euthanasia recovered from his nearly lethal illness (severe heart failure due to multiple pulmonary embolism) and during six years' follow-up never again mentioned the request he had made in a moment of despair. It is also generally known that, in reality, a request to die very often signifies something else, and can be a cry for help, for understanding, an attempt to dramatize the situation. Even when someone requests death emphatically and repeatedly, in writing or in the presence of witnesses, this does not preclude in the least that he is actually asking for help and attention.

EUTHANASIA IS NEVER "NECESSARY"

"Voluntary" euthanasia is to be rejected *because it is totally unnecessary*. In my many years of work as a hospital doctor, I attended thousands of patients and, much to my regret, many hundreds of them died. They needed support, relief from pain, breathlessness, or nausea. Until their last conscious moments they needed to belong, to share with all of us our common destiny, fears, uncertainties, and hopes. None of them needed euthanasia, and with a single exception in thirty-six years, none asked for it.

It is a most demanding task of the doctor to assist his patient to the very end, one that is very different from what vocal supporters of euthanasia expect and demand. Suffering should be alleviated as effectively as possible. The drugs used to relieve pain, or the anticonvulsants used on patients who have suffered cardiac arrest, may shorten a person's life by suppressing respiration, but this is a risk we take; it should never be our intention. . . .

FALLACIOUS REASONING

"Voluntary" euthanasia should also be rejected *because of the flaws in its philosophy*. Euthanasia advocates base their positions on the following line of reasoning: Seriously ill people who in the end will die neither wish to nor are able to endure their meaningless suffering. This has become an important social problem in connection with an aging population and the proliferation of old-age homes and homes for the chronically ill whose residents, cut off from their families and isolated from the rest of society, lose faith in the meaning of their lives. Moreover, as a result of medical and technical progress the lives—and the sufferings—of the seriously ill are extended and become unbearable. Like every important social problem, this one must be solved by society. The taboo on cutting short a person's life is at odds with a truly human attitude. A doctor who cuts short the life of a person experiencing terrible suffering acts out of higher necessity: he cannot act otherwise. People who want to die have a right to euthanasia. The individual's absolute right to self-determination must be acknowledged as fundamental.

However, rigorously applying the principle of voluntariness deprives infants, the mentally ill, paralytics who can neither speak nor write, and the comatose of the chance for a painless death. When a patient is inarticulate, but it can be assumed that if he were able to express his wish he would choose to die, euthanasia should be granted. In the case of the demented who "are beyond making their own decisions . . . someone else [should be given] the mandate to take over" and decide on euthanasia. As for the comatose, they are kept alive at great effort and expense to the despair of their families. Currently, no one dares to make a decision and cut short the lives of such people. But to keep a comatose person alive is also a decision that needs justification.

Anyone who intends to change the status quo must prove he is right; when the proposed change entails irreversible consequences, the arguments must be convincing beyond doubt and the proofs irrefutable. The philosophy of euthanasia does not meet these requirements.

Of course, the essential flaw lies in the attempt to justify both "voluntary" *and* involuntary euthanasia. "Voluntary" euthanasia is to be justified by the individual's right to self-determination. So absolute and inalienable is this right that we must overcome the obstacles of law and tradition, our habits of thinking and instincts, and kill people who request death. However, involuntary euthanasia also requires justification and then it turns out that the right to self-determination is not so absolute after all: some people—the newborn, the demented, the comatose—do not have this right, and will undergo euthanasia though some of them (the demented) obviously wish to live and the others never expressed a wish to die. . . .

Neither can present-day euthanasia be explained by the suffering of people whose lives are artificially prolonged by machines: in Holland, most acts of euthanasia are performed by general practitioners at patients' homes, on patients treated without any special techniques. The assertion that the growing need for euthanasia is due to the proliferation of homes for the elderly, where the isolation and the meaninglessness of existence prompt people to request death is false. The homes for the elderly are not natural disasters to which, with all their consequences, we must resign ourselves. These institutions are the result of our own conscious action. They were created as places where the elderly can *live*. Had our efforts produced only the opposite results, led only to people asking for death, then the logical conclusion would be to close the residences, not kill the inhabitants.

When used to justify involuntary euthanasia, the concept of killing a person in his own best interest is obviously illicit. People who feel quite happy in their lives are put to death "in their own interest" by doctors who know better. What a person feels, desires, and values are by definition that person's subjective attitudes; no one but he can pass judgment on them and certainly no one can know these better than he. Doctors who practice crypthanasia, or deny some patients life-saving help, assume a right to judge and decide on behalf of another person that it is "in his own interest" to die, but this is a right that cannot exist either morally or logically.

Moreover, the practice of euthanasia is often in an obvious way directed against the involved person's interest. Doctors who refused to treat acute pulmonary edema or insert pacemakers because of the patient's age, or to administer renal dialysis because the patient was unmarried, condemned these people to a particularly painful death. . . .

The concept of "quality of life," frequently used in the philosophy of euthanasia, implies an objective, impartial assessment, but its very point of departure is biased. The use of this concept assumes in advance that life as such, life independent of its "quality," has no intrinsic value. Then, the concept of "quality of life" is in turn used to justify the assertion that some lives are not worth living, which is an inadmissible error of logic *(circulus vitiosus)*. Such terms as "unbearable" or "senseless" suffering are value judgments that are inappropriate in logical argumentation. More important, reasoning that resorts to "unbearable" and "senseless suffering" is used to undermine the endurance, courage, and will to live of the severely handicapped or chronically ill. Such arguments are also used *instead* of adequate (and, indeed, attainable) alleviation of the sufferings of the gravely ill, thereby producing the very afflictions they decry.

"HIGHER NECESSITY"

The concept of euthanasia performed out of higher necessity was devised by the supporters of euthanasia among the judiciary and is now routinely used to justify medical killing. This is, however, an error of judgment. Higher necessity is not an independent and separate concept but depends on the actions considered admissible in a certain situation; actually it is an offshoot of those actions. . . .

Only those who assume a priori that a choice exists, that one can kill or not kill, can define leaving a person alive as a decision. Assertions that every person has the right to decide about his own life and death ("the right of self-determination"), or that nobody has this absolute right, are value judgments that cannot be proved or disproved by logical argumentation.

Traditional social practice, as well as legislation, considered human life the value worthy of the highest protection (at least in peacetime); all other values, including freedom, must be subordinate to the defense of life. It is important to notice that laws protecting a person's life, even against that person's will (for example, forcible hospitalization of the mentally ill who are in danger of committing suicide), are consistent with the deep belief we all share and which is a natural reaction: everyone rushes to help at the sight of a clothed person preparing to jump from a bridge into a river. Thus it cannot be argued that the right to self-determination is based on a general consensus among people. When confronted with attempted suicide, the great majority of people act in accordance with the belief that the community of people has the right and duty to intervene to save human life. Thus the individual's right to self-determination is not a self-evident one. It is a controversial concept proclaimed by many but rejected by all when ultimately tested. . . .

THE DANGER TO MEDICINE

"Voluntary" euthanasia should also be feared and rejected *because of the irreparable damage it causes to medicine*. It has become obvious that the practice of euthanasia interferes with doctors' performance as observers of nature and as helpers. The high occurrence of factual errors and oversights committed by doctors in the rush to euthanasia seems to be due to the excitement accompanying the socially and officially approved legalized killing. It has also been pointed out that it is the strong motivation of curative medicine that enables a doctor to grasp and memorize a great number of facts relevant to the case, while euthanasia dispenses the doctor from this necessity.

Desisting from potentially effective therapy because of the idea of euthanasia is a well-known phenomenon that is increasingly disabling the profession. Euthanasia does not just change medicine or extend its range; euthanasia *replaces* medicine. . . .

Euthanasia brings about the decline of medicine also by undermining the doctor-patient relationship.

The old confidence of the public in the medical profession, the old certainty that a doctor would do everything in his power to help the patient, that he would abandon nothing that could be of help, that he would never consciously do anything injurious—this certainty has vanished. Patients realize, too, that some of those doctors prepared to put patients to death at their own request will also be capable of doing it without a patient's knowledge. In the era of euthanasia, patients' attitudes toward doctors are increasingly marked by distrust, suspicion, and fear. . . .

At present, however, a generation of doctors is being raised who learn that a doctor may treat a patient or, sometimes, kill him. The thought of what's happening to the most humane profession is terrifying. Every society has learned to coexist with several dozen criminal killers. But no society knows how to live with an army of benevolent or casual killers, thousands strong.

PIETER V. ADMIRAAL

Euthanasia in The Netherlands

In recent years I have spoken on numerous occasions about various aspects of euthanasia practice in general hospitals. I always limit myself to that group of patients who are in the terminal phase of an incurable, usually malignant disease, and I have always placed emphasis upon the desirability of good terminal supportive care by a team of doctors, nurses, and pastors. At the same time I have repeatedly pointed out that the practice of euthanasia occurs only as a last resort and that the majority of patients die without recourse to euthanasia.

I shall limit myself to just two aspects of euthanasia. First, I wish to discuss what causes a patient to make a request for euthanasia to the doctor who is

Reprinted by permission of the publisher from Pieter V. Admiraal, "Euthanasia in the Netherlands," *Issues in Law & Medicine* 3 (1988), pp. 361–370. © 1988 by the National Legal Center for the Medically Dependent & Disabled, Inc.

treating him; and secondly, to address the question of what we are to understand by "passive euthanasia."

WHAT MAKES A PATIENT REQUEST EUTHANASIA

A patient in the terminal phase will only request euthanasia if he considers his suffering to be unbearable and chooses to die rather than to live under these circumstances. I assume that the request is the result of a lengthy decision process by a patient who is fully conscious of the consequences of his request to himself, to his relatives, and to the doctor to whom he directs his request. At the same time I assume that all persons involved are agreed that the suffering of the patient cannot be relieved in any way and that the performance of euthanasia is only and exclusively in the interest of the patient. Euthanasia then becomes the ultimate act of care for the dying.

What brings the patient to the point of requesting euthanasia from his doctor? Which factors cause the suffering of the patient to become unbearable? Objective considerations lead us to distinguish physical and psychological causes which are closely related to each other.

PHYSICAL CAUSES OF REQUESTS FOR EUTHANASIA

Loss of strength. Especially in cachectic patients, a serious loss of strength occurs as a result of greatly increased protein breakdown and poor peripheral circulation. As a result, the patient in a terminal phase no longer is capable of any physical exertion. The patient then becomes totally dependent on nursing care both day and night.

Fatigue. The loss of strength practically always is accompanied by extreme fatigue even without any physical effort at all. This fatigue cannot be influenced in any way at all and is experienced as exhausting by the patient.

Pain. Until recently pain was the most important cause of physical and psychological suffering. Nowadays, in most cases, pain can be adequately controlled without the normal psychological functions of the patient being adversely affected.

As examples of pain treatment one can mention pharmacotherapy with the administering of analgesics and psychopharmaceuticals, the continuous epidural application of morphine-like analgesics, and the fixed blocking of the sensitive nerve-paths of the sympathetic nervous system.

Unfortunately, the above methods of controlling pain are not yet known or applicable everywhere. Pain can then become unbearable. In a small number of instances pain cannot be subjected to acceptable control even with the most advanced techniques. One may be compelled to administer morphine and/or psychopharmaceuticals intravenously on a continuous basis in such high doses that it has serious harmful effects on the psychic functioning of the patient.

Shortness of breath. An increasing shortness of breath and belabored breathing often occurs in the terminal phase. . . .

Sleeplessness. Although sleeplessness may occur as a complaint all by itself, it is especially patients who suffer fatigue, shortness of breath, and pain who sleep badly, and this can result in exhaustion. When pain is the cause, one will have to administer an analgesic late in the evening or increase the dosage.

Persistent sleeplessness in patients without pain often necessitates the administering of barbiturates as a result of which the patient may be dull and drowsy during the daytime. Just as in the case of healthy people, waking periods appear to be longer at night than they actually are. Conversely, after a short period of sleep the patient can get the false impression that he has slept a long time, and that can be very disappointing and make the waking period seem even longer.

Nausea and vomiting. Nausea can be a side effect of analgesics or of cytotoxics. The administering of antiemetics is then indicated, but the effect is often disappointing. In the case of a total blockage of the stomach intestine, vomiting will be continuous, sometimes even when there is continuous suctioning by means of a stomach siphon. Vomiting is exhausting and disorients the patient.

Flow of saliva. When there is a total blockage of the esophagus or the throat cavity, the saliva produced must be spit out constantly and that is psychically burdensome.

Thirst. Thirst occurs when there is a disturbance of the electrolyte content of the blood and with dehydration. Especially when the patient is being treated at home it can be difficult to administer sufficient liquids by means of an infusion or a stomach siphon. The routine (almost ritual) moistening of the lips does not then offer relief.

Incontinence. There are several causes which can lead to the patient being incontinent with respect to urine or to feces for a shorter or longer period during an illness. Incontinence requires constant intensive nursing care and is experienced by the patient as humanly degrading.

Decubitis. Bedsores will easily develop in patients as a result of bad blood circulation in the skin, and definitely so in the case of cachectic patients who can no longer move themselves because of the loss of strength and the increase of fatigue. If the patient in addition is incontinent, then bedsores can scarcely be averted in intensive nursing. Through tissue deterioration and secondary infections the bedsores are often accompanied by a very penetrating unpleasant odor. . . .

The most important psychic causes are as follows:

Somatic deviations. This includes psychic suffering as a result of the above described somatic problems. All of the somatic deviations mentioned above can become a serious psychic burden to the patient.

Many of the above deviations last during an extended period of the illness, and almost all of them get increasingly worse, often to the very time of death, which in the long run leads to the psychical exhaustion of the patient, despite all nursing and spiritual care. It is especially incontinence, decubitis, and the loss of all strength which the patient in the end experiences as humanly degrading. Under these circumstances many patients consider this last phase as an affront to human dignity, as suffering without any use or purpose, as undeserved and as the disintegration of their humanness.

Anxieties. Practically every patient is plagued by anxiety during the course of his illness. From the very beginning, from the moment that an unfavorable diagnosis has been made and death is inevitable, many patients develop a fear of pain and grievous suffering. This anxiety is based on hearsay or on one's own experience, and even today is seemingly confirmed by the texts of some obituary announcements. [For example: after long and painful suffering, patiently endured, the Lord called home to his eternal rest, our dearly beloved. . . .] But information provided by laypersons is often not very encouraging. Whereas, many doctors betray their task as physicians by providing poor information or by falling short in the doctor-patient relationship. Regrettably, many doctors still talk and publish about "the pain of cancer" as something that is worse than any other pain.

Much more difficult to combat or to refute is the anxiety about spiritual and physical decay and deformation. After all, we cannot guard the patient against these. The only help we can give here is the promise to alleviate suffering when possible or if necessary to end it. The same thing holds for the anxiety about

needing total nursing care and becoming totally dependent. Loneliness and isolation are also anxious threats and indeed many patients are lonely in long nights of waking, alone with their thoughts and fearful expectations. Isolated nursing in the end phase, however much needed from a nursing perspective, encourages this loneliness at home or in the hospital. Only the experience of a warm shared humanity can afford relief in this situation.

Anxiety about dying itself can have various causes. In dying there comes, of course, the inevitable parting from this life, the world in which one has lived and worked, and from beloved relatives. But there can also be anxiety about the moment of dying, the anxiety that then "something" will happen that is unpleasant and threatening without your having any definite idea of what that might be. It is certain that the theatrical portrayal of dying on the stage, or on the screen, usually is far removed from reality. The death scene in an opera is a flagrant example of this.

Anxiety about what comes after death is culturally and religiously determined and can vary from a vague anxiety about the unknown to a literal deathly fear of punishment, which may or may not be eternal. Fortunately, many persons also die in the firm conviction of another, blessed life, united with those who went before. There are also more and more people who, in consequence of the present Western cultural pattern, no longer believe in a hereafter and consequently do not have any anxiety about the hereafter. Fears about dying can be discussed with both the spiritual counselor and the doctor.

As a result of intoxications from one's own body or from various pharmaceuticals, anxious hallucinations or confusions can occur. It requires competent medical and professional knowledge to prevent or to combat these anxieties.

Grief. However much we all realize that death is inevitable and unbreakably linked to life, the certainty of the approaching end of our lives makes us sorrowful. Grief can be about the loss of family and friends or about the loss of earthly things, the possession of which has now become so useless.

Grief will become worse in the measure that less expression can be given to it. Especially in the beginning of the illness process, when the diagnosis is just received, it often happens that the patient, his family and his friends, conceal their grief from each other; and sometimes, out of fear to show their own grief, they are not open to the grief of the other. Grief is then crowded out and bottled up. Grief then becomes sorrow and it would be better to listen to each other's grief and to give each other the opportunity to cry out one's feelings. Mutual understanding is after all the basis of the saying: "Company in distress, makes sorrow less." Grief becomes unbearable when it is not recognized, and the patient is left alone with it, and not understood [by others]. . . .

Such a grief can easily turn into rancor, revolt, and aggression. There can also be grief about the grief of those left behind or about the uncertain, perhaps even precarious future which confronts those left behind. Cares, for example, about less income when the provider dies, or cares about the further nurturing of children when the mother dies young. Such grief depresses the patient and can easily turn into a serious depression.

Some strict believers can experience their grief as wrong in the sight of God who "proposes and disposes," and they may feel guilty about the fact that they do not accept and cheerfully bear their grief.

Rancor, resistance, aggression, and denial but also acceptance and acquiescence play an important role in the terminal phase. They were clearly described for the first time by Kubler-Ross and it is to her great merit that she prepared the way for meaningful terminal care of the dying. Without in any way minimizing her work, I must point out that her observations are for the most part based on observations of American patients with a different life style and a different cultural pattern from that of the European. The above physical and psychological problems can become unbearable suffering for the patient and create the occasion for a request for euthanasia.

Suffering is specific for each human being: an animal does not suffer in the sense that we mean here. An animal feels pain, a human being suffers pain. Only that person can suffer who is capable of deliberate comparative retrospective and prospective contemplation in which one compares, weighs, and evaluates. Suffering therefore includes grief, depression, concern, and anxiety. But fortunately, there is also hope, acquiescence, and acceptance. These too are specifically human.

The suffering of a human being is strictly individual and is determined by the psychological tension and inner resources of that person in enduring dire distress. The suffering of the other is largely withdrawn from our objective observation and consequently it is difficult to weigh and to judge.

It is therefore just as wrong to admiringly attribute to one heroism or martyrdom and to reproach the other for a cowardly attitude toward life. We must seriously ask ourselves where some among us derive the right to judge the suffering of another to be bearable when that person tells us that his suffering is unbearable.

In my honest opinion, it is the inalienable right of each person to make the judgment that his individual suffering is no longer bearable and to request euthanasia from the doctor who is treating him. But then that doctor may not and cannot refrain from making a judgment about the suffering of the person who requests euthanasia. After all, a request for euthanasia, by itself, does not legalize its application. The doctor must then attempt, on the basis of observable facts and on the basis of feeling his way into the situation of the patient, apart from his own emotions, arrive at a judgment which is as honest as possible. He shall have to try to realize in his own mind why the patient under these circumstances prefers death to life. Above all he will have to ask himself whether the circumstances can be improved. His judgment will become more mature and more balanced as his experience in providing terminal care to the dying increases. He must always remain aware that he continues to bear the final responsibility for his decision. It is therefore desirable and necessary that the doctor seek the counsel and assistance of others so that he may in this way constantly test his opinion against that of others.

It is my opinion that every doctor has the right and the duty after prolonged and thorough deliberation to carry out euthanasia; at the request of the other person and in his interest, knowing that he is responsible to himself, to the other, and to the law. Similarly, every doctor has the unassailable right under any circumstance to refuse to carry out euthanasia, knowing that he is responsible to himself and to the other.

The carrying out of euthanasia can only be based on the acknowledgment of unbearable suffering. Here I wish consciously to pass over the Christian view that suffering purifies or, in a broader sense, that suffering is part of life and therefore must be accepted. Many do not subscribe to these views and I think it absolutely wrong to impose such a value judgment on another person or to make him dependent on it. A doctor can refuse to carry out euthanasia on those grounds, provided he does not block the way for a doctor who is prepared to act on the request of the patient.

It would be wrong to give the impression that the request of a patient who is terminally ill with cancer must always and only be based on the above examples of unbearable suffering. Thus, a patient who has arrived at the point of acceptance and acquiescence may no longer attach any value to his life, his relatives, or to his environs. We then speak of a total detachment, one that is especially difficult for relatives to understand and accept. Such a patient only longs for the end. We see this with some frequency in patients of advanced age who have lost all their relatives and friends. As indicated earlier, the desire for reunion can play a role in believing patients.

CARRYING OUT "PASSIVE EUTHANASIA"

In the Netherlands the political discussion about the legalization of euthanasia is to a large extent controlled by the confessional parties which find themselves confronted with a dilemma: on the one hand the practice of euthanasia is considered acceptable by a large majority of the population, including the confessional part, but on the other hand, the Roman Catholic Church and some Protestant churches forbid the practice of active euthanasia.

In order to get out of this impasse, the term "passive euthanasia" has been introduced in recent years. In general, it is defined as "the discontinuance of life sustaining means or treatment as a result of which the patient dies after a shorter or longer period." This can be clarified by means of two examples:

1. Stopping existing [life support] medications such as antibiotics, cytotoxins, antiarrythmia's [heart regulating medications], medications for increasing blood pressure, diuretics, corticosteroids, or insulin.
2. Stopping existing nonmedication treatments such as kidney dialysis, blood transfusions, intravenous or tube feeding, reanimation, physiotherapy, or antidecubitis treatment.

Under passive euthanasia one could also place the carefully considered decision not to begin one of the above treatments or an agreement not to reanimate when breathing is arrested or the heart stops beating.

In passive euthanasia there is therefore a conscious decision by the doctor either to discontinue an existing treatment or not to initiate a possible treatment. Only fifty years ago the problems were not so great. The number of possible treatments was small and just about all were exclusively symptomatic so that the treating physician, already in an early stage of the illness, was compelled and justified in saying to the patient that he, as a doctor, could do no more.

Today it is quite different. Our therapeutic arsenal is very extensive, every year new medicines and methods are discovered so that the number of patients to whom the doctor must say, "I can do nothing more for you," is becoming smaller and smaller.

As we have discussed earlier, a number of these therapies cause so many unpleasant side effects that the continuance of the treatment becomes unacceptable to the patient and he asks his doctor to discontinue the treatment. Obviously in reaching this decision, other factors, for example, the hopeless prospect of symptomatic treatment without any chance of a definite cure, also plays an important role. Whereas in the past, it was a matter of necessity that the doctor himself had to discontinue a treatment, it now will be difficult for many doctors to discontinue a treatment at the patient's request. Indeed, there has been a case where the patient had to sign a declaration demanding the discontinuance of further treatment.

One thing is clear: if the doctor discontinues treatment and does no more the patient will die from the direct consequences of his disease. Using the example cited above, death will be the result of a serious sepsis, cardiac arrest, diabetic or uremic coma, anemia, malnutrition, breathing insufficiency, etc. This means that with passive euthanasia most patients will die only after a long pathway of suffering.

Under these circumstances the word euthanasia is completely mistaken and misleading. This is not at all the "gentle death" which is desired by the patient. The word "passive" here refers altogether to the attitude of the doctor.

Passive euthanasia is nothing but abstention. And abstention, doing nothing, is surely the very last thing a patient making a request [for euthanasia] is entitled to.

Of course, after abstention [nontreatment] it is possible to make dying easier in various ways. But if this occurs with analgesics and psychopharmaceuticals in high doses, then I see no difference at all with active euthanasia. The concept "passive euthanasia" then becomes a cover for the active euthanasia which is not allowed.

Even more dangerous, in my judgment, is the standpoint taken by some church people in the Netherlands who say that there is no euthanasia when a patient dies sooner than normal as a result of high doses of morphine-like analgesics. That opens the door to abuses!

First of all, the number of patients whose pain is untreatable is getting smaller and smaller; and secondly, to carry out euthanasia with morphine in patients who have been treated with morphine for a considerable period of time already, just will not work, because of the swiftly developing tolerance to the breath depressant effect. What must be prevented is that under the guise of controlling pain the lives of patients can be terminated in a wrong and uncontrolled manner without even calling this euthanasia.

In summary, I wish to posit that passive euthanasia is a hypocritical euphemism and not in the interest of the patient who is in a terminal phase.

SUGGESTED READINGS

American Geriatrics Society. Public Policy Committee. "Voluntary Active Euthanasia." *Journal of the American Geriatrics Society* 39 (August 1991).

American Medical Association. Council on Ethical and Judicial Affairs. *Euthanasia: Report C,* in *Proceedings of the House of Delegates.* Chicago: American Medical Association, June, 1988, 258–60; *Current Opinions,* § 2.20, 1989; "Decisions Near the End of Life." *Report B.* Adopted by the House of Delegates (1991), 11–15; and "Decisions Near the End of Life." *Journal of the American Medical Association* 267 (April 22/29, 1992), 2229–2233.

Anscombe, G. E. M. "Ethical Problems in the Management of Some Severely Handicapped Children." *Journal of Medical Ethics* 7 (1981), 122.

———. "Action, Intention, and Double Effect." *Proceedings of the American Catholic Philosophical Association* 54 (1982), 12–25.

Anonymous. "It's Over, Debbie." *Journal of the American Medical Association* 259 (1988), 258–272.

Battin, Margaret. "Voluntary Euthanasia and the Risks of Abuse: Can We Learn Anything from the Netherlands?" *Law, Medicine & Health Care* 20 (Spring–Summer, 1992), 135.

Beauchamp, Tom L., "Suicide." In Regan, Tom, ed. *Matters of Life and Death.* 3d ed. New York: Random House, 1992.

Beauchamp, Tom L., and Childress, James F. *Principles of Biomedical Ethics.* 4th ed. New York: Oxford University Press, 1994. Chap. 4.

Beauchamp, Tom L., and Perlin, Seymour, eds. *Ethical Issues in Death and Dying.* Englewood Cliffs, N.J.: Prentice-Hall, 1976.

Brody, Baruch A. *Suicide and Euthanasia: Historical and Contemporary Themes.* Dordrecht, Holland: Kluwer Academic Publishers, 1989.

Browne, Alister. "Assisted Suicide and Active Voluntary Euthanasia." *Canadian Journal of Law and Jurisprudence* 2 (1989), 35–52.

Callahan, Daniel. *The Troubled Dream of Life: Living with Mortality.* New York: Simon and Schuster, 1993.

Cantor, Norman L. *Legal Frontiers of Death and Dying.* Bloomington, IN: Indiana University Press, 1987.

Caplan, Arthur, Merrick, Janna, and Blank, Robert H., eds. *Compassion: Government Intervention in the Treatment of Critically Ill Newborns.* Totowa, N.J.: Humana Press, 1992.

Cassel, C. K., and Meier, D. E. "Morals and Moralism in the Debate Over Euthanasia and Assisted Suicide." *New England Journal of Medicine* 323 (1990), 750–752.

Conwell, Yeates, and Craine, Eric D. "Rational Suicide and the Right to Die." *New England Journal of Medicine* 325 (1991), 1100–1102.

Doerflinger, Richard. "Assisted Suicide: Pro-Choice or Anti-Life?" *Hastings Center Report* 19 (January/February, 1989), S10–S12.

Engelhardt, H. Tristram, and Malloy, Michelle. "Suicide and Assisting Suicide: A Critique of Legal Sanctions." *Southwestern Law Journal* 36 (1982), 1003–1037.

Foot, Philippa. "Euthanasia." *Philosophy & Public Affairs* 6 (1977), 85–112.

Glover, Jonathan. *Causing Death and Saving Lives.* Penguin Books, New York, 1977.

Gomez, Carlos. *Regulating Death: Euthanasia and the Case of the Netherlands.* New York: Free Press, 1991.

Journal of Medicine and Philosophy 17 (1992). Special issue on the "Cruzan Case."

Kamisar, Yale. "When Is There a Constitutional 'Right to Die'? When Is There No Constitutional 'Right to Live'?" *Georgia Law Review* 25 (1991), 1203–1242.

Kass, Leon R. "Neither for Love Nor Money: Why Doctors Must Not Kill." *Public Interest* (1989), 25–46.

Kevorkian, Jack. *Prescription: Medicide—The Goodness of Planned Death.* Buffalo, N.Y.: Prometheus Books, 1991.

King, Patricia. "The Authority of Families to Make Medical Decisions for Incompetent Patients after the *Cruzan* Decision." *Law, Medicine & Health Care* 19 (1991), 76–79.

Koop, C. Everett. "Ethical and Surgical Considerations in the Care of the Newborn with Congenital Abnormalities." In Horan, D. J., and Delahoyde, M., eds. *Infanticide and the Handicapped Newborn.* Provo, Utah: Brigham Young University Press, 1982.

Koop, C. Everett, and Grant, Edward R. "The 'Small Beginnings' of Euthanasia." *Journal of Law, Ethics & Public Policy* 2 (1986), 607–632.

Kuhse, Helga, and Singer, Peter. *Should the Baby Live?* Oxford: Oxford University Press, 1985.

Lifton, Robert. *The Nazi Doctors: Medical Killing and the Psychology of Genocide.* New York: Basic Books, 1986.

Law, Medicine, and Health Care 17 (1989). Special issue on the "Linares Case."

Lynn, Joanne, ed. *By No Extraordinary Means.* Bloomington, IN: Indiana University Press, 1986.

———. "The Health Care Professional's Role When Active Euthanasia Is Sought." *Journal of Palliative Care* 4 (1988).

Marquis, Donald B. "Four Versions of Double Effect." *Journal of Medicine and Philosophy* 16 (1991).

McMillan, Richard C., Engelhardt, H. Tristram, Jr., and Spicker, Stuart F., eds. *Euthanasia and the Newborn: Conflicts Regarding Saving Lives.* Dordrecht: D. Reidel, 1987.

Meisel, Alan. *The Right to Die.* New York: John Wiley and Sons, 1989, § 5.10.

Misbin, Robert I. "Physicians' Aid in Dying." *New England Journal of Medicine* 325 (October 31, 1991), 1307–1311.

Pence, Gregory. *Classic Cases in Medical Ethics.* New York: Mc-Graw-Hill, 1990.

Quill, Timothy. "Death and Dignity: A Case of Individualized Decision Making." *New England Journal of Medicine* 324 (March 7, 1991), 691–94. Reprinted with additional analysis in Quill. *Death and Dignity.* New York: W. W. Norton, 1993.

Rachels, James. *The End of Life: Euthanasia and Morality.* Oxford: Oxford University Press, 1986.

Robertson, John. "Cruzan and the Constitutional Status of Non-Treatment Decisions for Incompetent Patients." *Georgia Law Review* 25 (1991).

Rosenblum, Victor G., and Forsythe, Clarke D. "The Right to Assisted Suicide: Protection of Autonomy or an Open Door to Social Killing?" *Issues in Law & Medicine* 6 (1990), 3–31.

Sacred Congregation for the Doctrine of the Faith. *Declaration of Euthanasia,* June 26, 1980.

Siegler, Mark, and Weisbard, Alan J. "Against the Emerging Stream: Should Fluids and Nutritional Support Be Discontinued?" *Archives of Internal Medicine* 145 (1985), 129–32.

Society for the Right to Die. *The Physician and the Hopelessly Ill Patient.* New York: Society for the Right to Die, 1985, 39–80, and *1988 Supplement,* 17–34.

Steinbock, Bonnie. "The Intentional Termination of Life." *Ethics in Science and Medicine* 6 (1979), 59–64.

Thomasma, David C., and Graber, Glenn C. *Euthanasia: Toward an Ethical Social Policy.* New York: Continuum, 1990.

van der Maas, Paul J., et al. "Euthanasia and Other Medical Decisions Concerning the End of Life." *Lancet* 338 (September 14, 1991), 669–74.

Walton, Douglas. *Slippery Slope Arguments.* Oxford: Clarendon Press, 1992.

Wanzer, S. H., Federman, D. D., Edelstein, S. T., et al. "The Physician's Responsibility Toward Hopelessly Ill Patient: A Second Look." *New England Journal of Medicine* 320 (1989), 844–849.

Wolf, Susan. "Holding the Line on Euthanasia." *Hastings Center Report* 19 (January–February 1989), S13–S15.

Withholding or Withdrawing Nutrition or Hydration (1992); *Living Wills and Durable Powers of Attorney: Advance Directive Legislation and Issues* (1992); *Active Euthanasia and Assisted Suicide* (1992). Bibliographies available from the National Reference Center for Bioethics Literature, Kennedy Institute of Ethics, Georgetown University, Washington, D.C. 20057. Beginning 1991, all except revised bibliographies are published in the *Kennedy Institute of Ethics Journal.*

Part V

PUBLIC HEALTH, BIOMEDICAL RESEARCH, AND BIOMEDICAL TECHNOLOGIES

8.

The Global Aids Epidemic

INTRODUCTION

No public health problem of the twentieth century is as threatening to human welfare as the global epidemic of AIDS. From small beginnings in a few sites about 1980, this epidemic has spread to every continent on earth. By early 1992 almost 13 million people worldwide were infected with the human immunodeficiency virus (HIV), the virus that causes AIDS. Of these 13 million people, almost 3 million were estimated to have advanced to the end-stage of HIV infection, the life-threatening clinical diagnosis of AIDS. By 1995, another 6.9 million people are likely to be infected with HIV, bringing the world total to 19.8 million infected people. By the year 2000, the most conservative estimate is that 38 million adults will be HIV-infected; a more realistic projection is that the number of adults infected by the year 2000 will be much higher, perhaps reaching 110 million.[1]

How is this virus transmitted, and why has the epidemic been so difficult to control? The simplest answer is that HIV infection is predominantly a sexually transmitted disease. Thus, it is associated with one of the strongest drives in human beings and with a sphere of behavior that is both intimate and private in most people's lives. There are, of course, other sexually transmitted diseases, but the power of twentieth-century medicine has conquered infections like syphilis and gonorrhea, if they are diagnosed early, and helped infected people to cope with the discomfort of herpes. Unlike these other sexually transmitted diseases, however, HIV infection is at present incurable and uncontrollable; its long-term effect, over the course of 10–15 years, is to weaken the infected person's immune system until he or she becomes susceptible to a life-threatening secondary infection.

There are, it is true, other modes of transmission for this potent virus. For example, in the early years of the epidemic, many hemophiliacs were infected through their use of clotting factor made from the blood products of HIV-infected people. Similarly, several thousand patients were infected through receiving HIV-infected blood transfusions. These modes of transmission have virtually ceased in industrialized countries because of new tests for antibody to the virus in blood and new methods of treating clotting factor that kill the virus. Still important as a mode of infection in some countries is the sharing of needles among injecting drug users. Because injecting drug use occurs despite being illegal in most of these countries, and because some injecting drug users are addicted to the drugs they inject, this mode of transmission is also quite difficult to control. A final important mode of transmission is from pregnant women to the fetuses they are carrying. In the United States the average rate of maternal–fetal transmission is estimated to be 30 percent.

The following essays represent the effort of people in numerous academic fields to respond to this major epidemic. Among the fields of training represented by the authors are philosophy, theology, medicine, law, political science, and public health. All of the authors whose works are reprinted here share the goal of fighting and eventually defeating the global epidemic of AIDS but, at the same time, of achieving this goal in a manner that is compatible with our other moral obligations and with human rights.

GENERAL ISSUES

How does one approach a problem as large and seemingly intractable as AIDS, philosophically and politically? The authors of the four selections in this section reflect diverse approaches. The first selection applies three general ethical principles—beneficence, justice, and respect for autonomy—to the major problems raised by the epidemic. The author concludes that these principles may require supplementation. The second and third selections seek to assess the probable social impact of the AIDS epidemic by comparing it with past epidemics. However, the authors of these selections select different analogies and reach incompatible conclusions. The final selection looks back on more than a decade of public health policies on AIDS and asks: Did public health officials in the United States assign too high a priority to the protection of individual rights during the early years of the epidemic? The author's answer is a qualified yes.

The first essay in this section, by LeRoy Walters, surveys major issues in the prevention and treatment of HIV infection and AIDS in three distinct spheres: public health, the delivery of health care, and biomedical research. In the public health sphere, Walters advocates a voluntary rather than a mandatory approach, with major emphasis on educating people at risk of infection about ways to reduce the probability of their infecting others and, simultaneously, their risk of being infected. In the author's view, only the screening of blood, semen, and tissues or organs should be required by law. In the health care sphere, Walters argues that health providers have a moral obligation to care for people with HIV infection but that policies should be implemented to insure that the health risks to such providers remain at a reasonable level. Further, at the level of the health care system, better access to timely health care should be provided to all HIV-infected people. Biomedical research will also raise important ethical questions, especially when researchers initiate large-scale clinical trials of vaccines for the prevention of HIV infection.

The next two selections in this section seek to assess the social impact of the AIDS epidemic, especially in the United States. In their introduction to the book *A Disease of Society*, Dorothy Nelkin, David Willis, and Scott Parris argue that the epidemic is more than a "passing tragedy" and that it will have "long-term, broad-ranging effects on personal relationships, social institutions, and cultural configurations." The authors compare the current epidemic to the nineteenth-century cholera epidemic in Europe, which had a profound effect on the literature, preaching, and politics of the time. The excerpt from a National Research Council panel report on *The Social Impact of AIDS in the United States* takes a somewhat different tack. The panel compares the current AIDS epidemic with the "forgotten" influenza epidemic of 1918, which killed perhaps 30 million people worldwide but arguably had no major impact on the social institutions and practices of the time. In a similar fashion, the panel notes, AIDS is increasingly affecting the most marginalized groups in the United States, especially the urban poor, many of whom belong to ethnic minorities. Thus, if the current pattern of the epidemic holds, the threat of AIDS may seem to disappear in the United States not because the virus has been controlled or eliminated but "because those who continue to be affected by [the epidemic] are socially invisible, beyond the sight and attention of the majority population."

In the final essay in this section Ronald Bayer traces changes in public health policy regarding AIDS that occurred in the United States in the late 1980s and the early 1990s. On such issues as routine or mandatory screening, partner notification, and the criminalization of practices that recklessly endanger other persons, AIDS ceased to be exceptional and began to be treated more like a classic infectious disease. Bayer notes that this reversion to a more typical mode of public policy making coincided with several important social and medical developments, including new therapies that at least slowed the rate of disease progression and a more intensive focus on the epidemic's spread among poor people living in cities. On the whole, the author applauds the end of AIDS exceptionalism, though he expresses the hope that the new emphasis on respect for individual autonomy will have lasting positive effects on both public health and the practice of medicine.

THE DUTY TO WARN AND THE DUTY NOT TO HARM

The duty to warn and the duty not to harm apply not just to health professionals, but to everyone. The authors of the three essays in the second section of this chapter examine the moral obligations of actual or potential sexual partners to each other and the obligations of health professionals to at-risk third parties.

The letter entitled "Sex, Lies, and HIV," by Susan Cochran and Vickie Mays, surveyed 665 college students from southern California. The students reported on their past practice of withholding information from, or lying to, sexual partners, as well as on their willingness to deceive in the future. Of particular importance for the topic of this chapter was the prospective willingness of 20 percent of the men and 4 percent of the women surveyed to lie about their HIV-antibody status. Also important was the willingness of almost half of the men and more than 40 percent of the women to understate the number of previous sexual partners.

Ferdinand Schoeman discusses the "standards of care" that should be employed in intimate sexual relationships by a person who knows that he or she is, or might be, HIV-infected. While acknowledging the difficulty of fulfilling such a moral obligation in practice, the author asserts that an HIV-infected person has a clear moral obligation to disclose his or her HIV status to the potential partner. At least two arguments are advanced to justify this position. The first argument concerns the seriousness of the potential harm to the partner: HIV infection is a life-threatening disease. The second relies on Annette Baier's notion of trust; according to Schoeman, conditions of trust and intimacy that are worth respecting should be characterized by openness and honesty between the parties to the relationship. Schoeman notes that there are questions of *legal* accountability in intimate relationships, as well. Thus, a male who, contrary to fact, asserted to a female that he was free of sexually transmitted disease and who subsequently transmitted his herpes infection to her was not allowed by a California court to hide behind an asserted constitutional right of privacy. Whatever the right of privacy may mean, the court found, it does not include misrepresenting the facts about one's health status in a way that leads to serious harm to another person.

There are two contexts in which health professionals may also face the questions of warning and not harming. The first involves patients who refuse to disclose their HIV infection to sexual partners. Do health professionals have a moral or legal obligation to warn such at-risk third parties in this life-and-death context? Schoeman argues that a therapeutic relationship aims to promote a patient's welfare "within the context of social responsibility." Therefore, in his view, the professional has a clear moral obligation to warn. Karen Rothenberg and Richard North caution that the answer to this question is not so simple, particularly when the HIV-infected person is a woman. In their view, there are two potential "foreseeable victims" in these tragic cases: the sexual partner if no warning occurs and the patient if a warning leads to physical abuse, abandonment, or even death. The authors recommend flexible legislation that allows health professionals to make a careful risk assessment in each case involving third parties who may be harmed.

TESTING AND SCREENING PROGRAMS

The essays in this section ask the questions: Under what circumstances should people be tested for HIV infection (through an antibody test), and should such testing be mandatory or voluntary? Debate about these questions has been a central feature of the AIDS policy discussion since a reasonably accurate antibody test became available in mid-1985. Note that the answers to the questions depend in part on the *facts* about how HIV infection is transmitted. That is, if HIV infection were transmitted through the air like the common cold or influenza, the risk of transmission to bystanders and casual acquaintances would be considerably higher and the argument for widespread testing and screening correspondingly stronger. In addition, the *facts* about whether an effective treatment for an infection exists may also influence one's judgments about the moral justification for testing and screening programs.

In his overview, James Childress accents the ethical principle of respect for persons and cites three types of rules that can be derived from this principle: rules of liberty, rules of privacy, and rules of confidentiality. The author then asks what set of conditions could justify overriding this principle and these prima facie rules. He suggests five conditions which, in his view, would be individually necessary and jointly sufficient to justify infringements of the rules. Childress's formal analysis is then applied to an interesting variety of potential screenees: hospital patients, couples applying for marriage licenses, pregnant women and newborns, prisoners, and immigrants. In general, Childress concludes that mandatory testing and screening of these groups is not justified, given the current fact-situation.

The remaining essays in this section discuss more specific topics. Carol Levine and Ronald Bayer ask whether public policies on screening at-risk populations should be changed because drugs have been developed that at least slow the rate of progression in HIV disease. The authors' nuanced answer is that more vigorous programs of voluntary testing and screening are morally justifiable in this new situation, if those programs are accompanied by appropriate follow-up and protection against discrimination for people whose test is positive. The essay by an interdisciplinary working group examines the closely related questions of testing pregnant women and newborns for HIV infection. Three important factual aspects of the working group's analysis are that approximately 30 percent of HIV-infected women in the United States give birth to HIV-infected infants, that no prenatal test can determine which infants will be infected, and that a positive test in an infant also discloses the HIV status of the infant's mother. After carefully weighing alternatives, the working group concludes that the test for HIV infection should be *offered* to all pregnant women and new mothers but that a mandatory approach to testing either newborns or pregnant women should be rejected.

A GLOBAL PERSPECTIVE

It is easy for North Americans to forget that the AIDS epidemic affects millions of people worldwide. In the final selection of this chapter, the Global AIDS Policy Coalition attempts to sound an alarm about the international scope and uncontrolled pace of the epidemic. For example, in three countries of Southeast Asia, the coalition reports, more than a million new people have been infected with HIV in the past few years alone. In sub-Saharan Africa, which already has a larger number of cases than any other part of the world, the epidemic is steadily moving from urban to rural areas. The authors of this essay speak of a "plateauing of efforts" to combat the epidemic and of a world that is "lagging behind in its response to AIDS." In short, they argue, we and our children must now confront "a global epidemic spinning out of control."

NOTE

1. For further detail on these estimates, see the excerpt from *AIDS in the World* reprinted as the last selection in this chapter.

General Issues

LEROY WALTERS

Ethical Issues in the Prevention and Treatment of HIV and AIDS

An adequate ethical framework for evaluating public policies regarding infection with the human immunodeficiency virus (HIV) will include the following considerations: (i) the outcomes, often categorized as benefits and harms, of the policies; (ii) the distribution of these outcomes within the population; and (iii) the liberty-rights, or freedoms, of those who are affected by the policies. A recent presidential commission on bioethics called these three considerations well-being, equity, and respect (*1*). In their *Principles of Biomedical Ethics*, Beauchamp and Childress designate these considerations beneficence and nonmaleficence, justice, and respect for autonomy (*2*).

As we and other societies attempt to confront the AIDS epidemic, the central problem we face is the following: How can we control the epidemic and the harm that it causes without unjustly discriminating against particular social groups and without unnecessarily infringing on the freedom of individuals? This formulation accepts the importance of halting the transmission of HIV infection but recognizes that the achievement of that goal may at times be in tension with other moral constraints, namely, constraints based on justice or respect for autonomy. At the same time, however, these three considerations, or moral vectors, may all point in the same direction, for example, if a particular policy is simultaneously counterproductive, discriminatory, and intrusive.

In this [essay] I will indicate how the ethical principles of beneficence, justice, and respect for autonomy relate to the epidemic of HIV infection in the United States (*3*). I will argue that, because these three principles are all of importance, none of them should be ignored in the formulation of public policy. While one principle may predominate in a given situation or

LeRoy Walters, "Ethical Issues in the Prevention and Treatment of HIV Infection and AIDS," *Science* 239 (February 5, 1988), 597–603. © 1988, American Association for the Advancement of Science.

sphere, it should not be allowed to overwhelm or displace the other two.

Three types of policies will be considered: public health policies, policies for the delivery of health care to people with HIV infection, and research policies.

PUBLIC HEALTH POLICIES

PUBLIC EDUCATION

Until more effective medical therapies and preventive measures are developed, public education is likely to be one of the most important means for controlling the epidemic. If the education appeals to the rational capacities of the hearer, it respects his or her autonomy. If public education simultaneously leads to risk-reducing behavioral change, it also promotes the health of the hearer and his or her associates.

Imaginative public education will be moral education in the sense that it helps the hearer to see clearly the possible effects of his or her behavior on others. One possible approach to such education involves the use of ethical if-then statements such as the following. "We have discussed the pros and cons of engaging in behavior X. If you choose to do X, then, in order to avoid harming others, you should adopt measures A, B, and C." Fortunately, many of the measures that protect others are also self-protective. Thus, public educators can simultaneously appeal to both the self-interested and altruistic sentiments of their audiences.

While everyone who is at risk of contracting or transmitting HIV infection should be educated, there are strong moral arguments for targeting educational efforts especially toward people who are most likely to engage in risky behaviors — for example, behaviors like receptive anal intercourse, intravenous (IV) drug use with shared needles, or vaginal intercourse with IV drug users. Such targeted programs can be justified on either or both of two grounds. Intensive coverage of the groups most at risk for infection is likely to be more efficient in controlling the epidemic than general educational programs alone will be. It can also be argued that groups at higher than average risk need, or even deserve, stronger than average warnings of the risks to which they may be exposed (4).

MODIFIED APPROACHES TO IV DRUG USE

Twenty-five percent of clinical AIDS cases involve the illegal use of IV drugs (5). The sharing of needles and syringes, sometimes a ritual in settings where multiple drug users self-inject together, seems to be the principal mode of transmission among IV drug users. People who become infected through sharing contaminated needles and syringes may, in turn, infect nondrug-using people through sexual intercourse.

Members of ethnic and racial minority groups are represented in disproportionate numbers among U.S. IV drug users who have AIDS. In AIDS cases involving IV drug use as the sole risk, 51% of patients are black and 28% are Hispanic (5). Among minority group women, the correlation between IV drugs and AIDS is particularly strong: 70% of black women with AIDS and 83% of Hispanic women with AIDS are either IV drug users or the sexual partners of IV drug users. Two-thirds of black children and three-fourths of Hispanic children with AIDS contracted their infections from mothers who were members of the same two risk groups (6,7).

It is clear that current programs for IV drug users in the United States are failing in many respects and that new and bold measures are needed. These measures may not be politically popular, given the misunderstanding and fear that frequently surround drug use and given our society's traditional neglect of IV drug users. But the initiatives will be essential for controlling the epidemic, for meeting the needs of people who are often stigmatized, and for enabling IV drug users to make autonomous choices about their lives.

The first initiative that should be undertaken is the expansion of drug-treatment programs to accommodate, on a timely basis, all IV drug users who desire treatment. Reports of 3-month waiting lists in U.S. drug-treatment programs are commonplace (8, pp. 108–109; 9). Our failure to provide treatment to people who indicate an interest in discontinuing drug use is both short-sighted and counterproductive. It is encouraging to note that the Presidential Commission on Human Immunodeficiency Virus Epidemic is making the lack of programs to treat IV drug users one of four major areas for initial study (10, pp. 22–23).

A second initiative that will probably be necessary to control the epidemic among IV drug users is the establishment of public programs for the exchange of sterile needles and syringes for used and possibly contaminated equipment. Three countries—the Netherlands, the United Kingdom, and Australia—have experimented with free needle-exchange programs and have reported initially encouraging results—although it is too early to know for certain that the exchange programs actually reduce the rate of infection transmission (9, 11, 12). Proposals to initiate needle-exchange programs in the United States have not yet been implemented, in part because they appear to condone or even to encourage IV drug use. Perhaps for this reason U.S. law-enforcement officials have generally opposed such programs (8, pp. 109–110; 9). However, the ethical if-then statements discussed above may also pertain here. Moral and legal prohibitions of IV drug use have not achieved universal acceptance in our society. Given that fact, one seeks to formulate rules of morally responsible drug use: "If you choose to use IV drugs, then you should take steps, including the use of sterile needles and syringes, to minimize the chance of your becoming infected and infecting others with HIV."

If the foregoing measures, coupled with targeted education for IV drug users, are insufficient, more radical initiatives will need to be contemplated. One of the most controversial initiatives, at least among law-enforcement officials, would be the provision of controlled access to injectable drugs by IV drug users in an effort to bring addiction and its social context above ground. Such a policy was endorsed editorially in May 1987 by the British journal *The Lancet* (13). Pilot programs of controlled access to injectable drugs, with simultaneous decriminalization of IV drug use, could provide valuable data on the potential effectiveness of this initiative.

MODIFIED APPROACHES TO PROSTITUTION

Male or female prostitutes who have unprotected intercourse with multiple sexual partners expose themselves to considerable risk of HIV infection in areas of moderate to high seroprevalence. This theoretical risk has been actualized among female prostitutes who have been studied epidemiologically in both the United States and equatorial Africa. For example, a recent cross-sectional survey of female prostitutes in the Newark, New Jersey, area indicated that 51.7% tested positive for antibody to HIV in 1987; in Miami the seroprevalence rate among incarcerated female prostitutes was 18.7% (14). A high infection rate among prostitutes imperils not only their own health but also the health of their clients and their clients' other sexual partners.

Official policies on prostitution in this country are set by states and localities. In most U.S. jurisdictions the general approach has been to criminalize the practice of prostitution; in some jurisdictions, the patronizing of a prostitute is also a crime. In contrast, many European countries and several counties in Nevada have adopted a licensing or regulatory approach that includes periodic screening of prostitutes for infectious disease (14; 15, pp. 2–20).

An ethically appropriate response to prostitution will be based not simply on our evaluation of prostitution as a practice but also on careful assessment of the extent to which alternative public policies on prostitution are compatible with the principles of beneficence, respect for autonomy, and justice. Although the intervening variables are numerous, the available evidence from Nevada and Europe suggests that, compared with the outlaw and arrest approach, the licensing and regulatory approach to prostitution is at least correlated with lower rates of infection with several other sexually transmitted diseases among prostitutes (14, 16, 17). At the same time, a licensing and regulatory approach displays greater respect for the autonomy of adult persons to perform acts that affect chiefly the persons themselves, especially if the transmission of disease is prevented through the use of condoms and through regular health examinations.

Again in this case we should be willing to become pragmatic and experimental in our approach to controlling the epidemic. The legal prohibition of prostitution has not been notably successful in preventing a rapid rise in seropositivity among prostitutes, at least in some cities. Pilot studies of less restrictive approaches in selected localities, taken together with evidence from Nevada and Western Europe, might reveal that alternative policies are, on balance, ethically preferable (18).

MODIFIED APPROACHES TO HOMOSEXUAL AND BISEXUAL SEXUAL ACTIVITY

As of December 1987, 65% of AIDS cases in the United States involve homosexual or bisexual males; an additional 8% of cases involve homosexual or bisexual males who also admit to IV drug use (5). Thus, in a substantial fraction of U.S. AIDS cases to date, HIV seems to have been transmitted through sexual intercourse between males. Receptive anal intercourse is one of the principle modes of viral transmission (19, 20).

Many homosexual and bisexual males with AIDS or HIV infection became infected before AIDS was described as a clinical syndrome and before the primary modes of transmission were identified. Thus, while they may have known that they were at increased risk for a series of treatable sexually transmitted diseases, for example, gonorrhea or hepatitis B, they could not have known that they were at risk for contracting an infection that might lead to AIDS. Since the facts about HIV transmission have become well known, homosexual and bisexual men have been heavily involved in targeted public education programs and in humane health care programs for people with AIDS. There is also substantial evidence to indicate that considerable numbers of homosexual and bisexual males have altered their sexual practices to reduce their probability of becoming infected and infecting others with HIV (21–23).

It might seem that, short of traditional public health measures such as increased testing and screening, little more can be done to encourage the cooperation of homosexual and bisexual males in controlling the epidemic. However, two public policy initiatives might conceivably have a salutary effect: (i) in jurisdictions that currently outlaw such acts, the decriminalization of private homosexual acts between consenting adults; and (ii) in jurisdictions that currently lack such antidiscrimination statutes, the legal prohibition of discrimination against people who engage in private consensual homosexual acts.

There would be strong moral arguments for these legal changes even in the absence of a major epidemic (24–27). However, in the midst of an epidemic that has already affected large numbers of homosexual and bisexual men, the following additional arguments can be advanced. First, decriminalization and antidiscrimination initiatives would encourage homosexual and bisexual males to disclose their patterns of sexual activity to health providers and hospitals without fear that a breach of confidentiality could lead to criminal prosecution. Such open disclosure could, in turn, lead to the discussion of risk-reducing practices such as the use of condoms or the avoidance of anal intercourse. Second, the legal changes could facilitate the gathering of more accurate data on current patterns of sexual activity in the United States—patterns that have not been studied in depth since the research of Alfred Kinsey and associates in the 1940s (28). By reducing respondents' fears about being stigmatized, the proposed legal changes could enhance the accuracy of data that would then be used for educational and epidemiological purposes. Third, the proposed legal changes would send a clear signal to homosexuals and bisexuals that heterosexuals intend to treat them with what Ronald Dworkin has termed "equal concern and

respect (29). More specifically, these policies would help all of us, regardless of sexual orientation or pattern of sexual practice, jointly to reassess whether the magnitude of our national effort to control the current epidemic has been proportionate to the gravity of the threat posed by the epidemic.

TESTING AND SCREENING PROGRAMS

The moral and legal justification for testing individuals or screening populations for antibody to HIV has been extensively debated (8, pp. 112–130; 15, chap. 2; 30–35). James Childress has proposed a helpful taxonomy of screening programs (31):

	Degree of Voluntariness	
Extent of screening	Voluntary	Compulsory
Universal	1	2
Selective	3	4

A recent amendment to the voluntary category in this matrix is "routine" counseling and testing, which is defined in Public Health Service guidelines as "a policy to provide these services to all clients after informing them that testing will be done." The Public Health Service guidelines add that "Except where testing is required by law, individuals have the right to decline to be tested without being denied health care or other services" (34).

There is scant justification and little public support for universal HIV antibody screening programs, whether voluntary or compulsory. The principal arguments against such programs are consequential. The usual screening test has poor predictive value in populations where the prevalence of seropositivity is low; thus, large numbers of people who are in fact antibody-negative would be falsely identified as positive during initial screening (36). Further, the cost of universal screening would be high, especially given the fact that screening would need to be repeated at regular intervals to track changes in antibody status. In short, universal screening is incompatible with the principle of beneficence. Mandatory universal screening would involve a massive violation of the respect for autonomy principle, as well.

The crux of the current debate is whether selective screening for HIV antibody should be undertaken and, if so, whether the screening should be compulsory or voluntary. To date, most commentators on the ethics of HIV antibody screening have argued that only carefully targeted, voluntary screening programs are morally justifiable and that such programs are morally justified only if they fulfill three conditions: (i) the programs include adequate counseling of screenees; (ii) they protect the confidentiality of information about individuals, except in carefully specified exceptional circumstances; and (iii) they are conducted in a context that provides guarantees of nondiscrimination to seropositive individuals (30–34). Categories of persons often nominated for selective, voluntary screening programs include hemophiliacs, IV drug users, homosexual and bisexual men, prostitutes, patients at clinics for sexually transmitted diseases, heterosexual sexual partners of infected persons, prisoners, military recruits and personnel, applicants for marriage licenses, and hospital patients, especially patients undergoing surgery or hemodialysis.

It is not possible here to discuss each of these population groups (37). I will, however, comment on the three conditions for ethically acceptable voluntary screening programs. The provision of face-to-face counseling to all persons participating in a large-scale, voluntary screening program may be infeasible on financial grounds. Thus, it might at first glance seem reasonable to reserve counseling for screenees who are confirmed to be HIV antibody positive. However, if voluntary screening programs are targeted to selected groups with much higher than average prevalence, then the screening context would seem an ideal setting for carefully tailored education regarding risk reduction. Such counseling demonstrates a program's respect for the autonomy of screenees and should help to slow the progress of the epidemic, as well.

The protection of patient confidentiality in all but carefully delineated circumstances also demonstrates respect for the autonomy of screenees (15, chap. 4; 38). Guarantees of confidentiality can be strengthened by statutes that impose criminal sanctions for unauthorized, medically nonindicated disclosure of antibody status. At the same time, however, guarantees of confidentiality should not be absolute. Several commentators have argued, for example, that health care providers have a moral duty to warn known intimate associates of an antibody-positive person who refuses to inform the associates of his or her antibody status and who continues to place those associates at risk (31, 32, 34, 39). In this case, the health provider cannot simultaneously respect the autonomy of both the screenee and the associates.

The level of participation in voluntary screening programs is likely to be higher if legal guarantees against discrimination are provided to antibody-positive persons (15, chap. 5; 40, pp. 347–350; 41). These guarantees would complement the general guarantees of nondiscrimination discussed above. One formulation of such a guarantee in a major federal bill reads as follows:

A person may not discriminate against an otherwise qualified individual in employment, housing, public accommodations, or governmental services solely by reason of the fact that such individual is, or is regarded as being, infected with the etiologic agent for acquired immune deficiency syndrome (42).

In a democratic society, the presumption should be in favor of voluntary rather than mandatory public health programs. This presumption should be overridden only as a last resort, after voluntary alternatives have been vigorously employed and have failed, and only if there is a reasonable hope that a mandatory program would succeed (43). In my judgment, voluntary screening programs that include adequate counseling and appropriate guarantees of confidentiality and nondiscrimination have not yet received a sufficient trial in the United States. Such screening programs, coupled with anonymous testing for those who desire it and with the other public health strategies outlined above offer us a reasonable hope of bringing the AIDS epidemic under control. Thus, I conclude that mandatory screening programs—other than those involving persons who voluntarily donate blood, semen, or organs—are not morally justifiable at this time (44).

POLICIES FOR THE DELIVERY OF HEALTH CARE

Even as public health efforts to prevent the further spread of HIV infection proceed, some of the approximately 1.5 million already infected people in the United States will experience initial symptoms, become ill, develop full-blown AIDS, or die. As of 7 December 1987, 47,436 infected adults and 703 infected children had been diagnosed as having clinical AIDS; 26,816 (60.3%) of the adults and 419 (59.6%) of the children had died (5). HIV infection produces a broad clinical spectrum that includes, at its extremes, asymptomatic status and terminal illness.

The health care delivery issue is currently focused on people who are symptomatic as a result of HIV infection and who know that they are infected with HIV. Increasingly, however, people at risk for HIV infection are likely to call on the health care system for help in clarifying their antibody status. Further, the health care system may be able to offer medical interventions to asymptomatic infected people that will prevent, or at least delay, some of the possible sequelae of HIV infection (45).

THE DUTY TO PROVIDE CARE

This issue can be considered at two levels: the level of the individual health care worker and the level of health-related institutions and the health care system.

Surveys of attitudes toward caring for AIDS patients in one high-prevalence area have revealed considerable anxiety among physicians and nurses. A study conducted at four New York residency programs in 1986 noted that 36% of medical house officers and 17% of pediatric house officers reported needlestick exposure to the blood of AIDS patients. Twenty-five percent of respondents indicated that they "would not continue to care for AIDS patients if given a choice" (46). A 1984 survey of nurses at the Westchester (New York) County Hospital found that 39% would ask for a transfer if they had to care for AIDS patients on a regular basis (47).

Studies suggest that the probability of infection transmission from patient to health care worker is very low. Yet ten reasonably well-documented cases of seroconversion in health care workers have been reported, with six of these workers having been exposed by accidental needlesticks and the remainder by exposure of the eyes, mouth, or hands and arms to infectious body fluids (48, 49). HIV seems to be much less infectious than the hepatitis B virus. Yet this comparison is not entirely pertinent; hepatitis B is not usually a lethal disease, and an effective vaccine against the disease is available. Thus, there remains a very small but nonetheless real probability that health care workers will acquire HIV infection from the blood or other body fluids of people with HIV infection. In an unknown proportion of these workers, the infection will have lethal consequences.

Despite these attitudes and risks, it might seem at first blush that the ethical obligation of health care workers to care for people with HIV infection is clear. The words "profession" and "professional" leap read-ily to mind, as do images of real or fictional heroines and heroes such as Florence Nightingale, Benjamin Rush, or Bernard Rieux (50). Yet the scope of the term health care worker is broad and includes the medical technologist, the phlebotomist, and the person who transports infective waste to the incinerator. Further, the basis for and the extent of the health care worker's obligation to provide care for patients are matters of dispute—despite several vigorous reassertions of the physician's moral duty to treat people with HIV infection (51).

A reasonable ethic for health care workers will not require of them heroic self-sacrifice or works of supererogation. Such a requirement would violate both the principles of autonomy and beneficence. On the other hand, a reasonable ethic will not allow people who are in need of care to be refused treatment or abandoned solely because they are infectious. Such refusal and abandonment would violate the principle of beneficence. Universal infection-control precautions such as those suggested by the Centers for Disease Control (CDC) (49) are likely to reduce substantially the risks to health care workers; thus, heroic self-sacrifice will not be required. If these measures are insufficient in certain high-risk settings, or if the universal precautions seriously impede patient care, testing of selected categories of patients—for example, surgical patients—may be justifiable. This testing should be carried out only with the prior knowledge and consent of patients and should include counseling for seropositive persons. Patients who decline testing will be presumed to be antibody-positive. Testing measures will seem less threatening to patients when carried out in a social context that respects confidentiality and opposes discrimination.

At the level of health care institutions and the health care system, the AIDS epidemic has exacerbated already existing problems regarding access to health care. The access problems faced by people with AIDS or HIV infection do not differ qualitatively from those faced by many other U.S. citizens with chronic or terminal illness. However, because people with HIV infection are almost always under 65 years of age, their health care needs graphically illustrate major deficiencies in the current U.S. system for providing health care to the nonelderly.

Even before the AIDS epidemic became a major factor in health care financing, it was almost commonplace to assert that 15 to 17.5% of U.S. residents under age 65 lack both public and private health insurance. These percentages translate into 30 to 35 million

Americans (52). An additional 10 to 15% of these under age 65 who are insured are not adequately protected against chronic or catastrophic illness (53). Of the 150 million Americans under 65 who are privately insured, at least 80% have their health insurance tied to group plans at their place of employment (54).

People with HIV infection who are currently employed and who have group health insurance coverage through their employers are in the best position to cope with the medical costs that may result from their infection. However, even for these most well-off people a double threat looms. If they become so ill that they can no longer continue employment, they face the prospect of losing both their source of income and their group health insurance coverage. Although federal legislation enacted in 1985 provides for continuing individual health insurance coverage for 18 months after the termination of employment, the cost of such coverage may be prohibitive for an unemployed person. Other people with HIV infection who become symptomatic—the underinsured, the uninsured, and the unemployed—are likely to rely on Medicaid for assistance, if they can meet complex eligibility requirements. Actuaries from the Health Care Financing Administration estimate that 40% of patients with clinical AIDS are assisted by Medicaid with their direct medical care expenses and that an average of 23% of such expenses are born by Medicaid. In fiscal year 1987 federal and state Medicaid expenditures for AIDS patients were estimated at $400 million (15, p. 6–5).

The future looks bleak, both in terms of costs and in terms of shortages of needed services for chronically and terminally ill patients. In the cost projections made to date, the estimates of personal medical costs for AIDS patients alone in 1991 range from a low of $3.5 billion to a high of $9.4 billion (in 1984 dollars) (55). Already in 1988, there are shortages of nursing home facilities, home care programs, hospice facilities, and counseling services for clinically ill people with HIV infection (8, chap. 5; 10, pp. 19–21; 15, chaps. 6 and 8).

Divergent views exist about the appropriate role of the private sector in the provision of health care to people infected with HIV, as well as to other people with health care needs (8), 162–173; 56). What is clear, however, is that we as a society cannot expect private hospitals and nursing homes to operate at a loss. Nor can we expect private health insurers or self-insuring employers to ignore the financial impact of an unanticipated epidemic.

The central ethical question confronting the U.S. health care system was evident long before HIV was discovered or named. That question is: Does our society have a moral obligation to provide a basic level of health care to every one of its members? Several commentators on the ethics of health care allocation have argued that our society does have such an obligation (57). They have based their argument on the principles of beneficence (the unpredictability of health care needs and the harms caused by lack of access) and justice (the inequities that result from current differentials in access). They assert that the principle of respect for autonomy must take second place, as those of us who are financially well off are called upon to share in meeting the needs of the less well off, presumably through the payment of increased premiums and taxes.

This judgment seems to me to be correct. If so, the major policy question is no longer whether we should attempt to meet the needs of the medically less well off. Rather, we should address the questions "What constitutes a basic level of care?" and "How can this level best be provided to everyone, including people infected with HIV?"

NEUROLOGICAL INVOLVEMENT AND CONSENT TO CARE

An unknown proportion of people with HIV infection experience involvement of the central nervous system, including the brain (58). Indeed, the CDC has recently expanded the clinical definition of AIDS to include such neurological complications (59). The extent of neurological involvement may range from minor symptoms of cognitive impairment to totally disabling dementia.

Brain involvement resulting from HIV infection, like brain involvement due to other causes, inevitably complicates the relation between patient and health provider. Two methods of extending patient autonomy forward in time have proved helpful in other health care settings and may also be beneficial in the treatment of HIV-infected patients with early symptoms of neurological deterioration. Advance directives about preferred modes of care of nontreatment are now expressly recognized by the statutes of 38 states and the District of Columbia (60). In addition, 18 states make legal provision for a patient's appointment of a spokesperson with durable power of attorney, who can express the patient's wishes if the patient should become incapacitated or be adjudged legally incompetent (*61*). The patient's spokesperson is usually a trusted friend or family member. Both modes of anticipatory decision-making were strongly endorsed by the President's Commission on Bioethics in 1983 (*62*) and both seem well adapted to the needs of HIV-infected patients with neurological symptoms (*63*).

THE CARE OF DYING AIDS PATIENTS

When treatment fails and death within a few months becomes inevitable, people with AIDS deserve compassion and support. Individual patient preferences vary, but many terminally ill patients have expressed a desire to die at home in the company of friends or in a hospice-like institutional setting. These alternatives should be provided by an upgraded system of care for all terminally ill patients.

A central role in patient management should be played by the patient's own directives and, if the patient becomes mentally incapacitated, by the patient-designated proxy. If at all possible, future decisions about resuscitation and the use of artificial nutrition and hydration measures should be explicitly discussed with the competent AIDS patient (*64*). Like other terminally ill patients who face the probability of severe physical deterioration and the possibility of a painful death, some AIDS patients will also want to discuss the options of suicide or voluntary active euthanasia. Both of these topics have received intensive study, especially in the Netherlands, the United Kingdom, and the United States (*65*). Respect for the autonomy of terminally ill patients would seem to require us to place these difficult issues on the agenda for sustained local and national discussion.

RESEARCH POLICIES

In the long term, the best hope for controlling the AIDS epidemic lies in biomedical research. A vaccine against HIV would seem to be the ideal solution but if immunization strategies prove to be infeasible, chemoprophylactic measures may succeed. For people already infected with HIV, new interventions are under development, but progress has been slow. Epidemiological, social-scientific, educational, and social-intervention studies will also be key elements in an overall research strategy.

A general question that has been raised about the U.S. research effort is whether it has been proportionate to the gravity of the threat posed by the current epidemic. A 1986 report from the Institute of Medi-

cine and the National Academy of Sciences concluded that at that time the response was inadequate (*8*, pp. 28 and 238–249). A less than adequate response to the epidemic violates both the principle of beneficence and the principle of justice. It fails to prevent avoidable harm to thousands if not millions of people, and it conveys the impression that policy-makers do not care about the welfare of the groups most at risk. Even in the best of times, members of several groups at increased risk for HIV infection experience neglect or even stigmatization by many of their fellow-citizens. These are not the best of times.

Clinical trials of various treatments are being conducted in asymptomatic and symptomatic people with HIV infection as well as in patients with clinical AIDS. The usual practice in early trials is to use a placebo-controlled design with each subgroup of people until an effective therapy for that group is discovered. When the efficacy of an agent has been demonstrated, placebos are no longer given; rather, various dosages of the effective agent are compared, or a new candidate therapy is compared against the older, effective therapy.

Some critics have questioned whether it is ethical to conduct placebo-controlled trials with HIV-infected patients. They have suggested that all symptomatic people with HIV infection should be given immediate access to potentially promising therapies that have not been validated in randomized controlled trials (*66*). Here one can, in my view, make a justice-based argument for subjecting potential treatments for HIV infection to the same kind of rigorous study that other new treatments must undergo. Further, from the perspective of beneficence, unnecessary suffering would be visited on people with HIV infection if they were provided immediate access to ineffective "therapies" or treatments with toxic effects that far outweigh their therapeutic benefits.

The testing of vaccines for the prevention of HIV infection will also raise important ethical questions. For example, it will be necessary for uninfected volunteers to be exposed to inoculations that will make them antibody-positive by ELISA and Western blot tests. Further, research subjects who participate in unsuccessful vaccine trials may thereby be made more susceptible to HIV or other infections than they would have been had they not taken part in the trials. Equally disturbing is the possibility that some subjects, having received an ineffective vaccine, may be rendered incapable of being immunized by subsequently developed effective vaccines. Because the numbers of participants in early trials may reach into the thousands or tens of thousands, they could constitute a serious additional public health problem for society.

The risks associated with vaccine trials have prompted some researchers to consider testing vaccines against HIV in countries of equatorial Africa, where the prevalence of infection is known to be higher than in the United States and where the number of trial participants could therefore be lower. In addition, the risk of litigation for research-related injury might be reduced in a non-U.S. setting. However, the proposal to export research risks raises questions of fairness in its own right.

Partial solutions to the ethical quandaries presented by vaccine trials can be found in policies that exemplify the principles of respect for autonomy, beneficence, and justice. The autonomy of participants in vaccine trials will be respected if they are warned clearly and in advance of the potential physical and social harms to which they will be exposed. The careful planning and foresight of researchers can also reduce the harms associated with vaccine-induced seropositivity. For example, in a vaccine trial sponsored by the National Institutes of Health, volunteers will be provided with official documentation certifying that their antibody status had been negative before they participated in a vaccine trial (67). Nonetheless, if participants in vaccine trials are injured as a result of their participation, they may have a legitimate claim to compensation for disabilities incurred in a publicly declared war on a major disease. Indeed, the principle of justice may require the establishment of a compensation program for research-related injuries (8, pp. 228–229; 68).

OTHER TYPES OF RESEARCH

Epidemiologic research will provide a scientific basis for policies in public health and health care delivery. Longitudinal studies among members of at-risk groups will help to clarify the natural history of HIV infection and the role of cofactors in the development of clinical symptoms. Homosexual and bisexual men, in particular, have been active participants in published longitudinal studies (23, 69). Cross-sectional studies of demographic groups—newborn infants, patients in "sentinel" hospitals, and residents in selected metropolitan areas—will facilitate more refined estimates of the number of people infected with HIV (70). One of the major ethical questions in cross-sectional studies has been whether to retain the identifying links between blood samples and the individuals from whom the samples were taken. Anonymous, unlinked testing without consent seems to be emerging as the method of choice, in part because a recent interview survey indicated a likely refusal rate of about 30% among adult Americans if they were invited to be tested in a national seroprevalence study (71). The advantages of anonymous epidemiologic studies are that no identifiable subjects are placed at risk and that the research results are not skewed by refusals. The disadvantage is that seropositive individuals cannot be identified, notified, and counseled.

Other types of research can also play important roles in understanding and coping with the current epidemic. Social science and behavioral research will help to elucidate such questions as the extent of homosexual sexual activity among U.S. adults—a topic that has not been studied in large, rigorously selected samples since the 1940s. Educational research will assist public health officials and counselors in communicating more effectively about lifesaving alternatives in the most intimate realms of human behavior (8, pp. 230–238; 72). Finally, social-intervention research can provide public policy-makers with essential information about the effects of innovative approaches to social practices such as IV drug use and prostitution (73).

CONCLUSION

At the beginning of this [essay] I mentioned three ethical principles that are thought to be of central importance in contemporary biomedical ethics: beneficence, justice, and respect for autonomy. These principles have informed the preceding analysis. However, as I have reflected on the complexities of the current epidemic, it has occurred to me that a fourth ethical principle may be required to guide our actions and policies in response to this major threat to the public health. I do not have a precise name for this additional principle, but I will venture to suggest some first approximations: mutuality, solidarity, or community (74).

REFERENCES AND NOTES

1. President's Commission for the Study of Ethical Problems in Medicine and Biomedical and Behavioral Research, *Summing Up* (Government Printing Office, Washington, DC, March 1983), pp. 66–71.

2. T. L. Beauchamp and J. F. Childress, *Principles of Biomedical Ethics* (Oxford Univ. Press, New York, 2d ed., 1983), chaps. 3–6.

3. Although the focus of this article is limited to the situation in the United States, I think that the same general ethical principles are also applicable elsewhere. However, the discussion of alternative public policy options would not necessarily fit other social and cultural settings. Other essays on ethics and HIV infection or AIDS include: A. R. Jonsen, M. Cooke, B. A. Koening, *Issues Sci. Technol.* **2**, 56 (1986); R. Bayer, *Milbank Mem. Fund Q.* **64** (Suppl. 1), 168 (1986). See also two special supplements to the *Hastings Center Report*, one published in August 1985, the other in December 1986; and C. Pierce and D. VanDeVeer, Eds., *AIDS: Ethics and Public Policy* (Wadsworth, Belmont, CA, 1988). On legal aspects of the epidemic and its control, see (*15*) and (*40*) below; H. E. Lewis, *J. Am. Med. Assoc.* **258**, 2410 (1987); and two special issues of *Law Med. Health Care* published in December 1986 and summer 1987.

4. For discussions of general and targeted public education in the context of the current epidemic, see (*8*, pp. 96–112 and 130–133) and (*15*, chap. 9). The illustrated version of the *Surgeon General's Report on Acquired Immune Deficiency Syndrome* (Department of Health and Human Services, Public Health Service, Washington, DC, 1986) is a model of factual, explicit general education about HIV infection and AIDS.

5. Centers for Disease Control (CDC), *AIDS Weekly Surveillance Report United States,* 7 December 1987.

6. L. Thompson, *Washington Post*, 11 August 1987, Health, p. 7.

7. D. S. Weinberg and H. W. Murray, *N. Engl. J. Med.* **317**, 1469 (1987).

8. Institute of Medicine, National Academy of Sciences, *Confronting AIDS: Directions for Public Health, Health Care, and Research* (National Academy Press, Washington, DC, 1986).

9. D. C. Des Jarlais and S. R. Friedman, *AIDS* **1**, 67 (1987).

10. Presidential Commission on the Human Immunodeficiency Virus Epidemic, *Preliminary Report* (The Commission, Washington, DC, 2 December 1987).

11. A. R. Moss, *Br. Med. J.* **294**, 389 (1987).

12. A. Wodak *et al.*, *Med. J. Australia* **147**, 275 (1987).

13. Anonymous, "Management of drug addicts: Hostility, humanity, and pragmatism," *Lancet* **1987-I,** 1068 (1987). See also J. B. Bakalar and L. Grinspoon, *Drug Control in a Free Society* (Cambridge Univ. Press, Cambridge, 1984) and A. S. Trebach, *The Heroin Solution* (Yale Univ. Press, New Haven, CT, 1982).

14. CDC, *J. Am. Med. Assoc.* **257**, 2011 (1987).

15. U.S. Department of Health and Human Services, Public Health Service, *AIDS: A Public Health Challenge* (Intergovernmental Health Policy Project, George Washington University, Washington, DC, October 1987), vols. 1–3.

16. G. L. Smith and K. F. Smith, *Lancet* **1987-II**, 1392 (1987).

17. G. Papaevangelou, A. Roumeliotou-Karayannis, G. Kallinkos, G. Papoutsakis, *ibid.* **1985-II**, 1018 (1985).

18. For a general discussion of regulatory policy on prostitution, see F. M. Shaver, *Can. Public Policy* **11**, 493 (1985).

19. L. A. Kingsley *et al., Lancet* **1987-I,** 345 (1987).

20. J. S. Chmiel *et al., Am. J. Epidemiol.* **126**, 568 (1987).

21. CDC, *Morbid. Mortal. Weekly Rep.* **34**, 613 (1985).

22. L. W. McKusick, W. Horstman, T. J. Coates, *Am. J. Public Health* **75**, 493 (1985).

23. W. Winkelstein, Jr., *et al., ibid.* **76**, 685 (1987).

24. J. Feinberg, *The Moral Limits of the Criminal Law,* vol. 2, *Offense to Others* (Oxford Univ. Press, New York, 1985).

25. D. A. J. Richards, *Sex, Drugs, Death, and the Law: An Essay on Human Rights and Overcriminalization* (Rowman and Littlefield, Totowa, NJ, 1982), pp. 29–83.

26. U.S. Supreme Court, "Bowers v. Hardwick," *S. Ct.* **106**, 2841 (1986), dissents by Justices Blackmun and Stevens.

27. R. Mohr, *Bioethics* **1**, 35 (1987).

28. A.C. Kinsey, W. B. Pomeroy, C. E. Martin, *Sexual Behavior in the Human Male* (Saunders, Philadelphia, 1948.)

29. R. Dworkin, *Taking Rights Seriously* (Harvard Univ. Press, Cambridge, MA, 1977), chaps. 6 and 7.

30. R. Bayer, C. Levine, S. M. Wolf, *J. Am. Med. Assoc.* **256**, 1768 (1986).

31. J. F. Childress, *AIDS Public Policy J.* 28 (1987).

32. L. Gostin and W. J. Curran, *Am. J. Public Health* **77**, 361 (1987).

33. D. P. Francis and J. Chin, *J. Am. Med. Assoc.* **257**, 1357 (1987); L. O. Gostin, W. J. Curran, M. E. Clark, *Am. J. Law Med.* **12**, 7 (1987); CDC, *Recommended Additional Guidelines for HIV Antibody Counseling and Testing in the Prevention of HIV Infection and AIDS* (CDC, Atlanta, 30 April 1987).

34. CDC, *Morbid. Mortal. Weekly Rep.* **36**, 509 (1987).

35. P. D. Cleary *et al., J. Am. Med. Assoc.* **258**, 1757 (1987).

36. K. B. Meyer and S. G. Pauker, *N. Engl. J. Med.* **317**, 238 (1987).

37. For an original approach to casuistic analysis in situations like these, see A. R. Jonsen and S. Toulmin, *The Abuse of Casuistry* (Univ. of California Press, Berkeley, 1988).

38. R. Gillon, *Br. Med. J.* **294**, 1675 (1987).

39. American Medical Association, Board of Trustees, *J. Am. Med. Assoc.* **258**, 2103 (1987).

40. G. W. Matthews and V. S. Neslund, *ibid.* **257**, 344 (1987).

41. The decision of the U.S. Supreme Court in "School Board of Nassau County, Florida v. Arline," seems clearly to extend the antidiscrimination protections contained in Section 504 of the Rehabilitation Act of 1973 to *symptomatic* people with HIV infection. The Court explicitly reserved judgment on the status of asymptomatic carriers of contagious disease (fn. 7 in the decision). The Rehabilitation Act applies only to programs receiving federal financial assistance. See *S. Ct.* **107**, 1123 (1987).

42. U.S. Congress, House, 100th Congr. 1st Sess., H.R. 3071; see Appendix 10, p. 437.

43. These formal conditions closely resemble the criteria of the just-war tradition. See L. B. Walters, Jr., *Five Classic Just-War Theories: A Study in the Thought of Thomas Aquinas, Vitoria, Súarez, Gentili, and Grotius* (unpublished dissertation, Yale University, 1971).

44. If substantial neurological compromise were conclusively demonstrated to be present in, say, 25% of asymptomatic people with HIV infection, then a strong case could be made for mandatory screening of people who are responsible for the lives of large numbers of other people, for example, airline pilots or public officials with decision-making authority over the use of nuclear weapons. However, strictly speaking, this would be a public safety rather than a public health justification. For recent data on HIV infection and neurological status, see I. Grant *et al., Ann. Intern. Med.* **107**, 828 (1987); and D. Price, *Science* **239**, 586 (1988). . . .

45. Clinical trials of zidovudine (AZT) among asymptomatic people with HIV infection are currently in progress.

46. R. N. Link, A. R. Feingold, M. H. Charap, K. Freeman, S. Shelov, *Third Int. Conf. on AIDS, Washington, DC, Abstr.* (U.S. Dept. Health and Human Services and WHO, Washington, DC 1987).

47. M. Blumfield *et al, Gen. Hosp. Psychiatry* **9,** 58 (1987).

48. CDC, *J. Am. Med. Assoc.* **257,** 3032 (1987).

49. *Ibid.* **258,** 1293 (1987); *ibid.,* p. 1441.

50. L. H. Butterfield, Ed., *Letters of Benjamin Rush* (Princeton Univ. Press, Princeton, NJ, 1951), vol. 2, p. 664; F. Nightingale, *Notes on Nursing* (Dover, New York, 1969 repr. of 1860 ed.), pp. 33–34; A. Camus, *The Plague,* S. Gilbert, translator (Knopf, New York, 1948).

51. R. Gillon, *Br. Med. J.* **294,** 1332 (1987); A. Zuger and S. H. Miles, *J. Am. Med. Assoc.* **258,** 1924 (1987); E. D. Pellegrino, *ibid.,* p. 939; American Medical Association, Council on Ethical and Judicial Affairs, *Report: A (I-87): Ethical Issues Involved in the Growing AIDS Crisis* (American Medical Association, Chicago, November 1987).

52. U.S. Bureau of the Census, Current Population Reports, Series P-60 (no. 155), *Receipt of Selected Noncash Benefits: 1985* (Government Printing Office, Washington, DC, 1987), pp. 15 and 19; D. Chollet, "A profile of the nonelderly population without health insurance," *Employee Benefit Research Institute Issue Brief,* no. 66, May 1987.

53. K. Davis and D. Rowland, *Milbank Mem. Fund Q./Health and Society* **61,** 149 (1983).

54. U.S. Bureau of the Census, Current Population Reports, Series P-70 (no. 8), *Disability, Functional Limitation, and Health Insurance Coverage: 1984/85* (Government Printing Office, Washington, DC, 1986), pp. 36–37.

55. A. A. Scitovsky and D. P. Rice, *Public Health Rep.* **102,** 5 (1987).

56. American Council of Life Insurance and Health Insurance Association of America, *AIDS Public Policy J.* **2,** 32 (1987); J. E. Harris, *Technol. Rev.* **90,** 59 (1987); J. K. Iglehart, *N. Engl. J. Med.* **317,** 180 (1987); D. P. Andrulis, V. S. Beers, J. D. Bentley, L. S. Gage, *J. Am. Med. Assoc.* **258,** 1343 (1987).

57. President's Commission for the Study of Ethical Problems in Medicine and Biomedical and Behavioral Research, *Securing Access to Health Care* (Government Printing Office, Washington, DC, March 1983), vols. 1–3; N. Daniels, *Just Health Care* (Cambridge Univ. Press, New York, 1985); A Buchanan, *Phil. Public Aff.* **13,** 55 (1984).

58. B. A. Navia, B. D. Jordan, R. W. Price, *Ann. Neurol.* **19,** 517 (1986); S. W. Burton, *Br. Med. J.* **295,** 228 (1987).

59. CDC, *J. Am. Med. Assoc.* **258,** 1143 (1987). . . .

60. *Handbook of Living Will Laws: 1987 Edition* (Society for the Right to Die, New York, 1987).

61. E. N. Cohen, *Appointing a Proxy for Health-Care Decisions: Analysis and Chart of State Laws* (Society for the Right to Die, New York, October 1987).

62. President's Commission for the Study of Ethical Problems in Medicine and Biomedical and Behavioral Research, *Deciding to Forego Life-Sustaining Treatment* (Government Printing Office, Washington, DC, March 1983), pp. 136–153.

63. In cases involving the use of experimental therapeutic procedures, the patient's proxy may also be called upon to give consent to research. On this issue, see J. C. Fletcher, F. W. Dommel, Jr., D. D. Cowell, *IRB: A Review of Human Subjects Research* **7,** 1 (November/December 1985).

64. R. Steinbrook et al., *N. Engl. J. Med.* **314,** 457 (1986).

65. J. Rachels, T*he End of Life: Euthanasia and Morality* (Oxford Univ. Press, New York, 1986); A. B. Downing and B. Smoker, Eds., *Voluntary Euthanasia* (Humanities Press, Atlantic Heights, NJ, rev. ed., 1986); J. K. M. Gevers, *Bioethics* **1,** 156 (1987).

66. E. Eckholm, *New York Times,* 13 July 1986, p. E30; R. Macklin and G. Friedland, *Law Med. Health Care* **14,** 273 (1986).

67. B. Merz, *J. Am. Med. Assoc.* **258,** 1433 (1987).

68. President's Commission for the Study of Ethical Problems in Medicine and Biomedical and Behavioral Research, *Compensating for Research Injuries* (Government Printing Office, Washington, DC, June 1982), vols. 1 and 2.

69. J. J. Goedert *et al., Science* **231,** 992 (1986).

70. E. Eckholm, *New York Times,* 10 January 1987, p. 6; P. M. Boffey, *ibid.,* 3 December 1987, p. A20.

71. W. Booth, *Science* **238,** 747 (1987).

72. M. Barinaga, *Nature (London)* **330,** 99 (1987).

73. A. Rivlin and M. P. Timpane, Eds., *Ethical and Legal Issues of Social Experimentation* (Brookings Institution, Washington, DC, 1975).

74. I thank M. Stanley and C. Williams for assistance in manuscript preparation and E. Meslin, S. Meinke, P. M. McCarrick for bibliographic assistance. I also thank the following people for helpful comments: L. B. Andrews, T. L. Beauchamp, J. F.Childress, R. M. Cook-Deegan, M. A. G. Cutter, B. M. Dickens, R. R. Faden, E. Locke, A. R. Jonsen, C. R. McCarthy, E. Meslin, J. Porter, E. E. Shelp, R. M. Veatch, and three anonymous reviewers for *Science.* This article is dedicated with gratitude to Jane M. Walters, my wife, who died on 15 January 1988 after open heart surgery.

DOROTHY NELKIN, DAVID P. WILLIS, AND SCOTT V. PARRIS

A Disease of Society

AIDS is no "ordinary" epidemic. More than a devastating disease, it is freighted with social and cultural meaning. More than a passing tragedy, it will have long-term, broad-ranging effects on personal relationships, social institutions, and cultural configurations. AIDS is clearly affecting mortality and morbidity—though in some communities more than others. It is also costly in terms of the resources—both people and money—required for research and medical care. But the effects of the epidemic extend far beyond medical and economic costs to shape the very ways we organize our individual and collective lives.

Social historians in recent years have pursued their studies of epidemics beyond the charting of pathogenesis and mortality to explore how diseases both reflect and affect specific aspects of culture. In writing about nineteenth-century cholera, for example, historian Asa Briggs (1961) called it "a disease of society in the most profound sense. Whenever cholera threatened European countries it quickened social apprehensions. Wherever it appeared, it tested the efficiency and resilience of local administrative structures. It exposed relentlessly political, social, and moral shortcomings. It prompted rumors, suspicions, and at times, violent social conflicts." Similarly, historian Gordon Craig (1988) observed: "It was no accident that preoccupation with the disease [cholera] affected literature and supplied both the pulpit and the language of politics with new analogies and symbols."

The literature describing the impact of AIDS is burgeoning. But most studies have focused on the medical and social epidemiology of the disease: how, for example, the virus entered the population and how it spread to different groups. Those analyses that deal with institutional responses suggest how norms and values have influenced various aspects of AIDS epidemiology and the efforts to control and to treat the disease; that is, the ways in which social values have shaped specific efforts to deal with the disease and its consequences. These contributions—for example, on public health agencies (Bayer 1989), public schools (Kirp 1989), the U.S. Public Health Service (Panem 1988)—have been central to our understanding of the past and present forms of the epidemic.

But AIDS will also *reshape* many aspects of society, its institutions, its norms and values, its interpersonal relationships, and its cultural representations (Bateson and Goldsby 1988). Just as the human immunodeficiency virus mutates, so too do the forms and institutions of society. Current clinical, epidemiologic, demographic, and social data about AIDS suggest that the future will be unlike both the present and the past.

How can we grasp the complexity of a society's response to disease? We need, surely, to avoid the tendency among many contemporary scholars and analysts to approach social problems by relying on public opinion polls or surveys, which may "confuse . . . cultural history with market research" (Lasch 1988). Rather, we must explore the accommodative process between disease and social life in its multiple dimensions, and the language and images that mediate their interaction. As the effects of the epidemic—and the numbers of persons infected—widen over the next

From Dorothy Nelkin, David P. Willis, and Scott V. Parris, eds., "A Disease of Society: Cultural Responses to AIDS: Introduction," *Milbank Quarterly* 68 (1990), 1–3. © 1990, Milbank Memorial Fund. Reprinted by permission of the Editor, *Milbank Quarterly,* and the authors.

five, ten, or twenty years, there will be many changes in our social institutions. Some will be adaptive and temporary, likely to change again; others will be more permanent, structural, and likely to persist.

Our intention in this [essay] is to explore the impact of AIDS on American culture and institutions from the perspective of the humanities and social sciences. The notion of culture, as we embrace the term, is an elusive concept. In past decades culture has been conceptualized as a complex but relatively coherent and enduring "web" of beliefs, meanings, and values. Recently, however, scholars have emphasized the truly volatile nature of cultural constructs. Political scientists write of "fragile values," referring to the very tentative and recent cultural acceptance of the rights of homosexuals, women, and various ethnic groups (McKlosky and Brill 1983). Sociologists studying the social construction of knowledge reject the concept of "enduring values," arguing that situations, interests, and organizational pressures influence cultural definitions (Berger and Luckmann 1966). Contemporary anthropologists write of the "predicament of culture," thinking of culture "not as organically unified or traditionally continuous, but rather as negotiated present process" (Clifford 1988). They argue that changes in technology and communication affecting patterns of social mobility and migration have substantively reshaped culturally accepted ways of thinking and acting.

AIDS demonstrates how much we as a "culture" struggle and negotiate about appropriate processes to deal with social change, especially in its radical forms. . . . [T]he institutions we have created to provide social and health services, make laws, enforce regulations, and represent ourselves in the arts and media are less monolithic and more malleable than we generally suppose. In confronting AIDS and its sequelae, these institutions are compelled by external and internal pressures to re-examine their objectives, operations, or methods, and to adapt in order to remain functional, effective, or meaningful. Clearly, no change stemming from this process is permanent. Rather, AIDS induces us to keep appraising the complex and fluid array of benefits and risks that may result from pursuing particular courses of action.

• • •

REFERENCES

Bateson, M.C., and R. Goldsby. 1988. *Thinking AIDS*. Reading, Mass: Addison-Wesley.

Bayer, R. 1989. *Private Acts, Social Consequences*. New York: Free Press.

Berger, P.L., and T. Luckmann, 1966. *The Social Construction of Reality*. New York: Doubleday.

Briggs, A. 1961. Cholera and Society in the Nineteenth Century. *Past and Present: A Journal of Historical Studies* 19 (April): 76–96.

Clifford, J. 1988. *The Predicament of Culture: Twentieth-Century Ethnography, Literature, and Art*. Cambridge: Harvard University Press.

Craig, G.A. 1988. Politics of a Plague. *New York Review of Books* 35 (11):9–13.

Kirp, D.L. 1989. *Learning by Heart*. New Brunswick: Rutgers University Press.

Lasch, C. 1988. Reagan's Victims. *New York Review of Books* 35 (12):7–8.

McKlosky, H., and A. Brill. 1983. *Dimensions of Tolerance: What Americans Believe about Civil Liberties*. New York: Russell Sage.

Panem, S. 1988. *The AIDS Bureaucracy*. Cambridge: Harvard University Press.

NATIONAL RESEARCH COUNCIL, PANEL ON MONITORING THE SOCIAL IMPACT OF THE AIDS EPIDEMIC

The Social Impact of AIDS in the United States

An epidemic is both a medical and social occurrence. Medically, it is the appearance of a serious, often fatal, disease in numbers far greater than normal. Socially, it is an event that disrupts the life of a community and causes uncertainty, fear, blame, and flight. The etymology of the word itself suggests the broader, social meaning: *epi demos*, in ancient Greek, means "upon the people or the community."

The epidemic of acquired immune deficiency syndrome (AIDS)—which was recognized in the United States in 1981, continues today, and will continue into the foreseeable future—mirrors epidemics of the past. The medical meaning of the epidemic has been revealed in the sobering numbers reported in epidemiologic studies. During 1991, 45,506 new AIDS cases were reported to the Centers for Disease Control (CDC), which brought the cumulative total of cases in the United States to 206,392; 133,233 (65 percent) deaths have been tallied (Centers for Disease Control, 1992). It is estimated that 1 million people are currently infected with the human immunodeficiency virus (HIV), which causes AIDS (Centers for Disease Control, 1990), but this number is very uncertain. . . .

These numbers identify the first and most obvious impact of the HIV/AIDS epidemic on American society: the large population of infected, sick, and dying persons attacked by a previously unknown disease.

Behind the epidemiologic reports and the statistical estimates lies the social disruption of the epidemic: the destroyed life for which each of the numbers stands and the changed lives of many others touched by the disease. And behind the individual lives are the manifold ways in which a variety of institutions and practices have been affected by the epidemic.

• • •

EPIDEMICS, IMPACTS, AND RESPONSES

. . . It is common to find references to the impact of AIDS and HIV. It is also rather common to find such references expressed in quite strong terms. For example, *Milbank Quarterly's* two-volume study, *A Disease of Society: Cultural Responses to AIDS*, opens with these words (Nelkin et al., 1991:1):

AIDS is no "ordinary" epidemic. More than a devastating disease, it is freighted with profound social and cultural meaning. More than a passing tragedy, it will have long-term, broad-ranging effects on personal relationships, social institutions, and cultural configurations. AIDS is clearly affecting mortality—though in some communities more than others. It is also costly in terms of the resources—both people and money—required for research and medical care. But the effects of the epidemic extend far beyond their medical and economic costs to shape the very ways we organize our individual and collective lives.

It is not clear what an "ordinary" epidemic would be. No epidemic seems ordinary to those who experience it. The AIDS epidemic has invoked comparison with many epidemics of the past. Most commonly, the bubonic plague (the Black Death) that devastated Europe in the fourteenth century is recalled: between 1348 and 1350, some 20 million people, one-third of the population of Europe, died. (Additional tens of millions had died in Asia during the preceding decade [McNeil, 1976].) This epidemic had unquestionable impacts. Historians attribute to it, at least in part, the emergence of nation states, the rise of mercantile economies, and the religious movements that led to the Reformation (Campbell, 1931; McNeil 1976; Tuchman, 1978). As Anna Campbell (1931) noted, the Black Death "changed the minds of men" bringing new ways of understanding God, the meaning of death, the place of tradition, and the role of authority in religious and social life. Changes in the collective mind of a society might be the most profound of all impacts, for the new ideas generated by a major social tragedy can propel institutional change and outlast immediate changes to affect lives far in the future. Difficult though it might be to predict the future import of the present impact of the HIV/AIDS epidemic, one should not shrink from the task, especially when one must plan for that future.

AIDS has been compared with other epidemics, too: the resurgence of bubonic plague in England in the mid-seventeenth century, the cholera epidemics of the nineteenth century, the venereal disease epidemics of the sixteenth century and the early twentieth century, and the polio epidemics of the twentieth century (Brandt, 1988; Risse, 1988; Slack, 1988). AIDS has its analogies to each of these epidemics—number of deaths, methods of prevention, stigmatization of sufferers and presumed carriers, and responses of authorities—all can be compared in general or in detail. The comparisons are often illuminating, but sometimes misleading (Fee and Fox, 1988). It can be said with some assurance, however, that none of the historical epidemics was "ordinary." Each had impacts that struck its sufferers and subsequent commentators as "extraordinary."

The comparison with epidemics of the past invokes the features that are remembered about those plagues. They have, in this respect, had an impact on history or, as Campbell wrote (1931), "on the minds of men." They also left social institutions that sometimes affect present-day thinking about the AIDS epidemic: cholera, for example, left a public health approach to epidemic disease that stressed quarantine; venereal diseases gave rise to the public health approach of contact tracing. These established public health prac-

tices have had to be reconsidered in the current epidemic. Many of the prominent, even dramatic impacts of past epidemics, however, have so melded into the social fabric that people are often astonished to hear of them today, and some, interesting though they be, seem of little relevance to the current problem. For example, to attribute the existence of Protestant Christianity to the effects of the Black Death on religious ideas and sentiments has little influence on the ways in which people today think about religion or about epidemics. Similarly, to attribute the existence of Canada as an independent nation to the fact that British troops had been vaccinated against smallpox before the Battle of Quebec, but American troops were decimated by the disease, is certainly to point to an effect of epidemic and, indeed, an impact. Yet that impact has been of little relevance to subsequent citizens and governments, except that "some Canadians to this day worship smallpox as the deliverer from United States citizenship" (Foege, 1988:332).

Many features of epidemics are no longer remembered and have left little imprint on the societies that they ravished for a time. Indeed, one of the greatest of epidemics, the influenza [outbreak] of 1918–1920, has been called by its historian "the forgotten epidemic" (Crosby, 1989). Worldwide, perhaps 30 million people died; in the United States, 675,000 people died, most of whom were not the usual victims of influenza (the very old, infants, and children), but men and women in their 20s and 30s. This terrible scourge might have had a great impact, but it passed and left almost no mark on the social institutions and practices of the time. Many people were mourned, but life quickly returned to normal. Even the absence of impact has a lesson for this study: it is possible that many of the effects currently taken as important and lasting will pass or be absorbed into the course of American life and culture. It is not entirely clear how confidently one should accept the words of *Milbank* editors Nelkin, Willis, and Parris (1991:1,2):

More than a passing tragedy, it [AIDS] will have long-term, broad-ranging effects on personal relationships, social institutions, and cultural configurations . . . AIDS will reshape many aspects of society, its norms and values, its interpersonal relationships and its cultural representations . . . [T]he future will be [unlike] both the present and the past.

Our report *[The Social Impact of AIDS in the United States]* suggests that, in some respects, the AIDS epidemic may be more like the influenza [outbreak] of 1918 than the bubonic plague of 1348: many of its most striking features will be absorbed in the flow of American life, but, hidden beneath the surface, its worst effects will continue to devastate the lives and cultures of certain communities.

GENERAL FINDINGS AND CONCLUSIONS

Historically, certain epidemics have done great damage to social institutions: the Black Death in a 3-year sweep through Europe wiped out enough laborers to cause a major restructuring of the economy of the continent. The HIV/AIDS epidemic, although often compared to the Black Death, has not affected U.S. social institutions to any such extent. Although it had by the end of 1991 infected perhaps 1 million people, brought devastating sickness to 206,392, and death to 133,233, it had not significantly altered the structures or directions of the social institutions that we studied. Many of the responses have been ad hoc and may be reversed when pressures subside. Others may be more lasting, but only because they reinforced or accelerated changes already latent or budding within the institutions.

It is the panel's opinion that the limited responsiveness of institutions can in part be explained because the absolute numbers of the epidemic, relative to the U.S. population, are not overwhelming, and because U.S. social institutions are strong, complex, and resilient. However, we believe that another major reason for this limited response is the concentration of the epidemic in socially marginalized groups. The convergence of evidence shows that the HIV/AIDS epidemic is settling into spatially and socially isolated groups and possibly becoming endemic within them. Many observers have recently commented that, instead of spreading out to the broad American population, as was once feared, HIV is concentrating in pools of persons who are also caught in the "synergism of plagues" (see Wallace, 1988): poverty, poor health and lack of health care, inadequate education, joblessness, hopelessness, and social disintegration converge to ravage personal and social life. These coexisting conditions foster and aggravate HIV infection and AIDS. Our study of New York City . . . illustrates this dramatically for one epicenter of the epidemic. We believe that the patterns shown there are repeated

throughout the country: many geographical areas and strata of the population are virtually untouched by the epidemic and probably never will be; certain confined areas and populations have been devastated and are likely to continue to be.

This epidemiological direction reveals the disconcerting implications of our major conclusion. The institutions that we studied are particularly weak at those points at which the epidemic is likely to be most destructive. For example, the health care system, which responded to the appearance of a new disease with some alacrity, is weakest organizationally and economically in those places where the affected populations are concentrated. The problems of caring for those who are infected are magnified by the particular configuration of the U.S. health care system, which emphasizes to a greater extent than other developed countries private insurance and ability-to-pay criteria. Providers, hospitals, and public health mechanisms can [respond] and have responded to a flood of patients with AIDS, but those responses were most successful where health care was better organized and financed and where the populations to be served had sufficient knowledge to understand the disease and its modes of transmission and were capable of organizing themselves in ways that supported and supplemented the health care system.

Thus, our most general conclusion about the epidemic is that its impact has hit institutions hardest where they are weakest: serving the most disadvantaged people in U.S. society. Predictions of the imminent collapse of the health care system due to the epidemic, for example, now look shrill, but, conversely, hopes that the epidemic would force the country toward more rational and equitable reform of the system now also seem unrealistic. In the panel's judgment, the HIV/AIDS epidemic has effected many transient changes in the institutions that we studied and relatively few changes that we expect to be permanent. Among the more permanent, however, two are particularly noteworthy.

First, the institutions of public health, of health care delivery, and of scientific research have become more responsive to cooperation and collaboration with "outsiders." Policies and practices have been modified in these three institutions under pressure from and in collaboration with those who are affected by the epidemic and their advocates. Many of these changes are positive and will contribute to the efficiency and efficacy of the institutions. Similarly, volunteer organizations stimulated by the challenge of the epidemic not only have discovered ways of supplying help where extant institutions were lacking, they have also influenced the policies and practices of those institutions.

Second, even in institutions with very defined purposes and strong constraints — institutions as different as religious groups and correctional agencies — the response to the epidemic has reflected awareness of the scientific realities, as well as the social implications, of HIV/AIDS. Traditionally based doctrinal constraints in the case of religious groups and the stringent requirements of civil punishment in the case of correctional agencies are powerful forces that could and did dictate rigid and narrow response. Yet, powerful as those forces were, they did not negate more reflective responses that contributed to containment of the epidemic and respected the rights of individuals. We are concerned, however, that as the epidemic strikes with greater force in socially and economically deprived communities, the directions toward more communal involvement and respect for civil and personal liberties might be constricted and diverted.

The panel believes that a failure by scientists and policy makers to appreciate the interaction between social, economic, and cultural conditions and the propagation of HIV/AIDS disease has often led to public misunderstanding and policy mistakes about the epidemic. Although in the beginning of the epidemic, gay life and behavior were certainly at the center of attention, even then they were noted primarily as "modes of transmission" and not as social contexts in which the disease had particular meanings around which strong forces for care, prevention, and political action could rally. Similarly, intravenous drug use was understood as a social behavior that could transmit infection, but its place in a matrix of social, cultural, and economic conditions was ignored.

A constant theme of this report and of the AIDS literature is the stigma, discrimination, and inequalities of the AIDS epidemic. At its outset, HIV disease settled among socially disvalued groups, and as the epidemic has progressed, AIDS has increasingly been an affliction of people who have little economic, political, and social power. In this sense, AIDS is an undemocratic affliction. In "democratic epidemics" (Arras, 1988), communicable illnesses cut across class, racial, and ethnic lines and threaten the community at large. In traditional societies with limited medical knowledge and technology, epidemics fall on most, if not all, of the people. In the modern world, particularly in industrial societies, inequalities in morbidity and mortality are often more social than biological

phenomena. With HIV/AIDS, the concentration of the epidemic from its beginnings was among those who were, for a variety of reasons, members of marginalized social groups. In this case, the biology of viral transmission matched existing social inequalities and resulted in an unequal concentration of HIV/AIDS in certain regions and among certain populations (see Grmek, 1990). This pattern has created tension between the social and geographical localization of the epidemic and the need to mobilize resources to deal with the epidemic from among individuals, groups, and institutions that are removed from the social groups that are at the epicenter of the epidemic. As the epidemic becomes endemic in already deprived and segregated populations, this tension will be intensified.

If the current pattern of the epidemic holds, U.S. society at large will have been able to wait out the primary impact of the epidemic even though the crisis period will have stretched out over 15 years. HIV/AIDS will "disappear," not because, like smallpox, it has been eliminated, but because those who continue to be affected by it are socially invisible, beyond the sight and attention of the majority population. . . .

REFERENCES

Arras, J.D. (1988) The fragile web of responsibility: AIDS and the duty to treat. *Hastings Center Report* 18(Suppl.):10–20.

Brandt, A.M. (1988) AIDS and metaphor: toward the social meaning of epidemic disease. *Social Research* 55:413–432.

Brookmeyer, R. (1991) Reconstruction and future trends of the AIDS epidemic in the United States. *Science* 253:37–42.

Campbell, A.M. (1931) *The Black Death and Men of Learning.* New York: Columbia University Press.

Centers for Disease Control (CDC) (1990) HIV prevalence and AIDS case projections for the United States: report based on a workshop. *Morbidity and Mortality Weekly Report* 39:(RR-16):1–31.

Centers for Disease Control (CDC) (1991) Mortality attributable to HIV infection/AIDS—United States, 1981–1990. *Morbidity and Mortality Weekly Report* 40:41–46.

Centers for Disease Control (CDC) (1992) *HIV/AIDS Surveillance Report.* Atlanta, Ga.: Centers for Disease Control.

Crosby, A.W. (1989) *Epidemic and Peace, 1918: America's Forgotten Pandemic.* New York: Cambridge University Press.

Fee, E., and D. Fox (1988) *AIDS: The Burdens of History.* Berkeley, Calif.: University of California Press.

Foege, W.H. (1988) Plagues: perceptions of risk and social responses. *Social Research* 55:331–342.

Grmek, M.D. (1990) *The History of AIDS: Emergence and Origin of a Modern Pandemic.* Princeton, N.J.: Princeton University Press.

Harris, J. (1990) Reporting delays and the incidence of AIDS. *Journal of the American Statistical Association* 85:915–924.

McNeil, W.H. (1976) *Plagues and Peoples*. New York: Doubleday.

Miller, H.G., C.F. Turner, and L.E. Moses, eds. (1990) *AIDS: The Second Decade*. Committee on AIDS Research and the Behavioral, Social, and Statistical Sciences, Commission on Behavior and Social Sciences and Education, National Research Council. Washington, D.C.: National Academy Press.

Nelkin, D., D.P. Willis, and S.V. Parris (1991) Introduction. In D. Nelkin, D.P. Willis, and S.V. Parris, eds., *A Disease of Society: Cultural Responses to AIDS*. New York: Cambridge University Press.

Risse, G.B. (1988) Epidemics and history: ecological perspectives and social responses. In E. Fee and D.M. Fox, eds., *AIDS: The Burdens of History*. Berkeley, Calif.: University of California Press.

Slack, P. (1988) Responses to plague in early modern Europe: the implications of public health. *Social Research* 55:433–453.

Tuchman, B. (1978) *A Distant Mirror. The Calamitous 14th Century*. New York: Knopf.

Turner, C.F., H.G. Miller, and L.E. Moses, eds. (1989) *AIDS: Sexual Behavior and Intravenous Drug Use*. Committee on AIDS Research and the Behavioral, Social, and Statistical Sciences, Commission on Behavioral and Social Sciences and Education, National Research Council. Washington, D.C.: National Academy Press.

Wallace, R. (1988) A synergism of plagues: "planned shrinkage," contagious housing destruction and AIDS in the Bronx. *Environmental Research* 47:1–33.

RONALD BAYER

Public Health Policy and the AIDS Epidemic: An End to HIV Exceptionalism?

In the early and mid-1980s, when democratic nations were forced to confront the public health challenge posed by the epidemic of the acquired immunodeficiency syndrome (AIDS), it was necessary to face a set of fundamental questions: Did the history of responses to lethal infectious diseases provide lessons about how best to contain the spread of human immunodeficiency virus (HIV) infection? Should the policies developed to control sexually transmitted diseases or other communicable conditions be applied to AIDS? If AIDS were not to be so treated, what would justify such differential policies?

To understand the importance of these questions, it is necessary to recall that conventional approaches to public health threats were typically codified in the latter part of the 19th or the early part of the 20th century. Even when public health laws were revised in subsequent decades, they tended to reflect the imprint of their genesis. They provided a warrant for mandating compulsory examination and screening, breaching the confidentiality of the clinical relationship by reporting to public health registries the names of those with diagnoses of "dangerous diseases," imposing treatment, and in the most extreme cases, confining persons through the power of quarantine.

As the century progressed, the most coercive elements of this tradition were rarely brought to bear, because of changing patterns of morbidity and mortality and the development of effective clinical alternatives. Nevertheless, it was the specter of these elements that most concerned proponents of civil liberties and advocates of gay rights as they considered the potential direction of public health policy in the presence of AIDS.[1] Would there be widespread compulsory testing? Would the names of the infected be recorded in central registries? Would such registries be used to restrict those with HIV infection? Would the power of quarantine be used, if not against all infected persons, then at least against those whose behavior could result in the further transmission of infection?

Although there were public health traditionalists in the United States and abroad who pressed to have

From *New England Journal of Medicine* 324 (1991), 1500–1504. Reprinted by permission of the *New England Journal of Medicine*.

AIDS and HIV infection brought under the broad statutory provisions established to control the spread of sexually transmitted and other communicable diseases, they were in the distinct minority. Typically, it was those identified with conservative political parties or movements who endorsed such efforts—e.g., the Christian Social Union of Bavaria—although not all conservatives pursued such a course.[2] Liberals and those identified with the democratic left tended to oppose such efforts. There were striking exceptions, such as the Swedish Social Democrats,[3] but in the end it was those who called for "HIV exceptionalism" who came to dominate public discourse.

In the first decade of the AIDS epidemic, an alliance of gay leaders, civil libertarians, physicians, and public health officials began to shape a policy for dealing with AIDS that reflected the exceptionalist perspective. As the second decade of the epidemic begins, it is clear that the potency of this alliance has begun to wane. The evidence of this change with regard to HIV testing, reporting, partner notification, and even quarantine is most visible in the United States, but it may begin to appear in other democratic nations as well. What follows is drawn from the American experience, but it most certainly has parallels in other countries.

TESTING AND SCREENING

The HIV-antibody test, first made widely available in 1985, was the subject of great controversy from the outset. Out of the confrontations emerged a broad consensus that, except in a few well-defined circumstances, people should be tested only with their informed voluntary and specific consent. When the clinical importance of identifying those with asymptomatic HIV infection became clear in mid-1989, the political context of the debate over testing underwent a fundamental change. Gay organizations began to urge homosexual and bisexual men to have their antibody status determined under confidential or anonymous conditions. Physicians pressed for AIDS to be returned to the medical mainstream and for the HIV-antibody test to be treated like other blood tests—that is, given with the presumed consent of the patient.

Thus, four clinical societies in New York State, including the New York Medical Society, unsuccessfully sued the commissioner of health in 1989 to compel him to define AIDS and HIV infection as sexually transmitted and communicable diseases.[4] Among the goals of the suit was the liberalization of the stringent consent requirements for HIV testing. In December 1990 the House of Delegates of the American Medical Association called for HIV infection to be classified as a sexually transmitted disease. Although the delegates chose not to act on a resolution that would have permitted testing without consent, their decision on classification had clear implications for a more routine approach to HIV screening, one in which the standard of specific informed consent would no longer prevail.[5]

The movement toward routine or mandatory testing has been especially marked in the case of pregnant women and newborns. Pregnant women are already tested in this way for syphilis and hepatitis B. The screening of newborns for phenylketonuria and other congenital conditions is standard. Although as of this writing a deeply divided AIDS task force of the American Academy of Pediatrics had not recommended mandatory HIV screening of newborns, that decision was a function of the lack of specificity of the test and the lack of a definitive clinical regimen for seropositive newborns. The publication in the *Morbidity and Mortality Weekly Report* on March 15, 1991,[6] of recommendations for the prophylaxis of *Pneumocystis carinii* pneumonia in newborns will undoubtedly affect future discussion of the importance of identifying infants born to mothers with HIV infection.

REPORTING OF NAMES

Clinical AIDS has been a reportable condition in every state since 1983. But since the inception of HIV testing, there has been a sharp debate about whether the names of all infected persons should be reported to confidential registries of public health departments. Gay groups and their allies have opposed HIV reporting because of concern about privacy and confidentiality. Many public health officials opposed such a move because of the potential effect on the willingness of people to seek HIV testing and counseling voluntarily. By 1991 only a few states, typically those with relatively few AIDS cases, had required such reporting.[7]

Divisions have begun to appear in the alliance against the reporting of names in states where the prevalence of HIV infection is high and where gay communities are well organized. In New York State, as noted above, four medical societies have demanded that HIV infection be made a reportable condition.[4] In 1989, Stephen Joseph, then commissioner of health in New York City, stated that the prospects of early clinical intervention warranted "a shift toward a disease-control approach to HIV infection along the lines of classic tuberculosis practices," including the "reporting of seropositives."[8] Although political factors thwarted the commissioner, it is clear that his call represented part of a national trend.

At the end of November 1990, the Centers for Disease Control declared its support for reporting. In a carefully crafted editorial note in the *Morbidity and Mortality Weekly Report*, the agency stated that

by using measures to maintain confidentiality, the implementation of a standardized system for HIV reporting to state health departments can enhance the ability of local, state, and national agencies to project the levels of required resources . . . [and aid] in the establishment of a framework for providing partner notification and treatment services. . . .[9]

Within a week, the House of Delegates of the American Medical Association endorsed the reporting of names as well.

NOTIFICATION OF PARTNERS

Most important in the move toward the reporting of names has been the belief on the part of public health officials that effective programs of partner notification require reporting the names of persons with HIV infection as well as the names of those with a diagnosis of AIDS. Despite its long-established, though recently contested, role in the control of other venereal diseases, notification of the sexual and needle-sharing partners of patients with HIV infection or AIDS has been the exception rather than the rule. Opponents of such notification or contact tracing have denounced it as a coercive measure, even though it has always depended on cooperation with the index patient and protection of that patient's anonymity.

The early opposition to partner notification by gay and civil-liberties groups has begun to yield, as a better understanding of the practice has developed. Since 1988 the Centers for Disease Control has made the existence of partner-notification programs in states a condition for the granting of funds from its HIV-prevention program.[10] Such programs have also been endorsed by the Institute of Medicine, the National Academy of Sciences,[11] the Presidential Commission on the HIV Epidemic,[12] The American Bar Association,[13] and the American Medical Association.[14]

Many of the early strict-confidentiality statutes relating to HIV infection and AIDS appeared to prevent physicians from acting when confronted with infected patients who indicated that they would neither inform their partners nor alter their sexual practices. More recent acknowledgment of clinicians' ethical responsibilities under such circumstances has led to modifications of the stringent prohibitions on breaches of confidentiality. Both the American Medical Association[15] and the Association of State and Territorial Health Officials[16] have endorsed legislative provisions that would permit disclosure to people placed at risk by the HIV infection of a partner.

As of 1990, only two states had imposed on physicians a legal duty to warn spouses that they were at risk for HIV infection. Approximately a dozen states had passed legislation granting physicians a "privilege to warn or inform" sexual and needle-sharing partners, thus freeing clinicians from liability whether or not they issued such warnings.[17] In a remarkable acknowledgment of the extreme sensitivity of the issues involved, some of the legislation stipulated that the warnings could not involve revealing the identity of the source of the threat to the person being warned.[18]

QUARANTINE AND CRIMINALIZATION

On epidemiologic, pragmatic, and ethical grounds, there has been virtually no support for extending the power to quarantine to apply to all HIV-infected persons. There has, however, been periodic discussion of whether the tradition of restricting liberty in the name of the public health should be invoked when a person's behavior poses a risk of HIV transmission.[1] Although bitter opposition has greeted all attempts to bring such behavior within the scope of existing quarantine statutes, more than a dozen states did so from 1987 through 1990. When such measures have been enacted, they have generally provided an occasion to revise state disease-control laws to reflect contemporary constitutional standards of due process (Intergovernmental Health Policy Project: unpublished data). There have been a few well-reported instances of efforts to impose control over recalcitrant persons for reasons of public health. Almost always, states have used the existence of the authority to quarantine to warn those who persist in unsafe sexual practices and to counsel them aggressively about the need for a change in behavior.

More common, though still relatively rare, has been the use of the criminal law under such circumstances. From 1987 through 1989, 20 states enacted statutes permitting the prosecution of persons whose behavior posed a risk of HIV transmission (Intergovernmental Health Policy Project: unpublished data), a move broadly endorsed by the Presidential Commission on the HIV Epidemic.[19] The 1990 Ryan White Comprehensive AIDS Resources Emergency (CARE) Act requires that all states receiving funds have the statutory capacity to prosecute those who engage in behavior linked to the transmission of HIV infection to unknowing partners. Perhaps more crucial, aggressive local prosecutors have relied on the general criminal law to bring indictments against some people for HIV-related behavior, even in the absence of statutes specifically defining such behavior as criminal.

In the vast majority of instances, such prosecutions have resulted either in acquittal or in a decision to drop the case. When there have been guilty verdicts, the penalties have at times been unusually harsh.[20]

THE ROOTS OF THE CHALLENGE TO HIV EXCEPTIONALISM

What accounts for the pattern of changes described above? When the communal welfare is threatened, public health policy always requires more than the application of a repertoire of standard professional practices. Inevitably, public health officials must contend with a range of extraprofessional considerations, including the prevailing political climate and the unique social forces brought into play by a particular public health challenge. In the first years of the AIDS epidemic, U.S. officials had no alternative but to negotiate the course of AIDS policy with representatives of a well-organized gay community and their allies in the medical and political establishments. In this process, many of the traditional practices of public health that might have been brought to bear were dismissed as inappropriate. As the first decade of the epidemic came to an end, public health officials began to reassert their professional dominance over the policy-making process and in so doing began to rediscover the relevance of their own professional traditions to the control of AIDS.

This process has been fostered by changing perceptions of the dimensions of the threat posed by AIDS. Early fears that HIV infections might spread broadly in the population have proved unfounded. The epidemic has been largely confined to the groups first identified as being at increased risk. As the focus of public health concern has shifted from homosexual men, among whom the incidence of HIV infection has remained low for the past several years, to poor black and Hispanic drug users and their sexual partners, the influence of those who have spoken on behalf of the gay community has begun to wane. Not only do black and Hispanic drug users lack the capacity to influence policy in the way that homosexual men have done, but also those who speak on their behalf often lack the singular commitment to privacy and consent that so characterized the posture of gay organizations. Furthermore, policy directed toward the poor is often characterized by authoritarian tendencies. It is precisely such authoritarianism that evokes the traditions of public health. Finally, in the United States as in virtually every Western democracy, the estimates of the level of infection put forth several years ago have proved to be too high.[21] As AIDS has become less threatening, the claims of those who argued that the exceptional threat would require exceptional policies have begun to lose their force.

The most important factor in accounting for the changing contours of public health policy, however, has been the notable advances in therapeutic prospects. The possibility of managing HIV-related opportunistic infections better and the hopes of slowing the course of HIV progression itself have increased the importance of early identification of those with HIV infection. That, it turn, has produced a willingness to consider traditional public health approaches to screening, reporting, and partner notification.

CONCLUSIONS

As of the end of 1990, 11 states had classified AIDS and HIV infection as sexually transmitted or venereal diseases. Twenty-two states had classified them as communicable diseases, infectious diseases, or both. Strikingly absent from this group are New York, California, and New Jersey, the three states that have borne the heaviest burdens during the epidemic (Intergovernmental Health Policy Project: unpublished data). Whether they and other states will follow will depend on epidemiologic and clinical developments. But more important will be the balance of political forces.

The pattern that has begun to emerge so clearly in the United States may not be replicated in every respect in other democratic nations where HIV exceptionalism has held sway in the first years of the epidemic. Much will depend on the tradition of public health practice with regard to sexually transmitted and communicable diseases and on the relative strength and viability of the alliances forged in the phase of the epidemic marked by therapeutic impotence. But what is clear is that the effort to sustain a set of policies treating HIV infection as fundamentally different from all other public health threats will be increasingly difficult. Inevitably, HIV exceptionalism will be viewed as a relic of the epidemic's first years.

Finally, the broad political context within which decisions will be made about the availability of resources for prevention, research, and the provision of care will be affected by the changing perspective on AIDS. The availability of such resources has always been the outcome of a competitive process, however implicit. In the beginning, the desperate effort to wrest needed resources from an unresponsive political system in the context of a health care system that failed to provide universal protection against the cost of illness compelled AIDS activists and their allies to argue that AIDS was different and required funding commitments of a special kind. However late these funds were in coming, and however grudgingly they were provided, it was inevitable that in a resource-constrained climate there would be challenges to the allocations that were made. Thus, in 1990 the Office of Technology Assessment was compelled to address the question of whether the resources made available for AIDS research had distorted the funding allocated for other medical conditions.[22] Winkenwerder et al. argued in 1989 that further increases in federal expenditures for AIDS would be disproportionate to the burden of disease in the population.[23] Such concern has begun to find expression in the popular media as well.[24] The erosion of the exceptionalist perspective on HIV infection will inevitably foster the further expression of such doubt, precisely when greater resources are required to treat those with HIV disease.

That the difference between the public health response to the HIV epidemic and the response to other conditions has been eroding does not necessarily mean that public health traditionalists will inevitably win out over those who have argued for a new public health practice. In Denmark, for example, the experience with AIDS has led to a reconsideration of the traditional approach to venereal disease.[25] Indeed, there are many reasons, both pragmatic and ethical, that some of the practices that have emerged over the past decade in response to AIDS should inform the practice of public health more generally. There are good reasons, for example, to argue that the principle of re-

quiring informed consent for HIV testing ought to apply to all clinical tests to which competent adults may be subject. Furthermore, the lessons learned—about mobilizing an effective campaign of public health education, about the central importance of involving in the process of fashioning such efforts those who speak on behalf of those most at risk, and about the very limited and potentially counterproductive consequences of recourse to coercion in seeking to effect a radical modification of private behavior—could be applied profitably to the patterns of morbidity and mortality that represent so much of the contemporary threat to the public health.

Were the end of HIV exceptionalism to mean a reflexive return to the practices of the past, it would represent the loss of a great opportunity to revitalize the tradition of public health so that it might best be adapted to face the inevitable challenges posed not only by the continuing threat of AIDS but also by threats to the communal health that will inevitably present themselves in the future.

Supported by the American Foundation for AIDS Research, the Conanima Foundation, and the Josiah Macy Jr. Foundation.

REFERENCES

1. Bayer R. Private acts, social consequences: AIDS and the politics of public health. New Brunswick, N.J.: Rutgers University Press, 1991.

2. Frankenberg G. In the beginning all the world there was America: AIDS policy in West Germany. In: Bayer R, Kirp D, eds. Passions, politics and policy: AIDS in eleven democratic nations. New Brunswick, N.J.: Rutgers University Press (in press).

3. Henriksson B., Ytterberg H. Swedish AIDS policy: a question of contradictions. In: Bayer R, Kirp D, eds. Passions, politics and policy: AIDS in eleven democratic nations. New Brunswick, N.J.: Rutgers University Press (in press).

4. New York State Society of Surgeons et al. v. Axelrod, 1989.

5. Jones L. HIV infection labeled as STD; board to clarify testing policy. American Medical News. December 14, 1990:3, 28.

6. Working Group on PCP Prophylaxis in Children. Guidelines for prophylaxis against *Pneumocystis carinii* pneumonia for children infected with human immunodeficiency virus. MMWR 1991; 40(RR-2):1–13.

7. Intergovernmental Health Policy Project. HIV reporting in the states. Intergovernmental AIDS Reports. November–December 1989:1–3.

8. Joseph SC. Remarks at the Fifth International Conference on AIDS, Montreal, June 4–9, 1989.

9. Update: public health surveillance for HIV infection—United States, 1989 and 1990. MMWR 1990; 39:861.

10. Fed Regist 1988; 53:3554.

11. Altering the course of the epidemic. In: Institute of Medicine, National Academy of Sciences. Confronting AIDS: update 1988. Washington, D.C.: National Academy Press, 1988:82.

12. Report of the Presidential Commission on the Human Immunodeficiency Virus Epidemic: submitted to the President of the United States. Washington, D.C.: Presidential Commission on the Human Immunodeficiency Virus Epidemic, 1988:76.

13. American Bar Association, House of Delegates. Report from the House of Delegates, August 1989: annual meeting. Chicago: American Bar Association, 1989:23–5.

14. Abraham L. AIDS contact tracing, prison test stir debate. American Medical News. July 8–15, 1988:4.

15. American Medical Association Board of Trustees. Report X: AMA HIV policy update. In: AMA Proceedings of the House of Delegates. December 3–6, 1989, 43rd interim meeting. Chicago: American Medical Association, 1989:76–95.

16. Association of State and Territorial Health Officials, National Association of County Health Officials, Conference of Local Health Officers. Guide to public health practice: HIV partner notification strategies. Washington, D.C.: Public Health Foundation, 1988.

17. Intergovernmental Health Policy Project. 1989 legislative overview. Intergovernmental AIDS Reports. January 1990:3.

18. New York State Public Health Law, Article 27-F.

19. Report of the Presidential Commission on the Human Immunodeficiency Virus Epidemic: submitted to the President of the United States. Washington, D.C.: Presidential Commission on the Human Immunodeficiency Virus Epidemic, 1988:130–1.

20. Gostin LO. The AIDS litigation project: a national review of court and human rights commission decisions, part 1: the social impact of AIDS. JAMA 1990; 263:1961–70.

21. Estimates of HIV prevalence and projected AIDS cases: summary of a workshop, October 31–November 1, 1989. MMWR 1990; 39:110–9.

22. Office of Technology Assessment. How has federal research on AIDS/HIV disease contributed to other fields? Washington, D.C.: Government Printing Office, 1990.

23. Winkenwerder W, Kessler AR, Stolec RM. Federal spending for illness caused by the human immunodeficiency virus. N Engl J Med 1989; 320:1598–603.

24. Krauthammer C. AIDS getting more than its share? Time. June 25, 1990:80.

25. Alback E. AIDS: the evolution of a non-controversial issue in Denmark. In: Bayer R, Kirp D, eds. Passions, politics and policy: AIDS in eleven democratic nations. New Brunswick, N.J.: Rutgers University Press (in press).

The Duty to Warn and the Duty Not to Harm

SUSAN D. COCHRAN AND VICKIE M. MAYS

Sex, Lies, and HIV

To the Editor: Reducing the risk of human immunodeficiency virus (HIV) transmission among sexually active teenagers and young adults is a major public health concern.[1] Young people are advised to select potential sexual partners from groups at lower risk for HIV,[2] in part by asking about partners' risk histories.[3] Unfortunately, this advice overlooks the possibility that people may lie about their risk history.[4]

In a sample of 18-to-25-year-old students attending colleges in southern California (n = 665), we found strong evidence that undermines faith in questioning partners as an effective primary strategy of risk reduction. The young adults, of whom 422 were sexually active, completed anonymous 18-page questionnaires assessing sexual behavior, HIV-related risk reduction, and their experiences with deception when dating.

We found that sizable percentages of the 196 men and 226 women who were sexually experienced reported having told a lie in order to have sex. Men reported telling lies significantly more frequently than women (Table 1). Women more often reported that they had been lied to by a dating partner. When asked what they would do in hypothetical situations, both men and women frequently reported that they would actively or passively deceive a dating partner, although again, men were significantly more likely than women to indicate a willingness to do so.

Although we cannot be certain that our subjects were fully forthcoming in their responses (e.g., they reported more frequent dishonesty from others than they admitted to themselves), one can probably assume

From *New England Journal of Medicine* 322 (1990), 774–775. Reprinted by permission of the *New England Journal of Medicine*.

Table 1.   Dishonesty in Dating.

Variable	Men (N = 196)	Women (N = 226)
	percent	
History of disclosure		
Has told a lie in order to have sex	34	10[*]
Lied about ejaculatory control	38	
or likelihood of pregnancy		14
Sexually involved with more than one person	32	23[†]
Partner did not know	68	59
Experience of being lied to		
Has been lied to for purposes of sex	47	60[‡]
Partner lied about ejaculatory control		46
or likelihood of pregnancy	34	
Willingness to deceive[§]		
Would lie about having negative HIV-antibody test	20	4[*]
Would lie about ejaculatory control	29	
or likelihood of pregnancy		2[*]
Would understate number of previous partners	47	42
Would disclose existence of other partner		
to new partner		
Never	22	10
After a while, when safe to do so	34	28
Only if asked	31	33
Yes	13	29
Would disclose a single episode of sexual infidelity		
Never	43	34
After a while, when safe to do so	21	20
Only if asked	14	11
Yes	22	35

[*]$P<0.001$ by chi-square test.

[†]$P<0.05$ by chi-square test.

[‡]$P<0.01$ by chi-square test.

[§]Hypothetical scenarios were described in which honesty would threaten either the opportunity to have sex or the maintenance of a sexually active relationship.

that their reports of their own dishonesty underestimate rather than overestimate the problem. The implications of our findings are clear. In counseling patients, particularly young adults, physicians need to consider realistically the patients' capacity for assessing the risk of HIV in sexual partners through questioning them.[5] Patients should be cautioned that safe-sex strategies are always advisable,[5-7] despite arguments to the contrary from partners. This is particularly important for heterosexuals in urban centers where distinctions between people at low risk and those at high risk may be less obvious because of higher rates of experimentation with sex and the use of intravenous drugs and undisclosed histories of high-risk behavior.

NOTES

1. Koop CE. Surgeon General's report on acquired immune deficiency syndrome. Washington, D.C.: Public Health Service, 1986.

2. Hearst N, Hulley SB. Preventing the heterosexual spread of AIDS: are we giving our patients the best advice? JAMA 1988; 259:2428–32.

3. Fox M. Asking the right questions. Health 1988; February:38–9, 98–100.

4. Potterat JJ, Phillips L., Muth JB. Lying to military physicians about risk factors for HIV infections. JAMA 1987; 257:1727.

5. Schulman K. Preventing the heterosexual spread of AIDS. JAMA 1988; 260:1879–80.

6. Padian NS, Francis DP. Preventing the heterosexual spread of AIDS. JAMA 1988; 260:1879.

7. Goedert JJ. Preventing the heterosexual spread of AIDS. JAMA 1988; 260:1880.

FERDINAND SCHOEMAN

AIDS and Privacy

Issues of privacy surface in nearly every dimension of AIDS, from diagnosis, to treatment, to epidemiology, to prevention. A sampling of issues includes topics like reporting human immunodeficiency virus (HIV) infection to public health agencies, confidentiality of the therapist-patient relationship, and the duty, on the part of the individual or public health authorities, to disclose one's condition to a sexual partner, surgeon, employer, or insurance provider. No group in society is more vulnerable to both biological and social repercussions of a disease than those infected with HIV. Tragically, some aspects of protecting the privacy of those who are HIV infected have frightening potential for others who understandably wish to avoid contagion, as well as for those who recognize the social costs of the increasing numbers and changing profile of AIDS victims. AIDS, as we will see, is destined to have as much impact on the contours of our notion of privacy as computerization of records and the legalization of abortion did.

Conflict and the inevitability of unmet and haunting needs is nowhere more manifest than in the case of AIDS. AIDS is a lethal disease that is communicable in controllable ways. To think of it as a fatal disease invokes one pattern of normative responses: sympathetic and protecting attitudes. To think of it as a condition that is communicable in a controllable way invokes another set of normative responses: those attributing accountability for harming others. Being sick diminishes one's accountability for some things — things over which one has impaired capacity. The negligence or recklessness involved in infecting another with HIV is *not*, however typically the result of impaired capacity (*United States* v. *Sergeant Nathaniel Johnson, Jr.*).[1] A person who deserves compassion for having a disease *may* also deserve admonition for acquiring or condemnation for transmitting it. Spouses or partners of those HIV infected may have cause for complaint on either ground.

People infected with HIV have much to fear besides the disease. Because of the association of AIDS with promiscuity, primarily homosexual but also heterosexual, or the self-abandonment connected with intravenous (IV) drug usage, any adult with AIDS is suspected of degeneracy. One in five Americans regard those with AIDS as deserving their suffering because of their immorality (Blendon and Donelan 1988). Homophobia is widespread in the United States, and the intrusion of AIDS as a public health problem has in many people's minds lent legitimacy to hostility toward gay individuals (Goleman 1990). The level of public ignorance about the disease, the deficiency of scientific understanding surrounding aspects of its transmission, and the general hysteria about AIDS mean that people diagnosed as HIV positive must face social, economic, and medical hurdles no one with such dire medical prospects should have to confront. These prejudices extend to those who care for AIDS victims and even to the dwellings of those with AIDS. A diagnosis of HIV infection, or even a suspicion of this, is sufficient in some cases to deprive people of housing, employment, life and health insurance, social tolerance, routine and even emergency medical treatment like mouth-to-mouth resuscitation, schooling, social contacts, friendships, the right to travel in and out of countries — a social identity. Studies of public attitudes toward those with AIDS make crystal clear the social consequences AIDS sufferers will confront (Blendon and Donelan 1988). One in four questioned in a survey indicated that he or she would refuse to work with someone with AIDS; the same percentage believe that employers should be able to fire employees with AIDS; 39 percent of people surveyed agreed that public school employees should be dismissed if found to have AIDS. In 1988, 18 percent felt that children with AIDS should be barred from school. Nearly one-third indicated that out of concern for their own children's health they would keep their children from attending schools that admitted children with AIDS. In surveys conducted in 1987, a substantial minority (between 21 and 40 percent, depending on the wording) favored isolating people with AIDS from the general community, from public places, and from their own neighborhoods. Panic over the prospect of becoming contaminated is even widespread among health professionals (see Zuger's essay in [Frederic G. Reamer, ed., *AIDS and Ethics* (New York: Columbia University Press, 1991), chapter 9]. Also widespread is skepticism about the accuracy of risk assessments promulgated in the best medical journals. Tragically, fear of discrimination is itself an important obstacle to both greater epidemiological understanding of HIV transmission and implementation of public health measures aimed at minimizing HIV infection.

Further complicating the terrifying social and medical dimensions of HIV infection is the awareness of having been infected by and/or potentially infecting those with whom one is most intimate. This is a moral burden few could find anything but crushing. And yet, discovering and revealing one's own HIV status threatens this source of meaning and support perhaps more than any other.

CONCEPTUAL FOUNDATIONS OF PRIVACY

Because of the way AIDS is transmitted and because of the social, financial, and medical consequences of being identified as HIV positive, it is no wonder that AIDS and privacy intersect at every dimension of the disease. Let us turn our attention to some of the foundational issues related to privacy, beginning with the meaning of privacy.[2] There are broader and narrower conceptions of privacy. On the narrower range of conceptions, privacy relates exclusively to information of a personal sort about an individual and describes the extent to which others have access to this information.[3] A broader conception extends beyond the infor-

mational domain and encompasses anonymity and restricted physical access. Thus far the characterizations allow a sharp contrast between privacy and autonomy. Embracing some aspects of autonomy within the definition of privacy, it has been defined as control over the intimacies of personal identity. At the broadest end of the spectrum, privacy is thought to be the measure of the extent an individual is afforded the social and legal space to develop the emotional, cognitive, spiritual, and moral powers of an autonomous agent. An advocate of one of the narrower conceptions can agree about the value of autonomous development but think that privacy as properly defined makes an important but limited contribution to its achievement.

Privacy is important as a means of respecting or even socially constructing moral personality, comprising qualities like independent judgment, creativity, self-knowledge, and self-respect. It is important because of the way control over one's thoughts and body enables one to develop trust for, or love and friendships with, one another and more generally modulate relationships with others (Fried 1960). It is important too for the political dimensions of a society that respects individual privacy, finding privacy instrumental in protecting rights of association, individual freedom, and limitations on governmental control over thoughts and actions (Benn 1971). Finally, it has been argued that privacy is important as a means of protecting people from overreaching social (as opposed to legal) pressures and sanctions and is thus critical if people are to enjoy a measure of social freedom. This is a dimension of privacy I return to below.

Respecting privacy does not commit us to elevating it above all other concerns. We respect privacy even when we abridge it provided we do so for good reason. What I shall be arguing as we proceed is that HIV status is to be regarded as private information about a person, deserving protection, unless there is "a need to know" on someone's part that in the circumstances makes withholding information unreasonable. In assessing the need to know, we have a responsibility to use the best available information about risk factors. What is protected in one informational context may be unprotected in another. Assessing whether a risk is reasonable is not just a function of the probability of harm. Relevant too are the consequences of abstaining from that behavior and the alternatives available for achieving similar objectives.

In assessing the need to know, many factors depend for their strength on social perceptions, ones that can vary over cultures and within a culture over time and circumstance. They can also vary over class and gender within a culture. By offering some examples of the variability of these standards, we can recognize that many acts we would regard as intrusive, others would not so regard. For instance, in some cultures that place a high premium on the virginity of brides and consummation of marriage as initiating the married state, the first act of intercourse between the man and woman is publicly monitored (Stone 1979). In colonial New England, people were required to live within a household, thinking it improper that a person not be supervised in his private affairs. There was a village officer, the tithingsman, whose role was to pry into the private lives of people to ensure compliance with local social standards (Flaherty 1972). In some communities within the contemporary United States, having a child out of wedlock would be something important to conceal. In other communities, it is the norm. We can and should be sensitive to the class, cultural, and even gender differences in attitudes toward the importance of treating something as private. Inevitably, policies in a pluralistic society will grate against some sensibilities, however judicious the policies are.

PRIVACY AND SEXUALLY TRANSMITTED DISEASES

As the discussion of AIDS and privacy proceeds, some additional theoretical categories will be introduced. AIDS is not the first disease to raise privacy issues. Most states require that a test for venereal diseases be made prior to marriage (Krause 1986:43–44) and that a doctor certify that the partners either are free of disease or have it in noncommunicable stages. All states have public health laws that require reporting sexually transmitted diseases (STDs). Most states do not deal with AIDS or the presence of the HIV antibody as falling under public health regulations pertaining to STDs proper, though they usually have equivalent regulations for AIDS.

As of July 1989, a total of 28 states required health care providers to report cases of persons infected with HIV to their state public health departments. The clear trend is toward reporting of HIV infection, with many states having such proposals before their legislatures (Gostin 1990a:1962).

Although it is certain that one major route of infection is through sexual contact, there is concern that if AIDS or HIV infection is treated as an STD, requiring reporting, those who are infected with HIV will face additional social, medical, and economic isolation in addition to the ravages of the disease (Gostin 1990a). Ironically, treating AIDS as an STD would automatically engage those confidentiality requirements associated with the relevant public health laws.

PRIVACY AND AIDS

The range of privacy issues that arise in the AIDS environment is bewildering (Gostin 1990a). These include confidentiality in relationships with health professionals and disclosure of HIV status to insurers and employers, to state health agencies, to family members or sexual or other partners where transmission is a possibility, to schools, and to residential settings of almost any kind, including correctional facilities. Privacy arises as an issue in considering proposals for HIV screening and in partner notification.

AIDS also has an impact on consideration of public norms that govern private relationships. AIDS and privacy intersect not only for the health care provider, the state, and the HIV-infected person but also for people in their ordinary and informal contact with others. The law both reflects and influences the moral and social rules governing these ordinary and informal contacts. Because AIDS is typically transmitted under circumstances that lie somewhere between the intimate and the private, we tend to think that enforceable public standards are not quite the appropriate levers for directing conduct. This attitude about public standards in private relationships is something I will reconsider. Especially I will want to consider how privacy norms operate vis-à-vis moral norms in general. Clarifying this relationship will help us discern which norms are applicable and what they impose or permit.

The standards I employ are those associated with our responsibility not to harm people, the state's responsibility to maintain public health, and our responsibility as members of society for maintaining practices of social trust and caring. At times the consequences of being guided by one of these standards frustrate the influence of the others.

• • •

PRIVACY AND THE THERAPEUTIC CONTEXT

In discussing limitations on the confidentiality privileges thought appropriate in the therapist-patient relationship, various forms of disclosure could be at issue. There could be disclosure to governmental health agencies, local, state, or federal. There could be disclosure to those who might help the patient, like physician or parent. There could be disclosure to those who might be or might have been endangered by the patient, like a sexual partner. Finally, there could be disclosure to courts, various criminal justice agencies, or those who might threaten the patient's welfare in other respects, like a health insurance provider or people seeking civil damages in court. In the discussion that follows, I am primarily concerned with disclosures to those medically endangered by contact with a patient. Here a case can be made for abridging the patient's privacy on the basis of someone else's need to know of her own risks.

Therapists counseling patients at various stages of HIV infection are aware of dangers their patients at times have posed for others. While some would maintain that the confidentiality of the therapist-patient relationship insulates the therapist from responsibility for those endangered, others would argue that such a restriction would violate the therapist's social responsibility. In this section I discuss the responsibility of the therapist in the context of a relationship with an HIV-infected patient who poses a danger for others. This issue brings us right to the heart of the conflict discussed in the beginning of this paper between seeing a person as ill and seeing a person as a threat to others.

Apparently, a person who confesses to his priest that he has contracted a contagious disease that he might infect his fiancée with is not entitled to confidentiality vis-à-vis his priest's communications with his fiancée.

Catholic teaching holds that a man forfeits any vow of professional secrecy about an incurable and contagious venereal disease through his intent to act in a way that might gravely injure his bride (Regan 1943).

Analogously, the *Tarasoff* cases (*Tarasoff* v. *Regents of the University of California* 1974, and *Tarasoff* v. *Regents of the University of California* 1976) and subsequent others that have raised similar issues establish a duty to warn and protect potential victims of patients undergoing therapy (Lewis 1986, Fulero 1988). Is this a reasonable basis for uprooting a profoundly significant confidential relationship? To address this question and apply it in the therapeutic relationship, we will consider some additional material on the foundations of respect for privacy. I will draw some distinctions whose relevance for the scope and limit of therapist-patient confidentiality will become clear.

There is no one answer to why privacy is important; in different settings, privacy is important for different reasons. Some of our activities, particularly those connected with bodily or biological functioning or malfunctioning, are associated with privacy norms: elimination, sexual reproduction, illness. Such norms, though widespread and diverse, are not universal. Still, for us they are associated with respect for people, perhaps connected with practices that obscure some of what we share with lower animals.

Privacy norms governing such activities or areas of life are not typically directed to providing those carrying out these functions discretion about how to manage. Instead, these functions, though carried out in private, are traditionally strictly governed by norms that were internalized when young and vigorously sustained on pain of shame. Let us call the privacy norms that are so regulated *discretionless privacy norms*. In the case of discretionless privacy norms one has a duty *not* to present certain faces of oneself in public. The point of this restriction is decidedly not liberation from social control.

Next comes an area of life that is highly regulated but one in which the discretion of how to carry out the objectives is left to the agents. Parent-child relationships characteristically fall into this category. The authoritative discretion parents are accorded in raising their children is rationalized on the grounds that it is to be exercised solely for the purpose of promoting the child's best interest. People will disagree about what does promote the child's interest, and it is in this area of interpretation that a parent is afforded her discretion. Let us call the privacy norms that permit discretion in the achievement of a given objective *narrow privacy*.

Finally, norms that restrict access of others to a person or to a sphere of life may be in place to enable wide discretion in behavior and interpretation of roles. This discretion encompasses discretion both in the ends to be achieved, something lacking in the narrow privacy domain, and in the means by which the ends are to be reached, something shared with the narrow privacy domain. Today we think of the privacy associated with intimate adult relationships as entitled to this full measure of discretion. It is not merely that gratuitous surveillance by others is regarded as out of bounds, as is the case in the discretionless and narrow discretion domains. It is that the couple is thought to be at liberty to develop the relationship as they see fit and to explore possibilities that suit the contours of their individual personalities. Let us call such privacy norms *wide privacy norms*.[4]

Now we can locate the therapist-patient relationship on this spectrum of privacy norms. I argue that therapeutic relationships fall into the middle region, the region of narrow privacy norms. The privacy and discretion afforded the therapist-patient relationship must be exercised to serve specific goals, and it is not up to the therapist and patient to develop other goals or interpret the goals already embraced in eccentric ways. Or at least, it is only within these confines that the relationship becomes socially and legally privileged. Lest one think this is too confining a restriction, recall that this is no narrower discretion than that regulating the parent-child relationship, one that offers considerable latitude in interpreting where the child's good lies and that allows the development of considerable personal and interpersonal meaning within its confines (Schoeman 1989).

In the therapist-patient relationship, anything that does not serve the patient's interest within the general bounds recognized as socially responsible is out of line, a misuse of the discretion, a violation of the relevant norms. Though privacy norms protect many violations from public exposure, this does not redeem their character as violations.

Another consideration that the parent-child relationship shares with therapist-patient relationship has to do with the notion of social responsibility. Parents are entrusted to use their discretion to promote their children's welfare. But parents are also responsible for raising their children to be decent and law-abiding citizens. Just as a person's own welfare can conflict with what is right for her to do, so a parent's regard of her child's welfare can conflict with her attitude about what it is right for the child to do or to become. It could be, for instance, in a child's long-term best interest to be coached on how to cheat in certain endeavors. Nevertheless, we think it wrong for parents to promote the child's interest through such advice. This illustrates that there is a complex goal or a complex set of side constraints that govern parents in the discharge of their responsibilities to promote their children's welfare.

A therapist operates also to promote the welfare of the patient in the context of standards of social decency. Central to our understanding what it is to help someone is a compatibility with a measure of social responsibility. The way the notion of helping works, we are helping only when we do so in a way that is socially responsible. We do not "help" a child molester by teaching him how to get away with abusing children, even if that is the advice he seeks. People for whom helping them is actually inconsistent with respect for others are people we are willing to change but not willing to serve. We tell them, and sincerely believe, that changing them will help them, but that claim is beside the point. For whether it helps them or not, changing them is the first priority.

This distinction between the patient's welfare and social welfare applies very directly to AIDS counseling. The therapist-patient relationship may take on a value in its own right, independent of the relationship serving the patient's narrowly therapeutic interests. But the privacy and confidentiality privileges associated with the relationship are not warranted because of this additional meaning. Confidentiality privileges are afforded because it is presumed that in this way the patient's welfare is promoted in a socially responsible manner.

In claiming that therapists are bound by principles of social responsibility, am I also saying that therapists are best thought as of agents of the state?[5] The question suggests a conflation between the political and the moral. Principles of social responsibility may require therapists to circumvent political requirements, as when a therapist illegally informs a patient about birth control or abortion. Nevertheless, ideally we would hope that the standards that the state expects therapists to adhere to are morally appropriate. If there is no discrepancy, then acting in a way that is socially responsible is coincidentally acting in a way that the state endorses or requires. Furthermore, the therapist is there to assist the patient. To discuss constraints on this does not undermine the point of the relationship, though the constraints do reveal something about it. What they reveal is that a therapeutic relationship requires a sense of distance from the patient. This distance is required for professional judgment and presupposed in our practices of according professional privileges.

So now we recognize some structure in the account of privacy that pertains to patient-therapist relationships. Unlike spousal intimacy, the patient-therapist relationship is not primarily an end in itself but a vehicle to enable the patient to respond to problems with professional help in the context of limitations on the costs to others that providing such help can exact.

One might object on the grounds that parent-child privacy is not just there for the purpose of promoting the child's interests but has an independent dignity founded on the intimacy of the parent-child bond (Schoeman 1980). So similarly, one might extrapolate, the therapist-patient relationship can also involve intimate sharing, and insofar as it does so, it deserves the respect with which norms of privacy can grace a relationship.

There is something to be said for this objection, but it goes only so far as there is consensus between therapist and patient, just as it extends in the parent-child relationship only so far as there is consensus between parent and child. For if there is discord between parental and child will, then the parent is accorded authority only insofar as the parent acts in (her interpretation of) the child's best interest. That is why in many contexts children can obviate the requirement of parental consent by establishing to another objective evaluator that the child's interest is served by not involving the parent.

So in the therapist-patient relationship, it is assumed that there is a convergence of interest *and* that this convergence has already passed whatever moral thresholds responsible social agents will recognize. Therapists are not entitled to help patients shirk fundamental social responsibilities.

Someone might object to this bald claim, suggesting that lawyers are entitled to benefit their clients and work with unconditional confidentiality rules that seem blind to standards of social responsibility. To the extent that lawyers are at liberty to act as "hired guns," their practice has been subjected to intense criticism (Luban 1988). But independent of that, the comparison is more complex than suggested.[6] The therapist, we are presuming, is required to breach confidentiality, to prevent a serious harm that threatens. Rule 1.6 of The American Bar Association Model Rules of Professional Conduct allows (though does not require) lawyers to breach confidentiality "to prevent the client from committing a criminal act the lawyer believes is likely to result in imminent death or substantial bodily harm." Rule 3.3 of this same code makes lawyers responsible for assuring that false evidence is not presented to a court. If the lawyer is not effective at persuading the client to withdraw false testimony, the lawyer is then duty bound to disclose the fraud to the court.

Still, unlike psychotherapists, it is *not* clear that attorneys are required to act to protect potential victims of their client's violent intentions. In *Hawkins* v. *King County* an attorney was held not liable for failure to notify officials at his client's bail hearing of his client's dangerousness and was held not liable for failure to notify his client's mother, a victim of his client's dangerousness. Nevertheless, *Hawkins* is different from *Tarasoff* v. *Regents* in three important respects. The defendant in *Hawkins* did not have specific indications of the direction of his client's dangerousness. He only knew that he was dangerous to himself and others. The defendant in *Hawkins* was not in a position to make a specific evaluation of his client's dangerousness; it is something he learned from others. Third, the victim of the client's aggression was as much aware of the client's dangerousness as the attorney was. If the fact situation had been different in *Hawkins*, the outcome might also have been different.

A difference between the lawyer-client relationship and the therapist-patient relationship is that the right to representation at a criminal trial is a constitutional right. No similar constitutional right is recognized for medical or psychological services. Furthermore, a lawyer's client faces criminal prosecution wherein the full power of the state is aimed at convicting and then punishing him. The therapist in reporting an endangering of others is not acting in response to a threat to her patient posed by the state. Though there may be consequences of the disclosure for her patient, the point of the disclosure is not to hurt the patient. Reporting statutes and judicial decisions require that health agencies and endangered persons be notified, not that the police or prosecutors be notified.

Above, we established that the privacy accorded a therapeutic relationship is aimed at an outcome: promoting the patient's welfare within the context of social responsibility. Realizing this aim helps us situate the confidentiality privileges associated with therapy. The confidentiality of the patient's condition does not preclude the therapist from taking steps to ensure notification of those endangered by the patient. Therapists should notify public health officials who in turn would notify those put at risk. Those endangered have a need to know of their vulnerability, and this need warrants breach of confidentiality.

Which behaviors constitute a risk that therapists must take responsibility for notifying others of their risks? Here we can use as a standard the following: if it is unreasonable for a patient to fail to inform others of a life-threatening risk, then the therapist owes it to these other persons to notify them of the risk. In [the next section of this essay] I discuss when it is unreasonable for people not to inform others of risks they pose to them.

• • •

THE INDIVIDUAL'S DUTY TO WARN

In the last [section], I addressed the question of what responsibilities therapists have to breach confidentiality and protect those endangered by patients with AIDS. . . . In this section, I discuss what responsibilities a person has to warn others whom he may be endangering because of his HIV infection. Since this often arises in the context of a sexual relationship, I focus here on standards of care that are enforceable despite arising in a private setting. . . .

Conditions of trust and intimacy that are worth respecting should be transparent, in that if partners were to be more fully informed of the other, the basis of the trust and intimacy would not be undermined (Baier 1986). Should this ideal be imposed by those not party to the relationship? Could not the information be misleading, or might not it be aberrational, or does it presuppose too much rationality in the agents? How does it affect matters when the behavior in question is life threatening?

What responsibilities does a person who knows he is or might be HIV infected have toward those he might transmit the virus to? Let us restrict our attention here to those who would not willingly be part of an interchange in which HIV might be transmitted. As this relates to privacy, we might ask more specifically whether the intimacy or privacy of the relationship might bar public or legal accountability on the part of someone who transmits the virus.

A further refinement of the question is in order. What we are here concerned with is what standard the state will impose if it is addressed to resolve a dispute between parties disagreeing over the proper standard of care. This involves, not surveillance on the part of the state into relationships where it is not invited, but a response to a complaint brought by people who were sexually intimate, even within the context of marriage.

Although not dispositive of the moral, the legal framework for assessing liability between sexual partners for transmission of disease is relevant. The leading relevant case here is *Kathleen K. v. Robert B.* (1984). The California Court of Appeals held that the constitutional right of privacy does not "insulate one sexual partner who by intentionally tortious conduct causes physical injury to another."

Kathleen K. alleged that she contracted genital herpes, a contagious and debilitating condition for which there is at present no cure, as a result of sexual intercourse with Robert B. at a time when he knew or should have known that he was a carrier. She also alleged that Robert B. misrepresented to her that he was free from venereal disease and that she relied on his assertion. Robert B. alleged that his right to privacy precluded a court's intrusion into the case, its jurisdiction in this domain.

The court found that Robert B.'s right to privacy was not absolute and was subordinate to the state's fundamental right to enact laws that promote public health, welfare, and safety. The court cited penal statutes covering consensual sexual acts, registration of convicted sex offenders, laws relating to paternity, even to marital rape legislation, to illustrate its jurisdiction in the private domain.

Recent Minnesota and New Jersey cases, *R.A.P.* v. *B.J.P.*, and *G.L.* v. *M.L.*, respectively, would allow a person to claim damages against a former spouse for transmitting genital herpes *during the tenure of the marriage*. Recovery is permitted on the basis of a duty to refrain from acts that might transmit a disease or minimally warn the spouse of her contagious condition. The New Jersey court endorsed the position that courts were instrumental in defining the level of care spouses owe one another.

The Supreme Court of Ohio (*Mussivand* v. *David*) held that if person A has a venereal disease and is having an affair with a married person B but has not informed B of his condition, A owes *B's spouse* notification of his, B's spouse's, vulnerability to the disease. (The duty A owes *B* was not an issue in this case.) Anything less subjects B's spouse to an unreasonable risk of contracting the disease, making A liable for damages.

These cases illustrate that sexual intimacy brings with it an enforceable standard of care despite being located within the private precincts of life. Most of the cases mentioned involved a risk of contracting genital herpes. Because the risks associated with AIDS are so much more threatening than those associated with herpes, there is every reason to think that the standard of care expected of those who might transmit AIDS will be more vigorously applied than that expected of those who might transmit herpes (Gostin 1990a; Lambert 1990).[7]

The standard of care required by law is implicit in public attitudes toward what people in intimate relationships owe one another. In one study of people who presented themselves at an STD clinic, when offered confidential HIV testing, 79 percent accepted; 71 percent of those accepting the test offered as a reason concern for transmitting HIV to their sexual partner(s).[8]

The intimate or delicate nature of many aspects of AIDS transmission is a real barrier to frank discussion of risk factors. Not surprisingly many people about to embark on a sexual relationship would not regard it as fitting to discuss prospects for transmission of venereal disease in general or HIV in particular. The more such issues are discussed in public contexts, the more people will in fact feel comfortable in raising them in private contexts without feeling as if they are doing something offensive and unreasonable. Very clearly people need more incentives or fewer inhibitions in taking safety precautions related to sexual behavior and frank sexual conversations. Much about our social upbringing disposes us to feel skittish about broaching such topics even with people we know well. More open discussion of such issues in schools, homes, churches, and other settings of exemplary social norms will go some way toward facilitating open expressions of concern when it is important to do so in sexual settings. The less prevalent the ravages of AIDS are within a community, the less awareness there will be that such privacy barriers are dangerous.

• • •

I mentioned at the outset that in cases of real moral conflict we are haunted by needs and concerns that cannot be addressed because of the pressing nature of the other values involved. Tragically, this is what we confront commonly when we consider the needs of those infected with HIV in cases where people legitimately raise privacy concerns.

The fact that people infected with HIV may be thought to be living under a death sentence, both physically and socially, argues in favor of respecting the privacy interests of these people to the extent possible. Being so fated, however, does not release these people from standards of decency and care they owe others. After all, if AIDS is horrible to endure, it is

horrible to transmit. A person's right to privacy concerning his HIV-positive status is properly abridged when doing so represents the least invasive and most efficient means of protecting others from contracting or spreading the disease.

We cannot afford to be anything but compassionate in our policies toward those infected with HIV. But because of the physical and social ruin this infection occasions, we cannot afford to be ambivalent toward those who unreasonably risk infecting others or who will not share information that can literally save lives. . . .

ACKNOWLEDGMENTS

I express appreciation to Robert Ball, Nora Bell, Nathan Crystal, Patricia Conway, Linda Kettinger, Susan Lake, Robert Post, Bosko Postic, Frederic Reamer, Laurence Thomas, and Deborah Valentine for valuable discussions and resource materials that helped me develop an understanding of issues related to AIDS. Frederic Reamer has been an ideal editor, offering wise comments and constructively prodding me on numerous issues that arose in the myriad versions of this paper. The paper owes much to his care and commitment to making it the most valuable contribution it can be. . . .

NOTES

1. *United States* v. *Sergeant Nathaniel Johnson, Jr.* upholds Sergeant Johnson's conviction for aggravated assault for attempting to engage in anal sex while knowing his condition to be HIV positive — making his semen deadly.

2. For a collection of much of the best writing on privacy along with a philosophical overview of this literature, see Schoeman (1984a). For a review of the philosophical dimension of central privacy issues, see Schoeman (1984c).

3. There is an even narrower conception, one that limits the range of privacy to personal information that is "undocumented."

4. One criterion of the difference between the narrow and the wide privacy norms can be phrased in terms of the distinction between a role and a relationship. While a role is relatively limited in the range of responses thought appropriate and the ends to be achieved, a relationship is treated as more flexible on both counts. Our standing as a parent is role governed insofar as we owe our children certain attitudes almost independently of how they behave; our standing as a spouse is much more responsive to the actual behavior of the partner (Greenhouse 1986).

5. I am indebted to Robert Post for suggesting that I address this question.

6. I am indebted to Nathan Crystal and Robert Post for coaching me on the intricacies of the lawyer-client confidentiality privilege.

7. Marc Christian, Rock Hudson's long-term companion, "won a multimillion-dollar award from Rock Hudson's estate in a suit alleging that the movie star lied about his illness and continued having unsafe sex" (Lambert 1990:15A). Because Mr. Christian was not HIV infected, the basis of the award must have been inflic-

tion of emotional distress and violation of a duty to inform (*Christian* v. *Sheft*).

8. Personal communication, Dr. Jeffrey Jones, Disease Control Division, South Carolina Department of Health and Environmental Control.

REFERENCES

Baier, A. 1986. Trust and Antitrust. *Ethics* 96:231–260.

Benn, S. 1971. Privacy, Freedom, and Respect for Persons. In F. Schoeman, ed., *Philosophical Dimensions of Privacy: An Anthology*, pp. 223–244. New York: Cambridge University Press, 1984.

Blendon, R. and K. Donelan. 1988. Discrimination Against People with AIDS. *New England Journal of Medicine* 319:1022–1026.

Christian v. *Sheft*. 1988. Super Ct. LA City: *AIDS Literature Reporter* (June 24).

Flaherty, D. 1972. *Privacy in Colonial New England*. Charlottesville: University Press of Virginia.

Fried, C. 1960. Privacy. In F. Schoeman, ed., *Philosophical Dimensions of Privacy*, pp. 203–222.

Fulero, S. 1988. *Tarasoff*: 10 Years Later. *Professional Psychology: Research and Practice* 19: 184–190.

G.L. v. *M.L.* 1988. 550 A.2d 525 (N.J. Super. Ch.)

Goleman, D. 1990. Studies Discover Clues to the Roots of Homophobia. *New York Times* (July 10), p. B1.

Gostin, L. 1990a. The AIDS Litigation Project: A National Review of Court and Human Rights Commission Decisions. Part I: The Social Impact of AIDS. *JAMA* 263:1961–1970.

Greenhouse, C. 1986. *Praying for Justice: Faith, Order, and Community in an American Town*. Ithaca, N.Y.: Cornell University Press.

Hawkins v. *King County*. 1979. 602 P.2d 361.

Kathleen K. v. *Robert B.* 1984. 198 *California Reporter* 273.

Krause, H. 1986. *Family Law*. St. Paul: West Publishing.

Lambert, B. 1990. AIDS: Keeping Track of the Infected. *New York Times* (May 13), p. 15A.

Lewis, M. 1986. Duty to Warn Versus Duty to Maintain Confidentiality: Conflicting Demands on Mental Health Professionals. *Suffolk Law Review* 20:579–615.

Luban, D. 1988. *Lawyers and Justice: An Ethical Study*. Princeton, N.J.: Princeton University Press.

Mussivand v. *David*. 544 N.E. 2d 265.

R.A.P. v. *B.J.P.* 1988. 428 N.W.2b 103 (Minn. Ct. App.)

Regan, R. 1943. *Professional Secrecy in Light of Moral Principles*. Washington, D.C.: Augustinian Press. Cited in S. Eth. 1988. The Sexually Active, HIV Infected Patient: Confidentiality Versus the Duty to Protect. *Psychiatric Annals* 18:571–576.

Schoeman, F. 1980. Rights of Children, Rights of Parents, and the Moral Basis of the Family. *Ethics* 91:6–19.

Schoeman, F., ed. 1984a. *Philosophical Dimensions of Privacy*. New York: Cambridge University Press.

Schoeman, F. 1984c. Introduction. In F. Schoeman, ed., *Philosophical Dimensions of Privacy*, pp. 1–33.

Schoeman, F. 1989. Adolescent Confidentiality and Family Privacy. In G. Graham and H. LaFollette, eds., *Person to Person*, pp. 213–234. Philadelphia: Temple University Press.

Stone, L. 1979. *The Family, Sex, and Marriage in England, 1500–1800*. New York: Harper & Row.

Tarasoff v. *Regents of the University of California*. 1974. 118 *California Reporter* 129.

Tarasoff v. *Regents of the University of California*. 1976. 17 Cal.3d 425.

United States v. *Sergeant Nathaniel Johnson, Jr.* 27 M.J. 798.

KAREN H. ROTHENBERG
AND RICHARD L. NORTH

The Duty to Warn "Dilemma" and Women with AIDS

Janet, a 28-year-old with four children, comes to the obstetrics/gynecology clinic of a large urban teaching hospital. She is not married but lives with John, who is the father of two of her children. Janet and John would like to have more children. She seeks advice

From *Courts, Health Science & the Law* 2 (1991), 90–94, 96–98. © 1991, Georgetown University. Reprinted by permission of the authors and publisher.

because she fears that she might have a sexually transmitted disease. She has a history of intravenous drug abuse but she denies present use. She admits to consuming at least a bottle of wine a day. She also reports that John is an IV drug abuser.

After counseling, Dr. Smith convinces Janet to be tested for the human immunodeficiency virus. The test is positive, but Janet has not told John of her infection.

Dr. Smith offers to help her in telling John, but Janet refuses. With further counseling, Janet admits that she fears that John will leave her if he learns she is infected and without him she cannot support herself and her children. She also reports that during her last pregnancy, she sought emergency care after John kicked her in the stomach. It becomes clear that Janet is afraid that John will become violent and hurt her if he is told that she is HIV positive.

Dr. Smith is faced with the duty to warn "dilemma"[1] which invariably surfaces in discussions about the ethical and legal implications of the acquired immunodeficiency syndrome (AIDS) epidemic.[2] Most often, the duty to warn dilemma is posited as a series of tensions which exist among principles of confidentiality, public health strategies, and legal duty to warn obligations. Health professionals and legal experts often conclude that these tensions are irreconcilable and place professionals in a "no win" position when confronting a patient like Janet.

Nurses,[3] dentists,[4] social workers,[5] psychologists,[6] psychiatrists,[7] and primary care physicians[8] all debate the existence of a duty to warn. The Centers for Disease Control (CDC), the American Medical Association (AMA), and the American Hospital Association all have taken positions with respect to third party notification.[9] Interest in the topic is not limited to the United States, but has been the subject of articles and conferences worldwide.[10]

In spite of all this interest, the changing demographics of AIDS requires us to re-examine the duty to warn debate. The Centers for Disease Control report that women constitute the fastest growing group of persons with AIDS. Women now represent 11% of reported cases. Nationwide, HIV/AIDS is among the top five leading causes of death in women of childbearing age (ages 15 to 44). It is estimated that 80,000 women of childbearing age may be HIV-infected. The epidemic of HIV among women of color is growing at alarming rates. Over 70% of infected women are women of color; African American are 51% of reported cases and Latina women are almost 20%. In New York City and New Jersey, AIDS is the leading killer of African American women of childbearing age. Latina women are disproportionally affected as well. Intravenous drug use is the mode of transmission of infection for women in over 50% of the cases reported, while 30% of women are infected through sexual contact with an HIV-infected partner.[11]

As the epidemic grows, more and more women are being tested for HIV at clinics for family planning, sexually transmitted diseases, prenatal care, and drug treatment. As a general rule, it is assumed that it makes good public health sense for a patient to notify sexual partners of HIV status.[12] A patient's refusal to notify partners is what has raised the duty to warn dilemma for the health care provider. However, a re-examination of the duty to warn debate is critical when considered in the wake of another epidemic against women—the threat of domestic violence.

Experts predict that the number of women battered each year ranges from 1.6 million to 12 million.[13] Studies report that 25 to 63% of women who have been battered experience abuse during pregnancy with blows to the abdomen, injuries to the breast and genitals, and sexual assault.[14] In fact, the Surgeon General's Workshop on Violence identified pregnancy as a high-risk period for battering, in which women are at increased risk of severity of injury and adverse health consequences.[15] In a recent study on violence and substance use during pregnancy, it was reported that a pregnant woman's risk of being battered was associated with her alcohol use during pregnancy and illicit drug use by her partner, even when controlling for socioeconomic factors and prior history of violence.[16] Based on this strong evidence, it is recommended that health care providers evaluate a woman's risk of violence, particularly when there is alcohol and drug abuse present.[17]

The health care provider who counsels the HIV-infected woman must be sensitive to her fear that telling a sexual partner that she is infected may trigger physical abuse.[18] In fact, the CDC notes in its brochure on patient counseling that one should anticipate a "hostile" reaction from a partner upon learning that he or she has been exposed to infection.[19] Nonetheless, they continue to urge that all partners be notified of a likely exposure. In certain cases, the risk of physical harm by a sexual partner to the female patient infected with HIV may be greater than the potential benefit of warning the sexual partner. In fact, the HIV-infected woman may be the "foreseeable victim" of violence by a sex or needle-sharing partner. . . .

CONFIDENTIALITY: THE ETHICAL AND LEGAL PRINCIPLES

Many professionals in the duty to warn debate believe that there is a tension between the tradition of confidentiality and the desire to protect identifiable individuals from harm. Confidentiality is rooted in the physician-patient relationship and arises out of the contractual and fiduciary nature of that relationship.[20] "Protected by no greater guaranty of secrecy than [the promise of confidentiality], countless generations of men and women, freely and confidently, have entrusted their most intimate and delicate secrets to their medical advisers."[21] Breaches of confidentiality are viewed as a violation of a patient's privacy and an assault on the patient's integrity as a person.

In spite of its prominence, the professions recognize exceptions to absolute confidentiality, even in the Hippocratic Oath:

Whatsoever things I see or hear concerning the life of men, in my attendance on the sick or even apart therefrom, *which ought not to be noised abroad*, I will keep silence thereon, counting such things to be as sacred secrets [emphasis added].[22]

Hippocrates gave little guidance about what could be "noised abroad" but this exception to absolute confidentiality has been preserved in almost every ethical code published thereafter. For example, Thomas Percival, writing in 1803, includes the following: "Secrecy and delicacy, when required by particular circumstances, should be strictly preserved."[23] In 1847, the American Medical Association published its first code stating that a physician should never divulge a secret "except when he is imperatively required to do so."[24] Most recently, the AMA has reviewed its position in light of the AIDS epidemic and has declared that "[confidentiality] rights are absolute until they infringe in a material way upon the safety of another person or persons."[25]

Similar exceptions to absolute confidentiality can be found in the Ethical Principles of Psychologists,[26] the Social Workers' Code of Ethics,[27] the International Council of Nurses Code for Nurses,[28] the guidelines of the American Psychiatric Association,[29] and the Model Rules of Professional Conduct for lawyers.[30] Most ethicists also agree that in extraordinary circumstances there may be justification for overriding confidentiality to protect another from death or severe harm; but when in doubt, they argue, priority should be given to confidentiality.[31]

Out of this ethical tradition has come a legally protected right of confidentiality, found in both statutes and common law. The common law duty to maintain client confidences has arisen only recently as notions of privacy have emerged as rights.[32] Courts rely upon various sources for the creation of this common law

duty including: professional disciplinary statutes, medical record confidentiality statutes, the fiduciary physician-patient relationship, contract theory, the tort of intentional infliction of emotional distress, testimonial privilege statutes, and malpractice based upon negligence or upon statute.[33] No matter what the source of the duty, all of the cases creating it recognize that disclosure of a patient's confidence is warranted "to meet a serious danger to the patient or to others."[34]

Many states have medical record confidentiality statutes which predate and do not mention AIDS or HIV infection. These statutes vary widely from state to state. For example, Maryland's law, which is based upon a model act of the American Medical Association, prohibits disclosure without written consent of the patient.[35] Tennessee is more vague, providing that records are "the property of the various hospitals . . . [however,] nothing contained in this part shall be deemed to impair any privilege of confidentiality conferred by law on patients."[36]

Some state statutes make it unlawful to disclose the HIV status of a patient except to the health department and other care providers.[37] Federal law provides for confidentiality of medical records maintained in connection with the performance of any alcohol abuse or drug abuse prevention function conducted, funded, authorized, or assisted by the federal government.[38]

Many states have made it permissible to disclose HIV status to a spouse.[39] A few states allow notification to the sex or needle-sharing partner (some only to the partner of a deceased AIDS patient)[40] or to a sex or needle-sharing partner where the patient will not make a disclosure.[41] These laws merely allow for the physician to disclose a patient confidence. They do not require warnings in the face of foreseeable danger to a specifically identifiable victim.[42] The growing statutory trend allows for the reporting of individuals to state health departments which, in turn, are given authority to carry out contact tracing in appropriate circumstances.[43] These statutes resolve concerns about untrained physicians carrying out warnings and create a mechanism, supposedly, for the counseling of the person receiving the bad news.

Breaches of confidentiality for the protection of others or the larger social good have long been part of the professional tradition and have been incorporated into the law. The more difficult questions arise when deciding if a disclosure is appropriate. We suggest that in the context of women with HIV infection, the decision to breach confidentiality is even more problematic both because it might frustrate the public health strategy employed to combat the AIDS epidemic and because it may increase the risk of violence to women.

PUBLIC HEALTH STRATEGIES

Public health advocates routinely argue that confidentiality must give way to the need to protect society as a whole in the face of an epidemic or other public health threat. As the medical profession has made important improvements in preventive medicine, arguments based on science and the ethics of collective responsibility have been offered to justify mandatory reporting, surveillance, and partner notification laws.[44] During the syphilis and tuberculosis epidemics, public health laws required the reporting of carriers and their contacts and included the authority to arrest, confine, or quarantine *until treated and cured*. In the context of AIDS, the traditional public health model would support partner notification as necessary to promote testing and counseling, education on risk prevention, and early medical intervention.

However, many public health experts have questioned the traditional public health model and argue strenuously for the maintenance of strict confidentiality.[45] They fear that disclosure to third parties will discourage persons at risk of infection from seeking testing and receiving the counseling that can lead to modifications of behavior. "Every time a professional breaks confidentiality, he or she risks the further reduction of trust in the profession which, while it exists, can itself be reasonably expected to help reduce the spread of the disease."[46] The possibility of driving underground the exact persons the profession wishes to attract is increased, they argue, by reporting laws. This may be the case with both HIV and domestic violence.

There is also debate within the public health community over the design of laws allowing or requiring disclosure. This debate concerns whether individual physicians rather than health officers should be charged with the duty to give warnings. Traditional practitioners seem to want mandatory reporting laws to relieve themselves of personal dilemmas and the discomfort associated with discussing intimate or illegal behavior with a patient. They want health departments to carry out the notice and contact tracing and they point to public health responses to past epidemics as models.

Compliance with mandatory reporting laws, however, would mean that each case must be evaluated to determine if additional steps are required to discharge a physician's legal obligations to both her patients and third parties. Such an evaluation must consider the prevailing public health strategies to combat both the epidemics of AIDS and violence against women.

THE LEGAL DUTY TO WARN

The legal analysis of the duty to warn begins with the principle that generally "a person has no legal obligation to care for or look after the welfare of a stranger, adult or child."[47] "A moral duty to take affirmative action is not enough to enforce a legal duty to do so."[48] Section 315 of the Restatement (Second) of Torts carves out an exception to the general rule and states that when a "special relationship" exists between the actor (Dr. Smith) and the other (Janet) or the third person (John or a fetus), then the actor has a duty to prevent that harm.[49]

This "special relationship" analysis was applied by the Supreme Court of California in the oft cited case of *Tarasoff v. California Board of Regents*.[50]

> [W]hen the avoidance of foreseeable harm requires a defendant to control the conduct of another person, or to warn of such conduct, the common law has traditionally imposed liability . . . if the defendant bears some special relationship to the dangerous person or to the potential victim.[51]

Most commentators attempting to apply the *Tarasoff* standard to the AIDS debate find it exceedingly problematic. The test requires a determination of whether the relationship between the professional and patient is significantly "special" to give rise to the duty. Section 319 of the Restatement (Second) of Torts provides one answer to this question. It imposes a duty on those in charge of persons having dangerous propensities. Specifically it provides that:

> One who takes charge of a third person whom he knows or should know to be likely to cause bodily harm to others if not controlled, is under a duty to exercise reasonable care to control the third person to prevent him from doing such a harm.[52]

The operative words of "take charge" and "control" are ambiguous at best. In *Tarasoff*, the court found that the relationship between a psychotherapist and patient was sufficiently "special" and that the psychotherapist had sufficient "control" to give rise to a duty to a third party who was threatened with harm. Some commentators, noting the absence of control, argue persuasively that the relationship between an HIV-infected patient and a treating physician is not so "special" to give rise to the legal duty under *Tarasoff*.[53]

The requirement of "foreseeability" of harm raises a second problem in applying *Tarasoff* to an AIDS case. Foreseeability of harm is factually complicated in each HIV case and is only clouded by the scientific data available. For example, one report concluded that "a single act of vaginal sex without using a condom with a partner who is known to be infected with HIV carries a 1 in 500 risk of infection."[54] The use of a condom lowers the risk to 1 in 50 million.[55] The risk of female to male transmission of the HIV is probably lower than from male to female and anal intercourse is more significantly associated with HIV infection than vaginal or oral sex.[56] There are questions about the number of exposures to the virus and an increase in the risk of infection,[57] increased risks if cofactors exist, such as other sexually transmissible diseases,[58] and questions about periods when infected persons may be more contagious.[59]

Rather than focusing on problems of foreseeability, most commentators attempting to apply *Tarasoff* to AIDS vacillate between the common law duty to warn a potential victim and patient common law rights to confidentiality. They perceive a tension of dilemma that does not really exist. As mentioned earlier, the courts balance the common law duties (to warn and to maintain confidences) and allow the greater societal good to predominate.[60]

In spite of such judicial accommodation, commentators continue to urge further legislative action in the face of the AIDS epidemic.[61] The most popular legislative proposal to resolve the alleged duty to warn dilemma is a grant of immunity to physicians for breaching confidentiality or immunity from liability to a third party for a failure to warn. For example, the AMA Council on Ethics and Judicial Affairs proposes:

Specific statutes must be drafted which, while protecting to the greatest extent possible the confidentiality of patient information, (a) provide a method for warning unsuspecting sexual partners, (b) protect physicians from liability for failure to warn the unsuspecting third party but, (c) establish clear standards for when a physician should inform the public health authorities, and (d) provide clear guidelines for public health authorities who need to trace the unsuspecting sexual partners of the infected person.[62]

These legislative proposals skew the delicate balance between confidentiality and affirmative duties to protect others from harm. The grant of immunity merely encourages professionals to warn when they should not and to remain silent when they should disclose, because with immunity there is no pressure to resolve the difficult factual and ethical questions. Immunity from liability for warning third parties may only encourage professionals to warn persons they believe at risk, since the warning entails no risk to the professional. Wholesale warning may discourage persons from seeking testing and counseling, driving them underground and frustrating public health goals.

Professionals also should not be lulled into a false sense of security if one of these immunity statutes exists in one's state. Some of these statutes grant immunity to civil or criminal liability only in actions related to a breach of patient confidentiality or for failure to warn third parties.[63] Others are ambiguous granting immunity "for the disclosure of otherwise confidential information."[64] This does not necessarily insulate a professional from liability for a disclosure that leads to the foreseeable injury to a patient from her abusive partner.

In our case study, Dr. Smith's conduct may be affected if she is protected by legislated immunity. It may be less likely that she will spend the extraordinary time necessary to counsel Janet. Rather than incurring costs and discussing uncomfortable sexual and drug use behavior, Dr. Smith may choose to remain silent or to warn John without a thoughtful examination of the circumstances. Believing (maybe falsely) she has no legal liability exposure, the quick and least messy solution may be the solution of choice, that is, silence. On the other hand, a precipitous warning could lead to physical harm to Janet. Thus, immunity which encourages warning could result in greater harm than silence. Furthermore, since Dr. Smith has a legal and ethical duty to do no harm to her patient, she should not place Janet in a position of harm if it is foreseeable that John may abuse her following notification.[65]

Interestingly enough, the *Tarasoff* court did not inquire into the foreseeability of harm to the psychotherapist's patient in determining there was a duty to warn in that case. Rather, the court followed a long line of older cases in weighing the confidentiality principle,[66] along with other considerations to find a common law duty. A duty is imposed only after weighing "the sum total of those considerations of policy which lead the law to say that a person is entitled to protection."[67] These policy considerations are:

the foreseeability of harm to the [third party], the degree of certainty that the [third party] suffered injury, the closeness of the connection between the [actor's] conduct and the injury suffered, the moral blame attached to the [actor's] conduct, the policy of preventing future harm, the extent of burden to the [actor] and the consequences to the community of imposing a duty to [protect], and the availability, cost, and prevalence of insurance for the risk involved.[68]

Rather than creating a dilemma, tort theory, *Tarasoff*, and its progeny can best be read as proposing a balancing exercise to resolve conflicts of competing values.

We believe that thoughtful professionals rather than rigid legislative solutions should be relied upon to resolve these conflicts, especially where the factual questions are likely to be complex and the science is uncertain. Professionals have a primary duty to protect their patients and they are likely to be in the best position to weigh the likelihood of harm to their patients with the likelihood of harm to others. They should do so without the prod of mandatory laws or the shield of legislated immunity. Our reliance upon the professions to act ethically in interpreting these values while reconciling individual and social goals is what elevates them from mere trades to what we call professions.[69] This trust and responsibility that distinguishes the professions also places upon them burdens to use judgment without exacting regulation.

To date, no state has passed a comprehensive statute that dictates the process which a physician must follow in resolving a duty to warn question. Nor are there any laws, as noted earlier, that mandate that physicians warn their patients' sexual or needle-sharing partners of their potential risk for exposure to HIV, although a number give them the discretion to do so.[70] Many of these same states limit a physician's liability if she warns a third party and release providers from such liability if they fail to make such disclosures.[71]

While it is seductive to have a law with a capital "L" telling one what must be done in resolving these difficult questions, state laws give only minimal guidance to reconcile the competing values inherent in the question to warn. Ethicists argue that there are times when the moral obligation might even trump the laws which do exist. The professional should weigh the relative value assigned to confidentiality by state law and her professional code to determine if disclosure is prohibited or allowable to prevent serious bodily harm to another. If a confidentiality statute exists which specifically prohibits disclosure of a patient's HIV status or generally is clear about the confidential nature of such information, then a physician may not warn a third party who is within the "zone of danger" of infection. The more likely case is that the AIDS statute is merely permissive and allows for a warning, or ambiguous, which makes the need for a full risk assessment more apparent. In such circumstances medical ethicists argue that the burden of persuasion falls upon one who wishes to disclose a patient confidence.[72]

• • •

CONCLUSION

In the 1990s, the epidemics of AIDS and domestic violence will intersect and create new challenges for society. Clearly, health care professionals must recognize that the HIV-infected woman will be a "foreseeable victim." To meet the challenge, physicians and other professionals must be prepared to balance the risks to each identifiable party in making the decision to warn or to maintain confidentiality. . . .

The duty to warn debate is really about complex and hard to solve factual questions and value judgments. Legislation cannot resolve Dr. Smith's dilemma or all the factual and value-laden questions in the duty to warn equation. These questions are best left to skilled and ethical professionals for resolution on a case by case basis.

Sections of this paper are adapted from North, R. L. and Rothenberg, K. H. (1990). The duty to warn "dilemma": A framework for resolution. *AIDS and Public Policy Journal, 4(3)*, 133–141.

NOTES

1. The Council on Ethical and Judicial Affairs of the AMA in its report "Ethical Issues Involved in the Growing AIDS Crisis" states, "[A] physician who knows that a seropositive patient is endangering a third party faces a *dilemma*. . . ." [Emphasis added]; cited in Labowitz, infra note 9 at 514.

2. The "duty to warn" means the legally enforceable or moral duty of a physician, health care worker, or other professional to protect a third party. A warning to an individual that he is at risk of acquiring HIV infection from a patient of the professional is only one means of attempting to discharge the legal duty to protect. Typically, most debates on the duty to warn pose a bisexual male who refuses to tell his spouse or fiancee of his infection. See, e.g., Winston, M. (1987). AIDS and the Duty to Protect. *Hastings Center Report 17,* 22–23. The problems posed by intravenous drug abusers may be even more complex.

3. Northrop, C. E. (1988). Rights versus regulation: confidentiality in the age of AIDS. *Nursing Outlook, 36,* 208.

4. Rogers, V. C. (1988). Dentistry and AIDS: Ethical and legal obligations in provision of care. *Medicine and Law, 7,* 57–63. Laskin, D. M. (1988). Treatment of patients with AIDS: A matter of professional ethics (Editorial). *Journal of Oral and Maxillofacial Surgery, 46,* 719.

5. Reamer, F. G. (1988). AIDS and Ethics — The agenda for social workers. *Social Work, 33,* 460–464.

6. Melton, G. B. (1988). Ethical and legal issues in AIDS-related practice. *American Psychologist, 43,* 941–947.

7. Dyer, A. R. (1988). AIDS, ethics, and psychiatry. *Psychiatric Annals, 18,* 577–581.

8. Dickens, B. M. (1988). Legal limits of AIDS confidentiality. *Journal of the American Medical Association, 259,* 3449–3451.

9. See Labowitz, K. E. (1990). Beyond Tarasoff: AIDS and the obligation to breach confidentiality. *St. Louis University Public Law Review, 495,* 512–516 (discussing these policy statements).

10. See, e.g., Gillon, R. (1987). AIDS and medical confidentiality, *British Medical Journal, 294,* 1675–1677 (United Kingdom); Berger, P. B. (1988). AIDS and ethics — An analytical framework. *Canadian Family Physician, 34,* 1787–1791 (Canada); Gerber, P. (1987). AIDS and the ethics of disclosure [letter]. *Medical Journal of Australia, 147,* 199, 202 [letter] AIDS and the Ethics of Disclosure, *Medical Journal of Australia, 147,* 522 (Australia); Zimmerli, W. C. (1988). AIDS, ethical considerations. *Zeitschrift Für Evangelische Ethik, 32,* 190–198 (Germany).

11. Centers for Disease Control (CDC), Department of Health and Human Services, HIV/AIDS Surveillance Report-August 1990; Center for Women Policy Studies (May 1990). *The Guide to Resources on Women and AIDS,* Introduction; Gwinn, M., et al., (1991) Prevalence of HIV infection in childbearing women in the United States. *Journal of the American Medical Association, 265,* 1704–1708; Chu, S. Y., Buehler, J. W. and Berkelman, R. L. (1990). Impact of the human immunodeficiency virus epidemic on mortality in women of reproductive age, United States. *Journal of the American Medical Association, 264,* 225–229. Although these figures are alarming, experts at the National Resource Center on Women and AIDS (Center for Women Policy Studies) point out that it is likely that these statistics underestimate the growth in the AIDS epidemic among women. Women in low income areas may not survive long enough to be diagnosed. Symptoms of infection in women may often go unrecognized. Many women fear that care will be denied if they are HIV-infected. Furthermore, women are often the primary care givers for partners and children with AIDS and do not have the time, means, or strength to seek care for themselves.

12. See, e. g., Centers for Disease Control (CDC), Department of Health and Human Services. (October 1990). Voluntary HIV counseling and testing: Facts, issues and answers. HIV/NAIEP/10-90/11 at pp. 19, 24.

13. Helton, A. S., McFarlane, J., and Anderson, E. T. (October 1987). Battered and pregnant: A prevalence study. *American Journal of Public Health, 77,* 1337–1339.

14. Id.

15. Id. at 1338. See *Surgeon General's Workshop on Violence: Recommendations on Spouse Abuse* at 19–21 (1986).

16. Amaro, H., Fried, L. E., Cabral, H., and Zukerman, B. (1990). Violence during pregnancy and substance use. *American Journal of Public Health, 80,* 575–579.

17. Id. at 578.

18. To the best of our knowledge, there has not been a study done on battering or threats of violence following notification of HIV status to a sexual partner. However, it has been reported by prevention and intervention programs, including the National Institute on Drug Abuse, that women at risk for HIV do not discuss condom use with sexual partners for fear of physical violence and the imbalance in power in the relationships between women and their partners. Briefing on Women and AIDS for U.S. Congress, National Resource Center on Women and AIDS and the Women's Congressional Caucus, April 11, 1991. See also Worth, D. (1989). Sexual decision-making and AIDS: Why condom promotion among vulnerable women is likely to fail. *Studies in Family Planning, 20,* 297–307; Kane, S. (Aug. 1990). AIDS, addiction and condom use: Sources of sexual risk for heterosexual women, *Journal of Sexual Research, 27,* 427–444; discussions with G. Weissbaum, NIDA, April 11, 1991.

19. See CDC, supra, note 12.

20. Gellman, R. M. (1984). Prescribing privacy: The uncertain role of the physician in the protection of patient privacy. *N. C. Law Review, 62,* 255 (citations omitted).

21. Dewitt, C. (1958). *Privileged Communications between Physician and Patient.* Charles C. Thomas, Inc., p. 23.

22. Campbell, A. V. (1984). *Moral Dilemmas in Medicine.* London: Churchill Livingstone Co., p. 167.

23. Percival, T. (1803). Medical Ethics. reprinted in Reiser, S. J., Dyck, A. J., and Curran, W. J. (1987). *Ethics in Medicine: Historical Perspectives and Contemporary Concerns.* Cambridge, MA: MIT Press.

24. Id. The AMA Code of Ethics was revised in 1912, 1957, and 1980, and each version retained an exception to absolute confidentiality. In 1912 the code stated that "a physician must determine whether or not his duty to society requires him to take definite action to protect a healthy individual from becoming infected . . . [and to] know the civil law of his commonwealth concerning privileged communications." In 1957 the code stated that a physician may not reveal a confidence "unless he is required to do so by law or unless it becomes necessary in order to protect the welfare of the individual or of the community." In 1980 a new shortened version read "[a physician] shall safeguard patient confidences within the constraints of the law." Id.

25. Current Opinions of the Council on Ethics and Judicial Affairs of the American Medical Association, (January 1987); see also Labowitz, supra note 9 at 514–515.

26. American Psychological Association Principle no. 5 (1981).

27. National Association of Social Workers. (1965). *The Social Workers' Code of Ethics: A Critique and Guide,* New York: National Association of Social Workers.

28. International Council of Nurses Code for Nurses: Ethical Concepts Applied to Nursing. (1973). Reprinted in Beauchamp, T. L. and Childress, J. F. (1985). *Principles of Biomedical Ethics.* New York: Oxford University Press, p. 296.

29. Reprinted in *Psychiatric News,* Jan. 15, 1988 p. 27.

30. American Bar Association Model Rules of Professional Conduct, Rule 1.6 (1986).

31. Beauchamp, T. L. and Childress, J. F. (1985). *Principles of Biomedical Ethics.* New York: Oxford University Press, 2nd; Harvard, J.D.J. (1985). Medical confidence. *Journal of Medical Ethics, 11(1),* 8–11.

32. See, e.g., *Alberts v. Devine,* 479 N.E.2d 113 (Mass. 1985); *Humpers v. First Interstate Bank,* 298 Or. 706, 696 P. 2d 527 (1985); *Horne v. Patton,* 291 Ala. 701, 287 So.2d 824 (1974).

33. 48 ALR 4th 651.

34. *Alberts v. Devine,* supra note 32 at 119; see generally 48 ALR 4th 651. The only caveat is that courts find that any disclosure must be made in a fashion so as to preserve the patient's privacy to the extent possible. See, e.g., *Tarasoff v. California Board of Regents,* 17 Cal.3d at 442, 131 Cal. Rptr. at 27, 551 P.2d at 347 (1976).

35. Md. Health Gen. Code Ann. §4–301 (Supp. 1990). The statute provides for eleven exceptions.

36. Tenn. Code Ann. §68–11–304 (Supp. 1990).

37. See, e.g., Fla. Stat. Ann. Ch. 88–380, §381.609 Fla. Sess. Law service (West 1988); Mass. Gen. Laws Ann. ch. 111 §70F (Supp. 1991); N.H. Rev. Stat. Ann. §141–F:8 (1990).

38. 42 U.S.C.A. §290dd-3 (Supp. 1990) and 42 U.S.C.A. §290ee-3 (Supp. 1990).

39. See, e.g., Mo. Ann. Stat. §191.656 (Vernon Supp. 1990); Tex. Rev. Civ. Stat. Ann. art. 4419b–1, §9.03 (b) (7) (Vernon Supp. 1991); Va. Ann. Stat. §32.1–36.1 (Supp. 1990). See also note 70, infra.

40. See, e.g., Wis. Stat. Ann. §146.025(5) (a) (14) (West 1989).

41. See, e.g., Cal. Health & Safety Code §199.25 (West Supp. 1989); N.Y. Pub. Health law §2782(4) (Supp 1991) (This law, however, prohibits the physician from disclosing the identity of the patient.) R. I. Gen. Laws §23–6–14 (1989).

42. For a critique of the new law in New York see, Comment, confidentiality, warning, and AIDS: A proposal to protect patients, third parties, and physicians. *Touro Law Review, 4,* 301 (1988).

43. See, e.g., Minn. Stats. §144.4171 et. seq. (1989).

44. Fox, D. M. (1986). From TB to AIDS: Value conflicts in reporting disease, *Hastings Center Report, 16,* 11–16.

45. Gostin, L. (1989). Public health strategies for confronting AIDS: Legislative and regulatory policy in the United States. *Journal of the American Medical Association, 261,* 1621–1630.

46. See Gillon, supra note 10.

47. Prosser and Keeton (1984). *Law of Torts, 375* (5th ed.). See, e.g., *Pope v. State* 284 Md. 309, 396 A.2d 1054 (1979).

48. LaFave, W. and Scott, A. (1986). *Criminal Law, 203.*

49. Section 315 of the Restatement (Second) of Torts, provides:

There is no duty so to control the conduct of a third person as to prevent him from causing physical harm to another unless

(a) a special relation exists between the actor and the third person which imposes a duty upon the actor to control the third person's conduct, or

(b) a special relation exists between the actor and the other which gives to the other a right to protection.

Restatement (Second) of Torts § 315 (1965).

50. 17 Cal.3d 425, 131 Cal. Rptr. 14, 551 P.2d 334 (1976).

51. Id. at 17 Cal.3d at 435, 551 P.2d at 342–43, 131 Cal. Rptr. at 22–23.

52. Restatement (Second) of Torts § 319 (1965).

53. See, e.g., Rothenberg et al. (1989). The AIDS project: Creating a public health policy—Rights and obligations of health care workers. *Maryland Law Review, 95,* 187. This article also argues that the relationship between the patient and psychotherapist is different because of the availability to the psychotherapist of civil commitment procedures.

54. *N. Y. Times,* Apr. 22, 1988, at A-18, col. 1.

55. Id.

56. Rosenberg, M. J. and Weiner, J. M. (1988). Prostitutes and AIDS: A health department priority? *American Journal of Public Health, 78,* 418–423.

57. Handsfield, H. H. (1988). Heterosexual transmission of human immunodeficiency virus, *Journal of the American Medical Association, 260,* 1943–1944.

58. Quinn et al. (1988). Human immunodeficiency virus infection among patients attending clinics for sexually transmitted diseases. *New England Journal of Medicine, 318,* 197–199.

59. Kim, H. C. et al. (1988). HIV in wives of hemophiliacs. *American Journal of Medicine, 85,* 472–476; Van der Ende, M. E., Rothbarth, P., and Stibbe, J. (1988). Heterosexual transmission of HIV by hemophiliacs. *British Medical Journal, 297(6656),* 1102–3.

60. See supra note 34 and accompanying text.

61. See, e.g., Piorkowski, J. D. (1987). Between a rock and a hard place: AIDS and the conflicting physician's duties of preventing disease transmission and safeguarding confidentiality. *Georgetown Law Review, 76,* 169.

62. Report of Council of Ethics and Judicial Affairs of the American Medical Association (Nov. 1987). One author comments that this proposal is easy to suggest but difficult to effectuate. Comments. (1988). Doctor-patient confidentiality versus duty to warn in the context of AIDS patients and their partners. *Maryland Law Review, 47,* 675, 699.

63. See, e.g., Md. Health Gen. Code Ann. §18–337 (1990).

64. Fl. Professions and Occ. §455.2416 (1989).

65. Hunt, D. M. (1990). Spouse abuse: Care goes beyond the office door. *Postgraduate Medicine, 87(2),* 130–135.

66. See, *Edwards v. Lamb,* 69 N.H. 599, 599–600, 45 A. 480, 480–81 (1899) (infectious open wound); *Skillings v. Allen,* 143 Minn. 323, 173 N.W. 663 (1919) (scarlet fever); *Davis v. Rodman,* 147 Ark. 385, 227 S.W. 612 (1921) (typhoid fever); *Jones v. Stanko,* 118 Ohio St. 174, 160 N.E. 456 (1928) (smallpox); *Wojcik v. Aluminum Co. of Amer.,* 18 Misc. 2nd 740, 183 N.Y.S. 2d 351 (Sup Ct. 1959) (tuberculosis); *Hofmann v. Blackmon,* 241 So.2d 752, 753 (Fla. Dist. Ct. App. 1970) (tuberculosis); *Derrick v. Ontario Community Hosp.,* 47 Cal. App.3d 145, 154, 120 Cal. Rptr. 566, 571 (1975). All of these cases dealt with diseases far more contagious than HIV infection. Therefore, foreseeability of harm was less problematic. Most were misdiagnoses rather than duty to warn cases.

67. *Tarasoff v. Regents of Univ. of Cal.,* 17 Cal. 3rd at 435, 551 P.2d at 342, 131 Cal Rptr at 22.

68. 17 Cal.3d 425, 131 Cal. Rptr. 14, 551 P.2d 334 (1976); Prosser and Keeton (1984). *Law of Torts* (5th ed.) at 359.

69. Jennings, B., Callahan, D., and Wolf, S. (1987). The professions: public interest and common good. *Hastings Center Report, 17,* 3–11.

70. Rowe and Bridgham (1989). Executive Summary and Analysis: Laws Governing Confidentiality of HIV-Related Information—1983–1988, The George Washington University Intergovernmental Health Policy Project, 1–10; AIDS Policy Center, Intergovernmental Health Policy Project, April 1991 Update.

71. Id.

72. See Beauchamp, supra note 31.

JAMES F. CHILDRESS

Mandatory HIV Screening and Testing

Faced with epidemics, societies frequently curtail individual rights and liberties, often in ways later considered to be excessive and unnecessary. Even liberal societies have protected the public health by such measures as compulsory screening and testing, quarantine and isolation, and contact tracing. For a liberal society—that is, a society that recognizes and protects individual rights and liberties—the difficult question is, When does the public health justify overriding these rights and liberties? For several years—roughly from the late 1950s to the early 1980s—the United States considered itself largely immune to major public health crises; even though debates lingered about policies to control sexually transmitted diseases, these diseases were not viewed as major threats to individual or communal survival. During the same period, law, public policy, and social practice, including health care, provided additional protections for various individual rights and liberties. Then came AIDS with its threat to the public health, and, with the development in mid-1985 of tests for antibodies to the human immunodeficiency virus (HIV), calls to use these diagnostic tools to identify seropositive individuals through consensual and/or mandatory screening and testing (Osborn, 1987). Numerous bills were introduced in state legislatures to require testing in various contexts, such as applicants for marriage licenses, and the federal government instituted mandatory screening of immigrants, inmates in federal prisons, military personnel, etc.

Advocates of mandatory screening and testing, who often invoke the metaphor of war against AIDS, frequently leave unclear what actions would follow from the identification of HIV-antibody-positive individuals. Yet it is not possible to isolate mandatory (or even consensual) screening and testing from other possible interventions because, in contrast to vaccines, they have no impact on an epidemic. What is done with the information and with the people who test positive will determine the effect on the AIDS epidemic. Hence, a first question for all proposed HIV-antibody tests is, Why is the information wanted and what will be done with that information (as well as with the people who test positive)? There have been debates about whether sexual contacts should be traced, whether current sexual partners should be warned, whether certain employers should be notified, whether seropositive individuals should be quarantined, etc. Such questions provide the backdrop for much of the debate about mandatory screening and testing (Walters, 1988).

In this essay I assume the social ethics or political morality of a liberal society and then try to determine when such a society, under the threat to the public health from AIDS, may justifiably resort to mandatory screening and testing for HIV antibodies, thereby overriding some of its important principles and rules. After sketching the major presumptive or prima facie principles and rules that may constrain public health efforts in a liberal society, I identify some conditions that need to be met to justify infringing those principles and rules in the pursuit of public health. Then I develop a typology of screening/testing policies, and examine the issues raised by different policies. I stress throughout this discussion the central role of analogical reasoning, and I conclude with an analysis of the impact of the metaphor "war against AIDS" on our society's debates about mandatory screening and testing.

AN ETHICAL FRAMEWORK FOR ASSESSING POLICIES OF SCREENING AND TESTING

It is not necessary to belabor why control of HIV infection and AIDS is a public health concern, rather than a private, individual matter. AIDS is an infectious disease; people may be infected and infectious for many years before they are aware of their condition; there is no known cure for AIDS, which has an extremely high death rate; the suffering of AIDS patients and others is tremendous; the cost for AIDS patients is very high; and so on. Protection of the public health, including health of individuals, is a legitimate moral concern—even a moral imperative—based on the fundamental moral principles affirmed by a liberal society, including beneficence, nonmaleficence, and justice, as well as respect for persons and their autonomy (Bayer, Levine, and Wolf 1986; Beauchamp and Childress 1989; Levine and Bayer 1989). "Public health is what we, as a society, do collectively to assure the conditions in which people can be healthy. This requires that continuing and emerging threats to the health of the public be successfully countered" (Committee 1986:1). AIDS is a paradigm instance of the public health threats that must be effectively countered.

If the goal of controlling AIDS is a strong moral imperative for the society, as well as for individuals, we still have to determine which measures may and should be adopted to achieve this goal. "The AIDS virus has no civil rights"—that rhetoric often suggests that the moral imperative to control AIDS cancels all other moral imperatives. Of course, few who use this rhetoric try to justify compulsory universal screening accompanied by mass quarantine or even mass slaughter. Even so, their position rarely takes seriously enough other significant moral principles and rules. I examine some of those principles and rules and sketch what they imply for public policies to control this infectious disease. This argument hinges on the best available medical information, including evidence that the spread of AIDS usually involves consensual, intimate contact, in the form of sexual ac-

tivity or sharing intravenous (IV) drug needles and syringes, and that casual contact is not a mode of transmission. A different set of facts could justify different screening and testing policies.

The principle of respect for persons is a primary principle in the ethical framework of a liberal society (Childress 1982a,b, 1987, 1990). It implies that we should not treat people merely as means to ends. From this principle (and others) we can derive more specific rules that also direct and limit policies. Three such rules are especially important for this analysis: rules of liberty, including freedom of association; rules of privacy, including bodily integrity and decisional space; and rules of confidentiality. The principle of respect for persons and its derivative rules can be stated as individual rights or as societal obligations and duties—for example, the individual's right to privacy or the society's obligation not to violate an individual's privacy. Even if some of these rules are independent rather than derived, they are closely related to personal autonomy, for the individual can autonomously waive the rights expressed in the rules or, perhaps more accurately, can exercise those rights by yielding liberty or privacy or by granting access to previously confidential information. Furthermore, in a liberal society, overriding the principle or respect for autonomy and these rules can be justified more easily to protect others than to protect the agent himself or herself. Thus, there is a strong suspicion of paternalism, which infringes these principles and rules to protect the agent rather than others (Childress 1982a). (Of course, the goals of intervention are often mixed.) Rather than offer a theoretical foundation for the principle of respect for autonomy and the various derivative rules, I assume that they can be discerned in our constitution, laws, policies, and practices—in short, in the social ethics or political morality of a liberal society.

CONDITIONS FOR OVERRIDING PRIMA FACIE PRINCIPLES AND RULES

My task is to try to determine which, if any, policies of mandatory screening and testing for HIV antibodies can be ethically justified in a liberal society in view of the moral imperative to control AIDS and these other moral principles and rules. We have to determine both what these principles and rules mean and how much weight they have relative to other principles and rules. (For brevity I sometimes use "principles" or "rules" to cover both principles and rules.) Some apparent violations of rules may not really be violations; upon closer inspection they may turn out to be consistent with the rules properly interpreted. And none of these rules is absolute; each one can be justifiably overridden in order to protect the public health under some conditions. However, in a liberal society these rules are more than mere maxims or rules of thumb, which yield to any and every utilitarian objection. If these rules are not absolute or mere maxims, is there an alternative conception of their weight or stringency? They may be construed as *prima facie* binding; that is, in and of themselves they have heavy moral weight or strong binding power. Because they are prima facie binding, it is necessary to justify any departures from them, and the process of justification involves meeting a heavy burden of proof (see Beauchamp and Childress 1989).

At least five conditions must be met to justify infringements of these rules (see Childress 1987, from which some of this discussion has been drawn). These conditions, which are called *justificatory conditions*, are effectiveness, proportionality, necessity, least infringement, and explanation and justification to the parties protected by the rules. These conditions express the logic of prima facie duties or rights, i.e., how principles and rules with such weight or stringency are to be approached, as well as the substance of the liberal principles and rules. A presupposition of these conditions is that the goal—both expressed and latent—is to protect public health, that is, the health of the community and the individuals within it, rather than to express moralistic judgments about individuals and their conduct or to exclude seropositive individuals from the community by subjecting them to discrimination or denying them access to needed services (Field 1990:54; see also Bayer, Levine, and Wolf 1986; Levine and Bayer 1989).

First, it is necessary to show that a policy infringing these rules will probably realize the goal of protecting public health. This first condition is one of effectiveness. A policy that infringes the moral rules but is ineffective simply has no justification; it is arbitrary and capricious. An ineffective policy to control HIV infection that infringes no moral rules may be wasteful, unwise, and even stupid, but if it infringes moral rules, there is a decisive moral argument against it.

Second, it is necessary to show that the probable benefits of a policy infringing rules outweigh both the moral rule(s) infringed and any negative consequences. This condition, which may be called proportionality, is complex, for it involves considering not only the weight of the infringed moral rule but also other harms, costs, and burdens that may flow from the infringement. For example, it is necessary to consider not only the weight of the rule of privacy but also other probably negative effects, such as discrimination, that may befall the one whose privacy is infringed. (As I argue later, to justify policies that *impose* community, it may also be essential to *express* community through protections against such negative consequences. Indeed, if community is expressed through such protections, imposition may be less necessary.)

Third, it is not sufficient to meet the first two conditions of effectiveness and proportionality and thus to show that infringement of these rules will produce better consequences for more people. As prima facie binding, these rules direct us to seek alternative ways to realize the end of public health, short of infringing the rules. For example, if it is possible to protect the public health without infringing liberty and privacy (and other moral rules), then the society should do so. This condition is one of necessity, last resort, or lack of a feasible alternative. Priority belongs to policies that do not infringe the rules of liberty, privacy, and confidentiality. For example, policies that seek to educate people about acting in certain ways have moral priority over policies that force people to act in certain ways. Under some circumstances, however, where coercive policies would be effective and proportionate, they can be justified if they are also necessary means to protect the public health. Many of the proposed policies of mandatory screening fail this third test.

Fourth, even when a liberal society is justified in infringing its moral rules to protect the public health, it is obligated to seek policies that least infringe its rules, for only the degree or extent of infringement that is necessary to realize the end that is sought can be justified. For example, when liberty is at stake, the society should seek the least restrictive alternative; when privacy is at stake, it should seek the least intrusive and invasive alternative; and when confidentiality is at stake, it should disclose only the amount and kind of information needed for effective action. This fourth condition may be called that of least infringement.

Finally, even when a public policy that infringes one or more moral rules satisfies all four prior conditions, the principle of respect for persons may generate additional requirements. This principle may require that the society inform those whose liberty, privacy, and confidential relations have been infringed. In many cases, such as coercive screening for HIV antibody, the infringements will be evident to the parties affected, but this may not be true in all cases, especially if secrecy or deception is involved. As Sissela Bok (1978) notes, in some contexts, secret or deceptive actions may be more disrespectful and insulting to the parties affected than coercive actions. Hence, the society may have a duty to disclose, and even to justify, the actions to the person and even in some contexts to undertake compensatory measures. Even if it is essential to infringe a person's rights in order to protect the public health, that person should not be reduced to a mere means to the goal of public health. The crucial point can also be stated through an image drawn from Robert Nozick (1968): Overridden moral principles and rules leave "moral traces." They do not evaporate or simply disappear when they are overridden; they are outweighed, not canceled.

As is true of much moral, political, and legal reasoning, this process of reasoning about the justification of mandatory HIV-antibody tests is to a great extent analogical. The principle of universalizability or formal justice requires treating similar cases in a similar way. Hence it is necessary to consider the relevant similarities and differences among candidate targets for screening, not only for HIV antibodies but also for other conditions, such as genetic ones. Reasoning in a liberal society not only considers precedent cases—for example, the relevant similarities and differences between HIV-antibody screening and other mandatory screening policies that have been held to be justifiable—but also the precedents mandatory HIV-antibody screening would create. As Margaret Somerville (1989) argues, "HIV and AIDS must not be treated in isolation; comparison with analogous situations is mandatory."

MAJOR TYPES OF SCREENING/TESTING POLICIES

In order to apply the principle of respect for personal autonomy and its derivative rules, all conceived as prima facie binding, along with the conditions for justifying their infringement, it is necessary to identify the range of proposed policies of mandatory screening and testing for HIV antibodies. The following chart indicates some of the most important options: policies of screening/testing may be consensual or compulsory and universal or selective. [See Table 1.]

The term "screening" usually refers to testing groups, while the term "testing" usually refers to testing individuals. However, even in mass screening, the individual is tested as part of the targeted group. Thus, I continue to use both terms as appropriate without drawing a sharp distinction between them. A more important distinction concerns the *scope* of the screening or testing: Is it universal or selective?

UNIVERSAL SCREENING

There is simply no adequate justification for *universal screening*, whether voluntary or compulsory (numbers 1 and 2). Even serious proposals for widespread screening usually fall short of universal screening. For example, Rhame and Maki (1989: 1253) recommend "HIV testing vigorously to all U.S. adults under the age of sixty regardless of their reported risk history." Universal screening is not necessary to protect the public health; HIV infection is not widespread outside groups engaging in high-risk activities; screening in groups or areas with low seroprevalence produces a high rate of false positives; universal screening would be very costly and would not be cost effective—the funds could be spent more effectively on education; and its potential negative effects, including discrimination, would outweigh any potential benefits. It is not even justifiable to encourage everyone to be tested.

If universal consensual screening is not justifiable, there is, a fortiori, no justification for universal

		Table 1. Screening/Testing Policies	
		Degree of Voluntariness	
		Consensual	**Compulsory**
Extent of Screening	Universal	1	2
	Selective	3	4

compulsory screening, which would also violate respect for autonomy and rules of liberty, privacy (and probably confidentiality), without compensating benefit. The main rationale for compulsory universal screening is that seropositive individuals can then reduce risks to others. There is evidence of some individual behavioral change following disclosure of seropositivity, especially with counseling (Cates and Handsfield 1988; McCusker et al. 1988), but there is no evidence that mandatory testing would produce the same level of voluntary changes in risk taking and risk imposition (Field 1990:58–59; Gostin 1987: 9–10).

Identification of and disclosure to the individuals who are seropositive do not necessarily translate into benefits for others, apart from additional interventions. And appropriate education and counseling, apart from mandatory testing, could be effective ways to realize the same end, especially because universal precautions are recommended whether the individual is seropositive or seronegative (for a survey of published reports, see Becker and Joseph 1988). In view of the current scientific and medical evidence, compulsory universal screening fails to meet the five conditions identified earlier for justified breaches of the relevant moral principles and rules. Universal precautions, pursued through education, are morally preferable to mandatory universal screening, and the latter is not demonstrably more effective and would produce serious negative consequences.

SELECTIVE SCREENING

Consensual or voluntary selective screening may appear to pose no moral problems, but who should be encouraged to be tested, who should bear the costs, what sort of pretest and posttest counseling should be provided, and what conditions make the decision to have the test a rational one? Individuals making rational choices will consent to testing only when they perceive a favorable risk-benefit ratio. And "more than most medical tests, HIV screening has major benefits and harms that must be weighed" (Lo et al. 1989:730). In all risk-benefit analyses, including assessments of policies, the comparison is between the probability of a harm of some magnitude and the probability of a benefit of some magnitude (O'Brien 1989). Since "risk" is a probabilistic term, while "benefit" is not, the necessity of determining both probability and magnitude of both benefits and harms is sometimes neglected.

If we assume the accuracy of the test results, the possible *benefits* of testing to *seronegative* individuals include reassurance, the possibility of making future plans, and the motivation to make behavioral changes to prevent infection, while the possible *benefits* to *seropositive* individuals include closer medical follow-up, including prognoses of various stages, earlier use of azidothymidine (AZT) (and other treatments), prophylaxis or other care for associated diseases, protection of loved ones, and clearer plans for the future. There appears to be a very *low risk* of harm to *seronegative* individuals, even though there have been occasional reports of discrimination against individuals who have voluntarily taken the HIV-antibody test but with negative results. There are, however, *major risks* to *seropositive* individuals. (For these risks and possible benefits, see Lo et al. 1989). These risks may be identified as psychological and social (with considerable overlap and interaction). The psychological risks include anxiety and depression—followed by a higher rate of suicide than for the population at large (Marzuk et al. 1988)—while the social risks include stigma, discrimination, and breaches of confidentiality.

Clearly the society can have a major impact on the risk-benefit analyses of potential candidates for voluntary testing. On the one hand, the medical benefits are possible only if seropositive individuals can gain access to them. Hence, even on the benefit side, the problem is not merely medical because of the social problem of access to health care. On the other hand, the risks can be greatly reduced by societal decisions to allocate funds and to establish strong rules to protect individual rights and liberties. The society should provide resources for pretest and posttest counseling both to help the individual and also to reduce risks to others, and it should protect seropositive individuals from breaches of privacy and confidentiality and from discrimination in housing, employment, insurance, health and social services, etc. Without societal support and protection, the social risks may outweigh the benefits, including any medical benefits, of the test for rational individuals.

If voluntary or consensual testing of selected groups can be effective, in some contexts, then there is no justification for compulsory screening of those groups. The liberal justificatory framework imposes this necessary condition: moral principles and rules are not to be infringed if the same important ends—in this case, the public health—can be realized without their infringement. Furthermore, the society may even have to bear additional costs to protect its important principles and rules.

The requirement, expressed by the terms "mandatory" and "compulsory," may be imposed on the one to be tested or on the tester or on both. For example, in the context of screening donated blood for transfusions, the term "mandatory" refers in the first instance to the obligation imposed on the organizations collecting blood. And such "mandatory" screening may be imposed or permitted by the state. The one area of mandatory selective screening that is morally settled and uncontroversial is screening all donated (or sold) blood, organs, sperm, and ova, in part because recipients cannot take other measures to protect themselves. In this area universal precautions cannot work without screening and testing.

As is evident in programs of screening donated blood, many policies of screening are actually mixes of voluntary actions and compulsory actions. While individuals can choose to donate blood or not, their blood will be tested if they do donate. Another good example is the policy of screening recruits into the military (Bayer 1989:158–161). The U.S. armed forces consist of volunteers, who are tested for HIV antibodies upon entry (and then again at least once a year). It could be argued that volunteers for the armed forces consent to HIV testing, because they voluntarily enter an institution where screening is compulsory, and that the mandatory screening thus does not violate any of the volunteers' rights. This argument has merit, but it does not adequately address the question whether the society can justify its policy by the conditions identified earlier. The major express rationale is that each member of the armed forces is a potential donor of blood for transfusions on the battlefield; hence the rationale is comparable to the one that governs screening donated blood. Even if this rationale is solid, along with the rationale of protecting HIV-infected people from live virus vaccines used in the armed forces, there is also reason to suspect that the military's homophobia was a factor in the decision. Furthermore, there is concern about the precedent this mandatory screening creates, especially in the invocation of the cost of future health care (Bayer 1989:160).

Voluntariness may be compromised in various ways. We tend to think of coercion as the major compromise of voluntariness—for example, forcing someone to undergo a test for HIV antibody. However, conditional requirements—if you want X, then you have to do Y—may also be morally problematic. For example, requiring HIV antibody testing as a condition for obtaining some strongly desired benefit, such as a marriage license, may constitute an undue incentive, even if it is not, strictly speaking, coercive because the person can choose to decline the benefit (for an important discussion of coercion, see Wertheimer 1987). One important question then is whether it is fair to impose the condition, even if the person is free to take it or leave it. This question expresses the important general point that selection of targets for mandatory screening—or even for voluntary screening—is in part a matter of justice in the distribution of benefits and burdens (see Fletcher 1987) and that not all important moral issues are reducible to voluntary choices. The justificatory conditions identified earlier serve as important selection criteria.

Nevertheless, because of the centrality of the principle of respect for personal autonomy in a liberal framework, it is not surprising that consent plays such an important role in the analysis and assessment of screening policies. When an individual gives valid consent to testing, there is no violation of his or her personal autonomy and liberty of action. Nor does consensual testing violate the rule of privacy, for the individual voluntarily chooses to surrender some of his or her privacy. And, finally, if a person grants others access to information about his or her HIV-antibody status, the rule of confidentiality is not violated. In a liberal framework, valid consent creates rights that did not previously exist. I use the terms "voluntary" testing and "consensual" testing interchangeably to refer to testing with the individual's voluntary, informed consent. It is irrelevant whether he or she requested a test or only accepted a recommended test.

What counts as consent? This question becomes important because people have been held to consent in various ways, not simply by express oral or written statements. And some varieties of consent have been invoked to override a person's express wishes and choices. I discuss this topic in the context of selective screening of hospital patients for HIV antibodies. The question is whether the institutional rules of consent should be structured to authorize HIV antibody testing without express, specific consent.

The term "routine" often covers several types of screening and testing. However, this term is seriously misleading without further qualification, for its ethical significance is unclear until we can determine whether the screening will be done routinely, without notice or the possibility of refusal, or whether it will be offered routinely with the possibility of refusal (see Walters 1990).

When a hospital patient consents to HIV-antibody testing after being informed about the risks and benefits of the test—including whether the intended benefits are primarily for the patient or for the caregivers—there is no breach of moral principles. But are there forms of consent in addition to express and specific oral or written consent that can create rights on the part of hospitals to test patients?

First, *tacit consent*, a favorite tool of political theorists in the contract tradition, is expressed silently or passively by omissions or by failure to indicate or signify dissent (see Simmons 1976; for an analysis of varieties of consent in bioethics, see Childress 1982a). If a newly admitted hospital patient is silent when told that the HIV-antibody test will be performed, along with other tests, unless he objects, his silence may constitute valid (though tacit) consent, if there is understanding and voluntariness—the same conditions that are important for express oral or written consent. But if the question is not asked, the patient's failure to dissent from the test, without any notice or additional information, is *presumed* to be consent on the basis of a presumed general understanding of hospital testing policy. And its validity as consent is suspect, despite the patient's right to dissent or opt out.

Whereas tacit consent or presumed consent is expressed through failures to dissent, *implied* or implicit consent is, in part, inferred from actions. Consent to a specific action may be implied by general consent to professional authority or consent to a set of actions. Does a person's voluntary admission to the hospital imply consent to the HIV-antibody test without express consent? Again much will depend on the patient's understanding. However, rather than rely on general consent or consent to several tests, hospitals should be obligated to seek specific express consent for HIV-antibody tests because of the psychological and social risks of the tests and their results.

There are two major reasons for specific disclosure and explicit consent. On the one hand, the diagnostic or therapeutic procedure may be invasive—e.g., drawing blood. But if a patient has consented to blood drawing for various tests to determine his or her medical condition, there is no additional invasion of his or her body to test that blood for HIV antibodies. Then the second major reason for specific disclosure and consent enters—the risk to the patient. Even where the blood has already been drawn, the test has the psychological and social risks noted above, and explicit, specific consent should be sought (Swartz 1988). (This argument does not exclude the possibility and justifiability of unlinked testing of blood samples in the hospital in order to determine seroprevalence as part of epidemiological studies because of the absence of psychological and social risks.)

A recent Virginia law (Virginia Code 32.1–45.1) invokes "deemed consent" in permitting a health care provider to test a patient's blood, without specific consent, following the provider's exposure to the patient's body fluids under circumstances where HIV infection might be spread. In that case, "the patient whose body fluids were involved in the exposures shall be deemed to have consented to testing for infection with human immunodeficiency virus [and] to have consented to the release of such test results to the person who was exposed." The law assigns to health care providers the responsibility to inform patients of this provision of deemed consent prior to the provision of health care services, in other than emergency circumstances. Presumably, the patient's acceptance of health care following disclosure of this statutory provision counts as consent (deemed consent). Even if the consent is valid, the fairness of imposing this condition is still an important question.

Because consent is so important an implication of the principle of respect for personal autonomy, we often resort to fictions such as deemed consent or one of the other varieties of "consent" even when they do not appear to constitute valid consent. We extend the meaning of rules of consent and the principle of respect for personal autonomy in order to avoid conflicts with our other moral principles. But such fictions may obscure important moral conflicts. It may be more defensible to indicate that the society believes it can justifiably override a patient's autonomy, liberty, privacy, and confidentiality in order to obtain and provide information about an individual's HIV-antibody status to a health care provider who has been exposed to the risk of infection in the provision of care. The most attractive argument in favor of deemed consent is that it incorporates the patient into a larger moral community of shared concern, but this does not negate the cost of the fiction.

There is evidence that hospitals sometimes test patients for HIV antibodies without their consent (and without providing information about actions to reduce risks) (see Henry, Maki and Crossley 1988; Sherer 1988). In general, hospitals are not justified in testing patients for HIV antibodies without their specific consent, either to benefit the patients themselves or to warn caregivers to take additional precautions. Information that a patient is seronegative may create a false sense of security on the part of professionals, in view of the long time that may elapse between exposure to HIV and the development of antibodies. Thus, the best protection, though not an inexpensive or perfect one, is offered by universal precautions. In one recent study there was no evidence "that preoperative testing for HIV infection would reduce the frequency of accidental exposures to blood" (Gerberding et al. 1990: 1788).

Where exposure has already occurred, and the blood is not available for testing, it is very difficult to justify forcible extraction of the patient's blood to test for HIV antibodies to reduce the caregiver's anxieties. Where the blood is already available, it is easier to justify testing after exposure, even against the patient's wishes. However, the analogy with the hepatitis B virus argues against mandatory testing, whether before or after exposure (Field 1990:104). One ethically acceptable possibility would be to obtain patients' advance express consent—not merely deemed consent—to testing if accidental exposure occurs. (I discuss testing health care professionals below.)

PREMARITAL SCREENING

State-mandated premarital screening for HIV antibodies is another mix of voluntary choices and compulsory screening; individuals choose to apply for marriage licenses, but the test is required as a condition of application. Historical analogies play an important role in debates about this public health policy. For example, Gary Bauer, former assistant to President Reagan for policy development, uses mandatory premarital screening as an example of the "routine testing" that is similar to measures taken in the past to deal with threatening epidemics. He ar-

gues that mandatory premarital screening for syphilis contributed to a "sharp reduction in the infant mortality rate from syphilis" (Bauer 1987:1). However, Larry Gostin contends that "statutes for syphilis screening were largely regarded as a failed experiment" (1987:16) and notes they have been repealed by most states.

The analogy with screening for syphilis is interesting in part because, in contrast to HIV infection, syphilis is treatable and infected individuals can be rendered noninfectious. Many argue that it is even more imperative to require premarital HIV tests as a condition for marriage licenses because there is no cure for AIDS, a fatal disease. By contrast, opponents contend that the absence of effective treatment is a good reason not to require the tests. Because antibiotics can cure syphilis, it is justifiable to withhold a marriage license until there is proof of a cure, but "it would be contrary to public policy to bar marriage to seropositive individuals," who cannot now be cured (Gostin 1987:17).

The legislatures (Illinois and Louisiana) that passed statutes mandating premarital screening subsequently rescinded those statutes, largely on grounds that they were not cost effective. A report (Turnock and Kelly 1989) on the first six months of experience in Illinois indicated that only 8 of 70,846 applicants for marriage licenses were found to be seropositive, while the cost of the testing program for that period was estimated at $2.5 million, or $312,000 for each seropositive individual identified. Furthermore, half of those identified as seropositive admitted having engaged in risky behavior and could probably have been identified more efficiently through voluntary programs aimed at populations with a higher seroprevalence rate. Illinois also experienced a 22.5 percent decrease (a total of approximately 10,300) in the number of marriage licenses, while neighboring states granted licenses to a significantly larger number of Illinois residents than usual. Since the applicants had to cover the costs of the tests, the state of Illinois did not have to determine the most cost-effective ways to spend public money and make trade-offs (Field 1990). Illinois did, however, lose the revenue from marriage licenses, estimated at $77,250 for six months. The authors conclude what policy analysts had predicted prior to the experiment: "The Illinois experience with premarital testing provides a strong argument against widespread or publicly supported HIV antibody screening of low prevalence populations" (Turnock and Kelly 1989; see also Cleary et al. 1987).

While many of the proposed policies of compulsory selective screening fail the test of necessity, because there are viable alternatives, the policy of mandatory premarital screening also fails the prior conditions of effectiveness and proportionality. There is no evidence that the screening program prevented any additional illnesses and that it was a "rational or effective public health policy" (Belongia, Vergeront, and Davis 1989:2198). It mistakenly assumed that sex begins only after the marriage, and it may even have been counterproductive in driving some away from the institution of marriage. Furthermore, the costs may have kept some low-income people from applying for marriage licenses. Finally, the important public health objective of protecting spouses (and future offspring) can be pursued in other ways that will not compromise respect for personal autonomy and yet will probably be more effective and cost effective — provision of information about HIV risks and provision of voluntary testing with counseling, perhaps free of charge, to all applicants for marriage licenses. It appears that the marriage license setting is an appropriate one "for promoting individual HIV risk assessment with educational materials" (Joseph 1989:3456).

SCREENING PREGNANT WOMEN AND NEWBORNS

One major goal of premarital screening is to prevent infected offspring of the marriage. Because mandatory premarital screening programs are failures, voluntary premarital screening is limited, and HIV infections may occur after marriage, there has been interest in screening pregnant women and newborns at least in selected settings. Since all fifty states and the District of Columbia mandate neonatal screening for several diseases, the question arises, Why not treat HIV "just like any other disease?" However, as Kathleen Nolan (1989:55) notes, even if HIV infection were strictly analogous to these other medical conditions, such as phenylketonuria (PKU), it would be difficult to determine what it would mean to treat HIV infection "just like any other disease," because the states have various laws — for example, there is no condition for which all states mandate screening, and many states allow parental refusal. Furthermore, HIV infection differs from other diseases because of its social risks. For example, there are "boarder babies" who cannot leave the hospital because no one will take these HIV-infected babies. Hence, HIV infection, Nolan (1989:56) argues, is best viewed as a "separate case."

Still affirming the importance of analogical reasoning, Nolan (1989) identifies three criteria for justifying neonatal *genetic* screening: (1) the seriousness of the genetic condition, (2) availability of presymptomatic interventions that effectively prevent serious injury, and (3) an acceptable benefit-cost ratio. While HIV infection satisfies the first criterion, it does not clearly satisfy the other two in neonatal cases, except where there are specific reasons for testing, and then the parents will usually consent. (Furthermore, there is the problem that neonatal and infant screening, for over a year, will reflect maternal antibodies without specifically reflecting neonatal or infant infection.) In summary, Nolan argues, "calls for mandatory neonatal screening emerge primarily from beneficent clinical attitudes towards newborns, and they are rejected primarily on the grounds that not enough benefit accrues at present to justify overriding parental autonomy and family values" (1989:59) (see also Levine and Bayer 1989:1665).

But do similar arguments apply to *prenatal testing*? According to LeRoy Walters (1990), HIV testing in pregnancy should be handled in a way similar to the ways we have handled prenatal diagnosis for fetal genetic conditions or anatomic abnormalities. Prenatal HIV testing involves screening the pregnant woman, especially on behalf of her future offspring or the society, including the professionals involved in her care. Even though there may be some potential medical benefits to the pregnant woman, she also bears the social risks identified earlier. In view of the risk of transmission of HIV infection to her offspring — in the range of 25 to 50 percent — there are debates about whether it is morally responsible to continue or to terminate pregnancy and thus what counselors should recommend if they are directive (Nolan 1989; Walters 1990). Once a woman is pregnant, the test for HIV antibodies "can help contain HIV only if it leads to abortion" (Field 1990:95).

Even if the society could agree on the morally responsible choice, which is highly unlikely in view of the abortion controversy, there are further moral questions about the legal enforcement of moral obligations. Efforts to mandate prenatal testing would probably be ineffective and even counterproductive. For example, mandatory prenatal screening of all pregnant women who appear at clinics in high seroprevalence areas would put them at social risk if they were seropositive. Thus, there is "the very real possibility that mandated or universal testing during pregnancy could result in marked decreases in the number of disadvantaged women to seek prenatal care" (Nolan 1989:64). Thus, the most defensible policy, because the most respectful of pregnant women's autonomy and also the most productive of desirable consequences, is to offer pregnant women, in high seroprevalence areas or with risk factors, prenatal testing for HIV with adequate information so that they can make their own decisions, with appropriate pretest and posttest counseling and support services.

It is also important, as Nolan (1989) reminds us, to consider whether we are following defensible precedents (historical analogies) for genetic diseases and what precedents our policies regarding HIV testing may set for other genetic diseases that in the future can be detected in utero. Indeed, she suggests, our different responses to cystic fibrosis and HIV infection suggest that morally extraneous factors such as race and geography play significant parts in our societal and professional judgments, particularly in the movement from nondirective to directive counseling (for example, counselors appear to be more directive in urging HIV-infected women to abort).

In summary, mandatory prenatal testing to protect offspring appears relatively ineffective because nothing can be done to prevent the infection of the fetus; morally controversial because abortion is the only way to prevent another HIV-infected infant, and yet fetuses are infected in only 25 to 50 percent of the cases of HIV-infected pregnant women; and counterproductive in driving pregnant women away from settings where HIV screening is compulsory.

PRISONERS AND OTHERS IN STATE CUSTODY

There are several institutional settings in which mandatory screening might appear to be justified. These are mainly custodial settings, such as prisons and institutions for the mentally infirm or mentally ill. I concentrate on prisoners, with brief attention to arrested prostitutes and patients in public psychiatric facilities. Many prisoners have been subjected to mandatory screening, because of the risk of rape and the frequency of consensual sexual intercourse in prisons where there is also high seroprevalence. Even if mandatory screening of prisoners, followed by quarantine or isolation, could reduce the spread of HIV infection, it is not clearly cost-effective and it imposes risks of injustice on seropositive prisoners, "ranging

from unequal facilities for inmates to violations of a number of hard-won rights of prisoners" (Macklin 1986:22). Furthermore, it is not the least intrusive or restrictive alternative. Indeed, on grounds of respect for persons, as well as other moral principles, it is crucial for the society to reduce nonconsensual sexual intercourse in prisons (Gostin 1987:21; Field 1990:81–91). It is also important to educate prisoners and perhaps even to provide condoms to reduce the risk of transmission of HIV through consensual sexual activities. Even the provision of voluntary testing may be useful; in one study in Oregon, "Two-thirds of all inmates, including those at highest risk for HIV, sought HIV counseling and testing when given the opportunity" (Andrus et al. 1989). Nevertheless, as Ruth Macklin argues, "it would not be unethical to subject to a blood test any prisoner who has sexually assaulted another inmate, and if he is found seropositive, to isolate him permanently from the general prison population" (1986:22).

Similarly, it would not be unethical, in terms of the principles of a liberal society, to confine a recalcitrant prostitute who puts others at serious risk, for example, by continuing to practice unsafe sex. A more difficult question is whether it is justifiable to require prostitutes to undergo HIV testing. Although prostitution is widely viewed as a major route for the spread of HIV infection among heterosexuals, Martha Field (1990) argues that the overall HIV infection rate among prostitutes does not justify targeting them for mandatory testing, that prostitutes tend to be well informed about safe sex practices, and that more than 99 percent of all prostitutes are never arrested. Thus, mandatory testing of prostitutes does not appear to satisfy the conditions identified earlier. However, if states pass laws to require prostitutes to be tested when in state custody, Field views two conditions as essential. First, testing should be required only of those who are convicted, not those who are arrested, because of the legal presumption of innocence. Second, patrons should be tested if prostitutes are tested; "although patrons are seldom arrested or convicted, both parties are guilty of criminal behavior that is capable of transmission" (1990:94).

Patients in state psychiatric institutions may be at risk of transmitting HIV infection through sexual intercourse. As in the case of prisoners, the state should attempt to prevent rape in psychiatric institutions—and not only because of the risk of HIV infection. Since many psychiatric patients are unable to benefit from efforts to educate them about HIV infection and safe sex, there may be a stronger argument for identi-fying and isolating HIV-infected patients. Even so it is necessary to make sure that there are no other alterna-tives and that the least restrictive alternative is chosen.

IMMIGRATION AND INTERNATIONAL TRAVEL

"Seeking to secure our national borders against an 'in-vasion' of AIDS, the United States now requires HIV-antibody testing of 500,000 immigrants, nonimmi-grants, and refugees annually. In addition, in what may be the most massive use of HIV testing in this country, more than 2.5 million aliens living in the United States must be tested in order to qualify for le-gal residence" (Wolchok 1989:128). Historically, soci-eties have responded to epidemics by closing their borders, but the current U.S. policy is ironic because the United States is probably a net exporter of HIV in-fection. Yet HIV infection was added to the list of des-ignated diseases (now eight, including infectious lep-rosy, active tuberculosis, gonorrhea, and infectious syphilis) for which aliens can be excluded from the United States. In view of the precedent set by listing the other exclusionary diseases, it did not seem to many to be unreasonable to add HIV infection. Now temporary visitors to the United States have to indi-cate their HIV-antibody status when they apply for a visa, and the immigration officer may require a test. Applicants for permanent residence must undergo a serologic test for HIV infection (and syphilis) and if positive cannot receive permanent residence. Because the costs of the program fall on the applicants, the so-ciety does not have to face the question of trade-offs in the use of public funds.

Analogical reasoning is also critical here, not only in considering historical precedents but also in consid-ering the implications of the mandatory screening of aliens for other groups. Margaret Somerville notes that viewing prospective immigrants who are HIV in-fected as "a danger to public health and safety would necessarily set a precedent that all HIV-infected peo-ple (already in the country) could be similarly charac-terized" (1989:891). In addition, it sets precedents for genetic screening as more and more tests become available.

Larry Gostin and his colleagues argue that "a just and efficacious travel and immigration policy would not exclude people because of their serologic status unless they posed a danger to the community through casual transmission" (Gostin et al. 1990:1745–1746). Indeed, the list of excludable conditions should be re-vised because only active tuberculosis poses a threat

of casual transmission. Immigrants are thus not a ma-jor threat to the public health, and screening them will have only a modest impact on the course of the epi-demic in the United States, which already has more than one million HIV-infected persons. In addition, the screening program discourages travelers from be-ing tested and "drives further underground undocu-mented aliens who live in the United States and re-duces their incentive to seek counseling and preventative care" (Wolchok 1989:142). Finally, cur-rent U.S. policy does not contribute to efforts to con-trol HIV infection in the international community (Gostin et al. 1990).

Since the current screening program does not con-tribute significantly to public health objectives, the major argument for excluding seropositive immigrants appears to be the cost to the society of providing health care. It may not be intrinsically unjust for a so-ciety to exclude immigrants on grounds of the costs of providing health care, but several commentators co-gently argue that "it is inequitable . . . to use cost as a reason to exclude people infected with HIV, for there are no similar exclusionary policies for those with other costly chronic diseases, such as heart disease or cancer" (Gostin et al. 1990:1746). Their argument rests on the requirement of justice to treat similar cases in a similar way. And, as is true of each pro-posed screening target, screening immigrants raises larger philosophical and ethical questions about the boundaries of the moral community.

OTHER AREAS OF SELECTIVE SCREENING

I have concentrated on a few areas to indicate how the liberal framework of principles, rules, and justifica-tory conditions applies to proposed policies of manda-tory HIV-antibody screening and testing. The argu-ments extend, *mutatis mutandis*, to other proposed policies. For example, what we know about the trans-mission of HIV renders mandatory screening in the workplace inappropriate, unless there is exposure to body fluids under circumstances that could transmit the virus.

Concern has been expressed about the possibility that health care professionals, particularly dentists and surgeons, might transmit the virus to their patients during invasive procedures. In July 1990, the Centers for Disease Control (CDC) reported a case of "possi-ble transmission" of HIV to a patient during the re-moval of two of her teeth by a dentist who had AIDS.

Although "the possibility of another source of infection cannot be entirely excluded," the CDC noted the absence of any other reported risk factors and a close relation between the viral DNA sequences from the patient and the dentist ("Possible Transmission" 1990:489). During the same week, researchers reported that there was no evidence that a Tennessee surgeon with HIV infection had infected any of his surgical patients, many of whom consented to HIV tests (Mishu et al. 1990). In view of the mode of transmission of HIV "it would be unexpected if HIV transmission" does not occur in surgical procedures (Rhame 1990:507). It is important, however, to keep the risk of such transmission in perspective. The probability is very low, perhaps between one in 100,000 to one in one million operations (Rhame 1990). While the risk is "exceedingly remote" of infection for any single patient, "the cumulative risk over a surgical career is real" (Gostin 1990b). The main risks appear to be in seriously invasive procedures, particularly vaginal hysterectomies or pelvic surgery, where there is "blind" (i.e., not directly visualized) use of sharp surgical tools (Rhame 1990). If there are grounds for restricting the activities of any surgeon—or dentist—who is known to be HIV infected, then there are probable grounds for mandatory testing to determine which ones are HIV infected. This area requires further careful attention, and the conclusions—at least for some forms of surgery—are likely to be applicable to both health care professionals and patients, since each party may put the other at risk of HIV infection.

Sometimes the goal of testing is to reduce costs rather than to prevent transmission of HIV infection. Both goals are present in some screening policies—for example, immigration and military screening. The goal of saving funds is often primary in workplace screening, and it is clearly the only concern in insurance screening. It is not unreasonable or even unjust for insurance companies to screen and for states to allow them to screen life and health insurance applicants for HIV antibodies, just as they screen for other conditions. It is, however, a failure of justice, compassion, and care for the society, through the federal and state governments, not to provide funds so that HIV-infected individuals and other sick people can obtain needed health care. In short, the fundamental problem is not the actions of insurance companies but rather the larger societal response to the health care needs of its citizens, including those with HIV infection.

CONCLUSION:
THE WAR AGAINST AIDS

Not only do societies often react (and, at least in retrospect, overreact) through coercive measures to epidemics of communicable disease, they frequently do so in the name of *war* against the diseases. The metaphor of "the war against AIDS" has been very prominent in justifications of mandatory screening and testing. "Under the guise of a war against AIDS," one commentator notes, "American politics have recently become enamored of an argument over testing citizens" for HIV antibody (Wood 1987:35). Reflecting the prominence of military metaphors, Larry Gostin observes that it often appears that "the first line of defense in combatting AIDS is to identify carriers of the virus by systematic screening" (1987:21). And, in a sensitive discussion of major vocabularies of concern about AIDS, Monroe Price notes that "the crisis of epidemic is a natural substitute for the crisis of war," and "the question is whether the AIDS epidemic will become such a serious threat that, in the public's mind, it takes on the stature of war" (1989:81,84).

The metaphor of war is natural in our sociocultural context when a serious threat to a large number of human lives requires the mobilization of societal resources, especially when that threat comes from biological organisms, such as viruses, that attack the human body. For example, the military metaphor is one way to galvanize the society and to marshal its resources for an effective counterattack, and AIDS activists may even appeal to it for this purpose (Kramer 1990). The metaphor has, however, other entailments that need to be questioned and perhaps even opposed, especially in our sociocultural context. (On the war metaphor, see Childress 1982a; Ross 1989a and 1989b; Sontag 1990).

From the beginning of the war against AIDS, identification of the enemy has been a major goal. Once the virus was identified as the primary enemy, it became possible to develop technologies to identify human beings who carry or harbor the virus. This led to what Ronald Bayer calls the "politics of identification" (1989). How are antibody-positive individuals to be viewed? As carriers of HIV, are they enemies to be fought? Should the society try to identify them? And how should it act on the information that a particular individual carries or harbors the virus? The line between the virus and the carrier becomes very tenuous, and the carrier tends to become an enemy just as the virus he or she carries. However much Surgeon General Everett Koop could argue that this war is against the virus, not against the people, that distinction is too subtle for many in the community. Furthermore, because the society does not consider many actions that lead to exposure to HIV as "innocent" and even views the associated life-styles as a threat to dominant social values, it is not surprising that this metaphor of war often coexists with metaphors of AIDS as punishment and as otherness (Price 1989; Ross 1989a and 1989b).

The military metaphor tends to justify coercive measures, such as quarantine and isolation of internal threats. In World War II the United States sent Japanese-Americans to internment camps, without due process, and with the approval of the U.S. Supreme court in *Korematsu v. United States* in 1944. These coercive policies were later discredited, and Congress even approved reparations to those who were interned. However, the coercive policy of identification and internment "demonstrates how, in times of war, like times of public health crisis, the actions of government become clothed with an unusual inviolability" (Price 1989:82). And it is even worse when the public health crisis is itself construed as warfare, because of the disjunction between "peacetime procedures" and "wartime needs" (Justice Douglas, quoted in Price 1989:84).

The metaphor of war against AIDS would not be so dangerous if our society had a better appreciation of the moral constraints on resort to and conduct of warfare, represented in the just war tradition (Childress 1982b). The justification and limitation of war, including the means employed, follow the pattern of the prima facie principles and conditions for justified infringements identified earlier. In general, like a dinosaur, the United States has been slow to engage in war but then hard to control once it starts to act. After AIDS appeared, the early societal response was limited in part because the disease was viewed as a threat mainly to those on the margins of society, especially gays, but then when AIDS was viewed as a threat to the larger society, the response was conceived in terms of war. In general, the United States has tended to engage in total war, with unlimited objectives and unlimited means, as expressed in our willingness to destroy cities in Vietnam in order to save them. In the war against AIDS it is important to recognize both limited objectives and limited

means. In contrast to Susan Sontag (1990), I do not believe that the metaphor of war should be retired, but its logic must be carefully explored and its application limited by "just war" criteria and supplemented by other metaphors.

In discussions of the war against disease, caring has often been viewed as an alternative metaphor. If the military metaphor tends to conflate the virus and the carriers of the virus, the caring metaphor tends to focus on concern for individuals who carry the virus. Even a liberal society need not be a society of mere strangers; it can at least be a society of "friendly strangers." This friendliness can be expressed in care, compassion, and empathy. If the metaphor of war against AIDS tends to divide the community insofar as HIV-infected individuals are viewed as enemies, it thereby undermines some of the conditions that could make voluntaristic policies work. Trust is indispensable, and it presupposes communal commitments to provide funds for health care and to enforce rules against discrimination, breaches of confidentiality, etc.

These communal efforts are critically important, because the groups most affected by AIDS—gay men and intravenous drug users—exist on the "margins" of the community (Price 1989). Thus, they tend to view coercive policies of identification of antibody-positive individuals as analogous to the Nazi efforts to identify Jews and others for nefarious purposes (Collins 1987:10). When the "politics of identification" appeals to the sociocultural metaphor of war, it is easy to understand the fears of HIV-infected individuals, especially when they live in marginalized subcommunities. The war metaphor tends to exclude HIV-infected individuals as enemies from the larger community, while the metaphor of care tends to include them in the community. Compulsory measures, such as mandatory screening, appear to impose community, but, without the expression of community—for example, through the allocation of funds for health care and the protection of individual rights and liberties—they largely exclude coerced individuals from the community. If the society expresses solidarity with HIV-infected individuals, it is less likely to need coercive policies to replace voluntaristic ones. If the society denies solidarity, coercive policies are likely to be ineffective and even counterproductive, because they too presuppose voluntary cooperation at many points, often to enter situations where testing is encouraged or required, and generally to carry out measures to protect others.

Mandatory HIV screening, in most settings, would set a precedent of overriding rights in a crisis — in a war against disease — even when it produces no benefits, or the burdens outweigh the benefits, or there are alternative ways to protect the public health. We need to respond out of metaphors other than (or at least in addition to) war, with careful attention to the moral commitments of a liberal society and the justificatory conditions for overriding prima facie principles and rules. How we respond will shape and express our "identity and community in a democracy under siege" (Price 1989:5).

REFERENCES

Andrus, Jon K., David W. Fleming, Catherine Knox et al. 1989. HIV Testing in Prisons: Is Mandatory Testing Mandatory? *American Journal of Public Health* (July), 79(7):840–842.

Bauer, Gary L. 1987. AIDS Testing. *AIDS & Public Policy Journal* (Fall–Winter), 2(4):1–2.

Bayer, Ronald. 1989. *Private Acts, Social Consequences: AIDS and the Politics of Public Health*. New York: Free Press.

Bayer, Ronald, Carol Levine, and Susan M. Wolf. 1986. HIV Antibody Screening: An Ethical Framework for Evaluating Proposed Programs. *JAMA* (October 3), 256(3):1768–1774.

Beauchamp, Tom L. and James F. Childress. 1989. *Principles of Biomedical Ethics,* 3d ed. New York: Oxford University Press.

Becker, Marshall H. and Jill G. Joseph. 1988. AIDS and Behavioral Change to Reduce Risk: A Review. *American Journal of Public Health* (April), 78(4):394–410.

Belongia, Edward A., James M. Vergeront, and Jeffrey P. Davis. 1989. Premarital HIV Screening (Letter to Editor), *Journal of the American Medical Association* (April 21), 261(15):2198.

Bok, Sissela. 1978. *Lying: Moral Choice in Public and Private Life*. New York: Pantheon Books.

Cates, Willard, Jr. and H. Hunter Handsfield. 1988. HIV Counseling and Testing: Does It Work? *American Journal of Public Health* (December), 78(12):1533–1534.

Childress, James F. 1982a. *Who Should Decide? Paternalism in Health Care*. New York: Oxford University Press.

Childress, James F. 1982b. *Moral Responsibility in Conflicts*. Baton Rouge, La: Louisiana State University Press.

Childress, James F. 1987. An Ethical Framework for Assessing Policies to Screen for Antibodies to HIV. *AIDS & Public Policy Journal* (Winter), 2(1):28–31.

Childress, James F. 1990. The Place of Autonomy in Bioethics. *Hastings Center Report* (January/February), 20:12–17.

Cleary, Paul D., et al. 1987. Compulsory Premarital Screening for the Human Immunodeficiency Virus: Technical and Public Health Considerations. *JAMA* (October 2), 258(13):1757–1762.

Collins, Christopher J. 1987. The Case Against AIDS Testing. *AIDS & Public Policy Journal* (Fall–Winter), 2(4):8–11.

Committee for the Study of the Future of Public Health, Division of Health Care Services, Institute of Medicine. 1988. *The Future of Public Health*. Washington, D.C.: National Academy Press.

Field, Martha A. 1990. Testing for AIDS: Uses and Abuses. *American Journal of Law and Medicine* 16(2):33–106.

Fletcher, John C. 1987. AIDS Screening: A Response to Gary Bauer. *AIDS & Public Policy Journal* (Fall–Winter), 2(4):5–7.

Gerberding, Julie Louise et al. 1990. Risk of Exposure of Surgical Personnel to Patients' Blood During Surgery at San Francisco General Hospital. *New England Journal of Medicine* (June 21), 322(25):1788–1793.

Gostin, Larry. 1987. Screening for AIDS: Efficacy, Cost, and Consequences. *AIDS & Public Policy Journal* (Fall–Winter), 2(4):14–24.

Gostin, Larry. 1990a. A Decade of a Maturing Epidemic: An Assessment and Directions for Future Public Policy. *American Journal of Law and Medicine (16)* (1 and 2):1–32.

Gostin, Larry. 1990b. Letter to Editor. *JAMA* (July 25), 264:452–453.

Gostin, Larry O. et al. 1990. Screening Immigrants and International Travelers for the Human Immunodeficiency Virus. *New England Journal of Medicine* (June 4), 322(24):1743–1746.

Henry, Keith, Myra Maki, and Kent Crossley. 1988. Analysis of the Use of HIV Antibody Testing in a Minnesota Hospital. *JAMA* (Jan. 8), 259(2):229–232.

Joseph, Stephen C. 1989. Premarital AIDS Testing: Public Policy Abandoned at the Altar. *JAMA* (June 16), 261(23):3456.

Kramer, Larry. 1990. A 'Manhattan Project' for AIDS. *New York Times* (July 16).

Levine, Carol and Ronald Bayer. 1989. The Ethics of Screening for Early Intervention in HIV Disease. *American Journal of Public Health* (December), 79(12):1661–1667.

Lo, Bernard, Robert L. Steinbrook, Molly Cooke, et al. 1989. Voluntary Screening for Human Immunodeficiency Virus (HIV) Infection: Weighing the Benefits and Harms. *Annals of Internal Medicine* (May), 110(9):727–733.

Macklin, Ruth. 1986. Predicting Dangerousness and the Public Health Response to AIDS. *Hastings Center Report* (December) 16:16–23.

Marzuk, Peter M., Helen Tierney, Kenneth Tardiff, et al. 1988. Increased Risk of Suicide in Persons with AIDS. *JAMA* 259:1333–1337.

McCusker, Jane, Anne M. Stoddard, Kenneth H. Mayer, et al. 1988. Effects of HIV Antibody Test Knowledge on Subsequent Sexual Behaviors in a Cohort of Homosexually Active Men. *American Journal of Public Health* (April), 78(4):462–467.

Mishu, Ban, William Schaffner, John M. Horan et al. 1990. A Surgeon with AIDS: Lack of Evidence of Transmission to Patients. *JAMA* (July 25), 264:467–470.

Nolan, Kathleen. 1989. Ethical Issues in Caring for Pregnant Women and Newborns at Risk for Human Immunodeficiency Virus Infection. *Seminars in Perinatology* (February), 13(1):55–65.

Nozick, Robert. 1968. Moral Complications and Moral Structures. *Natural Law Forum* 13:1–50.

O'Brien, Maura. 1989. Mandatory HIV Antibody Testing Policies: An Ethical Analysis. *Bioethics* 3(4):273–300.

Osborn, June E. 1987. Widespread Testing for AIDS: What Is the Question? *AIDS & Public Policy Journal* (Fall–Winter), 2(4):2–4.

Possible Transmission of Human Immunodeficiency Virus to a Patient During an Invasive Dental Procedure. 1990. *Morbidity and Mortality Weekly Report* (July 27), 39(29):489–493.

Price, Monroe E. 1989. *Shattered Mirrors: Our Search for Identity and Community in the AIDS Era*. Cambridge, Mass.: Harvard University Press.

Rhame, Frank S. 1990. The HIV-Infected Surgeon. *JAMA* (July 25), 264:507–508.

Rhame, Frank S. and Dennis G. Maki. 1989. The Case for Wider Use of Testing for HIV Infection. *New England Journal of Medicine* (May 11), 320(19):1248–1253.

Ross, Judith Wilson. 1989a. Ethics and the Language of AIDS. In Eric T. Juengst and Barbara A. Koenig, eds., *The Meaning of AIDS: Implications for Medical Science, Clinical Practice, and Public Health Policy*. New York: Praeger.

Ross, Judith Wilson. 1989b. The Militarization of Disease: Do We Really Want a War on AIDS? *Soundings* (Spring), 72:39–58.

Sherer, Renslow. 1988. Physician Use of the HIV Antibody Test. *JAMA* (Jan. 8), 259(2):264–265.

Simmons, A. John. 1976. Tacit Consent and Political Obligation. *Philosophy and Public Affairs* (Spring), 5:274–291.

Somerville, Margaret A. 1989. The Case Against HIV Antibody Testing of Refugees and Immigrants. *Canadian Medical Association Journal* (Nov. 1), 141:889–894.

Sontag, Susan. 1990. *Illness as Metaphor and AIDS and Its Metaphors*. New York: Anchor Books.

Swartz, Martha S. 1988. AIDS Testing and Informed Consent. *Journal of Health Politics, Policy, and Law* (Winter) 3(4):607–621.

Turnock, Bernard J. and Chester J. Kelly. 1989. Mandatory Premarital Testing for Human Immunodeficiency Virus: The Illinois Experience. *JAMA* (June 16), 261(23):3415–3418.

Walters, LeRoy. 1988. Ethical Issues in the Prevention and Treatment of HIV Infection and AIDS. *Science* (Feb. 5), 239: pp. 597–603.

Walters, LeRoy. 1990. Ethical Issues in HIV Testing During Pregnancy. [In Ruth Faden, Gail Geller, and Madison Powers, eds., *AIDS, Women and the Next Generation*. New York: Oxford University Press, 1991].

Wertheimer, Alan. 1987. *Coercion*. Princeton, N.J.: Princeton University Press.

Wolchok, Carol Leslie. 1989. AIDS at the Frontier: United States Immigration Policy. *Journal of Legal Medicine* 10: 128–142.

Wood, Gary James. 1987. The Politics of AIDS Testing. *AIDS & Public Policy Journal* (Fall–Winter) 2(4):35–49.

CAROL LEVINE AND RONALD BAYER

The Ethics of Screening for Early Intervention in HIV Disease

The treatment of AIDS (acquired immunodeficiency syndrome) and HIV (human immunodeficiency virus) infection has entered a new, more hopeful era, marked by incremental advances in therapy rather than heralded by a single, dramatic breakthrough. For those ill with AIDS itself, the prognosis remains grim. But many clinicians, public health officials, patients, and AIDS activists are now convinced that early treatment of asymptomatic HIV infection is beneficial in preventing or delaying the onset of illness.

The voices supporting this view are many and varied. Drs. Robert R. Redfield and Donald S. Burke, of the Walter Reed Army Institute of Research in Washington DC, were early advocates of HIV antibody testing for prompt diagnosis of HIV infection. In a recent summary, they stated: "Prompt diagnosis of HIV infection enables the patient to receive optimal medical care from the earliest moments of the disease. Such care can often prevent complications from developing or getting unnecessarily out of hand."[1]

From a community-based perspective, Project Inform, a San Francisco information and advocacy group, gives its constituents this remarkably similar "Basic Message":

Get tested, anonymously.
If positive, consider anti-viral treatment.
Monitor T4 cells quarterly, charting the trend.
If the trend of T4 cells is downward or falls consistently below 500, consider both anti-viral therapy and immune boosting therapy.

Carol Levine and Ronald Bayer, "The Ethics of Screening for Early Intervention in HIV Disease," *American Journal of Public Health* 79 (1989), 1601–1607. © 1989, American Public Health Association.

If the trend of T4 cells falls below 200, consider prophylactic (preventive) treatment against *pneumocystis* (aerosol or oral forms).[2]

After a review of available evidence, the United States Public Health Service has issued the same advice.[3] The San Francisco AIDS Foundation and the Gay Men's Health Crisis in New York launched campaigns to encourage everyone at risk to be tested voluntarily in order to take advantage of early medical intervention.[4] Dr. Anthony S. Fauci, director of the National Institute of Allergy and Infectious Diseases, has said that there is "no question" that it is now medically advantageous to know one's HIV status.[5] In the most sweeping recommendation, Drs. Frank S. Rhame and Dennis G. Maki recommended HIV testing "to all U.S. adults under the age of 60 regardless of their reported risk history."[6]

Testing patients with symptoms suggestive of HIV disease under conditions of informed consent as part of a diagnostic workup has never posed ethical problems. However, when HIV antibody testing became available in 1985, there were no clinical grounds for testing asymptomatic individuals, although there were public health reasons to encourage testing. Substantial changes in therapeutic prospects and the anticipation of even greater advances to come have fundamentally altered the context of the discussion about HIV antibody testing. Because of these changes, it is critical at this point to reconsider the ethics of screening for HIV infection.[7]

It is precisely when medicine's capacity to enhance patient welfare appears to be increasing that there is a danger that important ethical concerns can be overridden or disregarded. This is especially so in the case of AIDS — a disease that will continue to exact an enormous toll in human suffering for the foreseeable future and that continues to have a social and cultural impact far beyond the numbers of people affected.

In this [essay] we discuss the ethical aspects of screening and testing to detect asymptomatic HIV-infected individuals for clinical purposes. Adopting customary usage, we define "screening" as the application of the HIV antibody tests to populations and "testing" as the application of that procedure to individuals on a case-by-case basis.[8] It is important to distinguish among the many potential justifications for screening such as prevention of transmission, infection control, epidemiological surveillance, and medical care. We believe that all justifications for screening should be evaluated independently and should not be masked by the language of potential therapeutic benefit to the individual.

EVIDENCE FOR EARLY INTERVENTION

Earlier, more accurate identification of seropositive individuals would ideally make it possible to offer them the benefits of: (a) inhibition of viral replication or improvement of immunological status; (b) better management of symptoms or prevention of the onset of opportunistic infections; (c) better general health care.

IDENTIFICATION OF TRUE SEROPOSITIVES

The combined ELISA* HIV antibody test and the supplementary Western blot provide a high but not absolute level of accuracy in identifying seropositive individuals. Indeterminate Western blots occur in a small percentage of samples that are repeatedly reactive on ELISA tests, making necessary further testing for viral culture.[9] Recent evidence has indicated that antibody response may be delayed, in some cases as long as 35 months, in some unknown proportion of infected individuals, leading to false negative results.[10]

The level of accuracy that can be obtained with adults does not yet apply to infants. Infants born to infected mothers have maternal HIV antibodies, which may indicate true infection or which may disappear up to 15 or 16 months after birth. Recent studies indicate that from 20 to 50 percent of infants with HIV antibodies are truly infected, a decrease from earlier estimates.[11] Dr. Stephen C. Joseph reported during the Kenneth D. Blackfan Lecture in June 1989 that the most recent evidence from New York City shows a 29 percent transmission rate from infected mother to fetus.

New techniques for the direct identification of viral infection have been reported, primarily the polymerase chain-reaction technique (PCR).[12] This technique can detect the presence of HIV provirus DNA (deoxyribosenucleic acid) sequences as long as six months prior to seroconversion from negative on a Western blot. PCR may be of assistance in clarifying the meaning of indeterminate Western blots, but it is still highly experimental, expensive, and difficult to perform except under specialized laboratory conditions. Limited studies with infants show promise; in one study of seven infants, positive results proved reliable (the babies later developed AIDS or symptoms

---

*Enzyme-linked immunosorbent assay.

of HIV infection), but negative results are much less reliable and may miss as many as 60 percent of infected infants.[13] PCR is not, and may never be, useful as a mass screening tool. An enhanced ability to detect truly infected individuals is relevant because of the potential to provide early therapeutic benefit. At this juncture infected adults but not infected infants can be reliably identified.

INHIBITION OF VIRAL REPLICATION

Recent evidence indicates that early intervention may inhibit viral replication in some people. A group led by Frank de Wolf and Jan Mulder of the University of Amsterdam reported in February 1988 on the treatment of 18 asymptomatic men with longstanding HIV infection with low doses of zidovudine (AZT), either alone or in combination with acyclovir. They found that zidovudine has "an inhibitory effect on viral replication . . . in blood and (in one subject) the central nervous system. . . ."[14] Later that year they reported that only two of 24 health seropositive men treated with AZT needed blood transfusions, compared with 20 to 50 percent of patients with AIDS. Furthermore, the side effects of zidovudine in asymptomatic patients were "mild, transient, and infrequent."[15] In a study presented at the V International Conference on AIDS in June 1989, the Amsterdam group reported that "even with early zidovudine treatment and considerable suppression of HIV-Ag production disease progression can still occur."[16] In August 1989 an AZT trial was stopped after data showed that the drug retarded the development of AIDS in mildly symptomatic people.

Several studies of asymptomatic, HIV-positive persons are underway at the National Institutes of Health (NIH) and in the United Kingdom and France.[17] The largest NIH study is a Phase III, placebo-controlled study consisting of two doses of AZT. This trial, which began recruiting subjects in 1987, is a three-year study; it originally expected to enroll 1,562 subjects, but that number was increased to 3,000. Two weeks after the AZT trial with mildly symptomatic people was stopped, the arm of the trial testing AZT in people with mildly impaired immune systems was also halted, when data showed that those taking the drug were half as likely to develop symptoms as those taking a placebo.[18] Other smaller NIH studies are also underway, involving zidovudine as well as other drugs.

In his review of the development of early intervention strategies against HIV infection, Dani Bolognesi

concluded on a hopeful note. Nevertheless he cautioned that "the emerging picture is far from clear . . . One can [however] begin to visualize certain lines of investigation to pursue" for more definitive answers.[19]

PREVENTION OF OPPORTUNISTIC INFECTIONS

Clearly the symptoms of the opportunistic infection associated with AIDS are better managed today than in earlier years. The most dramatic difference is in the management of *Pneumocystis carinii pneumonia* (PCP), the most common infection and the one most often associated with early death. Sulfa-based drugs are used to prevent recurrences. However, many patients have allergic reactions to this class of drugs.

Aerosolized pentamidine had been widely used to prevent the recurrence of *Pneumocystis*, even before the Food and Drug Administration (FDA) approved its use under a Treatment IND (investigational new drug) for this purpose. The FDA also approved the drug for patients with 200 or fewer T4 helper cells per cubic millimeter, who are at high risk for developing PCP.[20] The US Public Health Service recommendations on primary prophylaxis (for individuals who have not had an episode of *Pneumocystis*) are largely based on extrapolations from evidence from trials of secondary prophylaxis.

IMPROVED GENERAL HEALTH STATUS

A clear benefit of early identification of HIV infection is the opportunity to test for other diseases, such as tuberculosis and syphilis, and to institute appropriate prophylaxis or therapies. Moreover, many persons who learn they are HIV positive are motivated to engage in healthier lifestyles, changing their diets, exercising more, and reducing cigarette, alcohol, and drug use. There are no studies to support the belief that these changes affect the progression of HIV disease, but many people who have altered their lifestyles report an enhanced feeling of control over their lives and higher energy levels.

POTENTIAL BENEFITS AND RISKS

Since HIV becomes part of the individual's genetic material, only a therapy that eliminated the virus from DNA or that permanently inhibited viral expression could be considered a cure. At best, early therapeutic intervention at this point can offer an individual longer disease-free intervals, a better quality of life through symptom management, and the hope that the longer one lives the greater the likelihood that even better therapies will be available. These are substantial benefits.

As is the case in adults, there is no proven therapy for asymptomatic HIV infection in newborns. However, knowing that an infant is potentially infected may make possible the aggressive treatment of infections that might otherwise be treated routinely. The more vigilant medical monitoring of such infants could prove especially beneficial since the majority of them are from poor and minority backgrounds and thus vulnerable to many other ailments that are common in economically deprived areas. Moreover, special vigilance can act as a counterbalance to some of the more general problems of health care in poor communities, including access and the lack of a single primary caregiver who can follow the infant's progress.

Providing patients or their guardians with such medically relevant information enhances autonomy. However, the uncertain nature of the information about possible infection can also create situations in which healthy, uninfected infants are subjected to aggressive and potentially risky interventions. In addition, there is no assurance that identified infants will actually receive special attention; according to the New York City Human Rights Commission, some mothers have encountered difficulties in obtaining health care for HIV-infected babies.

Innovative therapies currently available carry substantial risks. Early intervention in HIV infection is not analogous to a short course of penicillin to treat syphilis. All the drugs that are believed to have an anti-viral effect also have toxicities. These may be mild or moderate in low doses; long-term toxicities are unknown. Furthermore, some viral strains are already becoming resistant to drugs.[21] Because there are so many unanswered questions about the long-term consequences of taking anti-viral drugs and because not everyone is benefited, all such regimens must be evaluated on a continuous basis.

The method of administration may also be a burden. Drugs may have to be taken orally every few hours or intravenously. Over time, this regimen can become onerous to a healthy person. Presumably, any regimen that was effective would have to be continued for an indefinite period. The asymptomatic person may also find the psychological burdens of becoming a "patient" restrictive. All the regimens will require frequent monitoring by physicians or nurses as well as accurate self-reporting by the patient. Administration of some therapies to newborns may require hospitalization, intravenous infusions, and the attendant medical and psychological risks.

There are also potential, well-documented social risks to being identified as HIV-positive. These include the risks of loss of health insurance (especially significant to a person entering a lengthy regimen of expensive treatment), loss of job or housing, and isolation from friends and relatives who may reject the individual known to be infected. Maintaining confidentiality about HIV status is difficult enough for a healthy person; it is much harder for a healthy person undergoing regular medical treatment.

Treatments will be costly. For example, if zidovudine were to be administered to an asymptomatic patient at half or full dosage currently prescribed for AIDS patients, the annual costs would be between $4,891 and $10,382.[22] Aerosolized pentamidine costs about $1,500 to $2,500 annually, plus the costs of the nebulizer and office visits.[23] Monitoring of T-cell counts, recommended at six-month intervals, costs $150. On the other hand, there would be savings in hospital costs for patients who did not get *Pneumocystis*. However, patients would still be vulnerable to other opportunistic infections requiring hospitalization. Furthermore, treatment for asymptomatic patients during the next few years will primarily involve experimental interventions or drugs, which are not covered by most private insurance companies or Medicaid programs. Many policies also do not fully reimburse the costs of drugs or treatment given in outpatient settings.

Finally, seropositive patients may have a very difficult time locating physicians willing to treat them. Few community physicians will care for AIDS patients, and there are even fewer willing to undertake still unproven therapeutic regimens for asymptomatic HIV-infected persons.

In sum, the benefit-risk calculus has many elements. Treatment for asymptomatic HIV infection is still evolving, costly, and with potential long-term risks. But AIDS is still ultimately a fatal disease, and early intervention offers both the potential of prolonging life and the psychological benefit of giving individuals a sense of control over their destinies. Given such uncertainty, patients, in consultation with their physicians, will weigh the various elements differently. Some will choose an aggressive, all-out approach; others will select certain treatments and not others; and some may prefer to watch and wait.

In our ethical analysis, we draw on the principles of respect for persons, the harm principle, beneficence, and justice.[7] These four widely accepted ethical principles are derived from secular, religious, and constitutional traditions and are commonly applied to medicine, research, and public health.

Respect for persons requires that individuals be treated as autonomous agents who have the right to control their own destinies. Respect for persons requires that persons be given the opportunity to decide what will or will not happen to them. The right to privacy and the requirement of informed consent flow from this principle. A corollary — requiring persons with diminished autonomy to be given special protections — may also apply to some populations such as children and prisoners.

The *harm principle* permits limitations on an individual's liberty to pursue personal goals and choices when others will be harmed by those activities.

Beneficence requires that we act on behalf of the interests and welfare of others. The obligations of beneficence apply to actions affecting both individuals and the community. Potential risks must be weighed against potential benefits and the actions with the most favorable risk-to-benefit ratio adopted. The justification for public health authority derives from both the harm principle and beneficence.

Justice requires that the benefits and burdens of particular actions be distributed fairly. It also prohibits invidious discrimination.

These ethical principles may sometimes conflict. For example, the principle of beneficence and the harm principle may outweigh the need to obtain consent in some situations, but they never outweigh the obligation to treat persons with respect for their intrinsic worth and dignity. Considering both benefits and risks, and drawing on the ethical principles of autonomy, beneficence, and justice, we reach several conclusions:

1. *There are now clinical and ethical grounds for establishing voluntary anonymous or confidential screening programs in settings where individuals who may have been infected with HIV are treated.*

Defining the populations for whom such routinely offered screening would represent a benefit will not be simple. Certainly those who report a history of high-risk sexual or drug-using behavior could benefit from early identification. On the other hand, some investigators have observed that self-reported behavior may fail to identify all those at increased risk for HIV infection.[24] Therefore, it will be necessary to recommend HIV testing to persons seen in clinical settings, such as STD (sexually transmitted disease) clinics where the level of HIV infection is high, and to others — pregnant women, for example — in geographic areas where there is an elevated level of infection.

Private physicians should discuss HIV testing with their patients and recommend it to those whose sexual or drug-using history reveals risk behaviors and those who are not sure about their past risks. Recommending testing to all adults, regardless of their history, as suggested by Rhame and Maki, would result in a massive diversion of resources with few benefits.

Adolescents who may be at high risk of HIV infection should also be offered counseling and testing. Adolescents at highest risk because of sexual or drug-using behavior are often alienated from their families. Ideally parents or another family member or trusted adult should be involved in the decision, both to provide emotional support for the adolescent and to facilitate therapeutic follow-up.

2. *Testing of competent adults for clinical purposes should be based on explicit informed consent.*

As the clinical justification for offering HIV testing increases, there will inevitably be a trend toward incorporating testing into the standard panel of "routine" tests. We use the term "routine" to mean that physicians should as a matter of good medical practice and beneficence initiate discussions about HIV antibody testing with their patients.[25] We reject any use of "routine" that involves testing first and talking about it later.[26] HIV testing should not be performed under the conditions of general or presumed consent that governs many other, but not all, medical tests. Presumed consent is an unwritten contract by which the patient, by supplying urine or allowing blood to be drawn, agrees to the routine testing of these materials. If the tests for HIV antibodies were not blood tests, but procedures that involved patient cooperation such as tests for colorectal cancer or mammograms, there would be no question that specific consent would be required. HIV infection is not like other clinical conditions, even those that are potentially lethal. It carries not only great psychological burdens but the possibility of severe stigma and discrimination, including rejection or avoidance by health care workers and poor-quality treatment.

The consent procedure preceding testing should carefully define the benefits and risks of testing. An honest appraisal of the situation enhances patient autonomy. When the possible benefits of testing are inflated, when the limited therapeutic possibilities are exaggerated, the difficulty of enrolling in clinical trials overstated, or the fact that such trials may be placebo-controlled omitted from the discussion, the patient's right to an informed choice is undermined.

Some mothers, because of illness or drug addiction, may be unable to make decisions on testing for their children. However, many others are competent to do so. Competence is not a single standard; the determination in this case should focus on the specific question of decision-making for children, and not on other issues such as competence to make financial decisions or even decisions about the women's own health care. Mothers' consent for testing is critical since their involvement in monitoring the health status of their children will be especially important. In addition, newborn screening will also carry significant psychological and social consequences for mothers identified as infected. For some infants, who have no parent present or competent to give consent, there are significant barriers to testing, treatment, and enrollment in experimental protocols. These questions are beyond the scope of this [essay] but should be addressed by policy-makers to find ways to both protect vulnerable infants and offer them whatever benefits exist for their conditions.

Individuals with diminished capacity to consent—those with mental illness or retardation, for example—should be considered on a case-by-case basis, with the involvement of guardians or other representatives. Here too the absence of a guardian may result in the denial of some kinds of care because of concern about the individual's competence to consent. Those with diminished capacity to consent should not be denied the benefits of potential therapeutic intervention. Procedures should be established to review individual cases of guardians' refusal to permit testing, or the absence of a guardian to give consent.

In the case of adolescents, clinicians will have to determine, again on a case-by-case basis, if an adolescent is mature enough to make the decision about testing, either alone or in consultation with a responsible adult. If so, parental consent ought not be required, even though it is clearly desirable. The notification of parents should be determined on a case-by-case basis, weighing the crucial role that they may be called upon to play in their children's health care against the possibility that they may harm the adolescent. There is no cure or effective treatment for HIV infection. Since long-term follow-up is required, with significant medical interventions, parental involvement is more essential than in STDs. In addition, very few teenagers will be able to pay for treatment on their own.

3. *There is no justification for mandatory screening on the grounds of therapeutic benefit.*

A. Competent adults—Mandatory (i.e., legally required or institutionally enforced) screening for early intervention for competent adults would be a major departure from the accepted standards of medical practice. In our legal and ethical systems, competent adults have the ultimate decision-making authority over their medical care. Despite the well-documented clinical benefits of screening for other potentially fatal diseases (breast cancer, for example) screening programs are entirely voluntary. Changing this standard because of the infectious and stigmatized nature of HIV disease would be a grave mistake.

The few situations in which mandatory screening for individual benefit occur (for example, screening for lead toxicity in the workplace) are narrowly construed and result in beneficial responses, such as offering affected persons different jobs without loss of salary or benefits. Even premarital syphilis screening, which many states have in recent years rescinded on grounds of cost-effectiveness, has as its primary goal the prevention of transmission, not the treatment of an affected individual. While many types of mandatory screening such as drug screening in some narrowly defined employment settings may be constitutional, their stated justification is the prevention of harm to others.[27] Proposals for mandatory HIV screening on clinical grounds do not fall into this category.

Because of the limitations of screening based on well-defined patient characteristics or community prevalence rates, the Centers for Disease Control recommended in 1988 that all pregnant women be "routinely" screened for hepatitis B surface antigen in order to initiate the available prophylactic treatment.[28] Such a universal, quasi-mandatory approach to screening pregnant women cannot be justified in the case of HIV.

If there were an intervention that both benefited an infected person and also prevented transmission by rendering him or her noninfectious, mandatory screening might be considered and might be justified on the basis of the harm principle. But even in that entirely hypothetical situation, the likelihood of public health benefit would have to be weighed against the possible side effects and the intrusive and long-term nature of the intervention. Since HIV is transmitted through behavior that can be modified, clinical intervention is not the only possible means of controlling the spread of infection.

Even those who acknowledge that mandatory screening is not justified for prevention of transmission, infection control, or therapeutic benefit might argue that the three purposes, when combined, may indeed create a justification. We reject such a claim. These three weak arguments do not make a strong one. It is ethically unacceptable to require or encourage testing on grounds of potential therapeutic advantage when in fact the purpose of screening is entirely different.

B. Newborns — The case of newborns presents a more complex situation. Infants cannot consent for themselves, and society has an obligation to assure that they are not deprived of potentially life-saving therapeutic benefits. Nevertheless, the welfare of children is assumed in general to be more effectively protected by deferring to parents. While respect for persons is usually considered to be a principle affecting individuals, family autonomy has a long legal and moral tradition as well.

Unlike the situation with competent adults, there are mandatory or quasi-mandatory newborn screening programs in place for a few conditions. Screening for phenylketonuria (PKU), for example, is mandated in most states. In the case of PKU, there is a definitive test to identify the rare infant with the genetic enzyme deficiency that prevents the metabolization of phenylalanine. There is a well-established therapeutic regimen — a diet low in phenylalanine — that is highly effective in preventing retardation. It must be initiated early in infancy and continued until the child is age 5 or older.

But even here there is controversy. Ruth Faden and others have argued that "there are cogent moral arguments against requirements of parental consent for PKU screening" and "compelling moral arguments against a policy of honoring parental refusals of PKU screening.[29] However, George Annas has asserted that *voluntary* screening for PKU can be equally effective and that the focus should be on improving the consent

process and not on those few parents who withhold consent.[30]

In 1987, a National Institutes of Health consensus conference concluded that states should mandate the routine offering of sickle cell disease screening to newborns.[31] Sickle cell screening programs had been championed in the early 1970s but were beset by problems caused by the resulting stigmatization of those identified, the confusion between sickle cell disease and trait, and the absence of therapeutic interventions. The NIH consensus conference reviewed new evidence that prophylactic penicillin treatment of affected newborns prevented serious episodes of disease and, in some cases, death. Despite the clear potential benefits, the conference report called upon states to "mandate the availability of these services while permitting parental refusal." According to Dr. Marilyn Gastin of the National Institutes of Health, at present about 20 states are implementing, or planning to implement, sickle cell newborn screening programs. Some of these allow parental refusal; many do not provide any mechanism to inform parents about their right to refuse.

Unlike the cases of PKU and sickle cell screening, however, there [are] at present no definitive screening test to identify the HIV-infected infant, no proven therapy, and no proven benefits to early intervention. There are also strong arguments *against* mandatory HIV screening at present. Mandatory screening of all newborns would entail the coercive identification of infected mothers, since the HIV antibodies in the infant reveal infection in the mother. These women are typically from minority communities. Often they are poor and have a history of drug use. They are particularly subject to attempts to override their parental rights. Unless specifically demonstrated to be unable to act in their child's best interests, mothers at high risk for HIV infection should have the power to exercise the rights accorded to other parents, including the right to refuse HIV testing for their infants.

Only when a definitive test that accurately identifies HIV-infected infants becomes available, and when a treatment has been demonstrated to be safe and effective in prolonging life and improving its quality for the child, will overriding parental refusal for HIV testing be ethically defensible on the basis of the harm principle. This position conforms to the conclusion of the President's Commission for the Study of Ethical

Problems in Medicine and Biomedical and Behavioral Research that "programs requiring the performance of low-risk, minimally invasive procedures may be justified if voluntary testing would fail to prevent an avoidable, serious injury to people — such as children — who are unable to protect themselves."[32]

4. *Mandatory named reporting of those diagnosed with HIV infection is unnecessary for clinical purposes and may be counterproductive.*

The potential benefits that can follow from the early identification of infection has led some officials to reconsider their earlier opposition to the reporting by name of individuals with HIV infection to public health registries.[33] Such reporting, they have asserted, would permit careful follow-up and counseling regarding the importance of early clinical intervention and would facilitate partner notification to provide the same benefits to individuals reached through public health programs. In the first years of the AIDS epidemic the issue of reporting was the source of bitter controversy, especially in states with relatively low levels of HIV infection.[34] When the Institute of Medicine and the National Academy of Sciences considered the question in 1988 [they] declared that "although some arguments for mandatory reporting have merit . . . the costs far outweigh the benefits, especially if mandatory reporting discourages individuals from seeking voluntary testing."[35]

Now that the prospects for early clinical intervention are emerging and more people at risk are voluntarily seeking testing, it is especially critical to avoid public health measures that may foster anxiety about breaches of confidentiality. That is true regardless of the exemplary record of state health departments in maintaining the confidentiality of the records of those reported with AIDS and other diseases. To assure the proper counseling of HIV-infected individuals about the possibilities of early clinical intervention, it would be wiser to launch aggressive education campaigns targeted at both physicians and those at risk of infection. Partner notification is not dependent on named reporting. Counselors working with HIV-infected people should emphasize the importance of partner notification for clinical and public health reasons, and programs should be in place to assist in notification when the infected individual is unwilling or unable to do it personally.

5. *High-quality laboratory services must be used.* Beneficence requires that persons not be subjected to

any risk — whether social, psychological, or medical — if the information about them to be generated in screening does not meet the current standard levels of accuracy. According to Lawrence Miike, testifying before a House subcommittee in October 1987,[36] studies by the Office of Technology Assessment have found extremely wide variability in laboratory performance. High-quality laboratory services will be essential not only for HIV antibody testing but also for T-cell monitoring, and as consideration is given to wider reliance on PCR techniques.

6. *HIV-infected individuals should be protected against discrimination.*

Fear of the discriminatory consequences of being labeled as HIV-infected continues to affect decisions regarding the willingness to be tested for clinical purposes.[37] Despite some advances of the past two years in providing statutory protections against the unconsented disclosure of HIV status, and in protecting the civil rights of infected individuals, patients must be informed that whatever benefits may currently flow from the early identification of HIV infection may be compromised by violations of confidentiality and acts of discrimination. This underscores the importance of the protection of the rights of HIV-infected persons, which should be enacted in federal law, as recommended by the Presidential Commission on the HIV Epidemic.[37]

7. *Screening programs to identify asymptomatic individuals for clinical purposes which do not at the same time plan for appropriate follow-up services fail to meet the ethical standards of justice or beneficence.*

The demands of justice go beyond a prohibition of discrimination. They require a systematic and full-scale commitment to planning for and providing the medical and social services that will be required to meet the needs of HIV-infected individuals.

With over 100,000 cases of CDC-defined AIDS reported in the US so far, one-third of them in the New York City-northern New Jersey region, the health care systems in heavily affected areas have been severely strained. Providing experimental and therapeutic regimens as well as careful monitoring of the estimated 1.5 million asymptomatic individuals with HIV infection will require a dramatic expansion of services.[38] If the majority of asymptomatic seropositive people were treated on the basis of the current Public Health Service recommendations, costs would run into the billions of dollars.

The need for such a commitment has been recognized by the Public Health Service as well as by some public health officials who are now pressing for more aggressive programs to identify individuals infected with HIV. Thus Dr. Stephen C. Joseph, Commissioner of Health for New York City, has stated, "[The] shift toward a disease control public health approach must be accompanied by ensured availability of needed clinical and social services."[33] But more than assertions will be necessary. The next phase of the epidemic will require a major infusion of public resources and a willingness to mobilize and organize the services that will so clearly be necessary.

Following the principles of justice and beneficence, the economic barriers that could restrict access to therapeutic agents that may retard the progress of HIV infection must be eliminated. This is an especially critical issue since so many of the infected are poor, uninsured, underinsured, and medically underserved. Only a last-minute intervention by Congress assured that individuals clinically eligible for zidovudine would continue to get it regardless of their ability to pay. But the willingness of the federal government to continue to fund such special AIDS-specific programs is not at all certain.

In its report on genetic screening and counseling, the President's Commission for the Study of Ethical Problems in Medicine and Biomedical and Behavioral Research declared that "Screening programs should not be undertaken unless accurate results will be produced and a full range of prescreening and follow-up services are available."[39] That conclusion applies with equal force to screening for HIV infection. It is not ethically defensible to encourage individuals to undergo HIV testing for clinical purposes unless they will have access to available therapies regardless of ability to pay.

Some public health officials who acknowledge the critical shortage of affordable services nevertheless have objected to this conclusion. They have argued that only when individuals are identified through testing and begin to demand access to services will the resources be made available. Whatever the validity of such claims — and there is reason to doubt that the demands of the poor and disenfranchised would have such a desired impact in this case any more than they have had in the case of drug treatment and primary care — they are irrelevant from the perspective of this analysis. To encourage HIV testing for clinical benefit without informing individuals without insurance and primary health care that the necessary follow-up clinical services are virtually inaccessible would represent a breach of the principles that govern the process of informed consent. As Dr. June Osborn, dean of the University of Michigan School of Public Health, declared at the V International Conference on AIDS, "We must not use the cruelly false lure of access to inaccessible care to justify abandoning principles we have learned so dearly about the fundamental importance of confidentiality and human rights."

The challenge posed by AIDS is not unique: it simply underscores dramatically and urgently the importance of addressing the systemic failures of the American health care system, noted by every major organization and institution that has studied this question. Resolution of those problems is integral to any ethically justified clinical program of screening for HIV infection.

CONCLUSIONS

When HIV antibody testing first became available in mid-1985, its primary function was to prevent the spread of infection through the screening of blood, and, in conjunction with counseling, to foster behavior change. Out of the many sharp debates that surrounded the test at that time, a broad alliance of clinicians, public health officials, political leaders, and AIDS activists forged a consensus that emphasized the importance of specific informed consent for testing and the protection of the confidentiality of the test results. That consensus emerged in the context of relative therapeutic impotence.

Now that the clinical options for those with HIV infection have improved, and in light of the prospects for further advances, that consensus will be subject to challenge. The next phase of the HIV epidemic will thus be marked by improvements in therapies and by profound challenges to the ethical principles that should govern the practice of medicine and public health. Only if careful consideration is given to the rights of individuals, to respect for their privacy, and to society's obligations to provide the needed clinical and social services will it be possible to assure that the cautious optimism that is now medically justified will be translated into policies that are ethically justified.

REFERENCES

1. Redfield RR, Burke DS: HIV infection: The clinical picture. Sci Am October 1988; 90:1769.

2. PI Perspective, April 1988; 7.

3. US Public Health Service: Guidelines for prophylaxis against *Pneumocystis carinii pneumonia* for persons infected with

human immunodeficiency virus disease. MMWR June 16, 1989; 38(suppl #5).

4. Wall Street Journal, April 21, 1989; New York Times, August 16, 1989.

5. New York Times, April 24, 1989.

6. Rhame FS, Maki DG: The case for wider use of testing for HIV infection. N Engl J Med 1989; 320(19):1248–1254.

7. Bayer R, Levine C, Wolf S: HIV antibody screening: An ethical framework for evaluating proposed programs. JAMA 1986; 256:1768–1774.

8. Last JM: Dictionary of Epidemiology. New York: Oxford University Press, 1982; 32–33.

9. The Consortium for Retrovirus Serology Standardization: Serological diagnosis of human immunodeficiency virus infection by Western blot testing. JAMA 1988; 260:674–679.

10. Imagawa DT, Lee MH, Wolinsky SM, et al: Human immunodeficiency virus Type 1 infection in homosexual men who remain seronegative for prolonged periods. N Engl J Med 1989; 320:1458–1462.

11. European Collaborative Study: Mother-to-child transmission of HIV infection. Lancet November 5, 1988; 1039–1043.

12. Hart C, Spira T, Moore J, et al: Direct detection of HIV RNA expression in seropositive subjects. Lancet August 20, 1988; 418–421.

13. Rogers MF, Ou C-Y, Rayfield M. et al: Use of the polymerase chain reaction for early detection of the proviral sequences of human immunodeficiency virus in infants born to seropositive mothers. N Engl J Med 1989; 320:1649–1654.

14. de Wolf F, Gouldsmit J, deGan J, et al: Effect of zidovudine on serum human immunodeficiency virus antigen levels in symptom-free subjects. Lancet February 20, 1988: 373–376.

15. Reported in Campbell D: AIDS: Patient power puts research on trial. New Sci November 12, 1988; 27.

16. Lange J, Mulder J, de Wolf F, et al: Disease progression despite antigen decline during zidovudine treatment of asymptomatic HIV-infected subjects: Need for placebo-controlled trials. Abstracts of the V International Conference on AIDS, 1989; M.B.P. 352. p. 280.

17. Zidovudine in symptomless HIV infection. Lancet February 25, 1989; 415–416.

18. New York Times, August 17, 1989; 1:13.

19. Bolognesi DP: Prospects for prevention of an early intervention against HIV. JAMA 1989; 261(2):3007–3013.

20. 'Treatment IND' for aerosolized pentamidine. JAMA 1989; 261:1398.

21. Larder BA, Darby G, Richman DD: HIV with reduced sensitivity to zidovudine (AZT) isolated during prolonged therapy. Science 1989. 243 (4899): 1731–1734.

22. Citizens Commission on AIDS: The Crisis in AIDS Care: A Call to Action. New York: The CCAIDS, March 1989.

23. State of New York Department of Health, Albany, news release dated June 15, 1989.

24a. Landesman S, Minkoff H, Holman S, McCalla S, Siijin O: Serosurvey of human immunodeficiency virus infection in parturients: implications for human immunodeficiency virus testing programs of pregnant women. JAMA 1987; 258:2701–2703.

24b. Krasinski K, Borkowsky W, Bebenroth D, Moore T: Failure of voluntary testing for human immunodeficiency virus to identify infected parturient women in a high-risk population. N Engl J Med 1988; 318:185.

25. American Medical Association: HIV blood testing counseling: AMA physician guidelines. Chicago: AMA, 1988.

26. Sherer R: Physician use of the HIV antibody test: The need for consent, counseling, confidentiality, and caution. JAMA 1988; 259:264–265.

27. Annas GJ: Crack, symbolism, and the Constitution. Hastings Center Report 1989; 19(3):35–37.

28. Centers for Disease Control: Prevention of perinatal transmission of hepatitis B virus: Prenatal screening of all pregnant women for hepatitis B surface antigen. MMWR 1988; 37:341–346.

29. Faden R, Holtzman N, Chwalow A: Parental rights, child welfare, and public health: The case of PKU screening. Am J Public Health 1982; 72:1396–1400.

30. Annas GJ: Mandatory PKU screening: The other side of the looking glass. Am J Public Health 1982; 72:1401–1403.

31. NIH Consensus Conference: Newborn screening for sickle cell disease and other hemoglobinopathies. JAMA 1987; 258: 1205–1209.

32. President's Commission for the Study of Ethical Problems in Ethics in Medicine and Biomedical and Behavioral Research: Screening and Counseling for Genetic Conditions. Washington DC: The Commission, 1983.

33. Joseph SJ: Premarital AIDS testing: Public policy abandoned at the altar. (Editorial) JAMA 1987; 261:3456.

34. Bayer R: Private Acts, Social Consequences: The Politics of Public Health. New York: Basic Books, 1989; 101–136.

35. Institute of Medicine, National Academy of Sciences: Confronting AIDS: Update 1988. Washington, DC: National Academy Press, 1988; 11.

36. US House of Representatives, Subcommittee on regulation and business opportunities: Testimony of Lawrence Miike, at hearings held October 19, 1987.

37. Report of the Presidential Commission on the Human Immunodeficiency Virus Epidemic. Washington DC: The Commission, June 1988; 74.

38. Arno PS, Shenson D, Siegel NF, et al: The economic and policy implications of early intervention in HIV disease. JAMA (in press).

39. President's Commission for the Study of Ethical Problems in Medicine and Biomedical and Behavioral Research, Summing Up; Washingtron, DC: The Commision, 1983; 25.

WORKING GROUP ON HIV TESTING OF PREGNANT WOMEN AND NEWBORNS

HIV Infection, Pregnant Women and Newborns: A Policy Proposal for Information and Testing

Among the many tragic dimensions of the human immunodeficiency virus (HIV) epidemic as it moves into the 1990s is the growing number of infected women, infants, and children.[1] Women now constitute approximately 10% of the acquired immunodeficiency syndrome (AIDS) cases thus far reported to the Centers for Disease Control.[2] Most of these women are of reproductive age. The US Public Health Service has projected that there will be approximately 3000 cases of pediatric AIDS by the end of 1991.[3] In most of these cases, infants will have acquired the infection through vertical transmission from their mothers.

As the public health impact of HIV infection in women and children has increased, so has interest in screening pregnant women and newborns for evidence of HIV infection. Currently, however, knowing that a pregnant woman is seropositive does not necessarily indicate that her fetus is or will be affected. Human immunodeficiency virus testing of the newborn reveals only the presence or absence of maternal antibodies and thus establishes if mothers are infected, not if the infants themselves are infected. It is currently estimated that in the United States about 30% of HIV-positive mothers transmit HIV to their newborn infants.[4]

Whether among pregnant women or newborns, HIV disproportionately affects disadvantaged women and children of color, adding yet another layer of complexity to the policy problem of who should be screened. Currently, the Centers for Disease Control reports that over 70% of women with AIDS in the United States are African-American or Hispanic.[2] The mode of transmission in most of these cases is intravenous drug use or sexual intercourse with an intravenous drug user.

Screening of pregnant women and newborns raises profound moral, legal, and policy issues. To date, no national professional association or committee has called for the mandatory screening of either pregnant women or newborns, although arguments favoring mandatory policies have appeared in the literature (Krasinski et al[5] and *Village Voice*. October 31, 1989: 18). Numerous national groups have advocated offering testing to either all pregnant women or all "high-risk" pregnant women.[6-10] In addition, some organizations and commentators have called for directive counseling to discourage HIV-infected women from becoming pregnant or bearing children.[11-13]

This article presents a detailed 10-point program of policy recommendations for both pregnant women and newborns, and develops its rationale through the examination of potential objections and criticisms.

Members of the Working Group on HIV Testing of Pregnant Women and Newborns are as follows: From the Departments of Health Policy and Management (Ruth R. Faden, PhD, MPH; Gail Geller, ScD; Katherine Acuff, JD, MPH) and Epidemiology (Alfred Saah, MD, MPH), The Johns Hopkins University School of Public Health, Baltimore, Md; Departments of Obstetrics/Gynecology (Timothy Johnson, MD; John Repke, MD) and Pediatrics (Nancy Hutton, MD; John Modlin, MD; Lawrence S. Wissow, MD, MPH), The Johns Hopkins Hospital, Baltimore, Md; Georgetown University Law Center, Washington, DC (Anita Allen, PhD; Judith Areen, JD; Patricia King, JD); and the Kennedy Institute of Ethics, Washington, DC (Madison Powers, JD, DPhil; Nancy Kass, ScD; LeRoy Walters, PhD; Ruth R. Faden, PhD, MPH).

The opinions expressed herein are solely those of Working Group members and do not necessarily reflect the policies or positions of their respective institutions.

From *Journal of the American Medical Association* 264 (1990), 2416–2420. Copyright 1990, American Medical Association.

POLICY RECOMMENDATIONS

We advocate a policy of informing all pregnant women and new mothers about the epidemic of HIV infection and the availability of HIV testing. Although screening of either pregnant women or newborns is not the central focus of our policy, because we defend a consent requirement for testing our position can be interpreted as a policy of voluntary screening. In our view, a policy of mandatory screening either for pregnant women or for newborns is not justified in the current situation on traditional public health criteria or other grounds. Moreover, we reject implementation of counseling and screening policies that interfere with women's reproductive freedom or that result in the unfair stigmatization of vulnerable social groups. Our specific policy recommendations are as follows:

1. All pregnant women and new mothers should be informed about HIV infection and the availability of HIV testing for themselves and their newborns. Informing of pregnant women should take place at the time of registration for prenatal care. Topics to be addressed are presented in the Table. (Ideally, all women should be informed about the HIV epidemic and HIV testing in advance of pregnancy, as part of preconception care. In addition, it may shortly be advisable, either because an intrapartum intervention becomes available or because it becomes desirable to manage third trimester HIV-positive women differently, to discuss HIV testing again late in pregnancy.)

2. The information to be presented to pregnant women and new mothers may be provided through printed or audiovisual materials. However, in communities with a significant degree of HIV infection or drug use, a personal discussion is of particular importance and should be conducted. Whatever method is selected, the information disclosed should cover the same topics and content (see Table) and should be presented in a manner and language that is meaningful and understandable to the women served.

3. The information conveyed under recommendations 1 and 2 does not substitute for either pretest or posttest counseling. All women who express an interest in HIV testing for themselves or their newborns should receive personal pretest counseling; those tested should receive personal posttest counseling.

4. Both prenatal and newborn testing are to be voluntary, with a requirement of informed consent or parental consent. Consent for testing should be solicited only after pretest counseling.

5. The involvement of state and local health departments is essential to the successful implementation of this policy. Health departments should assume responsibility for developing and updating the educational materials referred to above, assuring the availability of materials in several languages, providing protocols and training for pretest and posttest counseling, and developing evaluation mechanisms to assume the proper conduct of the program. (State government may seek regulatory or legislative means to mandate the obligations of providers of prenatal and newborn

---

[Table.]   Informing Pregnant Women and New Mothers About Human Immunodeficiency Virus (HIV) Infection and the Availability of HIV Testing: Topics to Be Addressed.

- Risk factors associated with HIV infection
- Personal behaviors that afford protection against contracting or transmitting the infection
- Risks and potential benefits of being tested for both mother and baby, including limits on confidentiality, associated social risks, available antidiscrimination protections, the issue of pregnancy termination (for pregnant women), medical benefits of early clinical intervention in HIV infection, and any constraints or obstacles to access to abortion or medical services for HIV-infected women and children
- Prevalence of HIV infection in the local community, and impact on test results (where appropriate)
- Availability of anonymous or alternative testing sites
- Reassurance that testing is voluntary, in particular that the woman's decision about testing will not affect access to or quality of her prenatal care (for pregnant women) or the care the baby receives during this hospitalization (for new mothers)
- Acknowledgment of the detail and complexity of the information presented; that personal, pretest counseling is conducted with women interested in HIV testing before they have to make a final decision
- Relationship between HIV infection in pregnancy and prospects for the fetus/newborn, including the likely maternal-fetal/vertical transmission rate
- Limits of the technology of HIV testing in newborns (eg, that testing in newborns identifies maternal infection, not newborn infection; and that if the mother is/was tested in pregnancy, testing the newborn generally does not provide any additional information)
- Testing of a newborn necessarily reveals the HIV status of the mother

care to inform pregnant women and new mothers about the HIV epidemic and the availability of HIV testing. Alternatively jurisdictions may choose not to mandate these obligations by regulation or legislation unless mechanisms for guiding professional conduct fail, over a reasonable period of time, to ensure adoption of the practice.)

6. Health departments should also establish standards for laboratory procedures, including a requirement that all positive tests be confirmed on an independently drawn, second blood specimen prior to communicating results to the pregnant woman or new mother.

7. Every effort should be made to secure specialized medical interventions for the management of HIV infection, appropriate social services and supports, intensive primary care and abortion services (where requested by pregnant women) for all women and infants identified as HIV positive as a result of prenatal or newborn testing. All women should be informed of any difficulties in obtaining these interventions or services for themselves or their newborns. Specific obstacles to treatment or services should be discussed during pretest counseling with any woman interested in HIV testing for herself or her newborn.

8. Once it is established whether or not infants born to mothers who are HIV positive are infected with HIV, any medical or other records including information about HIV test results should be corrected to verify either that the infant has been diagnosed as infected or that the infant is not HIV-infected.

9. To assure recommendation 7, regional networks or referral services for HIV-positive women and their infants should be established. Each network should assist health care providers with the medical management and counseling of HIV-positive women and their infants, and should offer supportive social services directly to pregnant women and new mothers.

10. Existing laws regarding medical confidentiality and antidiscrimination protections should be strengthened and specifically extended to persons with HIV infection to combat the harmful consequences associated with unavoidable disclosures or public identification of HIV status. The variation between state confidentiality and antidiscrimination protections should be replaced by a uniform, national policy.

MAJOR OBJECTIONS TO
POLICY RECOMMENDATIONS

Our position is subject to several powerful criticisms or objections, both from the perspective of those who favor an aggressive screening policy and from those who have serious reservations about the propriety of any type of maternal or neonatal screening or testing.

WHY PREGNANT WOMEN?

Why do we need a public policy on HIV screening of pregnant women? The justification for our policy proposals reflects the importance of four goals: (1) to advance the national campaign to educate the public about HIV disease and how it can be prevented; (2) to enhance the current and future reproductive choices of women; (3) to identify women and newborns who can benefit from medical advances in the clinical management of HIV infection; and (4) to allow proper obstetrical treatment of women infected with HIV. Goal 1 is intended to contribute to the long-term, public health objective of controlling the HIV epidemic through education and voluntary modification of behavioral risk factors. Goals 3 and 4 are intended to advance the public health interest in reducing morbidity and improving quality of life for persons with HIV infection made possible by therapeutic advances in early clinical intervention. Thus, goals 1, 3, and 4 contribute, either in the short term or the long term, to the reduction of morbidity and mortality and thus are justifiable on public health grounds. By contrast, goal 2 does not appeal to short-term or long-term public health benefits for its foundation, but looks to the interest of women in reproductive freedom for its justification.

With the exception of our fourth goal, the goals of our policy are not specific to pregnant women. Goals 2 and 3 apply to all sexually active women, and goal 1 to all persons. Nonetheless, we have focused on pregnant women in this project for several reasons. First, the issue of vertical transmission has put pregnant women into the policy spotlight. In the near future, interventions may be available to reduce the rate of vertical transmission. We were motivated to head off policy directives that viewed pregnant women as mere vessels for the unborn or vectors of disease by developing policies respectful of the reproductive rights and interests of pregnant women. Second, we believe that primary medical care is a desirable setting for educating individuals about HIV disease and the availability of HIV testing. For many women, pregnancy is the only time when they have access to comprehensive primary care services. Among women who do not receive prenatal care — which often is the situation for women who are at particular risk for HIV disease—the postpartum hospital stay is, unfortunately, often the only opportunity afforded health care providers to discuss HIV infection and to attempt referral to appropriate medical services.

WHY THE REQUIREMENT OF CONSENT?

Currently, it is common practice in obstetrics to order numerous screening tests without informing the patient or obtaining informed consent. Why should testing for evidence of HIV infection be treated differently?

There are important ways in which HIV testing differs from testing for other conditions. Unlike most routine screening tests in pregnancy, HIV testing identifies a potentially fatal illness. Perhaps most important, HIV testing raises special issues of privacy, reproductive choice, and social risk that are not applicable to most other screening tests ordered in pregnancy, with the exception of toxicological screening. Unlike, for example, prenatal testing for Rh factor, it cannot be argued that testing is clearly in the best interests of pregnant women and thus that proceeding based on clinical judgment without informed consent is justified. Although the nature and extent of the harms experienced by HIV-positive women have not been well documented, recent evidence suggests that poor, minority women risk the devastation of their personal and family relationships, the loss of social and medical services, the loss of control of their own medical decisions, and even the loss of their children.[14]

There is also no public health justification for mandatory screening of pregnant women. Although the state clearly has a legitimate interest in reducing the rate of transmission of HIV infection, it is not clear how mandatory screening in general, let alone mandatory screening of pregnant women, relates to this interest.

With regard to horizontal transmission, prevention is largely a function of voluntary changes in the behavior of individuals; there is no evidence that mandatory screening alters behavior more effectively than voluntary programs of education, counseling, and the offer of testing.

We specifically did not include prevention of vertical HIV transmission among the goals for our policy. The goal of reducing vertical transmission is ethically problematic, either in the case of policies designed to prevent future pregnancies or in policies aimed at terminating current pregnancies.

Achieving the public health goal of reducing vertical transmission through the promotion of abortion is morally unacceptable, even if it is argued that an HIV-infected woman's personal decision to terminate a pregnancy is morally permissible. The question of whether to terminate a pregnancy is among the most private and significant of life's choices. The decision should clearly be made by the HIV-positive woman, in consultation with her family if she chooses, but certainly without interference by the state and without unsolicited advice or other undue influence from health professionals. Promoting abortion to achieve public health goals also is imprudent and (we believe) inappropriate public policy for a society deeply divided about the morality of abortion.

Apart from the implications of our society's divisive abortion debate, we have serious reservations about the use of abortion as a means of achieving public health goals of prevention. Preventing the birth of someone who would have an illness or disability is morally different from preventing illness or disability in persons already living. Two morally relevant differences merit greater attention.

First, a public health perspective that sees the two as equivalent—a case averted is a case averted—focuses too narrowly on the moral importance of health outcomes to the exclusion of the relevance of the means to their achievement. Ronald Bayer, for example, argues that while it may be rational for an HIV-infected woman to bear children when she knows that there is an approximately 70% chance that the infant will not be infected, it may not be rational from a social point of view to treat the woman's decision as one in which society must remain neutral.[11] He concludes that, from the social or public health perspective, the fiscal and human costs associated with pediatric AIDS provides strong arguments for a policy that urges infected women not to become pregnant. However, an argument that proceeds solely from an appeal to overall social outcomes is in danger of proving too much. Although the conclusion Bayer draws is limited, his appeal to overall social consequences, without more, forces us to judge alternative public policies only on one dimension—aggregate public health benefits. It is therefore indifferent to differences in the means to the production of public health benefits and can be used equally well to argue for policies prohibiting infected women from becoming pregnant or for recommending or compelling abortion, policies that Bayer does not appear to endorse. Although attention to comparative health outcomes is a central tenet of any public health perspective, it should not be the exclusive focus.

A second objection to treating the prevention of the birth of someone who would have an illness or disability as morally equivalent to preventing illness or disability in persons already living involves a morally unacceptable view of the social worth of such persons.[15] Public policies aimed at discouraging persons with inheritable disabilities or illnesses from having children embody highly objectionable social affirmations of individual inequality. First, it denies that such persons have an equal right to participate in a highly valued aspect of the human experience — the begetting and raising of children. Second, it says to disabled and ill persons generally that the lives of some are not worth living and hence not entitled to a share of the social resources necessary for human flourishing. Third, it conveys the message that the presence of persons with disability or illness within society is to be understood only as an economic and social drain on the aggregate and never as a source of enrichment for the lives of others.

Some of these same concerns cause us to have moral reservations about a public policy of reducing vertical transmission by attempting to influence HIV-positive pregnant women to delay or forgo future childbearing. Although the issue of abortion is removed, the importance of protecting reproductive choice from state interference remains, as do concerns about the propriety of preventing disease by preventing the birth of people who would have the disease. Although we recognize the importance of social interests in preventing vertical transmission, and the tragic lives many infants who have AIDS experience, on balance we are not persuaded that these interests override the opposing interests of women, minorities, and persons with disabilities in restricting the state from involvement in matters of reproductive choice.[16]

Turning from prenatal to neonatal screening, there again is no clinical or public health justification for a mandatory policy. Currently, and for the foreseeable future, programs of newborn screening are de facto programs testing for HIV infection in the mother, not the infant. Thus, any policy for newborn screening must take into account the mother's privacy and autonomy interests. In addition, newborns and their mothers are a family unit; when HIV-infected mothers experience social or institutional discrimination, their infants suffer as well. Human immunodeficiency

virus–positive newborns — 70% of whom are not themselves infected — face the further risk of being abandoned by their mothers, difficulties with adoption and foster home placements, and difficulties in access to day care.

At present, the expected benefits to newborns from HIV testing do not clearly outweigh these risks or the privacy and autonomy interests of their mothers. Although there are few experimental data on this point, we are persuaded that for the approximately 30% of newborns who are infected, the prospects for medical benefits are significant and would be enhanced by early identification of "at risk" status. Currently available benefits include the prevention or delay of death through *Pneumocystis carinii* pneumonia prophylaxis and the prospect that antiviral treatment may lengthen and improve the quality of life, particularly with regard to cognitive development.[17,18] However, for the approximately 70% of newborns who would be identified as being at increased risk because maternal antibodies are detected but who turn out not to be infected, the benefit-to-harm calculus may well tip in the opposite direction. For both groups of newborns, access to adequate medical care is by no means guaranteed. Where the interests of newborns are so difficult to discern and evaluate, there is no moral justification for substituting the judgment of the state or the health professional for that of the parent.

BUT SERVICES ARE NOT AVAILABLE. . . .

It is a central requirement of any screening program acceptable from a public health standpoint that such programs, even if voluntary, are not justified unless tangible benefits can be expected from undertaking screening. Currently, many women infected with HIV have no meaningful access to either general medical care or specific interventions for the management of HIV disease such as antiviral medications or prophylaxis for *P carinii* pneumonia. Also, it is increasingly being argued that women are denied access to abortion services, treatments for HIV infection, and involvement in clinical trials (Margaret McCarthy, unpublished data, May 1990). Problems of access to services occur as well for newborns, and access to adequate social services for both mothers and babies, especially drug treatment and family support services, also is woefully inadequate.

Why then, recommend that health providers inform women about the availability of HIV testing if there is no guarantee of treatment? We believe to do otherwise is to compound the moral problem of unjust access and rationing of treatments with the further moral wrong of deceiving or misleading those for whom such treatments are difficult to secure. Women need to know that adults and children infected with HIV can benefit from medical intervention. They also need to know about obstacles they might face in attempting to secure these benefits for themselves or their children.

IS NOT A 'TARGETED' PROGRAM MORE APPROPRIATE?

As noted earlier, HIV infection in women and children is a highly focal epidemic. It occurs disproportionately in poor women and children of color living in the inner cities of a few metropolitan areas. Would it not be more appropriate to target information and screening resources where there is the highest concentration of infection?

We reject a "targeted" policy for several reasons. Basing the offering of testing to pregnant women on an assessment of individual risk factors has been shown to be inefficient for both hepatitis and HIV infection.[19,20] As a result, targeting would need to be based on proxies for individual risk such as sociodemographic criteria. Targeting by sociodemographic criteria is, however, invidiously discriminatory on its face. Unlike certain genetic conditions, there is no biological basis for targeting HIV programs by ethnicity. Although our program only calls for informing women about the HIV epidemic and the availability of voluntary testing, the targeting of this program to only poor women of color would send the false and dangerous message that, among women, only persons of this racial and ethnic description are at risk for HIV infection. Moreover, it labels all such women — the overwhelming majority of whom are not and never will be infected — as sources of contagion. The fact that groups identified as "carrying the virus" for AIDS suffer discrimination, social prejudice, and hardship has been well documented with regard to gay men. Poor women and children of color already suffer these burdens disproportionately. Thus, to add the stigma of AIDS contagion to poor women of color is to further harm a group of persons who are already unfairly disadvantaged.

Targeting based on community prevalence rates, rather than sociodemographic criteria, is also morally problematic. Substantial efficiency is not likely to occur unless "high prevalence areas" are narrowly defined. The more narrow this definition is, the greater the potential that community prevalence rates become merely thinly veiled proxies for ethnicity and poverty. Targeting by prevalence rates would also place an inappropriate burden on women in "low prevalence areas" who have risk factors for HIV infection and for whom testing may be beneficial. In the absence of a policy such as we propose, these women may be unaware either of being at increased risk or of how to obtain testing. Certain women, such as migrant workers, might be particularly ill served.

There are also public health arguments against targeting. As noted previously, targeting may serve to create or reinforce in women who are outside the targeted group the dangerous view that they are invulnerable to HIV. Targeting thus could undermine the public health objective of universal adoption of safer sex and drug use practices. In addition, informing women about the HIV epidemic is of value in all areas of the country. There is some reason to suspect that the current epidemiological pattern of HIV infection among women and children may be shifting (Tim Donders, MD, HIV Seroepidemiology Branch, oral communication, May 1990). An informed public is our best defense against today's low-prevalence community becoming tomorrow's newest area of outbreak. Of particular concern are communities with significant drug use problems but as yet no significant HIV infection.

It might be argued that in rejecting targeting we have failed to understand what justice requires in the case of poor and minority women. Specifically, in this instance, justice may require not equal treatment but the provision of greater benefits to the worst-off members of society. Targeting, because it is more efficient, would presumably provide greater benefits to the women in the program. In order for this claim to be substantiated, however, it would first have to be established that the benefits of a targeted program to poor women of color outweigh the harms of stigma and labeling discussed earlier. Given our nation's unfortunate history with regard to the treatment of minorities, women, and the poor, it is not surprising that some read in a policy of targeting not a desire to do good, but an agenda of genocide.

Perhaps the two best arguments for targeting are the problems of nondiagnostic or false-positive results associated with testing in low-prevalence areas and the attendant costs incurred by an expanded program. In low-prevalence areas, there will be more false-positive test results.[21,22] As a practical manner, the false-positive issue can be accommodated by requiring that a confirmatory test on a separate blood sample be performed before disclosing results to patients. Nondiagnostic results also should not pose significant problems if protocols for short-term resolution of infection can be agreed on. Nondiagnostic results have not been associated with HIV infection in a large group of blood donors from a region of the country with a very low prevalence of HIV infection.[23] It appears that nondiagnostic results, in the absence of known risk behaviors, are not associated with HIV-1 infection in such communities. Because the ambiguity surrounding nondiagnostic results may cause women some lingering anxiety, women living in low-prevalence communities should be informed about this problem in advance of testing.

The cost issue is more complex and is discussed in detail elsewhere.[18] Briefly, we view the educational costs associated with recommendation 1 of our policy to be unproblematic. More troubling are the costs associated with counseling and testing. If a minority of women request testing, the implications are quite different than if all women request testing. At present, there is no reliable way to estimate how many women will elect to be tested. Underlying the question whether our policy represents a "good use" of funds are seemingly intractable allocation issues concerning how best to distribute limited resources; how even to frame the question is problematic. Should we be comparing the worthiness of implementing our policy against the worthiness of implementing other HIV-related interventions that are currently unfunded or underfunded? Alternatively, is the relevant comparison unfunded or underfunded interventions that could improve the prospects for pregnant women and newborns in areas other than HIV disease?

We cannot presume here to recommend to every jurisdiction in the nation how resources ought to be allocated. The hierarchy of unmet needs varies widely across the country, as does the political backdrop against which allocation decisions must be made. We recognize that some states may choose to concentrate their resources on other interventions, and that such allocation decisions may be just and right. What would be unjust, based on the arguments presented above, is for any state to structure programs in such a way as to explicitly or implicitly target poor women of color. In most instances, we believe that a prudent course would be the creation of statewide programs in which all women are informed about the HIV epidemic and the availability of testing. As noted in recommendation 3, the intensity of the educational effort—for example, whether this information is communicated by printed material or personal discussion—may vary by the significance of HIV infection and drug use in local communities.

CONCLUSION

In the face of the complex issues and uncertainties that surround HIV infection and diagnosis in pregnant women and infants, any policy proposal is likely to be controversial and in some respects unsatisfactory. We have presented the 10 core elements of a policy that we believe represents the best compromise of competing interests and social goals. This policy is sensitive to the current medical and social facts; we examine the implications of anticipated future developments on our recommendations elsewhere.[18]

We do not expect our policy recommendations to have any immediate or isolated effect on HIV transmission rates. It is unrealistic to expect any program of information about HIV infection and the availability of testing to, by itself, affect transmission rates, let alone a program directed at women, given the history of inequality of power and the legacy of sexual subordination that all too often still characterize relations between men and women in our society. We do believe, however, that educational programs can make a difference. With regard to smoking, it has been established that while individual educational efforts were largely ineffective, the cumulative impact of multiple educational efforts in a sustained national antismoking campaign dramatically altered cultural values and reduced the prevalence of smoking.[16] It is to be hoped that, over time, our nation will have a similar experience with HIV infection.

Nevertheless, a comprehensive policy response to controlling the HIV epidemic requires a broader focus than we have adopted herein. Human immunodeficiency virus disease in women and children is a disease of families and, as noted above, is intimately connected to relations between men and women. Any comprehensive policy must address the needs and interests of men as well [as] women and must address the root of the problem of HIV infection in women—drug dependency and the poverty and social isolation that make the use of drugs attractive. Without adequate drug rehabilitation services and social policies and programs that can empower both disadvantaged women and men to break the cycle of poverty that links them to drug use, policies of public information and the availability of HIV testing cannot be expected to significantly affect the pace of the HIV epidemic.

We are indebted to the American Foundation for AIDS Research for its support of this project. In developing our policy recommendations, we discussed HIV testing in group sessions with women receiving prenatal care at The Johns Hopkins Hospital Obstetrical Clinic; additionally, several of us interviewed over 50 clinic patients about their opinions regarding HIV testing. Although these exchanges with clinic patients were not in themselves determinative of our policy recommendations, learning about the experiences, opinions, and policy preferences of these women—who are among those likely to be most affected by the policy—significantly advanced our understanding of the policy problems. We are indebted to these women for their willingness to share this information with us. We also discussed policy options with advocates for African-American and Hispanic women as well as representatives of state and city health departments. We gratefully acknowledge the comments of Mark Barnes, Patrick Chaulk, Curtis Decker, Dazon Dixon, Iris Garcia, Sam Grosclose, George Halpin, Laura Hardesty, Lynne Mofenson, Audrey Rogers, Patricia Tyson, and Neil Williams on versions of our policy proposal.

REFERENCES

1. Guinan ME, Hardy A. Epidemiology of AIDS in women in the United States: 1981 through 1986. *JAMA*. 1987;257:2039–2042.

2. Centers for Disease Control. *HIV/AIDS Surveillance Report*. Atlanta, Ga: Centers for Disease Control; August 1990:1–18.

3. Coolfront report: a PHS plan for prevention and control of AIDS and the AIDS virus. *Public Health Rep*. 1986;101:341–348.

4. Modlin, J, Saah A. Public health and clinical aspects of HIV infection in women and children in the United States. In: Faden R, Geller G, Powers M, eds. *AIDS, Women and the Next Generation*. New York, NY: Oxford University Press Inc. In press.

5. Krasinski K, Borkowsky W, Bebenroth D, Moore T. Failure of voluntary testing for HIV to identify infected parturient women in a high risk population. *N Engl J Med*. 1988;318:185.

6. American College of Obstetricians and the American Academy of Pediatrics. *Guidelines for Perinatal Care*. 2nd ed. Washington, DC: American College of Obstetricians and the American Academy of Pediatrics; 1988.

7. American College of Obstetricians and Gynecologists. *Human Immune Deficiency Virus Infections*. Washington, DC: American College of Obstetricians and Gynecologists; 1988. ACOG Technical Bulletin 123.

8. *Final Report, Secretary's Work Group on Pediatric HIV Infection and Disease*. Washington, DC: US Dept of Health and Human Services; 1988.

9. American Academy of Pediatrics Task Force on Pediatric AIDS. Perinatal human immunodeficiency virus infection. *Pediatrics*. 1988;82:941–944.

10. US Public Health Service. *Caring for Our Future: The Content of Prenatal Care: A Report of the Public Health Service Expert Panel on the Content of Prenatal Care*. Washington, DC: US Public Health Service; 1989.

11. Bayer R. Perinatal transmission of HIV infection: the ethics of prevention. In: Gostin LO, ed. *AIDS and the Health Care System*. New Haven, Conn: Yale University Press; 1990:62–73.

12. American College of Obstetricians and Gynecologists. *Prevention of Human Immune Deficiency Virus Infection and Acquired Immune Deficiency Syndrome*. Washington, DC: American College of Obstetricians and Gynecologists; 1987:1–4.

13. Centers for Disease Control. Recommendation for assisting in the prevention of perinatal transmission of HTLV-III/LAV and acquired immunodeficiency syndrome. *MMWR*. 1985;34:721–731.

14. Hunter ND. *Report of the American Civil Liberties Union AIDS Project*. New York, NY: American Civil Liberties Union; July 1990.

15. Asch A. Reproductive technology and disability. In: Cohen S., Taub N, eds. *Reproductive Laws for the 1990s*. Clifton, NJ: Humana Press; 1989:69–107.

16. Warner KE. Cigarette smoking in the 1970s: the impact of the antismoking campaign on consumption. *Science*. 1981;211:729–731.

17. Pizzo PA, Eddy J, Falloon J, et al. Effect of continuous intravenous infusion of zidovudine in children with symptomatic infection. *N Engl J Med*. 1988;319:889–896.

18. Hutton, N., Wissow L. Maternal and newborn HIV screening: implications for children and families. In: Faden R, Geller G, Powers M, eds. *AIDS, Women and the Next Generation*. New York, NY: Oxford University Press Inc. In press.

19. Summers PR, Biswas MJ, Pastorek JG, Pernoll ML, Smith LG, Bean BE. The pregnant hepatitis B carrier: evidence favoring comprehensive antepartum screening. *Obstet Gynecol*. 1987;69:701–704.

20. Barbacci M, Dallabetta GA, Repke J, Polk F. HIV screening in an inner city prenatal population. Presented at the 28th annual meeting of the Interscience Conference on Antimicrobial Agents and Chemotherapy; October 24, 1988; Los Angeles, Calif.

21. Barry MJ, Mulley AG, Singer DE. Screening for HTLV-III antibodies: the relation between prevalence and positive predictive value and its social consequences. *JAMA*. 1985;253:3395.

22. Carlson JR, Bryant ML, Hinrichs, SH et al. AIDS serology testing in low- and high-risk groups. *JAMA*. 1985;253:3405–3408.

23. Jackson JB, MacDonald KL, Cadwell J, et al. Absence of HIV infection in blood donors with indeterminate Western blot tests for antibody to HIV-1. *N Engl J Med*. 1990;322:217–222.

A Global Perspective

THE GLOBAL AIDS POLICY COALITION

AIDS in the World

In the first decade of response to AIDS, remarkable successes in some communities contrast dramatically with a sense of threatening collective global failure. The course of the pandemic within and through global society is not being affected—in any serious manner—by the actions taken at the national or international level. This represents not only a problem of program development, but even more a failure of creativity and vision. An adequate response to AIDS requires reaching beyond traditional approaches to protecting public health; it engages—and challenges—the health and social system itself. Looking toward the mid-1990s and beyond, we see global vulnerability to the human immunodeficiency virus (HIV) increasing—not decreasing. We see, in fact, a failure to mobilize and respond to a common threat as a united global community. As we enter the second decade of AIDS, it is time to ask: Is the AIDS pandemic now out of control?

It is extraordinary that we still lack basic information about this global epidemic and the worldwide response. More than 10 years into the pandemic and 6 years after AIDS was proclaimed to the world as a new health threat of massive proportions, future vulnerability to HIV/AIDS is becoming more pronounced each day. . . . A global vision of AIDS is as important to the local, national, and international future as is global thinking about the Earth's physical environment. Indeed, if we were unaware how interdependent our world has become in the past 25 years—in political, economic, and social terms—AIDS would have taught us this great lesson.

A PANDEMIC OUT OF CONTROL?

The global HIV/AIDS epidemic is volatile, dynamic, and unstable, and its major impacts are yet to come. By early 1992, 12.9 million people around the world (including 4.7 million women, 7.1 million men, and 1.1 million children) have been infected with HIV. About one-fifth (2.7 million; 21 percent) have thus far developed AIDS; of these, over 90 percent (nearly 2.5 million) have died. The numbers become increasingly uncertain as we look ahead. Yet the basic features of the pandemic are now clear.

1. *No community or country is the world already affected by AIDS can claim that HIV spread has stopped.* In 1991, an estimated 75,000 new HIV infections occurred in Europe. Among adults in Abidjan, capital of the Côte d'Ivoire in West Africa, HIV prevalence increased from about 1 percent in 1987 to over 7 percent in 1991. Among pregnant women in São Paolo, Brazil, the rate of HIV infection increased over sixfold in just three years (1987–1990). In the United States, at least 40,000 to 80,000 new HIV infections are anticipated during 1992.

2. *HIV is spreading—sometimes quite rapidly—to new communities and countries around the world.* In Poland, the first HIV-infected drug

user was detected in late 1988; by early 1991, 70 percent of HIV-infected people in Poland were drug users. Ominously, HIV is spreading from urban to rural Africa, where most of the African population lives. An explosion of HIV has recently occurred in Southeast Asia, in Thailand, Burma, and India, where within only a few years more than 1 million people have already been infected. HIV/AIDS is now reported from areas that had earlier been left relatively untouched, such as Paraguay, Greenland, and the Pacific island nations of Fiji, Papua New Guinea, and Samoa. *The global lesson is that HIV will reach most, if not all, human communities: geography may delay, but it will not protect against, the introduction and spread of HIV.*

3. *The epidemic becomes ever more complex as it matures: the global epidemic is composed of thousands of smaller, complicated epidemics.* Most important, the impact of the pandemic on women—both directly and indirectly—is increasing dramatically. For example, in Mexico, the rate of HIV-infected men to women decreased from 25:1 in 1984 to 4:1 by 1990. In the United States, HIV/AIDS among women is growing more rapidly than among men. Within each community, HIV exploits every potential avenue for spread; in Brazil, the proportion of HIV infections linked with injection drug use has increased over tenfold since the early 1980s; in the Caribbean, heterosexual transmission is becoming the major mode of HIV spread. In one large metropolitan area in the United States, Dade County, Florida (in which Miami is located), at least five distinct subepidemics of HIV/AIDS are now under way. *Thus, HIV has repeatedly demonstrated its ability to cross all borders—social, cultural, economic, political— and the conditions that foster HIV spread are complex and changing.*

Against this background of a dynamic, evolving worldwide epidemic, the major impacts of HIV/AIDS are yet to come. By 1995, an additional 6.9 million people will become infected with HIV (5.7 million adults and 1.2 million children). In this short period, the cumulative total of adults infected with HIV will increase nearly 50 percent; during the same period, HIV infections among children will more than double (112 percent increase).

From 1992 to 1995, 3.7 million more people will develop AIDS than during the entire history of the pandemic through January 1, 1992. This 140 percent increase in the number of people with AIDS will include 2.8 million adults and over 900,000 children.

Projecting to the year 2000, the most conservative *AIDS in the World* estimates suggest that a minimum of 38 million adults will have become HIV infected: a more realistic projection is that this figure will be higher, perhaps up to 110 million. An increase to 108 million adults means that over six times more adults will have become HIV infected from 1995 to 2000 than became infected from the beginning of the pandemic until 1995. In this scenario, the number of cumulative AIDS cases by the year 2000 would reach nearly 25 million. Of great importance, the largest proportion of HIV infections by the year 2000 would be in Asia and Oceania (42 percent), compared with 31 percent in sub-Saharan Africa and 14 percent in Latin America and the Caribbean.

The impact [of AIDS] goes far beyond these statistics. AIDS is a unique pandemic. Unlike malaria, measles, or polio, it principally affects young and middle-aged adults; AIDS is a disease of human groups—families, households, couples—and its demographic and social impacts multiply from the infected individual to the group. In the most affected areas, infant, child, and adult mortality is rising, and life expectancy at birth is plummeting. The cost of medical care for each infected person—roughly estimated as equal to or greater than the annual per capita gross national product—overwhelms individuals and households.

• • •

A GLOBAL PERSPECTIVE: HOPES AND FEARS

Information is liberating. It helps us to ask the right questions, even where immediate answers are lacking. Information also improves accountability, not only in individual governments and international organizations, but also in our responses as a global community to the health and societal challenges of the HIV/AIDS pandemic.

Therefore, as people confront HIV/AIDS at the individual, community, and national levels, a clear global picture, a sense of how each part fits into the whole, is critical.

This global perspective, this capacity to sustain both a local and worldwide vision, is not an abstraction. First, local creativity and action inspire and motivate, even as we learn by observing others. Each affected community, each community responding to AIDS, is a laboratory of discovery in HIV/AIDS prevention and care. The capacity for accelerated global learning among communities is central to progress against AIDS, just as international sharing of scientific information from different research centers is fundamental to scientific advances.

Second, a series of global issues are now, or will become, critical to progress against HIV/AIDS. New drug developments, vaccine research, the role and status of women, and the reemerging tuberculosis pandemic are all issues of profound global and local significance.

Third, a global understanding helps us to escape the boundaries of our local environment—to recognize that our work against AIDS has the capacity to transcend our immediate horizon, linking people in distant cultures as colleagues.

Finally, the relative success of community organizations and the threatening collective failure of national and international leadership and institutions provide important insights about health and society. In confronting AIDS, national and international institutions are necessary but not sufficient. The societal implications of the definition of health promulgated by the World Health Organization—"a state of complete physical, mental and social well-being and not merely the absence of disease or infirmity"—have yet to be translated into a coherent vision of health and society.

This [essay] describes a global epidemic spinning out of control. The tone is pessimistic—and realistic, for the contradiction between the dynamic pace of the expanding pandemic and the plateauing of efforts against it dominates the global picture. . . . [T]he world is lagging behind in its response to AIDS. But beyond this harsh reality are hope and confidence. Individual knowledge, commitment, and action *can* make a difference. For AIDS is an intensely personal and local as well as national and global problem. The AIDS pandemic requires a new vision of health, not only to respond to an epidemic disease, but to guide and inspire individual, community, and global work for health into the next millennium.

SUGGESTED READINGS

GENERAL ISSUES

Allen, James R., et al. "AIDS: The Responsibilities of Health Professionals" [Special Supplement]. *Hastings Center Report* 18 (April–May 1988), S1–S32.

Almond, Brenda, ed. *AIDS: A Moral Issue—The Ethical, Legal and Social Aspects.* New York: St. Martin's Press, 1990.

Bayer, Ronald. *Private Acts, Social Consequences: AIDS and the Politics of Public Health.* New York: Free Press, 1989.

Blendon, Robert J.; Donelan, Karen; and Knox, Richard A. "Public Opinion and AIDS: Lessons for the Second Decade." *Journal of the American Medical Association* 267 (1992), 981–986.

Brandt, Allen M. "The Syphilis Epidemic and Its Relationship to AIDS." *Science* 239 (1988), 375–380.

Brennan, Troyen A. "The Challenge of AIDS." In his *Just Doctoring: Medical Ethics in the Liberal State.* Berkeley, CA: University of California Press, 1991, pp. 147–174, 264–268.

Cameron, Miriam E. *Living with AIDS: Experiencing Ethical Problems.* Newbury Park, CA: Sage Publications, 1993.

Daniels, Norman. "Insurability and the HIV Epidemic: Ethical Issues in Underwriting." *Milbank Quarterly* 68 (1990), 497–525.

Dickens, Bernard M. "Legal Rights and Duties in the AIDS Epidemic." *Science* 239 (1988), 580–587.

Gostin, Lawrence O. "The AIDS Litigation Project: A National Review of Court and Human Rights Commission Decisions" [Two Parts]. *Journal of the American Medical Association* 263 (1990), 1961–1970, 2086–2093.

Gostin, Lawrence O., ed. *AIDS and the Health Care System.* New Haven: Yale University Press, 1990.

Graubard, Stephen R., ed. *Living with AIDS.* Cambridge, MA: MIT Press, 1990.

Hastings Center. *AIDS: An Epidemic of Ethical Puzzles.* Brookfield, VT: Dartmouth, 1991.

Humber, James M., and Almeder, Robert F. *AIDS and Ethics.* Biomedical Ethics Reviews 1988. Clifton, NJ: Humana Press, 1989.

Institute of Medicine, Committee for the Oversight of AIDS Activities. *Confronting AIDS: Update 1988.* Washington, DC: National Academy Press, 1988.

Juengst, Eric T.; and Koenig, Barbara A., eds. *The Meaning of AIDS: Implications for Medical Science, Clinical Practice, and Public Health Policy.* New York: Praeger, 1989.

Kass, Nancy E.; Faden, Ruth R.; Fox, Robin, et al. "Homosexual and Bisexual Men's Perceptions of Discrimination in Health Services." *American Journal of Public Health* 82 (1992), 1277–1279.

Lo, Bernard. "Ethical Dilemmas in HIV Infection: What Have We Learned?" *Law, Medicine and Health Care* 20 (1992), 92–103.

Loewy, Erich H., ed. "Ethical and Communal Issues in AIDS:" [Topical Issue]. *Theoretical Medicine* 11 (1990), 173–226.

McKenzie, Nancy F., ed. *The AIDS Reader: Social, Political, Ethical Issues.* New York: Meridian, 1991.

Miller, Heather G.; Turner, Charles F.; and Moses, Lincoln E., eds. *AIDS: The Second Decade.* Washington, DC: National Academy Press, 1990.

Mohr, Richard D. *Gays/Justice: A Study of Ethics, Society, and Law.* New York: Columbia University Press, 1988.

Murphy, Timothy F. "No Time for an AIDS Backlash." *Hastings Center Report* 21 (March–April 1991), 7–11.

National Research Council, Commission on Behavioral and Social Sciences and Education, Committee on AIDS Research and the Behavioral, Social, and Statistical Sciences. *AIDS: Sexual Behavior and Intravenous Drug Use.* Edited by Charles F. Turner, Heather G. Miller, and Lincoln E. Moses. Washington, DC: National Academy Press, 1989.

National Research Council, Panel on Monitoring the Social Impact of the AIDS Epidemic. *The Social Impact of AIDS in the United States.* Washington, DC: National Academy Press, 1993.

Nelkin, Dorothy; Willis, David P.; and Parris, Scott V., eds. *A Disease of Society: Cultural and Institutional Responses to AIDS.* New York: Cambridge University Press, 1991.

Nicholas, Eve K., Institute of Medicine, National Academy of Sciences. *Mobilizing against AIDS.* Newly revised and enlarged ed. Cambridge: Harvard University Press, 1989.

Pierce, Christine, and VanDeVeer, Donald, eds. *AIDS: Ethics and Public Policy.* Belmont, CA: Wadsworth, 1988.

Reamer, Frederic G., ed. *AIDS and Ethics.* New York: Columbia University Press, 1991.

Shilts, Randy. *And the Band Played On.* New York: Penguin, 1988.

United States. "Americans with Disabilities Act of 1990" (Public Law No. 101–336). *[United States] Statutes at Large* 104, pp. 327 ff.

United States, National Commission on AIDS. *America Living with AIDS.* Washington, DC: U.S. Government Printing Office, 1991.

United States National Commission on AIDS. *AIDS: An Expanding Tragedy—The Final Report of the National Commission on AIDS.* Washington, DC: U.S. Government Printing Office, 1993.

THE DUTY TO WARN AND THE DUTY NOT TO HARM

Brennan, Troyen A. "Transmission of the Human Immunodeficiency Virus in the Health Care Setting—Time for Action." *New England Journal of Medicine* 324 (1991), 1504–1509.

Daniels, Norman. "HIV-Infected Professionals, Patient Rights, and the 'Switching Dilemma.'" *Journal of the American Medical Association* 267 (1992), 1368–1371.

Dickens, Bernard M. "Confidentiality and the Duty to Warn." In Gostin, Lawrence O., ed. *AIDS and the Health Care System.* New Haven: Yale University Press, 1990, pp. 98–112, 259–261.

Fleck, Leonard; and Angell, Marcia. "Please Don't Tell!" [Case Study]. *Hastings Center Report* 21 (November–December 1991), 39–40.

Freedman, Benjamin. "Violating Confidentiality to Warn of a Risk of HIV Infection: Ethical Work in Progress." *Theoretical Medicine* 12 (1991), 309–323.

Gostin, Larry. "The HIV-Infected Health Professional: Public Policy, Discrimination, and Patient Safety. *Law, Medicine and Health Care* 18 (1990), 303–310.

Lo, Bernard, and Steinbrook, Robert. "Health Care Workers Infected with the Human Immunodeficiency Virus: The Next Steps." *Journal of the American Medical Association* 267 (1992), 1100–1105.

Macklin, Ruth. "HIV-Infected Psychiatric Patients: Beyond Confidentiality." *Ethics and Behavior* 1 (1991), 3–20.

TESTING AND SCREENING PROGRAMS

Angell, Marcia. "A Dual Approach to the AIDS Epidemic" [Editorial]. *New England Journal of Medicine* 324 (1991), 1498–1500.

Brandt, Allan M.; Cleary, Paul D.; and Gostin, Lawrence O. "Routine Hospital Testing for HIV: Health Policy Considerations." In Gostin, Lawrence O., ed. *AIDS and the Health Care System.* New Haven: Yale University Press, 1990, pp. 125–139, 264–267.

Faden, Ruth; Geller, Gail; and Powers, Madison, eds. *AIDS, Women and the Next Generation.* New York: Oxford University Press, 1991.

Gunderson, Martin; Mayo, David J.; and Rhame, Frank S. *AIDS: Testing and Privacy.* Salt Lake City: University of Utah Press, 1989.

Hardy, Lelie M., ed. Institute of Medicine, Committee on Prenatal and Newborn Screening for HIV Infection. *HIV Screening of Pregnant Women and Newborns.* Washington, DC: National Academy Press, 1991.

O'Brien, Maura. "Mandatory HIV Antibody Testing Policies: An Ethical Analysis." *Bioethics* 3 (1989), 273–300.

Rogers, David E., and Osborn, June E. "Another Approach to the AIDS Epidemic." *New England Journal of Medicine* 325 (1991), 806–808.

A GLOBAL PERSPECTIVE

Mann, Jonathan; Tarontola, Daniel J. M.; and Netter, Thomas W., eds. *AIDS in the World.* Cambridge, MA: Harvard University Press, 1992.

Potts, Malcolm; Anderson, Roy; and Boily, Marie-Claude. "Slowing the Spread of Human Immunodeficiency Virus in Developing Countries." *Lancet* 338 (1991), 608–613.

BIBLIOGRAPHIES

Lineback, Richard H., ed. *Philosopher's Index.* Vols. 1–27. Bowling Green, OH: Philosophy Documentation Center, Bowling Green State University. Issued quarterly. See under "AIDS" and "HIV."

McCarrick, Pat Milmoe. "AIDS: Law, Ethics, and Public Policy." Addendum to Scope Note 8. Washington, DC: Kennedy Institute of Ethics, Georgetown University, 1991.

Walters, LeRoy, and Kahn, Tamar Joy, eds. *Bibliography of Bioethics.* Vols. 1–19. Washington, DC: Kennedy Institute of Ethics, Georgetown University. Issued annually. See under "AIDS." (The information contained in the annual *Bibliography* can also be retrieved from BIOETHICSLINE, an online database of the National Library of Medicine, and from *BIOETHICSLINE Plus,* a CD-ROM disc distributed by SilverPlatter.)

9.

Eugenics and Human Genetics

INTRODUCTION

This chapter discusses both historical and current issues in human heredity. In the first part of the chapter we examine two attempts to improve society by intervening in the reproductive decisions, or modifying the reproductive capacities, of human beings. The first of these eugenic programs emerged in the United States during the first half of the twentieth century; the second was enacted in Germany when that country was governed by Adolf Hitler and the National Socialists. The latter two parts of the chapter explore some of the ethical questions raised by human genetics, a field of science and medicine that began to emerge as a discrete discipline in the late 1940s and early 1950s. Three topics are considered: the human genome project, genetic testing, and human gene therapy.

EUGENICS PROGRAMS IN THE UNITED STATES AND GERMANY

The definition of eugenics is frequently controversial. One simple definition is that eugenics means "the study of human improvement by genetic means."[1] If this definition is accepted, one can discover eugenic proposals in writings as old as Plato's *Republic,* where selective breeding was proposed as a means of improving society.[2] The term "eugenics" was coined in 1883 by an English scientist, Francis Galton, who was a cousin of Charles Darwin. In his first major book, *Hereditary Genius,* published in 1869, and in later works Galton advocated a system of arranged marriages between men and women of distinction, with the aim of producing a group of gifted children and ultimately an improved British population.

In the eugenic programs of the twentieth century, the element of coercion by the state was added to the notion of eugenics as a social goal. The first systematic attempts to develop mandatory eugenic programs occurred in several states of the United States. The central aim of these programs was to prevent reproduction by people who were judged to be feeble-minded. The method by which this aim was to be achieved was involuntary sterilization. Philip Reilly's essay chronicles the history of eugenic sterilization in the United States. While several state courts struck down mandatory sterilization statutes as unconstitutional, the United States Supreme Court found Virginia's involuntary sterilization law to be compatible with the guarantees of the U.S. Constitution. The entire text of the court's famous *Buck v. Bell* decision in 1927 is reprinted in this chapter. In his essay "Carrie Buck's Daughter" paleontologist Stephen Jay Gould questions the factual premises on which the Supreme Court based its decision.

The eugenic programs undertaken in several states of the United States were closely monitored by academics and policy makers in other parts of the world, and especially in Germany. There the method of mandatory sterilization was found to be compatible both with the academic field called racial hygiene and with the political agenda of the National Socialists. Robert Jay Lifton traces the theory and practice of the Nazi sterilization program during the 1930s, when at least 200,000 persons deemed unfit to reproduce were sterilized. As is well known, this sterilization effort was but an initial step on the road that led eventually to the extermination of "unworthy" individuals and groups in Nazi concentration camps.[3]

THE HUMAN GENOME PROJECT AND GENETIC TESTING

There can be no doubt that we live in the golden age of genetics, especially human genetics. Even before the 1950s Gregor Mendel's classic work on various modes of inheritance was available as a framework for understanding how specific traits are transmitted from one generation to the next. However, Watson and Crick's discovery of the molecular structure of DNA in 1953 and the rapid advances made feasible by recombinant DNA techniques in the 1970s and 1980s have opened up entirely new possibilities for genetic diagnosis and therapy.

The genetic structure of human cells is incredibly intricate and complex. Within the nuclei of each human cell there are 46 chromosomes. These chromosomes, in turn, are comprised of 50,000–100,000 genes plus intervening sequences, the function of which is not yet well understood. The simplest units into which the genes and intervening sequences can be analyzed are individual nucleotides or bases, the familiar A, C, G, and T; two corresponding nucleotides form a base pair. It is estimated that each human cell contains approximately 3 billion base pairs.

Through the remainder of the twentieth century and well into the twenty-first, we will witness an intensive international effort to map and sequence the human genome. The initial fruits of this labor will undoubtedly be diagnostic: researchers will be able to locate and analyze the "errors" in genetic sequences that cause particular genetic diseases, or even susceptibilities to particular diseases. When tests are developed to identify these errors, new possibilities for prenatal diagnosis, newborn screening, and the counseling of couples considering reproduction will be at hand. Of course, the same tests will also be available for use by insurance companies, employers, or governments seeking to identify individuals who are afflicted with a particular genetic disease or who carry specific deleterious genes.

The essays by Victor McKusick, Alexander Capron, Paul Billings and associates, and Robert Proctor discuss the ethical questions that may be raised by the human genome project and genetic testing. McKusick provides a state-of-the-art review of the international human genome project, midway through its first five years. He notes with satisfaction the accelerating pace at which new knowledge about human genes and the location of those genes on particular chromosomes is being accumulated. In a more normative vein, Capron argues that the human genome project raises few novel ethical questions and that the project is not a major threat to human welfare. According to Capron, one of the technologies fostered by the new knowledge gained through the human genome project—namely, genetic testing—is more likely to be employed to the detriment of human beings. Capron is particularly concerned about the potential misuse of genetic testing to exclude the genetically affected, or even identifiable carriers of particular genetic traits, from employment or health insurance coverage.

That Capron's concerns are not merely speculative becomes clear in the essay by Billings and associates. From the small sample accumulated by the authors, it is difficult to know the frequency with which genetic discrimination in insurance or employment occurs. However, the kinds of potential problems that can be faced by the genetically affected are vividly depicted in a series of case studies. Proctor's essay returns to the theme of whether the human genome project or its technological spinoffs are likely to cause great harm to the human species. His nuanced answer is that this important project could lead to an undue emphasis on the genetic determinants of human disease—or human misery, more generally—to the neglect of other important factors like poverty, environmental pollution, unhealthy diets, and smoking. Further, Proctor argues that the hypothesis of genetic causation is unlikely to provide a simple explanation for complex human characteristics like criminality, addictive behavior, or sexual preference. In his view, the notion that human destiny can be reduced to biology was one of the fundamental flaws of the earlier, discredited eugenics movements. More detailed technical knowledge of the human genome should not mislead us into repeating the eugenicists' mistakes.

HUMAN GENE THERAPY

In the history of medicine, diagnosis is often the necessary prelude to a cure. It thus seems likely that the capacity to identify genetic diseases and susceptibilities will provide new impetus for already existing efforts to develop ways to correct, or at least to compensate for, genetic defects. The general name usually given to these therapeutic initiatives is *gene therapy,* or, more broadly, *genetic intervention.* In the early stages, gene therapy undoubtedly will be focused on relatively simple genetic disorders that involve errors in only a single gene within each cell. Examples of such disorders are cystic fibrosis, hemophilia, and some kinds of immune deficiency in children. Later, more complex disorders involving multiple genes may become better understood and may be amenable to gene therapy.

A central distinction in any discussion of gene therapy is the distinction between reproductive and nonreproductive cells, which are often called germ-line and somatic cells, respectively. Somatic cells, like our skin or muscle cells, contain the full complement of 46 chromosomes and cannot transmit genetic information to succeeding generations. Thus, the genetic information contained in somatic cells stops with us and is not passed on to succeeding generations. In contrast, germ-line cells, the egg and sperm cells, contain only 23 chromosomes and are capable of transmitting genetic information to our progeny in the next generation, as well as to their descendants in future generations.

A second important distinction in discussions of human gene therapy is that between the cure or prevention of disease, on the one hand, and the enhancement of human capabilities, on the other. A genetic approach to the treatment of cystic fibrosis clearly would be regarded as gene therapy. On the other hand, the attempt to increase stature or to improve the efficiency of long-term memory would probably be regarded by most observers as an effort to enhance capabilities rather than to cure disease. The two distinctions discussed in this and the preceding paragraph can be arrayed in the following two-by-two matrix:

	Somatic	Germ-line
Cure or prevention of disease	1	2
Enhancement of capabilities	3	4

In the present chapter, several of the ethical questions raised by gene therapy and genetic intervention are discussed. LeRoy Walters surveys ethical issues in somatic-cell and germ-line gene therapy (Types 1 and 2 in the above matrix) and describes how gene therapy proposals are currently reviewed in the United States. W. French Anderson, one of the pioneers in developing gene therapy as a treatment for human disease, reviews the worldwide experience with somatic-cell (Type 1) gene therapy as of early 1992. In the concluding section of his essay Anderson foresees the possibility that new and improved modes of somatic-cell gene therapy will be able to be administered to patients on a routine basis, as insulin is given to diabetics now. Further, Type 1 genetic intervention may also play a role in preventing disease. In that event, gene "therapy" would not be therapy in the strict sense of the word, for no disease would exist that required a cure. If a preventive role for so-matic-cell genetic intervention is achieved, we will need to invent a new phrase to describe this approach, perhaps "genetic health maintenance" or "genoprophylaxis."

The issue of germ-line intervention for the prevention or cure of disease (Type 2) has occasioned considerable debate in the 1980s and 1990s. The essay by Walters seeks to pro-vide a rationale for germ-line genetic intervention in specific cases, despite the technical obstacles that presently stand in the way of such an approach. Chief among these obstacles is the lack of a vector, or vehicle, that can reliably deliver a gene (with its control factors) to a predictable site within a cell. Ideally, such a vector would be equipped with a kind of radar that allowed it to find the normal site for a gene on a particular chromosome. In addi-tion, the vector would be equipped with a kind of molecular scissors or scalpel that en-abled it to snip out the malfunctioning gene and splice in the imported, properly function-ing gene in its place.

Another metaphor from the world of word processing may help to illustrate the major technical obstacle to germ-line genetic intervention. Current methods of somatic-cell gene therapy function like the *insert* function in word processing programs. Further, presently available vectors insert the genes that they carry into unpredictable locations on random chromosomes in the nuclei of the cells to which they are delivered. The method of gene in-sertion, or gene addition, seems to have worked in several somatic-cell therapy studies. In other words, the continuing presence of the malfunctioning gene in its original location does not seem to prevent the added gene from functioning in its random location else-where. For germ-line intervention, however, researchers would not simply want to add a properly functioning gene to a cell and leave the malfunctioning gene in its original site, for such a maneuver would result in the passing on of both genes to future generations. Thus, some of the individual's descendants would be likely to inherit the malfunctioning gene and pass it on, in turn, to their descendants. At some point the genetic disease would be likely to recur, depending on the genetic traits carried by the mates of those descen-dants. What researchers hope to be able to employ, instead, is what is called the *search-and-replace* function in word processing. This function would allow the user to look for a particular misspelled word or series of characters and to replace it with a properly spelled word (gene). Thus, unless a new mutation occurred, only the properly functioning gene at the repaired site would be passed on to posterity.

The essay by Walters illustrates how the general ethical principles of beneficence, jus-tice, and respect for autonomy could be applied to the evaluation of human germ-line in-tervention. In contrast, the position paper by the Human Genetics Committee of the Coun-cil for Responsible Genetics categorically opposes the use of germ-line modification in humans. The committee is concerned that the technique of germ-line genetic intervention could be used for eugenic purposes, especially the enhancement of human capabilities. Further, in the committee's view, the alternative strategy of prenatal diagnosis and selec-tive abortion is available as a method for preventing the inheritance of unwanted genes. Fi-nally, the committee emphasizes the limitations in our knowledge of how genes interact and the great harm that a botched intervention could have on many future generations.

like there isn't in the 1st place

L. W.

NOTES

1. Encyclopaedia Britannica, Micropaedia, "Eugenics," 1989, p. 593.

2. Plato, *Republic,* III (410), IV (456 to 461).

3. For the history of Nazi policies on the "unfit" and the "unworthy," see Lifton's entire book, *The Nazi Doctors* (New York: Basic Books, 1986), and Robert N. Proctor's more recent work, *Racial Hygiene: Medicine under the Nazis* (Cambridge, MA: Harvard University Press, 1988).

Eugenics Programs in the United States and Germany

PHILIP R. REILLY

Eugenic Sterilization in the United States

The most important event in the rise of state-supported programs to sterilize the feeble-minded, the insane, and criminals was the rediscovery in about 1900 of Mendel's breeding experiments. The elegant laws of inheritance were seductive, and a few influential scientists, convinced that even conditions such as pauperism were caused by defective germ plasm, rationalized eugenic programs.[1] But by the close of the nineteenth century, the science of eugenics was already well established.

The founding father was Francis Galton, who, in 1864, began to study the heredity of talent. His investigations of the accomplishments of the children of eminent British judges first appeared in the popular press in 1865.[2] Four years later his book *Heredity Genius: An Inquiry into Its Laws and Consequences*[3] provided a cornerstone for eugenics. A man obsessed with measuring, Galton returned to the problem of heredity many times throughout his long life.[4]

In the United States, evolutionary theory was complicated by the race problem. Some scientists argued that human races had degenerated from a common type and that color was a rough index of departure from the original (white) type.[5] Such notions accommodated the Old Testament and reinforced the convictions of Europeans and North Americans that the Negro was inferior. Particularly important was Morton's 1839 study of the cranial volume of 256 skulls from the five major races. He reported that the average Caucasian skull was 7 cubic inches larger than the average Negro skull—a powerful finding to explain "obvious" cultural superiority.[6]

Another important progenitor of eugenical theory was Cesar Lombroso, an Italian criminologist. Lombroso argued that the behavior of many criminals was the ineluctable product of their germ plasm. During the postmortem on a famous brigand, Lombroso noted a median occipital fossa, rarely found in human skulls, but commonly seen in rodents. That and similar findings convinced him that the criminal was "an atavistic being who reproduces in his person the ferocious instincts of primitive humanity and the inferior animals."[7] Late-nineteenth-century American criminology felt his influence. For example, a Pennsylvania prison official wrote that "everyone who has visited prisons and observed large numbers of prisoners together has undoubtedly been impressed from the appearance of prisoners alone, that a large portion of them were born to be criminals."[8]

Perhaps the single most important event in the rise of eugenics was a report written by Richard Dugdale, a reform-minded New York prison inspector. At one upstate prison, he was struck by the large number of inmates who were relatives. He eventually amassed a pedigree spanning five generations that included 709 individuals, the collective offspring of an early Dutch settler, all with a propensity for almshouses, taverns, and brothels. His study of "the Jukes" had an immediate success with the general public.[9] The family entered American folklore and came to symbolize a new kind of sociological study, one that eugenicists would repeat and refine in the early years of the twentieth century.

During the 1870s, there was a marked increase in the number of state institutions dedicated to the care of the feebleminded. But by 1880, lawmakers were re-assessing their relatively generous funding of these institutions. The U.S. Census of 1880 alarmed those who cared for defective persons; it reported that whereas the general population had grown by 30%, the apparent increase in "idiocy" was 200%.[10] By the 1880s, optimistic views on the educability of the feebleminded were fading, and there was a steady increase in the number of "custodial departments." The "Jukes" stimulated much interest in calculating the cost of providing for the nation's feebleminded, insane, or criminal.

The rediscovery of Mendel's laws was timed perfectly to reinforce the popular suspicion that the defective classes were the products of tainted germ plasm. It prompted a deluge of articles on eugenics in the pages of the popular press. Between 1905 and 1909, there were 27 articles on eugenics listed in *The Reader's Guide to Periodical Literature*. From 1910 to 1914, there were 122 additional entries, making it one of the most referenced subjects in the index. Not a few of them were alarmist in tone.

The popularity of this new subject owed much to Charles B. Davenport, the first director of the Station for Experimental Evolution at Cold Spring Harbor, New York. Trained in mathematics and biology (he took a Ph.D. from Harvard in 1892), young, and ambitious, Davenport was well placed to capture the dramatic implications of Mendelism.[11] After convincing the newly endowed Carnegie Institute to create a research facility, he embarked on genetic studies in domestic animals and plants. But the appeal of human studies was irresistible, and he was soon publishing papers on the inheritance of eye color and skin color.

In 1909, Davenport convinced Mrs. E. H. Harriman, the wealthy matron of a railroad fortune, to underwrite the creation of a Eugenic Record Office (ERO) for five years. His first task was to build a cadre of fieldworkers, young women trained to conduct family studies, to amass the raw data of eugenics. Progress was swift, and the ERO soon was publishing monographs arguing that degeneracy was highly heritable and that affected persons tended also to have large families.[12]

Significant as these works were, the major eugenics document of this century was probably Goddard's 1912 study of "the Kallikaks."[13] In 1907, Goddard, a psychologist doing research at the Vineland Training School, traveled to Europe. In Paris, he visited Simon and Binet and learned their new methods for testing intelligence. When he returned to New Jersey, Goddard, closely assisted by an ERO-trained fieldworker, used the methods to study the families of Vineland patients.

One family fascinated them. It was composed of two branches, both descendants of Martin Kallikak, a soldier in the Revolutionary War. While in the army, Martin had got a girl in the "Piney Woods" pregnant. After the war, he married a respectable Quaker maid and engendered a line of eminent New Jersey citizens. Goddard believed that this natural experiment proved the power of heredity. For generation after generation, the "Piney Woods" line produced paupers and feebleminded persons who, often unaware of their biological ties, sometimes worked as servants to their more eminent cousins.

The Kallikak Family was an immediate success. Written in clear language, embellished with many photographs of the moronic, sinister-looking family, and relatively short, the book hit home with the public. Reprinted in 1913, 1914, 1916, and 1919, it earned Goddard not a little celebrity. Only recently did Stephen Gould discover that the photographs had been altered, thus casting doubt on the integrity of the entire enterprise.[14] But in 1912 or 1919, one could hardly read *The Kallikak Family* without worrying about the consequences of childbearing by the weaker stock in the human family.

The climate of nativism made a large number of Americans particularly receptive to the argument that, if the wrong people had too many children, the nation's racial vigor would decline. No study of eugenic sterilization in the United States can ignore the impact of immigration. The history of the growth of nineteenth-century America is a history of immigration. The first of four great waves rolled across the land in the 1840s. During the 1890s, immigration exceeded the wildest predictions, rising from 225,000 in 1898 to 1,300,000 in 1907. Large-scale assimilation was painful, sometimes agonizing. Perhaps the most dramatic perturbation was competition for jobs. Despite their commitment to internationalism, even the great unions favored restrictive immigration laws. Several states passed laws excluding immigrants from the public works.[15]

Beginning about 1875 proposals to curtail the entry of aliens became a perennial topic before the U.S. Congress. The earliest laws were stimulated by fears in California that the importation of coolie labor had gone too far. Starting with the "Chinese Exclusion Acts," the federal government built the walls even higher. In 1882, a new law expressly excluded lunatics, idiots, and persons likely to become a public charge. During the late 1890s, the most ardent restrictionists sought to condition entry on a literacy test, but success in Congress was damped by President Cleveland's veto.

The early responses to fears of a rapidly growing number of defective persons were proposals that they be incarcerated. The first asylum dedicated to segregating feeble-minded women during their reproductive years was opened in New York in 1878. But by the 1890s, it was obvious that only a tiny fraction of feebleminded women would ever be institutionalized. This harsh reality engendered a successful campaign to enact laws to prohibit marriage by the feebleminded, epileptics, and other "defective" types. Beginning with Connecticut in 1895, many states passed eugenic marriage laws, but this solution was unenforceable. Even the eugenicists dismissed it as ineffective.[16]

Perhaps the most lurid alternative to proposals for lifetime segregation was mass castration. Although never legally implemented, proposals to castrate criminals were seriously debated in a few state legislatures during the 1890s.[17] With the development of the vasectomy, a socially more acceptable operation, procastration arguments (usually aimed at male criminals) faded.

THE SURGICAL SOLUTION

The first American case report of a vasectomy was by Albert Ochsner, a young Chicago surgeon. He argued that the vasectomy could eliminate criminality inherited from the "father's side" and that it "could reasonably be suggested for chronic inebriates, imbeciles, perverts and paupers."[18] Three years later, H. C. Sharp, a surgeon at the Indiana Reformatory, reported the first large study on the effects of vasectomy. He claimed that his 42 patients felt stronger, slept better, performed more satisfactorily in the prison school, and felt less desire to masturbate! Sharp urged physicians to lobby for a law to empower directors of state institutions "to render every male sterile who passes its portals, whether it be almshouse, insane asylum, institute for the feebleminded, reformatory or prison."[19]

In 1907, the governor of Indiana signed the nation's first sterilization law. It initiated the involuntary sterilization of any habitual criminal, rapist, idiot, or imbecile committed to a state institution whom physicians diagnosed as "unimprovable." Having operated on 200 Indiana prisoners, Sharp quickly emerged as the national authority on eugenical sterilization. A tireless advocate, he even underwrote the publication of a pamphlet, *Vasectomy.*[20] In it, he affixed tear-out post cards so that readers could mail a preprinted statement supporting compulsory sterilization laws to their legislative representatives.

Although the simplicity of the vasectomy attracted their attention to defective males, the eugenicists were also concerned with defective women. But the salpingectomy was not yet perfected, and the morbidity from intraabdominal operations was high. Eugenic theoreticians had little choice but to support the long-term segregation of feebleminded women. They were, however, comforted in their belief that most retarded women became prostitutes and were rendered sterile by pelvic inflammatory disease.[21]

Prosterilization arguments peaked in the medical literature in 1910, when roughly one half of the 40 articles published since 1900 appeared. The articles almost unanimously favored involuntary sterilization of the feebleminded. Appeals to colleagues that they lobby for enabling laws were commonly heard at meetings of state medical societies.[22] At the annual meeting of the American Medical Association, Sharp enthralled his listeners with reports on a series of 456 vasectomies performed on defective men in Indiana. After hearing him, a highly placed New Jersey official announced that he would seek a bill for the compulsory sterilization of habitual criminals in his state.[23] New Jersey enacted such a law 18 months later.

The most successful physician lobbyist was F. W. Hatch, Secretary of the State Lunacy Commission in California. In 1909, he drafted a sterilization law and helped convince the legislature (made highly sensitive to eugenic issues by the influx of "racially inferior" Chinese and Mexicans) to adopt it. After the law was enacted, Hatch was appointed General Superintendent of State Hospitals and was authorized to implement the new law. Until his death in 1924, Hatch directed eugenic sterilization programs in 10 state hospitals and approved 3,000 sterilizations, nearly half the nation's total.[24]

THE EARLY STERILIZATION LAWS

In studying the rapid rise of the early sterilization legislation, one is hampered by a paucity of state legislative historical materials.[25] Four small, but influential, groups lobbied hard for these laws: physicians (especially those working at state facilities), scientific eugenicists, lawyers and judges, and a striking number of the nation's richest families. There were, of course, opponents as well. But except for a handful of academic sociologists and social workers, they were less visible and less vocal.

The enthusiastic support that America's wealthiest families provided to the eugenics movement is a most curious feature of its history. First among many was Mrs. E. H. Harriman, who almost single-handedly supported the ERO in its first five years. The second largest financial supporter of the ERO was John D. Rockefeller, who gave it $400 each month. Other famous eugenic philanthropists included Dr. John Harvey Kellogg (brother to the cereal magnate), who organized the First Race Betterment Conference (1914), and Samuel Fels, the Philadelphia soap manufacturer. Theodore Roosevelt was an ardent eugenicist, who favored large families to avoid racial dilution by the weaker immigrant stocks.[26]

Of the few vocal opponents to the eugenics movement, Alexander Johnson and Franz Boas were the most important. Johnson, leader of the National Conference of Charities and Correction, thought that sterilization was less humane than institutional segregation. He dreamed of "orderly celibate communities segregated from the body politic," where the feebleminded and the insane would be safe and could be largely self-supporting.[27] Boas, a Columbia University anthropologist, conducted a special study for Congress to determine whether immigrants were being assimilated into American culture. His findings argued that Hebrews and Sicilians were easily assimiliable — a conclusion that was anathema to eugenicists.[28]

The extraordinary legislative success of proposals to sterilize defective persons suggests that there was substantial support among the general public for such a plan. Between 1905 and 1917, the legislatures of 17 states passed sterilization laws, usually by a large majority vote. Most were modeled after the "Indiana plan," which covered "conformed criminals, idiots, imbeciles, and rapists." In Indiana, if two outside surgeons agreed with the institution's physician that there was no prognosis for "improvement" in such persons, they could be sterilized without their consent. In California, the focus was on sterilizing the insane. The statute permitted authorities to condition a patient's

discharge from a state hospital on undergoing sterilization. California law was unique in requiring that the patient or the family consent to the operation, but as the hospitalization was of indeterminant length, people rarely refused sterilization; thus the consent was rendered nugatory.[29]

How vigorously were these laws implemented? From 1907 to 1921, 3,233 sterilizations were performed under state law. A total of 1,853 men (72 by castration) and 1,380 women (100 by castration) were sterilized. About 2,700 operations were performed on the insane, 400 on the feebleminded, and 130 on criminals. California's program was by far the largest.[30]

Sterilization programs ebbed and flowed according to the views of key state and institutional officials. For example, in 1909, the new governor of Indiana squashed that state's program. In New York, activity varied by institution. In the State Hospital at Buffalo, the superintendent, who believed that pregnancy exacerbated schizophrenia, authorized 12 salpingectomies, but in most other hospitals, no sterilizations were permitted despite the state law. Similar idiosyncratic patterns were documented in other states.[31]

The courts were unfriendly to eugenic policy. Between 1912 and 1921, eight laws were challenged, and seven were held unconstitutional. The first two cases were brought by convicted rapists who argued that sterilization violated the Eighth Amendment's prohibition of cruel and unusual punishment. The Supreme Court of the State of Washington, impressed by Dr. Sharp's reports that vasectomy was simple, quick, and painless, upheld its state law.[32] But a few years later, a federal court in Nevada ruled that the vasectomy was an "unusual" punishment and struck down a criminal sterilization law.[33] Peter Feilen, the appellant in the Washington case, was probably the only man ever forced to undergo a vasectomy pursuant to a law drafted expressly as a punitive rather than an eugenic measure.

In six states (New Jersey, Iowa, Michigan, New York, Indiana, and Oregon), constitutional attacks were leveled at laws that authorized the sterilization of feebleminded or insane persons who resided in state institutions. The plaintiffs argued that laws aimed only at institutionalized persons violated the Equal Protection Clause and that the procedural safeguards were so inadequate that they ran afoul of the Due Process Clause. All six courts invalidated the laws, but they were divided in their reasoning. The three that found a violation of the Equal Protection Clause did not clearly oppose eugenic sterilization; their concern was about uniform treatment of all feebleminded persons. The three that relied on due process arguments to reject the laws were more antagonistic to the underlying policy. An Iowa judge characterized sterilization as a degrading act that could cause "mental torture."[34]

From 1918 to 1921, the years during which these cases were decided, sterilization laws faded as quickly as they had appeared. One reason that the courts were less sympathetic to sterilization laws than the legislatures had been was that sterilization petitions (like commitment orders) touched the judiciary's historic role as protector of the weak. The judges demanded clear proof that the individual would benefit from being sterilized. Another important reason was that scientific challenges to eugenic theories about crime had appeared. For example, two physicians who studied 1,000 recidivists to determine whether inheritance was a factor in criminal behavior found "no proof of the existence of hereditary criminalistic traits."[35] But their voices were soon lost in the storm as another huge wave of immigrants swept across America.

THE RESURGENCE OF THE STERILIZATION MOVEMENT

Despite the judicial rejection of the earlier laws, after World War I arguments that mass eugenic sterilization was critical to the nation's "racial strength" resurfaced. Probably the major impetus was the sudden arrival of hundreds of thousands of southeastern European immigrants.[36] The xenophobia triggered by this massive influx had widespread repercussions. It reinforced concern about the dangers of miscegenation and helped to renew interest in biological theories of crime.

The concurrent concern about miscegenation reflected the weakening of southern white society's control over the lives of blacks. During the eighteenth and nineteenth centuries, the southern states forbade marriage between whites and Negroes. After the Civil War, the burgeoning "colored" population (largely a product of institutionalized rape before then) stimulated amendments that redefined as "negro" persons with ever smaller fractions of black ancestry.[37] This trend culminated when Virginia enacted a marriage law that defined as white "one who has no trace whatsoever of any blood other than Caucasian." It forbade the issuance of marriage licenses until officials had "reasonable assurance" that statements about the color of both the man and the woman were correct, voided all existing interracial marriages (regardless of whether they had been contracted legally else-

where), and made cohabitation by such couples a felony. Several other states enacted laws modeled on the Virginia plan. It was not until the 1940s that states began to repeal miscegenation laws, and only recently did the U.S. Supreme Court declare them to be unconstitutional.[38]

The early 1920s were also marked by an interest in biological theories of criminality somewhat akin to those legitimized by Lombroso. Orthodox criminologists were not responsible for this development.[39] The notion of biologically determined criminality was fostered largely by tabloid journalists and a few eugenically minded officials. For example, *World's Work,* a popular monthly, featured five articles on the biological basis of crime. One recounted the innovative efforts of Harry Olson, Chief Justice of the Chicago Municipal Court. Convinced that most criminals were mentally abnormal, Olson started a Psychopathic Laboratory and hired a psychometrician to develop screening tests to identify people with criminal minds.[40]

During the 1920s, many eugenics clubs and societies sprouted, but only two, the American Eugenics Society (AES) and the Human Betterment Foundation (HBF), exerted any significant influence on the course of eugenic sterilization. The AES was conceived at the Second International Congress of Eugenics in 1921. Dr. Henry Fairfield Osborn, President of the American Museum of Natural History, and a small group of patrician New Yorkers initiated the society. By 1923, it was sufficiently well organized to lobby against a bill to support special education for the handicapped, an idea that it considered dysgenic.

In 1925, the AES relocated to New Haven, Connecticut. For the next few years, its major goal was public education. The Great Depression caused a great fall in donations, and when Ellsworth Huntington, a Yale geographer, became president in 1934, the society was moribund. With the aid of a wealthy relative of the founder, Huntington breathed new life into the organization and realized that politically the AES would fare better if it pushed "positive" eugenics policies, such as family planning and personal hygiene. By 1939, the AES had dissociated itself from hardcore sterilization advocates.

The wealthiest eugenics organization was the Human Betterment Foundation (HBF), started by California millionaire Ezra Gosney, who in 1926 convened a group of experts to study the efficacy of California's sterilization program. This group eventually published over 20 articles confirming the safety of being sterilized and concluded that the state had benefitted. Gosney was convinced that a massive sterilization program could reduce the number of mentally defective persons by one half in "three or four generations."[41]

For five years after sterilization statutes were struck down by the courts, there was little legislative activity. Then, in 1923, four states (Oregon, Montana, Delaware, and Ohio) enacted new laws, and by 1925, eight other states had followed suit. The new statutes were drafted with much greater regard for constitutional issues. Besides frequently requiring the assent of parents or guardians, the laws preserved the right to a jury trial of whether the patient was "the potential parent of socially inadequate offspring." Despite concern about the Equal Protection Clause, most laws were still aimed only at institutionalized persons.

Opponents of sterilization quickly attacked the new laws. Battle was joined in Michigan and Virginia. In June 1925, the highest Michigan court ruled that the state's sterilization statute was "justified by the findings of Biological Science."[42] But the crucial case involved a test of the Virginia law. Dr. A. S. Priddy, Superintendent of the State Colony for Epileptics and Feeble-Minded, filed a sterilization petition to test the judicial waters. Carefully amassing a wealth of pro-eugenic testimony, he shepherded the case through the courts. His strategy paid off. In May 1927, Oliver Wendell Holmes, writing for the majority of the U.S. Supreme Court, upheld involuntary sterilization of the feeble-minded, concluding:

It is better for all the world, if instead of waiting to execute degenerative offspring for crime, or to let them starve for their imbecility, society can prevent those who are manifestly unfit from continuing their kind. The principle that sustains compulsory vaccination is broad enough to cover cutting the Fallopian tubes.[43]

YEARS OF TRIUMPH

The Supreme Court's decision to uphold the Virginia law accelerated the pace of legislation: in 1929, nine states adopted similar laws. As was the case before World War I, a small group of activists from influential quarters persuaded scientifically unsophisticated legislators that sterilization was necessary, humane, and just.

The lobbyists succeeded in part because of favorable views expressed in the medical profession. During 1927–1936, about 60 articles, the vast majority in favor of eugenic sterilization, appeared. In the general medical community, support was strong, but not uniform. Only 18 state medical societies officially backed sterilization programs.[44]

The legislative victories of the early 1930s were impressive, but the crucial measure of whether eugenic notions triumphed is to count the number of sterilizations. Data from surveys that were conducted by the Human Betterment Foundation and other groups permit minimal estimates of the extent of mass sterilization and compel some striking conclusions:

1. Between 1907 and 1963, there were eugenic sterilization programs in 30 states. More than 60,000 persons were sterilized pursuant to state laws.
2. Although sterilization reached its zenith during the 1930s, several states vigorously pursued this activity throughout the 1940s and 1950s.
3. At a given time, a few programs were more active than the rest. In the 1920s and 1930s, California and a few midwestern states were most active. After World War II, several southern states accounted for more than half of the involuntary sterilizations performed on institutionalized persons.
4. Beginning in about 1930, there was a dramatic rise in the percentage of women who were sterilized.
5. Revulsion with Nazi sterilization policy did not curtail American sterilization programs. Indeed, more than one half of all eugenic sterilizations occurred after the Nazi program was fully operational.

During 1929–1941, the Human Betterment Foundation conducted annual surveys of state institutions to chart the progress of sterilization. Letters from hospital officials indicate what factors influenced the programs. The most important determinants of the scope of a program's operation seem to have been the complexity of the due process requirements of the relevant laws, the level of funding, and the attitudes of the superintendents themselves. The HBF surveys strongly suggest that the total number of sterilizations performed on institutionalized persons was underreported. Respondents frequently indicated that eugenic operations were conducted outside the confines of state hospitals.[45]

Until 1918, there were only 1,422 eugenic sterilizations reportedly performed pursuant to state law. Ironically, the sterilization rate began to rise during the very period when the courts were rejecting the first round of statutes (1917–1918). From 1918 to 1920, there were 1,811 reported sterilizations, a fourfold increase over the annual rate during the prior decade. During the 1920s, annual sterilization figures were stable. But in 1929, there was a large increase in sterilizations. Throughout the 1930s, more than 2,000 institutionalized persons were sterilized each year, triple the rate of the early 1920s.

This rapid increase reflected changing concerns and changing policy. In the Great Depression years, the superintendents of many hospitals, strapped by tight budgets, decided to sterilize mildly retarded young women. Before 1929, about 53% of all eugenic sterilizations had been performed on men. Between 1929 and 1935, there were 14,651 reported operations, 9,327 on women and 5,324 on men. In several states, (e.g., Minnesota, and Wisconsin), virtually all the sterilized persons were women. This fact becomes even more impressive when one recognizes that salpingectomy incurred a relatively high morbidity and a much higher cost than did vasectomy. In California, at least five women died after undergoing eugenic sterilization.[46]

During the 1930s, institutionalized men were also being sterilized in unprecedented numbers, largely because of the great increase in the total number of state programs. Unlike the "menace of the feebleminded" that had haunted policy before World War I, the new concern was to cope with harsh economic realities. As the superintendents saw it, fewer babies born to incompetent parents might mean fewer state wards.

The triumph of eugenic sterilization programs in the United States during the 1930s influenced other nations. Canada, Germany, Sweden, Norway, Finland, France, and Japan enacted sterilization laws. The most important events took place in Germany, where the Nazis sterilized more than 50,000 "unfit" persons within one year of enacting a eugenics law.

The German interest in eugenics had roots that twined with nineteenth-century European racial thought, a topic beyond the scope of this [essay]. In the early years of this century, there was a spate of books that preached the need to protect Nordic germ plasm. A German eugenics society was formed in 1905, and in 1970, the first (unsuccessful) sterilization bill was offered in the Reichstag. The devastation of World War I halted the German eugenic movement, but by 1921, groups were again actively lobbying for eugenics programs. Hitler advocated eugenic sterilization as early as 1923.

When the Nazis swept to power, they quickly implemented a program to encourage larger, healthier families. Tax laws were restructured to favor childbearing. In 1933, a companion law was enacted to prevent reproduction by defective persons. The work of Gosney and Popenoe [see notes 24 and 41] was extremely influential on the Nazi planners.[47]

The law created a system of "hereditary health courts," which judged petitions brought by public health officials that certain citizens burdened with one of a long list of disorders (feeblemindedness, schizophrenia, manic-depressive insanity, epilepsy, Huntington's chorea, hereditary blindness, hereditary deafness, severe physical deformity, and habitual drunkenness) would be subjected to compulsory sterilization. In 1934, the courts heard 64,499 petitions and ordered 56,244 sterilizations, for a "eugenic conviction" rate of 87%.[48] In 1934, the German Supreme Court ruled that the law applied to non-Germans living in Germany, a decision that had special import for Gypsies. From 1935 through 1939, the annual number of eugenic sterilizations grew rapidly. Unfortunately, key records perished during World War II. But in 1951, the "Central Association of Sterilized People in West Germany" charged that, from 1934 to 1945, the Nazis sterilized 3,500,000 people, often on the flimsiest pretext.[49]

The Nazi program was eugenics run amok. In the United States, no program even approached it in scope or daring. But there is no evidence to support the argument, frequently heard, that stories of Nazi horrors halted American sterilization efforts.

THE QUIET YEARS

With the onset of World War II, there was a sharp decline in the number of eugenic sterilizations in the United States. Although manpower shortages (surgeons were unavailable) directly contributed to the decline, other factors were also at work. In 1939, the Eugenics Record Office closed its doors; in 1942, the Human Bettermen Foundation also ceased its activities. Later that year, the U.S. Supreme Court, considering its first sterilization case in 15 years, struck down an Oklahoma law that permitted certain thrice-convicted felons to be sterilized.[50] After the war, as the horror of the Nazi eugenics movement became more obvious, the goals of the lingering American programs became more suspect. Yet, despite these changes, many state-mandated sterilization programs continued, albeit at a reduced level of activity.

Between 1942 and 1946, the annual sterilization rate dropped to half that of the 1930s. Reports of institutional officials make it clear that this decline was largely due to a lack of surgeons and nurses.[51] There is little evidence to suggest that the Supreme Court decision had a major impact. Avoiding an opportunity to broadly condemn involuntary sterilization and overrule *Buck v. Bell*,[52] the justices demanded instead that such practices adhere to the precept of the Equal Protection Clause that like persons be treated in a similar fashion. The Oklahoma law was struck down because it spared certain "white-collar" criminals from a punitive measure aimed at other thrice-convicted persons, not simply because it involved sterilization.

During the late 1940s, there was no definite indication that sterilization programs were about to decline. After hitting a low of 1,183 in 1944, there were 1,526 operations in 1950. Slight declines in many states were balanced by rapid increases in North Carolina and Georgia. By 1950, however, there were bellwether signs that sterilization was in disfavor even among institutional officials. For example, during the 1930s and 1940s, 100 persons in San Quentin prison had been sterilized each year. But in 1950, new officials at the California Department of Corrections were "entirely averse" to the program.[53] During that year, sterilization bills were considered in only four states, and all were rejected.[54]

There were major changes in state sterilization programs in 1952. The California program, for years the nation's most active, was moribund, dropping from 275 sterilizations in 1950 to 39 in 1952. By that year, Georgia, North Carolina, and Virginia (having sterilized 673 persons) were responsible for 53% of the national total. General declines in most other states continued throughout the 1950s, and by 1958, these three states were responsible for 76% (574 persons) of the reported operations. The North Carolina program was unique in that it was directed largely at noninstitutionalized rural young women.[55] As recently as 1963, the state paid for the eugenic sterilization of 193 persons, of whom 183 were young women.[56] Despite the persistence, the southern programs must be seen as a local eddy in a tide of decline.

INVOLUNTARY STERILIZATION TODAY

During the 1960s, the practice of sterilizing retarded persons in state institutions virtually ceased. But the laws remained. In 1961, there were eugenic sterilization laws on the books of 28 states, and it was possible to perform involuntary sterilization in 26.[57] Between 1961 and 1976, five laws were repealed, six were amended (to improve procedural safeguards), and one state (West Virginia in 1975) adopted its first sterilization statute. Currently, eugenic sterilization of institutionalized retarded persons is permissible in 19 states, but the laws are rarely invoked. A few states have enacted laws that expressly forbid the sterilization of any persons in state institutions.

If the mid-1930s saw the zenith of eugenic sterilization, the mid-1960s saw its nadir. But the pendulum of policy continues to swing. The late 1960s saw the first lawsuits brought by the parents of noninstitutionalized retarded females arguing that sterilization was both economically essential and psychologically beneficial to their efforts to maintain their adult daughters at home.[58]

In 1973, the debate over sterilizing institutionalized persons whom officials had decided were unfit to be parents flared in the media. The mother of a young man whom physicians at the Partlow State School in Alabama wished to sterilize challenged the constitutionality of the enabling statute. When Alabama officials cleverly argued that they did not need statutory authority as long as consent was obtained from the retarded person, the federal judge not only overturned the law but decreed strict guidelines to control the process of performing "voluntary" sterilizations at Partlow. The key feature was the creation of an outside committee to review all the sterilization petitions.[59]

Also in 1973, the U.S. Department of Health, Education, and Welfare (HEW) became enmeshed in a highly publicized sterilization scandal. That summer, it was reported that an Alabama physician working at a family-planning clinic funded by HEW had sterilized several young, poor black women without their consent. The National Welfare Rights Organization joined with two of the women and sued to block the use of all federal funds to pay for sterilizations. This move prompted HEW to draft strict regulations governing the use of federal money for such purposes, but a federal judge struck them down and held that HEW could not provide sterilization services to legally incompetent persons.[60] Revamped several times, the

HEW guidelines were the subject of continuous litigation for five years. Late in 1978, "final rules" were issued that prohibited the sterilization of some persons (those under 21, and all mentally incompetent persons) and demanded elaborate consent mechanisms when a competent person requested to undergo sterilization to be paid for by public funds.[61]

During the last few years, the debate over sterilizing the mentally retarded, although no longer cast in a eugenic context, reheated. The key issue was to resolve the tensions between the society's duty to protect the incompetent person and the *right* of that person to be sterilized. Of course, exercise of this right presupposes that a family member or guardian is, in fact, properly asserting a right that the subject is incapable of exercising on her own (almost all requests are filed on behalf of retarded young *women*), a matter to which judges devote most of their attention. The court must be convinced that the operation will benefit the patient.

More than 20 appellate courts have been asked to consider sterilization petitions. This spate of litigation has resulted because physicians are now extremely reluctant to run the risk of violating the civil rights of the retarded. The courts have split sharply. In the absence of express statutory authority, six high courts have refused to authorize sterilization orders.[62]

In the more recent decisions, most appellate courts have ruled that (even without statutory authorization) local courts of general jurisdiction do have the power to evaluate petitions to sterilize retarded persons. In a leading case, the highest court in New Jersey held that the parents of an adolescent girl with Down syndrome might obtain surgical sterilization for her if they could provide clear and convincing evidence that it was in "her best interests."[63] Since then, high courts in Colorado, Massachusetts, and Pennsylvania have ruled in a similar manner. These decisions promise that, in the future, the families of some retarded persons will be able to obtain sterilizations for them, regardless of their institutional status.

The great era of sterilization has passed. Yet, grim reminders of unsophisticated programs that once flourished linger. In Virginia, persons sterilized for eugenic reasons decades ago have sued the state, claiming a violation of their civil rights. Although they lost their argument that the operations were performed pursuant to an unconstitutional law, litigation over whether the state failed in its duty to inform them of the consequences of the operations continues. From

pretrial discovery, it appears likely that not a few of the persons who were sterilized were not retarded.[64]

What of the future? Is the saga of involuntary sterilization over? Our knowledge of human genetics makes the return of mass eugenic sterilizations unlikely. However, it is more difficult to predict the future of sterilization programs founded on other arguments. During the 1960s, a number of state legislatures considered a bill to tie welfare payments to "voluntary" sterilization.[65] In 1980, a Texas official made a similar suggestion.[66] Unscientific opinion polls conducted by magazines and newspapers in Texas and Massachusetts found significant support for involuntary sterilization of the retarded.[67]

Although it is unlikely to happen in the United States, the pressing demands of population control in India and China have resulted in social policies that create strong incentives to be sterilized. Since launching the "one-child" program in 1979, China has rapidly altered the social fabric of 1 billion people.[68] As our resources continue to shrink and our earthly neighborhood becomes more crowded, compulsory sterilization may someday be as common as compulsory immunizations, but the eugenic vision will no longer provide its intellectual rationale.

REFERENCES AND NOTES

1. Estabrook, A., and Davenport, C. B., *The Nam Family: A Study of Cacogenics,* Eugenics Record Office, Cold Spring Harbor, NY, 1912.

2. Galton, F., Hereditary talent and character, *Macmillan's Magazine* 12:157–66 (1865).

3. Macmillan, London (1869).

4. Two other books by Galton, *English Men of Science: Their Nature and Nurture,* Macmillan, London (1874); and *Inquiries into Human Faculty and Its Development,* Macmillan, London, (1883), did much to legitimize eugenics.

5. Greene, J. C., Some early speculations on the origin of human races, *American Anthropologist* 56:31–41 (1954).

6. Morton, S. G., *Crania Americana,* John Pennington, Philadelphia (1839). After the Civil War, miscegenation took on new importance; the leading opponent of interracial marriages was a South Carolina physician: Nott, J. C., The mulatto a hybrid, *Am. J. Med. Sci.* 6:252–6 (1843).

7. Lombroso-Ferrerr, G., *Lombroso's Criminal Man,* Patterson-Smith, Montclair, NJ (1872).

8. Boies, H. M., *Prisoners and Paupers,* G. P. Putnam's Sons, NY (1893).

9. Dugdale, R. L., A record and study of the relations of crime, pauperism and disease, in *Appendix to the Thirty-first Report of the NY Prison Association,* NY Prison Assoc., Albany, NY (1875).

10. Kerlin, I., Report to the eleventh national conference on charters and reforms, *Proc. A.M.O.* (1884), 465.

11. Rosenberg, C. E., Charles Benedict Davenport and the beginning of human genetics, *Bull. Hist. Med.* 35:266–76 (1961).

12. See *supra* note 1; ERO workers also analyzed the inheritance of Huntington's chorea: Davenport, D. B., Huntington's Chorea in relation to heredity and eugenics, *Bull. No. 17,* Cold Spring Harbor, NY (1916); and early eugenic work was reported in a climate of scientific respectability.

13. Goddard, H. H., *The Kallikak Family,* Macmillan, New York (1912).

14. Gould, S. J., *The Mismeasure of Man,* Norton, New York (1981).

15. Higham, J., *Strangers in the Land,* Athenaeum, New York (1965).

16. Davenport, C. B., *State Laws Limiting Marriage Selection,* Eugenics Record Office, Cold Spring Harbor, NY (1913).

17. Daniel, F. E., Emasculation for criminal assaults and incest, *Texas Med. J.* 22:347 (1907).

18. Ochsner, A., Surgical treatment of habitual criminals, *JAMA* 53:867–8 (1899).

19. Sharp, H. C. The severing of the vasa deferentia and its relation to the neuropsychiatric constitution, *N.Y. Med. J* (1902), 411–14.

20. Sharp, H. C., *Vasectomy,* privately printed, Indianapolis (1909).

21. Ochsner, *supra* note 18.

22. Reilly, P. R., The surgical solution: The writings of activist physicians in the early days of eugenical sterilization, *Persp. Biol. Med.* 26:637–56 (1983).

23. Sharp, H. C., Vasectomy as a means of preventing procreation of defectives, *JAMA* 51:1897–1902 (1907).

24. Popenoe, P., The progress of eugenical sterilization, *J. of Heredity* 28:19–25 (1933).

25. But see Rhode Island State Library Legislative Research Bureau, *Sterilization of the Unfit,* Providence (1913); and Laughlin, H. H., *Eugenical Sterilization in the United States,* Chicago Psychopathic Laboratory of the Municipal Court, Chicago (1922).

26. Roosevelt, T., Twisted eugenics, *Outlook* 106:30–4, 1914; Eugene Smith, President of the National Prison Association, was a prominent lawyer pushing for sterilization laws—The cost of crime, *Medico-Legal J.* 27:140–9 (1908)—as was Judge Warren Foster, *Pearson's Magazine* (1909) 565–72.

27. Johnson, A., Race improvement by control of defectives, *Ann. Am. Acad. Penal Soc. Sci.* 34:22–29 (1909).

28. Report by the Immigration Commission, U.S. Government Printing Office, Washington, D.C. (1910).

29. See Laughlin *supra,* note 25.

30. *Id.*

31. *Id.*

32. *State v. Feilen,* 70 Wash. 65 (1912).

33. *Mickle v. Henrichs,* 262 F. 687 (1918).

34. *Davis v. Berry,* 216 F. 413 (1914).

35. Spaulding, E. R., and Healy, W., Inheritance as a factor in criminality, in *Physical Basis of Crime,* American Academy of Med. Press, Easton, PA (1914).

36. Ludmerer, K., *Genetics and American Society,* Johns Hopkins University Press, Baltimore (1972).

37. Mencke, J. G., *Mulattoes and Race Mixture: American Attitudes and Images, 1865–1918,* UMI Research Press, Ann Arbor, Mich. (1959).

38. *Loving v. Virginia,* 388 U.S. 1 (1967).

39. Parmelee, M., *Criminology,* Macmillan, New York (1918).

40. Strother, F., The cause of crime: Defective brain, *World's Work* 48:275–81 (1924).

41. Gosney, E. S., & Popenoe, P., *Sterilization for Human Betterment,* Macmillan, New York (1929). HBF was the leading source of prosterilization literature during the 1930s, sponsored a "social eugenics" column in the *Los Angeles Times,* aired radio programs, produced pamphlets, and underwrote lectures. It remained vigorous until Gosney's death in 1942.

42. *Smith v. Probate,* 231 Mich. 409 (1925).

43. *Buck v. Bell,* 274 U.S. 200 (1927).

44. Whitten, B. D., Sterilization, *J. Psycho-Asthenics* 40:56–68 (1935). But in some states, like Indiana, support was very strong. Harshman, L. P., Medical and legal aspects of sterilization in Indiana, *J. Psycho-Asthenics* 39:183–206 (1934).

45. See, e.g., Dunham, W. F., Letter to E. S. Gosney, *AVS Archive,* University of Minnesota (1936).

46. Gosney and Popenoe *supra,* note 41.

47. Kopp, M., The German sterilization program, *AVS Archive,* University of Minnesota (1935).

48. Cook, R., A year of German sterilization, *J. Heredity* 26:485–9 (1935).

49. *New York Herald Tribune* (Jan. 14, 1951), 12.

50. *Skinner v. Oklahoma,* 316 U.S. 535 (1942).

51. Taromianz, M. A., Letter to NJ Sterilization League, *AVS Archive,* University of Minnesota (1944).

52. 274 U.S. 200 (1927).

53. Stanley, L. L., Letter to the NJ Sterilization League, *AVS Archive,* University of Minnesota (1950).

54. Butler, F. O., Report, *AVS Archive,* University of Minnesota (1950).

55. Woodside, M., *Sterilization in North Carolina,* University of North Carolina, Chapel Hill (1950).

56. Casebolt, S. L., Letters to Human Betterment Association of America, *AVS Archive,* University of Minnesota (1963).

57. Landman, F. T., and McIntyre, D. M., *The Mentally Disabled and the Law,* University of Chicago Press, Chicago (1961).

58. *Frazier v. Levi,* 440 S.W. 2d 579 (TX 1968).

59. *Wyatt v. Aderholt,* 368 F. Supp. 1382 (Ala. D.C. 1973).

60. *Relf v. Weinberger,* 372 F. Supp. 1196 (1974).

61. *Fed. Reg.* 52146-75 (1978).

62. *In the Matter of S.C.E.,* 378 A. 2d 144 (1977).

63. *In re Grady,* 426 N.W. 2d 467 (NJ 1981).

64. *Poe v. Lynchburg,* 1981.

65. Paul, J., The return of punitive sterilization laws, *Law Soc. Rev.* 4:77–110 (1968).

66. *New York Times* (Feb. 28, 1980), A16.

67. *The Texas Observer* (March 20, 1981), 7; *Boston Globe* (March 31, 1982), 1.

68. *Intercom* 9(8):12–14, 1981.

UNITED STATES SUPREME COURT

Buck v. Bell (1927)

Argued April 22, 1927. Decided May 2, 1927.

On Writ of Error to the Supreme Court of Appeals of the State of Virginia to review a judgment affirming a judgment of the Circuit Court for Amherst County directing the sterilization of an inmate of a Colony for Epileptics and Feeble Minded. Affirmed. . . .*

The facts are stated in the opinion.

Mr. I. P. Whitehead argued the cause and filed a brief for plaintiff in error:

The act of assembly of Virginia does not provide due process of law guaranteed by the 14th Amendment to the Constitution of the United States. . . .

The act of assembly of Virginia denies to the plaintiff and other inmates of the State Colony for Epileptics and Feebleminded the equal protection of the law guaranteed by the 14th Amendment to the Constitution of the United States. . . .

Mr. Aubrey E. Strode argued the cause and filed a brief for defendant in error:

The act affords due process of law. . . .

The act is a valid exercise of the police power.

The statute may be sustained as based upon a reasonable classification. . . .

Mr. Justice Holmes delivered the opinion of the court:

This is a writ of error to review a judgment of the supreme court of appeals of the state of Virginia, affirming a judgment of the circuit court of Amherst county, by which the defendant in error, the superintendent of the State Colony for Epileptics and Feeble Minded, was ordered to perform the operation of sal-

pingectomy upon Carrie Buck, the plaintiff in error, for the purpose of making her sterile. 143 Va. 310, 51 A.L.R. 855, 130 S. E. 516. The case comes here upon the contention that the statute authorizing the judgment is void under the 14th Amendment as denying to the plaintiff in error due process of law and the equal protection of the laws.

Carrie Buck is a feeble minded white woman who was committed to the State Colony above mentioned in due form. She is the daughter of a feeble minded mother in the same institution, and the mother of an illegitimate feeble minded child. She was eighteen years old at the time of the trial of her case in the circuit court, in the latter part of 1924. An Act of Virginia approved March 20, 1924, recites that the health of the patient and the welfare of society may be promoted in certain cases by the sterilization of mental defectives, under careful safeguard, etc.; that the sterilization may be effected in males by vasectomy and in females by salpingectomy, without serious pain or substantial danger to life; that the Commonwealth is supporting in various institutions many defective persons who if now discharged would become a menace but if incapable of procreating might be discharged with safety and become self-supporting with benefit to themselves and to society; and that experience has shown that heredity plays an important part in the transmission of insanity, imbecility, etc. The statute then enacts that whenever the superintendent of certain institutions including the above named State Colony shall be of opinion that it is for the best interests of the patients and of society that an inmate under his care should be sexually sterilized, he may have the operation performed upon any patient afflicted with hereditary forms of insanity, imbecility, etc., on complying with the very careful provisions by which the act protects the patients from possible abuse.

---

*Editor's note: Some references to other court decisions are omitted or abbreviated.

From *United States [Supreme Court] Reports* 274 (1927), 1000–1002.

The superintendent first presents a petition to the special board of directors of his hospital or colony, stating the facts and the grounds for his opinion, verified by affidavit. Notice of the petition and of the time and place of the hearing in the institution is to be served upon the inmate, and also upon his guardian, and if there is no guardian the superintendent is to apply to the circuit court of the county to appoint one. If the inmate is a minor notice also is to be given to his parents if any with a copy of the petition. The board is to see to it that the inmate may attend the hearings if desired by him or his guardian. The evidence is all to be reduced to writing, and after the board has made its order for or against the operation, the superintendent, or the inmate, or his guardian, may appeal to the circuit court of the county. The circuit court may consider the record of the board and the evidence before it and such other admissible evidence as may be offered, and may affirm, revise, or reverse the order of the board and enter such order as it deems just. Finally any party may apply to the supreme court of appeals, which, if it grants the appeal, is to hear the case upon the record of the trial in the circuit court and may enter such order as it thinks the circuit court should have entered. There can be no doubt that so far as procedure is concerned the rights of the patient are most carefully considered, and as every step in this case was taken in scrupulous compliance with the statute and after months of observation, there is no doubt that in that respect the plaintiff in error has had due process of law.

The attack is not upon the procedure but upon the substantive law. It seems to be contended that in no circumstances could such an order be justified. It certainly is contended that the order cannot be justified upon the existing grounds. The judgment finds the facts that have been recited and that Carrie Buck "is the probable potential parent of socially inadequate offspring, likewise afflicted, that she may be sexually sterilized without detriment to her general health and that her welfare and that of society will be promoted by her sterilization," and thereupon makes the order. In view of the general declarations of the legislature and the specific findings of the court obviously we cannot say as matter of law that the grounds do not exist, and if they exist they justify the result. We have seen more than once that the public welfare may call upon the best citizens for their lives. It would be strange if it could not call upon those who already sap the strength of the state for these lesser sacrifices, often not felt to be such by those concerned, in order to prevent our being swamped with incompetence. It is better for all the world, if instead of waiting to execute degenerate offspring for crime, or to let them starve for their imbecility, society can prevent those who are manifestly unfit from continuing their kind. The principle that sustains compulsory vaccination is broad enough to cover cutting the Fallopian tubes. Jacobson v. Massachusetts, 197 U.S. 11. Three generations of imbeciles are enough.

But, it is said, however it might be if this reasoning were applied generally, it fails when it is confined to the small number who are in the institutions named and is not applied to the multitudes outside. It is the usual last resort of constitutional arguments to point out shortcomings of this sort. But the answer is that the law does all that is needed when it does all that it can, indicates a policy, applies it to all within the lines, and seeks to bring within the lines all similarly situated so far and so fast as its means allow. Of course so far as the operations enable those who otherwise must be kept confined to be returned to the world, and thus open the asylum to others, the equality aimed at will be more nearly reached.

Judgment affirmed.

Mr. Justice Butler dissents.

STEPHEN JAY GOULD

Carrie Buck's Daughter

The Lord really put it on the line in his preface to that prototype of all prescriptions, the Ten Commandments:

. . . for I, the Lord thy God, am a jealous God, visiting the iniquity of the fathers upon the children unto the third and fourth generation of them that hate me (Exod. 20:5).

The terror of this statement lies in its patent unfairness — its promise to punish guiltless offspring for the misdeeds of their distant forebears.

A different form of guilt by genealogical association attempts to remove this stigma of injustice by denying a cherished premise of Western thought — human free will. If offspring are tainted not simply by the deeds of their parents but by a material form of evil transferred directly by biological inheritance, then "the iniquity of the fathers" becomes a signal or warning for probable misbehavior of their sons. Thus Plato, while denying that children should suffer directly for the crimes of their parents, nonetheless defended the banishment of a personally guiltless man whose father, grandfather and great-grandfather had all been condemned to death.

It is, perhaps, merely coincidental that both Jehovah and Plato chose three generations as their criterion for establishing different forms of guilt by association. Yet we maintain a strong folk, or vernacular, tradition for viewing triple occurrences as minimal evidence of regularity. Bad things, we are told, come in threes. Two may represent an accidental association; three is a pattern. Perhaps, then, we should not wonder that our own century's most famous pro-nouncement of blood guilt employed the same criterion — Oliver Wendell Holmes's defense of compulsory sterilization in Virginia (Supreme Court decision of 1927 in *Buck* v. *Bell*): "three generations of imbeciles are enough."

Restrictions upon immigration, with national quotas set to discriminate against those deemed mentally unfit by early versions of IQ testing, marked the greatest triumph of the American eugenics movement — the flawed hereditarian doctrine, so popular earlier in our century and by no means extinct today . . . that attempted to "improve" our human stock by preventing the propagation of those deemed biologically unfit and encouraging procreation among the supposedly worthy. But the movement to enact and enforce laws for compulsory "eugenic" sterilization had an impact and success scarcely less pronounced. If we could debar the shiftless and the stupid from our shores, we might also prevent the propagation of those similarly afflicted but already here.

The movement for compulsory sterilization began in earnest during the 1890s, abetted by two major factors — the rise of eugenics as an influential political movement and the perfection of safe and simple operations (vasectomy for men and salpingectomy, the cutting and tying of Fallopian tubes, for women) to replace castration and other socially unacceptable forms of mutilation. Indiana passed the first sterilization act based on eugenic principles in 1907 (a few states had previously mandated castration as a punitive measure for certain sexual crimes, although such laws were rarely enforced and usually overturned by judicial review). Like so many others to follow, it provided for sterilization of afflicted people residing in the state's "care," either as inmates of mental hospitals and homes for the feeble-minded or as inhabitants of prisons. Sterilization could be imposed upon those judged insane, idiotic, imbecilic, or moronic, and upon convicted rapists or criminals when recommended by a board of experts.

By the 1930s, more than thirty states had passed similar laws, often with an expanded list of so-called hereditary defects, including alcoholism and drug addiction in some states, and even blindness and deafness in others. These laws were continually challenged and rarely enforced in most states; only California and Virginia applied them zealously. By January 1935, some 20,000 forced "eugenic" sterilizations had been performed in the United States, nearly half in California.

No organization crusaded more vociferously and successfully for these laws than the Eugenics Record Office, the semiofficial arm and repository of data for the eugenics movement in America. Harry Laughlin, superintendent of the Eugenics Record Office, dedicated most of his career to a tireless campaign of writing and lobbying for eugenic sterilization. He hoped, thereby, to eliminate in two generations the genes of what he called the "submerged tenth"— "the most worthless one-tenth of our present population." He proposed a "model sterilization law" in 1922, designed

to prevent the procreation of persons socially inadequate from defective inheritance, by authorizing and providing for eugenical sterilization of certain potential parents carrying degenerate hereditary qualities.

This model bill became the prototype for most laws passed in America, although few states cast their net as widely as Laughlin advised. (Laughlin's categories encompassed "blind, including those with seriously impaired vision; deaf, including those with seriously impaired hearing; and dependent, including orphans, ne'er-do-wells, the homeless, tramps, and paupers.") Laughlin's suggestions were better heeded in Nazi Germany, where his model act inspired the infamous and stringently enforced *Erbgesundheitsrecht,* leading by the eve of World War II to the sterilization of some 375,000 people, most for "congenital feeble-mindedness," but including nearly 4,000 for blindness and deafness.

The campaign for forced eugenic sterilization in America reached its climax and height of respectabil-

ity in 1927, when the Supreme Court, by an 8–1 vote, upheld the Virginia sterilization bill in *Buck* v. *Bell*. Oliver Wendell Holmes, then in his mid-eighties and the most celebrated jurist in America, wrote the majority opinion with his customary verve and power of style. It included the notorious paragraph, with its chilling tag line, cited ever since as the quintessential statement of eugenic principles. Remembering with pride his own distant experiences as an infantryman in the Civil War, Holmes wrote:

We have seen more than once that the public welfare may call upon the best citizens for their lives. It would be strange if it could not call upon those who already sap the strength of the state for these lesser sacrifices. . . . It is better for all the world, if instead of waiting to execute degenerate offspring for crime, or to let them starve for their imbecility, society can prevent those who are manifestly unfit from continuing their kind. The principle that sustains compulsory vaccination is broad enough to cover cutting the Fallopian tubes. Three generations of imbeciles are enough.

Who, then, were the famous "three generations of imbeciles," and why should they still compel our interest?

When the state of Virginia passed its compulsory sterilization law in 1924, Carrie Buck, an eighteen-year-old white woman, lived as an involuntary resident at the State Colony for Epileptics and Feeble-Minded. As the first person selected for sterilization under the new act, Carrie Buck became the focus for a constitutional challenge launched, in part, by conservative Virginia Christians who held, according to eugenical "modernists," antiquated views about individual preferences and "benevolent" state power. (Simplistic political labels do not apply in this case, and rarely in general for that matter. We usually regard eugenics as a conservative movement and its most vocal critics as members of the left. This alignment has generally held in our own decade. But eugenics, touted in its day as the latest in scientific modernism, attracted many liberals and numbered among its most vociferous critics groups often labeled as reactionary and antiscientific. If any political lesson emerges from these shifting allegiances, we might consider the true inalienability of certain human rights.)

But why was Carrie Buck in the State Colony and why was she selected? Oliver Wendell Holmes upheld her choice as judicious in the opening lines of his 1927 opinion:

Carrie Buck is a feeble-minded white woman who was committed to the State Colony. . . . She is the daughter of a feeble-minded mother in the same institution, and the mother of an illegitimate feeble-minded child.

In short, inheritance stood as the crucial issue (indeed as the driving force behind all eugenics). For if measured mental deficiency arose from malnourishment, either of body or mind, and not from tainted genes, then how could sterilization be justified? If decent food, upbringing, medical care, and education might make a worthy citizen of Carrie Buck's daughter, how could the State of Virginia justify the severing of Carrie's Fallopian tubes against her will? (Some forms of mental deficiency are passed by inheritance in family lines, but most are not—a scarcely surprising conclusion when we consider the thousand shocks that beset us all during our lives, from abnormalities in embryonic growth to traumas of birth, malnourishment, rejection, and poverty. In any case, no fair-minded person today would credit Laughlin's social criteria for the identification of hereditary deficiency—ne'er-do-wells, the homeless, tramps, and paupers—although we shall soon see that Carrie Buck was committed on these grounds.)

When Carrie Buck's case emerged as the crucial test of Virginia's law, the chief honchos of eugenics understood that the time had come to put up or shut up on the crucial issue of inheritance. Thus, the Eugenics Record Office sent Arthur H. Estabrook, their crack fieldworker, to Virginia for a "scientific" study of the case. Harry Laughlin himself provided a deposition, and his brief for inheritance was presented at the local trial that affirmed Virginia's law and later worked its way to the Supreme Court as *Buck* v. *Bell*.

Laughlin made two major points to the court. First, that Carrie Buck and her mother, Emma Buck, were feebleminded by the Stanford-Binet test of IQ then in its own infancy. Carrie scored a mental age of nine years, Emma of seven years and eleven months. (These figures ranked them technically as "imbeciles" by definitions of the day, hence Holmes's later choice of words—though his infamous line is often misquoted as "three generations of idiots." Imbeciles displayed a mental age of six to nine years; idiots performed worse, morons better, to round out the old nomenclature of mental deficiency.) Second, that most feeblemindedness resides ineluctably in the genes, and that Carrie Buck surely belonged with this majority. Laughlin reported:

Generally feeble-mindedness is caused by the inheritance of degenerate qualities; but sometimes it might be caused by environmental factors which are not hereditary. In the case given, the evidence points strongly toward the feeble-mindedness and moral delinquency of Carrie Buck being due, primarily, to inheritance and not to environment.

Carrie Buck's daughter was then, and has always been, the pivotal figure of this painful case. I noted in beginning this essay that we tend (often at our peril) to regard two as potential accident and three as an established pattern. The supposed imbecility of Emma and Carrie might have been an unfortunate coincidence, but the diagnosis of similar deficiency for Vivian Buck (made by a social worker, as we shall see, when Vivian was but six months old) tipped the balance in Laughlin's favor and led Holmes to declare the Buck lineage inherently corrupt by deficient heredity. Vivian sealed the pattern—*three* generations of imbeciles are enough. Besides, had Carrie not given illegitimate birth to Vivian, the issue (in both senses) would never have emerged.

Oliver Wendell Holmes viewed his work with pride. The man so renowned for his principle of judicial restraint, who had proclaimed that freedom must not be curtailed without "clear and present danger"—without the equivalent of falsely yelling "fire" in a crowded theater—wrote of his judgment in *Buck* v. *Bell:* "I felt that I was getting near the first principle of real reform."

And so *Buck* v. *Bell* remained for fifty years, a footnote to a moment of American history perhaps best forgotten. Then, in 1980, it reemerged to prick our collective conscience, when Dr. K. Ray Nelson, then director of the Lynchburg Hospital where Carrie Buck had been sterilized, researched the records of his institution and discovered that more than 4,000 sterilizations had been performed, the last as late as 1972. He also found Carrie Buck, alive and well near Charlottesville, and her sister Doris, covertly sterilized under the same law (she was told that her operation was for appendicitis), and now, with fierce dignity, dejected and bitter because she had wanted a child more than anything else in her life and had finally, in her old age, learned why she had never conceived.

As scholars and reporters visited Carrie Buck and her sister, what a few experts had known all along became abundantly clear to everyone. Carrie Buck was a woman of obviously normal intelligence. For example, Paul A. Lombardo of the School of Law at the University of Virginia, and a leading scholar of *Buck v. Bell,* wrote in a letter to me:

As for Carrie, when I met her she was reading newspapers daily and joining a more literate friend to assist at regular bouts with the crossword puzzles. She was not a sophisticated woman, and lacked social graces, but mental health professionals who examined her in later life confirmed my impressions that she was neither mentally ill nor retarded.

On what evidence, then, was Carrie Buck consigned to the State Colony for Epileptics and Feeble-Minded on January 23, 1924? I have seen the text of her commitment hearing; it is, to say the least, cursory and contradictory. Beyond the bald and undocumented say-so of her foster parents, and her own brief appearance before a commission of two doctors and a justice of the peace, no evidence was presented. Even the crude and early Stanford-Binet test, so fatally flawed as a measure of innate worth . . . but at least clothed with the aura of quantitative respectability, had not yet been applied.

When we understand why Carrie Buck was committed in January 1924, we can finally comprehend the hidden meaning of her case and its message for us today. The silent key, again as from the first, is her daughter Vivian, born on March 28, 1924, and then but an evident bump on her belly. Carrie Buck was one of several illegitimate children borne by her mother, Emma. She grew up with foster parents, J. T. and Alice Dobbs, and continued to live with them as an adult, helping out with chores around the house. She was raped by a relative of her foster parents, then blamed for the resulting pregnancy. Almost surely, she was (as they used to say) committed to hide her shame (and her rapist's identity), not because enlightened science had just discovered her true mental status. In short, she was sent away to have her baby. Her case never was about mental deficiency; Carrie Buck was persecuted for supposed sexual immorality and social deviance. The annals of her trial and hearing reek with the contempt of the well-off and well-bred for poor people of "loose morals." Who really cared whether Vivian was a baby of normal intelligence; she was the illegitimate child of an illegitimate woman. Two generations of bastards are enough. Harry Laughlin began his "family history" of the Bucks by writing: "These people belong to the shiftless, ignorant and worthless class of anti-social whites of the South."

We know little of Emma Buck and her life, but we have no more reason to suspect her than her daughter Carrie of true mental deficiency. Their supposed deviance was social and sexual; the charge of imbecility was a cover-up, Mr. Justice Holmes notwithstanding.

We come then to the crux of the case, Carrie's daughter, Vivian. What evidence was ever adduced for her mental deficiency? This and only this: At the original trial in late 1924, when Vivian Buck was seven months old, a Miss Wilhelm, social worker for the Red Cross, appeared before the court. She began by stating honestly the true reason for Carrie Buck's commitment:

Mr. Dobbs, who had charge of the girl, had taken her when a small child, had reported to Miss Duke [the temporary secretary of Public Welfare for Albemarle County] that the girl was pregnant and that he wanted to have her committed somewhere — to have her sent to some institution.

Miss Wilhelm then rendered her judgment of Vivian Buck by comparing her with the normal granddaughter of Mrs. Dobbs, born just three days earlier:

It is difficult to judge probabilities of a child as young as that, but it seems to me not quite a normal baby. In its appearance — I should say that perhaps my knowledge of the mother may prejudice me in that regard, but I saw the child at the same time as Mrs. Dobbs' daughter's baby, which is only three days older than this one, and there is a very decided difference in the development of the babies. That was about two weeks ago. There is a look about it that is not quite normal, but just what it is, I can't tell.

This short testimony, and nothing else, formed all the evidence for the crucial third generation of imbeciles. Cross-examination revealed that neither Vivian nor the Dobbs grandchild could walk or talk, and that "Mrs. Dobbs' daughter's baby is a very responsive baby. When you play with it or try to attract its attention — it is a baby that you can play with. The other baby is not. It seems very apathetic and not responsive." Miss Wilhelm then urged Carrie Buck's sterilization: "I think," she said, "it would at least prevent the propagation of her kind." Several years later, Miss Wilhelm denied that she had ever examined Vivian or deemed the child feebleminded.

Unfortunately, Vivian died at age eight of "enteric colitis" (as recorded on her death certificate), an ambiguous diagnosis that could mean many things but may well indicate that she fell victim to one of the preventable childhood diseases of poverty (a grim reminder of the real subject in *Buck* v. *Bell*). She is therefore mute as a witness in our reassessment of her famous case.

When *Buck* v. *Bell* resurfaced in 1980, it immediately struck me that Vivian's case was crucial and that evidence for the mental status of a child who died at age eight might best be found in report cards. I have therefore been trying to track down Vivian Buck's school records for the past four years and have finally succeeded. (They were supplied to me by Dr. Paul A. Lombardo, who also sent other documents, including Miss Wilhelm's testimony, and spent several hours answering my questions by mail and Lord knows how much time playing successful detective in re Vivian's school records. I have never met Dr. Lombardo; he did all this work for kindness, collegiality, and love of the game of knowledge, not for expected reward or even requested acknowledgment. In a profession—academics—so often marred by pettiness and silly squabbling over meaningless priorities, this generosity must be recorded and celebrated as a sign of how things can and should be.)

Vivian Buck was adopted by the Dobbs family, who had raised (but later sent away) her mother, Carrie. As Vivian Alice Elaine Dobbs, she attended the Venable Public Elementary School of Charlottesville for four terms, from September 1930 until May 1932, a month before her death. She was a perfectly normal, quite average student, neither particularly outstanding nor much troubled. In those days before grade inflation, when C meant "good, 81–87" (as defined on her report card) rather than barely scraping by, Vivian Dobbs received A's and B's for deportment and C's for all academic subjects but mathematics (which was always difficult for her, and where she scored D) during her first term in Grade 1A, from September 1930

to January 1931. She improved during her second term in 1B, meriting an A in deportment, C in mathematics, and B in all other academic subjects; she was placed on the honor roll in April 1931. Promoted to 2A, she had trouble during the fall term of 1931, failing mathematics and spelling but receiving A in deportment, B in reading, and C in writing and English. She was "retained in 2A" for the next term—or "left back" as we used to say, and scarcely a sign of imbecility as I remember all my buddies who suffered a similar fate. In any case, she again did well in her final term, with B in deportment, reading, and spelling, and C in writing, English, and mathematics during her last month in school. This daughter of "lewd and immoral" women excelled in deportment and performed adequately, although not brilliantly, in her academic subjects.

In short, we can only agree with the conclusion that Dr. Lombardo has reached in his research on *Buck* v. *Bell*—there were no imbeciles, not a one, among the three generations of Bucks. I don't know that such correction of cruel but forgotten errors of history counts for much, but I find it both symbolic and satisfying to learn that forced eugenic sterilization, a procedure of such dubious morality, earned its official justification (and won its most quoted line of rhetoric) on a patent falsehood.

Carrie Buck died last year. By a quirk of fate, and not by memory or design, she was buried just a few steps from her only daughter's grave. In the umpteenth and ultimate verse of a favorite old ballad, a rose and a brier—the sweet and the bitter—emerge from the tombs of Barbara Allen and her lover, twining about each other in the union of death. May Carrie and Vivian, victims in different ways and in the flower of youth, rest together in peace.

ROBERT JAY LIFTON

Sterilization and the Nazi Biomedical Vision

The Führer holds the cleansing of the medical profession far more important than, for example, that of the bureaucracy, since in his opinion the duty of the physician is or should be one of racial leadership.

—Martin Bormann

The *völkisch* state must see to it that only the healthy beget children. . . . Here the state must act as the guardian of a millennial future. . . . It must put the most modern medical means in the service of this knowledge. It must declare unfit for propagation all who are in any way visibly sick or who have inherited a disease and can therefore pass it on.

—Adolf Hitler

FIRST STEPS: POLICIES AND THE COURTS

Only in Nazi Germany was sterilization a forerunner of mass murder. Programs of coercive sterilization were not peculiar to Nazi Germany. They have existed in much of the Western world, including the United States, which has a history of coercive and sometimes illegal sterilization applied mostly to the underclass of our society. It was in the United States that a relatively simple form of vasectomy was developed at a penal institution around the turn of the century. This procedure, together with a rising interest in eugenics, led, by 1920, to the enactment of laws in twenty-five states providing for compulsory sterilization of the criminally insane and other people considered genetically inferior.

No wonder that Fritz Lenz, a German physician-geneticist advocate of sterilization (later a leading ideologue in the Nazi program of "racial hygiene"), could, in 1923, berate his countrymen for their backwardness in the domain of sterilization as compared with the United States. Lenz complained that provisions in the Weimar Constitution (prohibiting the infliction of bodily alterations on human beings) prevented widespread use of vasectomy techniques; that Germany had nothing to match the eugenics research institutions in England and the United States (for instance, that at Cold Spring Harbor, New York, led by Charles B. Davenport and funded by the Carnegie Institution in Washington and by Mary Harriman); and that Germany had no equivalent to the American laws prohibiting marriage both for people suffering from such conditions as epilepsy or mental retardation, and between people of different races. Lenz criticized America only for focusing too generally on preserving the "white race" instead of specifically on the "Nordic race"—yet was convinced that "the next round in the thousand year fight for the life of the Nordic race will probably be fought in America."[2]* That single reservation suggests the early German focus on a specific racial entity, the "Nordic" or "Aryan race," however unsupported by existing knowledge.

There had been plenty of racial-eugenic passion in the United States, impulses to sterilize large numbers of criminals and mental patients out of fear of "national degeneration" and of threat to the health of "the civilized races," who were seen to be "biologically plunging downward." Associated with the American eugenics movement was a biomedical vision whose extent is suggested by the following quotation from a 1923 book by A. E. Wiggam: "The first warning

---

*Lenz did not at this point infer anti-Semitism from his belief in racial differences. Citing him, among others, George L. Mosse has argued that "there is no warrant for the claim to see in the . . . doctrine of 'racial biology and hygiene' an immediate forerunner of the Nazi policy against the Jews."[2] But once the Jews came to be viewed as a race, the connection was readily made.

which biology gives to statesmanship is that the advanced races of mankind are going backward; . . . that civilization, as you have so far administered it, is self-destructive; that civilization always destroys the man that builds it; that your vast efforts to improve man's lot, instead of improving man, are hastening the hour of his destruction."[3]*

(A clear distinction must be made between genetics and eugenics. Genetics was, and is, a legitimate science, though one with limited development at the time [it began as a science with the recognition of Mendel's laws in 1900]; its principles were crudely, often falsely, applied by the Nazis. "Eugenics" is a term coined by Francis Galton in 1883 to denote the principle of strengthening a biological group on the basis of ostensible hereditary worth; despite its evolutionary claims and later reference to genetic laws, eugenics has no scientific standing.)

But the German version of eugenics had a characteristic tone of romantic excess, as in Lenz's earlier (1917) declaration, in a thesis written for his professor, Alfred Ploetz (a social-Darwinist and the founder, in 1904, of the German Society for Racial Hygiene), that "race was the criterion of value" and "the State is not there to see that the individual gets his rights, but to serve the race." Lenz understood his advocacy to be one of "organic socialism" and feared that, without a radical eugenics project, "our [Nordic] race is doomed to extinction."[5]

For Germans like Lenz in the 1920s, establishing widespread compulsory sterilization became a sacred mission—a mission that led them to embrace National Socialism, with its similar commitment. While American and British advocates of eugenics sometimes approached this German romantic excess, the political systems in the two countries allowed for open criticism and for legal redress. In Britain there was continual legal resistance to coercive sterilization; and in the United States, legal questions could be raised concerning individual rights and limited knowledge about heredity, which eventually led to the rescinding or inactivation of sterilization laws in the states where they had been passed.* In Nazi Germany, on the other hand, the genetic romanticism of an extreme biomedical vision combined with a totalistic political structure to enable the nation to carry out relentlessly, and without legal interference, a more extensive program of compulsory sterilization than had ever previously been attempted. Indeed, the entire Nazi regime was built on a biomedical vision that *required* the kind of racial purification that would progress from sterilization to extensive killing.†

As early as his publication of *Mein Kampf* between 1924 and 1926, Hitler had declared the sacred racial mission of the German people to be "assembling and preserving the most valuable stocks of basic racial elements [and] . . . slowly and surely raising them to a dominant position." He was specific about the necessity for sterilization *("the most modern medical means")* on behalf of an immortalizing vision of the state-mediated race *("a millennial future")*. And for him the stakes were absolute: *"If the power to fight for one's own health is no longer present, the right to live in this world of struggle ends."*[9]

Once in power—Hitler took the oath of office as Chancellor of the Third Reich on 30 January 1933—the Nazi regime made sterilization the first application of the biomedical imagination to this issue of collective life or death. On 22 June, Wilhelm Frick, the minister of the interior, introduced the early sterilization law with a declaration that Germany was in grave danger of *Volkstod* ("death of the people" [or "nation" or "race"]) and that harsh and sweeping measures were therefore imperative. The law was implemented three weeks later, less than six months after Hitler had become chancellor, and was extended by amendation later that year. It became basic sterilization doctrine and set the tone for the regime's medicalized approach to "life unworthy of life." Included among the "hereditarily sick" who were to be surgically sterilized were

---

*In a 1932 study of the sterilization movement in the United States, J. P. Landman spoke of "alarmist eugenics" and of "over zealous and over ardent eugenicists" who "regard the socially inadequate persons, i.e., the feeble-minded, the epileptics, the mentally diseased, the blind, the deformed and the criminals as inimical to the human race . . . [because] these peoples perpetuate their deficiencies and thus threaten the quality of the ensuing generations. It should be our aim to exterminate these undesirables, they contend, since a nation must defend itself against national degeneration as much as against the external foreign enemy."[4]

*In observing Nazi sterilization policies, the *Journal of the American Medical Association* did not so much express outrage as it contrasted America's "more gradual evolution of practice and principles" regarding sterilization.[6] Ardent American sterilizers, such as Dr. Joseph S. De Jarnette of Virginia, could even complain: "The Germans are beating us at our own game."[7]

†Thus Daniel J. Kevles reports: "Within three years, German authorities had sterilized some two hundred and twenty-five thousand people, almost ten times the number so treated in the previous thirty years in America."[8]

the categories of congenital feeblemindedness (now called mental deficiency), an estimated 200,000; schizophrenia, 80,000; manic depressive insanity, 20,000; epilepsy, 60,000; Huntington's chorea (a hereditary brain disorder), 600; hereditary blindness, 4,000; hereditary deafness, 16,000; grave bodily malformation, 20,000; and hereditary alcoholism, 10,000. The projected total of 410,000 was considered only preliminary, drawn mostly from people already in institutions; it was assumed that much greater numbers of people would eventually be identified and sterilized.

Special "Hereditary Health Courts" were set up to make decisions on sterilization, their composition reflecting the desired combination of medicalization and Nazi Party influence. Of the three members, two were physicians—one an administrative health officer likely to have close Party ties and the other ostensibly knowledgeable about issues of hereditary health; the third was a district judge, also likely to be close to the regime, who served as chairman and coordinator. There were also appeals courts, which made final decisions in contested cases and on which some of the regime's most recognized medical leaders served. All physicians were legally required to report to health officers anyone they encountered in their practice or elsewhere who fell into any of the preceding categories for sterilization, and also to give testimony on such matters unrestricted by the principle of patient-doctor confidentiality. Physicians also performed the surgical procedures. The entire process was backed up by law and police power.[10]

On 18 October 1935, a major ordinance regulating sterilization and the issuing of marriage licenses followed directly upon the notorious Nuremberg Laws (15 September), which prohibited marriage or any sexual contact between Jews and non-Jews. The Nuremberg lawmakers described themselves as "permeated with the knowledge that the purity of the German blood is a precondition for the continued existence of the German people, and filled with the inflexible determination to make the German nation secure for all future time."[11]

There were revealing discussions of method. The favored surgical procedures were ligation of the vas deferens in men and of the ovarian tubes in women. Professor G. A. Wagner, director of the University of Berlin's Women's Clinic, advocated that the law provide an option for removing the entire uterus in mentally deficient women. His convoluted argument was based on the principle of "hereditary health": mentally deficient women, after being sterilized, were especially likely to attract the opposite sex (who need not worry about impregnating them) and therefore to develop gonorrhea, which is most resistant to treatment when it affects the uterine cervix; the men who would then contract gonorrhea from these women would, in turn, infect other women with desirable hereditary traits and render them sterile. Other medical commentators, making a less genetic and more specifically moralistic argument, favored removal of the uterus in those candidates for sterilization who showed tendencies to promiscuity.* Still more foreboding was an official edict permitting sterilization by irradiation (X rays or radium) in certain specified cases "on the basis of scientific experiments."[13] These experiments, ostensibly in the service of improving medical procedures for specific cases, were a preliminary step toward later X-ray sterilization experiments conducted extensively, harmfully, and sometimes fatally on Jewish men and women in Auschwitz and elsewhere.

Directors of institutions of various kinds had a strong impulse to sterilize in order to eliminate the possible hereditary influence of a wide variety of conditions—blindness, deafness, congenital defects, and such "crippled" states as clubfoot, harelip, and cleft palate.[14] The genetically dominated worldview demanded of physicians led to discussions of the advisability of sterilizing not only the weak and impaired but their relatives, anyone who might be a "carrier" of these defects. Not surprisingly, Fritz Lenz carried the concept farthest in suggesting the advisability of sterilizing people with only slight signs of mental disease, though he recognized that a radical application of this principle would lead to the sterilization of 20 percent of the total German population—something on the order of twenty million people![15]

In that atmosphere, humane efforts were likely to take the form of pleas for restriction and exemption: for example, the recommendation by the distinguished anti-Nazi Berlin psychiatrist Karl Bonhoeffer that people who combined hereditary defects with unusual qualities or talents should not be sterilized; and the Munich psychiatrist Dr. Oswald Bumke's recommendation against sterilizing people who were schizoid rather than schizophrenic, along with his cautionary statement that schizophrenia itself could not be eliminated by sterilization because of the complexity of

---

*There was, indeed, concern that degenerate individuals might seek sterilization to pursue "unrestrained sexual gratification."[12]

hereditary influences.[16] (The eugenics courts sometimes did make exceptions for the artistically gifted.)

But the regime discouraged qualifications and employed a rhetoric of medical emergency: "dangerous patients" and "urgent cases" were people with hereditary taints still in the prime of life. Among "urgent cases" were mentally deficient but physically healthy men and women between the ages of sixteen and forty, schizophrenic and manic-depressive patients in remission, epileptics and alcoholics under the age of fifty, etc.[17] Once a petition was heard before a sterilization court, the die was pretty well cast. More than 90 percent of petitions taken before the special courts in 1934 resulted in sterilization (though a screening process eliminated some before they got to court); and fewer than 5 percent of appeals against sterilization made to higher courts, were upheld.[18] But the principle of legality was nonetheless extremely important, and the strict secrecy surrounding court deliberations lent power and mystery to this expression of medicalized authority.

The legal structure cloaked considerable chaos and arbitrariness in criteria for sterilization (especially concerning mental conditions, which resulted in the greatest number of sterilizations) and concerning alleged hereditary factors. Inevitably, too, political considerations affected diagnoses and decisions — as was made clear by a directive from Martin Bormann, Hitler's private secretary and close associate, instructing that the moral and political behavior of a person be considered in making a diagnosis of feeblemindedness. The clear implication was that one could be quick to label "feebleminded" a person seen as hostile to the Nazis, but that one should be cautious indeed about so labeling an ideologically enthusiastic Party member. Political currents and whims also affected the project in various ways; and, despite its high priority, there were undoubtedly periods of diminished enthusiasm for sterilization. No one really knows how many people were actually sterilized; reliable estimates are generally between 200,000 and 350,000.[19]

In association with the sterilization laws, and as a further expression of racial policy, steps were taken to establish a national card index of people with hereditary taints. Special research institutes for hereditary biology and racial hygiene were set up at universities — for example, the institute established by Otmar von Verschuer, a professor at Frankfurt. These institutes sought genetic information about individuals extending back over several generations, and made use of hospitals, courts, and local and national health institutions. The physician, as genetic counselor and policeman, could be the vigilant "protector of the family that is free from hereditary defects."[20] In other words, sterilization was the medical fulcrum of the Nazi biocracy.

FANATICAL GENETICS: THE ROLE OF ERNST RÜDIN

The predominant medical presence in the Nazi sterilization program was Dr. Ernst Rüdin, a Swiss-born psychiatrist of international renown. Originally a student of Emil Kraepelin, the great classical psychiatrist, Rüdin became a close associate of Alfred Ploetz in establishing the German Society for Racial Hygiene. Rüdin was an indefatigable researcher and saw as his mission the application of Mendelian laws and eugenic principles to psychiatry. A former student and associate of his told me that "the aim of his life" was to establish the genetic basis for psychiatric conditions, and that "he was not so much a fanatical Nazi as a fanatical geneticist."

But a Nazi Rüdin did become, joining the Party in 1937 at the age of sixty. From his prestigious position as director of the Research Institute for Psychiatry of the Kaiser Wilhelm Society in Munich, Rüdin worked closely with a regime whose commitment to genetic principles he applauded, and was one of the principle architects of the sterilization laws. He became a significant source of scientific legitimation for the regime's racial policies (including consultations with Hans F. K. Günther, the leading Nazi anthropologist-publicist on racial matters, whose intellectual repute was generally held to be very low). Rüdin was not involved in the direct medical killing of the "euthanasia" program; but a younger associate to whom I spoke had the impression that his teacher, though not without doubts about the program, could well have favored a version of it with careful medical control.

In a special 1943 issue of his journal, *Archive für Rassen-und Gesellschaftsbiologie* (Archive of Racial and Social Biology), celebrating ten years of National Socialist rule, Rüdin extolled Hitler and the movement for its "decisive . . . path-breaking step toward making racial hygiene a fact among the German people . . . and inhibiting the propagation of the congenitally ill and inferior." He praised both the Nuremberg Laws for "preventing the further penetration of the German gene pool by Jewish blood," and the SS for "its ultimate goal, the creation of a special group of medically superior and healthy people of the German Nordic type."[21]

A close relative, also a physician, told me that Rüdin felt it "necessary" to write those things and, in response to my question whether he had meant them at the time, answered, "Well, half and half." While Rüdin apparently did eventually become disillusioned with the regime, he could never (according to a former colleague) bring himself to resign his positions but sought always to work from within.*

No one I spoke to thought Rüdin a cruel person; to the contrary, he was seen as decent and dedicated to his work. Yet he not only served the regime but, in his person and scientific reputation, did much to effect the medicalization of racial policies—not quite those of killing but of suppressing in specific groups the continuity of life. He also demonstrates, in extreme form, the attraction of the Nazi biomedical vision for a certain kind of biologically and genetically oriented scientist.

OPPOSITION TO STERILIZATION

There did not seem to be much opposition to sterilization. The Catholic Church disapproved of it, but avoided confronting the issue and did little more than press for the exemption of Catholic judges and doctors from enforcing the law. One judge on a Hereditary Health Appeals Court raised the interesting question of the "burden of unusual responsibility" placed on doctors required to perform operations that "serve no therapeutic purpose." But Gerhard Wagner—then the leading Nazi medical authority and a zealous advocate of sterilization—denied any such moral conflict in doctors; and a Party newspaper ran a column with the significant heading "Life or Death," which made the simple point that the life of the nation took precedence over "dogma and conflicts of conscience," and also that opposition to the government's program would be met with strong retaliation.[23]

The great majority of the doctors I interviewed told me that they approved of the sterilization laws at the time. They believed the laws to be consistent with

prevailing medical and genetic knowledge concerning the prevention of hereditary defects, though a few of these doctors had some hesitation about the laws' compulsory features. The doctors all stressed their absolute distinction between those sterilization policies and later "euthanasia."

Decisions about sterilization were affected by bureaucratic struggles both between doctors and lawyers and between extremely ardent and less ardent advocates of the procedure. One doctor I interviewed, Johann S., who had been a leading organizer and high-level participant in Nazi medical programs including sterilization, thought that "the law was totally messed up by the legal people." He and his medical colleagues believed strongly that "it would have been more appropriate to leave this decision [about whom and when to sterilize] to a doctors' team." While psychiatrists later emphasized their restraint, Dr. S. related incidents in which they had to be restrained from sterilizing people with relatively benign psychological difficulties such as treatable depressions. He told how even Gerhard Wagner (whom he tended to glorify) had restrained a physician-health officer with the admonition, "This is not a rabbit hunt." While Dr. S. recognized that excessive zeal was widespread, he tended to excuse it as a product of the idealism of that time: "The great enthusiasm that carried through the developments between 1933 and 1939 cannot be denied. Everybody wanted to contribute. One of the first National Socialist laws to be enacted was the law on [hereditary] health. Thus the [state] health officers demonstrated their ambition to have as many people as possible sterilized."

THE NAZIFICATION OF MEDICINE

Nazification of the medical profession—a key aspect of the transition from sterilization to direct medical killing—was achieved by a combination of ideological enthusiasm and systematic terror. An influential manual by Rudolf Ramm of the medical faculty of the University of Berlin proposed that each doctor was to be no longer merely a caretaker of the sick but was to become a "cultivator of the genes," a "physician to the *Volk*," and a "biological soldier." While Ramm harked back to traditional forms of medical idealism ("inner calling, high ethics, profound knowledge . . . sacrifice and dedication"), he favored abandoning the old "liberal-materialistic spirit" (associated especially with the harmful influence of Jews in the profession) and acquiring instead "the idealistic

---

*Rüdin's defenders later claimed that he contested the "euthanasia" program from within. This is unlikely, as efforts in 1940 of two psychiatrists to enlist Rüdin, and through him the German Psychiatric Society, for opposition to the killing met with no success. . . . Rüdin received two high awards from Hitler as the "pathfinder in the field of hereditary hygiene."[22]

Weltanschauung of National Socialism." Thus, the physician could carry out what Gerhard Wagner identified as the task of his Public Health Office: the "promotion and perfection of the health of the German people . . . to ensure that the people realize the full potential of their racial and genetic endowment." [24] Ramm went on to speak of "breakthroughs in biological thinking" under National Socialism that enabled medical leaders to take an important part in projects to reverse racial decay such as the Nuremberg Laws and the sterilization program. To carry these programs out properly, the individual physician must become a "genetics doctor" *(Erbarzt)*. He could then become a "caretaker of the race" and a "politician of population." By following "public care" functions of preventing "bastardization through the propagation of unworthy and racially alien elements . . . and maintaining and increasing those of sound heredity," he could attain the national goal of "keeping our blood pure." [25]

Ramm also discussed the virtues of sterilization and labeled "erroneous" the widespread belief that a doctor should under no circumstances take a patient's life, since for the incurably sick and insane, "euthanasia" was the most "merciful treatment" and "an obligation to the *Volk*." That obligation was always central. The physician was to be concerned with the health of the *Volk* even more than with individual disease and was to teach them to overcome the old individualistic principle of "the right to one's own body" and to embrace instead the "duty to be healthy." [26] Thus, Johann S. spoke to me with pride about the principle of being "doctor to the *Volkskörper* ['national body' or 'people's body']" and of "our duty . . . to the collectivity."

Ramm's manual also specified that a doctor was to be a biological militant, "an alert biological soldier" living under "the great idea of the National Socialist biological state structure." . . . For it claimed that "National Socialism, unlike any other political philosophy or Party program, is in accord with the natural history and biology of man." [27]

Physicians could thrill to that message. Dr. S., for instance, described joining the Party immediately after hearing Deputy Party Leader Rudolf Hess say, at a mass meeting in 1934, "National Socialism is nothing but applied biology." And in his work of Nazi medical organizing, this doctor saw himself as primarily spreading a biological message: "We wanted to put into effect the laws of life, which are biological laws." His medical faction was disdainful of any politics that

did not follow that principle: "We understood National Socialism from the biological side — we introduced biological considerations into [Party] policies." He stressed the conviction that physicians alone possess the necessary combination of theoretical knowledge and direct human experience to serve as the authentic biological evangelists: "Every practitioner has much more knowledge about biology than a philosopher or what have you, because he has seen it."

At the same time, it was claimed that the desired identity of the Nazi physician evolved naturally from medical tradition — a tradition that now required "Germanizing" and "eugenicizing." One lavishly illustrated volume by two medical historians was entitled *The Face of the Germanic Doctor over Four Centuries*. It featured Paracelsus, the great sixteenth-century Swiss-German physician-alchemist, and praised him for both his scientific empiricism and his nationalism. He was quoted as saying, "Each country developed its own sickness, medicine, and its own doctor." More recent German scientists, especially Carl Correns who did pioneering work in plant genetics, were hailed as having "created the foundation for the eugenic and racial-biological measures of the National Socialist people's state." The authors' SS ranks are included;* and the introduction by Ernst Robert von Grawitz, chief physician of the SS, puts forward the concept of the physician, past and present, as the "protector of life" who "knows himself to be deeply obligated to the future of our *Volk*." [28†]

Another such introduction to a volume on medical ethics was written by Joachim Mrugowsky, a high-ranking SS doctor who became head of the Hygienic Institute, which was responsible for maintaining and distributing the Zyklon-B gas used at Auschwitz. Mrugowsky was put to death at Nuremberg in 1948 for his extensive involvement in fatal medical experiments. The book he introduced had been written a hundred years earlier by Christoph Wilhelm Hufeland, one of Germany's great modern physician-humanists.

---

*The SS (*Schutzstaffel*, or defense squadron) began as Hitler's personal guard unit. Particularly after 1929, under the control of Heinrich Himmler, it advertised itself as an élite corps whose members fit the ideal Aryan model. As such, it attracted considerable support from the aristocracy and professional classes, including physicians. . . .

†The concept of "Germanic" physicians included Austrians, Dutch, Belgians, and Scandinavians.

In his introduction, Mrugowsky focused upon the doctor's function as "the priest of the holy flame of life" (in Hufeland's words), and on the "art of healing" as the doctor's "divine mission." Partially anticipating his own future, he spoke of the National Socialist breakdown of the distinction between research and healing, since the results of the work of the researcher are for the benefit of the *Volk*.[29]

Inevitably, the Nazi medical ideal went back to Hippocrates and related itself to the Hippocratic oath. The claim was that medicine had been "despiritualized" mainly by what Gerhard Wagner identified as the "mechanically oriented spirit" of Jewish teachers. There was thus a need to "return to the ethics and high moral status of an earlier generation . . . which stood on [the] solid philosophical ground" of the Hippocratic oath.[30] Finally, the *Reichsführer* of the SS and overall head of the Nazi police system, Henrich Himmler himself embraced Hippocrates as a model for SS physicians. In a brief introduction to a series of short books for SS doctors under the overall title "Eternal Doctors," Himmler spoke of "the great Greek doctor Hippocrates," of the "unity of character and accomplishment" of his life, which "proclaims a morality, the strengths of which are still undiminished today and shall continue to determine medical action and thought in the future." The series was edited by Grawitz and possessed the ultimate imprimatur in being "authorized" by none other than Hitler himself.[31] In testimony at the Nuremberg Medical Trial, a witness referred to the Nazi embrace of Hippocratic principles as "an ironical joke of world history."[32] But this ultimate absurdity had an internal logic: the sense of recasting the medical profession — and the entire German nation — in the service of larger healing.

There was one area in which the Nazis did insist upon a clear break with medical tradition. They mounted a consistent attack upon what they viewed as exaggerated Christian compassion for the weak individual instead of tending to the health of the group, of the *Volk*. This partly Nietzschean position, as articulated by Ramm, included a rejection of the Christian principle of *caritas* or charity, and of the Church's "commandment to attend to the incurably ill person and render him medical aid unto his death."[33] The same position was expressed in the Nazi Party medical outlet *Ziel und Weg* (Aim and Road) from the time of its founding in 1931. The matter was put strongly by Dr. Arthur Guett, a high-ranking health official, who declared that "the ill-conceived 'love of thy neighbor' has to disappear. . . . It is the supreme duty of the . . . state to grant life and livelihood only to the healthy and hereditarily sound portion of the population in order to secure . . . a hereditarily sound and racially pure folk [Volk] for all eternity." He added the visionary-idealistic principle that "the life of the individual has meaning only in the light of that ultimate aim."[34] The doctor, like everyone in Nazi Germany, was expected to become "hardened," to adopt what Hitler himself called the "ice-cold logic" of the necessary.

The keynote of the Nazi policy was transformation, in Ramm's words: "a change in the attitude of each and every doctor, and a spiritual and mental regeneration of the entire medical profession." The true physician, moreover, "must not only be a Party member on the outside, but rather must be convinced in his heart of hearts of the biological laws that form the center of his life." He was also to be a "preacher for these laws."[35] Dr. S. believed that Nazi medicine had achieved some of this transformation: that is, it had overcome the exaggerated stress on "technical things," reversed the prior tendency to "know only cases and not people," and "put in the foreground the questions of the psyche that had been neglected."

But the Nazis sought something more than mere psychosomatic inclusiveness or "holistic" medicine: their quest had the quality of *biological and medical mysticism*. Mrugowsky, for instance, wrote, in the introduction mentioned earlier, that "today the [German] *Volk* is holy to us." Of the physician's relationship to the *Volk*, or "community of fate," Mrugowsky added that "only in the art of healing does he find the myth of life."[36] Other writers had viewed the Third Reich as "immanent in all German history, which strives toward that moment when the *Volk* becomes the vessel of God."[37] But in the vision I am describing, the physician-biologists saw themselves as the core of the mystical body of the *Volk*.

There had to develop, as one Nazi doctor put it, "a totality of the physicians' community, with physicians having total dedication to the *Volk*." This doctor's term for his biological mysticism was "biological socialism." The Nazis, he insisted, had been able to bring together nationalism and socialism because of their "recognition of the natural phenomena of life." Thus, "for the first time, the mind begins to understand that there are powerful forces over it which it must acknowledge"; that "the human being becomes . . . a working member in the kingdom of the living; and that his powers will be fulfilled when working within the balanced interplay of natural forces." We may say that mysticism, especially communal mysticism, was given a biological and medical face.

NOTES

(The numbers in brackets refer to the original, complete citation of a particular reference in each chapter. The dates in brackets denote original publication of a title.)

1. Fritz Lenz, *Menschliche Auslese and Rassenhygiene,* vol. II of Erwin Bauer, Eugen Fischer, and Lenz, *Grundriss der menschlichen Erblichkeitslehre und Rassenhygiene* (Munich: J. F. Lehmanns Verlag, 1923), p. 147. See the expanded version of this joint work's third (1927) edition, especially for American readers: *Human Heredity* (New York: Macmillan, 1931). On Davenport and Cold Spring Harbor, see Daniel J. Kevles, *In the Name of Eugenics: Genetics and the Uses of Human Heredity* (New York: Alfred A. Knopf, 1985), pp. 44–56.

2. George L. Mosse, *Toward the Final Solution: A History of European Racism* (New York: Harper & Row, 1978), p. 81.

3. Albert Edward Wiggam, *New Decalogue of Science* (Indianapolis: Bobbs-Merrill, 1923), pp. 25–26.

4. J[acob] P. Landman, *Human Sterilization: The History of the Sexual Sterilization Movement* (New York: Macmillan, 1932), pp. 4–5.

5. Helmut Krausnick, "The Persecution of the Jews," in Krausnick et al., *Anatomy of the SS State* (New York: Walker, 1968 [1965]), pp. 16–17.

6. "Human Sterilization in Germany and the United States," *JAMA [Journal of the American Medical Association]* 102 (1934): 1501–2; see Kevles, *Eugenics* [1], pp. 113–17.

7. Kevles, *Eugenics* [1], p. 116.

8. Ibid., p. 117.

9. Adolf Hitler, *Mein Kampf* (Boston: Houghton Mifflin, 1943 [1925–26]), pp. 403–4, 257, respectively.

10. *JAMA* 101 (1933):866–67; 102 (1934):630–31, 1501; 103 (1934):849–50. W. W. Peter, "Germany's Sterilization Program," *American Journal of Public Health* 24 (1934):187.

11. *JAMA* 105 (1935):1999.

12. *JAMA* 104 (1935):2109 (Wagner); 101 (1933):867; 106 (1936):1582.

13. *JAMA* 106 (1936):1582.

14. *JAMA* 103 (1934):766–67, 850; 106 (1936):58, 308–09.

15. *JAMA* 104 (1935):2110.

16. *JAMA* 102 (1934):57; 103 (1934):1164; 104 (1935):2110.

17. *JAMA* 104 (1935):1183.

18. *JAMA* 105 (1935):1051.

19. W[alter] von Baeyer, "Die Bestätigung der NS-Ideologie in der Medizin unter besonderer Berücksichtigung der Euthanasie," *Universitätstage* 5 (1966):64; Ernst Klee, *"Euthanasie" im NS-Staat: Die "Vernichtung lebensunwerten Lebens"* (Frankfurt/M.:

S. Fischer, 1983), p. 86. Much of my manuscript had been completed when this important book appeared, but I have used it to confirm and supplement information from other sources. Another important recent study is Gisela Bock, "Racism and Sexism in Nazi Germany: Motherhood, Compulsory Sterilization and the State," in *When Biology Became Destiny: Women in Weimar and Nazi Germany,* Renate Bridenthal, Atina Grossmann, and Marion Kaplan, eds. (New York: Monthly Review, 1985), pp. 271–96.

20. *JAMA* 105 (1935):1052–53.

21. Ernst Rüdin, "Zehn Jahre nationalsozialistischer Staat," *Archiv für Rassen- und Gesellschaftsbiologie* 36 (1942):321.

22. Robert Wistrich, *Who's Who in Nazi Germany* (New York: Macmillan, 1982), p. 261. See also B. Schultz, "Ernst Rüdin," *Archiv für Psychiatrie und Zeitschrift für Neurologie* 190 (1953):189–95.

23. Judge Goetz and Wagner quoted in *JAMA* 106 (1936):1582; party paper in *JAMA* 105 (1935):1051.

24. Rudolf Ramm, *Ärztliche Rechts- und Standeskunde: Der Arzt als Gesundheitserzieher,* 2d. rev. ed. (Berlin: W. deGruyter, 1943), pp. iv, 43, 79–80.

25. Ibid., pp. 101, 135.

26. Ibid., pp. 154–56.

27. Ibid. See Kurt Blome, *Arzt im Kampf: Erlebnisse and Gedanken* (Leipzig: J. A. Barth, 1942).

28. Bernward J. Gottlieb and Alexander Berg, *Das Antlitz des Germanischen Arztes in vier Jahrhunderten* (Berlin: Rembrandt-Verlag, 1942), pp. 3, 51–52.

29. Joachim Mrugowsky, "Einleitung," Christoph Wilhelm Hufeland, *Das ärztliche Ethos: Christoph Wilhelm Hufelands Vermächtnis einer fünfzigjährigen Erfahrung* (Munich and Berlin: J. F. Lehmann, 1939), pp. 14–15, 22; see pp. 7–40.

30. Hanns Löhr, *Über die Stellung und Bedeutung der Heilkunde im nationalsozialistischen Staate* (1935), quoted in George L. Mosse, ed., *Nazi Culture: Intellectual, Cultural and Social Life in the Third Reich* (New York: Grosset & Dunlap, 1968), p. 229.

31. Ernst Grawitz, ed., *Hippokrates: Gedanken ärztlicher Ethik aus dem Corpus Hippocraticum,* vol. I: *Ewiges Arzttum* (Prague, Amsterdam, Berlin, and Vienna: Volk und Reich Verlag, 1942), p. 5.

32. Werner Leibbrandt, 27 January 1947, *Nuremberg Medical Case,* vol. II, p. 81.

33. Ramm, *Ärztliche Standeskunde* [24], p. 19. On the Nazis' related elevation of pain, see Michael H. Kater, "Medizinische Fakultäten und Medizinstudenten: Eine Skizze," in Fridolf Kudlien, ed., *Ärzte im Nationalsozialismus* (Cologne: Kiepenheuer & Witsch, 1985), p. 93.

34. *Nuremberg Medical Case* [32], vol. I, p. 58.

35. Ramm, *Ärztliche Standeskunde* [24], pp. 80–83.

36. Mrugowsky, "Einleitung" [29], pp. 9–10, 14.

37. George L. Mosse, *Masses and Man: Nationalist and Fascist Perceptions of Reality* (New York: Fertig, 1980), p. 81.

VICTOR A. McKUSICK

The Human Genome Project: Plans, Status, and Applications in Biology and Medicine

The Human Genome Project aims to map and sequence completely the human genome. The sequence is the ultimate map. The National Research Council/National Academy of Sciences (NRC/NAS) committee, which concluded that the Human Genome Project was worthwhile and could be done in a reasonable time frame and budget, suggested "map first, sequence later."[1] No absolute stepwise dichotomy was in the mind of the committee, but this order was considered advisable because both the gene map and the "contig [adjacent DNA segments] map" are necessary for most efficient sequencing, and the technology for sequencing requires improvement.

Given adequate funding (an estimated $200 million a year for the worldwide effort, in 1988 dollars), the Project should be completed by 2005. Spinoff in applications to medicine, in particular, will occur continuously during that period. The end product of the project is: a reference map (and sequence)—a source book for human biology and medicine for centuries to come. Two broad areas—variation and function—will occupy scientists for many years. It is urged by some that studies of variation in populations worldwide begin immediately because the disappearance of some populations through assimilation or attrition is erasing the history of evolution. Important as these studies are, it seems clear that the extent of variation is not such that confusion will arise in assembling the reference map. The journalist's question "Whose genome will be mapped and sequenced?" is irrelevant. Although the source of DNA used in sequencing should be recorded, the final map and sequence will be a composite of information from many individuals. The extent of variation of the human genome will need to be studied later. Variation and function are the essence of biology and genetics; it is ridiculous to expect the Human Genome Project to do it all and it would be imprudent to diffuse the effort. It will be important to "keep our eyes on the ball" if the main objective of a complete map and sequence is to be achieved in a timely manner and within the budget limits set.

Doing the entire job will represent economy of scale, and having the map/sequence information will facilitate greatly the elucidation of genetic disease. Cystic fibrosis is a case in point: identification of the gene was an expensive project and would undoubtedly have been much less expensive (how much less is also hard to say) if the complete sequence had been available.

TYPES OF MAPS

Gene mapping subsumes both genetic linkage maps, which are derived from meiotic recombination frequencies and measured in centimorgans (cMs), and physical maps, which are based on various experimental methods. . . . The large-fragment clones that are produced by yeast artificial chromosome (YAC)

From "The Human Genome Project: Plans, Status, and Applications in Biology and Medicine," by Victor A. McKusick, in George J. Annas and Sherman Elias, eds., *Gene Mapping: Using Law and Ethics as Guides* (New York: Oxford University Press, 1992), pp. 18–21, 24, 26–27, 36–42. Copyright © 1992 by Oxford University Press, Inc. Reprinted by permission.

Total Number of Entries in *Mendelian Inheritance in Man*

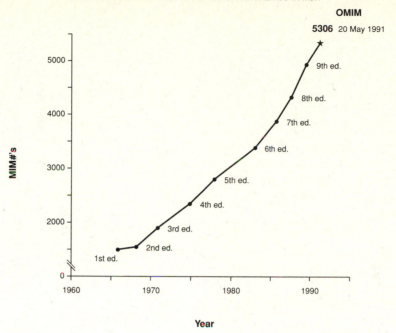

Figure 1.   Total number of entries in successive editions of *Mendelian Inheritance in Man* and in the online version (OMIM).

cloning are permitting the creation of "contig maps" for each chromosome, that is, maps of overlapping, and therefore contiguous, DNA segments. Smaller segments, cosmid clones, have been used for the same purpose but are less efficient. These mapped segments can be used for mapping genes of unknown location by hybridization. They are also the raw material for nucleotide [bases; the smallest units in DNA or RNA] sequencing. The contig map is the penultimate physical map; the nucleotide sequence is the ultimate map.

The correlation of the genetic map (based on the location of cloned genes and anonymous DNA segments through family linkage studies) and the physical map (as represented by the contig map, for example) is likely to be aided by the use of sequence-tagged sites (STSs).[2] They may obviate, to a considerable extent, the need to store and distribute cloned DNA segments for study by investigators in many laboratories. If the STS identifier of a particular segment is known, the researcher can clone that segment and not require it as a clone from a repository. One will store information, not DNA, related to each part of the genome. STSs are a sort of Esperanto for scientists using diverse genetic and physical methods.

Finding all the genes could be helped by a concerted effort to create the cDNA [complementary DNA] map—the map of probes made by reverse transcription of messenger RNAs that have tissue and developmental stage specificity. The cDNA (or exon) map would provide candidate genes for diseases mapped by phenotype. Since by definition the exons are "where the action is," sequencing could logically and efficiently start with them.

The Human Genome Project is getting underway against a background of human genetics research that has assembled at least some information on more than 5,000 of the 50,000 or more expressed genes in the human genome. The figure 5,000 comes from *Mendelian Inheritance in Man*,[3] a gene catalog that purports to carry one entry for each gene that has been characterized to any extent (Fig. 1). Furthermore, proposing to map all the genes, the project gets underway at a point where about 2,000 of the genes (4 percent or less) have been located to specific chromosomes and,

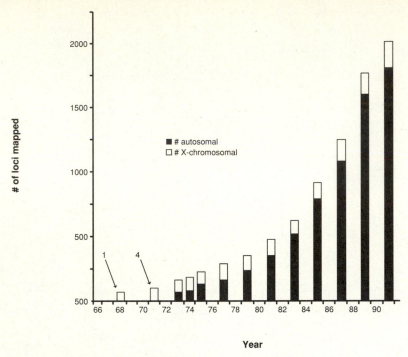

Figure 2. Growth [in number] of genes mapped to specific chromosomes.

in the case of most of them, to specific chromosomal regions (Fig. 2).

THE STATUS OF THE HUMAN GENE MAP

At the Human Gene Mapping Workshop in Oxford early in September 1990, the available information on the human gene map was collated, with results that are tabulated in Table 1 and Figure 4. Almost 1,900 genes had been mapped to specific chromosomal locations. In addition, over 4,500 DNA segments, so-called anonymous DNA segments because their function, if any, is not known (indeed most are known not to be expressed), had been mapped to specific chromosomal sites. About half these segments had been shown to be polymorphic, and many of them were sufficiently variable to make them useful as linkage markers.

The human is estimated to have about 50,000 genes, almost certainly not more than 100,000. Based on indirect arguments, estimates of this order were arrived at in the past; in more recent times, studies of the density of genes on the chromosomes and information on the range of sizes of genes support these estimates.

Many more genes have been assigned to some chromosomes than to others, if one examines either the absolute numbers (Fig. 3A) or the relative numbers, derived by dividing the absolute number by the length of the chromosome expressed as a percentage of the length of the haploid set of autosomes [one of each pair of chromosomes except for X or Y] (Fig. 3B).

• • •

THE ROLE OF GENE MAPPING IN HUMAN BIOLOGY AND MEDICINE

As Sir Walter Bodmer pointed out, what seemed like a rather recondite activity when the human gene mapping workshops were initiated in 1973 has achieved a central role in both human biology and scientific medicine. Charles Scriver of Montreal suggested that gene mapping is providing a neo-Vesalian basis for medicine. Beginning in the 1950s, the availability of relatively easy methods for microscopic study of the human chromosomes gave the clinical geneticist "his organ" and abetted the development of human genetics as a clinical specialty. Continually improving

Table 1. Number of Expressed Genes Assigned to Each Chromosome (Human Gene Mapping Workshop 10.5, Oxford, England, September 10, 1990)

Chromosome	Number of genes
1	194
2	110
3	68
4	74
5	72
6	104
7	107
8	53
9	59
10	58
11	132
12	100
13	24
14	60
15	51
16	68
17	107
18	23
19	91
20	34
21	36
22	58
X	187
Total	1868

The approximately 2,000 expressed genes that have been mapped to specific chromosomes, and in most instances to specific chromosome regions or bands (Table 1), code for blood groups, enzymes, hormones, clotting factors, growth factors, receptors (for example, for hormones and growth factors), cytokines, oncogenes, structural proteins (for example, collagens and elastin), and so forth. They also code for a large number of disease genes for which the biochemical basis is not known or was not known before the mapping. . . .

In all, the chromosomal location of more than 500 genetic disorders ("the morbid anatomy of the human genome") has been determined. Said differently, and perhaps more accurately, at about 500 of the 2,000 mapped loci, at least one disease-producing mutation has been identified. In the case of some disorders, the mapping has been done by locating the "wild-type" gene, such as that for phenylalanine hydroxylase, which is deficient in PKU and maps to 12q. In other disorders, the Mendelizing clinical phenotype has been mapped by family linkage studies using anchor markers such as RFLPs [restriction fragment length polymorphisms; used to detect differences in genetic sequences]; examples are Huntington disease, polycystic kidney disease, and Marfan syndrome. In yet other disorders, mapping has been done by both approaches; for example, elliptocytosis, type I, was mapped to the distal region of the short arm of chromosome 1 by linkage to Rh and other markers situated there and also by mapping of the gene for protein 4.1 (which is mutant in that disorder) to the same region.

To date, the *applied anatomy* of the human genome has related particularly to those disorders for which the basic biochemical defect was not yet known (Fig. 4). Because of this "ignorance," it was impossible to devise a fully specific diagnostic test or to design rational therapy. Once the chromosomal location of a disease-producing gene is known, together with its proximity to other genes and especially DNA markers, one can make a diagnosis (prenatal, presymptomatic, and carrier) by the linkage principle. Furthermore, one can expect to determine the fundamental nature of the genetic lesion by "walking" or "jumping" in on the gene, a process often labeled, with questionable appropriateness, reverse genetics. Then, knowing the nature of the wild-type gene, one can work out the pathogenetic steps that connect gene to

methods of chromosome study, particularly the methods for mapping genes on chromosomes, have given all of medicine a new paradigm. Specialists in all medical areas approach the study of their most puzzling diseases by first mapping the genes responsible for them. Thus, just as Vesalius's anatomical text of 1543 formed the basis for the physiology of William Harvey (1628) and the morbid anatomy of Morgagni (1761), gene mapping is having a widely pervasive influence on medicine.

In examining the significance of mapping information in clinical medicine, it may be useful to substitute the anatomical metaphor ("the anatomy of the human genome") for the cartographic metaphor ("the human gene map"). The anatomical metaphor prompts one to think in terms of the morbid anatomy, the comparative anatomy and evolution, the functional anatomy, the developmental anatomy, and the applied anatomy of the human genome.

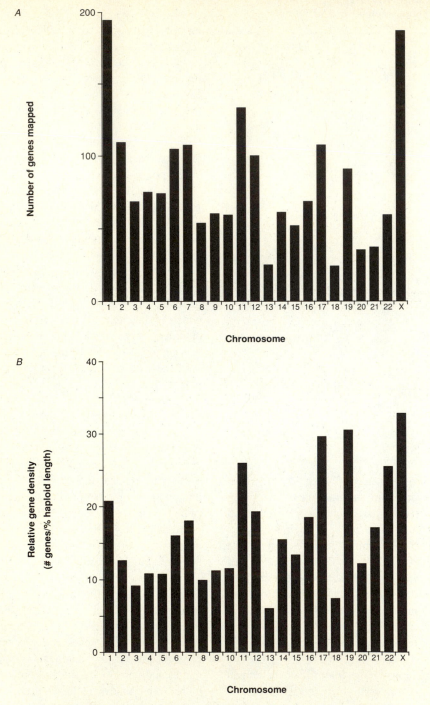

Figure 3. (A) Number of genes mapped to each chromosome. (B) Relative gene density (number of genes mapped to the chromosome/percent haploid length represented by that chromosome).

The Clinical Application of

GENE MAPPING

(location of genes to specific chromosome sites and/or
identification of their near neighbors)

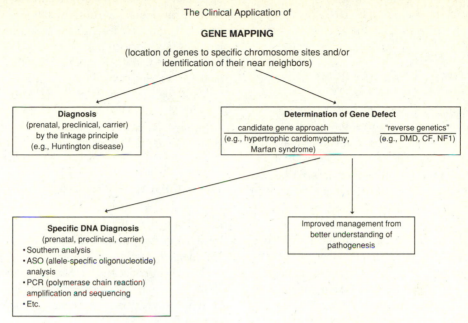

Figure 4. The clinical application of gene mapping.

phene, mutation to clinical disorder. Secondary prevention and therapy through modification of those steps can be developed. In many instances gene therapy will probably find gene mapping information useful background [note omitted].

In connection with the *morbid anatomy* of the human genome, mapping, perhaps more than any other single factor, has been responsible for the establishment of the chromosome basis of cancer: by the demonstration of specific, microscopically evident chromosomal aberrations in association with specific neoplasia [cancers], by the mapping of oncogenes [cancer-causing genes] and antioncogenes (recessive tumor suppressor genes), and by the correlation of the two sets of observations. Somatic cell genetic disease, as the basis not only of all neoplasia but also of some congenital malformations and probably of autoimmune diseases, joins the three cardinal categories of disease as to genetic factors: single-gene disorders, multifactorial disorders, and chromosomal disorders.

Mitochondrial genetic disease is a fifth category. The mitochondrial chromosome, the twenty-fifth chromosome, was completely sequenced by 1981 in the laboratory of Fred Sanger at Cambridge, and its

genes were mapped in the six years that followed. Deletions and point mutations in the mitochondrial chromosome were then identified as the basis of Leber optic atrophy, myotonic epilepsy/ragged red fiber disease, Pearson pancreas–bone marrow syndrome, oncocytomas, and, in cultured cells, chloramphenicol resistance. This sequence of discovery is the opposite, for the most part, of that pursued to date in the delineation of the nuclear genome, where the progression has been from study of diseases, then to their mapping, and finally to the sequencing of the genes. The mitochondrial chromosome, with its mere 16,569 base pairs, can be considered a paradigm for what the Human Genome Project hopes to achieve for the nuclear genome (which is approximately 200,000 times larger in terms of nucleotides). Indeed, complete sequencing may help greatly in identification of all the nuclear genes, just as it did in the case of the mitochondrial genes. At present, we have information, as cataloged in *Mendelian Inheritance in Man,* on more than 10 percent of the genes, or gene loci (Fig. 1). Walter Gilbert suggested that complete sequencing may be the best way to find the rest. Thereafter, one can determine the function of the genes and the disorders caused by mutations therein, as has been done for the mitochondrial chromosome. The cDNA map may be especially useful in "finding all the genes."

COUNTER-ARGUMENTS
AND COUNTER-COUNTER-ARGUMENTS
CONCERNING THE HUMAN GENOME PROJECT

Among scientists, the main arguments against the Human Genome Project seem to be four: that it is bad science; that it is big science (with the implication that it is not the way science is most effectively done); that it creates an improper milieu for doctoral training in science; and that it is taking money away from other worthy (in the opinion of some, more worthy) projects.*

The purpose of the Human Genome Project is to create a tool for science—the source book referred to earlier. A good deal of applied science and engineering will go into the Genome Project, but it may not be appropriate to criticize the Project through a comparison with biological science as it has been pursued traditionally.

The Human Genome Project is not so much big science as it is coordinated, interdisciplinary science. Especially in the sequencing part of the project, both the generation of the data and particularly their interpretation will require the recruitment of experts from disciplines that have had little involvement in biology to date. It seems clear that handling the information, validating, storing, and retrieving it, searching it for patterns indicative of functional domains, and identifying the coding portions will require much computer-assisted expertise. This represents a formidable challenge to the information scientist.

Regarding the argument that an institution where genomics (a generic term for mapping and sequencing) is being done is a poor site for graduate training and that the Human Genome Project will have a major adverse effect on graduate programs in biology, reality may be quite the contrary. With the full map and sequence, graduate students will be spared the drudgery of cloning and sequencing particular genes before they can get down to the much more interesting and intellectually demanding work of studying variation, function, regulation, and so on. The genomics labora-

tories will be superb settings for training a new breed of scientist—one who is prepared to capitalize on both the molecular genetics revolution and the computation revolution. These will be the leaders in biology in the twenty-first century.

It appears that the Human Genome Project is being made a scapegoat by those frustrated by the tight funding for research. If it [were] discontinued, the funding situation would not change perceptibly. Indeed, the excitement stimulated by discussion of the Human Genome Project has had and can continue to have a beneficial effect on science funding generally.

THE SOCIETAL IMPLICATIONS
OF THE HUMAN GENOME PROJECT

Attention to the ethical, legal, and social issues (ELSI) involved in the Human Genome Project has been unprecedentedly early and intensive—and appropriately so. The main concerns surround the use, misuse, and abuse of the information generated by the Human Genome Project and the power it provides for discerning the genetic makeup of individuals. . . . I will here make only some general statements.

It is my impression that the "problems" potentially created by the information of the Human Genome Project are not qualitatively different from those encountered every day in the practice of clinical genetics. They are, however, much greater in scope and significance. There are two generic risks. First, the information from the Human Genome Project and its ancillary endeavors will widen the gap between what we can diagnose and what we can do anything about (treat). This is already a problem in relation to Huntington disease and many other genetic disorders. A second hazard is that the gap will be widened between what we (physicians, scientists, and public alike) think we know and what we really know. In the years to come, weak associations will be found between particular genomic constitutions and specific behavioral peculiarities or susceptibilities to disease. Many of these, in the last analysis, will prove spurious. The significance of others, although statistically validated, will be blown out of all proportion, to the disadvantage of individuals and society as a whole.

The increasing gap between what we think we know and what we really know relates also to the hazards of reductionism and determinism.[4] Absurd as it may sound, the impression may become prevalent that when we know the sequence of the human genome down to the last nucleotide, we know all it

---

*I am indebted to Leroy E. Hood for this listing of counter-arguments and, in part, for the formulation of counter-counter-arguments..

means to be human—the ultimate of reductionism. Furthermore, it may become generally assumed that there is a direct one-to-one relationship between genomic constitution *and* all aspects of human health, disease, and behavior—the ultimate of determinism and hereditarianism.

NOTES

1. National Research Council, Committee on Mapping and Sequencing the Human Genome, *Mapping and Sequencing the Human Genome,* National Academy Press, Washington, D.C., 1988.

2. M. Olson, L. Hood, C. Cantor, and D. Botstein, "A Common Language for Physical Mapping of the Human Genome," *Science* 245:1434–5, 1989.

3. V. A. McKusick, *Mendelian Inheritance in Man: Catalogs of Autosomal Dominant, Autosomal Recessive, and X-Linked Phenotypes,* 9th ed. Johns Hopkins University Press, Baltimore, 1990.

4. Discussed in detail by E. Shuster [in George J. Annas and Sherman Elias, eds., *Gene Mapping: Using Law and Ethics as Guides* (New York: Oxford University Press, 1992), Chapter 6].

ALEXANDER MORGAN CAPRON

Which Ills to Bear?:
Reevaluating the "Threat" of Modern Genetics

[I.] THE CURRENT THREAT:
THE HUMAN GENOME PROJECT

The human genome—that is, the complement of 50,000 to 150,000 genes estimated as the molecular basis for human life—is now the object of concerted scrutiny by thousands of biological cartographers around the world. The largest effort is underway in the United States (with principal sponsorship coming from a new "center" at the National Institutes of Health headed by James Watson and from a special program in the Department of Energy), but many other countries are linked together in a cooperative/competitive arrangement coordinated by the international Human Genome Organization (HUGO).

The objective is first to produce a list of DNA "markers," sequences of DNA, with or without known biological effect, which are polymorphic, that is, which vary slightly, making it possible to differentiate their location. The list must be large enough so that every gene could be located on a chromosome between two markers with a high degree of accuracy

(say, 90% or higher).[1] Developing and using markers requires painstaking study of large pedigrees (the patterns of inheritance over several generations in families with many living relatives). Different restriction enzymes cause the genetic material drawn from these families to be cut at different sites, which produce different markers, referred to as RFLPs (restriction fragment length polymorphisms). Several different sets of markers have been produced by different research teams. When the information is combined, chromosome by chromosome, the result should be genetic linkage maps.[2]

In addition to these genetic maps, physical maps are also being constructed. These also rely on cutting up pieces of DNA with restriction enzymes and cloning the resulting fragments; the DNA sequences of the clones are then analyzed to see where they overlap, thus allowing the order of the clones to be determined. The result is a "contig map," the detail of which is determined by the amount of DNA being studied and the number of fragments produced.

The final stage in mapping will be to produce a listing of the sequence of DNA base-pairs for the entire human genome, approximately 2,800,000,000

From *Emory Law Journal* 39 (1990), 678–682, 684–696. Reprinted by permission of the author and the publisher.

base-pairs in all. This is plainly a time-consuming process. To be completed in full, it will require further advances in the automated techniques for reading the DNA sequences.

The large appropriations being requested from (and largely supplied by) Congress for this process of mapping and sequencing the human genome give it the aura of a massive project, the sort of "big science" associated with high energy physics and moon rocket launches. While the wisdom of making the Genome Project a scientific priority at this time has been sharply debated by scientists over the past several years, it is generally recognized that the "big science" image is somewhat misleading. Even granted that a good deal of the research is being carried out at the "national laboratories" affiliated with the Department of Energy, which have previously carried on physics studies requiring a major concentration of resources and personnel, most of the work is decentralized and a good deal of it derives from studies being carried out for other purposes besides mapping the human genome.[3]

Thus far, conflicts over the appropriate strategy to follow in mapping and sequencing the human genome (e.g., how much to spend, how fast, and in what fashion)[4] have overshadowed the ethical controversy. The project is regarded rather banefully by some lawyers and ethicists, who seem to think that any major undertaking involving genetics must be loaded with ethical issues.[5] Yet only one novel ethical-legal topic has emerged from the Genome Initiative, the issue of ownership and control of use over the information generated.[6]

This is not to say that the conventional issues do not take on a novel twist in the context of the Genome Project. As mentioned, large pedigrees are a requisite of map-building; through them, researchers can study patterns of inheritance by determining how frequently particular DNA sequences, located within certain distances of each other, are inherited together. The most obvious concern is that a great deal of information about the people who participate in genetic registries—including "information" in the form of genetic material—must be collected, stored, and then sent out to researchers. Care must be taken that the confidentiality of registry participants is ensured.[7] As with all records in an era of computerization, such assurances are difficult to fulfill.

A more subtle issue is the risk that the decision of any particular person to participate in a family linkage registry may not be truly voluntary. If the success of the registry is dependent upon a high degree of cooperation of families that are included in the registry, the risk is that any particular individual's reluctance will be overcome by pressure from others in the family or by researchers themselves, particularly when the initial involvement of the family with a genetics center arose because of the occurrence of a genetic disease in the family. In such a situation, failure to allow oneself to be studied might either seem a form of ingratitude or, worse, an impediment to the development of a medical response to the disease that burdens the family (even if the likelihood that the genetic mapping project will provide anything of direct value to understanding, much less correcting, the familial genetic disease is extremely remote).

•   •   •

[II.] THE REAL THREAT: GENETIC SCREENING

. . . [T]he real "threat" of modern genetics has been misperceived, first and rather dramatically, as coming from genetic engineering, particularly human gene therapy, and second and somewhat inchoately, as flowing from the Human Genome Initiative. While attention has focused on these highly technical areas, the less flashy field of genetic screening actually poses more significant issues. Perhaps, however, with the long-awaited ability close at hand to screen for carrier status (i.e., heterozygotes) for cystic fibrosis, the most common fatal autosomal recessive disease in the American population, the ethical and legal issues in genetic screening will begin to receive renewed attention.

The past lack of attention may have originated in the belief that all issues in genetic screening were well disposed of by that familiar bioethical triumvirate, the principles of autonomy, beneficence, and justice. From the principle of autonomy, for example, are derived rules about informed consent to testing; the right to refuse to be informed about test results; and rights of privacy and confidentiality regarding dissemination of test results. But none of these are absolutes. Just as consent and confidentiality are particularly important in this context because one is dealing with *genetic* information which is, after all, *inherent in*—and, indeed, one may say, *constitutive of*—an individual and thus is a matter of unusual sensitivity for many people, so too one must recognize that the genetic nature of the data may place limits on the usual rules. For example, might individuals have a moral (even if not usually a legal) obligation of beneficence to cooperate in a family linkage study—even at the risk of learning unwanted information—if the individual's tissue sample is necessary to establish the pattern of inheritance that other family members need to know so that they can safeguard their health or that of potential offspring?[8]

Putting flesh on the bones of the principles of beneficence and justice is of particular importance. Specifically, what is the definition of "doing good" in the area of genetic mapping or genetic therapy? And how is justice manifested when one is dealing with rare diseases that in an earlier era might have been explained as manifestations of fate or of God's judgment? How do we behave justly in selecting patients to treat or diseases to study, or indeed, in allocating resources to this exciting and challenging field of biomedicine that may some day have great benefit for future sufferers, when the alternative is to spend these funds to address the unmet needs of present sufferers?

A. FOUR VARIETIES OF GENETIC SCREENING

The fact that these topics elicit more questions than well-defined public policy answers probably reflects the relatively low level of visibility that genetic screening has had until [recently].[9] Indeed, one might even say that the most prominent instances of genetic screening were not really conceived or described by those who promoted them as instances of genetic testing. Although genetic tests have gotten public attention in certain legal settings—such as the recent, and still controversial use of DNA analysis to create "genetic finger prints" for forensic purposes, or the use of genetic tests to resolve paternity disputes—the more widespread use of genetic screening has gone largely unremarked and perhaps even unnoticed by millions of people who are subjected to it.

Genetic screening—that is, the search in an asymptomatic population for persons at elevated risk of genetic disease in themselves or their offspring—first came into general use in the early 1960s with the development of tests for several inborn errors of metabolism, particularly the Guthrie test of newborns for phenylketonuria (PKU), a condition that causes mental retardation unless the affected child is placed on a special diet that severely restricts intake of phenylalanine, a normal (indeed, essential) component of the human diet. These metabolic errors are rare (PKU occurs approximately once in every 14,000 births among Americans of European ancestry) and are typically autosomal recessive conditions, meaning that they arise when two people who carry the deviant gene mate; with each pregnancy, they have a one-in-four chance of producing a child who inherits the deviant gene from both of them and manifests the disease. In the case of PKU, Dr. Robert Guthrie developed a simple and inexpensive means of testing a small sample of blood from newborn children, taken at several days of age from a heel prick and sent on filter paper to the laboratory for automated testing.

In order to ensure that the test would be performed on all babies, most states—beginning with Massachusetts in 1963—adopted mandatory screening laws.[10] Although in some ways this was a "genetic" test, it was not generally so perceived. The statutes were championed by the state chapters of the Association for Retarded Persons as a means of preventing mental retardation, not by medical geneticists; furthermore, the true genetic nature of the condition, including its variations, was not well understood at the time, which led to a number of problems in screening and diagnosing some cases. Finally, because they were not thinking in genetic terms, the potential effects of the disease on the offspring of the children treated were neglected; only in recent years has it become apparent that girls who suffer from PKU should be urged to go back on the special low-phenylalanine diet (which the children ordinarily stop following by adolescence) before becoming pregnant, lest their metabolic problem damage the brain of their developing fetus.

From a legal vantage point, the major issue in newborn screening has been that the PKU statutes—and those adopted in some states that encompass a wider range of inborn metabolic problems—make screening mandatory, with some legal sanction. Even when these statutes provide that parents may exercise a religious or conscientious objection to testing, the right to do so is often not conveyed in a timely fashion.[11] Yet mandatory laws seem difficult to justify, both in light of the principle of autonomy and because a voluntary program, with good information and education of parents and health care providers, produces as high a rate of screening as mandatory programs.[12] Furthermore, screening by itself offers no benefit to children affected with PKU: first, a positive screening result must be confirmed through diagnostic testing, and then, affected children must receive the special diet. Yet neither of these additional steps is either required or guaranteed by legislation in most states.

Although screening of newborns in order to determine which ones may need treatment is the most common form of genetic testing today, two other types of screening related to reproduction are likely to become more prevalent in the near future, testing for carrier-status and prenatal tests. The best examples of such screening now are testing for Tay-Sachs disease among Ashkenazi Jews and for sickle-cell disease among African-Americans. The tests for the genetic defects that cause cystic fibrosis, while still not ready for use in screening the general population,[13] may soon generate screening programs with orders of magnitude larger than any heretofore.

Tay-Sachs disease causes progressive neurological deterioration and early death in affected children. About one Jew in thirty of East European extraction is a carrier of the gene (four times the rate of PKU carriers); for two decades, screening programs that employ a relatively simple blood test have been carried out in Jewish communities in the United States, initially with sponsorship by local Jewish organizations and today usually through ordinary medical channels. Since the condition is recessive, "carrier couples" face a one-in-four chance of producing an affected child with each pregnancy, but prenatal screening permits diagnosis of affected fetuses (usually before the end of the second trimester). One of the issues that arose in the initial screening programs was whether testing should be limited to couples of reproductive age (excluding not merely older persons but younger ones as well and persons who were not yet married), to avoid the risk that anyone would become the victim of discrimination or rejection.

Also beginning two decades ago, sickle-cell testing was widely promoted in the black community (where one-in-twelve Americans of African extraction carries the gene). It did not, however, achieve comparable acceptance to Tay-Sachs screening, in part because prenatal diagnosis was not then feasible, so that a person found to be a carrier faced the choice either to attempt to marry a non-carrier, not to have children if married to another carrier of the gene, or to risk giving birth to a child with the disease. Today, molecular medicine makes prenatal diagnosis possible, which in turn increases people's interest in learning whether they carry the gene and ought to consider prenatal testing. Another reason why sickle-cell testing has met with resistance is that, especially in its early years, some employers (including the United States Armed Services) and others (such as schools) excluded or placed restrictions on persons found to be carriers, despite the lack of evidence that being heterozygous for the sickle-cell gene elevated the risk of health problems. Since few employers or others ran their own screening programs,[14] the best way to avoid suffering this discrimination was thus not to have oneself tested.

A fourth type of screening now coming into prominence is susceptibility testing. In effect, a good deal of medical monitoring could be described as testing for genetic susceptibilities—for example, screening for serum lipid levels, as a means to predict atherosclerosis and other risks. Yet, despite the fact that some physicians may point to the relationship between test results and familial patterns of heart disease and stroke, this testing is not typically described as "genetic screening." The development of the genome map and other tools from genetic engineering will greatly increase the number of tests available to reveal one's personal risk of experiencing particular diseases and disabilities, ranging from small percentage risks to virtual certainty of certain late-onset conditions (such as Huntington's disease) that are inherited in a dominant fashion.

B. SCREENING, INSURABILITY, AND EMPLOYABILITY

Newborn screening aimed at detecting who is in need of protective interventions (e.g., PKU screening) is relevant to present discussions mostly as an historical precedent for the ease with which genetic testing became a part of common practice and accepted public policy with little thought having been given to the implications. Turning now to screening relevant to reproduction (i.e., carrier screening and prenatal testing) and to personal susceptibility, this earlier history suggests several concerns that deserve careful attention before these other types of screening move from their present place within medical practice into more widespread use by public and private authorities and institutions. Of particular interest are the issues of insurability and employability that may arise more often as accurate and inexpensive means are developed for a larger number of genetic conditions.

What makes this field complicated is that there are strong reasons that a person would want the information that can be gained from both reproductive and susceptibility-type screening, while at the same time the results of such screening will also be of interest to others with whom the person has voluntary relationships (such as employment) and who might wish to take actions that would be harmful to the person (such as denial of insurance). Several tensions are thus created: between the rights or interests of the individual screened and the rights or interests of others, and between failing to obtain or ignoring potentially useful information and having that information become the only factor guiding important decisions.

These tensions are exacerbated by another, inescapable reality, namely that discoveries and developments do not occur evenly across the whole of genetics nor do they necessarily touch first on those genetic conditions that are most common in the population. Instead, both the potential benefits and possible risks of genetic screening and diagnosis will attach very unevenly across the population. Although all of us carry five to seven lethal recessive genes as well as a still undetermined number of genes that make us susceptible to developing diseases based on interactions with the environment (e.g., through work, diet, etc.), persons who carry those particular genes for which screening first becomes available are in greater danger of suffering discrimination because of their apparent singularity. Once the widespread and basically random nature of genetic risks becomes more apparent, the need for concern about stigma—and specifically about loss of insurability and employability—may be lessened, even though it will never be the case that all people face identical genetic risks (defined in terms of the probability and severity of ourselves or our children suffering a disease of genetic origin).

Thus, the central question in my view involves the degree to which inborn differences should be regarded as ethically and legally relevant. To ignore them totally would not only be foolhardy but would also amount to a radical departure from our traditions—after all, the measurements of "merit" on which many decisions in our society rest do not equate merit with effort alone (indeed, they often separate aptitude from achievement). On the other hand, permitting inborn differences to play a decisive role in allocating a variety of benefits, such as access to employment and insurance, risks blaming the victim. Furthermore, to the extent that genetic screening is either inaccurate or partial (in the sense of uncovering some but not all genetic risks), too heavy a reliance on this one method in framing policy will lead to nonoptimal outcomes.

The tensions that need to be addressed can be seen in the relationship between reproductive screening and insurance and between susceptibility screening and employment. Regarding the former, suppose that tests are developed that can identify persons who carry a rare gene that causes a severe, crippling illness when inherited from both parents; further suppose that besides carrier testing, prenatal diagnosis can also be performed for the disease during the first trimester of pregnancy. If the carrier test is inexpensive enough and the costs of treating the illness are heavy enough, it may well be financially advisable for health insurance companies to provide the test. Focusing for the moment solely on persons who are already enrolled in a particular health insurance plan and who agree to undergo carrier screening voluntarily, what should be the insurance company's response when an identified "carrier couple" declines to undergo prenatal diagnosis? Under many indemnity insurance plans, coverage is not provided for "preexisting conditions." Could treatment of the genetic disease in an affected child be excluded on this ground? Alternatively, could the plan's exclusion from coverage for "self-inflicted" conditions be invoked? Though both of these limitations have themselves been criticized, both can also be defended on moral as well as prudential grounds. And both have at least some applicability to the hypothetical case, since insurance is meant to spread the risk of unexpected and inescapable harms, and the birth of an affected child is both foreseeable to, and avoidable by, the insured couple. Yet requiring prenatal diagnosis and abortion would deeply intrude into a protected realm of personal, private decisionmaking. Furthermore, if generalized, it would amount to a eugenics program by the insurance company, as it decided which children it thought fit enough to allow to be born.

Thus far, insurers have, to the best of my knowledge, not yet adopted such draconian measures. Indeed, it is unlikely for competitive reasons that a single company would dare to act alone toward a mandatory approach. But, by being willing to pay for genetic testing and by encouraging its use in appropriate cases, companies are able to achieve many of the results that they would want, even though there is no legal compulsion on prospective parents to use such tests, much less to act on their results.[15] As genetic tests become more widespread, it does not exceed the bounds of credibility to suppose that insurers will insist that their enrollees at least avail themselves of the tests, even if acting on the results is left up to them.

For most people, the door to health insurance is found in the workplace; thus, the question of insurability is in part a question of employability. Moreover, since they bear a portion of the cost of their employees' health care (which looms as an ever increasing portion of the cost of doing business), employers have the same interest as insurance carriers in excluding high-cost patients or at least in avoiding having to pay certain costs such patients generate.

Besides the interest they have in the risk that their employees and prospective employees will produce children burdened with genetic disorders, employers have an additional concern with their workers' own susceptibility to illness and injury. First, an employee who is prone to get sick will generate expenses: medical treatment costs, sick days, and potentially even disability benefits. Second, if the problem might be described as job-related, then the genetic condition could lead directly to workers compensation payments — for instance, a genetic predisposition to a bad back in an employee who has to do a lot of lifting. Finally, employers generally want to avoid hiring persons who are going to be sick a great deal because such persons cannot be relied upon to be present when needed and the expense of training them may thus be wasted if they become totally disabled.

Again, employers have yet to turn heavily to genetic testing, although some of the screening done in pre-employment physical exams is aimed at uncovering conditions in which genetics plays an important role. But as more genetic screens for disease susceptibility are perfected and made available at reasonable prices, it is likely that employers will be inclined to use them, especially if these tests identify employees who are at higher than average risk in particular work environments, from which they can therefore be excluded.[16]

[III.] IF WE WERE CLEAR ON THE THREAT, WHAT SHOULD WE DO?

I have argued in this essay that the "threat" of modern genetics has largely been misidentified with technologically glamorous developments such as human genetic engineering and the major effort to map and sequence the human genome, thereby overlooking the problems generated by genetic screening. The latter is the route through which the findings of the more glamorous areas of genetic engineering and genome mapping will probably first affect the lives of most Americans. In particular, I have suggested that a rapid increase in the number and technical capacity of screening methods for inherited conditions will affect two important relationships: between insured and insurer, and between employee and employer.

Plainly, some specific legal responses are possible, such as the passage of legislation to protect the confidentiality of genetic information and to prevent discrimination against those who have — or who are believed to be at high risk of developing — a genetic disability. Indeed, the report of the House-Senate conference committee on the recently adopted Americans With Disabilities Act makes clear that the scope of its protections encompasses genetic discrimination.[17]

Yet such responses, valuable as they may be, only address symptoms and do not respond to the underlying problems that the genetic techniques uncover. If we are to address the fundamental issues, we need to elevate them to a level of much greater public visibility. This is more than just the usual prescription for openness in a democracy, for it seems to me that if the deeper problems are going to be overcome, some collective redefinitions of concepts and standards will be required.

Plainly . . . some of that simply relates to reorienting how we think about normality and abnormality. Genetics, by illuminating the ways in which the line of difference between the two may be nothing more than the rearrangement of a single DNA base-pair (out of the billions in every cell), may make abnormalities less strange and "different." Some of the needed rethinking will have to extend to the concepts by which we describe our relationships and duties. For example, in light of the genetic connections that bind people to one another, in terms not only of inheritance but also of molecular diagnostics, what are the proper meanings of "autonomy" and "privacy"?

To be successful, what will be needed is a true social reexamination of the use that these concepts have in people's lives, not a mere "redefinition" by lawyers, who are capable of changing the meaning of any word, within the confines of a statute or contract. A further, more practical predicate, is the kind of legal protection already mentioned: people will only be able to think about a less restrictive view of "privacy" if they are assured that they have been protected from any repercussions of sharing a genetic diagnosis.

A second task — somewhat more pragmatic but grounded also on principles — will be to reexamine our notions of insurance and employment. Especially in the field of health insurance, we have moved from a risk-sharing model to a group-narrowing model — in other words, from seeing ourselves as all being in roughly the same situation (thereby making it morally desirable to spread risks as broadly as possible) to seeking our individual advantage in placing ourselves in a group from which we have excluded people who are at higher risk than ourselves. When the exclusions are based on voluntarily acquired risks (such as from smoking), they do not seem very pernicious, so long as we apply a fairly relaxed understanding of the term "voluntary." But exclusions grounded in genetic differences are less benign. Nonetheless, the acceptability of one practice or the other depends not on abstract ethical principles but on our conception of the purpose of insurance. If the purpose is simply to spread out the costs of paying for illness across a lifetime, then narrow groupings of people at comparable risk make sense; if, on the other hand, the purpose is to manifest solidarity in the face of misfortunes (which do not strike all people equally) then narrowing of insurance pools based on ever-finer genetic differentiations would be unacceptable.

Another issue raised already by genetic screening that probably remains many years off in genetic engineering or genome mapping is the issue of mandatoriness. It strikes me as unlikely that laws will soon be passed requiring anyone to undergo gene therapy or to provide personally identifiable genetic material for purely scientific uses. Yet mandatory laws already exist in the area of genetic screening, and private parties (insurers and employers), who already border on compelling the use of such tests, are likely to move even further and faster in this direction.

We begin with a strong predisposition to protect free choice in private matters generally and in medical care in particular. Yet the consequences for other people in the choices we make cannot be totally ignored. If taking those consequences into account means putting the costs of the choices onto the shoulders of those who make the choices, then voluntariness has a very different meaning — closer, perhaps, to the sense in which one has the "choice" to violate a criminal statute, provided that one is willing to be penalized. Yet the alternate — totally insulating a person making a choice in the face of a known genetic risk from having to shoulder any of the consequences of that choice — seems equally undesirable.

Thus, more than a reexamination of voluntariness and mandatoriness will be needed: along the way, we will need to examine what we mean by such concepts as "responsible parenthood." Again, we have traditionally regarded reproductive decisions as appropriately made within the family; the state gets involved only when there is family breakdown (divorce), when children are at risk (child abuse and neglect), or when family status is rearranged (marriage, adoption). My personal preference is to preserve family choice as much as possible. In many ways, it seems a bedrock of diversity in other spheres in society because, by bolstering the integrity of the family unit, choice about reproduction supports an institution that is important for individual self-definition, for the fostering of varied cultural and religious viewpoints, and the like.

Yet individuals are also members of their society, and they depend on the larger community in many ways. For some individuals, the choices made by their families have disastrous consequences. Rather than being solely concerned with not having to bear the costs of correcting those consequences after-the-fact, might not the community assert an interest in avoiding them in the first place? Regarding some consequences, the answer adopted by society already is "yes" — for example, through removal of children from abusive or neglectful homes. The implications of genetic screening go much further, however, because it may provide information about the risk to certain children in even being conceived or born.

I have argued against the use of tort law to restrict the choices of parents about whether to reproduce in the face of genetic risks.[18] Yet it seems inevitable that such a position will need to be reexamined and redefended in the light both of increased medical capabilities and other pressures in society.

That such reexamination of a wide range of practical issues and fundamental principles seems inevitable strikes me as a good rather than a bad thing. It is much more likely to occur if we reevaluate the "threat" of modern genetics and spend less time on distant prospects involving genome mapping and genetic engineering and more time thinking about genetic screening.

NOTES

1. An excellent introduction to the technologies for mapping the genome is provided by Chapter Two of Office of Technology Assessment, U.S. Congress, *Mapping Our Genes: The Genome Project: How Big, How Fast?* 19–51 (1988).

2. See Roberts, *The Genetic Map Is Back on Track After Delays,* 249 *Science* 805 (1990).

3. See, e.g., the description of the project, originated by Sydney Brenner of Cambridge University in 1963, "to learn everything there is to know about the nematode *Caenorhabditis elegans*"—a project that is now culminating in an effort "to decipher its complete genetic instructions." Roberts, *The Worm Project,* 248 *Science* 1310 (1990).

4. See, e.g., Roberts, *Genome Backlash Going Full Force,* 248 *Science* 804 (1990).

5. See, e.g., Annas, [*Who's Afraid of the Human Genome?* 19 Hastings Center Rep., July/Aug. 1989, at 19, 21.] The sense that important ethical problems are at hand is probably magnified by the unprecedented plan of NIH's National Center for Human Genome Research to allocate from one to three percent of its funds for ethical analysis; perhaps this is nothing more than the formula under which one percent of the construction costs of new buildings is set aside in some cities to purchase works of art—it does not guarantee more aesthetic buildings, but it does ensure that artists will be kept busy producing ornaments for what gets built.

6. See, e.g., Eisenberg, *Patenting the Human Genome,* 39 *Emory L. J.* 721 (1990).

7. From a scientific standpoint, researchers do not need to know the personal identity of the people from whom DNA samples come. In generating their maps, the genetic cartographers will use samples from many people; while each person's DNA differs slightly from other people's, any two people share about 99% of their genetic makeup.

Referring to the donor of the X-chromosome region [David] Schlessinger's group [at the Center for Genetics in Medicine at Washington University in St. Louis] is studying, he states, "The identity of the donor is locked away. . . . [T]hat individual is the genetic equivalent of the unknown soldier."

Fink, *Whose Genome Is It, Anyway?* 2 *Human Genome News,* July 1990, at 5.

8. Cf. President's Commission for the Study of Ethical Problems in Medicine and Biomedical and Behavioral Research, *Screening and Counseling for Genetic Conditions* 44 (1983) (discussing circumstances in which professional's ethical duty of confidentiality may be overridden by the need to prevent harm to relative of person who has undergone genetic testing).

9. After an initial flurry of ethical and legal analysis nearly two decades ago, the subject receded to a less prominent status. See, e.g., *National Research Council, Committee for the Study of Inborn Errors of Metabolism, Genetic Screening: Programs, Principles and Research* (1975) [hereinafter *Genetic Screening*]; *Genetic Counseling: Facts, Values, and Norms* (A. Capron, M. Lappé, R. Murray, T. Powledge, S. Twiss & D. Bergsma eds. 1979); Research Group on Ethical, Social and Legal Issues in Genetic Counseling and Genetic Engineering of the Institute of Society, *Ethical and Social Issues in Screening for Genetic Disease,* 286 *New Eng. J. Med.* 1129 (1972). One report by the President's Commission (*supra* note 8), and an OTA report, *Office of Technology Assessment, U.S. Congress, The Role of Genetic Testing in the Prevention of Occupational Disease* (1983) [hereinafter *Role of Genetic Testing*], both in 1983, stimulated some interest, but only recently has genetic screening again begun to receive concerted analysis. See, e.g., N. Holtzman, *Proceed with Caution* (1989); *Netherlands Scientific Council for Government Policy, The Social Consequences of Genetic Testing, Preliminary and Background Studies* 64 (1990).

10. See generally *Genetic Screening,* supra note 9, at 44–87.

11. Id.

12. See Faden, Chalow, Holtzman & Horn, *A Survey to Evaluate Parental Consent As Public Policy for Neonatal Screening,* 72 *Am. J. Pub. Health* 1347 (1982).

13. *Statement from the National Institutes of Health Workshop on Population Screening for the Cystic Fibrosis Gene,* 323 *New Engl. J. Med.* 70 (1990).

14. See *Role of Genetic Testing,* supra note 9, at 34. The OTA found that, despite a good deal of hype on the subject, few employers were actually using genetic tests to screen workers, but the perception that technical improvements have lately increased employers' interest in using genetic screening has recently led the OTA to update its survey of practices.

15. Some courts have recognized an obligation in medical professionals to offer appropriate genetic tests, the breach of which obligation can result in civil liability under the confusing labels of "wrongful birth" and "wrongful life," but no court has yet held parents liable to an affected child for failing to take steps to prevent the child's birth. See Capron, *Wrongful Life: Will Common Sense Prevail?* 3 *Bioethics Rptr.,* Commentary 23–27 (1985).

16. Employers have already been permitted to take one comparable factor (namely, the risk to fetuses of women workers exposed to lead) into account in excluding certain employees from certain types of work. The Supreme Court is now reviewing a Seventh Circuit ruling under Title VII of the Civil Rights Act of 1964 (which forbids discrimination on gender grounds) upholding an automobile battery manufacturer's policy that bars women from certain positions unless they can provide evidence of infertility. The circuit court found the policy "well reasoned and scientifically documented" and thus justified either as a "bona fide occupational qualification" or as a "business necessity." International Union, UAW v. Johnson Controls, Inc., 886 F.2d 871 (7th Cir. 1989), *cert. granted,* 58 U.S.L.W. 3609 (U.S. Mar. 27, 1990) (No. 89-1215).

17. See *Conference Report on S.393, Americans With Disabilities Act of 1990,* 136 *Cong. Rec.* H4614, H4627 (1990).

18. See, e.g., Capron, *Informed Decisionmaking in Genetic Counseling: A Dissent to the "Wrongful Life" Debate,* 48 *Ind. L. J.* 581 (1973); Capron, *Tort Liability in Genetic Counseling,* 79 *Colum. L. Rev.* 618 (1979).

PAUL R. BILLINGS, ET AL.

Discrimination as a Consequence of Genetic Testing*

INTRODUCTION

The accelerating development of biochemical and DNA-based diagnostic tests for human genetic conditions in the last decade has engendered a revolution in genetic diagnosis. Numerous families faced with agonizing clinical or family planning decisions have been aided by information obtained through these tests (Phillips 1988). With further refinement of the human genetic map (Donis-Keller et al. 1987; McKusick 1988), the limited repertoire of genetic tests for the predisposition to common conditions such as cancer, cardiovascular diseases, and mental disorders may markedly expand (Lander and Botstein 1986; Scott 1987).

Insurance companies, private employers, governments and educational institutions all have an immediate or potential interest in promoting large-scale genetic screening to identify individuals carrying disease-associated genes (Motulsky 1983; Murray 1983; Uzych 1986; Hewitt and Holtzman 1988; Holtzman 1988, 1989; Nelkin and Tancredi 1989; Office of Technology Assessment 1990; Natowicz and Alper, in press). In addition, economic pressures to apply genetic tests to broader sections of the population may increase as biotechnology companies develop and sell genetic testing products and services (Hewitt and Holtzman 1988). Finally, the pace of development and application of DNA and biochemical

genetic tests and their acceptance by the public may be accelerated by the recent widespread media coverage of the work of human geneticists.

As a result of the pressures to implement genetic technologies, problems engendered by their application may be overlooked. For example, with relatively few exceptions, our knowledge of how genes produce clinical illnesses is still quite limited. Yet an evaluation of the predictive value for clinical disease, utility, and impact is necessary before general use of genetic tests can be endorsed. In addition, some authors fear that an uncontrolled use of the tests may lead to a revival of social policies based on eugenics (Kevles 1985).

While there have been theoretical concerns about prejudices and discrimination surrounding genetic conditions, few investigations of these issues have been published (Hampton et al. 1974; Motulsky 1974; Kenen and Schmidt 1978; Murray 1991). Studies on the impact of genetic counseling have generally focused on subjects' understanding of genetic information and on family planning decisions (Leonard et al. 1972; Evers-Keibooms and van den Berghe 1979); evaluations of the impact of genetic screening programs are typically concerned with issues of diagnostic sensitivity and specificity, medical efficacy, and cost-effectiveness and have usually not assessed long-term nonclinical outcomes. The personal costs of consenting to genetic testing and screening have not been studied and raise many issues of considerable significance.

Given this situation—powerful and attractive new techniques, social and economic forces pressing for their application, and an incomplete understanding of the potential negative social and personal consequences of genetic testing—concern about the burdens engendered by widespread utilization of genetic

*The coauthors of this essay are Mel A. Kohn, Margaret de Cuevas, Jonathan Beckwith, Joseph S. Alper, and Marvin R. Natowicz.

Paul R. Billings, et al., "Discrimination as a Consequence of Genetic Testing," *American Journal of Human Genetics* 50 (1992), 476–482. © 1992 by the American Society of Human Genetics. Reprinted by permission of the author and the publisher, the University of Chicago Press.

tests seems justified. One such issue is the problem of genetic discrimination.

This [essay] describes the results of a preliminary study of individuals labeled with genetic conditions. This study is not a survey; it does not purport to give statistically significant information about the extent of genetic discrimination. Instead, the aim of the study was to discover whether incidents which may reflect genetic discrimination are occurring in the workplace, in access to social services, in insurance underwriting, and in the delivery of health care. If the existence and range of genetic discrimination revealed by this study are confirmed by other investigations, then current policies and practices regarding the application of genetic testing and utilization of information obtained from such testing may need to be reconsidered.

METHODS

A definition of genetic discrimination was developed for this preliminary study based in part on the work of the Genetic Screening Study Group, a Boston-based public interest group (Dusek 1987; Billings 1989; Beckwith 1991; Natowicz and Alper, in press). Discrimination stemming from supposed hereditary transmission of a condition can be obvious, as in the case of an individual who was denied a job because a health record noted that the applicant's mother was "schizophrenic." In other instances, the distinction between discrimination based on clinical disability or illness, and that arising from genetic aspects of a condition, may be more difficult to determine. For the purposes of this study, genetic discrimination is defined as discrimination against an individual or against members of that individual's family solely because of real or perceived differences from the "normal" genome of that individual. Genetic discrimination is distinguished from discrimination based on disabilities caused by altered genes by excluding, from the former category, those instances of discrimination against an individual who at the time of the discriminatory act was affected by the genetic disease.

An advertisement to solicit cases of possible genetic discrimination was mailed to 1,119 professionals working in the fields of clinical genetics, genetic counseling, disability medicine, pediatrics, and social services in New England. This solicitation was also published in the American Journal of Human Genetics (Billings 1988). Similar appeals were reprinted in newsletters of organizations of individuals with ge-

netic conditions, such as associations for persons with Friedreich ataxia, Charcot-Marie-Tooth disease (CMT), and muscular dystrophy.

Many responses included supporting documentation. Each described incident was reviewed independently by two of the authors (P.R.B. and M.A.K.), and a decision was reached as to whether it met the standard for inclusion in our study. This preliminary investigation was closed after receiving responses for 7 months.

The most common reasons for excluding responses in this study were that (1) the differential treatment was based on a physical variation or disability (for example, individuals with Turner syndrome who were discriminated against in employment because of short stature), (2) there was a lack of evidence that the differential treatment arose from the hereditary nature of the condition, and (3) there was inadequate information submitted to determine whether discrimination had occurred.

RESULTS AND DISCUSSION

Of the 42 responses received, 13 (31%) were excluded from further study because of failure to meet our strict criteria for genetic discrimination or because insufficient information was provided to enable an accurate assessment. The remaining 29 responses came from all regions of the United States and Canada. A variety of genetic conditions were represented in the study group, including Huntington disease [a late-onset disease that causes degeneration of mental and motor functioning], Friedreich ataxia [a disease of the spinal cord that leads to reduced muscular coordination], CMT [Charcot-Marie-Tooth disease, a neuromuscular condition], hemochromatosis [a disease characterized by excessive iron intake], phenylketonuria (PKU) [a biochemical disorder that causes brain damage], and others. Most of the responses were elicited by the advertisement reprinted in newsletters.

The 29 evaluated responses described 41 separate incidents of possible discrimination. Of these 41 incidents all but two involved insurance or employment. Thirty-two incidents involved insurance (applications or coverage changes for health, life, disability, mortgage, and auto insurance), and seven involved employment (hiring, termination, promotion, and transfer).

The respondents described difficulties in obtaining desired insurance coverage, in finding or retaining employment, and in interactions with adoption agencies. Problems with insurance companies rose when individuals altered existing policies because of relocations or changes of employers. New, renewed, or upgraded policies were frequently unobtainable even if individuals labeled with genetic conditions were asymptomatic. Assessment of the natural history of the genetic condition or evaluation of the fitness of the individual by physicians had little or no influence on the adverse outcomes presented by the respondents. Because of fear of discrimination, several respondents reported that they withheld or "forgot" to mention potentially important medical or family history information to physicians, employers or insurers. Others reported that their insurance agents suggested that they give incomplete or dishonest information on insurance application forms.

The responses excerpted below illustrate several themes that appeared repeatedly in the data. These themes can be grouped into three categories: (1) "The Asymptomatic Ill," (2) "The Problem of Variability," and (3) "The At-Risk: to Test or Not to Test? Dilemma." While the incidents suggest discrimination by specific institutions such as insurance companies, the cases and types of genetic discrimination described below may reflect the attitudes and practices of an array of business, social, and political institutions.

THE ASYMPTOMATIC ILL

Many individuals identified as having a hereditary condition are healthy. Some have undergone testing only because other affected family members have been identified with a genetic condition. As the number of genetic tests increases, and [the tests] are widely applied, an increasing number of individuals will discover that they harbor a disease-associated gene but have no identifiable clinical illness.

A respondent from a family with hereditary hemochromatosis wrote: "In 1973, at age 27 and 1/2, I was diagnosed as having excessive iron storage and was put on a regime of phlebotomies. . . .

"[After several years] I have never had the slightest symptom, in part because early detection [and appropriate treatment] of iron overload in my case avoided damage. . . .

"[After failing to get insurance because of my hemochromatosis] I have supplied doctor's testimonies to no avail. I might as well have AIDS. Even though I have proven that I prevented health problems by early detection and prophylaxis, they condemn me to the same category as lost causes. I run 10 Km races, etc. I am not a basket case, and will not be one, ever, because of iron overload."

With respect to a second case, a physician reported that "an individual was found to have Gaucher Disease. His brother was screened and the results were consistent with unaffected carrier status [heterozygote]. The brother applied for a governmental job and included the history of his testing in the application. He was denied the job because of his being a 'carrier, like a sickle cell'."

With respect to a third case, a clinical geneticist caring for individuals with PKU wrote: "[Name withheld] is an 8 year old girl who was diagnosed as having PKU at 14 days of age through the newborn screening program. . . . A low phenylalanine diet was instituted at that time. . . .

"Growth and development have been completely normal. Height, weight, and head circumference all follow the 25th percentile. Routine developmental assessments done at 26 weeks, 53 weeks, and 54 months revealed skills solidly appropriate for age, and in many instances skills were above age-expected levels. The child continues to be developmentally normal and be healthy. The circumstances of the discrimination that this child has experienced involve rejection for medical insurance. She was covered by the company that provided group insurance for her father's previous employer. However, when he changed jobs recently, he was told that his daughter was considered to be a high risk patient because of her diagnosis, and therefore ineligible for insurance coverage under their group plan. She is currently being covered at the expense of her family, but this is a temporary solution at best. The family has written to the agency that administers the group insurance plan to obtain details of the decision to deny coverage and also plans to write to the chairman of the large corporation for which the father works. All information will also be submitted to the [state] insurance commissioner."

COMMENT

The first case illustrates both the promise and the burden of genetic testing. It was through genetic testing that this individual was diagnosed and successfully treated. Yet, because of his test results, he has been stigmatized and denied insurance as if he were severely ill. Similarly, the individual described in the second case was denied employment because of his genotype, despite the fact that he was asymptomatic and a heterozygote for an autosomal recessive condition.

The third case illustrates both the benefits of genetic testing in enabling the early detection and successful treatment of many children with PKU and constraints that can be imposed by genetic labeling. The cost of a phenylalanine-restricted diet, an effective treatment for PKU, is high. Without insurance, it is possible that the family would not be able to afford treatment for their child, with the consequent risk of developmental delays and permanent impairment. The family's life is restricted by the necessity for the father to maintain employment in the same state and at the same job in order to have access to insurance. Thus, the child's diagnosis has a major impact on the geographic and job mobility of other family members. These constraints, in turn, could cause economic or other potentially significant limitations.

By preparing to take their situation to a state agency, this family demonstrated "self-advocacy" abilities. The poor, the uneducated, foreign nationals, or those with fears about their job security may not be as willing or able to negotiate the complexities of our legal and regulatory systems in order to secure their rights.

All three cases illustrate instances of discrimination against individuals who are completely asymptomatic; their only "abnormality" lies in their genotypes. As large numbers of individuals submit to or are coerced into testing in order to obtain employment or insurance coverage, a new social class and category—the "asymptomatic ill"—may be constructed. Although they are healthy, persons in this new group may find that they are treated as if they were disabled or chronically ill by various institutions of our society (Marx and Sherizen 1986; Nelkin and Tancredi, 1989).

All of the cases suggest that access to jobs, insurance, or social entitlements may be limited because of genetic discrimination. Stigmatization and frustration ("I might as well have AIDS") may accompany the test result. The financial and legal burdens of maintaining a reasonable standard of living and basic entitlements as a result of genetic discrimination could be significant.

THE PROBLEM OF VARIABILITY

Several responses described situations in which people were victimized because of a misunderstanding of the clinical variability of many genetic conditions. One respondent with CMT, a nonfatal, clinically variable, and genetically heterogeneous neuromuscular condition, wrote: "I have been rejected for life insurance many times, but only once was CMT cited [explicitly] as the reason. . . . [I appealed, informing the insurance company] that people do not die from CMT and that they had declared me automatically eligible for accidental death insurance—the one risk that can be assumed might be greater for people with CMT. . . . [The insurance company's reply] repeated the statement that CMT is the reason for rejecting my application.

"In 1979 my daughter was denied employment by the [name omitted] Company because she has CMT even though the case is not really noticeable. She had indicated on the form that she had CMT and the examiner asked her what it stood for; then, he looked it up in a medical book and denied her a job which had been offered to her by the recruiter."

Another respondent stated: ". . . My husband has a genetic disorder, Charcot-Marie-Tooth. We have just been turned down for automobile insurance with [name omitted] because of his disease. I have just recently sent them a letter from my husband's doctor . . . explaining that my husband is a far better driver than anyone I know. . . . My husband has had NO accidents, or traffic violations since he has been driving from the age of seventeen [twenty years of driving]."

COMMENT

In these examples, involving CMT, the individual does suffer from a disease, but the symptoms are mild. The decisions regarding life and automobile insurance, and employment, were based solely on a diagnostic label, without regard to the severity of the condition for each individual. In these and other cases, having a particular genotype is equated with the presence of a severe illness and the lack of effective treatments. This evaluation of genetic conditions illustrates a lack of understanding of the concepts of incomplete genetic penetrance, variable expressivity and genetic heterogeneity. In many cases, the worst possible scenario seems to be the standard used for policy decisions regarding at-risk individuals. Yet wide variation in clinical manifestations of a gene-associated disorder—individuality—is common. As highlighted in these examples, an individual may suffer serious consequences as a result of the inaccurate and unfair simplification of genetic conditions.

The third category includes those individuals who are currently healthy but who may be at risk for a genetic disease. Discrimination may ensue as a result of a decision to forego testing and thereby not determine whether they (or their future children) will develop the disease. Discrimination may also occur if they opt for such testing and the results reveal a genotype associated with disease.

A respondent wrote: "I am at risk for Huntington Disease [age 31]. After many years of consideration, my husband and I decided not to bear our own children, but rather to adopt children, so as not to take the chance of passing on the Huntington gene.

"In 1987 we began investigating adoption. We encountered restrictions due to religion and availability of infants, but were finally invited to make application with [name and location of agency omitted]. We began our counseling process and our home visits, at which point the issue of my being at risk was discussed (I had disclosed in my original application the possibility of my developing the disease and why we had chosen adoption). Before completion of our home study, we were asked to withdraw our application, because of the Huntington Disease situation. . . .

"We understand the right to choose the BEST 50 couples out of some 500 applicants per year for placement. Availability of children is incredibly limited. And yet, should I be judged by a disease that I am only at risk for and that may not develop for some years to come? Does this make me different than anyone with diabetes or cancer, for example, in their ancestry?"

Another couple at risk for Huntington Disease sent a letter they received from an adoption agency: "We have decided, in your situation, not to proceed with your application because there is a fifty-fifty chance of your getting Huntington Disease. Though you would be likely to get the disease around the age of fifty, it could be sooner. You would not receive a child from us, if we could proceed with your application, for several years, and therefore we would be risking the likelihood of not having you available to the child until he/she has reached adulthood. We feel that a fifty-fifty chance of getting a disease as serious as Huntington Disease is too great a risk, for our purposes and circumstances."

In a third case, a physician informed us that "a family with a child who has cystic fibrosis received health care through an HMO. When a second pregnancy occurred, prenatal diagnosis using DNA analysis was instituted. Fetal DNA tested positively for two copies of a mutation associated with cystic fibrosis. Nevertheless, the family decided to proceed with pregnancy. After disclosure of the test result, the HMO considered withdrawal of our financial limitations on the health care coverage for the pregnancy, postpartum and pediatric care, as well as for the already affected child. Threats of legal action were required before this situation was resolved."

COMMENT

In the first two cases, the adoption agencies' attitude illustrates how certain conditions categorized as "genetic" are viewed as special and handled differently in terms of social decision making. The use of genetic tests to ascertain the genotype in such at-risk individuals will not necessarily lessen the chances of subsequent discrimination, since a positive test will not be an infallible predictor of the burden a genetic trait may place on an individual, nor does it predict the abilities of affected individuals as parents or the qualities of a potential home.

These incidents also illustrate a large eugenic prejudice — the myth of genetic perfection (Billings 1989; Suzuki and Knudtson 1989). The agencies assume that the best possible family is the one least likely to face medical adversity — the "perfect" family with a disease-free genome. Unfortunately, all families are at risk. The comparison made by one respondent, of being at risk for Huntington disease with susceptibility to diabetes or cancer, highlights a prejudice — that the chance of developing a genetic condition is perceived differently from a similar probability of contracting an illness not produced primarily by a gene.

The third case raises several social and ethical problems. The family was faced with the possibility that bearing a child with a certain genotype might reduce their access to necessary health care benefits. These circumstances constitute a strong incentive for aborting a fetus on the basis of its genotype, a practice that might be interpreted as a form of eugenics. Finally, the couple was forced to threaten legal action to avoid the abortion and loss of benefits, an alternative not available to people who cannot afford an attorney. In addition, pressuring a couple to have an abortion seems to infringe on a right many believe to be fundamental, the right to bear children.

CONCLUSIONS

This pilot study identifies multiple facets of genetic discrimination. It does not document the full range of the prejudices faced by individuals with genetic diagnoses, nor does it establish the prevalence of these attitudes or discriminatory practices. A comprehensive study of the significance and varieties of genetic discrimination is critical to design strategies to ensure the ethical and appropriate use of genetic testing in the future. The need for such studies is underscored by the large number of genetic tests currently performed each year. In addition, powerful business interests support larger applications of genetic techniques because of the revenues that tests and kits generate directly and indirectly.

The dominant theme noted in the responses in this study is that genetic conditions are regarded by many social institutions as extremely serious, disabling, or even lethal conditions without regard to the fact that many individuals with "abnormal" genotypes will either be perfectly healthy, have medical conditions which can be controlled by treatment, or experience only mild forms of a disease. As a result of this misconception, decisions by such institutions as insurance companies and employers are made solely on the basis of an associated diagnostic label rather than on the actual health status of the individual or family. The appropriate use of genetic testing information to restrict or limit access to public entitlements such as health care or employment has not been established and may not exist. The cost of such labeling is magnified by the fact that errors in testing and interpretation do occur.

Once labeled (possibly erroneously), an individual may suffer serious consequences, as highlighted in the examples. These include the inability to get a job, health insurance, or life insurance, being unable to change jobs or move to a different state because of the possibility of losing insurance, and not being allowed to adopt a child.

Furthermore, information related to genetic labeling may enter large-scale data banks now used to store personal health-related information. Individuals' health profiles, which can include genetic conditions, are available privately and are generated in a manner similar to the ubiquitous credit checks encountered in business. Breaches of confidentiality and unauthorized uses of this information may arise (Dezell 1984; Norton 1989; Billings 1990; DeGorgey 1990). Genetic data on certain groups within our society are already being stored by governmental agencies (DeGorgey 1990).

These incidents suggest that there are very important nonmedical reasons why individuals may wish to avoid genetic testing. It is clear that the option not to know is being exercised now. Many persons at risk for Huntington disease, for example, have refused to be tested (Meissen et al. 1988; Brandt et al. 1989). The choice to refuse testing will become more difficult if such testing is required for employment, to obtain affordable medical care, or to obtain or renew health or life insurance. The personal decision to undergo genetic testing certainly requires accurate information about the clinical predictive value of genetic tests (data which may not be available currently), but the widespread utilization of genetic testing as a prerequisite for obtaining social entitlements may also influence an individual's right to choose not to know his or her genetic predispositions.

Various constraints exist to prevent or limit abuses made possible by access to genetic information. These include, for example, laws affecting privacy and civil rights (Russell-Einhorn and Rowe 1989; Natowicz et al. 1992). In addition, limitations exist on the uncontrolled expansion of genetic testing and screening. These include opposition by individuals and interest groups (such as labor unions and disability advocates) sensitized by the dismal history of eugenics movements and suspicious of genetic and scientific incursions into normal daily life, economic constraints (i.e., the poor profit yield of some tests), and state and federal regulations regarding testing and screening.

Nevertheless, it is clear that unfair and discriminatory uses of genetic data already occur under current conditions. Enacted state and federal laws are inadequate to prevent some forms of genetic discrimination, particularly that due to the health insurance industry (this report; Natowicz et al. 1992). The implementation of carefully considered legislation regarding, for example, the privacy of genetic information and the imposition of meaningful penalties on social institutions such as insurers that are found guilty of genetic discrimination are mechanisms to address aspects of genetic discrimination. Consideration of alternative medical care systems is another potential approach toward solving some of these issues. Any approach should include the reaching of a broad-based public consensus on the appropriate use of genetic tests. Without further changes in social attitudes, legal protection, and/or changes in the prevailing American health care system, many healthy and potentially productive members of our society will suffer genetic discrimination.

ACKNOWLEDGMENTS

The authors thank members of the Genetic Screening Study Group for stimulating this study and for thoughtful criticisms. We also thank Phil Bereano, Sherri Broder, Parris Burd, Wylie Burke, Marsha Lanes, Arno Motulsky, and Paul Slovic for contributing information or helpful comments and Denise Brescia for her assistance in the preparation of this manuscript.

REFERENCES

Beckwith J (1991) The Human Genome Initiative: genetics' lightning rod. Am J Law Med 40:1–13.

Billings P (1988) Research in genetic discrimination. Am J Hum Genet 43:225.

_____ (1989) Debunking the genetic myth. Technol Rev 6: 75–76.

_____ (1990) Brewing genes and behavior: the potential consequences of genetic screening for alcoholism. In: Banbury conference 33: The molecular biology and genetics of alcoholism. Cold Spring Harbor Publications, New York.

Brandt, J, Quaid KA, Folstein SE, Garber P, Maestri NE, Abbott MH, Slavney PR, et al (1989) Presymptomatic diagnosis of delayed-onset disease with linked DNA markers: the experience with Huntington's disease. JAMA 261: 3108–3114.

DeGorgey A (1990) The advent of DNA databanks: implications for information privacy. Am J Law Med 41:381–398.

Dezell M (1984) It's 1984: do you know where your medical records end up? Boston Business J 4:1, 12–13.

Donis-Keller H, Green P, Helms C, Cartinhour S, Weiffenbach B, Stephens K, Keith TP, et al (1987) A genetic linkage map of the human genome. Cell 51:319–337.

Dusek V (1987) Bewitching science. Sci People 19:163–168.

Evers-Kiebooms G, van den Berghe H (1979) Impact of genetic counseling: a review of published follow-up studies. Clin Genet 15:465–474.

Hampton ML, Anderson J, Lavizzo BS, Bergman AB (1974) Sickle cell "nondisease": a potentially serious public health problem. Am J Dis Child 128:58–61.

Hewitt M, Holtzman N (1988) The commercial development of tests for human genetic disorders. U.S. Congress, Office of Technology Assessment, Washington, DC.

Holtzman NA (1988) Recombinant DNA technology, genetic tests, and public policy. Am J Hum Genet 42:624–632.

_____ (1989) Proceed with caution: predicting genetic risks in the recombinant DNA era. Johns Hopkins University Press, Baltimore.

Kenen RH, Schmidt RM (1978) Stigmatization of carrier status: social implications of heterozygote genetic screening programs. Am J Public Health 68:1116–1120.

Kevles D (1985) In the name of eugenics: genetics and the uses of human heredity. University of California Press, Berkeley and Los Angeles.

Lander E, Botstein D (1986) Mapping complex genetic traits in humans: new methods using a complete RFLP linkage map. Cold Spring Harbor Symp Quant Biol 51:49–62.

Leonard CO, Chase, GA, Childs B (1972) Genetic counseling: a consumer's view. N Engl J Med 287:433–439.

McKusick V (1988) Mendelian inheritance in man, 8th ed. Johns Hopkins University Press, Baltimore.

Marx G, Sherizen S (1986) Monitoring on the job: how to protect privacy as well as property. Technol Rev 8:63–72.

Meissen G, Myers R, Mastromauro CA, Koroshetz WJ, Klinger KW, Farrer LA, Watkins PA, et al (1988) Predictive testing for Huntington's disease with use of a linked DNA marker. N Engl J Med 318:535–542.

Motulsky A (1974) Brave new world? Science 185:653–663.

_____ (1983) Impact of genetic manipulation on society and medicine. Science 219:135–140.

Murray TH (1983) Warning: screening workers for genetic risk. Hastings Cent Rep 2:5–8.

_____ (1991) Ethical issues in human genome research. FASEB J 5:55–60.

Natowicz M, Alper JK, Alper JS (1992) Genetic discrimination and the law. Am J Hum Genet 50:465–475.

Natowicz MR, Alper JS. Genetic screening: triumphs, problems and controversies. J Public Health Policy (in press).

Nelkin D, Tancredi L (1989) Dangerous diagnostics: the social power of biological information. Basic, New York.

Norton C (1989) Absolutely not confidential. Hippocrates 2:53–59.

Office of Technology Assessment (1990) Genetic monitoring and screening in the workplace. U.S. Government Printing Office, Washington, DC.

Phillips JA III (1988) Clinical applications of gene mapping and diagnosis. In: Childs B, Holtzman NA, Kazazian HH Jr, Valle DL (eds) Molecular genetics in medicine. Elsevier, New York, pp 68–99.

Russell-Einhorn M, Rowe M (1989) Employer screening for genetic disease: current legal problems. In: Foulkes F (ed) Current issues in strategic human resources. Prentice-Hall, New York.

Scott J (1987) Molecular genetics of common diseases. Br Med J 295:769–771.

Suzuki D, Knudtson P (1989) Genethics. Harvard University Press, Cambridge, MA.

Uzych L (1986) Genetic testing and exclusionary practices in the workplace. J Public Health Policy 7:37–57.

ROBERT N. PROCTOR

Genomics and Eugenics: How Fair Is the Comparison?

BIOLOGICAL DETERMINISM

Central to eugenics ideology was the view that biology is destiny—that human talents and institutions are largely the product of our anatomical, neurological, hormonal, genetic, or racial constitution. Eugenicists exaggerated the role of genetics predisposing one toward a life of alcoholism, crime, or other human defects or talent. At the root of the movement was a set of fears: that the poor were outbreeding the rich, that feminists were having too few babies, that the mentally ill and criminal were about to swamp the superior elements of the population with their high birth rates. Eugenics policies were designed to combat those fears.

Among all the potential dangers of human genomics, to my mind the most all-encompassing is the danger of its confluence with a growing trend toward biological determinism. Biological determinism is the view that the large part of human talents and disabilities—perhaps even our tastes and institutions—is anchored in our biology. The Human Genome Project has already been criticized by groups who fear that the ultimate rationale for the project is a biological determinist one. James Watson did little to dispel this concern, defending the Project as providing us with "the ultimate tool for understanding ourselves at the molecular level. . . . We used to think our fate was in our stars. Now we know, in large measure, our fate is in our genes."[1] Critics point to the long, seamy tradition of eugenicists exaggerating the role of genes in human behavior; even without the impositions of a heavy-handed state, there are dangers of seeing biology as destiny. Genes have become a near-universal scapegoat for all that ails the human species. Even where genetic influence is well established, critics worry that aggressive promoting of genetic testing may generate fears out of proportion to actual risks. In the rush to identify genetic components to cancer or heart disease or mental illness, the substantial environmental origins of those afflictions may be slighted.

I want to emphasize this danger of exaggerating the role of genetics in the development of disease. Take the example of cancer. A number of rare cancers are known to be the result of heritable genetic defects. Highly heritable cancers include retinoblastoma [a cancer of the retina] (associated with a deletion in chromosome 13), certain leukemias, xeroderma pigmentosum (which predisposes one toward skin cancer), and a number of rare malignancies associated with a deletion in the recently discovered p53 gene (linked to the Li-Fraumeni syndrome). These are all germline defects—in other words, the genes causing these cancers can be passed from generation to generation.[2] A number of genes have also been found that predispose the carrier to more common kinds of cancers. In the spring of 1991 a research team headed by Bert Vogelstein at Johns Hopkins announced the discovery of a tumor suppressor gene on chromosome 5, the deletion of which seemed to be implicated in the onset of colon cancer.[3] A great deal of research has also gone into the search for predisposing genes for breast cancer.[4] E. B. Claus, N. Risch, and W. D. Thompson estimate that as many as 5 to 10 percent of all cases of breast cancer can be accounted for by inherited factors, and that the distribution of breast cancers is consistent with the existence of an autosomal (non-sex-linked) dominant gene affecting about one-third of 1 percent of all women.[5] Still other studies have tried to demonstrate differential susceptibilities to lung cancer. Smoking is clearly a cause of small-cell carcinoma of the lung, but only a fraction of those who smoke heavily do in fact develop lung cancer.[6] Predisposing genes may provide an answer to the question posed by *Science* magazine reporter Jean Marx, "Why doesn't everybody get cancer?"[7]

Genetic differences no doubt account for at least part of the differential susceptibility to cancer, though assertions about their frequency and what this implies for social policy are politically charged. Popularizers are fond of providing estimates for the frequency of susceptibility genes: a front-page *New York Times* article reporting on the March 1991 discovery of a tumor suppressor gene for colon cancer states that "at least 20 percent" of all colon cancers ("and possibly many more") begin through the action of the newly discovered gene.[8] Mark Skolnick, coauthor of a widely cited *New England Journal of Medicine* report on the genetics of colon cancer, speculates that genes predisposing to colon cancer are inherited "by as many as one-third of all Americans." Skolnick draws clear policy implications from the work: if suitable markers can be found, "we could use a simple blood test to screen the entire U.S. population. Those with the gene or genes would know they are carrying within them a potentially dangerous genetic defect. They would be warned to get regular checkups, and avoid the kinds of high-fat foods thought to trigger the cancer." Skolnick also states that "one-third of Americans stand some risk of developing colon cancer, while the other two-thirds probably aren't at risk at all."[9]

Quite apart from the logistical difficulties of screening "the entire U.S. population," a number of questions can be raised about such statements. For one thing, the figures commonly given for predisposing genes for cancer are somewhat speculative. The statistical models used to generate such figures (most recently for breast and lung cancers) are designed to measure the extent to which cancer runs in families,[10] but they also have notorious problems controlling for the fact that families often share common exposures to mutagens (through the "heritability" of occupation or household environment, for example). Furthermore, the genes discovered in the 1991 *Science* study headed by Vogelstein are genes in the DNA of tumor cells, not in germ-line DNA. The finding of damaged or deleted genetic loci in tumors does not mean that the same defects will be found in the remaining cells of the body and that the defects are therefore heritable. Finally, there is little evidence for the claim that two-thirds of Americans "probably aren't at risk at all" for a disease such as colon cancer. Such a claim presumes a small number of predisposing genes when the actual number might be quite large, producing a continuum of differential susceptibility rather than a simple yes or no, "susceptible or not." There is no evidence that a sizable fraction of the American population is invulnerable to cancer.

The most serious objection to predisposition studies, though, is that they can [distract] attention from the epidemiological fact that cancer is a disease whose incidence varies according to occupation, diet, socioeconomic status, and personal habits such as smoking. Genetics can do little to explain such patterns. Rates of lung and breast cancer, for example — two of the three deadliest cancers — have both risen dramatically in recent years; genetic propensities can have little to do with such increases. Lung cancer rates for U.S. males rose from 5 per 100,000 in 1930 to 75 per 100,000 in 1985 — a fifteenfold increase.[11] Lung cancer rates for women rose some 420 percent over the last thirty years, and breast cancer rates have also grown. The American Cancer Society's 1991 *Cancer Facts and Figures* estimates that American women now face a one in nine chance of developing breast cancer — up some 10 percent from the risk calculated only four years earlier.[12] Such dramatic rises lead one to suspect environmental changes, rather than genetic propensities, as the primary culprit. Even Claus and his colleagues concede that "the great majority of breast cancers are nongenetic."[13]

A similar argument can be made for most of the systematic differences in cancer rates found between ethnic groups. Blacks, for example, have significantly higher cancer rates than do whites. But, as a National Cancer Institute study revealed in the spring of 1991, poverty — not race — is the primary cause of that difference.[14] And surely there are many other differences for which genetics will be irrelevant. Genetics is not going to explain the fact that asbestos miners have higher mesothelioma rates than people who work in air-conditioned offices, nor will it explain the fact that people who live in homes with radon seepage are more likely to contract cancer. Even if individuals vary in susceptibility to such agents, it may be wishful thinking to imagine that physicians will be able to assure people, from their genetic profiles alone, that they are or are not at risk for common diseases such as cancer. Nancy Wexler, president of the Hereditary Disease Foundation and chair of the ethics group of the Human Genome Project, has recently suggested that "[a]s geneticists learn more about diabetes or hypertension or cancer, at some point they will cross an important line. Instead of saying, as they do now, 'Lung cancer runs in your family and you should be careful,' physicians will be able to ask their patients, 'Would you like to take a blood test to see if you are going to get lung cancer?'[15] But if the majority of lung cancers are environmentally induced (and there is evidence that cigarette smoking alone accounts for as much as 90 percent of all lung cancers),[16] then physicians are unlikely ever to be able to predict cancers of this sort at an early age—except perhaps for the small percentage for whom a clear genetic defect can be discovered. It is misleading to suggest that physicians will ever have this power.[17]

Part of the confusion arises from the fact that cancers may be "genetic" in two very different senses. In one sense, all cancers are genetic. All cancer involves the runaway replication of cellular tissue; carcinogenesis invariably involves the switching on or off of genes that normally would not act in this fashion. Cellular replication involves genetic expression, and in this sense all cancers are genetic. Only a tiny proportion of cancers, however, are known to be heritable— that is, transmissible from generation to generation. There are thus two types of cancers, or rather two different ways cancers may originate: *somatic* cancers arise from genetic transformations in some particular bodily tissue (caused by exposure to mutagens or viruses, for example); *germline* or *heritable* cancers are passed from generation to generation through the genetic information in the germ cells (the sperm or eggs). The genetic defect is distributed differently in the two cases. In somatically induced cancers, the genetic malfunction lies only in the injured cells of the tumor. In heritable, germline cancers, the genetic defect will be found in every tissue of the body. The distinction is not always clear-cut: as already noted, some heritable genes confer an increased susceptibility to cancer, the ultimate trigger for which is some environmental mutagen. A given cancer (retinoblastoma, for example) may have both familial and sporadic (somatic) forms—the distinction being only in the timing and location of the mutation. The appropriate therapies for heritable and somatic cancers may be indistinguishable. Still, the root cause of cancer in the two extreme cases is quite different. Germline cancers may be expressed regardless of the environment to which one is exposed; somatic cancers are generally triggered by some postnatal environmental insult.

Knowledge of the genetic mechanisms involved in carcinogenesis has been growing rapidly in recent years. Since the late 1970s, several dozen different segments of the human genome have been discovered that, when mutated (sometimes by as little as one nucleotide, as in the case of human bladder cancer), produce cancer. "Oncogenes," as these segments are called, have been found associated with viruses that infect chickens, monkeys, and cats. Occurring naturally in certain animals, oncogenes may be picked up by these viruses and transmitted in the course of infection. Genes have also been discovered that, by contrast with oncogenes, allow cancer to flourish when the gene is absent. These "tumor suppressor genes" normally prevent the growth of cancer; when damaged or deleted, as seems to be required for the development of retinoblastoma, Wilms tumor (a kidney cancer), and certain forms of colon cancer, it is the absence or impairment of the gene that allows the malignancy to grow. How and why these growth-blocking genes are first activated or deactivated is not yet clear.[18]

The important question of policy interest, though, is: What causes a gene to mutate in the first place? Much has been made of the fact that carcinogenesis begins with genetic changes; Robert Weinberg of the Whitehead Institute (and one of the discoverers of oncogenes) states that "the roots of cancer lie in our genes."[19] Improved therapies may well emerge from investigating precisely what biochemical functions are curtailed by the loss of tumor suppressor genes. If, however, as most often appears to be the case, cancer begins through some kind of environmental insult— exposure to ionizing radiation, for example, or to one of the many chemical carcinogens in our air, food, or water—then the fact that oncogenes must be activated and suppressor genes turned off does not alter the fact that, from a long-run societal point of view, prevention is probably going to remain the best way to approach the problem of cancer.

One of the dangers of biological determinism, then, is that the root cause for the onset of disease is shifted from the environment (toxic exposures) to the individual (genetic defects). The scientific search shifts from a search for mutagens in the environment to biological defects in the individual. Geneticists sometimes argue that identification of persons especially at risk will allow us to determine "who will benefit maximally from treatments designed to manipulate the environmental causes of those conditions."[20] Critics, however, point out that susceptibilities may be used for less benevolent purposes. *Consumer Reports,* in its July 1990 cover story on genetic screening, warned, "The danger is that industry may try to screen out the most vulnerable rather than clean up an environment that places all workers at increased risk."[21]

The threat screening poses to individual workers is well known;[22] less well known may be the fact that a number of industry spokesmen have sought to play the genetic card to defend a particular product as safe. The Council for Tobacco Research has spent more than $150,000,000 on biomedical research since its founding in 1954; the overwhelming majority of its widely disseminated cancer studies have been devoted to genetic research.[23] Tobacco lobbyists have tried to argue that smoking causes cancer only in those persons for whom there is already a genetic predisposition.[24] The recent discovery of a gene triggering the onset of lung cancer (by converting hydrocarbons into carcinogens when exposed to cigarette smoke) prompted the discoverer to assert, "If we could identify those people in whom this gene is easily activated, then we could counsel them, not only not to smoke, but to avoid exposure to certain environmental pollutants."[25] Again, the danger in such arguments is that emphasis is placed on defects in the individual rather than defects in the industrial product or environment. The risk is what might be called an ideological one: if the (mis)conception grows that "nature" is more important than "nurture" in the onset of certain diseases, lawmakers may find themselves less willing to enact strong pollution prevention measures or consumer protection legislation.

It is not always easy, of course, to separate "nature" and "nurture" in such matters. Discoveries of genes for Alzheimer disease, manic depression, schizophrenia, Tourette syndrome, and lung cancer have all been announced with widespread media attention, only to be later found seriously flawed.[26] Even for diseases that are clearly heritable, genes may vary widely in their manner of expression. Five percent of men who have heart attacks before the age of sixty carry a gene that prevents the liver from filtering out harmful cholesterol. Not all of those men with the gene, however, suffer early heart disease—only about half do. Diet or some other factor can apparently ameliorate the negative effects of the disease. Neil Holtzman, professor of pediatrics at Johns Hopkins, points out that genetic tests may have little predictive value in cases where genetic expression is highly variable: "For the vast majority of people affected by heart disease, cancer and the like, the origin is so complex that it's a gross oversimplification to think that screening for a predisposing gene will be predictive."[27]

CONCLUSION

Popularizers and experts both often present the birth of genomics as heralding newfound technical and moral powers. The *Time* magazine cover story on the Human Genome Project of March 20, 1989, asserts that scientists are likely to be able eventually to predict an individual's vulnerability not just to diseases such as cystic fibrosis, but also for "more common disorders like heart disease and cancer, which at the very least have large genetic components."[28] Others imply sweeping moral transformations from the newfound knowledge of our nucleotides. An article in the *Hastings Center Report* envisions "a heightened societal attention to heritage, with DNA stored in banks becoming a new type of ancestral shrine"; the authors forecast a "renewed commitment to intergenerational relatedness." Daniel Koshland, in an editorial in *Science,* suggests that sequencing the human genome may result in "a great new technology to aid the poor, the infirm, and the underprivileged." George Bugliarello, of Brooklyn's Polytechnic University, states that human genome research may help us understand our "constitutional propensity to violence and aggression"; genome research is supposed to give us, for the first time, "a serious if distant hope of finding ways to change some of our dangerous ancestral traits."[29]

At the risk of dashing such fanciful hopes, it is important to keep in mind that there are not that many diseases that have a clear and simple genetic origin. Cystic fibrosis kills on the order of 500 Americans per year; death rates from Huntington disease are roughly comparable. These are not insignificant numbers, but they must be put into perspective. Cigarette smoking alone, for example, is estimated to cause the deaths of some 400,000 Americans per year—more, in other words, than all known genetic diseases combined.[30] Heart disease takes an even higher toll. If it is lives we want to save, where is the $3 billion antismoking initiative or the billion-dollar effort to reduce saturated fats or food additives? Where are the billions to reduce occupational exposures to toxins, or radon gas in homes? The U.S. infant mortality rate is among the worst for industrial nations; knowledge of genetics will do little to help change that. If improved health is our goal, then surely there is something wrong with the priorities of medical funding.

There is a great deal of concern about the "social control" likely to flow from the Human Genome Project. The argument I've made here is that there is an equal danger in the *illusion of control* that will flow from people assuming that everything is genetic. We are in the midst of an upsurge in biological determinism, and not just in areas such as cancer theory. There is little danger today of the kinds of abuses that 1920s and 1930s eugenicists foisted on the world. The emphasis today is on treating or preventing genetic disease, not on elevation of the health of the race. Efforts are aimed at voluntary therapy, not forcible sterilization or marital bans. Counseling is supposed to be self-consciously "nondirective," meaning that it is left to individual patients to decide what kind of therapy they (or their offspring) will or will not have. Unlike in the eugenics movement, those who have genetic diseases are often those in the vanguard pushing for therapy. The champions of genomics are among those calling for research into the social and ethical implications on the project: the NIH [National Institutes of Health] working group formed to monitor the "Ethical, Legal, and Social Issues Related to Mapping and Sequencing the Human Genome" has already begun to fund research into most of the concerns outlined here, as well as several others.[31] The DOE [Department of Energy] has begrudgingly agreed to support ethics research.[32] Most important, perhaps, is the fact that American society as a whole has changed. Civil rights advocates have successfully pushed for laws protecting the status of minorities; disability movements have resulted in guarantees of access for the handicapped. The increasingly powerful voices of women and minorities have made it harder to stigmatize groups in the fashion of the 1920s and 1930s. Times have changed.

The biological determinism that underlay the 1930s eugenics movement, however, has by no means disappeared. Genetics remains very much a "science of human inequality" insofar as the more we look for differences, the more likely we are to find them. In the face of unequal powers and unequal access, there is a great danger of exaggerating the extent to which human behavior is rooted in the genes. Scientists still work to prove that intelligence, alcoholism, crime, depression, homosexuality, female intuition, and a wide range of other talents or disabilities are the inflexible outcomes of human genes, hormones, neural anatomy, or evolutionary history.[33] Endocrinologists still pre-scribe hormonal therapies to prevent homosexuality; psychologists still try to prove that average differences in black-white IQ scores are genetic. It is not so long since sociobiologists suggested that women are unlikely ever to achieve equality with men in the spheres of business and science.[34]

Biology is a common and convenient explanation for intractable social problems. In 1979, amid growing fears of international terrorism, *Science* magazine reported research claiming that "most terrorists probably suffer from faulty vestibular functions in the middle ear." In 1989, with violence growing in the schools, the physician Melvin Konner wrote in the *New York Times* that the tendency for people to do physical harm to others was "intrinsic, fundamental, natural."[35] Genetics has been blamed for nearly every conceivable vice and folly of human life. . . .

Critics worry that science in such cases is being used as a proxy for deeply held social values—that women cannot compete, that blacks are inferior, that war or crime or homosexuality or poverty is a disease that must be combated by medical means. Critics point out that there is little evidence that terrorism, or sexual preference, or personality traits such as "shyness" or "bullying" are genetically anchored, and that it is easy to mistake the intransigence of human cultural qualities (aggression or rape, for example) for biological anchoring.[36]

If there is a disconcerting continuity between genomics and eugenics, it is the fact that both have taken root in a climate where many people believe that the large part of human talents and disabilities are heritable through the genes. The study of human biological differences is not an inherently malevolent endeavor,[37] but in late twentieth-century America, as in midcentury Germany, it is dangerous to assume that biology is destiny. Genetic disease is a reality, but the frequency of such disease should not be exaggerated. From the point of view of lives saved per dollar, monies would probably be better spent preventing exposures to mutagens, rather than producing ever more precise analyses of their origins and effects. Sequencing the human genome may be a technological marvel, but it will not give us the key to life. Pronouncements that "our fate is in our genes" may be good advertising for congressional support, but they may well exaggerate the benefit that will flow from knowledge of our nucleotides. The genome is not "the very essence" of what it means to be human, any more than sheet music is the essence of a concert performance.

But criticism must be concrete, not abstract. Critics sometimes warn about the "slippery slope" of technological development—that if you allow *x*, then what is to prevent you from doing *y?* The whole purpose of law, as of ethics, is to draw lines through the continuum of social space—lines that limit what can or should be done, independent of nature's continuum. Criticism of technologies must be rooted in understanding how specific harms and benefits are distributed over particular social groups; it is as easy (and as mindless) to slide down the slippery slope of criticism, condemning any and all manipulations as "playing God," as it is to plunge headstrong across new technological frontiers.

Optimists might like to imagine that old-style abuses are a thing of the past, but a bit of perspective reveals otherwise. Singapore has launched a eugenics program that rivals those of the 1930s; China in 1989 began a systematic effort to sterilize its mentally retarded.[38] In the United States many safety nets are in place, but new forms of technological acrobatics create ever-new pits into which people are likely to fall. We should keep in mind that the potential for abuse of any technology is largely dependent on the social context within which that technology is used. This is the kernel of truth behind the claims that the Human Genome Project is not likely to raise any new ethical questions. The questions most commonly raised concerning discrimination, unequal access to resources, knowledge in the face of impotence, and rationalizations of social inequality are all old ones in medical ethics. Abuses stem from powers unequally distributed. The danger, to my mind, is therefore not that people will try to improve the genetic health of their offspring, or even that the health of groups as well as individuals will be the target of health planners. The danger is that in a society where power is still unequally distributed between haves and have-nots, the application of the new genetic technologies—as of any other—is as likely to reinforce as to ameliorate patterns of indignity and injustice.

NOTES

1. Cited in L. Jaroff, "The Gene Hunt," *Time,* March 20, 1989: 62–7.

2. R. Weiss, "Genetic Propensity to Common Cancers Found," *Science News* 138:342, 1990.

3. K. W. Kinzler et al. (including Bert Vogelstein), "Identification of a Gene Located at Chromosome 5q21 That Is Mutated in Colorectal Cancers," *Science,* 251:1366–70, 1991. B. Vogelstein et al., "Genetic Alterations during Colorectal-Tumor Development," *New England Journal of Medicine* 319:525–32, 1988; L. A. Cannon-Albright et al., "Common Inheritance of Susceptibility to

Colonic Adenomatous Polyps and Associated Colorectal Cancers" in the same issue.

4. W. R. Williams, D. E. Anderson, "Genetic Epidemiology of Breast Cancer," *Genetic Epidemiology* 1:1–7, 1984; K. Wright, "Breast Cancer: Two Steps Closer to Understanding," *Science* 250:1659, 1990.

5. E. B. Claus, N. Risch, W. D. Thompson, "Genetic Analysis of Breast Cancer in the Cancer and Steroid Study," *American Journal of Human Genetics* 48:232–42, 1991. The authors estimate that 36 percent of all women with breast cancer aged twenty to twenty-nine are carriers of a gene predisposing them to the disease. Older women with the disease carry the gene with much lower frequency. The cumulative lifetime risk of developing the disease for carriers is estimated at 92 percent; noncarriers are estimated at 10 percent risk (the same as for the population as a whole).

6. N. Angier, "Cigarettes Trigger Lung Cancer Gene, Researchers Find," *New York Times,* August 21, 1990. Angier reports that only about 7 percent of those who smoke heavily develop lung cancer, but C. M. Pike and Richard Peto estimate that among men who smoke 25 or more cigarettes a day, 30 percent will develop lung cancer by age 75 in the absence of other causes of death. See *Lancet* 665–68, 1965.

7. J. Marx, "A New Tumor Suppressor Gene?" *Science* 252:1067, 1991.

8. N. Angier, "Crucial Gene Is Discovered in Detecting Colon Cancer," *New York Times,* March 15, 1991.

9. Cited in [J. E. Bishop and M. Waldholz, *Genome: The Story of the Most Astonishing Scientific Adventure of Our Time,* Simon & Schuster, New York,] 1990, pp. 156, 163. Similar generalizations accompanied the November 30, 1990, publication in *Science* of evidence for predisposing genes for a rare form of breast cancer. Commenting on his discovery, David Malkin of Boston's Massachusetts General Hospital Cancer Center asserted, "We'll be able to say, 'Yes, you carry this mutation . . . and you are at risk,' or 'No, you don't.'" See R. Weiss, "Genetic Propensity to Common Cancers Found," *Science News* 138:342, 1990.

10. Claus, Risch, and Thompson's "Genetic Analysis of Breast Cancer" is a recent example; compare also T. A. Sellers et al., "Evidence of Mendelian Inheritance in the Pathogenesis of Lung Cancer," *Journal of the National Cancer Institute* 82:1272–79, 1990.

11. E. Marshall, "Experts Clash Over Cancer Data," *Science* 250:902, 0.

12. American Cancer Society, *Cancer Facts and Figures— 1991,* American Cancer Society, Atlanta, 1991.

13. Claus et al., 1991, p. 241. In one sense, of course, breast cancer is overwhelmingly a genetic disease. More than 95 percent of all breast cancers occur in individuals with the XX rather than the XY karyotype—the disease strikes women far more often than men. Skin cancer is also genetic, insofar as populations with darker skin tend to suffer less from the disease. In both cases, however, genetic factors are incidental to the ultimate cause of the disease: males rarely get breast cancer because they don't have breasts; blacks suffer less from skin cancer because they are better protected from ultraviolet radiation. Predisposing genes for breast or skin cancer may well exist, but these are unlikely to have anything to do with either sex chromosomes or the genes controlling skin coloration.

14. "Poverty Blamed for Blacks' High Cancer Rate," *New York Times,* April 17, 1991. Adjusted for socioeconomic status, whites showed slightly higher rates than blacks for breast, rectal, and lung cancer; blacks showed greater risk for stomach, cervical, and prostate cancers.

15. Wexler is cited in R. M. Henig, "High-Tech Fortune Telling," *New York Times Magazine,* December 24, 1989, p. 20.

16. R. Doll, R. Peto, *The Causes of Cancer,* Oxford University Press, Oxford, 1981. The authors estimate that in the United States smoking accounts for about one third of *all* cancer deaths.

17. See E. S. Lander, "The New Human Genetics: Mapping Inherited Diseases," *Princeton Alumni Weekly,* March 25, 1987, pp. 10–16. Compare Natalie Angier's claim that "the study of oncogenes may not be the best hope of banishing cancer; it may be the only hope." More to the point may be the quip of Richard Rifkind, which Angier herself cites: "You want a cure for cancer? Tell the bastards to quit smoking." See her *Natural Obsessions,* Warner Books, New York, 1988, pp. 17, 141.

18. E. Fearon et al., "Clonal Analysis of Human Colorectal Tumors, *Science* 238:193–7, 1987; R. A. Weinberg, "Oncogenes and Tumor Suppressor Genes," in *Unnatural Causes: The Three Leading Killer Diseases in America,* edited by R. C. Maulitz, Rutgers University Press, New Brunswick, NJ, 1989.

19. R. A. Weinberg, "Finding the Oncogene," *Scientific American* 258:44–51, 1988.

20. The words are A. Motulsky's in the *American Journal of Human Genetics* 48:174, 1991.

21. "The Telltale Gene," *Consumer Reports,* July 1990, p. 485.

22. T. H. Murray, "Warning: Screening Workers for Genetic Risk," *Hastings Center Report,* February 1983, pp. 5–8.

23. *Report of the Council for Tobacco Research—U.S.A., Inc.,* Council for Tobacco Research, New York, 1988.

24. M. Lappé, *Genetic Politics: The Limits of Biological Control,* Simon & Schuster, New York, 1979, p. 120.

25. N. Angier, "Cigarettes Trigger Lung Cancer Gene, Researchers Find," *New York Times,* August 21, 1990.

26. In the early 1970s, for example, a number of researchers postulated that individuals might differ genetically in their ability to metabolize certain lung carcinogens. Subsequent studies, however, showed that such differences were not heritable. For a review and criticism, see B. Paigen et al., "Questionable Relation of Aryl Hydrocarbon Hydroxylase to Lung-Cancer Risk," *New England Journal of Medicine* 297:346–50, 1977.

27. [R. Green, "Tinkering with the Secrets of Life," *Health,* January 1990,] p. 84. See also N. Holtzman's extended discussion of these issues in his *Proceed With Caution: Predicting Genetic Risks in the Recombinant DNA Era,* Johns Hopkins University Press, Baltimore, 1990.

28. L. Jaroff, "The Gene Hunt," *Time,* March 20, 1989, p. 62.

29. K. Nolan, S. Swenson, "New Tools, New Dilemmas: Genetic Frontiers," *Hastings Center Report,* October/November 1988, p. 42; D. E. Koshland, "Sequences and Consequences of the Human Genome," *Science* 246:189, 1989; G. Bugliarello, "The Genetic and Psychological Basis of Warfare as a Challenge to Scientific Research," in [C. Mitcham and P. Siekevitz, eds., *Ethical Issues Associated with Scientific and Technological Research for the Military,* New York Academy of Sciences, New York, 1989], p. xvi. Compare also Marc Lappé's curious speculation that genomics may allow the establishment of files of persons "genetically at risk for acquiring AIDS following infection with the human immunodeficiency virus" ("The Limits of Genetic Inquiry," *Hastings Center Report,* August 1987, p. 6).

30. A recent article in *Circulation,* the official journal of the American Heart Association, estimates that more than 50,000 Americans may be killed each year by so-called "secondhand" or "environmental" smoke. See S. A. Glantz and W. W. Parmley, "Passive Smoking and Heart Disease," *Circulation* 83:1–13, 1991.

31. The Working Group's report has been published as an appendix in [U.S. Department of Health and Human Services and U.S. Department of Energy, *Understanding Our Genetic Inheritance: The U.S. Human Genome Project: The First Five Years, FY 1991–1995,* National Technical Information Service, Springfield, VA, 1990], pp. 65–73.

32. Benjamin Barnhart was reluctant to fund ethics as part of the DOE's Human Genome Project, despite the fact that Charles DeLisi had originally expressed an interest in this area. At a December 1989 meeting of the joint DOE-NIH advisor committee for the project, James Watson cautioned Barnhart that if the DOE did not fund ethical analysis, "Congress will chop off your head" (cited in [R. Cook-Deegan, *Gene Wars: Science, Politics, and the Human Genome Project,* W. W. Norton, New York, 1993].

33. R. C. Lewontin, S. Rose, L. J. Kamin, *Not in Our Genes: Biology, Ideology, and Human Nature,* Pantheon, New York, 1983.

34. G. Dorner et al., "A Neuroendocrine Predisposition for Homosexuality in Men," *Archives of Sexual Behavior* 4:1–8, 1975; T. Bouchard et al., "Sources of Human Psychological Differences: The Minnesota Study of Twins Reared Apart," *Science* 250:223–8, 1990; E. O. Wilson, "Human Decency Is Animal," *New York Times Magazine,* October 12, 1975, p. 50. For a recent and unabashed effort to prove that the average economic underperformance of blacks (compared to whites) is traceable to differences in black-white genetic endowments, see the essays in the December 1986 *Journal of Vocational Behavior.*

35. C. Holden, "Study of Terrorism Emerging as an International Endeavor," *Science* 203:33–35, 1979; "Math Genius May Have Hormonal Basis," *Science* 222:1312, 1983; M. Konner, "The Aggressors," *New York Times Magazine,* August 14, 1988, pp. 33–4.

36. Lewontin et al., 1983; A. Fausto-Sterling, *Myths of Gender: Biological Theories about Women and Men,* Basic Books, New York, 1985.

37. The presumption of human biological equality can be as misleading as the presumption of inequality. Take, for example, the case of cystic fibrosis (CF). Discovery of "the" CF gene was announced amid great fanfare in 1989, but it soon became apparent that while a majority of cases in the U.S. population could be traced to a simple three-base-pair deletion, the disease could also be caused by some sixty other mutations. Early hopes for a simple, comprehensive test were further set back by the discovery that human populations differ substantially according to how common the three-base-pair deletion is relative to other mutations causing the disease. Among Eastern European Jews, for example, the simple three-base-pair deletion appears to account for only about 3 percent of all CF cases. In Denmark, by contrast, the simple deletion accounts for about 88 percent of all CF cases. The usefulness of the test is therefore likely to vary greatly according to the genetic background of the population in question.

38. N. D. Kristof, "Chinese Region Uses New Law to Sterilize Mentally Retarded," *New York Times,* November 21, 1989; also his "Parts of China Forcibly Sterilizing the Retarded Who Wish to Marry," *New York Times,* August 8, 1991. For the case of India see Kaval Gulhati, "Compulsory Sterilization: The Change in India's Population Policy," *Science* 195:1300–5, 1977; for Latin America see Bonnie Mass, *Population Target, The Political Economy of Population Control in Latin America,* Latin American Working Group, Toronto, 1976; and for Singapore see C. K. Chan, "Eugenics on the Rise—Singapore," in *Ethics, Reproduction, and Genetic Control,* ed. R. Chadwick, Routledge, New York, 1987. The best recent U.S. review is Philip R. Reilly, *The Surgical Solution: A History of Involuntary Sterilization in the United States,* Johns Hopkins University Press, Baltimore, 1991.

In Britain, arguments have recently been put forward that DNA diagnostic laboratories should be judged in terms of how effectively they reduce the financial burden of caring for the handicapped. See, for example, J. C. Chapple et al., "The New Genetics: Will It Pay Its Way?" *Lancet* 1:1189–92, 1987. Angus Clarke of the University of Wales's Institute of Medical Genetics has pointed to a danger in the more general use of audits to evaluate diagnostic departments, especially insofar as "efficiency" is measured in terms of aborted fetuses per unit of diagnosed defects. The danger, as he sees it, is that cost-benefit analyses of this sort will re-introduce eugenic criteria under the guise of "social responsibility in reproduction": "It is not at all far-fetched to imagine finance for the care of the handicapped being reduced on the grounds that there will be fewer handicapped children if the genetics services operated more 'efficiently.' To encourage such services to meet targets in terms of terminations, our funding might depend upon 'units of handicap prevented,' which would pressurise parents into screening programmes and then into unwanted terminations with the active collusion of clinical geneticists anxious about their budgets. . . . There certainly is a role for public health genetics, but not for a system of eugenics by default, through the impersonal, amoral operation of a penny-pinching bureaucracy." See his "Genetics, Ethics, and Audit," *Lancet* 335:1145–47, 1990; also his further remark on "eugenics by accountancy" in *Lancet* 336:120, 1990.

Human Gene Therapy

LEROY WALTERS

Ethical Issues in Human Gene Therapy

There are four major types of potential genetic intervention with human beings. These four types of intervention, in turn, are based on two conceptual distinctions. The first distinction is rather clear-cut — the distinction between somatic (or nonreproductive) and germ-line (or reproductive) cells. A blood cell is an example of a somatic cell; an ovum is an example of a germ-line cell. The second distinction is more difficult to draw, at least in some cases. It is the distinction between the cure or prevention of disease, on the one hand, and the enhancement of capabilities, on the other.

These two distinctions can be employed to create the following matrix:

	Somatic	Germ-Line
Cure or prevention of disease	1	2
Enhancement of capabilities	3	4

Type-1 genetic intervention treats only somatic or nonreproductive cells in an effort to cure disease in an individual patient. Type-2 genetic intervention affects reproductive cells and, if successful, would reduce the incidence of a particular genetic disease — or perhaps prevent the occurrence of that disease entirely — in the descendants of the treated individual. Type-3 genetic intervention would enhance selected characteristics in the treated individual only. And type-4 genetic intervention would pass on such enhancements to future generations of a particular family through the germ line.

Only type-1 genetic intervention is currently being considered for use with human beings. I will devote most of this [essay] to a discussion of ethical issues raised by type-1 genetic intervention, that is, human gene therapy that targets somatic cells. In the latter part of the [essay], I will turn to the ethical questions that may arise if type-2 genetic intervention becomes sufficiently precise as a technique to justify contemplating its use in human beings.

THE EARLY HISTORY OF TYPE-1 GENETIC THERAPY: THE MARTIN CLINE EXPERIMENT OF 1980

In May 1979, Martin Cline of the University of California, Los Angeles (UCLA), submitted a proposal to his local institutional review board, in which he requested permission to perform type-1 genetic intervention in human beings. The extended review process, the treatment of two patients, and the clinical outcome are briefly reviewed in the following narrative, prepared by the author and based on a subsequent report by a committee at the National Institutes of Health (NIH).[1]

On 30 May 1979, Martin J. Cline, Professor of Medical Oncology at UCLA, and several collaborators submitted a protocol to the Human Subjects Protection Committee (HSPC) at UCLA. The protocol, entitled "Autologous Bone Marrow Transplantation in Sickle Cell Disease and Other Life-Threatening Disorders of Hemoglobin Synthesis," proposed to insert two linked genes into bone marrow cells that had been removed from each patient's body. One gene was from the herpes virus; the other gene produced one of the components of normal hemoglobin. After the bone marrow cells had been treated in an effort to insert the new genes into them, they would be intravenously infused into the body of the patient from whom they had been removed.

Following discussion of the protocol at meetings of the HSPC and the committee's receipt of written comments on the protocol from two UCLA consultants, Cline and his associates modified their protocol in September 1979 to exclude the use of the two-gene combination—a type of recombinant DNA—in patients. Instead, only the gene for producing a component of normal hemoglobin would be employed. This modification made review of the protocol by the UCLA Institutional Biosafety Committee unnecessary. THE HSPC reviewed the revised protocol, addressed further questions to Cline, considered his answers, and requested written comments on the revised protocol from four consultants outside of UCLA.

In July 1980, Cline traveled to Israel and Italy, where he treated one patient who was suffering from beta-zero-thalassemia (a form of thalassemia in which there is no synthesis of the beta chain of hemoglobin) in each country. In Israel, the proposed treatment, without the use of recombinant DNA, was approved

by the Human Subjects Protection Committee of Hadassah Hospital. The treatment was administered to a consenting twenty-one-year-old woman on 10-11 July 1980, using recombinant DNA. About the decision to employ recombinant DNA, Cline later wrote:

I decided to use the recombinant genes because I believed that they would increase the possibility of introducing beta-globin genes that would be functionally effective, and would impose no additional risk to the patient, since it was known that pieces of DNA are efficiently linked in all combinations once they are taken into cells. I made this decision on medical grounds.[2]

In Italy, Cline proposed performing a similar procedure for a sixteen-year-old woman suffering from beta-thalassemia major (a homozygous condition that causes severe anemia). Since no committee system for the review of human research exists in Italy, the protocol (including the use of recombinant DNA) was approved by the head of the appropriate clinical unit at the University Polyclinic in Naples. The study was performed on 15–16 July 1980, after the consent of the young woman's mother had been secured.

On 16 July 1980, the HSPC at UCLA voted to disapprove the revised protocol that had been submitted by Cline and his associates the previous year. Cline was informed of the disapproval in a letter dated 22 July 1980. Almost two years later, both research subjects were alive, apparently having been neither helped nor harmed by the gene-therapy procedures.

The *Los Angeles Times* broke the story of Cline's human gene-therapy studies on 8 October 1980.[3] Less than two months later, Cline and a colleague published an article on somatic-cell gene therapy in the *New England Journal of Medicine,* which included a long section entitled "Strategy, Timing and Ethics of Gene Transplantation in Human Beings."[4] The same issue of the journal also included the often-cited essay by W. French Anderson and John C. Fletcher entitled "Gene Therapy in Humans: When Is It Ethical to Begin?"[5]

Because Cline had attempted gene therapy in human patients without prior authorization by his local institutional review board, his actions were reviewed for possible disciplinary action by both UCLA and an ad hoc committee at NIH. As a result of these investigations, he was demoted from an administrative post at UCLA, and some of his NIH grants were either reduced in funding or terminated. In addition, for the three years after the completion of the NIH committee report, that report was required to be appended to all of Cline's new grant applications to NIH.[6] More than two years after he performed his gene therapy studies in Israel and Italy, Cline was invited to testify at a congressional hearing on "Human Genetic Engineering." He welcomed the opportunity to explain in public why he had attempted to employ this new technique despite the reservations about, and ultimate disapproval of, his proposal by the UCLA Human Subjects Protection Committee. One dramatic exchange between Cline and the subcommittee chairman, Congressman Albert Gore, Jr. (D-Tennessee), epitomized the divergent viewpoint of the researcher and his critics:

Dr. Cline: May I pose a question to you, Congressman? Suppose you had a child of 13 who was suffering from some incurable illness. Would you rather have someone like myself, presumably knowledgeable in clinical medicine, who has spent his life in caring for patients, making the judgments about what should be done next in the management of illness, or would you rather have a balanced committee composed of some professional people and lay individuals and lawyers making the judgment?

Mr. Gore: I am used to asking the questions, not answering them.

Let me depart from that practice and attempt to give you an answer.

I would, of course, advise anyone to rely upon the judgment of the physician chosen to exercise principal support for the care of the patient, be it a loved one or anyone else.

I would hope that individual physician was himself or herself making judgments that bore reference to the best science available and was not an individual who would recommend a procedure so experimental as to have no known chance of benefiting my child whatsoever.[7]

What problems in the review system for type-1 genetic intervention proposals had the experiences of Cline and UCLA revealed? In my view, at least three distinct problems emerged. First, even a university as prestigious as UCLA could find few qualified experts within the institution who were competent to review human gene therapy protocols. This difficulty occurred, in part, because Cline and his associates were probably the most knowledgeable faculty members at UCLA about the science relevant to human gene therapy. Second, in 1979 and 1980 there were no agreed-upon standards or guidelines for human gene therapy proposals. Third, because institutional review board meetings in most institutions are closed to the press and the public, policy makers and members of the public knew nothing about Cline's protocol until the

review process had been completed and, in this case, until after the studies had been performed. Thus, public information about the gene therapy proposals was available only after the fact, and public participation in the review process was precluded.

The unauthorized experiments of Martin Cline helped to create a momentum in favor of a national review mechanism for human gene therapy proposals. The *Splicing Life* report of the President's Commission for the Study of Ethical Problems in Medicine and Biomedical and Behavioral Research, unveiled at the November 1982 congressional hearing, strongly advocated the creation of a national oversight body for genetic intervention proposals.[8] On 27 April 1983, Congressman Gore translated one of the administrative alternatives suggested by the President's Commission into H.R. 2788, a bill that sought to create a President's Commission on the Human Applications of Genetic Engineering.[9] In the end, however, it was an already established and functioning committee at NIH, the Recombinant DNA Advisory Committee (RAC), that took action.

THE CREATION OF A NATIONAL REVIEW PROCESS FOR TYPE-1 HUMAN GENETIC INTERVENTION, 1983–87

The first moves toward creating a public national review process for somatic-cell human gene therapy occurred on 11 April 1983, less than five months after the congressional hearings on human genetic engineering and the publication of Splicing Life and just a few weeks before the introduction of the Gore bill. Robert Mitchell, a California attorney who was then chairing the RAC, suggested to the committee that it establish a working group to study and respond to Splicing Life, and especially the report's final chapter, "Protecting the Future." The RAC responded to Chairman Mitchell's initiative by appointing a working group to prepare a response to Splicing Life. The group, on which the author served as a member, met for the first time on 24 June 1983.[10]

After verifying that no existing agency or committee had current plans to oversee human gene therapy, the working group recommended to the RAC that the committee express its willingness, in principle, to review *specific proposals* to perform human gene therapy on a case-by-case basis. This recommendation was in line with the RAC's traditional mode of operation since its creation in 1974; the RAC deliberated primarily in response to research proposals put forward by scientists. At its 19 September 1983 meeting, the members of the RAC accepted the general proposal of the working group and asked for further specification of a review process.[11] On December 13, the working group met for a second and final time; the upshot of this meeting was the proposal that an interdisciplinary working group or subcommittee be created by the RAC to provide initial review of human gene therapy protocols for the RAC. This proposal was accepted by the RAC at its 26 February 1984 meeting, and by the NIH director on 17 April.[12]

The Working Group on Human Gene Therapy was created during the summer of 1984, appointed by Director of the NIH Office of Recombinant DNA Activities, William J. Gartland, after substantial consultation with Robert Mitchell, Chairman of the RAC; Bernard Talbot, Deputy Director of the National Institute of Allergy and·Infectious Diseases at NIH (the institutional home of the RAC at that time); NIH administrators and scientists; extramural experts in ethics, law, and public policy; and the author. The initial members of the working group included two laboratory scientists, five clinical researchers, three ethicists, three lawyers, two scholars of public policy, and a layperson.

The first three meetings of the Working Group on Human Gene Therapy in 1984 and 1985 were devoted primarily to the drafting of a guidance document for researchers entitled "Points to Consider in the Design and Submission of Human Somatic-Cell Gene Therapy Protocols."[13] The principal mode of discourse in "Points to Consider" was the question; in fact, the August 1985 version of the document contained over one hundred questions. This large number of specific questions can, however, be reduced to seven central queries.

1. What is the disease to be treated?
2. What alternative treatments for the disease exist?
3. What are the potential harms of gene therapy for the patients treated?
4. What are the potential benefits of gene therapy for human patients?
5. How will patients be selected in a fair and equitable manner?
6. How will the patients' voluntary and informed consent be solicited?
7. How will the privacy of patients and the confidentiality of their medical information be protected?

Several of these questions are closely related to a trio of ethical principles that received considerable attention in the 1970s and 1980s, particularly in a report of the National Commission for the Protection of Human Subjects of Biomedical and Behavioral Research[14] and a widely used textbook on biomedical ethics.[15] Questions 3 and 4 deal with the potential benefits and harms of somatic-cell gene therapy. They are thus closely related to the principle of *beneficence,* which examines the consequences or outcomes of an action or policy. The principle of *respect for autonomy* is embodied in questions 5 and 7, which deal with the voluntary and informed decisions of patients and with their control of information about themselves. The principle of *justice* underlies question 6, which asks investigators to set up procedures for choosing fairly among prospective patients if not all patients can be treated initially.

The Working Group on Human Gene Therapy labored vigorously to complete "Points to Consider" before the first gene therapy proposal was submitted. The group was surprised, therefore, when no proposals emerged in late 1985 or the entire year of 1986. In April 1987 the working group, now called the Human Gene Therapy Subcommittee, did receive a model proposal from W. French Anderson and associates entitled "Human Gene Therapy: Preclinical Data Document."[16] This extensive proposal for treating severe combined immune deficiency in children by genetically modifying bone-marrow cells received a thorough review at the December 1987 subcommittee meeting. However, the researchers and the subcommittee members understood that both the proposal and the review process were simulations—a dry run to prepare everyone for actual clinical protocols in the future.

THE REVIEW AND INITIATION OF THREE CLINICAL PROTOCOLS INVOLVING TYPE-1 GENETIC INTERVENTION IN HUMAN BEINGS, 1988–91

Almost three years elapsed between the completion of "Points to Consider" in September 1985 and the submission of the first clinical protocol in the summer of 1988. At its 29 July 1988 meeting, the Human Gene Therapy Subcommittee conducted the initial review of a protocol submitted by Steven A. Rosenberg and associates.[17] There were several surprises in this initial proposal. First, it involved cancer patients, especially patients afflicted with malignant melanoma, not patients suffering from genetic disease. Second, the researchers did not initially intend to provide gene-mediated therapy to the patients; rather, they sought approval to use human gene transfer as a method for *marking* certain somatic cells from patients, so that those cells, reintroduced into the patients' bodies, could be tracked during the succeeding months. (The marking of cells with radioactive isotopes allows such tracking for only a few days.) Third, the target cells in the human gene transfer proposal were not bone-marrow cells, as anticipated, but rather a type of lymphocyte, or white blood cell, called tumor infiltrating lymphocytes.

The gene transfer protocol submitted by Rosenberg and associates was not approved by the Human Gene Therapy Subcommittee at the 29 June 1988 meeting, pending the submission of additional data. The subsequent review process in 1988 and early 1989 was more complicated than anticipated. The subcommittee continued to withhold its approval in late September when the requested data were not submitted for review. However, after hearing an oral presentation of additional data on 3 October, the RAC voted, by a margin of eighteen to five, to approve the gene transfer proposal. NIH Director James Wyngaarden responded to the split vote of the RAC by requesting that the gene transfer protocol be resubmitted to the Human Gene Therapy Subcommittee, with the requested additional data in written form, for the subcommittee's review and approval. On 9 December 1988, the subcommittee reviewed the additional data provided by the researchers and unanimously aproved the gene transfer proposal. RAC members were then asked to reconfirm their 3 October approval by mail ballot in mid-December. Wyngaarden reported his approval of the gene transfer proposal at the RAC meeting held on 30 January 1989. However, initiation of the study was delayed until May 1989 because of a lawsuit filed by the Foundation on Economic Trends, which questioned the validity of a mail ballot in the review process.[18] The initial results of the human gene transfer study were published in August 1990.[19]

At long last, in 1990, two type-1 gene therapy protocols were submitted for review. The first protocol, submitted by R. Michael Blaese, W. French Anderson, and associates, was initially reviewed by the Human Gene Therapy Subcommittee and the RAC on 30 March 1990. Like the 1987 "Preclinical Data Document," this study was directed toward children with severe combined immune deficiency caused by the lack of a single enzyme, adenosine deaminase, or ADA. Unlike the 1987 simulation protocol, the actual protocol of 1990 envisioned using lymphocytes, or white blood cells, as the target cells, rather than bone-marrow cells.[20] The second protocol, proposed by Steven A. Rosenberg and colleagues, was initially reviewed by the Human Gene Therapy Subcommittee on 30 July 1990. This protocol was, in fact, a modification of the earlier gene transfer study; in addition to marking the tumor infiltrating lymphocytes genetically, the protocol sought to introduce into the lymphocytes the gene that produces tumor necrosis factor, a substance that kills tumor cells.[21] The review process for these studies was uneventful: the subcommittee approved both protocols on 30 July, and the RAC followed suit the next day. The first child with severe combined immune deficiency was enrolled in the Blaese-Anderson protocol in September 1990,[22] and several months later the first cancer patients were enrolled in the tumor necrosis factor gene therapy study of Rosenberg and associates.[23] The early results of the Blaese-Anderson study appear quite promising.[24]

Where does the review process for human gene therapy stand in 1991? With type-1 genetic intervention still in its infancy, it would be unwise to draw sweeping conclusions. However, when one compares the situation of 1991 with that faced by Martin Cline and UCLA in 1979 and 1980, it is quite clear that progress has been made. There is now in place a national public review process that allows both the press and the general public to follow the major steps toward somatic-cell human gene therapy. The technical, ethical, and legal expertise available to any single institutional review board has now been supplemented by a multi-institutional and interdisciplinary review committee and subcommittee, the RAC and the Human Gene Therapy Subcommittee. And the national public review process employs guidelines, the "Points to Consider," that have been published in the *Federal Register* for comment on three occasions.[25]

ETHICS AND GERM-LINE GENETIC INTERVENTION FOR THE CURE OR PREVENTION OF DISEASE (TYPE 2)

At some point within the next decade, it is likely that a proposal to perform type-2 genetic intervention will be put forward for consideration. It is therefore appropriate to undertake at least a preliminary ethical analysis, attempting to anticipate some of the ethical questions that will be discussed when such a proposal is submitted for review.

Important technical obstacles will need to be overcome before precise germ-line changes can be made. Currently available vectors for carrying new genes into cells are, in many ways, like unguided missiles. That is, the vectors, which are carefully domesticated retroviruses, deliver the genes to random sites in the chromosomes contained in the nuclei of cells. There the genes are simply *added* to the original set of genes and, if all goes well, begin to perform the function that is not being performed by the original set. Thus, in any genetically repaired cell, the original malfunctioning gene and the newly introduced properly functioning gene simply coexist, probably at very different sites on different chromosomes. If one were to compare the repair to the techniques used in word processing, the "insert" function is employed, and the simple insertion of a correctly spelled word is sufficient to overcome the deleterious effects of a misspelled word, even if the addition occurs in a very different part of the text.

What researchers hope to develop, for both type-1 and type-2 genetic intervention, is a guided missile — that is, a vector that can take its genetic payload to a precise target on a particular chromosome. Ideally, the vector would be able to assist in the process of splicing out the malfunctioning gene and *replacing* it with the properly functioning gene.[26] In word-processing terms, the search-and-replace function would be used: the misspelled word would be located, and the correctly spelled word would be substituted for the misspelled word.

Two lines of research that point toward the future feasibility of germ-line genetic intervention have moved ahead rather dramatically. The first is the actual repair of genetic defects through germ-line intervention in laboratory animals. In one study, a hereditary growth disorder in mice was corrected through the introduction of a new gene into the germ line.[27] In a second study, beta-thalassemia in mice was treated by similar means.[28] Two other germ-line experiments, also with mice, restored reproductive function to so-called hypogonadal animals[29] and cured a neurological defect that caused affected animals to "shiver."[30]

A second line of research that may be important for future type-2 proposals is recent work on the preimplantation diagnosis of genetic defects in early human embryos. Preimplantation diagnosis is increasingly employed by in vitro fertilization clinics to identify potential genetic or chromosomal abnormalities in the embryos. One or two cells are removed at the eight-cell cleavage stage, or a small group of cells is separated from the blastocyst (an embryo that is nearing the stage of development at which implantation occurs). The removed cells are then tested for evidence of chromosomal abnormalities (for example, trisomy 21, which produces Down's syndrome) or genetic conditions (for example, Duchenne's muscular dystrophy).[31] In the future, it seems likely that a test for the most prevalent mutations that cause cystic fibrosis will also be used at the preimplantation stage. If an early embryo is discovered to be affected with a genetic or chromosomal abnormality, the parents and their physicians usually agree that it should be discarded rather than transferred into the uterus of the genetic mother.

It is precisely in the context of preimplantation diagnosis that type-2 human genetic intervention may be initially proposed. Robert Cook-Deegan has suggested that because of their moral or religious beliefs about the sanctity of life, even in its earliest stages, some couples may prefer to have a genetically affected embryo treated by means of gene therapy rather than discarding it.[32] However, if gene therapy were performed on a preimplantation embryo, it is probable that *all* cells of the resulting fetus and child would be affected, including the reproductive cells. If the gene-replacement technique outlined above were available, gene therapy would allow the treated individual to avoid passing on the original, malfunctioning gene(s) to his or her offspring. At that site in the individual's genome, only the properly functioning gene(s) would remain, both in the somatic and the reproductive cells.

Type-2 genetic intervention would not be the only alternative for parents who discover through preimplantation diagnosis that an embryo is affected with a genetic abnormality. The embryo could be transferred into the uterus of the genetic mother in the hope that it would develop and be delivered as an infant. At the most appropriate time after birth, type-1 genetic intervention could be performed on the infant or child. Only if the genetic defect in question caused serious and irreversible harm during gestation would type-2 genetic intervention at the preimplantation stage be the clearly preferable alternative.

A second possible technique for effecting germ-line change has not yet been conclusively demonstrated in laboratory studies and may thus not be available for use in type-2 genetic intervention. This technique would focus on the reproductive cells of adults rather than on all the cells of early embryos. It would seek to replace defective genes in sperm or egg cells, either in vitro, after removal from the bodies of the adults, or in vivo, through the use of vectors that could carry the new genes directly to the proper cells in the reproductive organs of those adults. If germ-cell repair became a safe and effective technique, it would spare couples the discomfort and expense of the procedures associated with in vitro fertilization and preimplantation diagnosis.

The ethical principles that were applied to type-1 genetic intervention can also be applied to this more futuristic and hypothetical type of genetic intervention. In the following comments I will merely sketch a few of the ways in which these principles may apply to germ-line techniques. The principle of beneficence focuses on the potential benefits and harms of an action. In type-2 genetic intervention, because the effects would be directly transmitted to offspring, one will need to take into account the consequences both for the individual(s) treated and for future generations. A higher standard of safety and perhaps also of effectiveness will be required for type-2 than for type-1 genetic intervention, precisely because of these foreseen and (in the case of benefits) intended long-term consequences.

One argument that is likely to be advanced in favor of type-2 genetic intervention, as opposed to type-1, is based on efficiency. It will be easier and less expensive in the long run, so this argument goes, to deal with a genetic defect in a particular family line through germ-line intervention than to perform somatic-cell gene therapy in multiple members of multiple generations. Further, if type-2 genetic intervention is employed to treat both carriers of a genetic trait and individuals affected by the genetic condition, the long-term effect of the germ-line approach, when many families are treated, will be to reduce the incidence of the disease in the population. Against this efficiency argument could be counterposed the objection that a mistake in the attempt to perform germ-line intervention is much more difficult to rectify than an error in somatic-cell therapy that will not be passed on to the patient's descendants.

There is also a more comprehensive risk assessment that could be performed with type-2 genetic intervention. It would compare the potential health benefits of germ-line intervention with the social and political risk that this powerful new technology might be used for malevolent or competitive reasons unrelated to serious disease. If the probability of misuse were sufficiently low, or could be reduced to a reasonably low level through anticipatory policies, and if the potential health benefits of type-2 genetic intervention were both highly probable and exceedingly great, then the principle of beneficence alone might incline us to proceed with the use of this technique.

The principle of respect for autonomy is also relevant to type-2 genetic intervention. Here the primary focus will probably be on the family, and more specifically on parents making proxy decisions on behalf of their children, grandchildren, and more distant descendants. If type-2 genetic intervention becomes a safe and effective measure, future parents will in some cases be able to prevent foreseeable harms to their offspring—that is, they will be able to spare offspring from the ravages of a specific genetic disease or from the psychological burden of carrier testing or prenatal diagnosis. This type of familial autonomy would be a natural extension of the freedom that individuals and couples now enjoy in the context of genetic counseling.[33]

The principle of respect for autonomy would not automatically rule out mandatory programs of type-2 genetic intervention aimed at preventing a serious genetically transmitted disease. It would, however, place the burden of proof on policy makers to demonstrate that the same goal could not be achieved through noncoercive means and that the benefits of this new kind of public health program for near and distant generations are truly overwhelming. (The closest analogy in our current situation is mandatory screening of newborns for phenylketonuria and other inborn errors of metabolism. However, even in this context the need for a mandatory approach is controversial.[34])

The principle of respect for autonomy would readily undermine the rationale for any coercive program undertaken for racial, political, or competitive reasons. The term "eugenics" has often been applied to these programs, although it is sometimes unclear whether the term implies the use of coercive state power only, or the arbitrary use of that power against defenseless minorities.[35] Whereas earlier eugenic programs were based on crude methods like involuntary sterilization or selective breeding, new developments in molecular biology would allow for much more precisely targeted genetic change in a population. Ironically, the best defense against such eugenic programs may not be the discouragement or prohibition of certain lines of research, but rather the preservation of democratic institutions that embody respect for the autonomy of individuals and families.

The principle of justice will also be relevant to type-2 genetic intervention. As implied above, this principle should serve as a barrier to unjust discrimination against particular social or ethnic groups. If there is anything for which groups ought not to be held morally accountable, it is for the genes that are associated with those groups. More positively, if type-2 genetic intervention becomes a standard and accepted method for curing or preventing particular genetic diseases, it will inaugurate a new era in medicine — an era that parallels in some ways the new age in the treatment and prevention of most infectious diseases in the twentieth century. When that day comes, society will face new decisions about how to apply the principle of justice to the problem of access to health care. We do not know whether social reform will keep pace with technological progress as the twenty-first century unfolds. But as it does, we can hope for the day when germ-line genetic intervention becomes an integral part of an adequate level of health care, to which every member of society is entitled.[36]

ACKNOWLEDGMENTS

Substantial parts of this article were presented at the Nineteenth Annual Conference on Ethics, Humanism, and Medicine, held on 23 March 1991 at the University of Michigan Medical School in Ann Arbor. The author wishes to thank the sponsors of the conference for their kind invitation. The final part of the article is based on a symposium presentation at the February 1991 Annual Meeting of the American Association for the Advancement of Science in Washington, DC. This part of the article parallels the final section of the author's recent essay, "Human Gene Therapy: Ethics and Public Policy," published in *Human Gene Therapy* 2 (Summer 1991): 115–22.

The author wishes to thank Sharon J. Durfy, PhD, postdoctoral fellow at the Kennedy Institute of Ethics, for her helpful comments on an earlier draft of the article.

The research for this article was supported in part by Biomedical Research Support Grant S07RR07136-18 from the National Institutes of Health.

NOTES

1. US National Institutes of Health, *Report of the National Institutes of Health (NIH) Ad Hoc Committee on the UCLA Report Concerning Certain Research Activities of Dr. Martin J. Cline* (Bethesda, MD: NIH, 21 May 1981); see also US Congress, House, Committee on Science and Technology, *Human Genetic Engineering, Hearings Before the Subcommittee on Investigations and Oversight*, 97th Cong., 2nd sess., 16–18 November 1982, 543–45.

2. US National Institutes of Health, *Report*, 8.

3. P. Jacobs, "Pioneer Genetic Implants Revealed," *Los Angeles Times*, 8 October 1980, pp. 1, 26.

4. K. E. Mercola and M. J. Cline, "The Potentials of Inserting New Genetic Information," *New England Journal of Medicine* 303 (27 November 1980): 1297–1300.

5. W. F. Anderson and J. C. Fletcher, "Gene Therapy in Humans: When Is It Ethical to Begin?" *New England Journal of Medicine* 303 (27 November 1980): 1293–97.

6. US Congress, *Human Genetic Engineering*, 544–45.

7. *Ibid.*, 453.

8. President's Commission for the Study of Ethical Problems in Medicine and Biomedical and Behavioral Research, *Splicing Life: The Social and Ethical Issues of Genetic Engineering with Human Beings* (Washington, DC: Government Printing Office, 1982), 81–88; US Congress, *Human Genetic Engineering*, 181–89.

9. US Congress, House, *A Bill to Establish the President's Commission on the Human Applications of Genetic Engineering*, 98th Cong., 1st sess., 27 April 1983, H.R. 2788.

10. US National Institutes of Health, "Recombinant DNA Research: Actions Under Guidelines," *Federal Register* 50, no. 160, 25 April 1984, 17846.

11. *Ibid.*, 17847.

12. *Ibid.* For a more detailed chronology of these and subsequent events, see E. Milewski, "Development of a Points to Consider Document for Human Somatic Cell Gene Therapy," *Recombinant DNA Technical Bulletin* 8 (December 1985): 176–80; and L. Walters, "Human Gene Therapy: Ethics and Public Policy," *Human Gene Therapy* 2 (Summer 1991): 119–20.

13. US National Institutes of Health, "Points to Consider in the Design and Submission of Human Somatic-Cell Gene Therapy Protocols," *Federal Register* 50, no. 160, 19 August 1985, 33463–67.

14. National Commission for the Protection of Human Subjects of Biomedical and Behavioral Research, *The Belmont Report: Ethical Principles and Guidelines for the Protection of Human Subjects of Research* (Washington, DC: Government Printing Office, 1978).

15. T. L. Beauchamp and J. F. Childress, *Principles of Biomedical Ethics*, 3rd ed. (New York: Oxford University Press, 1989).

16. W. F. Anderson, R. M. Blaese, A. W. Nienhuis, and R. J. O'Reilly, "Human Gene Therapy: Preclinical Data Document," unpublished proposal submitted to the Human Gene Therapy Subcommittee, NIH Recombinant DNA Advisory Committee, 24 April 1987.

17. "N2-TIL Human Gene Transfer Clinical Protocol," *Human Gene Therapy* 1 (Spring 1990): 73–92.

18. *Ibid.*, 85–86.

19. S. A. Rosenberg, P. Aebersold, K. Cornetta, *et al.*, "Gene Transfer into Humans: Immunotherapy of Patients with Advanced

Melanoma, Using Tumor-Infiltrating Lymphocytes Modified by Retroviral Gene Transduction," *New England Journal of Medicine* 323 (30 August 1990): 570–78.

20. "ADA Human Gene Therapy Clinical Protocol," *Human Gene Therapy* 1 (Fall 1990): 327–29, 331–62.

21. "TNF/TIL Human Gene Therapy Clinical Protocol," *Human Gene Therapy* 1 (Winter 1990): 443–71, 473–80.

22. N. Angier, "Girl, 4, Becomes First Human to Receive Engineered Genes," *New York Times,* 15 September 1990, pp. 1,9; L. Thompson, "Human Gene Therapy Debuts at NIH," *Washington Post,* 15 September 1990, pp. A1, A10.

23. L. Thompson, "NIH Testing Gene Therapy on 2 Skin Cancer Patients," *Washington Post,* 30 January 1991, p. A2; N. Angier, "For First Time, Gene Therapy Is Tested on Cancer Patients," *New York Times,* 30 January 1991, pp. A1, A18.

24. C. Marwick, "Two More Cell Infusions on Schedule for Gene Replacement Patient," *Journal of the American Medical Association* 265 (8 May 1991): 2311–12.

25. US National Institutes of Health, "Points to Consider," *Federal Register* 50, no. 160, 19 August 1990, 33463–67; see also *Federal Register* 50, no. 60, 19 August 1985, 33463–67; and *Federal Register* 50, no. 14, 22 January 1985, 2940–45.

26. T. Friedman, "Progress Toward Human Gene Therapy," *Science* 244 (16 June 1989): 1275–81.

27. R. E. Hammer, R. D. Palmiter, and R. L. Brinster, "Partial Correction of Murine Hereditary Growth Disorder by Germ-Line Incorporation of a New Gene," *Nature* 311 (6 September 1984): 65–67.

28. F. Costantini, K. Chada, and J. Magram, "Correction of Murine Beta-Thalassemia by Gene Transfer into the Germ Line," *Science* 233 (12 September 1986): 1192–94.

29. A. J. Mason, S. L. Pitts, K. Nikolics, *et al.,* "The Hypogonadal Mouse: Reproductive Functions Restored by Gene Therapy," *Science* 234 (12 December 1986): 1372–78.

30. C. Readhead, B. Popko, N. Takahashi, *et al.,* "Expression of a Myelin Basic Protein Gene in Transgenic Shiverer Mice: Correction of the Dysmyelinating Phenotype," *Cell* 48 (27 February 1987): 703–12.

31. M. Monk, "Embryo Research and Genetic Disease," *New Scientist* 125 (6 January 1990): 56–59; Y. Verlinsky, E. Pergament, and C. Strom, "The Preimplantation Diagnosis of Genetic Diseases," *Journal of In Vitro Fertilization and Embryo Transfer* 7 (February 1990): 1–5.

32. R. M. Cook-Deegan, "Human Gene Therapy and Congress," *Human Gene Therapy* 1 (Summer 1990): 163–70.

33. President's Commission for the Study of Ethical Problems in Medicine and Biomedical and Behavioral Research, *Screening and Counseling for Genetic Conditions: The Ethical, Social and Legal Implications of Genetic Screening, Counseling, and Education Programs* (Washington, DC: Government Printing Office, 1983), 47–59.

34. R. R. Faden, A. J. Chwalow, N. A. Holtzman, and S. D. Horn, "A Survey to Evaluate Parental Consent as Public Policy for Neonatal Screening," *American Journal of Public Health* 72 (December 1982): 1347–52.

35. R. Proctor, *Racial Hygiene: Medicine Under the Nazis* (Cambridge: Harvard University Press, 1988); P. R. Reilly, *The Surgical Solution: A History of Involuntary Sterilization in the United States* (Baltimore: Johns Hopkins University Press, 1991).

36. President's Commission for the Study of Ethical Problems in Medicine and Biomedical and Behavioral Research, *Securing Access to Health Care: A Report on the Ethical Implications of Differences in the Availability of Health Services,* 3 vols. (Washington, DC: Government Printing Office, 1983).

W. FRENCH ANDERSON

Human Gene Therapy

Human gene therapy has progressed from speculation to reality in a short time. The first clinical gene transfer (albeit only a marker gene) in an approved protocol took place on 22 May 1989, almost exactly 3 years ago; the first federally approved gene therapy protocol, for correction of adenosine deaminase (ADA) deficiency, began on 14 September 1990. Now there are 11 active clinical protocols (Table 1) on three continents with nine more approved protocols about to begin and over a dozen additional protocols in various stages of development.

What are the objectives of these protocols? What are the scientific and clinical questions that they are asking? How safe are they? These are the questions that this review addresses. The extensive preclinical studies that support each clinical protocol are not covered.

W. French Anderson, "Human Gene Therapy," *Science* 256 (May 8, 1992), 808–813. Copyright © 1992 by American Association for the Advancement of Science.

Table 1. Gene marker and therapy clinical protocals.

Protocol	Institute	Diseases	Date initiated
Initiated: USA/RAC–approval			
Gene Marking			
NeoR/TIL	NIH, Bethesda, MD	Malignant melanoma	5/22/89
NeoR/bone marrow	St. Jude Children's Research Hospital, Memphis, TN	Pediatric AML	9/9/91
NoeR/bone marrow	St. Jude Children's Research Hospital, Memphis, TN	Neuroblastoma	1/16/92
NeoR/TIL	University of Pittsburgh, Pittsburg, PA	Malignant melanoma	3/3/92
Gene Therapy			
ADA/peripheral blood T cells	NIH, Bethesda, MD	ADA-deficient SCID	9/14/90
TNF/TIL	NIH, Bethesda, MD	Malignant melanoma	1/29/91
TNF/tumor cells	NIH, Bethesda, MD	Advanced cancer	10/8/92
IL-2/tumor cells	NIH, Bethesda, MD	Advanced cancer	3/12/92
Initiated: International			
Gene Marking			
NeoR/TIL	Centre Leon Berard, Lyon, France	Malignant melanoma	12/12/91
Gene Marking			
Factor IX/autologous skin fibroblasts	Fudan University and Changhai Hospital, Shanghai, China	Hemophilia B	12/3/91
ADA/peripheral blood T cells + progenitor-enriched bone marrow cells	Scientific Institute, San Raffaele, Milan, Italy	ADA-deficient SCID	3/9/92

(continued)

An unsuccessful attempt was made in 1980 to carry out gene therapy for ß-thalassemia [an inherited disorder of hemoglobin synthesis] with the use of calcium phosphate–mediated DNA transfer. Retroviral-mediated gene transfer [gene transfer that uses genetically altered retroviruses as vectors or vehicles] was developed in the early 1980s in animal models *(1)*. This technology is the principal procedure used today. Many recent reviews on retroviral vector development, packaging cell lines, and alternate gene delivery techniques *(2)* as well as on gene transfer and expression in cell cultures and in animal models *(3)* address the technical issues upon which human gene therapy relies.

NEOR/TIL GENE MARKING

The first federally approved human genetic engineering experiment, initiated in 1989, was for the transfer of gene-marked immune cells (specifically, tumor-infiltrating lymphocytes, or TIL) into patients with advanced cancer. The protocol had two primary objectives: (i) to demonstrate that an exogenous [originating outside the patient] gene could be safely transferred into a patient and (ii) to demonstrate that the gene could be detected in cells taken back out of the patient *(4)*.

The protocol asked a number of scientific and clinical questions, generated by several earlier experiments. In 1986, a clinical protocol for the treatment of advanced malignant melanoma [a type of cancer that usually originates in skin tissue] with the newly discovered class of immune cells called TIL was initiated at the National Institutes of Health (NIH) *(5)*. These lymphocytes [one kind of white blood cell] are T cells that are isolated directly from the tumor and that are then grown to large numbers in tissue culture in the

Table 1. *(continued)*

Protocol	Institute	Diseases	Date initiated
Approved (uninitiated) protocols			
Gene Marking			
NeoR/bone marrow	University of Texas, M. D. Anderson Cancer Center, Houston, TX	CML	
NeoR/hepatocytes	Baylor College of Medicine, Houston, TX	Liver failure	
NoeR/bone marrow	Indiana University, Indianapolis, IN	Adult AML and ALL	
NoeR/TIL	University of California at Los Angeles, Los Angeles, CA	Malignant melanoma and renal cell cancer	
Gene Therapy			
LDL receptor/ hepatocytes	University of Michigan, Ann Arbor, MI	Familial hypercholesterolemia	
Herpes simplex thymidine kinase/ ovarian cancer cells	University of Rochester, Rochester, NY	Ovarian cancer	
HLA-B7/melanoma in vivo	University of Michigan, Ann Arbor, MI	Malignant melanoma	
Herpes simplex thymidine kinase/ cytotoxic T lymphocytes	Fred Hutchinson Cancer Research Center and the University of Washington, Seattle, WA	AIDS	
ADA/bone marrow	Institute for Applied Radiobiology and Immunology (TNO) with University of Leiden, Leiden, the Netherlands	ADA-deficient SCID	

presence of the T cell growth factor interleukin-2 (IL-2). After expansion in culture several thousand times, approximately 2×10^{11} TIL are given to the patient intravenously in addition to high doses of IL-2 in several days of treatment. Even in those patients who did not respond to all other therapy (including treatment with IL-2 alone), 35 to 40% of patients responded to this protocol *(5)*.

The large-scale tissue culture and the large numbers of cells and Il-2 that are given to a patient make this procedure expensive and clinically difficult. Furthermore, 60 to 65% of patients fail to respond to this treatment, and even those who do respond will often fail after 6 to 12 months. It is likely that only a subset of the [heterogeneous] population of cells administered to a patient are effective in killing cancer cells in vivo; one goal of investigators is to determine which cells these are. It would be useful to be able to follow and study the administered cells in the patient's body to learn where they go and how long they survive. One approach would be to mark the TIL so that they could be tracked in the body. In[111] has been used to follow TIL in patients, but In[111] has a half-life of just 2.8 days, so that only short-term data could be obtained *(6)*.

The NeoR/TIL clinical protocol proposed to take an aliquot [a sample] of cells from TIL early in their culture, transfer into them a marker gene (the neomycin resistance gene NeoR obtained from *Escherichia coli*) with a retroviral vector *(7),* grow the marked cells in parallel with the unmarked cells, and then give both populations back to the patient. Periodic blood samplings would indicate how long the TIL survived in the bloodstream, periodic tumor biopsies would indicate if and roughly how many marked TIL were present in the tumors, and, if enough patients could be studied, perhaps a correlation could be drawn between the presence of marked TIL and the clinical response. . . .

The results from the first five patients have been published (8). Blood samples were taken before and during infusion, as well as 3 min, 1 hour, 24 hours, and on various days after infusion. Polymerase chain reaction (PCR) with NeoR probes (9) consistently detected marked TIL in the bloodstream from all patients for 21 days, from patient 3 on day 51, and from patient 5 on day 60. Patient 3 had a second TIL infusion on day 94, whereupon marked TIL were detected in the patient's blood samples up to day 189. The frequency of marked TIL was estimated to be 1 in 300 on day 3 in patient 5 (estimated with semiquantitative PCR), with values dropping to less than 1 in 10,000 cells in later samples. Marked TIL were detected in tumor biopsies taken from three of the five patients, including one taken on day 64 from patient 3. Thus, gene-marked TIL could consistently be detected (that is, more than one cell in 10^5 nucleated cells) in the bloodstream for 3 weeks, which is approximately the time span over which the patients received IL-2. Small numbers of gene-marked TIL were found in tumor samples as long as 9 weeks after infusion.

• • •

ADA GENE THERAPY

There were two objectives of the ADA [adenosine deaminase, an important enzyme] gene therapy protocol (10). The clinical objective was to evaluate the possible therapeutic efficacy of the administration of autologous [from the patient] lymphocytes transduced with a normal human ADA gene in an effort to reconstitute the function of the cellular and humoral immune system in patients with ADA-deficient severe combined immuno-deficiency (SCID). The scientific objective was to evaluate in vivo survival of culture-expanded autologous T cells [a type of white blood that is important for the functioning of the immune system] and the duration of expression of the inserted genes.

The rationale behind this protocol has a lengthy history. For many years, investigators had concentrated on ß-thalassemia as the most likely initial candidate for gene therapy. However, it became clear by 1984 that diseases of hemoglobin synthesis were going to be particularly difficult to correct by gene therapy because of the complex regulation involved (he-moglobin is composed of two chains that are made on two different chromosomes but in exactly the same amounts—a sophistication of regulation that is still not fully understood). For gene therapy, it seemed wiser to initially focus on a genetic disease in which corrected cells might have a selective growth advantage in the patient (11). In other words, find a disease where the mutation was involved in DNA metabolism so that cell division was inhibited by the defect. Correction of the defect should produce normal cell division of the corrected cells against a background of very slow division by the uncorrected cells.

Three diseases fit this description on theoretical grounds: ADA deficiency, PNP (purine nucleoside phosphorylase) deficiency, and HGPRT (hypoxanthine-guanine phosphoribosyltransferase) deficiency (known as Lesch-Nyhan syndrome). The three enzymes that are defective in these diseases catalyze sequential steps in purine metabolism. Of these three diseases, ADA deficiency had been cured by matched bone marrow transplantation, the first performed 20 years ago. One year after the transplant, patients who were successfully treated often had all of their own blood cells except for their T cells, which were exclusively from the donor. Thus, ADA-normal T cells alone are curative and are able to overgrow the patient's own ADA-deficient T cells. For these reasons, ADA deficiency was chosen as the first disease for gene therapy (11), although originally the proposal was to use transduction [genetic modification] of bone marrow cells rather than autologous T cells.

The plan for the ADA therapy protocol was to subject the patients to leukophoresis [a procedure for isolating white blood cells] once a month, to isolate the mononuclear cells by Ficoll gradient, and to grow these cells in culture under conditions that stimulated T lymphocyte activation and growth (OKT3 antibody stimulation with growth in IL-2). Once the T cells were dividing, they would be incubated with the retroviral vector LASN (which carries a normal ADA gene as well as the NeoR gene) and then grown for only a few days before infusion into the patient. . . .

The protocol was initiated in September 1990. A 4-year-old girl suffering from ADA deficiency received an intravenous infusion of her own gene-corrected T lymphocytes. She had been on enzyme replacement therapy, polyethylene glycol (PEG)-conjugated ADA, for 2 years, but after an initial improvement that lasted much of the first year, her T cell numbers decreased, she had frequent infections, and was anergic at the time the gene therapy treatment began. Over the next 10.5 months she received seven more infusions at 1- to 2-month intervals (together with the weekly PEG-ADA injections). Because of the improvement in her immune function studies and in her clinical condition as well as the presence of a significant number of gene-corrected T cells in her circulation (approximately 20 to 25%, on the basis of the amount of ADA in the mononuclear cell population and PCR analysis), she was followed without further gene therapy treatments for 6.5 months and then was begun on a program of maintenance infusions at 3- to 5-month intervals (12). A second patient, a 9-year-old girl, began treatment in January 1991 and has thus far received 11 infusions of gene-corrected autologous T cells (12). Both patients are maintained on weekly PEG-ADA injections.

The data from the protocol indicate that this therapy was clinically useful. Both patients have shown improvement in their clinical condition after gene therapy was begun as well as in a battery of in vitro and in vivo immune function studies (12). Both attend regular public schools and now have no more than the average number of infections. There have been no significant side effects from the cell infusions and no detected side effects from the presence of the transferred ADA gene itself. Data from patient 1 suggest that the ADA-deficient T cell population has a survival half-life in vivo of 30 to 35 days on the basis of the decline in circulating T cells when an infusion was missed early in the treatment procedure. PCR analysis and ADA enzyme activity in the mononuclear cell fraction suggest that the survival half-life of the ADA-corrected T cell population is much longer, perhaps three to five times longer (12). The T cell fraction, isolated from freshly drawn blood and tested for ADA expression, demonstrated a steady increase in the ADA level over the initial 10.5-month treatment period, starting under 1% of normal and reaching nearly 25% of normal after the eighth infusion (12, 13). This amount was maintained throughout the 6.5-month period without treatment. The assumption from these data is that the inserted ADA gene continues to be expressed in vivo for long periods of time, perhaps the lifetime of the T cell.

Even though both patients appear to be doing well, there is still a potential clinical concern. Because only mature T cells are being transduced, it is probable that holes are being left in their immune repertoires. In both children some of their immune function studies have not returned to normal, and positive skin tests are not observed for all antigens (12). To address this problem, the investigators propose an addition to the current protocol—to administer gene-corrected peripheral blood stem cells (that is, the CD34-enriched population) together with the gene-corrected mature T cells. A cell fraction highly enriched in hematopoietic progenitors and stem cells would be prepared by immunoselection with a CD34-specific antibody (14) and transduced with an ADA vector under culture conditions designed to facilitate retroviral-mediated gene transfer with preservation of repopulating stem cell activity (15). The two cell populations would be transduced with different ADA vectors (LASN, the vector presently being used, and G1NaSvAd, a new vector that can be differentiated from LASN by PCR probes). Thus, it should be possible to determine the contribution of CD34-enriched cells in comparison to that of mature T cells. Recent evidence in primates suggests that, under certain experimental conditions, it may be possible to transduce totipotent stem cells taken from the bone marrow by retroviral-mediated gene transfer (16). . . .

Investigators in Milan, Italy, have just begun a gene therapy protocol for ADA deficiency similar to the proposed addition described above. The rationale and questions asked are essentially identical. In the Milan protocol, ADA gene-corrected peripheral blood T cells (stimulated in culture with PHA, OKT3 antibody, and IL-2) were given to a 5-year-old boy in March 1992. In April, a mixture of ADA gene-corrected T cells and gene-corrected progenitor-enriched bone marrow cells (containing a vector that can be differentiated from the T cell vector) were given to the same patient (17). In addition, on the basis of their encouraging results in rhesus monkeys (16), investigators in the Netherlands have received approval for a bone marrow gene therapy protocol for ADA deficiency.

CANCER GENE THERAPY

The first cancer gene therapy protocol was a direct outgrowth from the NeoR/TIL gene marker protocol. After it was shown that gene-modified TIL could be safely given to patients, a new protocol was initiated in which the gene for tumor necrosis factor (TNF) was added to the vector (18). The objective was to make the TIL more effective against advanced malignant melanoma.

TNF itself is a powerful anticancer agent in mice. In humans, however, its toxic effects become profound at 8 μg per kilogram of body weight, whereas the effective dose in mice is 400 μg/kg (mice can tolerate the high dose) *(19)*. By putting a TNF gene into TIL, and then letting the TIL "home" to tumor deposits, it may be possible to develop effectively high doses of TNF in tumor sites and avoid systemic side effects. However, because the bulk of TIL cells are trapped (and probably destroyed) in liver, spleen, and lungs, and the production of TNF from the exogenous gene is from a heterologous promoter, production of large amounts of ectopic [literally, out of place] TNF with toxic effects is possible. Thus, a Phase I safety trial was needed to determine if toxic concentrations of TNF might develop in the liver or other organs.

The first patient began treatment in January 1991 and a number of patients are currently under treatment. There have been no side effects yet from the gene transfer and no apparent organ toxicity from secreted TNF, but it is still too early in the protocol to determine if the procedure is effective as a cancer therapy.

There are at least two ways to improve TIL immunotherapy by gene transfer: either add a gene to the TIL or tumor-specific T cells to make them more effective (as discussed above) or add a gene to the tumor cells in order to induce the body's immune system to make more effective TIL. Two protocols have begun in which either the TNF gene or the IL-2 gene is inserted into tumor cells that were isolated from a patient and grown in culture *(20)*. These approaches are based on animal studies that have shown that immunization with tumor cells transduced with certain cytokine [a soluble molecule that mediates interactions between cells] genes produces systemic antitumor immunity mediated by T cells. In these protocols, the cytokine-secreting autologous tumor cells are then injected subcutaneously and intradermally into the patient's upper thigh. Twenty-one days later the injection site and draining lymph nodes are removed, placed in culture, and grown under conditions to encourage T cell growth. The expanded lymph node T cells are given the patient with IL-2. Data from these "tumor vaccine" studies should be available later in the year.

Two other cancer gene therapy protocols have been approved by RAC and are awaiting FDA approval. These are the studies from the University of Michigan and from the University of Rochester (Table 1).

GENE THERAPY

Two additional gene therapy protocols have been approved but have not yet begun. The first, from the University of Michigan, proposes to insert a low density lipoprotein (LDL) [the "bad" type of cholesterol] receptor gene into hepatocytes [liver cells] obtained from patients suffering from familial hypercholesterolemia [very high cholesterol levels] (a result of a defective LDL receptor gene) *(21)*. The gene-corrected hepatocytes would be injected back into the portal circulation of the patient. The second, from the University of Washington, is really a cell therapy for a complication of acquired immunodeficiency syndrome (AIDS) in which a suicide gene is inserted into the therapeutic cytotoxic T cells to afford protection in case the T cells become too toxic *(22)*. Finally, a gene therapy protocol has been initiated in China for hemophilia B. A retroviral vector containing a factor IX [a blood factor used in treating hemophilia] gene has been used to transduce autologous skin fibroblasts [elongated cells] growing in culture. The factor IX-secreting autologous fibroblasts were then injected subcutaneously into the patients. The protocol was begun in December 1991 on two patients; results are not yet available.

GENE MARKING

Two types of gene marker protocols, in addition to those involving TIL, have been approved. The first category of protocol is for using gene marking to study bone marrow reconstitution and the mechanism of relapse in autologous bone marrow transplantation in patients with leukemia or neuroblastoma. Under way since September 1991 at St. Jude Children's Research Hospital, a study of children with acute myelogenous leukemia (AML) in first remission *(23)* is attempting to understand what happens when an AML patient who has received back his or her own purged bone marrow has a relapse. Does the relapse arise from residual cells in the transplanted marrow that were not killed by the purging techniques or does it arise from residual systemic disease in the patient that was not eradicated by the ablative therapy?

This question is of considerable clinical importance because, if the leukemia cells do come from the marrow implant, then harsher purging techniques would be necessary. Such techniques damage the healthy marrow cells, however, thereby preventing or delaying reconstitution in some cases. If relapse arises from cells in the patient's body, then more strenuous ablation [killing of cells in the patient's body] would be appropriate (with its toxic side effects), but the marrow transplant could be treated more gently. Because only the purged marrow would be gene-marked, a relapse composed of gene-marked cells would indicate that the marrow transplant was responsible for, or at least contributed to, the relapse. If marked tumor cells [are] found during relapse, the technique may also allow analysis of the efficiency of different purging techniques. The difficulty is that only some of the cells in the marrow will be gene-marked; therefore, the failure to detect gene-marked cells in a relapse would provide no useful information. Data from the first relapsed patient are now available, and gene-marked cells have been identified (24).

Also under way at St. Jude Children's Research Hospital is a similar marking study for pediatric patients with neuroblastoma (25). Marker protocols have been approved for the study of adult chronic myelogenous leukemia (CML) at the M. D. Anderson Cancer Center (26) and of adult AML and acute lymphocytic leukemia (ALL) at Indiana University (27).

The second category of gene marker protocol is where marking is to be used to study hepatocellular [with liver cells] transplantation in children with acute liver failure with no other medical or surgical options. The protocol, from Baylor College of Medicine, proposes to isolate heterologous [from a donor] hepatocytes from a donor liver, insert a marker NeoR gene by means of a retroviral vector, and inject the donor hepatocytes (some of them marked) into the diseased liver in order to provide essential hepatic functions (28). This protocol is scheduled to begin shortly.

SAFETY CONSIDERATIONS

How safe are these protocols? The safety considerations in retroviral-mediated gene transfer and therapy clinical protocols have been extensively reviewed (29). There is now experience from the equivalent of 106 monkey-years and 23 patient-years in individuals who have undergone retroviral-mediated gene transfer. Side effects from the gene transfer have not been observed, pathology as a result of gene transfer has not been found, and there has never been a malignancy observed as a result of a replication-defective retroviral vector.

Recently, however, investigators at NIH described three monkeys who developed malignant T cell lym-

phomas after a bone marrow transplantation and gene transfer protocol with a helper virus-contaminated retroviral vector preparation (30). The helper virus was probably directly responsible for these lymphomas. This finding strongly reaffirms the necessity for clinical protocols to use helper virus-free vector preparations, as is required for all protocols approved by RAC [the Recombinant DNA Advisory Committee of NIH] and by FDA [the Food and Drug Administration].

ETHICAL AND SOCIAL IMPLICATIONS

The ethical and social implications of somatic cell gene therapy have been discussed (31), and there is now a general consensus that somatic cell gene therapy for the purpose of treating a serious disease is an ethical therapeutic option. However, considerable controversy exists as to whether or not germline gene therapy would be ethical (32). The issues are both medical and philosophical.

The medical concern is that genetic manipulation of the germline could produce damage in future generations. Medicine is an inexact science; we still understand very little about how the human body works. Well-intentioned efforts at treatment with standard therapeutics can produce unexpected problems months or years later. Altering the genetic information in a patient's cells may result in long-term side effects that are unpredictable at present. Until the time comes that it is possible to correct the defective gene itself by homologous recombination (rather than just inserting a normal copy of the gene elsewhere in the genome), the danger exists of producing a germline mutagenic event when the "normal" gene is inserted. Therefore, considerable experience with germline manipulation in animals, as well as with somatic cell gene therapy in humans, should be obtained before considering human germline therapy.

Besides the medical arguments, there are a number of philosophical, ethical, and theological concerns. For instance, do infants have the right to inherit an unmanipulated genome, does the concept of informed consent have any validity for patients who do not yet exist, and at what point do we cross the line into "playing God"? The feeling of many observers is that germline gene therapy should not be considered until much more is learned from somatic cell gene therapy, until animal studies demonstrate the safety and reliability of any proposed procedure, and until the public has been educated as to the implications of the procedure. The NIH RAC plans to initiate the public debate.

There is also considerable concern about using gene transfer to insert genes into humans for the purposes of enhancement—that is, to try to "improve" desired characteristics *(33)*. The same medical issues arise: we have too little understanding of what normal function is to attempt to improve on what we think is "normal." Correction of a genetic defect that causes serious illness is one thing, but to try to alter a characteristic such as size (by administration of a growth hormone gene to a normal child, for example) is quite another. This area is further clouded by major social implications *(33)* as well as by the problem of how to define when a given gene is being used for treatment (or for preventing disease) and when it is being used for "enhancement."

THE FUTURE

How much impact will gene therapy have on medical practice in the future? Not a great deal so long as the technique is carried out as it is today, where cells are removed from a patient, the desired gene is inserted, and the gene-corrected cells are returned to the patient. This procedure is too dependent on specialized technologies, is too expensive, and requires too much scientific and medical expertise to be used extensively except in major medical centers. The many clever applications of gene transfer that investigators are devising ensure that gene therapy will be applied to a broad range of diseases over the next several years, but only thousands, not millions, of patients are treatable by current techniques.

Gene therapy will have a major impact on the health care of our population only when vectors are developed that can safely and efficiently be injected directly into patients as drugs like insulin are now. Vectors need to be engineered that will target specific cell types, insert their genetic information into a safe site in the genome, and be regulated by normal physiological signals. When efficient vectors of this type are produced—retroviral, viral, synthetic, or a combination of all three—then gene therapy will probably have a profound impact on the practice of medicine. As information from the Human Genome Project becomes available concerning the entire library of genetic information in our cells, then gene therapy will probably be used not only to cure an array of diseases, but also to prevent many disorders by providing protective genes before the diseases become manifest. Although the medical potential is bright, the possibility for misuse of genetic engineering technology looms large, so society must ensure that gene therapy is used only for the treatment of disease.

REFERENCES AND NOTES

1. A. D. Miller, D. J. Jolly, T. Friedman, I. M. Verma, *Proc. Natl. Acad. Sci. U.S.A.* **80**, 4709 (1983); R. Mann, R. C. Mulligan, D. Baltimore, *Cell* **33**, 153 (1983); A. Joyner, G. Keller, R. A. Philips, A. Bernstein, *Nature* **305**, 556 (1983), A. L. Joyner and A. Bernstein, *Mol. Cell. Biol.* **3**, 2191 (1983); A. D. Miller, R. J. Eckner, D. J. Jolly, T. Friedmann, I. M. Verma, *Science* **225**, 630 (1984); A. D. Miller, E. S. Ong, M. G. Rosenfeld, I. M. Verma, R. M. Evans, *ibid.*, p. 993; R. C. Willis *et al., J. Biol. Chem.* **259**, 7842 (1984); D. A. Williams, I. R. Lemischka, D. G. Nathan, R. C. Mulligan, *Nature* **310**, 476 (1984); G. Keller, C. Paige, E. Gilboa, E. F. Wagner, *ibid.* **318**, 149 (1985); M. A. Eglitis, P. Kantoff, E. Gilboa, W. F. Anderson, *Science* 230, 1395 (1985).

2. T. Friedman, *Science* **244**, 1275 (1989); A. D. Miller, *Hum. Gene Ther.* **1**, 5 (1990); J. R. McLachlin, K. Cornetta, M. A. Eglitis, W. F. Anderson, *Prog. Nucleic Acid Res. Mol. Biol.* **38**, 91 (1990); G. Y. Wu and C. H. Wu, *Biotherapy* **3**, 87 (1991); E. M. Karson, *Biotechniques* **16**, 189 (1991); R. C. Mulligan, in *Etiology of Human Disease at the DNA Level*, J. Lindsten and U. Pettersson, Eds. (Raven, New York, 1992), pp. 143–189.

3. D. J. Weatherall, *Br. Med. J.* **298**, 691 (1989); R. J. Akhurst, *J. Inherited Metab. Dis.* **12**, 191 (1989); D. B. Kohn, W. F. Anderson, R. M. Blaese, *Cancer Invest.* **7**, 179 (1989); T. Friedmann, L. Xu, J. Wolff, J. K. Yee, A. Miyanohara, *Mol. Biol. Med.* **6**, 117 (1989); S. S. Boggs, *Int. J. Cell Cloning* **8**, 80 (1990); D. Cournoyer et al., *Clin. Pharmacol. Ther.* **47**, 1 (1990); P. M. Lehn, *Bone Marrow Transplant.* **5**, 287 (1990); J. F. Apperley and D. A. Williams, *Br. J. Haematol.* **75**, 148 (1990); A. D. Miller, *Blood* **76**, 271 (1990); E. Beutler and J. Sorge, *Exp. Hematol.* (New York) **18**, 857 (1990); D. A. Williams, *Hum. Gene Ther.* **1**, 229 (1990); C. Hesdorffer, D. Markowitz, M. Ward, A. Bank, *Hematol. Oncol. Clin. North Am.* **5**, 423 (1991); R. C. Moen, *Blood Cells* **17**, 407 (1991); E. G. Nabel, G. Plautz, G. J. Nabel, *J. Am. Coll. Cardiol.* **17**, 189B (1991); R. Parkman and E. W. Gelfand, *Curr. Opin. Immunol.* **3**, 547 (1991); R. M. Blaese, *Clin. Immunol. Immunopathol.* **61**, S47 (1991); R. A. Fleischman, *Am. J. Med. Sci.* 301, 353 (1991); F. D. Ledley, *Int. Ped.* **7**, 7 (1992).

4. "Treatment of Patients with Advanced Cancer Using Cyclophosphamide, Interleukin-2, and Gene-Marked Tumor Infiltrating Lymphocytes," *Hum. Gene Ther.* **1**, 73 (1990).

5. S. Rosenberg et al., *N. Engl. J. Med.* **319**, 1676 (1988).

6. B. Fisher *et al., J. Clin. Oncol.* **7**, 1676 (1989); K. D. Griffith *et al., J. Natl. Cancer Inst.* **81**, 1709 (1989).

7. The vector originally proposed and approved for use in this protocol was N2 [D. Armentano *et al., J. Virol.* **61**, 1647 (1987)]; however, the vector ultimately used was a safety-modified version of N2 called LNL6 (M. A. Bender, T. D. Palmer, R. E. Gelinas, A. D. Miller, *ibid.*, p. 1639) together with the packaging cell line PA317 [A. D. Miller and C. Buttimore, *Mol. Cell. Biol.* **6**, 2895 (1986)].

8. S. Rosenberg *et al., N. Engl. J. Med.* **323**, 570 (1990).

9. R. A. Morgan, K. Cornetta, W. F. Anderson, *Hum. Gene Ther.* **1**, 135 (1990).

10. "Treatment of Severe Combined Immunodeficiency Disease (SCID) Due to Adenosine Deaminase (ADA) Deficiency with

Autologous Lymphocytes Transduced with a Human ADA Gene," *Hum. Gene Ther.* **1,** 327 (1990).

11. W. F. Anderson, *Science* **226,** 401 (1984).

12. M. Blaese *et al.,* unpublished data.

13. K. W. Culver, W. F. Anderson, R. M. Blaese, *Hum. Gene Ther.* **2,** 107 (1991).

14. R. G. Andrews, J. W. Singer, I. D. Bernstein, *Blood* **67,** 842 (1986); R. J. Berenson *et al., ibid.* **77,** 1717 (1991).

15. S. Karlsson, *ibid.* **78,** 2481 (1991); A. W. Nienhuis, K. T. McDonagh, D. M. Bodine, *Cancer (Philadelphia)* **67,** 2700 (1991); A. W. Nienhuis, R. D. Donahue, C. Dunbar, unpublished data.

16. V. W. van Beusechem, A. Kukler, P. J. Heidt, D. Valerio, *Proc. Natl. Acad. Sci. U.S.A.,* in press.

17. C. Bordignon, unpublished data.

18. "Gene Therapy of Patients with Advanced Cancer Using Tumor Infiltrating Lymphocytes Transduced with the Gene Coding for Tumor Necrosis Factor," *Hum. Gene Ther.* **1,** 441 (1990).

19. A. L. Asher, J. J. Mule, C. M. Reichert, E. Shiloni, S. A. Rosenberg, *J. Immunol.* **138,** 963 (1987); S. A. Rosenberg *et al., Ann. Surg.* **210,** 474 (1989).

20. "Immunization of Cancer Patients Using Autologous Cancer Cells Modified by Insertion of the Gene for Tumor Necrosis Factor," *Hum. Gene Ther.* **3,** 57 (1992); "Immunization of Cancer Patients Using Autologous Cancer Cells Modified by Insertion of the Gene for Interleukin-2," *ibid.,* p. 75.

21. "Ex Vivo Gene Therapy of Familial Hypercholesterolemia," *ibid.* **3,** 179 (1992).

22. "Phase I Study of Cellular Adoptive Immunotherapy Using Genetically Modified CD8$^+$ HIV-Specific T cells for HIV Seropositive Patients Undergoing Allogeneic Bone Marrow Transplant," *ibid.,* **3,** 319 (1992).

23. "Autologous Bone Marrow Transplant for Children with AML in First Complete Remission: Use of Marker Genes to Investigate the Biology of Marrow Reconstitution and the Mechanism of Relapse," *ibid.* **2,** 137 (1991).

24. M. Brenner, unpublished data.

25. "A Phase I Trial of High-Dose Carboplatin and Etoposide with Autologous Marrow Support for Treatment of Stage D Neuroblastoma in First Remission: Use of Marker Genes to Investigate the Biology of Marrow Reconstitution and the Mechanism of Relapse," *Hum. Gene Ther.* **2,** 257 (1991).

26. "Autologous Bone Marrow Transplantation for CML in Which Retroviral Markers Are Used to Discriminate Between Relapse Which Arises from Systemic Disease Remaining after Preparative Therapy Versus Relapse due to Residual Leukemia Cells in Autologous Marrow: A Pilot Trial," *ibid.,* p. 359.

27. "Retroviral-Mediated Gene Transfer of Bone Marrow Cells during Autologous Bone Marrow Transplantation for Acute Leukemia," *ibid.* **3,** 305 (1990).

28. "Hepatocellular Transplantation in Acute Hepatic Failure and Targeting Genetic Markers to Hepatic Cells," *ibid.* **2,** 331 (1991).

29. H. M. Temin, *J. Med. Virol.* **13,** 13 (1990); *Hum. Gene Ther.* **1,** 111 (1990); K. Cornetta, R. A. Morgan, W. F. Anderson, *ibid.* **2,** 5 (1991).

30. R. Kolberg, *J. NIH Res.* **4,** 43 (1992); A. Nienhuis, unpublished data.

31. J. C. Fletcher, *J. Med. Philos.* **10,** 293 (1985); L. Walters, *Nature* **320,** 225 (1986); *Hum. Gene Ther.* **2,** 115 (1991).

32. L. Kass, in *The New Genetics and the Future of Man,* M. Hamilton, Ed. (Eerdmans, Grand Rapids, MI, 1972), p. 61; P. Ramsey, *ibid,* p. 175; J. Fletcher, *The Ethics of Genetic Control* (Doubleday, Garden City, NY, 1974), pp. 14–15; President's Commission for the Study of Ethical Problems in Medicine and Biomedical and Behavioral Research, *Splicing Life* (Government Printing Office, Washington, DC, 1982); J. C. Fletcher, *Virginia Law Review* **69,** 515 (1983); W. F. Anderson, *J. Med. Philos.* **10,** 275 (1985); A. M. Capron, in *Genetics and the Law III,* A. Milunsky and G. J. Annas, Eds. (Plenum, New York, 1985), p. 24; G. Fowler, E. T. Juengst, B. K. Zimmerman, *Theor. Med.* **10,** 151 (1989); C. A. Tauer, *Hum. Gene Ther.* **1,** 411 (1990); E. T. Juengst, *J. Med. Philos.* 16, 587 (1991); B. K. Zimmerman, *ibid.,* p. 593; K. Nolan, *ibid.,* p. 613; M. Lappé, *ibid.,* p. 621; R. Mosely, *ibid.,* p. 641; A. Mauron and J. Thevoz, *ibid.,* p. 648; E. M. Berger and B. M. Gert, *ibid.,* p. 667; J. C. Fletcher and W. F. Anderson, in *Law, Medicine, and Health Care,* M. Kaitz, Ed. (American Society of Law and Medicine, Boston), in press.

33. W. F. Anderson, *J. Med. Philos.* **14,** 681 (1989); W. F. Anderson, *Hastings Cent. Rep.* **1990,** 21 (January–February 1990); B. Hoose, *Hum. Gene Ther.* **1,** 299 (1990); J. Porter, *ibid.,* p. 419.

COUNCIL FOR RESPONSIBLE GENETICS, HUMAN GENETICS COMMITTEE (FALL, 1992)

Position Paper on Human Germ Line Manipulation

THE POSITION OF THE COUNCIL FOR RESPONSIBLE GENETICS

The Council for Responsible Genetics (CRG) strongly opposes the use of germ line gene modification in humans. This position is based on scientific, ethical, and social concerns.

Proponents of germ line manipulation assume that once a gene implicated in a particular condition is identified, it might be appropriate and relatively easy to change, supplement or otherwise modify the gene by some form of therapy. However, biological characteristics or traits usually depend on interactions among many genes, and these genes are themselves affected by processes that occur both inside the organism and in its surroundings. This means that scientists cannot predict the full effect that any gene modification will have on the traits of people or other organisms. In purely biological terms, the relationship between genes and traits is not well enough understood to guarantee that by eliminating or changing genes associated with traits one might want to avoid, we may not simultaneously alter or eliminate traits we would like to preserve. Even genes that are associated with diseases that may cause problems in one context can be beneficial in another context.

Two frequently destructive aspects of contemporary culture are linked together in an unprecedented fashion in germ line gene modification. The first is the notion that the value of a human being is dependent on the degree to which he or she approximates some ideal of biological perfection. The second is the ideology that all limitations imposed by nature can and should be overcome by technology. To make intentional changes in the genes that people will pass on to their descendants would require that we, as a society, agree on how to identify 'good' and 'bad' genes. We do not have such criteria, nor are there mechanisms for establishing them. Any formulation of such criteria would necessarily reflect current social biases.

Moreover, the definition of the standards and the technological means for implementing them would largely be determined by the economically and socially privileged. By implementing a program of germ line manipulation these groups would exercise unwarranted influence over the common biological heritage of humanity.

WHAT IS "GERM LINE MANIPULATION"?

The undifferentiated cells of an early embryo develop into either germ cells or somatic cells. *Germ* cells, or reproductive cells, are those that develop into the egg or sperm of a developing organism and transmit all its heritable characteristics. *Somatic* cells, or body cells, refer to all other cells of the body. While both types of cells contain chromosomes, only the chromosomes of germ cells are passed on to future generations.

Techniques are now available to change chromosomes of animal cells by inserting new segments of DNA into them. If this insertion is performed on specialized or *differentiated* body tissues, such as liver, muscle, or blood cells, it is referred to as *somatic cell* gene modification, and the changes do not go beyond the individual organism. If it is performed on sperm or eggs before fertilization, or on the undifferentiated cells of an early embryo, it is called *germ cell* or *germ*

From *Human Gene Therapy* 4 (1993), 35–38. © 1992, Mary Ann Liebert, Inc. Reprinted by permission of the publisher.

line gene modification, and the changes are not limited to the individual organism. For when DNA is incorporated into an embryo's germ cells, or undifferentiated cells that give rise to germ cells, the introduced gene or genes will be passed on to future generations and may become a permanent part of the gene pool.

Deliberate gene alterations in humans are often referred to as 'gene therapy.' The Council for Responsible Genetics (CRG) prefers to use the terms 'gene modification' and 'gene manipulation' because the word 'therapy' promises health benefits, and it is not yet clear that gene manipulations are beneficial.

WHY MIGHT GERMLINE MODIFICATION BE ATTEMPTED IN HUMANS?

If one or both partners carry a version of a gene that could predispose their offspring to inherit a condition they want to avoid, genetic manipulation may appear to be a potential way to prevent the undesired outcome. The earlier during embryonic development the targeted gene or genes are replaced, the less likely is the resulting individual to be affected by the unwanted gene. But while the immediate goal of such a modification might be to alter the genetic constitution of a single individual, modifications made at the early embryonic stages would incidentally result in germ line modification, and so all the offspring of this person would have and pass on the modification.

Alternatively, germ line modification may be the intended consequence of the procedure. One goal might be to 'cleanse' the gene pool of 'deleterious' genes. For example, Daniel E. Koshland, Jr., a molecular biologist, and the editor-in-chief of *Science,* has written, "keeping diabetics alive with insulin, which increases the propagation of an inherited disease, seems justified only if one ultimately is willing to do genetic engineering to remove diabetes from the germ line and thus save the anguish and cost to millions of diabetics." (1) Another goal of germ line manipulation may be to avoid multiple treatments of somatic gene modification that would be required under proposed treatment protocols for certain conditions such as cystic fibrosis.

Some people may also look forward to the possibility of introducing genes into the germ line that can 'enhance' certain characteristics desired by parents or other custodians of the resulting offspring. In the article referred to above, Koshland raises the possibility that germ line alterations could be perceived to meet future 'needs' to design individuals "better at computers, better as musicians, better physically."

The attempt to improve the human species biologically is known as *eugenics,* and was the basis of a popular movement in Europe and North America during the first half of this century. Eugenics was advocated by prominent scientists across the entire political spectrum, who represented it as the logical consequence of the most advanced biological thinking of the period. In the U.S., eugenic thinking resulted in social policies that called for forced sterilization of individuals regarded as inferior because they were 'feeble minded or paupers.' In Europe, the Nazis took up these ideas, and their attempts at implementation led to widespread revulsion against the concept of eugenics. Today public discussion in favor of influencing the genetic constitution of future generations has gained new respectability with the increased possibility for intervention presented by in-vitro fertilization and embryo implantation technologies. Although it is once again espoused by individuals with a variety of political perspectives, the doctrine of social advancement through biological perfectibility underlying the new eugenics is almost indistinguishable from the older version so avidly embraced by the Nazis.

It is important to recognize that the dream of eliminating 'harmful' genes (such as those associated with cystic fibrosis or Duchenne muscular dystrophy) from the entire human gene pool could be realized only over time scales of thousands of years, and then only with massive, coercive programs of germ line manipulation. Such a program would be neither feasible nor morally acceptable. As a practical matter then, any presumed beneficial effects of germ line modification would pertain to individual families, not to the human population as a whole. This is in contrast to harmful effects, which would be widely disseminated.

Furthermore, parents who carry a gene which they would not want a child of theirs to inherit could arrange to have unaffected, biologically-related offspring *without* germ line modification. If a gene is well enough characterized to consider gene manipulation, there will always be a diagnostic test available to identify a fetus that carries that gene and parents, if they choose, may then terminate the pregnancy. Given that there are alternatives for avoiding the inheritance of unwanted genes, the main selling point of germ line modification techniques over the long term would appear to be the prospect of enhancement of desired traits.

WHAT IS THE FEASIBILITY OF MODIFYING THE GERMLINE OF HUMANS?

Both somatic and germ line modification are widely performed on laboratory animals for research purposes. Somatic gene modifications have already been performed on humans and additional experimental protocols are being approved by the National Institutes of Health in increasing numbers.

No published reports have yet appeared on germ line modification in humans, but there appear to be no technical obstacles to such experiments, and articles proposing these procedures are becoming more and more common in the literature (2,3,4). Germ line gene modification has actually proved technically easier than somatic modification in mice and other vertebrate animals which have been employed as 'models' for human biology in the past, because the cells of early embryos incorporate foreign DNA and synthesize corresponding functional proteins more readily than most differentiated somatic cells. A widely-reported example of the successful experimental use of the germ line technique was the introduction of an extra gene that specified growth hormone into fertilized mouse eggs. In the presence of the high levels of growth hormone produced, the mice grew to double their normal size. Germ line techniques are also being used in attempts to modify farm animals, with stated goals of increasing yields or enhancing nutritional quality of meat and other animal products.

Given what has been accomplished in animals, the only remaining technical requirements for germ line gene modification in humans are procedures for collecting a woman's eggs, fertilizing them outside her body, and implanting them in the uterus of the same or another woman, where they can be brought to term. These are already well established procedures for humans and are widely used in in-vitro fertilization clinics.

WHAT ARE THE TECHNICAL PITFALLS?

Current methods for germ line gene modification of mammals are inefficient, requiring the microinjection of numerous eggs with foreign DNA before an egg is successfully modified. Moreover, introduction of a foreign gene (even if there is a copy of one already present) into an inappropriate location in an embryo's chromosomes can have unexpected consequences. For example, the offspring of a mouse that received an extra copy of the normally present *myc* gene developed cancer at 40 times the rate of the unmodified strain of mice. (5)

Techniques to introduce foreign DNA into eggs, however, are constantly being improved and eventually will be portrayed as efficient and reliable enough for human applications. It may soon be possible to place a gene into a specified location on a chromosome while simultaneously removing the unwanted gene. This will increase the accuracy of the procedures, but does not eliminate the possibility that gene combinations will be created that will be harmful to the modified embryo, and its descendants in future generations. Such inadvertent damage could be caused by technical error, or more importantly, by biologists' inability to predict how genes or their products interact with one another and with the organism's environment to give rise to biological traits. It would have been impossible to predict, *a priori,* for example, that someone who has even *one* copy of the gene for a blood protein known as hemoglobin-S would be protected against malaria, whereas a person who has *two* copies of this gene would have sickle cell disease.

This unpredictability applies with equal force to genetic modifications introduced to 'correct' presumed disorders and to those introduced to enhance characteristics. Inserting new segments of DNA into the germ line could have major, unpredictable consequences for both the individual and the future of the species that include the introduction of susceptibilities to cancer and other diseases into the human gene pool.

WHAT ARE THE SOCIAL AND ETHICAL IMPLICATIONS OF GERM LINE MODIFICATION?

Clinical trials in humans to treat Adenosine Deaminase Deficiency — a life threatening immune disorder — and terminal cancer with somatic gene modification are already in progress and experiments to treat diabetes and hypertension are under development. It is important to distinguish the ethical problems raised by these protocols from the additional, and more profound, questions raised by germ line modification. While the biological effects of somatic manipulations reside entirely in the individual in which they are attempted, such treatments are not strictly analogous to other therapies with individual risk. Radiation, chemical or drug treatment can be withdrawn if they prove harmful to the patient, while some forms of somatic modification cannot. Thus, somatic gene modification requires a person to forfeit his/her rights to withdraw from a research study because the intervention cannot be stopped, whether harmful or not. Valid objections have also been raised to the fact that the first somatic gene modification experiments, involving Adenosine Deaminase Deficiency, were carried out on young children who were not themselves in a position to give informed consent. While it appears that somatic gene modification techniques will be used increasingly in the future, the CRG urges that they be used with greatest caution, and only for clearly life-threatening conditions.

Germ line modification, in contrast, has not yet been attempted in humans. The Council for Responsible Genetics opposes it unconditionally. Ethical arguments against germ line modification include many of those that pertain to somatic cell modification, as well as the following:

- Germ line modification is not needed in order to save the lives or alleviate suffering of existing people. Its target population[s] are 'future people' who have not yet even been conceived.
- The cultural impact of treating humans as biologically perfectible artifacts would be entirely negative. People who fall short of some technically achievable ideal would increasingly be seen as 'damaged goods.' And it is clear that the standards for what is genetically desirable will be those of the society's economically and politically dominant groups. This will only reinforce prejudices and discrimination in a society where they already exist.
- Accountability to individuals of future generations who are harmed or stigmatized by wrongful or unsuccessful germ line modifications of their ancestors is unlikely.

In conclusion, the Council calls for a ban on germ line modification.

REFERENCES

1. Koshland Jr., Daniel E., "The Future of Biological Research: What Is Possible and What Is Ethical?", *MBL* [Marine Biological Laboratory] *Science*, v. 3, no. 2, pp. 11–15, 1988.

2. Walters, LeRoy, "Human Gene Therapy: Ethics and Public Policy," *Human Gene Therapy*, v. 2, pp. 115–122, 1991.

3. Working Group on Genetic Screening and Testing, *Report of Discussions in Genetics, Ethics and Human Values,* XXIVth CIOMS Conference, Tokyo and Inuyama, Japan, 24–26 July 1990.

4. Buster, John E. and Carson, Sandra A., "Genetic Diagnosis of the Preimplantation Embryo," *American Journal of Medical Genetics,* v. 34, pp. 211–216, 1989.

5. Leder, A. et al, "Consequences of Widespread Deregulation of the c-myc Gene in Trangenic Mice: Multiple Neoplasms and Normal Development," *Cell,* v. 45, p. 485, 1986.

NOTES

This document was written by the Human Genetics Committee of the Council for Responsible Genetics (CRG). The Council is a Cambridge-based national organization of scientists, public health advocates, trade unionists, women's health activists and others who want to see biotechnology developed safely and in the public interest. The Council believes that an informed public can and should play a leadership role in setting the direction for emerging technologies. A fundamental goal of the CRG is to prevent genetic discrimination.

The Human Genetics Committee has 14 members with backgrounds in the biological sciences, public health, law, disability rights, occupational health and safety, and women's health. Members include: Abby Lippman, Professor of Epidemiology, McGill University, Chairperson; Philip Bereano, Professor of Engineering and Public Policy, University of Washington; Paul Billings, Chief of Genetic Medicine, Pacific Presbyterian Medical Center; Colin Gracey, Head of the Religious Life Office, Northeastern University; Mary Sue Henifin, Deputy Attorney General, State of New Jersey; Ruth Hubbard, Professor Emerita of Biology at Harvard University; Sheldon Krimsky, Associate Professor of Urban and Environmental Policy, Tufts University; Richard Lewontin, Alexander Agassiz Professor of Zoology, Harvard University; Karen Messing, Professor of Biology, University of Quebec in Montreal; Stuart Newman, Professor of Cell Biology and Anatomy, New York Medical College; Judy Norsigian, Co-Director, Boston Women's Healthbook Collective; Marsha Saxton, Director, Project on Women and Disability; Doreen Stabinsky, California Biotechnology Action Council and University of California at Davis; and Nachama L. Wilker, Executive Director, Council for Responsible Genetics.

SUGGESTED READINGS

GENERAL ISSUES

Andrews, Lori B., et al. "Genetics and the Law." *Emory Law Journal* 39 (1990), 619–853. Symposium.

Annas, George J., and Elias, Sherman, eds. *Gene Mapping: Using Law and Ethics as Guides.* New York: Oxford University Press, 1992.

Bankowski, Zbigniew, and Capron, Alexander Morgan, eds. Council for International Organizations of Medical Sciences. *Genetics, Ethics, and Human Values: Human Genome Mapping, Genetic Screening and Gene Therapy.* Geneva: Council for International Organizations of Medical Sciences, 1990.

David, Bernard D., ed. *The Genetic Revolution: Scientific Prospects and Public Perceptions.* Baltimore: Johns Hopkins University Press, 1991.

Fletcher, Joseph. *The Ethics of Genetic Control: Ending Reproductive Roulette.* Garden City, NY: Anchor Books, 1974.

Harris, John. *Wonderwoman and Superman: The Ethics of Human Biotechnology.* New York: Oxford University Press, 1992.

Hubbard, Ruth, and Wald, Elijah. *Exploding the Gene Myth.* Boston: Beacon Press, 1993.

Krimsky, Sheldon. *Biotechnics and Society: The Rise of Industrial Genetics.* Westport, CT: Praeger, 1991.

Miringoff, Marque-Luisa. *The Social Costs of Genetic Welfare.* New Brunswick, NJ: Rutgers University Press, 1991.

Muller, Hermann J. "The Guidance of Human Evolution." *Perspectives in Biology and Medicine* 3 (1959), 1–43.

Ramsey, Paul. *Fabricated Man: The Ethics of Genetic Control.* New Haven: Yale University Press, 1970.

Suzuki, David, and Knudtson, Peter. *Genethics: The Clash between the New Genetics and Human Values.* Revised and updated edition. Cambridge, MA: Harvard University Press, 1990.

United States Congress, Office of Technology Assessment. *New Developments in Biotechnology—Background Paper: Public Perceptions of Biotechnology.* Washington, DC: U.S. Government Printing Office, May 1987.

EUGENICS

Adams, Mark B., ed. *The Wellborn Science: Eugenics in Germany, France, Brazil, and Russia.* New York: Oxford University Press, 1990.

Duster, Troy. *Backdoor to Eugenics.* New York: Routledge, Chapman and Hall, 1990.

Haller, Mark H. *Eugenics: Hereditarian Attitudes in American Thought.* New Brunswick, NJ: Rutgers University Press, 1963.

Kevles, Daniel J. *In the Name of Eugenics: Genetics and the Uses of Human Heredity.* New York: Knopf, 1985.

Ludmerer, Kenneth M. *Genetics and American Society: A Historical Appraisal.* Baltimore: Johns Hopkins University Press, 1972.

Proctor, Robert N. *Racial Hygiene: Medicine under the Nazis.* Cambridge, MA: Harvard University Press, 1988.

Reilly, Philip R. *The Surgical Solution: A History of Involuntary Sterilization in the United States.* Baltimore: Johns Hopkins University Press, 1991.

Smith, J. David, and Nelson, K. Ray. *The Sterilization of Carrie Buck.* Far Hills, NJ: New Horizon Press, 1989.

Weindling, Paul. *Health, Race, and German Politics between National Unification and Nazism, 1870–1945.* Cambridge: Cambridge University Press, 1989.

THE HUMAN GENOME PROJECT

Boyle, Philip J., et al. "Genetic Grammar: 'Health,' 'Illness,' and the Human Genome Project." *Hastings Center Report* 22 (July–August 1992; Supplement), S1–S20.

Collins, Francis S. "Medical and Ethical Consequences of the Human Genome Project." *Journal of Clinical Ethics* 2 (1991), 260–267.

Cook-Deegan, Robert M. *The Gene Wars: Science, Politics, and the Human Genome.* New York: W. W. Norton, 1993.

Karjala, Dennis S. "A Legal Research Agenda for the Human Genome Initiative." *Jurimetrics Journal* 32 (1992), 121–222.

Kevles, Daniel J., and Hood, Leroy, eds. *The Code of Codes: Scientific and Social Issues in the Human Genome Project.* Cambridge, MA: Harvard University Press, 1992.

Lee, Thomas F. *The Human Genome Project: Cracking the Genetic Code of Life.* New York: Plenum Press, 1991.

Lewontin, Richard. "The Dream of the Human Genome: Doubts about the Human Genome Project." *New York Review of Books* 39 (May 28, 1992), 31–40.

National Research Council. *Mapping and Sequencing the Human Genome.* Washington, DC: National Academy Press, 1988.

Rothstein, Mark A., ed. *Legal and Ethical Issues Raised by the Human Genome Project.* Houston, TX: University of Houston, Health Law and Policy Institute, 1991.

United States Congress, Office of Technology Assessment. *Mapping Our Genes—The Genome Projects: How Big, How Fast?* Washington, DC: U.S. Government Printing Office, April 1988.

AAAS-ABA National Conference of Lawyers and Scientists and AAAS Committee on Scientific Freedom and Responsibility. *The Genome, Ethics, and the Law: Issues in Genetic Testing.* Washington, DC: American Association for the Advancement of Science, 1992.

American Medical Association, Council on Ethical and Judicial Affairs. "Use of Genetic Testing by Employers." *Journal of the American Medical Association* 226 (1991), 1827–1830.

Bartels, Dianne M.; LeRoy, Bonnie S.; and Caplan, Arthur L., eds. *Prescribing Our Future: Ethical Challenges in Genetic Counseling.* New York: Aldine De Gruyter, 1993.

Billings, Paul R., ed. *DNA on Trial: Genetic Identification and Criminal Justice.* Plainview, NY: Cold Spring Harbor Laboratory Press, 1992.

DeGrazia, David. "The Ethical Justification for Minimal Paternalism in the Use of the Predictive Test for Huntington's Disease." *Journal of Clinical Ethics* 2 (1991), 219–228.

Draper, Elaine. *Risky Business: Genetic Testing and Exclusionary Practices in the Hazardous Workplace.* New York: Cambridge University Press, 1991.

Gostin, Larry. "Genetic Discrimination: The Use of Genetically Based Diagnostic and Prognostic Tests by Employers and Insurers." *American Journal of Law and Medicine* 17 (1991), 109–144.

Holtzman, Neil A. *Proceed with Caution: Predicting Genetic Risks in the Recombinant DNA Era.* Baltimore: Johns Hopkins University Press, 1989.

Lippman, Abby. "Prenatal Genetic Testing and Screening: Constructing Needs and Reinforcing Inequities." *American Journal of Law and Medicine* 17 (1991), 15–50.

National Academy of Sciences, Committee on DNA Technology in Forensic Science. *DNA Technology in Forensic Science.* Washington, DC: National Academy Press, 1992.

National Research Council, Committee for the Study of Inborn Errors of Metabolism. *Genetic Screening: Programs, Principles and Research.* Washington, DC: National Academy of Sciences, 1975.

Natowicz, Marvin R., Alper, Jane K., and Alper, Joseph S. "Genetic Discrimination and the Law." *American Journal of Human Genetics* 50 (1992), 465–475.

Nelkin, Dorothy, and Tancredi, Laurence. *Dangerous Diagnostics: The Social Power of Biological Information.* New York: Basic Books, 1989.

Robertson, John A. "Ethical and Legal Issues in Preimplantation Genetic Screening." *Fertility and Sterility* 57 (1992), 1–11.

Rothman, Barbara Katz. *The Tentative Pregnancy: Prenatal Diagnosis and the Future of Motherhood.* New York: Viking Penguin, 1986.

United States Congress, Office of Technology Assessment. *Cystic Fibrosis and DNA Tests: Implications of Carrier Screening.* Washington, DC: U.S. Government Printing Office, August 1992.

United States Congress, Office of Technology Assessment. *Genetic Monitoring and Screening in the Workplace.* Washington, DC: U.S. Government Printing Office, October 1990.

United States Congress, Office of Technology Assessment. *Genetic Witness: Forensic Uses of DNA Tests.* Washington, DC: U.S. Government Printing Office, July 1990.

United States President's Commission for the Study of Ethical Problems in Medicine and Biomedical and Behavioral Research. *Screening and Counseling for Genetic Conditions.*

Washington, DC: U.S. Government Printing Office, February 1983.

Wertz, Dorothy C., and Fletcher, John C., eds. *Ethics and Human Genetics: A Cross-Cultural Perspective*. Berlin and New York: Springer Verlag, 1989.

HUMAN GENE THERAPY

Anderson, W. French. "Human Gene Therapy: Why Draw a Line?" *Journal of Medicine and Philosophy* 14 (1989), 681–693.

Fletcher, John C., and Anderson, W. French, "Germ-Line Gene Therapy: A New Stage of Debate." *Law, Medicine and Health Care* 20 (1992), 26–39.

Fowler, Gregory; Juengst, Eric T.; and Zimmerman, Burke K. "Germ-Line Gene Therapy and the Clinical Ethos of Medical Genetics." *Theoretical Medicine* 10 (1989), 151–165.

Friedmann, Theodore. "Progress toward Human Gene Therapy." *Science* 244 (1989), 1275–1281.

Glover, Jonathan. *What Sort of People Should There Be?* New York: Penguin Books, 1984.

Juengst, Eric T., ed. "Human Germ-Line Engineering." *Journal of Medicine and Philosophy* 16 (1991), 587–694. Topical issue.

Nichols, Eve K., and Institute of Medicine, National Academy of Sciences. *Human Gene Therapy*. Cambridge, MA: Harvard University Press, 1988.

United States President's Commission for the Study of Ethical Problems in Medicine and Biomedical and Behavioral Research. *Splicing Life: A Report on the Social and Ethical Issues of Genetic Engineering with Human Beings*. Washington, DC: U.S. Government Printing Office, November 1982.

Walters, LeRoy. "Human Gene Therapy: Ethics and Public Policy." *Human Gene Therapy* 2 (1991), 115–122.

Wivel, Nelson A., and Walters, LeRoy. "Germ-line Gene Modification and Disease Prevention: Some Medical and Ethical Perspectives." *Science* 262 (1993), 533–538.

BIBLIOGRAPHIES

Arizona State University Center for the Study of Law, Science and Technology. "The Human Genome Project: Bibliography of Ethical, Social, Legal, and Scientific Aspects." *Jurimetrics Journal* 32 (1992), 223–311.

Coutts, Mary Carrington. "Human Gene Therapy." *Scope Note 24.* Washington, DC: Georgetown University, 1994.

Durfy, Sharon J., and Grotevant, Amy E. "The Human Genome Project." *Scope Note 17.* Washington, DC: Kennedy Institute of Ethics, Georgetown University, 1991.

Goldstein, Doris Mueller. *Bioethics: A Guide to Information Sources.* Detroit: Gale Research Company, 1982. See under "Genetic Intervention."

Lineback, Richard H., ed. *Philosopher's Index.* Vols. 1–27. Bowling Green, OH; Philosophy Documentation Center, Bowling Green State University. Issued quarterly. See under "Genetic Engineering" and "Genetics."

McCarrick, Pat Milmoe. "Genetic Testing and Genetic Screening." *Scope Note 22.* Washington, DC: Kennedy Institute of Ethics, Georgetown University, 1993.

Walters, LeRoy, and Kahn, Tamar Joy, eds. *Bibliography of Bioethics.* Vols. 1–19. Washington, DC: Kennedy Institute of Ethics, Georgetown University. Issued annually. See under "Eugenics," "Gene Therapy," "Genetic Counseling," "Genetic Intervention," "Genetic Screening," and "Genome Mapping." (The information contained in the annual *Bibliography* can also be retrieved from BIOETHICSLINE, an online database of the National Library of Medicine, and from *BIOETHICSLINE Plus,* a CD-ROM disc distributed by SilverPlatter.)

Part VI

JUSTICE IN ACCESS TO HEALTH CARE

10.
Justice in the Distribution of Health Care

INTRODUCTION

Health care costs in the United States in 1965 were $1 billion. Today, health care costs are over $750 billion annually. Medicare payments for physicians alone account for more than $30 billion. In the 1980s and early 1990s, Medicare expenditures for physicians rose an average of 12 percent per year and were expected to increase at a rate of approximately 13 to 14 percent per year in the next decade. These costs have been subjected to intense study by the President and the Congress, who generally agree that Medicare's payment policies have fueled unacceptable increases in expenditures for health-care services.

The basic *economic problem* about health care is how to control costs and efficiently distribute resources in order to satisfy human needs and desires. The basic *ethical problem* is how to structure a health care system that fairly distributes resources and provides equitable access to health care at a manageable cost. These ethical and economic problems are often intertwined in the formation of public policy, which in this area is typically referred to as health policy.

The proper role of government is often at the center of health policy discussions. Most members of society agree that government is constituted to protect citizens against risks from the environment, risks from external invasion, risks from crime, risks from fire, risks from highway accidents, and the like. But the idea that health care should be similarly provided as a government service has long been controversial. Even if society decided that government has an obligation to provide health care, there are limits to what government can and should do. But what are those limits?

THE ALLOCATION OF HEALTH CARE RESOURCES

Many public policy and private corporate decisions aim at allocating resources fairly and efficiently. To allocate is to distribute goods and services among alternative possibilities for their use. However, the distribution need not be made by government officials. For example, the free market distributes goods and services through exchanges made by free agents acting in their own best interests. But when the decision is social or governmental rather than individual, decisions fall into two broad types: macroallocation and microallocation.

In macroallocation, social decisions are made about how much will be expended for health care resources, as well as how it will be distributed. These decisions are taken by Congress, state legislatures, health organizations, private foundations, and health insurance companies. At the microallocation level, decisions are made by particular institutions or health professionals concerning who shall obtain available resources—for example, which of several potential patients will be admitted to the last available bed in the intensive care unit. This chapter emphasizes the problem of macroallocation.

Two primary considerations are involved in macroallocation decisions about health care and research: (1) What percentage of the total available resources should be allotted to biomedical research and clinical practice, which compete for funding with other social projects such as defense, education, transportation, and the like? (2) How much budgeted to biomedicine should go to each specific project—for example, how much to cancer research, to preventive medicine, and to the production of technology for treatment facilities? An example of the second problem is whether funding for *preventive* medicine should take priority over funding for *crisis* medicine. From one perspective, the prevention of disease by improvements in unsanitary environments and dissemination of health information is cheaper and more efficient in raising health levels and saving lives than are kidney dialysis, heart transplantation, and intensive care units. But from another perspective, a concentrated preventive approach is morally unsatisfactory if it leads to neglecting needy persons who could directly benefit from available resources.

These problems of macroallocation are handled differently by competing systems of distribution. But which among these systems is the fairest?

DISTRIBUTIVE JUSTICE IN REDISTRIBUTING RESOURCES

In Chapter 1 we surveyed theories of justice. We can now examine how these theories have been used to gauge the justice of health care systems, including their macroallocation and microallocation decisions.

EGALITARIAN THEORY

In Chapter 1 we noted that John Rawls's *A Theory of Justice* has been a particularly influential work on social justice in the egalitarian tradition. Rawls argues that a social arrangement is a communal effort to advance the good of all in the society. Because inequalities of birth, historical circumstance, and natural endowment are undeserved, persons in a cooperative society should aim to correct them by making the unequal situation of naturally disadvantaged members more equal. Evening out disabilities in this way is, Rawls claims, a fundamental part of our shared conception of justice. His recognition of a positive societal obligation to eliminate or reduce barriers that prevent fair opportunity and that correct or compensate for various disadvantages has clear implications for discussions of justice in health care.

Rawls's analysis of justice deeply influenced the article in this chapter by Robert Veatch, who begins with the Rawlsian model of justice and then proposes two separate uses of egalitarian theory for health care. He believes that those individuals who are worst off in a society (that is, are at the minimum level) should be guaranteed access to a certain level of health care. In this way, the society improves the conditions of the least fortunate by increasing their level of care.

UTILITARIAN THEORY

One need not be an egalitarian to believe in an equitable social system that redistributes resources to improve the health care needs of all citizens. Utilitarians believe that society has an obligation to assist its members by preventing harms such as sickness and also that we are morally blameworthy if we do nothing at all. Utilitarians argue that *justice* is the name for the most paramount and stringent forms of social obligation created by the principle of utility. In the distribution of health care, utilitarians commonly view justice as involving trade-offs and partial allocations that strike a balance. In devising a system of public funding for health care, we must balance public and private benefit, predicted cost savings, the probability of failure, the magnitude of risks, and so on.

No author in this chapter explicitly defends a utilitarian system of distribution for health care. However, the article by the President's Commission for the Study of Ethical Problems adopts roughly the utilitarian approach. To the commission, society has an obligation to ensure equitable access to health care for all citizens, because of the special importance of relieving suffering and preventing premature death. It contends that creators of a health care distribution system must balance the issues of social responsibility, individual responsibility, and social resources. The commission report opts for a two-tiered system of health care in which those who wish to purchase more than is provided by the social scheme of insurance are free to do so at personal expense.

LIBERTARIAN THEORY

A perennial problem concerning the distribution of health care is whether justice requires any preplanned distribution of health care at all. Robert Nozick has raised the following question about our shared conception of justice:

Hearing the term "distribution," most people presume that some thing or mechanism uses some principle or criterion to give out a supply of things. . . . So it is an open question, at least, whether *redistribution* should take place; whether we should do again what has already been done once.[1]

In Chapter 1 we examined the libertarian theory of justice, for which Nozick is a spokesperson. These free-market theorists explicitly reject the conclusion that egalitarian and utilitarian patterns of distribution represent an appropriate normative ideal for distributing health care. People may be equal in many morally significant respects, but *justice* does not demand the collection and redistribution of economic resources such as the tax dollars required to fund government-distributed health care goods and services. For a libertarian, there is no pattern of just distribution independent of free-market procedures of acquiring property, legitimately transferring that property, and providing rectification for those who had property illegitimately extracted or otherwise were illegitimately obstructed in the free market.

A libertarian prefers a system in which health care insurance is privately and voluntarily purchased by individual or group initiative, because in this system no one has had property coercively extracted by the state in order to benefit someone else. This libertarian theory is defended in this chapter by H. Tristram Engelhardt, Jr., who relies heavily on the principle of respect for autonomy rather than a substantive principle of justice. Engelhardt argues that a theory of justice should work to protect our right not to be coerced; it should not propound a doctrine intended to regulate society through redistributive arrangements. Use of the tax code to effect social goals such as saving lives with advanced medical technologies is a matter of social *choice,* not social justice. Some disadvantages created by ill health, Engelhardt argues, should be viewed as merely *unfortunate,* whereas injury and illness caused by another person are correctly viewed as *unfair.* From this perspective, one will call a halt to the demands of justice where one draws the distinction between the unfair (and therefore obligatory in justice to correct) and the merely unfortunate.

THE RIGHT TO HEALTH CARE

These debates about justice and fair macroallocation have implications for the claim that we have a right to health care. If such a right exists, national allocations for health care would not be based on charity, compassion, and benevolence, but rather on rights grounded in justice. However, critics of the view that there is a right to health care respond that failures to allocate health care resources may be uncharitable, lacking in compassion, and even stingy—and therefore morally condemnable—yet not violations of anyone's rights. These critics themselves often find the U.S. system seriously inadequate, but they do not find the fault to lie in a failure to recognize a *right* to health care.

Positions in contemporary ethics on the right to health care range from a denial of any kind of right to strong egalitarian rights for all citizens. Typically utilitarians argue that the principle of utility determines whether a right to health care is supportable; egalitarians attempt to derive a right to health care from a principle of equality, such as fair equality of opportunity; and libertarians deny that there are any welfare rights, including rights to health care.

In this context a "right" is understood as an *entitlement* to some measure of health care; rights are thus to be contrasted with mere privileges, ideals, and acts of charity. In many nations there is a firmly established legal right to health care goods and services for all citizens. The prevailing legal view in the United States, by contrast, is that even if there are solid moral reasons for the enactment of a right to health care and no constitutional constraints against it, there is no *constitutional* right to health care. In 1965 Congress created Medicare to provide coverage for health care costs in populations that could not afford adequate coverage, especially the elderly. It has generally been successful in meeting this goal, but has proved to be economically inefficient. Medicare conferred a right to health care on a particularly vulnerable population and thereby stimulated discussion of whether all citizens have, or at least should have, a right to health care under similar conditions of need. There is no realistic legal basis to support such claims, but is there a moral basis?

It is often asked whether there is a right to a "decent minimum" of health care. The right to a decent minimum is supported by Ronald Bayer and his coauthors and also by James Todd, representing the American Medical Association. These proponents assert that each person should have equal access to an adequate (though not maximal) level of health care for all available types of services. The distribution proceeds on the basis of need, and needs are met by fair access to adequate services. Better services, such as luxury hospital rooms and expensive but optional dental work, can then be made available for purchase at personal expense by those who are able to and wish to do so.

However, Todd argues, the basic level of care to which all are entitled may have to be *funded* by multiple funding systems, not merely by a government agency. Todd argues against universal health insurance, but in favor of universal access. He appears to believe that universal insurance entails a government insurance plan. Some of these assumptions are challenged in the article by Alain Enthoven and Richard Kronick. They design a proposal for universal health insurance that relies not on government but rather on managed competition with a mixed public and private sponsorship. The idea is to locate some variety of insurance for all persons who do not already qualify for a public program such as Medicare and Medicaid (in which they suggest no major changes).

The President's Commission and Allen Buchanan argue that we have no *right* to this decent minimum of care but that there is nonetheless a social obligation to provide it. Engelhardt concludes that there is no right and no social obligation, although a society may freely choose to enact such a policy. From his perspective and Buchanan's, if needs are unfortunate they may still be ameliorated by benevolence or compassion; but only if they are unfair does the obligation of justice justify compensation to the disadvantaged by using state force to tax and redistribute resources. Maleficently or negligently caused setbacks to health justify the designation *unfair,* but other setbacks to health are matters of misfortune.

In light of this problem of a criterion of unfairness, the implications of the Rawlsian approach and the demands of the fair opportunity rule remain uncertain in biomedical ethics and health policy. However, Rawlsians like Veatch hold out for a different conclusion.

Veatch defends a right stronger than the right to a decent minimum. He proposes the distribution of health care based on the individual's health care needs, by using the yardstick of an "equal right to health care." The result is that "people have a right to needed health care to provide an opportunity for a level of health equal as far as possible to the health of other people." This application of the principle of justice to health care would result in a health care delivery system with only one class of services available, rather than a two-tiered system.

Even if one does not support either moral rights to health care or political obligations to supply it, one can still support legal entitlements to health care on grounds of charity, beneficence, or a sense of moral excellence in a community. Many appeals other than those to moral rights can be used to defend public distributions that confer legal rights, as Buchanan and the President's Commission in effect note. These appeals may also support a system of required contributions on grounds that it is the fairest system to those willing to cooperate and that it will be far more socially efficient.

UNIVERSAL HEALTH INSURANCE AND UNIVERSAL ACCESS

Many problems about justice in health care start with how to pay for and distribute limited social resources. The overarching problem in health policy — as Bayer and his associates argue in this chapter — is, "How can a health policy provide adequate and fairly distributed care to all subscribers at an affordable price?"

Many current problems stem from unequal resources and unequal access to care. Inequalities in access to health care and to health insurance continue to fuel debates in bioethics about social justice and forms of health care distribution. But does unequal access mean an inequity? And is *inequality* in the allocation of social resources a core problem about adequate access to care? Allen Buchanan argues, in the first part of his essay, that the idea of equality of health care is not even an appropriate criterion to use in moral evaluations of a health care system.

Several obstacles stand in the way of a more efficient, fair, and comprehensive access to health care in the U.S. system. Over thirty-five million U.S. citizens annually lack all health care coverage, largely because of the high cost of health insurance and a system in which access is generally obtained through an employer-based health plan. All but the most affluent citizens need some form of insurance to meet actual or potential health care needs, which are often unpredictable in onset, catastrophic if unmet, and too expensive for an individual's resources. Although more than two thousand dollars per person and over 12 percent of the gross national product are spent annually for health care in the United States, the poor and the uninsured often cannot afford or find access to even minimally adequate care. A small group of citizens turns out to be *uninsurable,* because they cannot pass physical examinations, present the kind of medical histories required for insurance, or are excluded because of their occupation.

There is also a major problem of underinsurance for over 20 million U.S. citizens who have seriously inadequate coverage. Costs require limiting coverage even in employer-based plans, and many exclusionary clauses deny access for types of treatment, as well as for specific diseases, injuries, or organ systems. A few people are both uninsured or underinsured. They experience gaps in insurance coverage that cannot be bridged because they move quickly from job to job or suffer from temporary but lengthy layoffs. More than a million laborers lose their insurance for some period of time during the year while they are unemployed, and more than 25 percent of the entire U.S. population changes insurance, with a resulting coverage gap, during the course of each year. Several of these problems are presented and proposed remedies provided in the essay by Alain Enthoven and Richard Kronick.

In the face of rapid rises in health care costs, the situation in U.S. health care is increasingly referred to as a "crisis." One generic issue concerns how to design or structure our basic health care institutions and forms of distribution for maximum coverage and efficiency. Various approaches produce different programs of health care services, who will have access to them, who may and should deliver those services, and how the services will be funded and distributed. Each author in the second section of this chapter has a vision of how to handle these and other questions about access to health care. Equitable and efficient access to care is the highest item on their agenda. Some approaches make direct appeals to the *right* to health care and some invoke one or more *theories* of justice; others make only an indirect appeal to rights and theories. Because there is neither a social consensus nor a paramount theory of justice at the present time, we should expect public policies to oscillate, now using the premises of one approach, later emphasizing another.

A health care system that draws support from all of the abovementioned theories of justice may in the end be the fairest approach to democratic reform of the health care system. Each has its attractive and unattractive features, and many citizens are appropriately fearful of the social consequences of adopting one of these philosophical ideals as the basis for public policy to the exclusion of others. Experience suggests that appeals to one of these accounts of justice works well in some contexts, but yields disappointing results in others. Compromises between these theories do not seem inappropriate in a democracy, where only a minority is likely to agree on the utility and acceptability of a general theory of justice.

RATIONING HEALTH CARE AND THE OREGON PLAN

Ethics and health policy have recently seen a rise in the language of *rationing* health care resources. This term often suggests financially stringent and critical circumstances that require social decisions to include some citizens while excluding others. However, the original meaning of rationing did not suggest austerity or an emergency. It meant a form of allowance, share, or portion, as when food is divided into rations in the military. Only recently has it been tied to limited resources and crisis management. If insurance coverage or ability to pay is a way of eliminating those who are uninsured from access to health care, then much of the U.S.'s health care system involves rationing by level of personal resources. There are many other forms of rationing, including forms of government reimbursement to hospitals, various forms of cost containment, restricting the elderly from some forms of care, and methods of disseminating new medical technologies.

Many now believe that the most important task of democratic political procedures for macroallocation is to establish priorities that distinguish the most important and the least important goals of a health care system. Determining which categories of injury, illness, or disease (if any) should receive a priority ranking in the allocation of public resources is a vital aspect of health policy. In trying to determine priorities among medical needs, policymakers justifiably take into account factors of various diseases such as communicability, frequency, cost, pain and suffering, and prospects for rehabilitation. It might be appropriate, for instance, to concentrate less on killer diseases, such as some forms of cancer, and more on widespread disabling diseases, such as arthritis.

A closely watched attempt to implement this strategy while extending health care to a wider set of citizens has taken place in the state of Oregon, which has been at the forefront of rationing decisions in the United States. Faced with skyrocketing costs and a restive population demanding more efficient and fairer access to quality health care, Oregon established a state committee in 1989 charged to rank hundreds of medical procedures for Medicaid, from most to least important, based in part on data about quality of well-being. State officials sought to extend coverage to a larger percentage of its citizens through its allocated Medicaid funds, and to do so both efficiently and fairly. The goal was to fund as many top priority–ranked services as possible.

In 1990, Oregon's Health Services Commission issued a list of 1,600 ranked medical procedures that formed the initial centerpiece of the plan. Procedures were ranked according to their respective costs and likely results on the patient's quality of well-being. A quality of life approach was used from the outset. This approach helps rank procedures by considering both the change in quality of life offered by the treatment to the average patient and its associated effect on the quality of life. Because the data collected for the ranking of treatments focus on how a treatment changes the quality of life for the average patient receiving it, and not on the quality of life at a given point in time after treatment, patients are not penalized for having serious debilitating diseases or injuries. The system is designed to ensure that the very sick are not discriminated against. (The elderly, the blind, and the disabled are excluded from the ranking scheme.) However, utilitarian concerns are also present because final rankings consider the life-sustaining impact of a treatment. The analysis of the Oregon Plan in this chapter by David C. Hadorn—"The Oregon Priority-Setting Exercise"—explores some of the utilitarian emphases in the plan, with a special emphasis on the role of quality-of-life judgments.

Oregon's plan is the first proposal for systematic allocation and rationing of health care funds in the United States. As such, it may mark the beginning of a new era in American medical care that brings it closer to the more systematic approaches adopted in other countries. In sacrificing high-cost operations that benefit only a few patients, in favor of a minimal level of health care for all residents, Oregon has at least implicitly relied on a theory of justice in making its determinations. Supporters of the scheme argue that only by such explicit and principled ranking and excluding of treatments can the state achieve a just system that overcomes the implicit and haphazard ranking system that has always been present in U.S. health care.

Critics contend that the Oregon plan discriminates against the poor and elderly and fosters an "us versus them" conception of health care through its emphasis on benefits to the poor. Critics also charge that the measures will damage the doctor–patient relationship. In reply, proponents of the plan point to the expanded coverage for all Medicaid-eligible citizens. The sensitive issue of who will suffer a setback under the Oregon plan has proved troublesome to resolve. Since the plan excludes the disabled and elderly from loss of eligibility, these groups will continue to receive the same benefits as before.

However, as Norman Daniels argues in his essay in this chapter, if current Medicaid recipients are made worse off, this fact by itself constitutes a serious objection to the Oregon plan. In his contribution to this chapter, Daniel Callahan argues that society should guarantee individuals care, i.e., decent and basic support in the face of illness and death, but not unlimited efforts to conquer illness and death. He sees criteria such as age as appropriate for setting limits to health care and its runaway expenditures. Callahan takes a favorable view toward the efforts in Oregon because they cope realistically with the major social problems, but he notes several moral problems about goals, means to those goals, and whether practical implementation can avoid unintended consequences.

JUST PROCEDURES AND JUST RESULTS

In the literature on distributive justice and health care an important distinction between just procedures and just results is often invoked. The term "distribution" may refer to the *procedure used to distribute,* or it may refer to the *result of some system of distribution.* Ideally it is preferable to have just procedures and just results, but it is not always possible to have both. For example, one might achieve a just result in macroallocation by meeting everyone's health care needs, but one might use an unjust procedure, such as undeserved taxation of certain groups, in order to achieve it. By contrast, just procedures sometimes produce unjust results, as occurs when a just procedure such as a fair trial reaches unjust results such as finding innocent parties guilty.

Many problems of justice and the distribution of health care that we must handle as a cooperative society involve designing a set of procedures that provides as much justice as possible. Once we agree on appropriate procedures, then as long as a person is treated according to those procedures, the outcome must be declared just. This conception is enthusiastically supported by Engelhardt in this chapter. However, because unfortunate (but not necessarily unfair) outcomes are inevitable in purely procedural systems, shifting the issue from results to procedures will not avoid all ethical controversy. The President's Commission lays strong emphasis on the use of democratic political procedures to make a choice among "just alternatives." But this conclusion requires that we have already delineated a range of just alternatives. Veatch's provocative arguments indicate how difficult this will be and why the controversy will persist. Moreover, the various traditional theories of ethics will likely provide competing criteria of just procedures. Thus, procedural justice may help us with some problems of distributing health care, but it will not resolve them all. No matter how strongly we believe in democracy, consensus, and negotiation, they do not seem capable of handling all questions about the justice of a system of health care distribution.

T. L. B.

NOTES

1. Robert Nozick, *Anarchy, State, and Utopia* (New York: Basic Books, 1974), pp. 149–50.

Just Health Care and the Right to Health Care

PRESIDENT'S COMMISSION FOR THE STUDY OF ETHICAL PROBLEMS IN MEDICINE AND BIOMEDICAL AND BEHAVIORAL RESEARCH

Securing Access to Health Care

The President's Commission was mandated to study the ethical and legal implications of differences in the availability of health services. In this Report to the President and Congress, the Commission sets forth an ethical standard: access for all to an adequate level of care without the imposition of excessive burdens. It believes that this is the standard against which proposals for legislation and regulation in this field ought to be measured. . . .

In both their means and their particular objectives, public programs in health care have varied over the years. Some have been aimed at assuring the productivity of the work force, others at protecting particularly vulnerable or deserving groups, still others at manifesting the country's commitment to equality of opportunity. Nonetheless, most programs have rested on a common rationale: to ensure that care be made accessible to a group whose health needs would otherwise not be adequately met.

The consequence of leaving health care solely to market forces — the mechanism by which most things are allocated in American society — is not viewed as acceptable when a significant portion of the population lacks access to health services. Of course, government financing programs, such as Medicare and Medicaid as well as public programs that provide care

directly to veterans and the military and through local public hospitals, have greatly improved access to health care. These efforts, coupled with the expanded availability of private health insurance, have resulted in almost 90% of Americans having some form of health insurance coverage. Yet the patchwork of government programs and the uneven availability of private health insurance through the workplace have excluded millions of people. The Surgeon General has stated that "with rising unemployment, the numbers are shifting rapidly. We estimate that from 18 to 25 million Americans — 8 to 11 percent of the population — have no health-insurance coverage at all." Many of these people lack effective access to health care, and many more who have some form of insurance are unprotected from the severe financial burdens of sickness. . . .

[W]hile people have some ability — through choice of life-style and through preventive measures — to influence their health status, many health problems are beyond their control and are therefore undeserved. Besides the burdens of genetics, environment, and chance, individuals become ill because of things they do or fail to do — but it is often difficult for an individual to choose to do otherwise or even to know with enough specificity and confidence what he or she ought to do to remain healthy. Finally, the incidence and severity of ill health is distributed very unevenly among people. Basic needs for housing and food are

From *Securing Access to Health Care,* Vol. 1. Washington, D.C.: U.S. Government Printing Office, 1983.

predictable, but even the most hardworking and prudent person may suddenly be faced with overwhelming needs for health care. Together, these considerations lend weight to the belief that health care is different from most other goods and services. In a society concerned not only with fairness and equality of opportunity but also with the redemptive powers of science, there is a felt obligation to ensure that some level of health services is available to all.

There are many ambiguities, however, about the nature of this societal obligation. What share of health costs should individuals be expected to bear, and what responsibility do they have to use health resources prudently? Is it society's responsibility to ensure that every person receives care or services of as high quality and as great extent as any other individual? Does it require that everyone share opportunities to receive all available care or care of any possible benefit? If not, what level of care is "enough"? And does society's obligation include a responsibility to ensure both that care is available and that its costs will not unduly burden the patient?

The resolution of such issues is made more difficult by the spectre of rising health care costs and expenditures. Americans annually spend over 270 million days in hospitals, make over 550 million visits to physicians' offices, and receive tens of millions of X-rays. Expenditures for health care in 1981 totaled $287 billion—an average of over $1225 for every American. Although the finitude of national resources demands that trade-offs be made between health care and other social goods, there is little agreement about which choices are most acceptable from an ethical standpoint. . . . The Commission attempts to lay an ethical foundation for evaluating both current patterns of access to health care and the policies designed to address remaining problems in the distribution of health care resources. . . .

THE CONCEPT OF EQUITABLE ACCESS TO HEALTH CARE

The special nature of health care helps to explain why it ought to be accessible, in a fair fashion, to all. But if this ethical conclusion is to provide a basis for evaluating current patterns of access to health care and proposed health policies, the meaning of fairness or equity in this context must be clarified. The concept of equitable access needs definition in its two main aspects: the level of care that ought to be available to all and the extent to which burdens can be imposed on those who obtain these services.

ACCESS TO WHAT?

"Equitable access" could be interpreted in a number of ways: equality of access, access to whatever an individual needs or would benefit from, or access to an adequate level of care.

Equity as Equality. It has been suggested that equity is achieved either when everyone is assured of receiving an equal quantity of health care dollars or when people enjoy equal health. The most common characterization of equity as equality, however, is as providing everyone with the same level of health care. In this view, it follows that if a given level of care is available to one individual it must be available to all. If the initial standard is set high, by reference to the highest level of care presently received, an enormous drain would result on the resources needed to provide other goods. Alternatively, if the standard is set low in order to avoid an excessive use of resources, some beneficial services would have to be withheld from people who wished to purchase them. In other words, no one would be allowed access to more services or services of higher quality than those available to everyone else, even if he or she were willing to pay for those services from his or her personal resources.

As long as significant inequalities in income and wealth persist, inequalities in the use of health care can be expected beyond those created by differences in need. Given people with the same pattern of preferences and equal health care needs, those with greater financial resources will purchase more health care. Conversely, given equal financial resources, the different patterns of health care preferences that typically exist in any population will result in a different use of health services by people with equal health care needs. Trying to prevent such inequalities would require interfering with people's liberty to use their income to purchase an important good like health care while leaving them free to use it for frivolous or inessential ends. Prohibiting people with higher incomes or stronger preferences for health care from purchasing more care than everyone else gets would not be feasible, and would probably result in a black market for health care.

Equity as Access Solely According to Benefit or Need. Interpreting equitable access to mean that everyone must receive all health care that is of any benefit to them also has unacceptable implications. Unless health is the only good or resources are unlimited, it would be irrational for a society—as for an individual—to make a commitment to provide whatever health care might be beneficial regardless of cost. Although health care is of special importance, it is surely not all that is important to people. . . .

"[N]eed" could be even more expansive in scope than "benefit." Philosophical and economic writings do not provide any clear distinction between "needs" and "wants" or "preferences." Since the term means different things to different people, "access according to need" could become "access to any health service a person wants." Conversely, need could be interpreted very narrowly to encompass only a very minimal level of services—for example, those "necessary to prevent death."

Equity as an Adequate Level of Health Care. Although neither "everything needed" nor "everything beneficial" nor "everything that anyone else is getting" are defensible ways of understanding equitable access, the special nature of health care dictates that everyone have access to *some* level of health care: enough care to achieve sufficient welfare, opportunity, information, and evidence of interpersonal concern to facilitate a reasonably full and satisfying life. That level can be termed "an adequate level of health care." The difficulty of sharpening this amorphous notion into a workable foundation for health policy is a major problem in the United States today. This concept is not new; it is implicit in the public debate over health policy and has manifested itself in the history of public policy in this country. In this [essay], the Commission attempts to demonstrate the value of the concept, to clarify its content, and to apply it to the problems facing health policymakers.

Understanding equitable access to health care to mean that everyone should be able to secure an adequate level of care has several strengths. Because an adequate level of care may be less than "all beneficial care" and because it does not require that all needs be satisfied, it acknowledges the need for setting priorities within health care and signals a clear recognition that society's resources are limited and that there are other goods besides health. Thus, interpreting equity as access to adequate care does not generate an open-ended obligation. One of the chief dangers of interpretations of equity that require virtually unlimited resources for health care is that they encourage the view that equitable access is an impossible ideal. Defining

equity as an adequate level of care for all avoids an impossible commitment of resources without falling into the opposite error of abandoning the enterprise of seeking to ensure that health care is in fact available for everyone.

In addition, since providing an adequate level of care is a limited moral requirement, this definition also avoids the unacceptable restriction on individual liberty entailed by the view that equity requires equality. Provided that an adequate level is available to all, those who prefer to use their resources to obtain care that exceeds that level do not offend any ethical principle in doing so. Finally, the concept of adequacy, as the Commission understands it, is society-relative. The content of adequate care will depend upon the overall resources available in a given society, and can take into account a consensus of expectations about what is adequate in a particular society at a particular time in its historical development. This permits the definition of adequacy to be altered as societal resources and expectations change.

With What Burdens? It is not enough to focus on the care that individuals receive; attention must be paid to the burdens they must bear in order to obtain it—waiting and travel time, the cost and availability of transport, the financial cost of the care itself. Equity requires not only that adequate care be available to all, but also that these burdens not be excessive.

If individuals must travel unreasonably long distances, wait for unreasonably long hours, or spend most of their financial resources to obtain care, some will be deterred from obtaining adequate care, with adverse effects on their health and well-being. Others may bear the burdens, but only at the expense of their ability to meet other important needs. If one of the main reasons for providing adequate care is that health care increases welfare and opportunity, then a system that required large numbers of individuals to forego food, shelter, or educational advancement in order to obtain care would be self-defeating and irrational.

The concept of acceptable burdens in obtaining care, as opposed to excessive ones, parallels in some respects the concept of adequacy. Just as equity does not require equal access, neither must the burdens of obtaining adequate care be equal for all persons. What is crucial is that the variations in burdens fall within an acceptable range. As in determining an adequate level of care, there is no simple formula for ascertaining when the burdens of obtaining care fall within such a range. . . .

A SOCIETAL OBLIGATION

Society has a moral obligation to ensure that everyone has access to adequate care without being subject to excessive burdens. In speaking of a societal obligation the Commission makes reference to society in the broadest sense—the collective American community. The community is made up of individuals, who are in turn members of many other, overlapping groups, both public and private: local, state, regional, and national units; professional and workplace organizations; religious, educational, and charitable organizations; and family, kinship, and ethnic groups. All these entities play a role in discharging societal obligations.

The Commission believes it is important to distinguish between society, in this inclusive sense, and government as one institution among others in society. Thus the recognition of a collective or societal obligation does not imply that government should be the only or even the primary institution involved in the complex enterprise of making health care available. It is the Commission's view that the societal obligation to ensure equitable access for everyone may best be fulfilled in this country by a pluralistic approach that relies upon the coordinated contributions of actions by both the private and public sectors.

Securing equitable access is a societal rather than a merely private or individual responsibility for several reasons. First, while health is of special importance for human beings, health care—especially scientific health care—is a social product requiring the skills and efforts of many individuals; it is not something that individuals can provide for themselves solely through their own efforts. Second, because the need for health care is both unevenly distributed among persons and highly unpredictable and because the cost of securing care may be great, few individuals could secure adequate care without relying on some social mechanism for sharing the costs. Third, if persons generally deserved their health conditions or if the need for health care were fully within the individual's control, the fact that some lack adequate care would not be viewed as an inequity. But differences in health status, and hence differences in health care needs, are largely undeserved because they are, for the most part, not within the individual's control. . . .

WHO SHOULD ENSURE THAT SOCIETY'S OBLIGATION IS MET?

THE LIMITATIONS OF RELYING UPON THE GOVERNMENT

Although the Commission recognizes the necessity of government involvement in ensuring equity of access, it believes that such activity must be carefully crafted and implemented in order to achieve its intended purpose. Public concern about the inability of the market and of private charity to secure access to health care for all has led to extensive government involvement in the financing and delivery of health care. This involvement has come about largely as a result of ad hoc responses to specific problems; the result has been a patchwork of public initiatives at the local, state, and Federal level. These efforts have done much to make health care more widely available to all citizens, but . . . they have not achieved equity of access.

To a large extent, this is the result of a lack of consensus about the nature of the goal and the proper role of government in pursuing it. But to some degree, it may also be the product of the nature of government activity. In some instances, government programs (of all types, not just health-related) have not been designed well enough to achieve the purposes intended or have been subverted to serve purposes explicitly not intended.

In the case of health care, it is extremely difficult to devise public strategies that, on the one hand, do not encourage the misuse of health services and, on the other hand, are not so restrictive as to unnecessarily or arbitrarily limit available care. There is a growing concern, for example, that government assistance in the form of tax exemptions for the purchase of employment-related health insurance has led to the overuse of many services of only very marginal benefit. Similarly, government programs that pay for health care directly (such as Medicaid) have been subject to fraud and abuse by both beneficiaries and providers. . . .

A RIGHT TO HEALTH CARE?

Often the issue of equitable access to health care is framed in the language of rights. Some who view health care from the perspective of distributive justice argue that the considerations discussed in this [essay] show not only that society has a moral obligation to provide equitable access, but also that every individual has a moral right to such access. The Commission has chosen not to develop the case for achieving equitable access through the assertion of a right to health care. Instead it has sought to frame the issues in terms of the special nature of health care and of a society's moral obligation to achieve equity, without taking a position on whether the term "obligation" should be read as entailing a moral right. The Commission reaches this conclusion for several reasons: first, such a right is not legally or constitutionally recognized at the present time; second, it is not a logical corollary of an ethical obligation of the type the Commission has enunciated; and third, it is not necessary as a foundation for appropriate governmental actions to secure adequate health care for all.

Legal Rights. Neither the Supreme Court nor any appellate court has found a constitutional right to health or to health care. However, most Federal statutes and many state statutes that fund or regulate health care have been interpreted to provide statutory rights in the form of entitlements for the intended beneficiaries of the program or for members of the group protected by the regulatory authority. As a consequence, a host of legal decisions have developed significant legal protections for program beneficiaries. . . .

Moral Obligations and Rights. The relationship between the concept of a moral right and that of a moral obligation is complex. To say that a person has a moral right to something is always to say that it is that person's due, that is, he or she is morally entitled to it. In contrast, the term "obligation" is used in two different senses. All moral rights imply corresponding obligations, but, depending on the sense of the term that is being used, moral obligations may or may not imply corresponding rights. In the broad sense, to say that society has a moral obligation to do something is to say that it ought morally to do that thing and that failure to do it makes society liable to serious moral criticism. This does not, however, mean that there is a corresponding right. For example, a person may have a moral obligation to help those in need, even though the needy cannot, strictly speaking, demand that person's aid as something they are due.

The government's responsibility for seeing that the obligation to achieve equity is met is independent of the existence of a corresponding moral right to health

care. There are many forms of government involvement, such as enforcement of traffic rules or taxation to support national defense, to protect the environment, or to promote biomedical research, that do not presuppose corresponding moral rights but that are nonetheless legitimate and almost universally recognized as such. In a democracy, at least, the people may assign to government the responsibility for seeing that important collective obligations are met, provided that doing so does not violate important moral rights.

As long as the debate over the ethical assessment of patterns of access to health care is carried on simply by the assertion and refutation of a "right to health care," the debate will be incapable of guiding policy. At the very least, the nature of the right must be made clear and competing accounts of it compared and evaluated. Moreover, if claims of rights are to guide policy they must be supported by sound ethical reasoning and the connections between various rights must be systematically developed, especially where rights are potentially in conflict with one another. At present, however, there is a great deal of dispute among competing theories of rights, with most theories being so abstract and inadequately developed that their implications for health care are not obvious. Rather than attempt to adjudicate among competing theories of rights, the Commission has chosen to concentrate on what it believes to be the more important part of the question: what is the nature of the societal obligation, which exists whether or not people can claim a corresponding right to health care, and how should this societal obligation be fulfilled?

MEETING THE SOCIETAL OBLIGATION

HOW MUCH CARE IS ENOUGH?

Before the concept of an adequate level of care can be used as a tool to evaluate patterns of access and efforts to improve equity, it must be fleshed out. Since there is no objective formula for doing this, reasonable people can disagree about whether particular patterns and policies meet the demands of adequacy. The Commission does not attempt to spell out in detail what adequate care should include. Rather it frames the terms in which those who discuss or critique health care issues can consider ethics as well as economics, medical science, and other dimensions.

Characteristics of Adequacy. First, the Commission considers it clear that health care can only be judged adequate in relation to an individual's health condition. To begin with a list of techniques or procedures, for example, is not sensible: A CT scan for an accident victim with a serious head injury might be the best way to make a diagnosis essential for the appropriate treatment of that patient; a CT scan for a person with headaches might not be considered essential for adequate care. To focus only on the technique, therefore, rather than on the individual's health and the impact the procedure will have on that individual's welfare and opportunity, would lead to inappropriate policy.

Disagreement will arise about whether the care of some health conditions falls within the demands of adequacy. Most people will agree, however, that some conditions should not be included in the societal obligation to ensure access to adequate care. A relatively uncontroversial example would be changing the shape of a functioning, normal nose or retarding the normal effects of aging (through cosmetic surgery). By the same token, there are some conditions, such as pregnancy, for which care would be regarded as an important component of adequacy. In determining adequacy, it is important to consider how people's welfare, opportunities, and requirements for information and interpersonal caring are affected by their health condition.

Any assessment of adequacy must consider also the types, amounts, and quality of care necessary to respond to each health condition. It is important to emphasize that these questions are implicitly comparative: the standard of adequacy for a condition must reflect the fact that resources used for it will not be available to respond to other conditions. Consequently, the level of care deemed adequate should reflect a reasoned judgment not only about the impact of the condition on the welfare and opportunity of the individual but also about the efficacy and the cost of the care itself in relation to other conditions and the efficacy and cost of the care that is available for them. Since individual cases differ so much, the health care professional and patient must be flexible. Thus adequacy, even in relation to a particular health condition, generally refers to a range of options.

The Relationship of Costs and Benefits. The level of care that is available will be determined by the level of resources devoted to producing it. Such allocation should reflect the benefits and costs of the care provided. It should be emphasized that these "benefits," as well as their "costs," should be interpreted broadly, and not restricted only to effects easily quantifiable in monetary terms. Personal benefits include improvements in individuals' functioning and in their quality of life, and the reassurance from worry and the provision of information that are a product of health care. Broader social benefits should be included as well, such as strengthening the sense of community and the belief that no one in serious need of health care will be left without it. Similarly, costs are not merely the funds spent for a treatment but include other less tangible and quantifiable adverse consequences, such as diverting funds away from other socially desirable endeavors including education, welfare, and other social services.

There is no objectively correct value that these various costs and benefits have or that can be discovered by the tools of cost/benefit analysis. Still, such an analysis, as a recent report of the Office of Technology Assessment noted, "can be very helpful to decisionmakers because the process of analysis gives structure to the problem, allows an open consideration of all relevant effects of a decision, and forces the explicit treatment of key assumptions."[1] But the valuation of the various effects of alternative treatments for different conditions rests on people's values and goals, about which individuals will reasonably disagree. In a democracy, the appropriate values to be assigned to the consequences of policies must ultimately be determined by people expressing their values through social and political processes as well as in the marketplace.

Approximating Adequacy. The intention of the Commission is to provide a frame of reference for policymakers, not to resolve these complex questions. Nevertheless, it is possible to raise some of the specific issues that should be considered in determining what constitutes adequate care. It is important, for example, to gather accurate information about and compare the costs and effects, both favorable and unfavorable, of various treatment or management options. The options that better serve the goals that make health care of special importance should be assigned a higher value. As already noted, the assessment of costs must take two factors into account: the cost of a proposed option in relation to alternative forms of care that would achieve the same goal of enhancing the welfare and opportunities of the patient, and the cost of each proposed option in terms of foregone opportunities to apply the same resources to social goals other than that of ensuring equitable access.

Furthermore, a reasonable specification of adequate care must reflect an assessment of the relative importance of many different characteristics of a given form of care for a particular condition. Sometimes the problem is posed as: What *amounts* of care and what *quality* of care? Such a formulation reduces a complex problem to only two dimensions, implying that all care can readily be ranked as better or worse. Because two alternative forms of care may vary along a number of dimensions, there may be no consensus among reasonable and informed individuals about which form is of higher overall quality. It is worth bearing in mind that adequacy does not mean the highest possible level of quality or strictly equal quality any more than it requires equal amounts of care; of course, adequacy does require that everyone receive care that meets standards of sound medical practice.

Any combination of arrangements for achieving adequacy will presumably include some health care delivery settings that mainly serve certain groups, such as the poor or those covered by public programs. The fact that patients receive care in different settings or from different providers does not itself show that some are receiving inadequate care. The Commission believes that there is no moral objection to such a system so long as all receive care that is adequate in amount and quality and all patients are treated with concern and respect. . . .

NOTE

1. Office of Technology Assessment, U.S. Congress, *The Implications of Cost-Effectiveness Analysis of Medical Technology. Summary,* U.S. Government Printing Office, Washington (1980) p. 8.

R O B E R T   M .   V E A T C H

Justice, the Basic Social Contract, and Health Care

The principle that each person's welfare should count equally is crucial if the community generated is to be a moral community. The moral community is one of impartiality. If the community employed an impartial perspective to draw up the basic principles or practices for the society, the principles would be generated without reference to individual talents, skills, abilities, or good fortune. Another way of formulating this condition is to say that the basic principles or practices established must meet the test of reversibility. That is, they must be acceptable to one standing on either the giving or the receiving end of a transaction.[1] The general notion is that the contractors must take equal account of all persons. It is only by such an abandonment of an egoistic perspective that common social intercourse is possible. As Plato wrote in Book I of the Republic, "the unjust are incapable of common action . . . and [the] utterly unjust, they would have been utterly incapable of action."

The most intriguing contractual theory of ethics that makes this commitment to impartiality or reversibility is that espoused by John Rawls.[2] In his version of social contract theory, Rawls asks us to envision ourselves in what he calls the original position. He does not pretend that such a position exists or ever could exist. Rather, it is a device for making "vivid to ourselves the restrictions that it seems reasonable to impose on arguments for principles of justice, and therefore on these principles themselves."[3]

From *A Theory of Medical Ethics,* © 1981. Reprinted by permission of the Kennedy Institute of Ethics.

The restrictions on the original position are that no one should be advantaged or disadvantaged in the choice of principles either by natural fortune or social circumstances. Persons in the original position are equal. To help us imagine such a situation, he asks us to impose what he calls a "veil of ignorance," under which "no one knows his place in society, his class position or social status, nor does any one know his fortune in the distribution of natural assets and abilities, his intelligence, strength, and the like."[4]

From that position one can derive impartially a set of principles or practices that provide the moral foundations for a society. Even if we cannot discover a universal basis for ethical decisions, perhaps we can create a community that accepts rules such as respect for freedom and the impartial consideration of interests; that is, one that adopts the moral point of view and thereby provides a common foundation for deciding what is ethical. Those who take this view believe it possible to generate some commonly agreed upon principles or practices for a society. The creation of a contractual framework could then provide a basis for making medical ethical decisions that would be commonly recognized as legitimate. . . .

There is . . . a moral community constituted symbolically by the metaphor of the contract or covenant. There is a convergence between the vision of people coming together to discover a preexisting moral order — an order that takes equally into account the welfare of all — and the vision of people coming together to invent a moral order that as well takes equally into account the welfare of all. The members of the moral community thus generated are bound together by bonds of mutual loyalty and trust. There is a fundamental equality and reciprocity in the relationship, something missing in the philanthropic condescension of professional code ethics. . . .

THE MAXIMIN THEORY

Some say that reasonable people considering alternative policies or principles for a society would not opt to maximize the aggregate benefits that exist in the society. Rather, they say that at least for basic social practices that determine the welfare of members of the moral community, they would opt for a strategy that attempts to assure fundamentally that the least well off person would do as well as possible. . . .

The implication is that those having the greatest burden have some claim on the society independent of whether responding to their needs is the most efficient way of producing the greatest net aggregate benefit. Holders of this view say that the commitment of a principle of justice is to maximize not net aggregate benefit, but the position of the least advantaged members of the society. If the principle of justice is a right-making characteristic of actions, a principle that reasonable people would accept as part of the basic social contract independent of the principle of beneficence, it probably incorporated some moral notion that the distribution of benefits and burdens counts as well as the aggregate amount of them. One plausible alternative is to concentrate, insofar as we are concerned about justice, on the welfare of the least well off. This is part of those principles of justice defended by Rawls as derived from his version of social contract theory. . . .

Since Rawls's scheme is designed to provide insights into only the basic practices and social institutions, it is very hard to discern what the implications are for specific problems of resource distribution such as the allocation of health care resources. Some have argued that no direct implications can be read from the Rawlsian principles. That seems, however, to overstate the case. At the least, basic social practices and institutional arrangements must be subject to the test of the principles of justice.

It appears, then, that this view will not justify inequalities in the basic health care institutions and practices simply because they produce the greatest net aggregate benefit. Its notion of justice, concentrating on improving the lot of the least advantaged, is much more egalitarian in this sense than the utilitarian system. It would distribute health care resources to the least well off rather than just on the aggregate amount of benefit.

There is no obvious reason why our hypothetical contractors articulating the basic principles for a society would favor a principle that maximized aggregate utility any more than one that maximized minimum utility. Our contract model, as an epistemological device for discovering the basic principles, views them, after all, as committed to the moral point of view, as evaluating equally the welfare of each individual from a veil of ignorance, to use the Rawlsian language. This perspective retains the notion of individuals as identifiable, unique personalities, as noncommensurable human beings, rather than simply as components of an aggregate mass. Faced with a forced choice, it seems plausible that one would opt for maximizing the welfare of individuals, especially the least well-off individuals, rather than maximizing the aggregate.

Nevertheless, the interpretation of justice that attempts to maximize the minimum position in the society (and is hence sometimes called the "maximin" position), still permits inequalities and even labels them as just. What, for example, of basic health care institutional arrangements that systematically single out elites with unique natural talents for developing medical skill and services and gives these individuals high salaries as incentives to serve the interests of the least well off? What if a special health care system were institutionalized to make sure these people were always in the best of health, were cared for first in catastrophies, and were inconvenienced least by the normal bureaucratic nuisances of a health care system?

It is conceivable that such an institutional arrangement would be favored by reasonable people taking the moral point of view. They could justify the special gains that would come to the elites by the improved chances thus created for the rest of the population (who would not have as great a gain as the favored ones, but would at least be better off than if the elite were not so favored). The benefits, in lesser amounts, would trickle down in this plan to the consumers of health care so that all, or at least the least advantaged, would gain. The gap between the elite of the health profession and the masses could potentially increase by such a social arrangement, but at least all would be better off in absolute terms.

So it is conceivable that reasonable people considering equally both the health professionals and the masses would favor such an arrangement, but it is not obvious. Critics of the Rawlsian principles of justice say that in some cases alternative principles of distribution would be preferred. Brian Barry, for example, argues that rational choosers would look not just at the welfare of the least advantaged, but also at the average or aggregate welfare of alternative policies.[5] On the other hand, Barry and many others suggest that in some circumstances, rational choosers might opt for the principle that would maximize equality of outcome.[6] At most, considering the institutionalization of advantages for a health care elite, they would be supported as a prudent sacrifice of the demands of justice in order to serve some other justifiable moral end.

From this perspective, favoring elites with special monetary and social incentives in order to benefit the poor might be a prudent compromise.[7] It might mediate between the demands that see justice as requiring equality of outcome (subject to numerous qualifications) and the demands of the principle of beneficence requiring maximum efficiency in producing good consequences. If that is the case, though, then there is still a fourth interpretation of the principle of justice that must be considered, one that is more radically egalitarian than the maximin strategy.

THE EGALITARIAN THEORY

Those who see the maximin strategy as a compromise between the concern for justice and the concern for efficient production of good consequences must feel that justice requires a stricter focus on equality than the maximin understanding of the principle of justice. The maximin principle is concerned about the distribution of benefits. It justifies inequalities only if they benefit the least well off. But it does justify inequalities — and it does so in the name of justice.

Rawls recognizes that there is an important difference between a right action and a just or a fair action. Fairness is a principle applying to individuals along with beneficence, noninjury, mutual respect, and fidelity. The list is not far removed from the basic principles I have identified. But, given this important difference between what is right in this full, inclusive sense and what is fair, if one is convinced that incentives and advantages for medical elites are justified, why would one claim that the justification is one based on the principle of fairness? One might instead maintain that they are right on balance because they are a necessary compromise with the principle of fairness (or justice) in order to promote efficiently the welfare of a disadvantaged group. It is to be assumed, given the range of basic principles in an ethical system, that conflicts will often emerge so that one principle will be sacrificed, upon occasion, for the sake of another.

The egalitarian understanding of the principle of justice is one that sees justice as requiring (subject to certain important qualifications) equality of net welfare for individuals.[8] . . .

Everyone, according to the principle of egalitarian justice, ought to end up over a lifetime with an equal amount of net welfare (or, as we shall see shortly, a chance for that welfare). Some may have a great deal of benefit offset by large amounts of unhappiness or disutility, while others will have relatively less of both. What we would call "just" under this principle is a basic social practice or policy that contributes to the same extent to greater equality of outcome (subject to restrictions to be discussed). I am suggesting that reasonable people who are committed to a contract model for discovering, inventing, or otherwise articulating the basic principles will want to add to their list the notion that one of the right-making characteristics of a society would be the equality of welfare among the members of the moral community.

THE EQUALITY OF PERSONS

The choice of this interpretation of the principle of justice will depend upon how the contractors understand the commitment to the moral point of view — the commitment to impartiality that takes the point of view of all equally into account. We certainly are not asserting the equality of ability or even the equality of the merit of individual claims. . . .

If this is what is meant by the moral point of view, taking into account equally the individuality of each member of the community, then in addition to the right-making characteristics or principles of beneficence, promise keeping, autonomy, truth telling, and avoiding killing, the principle of justice as equality of net welfare must be added to the list. The principle might be articulated as affirming that people have a claim on having the total net welfare in their lives equal insofar as possible to the welfare in the lives of others.

Of course, no reasonable person, even an egalitarian, is going to insist upon or even desire that all the features of people's lives be identical.[9] It seems obvious that the most that anyone would want is that the total net welfare for each person be comparable. . . .

If this egalitarian understanding of the principle of justice would be acceptable to reasonable people taking the moral point of view, it provides a solution to the dilemma of the tension between focusing exclusively on the patient and opening the doors to considerations of social consequences such as in classical utilitarianism. The principle of justice provides another basis for taking into account a limited set of impacts on certain other parties. If the distribution of benefits as well as the aggregate amount is morally relevant, then certain impacts on other parties may be morally more relevant than others. A benefit that accrues to a person who is or predictably will be in a least well-off group would count as a consideration of justice while a benefit of equal size that accrued to other persons not in the least well-off group would not. The hypothetical benefits of a Nazi-type experiment would not accrue to a least well-off group (while the harms of the experiment presumably would). They are thus morally different from, in fact diametrically opposed to, a redistribution scheme that produced benefits for only the least advantaged group.

EQUALITY AND ENVY

Critics of the egalitarian view of justice have argued that the only way to account for such a position is by attributing it to a psychology of envy.[10] Freud accounted for a sense of justice in this way.[11] They feel the only conceivable reason to strive for equality is the psychological explanation that the less well off envy the better off, and they hold that contractors take that psychological fact into account. Since they believe that envy is not an adequate justification for a commitment to equal outcome, they opt instead for an alternative theory of justice. . . .

The egalitarian holds that there is something fundamentally wrong with gross inequalities, with gross differences in net welfare. The problem is encountered when people of unequal means must interact, say, when representatives of an impoverished community apply to an elite foundation for funds to support a neighborhood health program. There is no way that real communication can take place between the elites of the foundation and the members of the low-income community. It is not simply that the poor envy the foundation executives or that the executives feel resentful of the poor. Rather, as anyone who has been in such a relationship knows, the sense of community is fractured. Not only do the less well off feel that they cannot express themselves with self-respect, but the elites realize that there is no way the messages they receive can be disentangled from the status and welfare differentials. Neither can engage in any true interaction. A moral relationship is virtually impossible. . . .

THE IMPLICATIONS OF THE EGALITARIAN FORMULA

It turns out that incorporating health care into this system of total welfare will be extremely difficult. Let us begin, temporarily, therefore, by considering a simpler system dealing only with food, clothing, and shelter. Fairness could mean, according to the egalitarian formula, that each person had to have an equal amount of each of these. No reasonable person, however, would find that necessary or attractive. Rather, what the egalitarian has in mind with his concept of justice is that the net of welfare, summed across all three of these goods, be as similar as possible. We could arbitrarily fix the amount of resources in each category, but nothing seems wrong with permitting people to trade some food for clothing, or clothing for shelter. If one person preferred a large house and minimal food and could find someone with the opposite tastes, nothing seems wrong with permitting a trade. The assumption is that the need of people for food, clothing, and shelter is about the same in everybody and that marginal utilities in the trades will be about the same. If so, then permitting people to trade around would increase the welfare of each person without radically distorting the equality of net overall welfare. Up to this point, then, the egalitarian principle of justice says that it is just (though not necessarily right) to strive in social practices for equality of net welfare. . . .

For health care and education, however, the situation is much different. Here it is reasonable to assume that human needs vary enormously. Nothing could be more foolish than to distribute health care or even the money for health care equally. The result would be unequal overall well-being for those who were unfortunate in the natural lottery for health, objectively much worse off than others. If the goal of justice is to produce a chance for equal, objective net welfare, then the starting point for consideration of health care distribution should be the need for it. Education (or the resources to buy education) initially would be distributed in the same way. The amount added to the resources for food, clothing, and shelter should then be in proportion to an "unhealthiness status index" plus another amount proportional to an "educational needs index."

However, that proposal raises two additional questions: Should people be permitted to use the resources set aside for health care in some other way? And who should bear the responsibility if people have an opportunity to be healthy and do not take advantage of it?

THE CASE FOR AN EQUAL RIGHT TO HEALTH CARE

Even for the egalitarian it is not obvious why society ought to strive for an equal right to health care. Certainly it ought not to be interested in obtaining the same amount of health care for everyone. To do so would require forcing those in need of great amounts of care to go without or those who have the good fortune to be healthy to consume uselessly. But it is not even obvious that we should end up with a right to health care equal in proportion to need, though that is the conclusion that many, especially egalitarians, are reaching. . . .

Is there any reason to believe that health care is any more basic than, say, food or protection from the ele-

ments? All are absolutely essential to human survival, at least up to some minimum for subsistence. All are necessary conditions for the exercise of liberty, self-respect, or any other functioning as part of the human moral community. Furthermore, while the bare minimum of health care is as necessary as food and shelter, in all cases these may not really be "necessities" at the margin. If trades are to be tolerated between marginal food and clothing, is there any reason why someone placing relatively low value on health care should not be permitted to trade, say, his annual checkups for someone else's monthly allotment of steak dinners? Or, if we shall make trading easier by distributing money fairly rather than distributing rations of these specific goods, is there any reason why, based on an "unhealthiness index," we could not distribute a fair portion of funds for health care as well as for other necessities? Individuals could then buy the health care (or health care insurance) that they need, employing individual discretion about where their limit for health care is in comparison with steak dinners. Those at a high health risk would be charged high amounts for health care (or high premiums for insurance), but those costs would be exactly offset by the money supplement based on the index.

Perhaps we cannot make a case for equal access to health care on the basis that it is more fundamental than other goods. There may still be reasons, though, why reasonable people would structure the basic institutions of society to provide a right to equal health care in the sense I am using the term, that is a right equal in proportion to need.

Our response will depend somewhat upon whether we are planning a health care distribution for a just world or one with the present inequities in the distribution of net welfare. . . .

But obviously we do not live in a perfectly just world. The problem becomes more complex. How do we arrange the health care system, which all would agree is fundamental to human well-being at least at some basic level, in order to get as close as possible to equality of welfare as the outcome? Pragmatic considerations may, at this point, override the abstract, theoretical argument allowing trades of health care for other goods even at the margin.

Often defenders of free-market and partial free-market solutions to the allocation of health care resources assume that if fixed in-kind services such as health care are not distributed, money will be. . . .

There is a more subtle case for an equal right to health care (in proportion to need) in an unfair world. Bargaining strengths are likely to be very unequal in a world where resources are distributed unfairly. Those with great resources, perhaps because of natural talents or naturally occurring good health or both, are in an invincible position. The needy, for example those with little earning power because of congenital health problems, may be forced to use what resources they have in order to buy immediate necessities, withholding on health care investment; particularly preventive health care and health insurance, while gambling that they will be able to survive without those services.

It is not clear what our moral response should be to those forced into this position of bargainers from weakness. If the just principle of distribution were Pareto optimality (where bargains were acceptable, regardless of the weaknesses of the parties, provided all gained in the transaction), we would accept the fact that some would bargain from weakness and be forced to trade their long-term health care needs for short-term necessities. If the principle of justice that reasonable people would accept taking the moral point of view, however, is something like the maximin position or the egalitarian position, then perhaps such trades of health care should be prohibited. The answer will depend on how one should behave in planning social policies in an unjust world. The fact that resources are not distributed fairly generates pressures on the least well off (assuming they act rationally) to make choices they would not have to make in a more fair world. If unfairness in the general distribution of resources is a given, we are forced into a choice between two unattractive options: We could opt for the rule that will permit the least well off to maximize their position under the existing conditions or we could pick the rule that would arrange resources as closely as possible to the way they would be arranged in a just world. In our present, unjust society distributing health care equally is a closer approximation to the way it would be distributed in a just society than giving a general resource like money or permitting trades. . . .

I see justice not just as a way to efficiently improve the lot of the least well off by permitting them trades (even though those trades end up increasing the gap between the haves and the have-nots). That might be efficient and might preserve autonomy, but it would not be justice. If I were an original contractor I would cast my vote in favor of the egalitarian principle of justice, applying it so that there would be a right to health care equal in proportion to health care need. The principle of justice for health care could, then, be stated as follows: People have a right to needed health care to provide an opportunity for a level of health equal as far as possible to the health of other people.

The principle of justice for health care is a pragmatic derivative from the general principle of justice requiring equality of objective net welfare. The result would be a uniform health care system with one class of service available for all. Practical problems would still exist, especially at the margins. The principle, for example, does not establish what percentage of total resources would go for health care. The goal would be to arrange resources so that health care needs would, in general, be met about as well as other needs. This means that a society would rather arbitrarily set some fixed amount of the total resources for health care. Every nation currently spends somewhere between five and ten percent of its gross national product (GNP) in this area, with the wealthier societies opting for the higher percentages. Presumably the arbitrary choice would fall in that range.

With such a budget fixed, reasonable people will come together to decide what health care services can be covered under it. The task will not be as great as it seems. The vast majority of services will easily be sorted into or out of the health care system. Only a small percentage at the margin will be the cause of any real debate. The choice will at times be arbitrary, but the standard applied will at least be clear. People should have services necessary to give them a chance to be as close as possible to being as healthy as other people. Those choices will be made while striving to emulate the position of original contractors taking the moral point of view. The decision-making panels will not differ in task greatly from the decision makers who currently sort health care services in and out of insurance coverage lists. However, panels will be committed to a principle of justice and will take the moral point of view, whereas the self-interested insurers try to maximize profits or efficiency or a bargaining position against weak, unorganized consumers.

NOTES

1. Kurt Baier, *The Moral Point of View:* A Rational Basis of Ethics (New York: Random House, 1965), p. 108.

2. John Rawls, *A Theory of Justice* (Cambridge, Mass.: Harvard University Press, 1971).

3. Ibid., p. 18.

4. Ibid., p. 12; cf. pp. 136–42.

5. Brian Barry, *The Liberal Theory of Justice: A Critical Examination of the Principal Doctrines in "A Theory of Justice" by John Rawls* (Oxford: Clarendon Press, 1973), p. 109; see also Robert L. Cunningham, "Justice: Efficiency or Fairness?" *Personalist* 52 (Spring 1971):253–81.

6. Barry, *The Liberal Theory;* idem. "Reflections on 'Justice as Fairness,'" in *Justice and Equality,* ed. H. Bedau (Englewood Cliffs, N.J.: Prentice-Hall, 1971), pp. 103–115; Bernard Williams, "The Idea of Equality," reprinted in Bedau, *Justice and Equality,* pp. 116–137; Christopher Ake, "Justice as Equality," *Philosophy and Public Affairs* 5 (Fall 1975):69–89; Robert M. Veatch, "What Is 'Just' Health Care Delivery?" in *Ethics and Health Policy,* ed. R. M. Veatch and R. Branson (Cambridge, Mass.: Ballinger, 1976), pp. 127–153.

7. Barry, "Reflections," p. 113.

8. See Ake, "Justice as Equality," for a careful development of the notion.

9. Hugo A. Bedau, "Radical Egalitarianism," in *Justice and Equality,* ed. H. A. Bedau, p. 168.

10. Rawls, *A Theory of Justice,* p. 538, note 9.

11. Sigmund Freud, *Group Psychology and the Analysis of the Ego,* rev. ed., trans. James Strachey (London: Hogarth Press, 1959), pp. 51f. (as cited in Rawls, *A Theory of Justice,* p. 439).

ALLEN E. BUCHANAN

The Right to a Decent Minimum of Health Care

THE ASSUMPTION THAT THERE IS A RIGHT TO A DECENT MINIMUM

A consensus that there is (at least) a right to a decent minimum of health care pervades recent policy debates and much of the philosophical literature on health care. Disagreement centers on two issues. Is there a more extensive right than the right to a decent minimum of health care? What is included in the decent minimum to which there is a right?

PRELIMINARY CLARIFICATION OF THE CONCEPT

Different theories of distributive justice may yield different answers both to the question 'Is there a right to a decent minimum?' and to the question 'What comprises the decent minimum?' The justification a particular theory provides for the claim that there is a right to a decent minimum must at least cohere with the justifications it provides for other right-claims. Moreover, the character of this justification will determine, at least in part, the way in which the decent minimum is specified, since it will include an account of the nature and significance of health-care needs. To the extent that the concept of a decent minimum is theory-dependent, then, it would be naive to assume that a mere analysis of the concept of a decent minimum would tell us whether there is such a right and what its content is. Nonetheless, before we proceed to an examination of various theoretical attempts to ground and specify a right to a decent minimum, a preliminary analysis will be helpful.

Sometimes the notion of a decent minimum is applied not to health care but to health itself, the claim being that everyone is entitled to some minimal level, or welfare floor, of health. I shall not explore this variant of the decent minimum idea because I think its implausibility is obvious. The main difficulty is that assuring any significant level of health for all is simply not within the domain of social control. If the alleged right is understood instead as the right to everything which can be done to achieve some significant level of health for all, then the claim that there is such a right becomes implausible simply because it ignores the fact that in circumstances of scarcity the total social expenditure on health must be constrained by the need to allocate resources for other goods.

Though the concept of a right is complex and controversial, for our purposes a partial sketch will do. To

From President's Commission, *Securing Access to Health Care,* Vol. II. Washington, D.C. U.S. Government Printing Office, 1983.

say that person A has a right to something, X, is first of all to say that A is entitled to X, that X is due to him or her. This is not equivalent to saying that if A were granted X it would be a good thing, even a morally good thing, or that X is desired by or desirable for A. Second, it is usually held that valid right-claims, at least in the case of basic rights, may be backed by sanctions, including coercion if necessary (unless doing so would produce extremely great disutility or grave moral evil), and that (except in such highly exceptional circumstances) failure of an appropriate authority to apply the needed sanctions is itself an injustice. Recent rights-theorists have also emphasized a third feature of rights, or at least of basic rights or rights in the strict sense: valid right-claims 'trump' appeals to what would maximize utility, whether it be the utility of the right-holder, or social utility. In other words, if A has a right to X, then the mere fact that infringing A's right would maximize overall utility or even A's utility is not itself a sufficient reason for infringing it.[1] Finally, a universal (or general) right is one which applies to all persons, not just to certain individuals or classes because of their involvement in special actions, relationships, or agreements.

The second feature — enforceability — is of crucial importance for those who assume or argue that there is a universal right to a decent minimum of health care. For, once it is granted that there is such a right and that such a right may be enforced (absent any extremely weighty reason against enforcement), the claim that there is a universal right provides the moral basis for using the coercive power of the state to assure a decent minimum for all. Indeed, the surprising absence of attempts to justify a coercively backed decent minimum policy by arguments that do *not* aim at establishing a universal right suggests the following hypothesis: advocates of a coercively backed decent minimum have operated on the assumption that such a policy must be based on a universal right to a decent minimum. The chief aim of this article is to show that this assumption is false.

I think it is fair to say that many who confidently assume there is a (universal) right to a decent minimum of health care have failed to appreciate the significance of the first feature of our sketch of the concept of a right. It is crucial to observe that the claim that there is a right to a decent minimum is much stronger than the claim that everyone *ought* to have access to such a minimum, or that if they did it would be a good thing, or that any society which is capable, without great sacrifice, of providing a decent minimum but fails to do so is deeply morally defective. None of the latter assertions implies the existence of a right, if this is understood as a moral entitlement which ought to be established by the coercive power of the state if necessary. . . .

THE ATTRACTIONS OF THE IDEA OF A DECENT MINIMUM

There are at least three features widely associated with the idea of a right to a decent minimum which, together with the facile consensus that vagueness promotes, help explain its popularity over competing conceptions of the right to health care. First, it is usually, and quite reasonably, assumed that the idea of a decent minimum is to be understood in a society-relative sense. Surely it is plausible to assume that, as with other rights to goods or services, the content of the right must depend upon the resources available in a given society and perhaps also upon a certain consensus of expectations among its members. So the first advantage of the idea of a decent minimum, as it is usually understood, is that it allows us to adjust the level of services to be provided as a matter of right to relevant social conditions and also allows for the possibility that as a society becomes more affluent the floor provided by the decent minimum should be raised.

Second, the idea of a decent minimum avoids the excesses of what has been called the strong equal access principle, while still acknowledging a substantive universal right. According to the strong equal access principle, everyone has an equal right to the best health-care services available. Aside from the weakness of the justifications offered in support of it, the most implausible feature of the strong equal access principle is that it forces us to choose between two unpalatable alternatives. We can either set the publicly guaranteed level of health care lower than the level that is technically possible or we can set it as high as is technically possible. In the former case, we shall be committed to the uncomfortable conclusion that no matter how many resources have been expended to guarantee equal access to that level, individuals are forbidden to spend any of their resources for services not available to all. Granted that individuals are allowed to spend their after-tax incomes on more frivolous items, why shouldn't they be allowed to spend it on health? If the answer is that they should be so allowed, as long as this does not interfere with the provision of an adequate package of health-care services for everyone, then we have retreated from the strong equal access principle to something very like the principle of a decent minimum. If, on the other hand, we set the level of services guaranteed for all so high as to eliminate the problem of persons seeking extra care beyond this level, this would produce a huge drain on total resources, foreclosing opportunities for producing important goods other than health care.

So both the recognition that health care must compete with other goods and the conviction that beyond some less than maximal level of publicly guaranteed services individuals should be free to purchase additional services point toward a more limited right than the strong access principle asserts. Thus, the endorsement of a right to a decent minimum may be more of a recognition of the implausibility of the stronger right to equal access than a sign of any definite position on the content of the right to health care.

A third attraction of the idea of a decent minimum is that since the right to health care must be limited in scope (to avoid the consequences of a strong equal access right), it should be limited to the 'most basic' services, those normally 'adequate' for health, or for a 'decent' or 'tolerable' life. However, although this aspect of the idea of a decent minimum is useful because it calls attention to the fact that health-care needs are heterogeneous and must be assigned some order of priority, it does not itself provide any basis for determining which are most important.

THE NEED FOR A SUPPORTING THEORY

In spite of these attractions, the concept of a right to a decent minimum of health care is inadequate as a moral basis for a coercively backed decent minimum policy in the absence of a coherent and defensible theory of justice. Indeed, when taken together they do not even imply that there is a right to a decent minimum. Rather, they only support the weaker conditional claim that if there is a right to health care, then it is one that is more limited than a right of strong equal access, and is one whose content depends upon available resources and some scheme of priorities which shows certain health services to be more basic than others. It appears, then, that a theoretical grounding for the right to a decent minimum of health care is indispensable. . . .

My suggestion is that the combined weight of arguments from special (as opposed to universal) rights to health care, harm-prevention, prudential arguments of the sort used to justify public health measures, and two arguments that show that effective charity shares features of public goods (in the technical sense) is sufficient to do the work of an alleged universal right to a decent minimum of health care.

ARGUMENTS FROM SPECIAL RIGHTS

The right-claim we have been examining (and find unsupported) has been a *universal* right-claim: one that attributes the same right to all persons. *Special* right-claims, in contrast, restrict the right in question to certain individuals or groups.

There are at least three types of arguments that can be given for special rights to health care. First, there are arguments from the requirements of rectifying past or present institutional injustices. It can be argued, for example, that American blacks and native Americans are entitled to a certain core set of health-care services owing to their history of unjust treatment by government or other social institutions, on the grounds that these injustices have directly or indirectly had detrimental effects on the health of the groups in question. Second, there are arguments from the requirements of compensation to those who have suffered unjust harm or who have been unjustly exposed to health risks by the assignable actions of private individuals or corporations—for instance, those who have suffered neurological damage from the effects of chemical pollutants.

Third, a strong moral case can be made for special rights to health care for those who have undergone exceptional sacrifices for the good of society as a whole—in particular those whose health has been adversely affected through military service. The most obvious candidates for such compensatory special rights are soldiers wounded in combat.

ARGUMENTS FROM THE PREVENTION OF HARM

The content of the right to a decent minimum is typically understood as being more extensive than those traditional public health services that are usually justified on the grounds that they are required to protect the citizenry from certain harms arising from the interactions of persons living together in large numbers. Yet such services have been a major factor—if not *the* major factor—in reducing morbidity and mortality rates. Examples include sanitation and immunization. The moral justification of such measures, which constitute an important element in a decent minimum of health care, rests upon the widely accepted Harm (Prevention) Principle, not upon a right to health care.

The Harm Prevention argument for traditional public health services, however, may be elaborated in a way that brings them closer to arguments for a universal right to health care. With some plausibility one might contend that once the case has been made for expending public resources on public health measures, there is a moral (and perhaps Constitutional) obligation to achieve some standard of *equal protection* from the harms these measures are designed to prevent. Such an argument, if it could be made out, would imply that the availability of basic public health services should not vary greatly across different racial, ethnic, or geographic groups within the country.

PRUDENTIAL ARGUMENTS

Prudent arguments for health-care services typically emphasize benefits rather than the prevention of harm. It has often been argued, in particular, that the availability of certain basic forms of health care make for a more productive labor force or improve the fitness of the citizenry for national defense. This type of argument, too, does not assume that individuals have moral rights (whether special or universal) to the services in question.

It seems very likely that the combined scope of the various special health-care rights discussed above, when taken together with harm prevention and prudential arguments for basic health services and an argument from equal protection through public health measures, would do a great deal toward satisfying the health-care needs which those who advocate a universal right to a decent minimum are most concerned about. In other words, once the strength of a more pluralistic approach is appreciated, we may come to question the popular dogma that policy initiatives designed to achieve a decent minimum of health care for all must be grounded in a universal moral right to a decent minimum. This suggestion is worth considering because it again brings home the importance of the methodological difficulty encountered earlier. Even if, for instance, there is wide consensus on the

considered judgment that the lower health prospects of inner city blacks are not only morally unacceptable but an injustice, it does not follow that this injustice consists of the infringement of a universal right to a decent minimum of health care. Instead, the injustice might lie in the failure to rectify past injustices or in the failure to achieve public health arrangements that meet a reasonable standard of equal protection for all.

TWO ARGUMENTS FOR ENFORCED BENEFICENCE

The pluralistic moral case for a legal entitlement to a decent minimum of health care (in the absence of a universal moral right) may be strengthened further by non-rights-based arguments from the principle of beneficence.[2] The possibility of making out such arguments depends upon the assumption that some principles may be justifiably enforced even if they are not principles specifying valid right-claims. There is at least one widely recognized class of such principles requiring contribution to the production of 'public goods' in the technical sense (for example, tax laws requiring contribution to national defense). It is characteristic of public goods that each individual has an incentive to withhold his contribution to the collective goal even though the net result is that the goal will not be achieved. Enforcement of a principle requiring all individuals to contribute to the goal is necessary to overcome the individual's incentive to withhold contribution by imposing penalties for his own failure to contribute and by assuring him that others will contribute. There is a special subclass of principles whose enforcement is justified not only by the need to overcome the individual's incentive to withhold compliance with the principle but also to ensure that individuals' efforts are appropriately *coordinated*. For example, enforcing the rule of the road to drive only on the right not only ensures a joint effort toward the goal of safe driving but also coordinates individuals' efforts so as to make the attainment of that goal possible. Indeed, in the case of the 'rule of the road' a certain kind of coordinated joint effort is the public good whose attainment justifies enforcement. But regardless of whether the production of a public good requires the solution of a coordination problem or not, there may be no *right* that is the correlative of the coercively backed obligation specified by the principle. There are two arguments for enforced beneficence, and they each depend upon both the idea of coordination and on certain aspects of the concept of a public good.

Both arguments begin with an assumption reasonable libertarians accept: there is a basic moral obligation of charity or beneficence to those in need. In a society that has the resources and technical knowledge to improve health or at least to ameliorate important health defects, the application of this requirement of beneficence includes the provision of resources for at least certain forms of health care. If we are sincere, we will be concerned with the efficacy of our charitable or beneficent impulses. It is all well and good for the libertarian to say that voluntary giving *can* replace the existing array of government entitlement programs, but this *possibility* will be cold comfort to the needy if, for any of several reasons, voluntary giving falters.

Social critics on the left often argue that in a highly competitive acquisitive society such as ours it is naive to think that the sense of beneficence will win out over the urgent promptings of self-interest. One need not argue, however, that voluntary giving fails from weakness of the will. Instead one can argue that even if each individual recognizes a moral duty to contribute to the aid of others and is motivationally capable of acting on that duty, some important forms of beneficence will not be forthcoming because each individual will rationally conclude that he should not contribute.

Many important forms of health care, especially those involving large-scale capital investment for technology, cannot be provided except through the contributions of large numbers of persons. This is also true of the most important forms of medical research. But if so, then the beneficent individual will not be able to act effectively, in isolation. What is needed is a coordinated joint effort.

First argument. There are many ways in which I might help others in need. Granted the importance of health, providing a decent minimum of health care for all, through large-scale collective efforts, will be a more important form of beneficence than the various charitable acts A, B, and C, which I might perform *independently,* that is, whose success does not depend upon the contributions of others. Nonetheless, if I am rationally beneficent I will reason as follows: either enough others will contribute to the decent minimum project to achieve this goal, even if I do not contribute to it; or not enough others will contribute to achieve a decent minimum, even if I do contribute. In either case, my contribution will be wasted. In other words, granted the scale of the investment required and the

virtually negligible size of my own contribution, I can disregard the minute possibility that my contribution might make the difference between success and failure. But if so, then the rationally beneficent thing for me to do is not to waste my contribution on the project of ensuring a decent minimum but instead to undertake an independent act of beneficence; A, B, or C — where I know my efforts will be needed and efficacious. But if everyone, or even many people, reason in this way, then what we each recognize as the most effective form of beneficence will not come about. Enforcement of a principle requiring contributions to ensuring a decent minimum is needed.

The first argument is of the same form as standard public goods arguments for enforced contributions to national defense, energy conservation, and many other goods, with this exception. In standard public goods arguments, it is usually assumed that the individual's incentive for not contributing is self-interest and that it is in his interest not to contribute because he will be able to partake of the good, if it is produced, even if he does not contribute. In the case at hand, however, the individual's incentive for not contributing to the joint effort is not self-interest, but rather his desire to maximize the good he can do for others with a given amount of his resources. Thus if he contributes but the goal of achieving a decent minimum for all would have been achieved without his contribution, then he has still failed to use his resources in a maximally beneficent way relative to the options of either contributing or not to the joint project, even though the goal of achieving a decent minimum is attained. The rationally beneficent thing to do, then, is not to contribute, even though the result of everyone's acting in a rationally beneficent way will be a relatively ineffective patchwork of small-scale individual acts of beneficence rather than a large-scale, coordinated effort.

Second argument. I believe that ensuring a decent minimum of health care for all is more important than projects A, B, or C, and I am willing to contribute to the decent minimum project, but only if I have assurance that enough others will contribute to achieve the threshold of investment necessary for success. Unless I have this assurance, I will conclude that it is less than rational — and perhaps even morally irresponsible — to contribute my resources to the decent minimum project. For my contribution will be wasted if not enough others contribute. If I lack assurance of sufficient contributions by others, the rationally beneficent thing for me to do is to expend my 'beneficence budget' on some less-than-optimal project A, B, or C, whose success does not depend on the contribution of others. But without enforcement, I cannot be assured that enough others will contribute, and if others reason as I do, then what we all believe to be the most effective form of beneficence will not be forthcoming. Others may fail to contribute either because the promptings of self-interest overpower their sense of beneficence, or because they reason as I did in the First Argument, or for some other reason.

Both arguments conclude that an enforced decent minimum principle is needed to achieve coordinated joint effort. However, there is this difference. The Second Argument focuses on the *assurance problem,* while the first does not. In the Second Argument all that is needed is the assumption that rational beneficence requires assurance that enough others will contribute. In the First Argument the individual's reason for not contributing is not that he lacks assurance that enough others will contribute, but rather that it is better for him not to contribute regardless of whether others do or not.

Neither argument depends on an assumption of conflict between the individual's moral motivation of beneficence and his inclination of self-interest. Instead the difficulty is that in the absence of enforcement, individuals who strive to make their beneficence most effective will thereby fail to benefit the needy as much as they might.

A standard response to those paradoxes of rationality known as public goods problems is to introduce a coercive mechanism which attaches penalties to noncontribution and thereby provides each individual with the assurance that enough others will reciprocate so that his contribution will not be wasted and an effective incentive for him to contribute even if he has reason to believe that enough others will contribute to achieve the goal without his contribution. My suggestion is that the same type of argument that is widely accepted as a justification for enforced principles requiring contributions toward familiar public goods provides support for a coercively backed principle specifying a certain list of health programs for the needy and requiring those who possess the needed resources to contribute to the establishment of such programs, even if the needy have no *right* to the services those programs provide. Such an arrangement would serve a dual function: it would coordinate charitable efforts by focusing them on one set of services among the indefinitely large constellation of possible expressions of beneficence, and it would ensure that the decision to allocate resources to these services will become effective. . . .

NOTES

1. Ronald Dworkin, *Taking Rights Seriously* (Cambridge, MA: Harvard University Press, 1977), pp. 184–205.

2. For an exploration of various arguments for a duty of beneficence and an examination of the relationship between justice and beneficence, in general and in health care, see Allen E. Buchanan, "Philosophical Foundations of Beneficence," *Beneficence and Health Care,* ed. Earl E. Shelp (Dordrecht, Holland: Reidel Publishing Co., 1982).

H. TRISTRAM ENGELHARDT, JR.

Rights to Health Care

A basic human right to the delivery of health care, even to the delivery of a decent minimum of health care, does not exist. The difficulty with talking of such rights should be apparent. It is difficult if not impossible both to respect the freedom of all and to achieve their long-range best interests. Rights to health care constitute claims against others for either their services or their goods. Unlike rights to forbearance, which require others to refrain from interfering, rights to beneficence require others to participate actively in a particular understanding of the good life. Rights to health care, unless they are derived from special contractual agreements, depend on the principle of beneficence rather than that of autonomy, and therefore may conflict with the decisions of individuals who may not wish to participate in realizing a particular system of health care. If the resources involved in the provision of health care are not fully communal, private owners of resources may rightly have other uses in mind for their property than public care. . . . [T]he principles of autonomy and beneficence that lie at the foundations of justice will spawn conflicts within any portrayal of a just allocation of health care resources.

THE LIMITS TO JUSTICE AS BENEFICENCE

These fundamental conflicts between respecting the freedom and achieving the best interests of persons are made worse by commitments to goals that, if pursued without qualification, lead to even more elaborate tensions within any concrete vision of a just health care system. Consider the following four goals that are at loggerheads.

1. The provision of the best possible care for all
2. The provision of equal care for all

From *Foundations of Bioethics* by H. Tristram Engelhardt, Jr. Reprinted by permission of Oxford University Press, 1986.

3. Freedom of choice on the part of health care provider and consumer
4. Containment of health care costs

One cannot provide the best possible health care for all and contain the cost of health care. One cannot provide equal health care for all and maintain freedom in the choice of health care provider and consumer. For that matter, one cannot maintain freedom in the choice of health services while containing the costs of health care. One also may not be able to provide all with equal health care that is at the same time the very best care because of limits on the resources themselves. These tensions spring not only from a conflict between freedom and beneficence, but from competing views of what it means to pursue and achieve the good in health care (e.g., is it more important to provide equal care to all or the best possible care to the least well-off class?). . . .

JUSTICE AND INEQUALITY

Interests in justice as beneficence are sustained in part because of inequalities among persons. That some have so little while others have so much properly evokes moral concerns of beneficence to provide help for those in need. . . . [T]he moral authority to use force to set such inequalities aside is limited. These limitations are in part due to the fact that the resources one could use to aid those in need are often already owned by other people. One is forced to examine the very roots of inequality to determine whether such inequality and need constitute a claim against those in a position to aid.

THE NATURAL LOTTERY

Natural lottery is used here to identify changes in individual fortune that are the result of natural forces, not the actions of persons. It is not used to identify the distribution of natural assets. The natural lottery contrasts with the social lottery, which is used here to identify changes in individual fortune that are not the result of natural forces but the actions of persons. The social lottery is not used to identify the distribution of social assets. The natural and social lotteries together determine the distribution of natural and social assets. The social lottery is termed a lottery, though it is the outcome of personal actions, because of the complex interplay of personal choices. They are both aptly termed lotteries because of the unpredictable character of their outcomes, which do not conform to an ideal pattern.

All individuals are exposed to the brutal vicissitudes of nature. Some are born healthy and by chance remain so for a long life, free of disease and major suffering. Others are born with serious congenital or genetic diseases, others contract serious crippling fatal illnesses early in life, and yet others are injured and maimed. These natural forces, insofar as they occur outside of human responsibility, can be termed the natural lottery. They bring individuals to good health or disease through no merit or fault of their own or others. Those who win the natural lottery will not be in need of medical care. They will live extraordinarily full lives and die painless and peaceful deaths. Those who lose the natural lottery will be in need of health care to blunt their sufferings and, where possible, to cure their diseases and to restore function. There will be a spectrum of losses, ranging from minor problems such as having bad teeth to major tragedies such as developing childhood leukemia, inheriting Huntington's chorea, or developing amyelotrophic lateral sclerosis.

These tragic outcomes, as the blind deliverances of nature, are acts of God for which no one is responsible (unless, that is, one wishes to impeach divine providence). The fact that individuals are injured by hurricanes, storms, and earthquakes is often simply no one's fault. Since no one is to blame, no one can be charged with the responsibility of making those whole who lose the natural lottery on the ground that they are accountable for the harm. One will need a special argument to show that the readers of this [article] should submit to the forcible distribution of their resources in order to provide health care for the individuals injured. It may very well be unfeeling or unsympathetic not to provide such help, but it is another thing to show that one owes others such help in a way that would morally authorize state force to redistribute resources, as one would collect funds owed in a debt. The natural lottery creates inequalities and places individuals at disadvantage without creating a straightforward obligation on the part of others to aid those in need.

THE SOCIAL LOTTERY

Individuals differ in their resources not simply because of outcomes of the natural lottery, but also due to the actions of others. Some deny themselves immediate pleasures in order to accumulate wealth or to leave inheritances to others. Through a complex web of love, affection, and mutual interest, individuals convey resources, one to another, so that those who are favored prosper, and those who are ignored languish. Some will grow wealthy and others will grow poor, not through anyone's maleficent actions or omissions, but simply because they were not favored by the love, friendship, collegiality, and associations through which fortunes develop and individuals prosper. In such cases there will be no fairness or unfairness, but simply good and bad fortune. In addition, some will be advantaged, disadvantaged, rich, poor, ill, diseased, deformed, or disabled because of the malevolent actions of others. Such will be unfair circumstances, which just and beneficent states should try to prevent and to rectify through retributive justice and forced restitution. Insofar as the injured party has a claim against the injurer to be made whole, not against society, the outcome is unfortunate from the perspective of society's obligations to make the actual restitution. Restitution is owed by the injurer.

When individuals come to purchase health care, some who lose the natural lottery will be able in part at least to compensate for that loss through their winnings at the social lottery. They will be able to afford expensive health care needed to restore health and to regain function. On the other hand, those who lose in both the natural and the social lottery will be in need of health care and without the resources to acquire it.

THE RICH AND THE POOR:
DIFFERENCES IN ENTITLEMENTS

If one owns property by virtue of just acquisition or just transfer, then one's title to that property will not be undercut by the needs of others. One will simply own it. On the other hand, if one owns property because such ownership is part of a system that ensures a beneficent distribution of goods (e.g., the greatest balance of benefits over harms for the greatest number, the greatest advantage for the least-well-off class), one's ownership will be affected by the needs of others. [There are] reasons why one should suspect that property is in part privately owned in a strong sense that cannot be undercut by the needs of others. In addition, it would appear that all have a general right to access to the fruits of the earth, if not the universe, which would constitute the basis for a form of taxation as rent in order to provide for fungible payments to individuals, whether or not they are in need. Finally, there are likely to be resources held in common by groups that will need to find reasonable and equitable means for their distribution. The first two forms of entitlements will exist independently of medical or other needs; the last form of entitlement, through the decision of a community, may be conditioned by need.

The existence of any amount of private resources is the basis of an inequality among persons. Insofar as one owns things, one will have a right to them, even if others are in need, and even if the taxation as rent on one's resources is far from excessive or onerous. The test of whether one should transfer one's goods to others will not be whether such a redistribution will prove onerous or excessive for the person subjected to the distribution, but whether the resources belong to that individual. Goal-oriented approaches to the just distribution of resources will need to be restricted to commonly produced and commonly owned goods. Therefore, one must qualify the conclusions of the President's Commission that suggest that excessive burdens should determine the amount of tax persons should pay to sustain an adequate level of health care for those in need.[1] One will need to face a more complicated moral world with three sources of goods for the support of health care.

DRAWING THE LINE BETWEEN THE UNFORTUNATE AND THE UNFAIR

How one regards the moral significance of the natural and social lotteries and the moral force of private ownership will determine how one draws the line between circumstances that are simply unfortunate and those that are unfortunate and in addition unfair in the sense of constituting a claim on the resources of others. Life in general and health care in particular reveal circumstances of enormous tragedy, suffering, and deprivation. The pains of illness and disease and the despair of deformity call upon the sympathy of all to provide aid and give comfort. Injuries and diseases due to the unconsented-to actions of others are unfair.

Injuries and diseases due to the forces of nature are unfortunate. As noted, unfortunate outcomes of the unfair actions of others are not necessarily society's fault. The horrible injuries that come every night to the emergency rooms of major hospitals may be someone's fault, even if they are not society's. Such outcomes, though unfair with regard to the relationship of the injured with the injurer, may be simply unfortunate with respect to society. One is thus faced with drawing the difficult line between acts of God and acts of malicious individuals that do not constitute a basis for societal retribution and injuries that provide such a basis. Such a line was drawn by Patricia Harris, the former secretary of the Department of Health, Education, and Welfare, when she ruled that heart transplantations should be considered experimental and therefore not reimbursable through Medicaid.[2] To be in need of a heart transplant and not have the funds available would be an unfortunate circumstance but not unfair. One was not eligible for a heart transplant even if another person had intentionally damaged one's heart. From a moral point of view, things could change if the federal government had in some culpable fashion injured one's heart. So, too, if promises of treatment had been made. For example, to suffer from appendicitis or pneumonia and not receive treatment reimbursable through Medicaid would be unfair, not simply unfortunate.

The line between the unfair and the unfortunate can be drawn because it is difficult if not impossible to translate all needs into claims against the resources of others. First it is hard to distinguish needs from mere desires. Is the request of an individual to have his life extended through a heart transplant at great cost and perhaps only for a few years a desire for an inordinate extension of life, or is it a need to be secure against a premature death? . . . Outside a particular view of the good life, needs do not create rights to the services or goods of others. Finally, there is a certain impracticality in seeing such circumstances as needs that generate claims. Attempts to restore health could indefinitely deplete societal resources in the pursuit of ever-more incremental extensions of life of marginal quality. A relatively limited amount of food and shelter is required to preserve the lives of individuals. But an indefinite amount of resources can be committed to the further preservation of human life. One is forced to draw a line between those needs that constitute claims on the aid of others and those that do not.

BEYOND EQUALITY

The line between the unfortunate and the unfair justifies certain social and economic inequalities. In particular, it justifies inequalities in the distribution of health care resources that are the result of differences in justly acquired resources and privileges. To this one must add that the very notion of equal distribution of health care is itself problematic, a point recognized in *Securing Access to Health Care,* the report of the President's Commission.[3]

1. Though in theory at least one can envisage providing all with equal levels of decent shelter and nutrition, one cannot restore all to or preserve all in an equal state of health. Health needs cannot be satisfied in the same way in which one can address needs for food and shelter.

2. If one provided all with the same amount of funds to purchase health care or the same amount of services, the amount provided would be far too much for many and still insufficient for some who could have always used more investment in treatment and research in the attempt to restore them to a level of function that would ensure equal opportunity.

3. If one attempts to provide equal health care in the sense of allowing individuals to select health care only from a predetermined list of available therapy, which would be provided to all so as to prevent the rich from having access to better health care than the poor, one would have confiscated a portion of the private property of individuals and have restricted the freedom of individuals to join in voluntary relationships. That some are fortunate in having more resources is neither more nor less arbitrary or unfair than some having better health, better looks, or more talents. If significant restrictions were placed on the ability to purchase special treatment with one's resources, one would need not only to anticipate that a black market in health care services would inevitably develop, but also to acknowledge it as a special bastion of liberty and freedom of association.

CONFLICTING MODELS OF JUSTICE

We will [now] turn to a comparison of two radically different understandings of what counts as justice in general and what should count as justice in health care in particular: justice as primarily procedural, a matter of fair negotiation, and justice as primarily structural, a pattern of distributions that is amenable to rational disclosure. As examples of these two contrasting approaches, John Rawls's *A Theory of Justice* and Robert Nozick's *Anarchy, State, and Utopia,* will be briefly examined. Rawls presumes that there is an ahistorical way to discover the proper pattern for the distribution of resources, and therefore presumably for the distribution of health care resources. Moreover, he presumes that societally based entitlements are morally prior to privately based entitlements. Nozick, in contrast, provides a historical account of just distributions. Justice in patterns for the allocation of goods, including health care services, depends on what individual men and women have agreed to do with and for each other. Nozick holds that privately based entitlements are morally prior to societally based entitlements. In contrast with Rawls, who argues that one can discover a proper pattern for the allocation of societal resources, Nozick argues that such a pattern cannot be discovered and that instead one can only identify the characteristics of a just process for fashioning rights to health care. . . .

This contrast between Rawls and Nozick can be appreciated more generally as a contrast between two quite different principles of justice, each of which would have remarkably different implications for the allocation of health care resources.

1. Freedom-based justice is concerned with those distributions of goods made in accord with the notion of the moral community as a peaceable community. It will therefore require the consent of the individuals involved in a historical, cultural nexus of justice-regarding institutions in conformity with the principle of autonomy. The principle of beneficence is pursued within constraints set by the principle of autonomy.

2. Goals-based justice is concerned with the achievement of the good of individuals in society, and where the pursuit of beneficence is not constrained by a strong principle of autonomy. Such justice will vary as one attempts to (a) give each person an equal share; (b) give each person what that person needs; (c) give each person a distribution as a part of a system designed to achieve the greatest balance of benefits over harms for the greatest number of persons; and (d) give each person a distribution as a part of a system designed to maximize the advantage of the least-well-off class within conditions of equal liberty for all and of fair opportunity. . . .

[A] market approach maximizes free choice in the sense of minimizing interventions in the free associations of individuals and in the disposition of private property. In not intervening, it allows individuals to choose as they wish and as they are able what they hold to be best for their health care. It makes no pretense at cost containment. Health care will cost as much and will receive as much commitment of resources as individuals choose. The percentage of the gross national product devoted to health care will rise to a level determined by the free choices of health care providers and consumers. If some element of health care becomes too expensive or not worth as much as a competing possible expenditure, individuals will engage in cost containment through not purchasing such health care, and its price will tend to fall. Finally, there will be no attempt to achieve equality, though there will be considerable room for sympathy and for the loving care of those in need. A free market economy, through maximizing the freedom of those willing and able to participate, may create more resources than any other system and thus in the long run best advantage those most harmed through the natural lottery. By creating a larger middle class, the market may tend to create greater equality at a higher standard of living and of health care than would alternative systems. Further, charity can at least blunt severe losses at the natural and social lotteries.

Whether one accepts a free market approach will depend on one's moral views regarding (1) the rights of individuals to create free associations, as occur in the market with physician–patient contracts; (2) the moral significance of the natural and social lotteries; and (3) the character and scope of private and communal ownership, as well as one's understanding of (4) the factual circumstances, that is, if and to what extent the market is in the long run the best provider of a high standard of living and of health care. If one holds that individuals and society have an obligation to provide a certain level of health care, which conforms to a particular market and that the obligation overrides rights to free choice and the use of one's property, one will need to abandon market mechanisms either in whole or in part. . . .

A two-tiered system of health care is in many respects a compromise. On the one hand, it provides at least some amount of health care for all, while on the other hand allowing those with resources to purchase additional health care. It can endorse the provision of communal resources for the provision of a decent minimal amount of health care for all, while acknowl-

edging the existence of private resources at the disposal of some individuals to purchase better care. This compromise character of a two-tiered system can find a number of justifications. The utilitarian may in fact find that this approach maximizes the greatest good for the greatest number because it is a compromise. In allowing free choice while providing some health care for all, the system supports two important human goals and sources of satisfaction (i.e., liberty and well-being). A two-tiered system can also be justified in Rawlsian terms insofar as health care is to be treated under the difference principle, that is, to the extent it is to be regarded as justly distributed if the distribution redounds to the benefit of the least-well-off class. One would then allow that amount of additional health care to be purchased by the affluent, which would maximize the quality of care for the least-well-off, or the general status of the least-well-off class.

[My] analyses of the principles of autonomy and beneficence and of entitlements to property support a two-tiered system of health care. Not all property is privately owned. Nations and other social organizations may invest their common resources in insuring their members against losses in the natural and social lotteries. On the other hand, . . . not all property is communal. There are private entitlements, which individuals may freely exchange for the services of others. The existence of a two-tiered system (whether officially or unofficially) in nearly all nations and societies reflects the existence of both communal and private entitlements, of social choice and individual aspiration. A two-tiered system with inequality in health care distribution would appear to be both morally and factually inevitable.

The serious task will be to decide how to create a decent minimum as a floor of support for all members of a society, while allowing money and free choice to fashion a special tier of services for the advantaged members of society. The problem will be to define what will be meant by a "decent minimum" or "minimum adequate amount" of health care. . . .

[T]he concept of adequate care will not be discoverable outside of an appeal to a particular view of the good life and a particular understanding of the charge of medicine. In general, smaller social groups, insofar as they share a common view of the good life, may be able to appeal to such a vision in order to discover what should count as a decent minimum of health care within that understanding. In nations encompassing numerous communities, an understanding of what one will mean by adequate level of health care or a decent minimum will need to be created through open discussion and fair negotiation. In some communities such as the BaMbuti, there may be little commitment of resources to the endeavors of modern health care. For such communities, a decent level of such care will be no care at all. In nations such as the United Kingdom, the decent minimum of care may not include hemodialysis for individuals over the age of fifty-five or coronary bypass surgery for any but the most promising candidates for surgical treatment (or at least there are informal ways of discouraging such treatment). For many, such a minimal level of investment may not count as a decent level. But one must remember that one creates through negotiation an amount of health care that becomes de facto the decent amount for the community as a whole, though it always remains open to further critique, discussion, and alteration. . . .

Rights are fashioned in terms of the content given to the duty to be beneficent to those in need. It is in terms of such visions of proper beneficent action that communities join together as nations to fashion large-scale webs of entitlements to health care and thus give content to beneficence through a system of rights to health care delivery. As always, however, particular communities may not wish fully to participate or may wish in various ways to have special health care systems with special rights and entitlements of their own (e.g., one might imagine Roman Catholics arguing that the provision of contraceptive, abortion, and sterilization procedures should not be provided through a national health insurance; on the other hand, one can easily imagine other communities wishing to provide such services through their communal insurance plans).

A web of concrete expectations is thus woven through the endorsement and negotiation of the men and women who constitute moral communities and who span moral communities through undertakings such as large-scale nations. In their weaving of patterns of commitment, they include certain goals and exclude others. Particular systems of health care are particular in choosing certain goals but not others, in ranking some goals higher and others lower. That patients in one system will receive care that they would not in another, that patients who would be saved in one system die for lack of care in another, is not necessarily a testimony to moral malfeasance. It may as well be the result of the different choices and visions of different free men and women. As we have seen, there are limits to our capacity as humans to discover correctly what we ought to do together. We humans must instead settle for deciding fairly what we will do together, when we cannot together discover what we ought to do. Even gods and goddesses must choose to create one world rather than another. So, too, must we.

NOTES

1. President's Commission for the Study of Ethical Problems in Medicine and Biomedical and Behavioral Research, *Securing Access to Health Care* (Washington, D.C.: U.S. Government Printing Office, 1983), Vol. 1, pp. 43–46.

2. H. Newman, "Exclusion of Heart Transplantation Procedures from Medicare Coverage," *Federal Register* 45 (Aug. 6, 1980): 52296. See also H. Newman, "Medicare Program: Solicitation of Hospitals and Medical Centers to Participate in a Study of Heart Transplants," *Federal Register* 46 (Jan. 22, 1981): 7072–7075.

3. President's Commission, *Securing Access to Health Care,* vol. 1, pp. 18–19.

RONALD BAYER, DANIEL CALLAHAN, ARTHUR L. CAPLAN, AND BRUCE JENNINGS

Toward Justice in Health Care

EQUITY AND EFFICIENCY: THE CHALLENGE OF JUSTICE

The American health care system is in crisis. It absorbs enormous economic and human resources and yet it fails all too often to meet the needs of millions of people. The challenge facing American health care today is to fashion a system that is at once just and affordable, a system in which both greater equity and greater efficiency prevail.

The annual rate of "medical inflation" has for many years exceeded the general rise in prices.[1] The proportion of the Gross National Product devoted to health care is more than twice the comparable figure in 1950. The Medicare Trust Fund has come close to bankruptcy.[2] Despite the extraordinary increase in health expenditures over the past three decades, and the rise in government financing through Medicare and Medicaid, significant and growing inequities continue to plague the health care system. Millions of Americans either have no health insurance at all or are inadequately protected by limited and intermittent coverage.[3] Millions still live in geographical regions that have been officially designated as "medically underserved."[4]

This state of affairs should be viewed as intolerable. Instead, it is scarcely visible as a public issue. With growing alarm about the rise in health care costs,

From Ronald Bayer, Daniel Callahan, Arthur Caplan, and Bruce Jennings. "Toward Justice in Health Care," *American Journal of Public Health* 78, No. 5, (May 1988). © American Public Health Assn. 1988. Reprinted by permission.

public attention has shifted from the social goal of securing equitable access for the unprotected to the issue of "cost containment." The reformist impulse of the 1960s which sought to create an equitable health care system has exhausted itself. In 1983, when the President's Commission for the Study of Ethical Problems in Medicine and Biomedical and Behavioral Research issued an important report, *Securing Access to Health Care*,[5] its call for governments to assume ultimate responsibility for ensuring equitable distribution of health care received only limited attention. An even more restrained response greeted the report of the National Citizens Board of Inquiry into Health in America, *Health Care USA: 1984.*[6]

In the face of such silence it is necessary to reassert the moral priority of equity. All Americans, rich, middle class, and poor alike, should be entitled to a decent level of health care. As a nation, it is our collective responsibility to provide all individuals with a level of care necessary to maintain and restore health, and to eliminate undue anxiety about and risk of future illness. Good health cannot be assured to everyone. But good health *care* can and should be guaranteed. Whether the demand for the reform of the health care system is framed in terms of a "right to health care" or a "societal obligation"[7] to guarantee access to health care is less important than recognizing a moral commitment to one overriding goal: All Americans must have access to the full range of necessary health care services. Objective criteria, professional judgment, and community consensus will all help to define that standard. In most instances there will be agreement. Where none exists, the difficult political task of determining what a just society must provide to its members will be unavoidable.

In both academic and public policy circles, the debate over health care reform often assumes that our society is on the verge of having to make tragic choices regarding the rationing of scarce medical resources.[8] When the situation is so characterized, the question of priorities in reform takes on an anguished form as efforts are made to determine the most acceptable distribution of resources among, for example, the young and the old and those with different diseases.

We do not believe that assertions about the necessity of making such choices are well grounded. Indeed, we believe that given the capacity of the American economy and the technical and professional development of the health care system, it is possible to undertake dramatic efforts at reform that will meet the challenge of inequity in the health care system and that will do so at a social cost that is tolerable. Furthermore, unlike those who argue that the issue of health care inflation must be met before efforts are made to expand access to the health care system, we believe that both goals can be pursued at the same time.

The highest priority for those who seek to fashion a just and adequate health care system must be the elimination of the prevailing pattern of economic barriers to access to needed medical services. A central feature of any such reform program must be the creation of a system of universal health insurance protection. Past efforts to provide such protection have centered on the creation of a national health insurance program. That was the goal of reformers in the Roosevelt and Truman Administrations[9] and in the 1960s as well. Although advocates of national health insurance maintain that such a program is the only way to protect the millions of Americans who are now vulnerable to the high cost of health care, and which would guarantee uniformity in the range of available services, it seems clear from recent political history that the prospects for the adoption of such a plan are remote.

Nevertheless, the creation of universal health insurance protection is a moral imperative. Without such protection, individuals will be dependent upon the charitable impulses of the community and the availability of public clinics and hospitals established to provide services to the poor and uninsured. Neither private philanthropy nor local governments alone can provide the foundation for a just and adequate health care system.

By its very nature, charity is a voluntary act. The level of effort and commitment is determined by those who believe they ought to share their resources with others who are less fortunate. Although modern hospitals developed as charitable institutions[10] and physicians historically offered their services free of charge in clinics, it is clear that the level of such provision has always been inadequate to meet the needs of the poor, the uninsured, and those whose insurance protection is inadequate.

Furthermore, the pattern of cross-subsidies through which hospitals have recently covered the costs of providing uncompensated "charity" care, by increasing the charges of those protected by insurance and of those who pay directly for their medical care, will be increasingly threatened under new prospective payment and preferred provider arrangements.

Much attention has been devoted recently to the moral implications of this threat to the institutional foundations of the provision of hospital service to the uninsured. This situation also forces us to recognize that cost-shifting practices have socially troubling dimensions. They are a morally inferior way of financing the care of the poor. The need to rethink the fiscal basis for guaranteeing care to the uninsured provides us with an opportunity to consider more equitable approaches to the problem, that would entail at the minimum universal protection by health insurance.

Finally, it is clear from the behavior of the uninsured that they are reluctant to seek out needed medical care that may be available on the basis of charity. They delay their use of medical services when they should not.[11] Sometimes they simply do without. In part, they may know that they may be compelled to make a "contribution" of their own that is simply too burdensome. In part, they may do so because they fear being turned away.

Historically, public hospitals have sought to provide access to health care for those who could not otherwise afford it. They continue to do so today. But under the pressure of fiscal crises local and state governments have found such institutions burdensome to maintain, so much so that at times they have made them expendable.[12] Both because of the resources available to them and because of the nature of their clientele, these institutions are in fact often inferior to hospitals in the voluntary, not-for-profit sector. A system of provision that is so profoundly characterized by the impoverished status of those whom it serves cannot provide care that meets the standards of equity. Though there are some striking exceptions—public hospitals that because they are great teaching institutions provide high quality care—separate in medicine can, in general, no more be equal than in the case of education.

There will obviously always be a role for public hospitals and clinics, especially in meeting the medical needs of those who live in underserved areas where physicians might not otherwise choose to establish their practices, and where voluntary associations might not otherwise choose to establish hospitals. But public clinics and hospitals are no substitute for the protection that would be provided by universal insurance. Indeed, the financial viability of such institutions, as well as their capacity to provide care to a broad case mix is dependent upon the existence of such insurance coverage.

Instituting a new pattern of universal health insurance coverage will thus be integral to any effort to create a just health care system. So, too, will be the development of a standard of "medical necessity" as a baseline for equitable care, and the development of better modes of technology assessment to guide social choices concerning the utilization and development of costly medical interventions.

UNIVERSAL HEALTH INSURANCE

The federal government bears the primary responsibility of assuring access to health care for all Americans. It is unlikely, however, that in the foreseeable future universal insurance coverage will be made available to the American people through a single national health insurance program under the aegis of the federal government. As a consequence, it will be necessary for policy makers at the federal level to fashion a program of universal protection based upon a mix of public and private insurance that in turn will require a further elaboration of the unique social arrangement through which employers have been assigned the responsibility of providing health insurance to those in their employ. However the details of such an arrangement are ultimately worked out, certain features will be necessary if the demands of justice are to be met.

ALL WORKERS MUST BE PROVIDED
BY THEIR EMPLOYERS WITH HEALTH INSURANCE
FOR THEMSELVES AND THEIR DEPENDENTS

Since the United States has chosen to rely primarily upon employment-based health insurance for the pro-

vision of protection against the cost of health care, the moral requirement that all Americans have such coverage dictates that as a matter of public policy all employers be required to provide their workers with insurance that includes the protection of their dependents. Where the imposition of such a requirement in certain marginal industries might produce economic hardships or threats to economic viability, it is the responsibility of the government to devise appropriate mechanisms that will assure workers in such industries of health insurance coverage, either through subsidies to employers or through direct provision.

UNEMPLOYMENT MUST NO LONGER RESULT
IN THE LOSS OF HEALTH INSURANCE PROTECTION

Because most health insurance is provided to Americans as a fringe benefit of employment, the loss of one's job typically resulted—until 1986—in a loss of health insurance, if not immediately, then shortly after the termination of employment. The loss of such protection at a moment when personal resources became constrained and when stress may actually increase the likelihood of episodes of illness represented an added burden to those who found themselves without work. In 1986, as a result of new legislation, employers were required to offer their terminated employees the option of *purchasing* continued health insurance. While an advance over the situation that had prevailed until then, this reform placed the primary burden of obtaining health insurance protection on the unemployed worker, at a cost that many would find too great. It is the government that ought to bear the responsibility for assuring the continuation of protection through either public or private insurance mechanisms.

FEDERAL STANDARDS
FOR MEDICAID ELIGIBILITY WILL BE REQUIRED

Millions of poor people are excluded from Medicaid.[13] In part, this failure stems from the eligibility provisions of the federal law, and in part from state-established standards that deny coverage to the medically indigent and that set eligibility standards far above the official poverty line. Medicaid must cover all those classed as poor and who are not employed or the dependents of insured employees. Whether such a shift in public policy will necessitate the federalization of Medicaid is an open question. But the principle that must undergird the new policy is that it is the responsibility of government to provide health insurance to those who otherwise would be without it, and that it is appropriate for the federal government to ensure adequate coverage, if necessary by providing the insurance itself.

These three measures are put forth for illustrative purposes, to demonstrate that far-reaching efforts and reforms will be necessary to create a system of universal health insurance coverage that will build upon the current pattern of public and private insurance coverage in the United States. While acknowledging that continued reliance upon employment-based programs is possible, these proposals place the primary responsibility upon government to mandate coverage in the private sector and to provide such coverage itself where private efforts do not seem feasible. It must also be borne in mind that there are considerable administrative costs associated with a system that relies upon a complex relationship between private and public payers, especially one that requires of the former that certain standards are met.[14]

STANDARDS OF HEALTH INSURANCE PROTECTION

The creation of a universal system of health insurance—one that will include coverage by Medicaid, Medicare, Blue Cross/Blue Shield, and other insurance programs—will inevitably require an assessment of the adequacy of the coverage thus provided. To mandate protection without establishing some uniform standards of what must be provided and under what terms of payment would be to create the illusion, rather than the substance, of equity.

These concerns grow out of the realities of current insurance coverage. Some policies include first-dollar coverage and a full array of ambulatory and hospital services. Others provide hospital coverage only and under conditions that require substantial insurance co-payments. Coverage for the cost of catastrophic illness is not available to many. "Preexisting conditions" clauses leave even the well-insured without protection against the costs of certain illnesses.[15]

The inadequacy of insurance coverage affects not only those insured by private carriers but those included in the Medicaid program. The states are free to restrict the range of "optional" services and the number of allowable hospital days.[16] The levels of reimbursement provided by Medicaid effectively preclude access to the services of many private practitioners.[17]

A just health care system must be built upon a foundation that provides a full range of medically necessary services under reimbursement criteria that provide equal access to all appropriate medical facilities regardless of the source of insurance. But how are we to define the appropriate range of covered services and adequate reimbursement procedures?

At the outset, it should be noted that considerable disagreement exists about what would constitute a morally acceptable level of coverage in a comprehensive insurance package. Some, following the broad World Health Organization definition of health,[18] would like to see a vast array of social and psychological services covered. There are others who feel, either for reasons of good scientific practice or on moral grounds, that the definition of a health care service should be considerably narrowed.[19] Some proponents of the "narrow" position have even argued that no coverage ought to be given for psychological or mental health services since these services do not constitute appropriate areas for medical or health professional interventions.[20] They buttress their argument by pointing out that these services are used disproportionately by the relatively advantaged in order to enhance the quality of their lives rather than as a remedy for illness.

Economic considerations also loom large in discussions of the scope of benefits to be provided under health insurance schemes. Some maintain that, although it may be legitimate to define health care services and health care problems broadly, to do so would result in insurance programs that would simply be too costly.[21] Questions about the scope of medicine, the efficacy of therapeutic and diagnostic interventions, and the social burden of providing certain types of care must be considered when decisions to establish standards are made. It will be critically important to identify which factors have been considered in the process. Only then can the agreed-upon standards be subjected to moral evaluation by both the public and the health care professions.

Historically, those concerned with the provisions of health care protection to the most vulnerable have spoken of "basic minimums." Such formulations have often implied a willingness to tolerate differential levels of care in which the poor and others dependent upon the public purse would have access to a range of services that differed in quality and kind from those available to individuals protected by private insurance. If we are committed to a just, equitable health care system, we cannot accept the distinctions that would be implied by reliance upon a standard that guaranteed only a "basic minimum."

Responding, in part, to such concerns, the President's Commission for the Study of Ethical Problems in Medicine and Biomedical and Behavioral Research elected, in its 1983 report *Securing Access to Health Care,* to frame its ethical standard for the evaluation of the health care system in terms of "adequacy".[22] While recognizing the essential ambiguity of this term, the Commission believed that its formulation provided a term of art that would acknowledge the importance of professional consensus and that would also incorporate broadly supported cultural standards of what the health care system ought to provide to those in need. Such a formulation represents an important step forward. Nevertheless, it may permit interpretations that allow for differences in access to health care that fail to meet our standard of justice. For that reason we have chosen to rely upon "medical necessity" as the criterion by which to judge the coverage provided by health insurance, whether public or private.

ETHICAL FOUNDATIONS
OF MEDICAL NECESSITY

The concept of "medical necessity"[23] has an important legislative history linked to the enactment of Medicaid. There also is an important judicially defined standard arising out of medical malpractice cases.[24] For us the term captures a deeper and broader moral concern—that of guaranteeing all Americans access to the health services which can reasonably be considered appropriate for meeting their medical needs.

We acknowledge that there is a fundamental problem in analyzing the notion of "medical necessity," since like the notion of adequacy it may lend itself to multiple interpretations. "Medical necessity" might on some readings include everything that clinical medicine can do regardless of the prospects for success and cost considerations, or it might be defined more narrowly to include only those interventions of proven efficacy which involve reasonable cost. Whether organ transplantation, artificial organs, or extremely costly forms of intervention aimed at extending the lives of the terminally ill should be available to all cannot be automatically determined by invoking the notion of "medical necessity".

As the powers of medicine have expanded and as the domain of physicians has increased, the issue of "medical necessity" and questions about the ends of medicine have become intertwined. Is a new neonatal intensive care unit "necessary," and what ought to be the criterion for "necessity of admission" to such a unit? Should age-based criteria ever be used in determining the access of individuals to costly life-sustaining therapies, out of the belief perhaps that "necessity" varies according to the age of different patients? Is the application of aggressive therapeutic intervention in the case of the terminally ill "necessary" and in what circumstances? How much potential progress must be expected from the application of rehabilitative technologies to make them worthwhile and therefore "necessary"? How much risk must exist to a given patient before a hospitalization is defined as "necessary?" Who should bear the burden of such uncertainty?

Answers to these questions require that we acknowledge that necessity in medicine is an extraordinarily complex notion, involving a mix of empirical findings regarding efficacy and moral judgments about social obligations. It is a notion that is bound to change over time, and one that is bound in some respects to reflect prevailing cultural values and the availability of resources. Societal resources, technological developments and, above all, matters of equity and fairness are thus involved. That no precise empirical or objective standard is presently available does not, however, mean that any substantive definition of the standard is morally tolerable. A standard that defined "necessity" so narrowly that many suffered or died would violate the most basic appreciation of what fairness and decency require.

Despite the disagreements noted above, sufficient consensus exists to make a standard of necessity useful. That problems remain at the margins, especially in cases of new and extraordinarily expensive technologies, should not obscure this fact. The matter of determining which of the clinical interventions at the margin of efficacy ought to be included in the definition of "necessity" will ultimately be a matter of political, scientific, and moral negotiation. The fact that negotiation is unavoidable underscores the importance of enhancing popular participation in the formulation of health policy. Such negotiation will be dependent upon sound empirical findings on the efficacy of not only innovative therapies, but of those that are part of current practice as well.

The adoption of a standard of medical necessity would have two major implications for the design of health insurance programs. In the first place, although experimental therapies or interventions of unproven efficacy could remain beyond "necessity," the current practice of excluding from coverage some medical services broadly deemed clinically appropriate given the health needs of the individual would be precluded. More important, all public and private health insurance programs would be bound by this common and basic standard.

Secondly, the current practice of establishing limits on the number of physician contacts, hospital days, and lifetime medical expenditures would no longer be morally acceptable. Such arbitrary limits can only function to shift the burden of health care onto patients themselves or onto hospitals and physicians who are forced to provide uncompensated care. Experience makes it clear that such limitations effectively create economic barriers to care that is unquestionably medically necessary.

The recent adoption of diagnosis-related groups (DRGs) as a system for the prospective payment of hospitalized Medicare patients underscores the problems that will be faced by any attempt to impose effective cost conscious limitations on medical care. There is no doubt that the establishment of typical treatment profiles can serve as an important guide to health care providers as they attempt to limit the unwise or excessive cost of care. Nevertheless, empirical studies have already begun to reveal that elderly patients are being discharged from hospitals before optimal, effective and necessary care has been provided, in order to stay within DRG limits.[25] Such financially imposed determinations not only raise disturbing questions about the willingness of the American health care system to provide medically necessary care, but about the financial wisdom of discharging patients who may require rehospitalization.

SHARING THE BURDEN OF COST

Over the past 20 years it has become abundantly clear that differential levels of allowable insurance reimbursements of hospitals and medical practitioners create a marked pattern of unequal access to health care.[26] For those who are inadequately protected, insurance co-payments require large out-of-pocket expenditures for needed medical care. When such individuals are poor and cannot supplement insurance reimbursements with out-of-pocket payments, the consequence may be exclusion from needed health care.[27] Medicare patients who are well-off thus experience fewer problems when they need medical care than the less well-off elderly who find the required out-of-pocket expenditures too burdensome.[28] In the case of Medicaid, where out-of-pocket payments are either prohibited by law or are very limited, the consequence has been a refusal to treat those covered by the program by some hospitals and many physicians.[29]

A just health care system cannot permit the continuation of this pattern. Indeed, a universal insurance program that failed to address this issue would not represent an effective social response to the current levels of inequity in the health care system. When the President's Commission for the Study of Ethical Problems in Medicine and Biomedical and Behavioral Research discussed the issue of the costs of care, it adopted the principle that access to adequate medical care ought not create "excessive burdens."[30] Individuals under such a formulation would be expected to bear some part of the burden of the costs generated by their "consumption decisions." We reject the view that personal health care services are a commodity, even a precious commodity. Therefore, we cannot accept as a perspective the argument that individuals ought to pay, at least in part, for what they "buy." Like education of the young, health services ought to be considered a community good, paid for out of communal resources.

We recognize that cost-sharing schemes, virtually a universal feature of insurance programs, may, however, be a defensible way of preventing the unwise use of medical resources. When they are so used, it is imperative that such devices not create obstacles to the use of necessary medical services. Furthermore, the combined impact of premiums and out-of-pocket expenditures should not result in regressively structured burdens for the poor and middle class.

When discussion of universal health insurance centered on the form that a governmentally sponsored national insurance program would take, it was possible to apply this standard of financial equity in a rather straightforward way. Progressive taxation was often deemed the appropriate source of general revenues to support the system. To the extent that premiums were deemed appropriate they too could be structured in a progressive fashion. Finally, the level of out-of-pocket payments could be adjusted to reflect the income of those who made use of the health care system.

To the extent that a universal system of health insurance will involve a mix of governmental and employer-based programs, the application of the principle of financial equity will require a complex set of policies that will permit the incorporation of the principle of progressivity. Among the possibilities might be the use of the income tax system to provide tax credits to compensate for the inevitable elements of regressivity that will characterize a system in which private insurance plays a central part. Governmental plans could with greater ease be adjusted to reflect the principle of progressivity. The experience of the elderly under Medicare makes it clear that a failure to adopt such a principle inevitably produces inequitable patterns of health care utilization.

TECHNOLOGY ASSESSMENT
AND MEDICAL NECESSITY

The prospect of the creation of a just health care system in which all Americans are provided access to medically needed services is haunted by the specter of high technology medicine. With the cost of each new advance viewed as yet another challenge to the fiscal integrity of the health care system, some have argued that we cannot afford equity.

There is some controversy over the extent to which the inflationary rise in health care costs can be attributed to rapid developments in high technology medicine, or to the widespread use of relatively inexpensive procedures—often of dubious efficacy—in countless clinical encounters.[31] No matter how this debate is resolved, it is clear that the accelerating pace of technological innovation has had a marked impact on the cost of health care.

The irony of our current situation is that at the very moment that the prospects for technological advances seem virtually limitless, we have become aware that our resources are finite. How will we confront this situation, and how will that confrontation affect the quality of the health care to which Americans will have access?

There are those who believe that, while the cost of the ensemble of predictable advances in medical technology will be significant, our society has the economic capacity to afford them. Indeed, they believe that if adequate measures were taken to control unwarranted expenditures on unproven diagnostic technology and therapies, the American health care system could absorb the costs of truly efficacious but costly technologies now being developed. For such

observers, the assertion that we now face the necessity of making tragic choices is at best premature.[32]

On this view, the creation of broadscale programs of technology assessment is a matter of urgency, not only for new medical procedures but also for those that are part of "customary practice."[33] The urgency of such assessment is underscored by the finding of the Office of Technology Assessment (OTA) of the US Congress that less than 20 percent of all existing medical technology has been subjected to any sort of controlled clinical trial or systematic study.[34] A reform priority must be the creation of both state and federal bodies that have the authority, resources, and expertise to collect standardized information about medical technologies, to analyze such data, and rapidly disseminate the results to guide policy decisions concerning access and reimbursement.

The optimistic view that technology assessment and the elimination of wasteful procedures can meet the challenge posed by health care costs is rejected by those who argue that we will soon have to choose among effective therapies.[35] For those who hold this view, no single technology or group of technologies is so expensive as to represent an unbearable burden for American society. It is clear to them, however, that not all of the potential advances of medicine can be afforded, especially if the demands of equity require access regardless of a person's ability to pay for treatment. In the not too distant future, they believe that choices will have to be made among the potential life-saving and life-enhancing technologies. For them, the question facing society will no longer be: Can this medical advance provide benefit to some individuals? Rather, they believe it will be necessary to ask: Does this potential advance meet the standard of medical necessity *at an acceptable social cost?* And in some cases, the decision is going to be that the cost of intervention is simply too great.

On this view, only a decision to forgo certain developments in medicine will preclude the necessity of developing rationing mechanisms that will either entail unconscionable choices about which individual lives are worth saving, or that will employ more subtle economic determinations masked by the language of medical suitability. These critics argue that the task of limiting the potential social cost of innovation must therefore begin early in the process of development, certainly before the pressure for dissemination can take hold. On a practical level, such efforts would have to take the form of restrictive decisions on the part of those public agencies that have played so central a role in the funding of biomedical research.

While techniques like cost-benefit analysis may help to clarify important aspects of the decision-making process, they cannot eliminate the need to face what are inherently moral and political questions. These decisions are the appropriate subject of broad-based discussions involving physicians, other medical experts, policy makers, and lay persons as well.

CONCLUSION

In this communication, we have stressed the moral priority that must be given to remedying the patterns of inequity that characterize the American health care system. This call for the necessary policy changes at the federal level comes, however, when in both the public and private sectors all energy seems devoted to cost containment, when government officials and leaders of industry have set a very different agenda for both discussion and action.

To control the level of public expenditure, Medicaid coverage has become subject to ever greater restrictions. The Medicare program has increased premiums and the requirements for out-of-pocket expenditures. In the private sector, efforts are being made to limit the scope of health insurance coverage as well as the extent to which insurance will reimburse for services. Proposals to tax employee health insurance benefits are designed to encourage the purchase of less costly, less comprehensive coverage.

In each of these cases the goals are twofold: to reduce social expenditure through the privatization of the cost of health care; and to make "consumers" cost-conscious, thus encouraging a reduction in the level of utilization of health care services. As Lester Thurow noted in his 1985 Shattuck Lecture before the annual meeting of the Massachusetts Medical Society: "No one is ever willing to come right out and say so, but the long-run aim is to return the system to the point where a large fraction of health care costs once again comes directly out of individual pockets. The goal is to make the patient the main cost container."[36]

While we acknowledge that the fiscal crisis of government and the overall cost of health care in America necessitate efforts at cost control, we believe that the measures now most prominently on the public agenda represent an unfortunate trend. Cost containment is being pursued in a manner that will exacerbate inequalities — multi-tier health care is no longer viewed as anathema but as unavoidable if the health care system is not to generate unacceptable burdens for American society. Furthermore, the privatization of health expenditures assumes that medical care is like other commodities rather than a basic social good which, like education and defense, ought to be viewed as a primary social responsibility.

Can we afford the cost of justice? We do not deny that the proposals set forth in this article will entail new costs for government and for American employers. In the short run, the creation of a just and decent health care system may force some economic dislocations. Inevitably, however, the costs generated by the decision to eliminate the inequities in the health care system will force American society to adopt firm but appropriate cost containment measures. Justice and fiscal responsibility are thus not necessarily incompatible; they will only be so if there is a failure of political nerve.

Rather than ask; "Can we afford the cost of justice?", we believe it is time to pose the question: "Can we any longer afford the moral price of inequity in health care?" Tales of patients being turned away from hospitals because they lack health insurance, of the poor, the elderly, and members of the middle class forgoing needed medical care because of its cost do and indeed ought to provoke disquiet among the American people. Our moral sentiments should serve as a critical force in the face of the numbing discussions of cost containment. The political determination to turn from equity because of cost may, however, have as its ultimate consequence the subversion of our capacity to respond with dismay when those who are in need are deprived of the health care which is their due. We may come to accept as inevitable that which should be the subject of our reformist impulse. If such a process occurs, we will be the worse for it as a political community.

The United States spends more on health care than virtually any of the advanced industrial democracies of Western Europe. There is no reason to believe that we cannot achieve the level of equity that exists in those societies. The question is not cost, but rather whether we have the moral imagination and political will to strive for justice.

1. Fuchs VR: The Health Economy. Cambridge, MA: Harvard University Press, 1986; 334–339.

2. Special Committee on Aging, United States Senate: Prospects for Medicare's Hospital Insurance Trust Fund. Washington, DC: Govt Printing Office, 1983.

3. Davis K., Rowland D: Uninsured and Underserved: Inequities in Health Care in the US. Milbank Mem Fund Q Spring 1983; 61(2):149–176.

4. Carpenter ES: Concepts of Medical Underservice: A Review and Critique. In: Securing Access to Health Care: The Ethical Implications of Differences in the Availability of Health Services, Volume III: Appendices—Empirical, Legal, and Conceptual Studies, President's Commission for the Study of Ethical Problems in Medicine and Biomedical and Behavioral Research. Washington, DC: Govt Printing Office, 1983.

5. President's Commission for the Study of Ethical Problems in Medicine and Biomedical and Behavioral Research. Securing Access to Health Care: The Ethical Implications of Differences in Availability of Health Services, Volume I: Report. Washington, DC: Govt Printing Office, 1983. (Hereafter President's Commission, Report.)

6. National Citizen's Board of Inquiry into Health in America. Health Care USA: 1984.

7. President's Commission, Report, 22–47.

8. Aaron HJ, Schwartz WB: The Painful Prescription: Rationing Hospital Care. Washington, DC: Brookings Institution, 1984.

9. Starr, P: The Social Transformation of American Medicine. New York: Basic Books, 1982.

10. Rosner D: A Once Charitable Enterprise: Hospitals and Health Care in Brooklyn and New York, 1885–1915. Cambridge: Cambridge University Press, 1982.

11. Davis and Rowland, op. cit.

12. Vladek C: Equity, Access and the Costs of Health Services. Med Care 1981; 19(12)(Suppl):69–80.

13. Institute for Medicaid Management: Data on the Medicaid Program: Eligibility, Services, Expenditures, Fiscal Years 1966–1978. Washington, DC: The Institute, 1978.

14. Himmelstein DB, Woolhandler S: Cost without benefit: Administrative waste in United States health care. N Engl J Med 1986; 314(7):441–445.

15. Oppenheimer GM, Padgug RA: AIDS: The risk to insurers, the threat of equity. Hastings Center Report October 1986; 16(5):18–22.

16. President's Commission, Report, 155.

17. Ibid., 88.

18. World Health Organization: Basic Documents, 26th Ed. Constitution of the World Health Organization. Geneva: WHO, 1976; 1.

19. Callahan D: The WHO Definition of Health. Hastings Center Studies 1973; 1(3):77–87.

20. See, for example, Daniels N: Health care needs and distributive justice. In: Bayer R, Caplan AL, Daniels N (eds): In Search of Equity: Health Needs and the Health Care System. New York: Plenum Press, 1983; 1–4.

21. Callahan D: Setting Limits: Medical Goals in an Aging Society. New York: Simon and Schuster, 1987.

22. President's Commission, Report, 35–43.

23. Sarro A: Determining medical necessity within Medicaid: A proposal for statutory reform. Nebraska Law Rev 1984; 63:835.

24. See, for example, Shuck PH: Malpractice Liability and the Rationing of Care. Texas Law Rev 1981; 59:1421–1427.

25. Dolenc DA, Dougherty CJ: DRGs: The Counterrevolution in Financing Health Care. Hastings Center Report June 1985; 15(3):19–29; Hospitals reduce costs, length of stay. Hospitals September 1984; 58(18):37; Gillock R, Smith H: Considerations for effectively managing DRGs. Hospital Topics March/April 1985; 63(2):6.

26. Huang LF, Koropecky O: The Effects of the Medicare Method of Reimbursement on Physicians' Fees and Beneficiaries' Utilization. Volume 2, Part 1. Washington, DC: Robert R. Nathan, Associates, 1973; Mitchell JB, Cromwell J: Physician Behavior under the Medicare Assignment Option. Final report submitted to the Health Care Financing Administration, January 1981.

27. Mitchell JB, Cromwell J: Access to Private Physicians for Public Patients: Participation in Medicaid and Medicare. In President's Commission, Volume III, op. cit., 121. (Hereafter, Access to Private Physicians).

28. President's Commission, Report, 152–153.

29. Mitchell and Cromwell, Access to Private Physicians, 105–130.

30. President's Commission, Report, 21–22.

31. Menzel P: Medical Costs: Moral Choices. New Haven: Yale University Press, 1983.

32. Angell M: Cost containment and the physician. JAMA 1985; 254(9):1203–1207.

33. Feinberg HV, Hiatt HH: Evaluation of medical practices: The case for technology assessment. N Engl J Med 1979; 301(20):1086–1091.

34. Office of Technology Assessment: The Implications of Cost-Effectiveness: Analysis of Medical Technology. Washington, DC: OTA, 1980.

35. Aaron and Schwartz, op. cit.

36. Thurow LC: Learning to say no. N Engl J Med 1984; 311(24):1569–1572.

JAMES S. TODD

It Is Time For Universal Access, Not Universal Insurance

An editorial by Relman proclaims, "Universal Health Insurance: Its Time Has Come."[1] Other recent *Journal* articles recommend various consumer-choice health care systems,[2,3] and the report of the National Leadership Commission on Health Care proposes what is essentially a national health insurance scheme.[4] I submit, instead, that the idea whose time has come is universal access to care — not through universal insurance that is funded from a central source or tightly controlled by forces other than medical need, but through a pluralistic delivery system.

Universal health insurance is not a good idea. To control goods or services through a single agency — especially when the driving force is economic — would fly in the face of the American way of doing things. We have tried central controls, and the results have been less than first-rate. Surely, for instance, we would not want to trust health care to a monolithic and monumentally ineffective monster like the postal service. Lost letters are one thing; lost lives are another.

What about the argument that we need government intervention to take care of those who are unable to care for themselves? Micromanagement in the health care system has become very much worse under the federal programs that exist today. And certainly our national experience with welfare and public housing has shown that a central bureaucracy fails miserably in addressing the heart of human need.

Rather than support such unworkable, soulless programs, I propose universal access through a pluralistic funding mechanism. Those who can take care of themselves should do so; those who need help should

receive it according to their need; and we should define a basic level of health care to which everyone is entitled, supported by multiple funding systems. Those who want special procedures (such as cosmetic surgery, the lack of which will cause no harm) or the ambience and comfort of "Cadillac care" should pay for them out of their own pockets.

The American Medical Association has made a series of proposals[5] whose implementation would not only increase access to health care but also go a long way toward providing appropriate, effective care in the proper setting. The proposals would expand eligibility and coverage under Medicaid to everyone below the poverty line and would create state risk pools with assistance, by means of vouchers, for uninsured people who are above the poverty line. The undergirding premise is to each according to his or her need and from each according to his or her means. When did this become undemocratic?

I am suggesting a pluralistic system because pluralism has made this country great in all respects — in large part because it offers built-in checks and balances that do not exist in monolithic systems of government. Turning the funding of health care over to the federal government, or any single entity, cannot seem a particularly reassuring or realistic idea to anyone. And dare we create a tax program that might or might not be used appropriately? Why do we keep getting bogged down in discussions of universal health insurance, ignoring the opportunity to do something really dramatic and humane?

Perhaps it is because so many countries now have such plans. But a look at universal health insurance programs in other countries inspires little confidence that a similar system here would solve the problem of access to care. The United States is unique, and our

From James S. Todd. "It Is Time for Universal Access, Not Universal Insurance," *New England Journal of Medicine* 321, No. 1 (July 6, 1989). Reprinted by permission of the publisher.

pluralistic approach is unique. There is no reason to think that an imported system would be successful here or that American citizens would accept its implicit restrictions.

Furthermore, no country has a system without major flaws. In many cases, the flaws would be particularly unacceptable to American consumers. For instance, despite recent favorable analyses of the Canadian experience,[6,7] the temporal rationing that occurs in that system—forcing patients to wait months or even years for what in this country are common medical procedures—is not the American way. Consider that in Vancouver there is a wait of two to four years for corneal transplantation, and up to three months for a psychiatric, neurosurgical, or routine orthopedic opinion.[8] Americans will not stand for temporal rationing or priorities by triage.

The problem with existing universal health insurance plans is that they focus primarily on paying for care. If cost is the only focus, it is easy to devise a plan that will at least function. Any budget can be controlled by making sure there is only one source of funds and then turning the spigot on and off according to what is available from that source. And this is essentially what has happened in every country with universal health insurance. Indeed, it is happening in this country, as the health care system continues to have a disproportionate role in the reduction of a federal budget deficit it did not create.

Other countries ignore appropriateness and effectiveness; they ignore the many complex elements of high-quality care that we in America demand; and they largely ignore the citizen's right to free choice, a concept we hold very dear. Americans will not stand for closing the spigot as long as there is a genuine need for care. In 1989 it is unrealistic to expect health care expenditures to level off, much less to decrease, in the absence of economic rationing. Instead, the level of health care activity will continue to grow as a result of various factors, including an aging population, increased demand (fostered in part by more consumer awareness of health issues), and the simple fact that medicine can do more for people now than ever before.

The American health care system at its best is universally acknowledged to be the best in the world, yet clearly that is not enough. Although we do need to address the enormous problems that exist in American health care, any plan that seeks to revamp completely a system that is working as well as ours is a dangerous proposition. We must not kill the can-do spirit that has

fostered what is best in American medicine—the breakthrough research, technological advances, and widespread availability of life-enhancing procedures. It would be tragic to jeopardize the best of this best-in-the-world system just because there are problems with it. These can be addressed in an evolutionary and equitable fashion if we have the resolve to do so.

What is the siren song of foreign programs? It is unrealistic to think we can import systems from different cultures—or try to revolutionize a system that has produced some of the greatest technology and physicians in the world—and expect success. Our political and economic climate is unique, and our pluralistic tradition is unique as well. Health care expenditures cannot be controlled by controlling the reimbursement of physicians or capping economic resources at some magic number, usually related to the gross national product.

Ignoring the demands or expectations of its patients dooms any monolithic system before it starts. To control health expenditures solely on the basis of economic targets does violence to all involved. Cost, access, and quality are interrelated; manipulating one has an astounding impact on the others.

So, we ought not to be talking about a universal health insurance scheme, but rather about universal access—access to needed care, on a timely basis, with controls on quality and use that have been accepted by everyone involved. The key principle of effective access and limited cost is the rationalization of care. In this age of high-technology medicine and miracle drugs, we must realize that we can no longer do everything for everybody just because it is possible. Rather, we should develop a system in which decisions about what we do, when, where, and to whom are based on reasonable expectations of the benefits involved and on sound medical principles communicated clearly to patients and their families.

Our only salvation lies in developing a greater sense of restraint and responsibility, ignoring the quick fix and the revolutionary brainchild of those who would control costs at the expense of patients and progress. What other countries have done is irrelevant to our problems. No country has reached a comfortable accommodation with its current system.

So universal access, not universal insurance, is an idea whose time has long since come. And if all of us—the health care community and our patients (those who do pay as well as those who should)—assume our rightful responsibilities, the idea can become a reality. We ought to be smart enough to devise in the United States a system of universal access at a cost that we can afford and in keeping with the principles of freedom we hold dear. This is the challenge before us; to improve the greatest health care system in the world, not to destroy it.

REFERENCES

1. Relman, AS. Universal health insurance: its time has come. N. Engl J Med 1989; 320:117–118.

2. Enthoven AC, Kronick R. A consumer-choice health plan for the 1990s; universal health insurance in a system designed to promote quality and economy. N. Engl J Med 1989; 320:29–37, 94–101.

3. Himmelstein DU, Woolhandler S, Writing Committee of the Working Group on Program Design. A national health program for the United States: a physicians' proposal. N Engl J Med 1989; 320:102–108.

4. For the health of a nation. Washington, D.C.: National Leadership Commission on Health Care, 1989.

5. Health policy agenda for the American People Ad Hoc Committee on Medicaid. American Medical Association Board of Trustees report UU, A-88. Presented at the Annual Meeting of the American Medical Association, Chicago, June 26–30, 1988.

6. Evans RG, Lomas J, Barer ML, et al. Controlling health expenditures—the Canadian reality. N Engl J Med 1989; 320: 571–577.

7. Relman AS. American medicine at the crossroads: signs from Canada. N Engl J Med 1989; 320:590–591.

8. Comment on the AARP study: the Canadian health care system: a special report on Quebec and Ontario. Chicago: Center for Health Policy Research, American Medical Association, 1988:2.

ALAIN ENTHOVEN
AND RICHARD KRONICK

A Consumer-Choice Health Plan for the 1990s: Universal Health Insurance in a System Designed to Promote Quality and Economy

WHY UNIVERSAL HEALTH INSURANCE?

THE PARADOX OF EXCESS AND DEPRIVATION

The health care economy of the United States is a paradox of excess and deprivation. We spend about 11.5 percent of the gross national product (GNP) on health care, much more than any other country.[1,2] And whereas other countries have stabilized the share of their GNP that is spent on health, ours has accelerated in recent years. Inflation-adjusted per capita spending for health care grew by 4 percent per year from 1970 to 1980, and by 4.6 percent per year from 1980 to 1986.[1] The Health Care Financing Administration (HCFA) recently projected that according to present trends, health care spending would reach 15 percent of the GNP by 2000.[1] These growing expenditures are adding greatly to deficits in the public sector, threatening the solvency of some industrial companies, and creating heavy burdens for many people.

At the same time, roughly 35 million Americans have no financial protection from the expenses of medical care—no insurance or other coverage, public or private.[3-6] This number is substantially higher than it was 10 years ago, as increasing numbers of employers find ways to avoid supplying coverage for employees and their dependents. Millions more have inadequate coverage that leaves them vulnerable to large financial risks.[7] And uncounted millions have cover-

From Alain Enthoven and Richard Kronick. "Universal Health Insurance in a System Designed to Promote Quality and Economy," *New England Journal of Medicine* 320, No. 1 (part 1 of 2 parts). Reprinted by permission of the publisher.

age that excludes preexisting medical conditions. Our present system of financing health care systematically denies coverage to many who need it most. Health insurers want to insure those who are the least likely to need medical care and to protect themselves and their policy holders from the costs associated with the care of the very sick.

The U.S. health care economy is inflationary. It is still dominated by fee-for-service payment of doctors and hospitals by third-party intermediaries with open-ended sources of finance. There is no total budget set in advance within which providers must manage the care of their patients. For the most part, there is no incentive to find and use medical practices that produce the same health outcome at less cost. And this method of payment leaves insured consumers largely unaware of the costs of the services they receive.

Health maintenance organizations (HMOs) and preferred-provider insurance (PPI), called "managed care plans," now cover more than 60 million Americans.[8,9] Such plans have the potential to create serious cost consciousness among consumers and providers. But they will not achieve it as long as potential subscribers do not have to pay the full extra cost themselves when they choose a more costly plan. (PPI contracts selectively with providers about price and use controls, and it reimburses patients at a higher rate when they see contracting providers, as a way of motivating patients to use such providers. In turn, access to patients is the incentive for providers to accept negotiated fees and controls.)

The employers of most insured people offer their employees a traditional insurance scheme by which all or most of their medical expenses are reimbursed after the payment of a deductible. If employers offer a less costly managed care plan, they often offer to pay its premium in full, as long as it does not exceed that of the traditional plan. Thus, the managed care plan has little or no incentive to reduce its price or improve its efficiency, because the employee making the choices sees little or no financial reward for choosing it. Some employers offer a fixed-dollar contribution and a cost-conscious choice of plan. In such cases, the managed care plan is motivated to reduce its price to attract subscribers. But even then, the Internal Revenue Code permits employees to characterize their premium contributions as nontaxable employer contributions and thus make the payment with pretax dollars. The effect is that if an employee chooses a health plan that is more rather than less costly, the government is likely

to be paying about one third of the difference in cost in the form of tax relief.[10,11] As a result, the employee's cost consciousness is attenuated, and the health plan has less need to cut its price to attract subscribers. In any case, health plans have little or no incentive to improve their efficiency in order to serve a few cost-conscious customers if most of their customers are not cost conscious; such plans need only shift costs from the former to the latter.

Moreover, most such "managed care" plans are really little more than traditional insurance arrangements that deal with physicians on an arms-length basis. It is unlikely that they will be able to achieve economical organization and delivery of care without obtaining the support of physicians and their commitment to that goal.

This inflationary financial environment reinforces other powerful cost-increasing factors: a growing supply of doctors looking for ways to make themselves useful; a professional culture that esteems the aggressive use of the most advanced technology without recognizing cost effectiveness as a virtue; the explosive growth of costly new forms of technology; the rising expectations of patients and malpractice litigation when expectations are not met; and an aging population. Little in this system promotes the cost-conscious use of resources or the efficient organization of the delivery system.

In addition, the present system of financing health care in the United States is unfair. It provides most people—those who are regularly employed by a medium-sized or large employer—with coverage either at no cost or at prices subsidized by the employer and the tax system. But the system denies the opportunity of coverage to millions of others for no good reason—to seasonal and part-time employees, self-employed persons, widows, divorcees, early retirees, the unemployed, and others whose employers choose not to provide health care coverage. Not all uninsured people are poor or unemployed. In fact, nearly two thirds of them are members of families with incomes above the poverty level; more than two thirds of uninsured adults belong to the labor force.[3] Viewed another way, when the uninsured are seriously ill (and most expenses are for seriously ill patients), taxpayers, insured persons, or both end up paying for most of their care. Voluntarily or involuntarily, some people are taking a free ride. Those who can do so ought to contribute their fair share to their coverage and be insured.

In the past, our open-ended financing system provided a ready source of financing for those who could not pay, even if it did not ensure equitable access to care. Hospitals simply raised their charges to those who could pay in order to cover the costs of those who could not. In recent years, efforts by employers and the government to contain costs have attacked this means of support for "uncompensated care." Hospitals have come under increased financial pressure to develop strategies to avoid caring for those who cannot pay—even to the point of closing their emergency rooms. Many who cannot pay turn to public providers of last resort, such as county hospitals. But these institutions are also under increasing financial pressure as public finances are strained and the numbers of the uninsured increase.

The present system is wasteful in many respects. We have spent little on evaluating medical technology, and there is much uncertainty about its efficacy.[12,13] Much care appears to be of unproved value.[14,15] There is considerable duplication and excess capacity in our medical facilities. The association between jobs and health insurance complicates and interferes with job mobility, because most people must change health plans when they change jobs. The presence of large numbers of uninsured persons imposes large costs on providers when they perform determinations of eligibility and coverage. The uninsured obtain much of their primary care in the outpatient departments and emergency rooms of public hospitals, instead of in the much less costly setting of a primary care physician's office. The deferment of care for conditions such as hypertension and diabetes adds to health risks and can cause much more expensive emergencies later. The lack of prenatal care can lead to very costly premature delivery and the birth of children with handicaps. The unavailability of insurance imposes heavy penalties on the uninsured: the postponement or denial of treatment, causing avoidable sickness and suffering, and the depletion of personal savings.

For all these reasons, our present system of health care does not reflect American values. We cherish efficiency and fairness, but we have a system that is neither efficient nor fair. Very few Americans believe that other Americans should be deprived of needed care or subjected to extreme financial hardship because of an inability to pay. There is widespread public outrage when a hospital turns away a delivering mother or an injured person for this reason. Congress has passed laws to punish hospitals that do this. But we have failed as a society to create institutions that assure all persons of the opportunity to obtain needed care, when they need it and without an excessive financial burden.

THE NEED FOR A COMPREHENSIVE STRATEGY TO PROMOTE EFFICIENCY AND EQUITY

To improve the health care system, we need a strategy that is comprehensive. Partial interventions can produce negative consequences or be rendered ineffective by developments elsewhere. Attempts to contain costs by the cost-conscious choice of managed care systems will be fruitless if, somewhere else, open-ended demand is bidding up the prices and standards of care that the managed care systems must meet. Why should doctors and hospitals accept serious cost containment by HMOs if there is plenty of open-ended demand for their services elsewhere? Partial "categorical" approaches leave people out and create enormous complexities as people change categories. And they can treat unequally people who appear similar but who actually fall into different categories.

The problems of achieving equity and efficiency are intimately related. Attempting to promote efficiency by making everyone conscious of costs conflicts with providing cross-subsidies for uncompensated care. On the other hand, we cannot afford to provide coverage for those who lack it without making the system efficient for all. The accelerating spiral of growth in expenditures has necessitated cutbacks in employer-provided coverage and Medicaid eligibility, and it is one of the main arguments used against universal coverage.

Thus, a satisfactory strategy for the health care economy in the United States must simultaneously address both sides of the paradox of excess and deprivation. We have designed our proposal with two main goals in mind. The first goal is to provide financial protection from health care expenses for all, either through enrollment in comprehensive health care financing and delivery plans or, for the irreducible minimum of people, through public providers of last resort. There will always be some—the homeless, undocumented aliens, and others whose life style does not include enrollment in a health plan, carrying a membership card, and making regular payments—whose needs will have to be addressed by public providers of last resort. But we can drastically reduce their numbers and so ease the financial burden on these institutions.

Our second goal is to promote the development of economical financing and delivery arrangements, by requiring consumers to be conscious of costs in choosing among health care organizations. There is ample evidence that efficient prepaid group practices can reduce the cost of care by 10 to 40 percent, as compared with open-ended fee-for-service practices, even without competition from other HMOs to serve cost-conscious purchasers.[16,17] There is good reason to believe that competition to serve cost-conscious purchasers could motivate cost-reducing innovation and slow the growth of health care spending. Our strategy would be to encourage the spread of HMOs and other efficient delivery arrangements by giving all consumers a choice of plans that requires a consideration of costs. Those who prefer to keep traditional "free choice of provider" arrangements and are willing to pay the extra costs associated with them would be free to do so.

THE NEED FOR A BROADLY ACCEPTABLE PLAN

Universal health insurance has not attracted overwhelming support in this country. Those who favor it should consider carefully the sources of opposition and seek to avoid designing a plan with features so objectionable to large numbers of American people or key interest groups that the plan would not be considered seriously in the political process. The idea of universal health insurance raises fears of socialized medicine or total dependence on the government for payment, of radical change or the disruption of satisfactory existing arrangements, of large-scale redistribution of income, or of excessive regulatory coercion. The causes of such fears can be avoided. We have designed a proposal for incremental change that is compatible with American cultural preferences and that should find broad acceptance. . . .

A UNIVERSAL HEALTH INSURANCE PLAN BASED ON MANAGED COMPETITION WITH MIXED PUBLIC AND PRIVATE SPONSORSHIP

Under this proposal, everyone not covered by an existing public program would be enabled to buy affordable subsidized coverage, either through their employers, in the case of full-time employees, or through "public sponsors," in the case of the self-employed and all others. We illustrate the general concepts with specific examples of tax rates, employer contributions, benefit packages, and other detailed features of the proposal. These should be understood as illustrative and, within limits, as "tunable dials" that can be adjusted in the political process. A supporting document provides more detail.[18]

STATE-LEVEL PUBLIC SPONSORS

Under this proposal, the federal government would enact legislation giving each state powerful incentives to create a "public sponsor" agency to act as sponsor for people otherwise unsponsored. A sponsor is an institution that ensures each member of its sponsored group financial coverage of health care expenses at a moderate price. In the competitive model we recommend, the sponsor serves as the broker, selecting the coverages to be offered, contracting with health plans and beneficiaries about rules of participation, managing the enrollment process, collecting premium contributions from beneficiaries, paying premiums to health plans, and administering both cross-subsidies among beneficiaries and subsidies available to the whole group. The main sponsors in this country are employers, Taft-Hartley trusts, and the HCFA. Public sponsors would aggregate the buying power of small employers and individuals. In a manner similar to that of very large employers such as the federal government, public sponsors would contract for a wide variety of managed care plans to be offered to the participating population in a competitive annual enrollment. (Whether to offer traditional indemnity insurance would be a management decision made by public sponsors.)

Public sponsors would offer to contract with any person or family not covered through employment who wished to abide by the conditions of participation, including enrollment during the annual open-enrollment period and a "lock in" for the full year. Such purchases of coverage would be subsidized: the public sponsor would pay 80 percent of the cost of the average qualified health plan, and the person or family covered would pay the rest.

Public sponsors would offer to act as brokers for employers who wished to obtain coverage through these agencies. Small employers and even many medium-sized employers are not large enough to manage competition among health plans effectively.[19] Moreover, small employers that buy insurance on their own are forced to pay higher rates, reflecting greater variability in small groups. A public sponsor could combine these risks and achieve economies of scale. States could achieve such economies in administration as well as greater bargaining power with the health plans by assigning this responsibility to the agencies that already buy coverage for public employees.

OBLIGATIONS OF EMPLOYERS

Under this proposal, employers would be required to cover all full-time employees (and their dependents not otherwise covered) and to pay an 8 percent payroll tax on the first $22,500 (i.e., half the Social Security wage base) of the wages and salaries of all employees not covered. In addition, employers would be required to offer all full-time employees (those working at least 25 hours per week) a choice of qualified plans, possibly including traditional insurance, and to contribute at least 80 percent of the average cost of the basic coverage, which would include the employees' dependents unless they were covered under a spouse's policy. (Some benefit plans would be more elaborate than others. For each health plan offered, the employer would obtain a quotation for the price of basic coverage, as defined below. The employer's required contribution would then be 80 percent of the weighted average of those prices.) The employees would be required to pay the difference between the employer's contribution and the cost of the health plan they chose.

Before the annual enrollment period, employers would designate each worker as full time, and thus covered automatically, or part time. (Part-time workers could also be designated as covered.) Detailed rules would be developed to specify which workers would have to be designated as full time and covered. Employers could choose to pay the 8 percent tax rather than cover seasonal or temporary workers.

Self-employed persons, early retirees, and everyone else not covered through full-time employment would be required to contribute through the income tax system. An 8 percent tax would apply to adjusted gross income up to an income ceiling related to the size of the household. The ceiling would be calculated to ensure that households with sufficient income paid for approximately the total subsidy that was available to them. The proceeds of the 8 percent tax would be used by public sponsors to subsidize the purchase of coverage by people not covered by an employer.

Why require employers to cover full-time employees and pay a tax on the earnings of workers not covered? Most health coverage in our country is based on employment, and there is no realistic prospect of changing that in the short run. We propose to spread the cost more evenly over all employment, and to fill in with publicly sponsored coverage where employment-based coverage cannot reasonably be expected to work. Publicly sponsored coverage for individuals has to be subsidized to create a strong incentive for even the healthy to subscribe. In the absence of a subsidy, consumers in apparently good health would seek to avoid paying for coverage until they got sick, or would rely on charity care or public providers because they know that our society is unwilling to let people suffer and die without care. Premiums would soar. The market would break down in a spiral of adverse risk selection, as the market for individual coverage in this country has in fact done.[20]

If publicly sponsored and subsidized coverage were available without the mandate or tax, employers would have a powerful incentive to stop providing coverage and send their employees to the public sponsor. People without coverage would demand it from the public sponsor, which would have to provide it without a source of revenue. Therefore, we propose to use the mandate to keep most coverage employment based. (An alternative model, publicly financed and sponsored, will be discussed in Part Two.) The tax on the earnings of workers not covered by employers would raise much of the funds needed for the public sponsor from those who would benefit. This approach would help avoid a large-scale redistribution of income. Also, it would minimize the otherwise strong incentives for employers to reduce the hours of workers to a level below 25 hours per week, to avoid providing health benefits. Viewed in another way, the 8 percent tax would be a means of aggregating premium contributions on behalf of the part-time, seasonal, and other workers whose attachment to a single employer is not strong enough to justify requiring the employer to provide full insurance coverage. Taft-Hartley trusts do this for unionized workers in specific industries; the proposed mechanism would generalize the Taft-

Hartley trust idea to everyone who was not employed full time by a single employer.

We recognize that there are good arguments against the employer mandate and the tax. Any tax distorts economic decision making. . . .

SUBSIDIES TO PREMIUMS FOR THE POOR

To encourage nearly universal coverage, individuals and families would be eligible for an additional federal subsidy toward the portion of the health insurance premium that they would have to pay if their adjusted gross income was below 150 percent of the poverty level for their family size. Without a subsidy, a family's share of an average premium would be approximately $500. For many families of four with an income equal to 100 percent of the poverty level—approximately $11,000—this would be a substantial expenditure that many would feel they could not afford.

For families with an income below 100 percent of the poverty line, the subsidy would equal the amount of the family's premium contribution (assuming the health plan chosen was no more expensive than the average cost of a basic health plan). For families whose income was between 100 and 150 percent of the poverty level, the subsidy would decrease to zero on a sliding scale as income approached 150 percent. This subsidy would be available both to full-time employees covered by their employers and to those buying coverage through the public sponsor, provided their income was low enough to qualify. The administration of the subsidies would be handled by the agency chosen by each state. We would prefer to see the public sponsors kept out of the process of income testing, because they are not meant to be welfare agencies. One possible approach would be for such testing to be carried out by public welfare agencies that would certify the eligibility of persons and families for subsidies.

SUBSIDIES FOR SMALL BUSINESSES

Small businesses are an important source of new jobs. We would suggest easing the burden of providing coverage for them in two ways. First, as noted earlier, they would be able to buy coverage through the public sponsor, thus realizing the benefits of the public sponsor's economies of scale. Second, small businesses (those with fewer than 25 full-time employees) that arranged coverage through the public sponsor would be required to pay no more than 8 percent of their to-

tal payroll for basic benefits for their employees. If the employer's 80 percent contribution for health insurance exceeded 8 percent of the payroll, the sponsor would subsidize the excess amount.

CREATING AN ENVIRONMENT WITH COST-CONSCIOUS CHOICE

Employers would be required to make a fixed contribution that would be independent of the health plan chosen. (As discussed below, this contribution would vary with the health-risk categories of the enrollees in each plan.) The amount of an employer's contribution that could be excluded from the employee's taxable income would be limited to 80 percent of the average cost of a qualified health plan in the employer's geographic area. The HCFA would offer employers a variety of approved risk-rating systems to translate this into individual tax-free amounts. Additional tax-free contributions under Section 125 of the Internal Revenue Code, which authorizes tax-favored "cafeteria benefit plans," would not be allowed.

The defined-contribution approach and the limitation on the amount of tax-free employer contributions are intended to promote both efficiency and equity. With these limitations, employees who chose more costly plans would have to pay the extra costs with their own net-after-tax dollars. This requirement should promote the choice of less costly plans. In addition, the limit on tax-free contributions would help make funds available to lower-income people not currently covered.

QUALIFIED HEALTH PLANS

Qualified health plans would have to include the basic benefits package specified in the HMO Act, possibly with tighter definitions and restrictions to reduce costs. This package would be updated periodically through legislation and regulation. Deductibles could be no higher than $250 per person in 1988, adjusted for inflation; health plans would pay at least 80 percent of the fees of contracting providers. We would prefer to allow only a small copayment or deductible for inpatient hospital services, because patients have relatively little influence over decisions about the use of such services. However, if more substantial cost sharing among patients were allowed, the premiums could be reduced and, with them, the overall cost of the scheme to taxpayers. Total out-of-pocket expenditures for deductibles and coinsurance for contracting providers' services covered by the health plan could not exceed 100 percent of the annual premium. Qualified plans could not exclude coverage for preexisting conditions for members who enrolled during an annual open-enrollment period. Our intent is to encourage the development of cost-effective managed care plans. Thus, health plans would be free to limit or exclude coverage of the services of nonparticipating providers, except in emergencies when participating providers were not available.

CONTINUITY OF COVERAGE

One goal of the proposal is to have everyone join a health plan during the annual enrollment period and stay in that plan for the subsequent year, unless a "qualifying event" occurred (such as divorce or a move to a new home). This provision would reduce administrative costs and new beginnings on annual deductibles, and would improve the ability of health plans to manage care. Everyone would start the year either covered by his or her employer in a health plan of the employer's arranging or covered by a health plan arranged by the public sponsor. The subsidy of 80 percent of the average cost of qualified health plans contracting with a public sponsor would come either from an employer or from the public sponsor (in the case of part-time employees or other uncovered workers).

People who moved from one part-time job to another would simply keep paying the public sponsor the difference between 80 percent of the average premium and the cost of the coverage they had chosen. Similarly, people who moved between part-time jobs (or unemployment) and full-time jobs with employers that arranged coverage through the public sponsor would feel no discontinuity. When a person was hired, the employer would simply pay 80 percent of the average premium to the public sponsor (as the employer would do for each of its other full-time employees). The subscribers would pay their shares either through the employer or through the sponsor.

When a person took or left a job with an employer that acted as an independent sponsor, there might be some discontinuity. In the detailed design of the program, a choice would have to be made between permitting changes in the health plan when they are caused by a job change and preventing them by complex rules. . . .

RELATION TO MEDICARE AND MEDICAID

We propose no initial change in Medicare and Medicaid. The public sponsors would have enough work to accomplish the objectives set out thus far. However, once this program was operating successfully, there would be opportunities to use the capabilities of the public sponsors to assist the Medicare and Medicaid programs. For example, Medicaid programs should consider contracting with the public sponsors to provide coverage for families on welfare, in order to ease the transition from welfare to work. The existence of the public sponsor would mitigate the work disincentive associated with losing eligibility for Medicaid because of an extra dollar earned, and a Medicaid–public sponsor agreement might mitigate this disincentive further. The existence of nearly universal coverage through the public sponsor should greatly reduce the number of people who "spend down" into Medicaid. As for Medicare, it might find an advantage in using the public sponsors as brokers for HMO enrollment.

MANAGED COMPETITION, TECHNOLOGY ASSESSMENT, AND MANAGEMENT OF OUTCOMES

Here we address the institutional framework within which consumers and providers decide about their participation in plans for health care financing and delivery and the incentives and constraints within which physicians and managers make their decisions about care and resource allocation.

The market for health plans is not inherently competitive. Market forces do not automatically lead it to produce an efficient, much less a fair, outcome.[19-22] In a free market, health plans could pursue profits or survival by using numerous competitive strategies that would destroy efficiency and fairness and that individual consumers would be powerless to counteract: risk selection, market segmentation, product differentiation, discontinuities in coverage, refusals of insurance for some people, biased information, and anticompetitive behavior. Consumers avoid buying coverage until they get sick, and health plans protect themselves with elaborate strategies, including medical review (e.g., testing for the human immunodeficiency virus) and the exclusion of coverage for preexisting conditions. For 35 million Americans to lack coverage is the sort of thing that happens when people are left to a free market.

The type of market structure that we believe can produce reasonable efficiency and fairness is one of managed competition in which intelligent collective agents, called sponsors, contract with competing health plans and continuously monitor and adjust the market to overcome its tendencies to failure. Managed competition has been discussed extensively elsewhere.[19-22] The key idea is that sponsors would manage a process of informed, cost-conscious consumer choice that would offer the reward of more subscribers to health plans whose providers delivered high-quality care economically. . . .

The sponsor could attenuate these incentives by "risk rating"—the process of identifying and grouping persons according to the characteristics that help predict medical expense, with a different price quoted to cover the people in each group. Then the incentive to discriminate against the sick could be reduced by allowing the health plans to charge higher prices for the care of people in high-cost groups. Unfairness to these people could be avoided by tying the sponsor's contributions to the costs in each category, thus protecting the sick from higher costs. For example, the sponsor should pay each health plan an amount equal to the expected cost of efficient care for each of its enrolled patients with the acquired immunodeficiency syndrome, in order to avoid a disincentive to the enrollment and care of such patients. Medicare uses a rudimentary risk-rating system in contracting with HMOs.[24] In addition, the sponsor might contract for standardized coverage in order to prevent the manipulation of the terms of coverage to select patients in particular risk groups. And the sponsor could manage the enrollment process, including contacts between beneficiaries and health plans that might be designed to select for risks. Finally, the sponsor could monitor performance with regard to risk selection and take corrective action as needed. In this way, sponsors could control economic incentives so that the health plans would produce efficient and fair service.

For managed competition to yield efficient, high-quality care, providers, sponsors, and consumers must all be well informed about the constituents of such care. Thus, it is essential that the institutional framework include effective, broad-based programs in technology assessment, the risk-adjusted monitoring of outcomes, and outcomes management. Bunker et al. have proposed the creation of an "institute for health care evaluation" that would establish a uniform data base, identify technologies for assessment, and carry out and disseminate the results of evaluations.[25,26] Blumberg has defined "risk-adjusted monitors of out-

comes" as statistical systems that measure outcomes continuously and enable comparisons to be made that take into account appropriately the differences in patient mix of the populations being compared.[27] This approach can be used, among other things, to identify specific providers whose outcomes are better or worse than expected. Ellwood has recently proposed "outcomes management . . . a common patient-understood language of health outcomes; a national data base containing information and analysis on clinical, financial, and health outcomes that estimates . . . the relation between medical interventions and health outcomes . . . and an opportunity for each decision-maker to have access to the analyses that are relevant to the choices they must make."[28]

Such information strategies are complementary to the process of managed competition; neither can have its intended effect without the other. The information enables sponsors and consumers to choose health plans wisely and to be informed about cost–quality tradeoffs. It enables physicians to avoid using their resources on treatments that do not improve outcomes and to save them for treatments that do. Managed competition rewards them for acting on such information.

In addition, such information is a public good. The profit incentive does not motivate the production of such information in socially optimal amounts. Substantial support by government is both necessary and a wise investment for taxpayers in the long run. All providers must participate in uniform systems of data reporting, because selective reporting on a voluntary basis will not produce credible data. Thus, action is required on the part of the states, the federal government, or both. Although large employers and government agencies (e.g., the HCFA) can gather, analyze, and publish much of this information, it will not have credibility with physicians until they participate actively in its development.

COVERAGE, COSTS, AND BUDGETS

The Congressional Budget Office, which makes such estimates for the Congress, has estimated the effects of our proposal on coverage, costs, and public-sector budgets.[29] Here we report their estimates, which are similar to our own.[18]

Of the 35 million people who are currently uninsured, according to Congressional Budget Office estimates, approximately 22 million would be covered by their employers under the proposed program, and the remaining 13 million would be eligible to purchase subsidized coverage from a public sponsor. . . . In addition to the 13 million currently uninsured people who would be eligible to buy coverage from the public sponsor, 6 million people currently purchasing nongroup insurance would be able to do so. Employers would purchase coverage for 43 million people in addition to those now covered by employer-sponsored insurance (this includes many self-employed people who currently purchase coverage).

Government needs money for five purposes under this proposal: (1) to subsidize 80 percent (50 percent from the federal government) of the cost of an average health plan for households in which no member is a full-time worker; (2) to subsidize small businesses arranging coverage through the public sponsor, whose unsubsidized costs exceed 8 percent of payroll; (3) to subsidize the individual's share of the premiums when family income is less than 150 percent of the poverty level; (4) to cover the increased cost to the federal employee's health benefits program; and (5) to cover the revenue lost from the reduction in taxable wages when employers contribute to the health insurance of previously uninsured employees.

This money would be raised in three ways. First, there would be an 8 percent tax on the first $22,500 of the wages of noncovered workers and a similar tax on self-employed persons and others. Second, there would be a limit on the amount of an employer's contribution to health insurance that could be excluded from an employee's taxable income. Third, the states would be required to fund part of the program, using monies saved because of the large reduction in the costs of hospital care that is publicly sponsored or uncompensated.

We think that the cost of the benefit package we have described would be approximately $2,400 per family per year.[18] The Congressional Budget Office estimates that with a $2,400 annual family premium our proposal would not have a significant effect on the federal deficit. . . . New federal expenditures (after accounting for offsets) would be approximately $12.8 billion; this would be balanced by approximately $12.4 billion in additional tax revenue. There is some uncertainty associated with all such estimates, but we believe that these are accurate enough to demonstrate that a proposal such as ours can be crafted that has no effect on the deficit. As we have shown, the proposal has been designed with a number of "tunable dials." Some marginal adjustments may be necessary to achieve deficit neutrality (or may be desirable for other reasons), but the proposal as currently formulated is close to "budget neutral."

REFERENCES

1. Division of National Cost Estimates, Office of the Actuary, Health Care Financing Administration. National health expenditures, 1986–2000. Health Care Financ Rev 1987; 8(4):1–36.

2. Schiebert GJ, Poullier JP. Recent trends in international health care spending. Health Aff (Millwood) 1987; 6(3):105–12.

3. Sulvetta M, Swartz K. The uninsured and uncompensated care: a chartbook. Washington, D.C.: National Health Policy Forum, George Washington University, 1986.

4. Wilensky GR. Filling the gaps in health insurance: impact on competition. Health Aff (Millwood) 1988; 7(3):133–49.

5. Ries P. Health care coverage by age, sex, race, and family income: United States, 1986. In: Advance data from Vital and Health Statistics of the National Center for Health Statistics. No. 139. Hyattsville, Md.: Public Health Service, 1987. (DHHS publication no. (PHS) 87–1250.)

6. Health insurance and the uninsured: background data and analysis. Washington, D.C.: Congressional Research Service, Library of Congress, May 1988.

7. Farley PJ. Who are the underinsured? Milbank Mem Fund Q 1985; 63:476–503.

8. Directory of preferred provider organizations and the industry report on PPO development. Bethesda, Md.: American Medical Care and Review Association, 1986.

9. InterStudy. The InterStudy edge. Excelsior, Minn.: InterStudy, 1988.

10. Enthoven A. A new proposal to reform the tax treatment of health insurance. Health Aff (Millwood) 1984; 3(1):21–39.

11. Idem. Health tax policy mismatch. Health Aff (Millwood) 1985; 4(4):5–14.

12. Eddy DM. Variations in physician practice: the role of uncertainty. Health Aff (Millwood) 1984; 3(2):74–89.

13. Wennberg JE. Dealing with medical practice variations: a proposal for action. Health Aff (Millwood) 1984; 3(2):6–32.

14. Siu AL, Sonnenberg FA, Manning WG, et al. Inappropriate use of hospitals in a randomized trial of health insurance plans. N Engl J Med 1986; 315:1259–1266.

15. Winslow CM, Solomon DH, Chassin MR, Kosecoff J, Merrick NJ, Brook RH. The appropriateness of carotid endarterectomy. N Engl J Med 1988; 318:721–727.

16. Luft HS. How do health-maintenance organizations achieve their "savings"? Rhetoric and evidence. N Engl J Med 1978; 298: 1336–1343.

17. Manning WG, Leibowitz A, Goldberg GA, Rogers WH, Newhouse JP. A controlled trial of the effect of a prepaid group practice on use of services. N Engl J Med 1984; 310:1505–1510.

18. Enthoven A, Kronick R. A consumer choice health plan for the 1990s: cost and budget estimates and supporting detail. Research paper no. 1023. Stanford, Calif.: Stanford University, Graduate School of Business, 1988.

19. Enthoven A. Theory and practice of managed competition in health care finance. Amsterdam: North-Holland, 1988.

20. Enthoven AC. Managed competition in health care and the unfinished agenda. Health Care Financ Rev 1986; Annu Suppl: 105–120.

21. Enthoven A. Managed competition of alternative delivery systems. J Health Polit Policy Law 1988; 13(2):305–321.

22. *Idem.* Assessing competition in health care: an agenda for action. Health Aff (Millwood) 1988; 7(2):25–47.

23. Newhouse JP. Is competition the answer? J Health Econ 1982; 1(1):109–115.

24. Langwell KM, Hadley JP. Capitation and the Medicare program: history, issues and evidence. Health Care Financ Rev 1986; Annu Suppl:9–20.

25. Bunker JP, Fowles J, Schaffarzick R. Evaluation of medical-technology strategies: effects of coverage and reimbursement. N Engl J Med 1982; 306:620–624.

26. *Idem.* Evaluation of medical-technology strategies: proposal for an institute for health-care evaluation. N Engl J Med 1982; 306:687–692.

27. Blumberg M. Risk-adjusting health care outcomes: a methodologic review. Med Care Rev 1986; 43:351–396.

28. Ellwood PM. Shattuck Lecture—outcomes management: a technology of patient experience. N Engl J Med 1988; 318: 1549–1556.

29. Long S, Rodgers J. Enthoven-Kronick Plan for Universal Health Insurance. Washington, D.C.: Congressional Budget Office, October 18, 1988.

ALLEN BUCHANAN

An Ethical Evaluation of Health Care in the United States

[A few] questions are widely thought to be crucial for evaluating any health care system from an ethical standpoint: (1) Does the system provide equal health care for all? . . . (2) Does the system control health care cost effectively? (3) Does the system maximize free choice for both patients and providers? . . . In this essay I first examine the meaning and presuppositions of each. . . . One conclusion reached is that the extent of freedom of choice in the U.S. health care system, as well as the moral value of some forms of this freedom, have been greatly exaggerated.

1. PROVIDING EQUAL HEALTH CARE FOR ALL

Before it can be determined whether this is an appropriate ethical criterion for evaluating health care systems it is necessary to clarify the meaning of the phrase 'equal health care for all.' It could mean either (a) all receive equal resources for health (i.e., equal amounts of money or services of equal monetary value), (b) all achieve, or have the opportunity to achieve, equal health status, or (c) all receive the same "level" of care (with respect to both "quantity" and "quality", who are in equal need of care).

The first two interpretations of the goal of equal health care for all may be dismissed rather quickly. Since individuals have widely differing needs (and preferences) for health care, pursuing the goal of providing equal amounts of resources for health care for all would not only be inefficient but would also lack an ethical rationale. The goal of achieving equal health status for all must also be rejected simply because it is impossible to achieve, quite independently of whether it would be ethically appropriate if it were possible: there are some unfortunate individuals for whom even the most minimally tolerable health status is unattainable.

The third interpretation, according to which all those who are in equal need of health care are to receive the same level of care, is a coherent goal. However, whether or not this criterion is ethically plausible will depend upon how the notion of *need* is

From Allen Buchanan. "An Ethical Evaluation of Health Care in the United States," in *Health Care Systems,* Hans-Martin Sass and Robert Massey, eds. Reprinted by permission of Kluwer Academic Publishers, 1988.

understood. On a broad interpretation of 'need', a health care need exists wherever the provision of health care services can reasonably be expected to produce net benefit for the patient: a need in this broad sense is simply a potential for net benefit. According to the broad interpretation of the criterion then, a system is ethically deficient if anyone lacks a health care service who could benefit from it as much as someone else who has that service, regardless of how large or small the benefit is. In spite of the fact that many people at least claim to subscribe to it, this broad interpretation of the goal of equal health care for those in equal need has little to recommend it from an ethical point of view, unless there are sound ethical grounds for attempting to arrange all social institutions so that benefits of all kinds are distributed in a strictly equal fashion among all citizens. Though I will make no attempt to rehearse them here, I believe there are a number of strong arguments against any such comprehensive egalitarian principle, not the least important of which is that even a modest attempt to implement such a principle would lead to intolerable restrictions on individual freedom, massive losses of productivity and hence of social welfare, and would obliterate not only individuality but also the social and personal recognition of all desert and merit.

Some who defend the broad interpretation of the goal of equal health care for those with equal health care needs might at this point attempt to dissociate it from a comprehensive equal benefits principle. The point, they might contend, is that *health care* is of such special importance that it requires egalitarianism even if other goods and services do not. Thus one may consistently espouse the goal of equal health care for those with equal potential for benefiting from it without embracing egalitarianism across the board with all of its undesirable consequences.

This reply, however, is inadequate as it stands. It is simply not true that *all* health care is of special importance, because it is not true that all benefits that can be gained from health care are of special importance. Some forms of health care (e.g., resuscitation of persons who will go on to live fulfilling lives) are extremely beneficial: other forms of health care (e.g., triple by-pass surgery or back surgery for some patients) are much less beneficial for those patients than alternative medical or non-medical uses of the same amounts of money would be. Once it is conceded that

not all forms of health care are especially beneficial relative to all other goods and services, it is quite arbitrary to ascribe to a strictly egalitarian principle for the distribution of health care while shrinking from strict egalitarianism for other goods, such as food.

A more charitable interpretation of the goal of equal health care for persons with equal health care needs would be to jettison the broad notion of needs as potentials for benefit and restrict 'needs' to 'potentials for exceptionally great benefits.' In other words *needs* would be understood as *especially important interests,* to be contrasted with mere preferences and with the mere potential for being benefited to some extent or other. But to interpret the equality criterion in this way is to restrict its scope very significantly: it no longer calls for equal health care for all who could benefit from care, but only that all receive equal health care with respect to the satisfaction of those especially important interests that count as health care needs. The great difficulty then, of course, is to determine what counts as a health care need or basic health care interest. Until health care needs in this narrow sense are at least roughly specified, it is impossible to determine how closely a given health care system approximates or falls short of the criterion of equality.

Assuming that the class of health care needs (in the narrow sense) can be roughly specified, the ethical basis for using the equality criterion for evaluating a health care system could be of either of two sorts. According to some ethical theories a system which fails to provide equal satisfaction of health care needs (i.e., basic health care interests) is *unjust*. Justice, however, is not the only ethical standard for institutions. According to some rather austere libertarian theories of justice, individuals have no general positive moral rights and hence, *a fortiori,* no general moral right to health care. Yet such a theory of justice is compatible with — and perhaps only plausible if conjoined with — a theory of ethical virtues, including the virtue of *beneficence* or *charity,* according to which a system which did not provide equal satisfaction of health care needs would be ethically defective, though not unjust.

It is important to understand that whether equal satisfaction of health care needs (construed narrowly as basic health care interests) is understood as an ethical requirement of justice or of charity, its fulfillment is perfectly compatible with inequalities in the provision of health care that satisfies preferences or interests that exceed the minimum constituting the set of health care needs. For example, if Jones and Smith receive equal amounts of health care of equal quality for the satisfaction of their basic health care needs, and if the potential for benefiting from cosmetic nose surgery is not a health care need, then the criterion of equality is satisfied, even if Jones and Smith could both benefit equally from cosmetic nose surgery but only Smith gets it.

Since the criterion that all are to receive equal health care who have equal health care needs is so ambiguous, and since the distinction between needs as especially important interests and needs as preferences or potentials for benefit is so unclear and in need of theoretical support, it is advisable to abandon this formulation altogether. Instead, what is plausible in the equal need criterion can perhaps best be reformulated as follows: everyone is to receive an "adequate level" or "guaranteed minimum" of care.

This formulation has several advantages. First, by requiring equality only with respect to the provision of some limited level of care, a floor or guaranteed minimum of services, it captures the idea that not all health care is of equal value or even of sufficiently high value to make strictly equal provision of it plausible. Similarly, even if there are sound ethical reasons for everyone's receiving some minimal provision of food or shelter, it does not follow that there are equally good reasons for preventing inequalities in the amounts or quality of food and shelter above that minimum. Second, unlike the term 'need' the qualifier 'adequate' here is explicitly normative. Thus the necessity of providing a theory of which health care interests are of special ethical importance is frankly acknowledged and the temptation to assume an objective scientific interpretation of 'needs' (as in 'physiological needs' or 'caloric needs') is avoided. In particular, it is important to preclude the erroneous suggestion that needs in 'equal health care needs' refers to some set of conditions that can be ascertained by the exercise of medical judgment alone.

In this less ambitious form the equality criterion — more accurately called the universal guaranteed minimum criterion — is a highly plausible standard for the ethical evaluation of health care systems, if sufficient content can be given to the notion of a 'guaranteed minimum' or 'adequate level' of care. . . .

Even without further specifying either the content of the universal minimum, without fleshing out the intuitive but vague notion that obstacles to utilizing the minimum are not to be excessive for anyone, and

without determining whether failure to meet this twin standard is a matter of injustice or a lack of charity, we can nevertheless conclude that the U.S. health care system is seriously ethically deficient. As a recent Presidential Commission on medical ethics has convincingly documented, there are at present between 22 and 25 million Americans who have neither private health care insurance nor coverage under Medicare or Medicaid.

Perhaps as many as another 20 to 22 million have coverage which fails to provide at least some of the least controversial elements of an adequate minimum. Moreover, the same Commission also documented the fact that many Americans, particularly in rural and inner city areas, face severe obstacles to utilizing care when it is available.

These figures should come as no surprise once two facts are noted. First, while many individuals whose incomes put them far above the official poverty line are unable to afford anything like comprehensive health insurance (especially if they are not eligible for group plans through their employer), less than 50% of those at or below the poverty line are covered by Medicaid.[1] Second, since Medicaid reimbursement rates are in some cases as low as 40% of prevailing private insurance reimbursement rates, many physicians refuse to treat those "covered" by Medicaid.[2]

It is important to qualify this rather bleak picture of the access problem with two points. First, approximately ninety percent of the American population does have some form of public or private health care insurance. Second, some of those who lack coverage nonetheless have been able to secure at least some forms of care, either through the explicit charity of public hospitals or through the hidden welfare system of "cross-subsidization," whereby a part of the surplus revenue from paying patients has been used to fund care for some of those who cannot pay. However, growing cost-containment competition and new prospective payment arrangements designed to limit charges for Medicare hospital care are making it very difficult for hospitals to continue the practice of cross-subsidization.

The American health care system and medical profession have received well-deserved praise for technological innovation and research, and for providing very high quality care for the majority of citizens. My purpose here is not to deny or to minimize these impressive accomplishments. Instead, I wish only to point out that serious ethical problems remain, especially in the area of access to care. . . .

2. CONTROLLING HEALTH CARE COSTS

One of the most distinctive features of health care in the U.S. has been the predominance of the third-party payment, fee-for-service system, the perverse incentives of which are well known. First, the physician has no effective economic incentive to restrain utilization of treatments and tests because the higher the utilization the higher his revenues. Second, what has traditionally been a fundamental tenet of medical ethics, the principle that the physician is to do the best he can for each patient, puts the moral seal of approval on the physician's urgings of self-interest. Third, fear of malpractice liability — whether that fear is realistic or not — also encourages the physician to order extra tests or treatments, even when they are of dubious value relative to their costs. Fourth, the physician can easily reconcile the provision of care that promises meager benefits relative to costs with his commitment to acting in the patient's best interests, because he knows that the insurance premium is already paid and that the cost of treating this particular patient are being spread over the entire insurance pool.

Similarly, quite aside from the fact that he is likely to defer to what the doctor orders in any case, the insured patient has no effective incentive to restrain utilization so long as the services in question promise any net benefit to him, since he has already paid his premium (unless his policy requires him to make a substantial copayment).

The goal of curbing health care costs can be viewed as a *public good* in the technical sense and, like other public goods such as energy conservation, clean air, and national security, may not be achieved through strictly voluntary efforts because of the free-rider problem. Although each consumer and physician may recognize that we would all benefit from lower health care costs, the incentives of the fee-for-service, third party payment system make it rational for each individual to act in ways which will prevent this goal from being reached. Each individual may reason that his own contribution to cost control will be so minimal as to be negligible and that either enough others will exercise restraint to achieve the goal or they will not, regardless of what he does. If the individual also believes that he will be able to reap the benefits of cost control regardless of whether he contributes to its achievement and if he views his own efforts at cost control to be a cost to him, then, so far as he behaves as an individual utility maximizer, he will not contribute and will attempt to take a "free-ride" on the contributions of others. If enough people act in this way the good will not be achieved — health care costs will continue to rise in spite of the fact that we all agree that curbing costs is necessary.

In addition to the "free-rider" problem, the *assurance problem* threatens to block voluntary action to control health care costs. Even if both the physician and the patient would be willing to exercise restraint in utilizing services *if they could be assured that others would do so as well,* neither may do so where such assurance is lacking. A physician may reason that whether or not health care costs are curbed will be determined not by his own rather insignificant behavior but rather by whether enough other physicians exercise restraint. Unless he can be assured that other physicians will also limit utilization, why should he unilaterally expose himself to malpractice liability (by falling below the "community standards of care" that determine what counts as malpractice), to a reduction of income, and to possible complaints from patients that he is not doing the best he can for them? Similarly, you and I as consumers of health care may bemoan rising costs, but may be unwilling to forego that extra laboratory test which has only a 0.005 probability of detecting cancer, unless we have assurance that others will exercise similar restraint. Even if each test is very inexpensive, the cost of this small added protection against misdiagnosis may be very great if many thousands of tests are done each year. Yet the cost of *my* having the test may be negligible, especially since the potential benefit to me of early detection of cancer is enormous. Granted this remarkable convergence of incentives, both for the provider and the consumer, it is not surprising that such a system generates increasing costs.

The final major contributor to the cost crisis in health care is the manner in which private insurers and government programs such as Medicare and Medicaid have paid for services provided by physicians and hospitals. Payment has been according to "reasonable and customary rates," and in a health care system in which organized medicine has approached a professional monopoly on the provision of reimburseable services, what is "reasonable and customary" has been determined largely by the providers of health care, in the absence of the restraints which price-competition provides in a genuine market.

It is important to understand the basis of the charge that the U.S. health care system has failed to satisfy the criterion of adequate cost containment. The fact that the percentage of the U.S. gross national product devoted to health care has more than doubled in the past dozen years is often taken as proof that there is a "cost-crisis" in health care. Such an inference, however, is invalid. There is no magic number which can be assumed to represent *the* correct proportion of social resources to be used for health care. It might be quite reasonable, for example, for a society as affluent as the U.S. to spend 20% rather than 11% of its G.N.P. for health care, *if* this allocation accurately reflected informed social priorities and if the allocation for health care were used efficiently. The real cost crisis in U.S. health care is not so much that we are spending too much, but that we are not getting our money's worth. . . .

Until quite recently, the same system that produced the cost crisis also supported a hidden welfare system for some of the millions of patients who lacked private insurance and who were not covered by government programs. By overcharging paying patients, hospitals were able to "cross-subsidize" some care for indigent patients. However, the main strategies for cost containment are making it increasingly difficult if not impossible for hospitals to continue the practice of cross-subsidization without exposing themselves to serious financial risk. . . .

So not only has the U.S. health care system failed to satisfy either the criterion that all are to be provided with at least a minimal level of basic health care services or the criterion of adequate cost-containment; even worse, current efforts to curb costs are exacerbating the problem of lack of access to care for millions of Americans.

3. MAINTAINING THE MAXIMUM AMOUNT OF FREE CHOICE FOR PATIENTS AND PROVIDERS

This fourth criterion for evaluating health care systems, if taken literally, contains a very controversial presupposition, namely, that the freedom, or rather, various freedoms, of different persons, in a given system can be individually quantified and then aggregated into a magnitude to be compared to similar aggregates of freedom in other systems. This presupposition is open to criticism on a number of grounds, not the least of which is that it may be difficult to spell out the notion

of an *amount* of freedom even for one person and for one kind of freedom. For example, do I have more freedom, in any morally interesting sense, in one situation than in another simply because I have one more option in the former than in the latter? Or does that depend upon how valuable the additional option is? Presumably we cannot always determine whether a person has greater freedom in one situation than another simply by counting his options, since to do so would be to overlook the fact that ultimately we are interested not merely in increasing opportunities for action (no matter how trivial or valueless) but in increasing the range of *significant options*.

Is the significance of options to be understood in a purely subjective way, as defined by the preferences of the agent, or is it to include an objective element? Further, in which situation do I have a great amount of freedom: in a situation of which I have fewer options, each of which I can avail myself of without great effort, or in a situation with more options, each of which would require more effort or costs on my part to realize? Instead of pondering further these and a number of other perplexities that lay behind the notion of 'maximum freedom,' I shall simply ask what kinds of freedoms are enjoyed by consumers and providers in the U.S. health care system, and then ask which freedoms are of greatest moral importance.

We can begin by considering freedoms which health care consumers have and do not have in the U.S. It is often said that one of the strong points of the U.S. system is that consumers have *the freedom to choose a physician* that meets their own standards. This, of course, is at best a very misleading half-truth. First of all, only those who are fortunate enough to have health care coverage have the freedom to choose a physician; those without coverage lack not only the freedom to choose among physicians but the ability to get any professional medical care at all for many of their problems, even in some cases of life-threatening emergencies. Second, many of those who are covered by government programs, in particular Medicaid, have little or no freedom to choose among physicians, and as was noted earlier may not even be able to find one physician in their region who will accept them, because of low Medicaid reimbursement rates. A more accurate statement, then, is that the U.S. health care system provides considerable freedom to choose a physician only for most of those who have private insurance or Medicare coverage but not for the more than 22 million who lack any form of coverage and not for many of the millions who have Medicaid coverage.

Nevertheless, the majority of people in the U.S., who are covered by Medicare or private insurance, have a good deal of freedom to choose a physician. And many seem to value this freedom highly.

There is one kind of freedom of choice concerning care, however, which largely has been lacking for those who have adequate health care coverage as well as those who do not: the freedom to show their preferences about the limited importance of health care (to them) relative to other valuable goods. In other words, the third-party payment, fee-for-service system that has dominated U.S. health care, as we have seen, has made it virtually impossible for consumers to control the amount of social and private resources that have been flowing into the health care system. . . .

Even if we set aside this lack of control over private and social resources as one important kind of freedom, it is difficult to justify the U.S. system on the grounds that the freedom to choose a physician enjoyed by the fortunate compensates for the lack of this freedom on the part of the unfortunate. The results of hypothetical choice or ideal contractarian or *ex ante* insurance decisions seem to support this conclusion. Given that he is behind a "veil of ignorance" that precludes him from knowing that he is a member of the fortunate group, a rational decision-maker whose aversion to risk falls within what can be considered the normal range would presumably choose a system in which he would be guaranteed access to progressional care, at least for serious problems, even if this system placed restrictions on his freedom to choose a physician, over a system which gave him greater freedom in the choice of a physician if he turned out to have coverage of the appropriate sort, but in which he might have no access to important forms of care at all.

Further, it is very implausible to maintain that we in the U.S. must choose between having a system in which some enjoy a wide freedom of choice among physicians while millions lack any access at all to some important health care services and a system in which everyone has access to important services but most or all have no freedom of choice among physicians. To assume that these are the only choices is to assume that the only alternatives are the current system or an extreme version of the National Health Service model in which the government not only provides all health care but does so in such a way that patients have little or no freedom to choose among physicians employed by the government. It is not at all clear, however, that even a National Health Service need be so restrictive. More importantly, there are several plausible options for increasing access to care while maintaining a wide freedom in the choice of physicians for all without introducing a National Health Service in the U.S. One of the most attractive of these is the idea of promoting greater competition in health care while providing the poor with health insurance vouchers subsidized from general tax revenues.[3] . . .

In addition to restricting the freedom of consumers to choose among alternative forms of health care and restricting the freedom of nurses and others to offer services independently of physicians, organized medicine in the United States has, of course, limited the freedom of all those persons who might have developed alternative forms of care had they been allowed to. Any attempt to characterize "the freedom of health care providers" in the U.S., then, must first distinguish among various sorts of providers and recognize that physicians have often used their freedom to curtail not only the freedom of consumers but also that of other, non-physician providers.

Physicians in the U.S. traditionally have enjoyed a great deal of freedom of several different sorts. Proposals aimed at providing wider access to health care, from the development of health maintenance organizations that offer more affordable services, to Medicare, National Health Insurance schemes, and more extreme plans for a National Health Service, have all met strong opposition from organized medicine in the U.S. in the name of preserving physicians' freedoms. Too often suggestions for improving access and for curbing costs have been dismissed on the grounds that they would unduly interfere with physicians' freedoms. What is needed is a careful account of what the relevant physician freedoms are, how various reforms would affect them, and, above all, what the moral status of those freedoms is. The latter question is of great importance because not all freedoms are of equal, or even of very significant, moral value. If an institutional change would violate a freedom or liberty which is so basic as to warrant talk of a *right* to that freedom, then that is a potent objection to making the institutional change in question. On the other hand, some freedoms do not deserve the strong protection provided by rights and others are themselves morally suspect, especially if they are enjoyed by some through interfering with the freedom of other persons.

It has been observed that physicians in the U.S. traditionally have enjoyed considerable freedom from interference by others in four areas: (1) the diagnosis and treatment of patients; (2) the entrance requirements to the profession; (3) the organization of medical practice; and (4) the financing arrangements for medical services.[4] Another freedom enjoyed by American physicians — and frequently declared to be worth preserving at almost any price — is (5) the freedom to choose one's specialty and practice where one wishes.

I have noted that (2), physicians' freedom in controlling the entrance requirements to the medical profession, has sometimes been exercised in ways which limit the freedom of consumers and non-physician health care providers or would-be health care providers. I have also suggested that at least in some cases these restrictions on freedom have not been justified, especially when they are imposed in the name of ensuring "the best possible health care," a goal which, I have argued, is neither rational nor ethical for a society to pursue at the cost of other important values. The special expertise to physicians does, of course, support a strong presumption that they are to play a major role in determining the requirements for entry into their professions. But the long record of self-serving behavior in this regard supports the conclusion that this freedom should be limited by regard for the public interest and the freedom of others.

Similarly, a great deal of physician freedom in the diagnosis and treatment of patients is desirable and justifiable on grounds of the physician's special expertise — and because of the vital need to prevent medical practice from becoming a tool (or rather a weapon) of state power and social control, as it has become in the Soviet Union. Nevertheless, as I have argued, the need to control costs is of sufficient gravity from both a rational-prudential and an ethical point of view to warrant some restrictions on this freedom as well. The trick, of course, will be to devise ways of limiting this physician freedom without undermining the patient's trust in the physician as his advocate, as someone whose primary concern is with the patient's well-being. . . .

The fifth physician freedom, the freedom to choose one's specialty and place of practice, is ambiguous. It could refer simply to the freedom of occupational choice which all Americans enjoy as a matter of legal right, the freedom to try one's hand at any legal occupation, but with no guarantee, of course, that one will succeed in the market. On this interpretation, the freedom to choose one's specialty and place of practice is compatible even with a National Health Service, so long as physicians are permitted to offer their services wherever they wish in a market which is allowed to exist alongside the government system, as in Great Britain. On the other hand, the fifth physician freedom could be understood, in a quite different way, to be the actual range of opportunities for choosing specialties and practice location *that will be economically viable or lucrative,* which American physicians now enjoy. There is little doubt that the establishment of a National Health Service, and, to a lesser extent, more modest proposals for improving access to care by limiting the number of training spots in over-supplied specialties such as general surgery, as well as other measures to encourage the movement of physicians into underserved locales, would limit *this* physician freedom.

The wide range of opportunities for selecting economically viable and even lucrative specialties and practice locations that American physicians now enjoy is, however, in part a result of lack of competition in health care, and in particular stems from questionable exercises of physicians' freedom in determining the entry requirements for the profession, the financing arrangements for medical practice, and the allocation of public monies among different specialty training programs. If a case could be made for arranging our social institutions in such a way as to guarantee physicians not only the freedom to choose an occupation (and to succeed or fail in the competitive market), which all Americans enjoy, but in addition the freedom to have an exceptionally broad range of economically viable occupational choices as a result of being protected, it could not rest upon the wildly implausible assumption that physicians have a basic moral right to such a privileged position. Instead, it would be necessary to show that the attainment of some especially important social good depended upon according physicians this special benefit. It is hard to imagine, however, that whatever social benefits might accrue to preserving the exceptional occupational opportunities which U.S. physicians have come to have as a result of a combination of massive public subsidies for medical education, research, and patient care and the monopolistic exercise of control over licensure and training could outweigh the fundamental goals of improving access and controlling costs.

In sum, any serious attempt to evaluate the U.S. health care system from the standpoint of consumer and provider freedom must yield mixed results. That system is not so bountiful in consumer freedom as its more enthusiastic celebrants have proclaimed. Moreover, the much-touted freedoms of American physicians are not plausibly viewed as basic moral rights and in any case have sometimes been secured and exercised in indefensible ways.

NOTES

1. ([1], I, p. 95).
2. ([1], I, pp. 86–87).
3. [3].
4. ([6], p. 98).

REFERENCES

1. Brock, D.: 1983, 'Distribution of Health Care and Individual Liberty,' President's Commission, *Securing Access to Health Care,* Government Printing Office, Washington, D.C., Vol. II, pp. 239–264.

2. Daniels, N.: 1981, *Just Health Care,* Cambridge University Press, Cambridge, England.

3. Enthoven, A.: 1980, *Health Plan: The Only Practical Solution to the Soaring Cost of Medical Care,* Addison-Wesley, Reading, Mass.

4. Friedman, M.: 1962, *Capitalism and Freedom,* University of Chicago Press, Chicago, Ill.

5. Shelp, E. (ed.): 1982, *Beneficence in Health Care,* D. Reidel, Dordrecht, Holland.

6. Stroman, D.: 1976, *The Medical Establishment and Social Responsibility,* Kennikat Press, Port Washington, New York, p. 98.

Rationing Health Care and the Oregon Plan

DAVID C. HADORN

The Oregon Priority-Setting Exercise: Quality of Life and Public Policy

In 1989 the Oregon State legislature passed the Oregon Basic Health Services Act, which created a Health Services Commission charged with "developing a priority list of health services, ranging from the most important to the least important for the entire population to be served."[1] The goal of this legislation was to permit the expansion of Medicaid to 100 percent of all Oregonians living in poverty by covering

only services deemed to be of sufficient importance or priority.

The Oregon Health Services Commission (OHSC) initially interpreted "for the entire population to be served" as suggesting the use of cost-effectiveness principles for developing the priority list. These principles are based on the utilitarian quest for "the greatest good for the greatest number" and tend to devalue adverse effects of a policy on specific individuals.[2] By the lights of cost-effectiveness, the "importance" of a health service depends not only on the expected outcomes of treatment (such as prolongation of life,

From David C. Hadorn. "The Oregon Priority-Setting Exercise: Quality of Life and Public Policy," *Hastings Center Report,* May–June, 1991. © 1991 The Hastings Center.

reduction of pain), but also on the cost of that service and on the number of patients who can benefit from it. Thus, even very beneficial treatments might not be considered important if the costs of providing those treatments are high or if only a few people benefit from them.

In keeping with their interpretation of the statute, the OHSC initially conducted a cost-effectiveness analysis of over 1,600 health services ranging from appendectomies to treatment of colds and flu. Predictably, the resulting draft list rated outpatient office visits for minor problems as the "most important" services; the cost of these visits was estimated at $98.51. Indeed, the first 94 items on Oregon's initial list were for office visits, for often self-limiting conditions such as thumb-sucking and low back pain. By contrast, certain life-saving surgeries, such as appendectomies, were rated relatively low because of their higher associated costs.

This counterintuitive priority order (and negative public reaction to it[3]) led the OHSC to abandon cost-effectiveness analysis for purposes of developing its final priority list.[4] Instead, the OHSC developed a set of seventeen health service "categories," which described either a specific type of service (for example, maternity care, preventive services) or, more generically, the expected outcomes of care (for example, "treatment of life-threatening illness where treatment restores life-expectancy and return to previous health"). Commissioners formally ranked these seventeen categories in order of importance according to three subjective criteria: value to the individual, value to society, and whether the category seemed "necessary."

Each treatment was then assigned to the single most appropriate category, based on Commissioners' judgment. Services were ranked within categories according to the degree of benefit expected from treatment. Finally, the OHSC rearranged apparently misplaced services "by hand," for example, moving obviously important services rated low by the method higher on the final list.

This alternative methodology produced a much more intuitively sensible final priority list than the earlier draft list, although more work may be needed before the "final" list can serve as the basis for public policy, particularly with respect to better specifying treatments and indications for treatment.[5]

At the time of this writing, independent actuaries are estimating the costs of providing services on the final list. The Oregon legislature will then decide whether to accept the list as the basis for expanding the State's Medicaid program, as per the Oregon Basic Health Services Act. If so, the legislature will draw a line somewhere on the list to separate the services that will be covered under Medicaid from those that will not. Finally, if this step is taken, Oregon will appeal to the federal government for a Medicaid waiver, which must be granted if the plan is to proceed.

ROLE OF QUALITY OF LIFE

The Oregon priority-setting process is significant in many ways, particularly with respect to its implications for social policy. Some of the most important of these implications, discussed in the accompanying article by Charles Dougherty, relate to questions of distributive justice, including Rawlsian attempts to identify the least advantaged members of society and to assess how the Oregon process affects them. (For my money, the uninsured poor are the worst off and the Oregon process improves their lot.) In addition, the fact that cost-effectiveness analysis failed to produce a reasonable priority list has significant implications for future efforts to set health care priorities.[6]

Another important story concerning the Oregon priority-setting exercise remains to be told, however. This story concerns the critical role played by quality of life judgments in constructing Oregon's final priority list. Estimates of how treatments affect quality of life were by far the single most important factor in determining the priority order on that list. Most of the service categories that constituted the principal method of prioritization were explicitly defined in terms of quality of life or, in what was generally treated as an equivalent term, "health status." Furthermore, the secondary (within-category) rank-ordering was performed by reference to the "net benefit" from treatment, which, as we shall see, was an explicit *numerical* estimate of the impacts of treatment on quality of life.

Lack of understanding about the role of quality of life in formulating the final priority list has already led to erroneous interpretations of the list. For example, a spokesperson for Children's Defense Fund in Washington, D.C., criticized the fact that treatment for extremely premature infants (less than 500 grams and less than 23 weeks gestation) was rated next to last on the list (just prior to treatment for infants born without a brain), saying, "If you're looking at it from a purely economic view, it makes sense not to cover those infants. Of course, we think it's completely unethical to do that."[7]

In fact, however, economic considerations had little or nothing to do with placement of this (or any other) treatment on the *final* list; rather, like most items near the bottom of the list, treatment of extremely premature infants was rated low because it had been assigned to the lowest-ranked service category: treatments offering "minimal or no improvment in QWB," or Quality of Well-Being, the OHSC's term for quality of life. It was a consideration of the *outcomes* (in this case, severe retardation and cerebral palsy) of treating extremely premature infants that led the OHSC to make this category assignment—and in turn determined placement on the final list.

Similarly, active medical or surgical treatments for terminally ill patients were rated near the bottom of the list by virtue of having been assigned to the same poor-outcome category just described. Terminally ill patients were defined (problematically, perhaps) as those with less than a 10 percent chance of surviving five years, even with treatment, and included patients suffering from "cancer with distant metastases" or "terminal HIV disease." Comfort care for these patients, including hospice programs and pain medication, was ranked relatively high, however—at 164 out of 709 total items—as was the longevity- and quality-of-life-enhancing during AZT for patients with HIV disease, at 158.

BACKGROUND

Before describing the method used by the OHSC to obtain explicit estimates of quality-of-life outcomes (the basis for within-category ranking of services) a little background is required, both historical and philosophical. The focus on quality of life as a principal factor in health care resource allocation has a long history in Oregon, most of which concerns the activity of a community grassroots bioethics project known as Oregon Health Decisions (OHD).[8] For several years preceding creation of the OHSC, OHD had held hundreds of citizen meetings around the state to discuss health care and resource allocation issues. In September 1988 a Citizens Health Care Parliament was held in Portland in which fifty delegates met for a day and a half to develop "a set of public policy principles which are intended to be guideposts for the state legislature and other policy-makers concerned with health

care resource allocation."[9] The principles developed by the parliament focused on quality of life to a remarkable extent. Indeed, the first six (of fifteen) principles contained explicit references to the importance of quality of life in making health care allocation decisions. Of particular interest are these:

1. The responsibility of government in providing health care resources is to improve the overall quality of life of people by acting within the limits of available financial and other resources.
4. Health care activities should be undertaken to increase the length of life and/or the health-related quality of life during one's life span.
5. Quality of life should be used as one of the ethical standards when allocating health care expenditures with insurance or government funds.
6. Health-related quality of life includes physical, mental, social, cognitive, and self-care functions, as well as a perception of pain and sense of well-being.

As part of the process of developing its priority list, the OHSC commissioned OHD to hold a series of public meetings to discuss people's values concerning the outcomes of care. OHD used a set of service categories similar to those ultimately adopted by the OHSC to elicit relative preferences for different treatments. Quality of life again emerged as a major priority.

ETHICAL CONSIDERATIONS

One final, critical clarification is required before describing the OHSC's approach to measuring quality of life. The use of quality of life information to develop public policy is potentially problematic from a couple of perspectives. First, the use of purely objective measures of quality of life, such as the degree of assistance required to walk or level of independence in self-care activities, does not correlate well with *perceived* quality of life. For example, Najman and Levine reviewed an extensive literature in which quality of life reports were obtained from patients who were "objectively" living restricted lives. Almost invariably, perceived quality of life was higher than might have been predicted.[10]

Second, judging others' quality of life may place us on a slippery slope. In the *Encyclopedia of Bioethics,* Reich notes that judgments of "unacceptable quality of life" are often determined by the "social acceptability" of various diseases or conditions.[11] Simi-

If for example some people were given life-saving treatment in preference to others because they had a better quality of life than those others, or more dependents and friends, or because they were considered more useful, this would amount to regarding such people as more valuable than others on that account. Indeed it would be tantamount, literally, to sacrificing the lives of others so that they might continue to live. . . . To discriminate between people on the grounds of quality of life . . . is as unwarranted as it would be to discriminate on the grounds of race or gender.[12]

There is, however, a key distinction between underestimating quality of life or using the concept to bring about invidious discrimination, on the one hand, and Oregon's use of it on the other. Specifically, the concerns expressed in the previous paragraphs involve judgments made about a person's quality of life at a given point in time—independent of any medical or surgical treatments. Such judgments are *inappropriate* bases upon which to ground resource allocation policy.

By contrast, the *appropriate,* non-discriminatory way to deal with quality-of-life information (and the approach adopted by the OHSC) is to focus on the *change* in quality of life expected with the use of a specific treatment or procedure. How much *better* or *worse* (if at all) is a patient's quality of life likely to be with application of a particular health service? This focus permits appropriate consideration to be given to the important impacts of treatments on quality of life which, as described earlier, are of considerable importance to the public in determining fair and rational systems of resource allocation. At the same time, the potential for discrimination is eliminated because treatments for handicapped or "poor quality of life" patients are evaluated on the same basis as are treatments for everyone else. It is the *change* in quality of life, or net benefit, realized from a *treatment* that matters, not the *point-in-time* quality of life of a *patient.*

QUALITY-ADJUSTED LIFE YEARS

After consulting with advisors at Oregon Health Decisions, the OHSC decided to incorporate quality of life considerations into the priority-setting process using the "quality-adjusted life year" (QALY) approach.[13] This method permits integration of the quality-of-life effects of treatment with its associated impacts on life expectancy. Some treatments, such as appendec-

tomies, are valued not for any improvements in quality of life, but rather for their substantial positive effects in life expectancy: in the case of appendicitis, going from perhaps two weeks to normal. Other treatments have significant impact on quality of life, but little or no effect on life expectancy—such as medication or surgery for arthritis, or prostatectomy for benign obstruction. Still other treatments involve trade-offs between quality and quantity of life, where a longer life expectancy may come at the expense of various side effects from treatment, resulting in a possible decrease in quality of life.

Use of the QALY approach requires the explicit estimation of "percentage of normal quality of life." One year of "normal" quality of life is considered equivalent in value to two years of "one-half normal" quality of life: moreover, two treatments offering these respective outcomes would be valued equally (other things being equal). The QALY concept is useful primarily because it reminds us of a few key principles:

Necessity. We have no choice but to consider both quality and quantity of life in some integrative fashion to properly evaluate health care services.

Common Sense. Other things being equal, treatments offering fewer net benefits in terms of either quality of life, longevity, or both, should be valued less highly than treatments offering more such benefits. Thus, if two treatments each offer about a year of additional life, the one that offers greater benefits in terms of quality of life should be favored.

Proportionate Value. Building on the last concept, treatments should be valued *roughly in proportion to the degree of benefit they offer to patients.* Thus, we should be able to distinguish between treatments that offer highly valued outcomes, such as comfort and the relief of pain that is characteristic of hospice programs, from treatments that provide less-valued outcomes, such as the marginal prolongation of life with severe side effects characteristic of many aggressive treatments for terminally ill patients. The QALY approach in theory permits this sort of distinction to be made.

Several problems with the QALY concept have so far caused it to remain merely a heuristic device, by limiting real-world application:

Questionable Assumption. The QALY method assumes that people see no difference between, say, one year of normal-quality life and ten years of life at one-tenth quality

Limitation or Symptom	Decrement Value
Moderate mobility limitation (e.g., unable to use transportation outside the home)	-.046
Major mobility limitation (e.g., hospitalized)	-.049
Moderate physical activity limitation (e.g., wheelchair)	-.373
Major physical activity limitation (e.g., bedbound)	-.560
Moderate social activity limitation (e.g., unable to work)	-.062
Major social activity limitation (e.g., unable to perform self-care activities)	-.106
Loss of consciousness such as seizure, fainting, or coma	-.114
Burn over large areas of face, body, arms, or legs	-.372
Trouble learning, remembering, or thinking clearly	-.367
Any combination of one or more hands, feet, arms, or legs either missing, deformed, paralyzed, or broken—includes wearing artificial limbs or braces	-.277
Sick or upset stomach, vomiting or loose bowel movement, with or without fever, chills, or aching all over	-.370
General tiredness, weakness, or weight loss	-.275
Coughing, wheezing, or shortness of breath, with or without fever, chills, or aching all over	-.318
Spells of feeling upset, being depressed, or of crying	-.326
Trouble talking, such as lisp, stuttering, hoarseness, or being unable to talk	-.188

Descriptions were slightly modified by the OHSC from Kaplan's QWB scale (Robert Kaplan and John Anderson, "A General Health Policy Model: Update and Applications," *Health Services Research* 23 [1988]: 203–35).

Decrement values were obtained as described in the text.

Figure 1   Descriptions of Limitations and Symptoms Used to Calculate Net Benefit from Treatment (Partial List).

(whatever *that* is). The QALY approach assumes that a short, good life is of equal value to a long, ailing one. This assumption seems unlikely to be valid.

Equity Problems. The QALY approach suffers from a limitation common to any purely utilitarian construct: our intuitive rejection of conclusions to the effect that one person should be treated rather than many. In particular, QALY logic supposes that if a choice comes down to treating one person who stands to gain ten QALYs, or nine people who each stand to gain one QALY, then the single person should be treated.

Measurement Problems. What does it mean to speak of someone having a "one-tenth normal" quality of life? How could we come up with such an overall numerical estimate? Anyway, how can we quantify a *quality,* especially one so amorphous and ill-defined as quality of life?

The first two of these problems speak to the fact that QALYs cannot be used as the sole basis for re-source allocation decisionmaking. This conclusion is hardly new; even the staunchest advocates of the QALY concept realize that the conflict between indi-vidual and societal preferences and issues of justice and equity must also be entered into the resource allo-cation equation.

It is the measurement problem that is responsible for the fact that QALYs have had so little impact on the health care system since their introduction almost twenty years ago. And it is here that the OHSC made its greatest methodological contribution to the goal of setting health care priorities. As such, the Oregon process represents the first large-scale effort in the United States to operationalize the QALY concept for purposes of resource allocation policy. . . .

NOTES

1. Oregon Senate Bill 27.

2. Milton Weinstein and William Stason, "Foundations of Cost-effectiveness Analysis for Health and Medical Practices," *NEJM* 296 (1976): 716–721.

3. T. Egan, "Problems Could Delay Proposal by Oregon to Ration Health Care," *New York Times,* 30 July 1990.

4. David Hadorn, "Setting Health Care Priorities in Oregon: Cost-Effectiveness Meets the Rule of Rescue," *JAMA* 265 (1991): 2218–25.

5. Hadorn, "Setting Health Care Priorities."

6. Hadorn, "Setting Health Care Priorities."

7. Dean Mayer and Merit Kimball, "Oregon Commission OKs Medicaid Pecking Order," *Healthweek,* 25 February 1991, pp. 1, 36.

8. Brian Hines, "Health Policy on the Town Meeting Agenda," *Hastings Center Report* 16, no. 2 (1986): 5–7; Bruce Jennings, "Community Health Decisions: A Grassroots Movement in Bioethics," *Hastings Center Report* 18, no. 5, Special Supplement (1988).

9. "Quality of Life in Allocating Health Care Resources," adopted by the Citizens Health Care Parliament, 23–24 September 1988, Portland, Oregon.

10. Jackob Najman and Sol Levine, "Evaluating the Impact of Medical Care and Technologies on the Quality of Life: A Review and Critique," *Social Science and Medicine* 15 (1981): 107–115.

11. Warren Reich, "Life: Quality of Life," *Encyclopedia of Bioethics* (New York: The Free Press, 1978), pp. 829–840, at 837.

12. John Harris, "QALYifying the Value of Life," *Journal of Medical Ethics* 13 (1987): 117–123, at 121.

13. Graham Loomes and Lynda McKenzie, "The Use of QALYs in Health Care Decision Making," *Social Science and Medicine* 28 (1989): 299–308.

N O R M A N   D A N I E L S

Is the Oregon Rationing Plan Fair?

The Oregon Basic Health Services Act mandates universal access to basic care, but includes rationing services to those individuals who are Medicaid recipients. If no new resources are added, the plan may make current Medicaid recipients worse off, but still reduce inequality between the poor and the rest of society. If resources are expanded and benefits given appropriate rankings, no one may be worse off; though inequality will be reduced, alternative reforms might reduce it even further. Whether the outcome seems fair then depends on how much priority to the well-being of the poor we believe justice requires; it also depends on political judgments about the feasibility of alternative strategies for achieving more egalitarian reforms. Oregon makes rationing public and explicit, as justice requires, but it is not clear how community values influence the ranking of services; ultimately, the rationing process is fair only if we may rely on the voting power of the poor.

From Norman Daniels, "Is the Oregon Rationing Plan Fair?" *Journal of American Medical Association* 265, No. 17 (May 1, 1991). © 1991, American Medical Association.

EXCLUDING PEOPLE VS. EXCLUDING SERVICES

In 1987, Oregon drew national attention when it stopped Medicaid funding of soft-tissue transplants. Officials justified the action by claiming that there are more effective ways to spend scarce public dollars than to provide high-cost benefits to relatively few people. They insisted that the estimated $1.1 million that would have been spent on such transplants in 1987 would save many more lives per dollar spent if invested in prenatal maternal care.[1] Rather than heartlessly turning its back on children in need of transplants, the state was making a "tragic choice" between two instances of rationing by ability to pay. The consequences of ignoring "invisible" pregnant women who cannot afford prenatal maternal care are much worse than are those of refusing to fund highly visible children in need of transplants.

The Oregan Basic Health Services Act boldly couples the rationing of health care with a plan to improve access.[2] It expands Medicaid eligibility to 100% for those individuals who are at the federal poverty level, creates an Oregon Health Services Commission (OHSC) to establish priorities among health services,

requires cutting low-priority services rather than excluding people from coverage when reducing expenditures is necessary, mandates a high-risk insurance
pool, and requires employers to provide health insurance or to contribute to a state insurance pool. Oregon
must obtain a federal waiver to implement the
changes in Medicaid.

Oregon explicitly rejects the rationing strategy that
predominates in the United States: our rationing system excludes whole categories of the poor and near-
poor from access to public insurance, denying coverage to *people,* rather than to low-priority *services.* In
contrast, the Oregon plan embodies the following
principles: (1) there is a social obligation to guarantee
universal access to a *basic level* of health care, (2) reasonable or necessary limits on resources mean that not
every beneficial service can be included in the basic
level of health care, and (3) a public process, involving consideration of social values, is required to determine what services will be included in the basic level
of health care.[1,3]

Though these principles are not a complete account
of justice for health care, they have considerable plausibility, derive support from theoretical work on justice and health care, and are, to varying degrees,
widely believed in by the US population.[4] Nevertheless, these principles permit rationing care to the poor
alone, with serious implications for equality. Thus,
critics attack the Oregon plan for making the poor,
specifically poor women and children, "bear the burden" of providing universal access.[5]

To evaluate this criticism, we must ask three questions: (1) Does the plan make the indigent groups
better off or worse off? (2) Are the inequalities the
plan accepts justifiable? (3) Is the procedure for determining the basic level of health care a just or fair
one? These questions raise issues of distributive justice that go beyond the principles underlying the Oregon legislation.

WHAT DOES THE OREGON PLAN DO
TO THE WORSE-OFF GROUPS?

Critics of Oregon's plan appeal to widely held egalitarian concerns when they argue that it makes the poor
bear the burden of this effort to close the insurance
gap. The strongest sense of "bear the burden" is "being made worse off." Does the plan, as the critics
charge, make the poor worse off instead of giving priority to improving their well-being?[6,7]

Consider the simplest case first, a zero sum game
with resources. For example, if extrarenal transplants
are removed from coverage and no higher-priority services, unavailable before the plan, are added, then current Medicaid recipients will lose some services and
the health benefits they produce. They will no doubt
then make this complaint: "We bear the burden of the
plan. Since we are already the most indigent group, or
close to it, we should not have to give up lifesaving or
other important medical services so that the currently
uninsured can get basic level health care."

It is important to grasp the moral force of this complaint. Notice that *aggregate* health status for *all* the
poor, including current Medicaid recipients and the
uninsured, can be improved by the plan, even though
current Medicaid recipients are made worse off. The
loss of less important services by current recipients is
more than counterbalanced by the gains of the uninsured. As a result, the plan reduces overall inequality
between the poor and the rest of society, albeit at the
expense of current Medicaid recipients. Therefore, the
complaint cannot be that the plan makes society less
equal; instead, it is that even greater reductions in inequality are possible if other groups sacrifice instead
of Medicaid recipients. It is unfair for current Medicaid recipients to bear a burden that others could bear
much better, especially since inequality would then be
even further reduced.

How stringent is the priority owed the poorest
groups when we seek to improve aggregate well-
being? Three positions are possible: (1) help the poor
as much as possible *(strict priority)*; (2) make sure the
poor get some benefit *(modified priority)*; or (3) allow
only modest harms to the poor in return for significant
gains to others who are not well off *(weak priority)*.
Critics of the Oregon plan insist that we should not
settle for weak priority, especially since feasible alternatives help the poor more. The Oregon plan leaves
the bulk of the health care system intact. By eliminating the inefficiencies it contains, e.g., by establishing a
low-overhead public insurance scheme (as in Canada),
or by developing treatment protocols that eliminate
unnecessary services, we might be able to avoid making current Medicaid recipients any worse off. Alternatively, by broadening rationing to cover most of society, as in Canada or Great Britain, we could avoid
the criticism that only the poor are being made to bear
the burden of improving access.

Proponents of the Oregon plan aim for a more
complex case than a zero sum game with services,
however, hoping to add either new services or new

revenue sources.[1,3,8] Suppose, for example, the plan makes available "high-priority" services that are currently not adequately provided, such as prenatal maternal care, mental health, and chemical dependency services, while "low-priority" services, eg, soft-tissue transplants, are not funded. Then current Medicaid recipients will have a *higher* expected payoff from the revised benefits. Since the currently uninsured are also made better off, and no one is made worse off (except that taxes may be increased), we have what economists call a *pareto superior* outcome. Of course, those particular Medicaid recipients who need the newly rationed services will be worse off, but it is reasonable to judge the effects of the system *ex ante,* and the poor as a whole are better off despite the loss to some individuals who would require soft-tissue transplants.

Thus, with appropriate revisions of Medicaid benefits, the poor will be better off than they are now. Nevertheless, current Medicaid recipients can object, "We achieve our gain in health status by giving up beneficial services that better-off groups receive; in that sense we 'bear the burden' of the Oregon plan. The poor would improve even more if better-off groups contributed more." The complaint is that social inequality could be reduced in a way that benefits the poor even more.

One version of this complaint appeals to long-term considerations: the Oregon plan makes the poor better off in the short run but worse off than they would be in the longer run if a national health insurance scheme were introduced. This claim depends on particular political assumptions about the likelihood of alternative scenarios for reform. In reply, some proponents see the current legislation in Oregon as but the first step in a comprehensive, incremental reform; ultimately, the state would become the major insurer and most powerful purchaser by substituting its basic insurance plan for many private insurance plans as well as for Medicare and long-term care under Medicaid (Sen. John Kitzhaber, verbal communication, January 1991). The debate then focuses on the means to health reform, not its ends; disagreement results from complex political, not moral, judgments.

A second complaint about reducible inequality derives from the Children's Defense Fund's charge that the Oregon plan "exempts" the elderly who are Medicaid recipients from the ranking of services.[5] Poor women and children, who constitute 75% of the Medicaid recipients, receive only 30% of the benefits in dollars. Much of the rest goes to the elderly who have

"spent down" their resources in order to be eligible for long-term care, but these services—as well as all acute care for the elderly who are covered under Medicare—are not included in the prioritization or rationing process. By not establishing priorities among health care services for the elderly, and by financing expansion of Medicaid coverage, primarily by rationing to women and children, the plan seems to suggest that any use of long-term medical services by the elderly is more important than short-term medical services for the young. This would be an irrational ranking on the face of it. If we did not know how old we were and had to allocate resources over our life span, taking our needs at each stage of life into account, we would not consider this ranking a prudent one.[9] A reasonable rationing plan would consider the importance of all health care services, short-term medical as well as long-term care, over an individual's life span, at each stage of life. To avoid what seems to be discrimination by age, rationing should include all age groups. In reply, and as noted, some Oregon proponents intend to expand the plan to cover Medicare and long-term Medicaid care.

Advocates for the Oregon plan argue that additional revenue, which would further reduce inequality, will be easier to obtain when the legislature must visibly cut beneficial services and cannot disguise rationing by raising eligibility requirements for Medicaid. This political judgment ignores evidence from the 1980s, when various states, as well as the federal government, cut important services to the poor, including prenatal maternal care and the Women, Infants, and Children's Program's distribution of food supplements to pregnant women and neighborhood mental health care services. Explicit rationing to the poor made neither politicians nor their constituents so uncomfortable that the cuts were stopped.

In short, we cannot answer the basic question about how the worse off will fare under the current legislation until we are told what they will get, that is, until the Medicaid benefit package is ranked by OHSC, is funded by the legislature, and is approved for a Medicaid waiver by the Department of Health and Human Services, sometime later in 1991. If the current Medicaid recipients are made worse off, there is a serious, though not necessarily fatal, objection to the Oregon plan. If we hold only a weak version of the requirement that we give priority to the worse off, we might still think the plan acceptable even though some of the poor bear the burden of reducing overall inequality. In any case, the Oregon planners hope that rationing will yield a result in which all the poor are better off than now. Political judgments differ about the likelihood of this preferred outcome.

ARE THE INEQUALITIES THE OREGON PLAN ACCEPTS JUSTIFIABLE?

By rationing lower-priority services to the poor, rather than excluding whole groups of the poor and near-poor from insurance, the Oregon plan reduces inequality in our society, even if current Medicaid recipients are, to some extent, worse off than they are now. Somewhat paradoxically, even under the scenario in which no one is worse off, there is still a sense in which the poor bear the burden of the plan, since the plan accepts as official policy an unjustifiable inequality in the health care system.

To see this point, contrast the kind of inequality the Oregon plan accepts with the inequality that arises in the heavily rationed British system.[10] Although about 10% of the British public buys private insurance coverage in order to procure various rationed services, the overwhelming majority abides by the consequences of rationing. This produces a more acceptable structure of inequality than would result if the bottom 20% of the Oregon population has no access to some services that are available to the great majority.[11]

To see why one structure of inequality seems worse than the other, consider how the poor would feel under both. Under the Oregon plan, the poor can complain that society as a whole is content not only to leave them economically badly off, but also to deny them medical services that would protect the range of opportunities that are open to them.[6] There is a basis here for reasonable regrets or resentment, for society as a whole seems content to shut the poor out of mainstream opportunities. They may reasonably feel that the majority is too willing to leave them behind under terms in which the benefits of social cooperation do not reflect their moral status as free and equal agents.[12,13] Alternatively, if health care protects opportunity in a way that is roughly equal for all, except that the most advantaged group has some extra advantages, then this may seem somewhat unfair, but no one group is then singled out for special disadvantages that are viewed as "acceptable" by the economically and medically advantaged majority. Conse-

quently, no group would have a basis for the strong and reasonable regrets that the poor have under the Oregon plan, despite their improvement relative to the current situation.

Thus, even if the poor are better off under the Oregon plan than now, the plan still accepts an inequality that is not ideally just. It is more just—perhaps much more just—than what we now have, but still not what justice requires. Does this mean we should not implement it? The answer seems to depend on political judgments about the feasibility of alternatives. If one thinks that a uniform, universal plan, like Canada's, is a political impossibility in the United States, or if one thinks that introducing the Oregon plan makes further reform in the direction of a uniform plan more likely, then the Oregon plan, even if it is not ideally just, seems reasonable. But if one thinks that introducing the Oregon reform makes more radical reform of the system less likely, then one might well prefer not to make a modest improvement in the justice of the system in order to facilitate a more significant improvement later.

IS THE PUBLIC PROCESS FOR DECIDING WHAT IS 'BASIC CARE' FAIR?

The Oregon plan involves public, explicit rationing; it disavows rationing hidden by the covert workings of a market, or buried in the quiet, professional decisions of providers. Its rationing decisions are the result of a two-step process involving separate, publicly accountable bodies. First (step 1), OHSC, which is charged with taking "community values" into consideration, determines priorities among services in a possible benefit package. Second (step 2), the legislature decides how much to spend on Medicaid, given competing demands on state funds. Some lower-priority services may thus not be covered, but the resulting Medicaid benefit package must still be approved by the Department of Health and Human Services. Assessing the fairness of the rationing process requires examining both steps.

Oregon's insistence on publicity is controversial. Calabresi and Bobbit[14] argue that "tragic choices" are best made out of the public view in order to preserve important symbolic values, such as the sanctity of life. Despite the importance of such symbols, however, justice requires publicity. People who view themselves as free and equal moral agents must have available to them the grounds for all decisions that affect their lives in fundamental ways, as rationing decisions do. Only with publicity can they resolve disputes about whether the decisions conform to the more basic principles of justice that are the accepted basis of their social cooperation.[15]

Actually, going beyond a concern for publicity, Oregon calls for broad public participation in the development of priorities. Public participation is desirable because it may yield agreement about how to resolve disputes among winners and losers in a fair way. It also makes it more likely that outcomes reflect the consent of those individuals who are affected and, since there may not be one uniquely fair or just way to ration services, participation allows the shared values of a community to shape the result. Is the public participation process itself fair, and does it have a real effect on outcomes?

OHSC held public hearings on health services and asked Oregon Health Decisions to hold community meetings throughout the state "to build consensus on the values to be used to guide health resource allocation decisions."[16] At 47 meetings that were held during the early part of 1990, citizens were asked to rank the importance of various categories of treatment and were asked, "Why is this health care service *important to us?*" From these discussions, an unranked list of 13 "values" was distilled. A tally was kept of how often each value was discussed, but we cannot rank the importance of the values on that basis.

One frequent criticism of the community meeting procedure is that it did not involve a representative cross section of Oregonians. Some 50% were health professionals; too many were college educated, white, and relatively well-off. Moreover, whereas 16% of Oregonians are uninsured, only 9.4% of community meeting participants were uninsured, and Medicaid recipients, the only direct representatives of poor children, were underrepresented by half.[5,16] Even if there was no evidence of bias in the meetings, the process is still open to the charge that it consisted of the "haves" deciding what is "important" to give the "have-nots." The charge is twofold. Not only is the composition of the meetings unrepresentative of the interests of those who will be affected, but the task set for the meetings presupposes that rationing will primarily have an impact on an underrepresented minority.

It is difficult to assess the importance of either charge of bias, for we have no way to compare the outcome with an unbiased alternative. Suspicions about the effects of compositional bias would be reduced, however, if there were no bias in the task, that

is, if the Oregon plan called for rationing services to the great majority rather than to the poor. We worry less about who is making a decision if it has an equal impact on everyone, including the decision makers.

The charge of bias is important only if the meetings actually influence the ranking of services (otherwise they are just window dressing). Contrary to public and media understanding, however, the community meetings do not yield a ranking of services, only a general list of community values. Moreover, the list of values cannot be used in any direct way in determining priorities among health services. Some of the "values" are really only categories of services, e.g., mental health and chemical dependency, or prevention. Other values, such as equity (guaranteeing access to all) or respecting personal choice, are things we desire of the system as a whole, not of individual services. And the values relevant to ranking services, such as quality of life or cost-effectiveness or ability to function, are not themselves ranked.

OHSC is well aware of this limitation and views the list of values only as a "qualitative check" on the process of ranking services (Paige Sipes-Metzler, personal communication, June and July 1990). Thus, it believes the community concern for equity is met because the system guarantees universal access to basic care. Community concerns about mental health and chemical dependency, or prevention, are met by making sure that these services are included in the ranking process. Although no weights were assigned to values such as quality of life or cost-effectiveness, they are included as factors in the formal ranking process. The only direct community input into the first attempt at ranking services, however, came from a telephone survey aimed at finding how Oregonians ranked particular health outcomes that affect their quality of life. By combining this information with expert judgments about the likely outcomes of using particular procedures to treat certain conditions, as well as with information about the costs of treating a population with those procedures, OHSC generated a preliminary cost-benefit ranking of services. Because this ranking drew extensive criticism (*New York Times.* July 9, 1990; sect A:17) and failed to match its own expectations about priorities, OHSC modified its procedure for ranking services. As a result, the OHSC commissioners themselves ranked general categories of services according to their importance to the individual, to society, and to the health plan and "adjusted" other items.[17] It remains unclear how this process reflects community values, and until we know just how the final rankings were "adjusted," we cannot know what influence public participation has had.

The rationing process involves two decisions, not one. Suppose that we have a fair procedure and a perfect outcome at step 1: the ranking of services captures relevant facts about costs and benefits and represents community values fairly. Unfortunately, fairness at step 1 does not assure it at step 2, because the voting power of the poor is negated in a political process that generally underrepresents them, judging from past voting patterns and outcomes. Therefore, even if there is a consensus at step 1 about what the basic, minimum package should be, there may be well-founded worries that the legislature will not fund it. Indeed, the situation is somewhat worse because OHSC only ranks services, it does not decide what is basic. The funding decision of the legislature determines what basic care is provided.

Clearly, political judgments diverge on how much we can trust the legislature. The crucial issue from the point of view of process, however, is this: because the Oregon plan explicitly involves rationing primarily for the poor and near-poor, funding decisions face constant political pressure from more powerful groups who want to put public resources to other uses. In contrast, if the legislature were deciding how to fund a rationing plan that applied to themselves and to all their constituents, then we might expect a careful and honest weighing of the importance of health care against other goods. The legislature would then have stronger reasons not to concede to political pressures to divert resources, and other groups would be less likely to apply such pressure. If the plan is expanded to include other groups, then the poor may find important allies.

Worries about fairness in the Oregon rationing process thus come from the plan's being aimed at the poor rather than at the population as a whole. Concerns about fairness in the process thus converge with concerns about the kinds of inequality the system tolerates. This does not mean that the Oregon experiment should not be tried; it may produce less overall inequality in health status than we now have. But we should recognize from the start that a system that rations only to the poor is less equitable and less fair than alternative systems that ration for the great majority of people. To the extent that the inequality ends up troubling many participants in the system, including physicians who will be able to do only certain things for some children and more for others, the strains of commitment to abiding by the rationing will be greater, and rationing may get a worse name than it deserves.

Oregon's plan retains the structure of inequality that it does because states must respond to the problems imposed by a highly inequitable and inefficient national health care system. The plan contains a bizarre irony: the state's Medicaid budget is in crisis because of rapidly increasing costs, largely the result of the burden of long-term care imposed by the elderly, yet the rationing plan focuses on poor children. Oregon did not design a Medicaid system that forces the most vulnerable children and the most vulnerable elderly to compete for scarce public resources. As long as states must respond to problems created by the national system, however, their solutions will inherit its major flaws. Uncoordinated responses by states cannot solve the problems caused by the continuing rapid dissemination of technology, inefficiencies in administering a mixed system, and a growing demand for services in our aging and acquired immunodeficiency syndrome-threatened society.

Oregon offers important lessons for any national effort to address these problems. Nationally, we should embrace Oregon's commitment to provide universal access to basic care and to making rationing a subject of open, political debate, but we should not simply expand the current legislation into a national plan. That would not only reproduce on a larger scale the unjustifiable inequality that the Oregon plan permits. It would also retain at the state level competition for funds between poor children and poor elderly, and it would leave unaddressed the basic problems of inefficiency and rapidly rising costs. In contrast, rationing within a single-payer, public insurance scheme that covered all age groups would more easily address these problems. Whether such a comprehensive scheme is best introduced all at once (on the model of the Canadian system), or is phased in (building on an Oregon-style starting point), is a complex issue. In any case, we have yet to see whether the Oregon plan gives us a clear model for how community values or public participation should influence the design of a national benefit package.

1. Golenski J. *A Report on the Oregon Medicaid Priority Setting Project*. Berkeley, Calif: Bioethics Consultation Group; 1990.

2. Senate Bills 27, 534, 935. 65th Oregon Legislative Assembly; 1989 regular sess.

3. Kitzhaber J. *The Oregon Basic Health Services Act*. Salem, Ore: Office of the Senate President; 1990.

4. Blendon RJ, Leitman R, Morrison I, Donelan K. Satisfaction with health systems in ten nations. *Health Aff*. Summer 1990:185–192.

5. *An Analysis of the Impact of the Oregon Medicaid Reduction Waiver Proposal on Women and Children*. Washington, DC: Children's Defense Fund; 1990:1–7.

6. Daniels N. *Just Health Care*. New York, NY: Cambridge University Press; 1985.

7. Rawls J. *A Theory of Justice*. Cambridge, Mass: Harvard University Press; 1971.

8. *Preliminary Report*. Salem: Oregon Health Services Commission; 1990.

9. Daniels N. *Am I My Parents' Keeper? An Essay on Justice Between the Young and the Old*. New York, NY: Oxford University Press Inc; 1988.

10. Aaron HJ, Schwartz WB. *The Painful Prescription: Rationing Health Care*. Washington, DC: The Brookings Institution; 1984.

11. Temkin L. Inequality. *Philosophy Public Aff*. 1986;15:99–121.

12. Cohen J. Democratic equality. *Ethics*. 1989;99:727–751.

13. Scanlon TM. Contractualism and utilitarianism. In: Sen AK, Williams B, eds. *Utilitarianism and Beyond*. New York, NY: Cambridge University Press; 1982:103–128.

14. Calabresi G, Bobbit P. *Tragic Choices*. New York, NY: WW Norton & Co Inc; 1978.

15. Rawls J. Kantian constructivism in moral theory: the Dewey Lectures. *J Phil*. 1980; 77:515–572.

16. Hasnain R, Garland M. *Health Care in Common: Report of the Oregon Health Decisions Community Meetings Process*. Portland: Oregon Health Decisions; 1990.

17. Kitzhaber J. *Summary: The Health Services Prioritization Process*. Salem: Oregon State Senate; 1990.

DANIEL CALLAHAN

Ethics and Priority Setting in Oregon

The past few years have been remarkable for the array of proposals advanced to address the American health care crisis. Their very quantity and diversity, however, suggest the intimidating range of the issues before us. We have difficulty agreeing on the nature of the problem; determining how to interpret the history and values that lie behind our affluent and advanced, yet inefficient and inequitable, health care system; and deciding how to devise a political strategy that can bring needed reform.

The great attraction of the Oregon initiative to prioritize state health spending is that it proposes a bold and integrated way of dealing with these daunting

From Daniel Callahan, "Ethics and Priority Setting in Oregon," *Health Affairs* 10, No. 2 (Summer 1991). Health Affairs Division of the University of Pennsylvania. Reprinted by permission.

problems. It challenges the widespread belief that health care can and should be an unlimited benefit. It rejects the common presumption that no rational way can be found to distinguish and set priorities among the bewildering array of individual health needs and claims. It embraces an open, democratic process to make painful policy choices. It questions the pervasive view that any plan that denies to the poor care available to the rich is of necessity unjust and unacceptable.

These premises are unsettling. They go against the grain of a number of values and practices that have marked the American health care system. For years, Americans have held fast to the belief that if we are just smart enough, and tough enough, and optimistic enough, we can give everyone the advantage of unlimited medical progress at a reasonable price. Unfortunately, reality has continually intruded into that

optimism, in a variety of forms: the high cost of continuing medical progress; the social and technical difficulties of (and resistance to) technology assessment;
unreasonable public and professional expectations for
improved health care; growing resistance to higher
taxes to pay for better health care, combined with a
deep distrust of government as the vehicle for a more
effective and equitable system; and, as a powerful historical legacy, a health care "system" that is not a system at all, at least if that term implies a coherent, organized set of institutions, practices, and values.

The Oregon initiative is an attempt to cope with
these realities and other problems, by targeting the
state Medicaid program. To meet the problem of access to health care, the plan provides coverage for all
persons under 100 percent of the federal poverty level.
To meet the problem of budget constraints within the
context of that universal coverage, a priority system
has been established. The priority system, based on
the analysis of a special commission, ranks the medical treatments that could be covered by the program;
additional cost figures will be developed to show the
financial impact of covering the ranked treatments.
The legislature then will establish an overall budget
figure, and these dollar amounts will determine how
far down the priority list of specific treatments the
program will be able to cover.

The results of the entire process will be highly visible, and the accountability clear. Public unwillingness
to pay higher taxes for better coverage, and legislative
unwillingness to vote higher budgets, will be reflected
directly in the level of coverage made available. Additional features of the program will provide incentives
for effective and appropriate care, avoidance of incentives for overtreatment, a plan for improved employer health care insurance, and a method of funding
designed to create an economically affordable system.
The long-term goal is a system of universal health
care for the state.

The ethical problems potentially raised by the
Oregon plan fall into four categories that require
scrutiny: (1) its moral context and political setting (including its ideological meaning); (2) its formal and
explicit goals; (3) its means of achieving those goals,
that is, its process of priority setting, public participation, and public accountability; and (4) its practical implementation, including possible unintended
consequences.

The context of the proposed Oregon plan is that of a
present Medicaid budget that, in responding to a
shortage of funds, has set its cutoff point for coverage
at 58 percent of the federal poverty line; those covered
by Medicaid, however, receive a full range of services. To date, the state has responded to its money
shortage by manipulating eligibility standards rather
than coverage of services. This is a common tactic
among states faced with this situation. Under the new
plan, by contrast, coverage will extend to everyone
below the poverty line, but the range of services provided will be limited.

THE EXISTENCE OF RATIONING

This history makes several salient moral points. First,
for those poor people whose income placed them
above the old 58 percent Medicaid eligibility level,
health care rationing was already a reality. The legislature had set the eligibility level by establishing a priority system based on income. It is thus hard to conclude that the new plan represents a radical departure
from the old in its background assumptions: that not
everyone can get all that they might need or want, and
that some system of priorities must be set. The Oregon plan remains a system of setting limits, only now
in a different way. The question to be asked is whether
it is a more rational, equitable way.

The main criticism of the new plan is that the
heaviest burden will fall upon mothers and children
in the Aid to Families with Dependent Children
(AFDC) program, the least powerful and most needy
group. Other needy groups (the blind, the disabled,
and the elderly) will be exempt from the priority system. The result will be to remove a significant number of mothers and children from their present privileged place in the Medicaid program and force them
to compete with everyone else. This is a serious and
telling deficit. But it is offset, in part, by the inclusion of additional previously excluded mothers and
children who will now be covered because of a federally mandated extension of the coverage up to 100
percent of the federal poverty line. It is not clear
whether the overall benefit to mothers and children
under the new plan will add up to a better balance of
health care for this group as a whole, but if the balance can be determined with any clarity, it would be a
relevant consideration in any final moral judgment
about the Oregon plan. It is also possible, of course,

that the Oregon plan could be amended to return AFDC mothers and children to a special place in the system.

COMPARING CARE OF THE POOR
TO CARE OF THE AFFLUENT

Second, it is obvious that the Oregon plan, as a Medicaid program, is designed for the poor, not those middle-class, affluent people covered more generously by employer health plans. It could thus be said, in the harshest construal of its meaning, that the Oregon plan is a targeted rationing program for the poor that sets limits for their care in a way that will not be borne by their more affluent fellow citizens. The Oregon plan's context is a two-tiered economic society, now matched by a two-tiered health care system.

The logic of this line of potential criticism is obvious. Unless Medicaid recipients are provided a level of health care equal to that of the more affluent, it can be seen as unjust and discriminatory. At least, this view will prevail if it is assumed that the poor have a basic right to equal access to the level of care that the affluent can buy or have provided them by private employer insurance plans. The obvious question is whether, in fact, our society has accepted as normative a right to equal access for all persons. The answer would seem to be no, at least in practice, even if public opinion polls find rhetorical support for the idea.

The most serious issue for debate is whether, by changing the Medicaid program, the actual result is to reinforce an unfair system, one that should not exist in the first place. Does the Oregon initiative wrongly legitimate the absence of a universal health care system in the United States? Does it also wrongly legitimate the idea of systematically (through the priority system) depriving the poor of some forms of health care they could have if they were more affluent? How these questions are answered will depend in part on two considerations. Is it wrong in all cases to use less-than-perfect programs to improve health care for the poor, and is working within the boundaries of public support a wrongful compromise for legislators?

What seems clear in response to these questions is that the Oregon legislators have little room to maneuver. The gap between aspirations for a one-tiered, ideal program and the political realities can be seen by the Oregon public's unwillingness to pay higher taxes to support a more generous Medicaid program. Thus it is the voters, not the legislature, who must bear the blame for the legislature's inability to provide support for Medicaid recipients equal to what the affluent can afford to buy (or get from their employers). A hard but obvious truth emerges: unjust or not, discriminatory or not, the legislature must work with the resources available to it. Its moral task, in that context, is to deploy resources in the fairest way possible. At the same time, we must not assume that because the affluent can obtain forms of health care not available to the poor under Medicaid, the poor have lost an *intrinsic* benefit. If the private sector has not learned how to set limits, must the public sector do likewise? That does not follow. In any case, the private sector is also working to set limits and priorities in its insurance and coverage practices. Increasingly, a restricted range of choices is being offered.

Are we to imagine that a government entitlement program could provide unlimited access to the highest-quality health care, regardless of cost? The possibilities for such care are infinite, and no other country—even those with universal health insurance plans—provides that level of care. The wealthy everywhere can buy better care than what is available to them under government programs, if only because of their ability to travel elsewhere to get what is denied them domestically.

What ultimately matters is not whether the new Oregon plan legitimates a two-tiered system—it surely does that, just as surely as does the present Oregon system, with its total exclusion of many thousands of poor people from the program—but whether the care provided under the new plan will be decent, humane, and reasonably adequate for most if not all legitimate medical needs of the poor. If that standard can be achieved (assuming we can define it with any precision), it could be judged reasonable and fair, even if the affluent do better.

GOALS OF THE OREGON INITIATIVE

The goal of the Oregon initiative is to provide a basic and adequate level of health care for all of the poor, but within the externally imposed constraints of a limited budget. These constraints in turn dictate that not all needed or desired care can be provided. There will be a ceiling on expenditures—a necessity in the case of a limited budget. The old ceiling was managed by limiting eligibility. The innovation in the new program is to manage the ceiling problem by making all of the poor eligible but then setting priorities to manage the available funds.

To the question of whether it is sensible and equitable to extend eligibility at the price of reducing coverage, no definitive answer can be given. It is a classic question of prudence, not fixed moral rules. The consequences of these two approaches can and should be evaluated: full eligibility and less coverage versus less eligibility and full coverage. To make this choice, various incommensurable goods will have to be compared, and no striking imbalances are likely to appear. Even if they do appear, none are likely to be so dramatic that they automatically condemn the plan of which they are the outcome.

One possibility, however, could make a real difference. Should it turn out that the coverage provided under the new plan systematically and continually deprived recipients of some crucial benefit or benefits that would drastically affect their health and lives, we might then conclude that it was unfair. But that could only be concluded if two conditions were met: first, that the program was unnecessarily deprived of funds by a stingy public; and second, that a reasonable effort was not made to balance the available resources to minimize that kind of outcome. Unhappily, of course, it could well be that even an otherwise rational priority-setting process might exclude some forms of care that are of intrinsic value and necessity to some individuals. Life-saving but expensive organ transplants might be an obvious example. If they end up as a low-priority item, they are not likely to make the budgetary cutoff point. Yet to limit coverage of such procedures for the sake of other important health care benefits would not necessarily be unfair. The right to a decent minimum level of health care need not entail coverage of each and every form of medical technology, no matter how expensive and how limited the number of beneficiaries. It is hard to see how any society could make that kind of promise for long without doing damage to other health and social needs.

Yet we are left with a terrible problem once we recognize that kind of limitation. Might it be said that a process that resulted in denial of certain forms of care would be a *prima facie* unjust process—because the right to those forms of care is so basic to human welfare that any system that jeopardizes them must be condemned? The way in which the denial of what Albert Jonsen has called "rescue technologies" (those necessary to save a patient's life) almost always re-

sults in acute public and professional discomfort illustrates both the moral and political issue here. The denial of some forms of care will be seen as both morally wrong and politically unacceptable. But, if that is so, that leaves us with a genuine dilemma. In addition to a fair political process, will we also need some independent moral criteria by which to judge the outcomes of the process? But, if so, will that not undermine the credibility of the process—making it subject, so to speak, to a moral veto if the results are unacceptable?

I see no way out of this dilemma other than to define a basic package of health care benefits available to all regardless of ability to pay. If the Oregon plan could be amended to guarantee such a package prior to the setting of priorities for additional care, the dilemma could be avoided. As matters now stand, it looks as if the priority system might deny some forms of care that seem imperative, and as if the price of avoiding such an outcome would be an arbitrary setting aside of the priorities. Some forms of care might be required to be available to all regardless of the priority they might receive if they had to compete with other forms in the political process; that is, they would be allowed to trump the priority-setting process. Of course, too much trumping would threaten the credibility of the process. Some therapies would be declared winners before the struggle over priorities even began. A basic health care package not subject to priority setting seems a preferable alternative, but it could of necessity exclude some important but expensive forms of acute care as the price of making that package financially tolerable.

THE PROCESS OF THE OREGON INITIATIVE

How might such a set of problems be decided? Ineluctably, consideration of the goals of the Oregon initiative must include consideration of the means to achieve them. Must the process of priority setting assume that a well-designed procedure will itself be tantamount to a just procedure, that is, that any outcome that results from a conscientious, scrupulous adherence to the procedure will be declared just, as if that is what "just" means? To come to grips with this question, two problems must be confronted. The first has been alluded to above: whether there are some health needs so preeminent that they must trump their way to the top of any priority list, or so important that their omission from any health care package based on the priority-setting process would tend to discredit the process altogether. Both possibilities could suggest a compromise of the integrity of the priority-setting procedure. Yet there may be no choice but to accept the need for such compromise.

The second problem is whether the design of the plan to set priorities is reasonable, organized to produce the fairest possible outcome. This is hard to say in the absence of any experience with such a procedure. The lack of any clear community historical tradition or present consensus on the setting of priorities, and the lack of any established method of determining the comparative importance to individual welfare of different procedures, make it problematic to evaluate the plan's design. A safe assumption is that there would be strong community support for the high priority of life-saving treatment, and a lower priority for treatments that affect the quality and comfort of a life. But it is less clear what the community, and the commission, will think of life-saving treatments that help a few people at a very high cost per person, or of a quality-enhancing treatment that can help many at a lower per capita cost.

A priority-setting process that neatly and deductively builds upon available ethical principles and community sentiment, and extracts from them a theoretically elegant and obviously acceptable set of priorities, is not wholly feasible. Instead, a more likely model is one that constructs a fresh way of looking at health care, one that will need to invent its own methods and set of standards. It will require a unique blend of principled equity, supportable preferences, and community sentiment. Only over a period of time, after the priorities have been put into practice, can this new approach pass the test of ethics. The final test can only be that of experience. The process must be found satisfactory in practice. It would, then, make most sense to look upon the process as a social experiment, the invention of a policy out of the less than whole cloth of existing preferences and values. Its tests will be its public acceptability and, independent of the process, whether the outcome is fair. Since there are no commonly accepted norms available to provide a wholly independent standard, there must be continuing public discussion and debate about the balance between good process and good outcomes. That is hard work, but a necessary part of life in a free society that strives for procedural justice and yet also recognizes that moral claims may on occasion transcend what can be achieved by procedural means alone.

One of the purposes of the Oregon process seems to be to serve as a goad to the public. If the public is told that the money they are willing to pay in taxes will determine how deep the coverage of individuals will be, that is, how far down the priority list the funds will allow the state to go, the public will ultimately be accountable for the welfare of Medicaid patients. No longer can the consequences of limited funds be hidden or obscured by administrative obfuscation. The winners and losers will be known. The citizens of Oregon are being asked to accept a priority-setting system as well as to accept the pressure it will (and should) put on them to be more generous in what they provide as taxpayers. It remains to be seen whether both the public and the legislators will be able to stand this bright, cold light of accountability.

PROBLEMS OF IMPLEMENTATION

Problems inevitably will abound when the Oregon plan is actually put into practice. One is the likelihood that powerful interest groups will feel aggrieved that the illness or condition for which they speak is not covered by the Medicaid coverage priority list. They will then mount a campaign to make an exception to the list, or, if that is unsuccessful, to claim that the method of setting priorities must, of necessity, be wrong or unfair because it ranked their condition too low. The attachments of riders to legislation, the meeting of "special" needs, and the specifying of exceptions to ordinary policy are staples of the American political process, however distasteful they may be. But too great a capitulation to such forces will sink the plan, the very essence of which is to cut through competing claims in the name of a reasonable ranking of priorities. (One reason, I am told, for initial resistance to a waiver for the Oregon Medicaid plan was that it would wipe out mandated coverage for many conditions, thus undoing the work of earlier reformers.)

A closely related possibility might also be not to deny the need for priorities but to say that severe cases of conditions otherwise ranked low would not be unreasonable exceptions, not in themselves subverting the idea of priorities. Again, some flexibility might be possible here, but not much without risking the plan as a whole. Indeed, a chief difficulty with a set of priorities for various illnesses and conditions is that it will not be responsible to individual patient variation. A severe case of a low-ranked illness might be as potent in its effect on an individual as a mild case of a more highly ranked condition. It is difficult, however, to justify exceptions of any magnitude, or the making of (otherwise valid) distinctions.

The greatest source of anguish in the implementation of the plan will come in learning how to live with, and to rationalize, its failure to cover some people whose condition will pull at our sympathies. This anguish will be all the greater when the victims are visible and when the accountability for their condition cannot be evaded. This is the greatest logical and emotional problem created by any set of priorities that set limits. We will, for one thing, always wonder if we are doing the right thing. We will always wonder, for another, if it might be possible to relieve the pain by some stratagem we have not yet devised.

The likely price, however, of letting that pain triumph over our reasonable efforts to be fair will be to move the injustice elsewhere, to stint on the need for education, or roads, or housing—where issues less momentous than life and health seem at stake. For just that reason, a resoluteness will be necessary to make the priority-setting plan work. There will always be what I have come to think of as a "ragged edge," a line that separates what we can in fact do from what we might in theory do. An ability to tolerate and accept that ragged edge is imperative to making the Oregon plan work.

SOME FINAL THOUGHTS

I have raised here what seem to me the most important moral problems in judging the Oregon initiative. The most obvious general problem is where to start. Ideally, we should have a universal health care system in the United States, complete with mandated federal and national standards. The present system is both unfair and administratively chaotic and expensive. Most of the maneuvering over the Oregon initiative should be seen as a response to those national shortcomings, yet both the old program and the proposed new ones partake of those shortcomings.

Should we then reject the Oregon plan as just one more patchwork effort to redeem and legitimate an inherently defective system? I confess to deep ambivalence here. There are yet no signs of a universal health care system in the immediate offing in the United States, even if pressures are growing in that direction. Does it hurt the cause of universal health insurance to tolerate interim, less-than-perfect solutions?

On the one hand, it might make it harder, not easier, to gain a decent universal system if we continue to find ways to slightly improve the present fragmented system. The 1965 Medicare and Medicaid programs

were meant to be the incrementalist precursors of a universal health insurance program for the United States. This did not happen, and, in fact, that approach may have backfired. The unexpected high costs of those programs dampened enthusiasm for a more comprehensive program. There is, then, reason to be wary of piecemeal approaches. On the other hand, at some point we must take better account of the present realities, not forever holding out for ideal solutions that may never appear. We will not in the near future find a way to assess all, or even most, of our technologies, introduce dramatic cost-saving efficiencies into the system, or persuade the public to radically increase their tax burden.

The popular idea that we should never put in place any rationing or priority scheme until all waste and inefficiency have been wrung from the system has two major flaws. One of them is that serious cost containment and waste reduction would themselves have to make use of many of the same techniques used in rationing and priority setting: tough discipline, guidelines and protocols for treatment, denial of some forms of care believed efficacious by many practitioners, and so on. The other flaw is that it amounts to little more than a subtle way of maintaining the status quo, particularly since we know that the historical record over twenty years shows an almost unbroken record of failure to significantly reduce health care costs. Given that record, why should we believe that it can or will work in any substantial fashion in the near future? To cling to such a hope in the face of that history guarantees continued paralysis.

If we can accept the idea, then, that there is a kind of folly in waiting until everything is ready for some ideal system before taking some reform steps now, then the Oregon initiative promises a helpful step forward. Its goal is to introduce immediate reforms into a bad system. If, as its proponents hope, those reforms have an effect on all forms of health care in the state, private as well as public, they will have put in place some important ingredients of an eventually decent system.

At the heart of the Oregon effort is a simple perception. If a Medicaid or any other health care budget must be limited, then it makes sense to set priorities as a way of most effectively using the available funds. It is hard to fault the theory of this approach. Indeed, the chaotic nature of the present system, with its erratic coverage and mixture of mandated and optional coverage, shows what happens when there is no priority system. I happen to believe, moreover, that we will never have universal health insurance until Congress is persuaded that there can be a way of controlling the costs of such a plan and a way of specifying some boundaries to what it will cover. Congress will have to start with the premise that it cannot provide coverage for all the health care that will be desired, or perhaps even needed. It will then have to know how to say "no"—effectively, rationally, and humanely. A priority method, based on some combination of technology assessment and public preferences and values, is one of the only conceivable ways of bringing that about.

On balance, my own inclination is to support the Oregon initiative. A number of practical problems are associated with it, and the potential harm it might do to women and children is a serious (but probably correctable) flaw. Assuming a genuine effort to make corrections and adjustments, we have few more promising routes open to us in this country. Universal health insurance is an important and imperative national need. Its absence is a national scandal, and it cannot come soon enough. In the meantime, however, we must work within the available limits of resources and public unwillingness to pay higher taxes. It is not enough, but it is the best we have. It deserves a chance.

SUGGESTED READINGS

American Geriatrics Society. Public Policy Committee. "Equitable Distribution of Limited Medical Resources." *Journal of the American Geriatrics Society* 37 (1989), 1063–1064.

Battin, Margaret P. "Age Rationing and the Just Distribution of Health Care: Is There a Duty to Die?" *Ethics* 97 (1987), 317–340.

Beauchamp, Tom L., and Childress, James F. *Principles of Biomedical Ethics*. 4th ed. New York: Oxford University Press, 1994. Chap. 6.

Bell, J. M., and Mendus, Susan, eds. *Philosophy and Medical Welfare*. New York: Cambridge University Press, 1988.

Binstock, Robert H., and Post, Stephen G., eds. *Too Old for Health Care? Controversies in Medicine, Law, Economics, and Ethics*. Baltimore: Johns Hopkins University Press, 1991, 92–119.

Blank, Robert. *Rationing Medicine*. New York: Columbia University Press, 1988.

Bole, Thomas J., and Bondeson, William B., eds. *Rights to Health Care*. Boston: Kluwer Academic Publishers, 1991.

Brock, Dan W. "Justice, Health Care, and the Elderly." *Philosophy & Public Affairs* 18 (1989), 297–312.

Buchanan, Allen. "Health-Care Delivery and Resource Allocation." In Veatch, Robert M., ed. *Medical Ethics*. Boston: Jones and Bartlett, 1989, 291–327.

Byrne, Peter, ed. *Health, Rights and Resources: King's College Studies 1987–1988*. London: Oxford University Press, 1988.

Callahan, Daniel. "Old Age and New Policy." *Journal of the American Medical Association* 261 (February 10, 1989), 905–906.

_____. "Rationing Medical Progress: The Way to Affordable Health Care." *New England Journal of Medicine* 322 (June 21, 1990), 1810–1813.

_____. *Setting Limits: Medical Goals in an Aging Society*. New York: Simon & Schuster, 1987.

_____. *What Kind of Life: The Limits of Medical Progress*. New York: Simon & Schuster, 1990.

Capron, Alexander Morgan. "Oregon's Disability: Principles or Politics?" *Hastings Center Report* 22 (November–December 1992), 18–20.

Cassel, Christine K., and Purtilo, Ruth B. "Justice and the Allocation of Health Care Resources." In Cassel, Christine K., et al., eds. *Geriatric Medicine*. 2d ed. New York: Springer-Verlag, 1990, 615–622.

Childress, James F. "Rights to Health Care in a Democratic Society." In Humber, James, and Almeder, Robert, eds. *Biomedical Ethics Reviews 1984*. Clifton, N.J.: Humana Press, 1984, 47–70.

Churchill, Larry M. *Rationing Health Care in America: Perceptions and Principles of Justice*. Notre Dame, IN: University of Notre Dame Press, 1987.

Daniels, Norman. *Am I My Parents' Keeper? An Essay on Justice Between the Young and the Old*. New York: Oxford University Press, 1988.

_____. "Cost Containment and Justice." *Mount Sinai Journal of Medicine* 56 (1989), 180–184.

_____. "Insurability and the HIV Epidemic: Ethical Issues in Underwriting." *Milbank Quarterly* 68 (1990), 497–525.

_____. *Just Health Care*. New York: Cambridge University Press, 1985.

Dougherty, Charles J. "Setting Health Care Priorities: Oregon's Next Steps." *Hastings Center Report* 21 (May–June 1991), S1–S10.

Eddy, David M. "The Individual vs. Society: Resolving the Conflict." *Journal of the American Medical Association* 265 (May 8, 1991), 2399–2401, 2405–2406.

_____. "Rationing by Patient Choice." *Journal of the American Medical Association* 265 (January 2, 1991), 105–108.

_____. "What's Going On in Oregon?" *Journal of the American Medical Association* 266 (July 17, 1991), 417–420.

Emanuel, Ezekiel J. *The Ends of Human Life: Medical Ethics in a Liberal Polity*. Cambridge, MA: Harvard University Press, 1991.

Fleck, Leonard M. "Justice, HMOs, and the Invisible Rationing of Health Care Resources." *Bioethics* 4 (1990), 97–120.

Fried, Charles. "Equality and Rights in Medical Care." *Hastings Center Report* 6 (February 1976), 29–34.

_____. "Rights and Health Care—Beyond Equity and Efficiency." *New England Journal of Medicine* 293 (July 31, 1975), 241–245.

Garland, Michael J. "Justice, Politics, and Community: Expanding Access and Rationing Health Services in Oregon." *Law, Medicine and Health Care* 20 (1992), 67–81.

Green, Ronald M. "The Priority of Health Care." *Journal of Medicine and Philosophy* 8 (1983), 373–380.

Hadorn, David C. "The Problem of Discrimination in Health Care Priority Setting." *Journal of the American Medical Association* 268 (September 16, 1992), 1454–1459.

Health Affairs 10 (1991). Special issue on "Rationing." See essays by Fox, Daniel M., Etzioni, Amitai, and Callahan, Daniel.

Hiatt, Howard H. *America's Health in the Balance: Choice or Chance?* New York: Harper & Row, 1987.

Jennings, Bruce, Callahan, Daniel, and Caplan, Arthur. "Ethical Challenges of Chronic Illness." *Hastings Center Report* 18 (March 1988), S1–S16.

Jones, Gary E. "The Right to Health Care and the State." *Philosophical Quarterly* 33 (1983), 278–287.

Journal of the American Geriatrics Society 40 (1992). Special issue on "Ethics and Rationing."

Journal of Medicine and Philosophy 4 (1979). Special issue on "The Right to Health Care."

Journal of Medicine and Philosophy 13 (1988). Special issue on "Justice Between Generations and Health Care for the Elderly."

Kapp, Marshall B. "Rationing Health Care: Will It Be Necessary? Can It Be Done Without Age or Disability Discrimination?" *Issues in Law & Medicine* 5 (1989), 337–351.

La Puma, John. "Quality-Adjusted Life Years: Ethical Implications and the Oregon Plan." *Issues in Law and Medicine* (1992), 429–441.

Lomasky, Loren E. "Medical Progress and National Health Care." *Philosophy & Public Affairs* 10 (1981), 65–88.

Mechanic, David. *From Advocacy to Allocation: The Evolving American Health Care System.* New York: Free Press, 1986.

Menzel, Paul T. "At Law—Oregon's Denial: Disabilities and Quality of Life." *Hastings Center Report* 22 (November-December 1992), 21–25.

_____. "Equality, Autonomy, and Efficiency: What Health Care System Should We Have?" *Journal of Medicine & Philosophy* 17 (1992), 33–57.

_____. *Medical Costs, Moral Choices.* New Haven, CT: Yale University Press, 1983.

_____. "Some Ethical Costs of Rationing." *Law, Medicine and Health Care* 20 (1992), 57–66.

_____. *Strong Medicine: The Ethical Rationing of Health Care.* New York: Oxford University Press, 1990.

Mooney, Gavin, and McGuire, Alistair, eds. *Medical Ethics and Economics in Health Care.* New York: Oxford University Press, 1988.

Morreim, E. Haavi. "Access Without Excess." *Journal of Medicine & Philosophy* 17 (1992), 1–6.

Moskop, John C. "Rawlsian Justice and a Human Right to Health Care." *Journal of Medicine and Philosophy* 8 (1983), 329–338.

Nelson, Robert M., and Drought, Theresa. "Justice and the Moral Acceptability of Rationing Medical Care: The Oregon Experiment." *Journal of Medicine and Philosophy* 17 (1992), 97–117.

Persaud, Rajendra D. "What Future for Ethical Medical Practice in the New National Health Service?" *Journal of Medical Ethics* 17 (1991), 10–18.

Powers, Madison. "Justice and the Market for Health Insurance." *Kennedy Institute of Ethics Journal* 1 (1991), 307–323.

President's Commission for the Study of Ethical Problems in Medicine and Biomedical and Behavioral Research. *Securing Access to Health Care.* Vols. I–III. Washington: U.S. Government Printing Office, 1983.

Reinhardt, Uwe E. "An American Paradox." *Health Progress* (November 1986).

Relman, Arnold S. "The Trouble with Rationing." *New England Journal of Medicine* 323 (September 27, 1990), 911–913.

Russell, Louise B. "Some of the Tough Decisions Required by a National Health Plan." *Science* 246 (November 17, 1989), 892–896.

Sass, Hans-Martin. "Justice, Beneficence, or Common Sense? The President's Commission's Report on Access to Health Care." *Journal of Medicine and Philosophy* 8 (1983), 381–388.

Sass, Hans-Martin, and Massey, Robert U., eds. *Health Care Systems: Moral Conflicts in European and American Public Policy.* Boston: Kluwer Academic, 1988.

Shelp, Earl, ed. *Justice and Health Care.* Boston: D. Reidel, 1981.

Smeeding, Timothy M., ed. *Should Medical Care Be Rationed by Age?* Totowa, N.J.: Rowman and Littlefield, 1987.

Veatch, Robert M. *The Foundations of Justice: Why the Retarded and the Rest of Us Have Claims to Equality.* New York: Oxford University Press, 1986.

_____. "Should Basic Care Get Priority? Doubts About Rationing the Oregon Way." *Kennedy Institute of Ethics Journal* 1 (1991), 187–206.

Veatch, Robert M., and Branson, Roy, eds. *Ethics and Health Policy.* Cambridge, MA: Ballinger, 1975.

Weinstein, Milton C., and Stason, William B. "Allocating Resources: The Case of Hypertension." *Hastings Center Report* 7 (October 1977), 24–29.

Winslow, Gerald R. *Triage and Justice.* Berkeley, CA: University of California Press, 1982.

BIBLIOGRAPHIES AND ENCYCLOPEDIAS
WITH BIBLIOGRAPHIES

The Aged and Allocation of Health Care Resources (1990); *A Right to Health Care* (1992). Bibliographies available from the National Reference Center for Bioethics Literature, Kennedy Institute of Ethics, Georgetown University, Washington, D.C. 20057. Beginning 1991, all except revised bibliographies are published in the *Kennedy Institute of Ethics Journal.*

Bioethicsline: Computer Retrieval Service.

Encyclopedia of Bioethics, ed. Warren Reich. New York: Macmillan, 1994.

Encyclopedia of Ethics, ed. Lawrence Becker and Charlotte Becker, New York: Garland, 1992.

Leatt, Peggy, et al. *Perspectives on Physician Involvement in Resource Allocation and Utilization Management: An Annotated Bibliography.* Toronto: University of Toronto; 1991.

Lineback, Richard H., ed. *Philosopher's Index.* Vols. 1–27. Bowling Green, Ohio: Philosophy Documentation Center, Bowling Green State University.

Walters, LeRoy, and Kahn, Tamar Joy, eds. *Bibliography of Bioethics.* Vols. 1–19. New York: Free Press. Issued annually.